Cybersecurity Blue Team Operations

Cybersecurity Blue Team Operations

Principles and Practices for Building Robust Defensive Operations

Jason Edwards
Texas

WILEY

This edition first published 2026

Registered Offices
John Wiley & Sons, Inc., 111 River Street, Hoboken, NJ 07030, USA
John Wiley & Sons Ltd. New Era House, 8 Oldlands Way, Bognor Regis, West Sussex, PO22 9NQ, UK

For details of our global editorial offices, customer services, and more information about Wiley products visit us at www.wiley.com.

The manufacturer's authorized representative according to the EU General Product Safety Regulation is Wiley-VCH GmbH, Boschstr. 12, 69469 Weinheim, Germany, e-mail: Product_Safety@wiley.com.

Wiley also publishes its books in a variety of electronic formats and by print-on-demand. Some content that appears in standard print versions of this book may not be available in other formats.

Library of Congress Cataloging-in-Publication Data applied for
Hardback ISBN: 9781394433179

Cover design: Wiley
Cover image: Angelica Zander/Getty Images

Set in 9.5/12.5pt STIXTwoText by Straive, Chennai, India

To my beloved family. To my mom and dad, who are no longer with us but whose love and guidance continue to inspire me every day. To my wife, Selda, and my children, Michelle, Chris, Ceylin, and Mayra, for your endless love, patience, and encouragement. To my close family members: Derek, Meltem, Nilos, and Ken. And to my sisters, Robin, Kelly, and Lynn. This book is dedicated to you, with all my love and gratitude.

Contents

Preface *xix*
Acknowledgments *xxi*
About the Companion Website *xxiii*

Part I Foundations, Governance, and Program Design *1*

1 The Foundations of Blue Team Operations *3*
Origins of Blue Teaming and Why It Matters *3*
Defensive Security as an Operational Discipline *4*
Differences Between Offensive and Defensive Security *5*
Core Principles of Defensive Security *7*
Blue Team Roles and Responsibilities in Modern Environments *8*
Balancing People, Process, and Technology in Defensive Programs *9*
Automation and AI-Assisted Workflows: Capabilities, Limits, and Accountability *11*
Defining Success in Defensive Operations *12*
Conclusion *14*
Recommendations *14*

2 Governance and Leadership for Defensive Security *17*
Why Governance Determines Defensive Outcomes *17*
Security Decision-Making and Accountability Models *18*
Policies, Standards, and Procedures: How They Differ *21*
Translating Risk into Executive Decisions and Investment Priorities *22*
Aligning Cybersecurity with Business Objectives *24*
Managing Competing Priorities and Tradeoffs *25*
Program Ownership, Delegation, and Operational Oversight *26*
AI-Enabled Decision Support: Validation, Evidence, and Avoiding False Confidence *27*
Leadership Behaviors That Improve Defensive Readiness *29*
Conclusion *30*
Recommendations *31*

3 Policy Frameworks and Operational Control *33*
Building a Policy Framework That Teams Can Use *33*
Policy Scope and Exceptions Without Losing Control *35*
Standards and Baselines for Consistent Execution *37*
Procedure Design: Making Security Repeatable *38*
Maintaining Policy Relevance Over Time *39*
Communicating Policy Changes Across the Organization *41*
Auditable Controls and Evidence Expectations *42*
Automation and AI in Control Execution: Where It Helps and Where It Must Not Decide *44*
Common Policy Failure Modes in Real Organizations *45*
Conclusion *47*
Recommendations *47*

4 Building a Blue Team Operating Model *49*
Defining Blue Team Services and Service Owners *49*
Operating Rhythms: Daily, Weekly, and Monthly Cadence *51*
Intake, Prioritization, and Work Management *53*
Escalation Paths, Authority Boundaries, and Decision Rights *54*
On-Call Practices and After-Hours Coverage *56*
Cross-Team Collaboration with IT and Engineering *57*
Documentation, Knowledge Transfer, and Continuity *59*
AI-Assisted Operations: Ticket Enrichment, Summarization, and Workflow Guardrails *61*
Scaling the Operating Model as the Organization Grows *63*
Conclusion *64*
Recommendations *64*

Part II Risk, Assets, and Defensive Architecture *67*

5 Identifying and Managing Risks *69*
Why Risk Is the Basis of Defensive Prioritization *69*
Risk Assessments: Scope, Inputs, and Outputs *70*
Identifying and Prioritizing Critical Business Functions *72*
Mapping Risk to Systems, Dependencies, and Trust Boundaries *73*
Evaluating Threat Landscapes and Attack Vectors *74*
Risk Treatment Options and Decision Tradeoffs *76*
Communicating Risk to Technical and Executive Audiences *77*
AI-Augmented Risk Analysis: Dependency Mapping, Scenario Modeling, and Control Validation *78*
Keeping Risk Assessments Current and Useful *80*
Conclusion *81*
Recommendations *81*

6 Asset Management as the Backbone of Defense *83*
Why Asset Awareness Controls Everything Downstream *83*
Building an Inventory of Physical and Digital Assets *85*

Defining Ownership and Accountability for Assets *87*
Classification and Prioritization for Defensive Focus *89*
Asset Lifecycle Management and Offboarding *90*
Handling Shadow IT and Unknown Assets *92*
Asset Data Quality, Maintenance Practices, and Drift *94*
Correlation and AI-Assisted Asset Discovery: Benefits, Risks, and Verification *95*
Using Asset Management to Drive Security Work *97*
Conclusion *99*
Recommendations *99*

7 Endpoint Security Management *101*
The Endpoint as a Primary Battleground *101*
Endpoint Baselines and Configuration Standards *102*
Managing Agents, Coverage, and Drift *104*
Managing Local Privileges and Administrative Access *106*
Endpoint Logging Strategy and Collection *107*
Endpoint Hardening and Operational Constraints *109*
Handling Exceptions Without Creating Blind Spots *110*
AI-Assisted Endpoint Triage: Behavioral Signals, Noise Reduction, and Analyst Controls *112*
Measuring Endpoint Control Effectiveness *114*
Conclusion *115*
Recommendations *116*

8 Network and Perimeter Defense Operations *119*
Network Defense Goals and Defensive Layers *119*
Segmentation Concepts and Practical Constraints *121*
Firewalls and Policy Management as Operations *123*
Remote Access, Exposure Reduction, and Authentication Constraints *125*
Visibility and Logging Across Network Boundaries *126*
Detecting Lateral Movement and Suspicious Connectivity *128*
Operational Change and Policy Drift in Networks *130*
AI-Assisted Network Analysis: Pattern Recognition, Alert Enrichment, and Validation *131*
Maintaining Network Defense in Hybrid Environments *133*
Conclusion *135*
Recommendations *135*

9 Designing a Defensive Security Architecture *137*
Principles of Layered Security in Practice *137*
Translating Risk into Architecture Decisions *139*
Architecture as a Set of Enforceable Patterns *141*
Integrating Controls Across Endpoint, Network, Identity, and Data *142*
Designing for Failure: Resilience and Recovery Thinking *143*
Security Architecture and Operational Reality *145*
Documenting Architecture Standards and Exceptions *146*

AI in Architecture: Automation Opportunities, New Attack Surface, and Control Requirements *147*
Keeping Architecture Aligned with Business Change *149*
Conclusion *150*
Recommendations *151*

Part III Identity, Access, and Data Protection *153*

10 Identity and Access Management Foundations *155*
Why Identity Is the New Control Plane *155*
Authentication Versus Authorization in Operations *157*
Role-Based Access Control and Organizational Fit *158*
Least Privilege as an Ongoing Process *160*
Managing Entitlements and Permission Sprawl *161*
Integrating Identity into Daily Operations *163*
Detecting Misuse Through Access Patterns and Behavioral Signals *164*
AI-Assisted Access Risk: Scoring, Explainability, and Human Approval Gates *166*
Common IAM Failure Modes and How They Appear *167*
Conclusion *169*
Recommendations *169*

11 Identity Lifecycle Operations *171*
Joiner, Mover, Leaver: The Operational Reality *171*
Provisioning Workflows and Approval Chains *173*
Deprovisioning as a Security and Audit Priority *175*
Handling Contractors, Vendors, and Temporary Access *177*
Managing Group Membership and Role Changes *178*
Identity Hygiene and Reducing Stale Access *180*
Access Reviews That Produce Real Outcomes *181*
AI Assistance for Identity Governance: Review Prioritization, Outlier Detection, and Evidence *183*
Ownership Models for Identity Processes *184*
Conclusion *186*
Recommendations *186*

12 Privileged Access Management and Administrative Control *189*
Why Privilege Is the Highest-Risk Access Category *189*
Defining Privileged Roles and Privileged Actions *191*
Approval Models and Administrative Workflow *193*
Break-Glass Accounts and Emergency Access *195*
Monitoring and Controlling Privileged Sessions *197*
Service Accounts and Non-Human Privilege *199*
Privilege Auditing and Evidence Collection *201*
AI-Assisted Privilege Monitoring: Session Signals, Anomaly Detection, and Override Controls *203*

Reducing Privilege Without Disrupting Operations *206*
Conclusion *207*
Recommendations *208*

13 Protecting Data and Systems *211*
Data Protection as a Business Requirement *211*
Data Classification and Practical Usage *212*
Encryption Concepts and Operational Implementation *214*
Protecting Data in Transit and at Rest *216*
Access Controls for Sensitive Information *218*
Preventing Unauthorized Movement and Exposure *219*
Monitoring Data Access for Abuse and Misuse *220*
AI in Data Protection: Classification Assistance, Leakage Risk, and Governance Constraints *222*
Common Data Protection Failure Modes *224*
Conclusion *225*
Recommendations *225*

14 Backup, Recovery, and Operational Resilience *227*
Why Recovery Is a Defensive Control *227*
Backup Scope, Coverage, and Retention *229*
Protecting Backups from Tampering and Loss *230*
Recovery Objectives and Realistic Expectations *232*
Restoration Testing and Operational Readiness *234*
Coordinating Recovery Across IT and Security *236*
Recovery During Active Incidents *237*
AI-Assisted Recovery Operations: Prioritization, Communication Support, and Validation Requirements *239*
Turning Recovery Lessons into Control Improvements *241*
Conclusion *242*
Recommendations *242*

Part IV Vulnerability Management and Threat Mitigation *245*

15 Vulnerability Management Program Foundations *247*
Defining What Vulnerability Management Is and Is Not *247*
Dependencies on Asset Management and Ownership *249*
Establishing Scope Across Systems and Environments *251*
Setting Frequency and Coverage Expectations *252*
Vulnerability Intake Beyond Scanning *254*
Prioritizing Work Based on Business Risk *256*
Handling Vulnerability Backlogs Without Losing Control *258*
AI-Assisted Vulnerability Prioritization: Inputs, Bias, and Decision Accountability *259*

Building Confidence in Program Outcomes *261*
Conclusion *263*
Recommendations *263*

16 Vulnerability Discovery and Exposure Reduction *265*
Scanning Approaches and Operational Fit *265*
Coverage Gaps and Blind Spot Management *267*
Identifying External Exposure and High-Risk Services *269*
Validating Findings and Reducing Noise *270*
Managing False Positives and Repeated Findings *272*
Coordinating Discovery with Change Management *274*
Tracking Vulnerabilities Across Asset Lifecycles *275*
AI to Reduce Noise: Deduplication, Clustering, and Verification Workflows *277*
Building a Repeatable Discovery Process *280*
Conclusion *281*
Recommendations *281*

17 Prioritization, Remediation, and Patch Operations *283*
Turning Findings into Actionable Work *283*
Prioritization Criteria and Decision Tradeoffs *285*
Patch Management as an Operational Program *287*
Coordinating with IT and Engineering Teams *289*
Maintenance Windows, Risk Acceptance, and Exceptions *291*
Compensating Controls When Patching Is Not Immediate *292*
Verifying Remediation and Preventing Regression *294*
AI-Assisted Remediation Operations: Routing, Fix Suggestions, and Validation Controls *296*
Managing Emergency Patching and Rapid Response *297*
Conclusion *299*
Recommendations *299*

Part V Visibility, Monitoring, and Threat Detection *301*

18 Logging Strategy and Telemetry Management *303*
Why Visibility Is the Foundation of Detection *303*
Defining What "Good Telemetry" Looks Like *304*
Log Sources: Endpoint, Network, Identity, and Cloud *306*
Collection, Normalization, and Retention Considerations *308*
Managing Gaps, Failures, and Quality Issues *310*
Operational Ownership for Logging Pipelines *312*
Access Control and Integrity for Log Data *314*
AI for Telemetry Operations: Enrichment, Entity Resolution, and Quality Monitoring *315*
Building Confidence in What You Can See *317*
Conclusion *318*
Recommendations *318*

19 Continuous Monitoring and Alerting Operations *321*
Monitoring Goals and Operational Constraints *321*
Establishing Baselines and Detecting Deviations *323*
Alerting Strategy: What Should Page Someone *324*
Alert Triage, Routing, and Escalation *327*
Managing Alert Fatigue and Noise *328*
Maintaining Monitoring Rules Over Time *330*
Handoffs Between Monitoring and Investigation *332*
AI-Assisted Triage: Summarization, Prioritization, and Guardrails Against Over-Trust *334*
Building a Sustainable Monitoring Cadence *336*
Conclusion *338*
Recommendations *338*

20 Detection Engineering and Anomaly Detection *341*
Detection as a Managed Capability *341*
Building Detections from Real Threat Behaviors *343*
Tuning Detections to Reduce False Positives *344*
Measuring Detection Quality Over Volume *346*
Anomaly Detection: Strengths and Limitations *347*
Detection Gaps and How They Persist *349*
Change-Driven Breakage and Detection Maintenance *350*
AI/ML in Detection Engineering: Modeling Choices, Drift, and Explainable Output *352*
Documentation and Versioning of Detection Logic *354*
Conclusion *356*
Recommendations *356*

21 Investigation Workflow and Incident Analysis *359*
From Alert to Hypothesis: The Analyst Mindset *359*
Evidence Collection and Preservation *361*
Scoping: Determining What Is Affected *362*
Timeline Construction and Narrative Building *364*
Confirming or Refuting Suspicious Activity *366*
Working with IT, Engineering, and Business Stakeholders *367*
Knowing When to Escalate to Incident Response *369*
AI-Assisted Investigations: Evidence Summarization, Correlation, and Verification Discipline *370*
Improving Investigation Quality Over Time *372*
Conclusion *374*
Recommendations *374*

Part VI Incident Response, Recovery, and Improvement *377*

22 Building and Maintaining Incident Response Plans *379*
Purpose and Scope of an Incident Response Plan *379*
Roles, Responsibilities, and Decision Authority *381*

Communication Pathways and Escalation Rules *383*
Playbooks, Runbooks, and Practical Usability *384*
Evidence Handling and Documentation Expectations *386*
IR Readiness Testing and Exercises *387*
Maintaining Plans Through Organizational Change *389*
AI Support in IR Planning: Playbook Maintenance, Documentation, and Control Boundaries *390*
Common IR Plan Failure Modes *392*
Conclusion *393*
Recommendations *394*

23 Incident Handling and Operational Containment *397*
Detect-to-Contain Workflows *397*
Containment Strategies and Business Tradeoffs *399*
Coordinating Actions Across Multiple Teams *401*
Managing Access During Active Incidents *403*
Isolation, Blocking, and System Stabilization *404*
Working Under Uncertainty and Partial Visibility *406*
Keeping an Incident Log and Operational Timeline *407*
AI-Assisted Containment: Decision Support, Change Discipline, and Avoiding Automated Harm *409*
Avoiding Containment Actions That Increase Risk *410*
Conclusion *412*
Recommendations *412*

24 Eradication, Recovery, and Business Restoration *415*
Eradication: Removing Access and Persistence *415*
Validation of Cleanup and Return-to-Service Decisions *417*
Recovery Planning Under Pressure *420*
Restoring Systems and Monitoring for Re-Infection *421*
Handling Credential Resets and Identity Risk *423*
Balancing Speed and Confidence During Recovery *424*
Executive Updates and Business Coordination *425*
AI-Assisted Recovery Coordination: Communication, Sequencing, and Verification Controls *426*
Closing an Incident with Defensible Evidence *429*
Conclusion *430*
Recommendations *430*

25 Post-Incident Learning and Program Improvement *433*
Lessons Learned as a Core Defensive Capability *433*
Root Cause Versus Contributing Factors *434*
Control Gaps and Corrective Action Tracking *437*
Updating Detections, Policies, and Procedures After Incidents *439*
Measuring Improvement Without Gaming the Metrics *440*
Sharing Lessons Across Teams Without Blame *442*
Building Institutional Memory from Incidents *443*

AI for Post-Incident Analysis: Clustering, Trend Detection, and Evidence Integrity *445*
Turning Incidents into Long-Term Resilience *446*
Conclusion *448*
Recommendations *448*

Part VII People, Training, and Organizational Resilience *451*

26 Security Awareness and Workforce Enablement *453*
Why Human Behavior Shapes Defensive Outcomes *453*
Security Awareness Versus Security Training *455*
Common Threats Addressed Through Awareness *456*
Designing Training That Changes Behavior *458*
Engagement Techniques and Practical Reinforcement *459*
Role-Based Training for Higher-Risk Functions *460*
Measuring Participation and Real-World Impact *461*
AI in Training Programs: Content Scaling, Personalization, and Misuse Risks *463*
Maintaining Awareness in Changing Organizations *464*
Conclusion *465*
Recommendations *466*

27 Building a Culture of Cyber Resilience *469*
Resilience as a Leadership Objective *469*
Collaboration Between Security, IT, and the Business *471*
Aligning Incentives to Encourage Secure Behavior *472*
Integrating Security into Everyday Work *473*
Communicating Security Without Fear or Fatigue *474*
Establishing Accountability Without Blame *476*
Sustaining Momentum Through Wins and Setbacks *477*
AI and Culture: Trust, Transparency, and Avoiding Automation-Driven Complacency *478*
Long-Term Maturity and Continuous Improvement *480*
Conclusion *481*
Recommendations *482*

Part VIII Cloud, Hybrid, and Proactive Defense *485*

28 Cloud and Hybrid Security Foundations *487*
Understanding Cloud Security Basics *487*
Shared Responsibility as an Operational Model *488*
Hybrid Complexity and Boundary Confusion *490*
Cloud Identity and Access Considerations *492*
Visibility and Logging in Cloud Environments *494*
Cloud Misconfigurations and Common Causes *495*
Integrating Cloud Security into Blue Team Work *497*

AI-Assisted Cloud Posture: Detection, Prioritization, and Validation in Large Environments *498*
Maintaining Consistency Across Environments *500*
Conclusion *502*
Recommendations *502*

29 Securing Cloud Workloads and Cloud-Native Operations *505*
Workloads, Services, and Operational Ownership *505*
Cloud-Native Application Considerations *508*
Protecting Data in Cloud Storage and Services *509*
Network Controls and Segmentation in Cloud Context *511*
Monitoring Cloud Activity and Behavior Patterns *513*
Responding to Cloud Incidents and Access Abuse *515*
Handling Multi-Account and Multi-Environment Complexity *516*
AI-Assisted Cloud Operations: Event Correlation, Misconfiguration Detection, and Human Controls *518*
Operationalizing Cloud Security Over Time *520*
Conclusion *522*
Recommendations *522*

30 Proactive Defense and Threat Intelligence *525*
What Threat Intelligence Provides to Blue Teams *525*
Converting Intelligence into Defensive Action *526*
Prioritizing Defenses Based on Likely Threats *528*
Collaboration with Red Teams for Defensive Improvement *530*
Testing Defensive Assumptions Through Exercises *531*
Deception Concepts and Defensive Deterrence *533*
AI in Threat Intelligence: Summarization, Clustering, and Analyst Verification *534*
Integrating Proactive Defense into Operations *535*
Sustaining Proactive Work Alongside Daily Demands *537*
Conclusion *539*
Recommendations *539*

Part IX AI Governance for Blue Team Operations *541*

31 Governing AI/ML in Defensive Security *543*
Defining Acceptable Use of AI/ML in Security Operations *543*
Data Handling, Privacy, and Retention for AI-Assisted Work *545*
Human-in-the-Loop Controls and Approval Gates *547*
Validation, Testing, and Measuring AI Output Quality *548*
Managing Drift, Bias, and False Confidence *549*
Securing AI Workflows Against Prompt Injection and Data Exfiltration *551*

Auditability, Evidence, and Change Management for AI-Driven Processes *553*
Operational Playbooks for Safe AI Adoption *555*
Conclusion *556*
Recommendations *556*

Glossary *559*
Index *567*

Preface

Cybersecurity is often described in terms of tools, threats, and headlines. But the day-to-day reality of defending an organization looks different: a steady stream of alerts, competing priorities, incomplete visibility, and decisions that must be made with imperfect information. Blue team operations is the craft of turning that chaos into disciplined, repeatable work—work that reduces risk, improves resilience, and gives leaders confidence that security is not just "installed," but actively functioning.

This book is written for the people responsible for outcomes. That includes security and IT leaders who need to understand what effective defense looks like in practice, as well as practitioners who are building or maturing a security program. If you've ever asked, "What should my team be doing every day?" "How do we know our detections are working?" "What does 'operational excellence' mean for a SOC?" or "How do we communicate risk and progress without drowning in metrics?"—this book is for you.

My goal is simple: help you run defense as an operation, not a collection of disconnected activities. Throughout the chapters, you'll see an emphasis on clarity of roles, consistent processes, and measurable outputs. Blue team work spans prevention, detection, response, and continuous improvement—but it only becomes reliable when it is operationalized: defined, practiced, measured, and refined. The concepts here are meant to be practical across organization sizes and industries, whether you are standing up capability for the first time or tightening an established program.

How to Use This Book

You can read the book straight through, but it is also designed to be used as a working reference.

- **If you're a leader:** focus on the "why," the decision points, and the mechanisms that turn effort into assurance—what good looks like, what to demand from reporting, and how to evaluate maturity without relying on theater.
- **If you're building or running operations:** treat the chapters as a checklist of operating concerns—visibility, triage, detection quality, response readiness, handoffs, documentation, and improvement loops.
- **If you're improving a specific capability:** jump directly to the relevant section, then work outward to confirm the upstream and downstream dependencies that make it sustainable.

You'll notice a consistent preference for operational language over vendor language. Tools matter, but tools are replaceable. The underlying discipline—how you decide, how you execute, how you verify, and how you improve—is what endures.

A Note on Scope and Expectations

This is not a book about fear, hype, or perfect security. It is about dependable security. You won't find promises of "stopping all attacks," and you won't find a single silver bullet. Instead, you'll find a defensible approach to organizing blue team work so that it holds up under pressure: when the alert volume spikes, when staffing is thin, when the incident is ambiguous, and when leadership needs answers that are both honest and actionable.

Some readers will use these pages to build a program. Others will use them to audit one, repair one, or scale one. However you apply it, I encourage you to treat the material as a set of operational commitments: choose what you will do consistently, define what "done" means, and measure whether reality matches intent. That is how blue teams earn trust—and keep it.

Dr. Jason Edwards

Acknowledgments

I am deeply grateful to all those who have contributed to the creation of this book. First and foremost, I would like to express my heartfelt appreciation to my family for their unwavering support and understanding throughout the writing process. To my wife, Selda, and my children, Michelle, Chris, Ceylin, and Mayra, your patience and encouragement have been my anchor. I am also thankful for the love and support from my extended family: Derek, Meltem, Nilos, Ken, and my sisters Robin, Kelly, and Lynn.

I am indebted to the organizations and the many fellow educators who have been pivotal in my professional development and the success of this book: Hallmark University, Moravian University, IronCircle, Cybrary, and the more than 100K LinkedIn subscribers who follow me.

To the millions of readers and listeners who follow my cybersecurity content each year on BareMetalCyber.com, your trust and engagement are the fuel that keeps this work moving forward. Thank you for making this journey possible.

I also encourage everyone reading this to support a cause close to my heart—the Beagle Freedom Project, which fights for the rights and rescue of animals used in laboratory testing. You can learn more about their work and my children's cybersecurity book series, starring Darwin the Cyber Beagle, at CyberBeagle.kids.

To find more of my books, check out CyberAuthor.Me

About the Companion Website

This book is accompanied by a companion website:

www.wiley.com/go/edwards/cybersecurityblueteamoperations1e

To access the website materials, click on the link under Related Resources on the book's page on wiley.com. You can also find this by searching www.wiley.com for the ISBN 9781394433179.

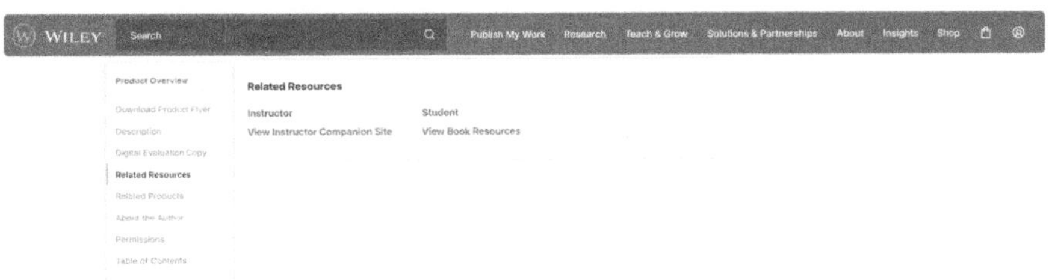

This website includes:

- Question and Answers

Part I

Foundations, Governance, and Program Design

1

The Foundations of Blue Team Operations

Defensive security is the operational practice of keeping an organization's systems and services trustworthy under constant change, persistent threat pressure, and inevitable mistakes. It draws a clear line between simply identifying risk and reliably managing it through repeatable monitoring, evidence-driven decisions, controlled containment, and disciplined recovery. In modern environments where identity is the primary control plane and telemetry arrives at overwhelming scale, success depends on balancing people, process, and technology while using automation and AI to accelerate work without surrendering accountability. The goal is not perfect prevention, but consistent defensive performance—detecting what matters, acting safely, learning quickly, and sustaining business continuity when real-world conditions are noisy and uncertain.

Origins of Blue Teaming and Why It Matters

Blue teaming emerged as an operational answer to a practical problem: organizations needed a dedicated function responsible for defending live systems, not just building them or auditing them after the fact. As networks expanded and business processes became inseparable from digital services, security failures stopped being isolated technical incidents and started becoming enterprise disruptions. The defensive role evolved from ad hoc "who can fix this?" response into a persistent capability with defined responsibilities, repeatable procedures, and measurable outcomes. Blue teaming became the umbrella for that capability, aligning people, process, and technology around keeping the business running safely.

A core reason blue teaming matters is that most organizations do not lose to dramatic, movie-style attacks; they lose to gaps in routine operations. Unpatched systems, weak authentication, misconfigurations, and inconsistent logging create a steady background of exploitable conditions that adversaries capitalize on. Blue teams reduce the time those conditions exist by creating accountability for detection, response, and hardening work that actually reaches production. The business value is straightforward: fewer outages, fewer high-impact incidents, and a smaller blast radius when something inevitably goes wrong.

Blue teaming also matters because it provides the operational bridge between risk statements and real defensive behavior. Executives may agree that ransomware, fraud, or data exposure are unacceptable, but that agreement is only meaningful when it translates into controls that function under stress. Blue teams operationalize security intent through day-to-day activities: monitoring, triage, containment, recovery, and continuous improvement of preventive controls. When those activities are run as a disciplined practice rather than an emergency reaction, the organization becomes less dependent on heroics and more resilient through routine.

The discipline of blue teaming is fundamentally about decision-making under uncertainty, and that is where consistent workflows become a force multiplier. Alerts are noisy, telemetry is incomplete, and incident narratives rarely arrive fully formed; defenders must decide what is real, what is urgent, and what is safe to ignore. Blue teaming establishes the handoffs, escalation paths, and evidence standards that prevent "gut feel" from becoming the primary control. That structure makes outcomes auditable and repeatable, which is essential in regulated environments and equally important in any organization that expects predictable operational performance.

Modern blue teams increasingly use AI/ML to improve speed and consistency in triage and correlation, but those gains only hold when the inputs and controls are sound. Models can summarize alerts, cluster related activity, and propose likely incident categories, but they are only as reliable as the underlying telemetry and labeling practices. Human-in-the-loop boundaries are non-negotiable for high-impact actions such as account disablement, network isolation, or production changes, where a confident model output can still be wrong. Failure modes include false confidence in plausible-sounding summaries, drift as environments change, bias introduced by incomplete training data, and inadvertent leakage if sensitive incident data is mishandled during model use or improvement.

Another reason blue teaming matters is that it reduces organizational fragility by treating defense as a lifecycle rather than a point-in-time assessment. Security reviews and compliance checks can identify issues, but blue teams close the loop by verifying that changes are implemented correctly, monitored effectively, and maintained over time. They provide the operational memory of the organization: what happened, how it was handled, what broke, and what needs to change to prevent recurrence. This feedback loop is one of the most effective ways to mature security because it ties lessons learned directly to engineering and operations realities.

Blue teaming also creates a shared language for security across technical and non-technical stakeholders by grounding discussions in observable events and defensible priorities. Instead of debating abstract threats, leaders can evaluate trends like incident frequency, time to detect, time to contain, and the impact of control improvements on business disruption. This enables informed tradeoffs, such as investing in better identity controls versus expanding monitoring coverage, based on operational evidence rather than intuition. When done well, blue teaming becomes a stabilizing function that increases trust in the organization's ability to withstand attacks without turning security into a blocker.

Ultimately, blue teaming matters because it is the mechanism by which an organization proves it can defend itself in the same environment it uses to operate. The goal is not perfection; it is controlled, measurable reduction of risk through prevention, detection, and response that work together under real conditions. A mature blue team is defined by clarity of responsibilities, disciplined execution, and the ability to learn faster than adversaries can iterate. That maturity directly supports business continuity by keeping incidents from becoming crises and by making the inevitable disruptions shorter, smaller, and easier to manage.

Defensive Security as an Operational Discipline

Defensive security becomes an operational discipline when it is treated as a daily production function rather than an occasional project or a periodic compliance exercise. The work is continuous because the environment is continuous: identities change, systems are patched and rebuilt, configurations drift, and business priorities shift. In that reality, defensive outcomes depend less on any single control and more on the reliability of routines that keep controls effective over time. The discipline is defined by repeatability, accountability, and the ability to execute under pressure without improvising the basics.

A disciplined defensive program starts with clear ownership of operational responsibilities and a shared understanding of what "normal operations" look like. That includes who monitors for issues, who is authorized to respond, who can change production settings, and how decisions are escalated when risk and availability collide. Without this clarity, incidents trigger confusion, duplicated effort, and delays that increase impact more than the adversary's technical sophistication ever could. Operational discipline turns security from a set of intentions into an organized capability that can be measured and improved.

Defensive operations rely on telemetry that is both intentionally collected and operationally usable, not just technically possible to generate. Logs, alerts, and contextual data are only valuable when they are timely, consistent, and tied to assets and identities the organization actually understands. A common failure mode is "observability theater," where large volumes of data exist but the team cannot answer basic questions during an incident because sources are incomplete or uncorrelated. Operational discipline prioritizes coverage and fidelity where it matters most, then enforces standards for retention, normalization, and access, so defenders can work efficiently and credibly.

Triage and prioritization are where defensive security most clearly resembles other mature operations functions: the objective is to reduce uncertainty quickly and route work appropriately. A well-run workflow distinguishes signal from noise using defined severity criteria, business impact context, and evidence thresholds that prevent overreaction. AI/ML can assist here by clustering related alerts, extracting key entities, and generating consistent summaries that reduce cognitive load during high-volume periods. Those benefits depend on disciplined feedback loops—analysts must correct model outputs, document why they overrode recommendations, and watch for drift when data sources or attacker behaviors change.

An operational discipline also requires controlled execution, especially when defensive actions can disrupt business services. Containment steps such as isolating hosts, disabling accounts, or blocking traffic must be gated by approvals and pre-defined runbooks that balance risk reduction with operational continuity. Human-in-the-loop controls are critical because automated or AI-assisted decisions can be confidently wrong, particularly when context is missing or when benign administrative activity resembles malicious behavior. The disciplined approach defines which actions can be automated safely, which require explicit authorization, and how to capture evidence, so the organization can justify decisions after the fact.

Handoffs and communication are not "soft skills" in defensive security; they are operational mechanics that determine whether incidents stay contained or spread. A disciplined team uses consistent terminology, tracks ownership through each phase of response, and ensures that escalation decisions are made with the right context at the right time. Miscommunication commonly shows up as delayed containment because operations teams fear breaking production, or as premature containment that creates outages because defenders did not understand dependencies. Operational discipline standardizes the interfaces between security, IT operations, engineering, and leadership, so decisions are faster and less error-prone.

Sustaining defensive security as an operational discipline requires measurement that reflects reality rather than vanity metrics. The most useful measures are tied to performance under real conditions: time to detect, time to contain, time to recover, recurrence of similar incidents, and the proportion of alerts that lead to meaningful action. Metrics also serve governance by making it clear where the organization is relying on luck, where coverage is thin, and where processes fail under load. When AI/ML is involved, auditability must extend to the model's role in decisions, including what data was used, how outputs were presented, and how frequently humans corrected or rejected recommendations.

Finally, an operational discipline assumes that failure will occur and treats every incident as input to improve the system rather than as an isolated event. That improvement is practical and specific: tuning detection logic, tightening access pathways, hardening configurations, and refining runbooks, so the next response is faster and safer. The defensive function matures when those improvements are integrated into normal operational change processes, not left as aspirational "lessons learned" that never translate into action. Over time, the organization becomes harder to surprise, not because threats disappear, but because defensive security behaves like a well-run operations team that continuously reduces risk through disciplined execution.

Differences Between Offensive and Defensive Security

Offensive and defensive security differ first in their objectives and therefore in how success is defined. Offensive work is designed to find and demonstrate ways a system can fail, often within a scoped engagement that has a defined start, end, and set of rules. Defensive work is designed to keep systems functioning safely every day, including during unexpected conditions, incomplete information, and competing business priorities. Where offense can declare victory by proving a path to impact, defense must sustain performance over time and under constant change.

The two disciplines also operate under different constraints of time and completeness. Offensive security can be deliberate, choosing targets, chaining steps, and refining techniques until a desired outcome is achieved within the engagement window. Defensive security rarely has the luxury of full context; it must act quickly with partial evidence, while adversaries can change tactics midstream. That asymmetry forces defenders to build workflows that tolerate ambiguity, including escalation paths, confidence thresholds, and mechanisms for reversing actions that might disrupt production.

Scope and surface area further separate the two. Offensive teams can focus on what is most likely to yield results—high-value targets, exposed services, or weak identity paths—because their job is to uncover risk, not to cover every corner. Defensive teams must assume that anything connected to business operations may become relevant, even obscure systems, legacy integrations, or rarely used accounts. This reality drives defensive emphasis on asset inventory, identity governance, logging coverage, and operational hygiene, because unknown or unmanaged components tend to become the easiest entry points.

Another key difference is the relationship to stability and change. Offensive work often benefits from novelty and flexibility: a new exploit path, a creative bypass, or an unusual chain of conditions can be the differentiator. Defensive work benefits from consistency: predictable processes, standardized configurations, and controlled change management reduce the number of exploitable states that exist at any moment. Defenders frequently prioritize reducing variance—closing exceptions, minimizing bespoke configurations, and enforcing baselines—because attackers thrive on the irregularities that operational sprawl creates.

The evidence standards and documentation expectations also diverge in important ways. Offensive engagements typically produce a narrative: what was found, how it was exploited, and what impact could occur, supported by artifacts like screenshots, logs, or proof-of-access. Defensive operations produce records that must stand up during real incidents: timelines, decisions, containment actions, recovery steps, and post-incident corrective work. That defensive record is not just for reporting; it is how teams coordinate across shifts, justify disruptive actions, and demonstrate due care to leadership and stakeholders.

AI/ML introduces different opportunities and risks on each side of the equation, largely because the incentives are different. Offensive operators can use AI to accelerate reconnaissance, summarize target documentation, generate plausible attack hypotheses, and prototype scripts faster, but the outputs still require expert validation because small errors can derail an operation. Defensive teams can use AI to reduce alert fatigue through clustering, enrichment, and summarization, but must be more cautious because automation can trigger outages or inappropriate access changes if it is wrong. Defensive AI use demands explicit human-in-the-loop approval boundaries, careful handling of sensitive telemetry, and monitoring for drift, so models do not become less reliable as environments and attacker behaviors evolve.

Operational tempo and staffing models reinforce the distinction. Offensive teams are often structured around planned engagements and deliverables, with a rhythm that supports deeper research and iterative testing. Defensive teams are built around continuous coverage and rapid coordination, including on-call rotations, incident command structures, and integration with IT operations and engineering. The defensive posture requires readiness and resilience: the ability to absorb surges in alert volume, execute containment safely, and return systems to stable operation without losing track of investigative rigor.

Finally, the two disciplines produce different kinds of organizational value, and misunderstanding that difference creates friction. Offensive security is invaluable for discovery—showing what can break, where assumptions fail, and how high-impact paths might look in practice. Defensive security is invaluable for control—reducing the probability of compromise, limiting blast radius, and ensuring that when incidents occur the organization responds with speed and confidence. The healthiest security programs treat these as complementary: offense informs defensive priorities, and defense validates whether improvements actually work in real operations.

Core Principles of Defensive Security

Defensive security rests on the principle of assumed breach: operate as if compromise is plausible today, not as a hypothetical future state. That mindset shifts attention from perfect prevention to resilient operations, where detection, containment, and recovery are treated as primary controls rather than emergency measures. It drives organizations to validate that identity controls, logging, and response workflows work under realistic conditions, including partial failures and degraded visibility. Assumed breach also reduces the cultural tendency to dismiss early warning signs because "that shouldn't be possible here."

Another core principle is coverage before sophistication, meaning foundational controls must be reliable across the environment before advanced techniques can be trusted. If asset inventory is incomplete, identity governance is inconsistent, or critical telemetry is missing, even the best detection logic will fail in practice because it cannot see what matters. Defensive maturity is often limited by basic gaps: unmanaged endpoints, unknown cloud resources, orphaned accounts, and brittle logging pipelines. The disciplined approach is to establish consistent baselines and expand coverage deliberately, rather than chasing complex detections that only work in ideal conditions.

Signal integrity is a defining principle because defensive decisions are only as good as the evidence supporting them. Logs and alerts must be time-synchronized, attributable to identities and assets, and retained long enough to reconstruct events without guesswork. Inconsistent parsing, missing fields, and unreliable timestamps create false narratives that slow response and increase business impact. Defenders prioritize telemetry that supports investigation and action, not just collection volume, and they treat monitoring pipelines as production services that require uptime, testing, and change control.

A practical defensive program also follows the principle of least privilege as an operational reality, not a static design goal. Access must be constrained to what roles require, but it must also adapt as teams, vendors, and systems change, or else privilege accumulates through exceptions and temporary grants. The most damaging compromises often leverage legitimate access paths, making identity hygiene as important as patching. Defensive teams succeed when they can rapidly answer who has access to what, how that access is used, and which changes are anomalous or unsafe.

Containment discipline is another core principle: actions that limit attacker movement must be executable quickly, safely, and consistently. Containment is not just a technical step; it is a controlled decision about interrupting activity without causing unnecessary outages or destroying evidence. Mature teams predefine what triggers containment, what approvals are required, and what rollback options exist if an action has unintended consequences. This discipline reduces the risk of both underreaction, where attackers persist, and overreaction, where defenders create the outage they were trying to prevent.

Human judgment remains central even as automation and AI/ML become more common, which makes governance a principle rather than an afterthought. AI can accelerate triage by summarizing alerts, linking related events, and proposing likely causes, but it can also introduce failure modes such as false confidence, bias toward familiar patterns, and degraded performance as systems and attack techniques evolve. Defensive use requires human-in-the-loop checkpoints for high-impact actions and a clear record of how model outputs influenced decisions. Auditability matters because leaders must be able to explain not only what was done, but why it was done and what evidence supported it.

Defensive security also depends on the principle of continuous improvement through feedback loops that connect incidents to concrete changes. Investigation is only half the work; the other half is translating lessons into configuration fixes, access tightening, detection tuning, and operational process changes that reduce recurrence. Without that loop, organizations relive the same incidents with slightly different indicators and gradually normalize failure. Effective teams treat post-incident work as operational debt repayment, prioritizing changes that eliminate entire classes of issues rather than patching symptoms.

Finally, defensive security is anchored in business alignment, not in abstract technical perfection. Controls exist to protect mission-critical services, sensitive data, and organizational trust, and decisions must reflect what the business can tolerate in terms of disruption and risk. That alignment shows up in how severity is defined, how response is authorized, and how investments are prioritized across prevention, detection, and recovery. When defensive principles are operationalized with this balance, security becomes a stabilizing capability that supports the organization's ability to operate safely under real-world pressure.

Blue Team Roles and Responsibilities in Modern Environments

Blue team roles exist to turn defensive intent into reliable daily operations across systems that are distributed, constantly changing, and deeply intertwined with business workflows. In modern environments, "the blue team" is rarely a single group sitting behind a console; it is a set of responsibilities that may be shared across security operations, cloud and platform teams, identity teams, and incident response leadership. The unifying thread is accountability for outcomes: the organization can detect meaningful threats, make sound decisions quickly, contain safely, and recover with evidence and learning intact. Clear role definition prevents two common failures—everyone assuming someone else owns a problem, or multiple teams acting independently and creating confusion during incidents.

The security operations function typically owns continuous monitoring, triage, and the initial coordination of response activities. That includes validating alerts against available telemetry, determining whether activity represents true compromise or benign behavior, and initiating containment actions when predefined thresholds are met. In practice, this role depends on disciplined queue management, consistent severity definitions, and a documented approach to evidence collection so that cases can be handed off without losing context. In high-volume environments, AI/ML can assist by deduplicating related alerts, extracting entities such as accounts and hosts, and generating structured summaries, but analysts must remain responsible for final classification and escalation decisions. Table 1.1 summarizes how modern blue team responsibilities map to operational outcomes across monitoring detection response and recovery.

Detection engineering and content development responsibilities focus on building and maintaining the logic that turns telemetry into reliable signal. This role is less about "writing rules" and more about understanding attacker behaviors, mapping them to available data sources, and validating that detections are both effective and maintainable as the environment evolves. Detection engineers also manage the operational lifecycle of detections: testing changes, tuning to reduce noise, and ensuring that alerts produce actionable context rather than vague warnings. When AI-assisted correlation or anomaly detection is used, this function must also govern training data quality, monitor for drift, and document model behavior, so the organization can explain why an alert was generated.

Table 1.1 Blue Team Roles and Responsibilities in Modern Environments.

Role	Primary Focus	Core Outputs	Key Handoffs
Security operations	Continuous monitoring and triage	Case creation and escalation decisions	Incident response leadership
Detection engineering	Detection logic lifecycle	Validated detections and tuned alerting	Security operations
Incident response leadership	Command and control during incidents	Decision authority and coordinated execution	IT operations and engineering
Identity and access	Identity control-plane operations	Session revocation and privilege changes	Security operations and incident response leadership
Platform endpoint cloud security	Hardening and recovery execution	Secure baselines and trusted rebuilds	Incident response leadership

Incident response leadership provides command and control when activity crosses the threshold from routine investigation to business-impacting event. This role establishes decision authority, sets incident objectives, coordinates cross-functional teams, and ensures that containment and recovery actions align with business priorities and legal or regulatory obligations. Effective incident leadership also ensures that parallel workstreams do not conflict—for example, that containment does not destroy evidence needed for root-cause analysis, and that recovery does not reintroduce compromised configurations. In modern hybrid environments, this role must be fluent in identity-driven incidents, cloud control-plane threats, and third-party access complications, because the most consequential decisions often involve access pathways rather than single endpoints.

Identity and access responsibilities are now central to blue team operations because identity has become the dominant control plane for both attackers and defenders. Whether this function sits within security or IT, it owns the processes that determine how accounts are created, authenticated, privileged, monitored, and revoked across workforce and non-human identities. During incidents, identity teams execute high-risk actions—credential resets, session revocation, privilege removal, and access policy changes—that can stop attacker movement but can also interrupt legitimate business activity. Modern environments amplify the need for discipline here: federated identity, single sign-on dependencies, and token-based access mean that responders must understand how to invalidate access safely and completely, not just change a password.

Platform, endpoint, and cloud security responsibilities translate defensive requirements into hardened, operable configurations across infrastructure that is increasingly managed as code. These roles ensure that systems are built with secure defaults, that patching and configuration management are reliable, and that monitoring hooks are present, so defenders can see and act when needed. They also play a critical role during recovery by rebuilding systems from trusted sources, validating that persistence mechanisms are removed, and ensuring that restored services do not reintroduce the original weakness. When environments rely on automation pipelines, these teams must ensure that blue team actions can be executed through controlled mechanisms rather than one-off manual changes that create drift and future risk.

Threat intelligence and threat-hunting responsibilities help the blue team prioritize and validate defensive focus, but their value is operational only when tied to concrete decisions. Intelligence functions translate external observations into internal relevance by identifying which threats match the organization's technology footprint and business context, then guiding collection and detection improvements accordingly. Hunting functions proactively search for evidence of compromise using hypotheses grounded in likely attacker behaviors and known gaps in detection coverage. AI/ML can accelerate both by summarizing large volumes of telemetry and identifying patterns across cases, but success still depends on disciplined scoping, careful interpretation, and a requirement to produce outputs that drive action—new detections, improved visibility, or validated absence of activity.

Across all roles, modern blue teaming requires explicit governance of decision boundaries, particularly where automation and AI influence outcomes. Teams must define which actions can be automated safely, which require human approval, and how to document the reasoning and evidence for decisions that affect production systems or user access. They must also manage failure modes: false positives that generate operational churn, false negatives that create complacency, and model-driven recommendations that sound authoritative but lack sufficient grounding. When roles and responsibilities are clearly defined, practiced, and audited, blue team operations scale with the environment rather than being overwhelmed by it, and defensive security becomes a reliable business capability instead of an episodic scramble.

Balancing People, Process, and Technology in Defensive Programs

Defensive programs fail most often when one pillar—people, process, or technology—outpaces the others and creates a brittle dependency. Organizations can buy capable tools, hire talented analysts, or publish polished procedures and still struggle if those elements are not integrated into a coherent operating model. Balance does not mean equal investment; it means that each pillar is strong enough to support the others under real operational stress. The practical test is whether the program can detect, decide, act, and recover predictably when conditions are noisy, incomplete, and time-sensitive.

People are the adaptive component of defense, and their effectiveness depends on clear roles, realistic workload, and a culture that rewards disciplined execution rather than heroics. Analysts and engineers need authority aligned to responsibility, including the ability to escalate quickly and the confidence that leadership will support evidence-based containment decisions. Training must be tied to the environment defenders actually operate, not generic scenarios that ignore identity dependencies, cloud-control planes, and business-critical service constraints. Retention and continuity matter operationally because institutional knowledge—how systems behave, where telemetry fails, and what past incidents looked like—often determines whether a team moves quickly or stalls.

Process converts individual skill into organizational capability by standardizing how work is performed and handed off. Strong processes define what constitutes an incident, how severity is assigned, what evidence is required for key decisions, and how containment and recovery actions are authorized. They reduce the cognitive load of "figuring it out" in the moment and prevent inconsistent outcomes across shifts or teams. Process should be treated as a living system that evolves through post-incident improvements, not as a static binder of procedures that no one consults until something breaks.

Technology provides scale and speed, but only when it is implemented and operated as part of a disciplined workflow. Telemetry collection, alerting, and response mechanisms must be engineered for reliability, including coverage validation, time synchronization, and controlled changes to detection logic. Tools that generate high volumes of low-quality alerts can consume the team's capacity and create a false sense of activity without meaningful risk reduction. Technology should reduce time to understanding and time to action, not merely increase the number of events the organization can store.

AI/ML can improve balance when used to amplify judgment rather than replace it, especially in triage, correlation, and case management. Models can group related alerts, extract key entities and timelines, and draft incident narratives that make investigations faster and more consistent across analysts. Those benefits depend on disciplined inputs—well-labeled outcomes, stable telemetry sources, and feedback loops where humans correct errors and document why they disagreed with model recommendations. Without governance, AI introduces failure modes that directly undermine balance, including overconfidence in fluent summaries, drift as the environment changes, and inadvertent leakage of sensitive incident data into model training or external services.

A balanced program also acknowledges that defensive work is a production workload with finite capacity, requiring explicit prioritization rather than an attempt to do everything. Processes should include a clear path for de-scoping low-value alerts, deferring non-critical investigations, and focusing effort where business impact is highest. People must be empowered to make those tradeoffs without fear that reducing noise will be perceived as lowering security, and technology must support it through suppression mechanisms, enrichment, and consistent severity criteria. When prioritization is absent, the team's attention becomes the scarce resource that adversaries exploit by creating distraction and forcing reactive behavior.

Cross-functional integration is where balance becomes visible, because defensive programs do not operate in isolation from IT operations, engineering, and leadership. People need established relationships and communication patterns, so security decisions do not stall in negotiation during an incident. Processes must define how changes are requested, reviewed, implemented, and verified across teams, especially when containment actions might disrupt production services. Technology must enable secure and efficient collaboration through shared case context and reliable access to evidence, while still enforcing least privilege and preserving chain-of-custody expectations for sensitive artifacts.

Sustaining balance requires measurement that reflects the health of all three pillars rather than focusing exclusively on tool outputs or staffing levels. Useful indicators include response timeliness, alert-to-action ratios, recurrence of similar incidents, and the stability of telemetry pipelines and detection content over time. Leadership should look for signs of imbalance—chronic backlog, frequent process bypasses, excessive

Table 1.2 Automation and AI-Assisted Workflow Boundaries.

Workflow Activity	Typical Method	Impact Level	Control Boundary
Case enrichment and normalization	Automation	Low	Preapproved run logic
Alert clustering and summarization	AI assisted	Low to medium	Analyst validation required
Severity recommendation	AI assisted	Medium	Human decides final severity
Account disablement	Automation optional	High	Explicit approval required
Host isolation	Automation optional	High	Explicit approval required
Production access policy change	Manual execution	High	Escalation and authorization required

false positives, or repeated outages from poorly governed actions—and treat them as operational risks, not as individual performance problems. When people, process, and technology reinforce each other, defensive security scales with modern environments and produces outcomes that are resilient, explainable, and aligned to business continuity. Table 1.2 distinguishes low-risk automated steps from high-impact actions that require explicit human approval.

Automation and AI-Assisted Workflows: Capabilities, Limits, and Accountability

Automation and AI-assisted workflows have become essential in defensive programs because modern environments generate more events than humans can triage manually with consistent quality. The value is not simply speed; it is repeatability under load, where routine enrichment and routing happen the same way every time regardless of staffing levels or alert spikes. Automation covers deterministic tasks such as collecting related telemetry, normalizing fields, opening cases, and triggering low-risk containment steps. AI assistance becomes useful where the inputs are messy and the output is a judgment aid—summarizing activity, correlating weak signals, and proposing likely next steps, so analysts can focus on decisions rather than data wrangling.

In practical terms, the strongest AI use cases in blue team workflows concentrate on triage acceleration and context building. Models can extract entities from alerts, build timelines from disparate events, and draft concise narratives that explain what happened in plain operational language. They can also cluster similar alerts across users or endpoints, helping teams identify campaigns, misconfigurations, or recurring failure patterns that would otherwise appear as isolated noise. These capabilities reduce cognitive load and improve consistency, particularly for organizations with multiple analysts, rotating shifts, or distributed teams.

The limits of automation and AI show up at the boundaries where incorrect actions create business disruption or destroy investigative value. Automated decisions can be confidently wrong because security signals are often ambiguous, and benign administrative activity can resemble malicious behavior at the event level. AI outputs are especially vulnerable to "false coherence," where a fluent summary implies certainty that the evidence does not justify. As a result, mature programs treat AI-generated conclusions as hypotheses that must be validated against raw telemetry and established evidence standards, not as authoritative findings.

Telemetry quality is the hidden dependency that determines whether automation and AI improve outcomes or amplify chaos. If timestamps are inconsistent, identities are not well resolved, or asset context is incomplete, automated enrichment will build misleading narratives and send responders down the wrong path. AI models trained or tuned on incomplete or biased data will reinforce those distortions, over-prioritizing familiar patterns while missing novel or underrepresented behaviors. Operationally, this means teams must manage data pipelines like production services: validated collection, consistent normalization, controlled schema changes, and routine checks that confirm the inputs are still fit for purpose.

Human-in-the-loop controls define the safety boundary between assistance and action. Low-risk steps—such as adding context to a case, tagging likely false positives, or requesting additional logs—can often be automated with minimal downside. High-impact steps—disabling accounts, isolating hosts, blocking network routes, or modifying production access policies—require explicit approvals, dual control, or escalation depending on business criticality. The goal is not to slow response; it is to ensure that disruptive actions are supported by evidence and aligned with authority, especially when AI suggests a course of action that sounds plausible but may be incomplete.

Accountability is the operational requirement that keeps automation from becoming a blame-shifting mechanism. Someone must own the decision chain for every meaningful action, even when the triggering event was automated or AI-assisted. That ownership includes defining what evidence thresholds are required for specific actions, documenting who approved them, and capturing what data and reasoning informed the decision at the time it was made. When AI is involved, accountability also means recording how the output was used—whether it merely summarized context, influenced severity, or directly recommended containment—so the organization can evaluate the tool's impact and refine its use.

Governance and auditability become more demanding when automation and AI are embedded in workflows because the organization must be able to explain outcomes to leadership, regulators, and internal stakeholders. Auditable systems preserve decision artifacts: the alert content, enrichment sources, model outputs, human notes, approvals, and subsequent actions, all tied to a consistent case record. This is particularly important when models change over time through updates or tuning, because drift can cause the same scenario to be interpreted differently month to month. A defensible program treats model configuration, prompt templates, and enrichment logic as controlled operational assets with versioning, change review, and rollback capability.

Finally, effective programs treat automation and AI as continuous improvement mechanisms rather than one-time deployments. Teams should measure whether automation reduces time to triage, improves alert-to-action ratios, and decreases recurrence by enabling more consistent follow-through on lessons learned. They should also actively monitor for negative effects, such as increased false positives, overreliance on AI summaries, or silent failures in telemetry pipelines that feed automated decisions. When capabilities, limits, and accountability are defined clearly, automation and AI become force multipliers that strengthen defensive operations without eroding trust, safety, or decision integrity.

Defining Success in Defensive Operations

Success in defensive operations is measured by reliable outcomes under real conditions, not by the presence of tools or the volume of activity. A mature program can detect meaningful threats in time to matter, make decisions that balance risk and business continuity, and execute containment and recovery with minimal collateral damage. This framing matters because defensive work is inherently asymmetrical: adversaries only need one path, while defenders must maintain coverage across many paths. Defining success as operational performance keeps the focus on what the organization can consistently do, even when information is incomplete and pressure is high.

The first practical indicator of success is whether the organization can distinguish signal from noise without exhausting its people. That does not mean eliminating false positives, which is unrealistic in complex environments, but it does mean that alert volume is manageable and that triage produces stable, evidence-based dispositions. When investigations repeatedly stall due to missing telemetry, poor asset context, or unclear severity criteria, the system is not operating successfully regardless of how many alerts it generates. Success shows up as predictable triage behavior: cases are enriched quickly, routed correctly, and either escalated with evidence or closed with defensible rationale.

Speed is part of success, but it must be the right kind of speed—time to understand and time to act, not time to click. Effective teams reduce time to detect and time to contain for incidents that matter, while avoiding premature actions that create outages or destroy evidence. This requires clear decision thresholds and practiced containment playbooks that can be executed safely, including rollback paths when business disruption is unavoidable. If

Table 1.3 Defining Success in Defensive Operations.

Success Indicator	What It Demonstrates	Common Failure It Prevents	Operational Emphasis
Manageable signal-to-noise ratio	Sustainable triage quality	Analyst burnout and missed incidents	Consistent evidence-based dispositions
Time to detect and contain	Timely interruption of attacker activity	Persistent adversary presence	Practiced containment workflows
Resilience under degraded conditions	Continuity during partial visibility	Paralysis during outages	Redundancy in process and staffing
Recurrence reduction	Learning translated into change	Repeat incidents of same class	Closed loop improvement
Telemetry pipeline reliability	Trustworthy investigation inputs	False narratives from bad data	Validation and controlled changes

containment consistently relies on improvisation or on a single individual's expertise, success is fragile and will not scale. Table 1.3 links practical success indicators to the common operational breakdowns they are meant to prevent.

Another defining element is resilience, meaning the program continues to function when conditions are degraded. Degraded conditions can include partial logging outages, misconfigurations introduced by urgent business changes, cloud service interruptions, or simultaneous incidents that compete for attention. Successful defensive operations have redundancy in people and process: multiple analysts can run the workflow, escalation paths are clear, and critical evidence sources are monitored as production dependencies. Resilience also includes the ability to recover services quickly and safely, restoring trusted states without reintroducing the weakness that allowed compromise in the first place.

Defensive success is also reflected in the program's ability to reduce repeat incidents through disciplined learning and follow-through. The point of investigation is not simply to close a ticket; it is to translate what was observed into durable improvements in prevention, detection, and response. When the same classes of failures recur—phishing-driven credential abuse, exposed remote access, misconfigured permissions—without measurable reduction, the program is operating reactively rather than effectively. Success includes a functioning feedback loop where lessons become changes, changes are validated, and the operational baseline actually improves over time. Figure 1.1 shows how defensive success is defined by operational outcomes and the concrete indicators that prove those outcomes in practice. It reinforces that success is not tool presence or alert volume, but reliable performance under real conditions including degraded visibility and competing incidents.

AI-assisted workflows can improve success metrics when they are governed and measured as part of operations rather than treated as a shortcut. Models can reduce time to triage by summarizing evidence, correlating related activity, and standardizing case narratives, but success requires that humans remain accountable for decisions and that model outputs are routinely validated. A key success criterion is whether AI reduces cognitive load without increasing error rates or producing false confidence that leads to inappropriate actions. If teams cannot explain how AI influenced a decision, cannot audit outputs, or cannot detect drift, then the apparent efficiency gain is masking risk.

Success must be defined in terms that leadership can understand without reducing it to purely financial or purely technical language. Leaders need to know whether the organization can keep critical services operating, protect sensitive data, and respond decisively when those priorities are threatened. Defensive teams support that understanding through a small number of stable performance measures that reflect operational reality, such as timeliness of detection and containment, recurrence rates, and the health of telemetry and response pipelines. The

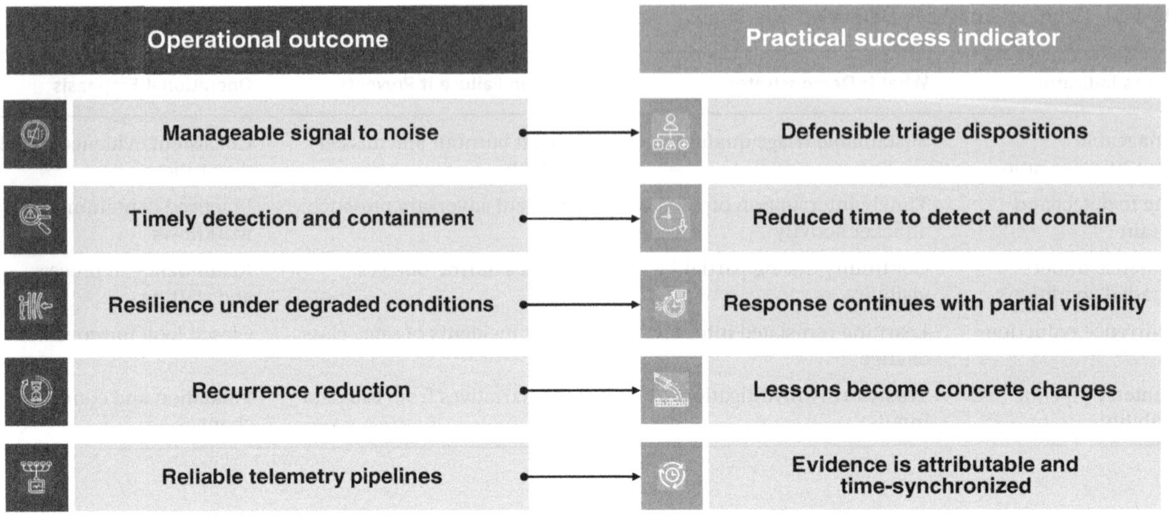

Figure 1.1 Defining Success in Defensive Operations.

most successful programs make those measures boring in the best sense: predictable, explainable, and improving in a way that demonstrates the organization is becoming harder to surprise.

Finally, success in defensive operations is demonstrated by trust—trust between security and operations teams, trust from leadership, and trust within the defensive team itself. That trust is built when decisions are evidence-based, actions are proportionate, and outcomes are documented well enough that the organization can learn and justify its response. It is strengthened when the program works consistently across shifts, when escalations are timely and clear, and when mistakes lead to improved controls rather than blame. When success is defined and measured this way, defensive operations become a dependable business capability, not an episodic reaction to incidents.

Conclusion

The foundations of blue team operations are ultimately about operational reliability: the ability to protect the business through consistent detection, disciplined decision-making, and controlled action under pressure. Clear roles and responsibilities prevent confusion during incidents, while well-engineered processes turn individual skill into repeatable outcomes that scale across shifts and teams. Automation and AI-assisted workflows can meaningfully reduce friction in triage and correlation, but only when grounded in high-quality telemetry, governed decision boundaries, and auditable accountability for every significant action. When defensive success is defined as sustained performance—lower recurrence, faster containment, safer recovery, and resilient operations—the organization becomes harder to surprise, quicker to stabilize, and better able to operate confidently in modern threat conditions.

Recommendations

1) Treat defensive security as a production operation, not an occasional project. Establish daily routines for monitoring, triage, containment readiness, and recovery coordination, so outcomes

remain consistent under load. Align ownership, so operational gaps do not get deferred indefinitely or bounced between teams. Review how well these routines held up after real incidents and adjust them as part of normal operations.

2) Define clear roles and decision authority across security, IT operations, engineering, and identity functions. Document who owns monitoring, detection content, incident command, and disruptive actions such as account disablement or host isolation. Make escalation paths explicit, so approvals do not become bottlenecks during high-impact events. Validate the model during exercises and real incidents by checking whether handoffs preserved context and accountability.
3) Prioritize coverage and reliability of foundational controls before pursuing sophistication. Confirm that asset awareness, identity hygiene, and telemetry collection are complete enough to support investigations in practice. Treat logging and enrichment pipelines as production services with uptime expectations and controlled changes. Use operational evidence to focus improvements where gaps most often prevent timely decisions.
4) Establish evidence standards for triage and escalation to reduce "gut feel" decisions. Require analysts to tie severity and recommended actions to observable telemetry, asset context, and identity attribution. Standardize how cases are documented, so they can be handed off without losing investigative value. Audit a sample of closed and escalated cases to ensure dispositions are defensible and consistent.
5) Implement containment discipline with predefined thresholds, approvals, and rollback paths. Specify which actions are low risk and can be executed quickly, and which actions require explicit authorization due to potential business disruption. Ensure containment preserves investigative value by avoiding unnecessary destruction of evidence. Practice these steps, so responders can act decisively without improvising during critical moments.
6) Use automation to eliminate repetitive work, not to outsource accountability. Automate deterministic enrichment, routing, and case creation where errors are low impact and benefits are immediate. Keep humans responsible for high-impact decisions and ensure every meaningful action has an identifiable owner. Track where automation fails or produces noise, and treat those failures as operational defects to fix.
7) Integrate AI assistance where it improves triage consistency, and gate it where it can cause harm. Use AI/ML for summarization, clustering, and timeline construction to reduce analyst cognitive load and improve case quality. Enforce human-in-the-loop boundaries for disruptive actions and require validation against raw telemetry when AI outputs imply certainty. Monitor for drift and false confidence by regularly reviewing cases where AI recommendations were accepted or rejected.
8) Protect signal integrity by enforcing consistent timestamps, attribution, and context across telemetry sources. Ensure events can be tied to specific identities and assets quickly, especially in identity-driven incidents. Treat missing fields, inconsistent parsing, and unreliable clocks as security-impacting operational issues. Verify that retention and access controls allow responders to reconstruct timelines without guesswork.
9) Build resilience for degraded conditions and competing incidents. Plan for partial telemetry outages, unexpected changes, and alert spikes by ensuring processes, staffing, and escalation paths still function. Avoid single points of failure in expertise by cross-training and documenting critical workflows. Evaluate resilience by looking at how performance changes when visibility is incomplete or when multiple investigations run in parallel.
10) Institutionalize a feedback loop that converts incidents into durable improvements. Translate investigative findings into concrete changes in configurations, access pathways, detection tuning, and response procedures. Track recurrence of similar incident patterns as a measure of whether improvements are actually reducing risk. Treat unresolved post-incident actions as operational debt and prioritize repayment where it most affects detection, containment, and recovery outcomes.

2

Governance and Leadership for Defensive Security

Governance and leadership determine defensive outcomes because they set the conditions under which security work is prioritized, funded, executed, and measured long before an incident begins. When decision rights, accountability, and operating expectations are explicit, blue teams can act quickly and consistently under pressure, and the business can make informed tradeoffs instead of absorbing risk by default. This chapter connects governance artifacts and leadership behaviors to real operational performance, showing how policies, standards, procedures, and oversight translate into durable control health and repeatable response. It also establishes how AI-enabled decision support can accelerate defensive work without eroding accountability, by insisting on evidence, validation, and human approval boundaries where business impact is material.

Why Governance Determines Defensive Outcomes

Defensive security succeeds or fails long before an alert fires. Governance is the mechanism that converts executive intent into operating conditions: what gets prioritized, what is funded, what is tolerated, and what is measured. Without it, teams default to local optimization—closing tickets, tuning tools, or "hunting" for interesting activity—while systemic exposure accumulates in identity, endpoints, cloud control planes, and third-party access. Strong governance does not slow responders down; it reduces ambiguity so that decisions made under pressure are consistent, defendable, and aligned to business risk. Figure 2.1 shows how executive intent becomes operational reality through governance artifacts and accountability. It reinforces that defensive outcomes are shaped by priorities, decision rights, and measurement long before an incident occurs.

Accountability is the first governance outcome that matters operationally. When ownership for telemetry, access controls, vulnerability remediation, and incident decision-making is unclear, gaps become "everyone's job," which means they become no one's job. Clear accountability also defines handoffs: who must be notified, who must approve disruption, and who is empowered to accept residual risk when a fix is not immediately feasible. This is especially critical in defensive work because the cost of delay is often invisible until it becomes an outage, breach, or regulatory disclosure. Executives do not need to know the mechanics of detection engineering to govern effectively, but they do need unambiguous responsibility lines and escalation thresholds.

Governance also determines the quality of defensive decisions by shaping the evidence the team can rely on. If logging, asset inventories, and identity records are incomplete or inconsistent, incident handling becomes guesswork and retrospectives become blame-oriented debates. A governed environment establishes minimum telemetry and data quality standards, along with ongoing checks that those standards are met as infrastructure changes. It also sets expectations for context enrichment—linking alerts to asset criticality, ownership, and exposure—so triage is driven by business impact rather than alert volume. In practice, better evidence reduces mean time to understand, not just mean time to respond.

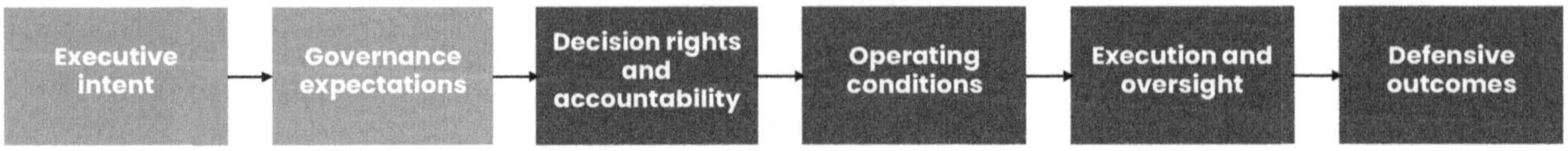

Figure 2.1 Governance to Defensive Outcomes Decision Chain.

Resource allocation is another place where governance decides outcomes, because defensive capacity is always finite. A governance model that funds only reactive work teaches the organization to accept chronic instability, where emergencies crowd out improvement. Conversely, governance that explicitly protects time for preventive maintenance—patching, hardening, detection tuning, identity cleanup, and tabletop exercises—creates compounding returns. The goal is not perfection but managed exposure: knowingly choosing which risks are carried and which are reduced, based on operational constraints and business priorities. When those tradeoffs are explicit, teams can stop treating every finding as a fire drill and start running a sustainable defense program.

Measurement is where governance becomes real, and poorly chosen metrics can quietly sabotage the entire program. Counting alerts, tickets closed, or tools deployed rewards activity, not outcomes, and it encourages teams to optimize for volume rather than risk reduction. Effective governance uses measures that reflect defensive performance and readiness, such as time to detect meaningful activity, time to contain credible incidents, coverage of critical assets, and the rate at which recurring failure patterns are eliminated. These measures must be interpretable by leaders and actionable by operators; otherwise, they become reporting theater. Good metrics also create a feedback loop where leaders see the operational cost of underfunded areas and can make informed investment decisions.

AI and machine learning can strengthen or weaken defensive governance depending on how they are controlled. AI-assisted triage, correlation, and summarization can help reduce analyst fatigue and speed decision-making, but only when the underlying telemetry is reliable and the model's outputs are treated as decision support rather than authority. Governance should define where human approval is mandatory, such as containment actions that disrupt business operations, changes to access entitlements, or incident severity declarations that trigger external communications. It should also anticipate failure modes: confident-sounding hallucinations in narrative summaries, drift when environments change, bias toward overrepresented alert types, and leakage risks when sensitive incident content is entered into systems without clear data-handling boundaries. Auditability matters here; leaders should expect traceable rationale for AI-influenced decisions, including what data was used, what outputs were generated, and who approved the resulting action.

Finally, governance sets the organization's tolerance for operational friction and ambiguity, which directly affects incident outcomes. If leaders have not pre-decided acceptable disruption levels—isolating a host, disabling an account, blocking a business-critical integration—responders either hesitate or act inconsistently, both of which increase impact. A governed response posture establishes decision rights, communication pathways, and pre-authorized actions so that teams can move quickly without improvising policy during a crisis. It also normalizes learning loops: recurring issues are treated as governance failures to correct, not individual mistakes to punish. In mature environments, governance is not paperwork; it is the steady pressure that keeps defensive work aligned, measurable, and resilient under stress.

Security Decision-Making and Accountability Models

Security decision-making is a practical discipline: it determines who can authorize changes, who can accept risk, and who is responsible when controls fail. In well-run organizations, decisions are not made by whoever is loudest or closest to the problem in the moment. They follow an accountability model that ties authority to business impact and operational responsibility, so security actions are consistent under pressure. This matters because defensive work is full of tradeoffs—speed versus certainty, containment versus availability, and immediate fixes versus durable remediation. When those tradeoffs are governed, responders spend less time negotiating and more time executing.

Accountability models start with a clear separation between control ownership and control operation. Ownership means being responsible for the effectiveness of a control domain—identity, endpoint hardening, logging, vulnerability remediation, cloud configuration—even if day-to-day tasks are delegated. Operation means running the control: implementing changes, monitoring health, and responding to exceptions. Without that separation, teams either centralize everything in security, which does not scale, or decentralize without guardrails, which creates inconsistent outcomes. The operational reality is that defensive security depends on infrastructure and application teams doing secure work as part of normal delivery, not as a favor to the security function. A strong model clarifies what security decides, what it advises, and what it verifies.

Decision rights must be aligned to the risk surface, not to org charts or historical habit. Routine decisions—standard patches, routine log forwarding, baseline access provisioning—should be delegated and automated where possible, because bottlenecks in basic hygiene create exploitable lag. High-impact decisions—disabling privileged accounts, isolating critical servers, blocking network paths, declaring an incident severity level—need defined authorities and escalation paths. The most common failure mode is leaving "who can approve disruption" ambiguous, which forces responders to seek permission in real time while adversaries continue operating. A mature model defines decision thresholds and the minimum evidence required to act, so decisive containment is not mistaken for recklessness. Table 2.1 shows how to assign decision rights evidence thresholds and documentation expectations for common defensive actions.

Good accountability models also define how risk acceptance works in practice. Risk acceptance is not a passive outcome; it is an explicit decision to carry exposure for a period of time, usually due to cost, feasibility, or business constraints. The decision must be owned by a business leader with authority over the impacted outcomes, not solely by security, because security does not own revenue targets or customer commitments. Operationally, this means risk acceptance should have a scope, a time boundary, and compensating controls when feasible, even if those controls are temporary. When risk acceptance is informal or perpetual, it becomes a governance loophole that quietly normalizes preventable exposure.

Incident decision-making requires its own accountability structure because time pressure changes behavior. Teams need clarity on who can declare an incident, who controls communications, and who authorizes disruptive containment actions. They also need to understand the difference between investigative certainty and operational necessity, because waiting for perfect attribution or complete timelines often increases damage. In practice, leaders should empower responders to execute pre-authorized actions when certain conditions are met, while reserving broader business decisions—like shutting down a customer-facing system or notifying external parties—for designated executives. That split keeps response fast and disciplined without pushing strategic risk decisions onto analysts.

AI can make decision-making faster, but it can also blur accountability if governance is not explicit. AI-assisted triage can summarize alerts, correlate signals across telemetry, and propose next steps, which helps reduce cognitive load during high-volume periods. The accountability model must still require humans to own the decision and document the rationale, especially when the action carries business impact. Failure modes include false confidence from well-written but incorrect summaries, model drift as environments change, and bias toward noisy alert classes that dominate training data. Governance should require traceability for AI-influenced decisions—what inputs were used, what output was generated, and who approved the action—so accountability remains clear and audit-ready.

The model must also address cross-functional friction, because defensive outcomes depend on coordinated action across teams. Security can identify a problem, but remediation typically belongs to platform, endpoint, identity, application, or vendor management owners. If accountability is unclear, security becomes a "nagging function," and operational teams treat fixes as optional. Effective models create predictable service expectations:

Table 2.1 Decision Rights and Accountability for Defensive Actions.

Decision Area	Typical Trigger	Decision Owner	Minimum Evidence Needed	Record Required
Routine hygiene prioritization	Backlog growth or missed timelines	Control domain owner	Asset criticality and exposure context	Change or ticket note
Nondisruptive containment	Confirmed suspicious activity on noncritical assets	Incident lead	Primary telemetry supports containment need	Incident log entry
Disruptive containment	Credible impact to critical service or privileged access	Designated executive authority	Validated indicators and business impact estimate	Incident decision record
Incident severity declaration	Material risk to operations data or trust	Incident commander with executive escalation path	Correlated signals and scope estimate	Severity and timeline entry
Risk acceptance	Remediation not feasible within required window	Business leader for impacted outcomes	Documented exposure and compensating controls	Risk acceptance record with time bound

response times for critical remediation, escalation channels for stalled work, and a shared understanding of what constitutes unacceptable exposure. When these mechanisms are consistent, security stops being a series of one-off negotiations and becomes an integrated part of operational reliability.

Finally, accountability models must be reinforced through routine review, not only after a major incident. Decision logs, post-incident analyses, and recurring control failures should be used to validate whether decision rights are placed correctly and whether escalation thresholds are realistic. If the same disputes occur repeatedly—who can isolate, who approves blocking, who owns patch deadlines—the model is signaling misalignment, not individual failure. Over time, the organization should see fewer "surprise" decisions during crises because authorities and expectations are already understood. That is the core promise of governance-driven accountability: faster, safer decisions that are consistent with business priorities and resilient under stress.

Policies, Standards, and Procedures: How They Differ

Policies, standards, and procedures are often treated as interchangeable paperwork, but they serve different operational purposes and fail in different ways. A policy expresses intent and non-negotiable expectations—what the organization requires and why it matters. A standard translates that intent into specific, measurable requirements that can be implemented consistently. A procedure describes how work is actually performed, step by step, by real people in real systems. When these are confused, organizations either create vague directives that no one can apply or overly detailed mandates that cannot survive change.

A policy should be durable and technology-agnostic, because it represents leadership's commitment to a control outcome rather than a particular implementation. For defensive security, policies establish what must be true: that access is controlled, logs are retained, vulnerabilities are managed, incidents are handled, and data is protected. The wording is intentionally firm, because policy is the artifact that anchors accountability and auditability. A strong policy also sets scope and authority: who it applies to, who owns it, and what happens when it is not followed. The most common failure mode is writing policies as wish lists—broad statements without enforcement mechanisms or ownership. Table 2.2 clarifies how policies standards and procedures differ in purpose specificity verification and maintenance cadence.

Standards exist to remove ambiguity from policy by defining "what compliant looks like" in concrete terms. Where a policy might require strong authentication, the standard defines minimum factors, approved methods, coverage expectations, and enforcement timelines. Standards should be testable, because they are the bridge between governance and engineering work; if a requirement cannot be verified, it will eventually be ignored. They also support consistency across teams, which matters in modern environments where different platforms and delivery teams would otherwise invent their own interpretations. A weak standard is either so generic that every team claims compliance or so brittle that it becomes obsolete with every architectural change.

Table 2.2 Governance Artifacts at a Glance Policy Versus Standard Versus Procedure.

Artifact	Primary Role	Specificity Level	How It Is Verified	Typical Update Rate
Policy	States intent authority and non-negotiables	Low	Leadership approval and scope review	Infrequent
Standard	Defines minimum requirements that are testable	Medium	Control checks and evidence review	Periodic
Procedure	Describes step by step execution and handoffs	High	Operational walkthrough and incident use review	Frequent

Procedures are the operational playbooks that make policies and standards executable at scale. They describe who does what, in what order, using what inputs, and what constitutes success or escalation. In defensive operations, procedures are critical for repeatability under stress—incident intake, triage, evidence preservation, containment actions, escalation to legal or communications, and restoration steps. Procedures also capture handoffs, because many security activities cross team boundaries and fail when responsibilities are implied rather than explicit. A common pitfall is writing procedures as idealized diagrams that do not match how systems are deployed or how teams actually work, making them irrelevant during real incidents.

The three layers must be aligned, but they should not duplicate one another. A policy that includes detailed configuration steps will be outdated quickly and will create disputes when teams follow the "spirit" but not the letter. A standard that reads like a policy will not provide the specificity needed for consistent implementation and verification. A procedure that tries to justify why the work matters will become bloated and harder to use under pressure. The clean separation is practical: policy defines outcomes and authority, standards define minimum requirements and measurement, and procedures define execution and escalation.

Governance depends on how these documents are controlled and maintained, not simply that they exist. Ownership should be clear, and review cycles should match the pace of operational change—procedures typically require more frequent updates than policies. Exceptions must be handled through a defined mechanism, because real environments include legacy systems, acquisitions, and business constraints that cannot always meet standards immediately. A well-run exception process documents the risk, identifies compensating controls, and sets a timeline for remediation or reevaluation. Without this, exceptions become informal and permanent, and standards quietly stop meaning anything.

AI and automation can improve how policies, standards, and procedures are applied, but they can also amplify confusion if governance is weak. AI-assisted analysis can map control requirements to system inventories, summarize compliance evidence, and flag gaps in telemetry or configuration drift, reducing manual effort and improving coverage. At the same time, AI-generated policy or procedure text can sound authoritative while embedding subtle inaccuracies, outdated assumptions, or untestable requirements, which undermines trust and auditability. Human review must remain mandatory for any governance artifact, with explicit approval boundaries and version control, so changes are traceable. The goal is to use AI to reduce friction in maintaining alignment, not to outsource accountability for what the organization claims it will do.

Operationally, the best indicator that these layers are working is predictability: teams know what is required, how it will be measured, and how to perform the work without negotiating every decision. Security leaders can explain requirements in plain language, engineers can implement them consistently, and auditors can verify them without inventing interpretations. When an incident occurs, procedures guide action while policies and standards support the authority to act quickly and consistently. When they are misaligned, the organization experiences constant rework—controls implemented inconsistently, incidents handled improvisationally, and governance reduced to paperwork that does not change outcomes. The difference is not documentation volume; it is whether these artifacts form a coherent operating system for defense.

Translating Risk into Executive Decisions and Investment Priorities

Risk translation is the act of turning technical exposure into business decisions that executives can own and fund. Security teams routinely see thousands of signals—vulnerabilities, misconfigurations, identity anomalies, third-party findings—but leaders cannot govern from raw detail. The goal is not to "scare the business" into spending; it is to describe credible loss scenarios, likelihood drivers, and control options in terms that map to revenue, operations, legal obligations, and brand trust. When this translation is done well, leaders can make tradeoffs explicitly instead of absorbing risk by default through inaction or ambiguity.

Effective translation begins by connecting exposures to business-critical services and data, not to tooling domains. A critical vulnerability on an isolated lab host is different from a moderate weakness on an externally exposed identity gateway that supports customer access. Executives need to understand what could stop the business from operating, what could trigger contractual penalties, and what could require customer notification, even if the root cause is "just" an IAM misconfiguration. That linkage also changes prioritization: teams focus on reducing risk in the paths attackers actually use to reach material impact. This is where asset criticality, data classification, and dependency mapping stop being theoretical governance and become decision-enabling context.

The next step is expressing risk as a limited set of decision-ready narratives rather than a spreadsheet of findings. A decision-ready narrative identifies the exposure, explains how it could be exploited, and describes the plausible impact in operational terms—service outage windows, fraud potential, data loss scope, recovery effort, and reputational consequences. It also calls out key assumptions, because executives must know what is known versus inferred, especially during fast-moving incidents or incomplete telemetry. The point is clarity and comparability: leaders should be able to look across multiple risks and understand which ones threaten the organization's mission and which ones are tolerable for now. Without that structure, risk discussions devolve into technical debates or worst-case speculation.

Investment priorities should be framed around reducing repeated classes of loss, not chasing one-off findings. Executives fund outcomes: fewer successful account takeovers, less time spent in incident response, fewer emergency patches, reduced downtime, and more predictable delivery of secure services. Security teams translate those outcomes into capabilities—stronger identity controls, better telemetry, faster patching, improved containment authority, and disciplined third-party access management—without getting trapped in tool-centric arguments. This is also where "run" versus "change" investment becomes visible: money spent on emergency response and firefighting is often a symptom of underinvestment in prevention and operational hygiene. A mature translation approach shows leaders that shifting resources toward durable controls reduces long-term cost and operational disruption.

Risk translation must also be honest about constraints, because unrealistic commitments erode credibility. Some risks cannot be eliminated quickly due to legacy systems, vendor dependencies, or business timelines, and pretending otherwise leads to broken promises and hidden exposure. In those cases, executives need options: accept the risk temporarily with compensating controls, reduce exposure by limiting attack paths, or invest in modernization with an understood timeline. The security leader's role is to present these options with clear consequences, not to demand a single "correct" choice. When leaders make the call, accountability becomes shared and documented, which is essential for governance and for resilience during future incidents.

AI and machine learning can help security teams translate risk at executive speed, but only when paired with disciplined controls and transparent assumptions. Models can summarize incident timelines, cluster related findings into themes, and correlate telemetry to highlight which exposures are active versus theoretical. However, these tools can also produce false confidence by generating polished narratives from incomplete data, and they can amplify bias by overemphasizing areas with more telemetry while underrepresenting blind spots. Human-in-the-loop review is non-negotiable for executive-facing risk statements, and governance should require traceability to underlying evidence and clear labeling of uncertainty. Risk translation is a trust exercise; if AI-generated output cannot be audited and defended, it should not be used to drive high-impact investment decisions.

Finally, translation must result in an operating cadence that keeps investment aligned with evolving exposure. Executives should receive concise, repeatable risk reporting that highlights material changes—new attack paths, degraded control health, emerging third-party issues, or shifts in adversary behavior—rather than fluctuating metrics that create noise. Security should be able to show how prior investments changed the risk posture, including what was reduced, what remains, and what new risks emerged as the environment changed. Over time, leaders learn which investments produce measurable resilience and which are merely reactive spending. That feedback loop is what turns risk translation into governance: a disciplined way to allocate attention and resources so defensive outcomes improve year over year.

Aligning Cybersecurity with Business Objectives

Alignment is not a slogan about "being a business partner"; it is the operational practice of ensuring security work protects what the organization is trying to achieve. Business objectives typically translate into a small set of priorities—revenue growth, service reliability, customer trust, regulatory compliance, and operational efficiency. Defensive security must map its activities to those priorities in ways leaders can see and teams can execute. When alignment is missing, security becomes a parallel program measured by internal outputs rather than business outcomes, and it is perceived as unpredictable friction. When alignment is strong, security decisions look like risk-informed operations: deliberate, timely, and proportional.

The first alignment mechanism is clarity on what the business cannot afford to lose or interrupt. For some organizations, the critical concern is availability of a customer platform; for others it is protection of regulated data, safety, intellectual property, or supply-chain continuity. Defensive priorities should flow from those realities, because they define impact severity and acceptable disruption thresholds. This directly influences decisions during incidents: isolating a non-critical service may be easy, while interrupting payment processing or a production control system requires higher-level approval and tighter coordination. Alignment begins when security can explain, in plain operational terms, which services are "must not fail" and which can tolerate controlled disruption.

Security must also align its work to the way the business builds and operates technology. If delivery teams release daily, security controls must fit into that cadence through repeatable standards, automated checks, and clear ownership rather than last-minute gatekeeping. If the organization relies on SaaS platforms and cloud services, alignment means governing identity, configuration, and data flows as primary control surfaces, not treating them as secondary to network perimeter controls. If third parties are central to operations, alignment means integrating vendor access and monitoring into normal operations, not only during contract negotiations. The consistent theme is that security must meet the business where it operates, because misaligned controls are bypassed, deferred, or resented until they fail catastrophically.

Alignment requires a shared prioritization model that connects defensive work to material business risk. That model should consistently elevate issues that affect critical services, privileged access, sensitive data, and high-trust integrations, even when they are not the noisiest. It should also recognize operational reality: teams cannot remediate everything immediately, so prioritization must be stable enough to guide work over weeks, not just hours. Leaders want to know why one item is urgent and another is scheduled, and alignment means those answers reference business impact and exposure windows rather than tool severity scores alone. Over time, a shared model reduces conflict because teams understand the rationale before the next emergency.

Governance is the practical backbone of alignment because it sets decision rights and acceptable risk boundaries. Business leaders must be able to approve tradeoffs, such as delaying a security improvement to meet a launch date, but those decisions need to be documented, time-bounded, and paired with compensating controls when feasible. Security leaders, in turn, must clearly state what is non-negotiable, such as minimum identity protections for privileged access or baseline logging for critical services. Without these boundaries, alignment devolves into ad hoc bargaining where security is pressured to "sign off" on risk without authority or accountability. A mature operating model makes risk acceptance a business decision with clear ownership, not a quiet compromise.

AI can support alignment by translating technical signals into business-relevant narratives and by reducing friction in routine security work. AI-assisted triage can help analysts rapidly identify which alerts touch critical services, correlate identity activity with business operations, and summarize incident context for leadership without drowning them in raw logs. AI can also be used to classify and route security work, but only if the underlying asset data and ownership records are accurate; otherwise, automation accelerates misrouting and missed accountability. Governance should establish approval boundaries for AI-influenced decisions, especially when recommendations could cause business disruption, and it should require audit trails for what the AI suggested versus what humans approved. Alignment depends on trust, and trust depends on transparency and predictable decision-making.

Finally, alignment is sustained through a cadence of communication that keeps security priorities synchronized with business change. As the organization acquires new companies, launches new products, or shifts infrastructure, the attack surface changes and defensive priorities must adjust without constant reinvention. Security leaders should provide leaders with clear status on control health for critical services and on the risks that could disrupt business objectives, not a rotating dashboard of internal metrics. Operational teams should receive actionable guidance—standards, procedures, and escalation paths—that helps them deliver securely without repeated negotiation. When alignment works, security is not a separate initiative competing with business goals; it is an enabling constraint that makes those goals achievable without accepting unmanaged exposure.

Managing Competing Priorities and Tradeoffs

Competing priorities are not a symptom of poor planning; they are the normal operating condition of defensive security. Blue teams must balance urgent alerts, long-term exposure reduction, operational uptime, and business delivery timelines, often with incomplete information and finite capacity. The organizations that perform well do not eliminate tradeoffs—they make them explicit, repeatable, and governed. When tradeoffs remain implicit, teams thrash between "firefighting" and "strategic improvement," and both sides of the mission suffer. Managing priorities is therefore a leadership discipline that determines whether defensive work is coherent or reactive.

The first practical problem is distinguishing urgency from importance. Urgent work typically arrives as alerts, incidents, and executive escalations, and it demands immediate attention even when impact is unclear. Important work includes patching, identity hygiene, detection engineering, and control maintenance that prevents future incidents but rarely produces daily drama. If leaders do not intentionally protect time for important work, urgent work expands to fill the calendar and the environment becomes increasingly fragile. Over time, the organization pays for that imbalance through recurring incidents, slow recovery, and elevated operational risk. A governed model ensures that important work has sustained capacity, even during high-alert periods.

Tradeoffs also arise from the tension between security rigor and operational continuity. Containment actions—isolating hosts, disabling accounts, blocking traffic, rolling back changes—can prevent adversary movement but may disrupt business operations and customer experience. Leaders must establish decision thresholds and pre-authorized actions, so responders are not forced to negotiate disruption during an active incident. The goal is proportionality: act decisively when the credible impact is material, but avoid reflexive disruption when evidence is weak or alternatives exist. Organizations that fail here tend to oscillate between overreaction that breaks business processes and hesitation that allows damage to spread.

Competing priorities are amplified by shared ownership across teams. Security may identify a high-risk exposure, but remediation often belongs to infrastructure, identity, application, or vendor owners who are already committed to delivery deadlines. When governance does not define service expectations—remediation timelines, escalation paths, and risk acceptance authority—security work becomes a sequence of one-off negotiations. That negotiation cost is invisible in most reporting, yet it is a major driver of delayed fixes and analyst burnout. A mature operating model turns these interactions into predictable workflows with clear accountability, making tradeoffs manageable rather than personal.

Managing tradeoffs requires decision quality, which depends on trustworthy context. Teams need asset criticality, business ownership, exposure data, and telemetry coverage to prioritize correctly; otherwise, they prioritize based on what is loudest or easiest. This is why "inventory" is not a compliance artifact but a leadership asset: it enables fast, defensible prioritization. It also reduces conflict because teams can see why certain issues outrank others, even when technical severity appears similar. In practice, better context turns prioritization into a shared judgment rather than a security-only edict.

AI can help manage competing priorities by compressing analysis time and improving consistency, but it must be constrained to avoid accelerating bad decisions. AI-assisted triage can cluster related alerts, propose likely root causes, and summarize evidence, allowing analysts to focus on decisions rather than manual correlation. These benefits depend on clean telemetry and accurate asset metadata; otherwise, the model will infer patterns from incomplete signals and may elevate the wrong work. Governance should require human approval for priority changes that drive disruptive actions or significant resource shifts, and it should treat AI output as a recommendation with confidence bounds, not as truth. Failure modes include false confidence from fluent summaries, drift as alert patterns change, and bias toward heavily instrumented systems while neglecting blind spots.

Another tradeoff is between local optimization and systemic risk reduction. Teams often celebrate closing individual findings, yet the business outcome improves most when recurring classes of exposure are eliminated—weak identity controls, inconsistent logging, unmanaged third-party access, or slow patch cycles. Leaders should steer investment toward capabilities that reduce the volume and severity of future work, even if the benefits are less visible in the short term. This requires resisting the temptation to measure success purely by throughput, because throughput can increase while systemic risk stays the same. The most effective organizations treat repeated incidents and recurring findings as signals of governance and control failures, not as normal background noise.

Finally, tradeoffs must be documented and revisited, because priorities that were reasonable in one context may become unacceptable as the environment changes. Risk acceptance decisions should have time boundaries, compensating controls where feasible, and clear owners who can re-evaluate when conditions shift. When teams capture why a tradeoff was made—what evidence was available, what alternatives were considered, and what was chosen—they reduce future confusion and blame during post-incident reviews. Over time, this builds organizational muscle: leaders learn how to make faster, higher-quality calls under uncertainty. That is the operational goal of managing competing priorities—turning unavoidable tradeoffs into controlled, accountable decisions that improve defensive outcomes.

Program Ownership, Delegation, and Operational Oversight

Program ownership is the commitment to outcomes, not the act of doing every task. In defensive security, ownership means someone is accountable for whether a control area works reliably across the organization—identity protections remain enforced, logging remains complete, vulnerabilities are remediated on time, and incident handling remains disciplined. Delegation is how that work is executed at scale, because most controls are implemented and operated by infrastructure, application, and platform teams. Operational oversight is the mechanism that ensures delegation does not become abdication, with visibility into control health, drift, and exceptions. When these three elements are balanced, security programs remain resilient as systems and teams change.

Ownership must be explicit about scope and authority, because defensive programs cut across business units and technologies. A named owner should be responsible for defining the minimum requirements, setting the operating cadence, and ensuring that risks and exceptions are managed consistently. Authority matters as much as responsibility; owners need the ability to escalate, to require corrective action, and to influence investment when systemic gaps appear. Without authority, program owners become coordinators who can report problems but cannot drive resolution. In practice, this is when security work turns into chronic follow-up rather than durable improvement.

Delegation works when responsibilities are assigned to the teams that control the underlying systems, with security providing clear expectations and verification. For example, endpoint teams can own hardening and patch deployment, identity teams can own access provisioning and privileged account controls, and platform teams can own logging pipelines and telemetry availability. Delegation should include defined service expectations—what must be done, how quickly, and what evidence proves it is done—so the work is operationally concrete. If delegation is informal, security requests are treated as best effort, and the most constrained teams become the least secure areas of the environment. Effective delegation turns security requirements into normal operational work, not special projects that compete for attention.

Operational oversight is where many programs fail because organizations mistake reporting for control. Oversight should provide an accurate view of control health and risk posture, including coverage gaps, backlog aging, and areas where standards are routinely missed. It should also identify leading indicators, such as a growing population of unmanaged assets, declining log completeness, or increasing time-to-remediate for critical systems. Oversight is not micromanagement; it is the feedback loop that allows leaders to intervene before failures become incidents. Without this loop, executives learn about problems only when business impact forces attention.

Oversight must also include a disciplined approach to exceptions and drift. Exceptions are sometimes necessary due to legacy constraints, vendor limitations, or operational realities, but they must be owned, time-bounded, and visible to program leadership. Drift is the gradual erosion of control effectiveness as environments evolve—new systems are deployed without telemetry, permissions expand, or patching processes degrade under delivery pressure. Mature oversight detects drift through recurring checks and reconciliations, not through assumptions that last year's compliance implies today's security. When exceptions and drift are unmanaged, the organization accumulates hidden exposure that surfaces as surprise incidents and emergency remediation.

AI can strengthen ownership and oversight by improving signal to noise and enabling more consistent monitoring of control health, but it must be governed carefully. AI-assisted analytics can identify patterns in ticket backlogs, correlate incidents to control gaps, and highlight areas where remediation repeatedly stalls, which helps owners target systemic constraints rather than chasing symptoms. These capabilities depend on accurate underlying data—asset ownership, ticket metadata, and telemetry coverage—otherwise, AI will produce misleading insights and false precision. Human-in-the-loop review is essential for any AI-driven prioritization that could reallocate resources or trigger escalations, because these actions have organizational consequences. Governance should require that AI outputs are explainable enough to be challenged and audited, especially when they influence investment decisions.

Program ownership also requires clarity on what security will do centrally versus what is embedded in delivery and operations teams. Central security typically defines standards, runs core detection and response functions, and provides subject-matter expertise for risk and incident decisions. Distributed teams operate controls in their domains, implement remediation, and maintain the environments that generate the telemetry security depends on. The handoffs must be explicit, because ambiguous boundaries create duplicated work in some areas and neglected work in others. Over time, organizations with clear boundaries see fewer "last-minute security surprises" because the responsibilities for prevention, detection, and response are understood and practiced.

Finally, operational oversight is sustained through routine review that produces corrective action, not just visibility. Leaders should be able to see where programs are healthy, where they are degrading, and what interventions are required—staffing, automation, process changes, or business-level risk decisions. When oversight identifies recurring failures, ownership must drive remediation at the system level, not simply demand more effort from already-constrained teams. The measure of success is not perfect compliance; it is predictable control performance and a steady reduction in preventable incidents. That outcome is only possible when ownership is clear, delegation is deliberate, and oversight is continuous enough to catch drift before it becomes damage.

AI-Enabled Decision Support: Validation, Evidence, and Avoiding False Confidence

AI-enabled decision support can make defensive teams faster, but it can also make them wrong more efficiently. In blue team operations, the value of AI is rarely in "finding" the incident by itself; it is in compressing analysis time by summarizing telemetry, correlating signals, and suggesting plausible next steps. The risk is that AI outputs are often fluent and confident even when the underlying evidence is partial, stale, or misinterpreted. Decision support must therefore be governed like any other control: it requires defined inputs, validation expectations, and clear boundaries on what it can and cannot authorize. When those conditions are met, AI becomes an accelerator rather than a source of operational debt.

Validation starts with an explicit distinction between evidence and inference. Evidence is what the organization can substantiate from logs, configurations, endpoint artifacts, identity records, and confirmed observations. Inference is a hypothesis about what likely happened or what should be done next, derived from patterns in the evidence. AI systems excel at producing plausible inferences, but they cannot be allowed to blur that line in incident records, executive updates, or remediation decisions. Operationally, teams should treat AI output as a starting point for verification, with human reviewers responsible for confirming key claims against primary telemetry. The practical goal is to prevent narrative momentum from outrunning what can be proven.

The quality of AI decision support is bounded by the quality of the data it can see. Missing logs, inconsistent timestamps, incomplete asset ownership, and weak identity correlation create gaps that AI will often paper over with assumptions. This is where teams fall into false confidence: the AI produces a coherent story, so responders assume the environment is observed more completely than it is. Mature programs make telemetry dependencies explicit—what log sources are required for certain decisions, what fields must be present for correlation, and what "unknown" means when evidence is absent. When those prerequisites are not met, AI output should be labeled as low confidence and treated accordingly, rather than being used to justify high-impact actions.

Human-in-the-loop controls are the practical boundary that keeps AI from silently becoming an unaccountable decision-maker. In blue team workflows, there are predictable points where approval must remain human: declaring incident severity, initiating containment that affects customer-facing services, disabling privileged access, authorizing data sharing, or committing to external statements. AI can propose, prioritize, and draft, but it should not be the final authority for actions with material business impact. This boundary should be enforced in process and in tooling, so it is not dependent on individual discipline during stressful events. When accountability is clear, AI becomes an assistant to decision-makers rather than a substitute for them. Table 2.3 defines practical guardrails that keep AI decision support evidence-based human-approved where needed and auditable.

Table 2.3 AI-Enabled Decision Support Controls for Validation and Auditability.

AI Use Case	Telemetry Dependency	Human Approval Boundary	Common Failure Mode	Audit Artifact
Alert summarization	Complete logs with consistent timestamps	Reviewer validates key claims	Hallucinated details or missing context	Summary with cited evidence links
Signal correlation and clustering	Asset identity and ownership enrichment	Analyst confirms relationship	False grouping or missed linkage	Correlation rationale note
Prioritization recommendations	Criticality and exposure data quality	Lead approves priority shifts	Bias toward noisy sources	Priority decision record
Containment recommendation	Endpoint identity and network evidence	Human required for disruptive action	False confidence under uncertainty	Containment approval entry
Executive update drafting	Validated incident timeline and scope	Leader approves external facing statements	Overstated certainty from inference	Approved update and assumptions list

Evidence handling and auditability are also non-negotiable, because incident response is both operational and governance work. If an AI tool summarizes an alert, proposes a root cause, or recommends containment, the organization should be able to trace that output back to inputs and show what was accepted, modified, or rejected. This is not about creating paperwork; it is about preserving defensibility when decisions are questioned by leadership, regulators, customers, or internal review. AI systems can introduce hidden variability—changes in model behavior over time, shifting thresholds, and different outputs for the same prompt—so versioning and change control matter. A disciplined program treats AI-assisted decisions as artifacts that must be reproducible enough to support learning and accountability.

Avoiding false confidence also requires recognizing specific failure modes common in security contexts. One is hallucination, where the system invents details such as process names, timelines, or attacker intent to complete a narrative. Another is overgeneralization, where the model assumes a common pattern—phishing leading to account takeover, for example—despite limited evidence in the case at hand. A third is confirmation bias acceleration, where responders ask the AI questions that reinforce an early hypothesis and receive increasingly confident answers that drown out alternative explanations. Teams mitigate these risks by requiring adversarial review: intentionally checking disconfirming evidence, validating key claims against raw telemetry, and documenting uncertainty rather than forcing premature certainty. The discipline is not to distrust AI reflexively, but to refuse to let it turn ambiguity into authority.

AI-enabled decision support must also be protected against data leakage and misuse, because the content it processes is often sensitive. Incident data can include credentials, internal architecture details, personal data, and proprietary business information, all of which have legal and operational implications if exposed. Governance must define what data is permitted for AI processing, how it is sanitized, and what retention and access controls apply to outputs. This includes managing prompt and output handling in tickets and collaboration systems, where sensitive details can persist beyond the incident. If the organization cannot confidently control the data, it should constrain AI usage to less sensitive functions, such as summarizing already-approved internal reports or classifying alerts using non-sensitive metadata.

Finally, AI decision support should be evaluated like any operational capability: measured, tested, and continuously improved. Teams should track whether AI reduces triage time without increasing error rates, whether it improves consistency across analysts, and whether it helps surface systemic control gaps that drive recurring incidents. Evaluation should include edge cases—noisy data, incomplete logging, unusual attack paths—because that is where false confidence is most dangerous. Over time, organizations that govern AI well see AI outputs become more reliable because telemetry, labeling, and feedback loops improve, not because models magically become infallible. The outcome executives should expect is disciplined speed: faster decisions that remain evidence-based, auditable, and accountable under real-world constraints.

Leadership Behaviors That Improve Defensive Readiness

Defensive readiness is not primarily a technology problem; it is a leadership problem expressed through day-to-day behavior. Leaders shape what teams prioritize, what gets funded, and what gets normalized when tradeoffs are required. In blue team operations, readiness is the ability to detect meaningful activity, make timely decisions, and execute containment and recovery without improvisation. That capability is built through consistent expectations, disciplined routines, and an environment where problems surface early instead of being hidden. Leadership behaviors determine whether security is practiced as a repeatable operating system or as an occasional crisis response.

One of the most consequential behaviors is insisting on clarity of ownership and decision rights. Readiness collapses when responders do not know who can approve disruptive actions, who owns a critical control, or who is accountable for remediation timelines. Leaders improve readiness by making responsibilities explicit and by reinforcing them in routine operations, not only during incidents. This includes setting escalation thresholds so that analysts are not forced to negotiate authority in the middle of a fast-moving event. It also includes holding owners accountable for control health, not merely for completing tasks, because controls that are "owned" but ineffective still fail in crisis. When ownership is clear, teams move faster and argue less under pressure.

Leaders also improve readiness by protecting time for operational hygiene and continuous improvement. Most readiness is built in unglamorous work: patching, identity cleanup, logging completeness, detection tuning, and documenting procedures that match reality. Without deliberate protection, urgent work will consume all capacity, and the environment will drift toward chronic fragility. Leaders who value readiness create predictable space for maintenance and corrective action, even when business delivery is busy. They also expect that recurring incidents or recurring control failures trigger systemic fixes, not just more heroic effort. This behavior steadily reduces the volume of preventable emergencies.

Another readiness behavior is demanding evidence-based decision-making without rewarding paralysis. In defensive operations, leaders should insist that claims are grounded in telemetry and that uncertainty is labeled honestly. At the same time, they must enable action when the evidence is sufficient to justify containment, even if the full story is not yet known. This balance is only possible when leaders define what "sufficient evidence" means for different classes of decisions, and when they pre-authorize actions for common scenarios. It prevents two common failures: rushing into disruptive actions based on speculation, and delaying containment until the incident grows. A readiness-focused leader makes it safe to act decisively when the risk is credible and the process is followed.

Communication behavior is another major determinant of readiness, because incidents are coordination problems as much as technical problems. Leaders improve readiness by establishing clear communication pathways and by modeling calm, concise updates that focus on impact, decisions, and next actions. They avoid demanding constant novelty—new theories, new culprits, new explanations—when the team is still building evidence. They also ensure that communications are consistent across stakeholders, so operational teams are not pulled into conflicting narratives by different executives. In practice, disciplined communication reduces distraction and prevents the incident response team from becoming a reporting factory. It keeps the organization aligned while technical work proceeds.

Leaders must also set expectations for how AI is used in defensive operations, because AI can either enhance readiness or erode it through false confidence. A readiness-focused leader encourages AI-assisted summarization and correlation when it reduces manual effort, but requires human validation for high-impact decisions and external statements. They demand traceability: what evidence supports the AI-generated narrative, what uncertainty remains, and who approved the resulting action. They also anticipate failure modes such as drift, biased prioritization, and fluent hallucinations, and they require routine evaluation to ensure AI is improving outcomes rather than merely speeding up reporting. This behavior preserves accountability while capturing the operational advantage AI can provide.

Finally, leaders improve readiness by creating a culture where learning is systematic and psychologically safe without becoming complacent. After-action reviews should identify control failures, decision bottlenecks, and process gaps, then drive concrete changes in standards and procedures. Leaders should reward early escalation and honest reporting of weaknesses, because hidden issues are the enemy of readiness. They should also resist blame-driven responses that teach teams to protect themselves rather than the organization, while still holding owners accountable for repeated neglect. Over time, these behaviors produce a stable defensive posture: teams practice, improve, and execute under stress with less drama and more reliability. That is what readiness looks like in an organization where leadership actively governs defensive outcomes.

Conclusion

Defensive outcomes are determined by the decisions leaders make about ownership, authority, and investment, and by whether those decisions are translated into repeatable operating conditions. When policies, standards, and procedures are aligned and actively governed, teams spend less time negotiating and more time executing, because expectations and escalation paths are already understood. Sustainable readiness comes from protecting capacity for hygiene and improvement, managing tradeoffs explicitly, and maintaining oversight that detects drift and forces corrective action before incidents become business-impacting events. AI-enabled decision support can strengthen that system when it is treated as assistance rather than authority, with evidence requirements, auditability, and human approval boundaries that preserve accountability while increasing speed.

Recommendations

1) Establish clear decision rights and accountability for defensive actions. Define who can declare incidents, authorize disruptive containment, and accept risk when remediation cannot be completed immediately. Ensure those authorities are practiced in normal operations, so they are not negotiated during an active event. Reinforce ownership by tying control health outcomes to named leaders rather than to shared committees or informal expectations.
2) Translate security risk into decision-ready narratives that executives can own and fund. Link exposures to business-critical services, sensitive data, and realistic loss scenarios rather than presenting raw vulnerability counts or alert volumes. Present options with consequences—reduce, accept with compensating controls, or invest in modernization—so tradeoffs are explicit and time-bounded. Document assumptions and uncertainty, so leaders understand what is proven versus inferred.
3) Separate policies, standards, and procedures and keep each artifact fit for purpose. Write policies as durable statements of intent and authority, define standards as testable minimum requirements, and maintain procedures as step-by-step operational playbooks. Align the three layers, so they reinforce each other without duplicating content or embedding brittle technical detail in policy. Assign clear owners and review cadences, so procedures evolve with operational reality while policies remain stable.
4) Protect capacity for preventive hygiene and continuous improvement alongside reactive response work. Reserve predictable time for patching, identity cleanup, logging completeness, detection tuning, and procedure maintenance. Treat recurring incidents and repeat findings as signals of systemic control failure that require durable fixes rather than repeated heroics. Use oversight to keep important work from being perpetually preempted by urgent noise.
5) Build operational oversight that measures control health and detects drift before it becomes incident impact. Monitor coverage gaps, backlog aging, and leading indicators such as unmanaged assets, incomplete telemetry, and stalled remediation in critical areas. Ensure oversight produces corrective action—staffing, process changes, or escalations—rather than passive reporting. Make exception handling visible, owned, and time-bounded, so standards do not erode through informal exemptions.
6) Delegate control operation to the teams that run the underlying systems while retaining accountable program ownership. Define what security owns centrally (requirements, verification, core detection/response) and what platform and delivery teams must operate (hardening, patching, logging pipelines, access administration). Specify service expectations for delegated work, including evidence of completion and escalation paths for missed timelines. Prevent delegation from turning into abdication by regularly validating outcomes, not just activity.
7) Manage competing priorities by making tradeoffs explicit and governed rather than ad hoc. Distinguish urgency from importance and ensure both receive sustained capacity through intentional planning. Predefine containment thresholds and minimum evidence requirements, so responders can act quickly without overreacting or hesitating. Capture the rationale for major prioritization decisions to reduce future disputes and improve learning.
8) Enforce evidence-based decision-making and require clear labeling of uncertainty. Validate high-impact claims against primary telemetry and avoid allowing coherent narratives to outrun what can be substantiated.

Define what constitutes sufficient evidence for different decisions, especially those with business disruption or external reporting implications. Treat missing telemetry as an operational risk in itself and address it as a control health issue.

9) Govern AI-enabled decision support with human approval boundaries and auditability expectations. Use AI to accelerate summarization, correlation, and routing while requiring humans to approve severity declarations, disruptive containment, and executive-facing narratives. Demand traceability of AI-influenced decisions by preserving inputs, outputs, and approver rationale in incident records. Actively manage failure modes such as false confidence, hallucinated details, drift, bias toward instrumented systems, and sensitive-data leakage.
10) Model leadership behaviors that sustain readiness under stress and through change. Normalize early escalation, calm and concise communication, and accountability without blame-driven reactions that suppress reporting. Reinforce the discipline of repeatable routines—ownership clarity, oversight cadence, and continuous improvement—so readiness is built daily rather than rediscovered during crises. Use after-action learning to drive concrete changes in standards and procedures, and ensure those changes are implemented across teams. Keep leadership attention focused on outcomes that reduce preventable incidents and speed recovery, not on superficial activity metrics.

3

Policy Frameworks and Operational Control

Strong policy programs turn security expectations into operational control that teams can execute consistently under real-world constraints. Clear scope, defined ownership, and disciplined exception handling prevent policies from becoming ambiguous guidance that varies by team or circumstance. Standards, baselines, and repeatable procedures translate intent into measurable actions, while evidence expectations ensure controls can be demonstrated, not merely asserted. Automation and AI can accelerate consistency, triage, and verification when grounded in reliable telemetry, but accountable humans must remain the decision point for risk acceptance and high-impact actions.

Building a Policy Framework That Teams Can Use

A usable policy framework starts by acknowledging that policy is an operational interface, not a compliance artifact. Security policies exist to shape day-to-day decisions: what teams are allowed to do, what they must do, and what they must not do. When policy is written for auditors instead of operators, it becomes ambiguous, overbroad, and disconnected from how work actually happens. A usable framework treats policy as a system of constraints and permissions that makes safe behavior the easiest behavior. It also assumes that people will act under pressure, with imperfect information, and often with competing business priorities.

Structure matters because teams read policies the way they read runbooks: scanning for what applies, what is required, and what the escalation path is. A practical framework defines scope explicitly, so teams know whether it applies to endpoints, cloud services, third parties, or all environments. It also uses stable, consistent vocabulary for roles and assets, so "system owner," "data owner," and "service owner" do not mean different things depending on which document you opened. Where policy needs definitions, they should be short and placed where the reader encounters the term, not buried in a glossary that nobody checks during a production incident. Clarity and consistency reduce the need for interpretation, which is where policy gaps turn into control gaps.

The most effective policies translate into controls that are observable, testable, and enforceable. If a requirement cannot be verified through evidence—such as configuration state, logs, tickets, approvals, or attestations—it becomes a matter of belief rather than control. Policies should therefore connect each obligation to what evidence looks like and who is accountable for producing it. This is where many organizations fail by writing requirements that are technically true but operationally unmeasurable, such as "systems must be secure" or "access must be appropriate." A usable framework forces requirements into statements that can be checked and defended, especially when exceptions are requested. Table 3.1 shows how policy intent becomes operational execution with clear artifacts and evidence at each layer.

Ownership is another difference between policies that exist and policies that work. Every policy needs a named accountable role for updates, interpretation, and exception decisions, as well as a defined review cadence tied to operational change velocity. If the environment changes faster than policy, teams will route around the policy

Table 3.1 Policy to Execution Traceability Map.

Control Objective	Policy Output	Standard Output	Procedure Output	Evidence Source
Privileged access safety	Access must be controlled	Privileged access requirements	Access request workflow	Approval record
Logging reliability	Events must be logged	Logging baseline settings	Logging validation steps	Telemetry receipt proof
Exception discipline	Deviations must be governed	Exception conditions defined	Exception request handling	Exception register
Drift control	Controls must remain effective	Baseline compliance targets	Periodic verification run	Validation report
Change accountability	Changes must be authorized	Change review requirements	Change approval routing	Change record

rather than wait for it to catch up. A clean ownership model also prevents "policy drift," where informal interpretations evolve across teams until enforcement is inconsistent. Consistency is not only a governance objective; it is also a security outcome, because attackers exploit uneven controls and ambiguous boundaries. Clear ownership makes it possible to decide, quickly and defensibly, what must change when risk changes.

Exception handling is where usability is tested, because the real world always produces edge cases. A mature framework treats exceptions as a controlled workflow with time bounds, compensating controls, and explicit risk acceptance by the right authority. Teams should not have to invent a process in the moment or negotiate informally with security to ship a release. If exceptions are too hard to obtain, teams will ignore them and proceed without visibility; if exceptions are too easy, policy becomes optional. The goal is a predictable path that balances delivery with risk and creates a paper trail that can be reviewed and learned from. Over time, exception trends should feed policy improvement rather than becoming a permanent shadow process.

Policies become operational when they align with the way work is planned, built, and changed. Requirements should map to recognizable activities such as onboarding, change management, access requests, incident response, and decommissioning, because that is where controls can be embedded without forcing parallel processes. When policy demands steps that are not represented in existing workflows, security either creates friction or creates paperwork that is ignored. A usable framework anticipates handoffs across teams, such as when engineering deploys, IT provisions, or procurement engages a vendor, and it makes responsibilities explicit at those seams. The result is a control model that supports delivery while still creating clear security guardrails. This also makes it easier for leaders to see where the organization is over-reliant on informal heroics instead of repeatable process.

AI/ML can improve policy usability when it is applied to reduce ambiguity and speed up correct decisions, but it must be governed like any other control. For example, organizations can use ML-driven classification to suggest the likely data sensitivity of repositories, or to flag policy-relevant changes such as broad access grants or unusual privilege escalations that should trigger review. These uses depend on clean telemetry—identity events, change logs, repository metadata, and access patterns—and they fail predictably when those inputs are incomplete, biased, or inconsistent across environments. Human-in-the-loop controls are essential: AI can recommend a classification, an approval route, or an exception risk rating, but a named accountable person must approve decisions that change access, exposure, or control posture. The most dangerous failure mode is false confidence, where a plausible recommendation is treated as correct without evidence, especially as models drift over time or learn from poor historical decisions. Good governance requires auditability: keep records of recommendations, inputs, approvals, and outcomes, so the organization can defend decisions and recalibrate when the system is wrong.

Finally, usability depends on how policies are published, maintained, and taught, not just how they are written. Teams need policies in places they already work—integrated into request forms, ticket templates, build pipelines, and operational playbooks—so the policy shows up at decision time rather than as a separate reading assignment. Policy updates must be communicated in terms of behavioral change and operational impact, not only in terms of revised language, and those updates should be paired with examples that reflect real workflows. When policy is treated as living operational guidance, it earns trust, because teams can see that it reflects reality and that it is responsive to constraints. When policy is treated as static documentation, it becomes an artifact to satisfy a requirement rather than a tool to reduce risk. A usable framework is ultimately one that teams can follow under stress, with clear accountability, measurable controls, and a path for evolving safely as the business changes.

Policy Scope and Exceptions Without Losing Control

Scope is the boundary that determines whether a policy is a guardrail or a guessing game. A well-scoped policy states exactly which systems, data types, users, and operational contexts it governs, and it avoids vague language that forces teams to interpret intent under pressure. Scope should be written in terms teams can recognize, such as corporate-managed endpoints, production cloud accounts, customer data stores, third-party access paths, and administrative interfaces. When scope is unclear, enforcement becomes inconsistent, and inconsistent controls are easier to bypass than weak controls. The goal is not to cover everything with the same language, but to ensure every important surface has a clear home in the policy set.

Over-scoping is as dangerous as under-scoping because it creates requirements that cannot be met consistently. If a policy claims it applies to "all systems everywhere" but the organization lacks visibility into shadow IT, inherited vendor platforms, or legacy networks, compliance becomes performative. Teams will either ignore the policy or create local interpretations that drift away from what security intends. A more resilient approach is to define scope tiers, even if informally in narrative form, by distinguishing managed versus unmanaged assets and production versus non-production contexts. That distinction allows leaders to demand stronger controls where risk concentrates while acknowledging reality elsewhere. The policy still sets expectations, but it does so in a way that can be enforced, audited, and improved.

Scope also must account for identities and access pathways, because most modern control failures are scope failures in disguise. Policies that mention "users" but do not explicitly include service accounts, API keys, automation identities, and vendor identities leave a gap large enough for attackers to operate in. The same is true for access channels such as VPN, SSO, local admin, break-glass accounts, and shared administrative tooling. If the policy scope does not explicitly cover privileged access workflows, exceptions will proliferate there first, and that is where mistakes are most expensive. A defensible scope uses consistent identity terms and makes privileged access an explicit part of the boundary. This ensures that exceptions are handled where the organization needs the most discipline, not where it is easiest to be permissive.

Exceptions are inevitable, but unmanaged exceptions are simply undocumented scope changes. A controlled exception process starts by defining what qualifies as an exception, who can request one, and who is authorized to approve it based on risk and business impact. Exceptions should be time-bound by default, because permanent exceptions are usually evidence that the policy is mis-scoped or that the organization has accepted a long-term exposure without acknowledging it. The request should require a specific description of what control cannot be met, why it cannot be met, what compensating controls will be used, and what evidence will be produced during the exception period. This turns an exception from a permission slip into an operational plan. It also creates a consistent artifact that can be reviewed, audited, and learned from. Table 3.2 reinforces the minimum information and evidence needed to keep exceptions time bound accountable and measurable.

Table 3.2 Exception Request and Approval Evidence Requirements.

Exception Element	Required Content	Accountable Role	Minimum Evidence
Control that cannot be met	Specific control statement	Requester	Linked request ticket
Reason and constraint	Why compliance is not feasible	System owner	Constraint description
Compensating controls	Specific measurable actions	Security owner	Control verification proof
Approval authority	Named risk acceptor	Approver	Approval record
Time bound expiry	End date for exception	Approver	Expiration field set
Renewal criteria	Conditions for renewal	Security owner	Review notes
Monitoring plan	Who reviews what signal	Operations owner	Review cadence record

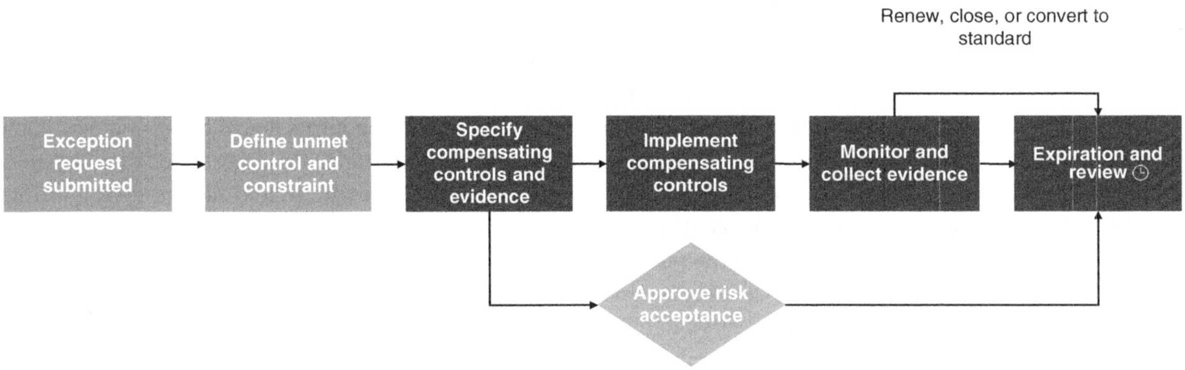

Figure 3.1 Exception Workflow Without Losing Control.

Compensating controls are where organizations either maintain control or quietly surrender it. If an exception removes a preventive control, the compensating controls must strengthen detection, response, monitoring, or segmentation enough to keep residual risk within tolerance. That means being explicit about what will be logged, who will review the evidence, and what triggers escalation if the compensating control indicates a problem. A common failure mode is accepting a compensating control that sounds reassuring but produces no actionable signal, such as "we will monitor the system" without stating what telemetry is available and who is accountable for review. Another failure mode is relying on manual checks with no cadence, no documentation, and no ownership, which collapses the moment staff rotates or priorities shift. Good exception handling keeps the control objective intact even when the original control implementation changes. Figure 3.1 visualizes a controlled exception path that preserves control intent through accountable approval, compensating controls, and expiration. It supports the chapter's point that unmanaged exceptions become undocumented scope changes.

AI/ML can support exception management by improving consistency and speed, but it cannot be allowed to become the decision maker for risk acceptance. In practice, ML-assisted triage can cluster similar exception requests, highlight patterns like repeated requests tied to the same team or system type, and flag requests that resemble prior incidents or known control failures. These capabilities depend on structured data from tickets, approvals, asset inventories, identity events, and outcomes from past exceptions, and they degrade quickly when requests are written inconsistently or when asset context is missing. Human approval boundaries must remain clear: AI can recommend a risk rating or suggest compensating controls based on history, but an accountable leader must make the final call and own the residual risk. The most dangerous failure modes are false confidence and bias, where the model learns that certain teams "always get exceptions" or treats well-written requests as safer than poorly written ones. Governance expectations should include audit logs of recommendations, approver decisions, and eventual outcomes, so the organization can detect drift and correct the process rather than institutionalize bad habits.

To avoid losing control, exception volume and exception aging must be treated as operational signals, not paperwork metrics. A rising exception count usually indicates that scope is too broad, controls are too hard to implement, or enabling services are missing, such as identity governance, logging, or standardized deployment pipelines. Aging exceptions indicate weak ownership, unclear renewal criteria, or a culture that treats time-bound approvals as optional. Reviews should focus on whether compensating controls are functioning, whether the original constraint still exists, and whether the exception should be closed, renewed with new conditions, or converted into an approved alternate standard. This is also where leaders can force hard prioritization: if exceptions are recurring in the same control area, the organization should either fund remediation or explicitly accept the risk at the right level. Control is maintained when exceptions drive improvement and accountability rather than becoming an invisible expansion of the attack surface.

Standards and Baselines for Consistent Execution

Standards and baselines are the practical layer that turns policy intent into consistent operational behavior. Policies state what must be true, but standards define how the organization will meet those requirements in repeatable ways that teams can implement without improvisation. A baseline is the minimum acceptable configuration or control set for a given class of assets, such as endpoints, servers, identities, or cloud accounts. When standards are missing, every team reinvents "secure enough," and security outcomes depend on individual expertise rather than organizational capability. Consistency is not bureaucracy here; it is how you reduce variance that attackers exploit and how you make security measurable at scale.

A usable standard is specific enough to be implemented and verified, but not so brittle that it breaks the moment the environment evolves. That balance typically comes from writing standards around controllable settings and observable behaviors, such as authentication requirements, logging expectations, patching timelines, network exposure rules, and administrative access constraints. Each standard should clearly state what evidence proves compliance, because otherwise verification becomes a debate rather than an operational check. Teams should be able to point to configuration state, identity logs, change records, and monitoring outputs that demonstrate the standard is being met. Where standards require exceptions, the exception path should be the same controlled workflow used elsewhere, not an informal workaround that erodes baseline credibility. The result is a set of rules that engineers can implement and security can validate without relying on trust or tribal knowledge.

Baselines work best when they are aligned to asset categories that match how the organization actually builds and manages technology. If a single baseline is applied to everything from developer laptops to internet-facing production workloads, it will either be too weak for high-risk systems or too strict to be adopted broadly. Practical baselines distinguish between managed and unmanaged assets, privileged and non-privileged identities, production and non-production environments, and systems with different data sensitivity. This does not require complex taxonomy, but it does require stable definitions, so teams know which baseline applies. When the baseline mapping is clear, onboarding new systems becomes predictable, and control gaps are less likely to appear during rapid growth or incident-driven change. Leaders benefit as well because baseline coverage becomes a meaningful metric instead of an abstract compliance claim.

Consistent execution depends on how standards are operationalized, not merely where they are documented. Standards should be embedded into the workflows teams already use for provisioning, configuration, and change, so meeting the baseline is the default outcome of normal work. If compliance requires manual steps that are easy to skip, the organization will accumulate drift over time, especially across acquisitions, legacy environments, and emergency changes. Drift is not always malicious; it is often the natural result of patch cycles, temporary troubleshooting changes, and incremental exceptions that never get revisited. A strong baseline program assumes drift will occur and designs for rapid detection and correction through routine verification. That mindset keeps the organization from confusing initial hardening with sustained control.

Verification is where standards become operational controls rather than hopeful guidance. Baseline compliance should be checked through a mix of periodic review and event-driven validation tied to change activity, because most configuration risk appears immediately after a change. Evidence collection should be consistent and attributable, so it is clear which system is being measured, when it was measured, and what configuration state was observed. When verification is inconsistent, teams learn that compliance depends on who is asking and how loudly, which quickly undermines credibility. A common pitfall is allowing verification to become a once-a-year audit exercise, which produces neat reports while leaving long windows where drift persists unnoticed. A baseline that cannot be continuously validated in practice is a baseline that will not hold under real operational conditions.

AI/ML can strengthen standards and baseline execution by improving how teams identify drift and prioritize remediation, but it must be treated as an assistive control with clear boundaries. For example, ML-driven anomaly detection can surface configuration patterns that deviate from normal for a given asset class, and correlation models can connect those deviations to identity changes or unusual access activity. These capabilities depend on reliable telemetry from configuration management, identity providers, endpoint or server logs, and change records, and they fail when data is incomplete or labels are inconsistent. Human review remains essential because models can mistake legitimate operational variance for risk, especially during migrations, incident response, or large-scale patching. False confidence is a common failure mode when an ML score is treated as proof of compliance rather than a signal to investigate, and drift can also occur as environments change faster than the model is retrained. Governance expectations should include traceable decision records for ML-driven prioritization, so leaders can audit why certain deviations were remediated quickly while others were deferred.

Standards also need a disciplined lifecycle, because the environment and threat landscape will outpace static documentation. Each standard should have a clear owner, a review cadence, and a controlled path for updates that accounts for business impact and implementation effort. When standards change without coordination, teams experience them as unpredictable mandates; when they never change, teams learn that standards are disconnected from reality. A mature approach treats standards as living operational contracts that can evolve while preserving predictability through versioning and communicated effective dates. The same rigor applies to retiring standards when technology changes, because outdated baselines become a source of confusion and accidental noncompliance. Consistent execution is sustained when standards remain current, verifiable, and integrated into daily work rather than treated as static reference material.

Procedure Design: Making Security Repeatable

Procedures are where security moves from intent to action, translating policy and standards into step-by-step execution that teams can follow under normal conditions and during stress. A well-designed procedure removes ambiguity by defining who does what, in what order, using which inputs, and producing which outputs. This matters because most security failures are not caused by missing policy, but by inconsistent execution when people interpret requirements differently. Procedures should assume limited time, partial information, and handoffs across roles, because that is how real operations function. When procedures are clear, repeatability replaces heroics, and outcomes become predictable.

Effective procedures are written from the perspective of the operator, not the author. They focus on decisions and actions rather than explanations of why security matters, which the reader already understands. Each step should be concrete enough that two different people following the same procedure would arrive at the same result, even if their experience levels differ. Inputs such as alerts, tickets, access requests, or change records should be explicitly named, so teams know when the procedure applies. Outputs should also be explicit, whether that is a configuration change, an approval, a documented decision, or an escalation to another role.

Scope discipline is critical in procedure design, because overly broad procedures are rarely followed end to end. A procedure should cover a single operational objective, such as onboarding a system, approving privileged access, responding to a specific alert class, or renewing an exception. When procedures try to handle every scenario, teams either skip steps or create informal shortcuts that undermine control. Narrow procedures also make it easier to update guidance as tools, environments, or risks change. This keeps procedures aligned with reality instead of turning them into static documents that nobody trusts during an incident.

Handoffs are the most common failure point in procedural execution, and good design addresses them directly. Each handoff should specify what information must be passed, what condition triggers the handoff, and who becomes accountable at that point. Ambiguous ownership leads to stalled tickets, duplicated work, or missed actions that attackers can exploit. Procedures should also define what happens when prerequisites are missing or when expected inputs are incomplete, because that is where teams tend to improvise. By anticipating failure paths, procedures reduce the likelihood that work simply stops or proceeds unsafely.

Verification and evidence collection should be built into the procedure rather than treated as an afterthought. Each critical action should naturally produce evidence, such as logs, approvals, screenshots, or automated records, without requiring extra effort from the operator. This not only supports audit and review, but also allows teams to self-check whether the procedure was followed correctly. A common pitfall is designing procedures that require separate documentation steps, which are often skipped under time pressure. When evidence is a byproduct of doing the work, repeatability and accountability reinforce each other.

AI/ML can improve procedural reliability by assisting with decision support and consistency, but it cannot replace defined steps or accountable ownership. For example, ML-assisted triage can suggest likely severity, related assets, or prior similar cases to guide operators through the correct procedural path. These capabilities depend on clean telemetry from alerts, asset inventories, identity systems, and historical outcomes, and they degrade when inputs are inconsistent or incomplete. Human-in-the-loop controls remain essential, because operators must validate recommendations and make judgment calls when context matters. Failure modes include automation bias, where suggested actions are accepted without scrutiny, and model drift, where outdated patterns no longer reflect current risk. Procedures should therefore define where AI input is advisory and where human approval is mandatory.

Procedures must be treated as living operational assets, not static documentation. They should be reviewed after incidents, near-misses, and major changes to identify where steps were unclear, skipped, or impractical. Feedback from operators is especially valuable, because it reveals friction that designers may not see from a governance perspective. Updates should be controlled and communicated, so teams know which version applies and when changes take effect. Making security repeatable is ultimately about designing procedures that people can and will follow consistently, even when conditions are imperfect and time is limited.

Maintaining Policy Relevance Over Time

Policy relevance decays unless it is maintained as deliberately as the systems it governs. Technology stacks shift, business processes evolve, and threat pressure changes faster than most documentation cycles. When policies lag reality, teams treat them as optional or interpret them locally, which produces inconsistent execution and hidden control gaps. A relevant policy set is one that continues to reflect how work is actually done while preserving the control intent leaders care about. Maintaining relevance is therefore an operational discipline, not a documentation exercise.

The first requirement is a clear ownership model that includes responsibility for updates, interpretation, and exception decisions. Without a named owner, policies drift into committee artifacts that only change after an incident or an audit finding. Owners need authority to resolve ambiguity quickly, because ambiguous language is where teams lose time and attackers gain opportunity. They also need structured input from the teams most affected by policy, including engineering, IT operations, and identity administration, so updates reflect real constraints. Accountability becomes credible when policy ownership includes measurable expectations, such as review cadence, update backlog management, and timely resolution of conflicts.

Review cadence should be tied to change velocity and risk concentration, not a one-size-fits-all annual schedule. Policies governing high-change areas such as identity, cloud access, and external exposure usually need more frequent review than policies governing stable physical controls. Reviews should consider not only whether requirements are still correct, but whether they are still implementable with current processes and telemetry. A policy can be technically sound and still be irrelevant if the organization cannot measure compliance or cannot execute the required steps at scale. The practical test is whether teams can follow the policy in the normal course of work without inventing side processes. If they cannot, the policy is already losing relevance, regardless of its wording.

Relevance also depends on tight coupling between policies, the standards that implement them, and the procedures that execute them. When these layers diverge, teams experience policy as aspirational while standards and procedures become the de facto reality. That divergence creates a hidden gap where leaders believe one thing is true and operators know another is true, which is a common precursor to high-impact incidents. Maintaining relevance therefore requires deliberate alignment checks: does the standard still satisfy the policy intent, and does the procedure still produce evidence that the standard is met. When alignment is treated as routine maintenance, policy becomes a reliable reference rather than an obstacle. When alignment is ignored, policy becomes a parallel universe that only matters during audits.

Telemetry is the feedback mechanism that tells you whether policies are still working. If policy requirements are not observable through logs, configuration state, access records, and workflow artifacts, the organization cannot tell whether it is operating within the intended guardrails. That lack of observability often leads to "checkbox compliance," where teams attest to adherence without reliable evidence. Mature programs treat telemetry gaps as policy risks because they undermine enforcement and accountability. When telemetry improves, policy can become more precise without becoming more burdensome, because verification becomes easier. Maintaining relevance therefore includes maintaining the measurement system that supports policy.

Exceptions are not just necessary compromises; they are a diagnostic signal about policy relevance. A growing volume of exceptions often indicates that policy scope is misaligned, standards are unrealistic, or enabling services are missing. Exception renewal patterns also reveal whether temporary constraints are being resolved or whether the organization is normalizing long-term exposures. A relevant policy program uses exception analysis to identify which requirements are frequently unworkable and why, then uses that data to drive targeted updates. This prevents the exception process from becoming a shadow policy system where real decisions occur without improving the underlying control model. Relevance is preserved when exceptions lead to refinement, not erosion.

AI/ML can help maintain policy relevance by detecting drift between stated requirements and observed operational reality, but it must be governed to avoid misleading conclusions. For example, models can identify policy-related anomalies such as repeated broad access grants, unusual exception clusters, or configuration deviations that correlate with incidents. These insights depend on high-quality structured data from identity systems, ticketing workflows, asset inventories, and monitoring telemetry, and they are vulnerable to bias if some teams document work better than others. Human review is necessary to validate signals and to distinguish meaningful drift from legitimate operational variance during migrations or incident response. Another failure mode is overfitting to past behavior, which can cause models to normalize insecure patterns simply because they are common historically. To remain trustworthy, AI-supported policy analytics must be auditable, with traceable inputs, explainable recommendations, and periodic recalibration.

Finally, policy relevance is sustained through disciplined communication and change management rather than passive publication. When policies change, teams need to know what behavior must change, what evidence will be expected, and what the transition timeline is. Silent updates create inconsistent adoption, especially in distributed organizations, and inconsistency undermines both security outcomes and leadership confidence. Effective communication treats policy updates as operational changes that require enablement, not as document revisions that require awareness. Over time, the program earns credibility when teams see that policy evolves in response to real conditions while still holding the line on control intent. That credibility is what keeps policy relevant when the organization is moving fast and attackers are moving faster.

Communicating Policy Changes Across the Organization

Policy changes fail most often at the point of communication, not at the point of writing. A policy can be technically correct and well-intentioned, yet still produce risk if teams learn about it late, interpret it differently, or cannot connect it to their day-to-day decisions. Communication is therefore part of the control, because it determines whether the organization actually changes behavior. Effective communication treats policy updates as operational change events with dependencies, rollout steps, and accountability. The objective is consistent adoption, not broad awareness.

The most important practice is communicating the "what changed" in operational terms rather than publishing revised text and assuming readers will infer impact. Teams need to understand which decisions must be made differently, which workflows are affected, and what evidence will be expected going forward. Changes should be framed in the language of work: access requests, deployment approvals, incident handling, vendor onboarding, and logging requirements. This reduces the chance that teams view policy updates as abstract governance and ignore them until an audit. Leaders also benefit because the operational framing makes it easier to assess cost, staffing implications, and implementation risk.

Communication should be audience-specific without changing the policy itself. Executives need to understand business impact, risk rationale, and any decisions required, such as funding, deadlines, or risk acceptance. Engineering and operations teams need implementation details, including timelines, required procedural changes, and how compliance will be validated. Support functions such as procurement, HR, and legal need to know when policy changes alter vendor requirements, employee responsibilities, or contractual terms. Sending the same message to everyone creates noise for some and insufficient detail for others, which is a reliable way to produce inconsistent adoption. Consistent execution depends on tailoring the message while keeping the underlying control intent stable.

A predictable change cadence reduces friction and builds trust. When policy changes arrive randomly and without context, teams treat them as surprises and respond defensively, which often turns security into a negotiation. A defined rhythm for updates—paired with emergency pathways for urgent risk—helps teams plan and reduces last-minute exceptions. Communication should also include clear effective dates and transition periods, because policies that are "effective immediately" often produce noncompliance simply due to operational inertia. Where phased rollout is needed, the phases should be tied to measurable readiness criteria, such as baseline coverage or telemetry availability. This makes adoption a managed process rather than an informal hope.

Policies are adopted when they show up inside existing workflows at decision time. Communication should therefore be paired with workflow updates, such as revised request forms, ticket templates, approval routing, and evidence expectations. If the policy changes but the workflow artifacts do not, teams will continue to behave as before, and the policy will exist only on paper. This is especially critical for controls that depend on consistent approvals or configuration changes, because missing workflow alignment creates silent bypass paths. Embedding policy changes into operational tooling also creates automatic traceability, which supports both enforcement and learning. Communication without integration tends to produce short-lived compliance followed by drift.

Training and enablement need to be practical and role-based rather than generic security awareness. When policy changes affect a technical control, teams need examples of correct implementation and common failure modes, expressed in the same vocabulary used in standards and procedures. This is where organizations often lose credibility by providing high-level statements like "use least privilege" without clarifying how that affects real access requests, service accounts, or break-glass processes. Enablement should also include guidance for exception requests during transition, so teams do not invent ad hoc workarounds when they encounter constraints. When enablement is treated as part of the change, exceptions become controlled and time-bound rather than chaotic. The result is smoother adoption and fewer operational surprises.

AI/ML can support policy-change communication by identifying who is affected and by monitoring adoption signals, but it must be used with careful governance. For example, models can analyze ticket categories, access requests, and change records to predict which teams will be most impacted and where adoption risk is highest. They can also summarize recurring questions and confusion points from support channels to refine messaging and update procedures quickly. These capabilities depend on complete and well-labeled workflow data, and they can introduce bias by over-weighting teams that document more thoroughly while under-detecting informal processes. Human review remains essential to validate impact analysis and to avoid exposing sensitive policy details through automated summaries. Auditability matters here as well: organizations should be able to trace what was communicated, to whom, and what signals indicated adoption or confusion.

Finally, communication should include a feedback mechanism and a way to measure whether the change actually landed. Feedback is not a democratic rewrite process, but it is a control improvement loop that identifies ambiguity, friction, and unintended consequences early. Measurement can include adoption indicators such as reduced exception volume after transition, consistent evidence in tickets, and fewer policy-related escalations due to misunderstanding. Without feedback and measurement, organizations confuse publication with implementation and only discover problems after an incident or audit. Policy change communication succeeds when it produces consistent behavior, predictable decision-making, and a shared understanding of what will be enforced. That consistency is what keeps the organization aligned when risk increases and operational tempo is high.

Auditable Controls and Evidence Expectations

Auditable controls are controls that can be demonstrated, not merely asserted. In operational security, "auditability" is less about preparing for an external audit and more about being able to prove, internally and continuously, that critical safeguards are in place and functioning. When leaders ask whether a control exists, the answer should come from evidence: configuration state, identity records, logs, approvals, and documented exceptions. Without evidence expectations, controls degrade into informal practice, and informal practice collapses under staff turnover, incident pressure, or organizational change. Evidence is the connective tissue between policy intent and operational reality.

Evidence expectations begin with defining what "proof" looks like for each control objective. If a standard requires MFA for privileged access, evidence might include identity provider configuration, enforcement logs, and records of any break-glass usage. If a baseline requires specific logging, evidence might include telemetry configuration, log retention settings, and demonstration that events are actually arriving and being reviewed. The key is that evidence must be attributable to a specific asset and time period, because generic statements like "we log everything" are not defensible. Evidence must also be reproducible, meaning another qualified person could retrieve the same proof using the same sources. This shifts the organization from trusting process to validating outcomes.

Operationally, evidence is strongest when it is generated automatically as part of normal work. Manual evidence collection is brittle because it depends on people remembering to capture screenshots, attach notes, or write explanations after the fact. Procedures should be designed so that approvals, changes, and validations leave a durable trail in the systems used to manage work. This includes consistent ticketing artifacts, approval routing, change records, and identity events that can be queried later. When evidence is a byproduct of execution, auditability improves without adding friction. When evidence is an extra step, it becomes optional in practice and unreliable in hindsight.

A common failure mode is confusing the existence of a document with the existence of a control. A written policy or standard is not evidence that the control is in place, and a completed checklist is not evidence that the control is functioning. Auditable controls require verification that the configured state matches the intended state and that it stays that way over time. This is where drift matters: systems change, exceptions accumulate, and emergency fixes introduce temporary weakening that becomes permanent. Evidence expectations should therefore include both point-in-time validation and time-bound continuity, such as proof of periodic checks or event-driven validation after changes. The organization is most exposed when it can prove what was true last quarter but cannot prove what is true today.

Evidence also needs quality standards to remain useful to leadership and defensible under scrutiny. Evidence should be clear about the source of truth, the time window, and the relationship between the artifact and the control objective. It should avoid ambiguity, such as screenshots with no context or logs with missing system identifiers. It should also be retained according to a realistic retention model, because evidence that expires before it is needed undermines incident investigations and compliance obligations. Over-retention can create cost and privacy issues, but under-retention creates operational blind spots that are difficult to recover from. Good evidence management treats retention as part of risk management, not as a storage problem.

AI/ML can improve auditability by detecting missing evidence and by prioritizing where verification effort should go, but it must be constrained by governance. For example, ML can identify patterns of control drift by comparing expected configuration states to observed telemetry across large asset populations, and it can highlight systems whose evidence trails are incomplete or inconsistent. These approaches depend on reliable telemetry pipelines, consistent asset identity mapping, and labeled outcomes that distinguish false alarms from true gaps. Failure modes include false confidence from incomplete visibility, where the model reports high compliance because it cannot see unmanaged assets or uninstrumented systems. Another risk is leakage, where evidence artifacts contain sensitive data that could be exposed through automated summarization or reporting if access controls are weak. Human review and access governance must remain central, with clear approval boundaries for automated findings that trigger enforcement actions.

Exception handling is inseparable from evidence expectations because exceptions are deliberate deviations from the standard control posture. A well-run exception process produces auditable artifacts: the justification, the approver, the compensating controls, the expiration date, and the evidence that compensating controls are functioning. Without these artifacts, exceptions become invisible policy rewrites that cannot be reviewed or revoked. Evidence expectations should also include renewal criteria, because a time-bound exception that is repeatedly renewed without change is effectively permanent and should be treated as such. Leaders should be able to see exception inventory by control area and risk level, because exceptions are often the clearest indicator of where enabling capabilities are missing. In a mature program, exception evidence informs prioritization rather than merely satisfying oversight.

Ultimately, auditable controls and evidence expectations enable accountability without slowing the business. They allow security teams to answer questions quickly, to detect drift early, and to focus remediation where it matters most. They also support incident response by providing reliable historical context about what controls were in place and when they changed. When evidence is designed into workflows, auditability becomes an operational benefit rather than a periodic burden. The organization gains confidence not because it claims to be secure, but because it can demonstrate control with clear, repeatable proof.

Automation and AI in Control Execution: Where It Helps and Where It Must Not Decide

Automation improves control execution when it reduces variance, shortens time-to-action, and makes the secure path the default path. In practical terms, automation is most valuable for controls that are repetitive, state-based, and measurable, such as enforcing configuration baselines, applying identity lifecycle rules, validating logging settings, and performing routine evidence collection. These are areas where human execution is often inconsistent due to workload and where drift accumulates quietly over time. Automation also strengthens resilience by operating continuously, not just during business hours, and by producing standardized artifacts that support auditability. The business value shows up as fewer preventable incidents and less operational friction from one-off enforcement.

A second category where automation helps is workflow orchestration, where controls depend on predictable handoffs and timely approvals. Automated routing can ensure requests reach the right approver, enforce required fields, and prevent implementation until prerequisites are met. This is particularly important for privileged access workflows, sensitive data handling, and changes that affect external exposure, because those are the seams where informal shortcuts are most common. Orchestration also reduces "silent bypass" by ensuring controls are applied consistently regardless of who submits the request or which team is executing the change. When the workflow system itself enforces the process, compliance becomes a property of the system rather than a memory test for busy operators. That shift is central to making controls durable.

AI-assisted execution adds value when it improves triage, correlation, and prioritization across high-volume signals. In many operations, the limiting factor is not a lack of alerts or findings but a lack of attention, and AI can help by grouping related events, highlighting anomalies, and suggesting likely root causes based on patterns in historical data. This is operationally appropriate when the AI output is treated as a recommendation that accelerates human judgment rather than replacing it. The data dependencies are non-negotiable: reliable identity telemetry, asset inventory context, change records, and consistent event logging are required for AI to provide meaningful guidance. Without that foundation, AI produces confident noise, and confident noise is worse than silence because it encourages misplaced trust. The goal is to reduce cognitive load while preserving accountability. Table 3.3 clarifies where automation and AI can accelerate execution and where human accountability must remain the decision point.

Where automation and AI must not decide is where the control outcome represents risk acceptance, legal exposure, or irreversible business impact. Decisions such as granting or expanding privileged access, approving exceptions that weaken a control, waiving security requirements for a release, or classifying data in ways that

Table 3.3 Automation and AI Decision Boundaries in Control Execution.

Control Activity	Automation Role	AI Role	Human Decision Required	Audit Record
Baseline enforcement	Apply required state	Flag deviations	Yes for disruptive actions	Change log entry
Evidence capture	Collect artifacts	Summarize gaps	No	Evidence repository record
Workflow routing	Enforce required fields	Suggest approver	Yes for exceptions	Ticket trail
Triage and correlation	Group-related events	Suggest severity	Yes for containment	Case notes
Privileged access grant	Block without approval	Suggest risk context	Yes always	Approval record
Exception approval	Track expiry and renewal	Suggest comparable cases	Yes always	Exception register

change access scope require accountable human authorization. AI can inform these decisions by surfacing relevant context, comparable prior cases, and likely outcomes, but it should not be the final authority. The failure mode here is automation bias, where a plausible recommendation becomes a de facto approval path, especially under time pressure. Another failure mode is policy drift, where the AI learns from a history of permissive decisions and begins to normalize risky behavior as "typical." Approval boundaries must therefore be explicit and enforced in workflow, not left to convention.

Control execution also has "must not decide" zones related to containment and response actions that can disrupt operations. Automated isolation, account disablement, or traffic blocking can be appropriate when conditions are well-defined and the blast radius is understood, but the threshold must be carefully governed. If automation triggers disruptive actions based on weak signals, the organization will quickly disable it, and the control will fail in the next true incident. Conversely, if thresholds are too conservative, automation becomes a reporting tool rather than an execution tool. A practical approach is to automate low-risk, reversible actions and require human confirmation for actions that could materially affect availability or customer experience. This preserves speed while ensuring that operational context remains part of the decision.

Evidence collection is one of the safest and highest-return areas for automation and AI, because it supports accountability without directly changing control posture. Automating evidence capture from configuration state, identity logs, and workflow records reduces the temptation to rely on attestations and makes audits and internal reviews less disruptive. AI can further help by summarizing evidence gaps, detecting inconsistent artifacts, and highlighting anomalies that suggest controls are not being executed as intended. The primary risks here are completeness and leakage: evidence systems can create false confidence if coverage is partial, and they can expose sensitive information if access controls are weak or summaries are shared too broadly. Governance must therefore define who can access evidence, how long it is retained, and how sensitive data is handled in automated reporting. Auditability should improve security posture, not create a new data-exposure problem.

Human-in-the-loop controls are not a slogan; they are a design requirement that must be implemented through explicit gates, approvals, and traceability. For AI-assisted recommendations, the system should record inputs, outputs, the human decision, and the rationale when decisions deviate from recommendations. This creates an audit trail and supports continuous improvement, because teams can analyze when AI was helpful, when it was wrong, and why. It also helps detect model drift by showing changes in performance over time as environments and attacker behavior evolve. If decisions are not traceable, the organization cannot defend them and cannot improve the system. Governance should treat AI outputs as part of the control system, subject to the same evidence expectations as any other mechanism.

Over time, the healthiest posture is to treat automation and AI as accelerators of disciplined process rather than replacements for it. Automation should enforce the known-good path, reduce manual error, and provide continuous verification. AI should reduce triage burden, improve signal-to-noise, and highlight context that humans might miss, while remaining subordinate to accountable decision-making. When the organization is clear about where machines act and where humans decide, controls become faster without becoming reckless. That clarity prevents both extremes: paralysis from fear of automation and overreach from delegating risk decisions to systems that cannot own consequences. In mature operations, the question is not whether to automate, but which decisions must remain human to preserve trust, accountability, and control.

Common Policy Failure Modes in Real Organizations

One of the most common policy failure modes is writing policy as an aspirational statement rather than an operational constraint. Policies that read like values—"systems must be secure," "access must be appropriate," "data must be protected"—signal intent but do not guide decisions. Teams are then forced to interpret what "secure" means in the context of a specific system, deadline, and set of tradeoffs, which guarantees inconsistent execution.

This ambiguity becomes a control gap because enforcement depends on who is involved and how much time they have. In practice, attackers benefit from the seams created by interpretation, especially where privileged access and external exposure intersect.

A second failure mode is scope inflation that outpaces visibility and capability. Policies are often written to cover "all systems" or "all data" while the organization lacks a complete asset inventory, consistent identity governance, or reliable telemetry. This creates a predictable pattern where compliance becomes symbolic: teams attest to requirements that cannot be measured, and security reports success based on incomplete coverage. Over time, unmanaged environments and inherited platforms become the real operating surface, while policy describes an idealized environment that does not exist. Leaders then make risk decisions using a distorted picture of control effectiveness. The result is not just noncompliance, but strategic miscalculation.

Policy fragmentation is another frequent failure mode, where different parts of the organization maintain overlapping policies with conflicting terms and requirements. This often happens after mergers, reorganizations, or rapid platform expansion, when teams copy and modify documents locally to solve immediate problems. The same role might be called "system owner" in one document, "service owner" in another, and "application steward" in a third, each with different responsibilities. Conflicts also appear in control requirements, such as inconsistent patch timelines or logging expectations across environments. Fragmentation forces teams to choose which policy to follow, and they will choose the least disruptive option under delivery pressure. In effect, fragmentation creates a "policy shopping" environment that erodes enforcement and accountability.

Another failure mode is treating exceptions as a release valve rather than a controlled workflow with time bounds and compensating controls. When exception requests are handled through informal approvals, chat messages, or undocumented agreements, they become permanent holes in the control model. Even when exceptions are documented, they often lack expiration dates or renewal criteria, which means risk acceptance is never revisited. Compensating controls are frequently described in vague terms like "monitoring will be increased," without specifying what telemetry exists, who reviews it, and what triggers escalation. Over time, the exception inventory becomes a shadow policy set that describes the real control posture, while the published policy becomes a formality. Attackers tend to find and exploit exactly these long-lived, undocumented deviations.

A fifth failure mode is policy that is disconnected from standards and procedures, creating a gap between governance language and operational execution. Security teams may believe a control exists because the policy requires it, while operators follow procedures that do not implement the requirement or cannot produce evidence. This is common when policies change but workflows and templates do not, so teams continue executing the old process with the new language sitting elsewhere. The disconnect is especially damaging for controls that rely on consistent approvals, identity lifecycle steps, or logging configuration, because these controls fail silently when not embedded into the work system. The organization then discovers the gap only during an incident, when it becomes clear that the control was never effectively implemented. This undermines trust in both security reporting and governance.

AI/ML introduces its own set of policy failure modes when organizations treat automated outputs as authoritative without governance. One pattern is allowing AI-generated risk scores or summaries to become de facto policy interpretation, especially when reviewers are overloaded and rely on recommendations as shortcuts. This creates automation bias, where plausible outputs are accepted even when telemetry is incomplete or context is missing. Another pattern is drift, where models trained on past decisions learn permissive norms or outdated operating conditions and continue recommending actions that no longer align with current risk. Leakage is also a risk when AI systems summarize sensitive exception rationales, security findings, or evidence artifacts into channels that are not access-controlled appropriately. Without auditability of inputs, outputs, and approvals, AI-supported policy execution becomes harder to defend than purely human decision-making.

Finally, policy often fails through neglect of maintenance and communication, even when the initial content is strong. Policies are published, referenced in onboarding, and then rarely updated, despite significant changes in architecture, identity platforms, and external exposure. Teams learn that policy is not a reliable guide to current expectations, so they stop consulting it and rely on local norms. When updates do occur, they are communicated as document revisions rather than operational changes, so adoption becomes uneven and enforcement inconsistent. The net effect is predictable: policy becomes a compliance artifact that does not shape behavior, while real risk decisions are made ad hoc. In mature organizations, policies remain relevant only when they are treated as living controls with ownership, telemetry, and disciplined change management.

Conclusion

A durable policy program is ultimately measured by consistent behavior, not by the volume or elegance of the documents that describe it. When scope is explicit, ownership is real, and exceptions are controlled, policy becomes a dependable operational interface that guides decisions at the pace the business moves. Standards, baselines, and procedures make that interface executable, while auditable evidence turns control claims into defensible facts that can be validated and improved. Automation and AI strengthen execution when they reduce variance and accelerate analysis, but control is preserved only when human accountability remains the final authority for risk acceptance, disruptive actions, and irreversible decisions.

Recommendations

1) Treat policy as an operational interface, not a compliance artifact. Write policies to guide real decisions under time pressure, using clear constraints and permissions that make the secure path the easiest path. Ensure each requirement can be understood and applied by the teams who execute it, not just reviewed by stakeholders. Validate usability by testing whether operators can follow the policy without needing informal interpretation.
2) Define policy scope explicitly to prevent inconsistent enforcement. Specify which systems, data types, identities, and access pathways the policy governs, including service accounts, API keys, vendors, and privileged workflows. Avoid "applies to everything" language when visibility and control coverage are incomplete, because it drives performative compliance. Align scope to asset realities so enforcement can be measured and defended.
3) Establish a controlled exception workflow that preserves control intent. Require exceptions to be time-bound, documented, and approved by an accountable authority with clear risk ownership. Demand compensating controls that are specific, observable, and assigned to an owner, rather than vague promises of "increased monitoring." Review exceptions regularly to close them, tighten conditions, or convert recurring needs into updated standards.
4) Translate policies into standards and baselines that are implementable and verifiable. Convert broad requirements into specific, testable expectations tied to recognizable asset classes and operational contexts. Ensure each standard defines what evidence proves compliance so validation is not a debate. Design baselines to reduce variance across teams and platforms while remaining adaptable to operational change.
5) Design procedures around repeatability, handoffs, and stress conditions. Build procedures that define inputs, roles, decision points, and outputs, so execution is consistent regardless of who performs the work. Make handoffs explicit, including what information must transfer and who becomes accountable at each step. Include failure paths for missing prerequisites, so teams do not improvise unsafe shortcuts.
6) Embed verification and evidence collection into normal workflows. Make approvals, changes, and validations produce durable artifacts automatically through the systems used to manage work. Define evidence expectations that are attributable to specific assets and time windows, and ensure another qualified person could reproduce the proof. Treat drift as inevitable and design for continuous validation rather than annual confirmation.

7) Align policy, standards, and procedures to prevent control gaps created by divergence. Regularly check that standards still satisfy policy intent and that procedures reliably implement the standards with measurable outputs. Update workflows and templates when policies change, so teams do not continue executing old processes with new language sitting elsewhere. Use misalignment as a signal that policy is losing operational relevance.
8) Communicate policy changes as operational change events with adoption requirements. Explain what changed in terms of decisions and workflows, state effective dates, and provide transition periods that reflect implementation reality. Tailor communication to audiences, so executives understand risk and impact while operators receive practical implementation guidance. Pair announcements with workflow updates, so policy shows up at decision time rather than as passive documentation.
9) Use automation to enforce consistency and reduce variance, not to outsource accountability. Automate repetitive, state-based controls like baseline enforcement, workflow routing, and evidence capture to reduce manual error and drift. Prefer automation for low-risk, reversible actions, and require explicit human confirmation for disruptive changes that could affect availability or customer experience. Treat automation outputs as part of the control system that must be observable and auditable.
10) Apply AI/ML to triage, correlation, and prioritization while keeping humans as the decision authority for risk acceptance. Use AI to group signals, suggest likely context, and highlight anomalies when supporting telemetry is reliable and coverage is understood. Define human-in-the-loop approval boundaries for privileged access, exceptions, and other high-impact decisions to avoid automation bias and false confidence. Maintain auditability of AI inputs, recommendations, and human outcomes, so drift, bias, and leakage risks can be detected and corrected.

4

Building a Blue Team Operating Model

A blue team operating model is what turns security effort into reliable security outcomes, especially as environments grow more complex and less forgiving. It defines the services the blue team delivers, the owners accountable for results, and the operating rhythms that keep work prioritized, visible, and continuously improved. It also establishes the practical mechanics that determine whether response is fast and controlled or slow and improvisational, including escalation paths, on-call coverage, cross-team collaboration, and the documentation that preserves continuity through change. Finally, it incorporates AI-assisted operational support where it improves speed and consistency while keeping human decision rights, auditability, and governance firmly in place.

Defining Blue Team Services and Service Owners

A blue team operating model becomes real when "security" is expressed as a defined set of services with clear entry points, outputs, and accountable decision-makers. A service is not a technology and it is not a team name; it is a repeatable capability that produces a measurable outcome for the organization. Leaders should be able to ask what the blue team provides, what "done" looks like for each offering, and how other parts of the business consume it. Services should be described in business language first, with technical mechanics and tooling treated as implementation details that can evolve without changing the promise. This framing reduces ambiguity in expectations and prevents the common failure mode where security work is perceived as a collection of ad hoc tasks rather than a reliable operational function.

Defining services starts with identifying stable demand signals and mapping them to operational outputs, not by inventorying tools. Security monitoring becomes a service when it has declared coverage goals, alert handling boundaries, escalation paths, and reporting cadences that stakeholders can rely on. Vulnerability management becomes a service when it includes prioritization logic, remediation coordination, exception handling, and verification of closure rather than simply generating scan results. Identity assurance becomes a service when it has provisioning standards, access review routines, and clear controls for privileged access beyond the presence of an IAM platform. When services are framed this way, the organization can distinguish between the service promise and the mechanisms used to deliver it, which keeps the operating model resilient through reorganizations and technology refreshes.

Service definitions also force clarity on interfaces, because every blue team service has customers, upstream dependencies, and downstream handoffs. Incident response depends on reliable telemetry, accurate asset inventories, and pre-negotiated legal and communications workflows, so its service definition must explicitly include those prerequisites and who provides them. Detection engineering depends on log collection standards, data normalization, and change control, so the service must include minimum logging requirements and a process for onboarding new data sources. Threat intelligence, if treated as a service, must define how intelligence is operationalized into detections, awareness, or control adjustments rather than existing as a passive reporting function.

The service catalog becomes the shared vocabulary for cross-team collaboration, making gaps visible as broken or missing interfaces instead of invisible organizational friction.

Once services are defined, ownership must be assigned in a way that matches decision authority to accountability. A service owner is not a coordinator who chases updates; they are the accountable leader for the service's outcomes, quality, and evolution, with the authority to set standards and make tradeoffs. Ownership includes defining success metrics, managing the service backlog, approving changes that affect service reliability, and negotiating priorities with stakeholders when demand exceeds capacity. The service owner also owns the service's risk posture, including which risks are accepted, which are mitigated, and which require escalation to business leadership. Without that authority, "ownership" devolves into a title without leverage, and services revert to informal best-effort delivery. This table shows how blue team work becomes measurable services with clear outcomes inputs outputs and accountable ownership. Table 4.1 shows how blue team work becomes measurable services with clear outcomes inputs outputs and accountable ownership.

Good service ownership also clarifies what work belongs where, which prevents duplication and reduces missed responsibilities at the seams. For example, the owner of monitoring and detection should be accountable for end-to-end signal quality, including alert fidelity, triage playbooks, and feedback loops from incident handlers back into detection tuning. The owner of vulnerability management should be accountable for prioritization and governance, including how exploitability and business criticality influence remediation expectations and how exceptions are documented and reviewed. The owner of identity services should be accountable for access assurance outcomes, including the integrity of privileged access processes and the reliability of access reviews, rather than delegating those outcomes to whichever team happens to administer the directory. This role clarity enables executives to resolve disputes quickly because accountability is explicit and aligned to outcomes rather than personalities.

Table 4.1 Blue Team Service Catalog Snapshot.

Service	Primary Outcome	Key Inputs	Key Outputs	Service Owner Accountability
Security monitoring and triage	Timely identification of actionable events	Telemetry alerts case queue	Triage decisions escalations case records	End-to-end signal quality and triage boundaries
Detection engineering	Actionable detections aligned to telemetry coverage	Log sources normalization requirements change context	Detection rules tuning notes test results	Coverage fidelity and tuning backlog decisions
Incident response	Controlled containment and recovery with preserved evidence	Alerts cases asset ownership escalation contacts	Containment actions evidence capture handoffs	Response speed decision rights and escalation execution
Vulnerability management	Sustained reduction of exploitable exposure	Scan results asset criticality remediation capacity	Prioritized remediation work exceptions verification	Prioritization logic exception governance closure verification
Identity assurance	Reduced access misuse and privileged risk	Provisioning events access reviews privileged activity	Access controls review outcomes revocations	Standards for access assurance and review reliability
Threat intelligence operationalization	Intelligence converted into defensive action	Intel inputs incident learnings detections gaps	Detection updates awareness inputs control adjustments	Operational use cases and measurable impact

Table 4.2 Operating Rhythm Cadence Map.

Cadence	Primary Focus	Core Artifacts	Key Decisions	Operational Intent
Daily	Situational awareness and fast triage	Case queue escalation log exposure changes	Containment triggers escalation initiation	Protect response time and reduce ambiguity
Weekly	Service health and improvement work	Backlog review tuning actions recurring issues list	Prioritization tradeoffs cross team commitments	Convert activity into managed improvements
Monthly	Risk posture and governance	Service outcomes trends sustained exceptions	Investment decisions risk acceptance scope changes	Keep operating model aligned to business change

AI/ML becomes operationally valuable inside service ownership when it is treated as an assistive capability governed like any other production dependency. In monitoring and triage, machine learning–based clustering and summarization can reduce alert noise, correlate related activity, and speed up case assembly, but it depends on clean, consistent telemetry and stable labeling signals from prior incident outcomes. Service owners must define human-in-the-loop approval boundaries, such as requiring analyst confirmation before a case is closed, before an indicator is promoted to blocking controls, or before an incident is escalated to executives. Failure modes must be anticipated, including false confidence when the model overgeneralizes from sparse data, drift when attacker behaviors change, and bias when training labels reflect inconsistent past decisions. Governance expectations should include auditability of AI-assisted decisions, retention of the underlying evidence used for model outputs, and a clear mechanism to roll back automation when quality degrades.

Finally, service definitions and service ownership provide the foundation for capacity planning and credible reporting, because the organization can measure work by service outcomes rather than by volume of activity. When leaders ask whether security is improving, the blue team can answer in terms of service reliability, coverage, and response performance, not just the number of alerts reviewed or tickets closed. Service owners can defend investment requests with concrete constraints, such as telemetry gaps limiting detection coverage or staffing levels constraining response time, and can show the operational impact of addressing those constraints. This structure also enables consistent prioritization across competing demands, because each request can be evaluated against the service promise and the risk it mitigates. The result is a blue team that behaves like an operating function with accountable owners, predictable outputs, and controlled change, rather than an always-on help desk reacting to the loudest problem of the day. Table 4.2 clarifies what each cadence is for what outputs it produces and what decisions it enables.

Operating Rhythms: Daily, Weekly, and Monthly Cadence

Operating rhythm is the discipline of turning security work into a predictable cadence of decisions, reviews, and handoffs, so outcomes do not depend on heroics or individual memory. A cadence is not a calendar of meetings for its own sake; it is the minimum set of recurring touchpoints that keep the blue team aligned to risk, capacity, and business priorities. When rhythms are well designed, they make the invisible visible by forcing teams to surface drift, debt, and emerging threats before they become incidents. They also reduce operational thrash by creating predictable “decision windows” instead of constant, unstructured interruptions. Executives benefit because progress becomes measurable and exceptions become explainable rather than mysterious.

Daily rhythms exist to preserve situational awareness and protect response time, especially where attackers move faster than organizational change. The daily cycle typically orients around incoming signals, new exposures, and

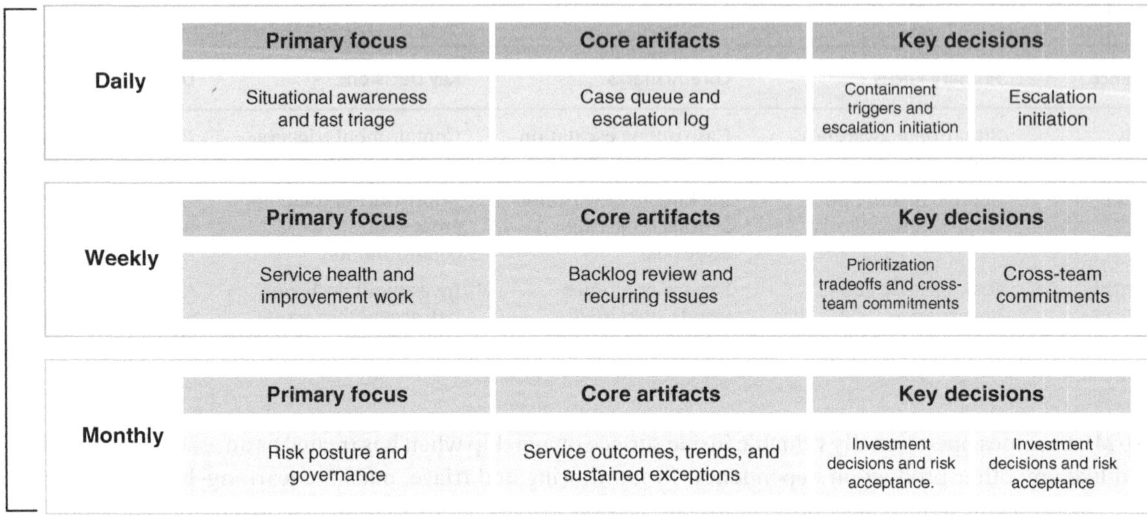

Figure 4.1 Operating Rhythms and Decision Windows Across Daily Weekly Monthly Cadence.

active investigations, with emphasis on what requires action within hours. Effective daily operations separate triage from response, ensuring the team does not confuse "acknowledging" an alert with actually containing a problem. Daily work should include short feedback loops that validate whether the right telemetry is arriving, whether detections are producing actionable fidelity, and whether escalations are flowing to the right owners. When AI-assisted triage is used to cluster related alerts or draft case summaries, daily rhythm must explicitly include human validation steps to prevent automation from quietly normalizing false positives or missing weak but meaningful signals. Figure 4.1 maps daily weekly and monthly cadence to the artifacts and decisions each rhythm is intended to produce. It supports the chapter's focus on predictable decision windows that reduce thrash and make progress measurable.

Weekly rhythms exist to convert operational activity into managed work, so the team continually improves rather than only reacts. Weekly cadence is where the blue team checks the health of services, reviews backlog, and resolves friction points with partners like IT operations, identity, and application teams. This is also the natural interval for reviewing near misses and lessons learned that do not rise to full incident postmortems but still reveal control gaps or brittle processes. Weekly rhythms should force prioritization decisions, particularly around detection tuning, vulnerability remediation coordination, and response playbook maintenance, because those tasks are otherwise perpetually deferred. If AI/ML is being used to recommend prioritization or to summarize trends, weekly review must include spot checks against raw evidence to guard against model drift and the tendency for summaries to obscure outliers.

Monthly rhythms exist to manage risk posture and governance, ensuring leadership receives consistent, decision-ready information and that the operating model stays aligned to business change. Monthly cadence is where the team reviews service-level outcomes, trends in exposure, incident patterns, and the effectiveness of response and recovery processes. It is also where the blue team should reconcile reality against stated policy, because policy-only compliance that is not reflected in operational performance is a warning sign of control theater. Monthly review is a good point to examine sustained exceptions, such as delayed patching for critical systems or recurring access review failures, and to force a decision on whether those exceptions are accepted risk or require investment. Leaders should see the delta between what the team is responsible for and what it can actually deliver at current capacity, without the team resorting to vague narratives or selective metrics.

A mature cadence makes work visible through stable artifacts and consistent handoffs, rather than through slides built on demand. Daily artifacts tend to be operational, such as case queues, escalation logs, and a concise record of what changed in exposure or threat activity since the prior day. Weekly artifacts tend to be improvement-oriented, such as lists of detection gaps, recurring failure modes, aging vulnerability exceptions, and operational debt that is compounding risk. Monthly artifacts tend to be executive-ready, such as service health indicators, risk trends tied to business units or critical systems, and decisions required from leadership to remove constraints. The point is not to generate documentation volume, but to preserve continuity so the organization can answer, with evidence, why a decision was made and what changed afterward.

Cadence must also account for the reality that security is a dependency-driven system, where many outcomes require coordinated effort outside the blue team. If the rhythm does not include predictable engagement with service owners in IT, identity, and application delivery, the blue team will accumulate unresolved findings that degrade trust and eventually reduce cooperation. Operating rhythms should include explicit escalation pathways for stalled remediation and repeated failures, with thresholds that trigger leadership involvement before risks become normalized. Done well, cadence reduces interpersonal conflict because it replaces ad hoc pressure with an agreed-upon process for prioritization and accountability. It also supports business continuity because critical decisions—like isolating a system, revoking access, or pausing a deployment—are executed through established channels rather than improvised during crisis.

The most common failure mode in operating rhythm is confusing activity with control, where the organization holds frequent meetings but cannot demonstrate improved outcomes. Another failure mode is overloading the cadence until it becomes performative, pulling key responders into recurring sessions that prevent them from doing the work the cadence is supposed to govern. Rhythm should be designed around operational constraints, with explicit protection of focus time for investigation, detection engineering, and remediation coordination. It should also be resilient to surge conditions, with rules for what gets deferred during active incidents and how the cadence is restored afterward. When cadence is treated as an operating system rather than a bureaucracy, it becomes the mechanism that makes blue team services reliable, improvable, and governable.

Intake, Prioritization, and Work Management

Intake is the control point where security demand becomes accountable work, and it determines whether the blue team operates deliberately or remains trapped in reactive churn. Without a defined intake process, requests arrive through informal channels, urgency is set by who asks loudest, and important work competes poorly against visible interruptions. A good intake model creates a single, predictable path for new work to enter the system, even if the work originates from many sources like detections, audits, vulnerability scans, incident follow-ups, or executive asks. It also establishes basic completeness standards, so teams are not forced to spend cycles reconstructing context, scope, and ownership. For executives, intake is what makes security delivery legible because it turns scattered requests into a managed portfolio of risk-reducing work.

Prioritization must be explicit because capacity is finite, and "do everything" is not an operating strategy. Effective prioritization considers impact, likelihood, and time sensitivity, but it also acknowledges practical constraints such as business criticality, operational windows, and dependencies on other teams. Work should be categorized by the type of outcome it drives, such as immediate risk containment, sustained risk reduction, or service quality improvement, because these classes compete differently for attention. When prioritization is implicit, teams tend to over-invest in visible activities like closing tickets while under-investing in foundational work like telemetry onboarding or detection quality, which quietly increases future risk. The goal is a repeatable decision process that stakeholders can understand, even when they disagree with the result.

Work management is where prioritization becomes execution, and it depends on defining what "ready" and "done" mean for security tasks. "Ready" includes enough information to act: affected assets, business owner, urgency rationale, constraints, and the expected outcome, not just a vague description of a problem. "Done" must be tied to verified outcomes rather than intent, such as confirming a vulnerability is actually remediated in production, validating a detection fires correctly under controlled conditions, or documenting a risk exception with an expiration and review path. If "done" is defined as "handed off," teams accumulate hidden backlog in other queues, and the blue team loses credibility when risks persist despite apparent activity. Operationally, this is where clear handoffs and accountability boundaries prevent security work from becoming an endless loop of rework.

Intake should also enforce routing to the correct service owner, because many security requests are misdirected by default. A request that looks like "monitor this" might actually be a telemetry onboarding problem, a logging standard issue, or an identity control gap, and routing it incorrectly creates wasted cycles and slow outcomes. Clear routing rules reduce contention between teams and prevent duplication, especially when multiple groups touch the same domain such as identity, endpoint controls, and cloud configuration. Where ambiguity is common, intake should include a lightweight triage function that is empowered to clarify scope and assign ownership quickly. This preserves responder time for true investigations while ensuring requests do not stall in limbo.

AI/ML can improve intake and prioritization, but only when its recommendations are treated as advisory signals grounded in evidence rather than as decision authority. Models can summarize request text, extract entities like systems and owners, cluster similar issues to expose recurring patterns, and suggest priority based on learned outcomes from past incidents and remediation performance. These capabilities are dependent on clean historical data, consistent labeling of severity and outcomes, and a stable taxonomy for services and work types; without those, the model will amplify inconsistency and produce persuasive but unreliable outputs. Human-in-the-loop controls are essential, including explicit approval boundaries for any automated re-prioritization, automated closure, or routing that affects response time and risk acceptance. The failure mode to watch is false confidence, where the team begins to trust prioritization scores without validating them against business context, leading to systematic under-prioritization of rare but high-impact scenarios.

A practical work management model also separates interrupt-driven work from planned work so that urgent signals do not consume all capacity and quietly degrade long-term posture. Triage and incident handling require responsiveness, but detection engineering, control hardening, and vulnerability program improvements require protected time and predictable throughput. If everything is treated as urgent, the team will oscillate between partial starts and abandoned tasks, creating operational debt that increases future alert volume and incident frequency. Work-in-progress limits, enforced informally through leadership discipline rather than bureaucracy, help keep the team finishing work rather than endlessly starting it. This balance is what allows blue teams to reduce risk over time instead of merely surviving.

Finally, intake and prioritization must produce transparency that leaders can use to make tradeoffs, especially when the organization asks for more than the team can deliver. A credible backlog shows what is being deferred and what risk that deferral carries, which enables informed decisions about resourcing, scope reduction, or acceptance of exposure. When stakeholders can see consistent prioritization logic and verified completion outcomes, friction decreases even when requests are declined or delayed. Conversely, when work management is opaque, security is perceived as arbitrary, and teams compensate by creating shadow channels that bypass intake entirely. A disciplined intake and work management system is therefore both an operational control and a trust mechanism, keeping the blue team accountable while protecting it from unsustainable demand.

Escalation Paths, Authority Boundaries, and Decision Rights

Escalation is the mechanism that prevents security operations from stalling when risk, uncertainty, or organizational friction exceeds the team's authority. In practice, most failures during incidents or sustained exposures are not caused by a lack of technical options, but by hesitation about who can approve disruptive actions and who owns the business impact. Clear escalation paths convert ambiguity into a predictable sequence of decisions, reducing time lost to debate and preventing decisions from being made by whoever happens to be available. Authority boundaries define what the blue team can do unilaterally, what requires peer coordination, and what requires executive approval. Decision rights make those boundaries enforceable by naming who decides, who must be consulted, and what evidence is required to act.

Authority boundaries should be explicit because many security actions are operationally invasive, even when they are technically simple. Isolating an endpoint, disabling an account, blocking a domain, or quarantining email can interrupt business operations, trigger customer impact, or create legal and compliance implications. The blue team needs pre-defined authority to take time-critical protective actions within agreed limits, especially when the alternative is uncontrolled attacker movement. At the same time, boundaries must acknowledge that business owners are accountable for mission impact, which is why authority is best expressed as a set of conditions and thresholds rather than as blanket permissions. When boundaries are unclear, teams either hesitate and allow harm to spread, or overreach and lose trust, both of which degrade response effectiveness.

Decision rights should be built around the kinds of decisions that recur under pressure, not around the org chart. Common recurring decisions include whether an event is declared an incident, whether to contain aggressively or monitor silently, whether to invoke legal counsel and external communications, and whether to take a critical system offline. Other decisions include whether to accept a vulnerability exception, whether to delay a release due to a security finding, and whether to require an emergency control change outside normal change windows. Each decision type should have an owner with authority to approve it, and that authority should be backed by a clear expectation of what evidence is required and what documentation must be produced afterward. This structure is what turns escalation into a control rather than a personal negotiation.

Escalation paths work best when they are tiered, time-bound, and tied to defined triggers. Tiered escalation means the first escalation is to an accountable operational owner who can act quickly, while subsequent escalations move to broader authority when impact or uncertainty increases. Time-bound escalation means that if action is not taken within a defined window, the decision moves upward automatically rather than waiting for consensus to form. Trigger-based escalation means teams do not have to argue about whether escalation is appropriate; conditions such as confirmed lateral movement, privileged credential exposure, regulated data risk, or repeated remediation failure initiate escalation by default. This design reduces the chance that critical decisions are delayed simply because the early symptoms looked ambiguous or inconvenient.

AI/ML can improve escalation quality by accelerating triage, summarizing evidence, and forecasting likely impact, but it must not become a substitute for decision accountability. Models can help analysts assemble a coherent narrative from noisy telemetry, correlate related activity across systems, and draft an escalation brief that includes the what, so what, and now what. These benefits depend on reliable telemetry pipelines, consistent incident labeling, and disciplined post-incident documentation, because poor historical data leads to confident but incorrect recommendations. Human-in-the-loop controls should require that a named decision-maker validate the underlying evidence and confirm that recommended actions align with authority boundaries and business constraints. The failure mode to guard against is automation-driven escalation that either floods leaders with low-value notifications or under-escalates meaningful risk because the model learned conservative patterns from past under-reporting.

Authority boundaries should include explicit "stop actions" that can be taken immediately to protect the organization, along with the expectation of rapid notification and documentation. For example, security operations may have authority to disable suspicious accounts, isolate hosts that show confirmed malicious activity, or block known-bad infrastructure at the network edge when confidence thresholds are met. Those actions should be reversible, logged, and accompanied by a clear path to restore business functionality safely, because containment that cannot be unwound becomes operationally toxic. Boundaries should also define what the blue team cannot do without approval, such as taking revenue systems offline, collecting sensitive employee communications, or engaging third parties, because these actions carry legal, privacy, and reputational implications. When these boundaries are agreed in advance, responders spend less time seeking permission and more time executing controlled response.

Decision rights must also address slow-burn risk, not just crisis response, because many damaging outcomes come from chronic delay rather than a single dramatic incident. Vulnerability exceptions that persist, repeated failures to complete access reviews, or telemetry gaps for critical systems should trigger escalation when they cross defined age or recurrence thresholds. In these cases, escalation is not about urgency in minutes, but about forcing a decision: invest, accept risk explicitly, or change scope. This prevents the operating model from silently tolerating risk because it is inconvenient to resolve or because accountability is diffuse. Executives should expect to see these escalations framed as tradeoffs with clear options and consequences, not as open-ended complaints about workload.

The most common pitfall is designing escalation as a social process instead of an operational control, where teams rely on informal relationships and personal judgment to move issues upward. That approach fails under stress, during staff turnover, and during off-hours, which is exactly when escalation matters most. Another pitfall is making authority boundaries overly rigid, which causes responders to waste time routing every decision upward even when the risk is obvious and the action is reversible. A resilient model defines enough autonomy to act quickly, enough structure to avoid overreach, and enough documentation to preserve accountability after the fact. When escalation paths and decision rights are treated as core operating mechanics, the organization responds faster, argues less, and makes risk decisions that are explicit, reviewable, and aligned to business ownership.

On-Call Practices and After-Hours Coverage

On-call coverage is a reliability function, not a hero system, and it should be designed to protect both business continuity and responder judgment under stress. Attackers do not respect business hours, and the operational impact of delayed containment often grows nonlinearly as compromise spreads or evidence expires. After-hours coverage is therefore less about doing every task at night and more about making the right decisions quickly: confirm whether something is real, contain what must be contained, preserve evidence, and initiate the correct escalation path. A mature on-call model defines what types of events warrant immediate action, what can safely wait, and how decisions are documented, so the daytime team inherits clean context. When on-call is undefined or informal, organizations drift into inconsistent response quality that depends on who happens to pick up the phone.

The foundation of on-call is clear scope, because "security emergency" is otherwise interpreted differently by every stakeholder and every analyst. Scope should specify the services that have after-hours responsibility, such as incident response, critical detection triage, privileged access abuse, and major service outages affecting security controls. It should also clarify what is explicitly out of scope, such as routine vulnerability remediation coordination, standard access provisioning, and non-urgent policy questions, unless those activities are required to contain an active threat. Defining scope protects responders from being pulled into routine work at night and ensures the business does not treat on-call as a general-purpose help desk. It also improves stakeholder behavior by setting expectations for what happens when they report an issue after hours.

Alerting must be engineered for after-hours reality, because an on-call system is only as good as the signals that page people. Paging criteria should be narrower than daytime triage criteria, emphasizing high-confidence detections, verified anomalies on crown-jewel systems, and events with rapid blast-radius expansion like privileged credential compromise. If paging is driven by noisy alerts, responders become conditioned to dismiss pages, which is functionally equivalent to having no coverage. Good practice is to treat every after-hours page as a reliability incident for the detection program, with follow-up tuning required when false positives occur. AI/ML can help by suppressing duplicates, clustering related alerts, and producing a concise evidence summary, but its outputs must be reviewed against raw telemetry to avoid false confidence and to prevent drift from quietly degrading page quality.

A structured on-call workflow reduces cognitive load when responders are operating with limited context and limited access to stakeholders. The first objective is rapid triage: determine whether the signal indicates a credible security event, a control failure, or benign activity that can be tracked. The second objective is containment within pre-approved authority boundaries, using reversible actions wherever possible, such as isolating an endpoint, revoking tokens, disabling suspicious accounts, or blocking known malicious infrastructure. The third objective is preservation of evidence, including capturing volatile artifacts when feasible and ensuring logs are retained and not overwritten. The last objective is clean handoff, leaving a well-formed case record that explains actions taken, evidence observed, and decisions made so that the daytime team can continue without redoing early work.

Coverage models should be matched to organizational risk and capacity rather than adopted as a one-size-fits-all rotation. Some organizations need true 24/7 staffed monitoring, while others can operate effectively with pager coverage that triggers a defined response tier when high-severity conditions are met. In either model, tiering matters: the first responder should be empowered to take immediate protective actions, while deeper specialists can be engaged through escalation only when technical depth or broader authority is required. Rotations must account for fatigue and sustainability, because chronic sleep disruption leads to poor decisions and eventual attrition, which degrades security more than any single missed alert. Leaders should treat on-call as a measurable operational cost and plan staffing accordingly, rather than assuming it can be absorbed indefinitely as invisible labor.

Authority boundaries are particularly important after hours because the business owners who normally approve disruptive actions may not be immediately reachable. On-call responders should have clearly defined permission to take time-critical, reversible actions that reduce harm, paired with an obligation to notify designated decision-makers as soon as practical. For actions with high business impact, such as taking critical systems offline or triggering external communications, the escalation path must be explicit and tested, so responders do not improvise governance at 2 a.m. This is where decision rights must be operationalized into contact trees, response thresholds, and documented approval rules that do not require negotiation. When these mechanics are missing, organizations either delay decisive action until morning or take drastic action without stakeholder alignment, both of which create avoidable damage.

AI/ML can improve after-hours effectiveness, but it must be governed carefully because errors at night are less likely to be caught quickly. Models can draft incident briefs, identify likely related systems, and propose response actions based on patterns learned from prior incidents, which can speed response when staffing is thin. These capabilities depend on high-quality historical incident data and consistent labeling of outcomes; otherwise, the model's recommendations will reflect past inconsistency and institutional bias. Human approval boundaries should be strict around any automation that blocks traffic, disables accounts, or closes cases, especially when the model's confidence is derived from incomplete telemetry. The key governance expectation is auditability: the responder must be able to show what evidence was present, what the model suggested, what they chose to do, and why.

After-hours coverage should include a deliberate recovery process that protects both operational quality and the people doing the work. Every page should produce a daytime review of what happened, whether paging criteria were appropriate, what actions were taken, and what improvements are required to reduce recurrence. That review is also where the team addresses systemic issues like missing telemetry, ambiguous escalation paths, or repeated false positives, turning on-call from a burden into a driver of operational maturity. Sustained performance requires humane rotation practices, clear compensatory time or workload adjustments, and leadership attention to burnout indicators, because exhausted responders make riskier choices and erode service reliability. When on-call is treated as a designed capability with clear boundaries, high-fidelity paging, and disciplined handoffs, after-hours coverage becomes a predictable extension of blue team operations rather than a fragile, personality-dependent safety net.

Cross-Team Collaboration with IT and Engineering

Cross-team collaboration is the difference between a blue team that detects problems and a blue team that changes outcomes. Most security controls are delivered through IT and engineering systems—identity platforms, endpoint management, network services, cloud infrastructure, and application delivery pipelines—so the blue team's effectiveness depends on how well it works through those owners. When collaboration is weak, security becomes a parallel organization that reports risk but cannot reliably drive remediation, and the business experiences security as friction rather than resilience. Collaboration should be treated as an operating discipline with defined interfaces, expectations, and escalation paths, not as an informal goodwill arrangement. Executives should evaluate collaboration the same way they evaluate operational dependencies: by reliability, response time, and the quality of handoffs.

The foundation is shared service language that makes it clear what the blue team provides and what it requires from IT and engineering to deliver those services. Monitoring and detection depend on predictable telemetry from endpoints, identity systems, network controls, and cloud services, so logging standards and onboarding processes must be negotiated and maintained. Incident response depends on reliable asset ownership information, access to containment mechanisms, and change control exceptions for emergencies, which require alignment with IT operations and application owners. Vulnerability and configuration risk management depend on patching capability, configuration baselines, and deployment practices, which live outside the blue team's direct control. When these dependencies are explicit, collaboration becomes structured problem-solving rather than repeated arguments about "who owns it."

Good collaboration reduces operational friction by making work requestable, routable, and trackable across team boundaries. The blue team should not rely on personal relationships to get critical work done; it should have established intake paths and service owners on the IT and engineering side who can accept, prioritize, and execute security-driven work. Handoffs must include enough technical and business context to act, including affected systems, evidence, risk rationale, constraints, and an expected outcome that can be verified. Conversely, the blue team should define what it will and will not do in support of remediation, such as providing validation steps, assisting with testing, or updating detections after a fix is deployed. This clarity prevents the common failure mode where security tickets circulate endlessly because each team assumes the other is responsible for confirming closure.

Operational rhythms are where collaboration becomes repeatable instead of episodic, especially in environments with continuous change. Daily collaboration is typically minimal and focused on active incidents, critical outages affecting security controls, and time-sensitive containment decisions. Weekly collaboration is where teams address recurring operational debt, such as missing logs, brittle detections, patching exceptions, and identity process failures that create repeated incidents. Monthly collaboration is where shared risk posture is reviewed, including trends in exposure, systemic gaps, and investments needed to remove constraints. The cadence matters because it establishes predictable windows for decision-making, reduces ad hoc escalations, and ensures that long-term posture work is not perpetually displaced by the urgent.

AI/ML can strengthen collaboration by improving the quality and speed of cross-team communication, but only if outputs are grounded in evidence and reviewed by accountable humans. Models can summarize incidents into engineering-friendly narratives, extract impacted components, correlate related tickets, and translate raw telemetry into actionable remediation hypotheses. These capabilities depend on consistent data structures, clean asset ownership metadata, and disciplined incident documentation; otherwise, the model produces plausible summaries that omit key constraints or overstate confidence. Human-in-the-loop controls should require that the blue team validates model-generated recommendations before they are treated as root cause, especially when proposed changes could destabilize production systems. Governance should also include safeguards against leakage, ensuring sensitive logs, customer data, or internal indicators are not inadvertently exposed through AI workflows or over-broad sharing.

Engineering collaboration often fails when security asks for "fix it" without framing the request in terms engineers can execute and verify. Effective requests identify the failing control or condition, provide reproduction or evidence where possible, and define a measurable end state, such as a logging pipeline producing a required event type, a misconfiguration corrected and confirmed, or an access path removed and tested. Security should also respect engineering constraints by proposing safe change strategies, acknowledging release windows, and aligning remediation to the systems' criticality and operational risk. When tradeoffs are real—such as a mitigation that introduces latency or reduces feature velocity—decision rights and escalation paths should be used rather than forcing engineers to absorb risk decisions informally. This preserves trust and keeps security from being perceived as an unfunded mandate.

IT collaboration is equally critical because IT operations control the mechanisms that often determine containment speed and investigative visibility. Endpoint isolation, device reimaging, account disablement, network segmentation changes, certificate rotations, and emergency patching are typically executed through IT-run systems and processes. If IT is not integrated into incident workflows, the blue team can identify compromise but cannot reliably stop it or restore integrity at scale. Collaboration should include pre-approved emergency procedures and access pathways that allow security to request time-critical actions without bypassing operational safeguards. The goal is controlled urgency: fast enough to reduce harm, disciplined enough to avoid creating outages or losing evidence through rushed remediation.

Sustained collaboration requires clear escalation when dependencies break down, because unresolved friction quietly becomes risk. Repeated failure to deliver required telemetry, chronic delays in patching critical exposures, or ongoing gaps in privileged access controls should trigger escalation based on defined thresholds, not based on individual frustration. Escalation should be framed as a decision request with options: invest, change scope, accept risk explicitly, or alter operational constraints that are preventing progress. When leadership sees collaboration as a measurable part of the operating model, teams are incentivized to maintain the interfaces and workflows that keep security reliable. Over time, the healthiest indicator is that security improvements appear as changes in IT and engineering systems and habits, not just as more alerts, more tickets, or more meetings.

Documentation, Knowledge Transfer, and Continuity

Documentation is the mechanism that turns security work from individual expertise into organizational capability. In blue team operations, the goal is not to write more documents, but to preserve the minimum information required to make decisions repeatable, investigations consistent, and handoffs reliable. When documentation is weak, teams waste time rediscovering context, repeating past mistakes, and rebuilding investigative narratives under pressure. When documentation is strong, the team's performance is less sensitive to turnover, vacations, and surge conditions, because critical knowledge is embedded in artifacts rather than trapped in people. For executives, this is continuity risk management: the organization's ability to sustain defense outcomes despite inevitable staffing and operational change.

Operational documentation should be anchored to services and workflows, because those are the stable units of the operating model. A detection program needs documented onboarding requirements for telemetry, definitions for alert severity, tuning expectations, and triage decision criteria, so analysts do not improvise under load. Incident handling needs documented escalation paths, authority boundaries, evidence collection expectations, and communication procedures, so response does not hinge on who is on call. Vulnerability and exposure management needs documented prioritization logic, exception processes, verification steps, and reporting routines, so remediation is consistent and auditable. These artifacts should be practical and actionable, designed to be used during work rather than only reviewed during audits.

Knowledge transfer is where documentation becomes operational, because a document that is never used is not continuity, it is shelfware. The blue team should treat every major event, near miss, and systemic failure as an opportunity to update the shared knowledge base with specific lessons that change future behavior. That includes updating playbooks to reflect what actually worked, adjusting triage criteria based on observed false positives and false negatives, and capturing new investigative techniques required by evolving attacker tradecraft. Knowledge transfer should be structured enough that new team members can become effective without shadowing a single expert for months, but lightweight enough that it does not slow response work. The objective is to shorten the time between discovering a lesson and embedding that lesson in the team's standard operating patterns.

Continuity depends on making critical information discoverable and trustworthy, not just written down. Discoverability means responders can find the relevant artifact quickly during an incident, with a clear path from a case record to the playbook, from the playbook to the escalation contact, and from the escalation contact to the decision authority. Trustworthiness means the artifact reflects reality, including the current environment, current access paths, and current dependencies on IT and engineering systems. A common failure mode is stale documentation that looks complete but contains broken links, outdated system names, and processes that no longer align with organizational structure. Continuity is improved when ownership for keeping artifacts current is explicit, and when review cadence is tied to operational rhythms rather than treated as optional housekeeping.

Case documentation deserves special attention because it is often the only durable record of what was observed, what was done, and why. A well-documented case captures key evidence and the reasoning behind decisions, including the conditions that triggered escalation, the scope of affected systems, containment actions taken, and the remaining uncertainties. It also records what information was missing, such as telemetry gaps or unclear asset ownership, because those gaps often represent the most important improvement opportunities. Case documentation should support downstream needs like legal review, compliance inquiries, and insurance claims without being written in legalistic language that hinders operational use. Done well, case records become training material and detection feedback sources, turning response activity into institutional learning.

AI/ML can strengthen documentation and knowledge transfer by reducing the burden of writing while improving consistency, but it must be governed to avoid subtle quality and security failures. Models can draft case summaries, normalize incident timelines, extract entities and affected assets, and suggest related prior cases or playbooks based on similarity. These benefits depend on clean telemetry, consistent labeling, and strong access controls, because the model's outputs are only as reliable as the data it sees and the guardrails around it. Human review is mandatory for any AI-generated artifact that will be relied upon for decisions, because plausible language can mask incorrect assumptions, missing evidence, or mis-scoped impact. Governance should also address leakage risk, ensuring sensitive data, internal indicators, or privileged operational details are not exposed through overly broad prompts, shared workspaces, or uncontrolled retention of generated content.

Continuity is also operationally tested through structured handoffs, particularly across shifts, on-call transitions, and cross-team escalations. Handoffs should communicate what is known, what is being done, what decisions are pending, and what constraints exist, so the receiving team does not restart the investigation from scratch. The best handoffs include explicit next actions and an agreed definition of "stable state," such as containment achieved, monitoring in place, and evidence preserved, even if root cause is not yet fully confirmed. Poor handoffs create duplicate work, increase the chance of contradictory actions, and can lead to avoidable outages when teams act on different assumptions. Continuity improves when handoffs are treated as a required operational control and when the artifacts used for handoff are standardized enough to prevent omission of critical context.

Finally, documentation and continuity are only sustainable when they are integrated into the operating model as routine work, not as a side project reserved for quiet weeks. Teams should allocate capacity to maintain playbooks, refresh system context, and curate lessons learned, because operational reality ensures quiet weeks rarely arrive. The strongest indicator of maturity is that documentation changes follow operational change: new systems come with onboarding guides, new detections come with triage notes, and every significant incident results in updated procedures and improved knowledge artifacts. When leadership reinforces that documentation is part of delivering the service—on par with triage, containment, and remediation coordination—knowledge stays current and defensible. The outcome is a blue team whose performance survives turnover and surge, because the organization, not the individual, retains the knowledge required to defend itself.

AI-Assisted Operations: Ticket Enrichment, Summarization, and Workflow Guardrails

AI-assisted operations are most valuable when they reduce friction in routine work while keeping humans accountable for decisions that carry risk. In a blue team context, the practical target is the "middle mile" of operations: the translation of raw signals into structured work items that can be triaged, routed, executed, and audited. Ticket enrichment and summarization can shorten time to understanding, reduce repetitive writing, and improve consistency across analysts and shifts. The risk is that automation introduces persuasive but incorrect narratives, or silently changes how work is prioritized and closed without clear accountability. Treating AI as an operational dependency means defining where it is allowed to act, what it is allowed to suggest, and how its outputs are validated. Table 4.3 reinforces where AI can assist the workflow and where humans must remain accountable for high-impact decisions.

Ticket enrichment is the process of adding missing context that responders and partner teams need to act quickly. For security work, enrichment typically includes asset identifiers, ownership, business criticality, environment tags, recent change history, and links to relevant telemetry or related cases. It can also include structured fields that reduce ambiguity, such as the suspected technique, the confidence level of the alert, and the recommended next action to confirm or refute the hypothesis. AI can accelerate this by extracting entities from unstructured alerts and notes, correlating identifiers across systems, and proposing likely owners or impacted services based on historical patterns. However, enrichment must be designed so that proposed context is clearly marked as inferred, because incorrect ownership or scope can cause delays, misrouted work, and inappropriate containment actions.

Summarization is valuable because security operations generate high-volume narrative data that is difficult to consume under time pressure. A good summary compresses what matters without hiding uncertainty: what was observed, why it matters, what has been done, what remains unknown, and what decisions are needed. AI can draft concise case narratives, timeline views, and handoff notes that improve continuity across shifts and reduce

Table 4.3 AI-Assisted Ticket Workflow Guardrails.

Workflow Step	AI Allowed Assistance	Human Required Decision	Required Provenance	Primary Failure Mode
Ticket enrichment	Extract entities suggest owner propose context	Confirm affected assets owner and scope	Inputs used output generated human edits	Incorrect scope or misrouting presented as fact
Case summarization	Draft narrative timeline and handoff notes	Validate summary against raw evidence	Links to supporting artifacts approval recorded	Plausible narrative that omits contradictions
Routing recommendation	Suggest service owner queue and category	Approve final routing for high-impact work	Recommendation and final route recorded	Sends work to wrong team and delays action
Prioritization suggestion	Cluster duplicates propose urgency signal	Set final priority and escalation threshold	Basis for priority and reviewer decision captured	False confidence and drift in scoring
Closure recommendation	Propose closure criteria and next steps	Approve closure and verify outcome	Closure reason evidence link approver	Premature closure leaves risk unresolved
Containment suggestion	Propose reversible actions and rationale	Approve disruptive actions within authority boundaries	Action taken decision maker and evidence	Overreach or under response based on weak evidence

the documentation burden that otherwise competes with response work. The operational requirement is that summaries remain tethered to evidence, with references to the underlying events, artifacts, and timestamps that support the narrative. Without that tether, summaries become story-shaped outputs that can be emotionally convincing while being operationally misleading.

Workflow guardrails are what prevent AI assistance from becoming uncontrolled automation that changes outcomes without accountable oversight. Guardrails should define which actions are permitted to be automated, which require human approval, and which are prohibited entirely. In most blue team environments, AI should be allowed to suggest routing, deduplication, correlation, and draft content, while decisions like incident declaration, case closure, blocking actions, account disablement, and risk acceptance remain human-owned. Guardrails should also include confidence thresholds and escalation triggers, so that low-confidence outputs do not silently steer work and high-impact cases receive additional scrutiny. This structure ensures the organization can benefit from speed and consistency without delegating judgment to a system that cannot be held responsible.

AI-assisted enrichment and summarization depend heavily on data quality and data access design. If asset inventories are incomplete, ownership data is stale, or telemetry is inconsistent, AI will produce outputs that reflect those gaps and may amplify them by presenting guesses as facts. If labeling of incident outcomes is inconsistent, models will learn inconsistent prioritization patterns and may institutionalize past bias, such as over-escalating noisy categories while under-escalating rare but high-impact events. Data access must be least privilege, because enrichment often touches sensitive information like user identities, privileged access events, and security control configurations. The more data an AI system can see, the more it can help, but the greater the blast radius if it leaks, is misconfigured, or is used inappropriately.

Human-in-the-loop controls must be operational, not ceremonial, because the main risk is false confidence and silent drift. Review steps should require that a responder validates key fields that drive downstream work, such as affected assets, suspected scope, and recommended next action. For high-impact items, review should include checking a small number of raw artifacts directly, such as authentication logs, endpoint process trees, or network connections, to confirm the summary is not omitting critical contradictions. Drift controls should include periodic sampling of AI-produced tickets to measure error rates, identify systematic failure patterns, and recalibrate prompts or models accordingly. If the organization cannot measure output quality over time, it will not notice when the system becomes less accurate as environments and attacker behaviors change.

Guardrails must also address security and governance expectations, because AI assistance changes the audit and accountability surface. Every AI-assisted ticket should preserve provenance: what inputs were used, what output was generated, whether a human edited or approved it, and what actions were taken afterward. This provenance supports investigations, compliance inquiries, and internal reviews, and it also prevents disputes about whether a decision was made by a person or suggested by automation. Policies should also define retention and sharing rules, especially when summaries contain sensitive details that could increase attacker advantage if exposed. An AI system that improves operational speed but undermines confidentiality, integrity of records, or accountability is a net negative in a security operating model.

Finally, AI-assisted operations should be introduced with a disciplined scope, so benefits are realized without destabilizing the existing workflow. The best early wins are narrow and measurable: faster enrichment for routing accuracy, better handoff summaries for continuity, and consistent case narratives that reduce rework across shifts. Over time, the system can expand to more complex assistance, but only when the organization has evidence that quality is stable and that responders understand how to validate and challenge outputs. When AI is treated as a controlled assistant embedded in ticketing and case management—bounded by clear approval rules, measurable quality checks, and auditable provenance—it becomes a force multiplier for the blue team rather than a new source of operational risk.

Scaling the Operating Model as the Organization Grows

Scaling a blue team operating model is fundamentally about preserving decision quality and service reliability as complexity increases. Growth introduces more systems, more users, more data, and more dependencies, all of which increase the surface area for failure if the operating model does not adapt. The mistake many organizations make is assuming scale is primarily a tooling or headcount problem, when it is actually an operating discipline problem. Without deliberate changes, processes that worked at small scale become brittle, opaque, and personality-driven as volume increases. Effective scaling keeps the model legible to leaders and usable by operators, even as the environment becomes more dynamic.

The first pressure point in growth is usually service clarity, because informal understandings break down when new teams and platforms are added. As organizations grow, blue team services must be revalidated to ensure their scope, inputs, and outputs still match reality. New business units, cloud environments, and third-party integrations often introduce demand that was never accounted for in the original service definitions. If services are not explicitly adjusted, teams compensate by absorbing unplanned work, which quietly degrades response times and increases backlog. Scaling well means periodically recalibrating service boundaries and making explicit decisions about what is included, what is deferred, and what requires new investment.

Organizational growth also strains ownership models, because decision rights that were once obvious become ambiguous across geographies, products, or regulatory regimes. Service owners must retain authority that scales with scope, or risk becoming coordinators without leverage as dependencies multiply. In practice, this often means introducing deputy ownership, regional accountability, or domain-specific leads who operate within a common service framework. What should not change is the principle that every service has a clearly accountable owner for outcomes, not just activity. When ownership fragments without a unifying model, escalation paths become unclear and risk decisions are delayed or inconsistently applied.

Operational rhythms must evolve with scale to prevent overload and loss of signal. As volume increases, daily operations should emphasize exception handling rather than comprehensive review, relying on defined thresholds to surface what truly requires attention. Weekly and monthly cadences become more important, not less, because they are where systemic issues are identified and addressed before they cascade. Scaling organizations often need to invest in better aggregation and filtering, so leaders are not overwhelmed by raw metrics that obscure trends. The goal is to maintain meaningful situational awareness while acknowledging that no individual can hold the entire environment in their head.

AI/ML becomes increasingly valuable as scale grows, but only when it is introduced with the same discipline as any other operational dependency. At higher volumes, humans cannot manually correlate all signals, summarize all cases, or consistently prioritize work without assistance. AI can help by clustering related activity, highlighting deviations from baseline behavior, and surfacing patterns that warrant investigation or escalation. These benefits depend on stable data pipelines, consistent labeling, and well-defined human approval boundaries, because errors at scale propagate faster and are harder to unwind. Governance expectations must increase with usage, ensuring that automation does not quietly reshape risk posture without visibility or accountability.

Scaling also requires deliberate investment in documentation and onboarding, because growth inevitably brings turnover, specialization, and distributed teams. Playbooks, service definitions, and escalation rules must be updated to reflect new architectures and operating realities, or they will quickly become misleading. Knowledge transfer mechanisms should be designed, so new team members can operate effectively within weeks, not months, without relying on informal tribal knowledge. This is especially critical when coverage expands across time zones, where handoffs and asynchronous work become the norm. Continuity at scale depends on shared artifacts being accurate, discoverable, and actively used.

Finally, scaling the operating model requires leadership to make explicit tradeoffs rather than assuming security can stretch indefinitely. Growth will surface constraints in telemetry coverage, response capacity, and cross-team dependencies that cannot be solved through process alone. A mature operating model makes those constraints visible, so leaders can choose to invest, narrow scope, or accept risk consciously. When scaling is treated as an intentional evolution of services, ownership, cadence, and decision rights, the blue team remains effective even as the organization changes shape. The result is not just a larger security function, but a more resilient one that can absorb growth without losing control.

Conclusion

A blue team operating model succeeds when it makes defensive work predictable, accountable, and resilient under real-world pressure. Clear services and service owners translate "security" into outcomes the business can request, measure, and improve, while operating rhythms keep the team aligned to the right work at the right time. Defined escalation paths, authority boundaries, and on-call practices ensure that urgent decisions are made quickly and responsibly, even after hours and even when tradeoffs are uncomfortable. Strong collaboration with IT and engineering, reinforced by disciplined documentation and governed AI-assisted workflows, creates continuity and scale, so the organization can grow without losing control of risk.

Recommendations

1) Define blue team services in outcome terms and publish clear interfaces. Treat each service as a repeatable capability with declared inputs, outputs, and minimum prerequisites, so stakeholders know how to engage it. Keep the description stable even as underlying tools and implementation details change. Use service definitions to expose dependency gaps like missing telemetry, unclear ownership, or unreliable escalation pathways.
2) Assign a named service owner for every blue team service and match authority to accountability. Give service owners the decision rights to set standards, manage backlogs, and negotiate tradeoffs when demand exceeds capacity. Require them to define success metrics and to own the service's risk posture, including how exceptions are handled and reviewed. Avoid "ownership" roles that can be blamed for outcomes without the leverage to change them.
3) Establish daily, weekly, and monthly operating rhythms that create predictable decision windows. Design daily cadence to preserve situational awareness and protect response time, weekly cadence to drive improvement work and resolve cross-team friction, and monthly cadence to manage risk posture and governance. Keep the cadence lean enough to preserve focus time for investigation and engineering work. Treat repetitive after-hours pages and recurring issues as signals that the rhythm must surface and fix.
4) Implement a single, disciplined intake path that turns demand into accountable work. Require minimum completeness for requests, so analysts are not forced to reconstruct scope, owners, and urgency during execution. Route work to the correct service owner quickly, especially when requests are misdirected by default. Define "ready" and "done" in outcome terms, so closure reflects verified results rather than simple handoff.
5) Make prioritization explicit and defensible, and separate interrupt work from planned work. Use a repeatable decision process that weighs time sensitivity, business criticality, and dependencies rather than letting urgency be set by the loudest requestor. Protect capacity for foundational work like telemetry onboarding, detection tuning, and response playbook maintenance, so posture improves over time. Use the backlog to communicate what is being deferred and what risk that deferral creates.
6) Codify escalation paths, authority boundaries, and decision rights before a crisis forces improvisation. Define which protective actions responders can take immediately, which require peer coordination, and which require executive approval, and tie escalation to clear triggers and time bounds. Ensure recurring decisions like incident declaration, aggressive containment, and risk exception approval have named accountable

decision-makers. Treat chronic risk drift, not just acute incidents, as escalation-worthy when thresholds are crossed.

7) Design on-call coverage as a reliability capability with narrow paging criteria and clean handoffs. Limit after-hours pages to high-confidence, high-impact conditions and treat false pages as detection program defects that require tuning. Ensure responders have pre-approved reversible containment options and a tested path to reach decision-makers for high-impact actions. Require structured handoff notes, so the daytime team inherits evidence, actions taken, and pending decisions without rework.
8) Operationalize cross-team collaboration with IT and engineering through stable interfaces and shared cadence. Negotiate logging standards, containment mechanisms, and remediation workflows as explicit dependencies rather than informal favors. Provide remediation requests in executable terms, including evidence, constraints, and a verifiable end state, so partner teams can act efficiently. Escalate recurring dependency failures based on thresholds to force investment, scope change, or explicit risk acceptance.
9) Treat documentation and knowledge transfer as part of service delivery, not optional housekeeping. Maintain practical artifacts that operators actually use during work, including triage criteria, escalation contacts, and response procedures that reflect current reality. Capture case records that preserve evidence and reasoning, including what was missing, to drive continuous improvement. Review and update critical artifacts on an operational cadence, so they remain discoverable and trustworthy through change.
10) Adopt AI-assisted ticket enrichment and summarization with clear workflow guardrails and auditability. Allow AI to propose routing, deduplication, correlation, and draft narratives, but keep humans accountable for incident declaration, case closure, blocking actions, and risk acceptance. Require validation of key fields that drive downstream decisions and sample outputs regularly to detect drift and false confidence. Preserve provenance for AI-assisted work, so the organization can show what evidence was used, what was generated, what was approved, and what actions followed.

Part II

Risk, Assets, and Defensive Architecture

5

Identifying and Managing Risks

Risk is the mechanism that turns defensive ambition into a realistic plan, because it forces security teams to choose what matters most under real constraints. Effective risk work connects business impact to technical pathways by tying critical functions to the systems, dependencies, and trust boundaries that enable or undermine them. It also establishes a disciplined approach to evaluating threat landscapes and attack vectors, so prioritization reflects what is plausible in the environment, not just what is loud in the market. Finally, it treats risk treatment decisions, communication, AI-augmented analysis, and continuous refresh as operational practices that must remain evidence-driven, auditable, and accountable to both technical teams and executive leadership.

Why Risk Is the Basis of Defensive Prioritization

Defensive teams never have enough time, people, or budget to treat every weakness as equally urgent, and pretending otherwise produces noise instead of security. Risk is the practical translation layer between an endless list of possible problems and the finite set of actions a team can execute this week. In operational terms, risk is the combination of likelihood and impact, with impact grounded in business consequences such as outage time, data exposure, safety, regulatory penalties, and reputational damage. When leaders ask "what should we do first," they are asking for a risk answer, not a technology answer.

Good prioritization starts with the reality that the same technical issue can represent radically different risk depending on where it lives. An unpatched service on an isolated lab subnet is not the same as the same service on an internet-facing system tied to revenue, privileged access, or sensitive data. Context like exposure, asset criticality, identity privileges, and downstream dependencies determines whether an issue is a nuisance or an incident waiting to happen. That context is what turns "we have 3,000 findings" into a defensible order of work that both security and the business can support. Use the context factors in Table 5.1 to turn raw findings into a defensible risk order of work based on how compromise would realistically occur and what it would affect.

Risk-based prioritization also forces clarity about what the organization is actually trying to protect. Defensive work is a sequence of tradeoffs: preventing disruption, preventing unauthorized access, preventing data loss, and maintaining trust with customers and regulators. A mature team can explain why a specific control improvement outranks a different one by tying it to concrete outcomes such as reducing the probability of ransomware spread, reducing blast radius in a compromise, or shortening time-to-containment. This is where defensive credibility is built, because priorities that track to business outcomes survive scrutiny during planning, audits, and post-incident reviews.

Operationally, risk becomes actionable when it is made visible, comparable, and reviewable across domains like vulnerabilities, identity, cloud posture, and third-party access. The goal is not a perfect score; the goal is a consistent decision process that can be repeated under pressure and explained after the fact. That process typically weighs factors such as exploitability, ease of weaponization, exposure to untrusted networks, privilege level involved, and

Table 5.1 Risk Prioritization Context Factors and Practical Signals.

Context Factor	What It Changes	Practical Signal to Check	Common Pitfall
Exposure	Increases likelihood	Internet reachable path exists	Assuming internal equals safe
Asset criticality	Increases impact	Supports critical business function	Labeling everything Tier 1
Privilege level	Increases blast radius	Admin or broad role access present	Ignoring service accounts
Downstream dependency	Amplifies cascading impact	Many services rely on component	Missing hidden integrations
Telemetry coverage	Improves confidence	Logs and alerts exist for pathway	Confusing silence with safety
Compensating control	Reduces likelihood or impact	Segmentation or multi factor authentication (MFA) enforced	Assuming intended equals enforced

the quality of existing compensating controls like segmentation, MFA, or monitoring. If a team cannot articulate the assumptions behind a priority decision, the organization is effectively prioritizing based on intuition and the loudest stakeholder.

Prioritization is where many programs fail quietly, because they confuse activity with risk reduction. Patching everything "high severity" can be the wrong move if the highest-risk pathway is actually identity abuse, over-privileged service accounts, or a brittle remote access path with weak monitoring. Similarly, chasing every alert can burn an Security Operations Center (SOC) while the underlying control gaps remain untouched, guaranteeing the same incidents repeat. Risk discipline means recognizing when the right work is hard, unglamorous, and cross-team, and still doing it because it changes the probability and impact of real failure modes.

AI and machine learning can improve prioritization when used as decision support rather than decision authority. Models can help correlate telemetry across systems, cluster similar findings, infer likely attack paths from observed access patterns, and estimate which combinations of weakness and exposure are most likely to be exploited in your environment. Those benefits depend on clean inputs—accurate asset inventories, identity and privilege data, network exposure, vulnerability state, and reliable alert history—because incomplete telemetry produces confident but wrong rankings. Human-in-the-loop controls matter here: analysts should be able to see why something was escalated, override the ranking, and record the rationale, because drift, bias toward well-instrumented systems, and leakage of sensitive operational details are real failure modes.

Governance is what keeps risk-based prioritization from becoming a one-time spreadsheet exercise that decays into politics. Decisions should leave an audit trail: what was prioritized, what was deferred, what assumptions were used, who approved risk acceptance, and when the decision must be revisited. Over time, the best programs can show a measurable shift: fewer repeat incidents, faster containment, fewer "unknown" assets, and a smaller set of truly critical exposures waiting on remediation. That is what it looks like when risk is not a slogan, but the operating system of defensive work.

Risk Assessments: Scope, Inputs, and Outputs

A risk assessment is a structured way to answer three questions that matter operationally: what could go wrong, how likely is it, and what happens if it does. The scope is the boundary that prevents the exercise from becoming an endless debate about every possible threat. Scope should be defined in terms leaders can recognize and teams

Table 5.2 Risk Assessment Inputs and Outputs by Evidence Type.

Evidence Type	Primary Purpose	Example from Practice	If Missing Then
Asset inventory	Establish ownership and scope	Accurate system and service list	Unknown assets drive uncertainty
Data classification	Clarify impact	Identify sensitive records handled	Impact becomes vague
Exposure context	Estimate likelihood	Internet facing versus internal only	Plausibility is misjudged
Identity and privilege	Reveal attack paths	Role and service account access graph	Lateral movement is underestimated
Config and vulnerability posture	Show weaknesses	Current state of known issues	Findings become stale noise
Operational telemetry	Validate assumptions	Auth logs endpoint coverage alert history	Controls cannot be verified

can execute, such as a business process, an application and its dependencies, a cloud account boundary, a user population, or a third-party integration. Without an explicit scope, assessments default to whichever systems are most visible, leaving the most consequential blind spots untouched. High-quality inputs produce risk outputs that are scenario-driven reviewable and tied to observable evidence instead of opinion as shown in Table 5.2.

The most useful scope statements are precise about what is included and what is deliberately excluded. "Customer payments platform including identity, APIs, and data stores" is actionable because it implies ownership, dependencies, and pathways an attacker would use. "All cybersecurity risks" is not actionable because it cannot be assessed with consistent depth or revisited on a predictable cadence. Scope should also identify the decision the assessment is meant to support, such as prioritizing remediation work, evaluating a control design, approving a go-live, or determining whether a compensating control is acceptable. When the decision is clear, the level of detail and the stakeholders needed become obvious.

Inputs are the raw material that turn risk assessment from opinion into evidence-driven analysis. At minimum, inputs include an accurate asset inventory, a data classification view of what the system handles, a map of trust boundaries and external exposure, and identity and privilege relationships for both humans and service accounts. Defensive teams also need known vulnerabilities and configuration posture, including whether issues are internet-reachable, authenticated-only, or constrained by segmentation and access controls. Operational telemetry—such as authentication logs, endpoint coverage, alert history, and incident records—adds realism, because it shows where controls actually work and where visibility gaps create uncertainty.

Threat inputs should be grounded in the environment rather than generic lists of adversaries. The relevant question is not whether a threat exists in the world, but whether a threat can plausibly traverse the organization's pathways and achieve meaningful impact. Inputs such as past incident patterns, common failure modes in similar architectures, and observed attacker behaviors in the organization's telemetry are often more valuable than theoretical scenarios. Where intelligence is used, it should be treated as prioritization context rather than a substitute for internal evidence. A team that cannot validate assumptions in its own logs is relying on narratives instead of signals.

Quality controls on inputs matter because bad inputs create false certainty, and false certainty produces bad decisions. Asset and identity data are the most common points of failure, especially in hybrid environments where ownership is unclear and ephemeral workloads change faster than inventories update. Vulnerability data is often noisy, with duplicates, stale findings, and missing context about exploitability in the actual configuration.

Telemetry can be misleading when coverage is uneven, because well-instrumented areas appear riskier simply due to higher visibility. A disciplined assessment explicitly notes uncertainty and treats unknowns as risk drivers rather than silently ignoring them.

Outputs are only useful if they drive action, and that requires outputs to be concrete, comparable, and decision-ready. The core output is a prioritized set of risks framed as scenarios that connect cause to consequence, not just a list of weaknesses. A scenario expresses the pathway, such as a credential compromise leading to privileged access, lateral movement, and data exposure, with the impacted assets and business outcomes made explicit. Each risk should include the primary contributing factors, the current controls that reduce likelihood or impact, and the residual risk that remains after those controls are considered. This structure makes it clear whether the problem is missing prevention, weak detection, slow response, or a combination.

A practical output set also includes remediation candidates and ownership alignment, even when the assessment is not a project plan. The point is not to prescribe specific tools, but to identify the control outcomes needed, such as reducing exposure, tightening privilege, improving monitoring coverage, or adding segmentation at a trust boundary. Good outputs specify what evidence would demonstrate improvement, because without measurable criteria, teams close tickets without reducing risk. Outputs should also capture accepted risk with an explicit decision owner, because risk acceptance is a business choice that must be reviewable. When acceptance decisions are undocumented, they become invisible debt that reappears during incidents.

AI-assisted analysis can strengthen both inputs and outputs when it is used to synthesize evidence at scale and highlight relationships humans would miss. Models can help normalize and deduplicate findings, correlate identity and network relationships into likely attack paths, and summarize control effectiveness from historical telemetry and incident outcomes. The dependencies are non-negotiable: the model needs consistent asset identifiers, clean privilege data, and trustworthy logs to avoid generating plausible but incorrect narratives. Human approval boundaries should require analysts to validate the highest-impact scenarios, especially those driving major spend or operational change, because failure modes like hallucinated dependencies, bias toward well-documented systems, and drift as the environment evolves can distort priorities. The expectation should be that AI accelerates sensemaking, while the organization retains accountable decision-making and an auditable rationale for every material risk call.

Identifying and Prioritizing Critical Business Functions

Critical business functions are the smallest units of work the organization must keep running to meet its obligations, protect revenue, and maintain trust. They are not the same as systems, applications, or departments, even though those things support them. A function is expressed as an outcome, such as taking customer orders, paying employees, fulfilling shipments, issuing refunds, supporting customers, or producing regulated reports. Defensive prioritization becomes far more accurate when it is anchored to these outcomes, because it ties technical decisions to what leadership actually values under stress.

The first operational step is to define functions in a way that can be owned and measured, rather than debated. A function should have a clear business owner, a clear set of consumers, and a clear indicator of failure that anyone can recognize. If the organization cannot agree on what "down" looks like, it will not agree on what "critical" means when tradeoffs appear. Useful definitions include time sensitivity, peak usage windows, and dependency on external parties like payment processors or logistics providers. This converts abstract importance into concrete operational requirements.

Once functions are named, the next task is mapping dependencies with enough precision to support defensive decisions. Dependencies include the obvious technology pieces—applications, data stores, identity providers, network paths, and endpoints—but also include people, vendors, and manual workarounds. Many organizations discover that a function depends on a few fragile "hidden" components, such as a single integration, a privileged service account, or a shared administrative portal. Those hidden dependencies are often the real risk concentrators, because compromise or outage there creates broad impact. The mapping does not need to be perfect, but it must be accurate enough to identify where an attacker would gain leverage.

Prioritization then becomes a matter of impact tolerance and recoverability, not just importance. Two functions can both be "critical" while having different failure consequences and different acceptable downtime. A function that supports safety, regulatory compliance, or direct revenue collection typically has low tolerance for disruption and high urgency for defensive hardening. Other functions may tolerate short interruptions if there are reliable workarounds and the data integrity can be preserved. This is where executives and technical teams meet: business owners define tolerances, and defenders translate them into control emphasis and response readiness.

In practice, teams should treat the prioritization as an input to daily security operations, not a one-time classification exercise. If a function is critical, then identity protections, logging coverage, incident response playbooks, and restoration procedures around its dependencies must be held to a higher standard. Vulnerabilities affecting function-critical components should move up the remediation queue, especially when they intersect with external exposure or privileged access. Monitoring should also be weighted toward early indicators of compromise in those pathways, because detection latency on critical functions creates outsized business impact. The goal is to make "critical" meaningful by changing what gets attention, not just what gets labeled.

AI and machine learning can help identify criticality and hidden coupling, but only when paired with governance and validated data. Models can analyze service maps, authentication patterns, network flows, and ticket histories to surface which systems are central to many workflows and which accounts act as privilege hubs. These inferences depend on strong telemetry, consistent asset identifiers, and reliable identity logs; otherwise, the model will overvalue what it can see and undervalue what it cannot. Human review must remain decisive, because the business definition of criticality includes contractual obligations, reputational stakes, and operational workarounds that may not exist in machine-readable data. Clear approval boundaries are necessary, so automated scoring informs prioritization without quietly redefining what "critical" means.

Common failures in this work usually come from treating critical business functions as a technology inventory problem or a politics problem. If the output is simply a list of "Tier 1 applications," teams lose the linkage to business outcomes and cannot defend why one remediation outranks another. If every stakeholder declares their function as most critical, the list becomes meaningless and the organization returns to prioritizing by urgency and noise. The remedy is disciplined criteria, visible tradeoffs, and documented tolerances that leadership can stand behind. When functions are identified and prioritized correctly, defensive work becomes more coherent: controls are strengthened where impact concentrates, incident response focuses on what must be restored first, and risk decisions become explainable in terms the business already uses.

Mapping Risk to Systems, Dependencies, and Trust Boundaries

Risk becomes operationally useful when it is attached to real pathways in the environment rather than abstract statements about threats and controls. Mapping risk to systems means identifying which specific components can be used to create business impact, and which failures would be merely inconvenient. This work starts by treating systems as part of an interconnected service chain, not as standalone assets with independent risk. A single weak component can become a leverage point if it sits on a path to privileged identity, sensitive data, or a critical business function. The practical objective is to understand how an attacker or a fault could move from an initial foothold to a meaningful outcome.

Dependencies are the connective tissue that turns isolated issues into systemic risk. They include application-to-application integrations, shared services like identity and DNS, cloud control planes, administrative portals, and the data pipelines that feed analytics and operations. They also include people and process dependencies such as privileged support workflows, break-glass accounts, and vendor-managed components that bypass standard change controls. A dependency map is valuable when it highlights concentration points, where many services rely on a small set of components. Those concentration points are where outages cascade and where attackers gain disproportionate blast radius.

Trust boundaries are where assumptions change and where defensive controls must be explicit. A trust boundary exists whenever data, code, or identity crosses from a context you control into one you do not fully control, or where the level of assurance changes. Common examples include the transition from the public internet to a perimeter service, from a user workstation to a server network, from an application runtime to a database, or from a corporate identity realm into a third-party SaaS integration. The boundary is not defined by a firewall icon on a diagram; it is defined by authentication strength, authorization enforcement, segmentation, and the monitoring visibility available at that crossing. When teams fail to articulate trust boundaries, they often assume a level of safety that is not actually enforced.

A risk map should connect assets and boundaries into credible scenarios that reflect how compromise and failure propagate. Rather than listing "web server risk" or "database risk," the map should show relationships like "public-facing endpoint leads to application token theft which leads to access to customer records." This is how likelihood becomes more than a guess, because pathway complexity, required privileges, and control coverage can be assessed. It is also how impact becomes concrete, because the scenario terminates at a business function, a data set, or a control plane capability. Executives can then see why certain weaknesses demand immediate action even if their technical severity appears similar to others.

Operational teams can make this mapping repeatable by anchoring it to a few consistent data sources. Asset inventories provide ownership and criticality, identity systems reveal privilege relationships, and network and cloud telemetry show which components actually communicate in production. Vulnerability and configuration posture data adds evidence of weakness, while detection coverage indicates whether a pathway can be seen and interrupted in time. The highest-value mapping work is often the reconciliation of these sources, because it exposes contradictions such as "this system is critical but has no logging," or "this integration exists in traffic but is not documented." Those contradictions are themselves risk indicators, because they imply unmanaged change and unknown exposure.

AI-assisted correlation can accelerate mapping by turning large volumes of telemetry into candidate dependency graphs and likely attack paths. Models can cluster services by communication patterns, identify anomalous trust relationships, and highlight accounts or systems that sit at the center of many interactions. The dependencies are strict: if identity telemetry is incomplete or asset naming is inconsistent, automated mapping will produce gaps and false edges that look plausible. Human-in-the-loop review should focus on validating the most critical paths and the boundaries that would change priority decisions, because those are the places where false confidence is most dangerous. Governance also matters, because mapping outputs often contain sensitive architectural details and must be handled with access controls and an audit trail of changes.

The most common pitfall is producing diagrams that look precise while failing to drive decisions. A map that stops at "network zones" without showing identity flows, service-to-service authorization, and data movement will miss how modern compromises spread. Another failure is assuming that a trust boundary exists because a control is intended, rather than confirming it is enforced and monitored under real operating conditions. Risk mapping is effective when it changes what teams do next: which remediation work rises to the top, which detection gaps get closed first, and where segmentation or privilege reduction will meaningfully reduce blast radius. When systems, dependencies, and trust boundaries are mapped with that decision intent, risk stops being a theoretical concept and becomes a daily tool for defensive prioritization.

Evaluating Threat Landscapes and Attack Vectors

A useful view of the threat landscape is not a catalog of scary actors; it is an operational understanding of how the organization is most likely to be harmed given its technology, people, and dependencies. Threat evaluation becomes practical when it starts with what is exposed, what is trusted, and what is valuable, then asks which attack vectors can realistically traverse those pathways. The objective is to reduce uncertainty in prioritization by distinguishing between plausible attack sequences and background noise. This framing keeps teams focused on conditions that produce incidents, rather than on headlines that may not map to their environment.

Attack vectors are the entry and movement mechanisms that connect an adversary to impact, and most environments have a small number of repeatable patterns. External exposure remains a primary driver, especially when internet-facing services, remote access paths, and third-party integrations are treated as convenience features rather than high-assurance control points. Identity-based vectors—credential theft, session token abuse, and misuse of privileged accounts—are often more reliable for attackers than pure exploitation, because they blend into normal access patterns. Endpoint vectors, including phishing-driven initial access and malicious execution, matter because endpoints are where human behavior intersects with trust. Cloud control plane vectors matter because a single compromised identity can change policy, create persistence, and reshape logging in ways that suppress detection.

Evaluating threat landscapes requires separating "can happen" from "likely to happen here," and that depends on evidence. Internal signals such as authentication anomalies, repeated exposure of the same misconfigurations, incident history, and near-misses provide a grounded baseline for what the organization struggles to control. External signals like public reporting, vulnerability exploitation trends, and common techniques observed across similar organizations provide context for what is being weaponized at scale. The most defensible evaluation ties external signals to internal conditions, such as "this class of exploit matters because we have that service exposed," or "this technique matters because our privilege model makes lateral movement cheap." Without that linkage, threat evaluation becomes an abstract exercise that produces vague action items.

Trust boundaries shape which vectors are highest risk because they determine where assurance changes and where monitoring may be weakest. A boundary that relies on a single factor of authentication, or that grants broad network access after a successful login, creates fertile ground for identity abuse. Boundaries between SaaS services and corporate identity, between production and engineering networks, or between vendor access and internal administration are common areas where assumptions are fragile. Attackers prefer vectors that minimize friction, and weakly governed boundaries offer a path that is both reliable and stealthy. Evaluating vectors therefore includes asking not only how an attacker gets in, but how they expand influence once inside.

A mature evaluation also considers the business timing of threats, because likelihood changes with operational cycles. Periods of heavy change—major releases, migrations, seasonal demand spikes, mergers, and urgent remediation sprints—create conditions where controls are bypassed and monitoring coverage lags. Attackers exploit these moments because defenders are overloaded and exceptions become routine. Similarly, reliance on third parties creates time-dependent exposure when vendors rotate staff, change access methods, or introduce new integrations. Threat evaluation that ignores timing treats risk as static, which is inconsistent with how incidents actually unfold.

AI and machine learning can strengthen threat evaluation by turning high-volume telemetry into prioritized hypotheses about active vectors. Models can detect patterns across authentication events, endpoint behavior, and network flows that indicate common intrusion sequences, and can summarize which tactics appear most frequently against critical assets. These benefits depend on comprehensive logging, consistent identity data, and clear baselines, because missing telemetry produces blind spots and biased conclusions. Human-in-the-loop controls are essential: analysts must validate model outputs against raw evidence, and approval boundaries should prevent automated systems from escalating speculative hypotheses into disruptive actions. Failure modes such as drift, where the environment changes faster than baselines update, and false confidence, where probabilistic outputs are treated as certainty, must be expected and governed.

The output of threat landscape evaluation should be a defensible set of prioritized vectors tied to explicit environmental conditions and control gaps. If a vector is high priority, the organization should be able to point to the specific exposures, privilege pathways, and monitoring limitations that make it so, and identify what would materially reduce the risk. Common pitfalls include over-rotating to rare but dramatic threats, treating vulnerability severity as a proxy for likelihood, and ignoring identity and trust relationships because they are harder to measure. The teams that consistently improve are the ones that treat threat evaluation as a living operational practice, continuously tested against telemetry and incident outcomes, and used to drive focused control improvements rather than broad, unfocused security activity.

Risk Treatment Options and Decision Tradeoffs

Risk treatment is the point where analysis becomes commitment, because every option represents a deliberate tradeoff rather than a purely technical choice. In practice, treatment options fall into a small set of patterns: reducing likelihood, reducing impact, transferring risk, accepting residual risk, or avoiding the activity entirely. What matters operationally is not the label, but whether the chosen treatment changes the conditions that produce incidents. Teams that skip this translation step often appear busy while leaving the underlying risk profile unchanged.

Reducing likelihood focuses on making successful compromise harder or less probable. This includes strengthening authentication, tightening authorization, removing unnecessary exposure, hardening configurations, and closing exploitable weaknesses along common attack paths. Likelihood reduction tends to be attractive because it aligns with preventative controls, but it can be expensive and slow when it requires architectural change or cross-team coordination. The tradeoff is that not all likelihood can be reduced to zero, especially in environments that rely on third parties, remote access, or rapid change. Effective decisions recognize diminishing returns and prioritize the controls that materially disrupt realistic attack vectors. Select treatment options by stating the explicit tradeoff and the specific scenario conditions that the choice changes as show in Table 5.3.

Reducing impact assumes that some compromises will occur and focuses on limiting blast radius and recovery cost. Techniques such as segmentation, least-privilege design, data isolation, and strong backup and restoration processes change the outcome even when an attacker gains a foothold. Impact reduction is often undervalued because its success is less visible in day-to-day operations, yet it consistently determines whether incidents become crises. The tradeoff is that impact controls may not prevent initial access and can be perceived as accepting failure, which requires leadership maturity to support. When done well, they provide resilience that complements prevention rather than replacing it.

Risk transfer shifts some consequences to another party, most commonly through contracts, insurance, or managed services. Transfer does not remove risk; it changes who bears certain costs and obligations when an event occurs. The decision tradeoff lies in coverage limits, exclusions, and dependencies on third-party response quality, all of which can create false confidence. Transfer is most appropriate for risks that are hard to reduce internally and where the organization can clearly define what is being transferred. Overreliance on transfer without internal controls often results in operational surprises during incidents, when contractual protections do not align with technical reality.

Table 5.3 Risk Treatment Options and Decision Tradeoffs.

Treatment Option	What It Changes	When IGt Fits	Key Tradeoff
Reduce likelihood	Harder to succeed	High exposure or common vectors	Can be slow and cross team
Reduce impact	Limits blast radius	Assume compromise is possible	Less visible day-to-day benefit
Transfer risk	Shifts some consequences	Hard to reduce internally	False confidence from exclusions
Accept residual risk	Documented decision	Cost exceeds benefit	Debt if not time bounded
Avoid the activity	Removes the driver	Low business value feature	Immediate user or revenue impact

Risk acceptance is an explicit choice to live with residual risk because further treatment is not justified by cost, feasibility, or strategic priorities. Acceptance must be bounded by clear conditions: what is being accepted, for how long, and under what assumptions about controls and monitoring. The tradeoff is governance-related rather than technical, because undocumented acceptance quietly accumulates and resurfaces during audits and incidents. Mature programs treat acceptance as time-limited and reviewable, with owners accountable for reassessment as conditions change. Acceptance without visibility is not a decision; it is unmanaged exposure.

Avoidance removes the risk by changing or discontinuing the activity that creates it, such as decommissioning a system, disabling a risky feature, or exiting a dependency. Avoidance can be the most effective treatment when a function or exposure no longer aligns with business value. The tradeoff is often immediate impact to users or revenue, which makes avoidance politically difficult even when it is technically straightforward. Clear articulation of business impact versus security exposure is essential to support these decisions. Avoidance decisions that are delayed tend to become forced decisions later, often under incident pressure.

AI-assisted decision support can help compare treatment options by modeling how different controls affect likelihood and impact across multiple scenarios. Models can estimate how reducing a privilege set or adding segmentation changes attack path viability, or how detection improvements shorten time-to-containment. These insights depend on accurate representations of the environment and on assumptions that must be transparent to decision-makers. Human approval boundaries are critical, because automated recommendations can overweight easily measurable factors and underweight strategic considerations like regulatory exposure or customer trust. Failure modes such as model drift, oversimplified cost assumptions, and unexamined bias toward certain control types must be actively governed.

The core discipline in risk treatment is making tradeoffs explicit and defensible. Every treatment option should be tied to a specific risk scenario, a clear rationale, and an expected change in likelihood or impact. When leaders can see why a control was chosen, what it costs, and what risk remains, prioritization becomes stable rather than reactive. The organizations that execute this well are not those that eliminate all risk, but those that consistently choose where risk is allowed to exist and can explain that choice under scrutiny.

Communicating Risk to Technical and Executive Audiences

Risk communication fails most often when it is treated as translation of jargon rather than alignment on decisions. Technical teams want specificity about conditions, controls, and failure modes, while executives want clarity about impact, likelihood, and what must be funded or changed. The same risk can be true in both languages, but it must be framed differently to be useful. Effective communication begins by anchoring on what decision the audience is expected to make, because without a decision, the discussion drifts into debating severity labels and hypothetical threats.

For executive audiences, risk should be expressed as a business scenario with consequences, not as a list of technical findings. The framing that lands is "If this happens, here is what breaks, how long it could be disrupted, what data could be exposed, and what obligations we trigger." Executives also need confidence intervals, because pretending certainty in an uncertain domain damages credibility when outcomes differ. Communicating uncertainty is not weakness when it is disciplined, such as explaining that visibility gaps or incomplete asset ownership increase risk because they widen the range of plausible outcomes. When the scenario and uncertainty are clear, executives can make tradeoffs that reflect strategy rather than fear.

For technical audiences, risk must remain actionable and falsifiable, with a clear chain from cause to impact. Engineers and operators need to know where the pathway exists, what assumptions are being made about exposure and privilege, and which controls are expected to interrupt the sequence. A technically useful message includes the trust boundaries involved, the dependencies that create blast radius, and the observability available to detect and contain the issue. It also clarifies what "done" means in evidence terms, such as reduced exposure, reduced privilege, improved logging coverage, or faster containment. Without this concreteness, technical teams interpret risk communication as subjective and deprioritize it in favor of visible operational demands.

A common failure mode is mixing audiences in a single message and satisfying neither. When an executive brief is filled with vulnerability identifiers, configuration details, and log artifacts, leaders disengage and default to asking for a score. When a technical remediation request is framed only as "high risk to the business," teams lack the information needed to plan, test, and validate. Effective programs produce two synchronized views: one that supports leadership decisions and another that supports engineering execution, both derived from the same underlying scenario. Consistency between these views is essential, because contradictions erode trust and create room for risk to be ignored.

Communication also must account for organizational incentives, because risk discussions are often negotiations about ownership, time, and budget. Teams will naturally minimize problems that fall outside their remit, especially when success metrics reward delivery speed and uptime over control quality. Risk messages should therefore clarify ownership boundaries and handoffs, including where security depends on platform teams, identity teams, cloud operations, and vendors. When handoffs are vague, risk becomes everyone's problem and therefore no one's priority. Clear accountability reduces defensiveness and shifts the conversation toward execution.

AI and machine learning can assist risk communication by summarizing complex evidence into coherent narratives and generating audience-specific versions of the same risk scenario. Models can help extract the salient facts from telemetry, highlight the most critical dependencies, and produce concise executive framing while preserving traceability to the underlying data. The dependencies are strict: if input data is incomplete or poorly labeled, AI-generated summaries can amplify errors and create persuasive but incorrect narratives. Human review must be mandatory for high-impact communications, and approval boundaries should require validation of the key claims and assumptions before they are shared. Governance expectations include auditability, so that the organization can show what evidence supported a risk statement and why a decision was made.

The strongest risk communication practices are iterative and outcome-driven rather than performative. After a remediation cycle or an incident, teams should revisit whether the communicated risk reflected reality and whether the chosen treatment reduced likelihood or impact as expected. Over time, this feedback loop improves the organization's shared understanding of what matters and which controls actually work in its environment. Risk communication then becomes a stabilizing force: it reduces reactive work, aligns technical effort with business priorities, and makes defensive decisions explainable under scrutiny.

AI-Augmented Risk Analysis: Dependency Mapping, Scenario Modeling, and Control Validation

AI-augmented risk analysis is most valuable when it accelerates the parts of risk work that are slow for humans: synthesizing large volumes of telemetry, reconciling inconsistent inventories, and surfacing relationships that are not obvious in any single dataset. The goal is not to replace risk judgment, but to improve the speed and quality of evidence that informs it. When used well, AI helps teams move from static snapshots to continuously refreshed views of how systems connect, where trust boundaries actually exist, and which controls measurably reduce risk. When used poorly, it creates a new layer of opaque scoring that feels authoritative while masking gaps and assumptions.

Dependency mapping is a natural starting point because modern environments are too dynamic for manual diagrams to stay accurate. AI can learn service-to-service relationships by analyzing network flows, API call patterns, identity token usage, and cloud resource metadata, producing a living map of what talks to what in production. It can also highlight central nodes such as identity providers, shared databases, and integration brokers that amplify blast radius if compromised or disrupted. The quality of this mapping depends on consistent asset identifiers and telemetry coverage across segments, cloud accounts, and third parties, because missing visibility produces

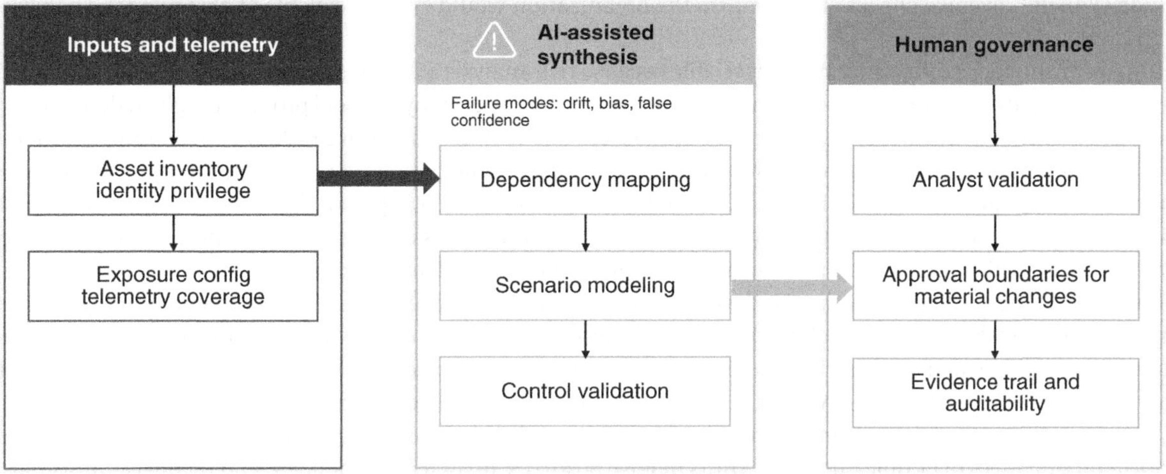

Figure 5.1 AI-Augmented Risk Analysis with Human Approval Boundaries.

false edges and false isolation. A responsible program treats AI-generated maps as hypotheses to validate, not as authoritative truth, and uses validation work to improve underlying inventories and logging.

Scenario modeling turns dependency maps into risk narratives by describing plausible paths from entry to impact. AI can generate candidate attack paths by combining exposure context with privilege relationships and observed communication patterns, effectively proposing "if-then" sequences that would allow an adversary to move laterally or escalate privileges. It can also cluster similar scenarios to reduce duplication, helping teams focus on systemic weaknesses rather than on thousands of individual findings. Scenario modeling is only as good as its assumptions about trust boundaries, authorization enforcement, and compensating controls, which are often misrepresented in data sources. Human analysts must review high-impact scenarios to confirm that the path is technically feasible, that the required privileges exist in reality, and that the impact statement matches what the business function would actually lose. Figure 5.1 shows how AI augments risk analysis by generating dependency maps, scenario models, and control validation signals, while humans retain accountability through validation and approval boundaries. It reinforces the chapter's emphasis on telemetry dependencies and failure modes such as drift, bias, and false confidence.

Data and telemetry dependencies determine whether AI-augmented analysis produces clarity or false confidence. The minimum viable inputs include accurate inventories, identity and privilege graphs, exposure data, configuration posture, and reliable logs that represent both normal behavior and past security events. Without identity fidelity, models routinely misjudge risk by underestimating privilege pathways through service accounts, delegated admin roles, and shared credentials. Without trustworthy exposure context, models can treat internal-only weaknesses as urgent while missing an internet-reachable chain that collapses the boundary assumptions. Teams should explicitly track data quality as a first-class risk factor, because uncertainty created by missing telemetry is itself a driver of residual risk.

Control validation is where AI-augmented risk analysis becomes operationally credible, because it ties risk treatment decisions to measurable outcomes. Rather than assuming a control works because it exists, AI can test control effectiveness by analyzing whether expected signals appear during exercises, whether alerts fire for known behaviors, and whether incident timelines show containment improving over time. It can also help detect control drift, where configurations degrade or coverage erodes due to change, by comparing current telemetry patterns to known-good baselines. Validation must be bounded by careful governance because models can mistake lack of evidence for evidence of absence, especially when logging gaps exist. The validation approach should therefore include explicit “coverage checks” that confirm the organization would even be capable of observing the behavior being validated.

Human-in-the-loop controls are non-negotiable because risk analysis affects resource allocation, operational priorities, and executive commitments. Analysts should be able to inspect why a model produced a given dependency, scenario, or control assessment, including the data sources and features that drove it. Approval boundaries should require human review for recommendations that trigger major remediation work, changes to critical access, or formal risk acceptance decisions. This protects against failure modes such as persuasive but incorrect scenario narratives, bias toward well-instrumented systems, and drift as architectures change. It also reinforces accountability, ensuring the organization can explain decisions without hiding behind an algorithm.

Governance and auditability must be designed in from the beginning because AI-augmented analysis often touches sensitive telemetry and architectural details. Access to model outputs should follow least privilege, and outputs should be treated as operationally sensitive artifacts rather than general documentation. Decision records should capture when AI was used, what it concluded, what was accepted or overridden, and why, so that the organization can reconstruct the reasoning during audits and post-incident reviews. Models should be monitored for performance changes over time, including shifts in false positives, missed dependencies, and inconsistent scenario rankings, because risk environments are not static. Without this governance, AI becomes a confidence engine rather than an evidence engine.

The practical standard for success is that AI makes risk work more repeatable, more current, and more defensible without reducing human accountability. Teams should see faster identification of high-leverage dependencies, clearer articulation of realistic attack paths, and earlier detection of control degradation before it becomes an incident catalyst. At the same time, the organization should avoid treating model outputs as a substitute for hard questions about scope, assumptions, and business impact. When AI is integrated as an assistive layer over strong telemetry, disciplined review, and clear decision rights, it improves the fidelity of prioritization and makes risk treatment decisions more resilient under real operational pressure.

Keeping Risk Assessments Current and Useful

Risk assessments lose value when they become documents that describe an environment that no longer exists. Modern systems change continuously through deployments, cloud scaling, identity updates, vendor integrations, and evolving business processes, and those changes quietly invalidate prior assumptions. Keeping assessments current does not mean rewriting them every week; it means designing them to be refreshed through evidence and revisited when key conditions shift. The operational aim is to preserve decision usefulness by ensuring the highest-impact risks remain tied to real pathways, real dependencies, and current control effectiveness.

A practical way to keep assessments current is to treat scope as stable while allowing inputs to update on a regular cadence. The scope should remain anchored to critical business functions and their supporting systems, because those do not change as often as the technical components beneath them. Inputs, however, must be refreshed from authoritative sources such as inventories, identity systems, configuration posture, and operational telemetry. When these sources are incomplete or inconsistent, the assessment should explicitly reflect that uncertainty rather than implying confidence. This is how assessments remain honest and defensible, even when the environment is imperfectly measured.

Change triggers are more reliable than calendar-driven reviews because they align reassessment effort with actual risk movement. Material changes include new external exposure, new privileged roles or access paths, major architecture shifts, onboarding of a third party with elevated access, or significant changes to monitoring coverage. Incident learnings and near-misses are also triggers, because they reveal where prior assumptions about likelihood, detection, or containment were wrong. A program that only revisits risk annually often discovers during an incident that its “top risks” were not the risks that mattered in practice. The discipline is to define what constitutes a material change and ensure there is a predictable process to re-evaluate affected scenarios.

Assessments stay useful when outputs remain tightly connected to decisions and actions rather than drifting into generic risk registers. A current assessment should still produce prioritized scenarios with clear contributing factors, mapped dependencies, and a view of residual risk after existing controls. It should also preserve the evidence trail: what data sources were used, what assumptions were made, and what is known to be uncertain. When remediation work is completed, the assessment should be updated to reflect what actually changed, such as reduced exposure, reduced privilege, or improved detection fidelity. If completed work never feeds back into the assessment, the organization cannot demonstrate risk reduction and will repeatedly fund the same categories of work without measurable progress.

AI and machine learning can help keep assessments current by automating evidence refresh and highlighting where assumptions no longer hold. Models can detect emerging dependencies, shifts in communication patterns, new concentrations of privilege, and changes in exposure that alter attack path feasibility. These capabilities depend on stable identifiers, consistent logging, and a governance model that prevents automated updates from silently rewriting risk narratives without review. Human approval boundaries should apply to changes that materially alter prioritization, because models can be biased toward what is most visible and can misinterpret temporary operational anomalies as structural shifts. The value of AI is in early warning and synthesis, not in unsupervised decision-making.

A common pitfall is letting "current" become synonymous with "more data," which creates bloated assessments that no one reads. The objective is relevance, not comprehensiveness, and that requires disciplined pruning of stale findings and consolidation of duplicate scenarios. The most useful assessments preserve a stable set of high-impact risk scenarios and update the evidence that supports them, rather than continuously inventing new categories of risk. When new risks are introduced, they should be integrated by mapping them to existing business functions and trust boundaries, so they can be compared consistently. This keeps leadership from experiencing risk as a rotating set of unrelated alarms.

Keeping risk assessments current is ultimately a governance and operating model problem, not a documentation problem. Ownership must be clear, reassessment triggers must be enforced, and the evidence sources must be maintained with the same seriousness as other operational dependencies. When teams treat inventories, identity graphs, and telemetry as foundational, risk assessments remain actionable because they reflect the environment that defenders actually operate. The result is not a perfect representation of risk, but a living decision tool that continues to guide prioritization, funding, and control validation as the organization evolves.

Conclusion

Risk management remains credible only when it produces repeatable decisions that hold up during incidents, audits, and budget cycles. When critical business functions are clearly defined, mapped to their supporting systems and trust boundaries, and evaluated against realistic attack vectors, defensive prioritization becomes consistent instead of reactive. Risk treatment choices then become explicit tradeoffs—likelihood, impact, transfer, acceptance, or avoidance—supported by evidence and communicated in a way that drives both executive decisions and technical execution. Over time, AI-augmented dependency mapping, scenario modeling, and control validation can sharpen this practice, but only when governed with clear approval boundaries, auditable rationale, and continuous refresh mechanisms that keep assessments aligned with how the environment actually operates.

Recommendations

1) Anchor defensive prioritization in explicit risk scenarios rather than severity labels or raw finding counts. Translate each priority into a likelihood-and-impact statement that names the business consequence and the

pathway that creates it. Use that framing to defend tradeoffs when time, budget, or staffing constraints force hard choices. Revisit priorities when exposure, privilege, or dependency conditions materially change.

2) Define the scope of each risk assessment in terms of a business function or decision you need to support. Specify what is included and excluded, so the assessment is executable and repeatable under pressure. Assign a clear owner for the scoped function and ensure they can confirm what "failure" looks like in operational terms. Avoid broad scopes that create shallow analysis and hide critical blind spots.
3) Build risk assessments on evidence by maintaining trustworthy inputs across assets, identity, exposure, and telemetry. Treat identity and privilege relationships as first-class inputs because they often define real attacker pathways. Validate that vulnerability and configuration data reflects current reality and is not stale, duplicated, or missing key context. Document uncertainty when visibility or inventory gaps prevent confident conclusions.
4) Map risks to systems, dependencies, and trust boundaries, so teams can see how compromise and failure propagate. Identify concentration points such as shared identity services, central integrations, and administrative portals that amplify blast radius. Validate trust boundaries by confirming assurance, authorization enforcement, segmentation, and monitoring at the crossing points. Use the resulting pathways to drive prioritization and remove guesswork from "what matters most."
5) Evaluate threat landscapes by linking external exploitation trends to internal conditions and exposure. Focus on vectors that can plausibly traverse your environment, especially those involving external access paths and identity misuse. Use internal telemetry, incident history, and observed anomalies to ground likelihood instead of relying on generalized narratives. Update evaluations when new exposure, privilege pathways, or monitoring gaps emerge.
6) Choose risk treatment options by explicitly stating the tradeoffs between reducing likelihood, reducing impact, transferring risk, accepting residual risk, and avoiding the activity. Tie each treatment decision to a specific scenario and explain what conditions it changes in the environment. Set review dates and owners for any accepted risk, so it does not become invisible debt. Ensure completed remediation work feeds back into updated residual risk rather than closing tickets without measurable change.
7) Communicate risk differently to technical and executive audiences while keeping the underlying scenario consistent. Present executives with outcome-focused narratives that describe disruption, data exposure, and decision implications without drowning them in implementation detail. Provide technical teams with actionable paths, affected boundaries, and evidence-based assumptions they can validate and remediate. Maintain a defensible audit trail that shows what evidence supported each risk statement and decision.
8) Use AI and machine learning to accelerate synthesis and correlation, not to replace accountable judgment. Start with dependency mapping and scenario generation as hypotheses that must be validated against real telemetry and ownership knowledge. Require human approval for changes that materially alter priority, remediation scope, or formal risk acceptance decisions. Monitor for drift, bias toward well-instrumented systems, and persuasive-but-wrong narratives when data quality degrades.
9) Validate controls by measuring whether they work in practice, not by assuming they work because they exist. Confirm that expected signals appear in telemetry, that detection coverage matches critical paths, and that response timelines improve where risk is highest. Treat missing logs and uneven coverage as risk factors that widen uncertainty and delay containment. Update risk scenarios based on observed control performance rather than static design intent.
10) Keep risk assessments current by defining material-change triggers and establishing a predictable refresh process for inputs and outputs. Refresh inventories, exposure context, privilege data, and monitoring coverage on a cadence that matches operational change velocity. Consolidate and prune scenarios, so the assessment remains readable and decision-ready instead of growing into an unmaintainable register. Ensure every major change, near-miss, or incident learning results in an updated scenario view and an updated prioritization stance.

6

Asset Management as the Backbone of Defense

Asset management is the operational foundation that makes every other defensive activity measurable, repeatable, and trustworthy. When teams can reliably identify what exists—physical devices, cloud resources, SaaS services, identities, and the relationships between them—they can set clear scope for patching, monitoring, access control, and incident response without relying on assumptions. The discipline is not limited to building a list; it requires durable ownership, meaningful classification, lifecycle controls that prevent orphaned exposure, and ongoing maintenance that limits drift as environments change. When these elements are in place, security work becomes faster and more precise because decisions are anchored to verified asset context rather than incomplete visibility and manual guesswork.

Why Asset Awareness Controls Everything Downstream

Asset awareness is the operational truth that every defensive control depends on, whether teams acknowledge it or not. You cannot harden what you cannot name, you cannot monitor what you cannot locate, and you cannot validate what you cannot inventory. In practice, "asset" must be broader than servers and laptops; it includes identities, endpoints, cloud workloads, network devices, SaaS tenants, code repositories, certificates, and the data stores that power business workflows. When asset awareness is weak, defensive decisions become inference and guesswork, and every downstream control inherits that uncertainty. Leaders often feel this as chronic friction: projects stall over "unknown owners," incidents take longer because responders cannot determine scope, and risk conversations drift into abstraction because nobody can anchor them to what actually exists.

Every meaningful control starts with scope, and scope is an asset question before it is a security question. Patch management depends on knowing which systems exist, which versions they run, and which of them are actually reachable and in production. Vulnerability management depends on knowing what should be scanned, what cannot be scanned, and what must be assessed through alternate means because of operational constraints. Configuration standards only matter if there is a way to measure conformance across all relevant assets, including ephemeral cloud resources that appear and disappear on demand. Even basic enforcement—like ensuring MFA coverage or disk encryption—requires confidence that the full population of accounts and endpoints is known and continuously reconciled. Without asset awareness, teams can report impressive percentages while quietly excluding the systems that are hardest to find and often the easiest to compromise.

Detection and response are where the cost of poor asset awareness becomes impossible to ignore. An SOC cannot reliably interpret alerts without understanding what an asset is supposed to do, who uses it, what network segments it belongs to, and which logs are expected from it. During an incident, scoping hinges on questions like "where else does this software run?" "which identities can access this data?" and "what other systems trust this host?" all of which are asset relationships rather than isolated facts. If responders must build this context from scratch under time pressure, containment becomes either timid and slow or overly aggressive and disruptive.

Asset awareness also determines whether telemetry gaps are visible; teams cannot notice missing logs from a critical system if they do not know that system exists or that it should be emitting logs at all. The practical outcome is that attackers gain time, defenders lose confidence, and leadership receives incomplete answers when they need clarity most.

Asset awareness also controls identity and access outcomes, even when organizations treat IAM as a separate discipline. Accounts are assets with lifecycle, ownership, and expected behavior, and they should be tracked with the same rigor as infrastructure. Service accounts, API keys, and OAuth tokens are often the most operationally powerful "assets" in modern environments, yet they frequently lack clear owners and expiration expectations. Entitlements drift when teams cannot continuously map who has access to what systems and which privileges are still justified by a current business need. When inventories ignore identities, the organization ends up hardening devices while leaving privileged paths open through stale accounts and over-broad roles. Good asset awareness ties identities to the systems, data, and business processes they support, which is what allows access reviews to move beyond checkbox exercises into meaningful risk reduction.

In modern environments, asset awareness must be continuous rather than periodic, because the infrastructure itself is dynamic. Cloud services, containers, and managed endpoints shift constantly, and the "inventory" is less a spreadsheet than an operational fabric of discovery, reconciliation, and ownership mapping. The hard part is not collecting raw lists from multiple systems; it is resolving conflicts, deduplicating identifiers, and deciding which source is authoritative for a given attribute like owner, environment, or business criticality. Asset records also need to capture relationships, such as dependencies between applications and databases, trust paths between accounts and services, and exposure points like internet-facing interfaces. When those relationships are missing, risk assessments collapse into generic severity labels that fail to reflect real blast radius. A defensible program treats the asset inventory as a living representation of the environment, maintained through operational processes rather than annual audits.

AI and machine learning can improve asset awareness, but only when their use is grounded in reliable telemetry and controlled decision boundaries. Pattern-based enrichment can correlate naming conventions, network observations, authentication logs, and configuration data to infer ownership and classify assets by function, such as "domain controller," "build server," or "point-of-sale endpoint." Similar techniques can cluster assets by behavior to reveal unmanaged devices, shadow SaaS usage, or systems that have drifted into anomalous communication patterns. These approaches depend on consistent identifiers and high-quality data feeds; when logs are missing, time is skewed, or sources disagree, the model will confidently "complete" the picture with incorrect assumptions. The human-in-the-loop control is critical: automated enrichment should propose, not dictate, and changes that affect scope, criticality, or ownership should require review and approval. Governance expectations should include auditability of what inputs drove the recommendation, how conflicts were resolved, and how the organization detects drift when the environment changes faster than the model's assumptions.

The failure modes of asset awareness programs are predictable, and they often look like success on paper. Teams focus on counting assets rather than proving coverage for the assets that matter most, which leads to inventories that overrepresent well-managed fleets and underrepresent the operational edge. Another common pitfall is treating "owner" as an email field instead of a real accountability relationship, leaving critical systems with nominal owners who cannot make decisions during incidents. Asset records also degrade when they are maintained manually without incentives or when processes allow systems to go live before ownership, classification, and telemetry expectations are met. In environments using AI-assisted enrichment, a particularly dangerous failure mode is false confidence—accepting plausible classifications without verifying the underlying evidence—followed by automation that expands scope or relaxes controls based on that unverified context. The organizations that perform best treat asset awareness as a prerequisite gate for downstream security work, with continual reconciliation, accountable ownership, and explicit handling for unknowns rather than hiding them in reporting.

Building an Inventory of Physical and Digital Assets

An effective inventory begins by defining what "asset" means in operational terms and then enforcing that definition consistently across the organization. Physical assets typically include end-user devices, servers, network appliances, removable media, and specialized systems like building controls and industrial equipment. Digital assets extend beyond "things you can touch" to include cloud workloads, SaaS tenants, virtual networks, applications, data stores, certificates, code repositories, and identities such as user accounts and service principals. The inventory must also distinguish between production and non-production, managed and unmanaged, and corporate and personal ownership models, because each category carries different control expectations. If the definition is too narrow, critical exposure remains invisible; if it is too broad without structure, teams drown in noise and stop trusting the inventory.

Discovery is the first practical hurdle, and it is rarely solved by a single source of truth. Physical endpoints may be observed through device management platforms, directory services, DHCP and DNS records, network access logs, procurement systems, and help desk tickets, each providing partial visibility with different failure modes. Cloud assets may be enumerated through cloud control planes, configuration repositories, workload orchestration layers, and identity platforms, where ephemeral resources appear and disappear faster than manual processes can track. SaaS assets often hide in plain sight because business units can provision them without central IT involvement, leaving security to infer usage through authentication logs and network egress patterns. A mature discovery approach treats each source as a sensor, continuously collecting candidates and then reconciling them rather than arguing about which system is "right." The goal is coverage with validation, not perfect cleanliness on day one. Table 6.1 summarizes the minimum asset record fields that make an inventory operationally useful for defense.

Reconciliation is where inventories become usable, because raw discovery outputs are filled with duplicates, stale records, and ambiguous identifiers. A single laptop might appear under multiple hostnames, IP addresses,

Table 6.1 Core Inventory Fields and Why They Matter.

Field	Operational Purpose	Downstream Security Impact
Stable asset identifier	Track continuity across renames rebuilds and migrations	Prevents duplicate scope and broken remediation routing
Owner team	Assign accountable action and incident decisions	Enables fast routing for patching response and telemetry fixes
Asset category	Distinguish endpoint server network cloud SaaS identity	Sets correct control expectations and monitoring coverage
Environment	Separate production from non-production	Prevents misprioritized remediation and reduces business disruption
Criticality	Link asset to mission impact and downtime tolerance	Drives patch timelines monitoring depth and containment posture
Exposure	Record external reachability and trust paths	Prioritizes high risk assets and improves scoping during incidents
Lifecycle state	Track active decommissioning retired	Prevents stale assets from inflating scope and hiding residual risk
Telemetry expectation	Define required logs and signals for the asset	Enables detection of dark assets and monitoring gaps

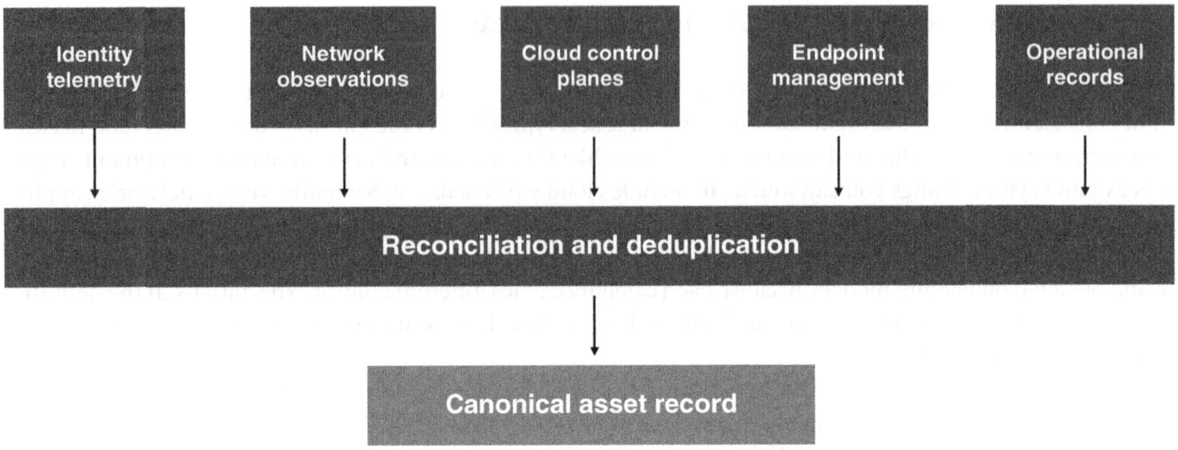

Figure 6.1 Multi-Signal Asset Discovery and Reconciliation Flow.

and directory objects over time, and cloud workloads may be represented by instance IDs, resource names, and tags that change across deployments. Practical inventories assign stable identifiers and maintain a mapping between observed attributes and the canonical record, so the organization can track an asset through name changes, reimaging, and lifecycle events. Just as important, reconciliation must incorporate a "confidence" concept, where assets with weak corroboration are flagged for follow-up instead of silently treated as fully known. When teams collapse uncertain records into certainty, downstream controls inherit that false precision and failures become harder to diagnose. Treating ambiguity as a first-class condition keeps the inventory honest and makes remediation measurable. Figure 6.1 shows how multiple partial discovery sources act as sensors that feed a reconciliation step to produce a canonical asset record. It reinforces the idea that coverage comes from continuous correlation and deduplication rather than relying on a single "source of truth.".

Ownership and classification are the minimum enrichment needed to turn an inventory into an operational control surface. Ownership is not simply a name; it is the accountable party who can approve changes, accept risk, and respond to incidents involving that asset. Classification includes environment, business function, data sensitivity, and criticality, which determine patch urgency, monitoring depth, and acceptable downtime during containment. These attributes should be derived from operational reality, not aspirational architecture diagrams, and they should be validated when assets move between teams or when business processes change. The inventory must also capture key relationships, such as what applications depend on a database, which identities administer a system, and which networks expose an asset to external traffic. Without relationships, risk scoring becomes generic and incident scoping becomes guesswork.

Lifecycle management is what prevents inventories from degrading into historical archives. Assets enter the environment through procurement, onboarding, and provisioning, and each entry point should include a step that establishes the asset record, assigns ownership, and sets baseline control expectations. Assets leave through decommissioning, offboarding, contract termination, and cloud teardown, and those exits must trigger record updates, access revocation, and evidence that data-handling requirements were met. The most common breakdown is orphaned assets: systems that remain reachable after their owners change roles, projects end, or vendors rotate, leaving residual access paths for attackers. A disciplined program ensures that lifecycle events are reflected quickly, and that stale records are surfaced as operational defects rather than tolerated as "inventory drift." The inventory becomes credible when it mirrors the environment's lifecycle cadence, not when it looks tidy at audit time.

AI and machine learning can accelerate discovery and enrichment, but only when the organization controls how suggestions become truth. Behavior-based clustering can group assets by typical communication patterns and authentication activity, helping identify unmanaged devices, shadow SaaS usage, and systems that do not match their declared purpose. Natural language processing can also normalize messy naming conventions and tag descriptions to propose classifications and likely owners, especially in large environments where humans struggle to keep labels consistent. These capabilities depend on high-quality telemetry—authentication logs, network flow data, configuration signals—and they fail when data is sparse, biased toward certain segments, or delayed. Human-in-the-loop review is essential for changes that affect scope, criticality, or ownership, because a confident model output can still be wrong in ways that materially increase risk. Auditability matters as well: teams should be able to explain which evidence drove an AI-assisted inference and how conflicts were resolved when sources disagreed.

An inventory becomes defensible when it is integrated into daily workflows and measured by coverage outcomes rather than by record counts. When patching, vulnerability management, and monitoring rely on the inventory to define scope, gaps become visible because controls fail loudly for missing or misclassified assets. When incident response procedures reference the inventory for owners, dependencies, and containment boundaries, responders can move faster with fewer disruptive guesses. When leadership asks, "Are we exposed?" the inventory enables a precise answer tied to known asset populations, not a probability statement. The fastest way to undermine the program is to allow exceptions that bypass inventory onboarding, because every bypass becomes an unmonitored attack path. Treating inventory accuracy as an operational reliability problem—continuously reconciled, validated, and owned—keeps physical and digital asset awareness strong enough to support everything else the defense team is trying to accomplish.

Defining Ownership and Accountability for Assets

Ownership is the mechanism that turns an inventory from a catalog into an operational control, because every meaningful security decision eventually requires a person or team to act. An asset record without a responsible owner is effectively unmanaged, even if it sits inside a well-funded environment with strong tooling. Ownership must be defined in terms of authority and obligation, not simply a name in a field, and it must map to real-world operational responsibility. In practice, this means the owner can approve configuration changes, prioritize remediation work, and make risk-based tradeoffs when controls conflict with uptime or business demands. When ownership is vague, security work becomes a series of escalations and delays, and the organization quietly normalizes exposure as "someone else's problem."

Accountability becomes clearer when ownership is split into distinct, complementary roles that match how modern environments are operated. Business ownership aligns the asset to a business process, budget, and mission impact, which is essential for setting criticality and deciding what downtime is acceptable during containment. Technical ownership aligns the asset to a team that can implement patches, adjust configurations, and maintain telemetry, which is essential for closing security gaps quickly. Operational custody addresses day-to-day administration, such as who handles access requests, monitors health, and coordinates maintenance windows, which is essential for keeping controls from degrading over time. These roles may be held by one team for some assets and by multiple teams for others, but the inventory must capture who is accountable for which decisions. When the organization collapses all of these responsibilities into a single ambiguous "owner," accountability breaks the moment tradeoffs are required. Table 6.2 clarifies how ownership responsibilities map to decisions defenders must execute quickly.

The most important ownership decision is who can say "yes" and who must say "no" when risk increases, because those boundaries determine how fast the organization can respond under pressure. Asset owners should have explicit authority to approve remediation actions that impact their systems, including emergency patching, credential resets, configuration rollbacks, and temporary access restrictions. At the same time, owners must accept the obligation to meet baseline security expectations, such as telemetry enablement, timely patching, and maintaining accurate classification data for criticality and data sensitivity. When owners cannot authorize change,

Table 6.2 Ownership Roles and Decision Boundaries by Asset Context.

Ownership Element	Primary Responsibility	Example Decision Enabled	Common Failure Mode
Business ownership	Align asset to mission impact and acceptable downtime	Approve disruptive containment for high-impact events	Criticality becomes politics not impact
Technical ownership	Implement patches configuration and telemetry	Execute emergency patching and logging restoration	Owner cannot make changes during incidents
Operational custody	Handle day-to-day administration and coordination	Schedule maintenance windows and validate control baselines	Work stalls in handoffs and escalations
Escalation path	Provide after hours authority for critical assets	Authorize access restrictions and account disablement	Delays while teams search for contacts
Access accountability	Validate admins' service accounts and tokens for the asset	Revoke stale privileges and constrain service identities	Privilege sprawl persists without review

security teams end up negotiating during incidents, and containment becomes slower and more disruptive. When owners are not obligated to maintain controls, the inventory fills with stale records that look compliant until an incident proves otherwise. Clear boundaries reduce both friction and blame, because responsibility is defined before a crisis.

Ownership must also be resilient to organizational change, because people move roles faster than assets change state. Assigning ownership to individuals rather than teams creates brittle accountability that collapses during vacations, turnover, and reorganizations. A more durable approach ties ownership to functional groups with defined escalation paths, so responsibility survives staffing changes and remains actionable during incidents. The inventory should record both the accountable team and the operational contact path, including how after-hours decisions are made for high-impact assets. This is not administrative overhead; it is the difference between containment in minutes and containment in days when an incident touches critical systems. When accountability is durable, security work is less dependent on heroics and more dependent on established operations.

Defining ownership is also how organizations prevent privilege sprawl and unclear access paths from becoming permanent risk. Owners should be accountable for validating which identities administer their assets and whether those privileges remain justified over time. That includes human administrators, service accounts, API credentials, and delegated access models that often outlive the projects that created them. Without a clear owner, access reviews become generic exercises that focus on directory-level groups while missing asset-specific privilege paths. Ownership also enables fast decisions during response, such as disabling a service account that appears compromised or restricting administrative interfaces that are being targeted. When owners understand that access is part of their accountability, identity risk becomes manageable rather than diffuse.

AI-assisted enrichment can help establish and maintain ownership signals, but it should not become an automated authority for assigning responsibility. Correlating authentication logs, change records, ticket activity, and deployment metadata can suggest likely owning teams for systems that lack clean labels, especially in large environments where assets outpace documentation. Models can also detect ownership drift by identifying assets whose activity patterns no longer match the expected business function or administrative population, prompting review before a gap becomes an incident. These methods depend on complete and trustworthy telemetry, and they can be biased toward teams that generate more visible signals, such as frequent deployers, while missing less active but highly critical systems. Human review is essential for final ownership assignments, because accountability is a governance decision with operational consequences, not merely a statistical inference. The audit expectation should be that any AI-derived suggestion is traceable to evidence and that assignment changes are recorded with rationale.

The practical test for ownership and accountability is whether routine security work can proceed without escalations and whether incident response can execute without confusion. When ownership is well defined, vulnerability remediation can be assigned and tracked to completion, exceptions can be explicitly granted and time-bounded, and telemetry gaps can be resolved by accountable teams rather than by broad requests to "IT." When ownership is weak, the organization compensates with informal networks, repeated outreach, and workarounds that hide gaps rather than closing them. Accountability also creates a healthier risk conversation, because leaders can connect exposure to specific business systems and decision-makers rather than treating risk as an abstract score. The objective is not to punish asset owners; it is to ensure that every asset has a responsible steward who can make timely, informed decisions that keep the environment defensible.

Classification and Prioritization for Defensive Focus

Classification is the discipline of describing assets in ways that are operationally meaningful for defense, and prioritization is the discipline of using that description to allocate finite security attention. Most organizations have more systems, identities, and integrations than they can monitor deeply or remediate immediately, which makes "treat everything the same" a guarantee of shallow coverage. A usable classification scheme captures what an asset is, what it supports, how exposed it is, and what would happen to the business if it were unavailable or compromised. This is not a paperwork exercise; it is the basis for deciding which assets get the fastest patch windows, the richest telemetry, and the most aggressive containment actions during incidents. When classification is vague or inconsistent, prioritization collapses into politics, urgency, and the loudest stakeholder.

Business criticality is the anchor attribute because it links technical reality to mission impact without requiring executives to become infrastructure experts. An asset that supports revenue capture, customer identity, or operational safety carries a different risk profile than a development sandbox, even if the same vulnerability exists in both places. Criticality should reflect actual dependency chains, including upstream identity providers, shared databases, and network services that many applications rely on. This is where teams often underestimate risk, because "supporting systems" feel indirect until a failure cascades across multiple business functions. A defensible approach ties criticality to concrete outcomes such as downtime tolerance, data sensitivity, regulatory exposure, and the operational cost of recovery. When those factors are embedded into classification, incident decisions become faster because responders already know which systems can be isolated aggressively and which require coordinated containment.

Exposure and accessibility are the next classification layer because they determine how quickly an attacker can reach an asset and how likely exploitation is to be observed. Internet-facing services, remote access pathways, externally reachable management interfaces, and publicly accessible SaaS tenants represent a different defensive surface than internal-only systems behind segmented networks. Exposure also includes trust relationships, such as assets reachable through vendor connections or systems that accept federated authentication from external identities. Organizations frequently misclassify exposure when they rely on intended architecture rather than observed reality, especially when legacy exceptions or temporary testing rules become permanent. A strong classification model treats exposure as an attribute that can change and therefore must be validated through continuous observation, not assumed from diagrams. When exposure is accurately captured, vulnerability remediation and detection engineering can focus first on the assets most likely to be targeted.

Data sensitivity must be integrated into classification because data often outlives systems and is the true target of many attacks. Systems that store, process, or provide access to sensitive data—customer records, authentication secrets, financial data, proprietary code, and operational plans—require tighter controls regardless of whether they are "important" to day-to-day operations. Sensitivity also applies to metadata and administrative artifacts, such as audit logs, configuration repositories, and credential vaults, which can enable lateral movement when compromised. A common failure is to classify data stores correctly while ignoring the applications, integrations, and identities that can access them, creating a false sense of containment. Effective classification captures both where sensitive data resides and the paths through which it can be reached. This enables defensible decisions like prioritizing identity hardening and monitoring around sensitive access paths even when the systems themselves are not externally exposed.

Prioritization becomes actionable when classification is mapped to specific defensive expectations that teams can execute and measure. High-criticality, high-exposure assets should have the most complete telemetry, the most aggressive patch timelines, the most rigorous configuration baselines, and the most rehearsed incident procedures. Lower-criticality assets may still be patched and monitored, but they can accept longer remediation windows and lighter telemetry when resources are constrained. This mapping prevents the two extremes that cause operational harm: applying maximum controls everywhere until teams burn out, or applying minimum controls everywhere until incidents become inevitable. The practical advantage is that security leaders can explain resource allocation in terms of business impact and attack likelihood, rather than personal preference. When prioritization is explicit, it also reduces conflict during incidents because responders can point to pre-established expectations when recommending isolation or access restrictions.

AI and machine learning can help refine classification and prioritization by synthesizing signals that humans struggle to reconcile at scale. Models can infer asset roles from behavioral telemetry, correlate identity usage patterns to identify high-value administrative paths, and detect anomalies that suggest a system's classification has drifted from its declared purpose. For prioritization, AI-assisted triage can combine vulnerability attributes, observed exploit activity, exposure indicators, and business criticality to propose remediation ordering that is more grounded than severity scores alone. These approaches depend on consistent, high-quality data such as authentication logs, network observations, configuration states, and dependency mappings, and they can fail when telemetry is incomplete or biased toward certain parts of the environment. Human-in-the-loop controls are essential for approval boundaries, especially when AI recommendations would change containment posture, accelerate emergency patching, or trigger broad access revocations. Governance should require that prioritization decisions remain explainable, that model-driven recommendations are auditable, and that teams monitor for drift when the environment changes faster than the model's assumptions.

The most reliable indicator that classification and prioritization are working is improved decision quality under stress. When a critical vulnerability emerges, teams should be able to identify the affected asset population quickly, determine which instances are most exposed, and sequence remediation in a way that reduces real risk first. When a detection fires, analysts should immediately know whether the alert touches a crown-jewel system or a low-impact environment, and they should have pre-aligned response playbooks that match that classification. Common pitfalls include overclassifying assets as "critical" to avoid scrutiny, underclassifying shared infrastructure because it is "just plumbing," and allowing classification attributes to become stale as systems evolve. Classification should be treated as a living operational model, validated through change management and reinforced through incident learnings, not a one-time categorization project. When done well, it creates a defensible basis for focus, speeds up response, and ensures that limited defensive resources protect what truly drives the business.

Asset Lifecycle Management and Offboarding

Asset lifecycle management is the practice of controlling how assets enter, change within, and leave the environment in a way that keeps security posture aligned with operational reality. Most security failures attributed to "misconfiguration" or "missed patching" are actually lifecycle failures: assets were created outside standard onboarding, ownership was never established, or decommissioning steps were skipped when a project ended. Lifecycle management must cover physical and digital assets, including endpoints, cloud workloads, SaaS tenants, identities, certificates, and automation credentials. The objective is not bureaucratic control; it is ensuring every asset has an owner, a classification, baseline controls, and verifiable telemetry from the moment it becomes reachable. When lifecycle processes are weak, the organization accumulates unmanaged systems that are invisible to monitoring and persistent long after their business purpose ends.

Onboarding is where defensive debt is either prevented or guaranteed, and it starts before an asset is powered on or a resource is provisioned. For physical assets, onboarding includes procurement tracking, asset tagging, enrollment into device management, assignment to a user or team, and baseline configurations that establish encryption, endpoint protection, and logging expectations. For digital assets, onboarding includes registration in authoritative inventories, assignment of ownership, application of environment and criticality classification, and configuration of access controls and network exposure. The most important operational concept is gating: an asset should not be considered "in service" until it meets minimum control requirements appropriate to its classification. When teams allow exceptions to onboarding gates, they create a parallel environment where assets exist but do not participate in patching, monitoring, or incident response workflows. That parallel environment becomes the attacker's preferred terrain because it is both reachable and neglected.

Change within the lifecycle is where assets drift, and drift is the silent killer of security assumptions. Systems get repurposed, moved between networks, migrated to new platforms, or inherited by different teams, often without updating ownership or classification. Cloud resources can change shape through autoscaling and redeployments, which can alter exposure and telemetry in ways that are hard to see if the inventory is not continuously reconciled. Identities and privileges drift as people change roles and service accounts become embedded in automation, leaving access paths that no longer map to current business needs. Lifecycle management must treat changes as events that trigger validation of controls, not just tickets that approve functionality. When drift is handled explicitly, defenders can maintain consistent monitoring and access boundaries even as the environment evolves.

Offboarding is the most consequential lifecycle stage because it is where organizations either remove attack paths or leave behind durable, low-visibility entry points. For physical assets, offboarding must address data handling, ensuring devices are wiped or destroyed according to sensitivity and that inventory records reflect their true disposition. For digital assets, offboarding must include disabling workloads, removing public exposure, revoking credentials, and validating that data is archived or deleted as required. The hardest part is not turning off a server; it is identifying and removing the residual dependencies—API keys, scheduled jobs, DNS records, certificates, and integration accounts—that keep the asset reachable or trusted. Offboarding is also where SaaS risk accumulates, because tenants and applications can persist after contracts end, still connected to identity providers and still holding sensitive data. A disciplined offboarding process treats these remnants as first-class risks and requires evidence that they were removed, not simply assumed.

Identity offboarding deserves special attention because it is the most direct way attackers exploit lifecycle gaps. Human account offboarding must be timely and complete, including disabling authentication, revoking sessions, removing group memberships, and addressing privileged access that could persist through cached tokens or delegated roles. Service accounts and automation identities require even more rigor, because they are often shared across pipelines and integrations and may not have a clear owner by the time a project ends. When a service account remains active without oversight, it becomes a stealthy persistence mechanism that can bypass many endpoint-focused controls. Lifecycle management should require explicit ownership for non-human identities, expiration expectations, and periodic validation that the account is still needed and still constrained to least privilege. Offboarding that overlooks identities and tokens is effectively offboarding theater, because the paths that matter to attackers remain open.

AI and machine learning can strengthen lifecycle management by detecting lifecycle anomalies and highlighting offboarding failures that humans miss at scale. Models can correlate inventory data with telemetry to identify assets that are still communicating or authenticating despite being marked as decommissioned, or assets that have become "dark" by disappearing from logging without a recorded retirement. Similar techniques can flag likely orphaned resources by spotting long-unused privileges, certificates nearing expiration with no owner, or SaaS applications that continue to receive authentications after a business unit claims they were retired. These capabilities depend on reliable data sources—inventory states, authentication logs, network observations, and configuration signals—and they can produce false confidence if telemetry is incomplete or if labels in the inventory are inaccurate. Human-in-the-loop controls are essential when AI suggestions would disable accounts, tear down resources, or revoke integrations, because the operational blast radius can be significant. Governance expectations should include audit trails for lifecycle state changes, evidence for offboarding actions, and periodic reconciliation between "expected" and "observed" asset activity.

Lifecycle management becomes operationally real when it is embedded into routine workstreams and measured by reduction in unmanaged exposure rather than by compliance checkmarks. Teams should be able to answer basic questions quickly, such as which assets are scheduled for decommissioning, which have no owner, and which are active but missing telemetry. Offboarding should produce observable outcomes, such as the absence of authentication activity and network communications for retired systems, and the removal of DNS and certificate artifacts that can be abused. Common pitfalls include treating decommissioning as a one-time action rather than a sequence, allowing "temporary" exceptions to persist indefinitely, and failing to account for third-party access and integrations that remain connected after projects end. A mature lifecycle program reduces incident scope, speeds containment decisions, and prevents attackers from exploiting the organization's own operational leftovers. When offboarding is executed with the same rigor as onboarding, the environment becomes harder to enter, harder to persist in, and easier to defend.

Handling Shadow IT and Unknown Assets

Shadow IT is not primarily a technology problem; it is a visibility and incentives problem that surfaces when teams can acquire capability faster than the organization can provide it. Business units adopt SaaS tools, create cloud resources, or integrate third-party services to meet real delivery timelines, often without malicious intent and sometimes with better user experience than sanctioned options. Unknown assets are the technical manifestation of that behavior: systems, accounts, and services that exist outside the organization's expected inventory and control plane. For defenders, the risk is not that these assets exist at all, but that they exist without ownership, classification, telemetry, and lifecycle management. When shadow assets become normal, the environment turns into a partial map where security controls provide comfort rather than coverage.

The first operational requirement is to treat "unknown" as a measurable condition and a routine workflow, not an embarrassment to hide. Unknown assets will always exist in dynamic environments, particularly in cloud and SaaS ecosystems, so the objective is rapid identification, triage, and disposition. Detection starts with multiple signals: network observations, authentication and authorization logs, DNS patterns, certificate issuance, email and collaboration platform integrations, and procurement and expense artifacts that hint at new services. The most common failure mode is relying on a single discovery source, which creates blind spots that shadow IT naturally exploits. A credible program continuously reconciles these signals and produces a backlog of candidates that must be investigated, rather than assuming inventory completeness. The organization's confidence should be based on how quickly unknowns are found and resolved, not on how clean the inventory looks.

Triage for unknown assets must balance security urgency with business empathy, because heavy-handed responses drive shadow IT deeper underground. The first questions are practical: what is it? who is using it? what data touches it? and how is it connected to corporate identities or networks? If an unknown SaaS application is federated with corporate SSO or receiving corporate email, it is already inside the trust boundary and must be treated as a real enterprise dependency. If an unknown host is communicating externally or receiving inbound traffic, it may represent immediate exposure that warrants containment while ownership is established. The triage process should assign temporary classification and provisional ownership quickly, even if imperfect, so that basic controls and monitoring can be applied while deeper evaluation happens. The objective is to convert unknowns into managed assets through a predictable pathway, not to shame teams for moving fast.

Converting shadow IT into managed IT requires a clear decision model that includes both adoption and retirement outcomes. Some shadow assets should be brought under governance because they meet a legitimate need and can be controlled, while others should be decommissioned because they duplicate capability, create unacceptable exposure, or violate data-handling requirements. The decision hinges on business criticality, data sensitivity, identity integration, and the feasibility of enforcing baseline security expectations such as access control, logging, and administrative accountability. If the organization cannot integrate a service into its identity and monitoring model, it should assume the service will become a persistent blind spot and treat that as an explicit risk decision rather than an accident. Conversely, if the organization can integrate and govern it, the fastest path is usually to formalize ownership, document allowed use, and enforce lifecycle controls without disrupting the business. Shadow IT becomes dangerous when it remains in limbo, neither adopted nor removed, because limbo assets accumulate privileges and data without scrutiny.

Unknown assets also expose the limits of traditional perimeter thinking, because shadow IT often lives in SaaS and cloud control planes rather than on corporate networks. A single employee can create a cloud project, deploy workloads, and expose services to the internet in minutes, and those resources may never appear in on-premises discovery. Similarly, SaaS tools can store sensitive data and integrate with corporate identities without ever touching a corporate endpoint in a way that triggers obvious alerts. Handling these realities requires defenders to treat identity telemetry as a primary discovery mechanism, because federated login events, token grants, and application consent flows reveal shadow adoption earlier than infrastructure scans. It also requires attention to administrative surfaces like OAuth app registrations, third-party integrations, and API keys, because those are often the real assets attackers exploit once a shadow service exists. When unknown assets are framed as "internet problems" rather than "identity and trust problems," organizations end up securing the wrong layer.

AI and machine learning can improve shadow IT detection and unknown asset handling by correlating weak signals into actionable leads, but only when organizations maintain disciplined controls on what automation is allowed to do. Models can flag anomalous authentication patterns that suggest new SaaS applications, cluster network destinations that resemble unsanctioned file sharing or collaboration platforms, and identify emerging asset populations that do not match known inventories. AI-assisted enrichment can propose likely owners by analyzing usage patterns, group memberships, and historical ticketing activity, which helps convert unknowns into accountable assets faster. These capabilities depend on high-fidelity telemetry, especially identity logs and network observations, and they can fail through bias or drift when business behavior changes, such as during reorganizations or new product launches. Human-in-the-loop review is essential for actions that would block access, revoke integrations, or disable accounts, because false positives can disrupt legitimate work and erode trust in the program. Governance expectations should include auditability of why an asset was flagged, what evidence supported the classification, and how decisions to adopt or retire were recorded.

The most sustainable way to reduce shadow IT is to align security controls with business velocity, so teams do not feel forced to choose between delivery and compliance. That includes providing sanctioned pathways for rapid adoption of common capabilities, clear intake processes for new SaaS tools, and default security baselines that can be applied quickly when something new appears. It also includes making ownership and accountability straightforward, so business units can take responsibility without being trapped in endless approval loops. Unknown assets should be treated as routine operational work, with service-level expectations for investigation and resolution, rather than as sporadic "cleanup campaigns" that never fully catch up. Common pitfalls include punitive responses that push adoption into personal accounts, focusing only on technology discovery while ignoring procurement and identity signals, and allowing exceptions to persist without time bounds. When the organization treats shadow IT as a predictable byproduct of modern operations and builds a disciplined conversion process, unknown assets stop being a chronic blind spot and become a manageable stream of work that strengthens overall defensive posture.

Asset Data Quality, Maintenance Practices, and Drift

Asset data quality is the difference between an inventory that supports operations and an inventory that merely exists. An asset record is only as useful as its accuracy, timeliness, and consistency, and those qualities degrade naturally as environments change. Drift is the gap that forms between "what the inventory says" and "what is actually running," and it expands whenever onboarding, change, or offboarding processes fail to update the authoritative record. In modern environments, drift is not a rare exception; it is a constant force driven by cloud elasticity, rapid deployments, reorganizations, and identity changes. If teams do not treat drift as an expected operational condition, they will unknowingly make control decisions based on outdated assumptions. The result is predictable: patch coverage overstatements, incomplete detection scope, and incident response confusion that consumes time when minutes matter.

High-quality asset data begins with a small set of attributes that are consistently populated and operationally meaningful. Stable identifiers matter because hostnames, IP addresses, and resource names change, while the organization still needs to track continuity across rebuilds and migrations. Ownership matters because remediation and response require accountable action, and records without a current owner become dead ends in workflows. Classification matters because criticality and data sensitivity determine defensive depth, and misclassification causes either wasted effort on low-impact assets or neglect of high-impact ones. State matters because assets move through lifecycle phases, and a retired system that still appears "active" in inventory will continue to be treated as in-scope noise. When inventories try to capture dozens of optional fields without enforcing the core attributes, completeness becomes cosmetic and the fields that matter most quietly rot.

Maintenance practices must reflect that inventories are fed by many sources that disagree, and reconciliation is a continuous discipline rather than a periodic cleanup. In practice, multiple systems provide partially authoritative truth: identity platforms know accounts and group memberships, device management knows endpoint posture, cloud control planes know resource existence, and ticketing systems know business intent and change history. Data quality improves when each attribute has an identified system of record and a defined precedence order for conflicts, rather than a "last write wins" model that allows random sources to overwrite critical fields. Deduplication is equally important, because duplicate records inflate asset counts and dilute accountability, and they are common when assets are reimaged, renamed, or moved between environments. A credible program tracks confidence and provenance, so teams can see which attributes are strongly supported and which are inferred or stale. When provenance is missing, analysts cannot tell whether a record is trustworthy, and they either ignore the inventory or treat it as gospel, both of which are dangerous.

Drift is often caused by normal operational change that was never designed to update security-relevant data. Teams deploy new versions, autoscale workloads, rotate certificates, and change network routes without touching inventory fields, especially when inventory updates are manual. Over time, asset purpose changes while labels remain frozen, and the system no longer matches its declared environment, criticality, or owner. Identity drift is particularly damaging because access paths change faster than infrastructure, and stale group memberships, delegated roles, and service account permissions become persistent privilege. A mature practice treats change events as triggers for asset validation, ensuring that ownership, classification, exposure, and telemetry expectations are rechecked when assets are modified. When this is not embedded into change management or deployment pipelines, drift becomes the hidden tax on every downstream control.

Operational controls must also account for "dark assets," which are assets that exist but stop producing expected signals. A system might be present in the inventory but missing from logging due to configuration changes, network segmentation, agent failures, or deliberate attacker interference. If the inventory does not include telemetry expectations—what signals should exist and from where—teams cannot distinguish "quiet" from "invisible." Dark assets are especially dangerous because they can appear compliant while being effectively unmonitored, and they often include the most critical systems where change is tightly controlled and therefore logging failures go unnoticed. Maintenance practices should include periodic reconciliation between inventory and observed telemetry, so missing logs are treated as operational defects with owners and remediation timelines. The most common pitfall is treating monitoring gaps as SOC issues rather than asset maintenance issues, which delays remediation and obscures accountability.

AI and machine learning can improve data quality by automating reconciliation and drift detection, but these methods must be governed carefully to avoid compounding errors. Models can normalize inconsistent naming, infer missing attributes from behavior, and identify records that likely represent the same underlying asset across different sources. They can also detect drift by spotting assets whose observed patterns no longer match their expected role, such as a system labeled "development" that begins handling production authentication traffic or a workstation that starts behaving like a server. These approaches depend on clean telemetry and stable identifiers, and they fail when the training data reflects historical labeling mistakes or when key sources are missing from certain segments. Human-in-the-loop review is critical for high-impact changes, especially those that would alter ownership, criticality, or exposure classifications, because those fields drive prioritization and incident decisions. Governance should require that AI-driven updates are explainable, that changes are logged with evidence, and that teams can roll back incorrect inferences without losing trust in the inventory.

Sustained data quality requires accountability and routine hygiene, not occasional remediation campaigns. Asset records should have defined freshness expectations, and fields that matter for defense—ownership, classification, lifecycle state, and exposure—should be periodically revalidated through operational workflows rather than through annual attestations. Organizations that do this well treat the inventory as a production system with reliability targets, monitoring, and defect backlogs, because inventory errors have real operational consequences. Common pitfalls include allowing exceptions to onboarding to persist, tolerating "temporary" assets that never get classified, and letting teams self-report criticality without verification, which quickly turns "critical" into a political label. When maintenance is disciplined, drift shrinks, and downstream controls become more reliable because they are operating on a map that reflects current reality. That reliability shows up everywhere: fewer surprise assets during incidents, faster remediation assignments, and security reporting that leaders can trust because it matches what is actually running.

Correlation and AI-Assisted Asset Discovery: Benefits, Risks, and Verification

Correlation is the practical act of turning many partial views of an environment into a defensible understanding of what exists and how it behaves. No single system sees all assets: identity platforms see accounts and sessions, network systems see communications, cloud control planes see provisioned resources, and endpoint management sees enrolled devices. Correlation links those perspectives, so the organization can resolve duplicates, surface unknown assets, and understand relationships such as which identities administer which systems and which applications depend on which data stores. AI-assisted asset discovery extends correlation by using models to infer missing context, cluster assets by behavior, and propose classifications or ownership where human effort does not scale. The benefit is speed and coverage, especially in environments with dynamic cloud resources and constant SaaS adoption. The risk is that inference can look like certainty, and once an inventory is wrong with confidence, downstream controls fail quietly.

AI-assisted discovery is most valuable when it accelerates the steps that are repetitive for humans but still evidence-driven. Models can normalize inconsistent naming, map multiple identifiers to a canonical asset record, and suggest that two seemingly different records actually represent the same asset across different sources. Behavior-based clustering can identify unmanaged endpoints, unexpected workload roles, or assets that do not fit their declared environment because their traffic patterns and authentication activity diverge from peers. Correlation can also reveal relationships that are hard to build manually, such as a service account that touches multiple applications, or a SaaS integration that appears across many user sessions. These outputs improve defensive focus by turning "we think this exists" into "here is the evidence that it exists and what it is connected to." The operational value is not just discovery, but improved scoping for patching, monitoring, and incident response because assets are better contextualized.

The quality of AI-assisted discovery is bounded by data quality and coverage, which makes telemetry dependencies a first-order concern. Identity logs are often the most reliable discovery signal because they reveal what applications are being accessed, which accounts are active, and where administrative actions occur. Network observations provide breadth by showing unknown destinations, lateral movement patterns, and assets communicating from unexpected segments, but they can be noisy without strong attribution. Endpoint and cloud management signals provide authoritative posture for enrolled devices and provisioned resources, but they miss unmanaged endpoints and shadow deployments that evade standard tooling. When these sources are incomplete, delayed, or inconsistent, models will still produce outputs, but those outputs will be biased toward what is visible rather than what is important. A mature program treats telemetry gaps as discovery risk and explicitly tracks which segments are under-observed, so AI outputs are interpreted with the right caution. Table 6.3 shows how to verify AI suggested asset facts before they drive scope or containment decisions.

Human-in-the-loop controls are non-negotiable because discovery outputs often drive high-impact decisions. Automated enrichment that suggests an owner or classification can be low risk when it only improves routing and labeling, but it becomes high risk when it changes scope for patching, monitoring, or containment. Approval boundaries should be explicit: AI can propose merges, ownership assignments, and criticality changes, but humans should confirm changes that would reclassify an asset into a higher enforcement tier or remove it from one. The most dangerous failure mode is false confidence, where teams accept AI outputs because they are plausible and because the inventory looks cleaner afterward. Drift and bias can also mislead, especially when models learn from historical labels that were wrong or when certain business units generate more telemetry and therefore dominate the model's view. A defensible approach assumes models can be wrong in systematic ways and designs review workflows that catch those errors before they propagate.

Verification is the discipline that prevents correlation from becoming self-referential and prevents AI from laundering uncertainty into certainty. Verification begins by establishing "ground truth" checks using authoritative signals, such as confirming that a discovered host appears in device management, that a cloud resource exists in the control plane, or that a SaaS integration is present in identity configuration. It also includes validation through

Table 6.3 Verification Checklist for Correlation and AI-Assisted Asset Discovery.

AI Suggested Output	Verification Evidence Source	Approval Boundary	If Verification Fails
Duplicate record merge	Confirm matching stable identifiers and corroborating telemetry	Human review when merge changes scope or ownership	Keep separate and flag for investigation
Owner assignment	Correlate identity usage tickets and change activity	Human approval required for owner of critical assets	Assign provisional owner and escalate
Role classification	Validate with network behavior and authentication activity	Human approval for criticality or exposure changes	Mark as unknown role and increase monitoring
Exposure status	Confirm external reachability and trust relationships	Human approval for containment or access restrictions	Treat as potentially exposed until proven otherwise
Lifecycle state change	Confirm control plane state and observed telemetry absence	Human approval when decommission triggers credential revocation	Rollback state and investigate residual activity
Telemetry completeness	Confirm expected logs are present and timely	Human approval for disabling assets or blocking access	Open defect with owner and track to resolution

independent perspectives, such as corroborating an inferred asset role with both network behavior and authentication activity rather than relying on one telemetry stream. For unknown assets, verification should include ownership confirmation and data flow assessment, because the most consequential unknown is not "what is it" but "what does it touch and who is responsible." The inventory should preserve provenance and confidence scores, so teams can distinguish verified facts from inferred attributes and prioritize verification work accordingly. When provenance is missing, errors become invisible and review becomes impossible to scale.

AI-assisted discovery also introduces governance and auditability expectations because it affects how the organization justifies risk decisions. Leaders should be able to explain how the organization knows what assets exist, what evidence supports critical classifications, and why certain assets were prioritized for remediation or monitoring. If AI outputs change asset records, those changes should be logged with the supporting evidence, the approving party, and the time of change, so incident teams can reconstruct what was believed at the time. This matters when responding to high-impact events, because inaccurate inventories can lead to incorrect scoping, delayed containment, and misleading reporting to stakeholders. Auditability also constrains model usage in sensitive contexts, such as when discovery relies on analyzing authentication and usage patterns that may include personal data. A disciplined program keeps model inputs and outputs aligned with access controls and data-handling expectations, and it avoids broad exposure of discovery data to systems or users that do not need it.

The risks of AI-assisted discovery are manageable when organizations treat it as decision support rather than decision replacement. Models can accelerate correlation, surface anomalies, and reduce manual effort, but they cannot own accountability, accept risk, or understand business intent without human confirmation. The most effective operational pattern is to use AI to generate a prioritized queue of verification work: suspected duplicates, likely orphaned assets, probable shadow SaaS, and assets with drift indicators that deserve review. Over time, verification outcomes can be fed back to improve both correlation logic and model performance, but that feedback loop must be controlled to avoid reinforcing errors. Common pitfalls include over-automating merges that erase important distinctions, relying on AI to fill missing fields rather than fixing the upstream process, and treating discovery coverage as complete when telemetry is uneven. When correlation and AI-assisted discovery are paired with disciplined verification, they expand visibility without sacrificing trust, and they create an inventory that supports reliable downstream defense rather than a polished artifact that hides uncertainty.

Using Asset Management to Drive Security Work

Asset management drives security work when the inventory is treated as the authoritative scope setter for what must be protected, measured, and operated. In mature programs, the first question for any control is not "what tool do we use" but "which assets does this apply to and how do we know we covered them." That posture forces clarity about population, ownership, and expected telemetry, which prevents teams from reporting progress based on partial visibility. Asset records become operational inputs: they define which systems are in patch cycles, which identities require stricter controls, which applications warrant deeper monitoring, and which environments can tolerate disruptive containment actions. When the inventory is not used this way, security work fragments into parallel spreadsheets and tribal knowledge, and the organization cannot reliably connect effort to risk reduction. Treating the asset inventory as a living operational system turns it into the backbone for prioritization and accountability across the defensive program.

Vulnerability and patch management are the clearest examples of asset-driven execution because they require precise population control and ownership routing. The inventory should define which assets are in scope for scanning, which cannot be scanned and therefore require alternate assessment, and which are exempt with time-bounded justification tied to business impact. Ownership fields drive assignment, while classification fields drive deadlines, maintenance windows, and escalation thresholds when remediation is late. Exposure and criticality attributes allow teams to prioritize vulnerabilities based on real risk, not just severity labels, and to focus first on assets that are both reachable and business-significant. This approach also surfaces gaps that otherwise remain hidden, such as unmanaged endpoints that never appear in scanning results or cloud resources that are created outside standard provisioning. Asset-driven vulnerability management turns remediation into a governed workflow with measurable coverage rather than a periodic scramble when reports look bad.

Detection engineering and monitoring become more effective when asset management defines what "normal" telemetry coverage should look like. An inventory that includes asset type, environment, and criticality can set clear expectations for which logs and security signals must be present and how quickly gaps must be resolved. Analysts can interpret alerts with more accuracy when they can immediately see an asset's owner, role, exposure, and dependency context, which reduces both false alarms and missed escalations. Asset relationships also enable better correlation during investigations, because responders can pivot from a compromised system to its administrative identities, peer systems, and downstream dependencies without building a map under pressure. When monitoring is not inventory-driven, teams often chase noisy alerts on low-impact systems while missing silent failures on critical assets that were never properly onboarded. Inventory-driven monitoring makes telemetry completeness a measurable operational requirement rather than a best effort aspiration.

Identity and access controls become more defensible when they are anchored to assets rather than treated as generalized directory hygiene. Privilege decisions should be tied to specific systems and data stores, with owners accountable for who has administrative access and which service accounts or tokens exist for automation. Asset classification informs access rigor, because administrative access to a critical, exposed system carries a different risk than access to a low-impact test environment. When identity is connected to assets, access reviews can focus on meaningful entitlements and high-risk paths instead of generic group membership lists that do not reflect actual access. This linkage also improves incident response, because responders can quickly identify which identities are "keys to the kingdom" for affected assets and prioritize containment actions accordingly. Without asset grounding, identity programs often produce volume and activity without reliably reducing the most consequential access risks.

Asset management also drives incident response by enabling fast scoping, confident containment, and accurate communications. When an incident begins, responders need to answer which assets are affected, which are likely adjacent, and which business processes are at risk, and those answers come from inventory relationships and classifications. Ownership and criticality enable quick engagement of the right teams and the right leaders, while exposure data supports decisions about isolating systems, blocking access paths, or disabling integrations. A reliable inventory reduces the chance of both under-containment, where compromised dependencies are missed, and over-containment, where unnecessary shutdowns harm the business. It also improves post-incident learning because teams can identify which asset data was missing or wrong and treat those gaps as remediation work rather than as vague "process improvements." Asset-driven incident operations turn response from improvisation into execution against known context.

AI-assisted triage and prioritization can amplify the value of asset management by helping teams route work and detect when effort is misaligned with risk. By combining inventory attributes with live signals such as exploit activity, authentication anomalies, and exposure changes, models can propose remediation ordering that reflects both business impact and attack likelihood. The same approach can flag work queues that are skewed toward low-impact assets, or identify critical assets that lack expected telemetry and therefore represent blind spots. These benefits depend on accurate asset data and clearly defined approval boundaries, because AI recommendations that adjust containment posture, accelerate emergency patching, or revoke access can create business disruption if wrong. Failure modes include bias toward well-instrumented parts of the environment, drift as asset classifications become stale, and false confidence when a model's rationale is not transparent. Human-in-the-loop controls should require evidence for high-impact recommendations and maintain an auditable trail of why decisions were made, especially when AI-assisted outputs influence executive reporting.

Security work becomes sustainable when asset management is integrated into planning, execution, and measurement rather than treated as a separate discipline owned by a single team. Operationally, this means teams use the inventory to define scope at the start of initiatives, route tasks to accountable owners during execution, and measure coverage and completeness at the end. It also means lifecycle gates prevent new assets from entering production without owners, classifications, and telemetry expectations, so security does not spend its time chasing unknowns created by normal delivery. Common pitfalls include using asset counts as a vanity metric, allowing exceptions that bypass onboarding, and relying on manual updates that guarantee drift under modern change velocity. When asset management is used to drive work, it becomes the common language that aligns executives, engineers, and responders around what exists, what matters most, and what must happen next. The defensive program stops being a collection of good intentions and becomes an operational system with clear scope, accountable action, and measurable outcomes.

Conclusion

A defensible blue team program ultimately rises or falls on whether it can translate intent into coverage, and coverage begins with assets that are known, owned, and continuously validated. When inventories capture the right attributes, reflect real lifecycle state, and resist drift, they become the control surface that drives remediation, monitoring depth, access discipline, and confident incident scoping. Correlation and AI-assisted discovery can expand visibility and speed enrichment, but only when outputs are verified, approvals are bounded, and provenance is preserved, so the organization can trust what it believes. When asset management is treated as an operational system rather than an administrative exercise, downstream security work becomes more predictable, faster to execute, and easier to defend to both technical teams and leadership.

Recommendations

1) Define assets broadly and consistently across the organization. Treat endpoints, servers, network devices, cloud workloads, SaaS tenants, identities, certificates, and data stores as first-class assets in the same inventory discipline. Ensure teams use a shared definition, so controls do not unintentionally exclude high-risk categories like service accounts or third-party integrations. Revisit the definition when operating models change, so the scope stays aligned with how the business actually runs.
2) Build discovery as a continuous, multi-signal process rather than a one-time inventory effort. Combine partial views from identity telemetry, network observations, cloud control planes, endpoint management, and operational records to surface candidates and reduce blind spots. Establish a routine reconciliation workflow that deduplicates records and resolves conflicts instead of debating which system is "right." Track unknowns as a backlog with clear ownership until they are verified and dispositioned.
3) Assign durable ownership that maps to real decision authority and response obligations. Tie ownership to accountable teams and escalation paths rather than to individuals who will inevitably rotate. Ensure owners have authority to approve remediation actions that may impact operations and accept responsibility for baseline control expectations like telemetry, patching, and accurate classification. Record ownership in the inventory in a way that incident responders can use immediately without hunting for contacts.
4) Classify assets using attributes that directly drive defensive decisions. Capture business criticality, exposure, environment, and data sensitivity in a consistent way, so prioritization is grounded in mission impact and attack likelihood. Treat supporting dependencies and trust paths as part of criticality, so shared services are not underweighted. Use the classification to set explicit expectations for remediation timelines, monitoring depth, and containment aggressiveness.
5) Enforce onboarding gates that prevent unmanaged assets from entering service. Require new assets to have an inventory record, assigned ownership, appropriate classification, and baseline control enrollment before they are considered production-ready. Apply the same discipline to cloud and SaaS provisioning, so "fast" does

not mean "invisible." Treat bypasses as operational defects that must be corrected quickly to avoid creating parallel environments outside governance.

6) Operationalize offboarding as a sequence that removes residual access and trust, not just the primary system. Revoke accounts, sessions, tokens, API keys, and integrations associated with retired systems and validate that exposure artifacts like DNS entries and certificates are removed. Ensure data-handling steps match sensitivity, including secure wipe, archive, or deletion outcomes that are verifiable. Use observed telemetry to confirm that "decommissioned" assets are truly inactive and no longer communicating.
7) Handle shadow IT by converting unknowns into managed decisions rather than defaulting to punitive reactions. Establish a triage path that rapidly identifies what the asset is, who is using it, what data it touches, and how it connects to corporate identities or networks. Make adoption versus retirement decisions based on criticality, sensitivity, integration feasibility, and control enforceability, then document the outcome with accountable ownership. Avoid heavy-handed blocking as a first move when it will drive usage into personal accounts and deepen invisibility.
8) Treat data quality and drift as reliability problems with measurable outcomes. Define a small set of core fields—stable identifiers, ownership, classification, lifecycle state, and exposure—that must remain accurate and current. Reconcile inventory records against observed telemetry to detect "dark assets" that stop producing expected signals and assign remediation to owners. Track provenance and confidence, so teams can distinguish verified facts from inferred attributes and prioritize validation work.
9) Use correlation and AI-assisted discovery as decision support with clear verification and approval boundaries. Allow models to propose merges, enrichments, and likely ownership based on evidence from identity and network signals, but require human confirmation for changes that affect scope, criticality, or containment posture. Preserve audit trails showing what evidence drove updates and who approved them, so incident teams can trust the inventory under pressure. Monitor for bias and drift by recognizing that uneven telemetry coverage can skew model outputs toward what is visible rather than what matters most.
10) Drive security execution through the inventory by making it the authoritative scope setter for downstream work. Use asset records to define populations for patching, vulnerability remediation, monitoring coverage, and access governance, so progress reflects real coverage rather than partial visibility. Route work to accountable owners and measure completion against the asset population, not against the tickets created. Make incident response faster and less disruptive by relying on inventory relationships and classifications to scope, contain, and communicate with confidence.

7

Endpoint Security Management

Endpoint security management is fundamentally about controlling the devices where users work, credentials are exercised, and adversaries most often gain their first durable foothold. In modern environments, endpoints are both the primary source of actionable security telemetry and the most common platform for execution, persistence, and privilege escalation. Effective programs treat endpoints as a governed fleet, built on consistent baselines, reliable agent coverage, disciplined privilege control, and logging that supports fast triage and confident investigation. The operational challenge is sustaining that control under constant change, including configuration drift, necessary exceptions, and the inevitable tradeoffs between hardening and business productivity.

The Endpoint as a Primary Battleground

The modern endpoint is where most meaningful security decisions are made in real time, often before a human ever sees an alert. Identity is exercised from endpoints, sensitive data is created and staged on endpoints, and privileged actions are initiated from endpoints even when the target is in a cloud control plane. Attackers understand this and treat endpoints as their most reliable foothold for establishing persistence, harvesting credentials, and moving laterally without touching hardened perimeter controls. That shift changes defensive priorities: protecting endpoints is not a hygiene task, it is a primary control surface for business continuity. When endpoint controls are weak or inconsistently deployed, every other layer inherits that fragility.

Endpoint compromise is rarely a single event; it is typically a sequence of small successes that accumulate into operational control. Initial access may come from phishing, drive-by downloads, malicious document macros, browser exploit chains, or abuse of legitimate remote access tools. Once code runs, adversaries will test local privileges, security settings, and available credentials, then pivot to persistence mechanisms such as scheduled tasks, services, registry run keys, or startup folders. They will also exploit "living off the land" techniques, using trusted binaries and administrative tools to blend in and avoid simple signature-based detection. The practical implication is that endpoint security must be designed to recognize behavior patterns and control execution pathways, not just block known bad files.

In a well-run environment, endpoint security management is built on consistency: the same baseline controls, telemetry, and response actions apply across laptops, workstations, servers, and virtual desktops, with justified exceptions documented and monitored. Asset inventory becomes a security requirement, because unmanaged or unknown endpoints are effectively unbounded risk that cannot be patched, monitored, or isolated. Configuration management matters as much as malware prevention, because attackers routinely succeed by finding the one machine with a relaxed policy, outdated agent, or local admin rights that were "temporary" and never removed. Patch discipline must be paired with configuration drift detection, since secure settings can be undone by imaging errors, user workarounds, legacy software requirements, or incomplete migrations. Endpoint security fails quietly when leadership assumes uniform coverage that does not actually exist.

Defensive control on endpoints depends on the ability to observe and constrain what executes, what connects, and what changes. Reliable telemetry should capture process creation, parent–child relationships, command-line arguments, network connections, authentication events, and security-relevant configuration changes, because these are the signals that reveal intent. This telemetry must be time-synchronized and consistently enriched with device identity, user identity, and organizational context, so teams can distinguish normal administrative activity from suspicious use of the same tools. Over-collection without purpose is a common mistake; the goal is not volume, but high-fidelity signals that support detection and response decisions. Equally important is ensuring endpoints can still report when offline or on hostile networks, because attackers often exploit those periods to operate unobserved.

Response on endpoints must be designed for speed, reversibility, and clear authority boundaries. The most valuable actions are the ones that can be taken quickly and safely: isolating a host from the network, killing a malicious process tree, quarantining artifacts, and collecting a minimal forensic package that preserves volatile evidence. Those actions require disciplined role design, because an overbroad ability to isolate devices or terminate processes can disrupt business operations if used incorrectly or by a compromised account. Good practice is to treat endpoint containment as a controlled power: it is pre-authorized for defined conditions, logged automatically, and subject to rapid review rather than slow approval chains. Endpoint response also depends on clean handoffs, where incident responders can translate endpoint findings into identity actions, network controls, and remediation tasks without losing context.

AI and machine learning can materially improve endpoint defense when used as an assistive capability tied to verifiable telemetry, not as an oracle. Models can help cluster related alerts, highlight unusual command lines, or prioritize endpoints exhibiting rare combinations of behaviors, which reduces triage time and helps teams focus on higher-risk activity. The value depends on data quality and coverage; if process telemetry is incomplete, if device identity is inconsistent, or if logging is suppressed under load, AI outputs become confidently wrong and can cause responders to miss the real compromise. Human-in-the-loop controls are essential: analysts should be able to trace why a recommendation was made, validate it against raw events, and override it with clear documentation when business context explains an anomaly. Governance expectations include auditability of automated actions, periodic validation against drift as endpoint software and user behavior change, and safeguards against data leakage when sensitive telemetry is used for model tuning or enrichment.

Endpoint security management ultimately succeeds when it treats endpoints as a governed fleet rather than a collection of individual machines. That means lifecycle controls that start at provisioning, include secure configuration and least privilege enforcement, and continue through patching, monitoring, incident response, and decommissioning. It also means designing for the hard cases: developers who need elevated tooling, executives who travel with intermittent connectivity, kiosks and shared devices with unique usage patterns, and servers that cannot reboot on demand. Attackers routinely exploit the seams between "IT operations" and "security operations," so the operating model must be explicit about ownership, escalation paths, and what happens when business requirements collide with risk. When that model is clear and consistently executed, the endpoint stops being the attacker's most dependable battleground and becomes a defensive advantage.

Endpoint Baselines and Configuration Standards

Endpoint baselines are the minimum set of configuration expectations that define what "normal" and "acceptable" looks like for every managed device class in the organization. They translate security intent into concrete settings across operating systems, browsers, productivity tools, and core security controls so that endpoints behave predictably under both routine use and attack pressure. Without a baseline, every endpoint becomes a unique snowflake shaped by ad hoc admin decisions, legacy installs, and user workarounds, which makes prevention inconsistent and detection unreliable. A baseline is not a static hardening checklist; it is a living contract between security, IT operations, and the business about which risks are being reduced and which exceptions are being consciously accepted. The goal is consistency at scale, because consistency is what makes control enforcement and incident response repeatable.

Configuration standards sit one level deeper than the baseline by specifying how settings are expressed, applied, and verified over time. That includes which controls are mandatory versus conditional, which settings are enforced centrally versus locally, and how deviations are handled when a device is offline, newly provisioned, or partially managed. Standards also define the shape of "secure by default," such as least privilege for day-to-day use, restricted administrative interfaces, and safe defaults for scripting and application execution. They should be written so that an endpoint team can implement them without interpretation, and so that an auditor or incident responder can assess them without guesswork. When standards are vague, enforcement becomes optional, and optional controls are rarely present on the endpoints that matter most.

A practical baseline starts with a clear endpoint taxonomy, because the right controls depend on the role and exposure of the device. A user workstation has different needs than a jump host, a server, a point-of-sale device, or a shared kiosk, and applying a single monolithic standard usually results in either broken workflows or widespread exceptions that hollow out the control set. The taxonomy should be narrow enough to be manageable and broad enough to cover real differences in risk, including factors like exposure to the internet, sensitivity of the data handled, and whether privileged administration occurs on the device. Standardization reduces noise in telemetry, because similar endpoints produce similar logs and behaviors, making anomalies more meaningful. It also reduces the attack surface, because attackers lose the easy wins that come from hunting for the one poorly configured endpoint class. Table 7.1 highlights the specific verification signals that demonstrate whether a baseline control is actually working in day-to-day operations.

Verification is the defining feature that separates aspirational baselines from operational ones. A baseline that cannot be measured will not be maintained, and in most environments configuration drift is inevitable due to updates, software installs, user privilege creep, and competing administrative tools. Standards should therefore include a small set of measurable controls that provide high assurance, such as local admin group membership, disk encryption state, host firewall posture, secure boot status where applicable, and the health and reporting status of endpoint security telemetry. Compliance should be assessed continuously or at least frequently enough to catch drift before it becomes an incident enabler. The key is to treat deviations as signals that trigger remediation workflows, not as passive reports that get reviewed only after a breach.

Baselines must also account for the reality that endpoints are part of a larger identity and access ecosystem. Many high-impact intrusions rely on credential theft from endpoints, token abuse, or session hijacking, so configuration standards should reinforce strong identity boundaries through least privilege, isolation of administrative

Table 7.1 Baseline Verification Signals by Control Outcome.

Control Outcome	What Is Verified	Operational Evidence	Failure Indication
Execution control	Unapproved code paths are blocked	Blocked execution events with full context	Unsigned or unexpected binaries run
Privilege boundaries	Elevation is controlled and attributable	Logged elevation with user and reason	Silent elevation or broad admin rights
Credential exposure	Credentials are not easily harvested	Reduced privileged auth on standard endpoints	Privileged logons from user workstations
Logging integrity	Endpoint telemetry is complete and reliable	Process lineage and command lines arrive	Missing fields or stale reporting
Containment readiness	Isolation and response actions work	Successful isolation and evidence capture	Isolation fails or is delayed

workflows, and reduction of credential exposure in memory and storage. Where privileged access is required, standards should constrain how it is used, including separating administrative accounts from daily accounts and limiting where privileged authentication can occur. Configuration standards should also ensure that endpoint authentication events and privilege changes are reliably logged and forwarded, because these are among the earliest indicators of escalation. When identity controls and endpoint baselines are designed in isolation, defenders end up with gaps that attackers exploit to turn a single compromised workstation into enterprise-wide access.

AI-assisted configuration management can improve baseline adherence when it is used to detect drift patterns and prioritize remediation rather than to invent policy. Models can help identify clusters of endpoints that are deviating in similar ways, distinguish between benign variance and suspicious change, and forecast which deviations correlate with higher incident rates or repeated operational failures. This only works when the underlying configuration and telemetry data is complete, normalized, and attributable to device and owner context; otherwise, the model will amplify measurement errors into misleading priorities. Human-in-the-loop controls are essential because configuration changes can disrupt business operations, and remediation actions must be reviewable, explainable, and reversible. Governance expectations should include audit logs of recommended and applied changes, clear approval boundaries for automated enforcement, and periodic reassessment to prevent "baseline creep" where security adds controls without validating operational impact.

Exception handling is where endpoint standards often fail, because exceptions accumulate until they effectively become the standard. A mature approach treats exceptions as time-bound, risk-scored, and owned, with explicit compensating controls when baseline settings cannot be applied. Exceptions should be rare for high-risk controls, and when they exist they should be discoverable in the same systems used to measure compliance so that incident responders can rapidly assess whether an affected endpoint was operating outside the baseline. The operational pattern is straightforward: define the baseline, enforce it, measure it, and remediate deviations, while forcing exceptions into a disciplined workflow that makes risk visible. When that cycle runs reliably, endpoints become predictable defensive terrain, and attackers lose the easy leverage that comes from configuration inconsistency.

Managing Agents, Coverage, and Drift

Endpoint security depends on agents because agents are how defenders apply controls and collect the telemetry that makes threats visible. Whether the function is telemetry collection, policy enforcement, vulnerability assessment, or remote response, an agent is only valuable if it is installed, healthy, current, and consistently configured. The uncomfortable truth is that most organizations believe they have "coverage" when they actually have partial deployment, intermittent reporting, and silent failures on the exact endpoints attackers prefer. Managing agents is therefore not a tooling task; it is an operational discipline that treats agent health as a production dependency. If an endpoint is unmanaged or unobservable, it should be assumed to be a high-risk blind spot until proven otherwise.

Coverage is not a single number, and treating it as a simple percentage invites self-deception. Useful coverage is segmented by endpoint class, business unit, geography, and connectivity profile, because a 95% overall install rate can still hide a 40% gap in a critical population like privileged workstations or remote laptops. Coverage must also consider "effective reporting," meaning the endpoint is not only enrolled but regularly sending the expected telemetry with stable identity and time synchronization. An agent that is installed but not reporting is operationally equivalent to no agent, except it can create false confidence and delayed detection. Mature programs define a small set of coverage metrics that executives can understand and that operations teams can action immediately. Table 7.2 shows how to distinguish nominal agent presence from effective coverage by using health and drift indicators defenders can act on.

Health management is where agent programs either stabilize or collapse under their own complexity. Agents fail for predictable reasons: conflicting software, corrupted updates, expired certificates, misconfigured proxies, resource constraints, user tampering, and operating system changes that break kernel-level components or

Table 7.2 Agent Coverage Health and Drift Indicators.

Indicator	What It Measures	What Good Looks Like	What to Do When It Fails
Enrollment status	Agent installed and enrolled	All managed endpoints enrolled	Trigger repair or reinstall workflow
Heartbeat freshness	Recent reporting cadence	Regular check-ins per policy	Investigate connectivity proxy or tampering
Policy enforcement	Controls actively applied	Policy current and enforced	Force policy refresh and validate settings
Version currency	Agent not falling behind	Current supported version fleetwide	Stage update and remediate stragglers
Telemetry completeness	Required fields present	Process lineage and command lines present	Fix collection gaps and confirm normalization

permissions. A practical approach establishes a heartbeat concept for each agent type, with thresholds that distinguish temporary disruptions from true failure requiring remediation. Health signals should flow to the same operational queues that handle endpoint support and security operations so that failures are treated as actionable work, not as dashboards that no one owns. The goal is rapid detection of agent degradation, because attackers exploit the window between a control breaking and the organization noticing.

Drift is the natural tendency of endpoints to diverge from intended configuration over time, and drift applies to agents as much as it applies to security settings. Version drift occurs when endpoints miss updates, remain pinned to older versions for compatibility, or fall behind due to intermittent connectivity. Policy drift occurs when configuration changes are made locally, when multiple management systems compete, or when emergency exceptions are granted and never removed. State drift occurs when an agent is present but its configuration is partially applied, its telemetry filters are incorrect, or its response features are disabled. Managing drift requires acknowledging that "set and forget" is a myth in endpoint environments that change daily.

The most dangerous drift is the drift you cannot see, which is why inventory and reconciliation matter. An authoritative asset inventory provides the list of endpoints that should exist, while agent consoles provide the list of endpoints they can see, and the gap between those lists is where risk concentrates. Reconciliation should be continuous enough that new devices, reimaged devices, and devices that fall out of management are detected quickly rather than weeks later during quarterly audits. This is operationally challenging in environments with contractors, bring-your-own-device arrangements, and multiple endpoint platforms, but the principle remains the same: known endpoints must be managed, and unmanaged endpoints must be addressed. When reconciliation is weak, attackers can persist on orphaned systems that are effectively invisible.

Response workflows for agent failure and drift must be designed like incident workflows, with clear ownership and escalation paths. When a high-risk endpoint stops reporting, the first decision is whether the business can tolerate continued operation without visibility, and the default answer should be "no" for privileged or sensitive systems. Remediation steps need to be scripted and repeatable, ranging from restart and repair actions to reinstall, re-enrollment, and where appropriate, forced policy refresh. For persistent failures, teams need the ability to quarantine the endpoint at the network level or restrict its access until management is restored, because the risk is not theoretical. The operational pattern is to treat loss of endpoint control as a security-relevant event, not a routine IT inconvenience.

AI can assist agent and drift management by turning noisy operational data into prioritized work, but it must be bounded by verifiable evidence and change controls. Models can identify which agent failures correlate with specific operating system builds, software conflicts, or network paths, and they can predict which endpoints are likely to fall out of compliance based on historical patterns. This is most useful when it reduces mean time to repair by routing issues to the right team with the right context, rather than flooding analysts with generic "unhealthy agent" alerts. Failure modes are common: incomplete telemetry can create misleading confidence scores, drift in model assumptions can over-prioritize non-issues, and bias can emerge when certain business units are overrepresented in training data. Human approval boundaries should be explicit for any automated remediation, and audit logs must capture what was changed, why it was changed, and what evidence supported the change.

Sustained success comes from treating endpoints like a fleet with service-level expectations rather than like individual machines managed by exception. Agent coverage becomes a measurable operational commitment, with targets that reflect risk, not convenience, and with consequences when critical endpoints fall out of visibility. Drift management becomes a continuous loop of measurement, remediation, and exception control, driven by reconciled inventories and clear ownership. When this discipline is in place, security teams spend less time arguing about whether they have coverage and more time using endpoint telemetry to detect and contain real threats. Attackers thrive in the cracks between systems, and managing agents, coverage, and drift is how those cracks get sealed.

Managing Local Privileges and Administrative Access

Local privileges are one of the most consistent force multipliers in endpoint compromise because they turn a foothold into control. When an attacker can elevate privileges on a workstation, they can disable protective controls, harvest credentials, install persistence mechanisms, and pivot to other systems with far less resistance. Even when the initial intrusion is limited to a single user context, local admin rights often provide the bridge to system-level access and broader enterprise impact. The operational reality is that privilege decisions made for convenience are repaid later as incident complexity and business disruption. Managing local privileges is therefore a governance and engineering problem as much as it is a technical setting.

Administrative access must be treated as a distinct workflow, not a variation of normal user behavior. An endpoint environment where users routinely operate as local administrators blurs the line between legitimate change and malicious change, which undermines both prevention and detection. A more defensible model separates daily activities from administrative tasks through least privilege and controlled elevation, ensuring administrative actions are deliberate, attributable, and auditable. This separation also reduces the attack surface available to commodity malware, which often assumes it can write to protected directories, register services, or modify security settings. When administrative access is treated as exceptional and controlled, attackers lose many of the low-friction options they rely on.

A practical privilege program begins with defining what constitutes administrative need, because "I need admin" is often shorthand for "my workflow is broken." Many admin requests are driven by legacy applications, drivers, developer tooling, or poorly designed installers that assume system-level write access. The right response is not to grant broad privileges permanently, but to identify the minimum capability required and apply it in a bounded way, such as by allowing specific installers, approving specific changes, or using time-limited elevation. This approach reduces standing privilege, which is the condition attackers exploit when they persist on a device and wait for a moment to act. It also forces a healthier feedback loop where applications that require unsafe access patterns are identified and remediated over time.

Local admin group membership is only the visible part of privilege management, and focusing solely on that list can create blind spots. Administrative capability can be granted through other pathways, including local security policy rights, scheduled task creation privileges, remote management permissions, and the ability to run powerful interpreters and scripting engines with elevated tokens. Endpoint standards should therefore define administrative access in terms of capabilities and actions, not just group membership, and they should ensure that privilege changes are logged and centrally monitored. Attackers frequently add accounts to local admin groups, but they also abuse token theft, pass-the-hash style credential reuse, and cached credentials to gain effective administrative control without obvious configuration changes. Defensive posture improves when teams monitor for the behaviors that indicate privileged execution, not just the configuration states that might enable it.

Administrative access is also a lateral movement problem because endpoints are where administrators authenticate to manage other systems. If privileged credentials are used routinely on standard workstations, a single compromised workstation can become a credential harvesting platform with outsized impact. A defensible approach limits where privileged authentication can occur and reduces credential exposure by ensuring administrative actions happen from controlled contexts and by separating administrative accounts from daily accounts. This also supports cleaner incident response, because responders can more quickly determine whether privileged credentials were at risk based on where and how they were used. When administrative access is scattered and informal, every compromise triggers a costly and often organization-wide credential reset exercise.

Operational controls must balance security with continuity, because overly rigid privilege restrictions can push teams into unsafe workarounds. The goal is to make the secure path the easy path, which requires clear processes for requesting elevation, fast approvals for legitimate needs, and predictable outcomes for users and support staff. Privilege decisions should be risk-tiered so that high-risk endpoints and privileged users receive stricter controls, while lower-risk populations can use streamlined workflows that still avoid standing admin rights. Exceptions must be time-bound and owned, with explicit compensating controls when a device must temporarily operate outside the standard model. A privilege program that creates friction without support capacity tends to collapse into blanket exemptions, which restores the very risk it was meant to reduce.

AI can assist privilege management by identifying abnormal elevation patterns and helping teams prioritize which privilege issues are most likely to lead to compromise. For example, models can flag unusual spikes in elevation requests, rare combinations of processes launching with elevated tokens, or new administrative tool usage on endpoints that do not typically perform admin work. This is effective only when the underlying telemetry includes reliable process execution data, privilege context, and user and device identity, and when the organization has defined what "normal administrative behavior" looks like for each endpoint class. Failure modes are predictable: models can learn the wrong baseline if privilege misuse is widespread, they can generate false confidence when telemetry is incomplete, and they can over-prioritize noisy but benign administrative activity. Human-in-the-loop review is essential for actions like revoking access, changing group membership, or triggering containment, and every automated recommendation should be explainable and traceable to observed events.

Sustained control comes from treating administrative access as a managed service with clear boundaries, measurable outcomes, and continuous validation. Standing local admin rights should be rare, justified, and periodically reapproved, while most administrative tasks should flow through controlled elevation with strong logging and rapid reversal capability. Endpoint teams should continuously monitor for privilege drift, including unauthorized group membership changes, unexpected local policy rights, and evidence of privileged execution outside approved workflows. When privilege management is executed with this level of discipline, endpoints become harder to repurpose for enterprise compromise, and incident response becomes faster because defenders can trust the integrity of their administrative boundary. Attackers rarely need creativity when privilege is freely available, and managing local privileges is how that free leverage gets removed.

Endpoint Logging Strategy and Collection

Endpoint logging is the foundation that turns isolated security events into an observable, defendable environment. Most high-impact incidents leave traces on endpoints first, because endpoints are where users click, where processes spawn, where credentials are accessed, and where adversaries establish persistence. A logging strategy is therefore not "turn on everything," but a deliberate decision about which endpoint events are essential for detection, investigation, and recovery. When teams collect too little, attacks blend into routine activity; when teams collect too much without structure, signal is buried under cost and noise. The operational objective is to capture high-fidelity endpoint telemetry that supports fast triage and reliable reconstruction of attacker actions.

A practical endpoint logging strategy starts with purpose and questions, not with log sources. Leaders should be able to ask whether defenders can answer basic operational questions such as which process created a suspicious child process, which user context executed it, what command-line arguments were used, and what network destinations were contacted. For investigation, teams need a defensible chain of evidence that ties endpoint activity to identity activity, including logon events, privilege changes, remote access sessions, and token use where visibility exists. For response, logs must support containment decisions, including whether a device shows signs of persistence, whether lateral movement tooling is present, and whether the endpoint has reached sensitive internal resources. Logging becomes strategically valuable when it reliably answers these questions across endpoint classes, not just on a handful of well-managed devices.

Collection design must treat endpoints as unreliable network participants, because laptops roam, VPN usage fluctuates, and endpoints are often offline at the worst times. A resilient collection approach ensures endpoints can buffer and forward logs when connectivity returns, with clear limits that prevent disk exhaustion or performance degradation. It also means choosing collection intervals and batching behaviors that reflect operational realities, so that defenders do not assume real-time visibility where none exists. Time synchronization is non-negotiable, because an investigation that cannot reliably align events across systems becomes guesswork, especially when correlating endpoint activity with network or identity signals. The difference between "we saw suspicious activity" and "we can prove what happened" is often nothing more than consistent timestamps and durable delivery.

Endpoint logs only become useful at scale when they are normalized and enriched in ways that preserve meaning. Process telemetry should capture parent–child relationships, executable paths, hashes where available, signing information where available, and the full command line, because attackers often differ from legitimate activity in the details. Network telemetry should tie connections to processes and users, because raw network destinations without process context are difficult to interpret and easier for adversaries to exploit. File and registry changes must be scoped to security-relevant locations to avoid overwhelming collection systems, while still preserving visibility into persistence mechanisms and configuration tampering. Standardizing fields such as device identifiers, user identifiers, and event categories enables reliable correlation and reduces the analyst time spent translating different formats into a coherent story.

Retention and cost management are part of the logging strategy, not an afterthought. Endpoint telemetry can be high-volume, and organizations that do not define retention tiers often end up cutting data reactively during budget pressure, right when logs are most needed. A more stable model aligns retention with operational needs, such as longer retention for high-value endpoints, privileged populations, and investigative artifacts, while using shorter retention for lower-value or noisier sources. Retention decisions must also consider incident dwell time, because investigations frequently reach back weeks or months to determine initial access and scope. The operational compromise is to retain the right detail for the right period, with the ability to increase collection temporarily during heightened threat activity or active incident response.

Detection engineering and logging strategy are inseparable because detectors can only be as good as the telemetry they rely on. If a detection depends on command-line visibility, then command lines must be collected consistently; if a detection depends on privilege context, then elevation events must be reliably logged. It is common for teams to build detections on data from a subset of endpoints, then discover during an incident that the compromised endpoints did not collect the necessary fields. A mature approach ties every high-value detection to a telemetry dependency list and validates coverage as part of ongoing operations. This is where "what good looks like" becomes measurable: detections are mapped to logs, logs are mapped to endpoints, and gaps are treated as priority defects.

AI can help make endpoint logging more operationally effective by reducing noise and accelerating correlation, but it cannot compensate for missing or low-quality data. Models can assist by clustering related endpoint events into coherent narratives, highlighting rare process chains, or prioritizing alerts that show strong indicators of malicious intent when combined with identity and network context. These benefits rely on consistent normalization, stable identifiers, and well-defined event semantics; otherwise, the model learns patterns that reflect logging quirks rather than attacker behavior. Failure modes include false confidence in summarized narratives, drift as endpoint software and user behavior change, and bias toward well-instrumented endpoint classes that produce cleaner data. Human-in-the-loop controls should require that AI-generated summaries link back to raw events, that analysts can challenge conclusions, and that any automated response triggered by AI is bounded by clear policy and auditability requirements.

Endpoint logging succeeds when it is treated as a core control plane that is continuously tested and maintained. Collection pipelines should be monitored like production services, with clear indicators for ingestion failures, field dropouts, abnormal volume changes, and endpoint populations that stop reporting. Logging standards should evolve deliberately as attacker techniques shift, but changes must be governed to avoid breaking downstream detections and investigative workflows. When endpoints are consistently instrumented and logs are reliably collected, defenders can move from reactive hunting to structured triage and confident containment. Attackers will still attempt to evade logging, but disciplined collection and validation make that evasion itself detectable and reduce the time they can operate unseen.

Endpoint Hardening and Operational Constraints

Endpoint hardening is the practice of deliberately reducing the attack surface of a device by constraining what can run, what can be modified, and how the system can be abused, while still enabling the business to function. Hardening is not a single control or checklist; it is the cumulative effect of configuration decisions that limit unnecessary exposure and remove entire classes of exploit paths. Attackers benefit from default behaviors, permissive settings, and rarely used features that remain enabled "just in case." Hardening challenges those defaults by forcing explicit choices about which capabilities are truly required. When done well, hardening raises the cost of compromise without turning endpoints into brittle or unusable systems.

The most effective hardening measures focus on execution control and privilege boundaries, because these are where most endpoint attacks succeed. Restricting which binaries, scripts, and interpreters can run, and under what conditions, removes a large portion of commodity malware and post-exploitation tooling. Constraining macro-execution, scripting engines, and unsigned code reduces abuse of trusted platforms that attackers rely on to blend in. Hardening also includes reducing available attack surface by disabling unused services, limiting exposed management interfaces, and enforcing secure defaults for browsers and document handlers. Each of these measures narrows the space in which an attacker can operate, even if initial access occurs.

Operational constraints are the counterweight to hardening, and ignoring them is how well-intentioned controls get bypassed. Endpoints support diverse workflows, including developers who compile code locally, analysts who run custom scripts, administrators who need deep system access, and executives who travel with intermittent connectivity. Applying uniform restrictions without understanding these realities often results in shadow IT, local exceptions, or complete disablement of controls to "get work done." A sustainable hardening program acknowledges these constraints explicitly and designs alternative secure paths rather than relying on blanket prohibitions. The objective is not maximal restriction, but risk-informed restriction aligned with how endpoints are actually used.

Hardening decisions must also account for reliability, performance, and user experience, because controls that degrade system stability quickly lose support. Kernel-level protections, aggressive behavior blocking, and tight execution policies can introduce compatibility issues, application crashes, or noticeable latency if not tested and tuned. These impacts are not just annoyances; they create operational pressure to roll back controls during peak business periods or under executive scrutiny. Mature teams stage hardening changes, validate them across representative endpoint classes, and measure impact before broad rollout. This discipline prevents the cycle of emergency disablement that attackers often exploit during organizational stress.

Change management is inseparable from endpoint hardening because the environment is constantly evolving. Operating system updates introduce new features and defaults, applications change their behavior, and threat actors adapt to controls that were effective six months earlier. Hardening standards must therefore be reviewed and adjusted regularly, with a bias toward removing obsolete restrictions and tightening controls where new abuse patterns emerge. Poor change management leads to "hardening drift," where endpoints appear hardened on paper but in practice accumulate exceptions and outdated rules that provide little real protection. Consistent validation and cleanup are what keep hardening meaningful over time.

AI can assist hardening efforts by identifying which controls produce the most risk reduction relative to their operational cost. By analyzing incident data, application usage patterns, and historical exception requests, models can help highlight which features are rarely used but frequently abused, or which restrictions consistently cause operational friction without clear security benefit. This allows teams to prioritize hardening measures that deliver disproportionate defensive value and to redesign or retire controls that do not. The effectiveness of this approach depends on accurate telemetry and honest exception tracking; biased or incomplete data can lead to false optimization. Human oversight remains essential, because hardening decisions are ultimately business decisions that balance risk, productivity, and resilience.

Successful endpoint hardening is characterized by predictability rather than severity. Users understand what is allowed and why, administrators have clear processes for requesting changes, and security teams can explain the rationale behind restrictions in operational terms. Hardening controls are enforced consistently, monitored for bypass attempts, and adjusted when legitimate needs change, rather than being silently eroded through ad hoc exceptions. When operational constraints are treated as design inputs instead of obstacles, hardening becomes a stabilizing force rather than a source of friction. Attackers thrive on inconsistency and confusion, and disciplined endpoint hardening removes both from the environment.

Handling Exceptions Without Creating Blind Spots

Exceptions are inevitable in endpoint security because real environments contain legacy systems, specialized workflows, and operational realities that do not fit neatly into standard baselines. The problem is not that exceptions exist, but that exceptions often become invisible over time, turning into permanent blind spots that attackers reliably exploit. An exception that disables a control, suppresses a log source, or relaxes execution policy changes the security posture of an endpoint in ways that must be deliberately understood and continuously monitored. When exceptions are informal, undocumented, or handled through side channels, the organization loses the ability to reason about risk at the device level. Handling exceptions well means treating them as managed risk decisions, not as ad hoc favors.

A disciplined exception process begins with clarity about what is being excepted and what the security impact is. It is not enough to say "this device can't run the agent" or "this application needs admin rights," because those statements hide important specifics about which control is affected and which attacker techniques become easier as a result. The exception record should capture the scope, the exact control change, the affected endpoint population, and the business justification in plain language that can be understood by both security and operations. This creates accountability and prevents the common failure mode where exceptions persist simply because no one remembers why they were granted. If the exception cannot be described precisely, it is usually a sign that the underlying requirement is not well understood.

Time-bounding is one of the most effective guardrails against exception sprawl. Most exceptions are granted during a project, a vendor engagement, a migration, or a troubleshooting period, and they should expire unless actively renewed with fresh justification. Expiration forces periodic review of whether the original constraint still

Table 7.3 Exception Guardrails to Prevent Endpoint Blind Spots.

Guardrail	What It Requires	Why It Matters	Responder Benefit
Precise scope	Exact control change and affected endpoints	Prevents vague permanent waivers	Fast understanding of lost capability
Time bound approval	Expiration and renewal checkpoint	Forces reassessment and cleanup	Reduces stale hidden risk
Compensating controls	Alternate visibility or restriction	Preserves detection and containment	Maintains investigative options
Operational discoverability	Visible in inventory monitoring and response	Stops exceptions from being invisible	Accurate triage and containment
Continuous validation	Periodic confirmation of need and state	Catches drift and changing risk	Prevents surprise gaps in telemetry

exists and whether the exception has become an unnecessary risk. It also provides a natural moment to reassess compensating controls and to verify that the endpoint remains visible and manageable. Without time-bounds, exception lists become a graveyard of outdated decisions that no one owns and no one monitors.

Compensating controls are how exceptions avoid becoming blind spots, and they should be selected based on what capability was lost. If an endpoint cannot run a standard security agent, compensating controls might emphasize stronger network restrictions, stricter identity controls, or enhanced logging through alternate mechanisms that preserve investigative value. If an application requires elevated privileges, compensating controls might constrain elevation to time-limited workflows, tighten monitoring of privileged execution, and restrict where the privileged account can authenticate. The point is not to invent new control regimes, but to ensure that visibility and containment options remain viable even when a standard control cannot be applied. An exception without compensating controls is not an exception, it is an unmanaged exposure. Table 7.3 summarizes the guardrails that keep necessary exceptions from turning into unmanaged exposure during incidents.

Exceptions must be discoverable in the same operational systems used for inventory, monitoring, and incident response. When responders are working an active incident, they should be able to see immediately whether the affected endpoint is operating under an approved exception and what that exception changes about expected telemetry and control behavior. If exceptions live in email threads, ticket comments, or informal chats, incident response loses time and confidence, and teams may make incorrect containment decisions based on assumptions that are no longer true. A mature approach links exception status to endpoint identity, so that dashboards, alert enrichment, and investigative queries reflect the endpoint's real security posture. This also enables more honest reporting, because "coverage" metrics can distinguish between endpoints that are fully controlled and endpoints that are controlled with documented gaps.

Exception handling must be paired with continuous validation, because the risk of an exception often changes as the environment changes. An exception that was low risk when a device was isolated on a restricted network can become high risk after a network redesign, a remote work expansion, or a change in how credentials are used. Validation should include confirming that the exception is still required, that compensating controls remain in place, and that the endpoint still produces the minimum telemetry required for detection and investigation. It should also include testing for unintended drift, because exceptions can create unique configurations that are more likely to break, fall out of management, or stop reporting. The operational goal is to keep exceptions from becoming unique, unmanaged snowflakes.

AI can help manage exceptions by detecting patterns of exception creation and highlighting where exceptions are creating correlated risk. For example, models can identify clusters of endpoints with similar exception profiles, relate those profiles to incident history, and prioritize which exceptions warrant review because they correlate

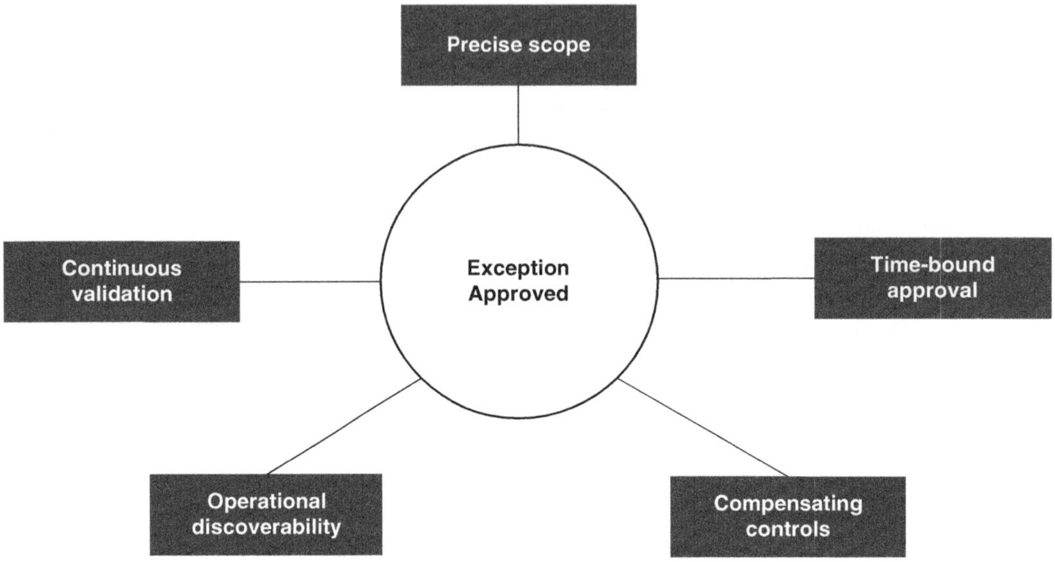

Figure 7.1 Exception Guardrails That Preserve Visibility and Containment.

with higher compromise rates or repeated control failures. AI can also assist with quality control by flagging exception requests that are vague, missing required fields, or inconsistent with prior decisions for similar use cases. These capabilities require clean exception data, reliable endpoint identifiers, and telemetry that reflects actual control state; otherwise, the model will reinforce incomplete records and provide misleading confidence. Human-in-the-loop governance remains essential, especially when the output drives decisions such as denying access, imposing network restrictions, or forcing expedited remediation.

Exceptions handled without creating blind spots share a consistent pattern: explicit scope, time limits, compensating controls, and operational visibility. They are treated as part of normal security operations, with ownership, review cadence, and integration into monitoring and response workflows. This approach reduces friction because stakeholders know how to request exceptions, what information is required, and what tradeoffs will be made to preserve visibility. It also reduces attacker advantage, because exceptions are no longer hidden weak points but known conditions with guardrails and monitoring. In endpoint security, the enemy of resilience is not the exception itself, but the invisible exception that quietly removes control where defenders least expect it. Figure 7.1 shows the guardrails that prevent necessary exceptions from turning into blind spots during incidents. It reinforces that exceptions must be precisely scoped time bound paired with compensating controls discoverable in operations and continuously validated.

AI-Assisted Endpoint Triage: Behavioral Signals, Noise Reduction, and Analyst Controls

AI-assisted endpoint triage is most valuable when it accelerates human decision-making without replacing it. Endpoint telemetry is dense, and even well-tuned detection programs generate a steady stream of alerts that include benign administrative activity, software updates, and user-driven anomalies. The practical goal of triage is to decide what needs immediate action, what needs deeper investigation, and what can be safely deprioritized, all while preserving an evidentiary trail. AI can help by ranking, grouping, and summarizing activity, but only when it is grounded in observable signals and bounded by analyst controls. When AI is treated as authoritative rather than assistive, it tends to amplify mistakes at scale.

Behavioral signals are the raw material for effective triage because attackers repeatedly rely on recognizable execution patterns. Process trees, parent–child relationships, command-line arguments, unusual binary locations, unexpected scripting activity, and rare privilege transitions often distinguish malicious behavior from routine operations. Network connections tied to processes, especially first-seen destinations or unexpected protocols for a given endpoint class, add high value when correlated with execution context. Persistence behaviors, such as scheduled task creation, service installation, registry run key modification, or tampering with security controls, should be treated as triage accelerators because they indicate intent to maintain access. AI works best when it is asked to interpret these specific features rather than loosely "judge suspiciousness" without a defined behavioral basis.

Noise reduction is not the same as suppression, and confusing the two is a common failure mode in AI-assisted workflows. Suppression hides alerts; noise reduction clarifies which signals matter in a given context and preserves the ability to reconstruct what happened. A strong approach uses AI to cluster related events across time and across a device population, so analysts see one coherent narrative instead of dozens of disconnected alerts. It can also prioritize alerts by identifying common benign patterns, such as known update behaviors or standard administrative tool chains, while elevating rare combinations that are statistically unusual for that endpoint class. The output should reduce cognitive load without deleting data, because the data you suppress today is often the data you need tomorrow when scope changes.

Data and telemetry dependencies determine whether AI triage improves outcomes or merely creates confident-looking summaries that are wrong. If process telemetry is inconsistent, command lines are missing, device identity is unstable, or timestamps drift, AI will infer relationships that do not exist and miss relationships that do. If alert enrichment lacks asset criticality, user role context, and ownership information, prioritization will skew toward noisy endpoints rather than business-relevant risk. Coverage gaps also matter: models trained on well-instrumented populations tend to perform poorly on under-instrumented endpoints, which can bias triage away from the very systems where attackers hide. Operationally, teams should treat telemetry quality as a prerequisite control and validate that the fields AI depends on are present and trustworthy across endpoint classes.

Analyst controls are the safety rails that keep AI triage from turning into automated error propagation. Analysts must be able to see why an item was prioritized, which signals drove the decision, and what evidence supports any narrative summary, with direct linkage back to raw events. Approval boundaries should be explicit for actions that change endpoint state, such as isolation, process termination, or credential revocation, because triage confidence is not the same as operational certainty. Analysts also need frictionless ways to override, reclassify, and annotate outcomes, because those human corrections are how the system improves and how governance is maintained. If the only interaction is "accept" or "ignore," the organization will accumulate hidden debt in misclassifications and will lose trust in the triage pipeline.

Failure modes in AI-assisted endpoint triage are predictable and should be planned for rather than discovered during a crisis. False confidence is the most dangerous, where summaries read plausible but omit key details like lateral movement steps, privilege context, or persistence indicators that were present in raw logs. Drift is inevitable as operating systems change, software behaviors evolve, and attackers adapt to known detection patterns, which means triage performance must be continuously measured against real outcomes. Bias can emerge when certain business units, geographies, or device types dominate the historical data used to tune triage, leading to under-prioritization of outlier populations such as executives, developers, or specialized systems. Leakage is also a risk when sensitive endpoint telemetry is used for training or enrichment without clear data handling rules, especially if the telemetry includes credentials, tokens, or proprietary content.

Governance and auditability are what make AI-assisted triage operationally acceptable in environments where decisions have real business impact. Triage outputs should be logged as decisions with provenance: what model or rule set produced the result, what data it saw, what confidence was assigned, and what action was taken by humans or automation. This supports accountability when disruptions occur, and it enables continuous improvement by linking triage recommendations to downstream outcomes like confirmed incidents, false positives, and remediation effectiveness. A mature program also sets clear thresholds for when automation is allowed, such as auto-closing low-risk items with strong supporting evidence, while requiring human approval for containment and credential-impacting decisions. When AI triage is implemented with transparent signals, noise reduction that preserves evidence, and analyst controls that enforce safe boundaries, it becomes a force multiplier rather than a source of opaque risk.

Measuring Endpoint Control Effectiveness

Endpoint control effectiveness is the difference between believing endpoints are protected and proving that protections actually work under real conditions. Many organizations measure activity, such as how many agents are installed or how many alerts were generated, and mistake that for effectiveness. Effective measurement focuses on whether controls are present, correctly configured, consistently enforced, and capable of producing the intended outcome when an endpoint is under attack. This distinction matters because attackers do not care how many controls you own; they exploit the endpoints where controls are missing, misconfigured, or unenforced. Measurement is therefore a leadership tool for risk clarity and an operational tool for continuous improvement.

A practical measurement approach starts by defining the outcomes that matter at the endpoint: preventing unauthorized execution, limiting privilege escalation, protecting credentials, maintaining visibility through logging, and enabling fast containment and remediation. Each of these outcomes maps to observable evidence, such as whether execution restrictions block unapproved code paths, whether administrative actions require controlled elevation, whether credential exposure is reduced by configuration, and whether telemetry arrives with the fields needed for investigation. Measuring effectiveness also means testing response capability, including whether isolation works when needed, whether an endpoint can be remediated at scale, and whether the organization can confidently re-image or restore a device without losing critical evidence. These outcomes are operational and measurable, and they are far more informative than generic "compliance" statements.

Coverage metrics must be treated as a multi-dimensional view rather than a single headline number. Control coverage should be segmented by endpoint class, risk tier, business unit, and connectivity profile, because the most important gaps often hide in specialized populations like privileged workstations, remote laptops, or high-value servers. Coverage should also include a health dimension, meaning the control is not only installed but reporting, enforcing policy, and not in a degraded state. A device that is enrolled but has stale telemetry, disabled protections, or broken update paths should be counted as an effectiveness failure, not a partial success. When coverage metrics reflect effective coverage rather than nominal coverage, they become actionable instead of cosmetic.

Configuration compliance is central to effectiveness because endpoints can appear protected while quietly drifting away from standards. Measuring configuration compliance requires identifying a small set of security-critical settings that serve as proxies for broader posture, such as privilege boundaries, logging enablement, and protections against common tampering behaviors. The measurement should distinguish between intentional exceptions and uncontrolled drift, because exceptions can be governed while drift indicates loss of control. This is also where change management becomes measurable: teams can see whether new baselines are being adopted predictably or whether implementation is fragmenting across the fleet. Compliance measurement that is not tied to remediation workflows tends to become a reporting exercise, so effectiveness programs must link findings to ownership and closure.

Detection effectiveness is often misunderstood, and measuring it requires more than counting alerts or tracking false-positive rates. Effective detection measurement asks whether the organization can reliably detect specific attacker behaviors on endpoints, such as suspicious process chains, credential access patterns, persistence creation, and security control tampering. That requires validating the telemetry dependencies behind detections and confirming that the detections fire consistently across endpoint classes, not just in well-instrumented pockets. It also means measuring timeliness, because a detection that triggers hours later may be technically correct but operationally irrelevant. Detection effectiveness should be evaluated alongside investigative effectiveness, which includes whether analysts can quickly pivot from an alert to the raw endpoint events needed to confirm scope and intent.

Response effectiveness is the most operationally revealing category because it tests whether controls can change the state of an endpoint when it matters. Teams should be able to measure mean time to contain for endpoint-driven incidents, including the time from alert to isolation, from isolation to evidence capture, and from evidence capture to remediation. They should also measure success rates for containment actions, because unreliable isolation, incomplete remediation, and failed re-enrollment are common reasons incidents recur. Response effectiveness includes the ability to handle scale, such as isolating dozens of endpoints during a widespread compromise without disrupting unrelated business operations. When response actions are measurable and repeatable, the organization builds confidence that endpoints are not only monitored but controllable.

AI can strengthen endpoint effectiveness measurement by highlighting patterns and predicting where controls are likely to fail before they fail in a high-impact incident. Models can correlate control health signals with incident outcomes, identify endpoint populations with persistent drift, and prioritize remediation by estimating which gaps produce the highest risk exposure. This is especially useful when operational data is noisy and fragmented, because AI can surface consistent failure modes, such as specific operating system versions that break protections or user populations that frequently trigger privilege exceptions. The same failure modes apply here: incomplete data can produce misleading priorities, drift in assumptions can degrade accuracy, and bias can emerge when well-managed endpoints dominate the dataset. Human oversight is required to validate findings, ensure remediation decisions remain aligned with business context, and maintain auditability of how measurement insights influenced changes.

Effectiveness measurement becomes a strategic advantage when it is treated as a continuous control loop rather than a periodic scorecard. Metrics should drive action by making gaps visible, assigning ownership, and confirming closure with evidence rather than assumption. Leadership should receive a small set of outcome-oriented indicators that reflect true posture, while operations teams should have detailed views that support remediation and validation. Over time, the organization should see a reduction in unmanaged endpoints, fewer high-risk exceptions, faster containment, and higher confidence investigations, because those are the tangible effects of effective endpoint controls. Measuring endpoint control effectiveness is ultimately how teams move from aspirational security to verified security on the battleground that matters most.

Conclusion

Endpoint security management succeeds when it moves from assumed coverage to verified control, where baselines are enforced, agent health is continuously validated, and drift is treated as a routine defect to be corrected rather than an acceptable state. Local privileges and administrative access must remain tightly governed because they are the most common bridge from a single compromised device to enterprise-wide impact, and that governance only holds when exceptions are time-bound, visible, and paired with compensating controls. Logging and collection discipline provide the investigative backbone that makes endpoint telemetry reliable at scale, while AI-assisted triage can reduce noise and accelerate decisions only when models are grounded in high-quality behavioral signals and bounded by analyst approval and auditability. Ultimately, the measure of maturity is practical: defenders can detect meaningful endpoint behaviors, contain compromised devices quickly, remediate consistently, and prove—through effectiveness metrics—that endpoint controls remain dependable even as the environment and adversary tactics continue to evolve.

Recommendations

1) Establish a measurable endpoint baseline for each endpoint class and enforce it consistently across the fleet. Define the minimum security settings that must be present and treat deviations as operational defects, not as normal variance. Validate baseline adherence continuously to catch configuration drift before it becomes an incident enabler. Ensure exceptions are explicit, documented, and tied to compensating controls, so the baseline remains meaningful.
2) Prioritize agent coverage as an operational dependency by tracking not just installation but also effective reporting and enforcement. Segment coverage metrics by endpoint class, risk tier, and connectivity profile, so critical gaps cannot hide inside aggregate numbers. Build a remediation workflow for unhealthy agents with clear ownership, escalation paths, and repeatable repair actions. Treat endpoints that stop reporting as high-risk blind spots until management is restored.
3) Implement a continuous drift management loop that reconciles authoritative asset inventory with what security controls can actually see. Detect endpoints that fall out of management quickly, especially after reimaging, device replacement, or extended offline periods. Close gaps through automated re-enrollment and repair processes wherever feasible, and restrict access for high-risk endpoints that remain unmanaged. Use drift findings to drive durable fixes in provisioning, imaging, and change management rather than repeating one-off repairs.
4) Enforce least privilege by separating daily user activity from administrative workflows and minimizing standing local admin rights. Require deliberate, attributable elevation for administrative tasks, so privileged actions are logged, reviewable, and reversible. Monitor privileged execution patterns and privilege changes as security-relevant events that warrant timely investigation. Design the secure path to be operationally usable, so teams do not bypass controls through informal workarounds.
5) Align administrative access with identity risk by controlling where privileged authentication can occur and by separating administrative accounts from daily accounts. Reduce credential exposure on endpoints by limiting the use of privileged credentials on standard workstations. Ensure authentication and privilege events are reliably logged and forwarded, so investigations can determine scope and impact quickly. Treat endpoints used for administration as higher-risk assets that require stronger controls and tighter exception handling.
6) Define an endpoint logging strategy around investigative questions and behavioral visibility rather than collecting everything indiscriminately. Ensure core telemetry reliably captures process lineage, command-line details, privilege context, and process-to-network relationships to support triage and reconstruction. Build collection resilience for offline endpoints through buffering and durable delivery, and enforce time synchronization to preserve event integrity. Normalize and enrich logs consistently, so correlation across endpoints and identities remains reliable at scale.
7) Apply endpoint hardening through execution control and attack surface reduction while explicitly accounting for operational constraints. Stage and validate hardening changes across representative endpoint populations to avoid destabilizing critical workflows. Avoid controls that are so brittle they require emergency disablement, because that creates predictable windows of exposure. Treat hardening as a living set of decisions that must be maintained as operating systems, applications, and attacker behaviors evolve.
8) Formalize exception handling to prevent security gaps from becoming invisible and permanent. Require precise scope, business justification, and time bounds for every exception, with renewal only after reassessment. Attach compensating controls based on what capability is being relaxed, so visibility and containment remain viable. Make exception status discoverable in inventory, monitoring, and response workflows, so responders can make accurate decisions under pressure.
9) Use AI-assisted endpoint triage to reduce analyst load by clustering related activity, prioritizing behavior-rich signals, and summarizing evidence with traceability. Validate that the telemetry fields AI depends on are complete and consistent across endpoint classes before relying on model-driven prioritization. Enforce human-in-the-loop controls for containment and credential-impacting actions, and require explainability

that links AI outputs back to raw events. Continuously measure for drift, bias, and false confidence, so AI augments judgment rather than replacing it.

10) Measure endpoint control effectiveness using outcome-based indicators that prove controls work under real conditions. Track effective coverage, configuration compliance, detection timeliness, and response success rates rather than relying on tool activity metrics. Test containment and remediation capabilities, so teams know isolation, evidence capture, and re-enrollment work at scale when needed. Use measurement results to drive ownership, remediation, and continuous improvement until verified control becomes the operational norm.

8

Network and Perimeter Defense Operations

Network and perimeter defense operations are about making connectivity deliberate, observable, and resilient under stress, because modern attacks routinely begin at exposed entry points and succeed through uncontrolled internal movement. This chapter treats the network as an operational system where defensive outcomes come from clear goals, layered enforcement, disciplined change control, and telemetry that supports fast investigation. It shows how segmentation, firewall policy management, and remote access controls work together to reduce exposure, constrain blast radius, and prevent exceptions from turning into permanent weaknesses. It also explains how visibility across boundaries and detection of suspicious connectivity depend on consistent logging, correlation, and validated analysis, including AI-assisted pattern recognition and alert enrichment with human approval boundaries. Finally, it addresses the realities of hybrid environments, where different control planes and change velocities create seams that must be governed intentionally, so defensive intent remains consistent and auditable across data center, cloud, and remote access paths.

Network Defense Goals and Defensive Layers

Network defense starts with clear goals that translate business risk into operational outcomes. The first goal is controlled connectivity: every allowed path into, out of, and within the environment should be intentional, reviewable, and reversible. The second goal is measurable visibility: defenders must be able to observe traffic patterns, authentication flows, and policy decisions with enough fidelity to investigate incidents without guesswork. The third goal is resilience under failure: when a control degrades or telemetry drops, the environment should fail in a predictable direction that preserves safety and preserves evidence. A fourth, often underappreciated goal is operational sustainability, because a control that cannot be maintained at scale will drift into exception handling and quietly become a liability.

Defensive layers exist because no single control is perfectly preventive, perfectly observable, and perfectly reliable. Layering allows prevention, detection, and response to reinforce one another while reducing the consequences of any one gap. In practice, a layer is not a product category; it is a set of decisions that shape how traffic is permitted, how identities are validated, and how changes are governed. Leaders should expect that each layer has an owner, a change process, and a defined "break glass" path for business continuity. Defenders should expect that layers are tested against real workflows, not idealized diagrams, because shortcuts and legacy paths are where attacks frequently land. When a layer is healthy, it is boring: it blocks what it should, it logs what it must, and it does not require heroics to keep it running. Figure 8.1 links the core network defense goals to the major defensive layers that implement them in practice. It reinforces that outcomes like controlled connectivity and measurable visibility depend on operational decisions and ownership across multiple layers rather than a single control.

The outermost layer focuses on exposure management at the boundary, where internet-facing services and remote access converge. The defensive goal here is to reduce the number of reachable entry points, constrain what

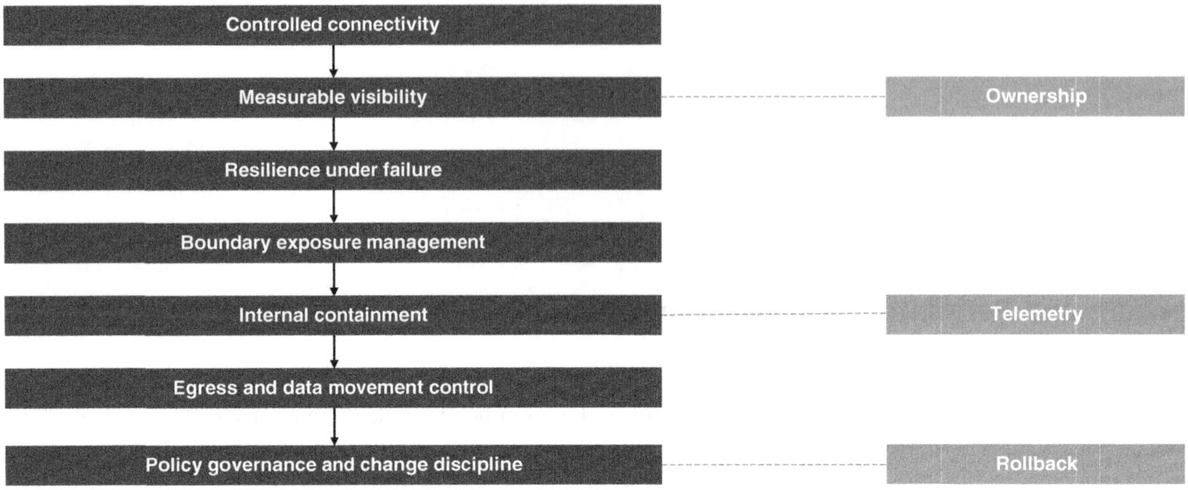

Figure 8.1 Network Defense Goals and Defensive Layers at a Glance.

those entry points can do, and ensure that each connection is strongly bound to an identity and a purpose. Control effectiveness depends on disciplined policy management, consistent authentication enforcement, and tight alignment between what the business believes is exposed and what is actually reachable. Telemetry at this layer is most valuable when it captures denied attempts, unusual negotiation patterns, and abrupt shifts in client behavior that suggest automation or credential misuse. A practical AI/ML use case here is behavioral baselining over connection metadata and authentication events to surface anomalies early, but it must be treated as a decision-support signal with human approval boundaries rather than an automated gate that can lock out critical access during false positives.

Inside the perimeter, the next layer is containment, which assumes that initial access can and will happen. The operational purpose of containment is to prevent a foothold from becoming a pathway, especially across administrative boundaries and high-value systems. That requires segmentation decisions that reflect trust zones and business functions, not just IP address convenience, and it requires enforcement points that are consistently managed over time. Containment also depends on controlling east–west movement through strict service exposure and limiting administrative access pathways so that routine operations do not rely on broad network reachability. Defenders should treat "flat" internal networks as a standing incident condition because lateral movement becomes easier, faster, and harder to attribute when everything can talk to everything. When AI/ML is applied to east–west traffic analysis, it must be anchored in high-quality flow data and identity context; otherwise, the model will confidently label noise as signal and erode trust when investigations repeatedly dead-end.

A separate but equally important layer is egress and data movement control, because many breaches become material only when data leaves or commands reach out. The goal is not to stop all outbound traffic, but to make outbound behavior deliberate, attributable, and constrained to approved destinations and protocols. Egress controls become practical when they are aligned with how workloads and users actually operate, including sanctioned cloud services and necessary update channels, rather than forcing broad exceptions that undermine enforcement. Telemetry must support investigation of unusual destinations, rare protocol use, and abnormal transfer volumes, and it should tie those observations back to the initiating identity or workload rather than only a source IP. AI/ML can add value by clustering outbound destinations and identifying novelty that is statistically meaningful, but it is vulnerable to drift when business activity changes, so governance must include periodic retraining review, change-driven baselining, and auditability of why an event was flagged.

Across all layers, the network control plane is only as strong as its policy governance and change discipline. Defensive layers degrade when rules accumulate without owners, when emergency exceptions become permanent, and when teams cannot explain why a pathway exists. Good operations treat network policy like production code: changes are reviewed, tested in context, documented with intent, and rolled back when outcomes diverge from expectations. The fastest way to lose confidence in network defense is to discover, during an incident, that logs are incomplete, time is inconsistent, or enforcement decisions are not traceable to configuration history. AI-assisted analysis can help triage noisy alerts and highlight rule changes correlated with new exposures, but it introduces its own failure modes, including false confidence, opaque reasoning, and inadvertent leakage if sensitive configuration artifacts are used in training or prompt contexts without strict handling controls. For that reason, human-in-the-loop approval and tight data-handling boundaries are not optional; they are the difference between assistance and amplified error.

Finally, defensive layers must be evaluated by how well they support incident handling under pressure. Prevention that blocks an attack but produces no usable evidence creates blind spots for the next attempt, while detection that floods responders with low-quality signals consumes the very time needed for containment. In mature operations, each layer contributes something specific during an incident: boundary controls constrain the blast radius, internal controls slow movement, egress controls reduce impact, and telemetry provides the narrative that guides response decisions. Weaknesses usually appear at handoffs, such as when network teams and endpoint teams use different naming, different timestamps, or incompatible severity language, making correlation slow and contentious. The practical expectation is not perfect security, but predictable behavior: when an attacker tries to move, they should collide with friction that is visible, attributable, and actionable. That is the operational meaning of layered network defense, and it is why goals must be explicit before layers can be built, maintained, and trusted.

Segmentation Concepts and Practical Constraints

Segmentation is the disciplined act of limiting where traffic can go and what it can reach, based on business function and trust assumptions rather than convenience. Done well, it turns "the network" from a single shared space into a set of controlled neighborhoods with clear rules of engagement. The defensive outcome is containment: when an attacker lands, the environment constrains movement, slows discovery, and reduces the number of systems that can be touched from any one foothold. Segmentation also reduces the operational blast radius of mistakes, such as misconfigurations and runaway automation, by preventing a single error from propagating across unrelated systems. Executives should think of segmentation as an availability and resilience control as much as a security control, because it reduces the scope of outages and accelerates recovery by narrowing what must be triaged.

At its core, segmentation depends on a repeatable way to group assets into zones that reflect real operational boundaries. Zones can map to sensitivity levels, business units, environments like production and development, or system roles such as user workstations, servers, and administrative planes. The exact taxonomy matters less than consistency, because enforcement and visibility both depend on stable definitions. A common failure mode is designing zones that look elegant on paper but do not align to how applications communicate, forcing endless exceptions that eventually hollow out the model. Another failure mode is defining zones purely by IP ranges while ignoring identity and workload context, which makes policy brittle in modern environments where systems move, scale, and change address. The practical goal is to choose groupings that remain meaningful as infrastructure evolves, and to treat changes in zone membership as a security-relevant event, not a routine networking chore. Table 8.1 summarizes zone intent and the expected connectivity boundaries that make segmentation operationally meaningful and contain lateral movement.

Enforcement points determine whether segmentation is real or just documentation. In practice, segmentation is implemented where decisions can be made consistently, such as at internal firewalls, routing boundaries, virtual

Table 8.1 Segmentation Zones and Expected Connectivity Boundaries.

Zone	Primary Purpose	Allowed Connectivity Pattern	Common Drift Trigger
User workstations	User productivity endpoints	Limited to required services and app tiers	Temporary troubleshooting access left in place
Application tier	Serve business applications	Only to dependent data and service tiers	New dependency introduced without review
Data tier	Store and process sensitive data	Only from approved application sources	Broad access opened for migration support
Administrative plane	Privileged management and control paths	Only from approved admin paths and systems	Shared admin access expanded for convenience
Identity infrastructure	Authentication and authorization services	Only from systems needing auth services	Legacy client exceptions bypass strong controls

network constructs, and host-level controls that can deny traffic even when the network path exists. Defenders should prioritize enforcing segmentation where it reduces the most risk with the least operational disruption, particularly around administrative access paths, authentication infrastructure, and high-value data stores. An important operational concept is the difference between "hard" boundaries that are difficult to bypass and "soft" boundaries that rely on conventions or incomplete controls. Hard boundaries are preferable for high-impact zones, but they require mature change control and strong monitoring because mistakes can interrupt business quickly. Soft boundaries can be useful early for visibility and learning, but they should not be treated as meaningful containment when threat activity is suspected.

Segmentation is often described as "deny by default," but the practical version is "deny by default with explicit, documented allowances." That means each permitted flow should have an accountable business reason, a defined source and destination scope, and a review cadence that removes obsolete access. Without these disciplines, segmentation devolves into a sprawling allow list that is harder to manage than a flat network, while still failing to stop attackers. The operational reality is that many flows are not well understood until they break, so teams need mechanisms to observe traffic, validate dependencies, and phase changes without guesswork. This is a natural place for AI/ML-assisted analysis, such as clustering observed flows to propose candidate allow rules or highlighting outlier communications that do not match typical service behavior. Those outputs must be treated as recommendations, because models can mistake noisy telemetry for legitimate dependencies and create permissions that quietly widen access.

Practical constraints are where segmentation succeeds or fails, and they show up most clearly in legacy systems and fragile applications. Older platforms may use hard-coded IPs, broad port ranges, or embedded trust relationships that assume flat reachability, making clean boundaries difficult. Some business-critical systems cannot tolerate latency, asymmetric routing, or interruptions caused by misapplied policies, which raises the stakes of enforcement changes. Vendor support limitations can also become a constraint when the provider's recommended architecture conflicts with the organization's segmentation goals, forcing compensating controls or staged modernization. In these cases, acknowledging constraints is not a concession; it is a planning input that dictates where to place boundaries, how to monitor exceptions, and how to prioritize refactoring efforts. The segmentation strategy should make room for technical debt while preventing it from defining the security posture indefinitely.

Identity and administration deserve special treatment because they shape the most dangerous paths in the environment. Segmentation that protects data but leaves administrative movement wide open often fails during real incidents, because attackers target privilege escalation and management planes to gain durable control. Administrative systems, identity providers, and management interfaces should be isolated so that routine user networks cannot reach them and so that administrative access is constrained to explicit, monitored paths. This is not only a security requirement but also an operational requirement, because it simplifies investigations by reducing the number of plausible routes an attacker could have used. AI/ML can help by correlating privileged authentication events with network path attempts and flagging unusual combinations, but it can also create false confidence if identity telemetry is incomplete or if time synchronization is inconsistent across data sources. Human review remains essential, especially for any automated response that would block administrative traffic and risk disrupting recovery actions.

Finally, segmentation must be managed as a living system with continuous validation, not a one-time project. Policies should be reviewed against observed traffic, exceptions should expire unless renewed, and zone definitions should be revisited when business processes change or systems migrate. The most reliable segmentation programs can answer basic questions quickly during an incident: which zones are involved, which paths exist between them, and which controls should have prevented movement. That requires documentation that matches reality, telemetry that reflects enforcement decisions, and an operating rhythm that keeps the model from drifting as teams change and infrastructure evolves. When teams use AI-assisted tools to summarize policy changes or to detect unexpected connectivity, those tools should produce auditable outputs that can be verified and traced back to underlying logs and configurations. Segmentation is ultimately a control over complexity, and its success depends less on perfect diagrams and more on operational discipline under real-world constraints.

Firewalls and Policy Management as Operations

Firewalls are most effective when they are treated as an operational system, not a deployed device. The technology enforces decisions about what is allowed to communicate, but the security outcome comes from how those decisions are made, reviewed, implemented, and monitored over time. In mature environments, firewalling is less about blocking "bad traffic" and more about maintaining controlled pathways that reflect business intent and risk tolerance. That requires consistent ownership, explicit policy standards, and a change process that balances speed with safety. When firewalls are treated as infrastructure plumbing with ad hoc rule edits, they accumulate exceptions, lose interpretability, and eventually become a high-risk dependency that no one feels confident touching.

Policy management begins with defining what a rule means in operational terms. A useful rule has a clear source scope, destination scope, protocol and port definition, and an accountable justification that connects back to an application dependency or business workflow. Justification is not bureaucracy; it is how teams avoid creating permanent "temporary" access that later becomes an attacker's easiest path. Rule definitions should be stable and readable, because responders will rely on them during incidents to understand what should be possible and what indicates misuse. Naming conventions, consistent object groupings, and documentation that explains intent are not cosmetic choices, they are the difference between a controllable environment and an opaque one. Executives should care about this because unclear firewall policy directly increases outage risk, incident duration, and the likelihood of overbroad access that expands the impact of compromise.

Operationally, firewall changes are production changes and should be handled with the same seriousness as changes to core business systems. A disciplined process includes request intake with sufficient context, technical validation against known dependencies, peer review to catch unintended consequences, and a plan to validate outcomes after deployment. The validation step matters because a change can be syntactically correct and still break a workflow or silently open a new path. Even in fast-moving environments, changes can be structured, so emergency access is time-bounded, logged, and reviewed as soon as the business pressure passes. The organizations that struggle most are those that conflate speed with bypassing controls, because that creates a cycle where every request becomes "urgent" and the rulebase grows without governance. Over time, teams lose the ability to distinguish critical flows from historical artifacts, and security becomes dependent on institutional memory rather

Table 8.2 Firewall Rule Lifecycle Checklist for Operational Policy Management.

Lifecycle Step	Required Rule Attribute	Operational Owner Outcome	Failure Mode if Skipped
Request intake	Business justification and scope	Traceable intent for each allow path	Temporary access becomes permanent
Technical validation	Source destination protocol defined	Reduced outages and overbroad exposure	Rule too broad or misapplied
Peer review	Naming and object consistency	Readable and auditable rulebase	Uninterpretable policy during incidents
Implementation	Versioned change record and rollback	Fast recovery from mistakes	No safe rollback under pressure
Post change verification	Functionality and intent validated	Confirms exposure did not expand silently	Business works but security intent breaks
Periodic review	Owner and review cadence	Removes obsolete or risky rules	Policy drift and rulebase sprawl

than documented intent. Table 8.2 reinforces firewall policy as an operational lifecycle with required attributes that prevent drift and preserve rollback safety.

Rulebase growth is a predictable operational problem, and it must be managed proactively. As environments evolve, rules that once supported a project often remain long after the project ends, creating unnecessary exposure and complicating troubleshooting. A sustainable program includes periodic review of rule usage and relevance, with a bias toward removing or tightening rules that are no longer needed. This is where high-quality telemetry becomes essential, because teams need evidence about which rules are used, by whom, and for what purpose. AI/ML can assist by summarizing usage patterns, identifying rules that appear redundant or shadowed, and flagging access paths that do not align with typical application behavior. Those recommendations must be reviewed by engineers who understand the environment, because models can misinterpret infrequent but legitimate activity as unused, and an automated cleanup can create outages that are costly and politically damaging.

Consistency across enforcement points is another practical requirement that is often overlooked. Organizations rarely have a single firewall, and inconsistent policy intent across perimeter, internal segmentation points, and cloud network constructs creates gaps and blind spots. Operational policy management treats the environment as a system, aligning rule logic and documentation across domains so that "allowed" and "blocked" mean the same thing everywhere. Without alignment, responders waste time reconciling conflicting enforcement decisions and chasing false leads that come from partial visibility. Centralizing decision standards does not require centralizing every action, but it does require shared definitions for zones, services, and risk-based exceptions. A common pitfall is allowing each team to build policies in isolation, which produces incompatible rule structures and makes enterprise-wide audits slow, expensive, and error-prone.

Logging and monitoring are not secondary features of firewall operations; they are the feedback loop that keeps policy trustworthy. Firewall telemetry should support both security detection and operational troubleshooting, with enough detail to reconstruct who initiated a connection, what was attempted, and what decision was made. Poor logging practices create two failure modes: defenders cannot detect meaningful abuse because events lack context, and engineers cannot troubleshoot business issues because the logs cannot explain why traffic failed. Time synchronization, log retention, and consistent parsing into the organization's monitoring pipeline are essential to make firewall events usable during incidents. AI-assisted triage can help prioritize spikes in denies, novel destinations, or suspicious protocol changes, but it can also generate false confidence if the underlying logs are incomplete or biased toward certain network segments. For that reason, teams should treat AI outputs as prioritization cues and preserve the ability to drill into raw events and configuration history for verification.

Finally, firewall operations must include resilience planning for when things go wrong. Mistakes will happen, and the difference between a controlled event and a crisis is whether teams can roll back quickly, understand the blast radius, and restore known-good policy without improvisation. That requires versioned configuration management, tested rollback procedures, and clear escalation paths between network operations, security operations, and application owners. In high-pressure moments, teams are tempted to "open it up" to restore service, but that response can turn a transient outage into a security incident if broad access remains in place. Mature operations anticipate this by defining break-glass pathways that are logged, time-limited, and reviewed, so business continuity does not require permanent exposure. Firewalls and policy management become reliable when they are run like operations: measured, governed, observable, and designed to recover gracefully under stress.

Remote Access, Exposure Reduction, and Authentication Constraints

Remote access is a business enabler that also concentrates risk, because it turns identity and connectivity into a single control plane exposed to the internet. The operational goal is not simply to allow users to connect from anywhere, but to make every remote session intentional, strongly authenticated, and constrained to the minimum access required. When remote access is treated as a convenience feature, organizations tend to accumulate multiple entry paths, inconsistent authentication policies, and legacy protocols that are difficult to monitor. Attackers exploit this complexity by targeting the most weakly governed path, not the most commonly used one. A resilient remote access posture starts by recognizing that remote connectivity is part of the perimeter, and the perimeter must be continuously managed rather than assumed stable.

Exposure reduction begins with minimizing what is reachable from the outside in the first place. Every internet-facing service expands the attack surface, and remote access services are especially attractive because they combine authentication, session establishment, and access to internal resources. Reducing exposure means consolidating entry points where possible, disabling unused services, and ensuring that any externally reachable interface is intentionally published and continuously inventoried. It also means removing "accidental exposure," such as management interfaces left open during troubleshooting or legacy access methods kept for a small set of users without ongoing review. Telemetry should support a simple operational question: what remote access paths exist today, who owns them, and what identities are permitted to use them. AI/ML can help by correlating external scan results, DNS records, certificate issuance, and authentication logs to surface unknown or newly exposed services, but only if those data sources are collected consistently and reviewed with clear accountability.

Remote access control is ultimately an identity problem, and authentication constraints shape what is possible in practice. Strong authentication requires more than turning on MFA, because MFA quality varies and can be undermined by fallback methods, weak enrollment practices, and session persistence that effectively bypasses reauthentication. Constraints appear when business workflows depend on non-interactive access, shared accounts, embedded credentials, or third-party integrations that were never designed for modern identity controls. Organizations often respond by carving out exceptions, which becomes dangerous when exceptions are not time-bounded, documented, and monitored. A practical remote access program treats authentication methods as tiers of assurance, aligning higher-risk access to stronger factors and tighter session controls. Executives should expect that authentication constraints are discussed openly, because hiding them behind vague statements about "MFA is enabled" creates a false sense of safety that collapses during a real incident.

Session management is where many remote access compromises become operationally significant. Even when initial authentication is strong, long-lived sessions, permissive device trust assumptions, and broad post-login access can allow a single successful login to translate into deep internal reach. Mature operations define how sessions are established, how long they persist, when reauthentication is required, and what contextual signals can restrict access, such as device posture, location risk, or unusual login timing. Constraints emerge when users expect uninterrupted access or when critical workflows break under frequent reauthentication, but those expectations must be balanced against the reality of credential theft and token replay. AI/ML can contribute by scoring session risk based on behavioral patterns across login events and network activity, but it must be implemented with human-in-the-loop controls that prevent automated lockouts from becoming a self-inflicted outage. Risk scoring also requires careful governance to avoid bias and to ensure that decisions are explainable during audits and incident reviews.

Third-party and vendor access is a recurring constraint that tests whether remote access controls are truly consistent. Vendors often require access during odd hours, from diverse networks, and across systems that internal staff rarely touch, which creates a perfect storm of unfamiliar behavior and broad permissions. If the only way to support vendors is to grant persistent access to internal networks, then remote access becomes a standing exception that attackers will eventually target. Operationally, vendor access should be bounded by scope and time, with explicit accountability for who approved it and what systems it can reach. Telemetry should make vendor activity easy to separate from employee activity, so investigations are not delayed by ambiguity. AI/ML can help by learning normal patterns for each vendor relationship and flagging deviations, but it can also amplify noise if vendor behaviors are inherently irregular, so alert thresholds and review workflows must be tuned to reduce fatigue.

Exposure reduction must also account for the reality that remote access is frequently used during incidents, outages, and change windows. If defenders cannot access systems safely under stress, teams will bypass controls to restore operations, and those bypasses can become permanent weaknesses. Resilient designs include a controlled break-glass mechanism that preserves strong identity binding, produces high-fidelity logging, and expires by default rather than requiring someone to remember to remove it later. Constraints often show up in incident response when privileged access is needed quickly and authentication systems are degraded, so planning should include tested recovery procedures for identity dependencies and remote access infrastructure. AI-assisted tools can support responders by summarizing recent authentication anomalies, enumerating active sessions, and correlating remote logins with lateral movement signals, but outputs must be auditable and verifiable to prevent decisions based on misleading summaries. Good remote access operations treat identity and connectivity as inseparable, reducing exposure, constraining sessions, and managing authentication constraints with disciplined exceptions rather than informal workarounds.

Finally, remote access controls must be continuously validated because drift is the default state in complex environments. New teams and projects introduce new access needs, and over time those needs create additional paths, broadened permissions, and forgotten configurations that quietly increase risk. Continuous validation means regularly reconciling who has access against who should, testing whether MFA and session controls are actually enforced for all remote paths, and reviewing logs to ensure that remote access behavior is observable and attributable. A common pitfall is assuming that a policy statement equals enforcement, only to discover that legacy clients, alternate portals, or inherited configurations bypass the intended controls. AI/ML can make validation more scalable by highlighting mismatches between policy intent and observed behavior, but it cannot replace ownership and accountability for closing gaps. Remote access becomes manageable when it is run like an operational service with clear inventory, strong authentication, disciplined exceptions, and consistent monitoring that treats every external entry path as a control that must earn and keep trust.

Visibility and Logging Across Network Boundaries

Network visibility is the practical ability to explain what happened, where it happened, and how it happened using evidence that survives scrutiny. It is not enough to know that "traffic was blocked" or "an alert fired" if teams cannot reconstruct the path, the initiating identity, and the enforcement decisions that shaped the outcome. The operational goal is to create a coherent story across boundaries that are often owned by different teams and implemented by different technologies. Those boundaries include perimeter controls, internal segmentation points, cloud network constructs, and service-to-service communication paths that may never traverse a traditional choke point. When visibility fails, investigations become guesswork, containment becomes overly broad, and leaders are forced to make high-impact decisions without reliable facts.

Logging across network boundaries starts with standardizing what "good evidence" looks like. At minimum, defenders need timestamps that are accurate and synchronized, identifiers that allow traffic to be tied back to a system and an owner, and event details that capture what was attempted and what decision was made. Network logs are most useful when they include both the technical attributes of a connection and the context required to interpret it, such as zone names, rule identifiers, and authentication outcomes. A common failure mode is collecting large volumes of low-context logs that are difficult to search and even harder to correlate, which creates cost without clarity. Another failure mode is inconsistent log formats and inconsistent retention, where one boundary provides high-fidelity data for a short window and another provides low-fidelity data for a long window, leaving gaps that attackers can exploit. Operationally, the goal is not maximum logging, but consistent and decision-relevant logging that supports detection, triage, and investigation.

Correlation is where boundary visibility becomes real, and correlation requires shared reference points. Teams should be able to align events using time, network identifiers, and identity signals so that a remote login, a policy decision, and an internal connection attempt can be traced as part of the same narrative. This is difficult when NAT rewrites addresses, when proxying obscures true sources, or when multiple egress points make outbound traffic appear to originate from the same place. Defenders should plan for these realities by ensuring that translation and proxy layers log the original source context and preserve traceability through stable identifiers. Without that, analysts see disconnected fragments and may misattribute activity to the wrong host or user, which delays containment and can harm trust with business stakeholders. AI/ML can help correlate large volumes of events across boundaries by linking likely related sessions and highlighting anomalous sequences, but those linkages must be explainable and supported by underlying evidence to avoid building investigations on fragile assumptions.

Boundary visibility also depends on understanding what is not visible and treating those blind spots as operational risks. Encrypted traffic, for example, reduces observable payload content and shifts visibility toward metadata such as destinations, certificates, protocol behavior, and timing. East–west traffic in flat networks may admit few meaningful choke points, and cloud-native communication can bypass traditional monitoring locations entirely. These realities do not eliminate the need for network logging, but they require deliberate choices about where to place sensors and what telemetry is realistic to collect. Leaders should expect security and network teams to be explicit about these limitations, because pretending that visibility is complete leads to overconfidence and brittle response plans. A mature approach uses multiple complementary data sources so that when one boundary provides limited detail, another boundary or system provides the missing context needed to interpret the event.

Log quality is as important as log presence, and quality is an operational practice, not a one-time configuration. Network logs must be consistently parsed into the organization's monitoring pipeline, normalized so that the same fields mean the same thing across sources, and tested to ensure that key event types are actually arriving as expected. Time synchronization is a foundational requirement because even small skews create false sequences that mislead analysts and complicate legal and compliance reporting. Retention must be aligned to how long investigations realistically take, including slow-moving intrusions where the initial access may have occurred weeks before detection. A common pitfall is optimizing retention only for cost, which forces teams to investigate with partial histories and encourages premature conclusions. AI-assisted analysis is only as good as the data it consumes, and poor log hygiene leads models to learn patterns that reflect collection artifacts rather than attacker behavior, producing confident but incorrect outputs.

Operational visibility also requires that logs can be acted on, which means routing, access, and ownership must be clear. If analysts cannot access network logs quickly, or if they do not know which team owns a boundary, response slows and accountability blurs. Access controls should protect log integrity without turning evidence into a ticket-driven bottleneck during incidents. Ownership should be explicit so that when an alert points to a policy decision at a boundary, responders know who can interpret it, modify it, and validate changes. This is where cross-team handoffs often fail, particularly between network engineering and security operations, because the two groups may use different language for the same concepts. AI/ML can reduce friction by summarizing boundary events in consistent terms and surfacing likely owners based on configuration metadata, but it must be governed so that summaries do not replace verification and do not leak sensitive configuration details into inappropriate workflows.

Finally, visibility across boundaries should be continuously validated through routine operational exercises, not discovered during crises. Teams should periodically trace a known flow end-to-end and confirm that the expected logs appear with the expected fields, timestamps, and identifiers. They should also test negative cases, such as denied connections and failed authentications, because those events often carry the most investigative value. When gaps are found, the fix should include both technical changes and process changes so that the gap does not reappear after upgrades or organizational transitions. AI/ML can help by continuously checking for telemetry regressions, unusual drops in event volume, or changes in field distributions that suggest a logging failure, but it must operate with clear thresholds and human review to avoid generating noise. Network visibility becomes reliable when it is treated as an operational product: engineered for traceability, maintained through hygiene, and proven through repeatable validation across every boundary that matters.

Detecting Lateral Movement and Suspicious Connectivity

Lateral movement is the attacker's process of turning a single foothold into meaningful access, and it is often the phase where early containment is still possible. The operational objective is to recognize when connectivity patterns shift from normal business communication into exploratory, opportunistic, or privilege-seeking behavior. This is difficult because many legitimate workflows involve remote administration, service-to-service communication, and automated scanning for availability. Defenders need to distinguish expected internal traffic from activity that indicates discovery, credential use outside normal patterns, or attempts to reach management interfaces. The most reliable programs treat lateral movement detection as an exercise in context: who is talking, to what, using which protocol, from which zone, and under what identity.

Suspicious connectivity typically shows up as novelty in paths, not necessarily in payloads. Attackers may use legitimate protocols and tools, but they use them in unusual sequences, at unusual times, and across unusual boundaries. A workstation suddenly initiating many connections to server subnets, a service account reaching systems it has never touched, or a burst of failed connection attempts across many destinations are common indicators that deserve attention. Internal scanning is particularly revealing when it crosses segmentation boundaries, because it suggests the actor is mapping reachable surfaces rather than executing a known workflow. The challenge is that novelty is not always malicious, especially during migrations, incident response activities, or administrative maintenance. Operational detection therefore needs both telemetry and a way to rapidly validate whether the behavior maps to an approved change or a plausible business event.

High-quality lateral movement detection depends on collecting connectivity data that is both broad and attributable. Flow records, firewall denies and allows, and authentication events become far more valuable when they can be linked to a host identity, a user identity, and a zone context. Without attribution, defenders see that "something" is scanning, but they cannot determine whether it is a vulnerability scanner, a management tool, or an attacker. Attribution can be complicated by NAT, proxies, shared jump hosts, and ephemeral infrastructure, which is why consistent logging at translation and enforcement points matters. Time synchronization and stable identifiers are foundational because lateral movement investigations are sequence-driven, and inconsistent clocks can turn a clear progression into apparent randomness. When these fundamentals are in place, suspicious connectivity is less about guessing intent and more about testing hypotheses against evidence.

Segmentation boundaries create natural detection points because they reflect intent and policy. When an internal control denies traffic, that denial is often more informative than an allow, because it indicates an attempt to reach something that policy says should not be reachable. A cluster of denies from a single source toward administrative networks, identity infrastructure, or database zones is a strong signal that warrants rapid triage. However, relying only on denies can miss successful lateral movement that stays within permissive zones, so detection must also examine unusual successful connections, especially first-time paths and sudden expansions in connection volume. Defenders should tune for behavior that is inconsistent with the source system's role, such as a user workstation initiating remote management protocols or a non-administrative server attempting to contact a wide range of peers. The goal is to surface connectivity that violates expectations, then confirm those expectations quickly with application owners and change records.

Authentication telemetry is a primary companion signal for lateral movement because many movement techniques involve credential use. Unusual authentication patterns such as repeated failures followed by a success, logins from hosts that do not typically initiate authentication, or privilege use outside normal administrative windows can provide early warning. When suspicious connectivity aligns with suspicious authentication, the confidence of the detection rises dramatically, and responders can act with fewer assumptions. Conversely, connectivity without identity context often leads to long investigations that end in "could not determine," which wastes time and reduces trust in the monitoring program. AI/ML can help by correlating connectivity sequences with authentication sequences across large datasets and flagging combinations that are statistically rare in that environment. Those systems must be governed carefully because rare does not always mean malicious, and models can drift as workflows change, producing false confidence or alert fatigue if they are not retrained and reviewed.

A practical detection workflow balances automation with human judgment, especially when the response action could disrupt business. Automated enrichment can add zone context, asset criticality, and recent change activity to an alert, so an analyst can rapidly assess plausibility. Automated suppression should be conservative, because suppressing an alert based on incomplete context can allow an attacker to operate under the cover of "normal noise." Human-in-the-loop review is essential for escalations that involve isolating systems, blocking internal protocols, or disabling accounts, because these actions can impair operations and complicate recovery if done prematurely. The strongest teams treat lateral movement signals as triggers for structured investigation steps, including scoping, validation of legitimacy, and containment planning, rather than as isolated alerts to be closed. AI-assisted triage can accelerate this by producing concise narratives of "what changed" and "what is unusual," but those narratives must be traceable back to raw evidence and should never become the sole basis for a disruptive action.

Common pitfalls in lateral movement detection often come from misaligned expectations and incomplete coverage. Flat networks reduce the number of meaningful choke points, making it harder to observe internal movement and easier for scanning to blend into legitimate traffic. Overly permissive administrative tooling can normalize patterns that look like attacker behavior, such as broad remote execution, widespread credential use, and shared management accounts. Inconsistent logging creates gaps that attackers can traverse, and poor asset inventory prevents defenders from understanding which systems should never be initiating certain connections. Another pitfall is treating "east–west detection" as purely a network problem, when it is actually a combined view of network paths, identity use, and system role. If the organization cannot confidently state what "normal" is for critical segments, it will struggle to detect deviations without generating overwhelming noise.

Effective lateral movement detection is ultimately a measure of how well the environment enforces and observes intent. When zones are meaningful, policies are clear, and telemetry is attributable, suspicious connectivity stands out as a deviation rather than as an ambiguous pattern. Detection improves when teams continuously learn from incidents and near-misses by refining expectations, tightening permissive paths, and improving logging where investigations stalled. AI/ML can make this learning cycle faster by highlighting emerging patterns and suggesting new baselines, but it must be paired with governance that documents why changes were made and how model outputs are validated. The operational aim is not perfect prediction; it is rapid recognition and confident action when internal movement starts to resemble adversary behavior. In environments where lateral movement is detected early and consistently, attackers are forced into noisier techniques, defenders gain time, and containment becomes a practical outcome rather than a late-stage aspiration.

Operational Change and Policy Drift in Networks

Network security posture is not a static design state; it is the product of daily operational change. Every project, outage, vendor request, acquisition, and modernization effort introduces new connectivity needs and new exceptions, often under time pressure. The defensive challenge is that networks are permissive by default unless deliberately constrained, and permissive decisions tend to accumulate faster than restrictive decisions. Over time, this creates policy drift, where the implemented ruleset no longer matches the organization's intent, risk tolerance, or architectural assumptions. Drift is rarely the result of negligence, but it becomes a security problem when it is invisible, unowned, and unmanaged.

Policy drift typically begins as well-intentioned exception handling. A rule is opened to unblock a deployment, to support a troubleshooting window, or to accommodate a legacy dependency that cannot be changed quickly. The exception is logged in a ticketing system, discussed in a meeting, or justified in an email, and then it quietly persists because the business moves on and no one is incentivized to remove it. As these exceptions compound, the rulebase becomes harder to interpret and harder to audit, which increases both security exposure and operational fragility. Attackers benefit because drift creates "soft spots" where access is broader than necessary and monitoring expectations are unclear. Defenders suffer because incident response becomes slower when responders cannot confidently determine whether a connection path is intended or accidental.

Operational change becomes risky when it outpaces the organization's ability to validate outcomes. Network changes often involve multiple dependencies, including routing, DNS, identity flows, and application behavior, and a seemingly narrow rule adjustment can have wide effects. Without reliable pre-change testing and post-change verification, teams may introduce new access paths unintentionally or break segmentation assumptions without noticing. Verification must include both service functionality and security intent, because a change can succeed operationally while still expanding exposure. Leaders should expect that network change control includes explicit risk consideration, not as a paperwork exercise but as a practical check that the organization still understands and owns its connectivity posture. When teams skip these steps for speed, they usually pay later through outages, emergency broadening of access, and prolonged incident investigations.

Drift is amplified by complexity and by fragmentation of ownership across network boundaries. Perimeter controls, internal segmentation points, cloud networks, and third-party connections may each have separate change processes, separate documentation, and separate mental models. When one boundary changes without coordinated review, the combined effect can create unexpected paths that no single team intended. This is especially common when cloud workloads scale dynamically or when infrastructure is managed through automation that can rapidly introduce new routes and security group rules. The operational fix is not to centralize every decision, but to standardize intent and visibility so that changes are understandable across teams and boundaries. Consistent naming, zone definitions, and policy documentation reduce the translation burden during reviews and incident response.

Telemetry provides the evidence required to detect drift, but only if it is tied to the change process. Logs that show new traffic patterns, increased rule hits, or new denied attempts across boundaries can indicate that a change has altered behavior in ways the request did not anticipate. This is a practical place for AI/ML to contribute by continuously comparing observed connectivity against historical baselines and flagging statistically meaningful deviations after policy updates. Those signals must be integrated into operational workflows, so they trigger follow-up reviews rather than becoming noise in an alert queue. Models can fail when business activity changes abruptly, such as during major migrations or seasonal demand, which means drift detection must incorporate change calendars and human context to avoid false confidence. Governance should also include auditability, where analysts can trace a drift signal back to the specific policy change and the underlying logs that support it.

Rule lifecycle management is the discipline that prevents drift from becoming permanent. Rules should have owners, and rules that exist to support temporary activities should have explicit expiration conditions, so they do not linger by default. Even long-lived rules benefit from periodic review that asks whether the business justification still exists, whether the source and destination scopes remain minimal, and whether the rule still aligns with segmentation intent. A common operational pitfall is reviewing only allows and ignoring denies, even though deny patterns can reveal misrouted traffic, failed deployments, or probing activity that tests boundaries. Another pitfall is treating rule cleanup as a rare project rather than a recurring operational task, which guarantees that the backlog will become politically and technically difficult to address. Drift is reduced when rule review is normalized as part of operations, not framed as a disruptive security initiative.

Emergency changes are where drift most often becomes entrenched because they are made under pressure and rarely revisited. During outages or incidents, teams may broaden access to restore service quickly, and if there is no structured follow-up, that broadened access can persist indefinitely. Mature operations create a break-glass path that is logged, time-bounded, and automatically flagged for review, so emergency access does not require heroics to unwind later. AI-assisted summarization can help by producing a clear list of emergency changes, their owners, and observed traffic impacts, enabling leaders to demand closure rather than accepting vague assurances. However, automated summaries must be verified against configuration history and change records because incomplete data or parsing errors can hide the very exceptions that matter most. The operational expectation is that emergencies are handled quickly without compromising long-term posture, which requires that the unwind process is as deliberate as the initial change.

Ultimately, managing drift is about preserving the integrity of intent over time. Networks change because the business changes, and the defensive task is to ensure that connectivity remains deliberate, attributable, and aligned with risk rather than evolving through uncontrolled accumulation. When teams can explain why a pathway exists, who approved it, how it is monitored, and when it will be reviewed, drift becomes manageable and audits become predictable. When they cannot, the network becomes a historical artifact shaped by past urgency rather than current design, and attackers inherit a maze of permissive routes and weakly observed boundaries. AI/ML can increase operational scale by highlighting drift earlier and by reducing manual analysis, but it cannot substitute for ownership, lifecycle discipline, and verification. A stable security posture is achieved not by freezing change, but by running change as an operational system that continuously reconciles what is implemented with what is intended.

AI-Assisted Network Analysis: Pattern Recognition, Alert Enrichment, and Validation

AI-assisted network analysis is most valuable when it accelerates human decision-making without obscuring the evidence behind those decisions. Networks generate high-volume, high-cardinality telemetry where meaningful signals are often subtle and distributed across boundaries. Pattern recognition can surface anomalies that are hard to see with fixed thresholds, while enrichment can reduce the time analysts spend assembling context from multiple sources. The operational goal is not to replace analysts, but to make analysis faster, more consistent, and less dependent on individual intuition. To be useful in a blue team environment, AI outputs must be tied to observable data and must support verification, because network defense fails quickly when teams act on confident but ungrounded conclusions.

Pattern recognition in network telemetry typically focuses on identifying deviations in behavior rather than identifying "bad packets." Useful patterns include new communication paths between zones, sudden increases in connection attempts, unusual protocol negotiation, changes in DNS behavior, and shifts in typical outbound destination profiles. Models can also detect sequence patterns, such as an initial remote access session followed by a burst of internal discovery and then authentication attempts against high-value systems. These detections work best when the environment has stable baselines and when telemetry includes enough context to distinguish business change from adversary activity. Pattern recognition is especially effective for lateral movement and egress monitoring because attackers often must create new paths or interact with destinations that are atypical for a given host or account. The operational constraint is that networks are dynamic, so the definition of "normal" must adapt without allowing the model to normalize attacker persistence.

Alert enrichment is where AI can deliver immediate operational value by shrinking the distance between detection and action. Enrichment should attach identity context, asset criticality, zone or segment labels, relevant policy decisions, and recent change activity to the alert, so an analyst can assess intent quickly. For example, a spike in denied internal connections is far more actionable when it is paired with the specific enforcement rule, the zones involved, and whether the source host recently changed posture or software. Enrichment should also include pivots, such as related sessions, nearby authentication events, and other hosts exhibiting similar behavior, so the analyst can scope the event without manual stitching. The best enrichment reads like a concise incident narrative, but it must remain evidence-backed and avoid speculative language that implies certainty. A common failure mode is enrichment that adds volume without clarity, burying the key decisions under generic summaries and unvalidated correlations.

Validation is the safeguard that makes AI assistance safe in operational environments. Every AI-generated conclusion should be treated as a hypothesis that must be tested against raw logs, configuration history, and known business context. Validation is not only about preventing false positives; it is about preventing false confidence, which is more dangerous because it encourages premature closure or disruptive response actions. A practical validation loop includes checking whether the observed pattern is truly novel for the asset, whether a change request or deployment could explain it, and whether other telemetry sources corroborate the same story. When models provide explanations, those explanations should point to specific events or features that can be independently confirmed, rather than opaque scores that cannot be interrogated. Leaders should expect that AI outputs are auditable, including the data sources used, the time window analyzed, and the rationale for any automated prioritization. Table 8.3 outlines practical AI guardrails showing the telemetry needed the approval boundary and the failure modes that must be governed.

Data and telemetry dependencies determine whether AI-assisted analysis improves outcomes or amplifies noise. Network models require consistent, high-quality inputs such as flow data, firewall decisions, DNS logs, remote access logs, and authentication events, ideally with stable identifiers and synchronized time. If telemetry is missing for certain segments, the model learns an incomplete picture and may treat blind spots as normal inactivity. If parsing and normalization are inconsistent, the model may detect artifacts of collection rather than genuine behavioral change. Retention matters because training and baseline building require enough history to capture routine variability, including maintenance windows and business cycles. The operational reality is that AI does not rescue poor visibility; it increases the penalty of poor visibility by producing confidently framed outputs from flawed inputs.

Table 8.3 AI Assisted Network Analysis Guardrails and Validation Requirements.

AI Use Case	Telemetry Dependency	Human Approval Boundary	Key Failure Mode to Watch
Pattern recognition for novel paths	Flow and firewall decisions with zones	Analyst validates novelty and scope	Model drift normalizes attacker behavior
Alert enrichment for faster triage	Identity context asset criticality change history	Analyst confirms evidence before action	Overconfidence from incomplete context
Cross boundary correlation	Consistent identifiers and synchronized time	Analyst verifies linked sessions	Opaqueness hides weak correlations
Connectivity anomaly scoring	DNS remote access and auth events	No auto blocks for high-impact zones	Bias toward familiar patterns
Telemetry regression detection	Stable log volume and field parsing	Engineer reviews and fixes collection gaps	Artifacts mistaken for attacker signals

Human-in-the-loop controls define the safe boundary between assistance and automation. AI can prioritize alerts, suggest likely root causes, and recommend investigative pivots, but decisions that alter connectivity or identity should require explicit human approval unless the action is narrowly scoped and low impact. When automated response is used, it should be constrained to reversible actions with clear rollback, strong logging, and alerting that signals what was changed and why. Approval boundaries should be aligned with business criticality, so the system is more conservative for administrative planes, identity infrastructure, and production-critical services. Analysts also need training on how to challenge model outputs, because a tool that is always "right" in perception will be accepted even when it is wrong in fact. The control objective is to prevent the automation of error, which is one of the fastest ways to convert an analytical aid into an outage generator.

AI-assisted analysis has predictable failure modes that must be planned for as part of operations. Models can drift as network behavior changes, causing alert rates to spike or meaningful signals to be suppressed because the model adapted to attacker persistence. Models can inherit bias from historical incidents and response decisions, focusing attention on familiar patterns while missing novel attacker approaches. Leakage is a serious concern when sensitive network details, internal hostnames, or access patterns are used in training or prompt contexts without strict handling, because those artifacts can reveal operational posture if exposed. Another failure mode is overfitting to a single data source, where the model appears accurate until that source degrades or changes format, at which point the model's outputs become unreliable. Operational governance must include monitoring of model health, periodic review of performance against real incidents, and a clear process for disabling or rolling back model-driven workflows when confidence degrades.

Governance and auditability are what allow AI-assisted network analysis to be adopted without cheerleading operations into a black box. Defenders should be able to explain, after the fact, why an alert was prioritized, what evidence supported a conclusion, and what actions were taken as a result. Model changes should be controlled and documented, with clear ownership and testing that validates behavior against representative scenarios. Audit expectations should include traceability from an AI summary back to specific log events and configurations, so investigators can reproduce the reasoning without trusting the model's narrative. When AI is integrated into network operations, it becomes part of the control environment and must be treated with the same rigor as any other security-relevant system. The outcome should be faster recognition, clearer context, and more confident validation, with human judgment preserved as the final authority for actions that affect availability and risk.

Maintaining Network Defense in Hybrid Environments

Hybrid environments combine different networking models, different control planes, and different operational assumptions into a single security problem. Traditional data centers emphasize centralized routing and perimeter enforcement, while cloud environments often distribute controls across virtual networks, service constructs, and workload-level policy. Remote users and SaaS traffic add additional paths that may never touch corporate network chokepoints. The operational goal is to maintain consistent defensive intent across these domains so that connectivity remains deliberate, segmentation remains meaningful, and investigations remain possible. Hybrid defense fails when teams treat each domain as a separate universe, because attackers will use the seams between universes as the easiest route to move and hide.

Consistency starts with defining network intent in terms that can be applied across platforms. Zones and trust boundaries should map to business function and sensitivity rather than to a particular network technology, so that a "production application zone" has the same meaning whether it resides in a data center segment or a cloud virtual network. Policy decisions should be expressed in a way that supports translation into domain-specific enforcement without changing the underlying intent. The practical challenge is that different domains expose different primitives, which can tempt teams to implement what is easy rather than what is intended. Over time, these compromises create uneven protection, where one domain is tightly controlled and another is permissive due to operational convenience. A resilient hybrid posture acknowledges these translation challenges upfront and invests in governance, documentation, and testing that keeps intent aligned even when implementations differ.

Visibility is the second foundational requirement, because hybrid environments fragment telemetry by design. Data center firewalls, cloud network logs, identity providers, and remote access gateways may each describe the same activity using different fields, different identifiers, and different timestamps. Investigations depend on being able to stitch these views into a single narrative that explains where a session originated, what it touched, and what enforcement decisions were applied along the way. Time synchronization, normalization, and consistent asset identity become more difficult when workloads are ephemeral and addresses change frequently. Without disciplined logging, teams will detect that something is happening but will struggle to scope it across boundaries quickly enough to contain it. AI/ML can help correlate these disparate telemetry streams by linking likely related sessions and highlighting cross-domain sequences, but those correlations must be verifiable and must not become a substitute for reliable identifiers and properly engineered logging.

Change management is where hybrid defense is most likely to drift, because change velocity is rarely uniform across domains. Cloud deployments and infrastructure automation can introduce new routes, new access paths, and new service dependencies faster than traditional network teams can review them. Conversely, data center changes may be slower and more controlled, creating the perception that "cloud is flexible" and "data center is strict," which becomes a structural imbalance attackers can exploit. Maintaining defense requires that high-velocity domains still have guardrails, including standardized change inputs, peer review for security-relevant changes, and post-change validation that confirms intent was preserved. Policy drift in hybrid environments often manifests as exceptions that proliferate in cloud networks because they are easy to create and hard to inventory across accounts and projects. AI-assisted drift detection can surface unexpected connectivity expansions and highlight anomalous rule changes, but only if it is coupled to ownership, escalation paths, and a process that can remove or tighten permissions without breaking critical services.

Segmentation in hybrid environments is as much about identity and workload role as it is about network location. In data centers, segmentation often assumes stable subnets and predictable east–west paths, while in cloud environments segmentation may rely on service boundaries and workload tags that can change with deployment pipelines. The defensive objective remains containment, but the implementation must reflect how traffic actually flows, including service-to-service calls that bypass traditional internal firewalls. Workload identity, service accounts, and administrative planes must be protected consistently, because attackers increasingly target control planes and management interfaces to gain durable access across domains. Practical constraints arise when legacy applications require broad reachability or when third-party integrations introduce opaque traffic patterns that are difficult to segment cleanly. AI/ML can assist by identifying typical service dependency graphs and flagging new or unusual edges, but those models are vulnerable to drift during migrations, so defenders must validate changes against deployment intent and maintain tight approval boundaries for new cross-zone paths.

Remote connectivity is a permanent component of hybrid defense, not an edge case, because users, contractors, and automated systems frequently interact with cloud-hosted services directly. This shifts some enforcement away from centralized network controls and toward identity, device posture, and application-layer access decisions. The operational constraint is that when identity becomes the primary gate, misconfigurations and exception handling in authentication and authorization can undermine network defenses across every domain. Teams should ensure that remote access paths, administrative access, and service-to-service authentication are logged with enough context to tie actions back to identities and to the systems they affected. Cross-domain incidents often hinge on whether defenders can connect a remote session to internal actions, and that is only possible when identity telemetry and network telemetry are intentionally aligned. AI-assisted enrichment can accelerate this correlation by attaching identity context to network events and highlighting atypical privilege use, but the outputs must be auditable and supported by raw logs to avoid decisions based on incomplete summaries.

Operational ownership and communication are the final determinants of whether hybrid defense holds together under stress. Hybrid environments naturally encourage specialization, and specialization can become fragmentation if teams do not share definitions, escalation paths, and a common view of exposure. Incidents move fastest when responders know which boundary controls exist in each domain, who can modify them, and how those modifications are validated. A common pitfall is discovering during an incident that cloud networking changes require a different approval chain, that logs reside in different systems with different access controls, or that critical telemetry is missing because logging was not enabled consistently across accounts. Maintaining defense means rehearsing cross-domain investigations and response actions, so the seams are understood before attackers exploit them. Hybrid security becomes sustainable when defensive intent is consistent, telemetry is correlatable, changes are governed despite velocity differences, and AI assistance is used to reduce analysis time while preserving validation and human authority over risk-bearing actions.

Conclusion

Network defense succeeds when connectivity is treated as a governed capability rather than an assumed utility, with clear intent that can be enforced and verified across every boundary that matters. Segmentation, firewall policy management, and remote access controls reduce exposure and contain impact only when exceptions are owned, time-bounded, and continuously reconciled against observed behavior. Visibility and logging turn those controls into operational leverage by making enforcement decisions traceable and investigations repeatable, especially when identity context and boundary telemetry can be correlated into a coherent timeline. AI-assisted analysis can accelerate pattern recognition and alert enrichment, but it must remain evidence-backed, auditable, and bounded by human approval, so automation does not amplify error or create outages. In hybrid environments, sustaining these outcomes requires consistent definitions, disciplined change practices, and cross-team operating rhythms that prevent policy drift at the seams where attackers most often move and hide.

Recommendations

1) Establish explicit network defense goals that translate business risk into operational outcomes. Define what "controlled connectivity," "measurable visibility," and "resilience under failure" mean in your environment, so teams can implement and verify them consistently. Align ownership and change processes to those goals, so the network does not drift into ad hoc exception handling. Use those goals to drive prioritization when enforcement decisions compete with availability pressures.
2) Treat defensive layers as operational decisions rather than product placements. Assign clear owners for each layer, define how changes are requested and reviewed, and ensure there is a tested rollback path when enforcement disrupts business workflows. Validate that layers reinforce each other by confirming that prevention, detection, and response signals are all supported by the same underlying policy intent. Regularly test that the environment fails in a predictable direction when a layer degrades or telemetry drops.
3) Reduce remote access exposure by minimizing externally reachable entry points and continuously inventorying what is published. Consolidate access paths where possible and remove accidental exposure such as leftover management interfaces or legacy access methods kept without review. Ensure every remote access path has an accountable owner and produces logs that can be tied to identities and systems. Treat unknown or newly exposed services as operational findings that require immediate triage and closure.
4) Strengthen authentication by addressing constraints that create bypasses, not just by enabling MFA. Review enrollment and fallback methods, session persistence, and exception patterns that undermine strong identity binding in practice. Align stronger authentication and tighter session controls to higher-risk access, including administrative paths and sensitive zones. Document and monitor exceptions with time bounds, so constraints do not become permanent weaknesses.

5) Implement segmentation using zone definitions that reflect real business and application boundaries, then enforce them at meaningful control points. Prefer stable, readable zone models over elegant diagrams that require constant exceptions to keep applications running. Treat administrative planes, identity infrastructure, and management interfaces as priority zones that should not be reachable from routine user networks. Use denied traffic and first-time successful paths across zones as high-value signals for investigation and tuning.
6) Run firewall policy management like production operations with disciplined change control and rule lifecycle practices. Require each rule to have clear scope, protocol definition, accountable justification, and a review cadence that supports tightening or removal. Include post-change verification that checks both service functionality and security intent, so changes do not silently expand exposure. Normalize periodic cleanup, so rulebases remain interpretable and audits remain predictable.
7) Standardize logging expectations across network boundaries to preserve traceability during investigations. Ensure timestamps are synchronized, key identifiers are stable, and enforcement decisions include the context needed to interpret them, such as zones and rule identifiers. Preserve original source context through translation and proxy layers, so correlation remains possible even when addresses change. Align retention to realistic investigation timelines, so responders can reconstruct sequences without missing early-stage evidence.
8) Build lateral movement detection around connectivity novelty and identity context rather than relying on payload inspection. Monitor for new paths between zones, bursts of denied connections, unusual protocol use from endpoints, and authentication patterns that suggest credential use outside normal workflows. Tune detection, so it distinguishes legitimate change activity from exploratory behavior by incorporating recent change context and asset role expectations. Use the combination of suspicious connectivity and suspicious authentication as a high-confidence trigger for structured investigation and containment planning.
9) Manage operational change to prevent policy drift by making exceptions visible, owned, and reversible. Time-bound emergency changes through break-glass practices that are logged and automatically flagged for follow-up review. Tie telemetry review to the change process, so unexpected connectivity expansions after updates are investigated rather than normalized. Treat drift as a lifecycle problem, ensuring rules and access paths are periodically reconciled against current business intent.
10) Apply AI-assisted network analysis as decision support with validation and clear human approval boundaries. Use AI to surface patterns, correlate sequences across boundaries, and enrich alerts with identity, zone, policy, and change context to speed triage. Validate AI outputs against raw logs and configuration history to prevent false confidence and to maintain auditability for prioritization decisions. Monitor for model drift, bias, and telemetry gaps, so AI assistance does not amplify noise or mask blind spots.

9

Designing a Defensive Security Architecture

Designing defensive security architecture begins with accepting that modern enterprises are dynamic systems where trust, access, and data movement are constantly changing. Effective architecture turns that reality into predictable, enforceable patterns that integrate endpoint, network, identity, and data controls, so failures are contained rather than catastrophic. It translates business risk into concrete design decisions about trust boundaries, policy enforcement points, telemetry requirements, and recovery behavior, ensuring security outcomes are measurable and repeatable. As automation and AI become part of the defensive toolkit, architecture must also account for new attack surface and governance needs, keeping humans in control of high-impact actions while using machine assistance to improve correlation and speed. Above all, architecture stays relevant only when it remains aligned with operational constraints and business change, so standards, exceptions, and resilience thinking evolve together instead of drifting apart.

Principles of Layered Security in Practice

Layered security is the discipline of assuming every control can fail and designing the environment so that failure does not become catastrophe. In practice, that means building multiple independent opportunities to prevent, detect, and contain attacker behavior as it moves from the outside edge to internal systems and data. The layers are not redundant copies of the same safeguard, but different kinds of friction applied at different points in the workflow. When a credential is phished, strong access control can still block misuse, endpoint policy can still constrain execution, and monitoring can still surface abnormal behavior quickly enough to contain impact. The business value is not theoretical "more security," but measurable reduction in blast radius, dwell time, and operational disruption.

Effective layers start with clean trust boundaries, because ambiguous boundaries create gaps defenders cannot see. A trust boundary is the point where an identity, device, or network segment transitions from less trusted to more trusted, such as internet to VPN, contractor to internal application, or user workstation to privileged admin system. Each boundary deserves explicit controls for authentication strength, device posture, and allowable actions, rather than relying on implicit trust because something is "inside." The more clearly these boundaries are drawn, the more reliably access decisions can be enforced and audited. When boundaries are fuzzy, layered security becomes performative: controls exist, but attackers route around them through inherited trust paths. Table 9.1 illustrates how independent layers work together so that common failures remain bounded and recoverable.

Layered security works best when it is anchored to identity as the primary control plane and treats the network as a transport rather than a permissioning system. Identity-driven access means decisions are based on who is requesting access, from what device, with what assurance, and to which resource, not simply whether the request originates from a particular subnet. That approach makes common failures easier to survive, because a compromised host does not automatically become a trusted host, and a trusted host does not automatically become an

Table 9.1 Layered Security Layers and Practical Failure Containment.

Layer	Primary Defensive Intent	Example Failure It Absorbs	Containment Outcome
Identity and access	Limit misuse of valid credentials	Phished password	Blocks or constrains session scope
Endpoint	Constrain execution and observe behavior	Initial workstation compromise	Prevents privilege spread and flags tampering
Network	Restrict paths and limit lateral movement	Bypassed edge control	Contains movement to approved routes
Data	Limit access and detect abnormal usage	Overbroad access granted	Surfaces unusual reads and reduces exposure
Monitoring and response	Detect correlate and contain quickly	Any single control bypass	Shortens time to containment

administrative host. In operational terms, it pushes teams to formalize privilege levels, separate administrative identities, and ensure strong authentication is required precisely where the consequences of misuse are highest. It also makes telemetry more coherent, because identities, sessions, and authorization outcomes can be correlated across systems.

The practical expression of "defense in depth" is to pair preventative controls with fast, reliable detection and response controls that assume prevention will be bypassed. Preventative controls include strong authentication, least privilege, hardened baselines, and segmentation, but they must be supported by visibility into authentication flows, process execution, and data access. Detection cannot be limited to obvious signatures, because modern intrusions often look like legitimate activity until late in the chain. This is where careful telemetry design matters: logs must be consistent, time-synchronized, and rich enough to reconstruct what happened without guesswork. When layered security is implemented well, a failure at one layer produces high-fidelity signals at another, enabling rapid containment rather than a slow forensic chase.

Operational layering also requires that controls fail safely, not silently, and that the organization knows what "normal" looks like at each layer. Fail-safe behavior means that when a policy cannot be evaluated, the system defaults to a conservative decision aligned with risk, such as requiring step-up verification or denying high-impact actions. In contrast, fail-open designs often arise from convenience, legacy integration pressures, or a desire to reduce user friction, and they turn minor outages into security incidents. Establishing baselines for normal authentication patterns, privileged actions, and sensitive data access gives defenders an anchor for distinguishing drift from attack. Without baselines, teams tend to either tune alerts into irrelevance or accept constant noise as inevitable.

AI and machine learning can strengthen layered security when they are treated as amplifiers of human judgment rather than replacements for it. In mature environments, models can help correlate weak signals across layers, such as unusual device posture combined with atypical access times and novel application behavior, producing prioritized triage rather than scattered alerts. The dependency is data quality: if identity logs are incomplete, endpoint events are inconsistent, or asset context is missing, the model will generate confident answers to poorly posed questions. Human-in-the-loop controls are essential, especially for automated containment actions like disabling accounts or isolating hosts, because false positives can cause business outage and erode trust in the program. Teams should also expect failure modes like drift, where changing user behavior or infrastructure updates degrades model performance, and they should design review and audit trails, so decisions can be explained and challenged.

The final test of layered security is whether handoffs and responsibilities are unambiguous when something breaks. Layers cross organizational seams, including identity teams, network teams, endpoint teams, application owners, and the security operations function, and attackers exploit the gaps between those seams. Good practice is to define ownership for each layer's control intent, telemetry, and response action, so that detection has a clear path to containment and containment has a clear path to recovery. Layered security is also a lifecycle discipline: as systems evolve, layers can thin out through exceptions, legacy dependencies, or unreviewed changes that create new implicit trust. A resilient architecture is one where layers are periodically validated, not just implemented, and where the organization can demonstrate that a single compromised credential, host, or control does not translate into uncontrolled lateral movement or unmanaged data exposure.

Translating Risk into Architecture Decisions

Risk becomes useful to architecture only when it is translated from abstract probability into concrete design pressure on systems, identities, and data flows. Security leaders often discuss risk in business language, while architects make decisions in technical language, and the gap between the two is where defensive intent gets lost. Translating risk means taking a threat scenario and expressing it as a requirement about trust boundaries, access constraints, visibility, and recovery behavior. Instead of "reduce breach likelihood," the architecture question becomes "what happens if a user credential is stolen" or "what is our blast radius if a workstation is compromised." When risk is expressed in operational terms, it naturally guides where to invest in stronger controls and where lighter controls are acceptable. Table 9.2 shows how risk becomes actionable when expressed as specific design questions with observable evidence.

A practical translation starts by identifying what must be protected and why, then mapping how it is actually used. The "what" is usually a mix of sensitive data, business-critical services, privileged control planes, and availability-dependent workflows that cannot tolerate disruption. The "how" includes the real access paths that exist in production, not the idealized diagrams, including vendor access, service accounts, automation pipelines, and emergency break-glass procedures. Risk is often underestimated because teams focus on the primary path and ignore alternate paths that attackers prefer because they are poorly monitored or loosely controlled. Architectural decisions are most defensible when they are grounded in these real usage patterns and the consequences of their compromise.

Once assets and flows are clear, risk translates into placement of trust boundaries and policy enforcement points. Trust boundaries are not only network segmentation lines, but also identity transitions, privilege transitions, and data classification transitions, such as moving from general collaboration systems into financial records or from

Table 9.2 Risk Translation from Scenarios to Concrete Architecture Pressure.

Risk Scenario	Architecture Question	Primary Control Focus	Operational Evidence
Stolen user credential	What stops misuse and limits impact	Privilege separation and access constraints	Authentication context and authorization outcomes
Compromised workstation	What prevents lateral movement	Segmentation and managed access paths	Endpoint execution signals and network attribution
Privilege misuse	How are admin actions constrained and audited	Separate admin identities and controlled elevation	Admin activity logs and session linkage
Legacy system constraint	How is risk contained when controls are weak	Isolation and compensating monitoring	Restricted paths and increased logging around seams
Data exposure pathway	How is abnormal access detected and limited	Approved access routes and behavior visibility	Data access logs showing bulk or unusual patterns

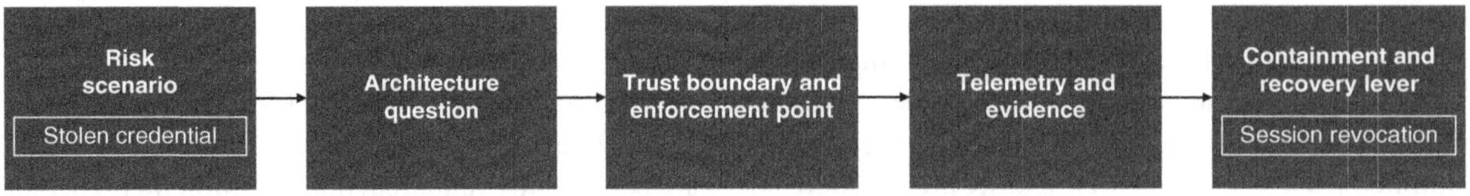

Figure 9.1 Translating Risk into Architecture Decisions.

standard user contexts into administrative tooling. High-risk transitions should demand higher assurance, tighter authorization, and stronger monitoring, while low-risk transitions can be optimized for usability and speed. This is where "least privilege" becomes an architectural property rather than a permissions exercise, because systems are built to make privileged actions rare, explicit, and observable. In well-run environments, the architecture makes the safe path the easiest path, reducing the operational pressure to create exceptions. Figure 9.1 depicts the workflow of converting a risk scenario into enforceable design choices and observable evidence. It supports the idea that risk becomes actionable when expressed as concrete questions tied to boundaries, enforcement points, telemetry, and recovery behavior.

Risk also determines what failure is tolerable and how systems should behave under stress. If the business cannot tolerate downtime for a customer-facing service, the architecture must avoid defensive designs that fail open in ways that enable abuse or fail closed in ways that create outages without a recovery path. Similarly, if the organization cannot tolerate loss of certain data, the architecture must enforce strong controls around exfiltration paths, including egress restrictions, data access monitoring, and segmentation that prevents broad lateral movement. The right design is rarely "maximum security everywhere," but rather a set of explicit tradeoffs where compensating controls are chosen intentionally. When this translation is done well, outages and incidents become bounded events with preplanned recovery options instead of uncontrolled cascades.

Telemetry and detection requirements should be treated as first-class architectural outcomes of risk decisions, not an afterthought delegated to operations. If a risk scenario involves misuse of valid credentials, then logging must capture authentication context, authorization decisions, and session behavior in enough detail to support both detection and investigation. If a scenario involves lateral movement or privilege escalation, endpoint and identity telemetry must be structured so that analysts can connect actions to identities, devices, and time windows without ambiguity. Architecture should also provide places to enforce containment, such as the ability to rapidly revoke tokens, disable accounts, isolate devices, or restrict network paths in a controlled way. Without these capabilities, risk discussions become performative because the organization has no reliable way to respond when the predicted failure mode occurs.

AI and machine learning can help convert risk statements into actionable architectural priorities by accelerating correlation and surfacing hidden dependency chains, but they must be governed carefully. Models can identify patterns like repeated access exceptions, unusual privilege use, or drift in authentication behavior that suggest the architecture is accumulating risk through operational shortcuts. These insights are only reliable when the underlying asset inventory, identity data, and policy events are complete and consistent; otherwise, the model tends to generate false confidence and incorrect prioritization. Human approval boundaries matter most when AI outputs are used to justify architectural changes, because models may overweight recent incidents, underrepresent rare but catastrophic scenarios, or inherit bias from incomplete historical data. To keep this usable, decisions influenced by AI-assisted analysis should be documented with the underlying evidence and assumptions, so the organization can audit why a boundary moved, why a control was strengthened, or why an exception was granted.

The most difficult part of translating risk into architecture is maintaining discipline over time as systems evolve and business demands change. Risk shifts when new vendors are added, when identities are federated, when cloud services introduce new access models, or when automation expands the use of non-human accounts. Every one of those changes can silently create new trust relationships and new exfiltration paths that were not present when the architecture was originally justified. Mature programs treat this as a continuous process: architectural guardrails are defined, exceptions are measurable, and risk acceptance is explicit rather than accidental. The result is an environment where risk does not just exist as a spreadsheet artifact, but actively shapes how systems are built, how access is granted, and how incidents are contained.

Architecture as a Set of Enforceable Patterns

Architecture becomes operational when it is expressed as patterns that can be repeated, verified, and enforced across teams and systems. Diagrams and principles are useful for direction, but they do not prevent drift when product teams move fast, vendors bring their own assumptions, and legacy systems resist change. Enforceable patterns translate architectural intent into concrete implementation expectations, such as how services authenticate, how data is accessed, and how administrative actions are performed. The point is not to constrain innovation, but to ensure that innovation happens inside guardrails that preserve security outcomes. When patterns are clear and enforced, security reviews become faster and more consistent because teams are measuring work against known standards rather than reinventing decisions per project.

A defensible pattern starts with a defined trust boundary and a policy enforcement point that is hard to bypass. The trust boundary might be an identity transition, an application gateway, a network segment, or a privileged administration plane, but it must be explicit and observable. The enforcement point is where the system can reliably decide "allow" or "deny" based on identity, context, and policy, rather than relying on informal conventions like "only IT knows that address." Patterns that depend on implicit trust tend to fail during incidents because they are not measurable and are difficult to validate under pressure. Enforceable patterns also specify the minimum telemetry required at the boundary so that the organization can prove policy was applied and investigate exceptions.

Patterns must include standard approaches to identity and access because identity is the common path through every modern environment. A strong pattern defines how users authenticate, how sessions are established, how authorization decisions are made, and how privileged activity is separated from normal work. It also defines how non-human identities operate, including service accounts and automation workflows, because these identities often have broad permissions and weak oversight. The operational test is whether the organization can revoke access quickly, understand who did what, and prevent privilege from spreading through convenience. When identity patterns are enforceable, least privilege becomes a property of the environment rather than a manual effort that degrades with time.

Segmentation patterns are another area where enforceability matters more than elegance. Segmentation is not merely dividing networks; it is defining which systems are allowed to talk to which other systems and under what conditions, then enforcing those rules in a way that survives change. Good patterns align segments to meaningful risk boundaries such as user endpoints, shared services, production workloads, and privileged administration, rather than arbitrary IP blocks. They also recognize that many environments are hybrid and that connectivity is expressed through routing, security groups, and application-layer permissions simultaneously. A pattern is enforceable when new systems can be placed into the correct zone with predictable connectivity and monitoring, without bespoke firewall exceptions that become permanent.

Secure patterns must account for the full lifecycle: provisioning, change, failure, and recovery. A pattern that only addresses steady-state operation will break the moment a certificate expires, an identity provider has an outage, or a critical patch requires an emergency access path. Enforceable architecture includes preplanned break-glass behavior that is tightly scoped, auditable, and time-bound, so operational continuity does not become an attacker's shortcut. It also includes standards for patching, baseline configuration, and dependency management so that systems do not slowly diverge into unique snowflakes that cannot be defended consistently. The best patterns anticipate how people actually work under stress and provide safe defaults that reduce the need for exceptions.

Telemetry and auditability are what make patterns enforceable at scale, because they allow verification without constant manual review. When patterns define required logs and event semantics, security operations can validate adherence continuously and detect drift early. This is where AI-assisted analysis can provide practical leverage, by clustering systems that look alike, highlighting outliers that violate expected behavior, and correlating policy decisions with incident data to reveal which patterns are actually reducing impact. The dependency is governance: models must be trained on representative, high-quality telemetry and must be evaluated for false positives that would otherwise generate churn and mistrust. AI should inform where to investigate and what to prioritize, while humans retain authority over decisions that could disrupt production systems or materially change access.

Enforcement ultimately requires that patterns are embedded into delivery workflows, not published as static documents. When patterns are implemented as repeatable components, validated configurations, and clear acceptance criteria, teams adopt them because they reduce friction rather than add it. Exceptions still exist, but they become explicit choices with an owner, an expiration, and compensating controls rather than silent architectural debt. Over time, this approach changes the nature of architecture from a set of ideals into a living system of controls that can be measured and improved. The result is not perfect uniformity, but consistent security outcomes that survive organizational growth, technology change, and the inevitable realities of day-to-day operations.

Integrating Controls Across Endpoint, Network, Identity, and Data

Integrated defense is the practice of making endpoint, network, identity, and data controls behave like a single system rather than four separate programs. Attackers do not respect organizational charts, and their most reliable advantage is the gap between teams and telemetry domains. When controls are integrated, each layer reinforces the others by sharing context, enforcing consistent policy, and producing correlated evidence that can survive investigation. This integration is not achieved by buying more tools, but by aligning control intent, defining clean handoffs, and ensuring signals and decisions can be connected to real identities, real devices, and real data. The business payoff is fewer blind spots, faster containment, and less operational disruption during incidents.

Endpoint controls are often the first layer to observe execution and user activity, but they only reach their potential when they are identity-aware and policy-aligned. A compromised workstation should not automatically grant access to high-value applications simply because the network path exists, and endpoint posture should influence what sessions are allowed. Integration means device health, configuration state, and security events are tied to the user session and access decision, so that risky devices face stronger constraints without treating every anomaly as a crisis. It also means administrative activity on endpoints is handled differently from normal user work, with stronger authentication, better auditing, and reduced exposure to phishing and token theft. When endpoint and identity are connected, defenders can answer basic questions quickly, such as whether an alert corresponds to a legitimate user action or an attacker operating under stolen credentials.

Network controls provide containment and path restriction, but integration requires shifting from static assumptions to policy-driven connectivity. In many environments, the network is treated as the primary enforcement layer, yet modern access patterns include cloud services, remote users, and encrypted traffic where traditional inspection is limited. Integration means network segmentation and egress controls are designed around identity and workload roles, not just IP space, and that network telemetry can be attributed to users, devices, and services. It also means that when identity detects an anomalous session, the network layer can participate in containment by restricting paths or limiting exposure without waiting for a manual firewall change. When network policy and identity policy conflict, the attacker gets the benefit of ambiguity, so integrated design insists on consistent decision logic and clear precedence.

Identity controls are the connective tissue that makes endpoint and network decisions meaningful, because identity is how access is granted and abuse is disguised. Integration requires consistent authentication strength, clear privilege separation, and well-defined authorization boundaries for both human and non-human identities.

Service accounts and automation identities must be treated as first-class citizens, with scoped permissions, monitored usage, and controlled credential handling, because attackers often target them to bypass user-focused defenses. Identity systems should also produce decision-grade telemetry, including authentication context, token issuance, policy evaluation outcomes, and administrative changes. When identity is integrated properly, it becomes possible to revoke access rapidly and consistently across applications, endpoints, and data stores, instead of performing a slow, error-prone cleanup across many disconnected systems.

Data controls are where impact becomes real, so integration must ensure data access decisions are aligned with identity context and environment state. Protecting data is not only about encryption and classification; it is about controlling who can access it, from where, and under what conditions, and detecting when normal access becomes abnormal. Integration means sensitive data repositories enforce access paths that require strong identity assurance and are reachable only through approved network routes and managed endpoints. It also means data access logs are rich enough to support detection of suspicious patterns like bulk reads, unusual query behavior, and access from atypical devices or geographies, without relying on brittle content inspection. When data controls are isolated from endpoint and identity context, organizations frequently discover exfiltration only after the fact because the "who" and "how" were not tied to the "what."

AI and machine learning can materially improve cross-domain integration by correlating weak signals that are individually ambiguous but collectively decisive. A model can connect a subtle endpoint anomaly, a slightly unusual authentication pattern, and a shift in data access behavior into a higher-confidence triage candidate, reducing both noise and missed incidents. This only works when telemetry is normalized, time-synchronized, and enriched with consistent identifiers, so events can be joined across domains without manual guesswork. Human-in-the-loop controls remain essential because AI systems can produce false certainty, particularly when data quality degrades, user behavior shifts, or the model is exposed to bias from incomplete histories. For integrated defenses, AI should assist prioritization and investigation while containment actions remain gated by explicit approval rules, especially when those actions could disrupt critical business workflows.

Operationally, integration is sustained through shared playbooks, common vocabulary, and engineering discipline around change management. When an alert fires, teams need predetermined handoffs: what identity actions are taken, what endpoint actions are taken, what network restrictions are applied, and what data access is reviewed, with accountability for each step. Integration also requires that control changes are traceable, because incidents often exploit recent exceptions, rushed migrations, or configuration drift that no one intended to create. If controls are integrated only during incident response, the environment will revert to fragmentation under normal delivery pressure. Integrated control design is therefore a day-to-day operating model where endpoint, network, identity, and data are treated as interdependent layers, measured together, and improved based on observed failure modes rather than assumed coverage.

Designing for Failure: Resilience and Recovery Thinking

Resilient security architecture assumes compromise is possible and designs systems so that compromise is survivable. The goal is not to accept failure, but to shape failure into contained, recoverable events rather than cascading outages or uncontrolled data loss. This mindset changes how teams evaluate controls, because the question becomes what happens after a control is bypassed, not whether a control is theoretically strong. Resilience requires that containment paths exist, that recovery steps are realistic under pressure, and that business-critical services can be restored without amplifying risk. It also requires honesty about dependencies, because the fastest way to turn a manageable incident into a crisis is to discover hidden coupling during response.

Failure-aware design begins by identifying the most damaging and most likely failure modes and ensuring there is a practical way to limit their blast radius. Credential theft, privilege misuse, and endpoint compromise are common starting points for intrusions, and resilient architecture treats each as an input condition rather than an exceptional event. For stolen credentials, the architecture should prevent a single account from becoming a universal key by enforcing privilege separation and limiting where the account can authenticate. For endpoint compromise, the environment should restrict lateral movement through segmentation and enforce that sensitive resources require stronger access conditions than simply being "reachable." For privilege misuse, administrative actions should be observable, time-bound, and difficult to perform from high-risk contexts like general-purpose user workstations.

Resilience also depends on designing systems that degrade safely when controls or dependencies fail. Authentication services can have outages, logging pipelines can drop events, and security enforcement points can become unavailable during network instability or cloud service disruptions. When these failures occur, the environment should not silently relax into permissive behavior that attackers can exploit, nor should it collapse into a state where business operations halt without a controlled fallback. Safe degradation often means defining explicit modes such as requiring step-up verification for high-risk actions, restricting administrative pathways, or limiting access to sensitive data until normal policy evaluation is restored. The architectural requirement is that these modes are planned, tested, and communicated, not invented in the middle of an incident.

Recovery thinking must be engineered into identity, endpoints, and data rather than treated as a separate operational concern. Identity recovery includes the ability to rapidly revoke sessions, rotate credentials, and restore confidence in administrative control without relying on manual, error-prone steps across many systems. Endpoint recovery requires standardized rebuild processes, known-good baselines, and the ability to rejoin devices to the environment without reintroducing compromised state. Data recovery requires that backups are protected from the same access paths used to reach production data, and that restoration can occur without overwriting evidence or enabling reinfection. If recovery is slow or uncertain, organizations often delay decisive containment, which increases dwell time and expands impact.

A resilient architecture also reduces "time to truth," meaning the time it takes to understand what is happening well enough to act confidently. During incidents, defenders need to know which identities are affected, which systems are involved, what data was accessed, and which controls were bypassed, and they need that clarity quickly. This requires robust telemetry that is correlated across domains and preserved through failure, including central logging that can survive partial outages and provide evidence even when endpoints are unstable. It also requires operational discipline around time synchronization and consistent identifiers so that events can be reconstructed without heroic effort. When time to truth is long, teams either take overly conservative actions that create unnecessary outage or overly permissive actions that allow the intrusion to continue.

AI and machine learning can support resilience and recovery by accelerating triage and helping teams choose response actions with an understanding of business impact, but governance is essential. Models can cluster affected systems, highlight likely intrusion paths, and identify anomalous access patterns that suggest which recovery steps should be prioritized. These capabilities depend on reliable asset context, identity telemetry, and change history; without them, AI will produce plausible narratives that collapse under scrutiny. Human-in-the-loop boundaries matter most when AI outputs recommend disruptive actions such as broad account disables, network isolation, or rollback of critical services. Resilient programs treat AI as decision support, require explainability sufficient for audit, and track model performance, so drift does not quietly undermine response quality.

Designing for failure also means practicing recovery as a repeatable operational capability, not an emergency improvisation. The architecture should support controlled isolation of affected segments, staged restoration of services, and validation steps that confirm integrity before returning systems to normal operation. Dependencies must be mapped well enough that recovery does not unintentionally break downstream services or force unsafe shortcuts like reusing compromised credentials to restore access quickly. Over time, incident learnings should feed back into architecture, so recurring failure modes are addressed structurally, not patched with procedural workarounds. When resilience and recovery thinking are embedded into design, security becomes less about avoiding every incident and more about ensuring incidents do not become existential events for the business.

Security Architecture and Operational Reality

Security architecture succeeds or fails on whether it can be operated day after day without heroics. A design can look flawless in a diagram and still collapse under the friction of deadlines, legacy constraints, vendor dependencies, and human behavior. Operational reality is the environment in which controls must be implemented, maintained, monitored, and recovered, often by different teams with competing priorities. The most reliable attacker advantage is not a missing control, but a control that exists only on paper or cannot be executed consistently. When architecture respects operational reality, it becomes a set of decisions that reduce ambiguity, prevent drift, and give defenders repeatable leverage.

The first operational constraint is that systems change constantly, and architecture must assume continuous change rather than periodic refresh cycles. Cloud services introduce new features, application teams ship updates, identities are added and removed, and exceptions accumulate as the fastest path around friction. If architecture is not expressed in enforceable patterns, those changes will slowly erode control intent until the environment is defended by tribal knowledge instead of policy. Operationally, this is why guardrails matter more than one-time reviews: teams need clear defaults, controlled exception processes, and automated checks that detect when reality diverges from design. Architecture that cannot be validated continuously is architecture that will be out of date before it is fully deployed.

The next constraint is that organizations run mixed estates where "modern" and "legacy" coexist, and the weakest integration points often become the primary intrusion paths. Legacy systems may not support strong authentication, modern logging, or granular authorization, and vendors may require access methods that do not align with the desired control model. Operational reality means the architecture must include compensating controls that are feasible, such as restricting access paths, isolating legacy systems, and increasing monitoring around the seams where modern and legacy meet. It also means accepting that some systems cannot be hardened quickly and designing containment boundaries, so their compromise does not become enterprise-wide compromise. A realistic architecture does not pretend legacy disappears; it treats legacy as a risk concentration and designs accordingly.

Identity and access decisions are where architecture most often clashes with operations, because the business experiences security primarily as friction. Strong controls that break workflows will be bypassed, delayed, or quietly weakened through exceptions that later become permanent. Operationally sustainable architecture makes high-assurance access the normal, supported path for high-value actions, while reducing unnecessary barriers for low-risk work. It also separates administrative work from general work in ways that operators can actually follow, such as using distinct admin identities, controlled access methods, and time-bound elevation. When access patterns are practical and consistent, teams spend less time negotiating exceptions and more time improving actual risk posture.

Visibility is another place where operational reality shapes outcomes, because monitoring is constrained by cost, complexity, and the limits of what can be collected reliably. Architecture should not assume perfect telemetry; it should define the minimum evidence required to detect and investigate the failure modes that matter most. That includes identity events that show authentication and authorization outcomes, endpoint signals that show execution and tampering, and data-access signals that reveal unusual usage patterns. The architecture must also account for the operational burden of log volume, retention, and normalization, because unusable data is equivalent to no data. If the monitoring strategy produces constant noise, teams will tune out the very signals needed during an incident.

Incident response is the moment when architecture meets operational reality at full speed, and designs that are not response-aware tend to magnify damage. If containment requires complex manual steps, access to too many consoles, or coordination across too many teams, response will lag and attackers will gain time. Architecture should provide simple, well-tested containment levers such as rapid session revocation, scoped network restriction, and endpoint isolation that can be applied with clear approval boundaries. Recovery must also be designed as a normal capability, with standardized rebuild processes and protected backups, because organizations routinely discover during incidents that their restoration path is either too slow or not trustworthy. A response-aware architecture reduces time to truth and gives responders controlled options that do not require improvisation.

AI and machine learning can help bridge architecture and operational reality by turning noisy, cross-domain telemetry into prioritized, explainable work, but only when used with disciplined governance. Models can surface drift, highlight unusual access paths, and correlate weak signals across identity, endpoint, and data domains, so teams focus on the highest-risk anomalies. The risk is that AI outputs can be treated as authoritative when they are actually sensitive to missing data, changing behavior, and biased training history, producing either false alarms or false reassurance. Operationally, this means AI must be constrained by approval boundaries, tested against known scenarios, and audited so that decisions influenced by models remain accountable. When used responsibly, AI can reduce analyst workload and increase consistency, but it cannot substitute for clear architecture patterns and the human responsibility to validate and act.

Ultimately, operationally real security architecture is the architecture that teams can execute without constant negotiation and that leaders can govern without relying on intuition. It aligns controls with how work actually happens, provides safe defaults that reduce exception pressure, and creates measurable signals that show whether the environment is drifting toward risk. It acknowledges constraints like legacy systems, staffing limits, and uptime requirements, then designs around them with containment and recovery in mind. Over time, this approach produces a stable defensive posture where change is absorbed through patterns rather than chaos. The difference is visible in incidents: instead of scrambling to rediscover how the environment works, responders operate within a design that anticipates failure and supports controlled recovery.

Documenting Architecture Standards and Exceptions

Architecture documentation is only valuable when it drives consistent implementation and reduces ambiguity during delivery and incidents. In operational environments, teams are constantly making small decisions that cumulatively determine security outcomes, and undocumented standards turn those decisions into guesswork. Good documentation translates architectural intent into clear, testable expectations that engineers can follow without a security translator in the room. It also creates a shared language across security, infrastructure, and application teams, which is essential when controls span identity, network, endpoint, and data. The objective is not to produce large documents, but to produce durable guidance that survives turnover, audits, and rapid change.

Standards should be written as enforceable patterns, not aspirational statements, so that teams can reliably determine whether they are compliant. An enforceable standard specifies what must be true, where it applies, and how it can be validated, such as required authentication strength for administrative access, required segmentation boundaries for sensitive systems, or required logging for authorization decisions. Documentation should also define the minimum acceptable controls and the rationale tied to risk, because teams are more likely to comply when they understand the consequence of deviation. Vague standards invite debates at the worst possible time, often late in a project when change is expensive and exceptions feel inevitable. Precise standards shorten review cycles and reduce the number of bespoke solutions that defenders must later learn and monitor.

Architecture documentation must reflect operational reality, which means capturing dependencies, ownership, and handoffs rather than focusing only on static diagrams. A standard is incomplete if it does not clarify who owns its implementation, who monitors it, and who has authority to approve changes when business needs conflict with control intent. It should identify enforcement points, such as where policies are evaluated and where access is granted, because standards that cannot be mapped to an enforcement mechanism tend to decay into best-effort behavior. Documentation should also include the expected telemetry and evidence artifacts that demonstrate compliance, since operational security is measured through observable behavior and logs. When ownership and evidence are defined, security becomes easier to govern because disagreements can be resolved through facts rather than interpretations.

Exceptions are not a failure of architecture; they are an expected outcome of constraints like legacy systems, vendor requirements, and transitional states during migrations. The problem is not that exceptions exist, but that they become invisible, permanent, and unmeasured. An effective exception process documents what is being waived, why the standard cannot be met, what compensating controls will be used, and how the exception will be monitored. It also defines an expiration or review trigger, because exceptions that outlive their business justification quietly become the architecture. When exceptions are treated as time-bound risk decisions rather than informal accommodations, leaders can see where risk is accumulating and allocate resources to reduce it.

Documentation must also make it easy to understand the impact of an exception on other layers, because layered security depends on integrated controls. If a system cannot support strong authentication, the exception record should indicate how segmentation, monitoring, and access path restrictions will compensate. If logging cannot meet the standard, the exception should specify how investigation will be supported, such as additional endpoint telemetry, stricter access constraints, or limited exposure to sensitive data. This cross-layer thinking prevents the common failure where one team grants an exception locally and unintentionally creates a gap that another team assumes is covered. Exception documentation is therefore a control in itself, because it forces explicit decisions about blast radius and detection capability.

AI and machine learning can improve documentation hygiene and exception governance by detecting drift and surfacing inconsistency, but they must be used carefully to avoid false certainty. Models can identify systems that resemble known compliant patterns but deviate in a few key signals, suggesting an undocumented exception or configuration drift. They can also cluster exception types and highlight recurring root causes, such as a specific legacy dependency or a frequent vendor access model, which helps architecture teams prioritize remediation efforts. The risk is that AI may miss issues when telemetry is incomplete or may over-flag benign differences that create review fatigue, so outputs must be treated as triage signals rather than definitive findings. Human approval boundaries remain essential when AI recommendations would change access policy, alter segmentation, or enforce remediation that could disrupt production workflows.

Finally, architecture documentation should be designed to support both steady-state operations and incident response, because incidents stress every ambiguity. During a response, teams need quick answers about expected access paths, privileged control boundaries, and where enforcement and logging occur, and documentation that is overly verbose or outdated will not be used. Standards and exceptions should therefore be maintained as living artifacts with version control, clear change history, and periodic review tied to material changes such as migrations, new identity providers, or major application deployments. When documentation is maintained with discipline, it becomes a force multiplier for both delivery and defense, enabling consistent builds and faster containment. When it is neglected, it becomes theater, and the real architecture exists only in the memories of a few people who are rarely available when they are most needed.

AI in Architecture: Automation Opportunities, New Attack Surface, and Control Requirements

AI can be a practical force multiplier in defensive architecture when it is used to automate high-volume, low-judgment work while preserving human authority over consequential actions. The most immediate opportunities tend to be in correlation, enrichment, and triage, where defenders are otherwise forced to stitch together identity events, endpoint signals, network flows, and data access logs by hand. Architecturally, this means designing data pathways that deliver timely, consistent telemetry into analysis pipelines and ensuring the outputs can drive operational workflows. Done well, AI reduces mean time to understand what is happening, not by magically detecting everything, but by making cross-domain context available at the point of decision. Done poorly, it becomes an expensive noise generator that accelerates wrong conclusions.

Automation opportunities become meaningful only when the architecture makes inputs trustworthy and outputs actionable. AI-assisted triage depends on clean identity resolution, accurate asset context, time-synchronized events, and consistent semantics for policy decisions and security events across systems. If the environment cannot reliably answer "who," "what device," "what resource," and "what action," the model will still produce confident-looking results, but those results will be brittle and hard to validate. Outputs must also be designed for operational use, such as producing explainable risk signals that map to containment levers and investigative steps. When AI is integrated as a workflow component rather than a dashboard, it can reduce queue depth and focus analysts on the events that actually change outcomes.

The same AI capabilities that improve defense also expand the attack surface by creating new interfaces, new dependencies, and new failure modes. Any system that accepts natural language instructions, summarizes logs, or recommends actions becomes a potential target for manipulation, including prompt injection where malicious content attempts to steer the system into unsafe behavior. Architecturally, this risk is amplified when AI systems are connected to privileged functions like account disablement, endpoint isolation, or network policy changes. Attackers can also exploit over-trust in AI outputs, crafting activity that looks "normal enough" to evade probabilistic judgments or to trigger false positives that exhaust responders. The net effect is that AI can shift risk from purely technical bypass to socio-technical exploitation of trust and automation. Table 9.3 summarizes how AI can help defenders while requiring strong data quality governance and human-in-the-loop controls.g

Data is both the fuel and the vulnerability for AI in security architecture, and control requirements must begin with data governance. Telemetry pipelines feeding AI models can be poisoned through crafted events, misleading labels, or manipulated baselines that gradually teach the system that attacker behavior is normal. Sensitive information can leak through prompts, retrieval mechanisms, or training data retention, especially when raw logs contain secrets, tokens, or personal data. Model and prompt configurations can also become targets for theft, tampering, or unauthorized replication, creating both security and intellectual property exposure. A defensive architecture should assume that AI inputs and outputs are sensitive assets that require integrity controls, access controls, and retention discipline just like any other high-value system.

Human-in-the-loop controls are the boundary that keeps automation from becoming automated harm, and the architecture must enforce those boundaries rather than relying on operator judgment alone. High-impact actions

Table 9.3 AI Integration Requirements in Defensive Architecture.

AI Use Case	Telemetry Dependency	Human Approval Boundary	Key Failure Mode	Audit Expectation
AI-assisted triage and prioritization	Time-synchronized enriched events	Analyst validates before action	False confidence from missing context	Record inputs rationale and outcome
Cross domain correlation	Consistent identity device and resource identifiers	Responder approves containment steps	Drift as behavior changes over time	Versioned logic and traceable joins
Automation recommendations	Decision grade identity and endpoint telemetry	Supervisor approval for disruptive changes	Bias from incomplete history	Document recommendation and final decision
Response acceleration	Reliable asset context and change history	Gate account disables and isolation actions	Over containment causing outage	Log who approved and when executed
Anomaly surfacing for drift detection	Baselines from normalized telemetry	Engineer confirms remediation plan	Over flagging benign differences	Track alerts to remediation and exceptions

should require explicit approval steps, defined escalation paths, and clear criteria for when automation is permitted versus when it must stop and ask. This is especially important for containment actions that can disrupt revenue-generating systems or lock out critical staff, because a single incorrect automated decision can create an outage that rivals an attack in business impact. Approval boundaries should be paired with guardrails that limit what AI can do, such as scoping it to recommendations, scoped remediation, or time-bound restrictions rather than irreversible changes. In practice, this ensures AI accelerates response without becoming a single point of failure.

Architectural control requirements also include auditability, because AI-driven decisions must be explainable enough to support incident review, accountability, and regulatory scrutiny. The environment should log not only the underlying security events, but also the AI inputs, the model or rule version used, the rationale signals produced, and the human decisions taken in response. This creates a chain of custody for decisions that otherwise devolve into "the system said so," which is operationally unacceptable during post-incident learning or dispute. It also enables performance monitoring, so teams can detect drift, degradation, or unexpected bias as the environment and attacker behavior change. Without an auditable trail, organizations either over-trust AI and take unsafe actions or under-trust it and waste the potential benefits.

Finally, AI integration must be designed as part of resilience and recovery rather than an always-on dependency that collapses under stress. During incidents, data pipelines may be incomplete, systems may be isolated, and normal behavior may be disrupted, which can cause models to misfire precisely when accuracy matters most. A resilient architecture defines fallback modes where analysts can operate with reduced automation, where critical decisions do not depend on an unavailable model, and where AI outputs are clearly marked when confidence is degraded due to missing inputs. It also limits the blast radius of AI failure by constraining privileges, segmenting AI infrastructure, and protecting service credentials and data stores from lateral movement. When these controls are in place, AI becomes a governed capability that improves defensive speed without creating a fragile new dependency that attackers can target or outages can disable.

Keeping Architecture Aligned with Business Change

Security architecture drifts when the business changes faster than the controls that shape technology decisions. Mergers, new product lines, cloud migrations, outsourcing, remote work, and accelerated delivery cycles all change the enterprise attack surface, often in ways that are not visible to security until after new access paths are already in production. Alignment is not achieved by slowing the business down, but by designing architecture standards that can absorb change while preserving core outcomes like bounded trust, least privilege, and detectable behavior. When architecture keeps pace, security becomes an enabler that reduces surprises and stabilizes delivery. When it lags, the organization accumulates hidden risk through exceptions, one-off integrations, and inconsistent identity and data handling.

The most reliable way to stay aligned is to treat architecture as a living set of enforceable patterns that are embedded into delivery workflows. Business change typically arrives as projects, migrations, and vendor decisions, so patterns must be available as defaults that teams can apply quickly without negotiating fundamentals each time. This includes standard access models, standard segmentation expectations, standard logging requirements, and standard recovery behavior for critical services. The pattern approach reduces the cognitive overhead of security, because engineers reuse known-safe designs rather than improvising under deadline pressure. When patterns are integrated into the way work is delivered, security reviews shift from subjective debate to objective verification.

Alignment also requires maintaining current visibility into what exists, because architecture decisions are only as good as the asset and dependency picture they are based on. Business change often creates shadow integrations, duplicate identity stores, new data repositories, and informal vendor access routes that bypass intended boundaries. Keeping up means continuously reconciling inventory across endpoints, identities, applications, and data flows, and treating discrepancies as operational issues rather than tolerable noise. This is where telemetry becomes more than detection; it becomes architectural feedback about where the environment is evolving. Without that feedback loop, the organization will believe it has one architecture while operating another.

Identity is usually the first pressure point during business change because new initiatives bring new users, new partners, and new systems that need access quickly. Alignment requires that identity standards are strong enough to handle rapid onboarding without resorting to shared accounts, unmanaged service identities, or permanently elevated roles. It also requires predictable privilege boundaries for administrative work, because business change tends to increase the number of people who need "temporary" elevated access that becomes permanent when no removal mechanism exists. If identity patterns are not scalable and operationally convenient, teams will create local workarounds that fragment authorization and weaken auditability. The result is a security posture that looks controlled on paper but cannot prove who had access to what and when it mattered.

Data movement is another area where business change creates architectural misalignment, especially when new analytics, automation, or AI initiatives demand broad data access. New pipelines often bypass existing controls, replicate sensitive data into new stores, or expand access to roles that were not previously exposed to that information. Alignment requires that data access patterns are standardized, that sensitive repositories remain reachable only through managed access paths, and that monitoring can detect abnormal usage without depending on ad hoc queries during incidents. It also requires that data governance keeps pace with new uses, so teams know what they are handling and can apply consistent protection expectations. When data architecture evolves without security alignment, exfiltration risk increases quietly because the number of effective "exit doors" grows.

AI and machine learning can assist alignment by identifying drift and predicting where architecture standards are being bypassed, but they must be treated as decision support rather than truth. Models can flag unusual access routes, detect emerging clusters of exceptions, and correlate changes in telemetry patterns with new business initiatives that are altering behavior. This capability depends on high-quality change signals and consistent identifiers across systems; otherwise, the model will confuse normal transformation with compromise or miss real divergence entirely. Human governance is critical because business change often creates legitimate anomalies, and automated enforcement based on AI outputs can disrupt operations if it acts on incomplete context. Used responsibly, AI can reduce the time between business change and architectural adaptation by surfacing where reality is moving.

Sustained alignment is ultimately a governance and operating model problem, not a documentation problem. Architecture standards need clear ownership, exception handling that is time-bound and measurable, and review triggers tied to material changes like acquisitions, major vendor onboarding, identity platform changes, and critical application migrations. Teams also need a cadence of validation, where key patterns are tested against reality through evidence and incident learnings rather than assumed to be working. When architecture is governed this way, business change becomes a driver for incremental improvement rather than a source of uncontrolled drift. The organization stays defensible not because it avoids change, but because the architecture is designed to adapt without sacrificing control integrity.

Conclusion

A defensible security architecture is ultimately measured by how well it holds up under pressure, when controls are bypassed, dependencies fail, and teams must act quickly with incomplete information. Layered security works when the layers are genuinely independent, integrated through shared context, and expressed as enforceable patterns that make secure behavior the default rather than an exception. Translating risk into architecture decisions keeps investment focused on blast radius reduction, credible containment levers, and telemetry that supports fast, confident action rather than retrospective reconstruction. As AI becomes embedded in defensive workflows, its value depends on disciplined data governance, human approval boundaries, and auditability that preserves accountability while improving speed and consistency. When standards and exceptions are documented as living operational artifacts and kept aligned with business change, architecture becomes a stabilizing force that enables growth without quietly expanding exposure. The result is not an environment that never fails, but one that fails in predictable ways, recovers with control, and improves with every change and incident rather than drifting into fragility.

Recommendations

1) Treat layered security as a deliberate design discipline rather than a checklist. Ensure each layer provides an independent opportunity to prevent, detect, or contain attacker behavior so that any single control failure is survivable. Validate that layers are not redundant copies of the same safeguard and that they meaningfully reduce blast radius and dwell time. Require evidence that containment and recovery can still function when a layer is bypassed.
2) Define and enforce clear trust boundaries across identity, network, endpoint, and data paths. Document where trust transitions occur and ensure each transition has explicit authentication, authorization, and monitoring expectations. Eliminate ambiguous "inside equals trusted" assumptions by anchoring access decisions to identity and context. Make boundary enforcement observable, so drift can be detected early.
3) Translate top-risk scenarios into specific architectural requirements and engineering acceptance criteria. Convert abstract risk statements into concrete decisions about privilege separation, segmentation, enforcement points, and recovery behavior. Use real production access paths, including vendors and automation identities, as the basis for design choices. Keep tradeoffs explicit, so compensating controls are intentional rather than accidental.
4) Standardize architecture as enforceable patterns that teams can reuse consistently. Express standards as measurable expectations that specify what must be true, where it applies, and how it is validated. Embed the safe path into normal delivery workflows, so engineering teams adopt it by default rather than through negotiation. Use patterns to minimize bespoke implementations that are difficult to monitor and defend.
5) Integrate endpoint controls with identity context to prevent a compromised device from becoming a trusted access broker. Ensure device posture and endpoint signals can influence access decisions and investigative prioritization. Separate administrative activity from normal user work, so privileged actions are harder to perform from high-risk contexts. Maintain audit-quality linkage between user sessions, devices, and high-impact actions.
6) Align segmentation and network policy to meaningful risk boundaries and containment needs. Design connectivity rules that restrict lateral movement and limit exposure of sensitive systems to only required paths. Ensure network telemetry can be attributed to identities, devices, and services, so investigation is not guesswork. Maintain containment levers that can be applied quickly without complex, error-prone change processes.
7) Treat identity systems as the control plane and ensure privileged actions are rare, explicit, and observable. Enforce privilege separation with distinct administrative identities and controlled methods for elevation. Apply clear authorization boundaries for both human and non-human identities, and ensure rapid revocation is feasible during incidents. Require decision-grade identity telemetry that captures authentication context and authorization outcomes.
8) Engineer data protections around access paths and behavior visibility, not just storage controls. Restrict sensitive repositories to approved access routes that depend on strong identity assurance and managed endpoints. Ensure data access logging is sufficient to detect abnormal patterns such as bulk reads or unusual usage without relying on ad hoc investigation. Design data controls, so exfiltration becomes difficult to perform quietly and easier to validate during response.

9) Use AI-assisted triage and correlation only where inputs are trustworthy and actions are governed. Ensure telemetry is consistent, time-synchronized, and enriched with reliable identifiers before relying on model-driven prioritization. Establish human approval boundaries for disruptive actions and require audit trails for AI-influenced decisions. Monitor for failure modes such as drift, bias, and false confidence, so automation strengthens operations rather than undermining them.
10) Document standards and exceptions as living operational artifacts with ownership, evidence, and expiration. Record what is being waived, why it cannot be met, what compensating controls apply, and how the exception will be monitored. Tie reviews to business change, so architecture adapts without silently expanding exposure through permanent exceptions. Use documented handoffs and containment options to reduce ambiguity during incidents and accelerate controlled recovery.

Part III

Identity, Access, and Data Protection

10

Identity and Access Management Foundations

Identity and access management is the foundation that determines who and what can interact with systems, data, and operational capabilities across the enterprise. As environments become more distributed and software-driven, identity increasingly functions as the control plane that governs access decisions, session behavior, and the practical blast radius of compromise. The distinction between authentication and authorization is central to operational security because proving an identity is not the same as constraining what that identity can do once it is admitted. When role design, least privilege, entitlement management, behavioral detection, and AI-assisted risk scoring are treated as daily operational disciplines with clear human approval boundaries, IAM becomes both easier to run and harder for adversaries to exploit.

Why Identity Is the New Control Plane

Modern environments are no longer organized around a clean network edge, and that reality changes what "control" looks like in practice. Workloads live in multiple clouds, users move between managed and unmanaged devices, and business applications are consumed as services rather than hosted on a single corporate network. In that model, the most consistent point of leverage is the identity presenting itself to each system at the moment of access. When identity becomes the common denominator, it effectively becomes the control plane that determines who can do what, from where, and under which conditions.

Identity becomes the control plane because it sits at the intersection of authentication, authorization, and session establishment. Authentication proves the subject is who it claims to be, while authorization decides what the subject is allowed to do once admitted. The session is where those decisions become real, because tokens, cookies, and other session artifacts translate "approved access" into ongoing capability. Attackers understand this and routinely pursue credentials, token theft, and session hijacking because these shortcuts often bypass traditional perimeter or endpoint assumptions. When identity is well governed, it can constrain blast radius even when a device is compromised; when it is not, compromise becomes scalable. Figure 10.1 shows how identity-driven control is realized through authentication, authorization, and sessions, with governance and telemetry reinforcing the entire access path. It reinforces why identity remains the most consistent enforcement point in distributed environments.

The "who" in access control is no longer limited to employees with laptops, and that expansion is a primary reason identity now governs the environment. Contractors, partners, and vendors require access paths that are difficult to normalize with static network rules, and business pressure often pushes teams toward convenience. In parallel, machine identities—service accounts, application identities, and automation credentials—frequently outnumber human users and operate continuously. These non-human identities are powerful because they can act at machine speed, and they are risky because they are easy to over-permission and hard to monitor with the

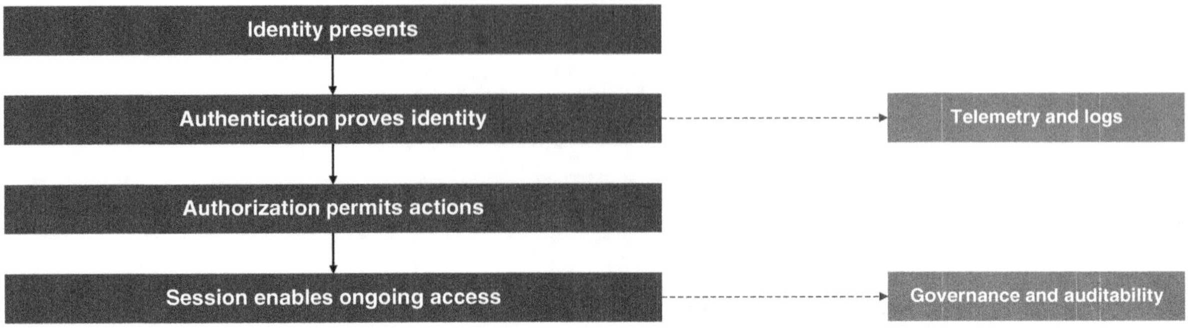

Figure 10.1 Identity as the Control Plane for Access Decisions.

same rigor as human logins. When identity is treated as the control plane, both human and machine access are governed through the same discipline: explicit permissions, traceable approvals, and verifiable signals.

A practical identity control plane depends on strong, consistent identity sources and the ability to enforce policy at the moment of access. Centralized identity providers, directory services, and federated authentication patterns are valuable primarily because they standardize enforcement and logging across applications. Single sign-on reduces password sprawl, but it also concentrates risk if the identity layer is weak or poorly monitored. Multifactor authentication strengthens initial access, yet it must be paired with controls that address token replay and session persistence, or else attackers simply shift to stealing what comes after the login prompt. When the identity layer is the decision point, "access" is not a one-time event; it is a continuously asserted state that must remain defensible.

The control plane concept also reframes how defenders think about privileged access, because privilege is where identity decisions translate into enterprise-wide impact. Administrative roles, delegated rights, and powerful groups are often created for operational convenience and then quietly accumulate permissions over time. Privileged access management is not only about vaulting credentials; it is about ensuring that powerful actions are intentional, time-bounded when possible, and attributable to a specific identity. Standing privilege invites misuse and makes incident containment harder because the difference between normal operations and adversary activity becomes ambiguous. Treating identity as the control plane means building friction deliberately around privilege while keeping routine access predictable and supportable.

Because identity decisions happen constantly, telemetry is what makes the control plane observable and defensible. Authentication logs, authorization failures, token issuance events, session creation, and privilege assignments are the raw material for detecting misuse and diagnosing incidents. Correlating identity events with device posture, geolocation anomalies, impossible travel patterns, and unusual access paths can reveal account takeover and misuse earlier than endpoint alerts alone. This is also where AI and machine learning can provide operational lift: anomaly models can surface subtle deviations in login behavior, session duration, and resource access that would be lost in high-volume logs. The value is highest when those models are grounded in clean identity telemetry and constrained by clear escalation rules, rather than treated as a substitute for access design.

AI-enabled analytics introduce their own failure modes, and identity is one of the places where false confidence can be most damaging. A model that learns "normal" from already-compromised behavior will drift into accepting attacker activity as baseline, and a model trained on incomplete logs will generate both blind spots and noise. Bias can surface when different user populations have different access patterns, leading to uneven alerting or excessive friction for specific teams, geographies, or job functions. Data leakage is also a real concern: identity logs can contain sensitive attributes, and any system that processes them must be governed with tight access controls and auditability. Human-in-the-loop controls matter here, with explicit boundaries on what can be automated versus what requires approval, especially when actions affect account lockout, privilege changes, or conditional access decisions.

Ultimately, identity as the control plane is less about philosophy and more about operational consequence. Incident response increasingly begins with questions like which identities were used, what tokens were issued, what privileges were exercised, and whether access paths were legitimate or coerced. Recovery often hinges on revoking sessions, rotating secrets, tightening policies, and rebuilding trust in the identity layer before business operations can safely resume. When identity is strong, the organization can make access decisions confidently and explain them after the fact; when identity is weak, every system becomes a potential side door and every investigation becomes a debate about whether the logs can be trusted. Blue teams that treat identity as the primary control plane build an environment that is easier to defend, easier to audit, and harder to exploit at scale.

Authentication Versus Authorization in Operations

Authentication answers the question of who or what is requesting access, and operational teams must treat it as the starting point rather than the security outcome. A successful login only establishes that a set of presented factors matched what the identity system expects, which is fundamentally a proof event, not a permission grant. In day-to-day operations, defenders need to remember that attackers are often excellent at producing valid proofs through stolen credentials, reused passwords, social engineering, or intercepted one-time codes. The practical implication is that authentication strength reduces risk, but it does not define what the identity can do once admitted. Treating authentication as "security achieved" is one of the most common reasons environments drift into preventable breach conditions.

Authorization determines what the authenticated identity is allowed to do, and it is where business intent gets translated into enforceable constraints. Authorization decisions are expressed through roles, group memberships, policies, and entitlements, and they apply to both human and non-human identities. In operations, authorization is the control that shapes blast radius: the difference between a compromised user account and a compromised administrator account is almost entirely authorization. When authorization is overly broad, every successful authentication becomes a potentially high-impact event. When authorization is too narrow or brittle, teams work around it with shared accounts, shadow access paths, or ad hoc exceptions that ultimately weaken control.

A key operational distinction is that authentication is often centralized while authorization is frequently distributed, and that mismatch creates real-world governance problems. Many organizations have a single identity provider that handles logins, but dozens or hundreds of applications each with their own role models and permission semantics. That distribution leads to inconsistent access patterns, orphaned entitlements, and unclear ownership for who can approve or revoke access. It also increases the likelihood that high-risk privileges persist simply because no one has full visibility into where authorization is defined. Effective IAM operations recognize that centralizing authentication without taming distributed authorization only solves half the problem.

Sessions are where authentication and authorization meet, and operational reality lives in the mechanics of tokens and session state. Most modern systems issue an access token or session cookie after authentication, and that artifact becomes the portable proof that allows calls to applications and APIs. If an attacker steals a token, they may bypass repeated authentication challenges entirely, which is why token theft and session hijacking are such high-return tactics. Authorization is typically enforced on each request using the claims in the token and the application's policy evaluation, which means mistakes in token scoping or claim design can turn a narrow permission set into something far broader. Operational teams should treat session management as part of authorization control, not merely an authentication afterthought.

In production environments, the difference between "logged in" and "allowed" becomes most visible during incidents and access reviews. During an investigation, a responder needs to know whether observed behavior is consistent with the account's entitlements, or whether the account is performing actions it should not be able to perform. That requires understanding both the authentication path that established the session and the authorization context that enabled specific actions. Access reviews that focus only on whether users exist and can log in miss the more important question of what those users can do across systems. In mature operations, authorization reviews are tied to business roles and operational needs, and revocation is treated as routine hygiene rather than a disruptive event.

Machine identities make the authentication versus authorization distinction even more operationally important because they rarely authenticate in the way humans do. Service accounts, workload identities, and automation credentials typically rely on long-lived secrets, certificates, or issued tokens that are used non-interactively. That makes authentication events less frequent and less obvious, while authorization risk can be extreme because machine identities often have broad access to data stores, messaging systems, and deployment pipelines. If a machine identity is over-permissioned, compromise can produce rapid, automated damage that is difficult to contain. Operationally, this is why least privilege and tightly scoped entitlements matter more for machine identities than almost anywhere else in the environment.

AI and machine learning can support operational clarity here, but only when the underlying identity and entitlement data is reliable and the decision boundaries are explicit. Models can help identify anomalous authorization usage, such as a user suddenly invoking rarely used administrative APIs, accessing unfamiliar datasets, or performing privilege-like actions outside normal patterns. They can also assist in entitlement hygiene by flagging unused permissions, detecting drift in role definitions, and highlighting access paths that no longer align with job functions. The failure mode is allowing models to become de facto decision-makers for access without guardrails, especially when training data reflects historical over-permissioning or incomplete logs. Human approval boundaries should be firm for any action that changes entitlements, disables accounts, or alters conditional access rules, and model outputs should be auditable as recommendations rather than silent automation.

Operational excellence comes from designing authentication and authorization to complement each other instead of compensating for each other's weaknesses. Strong authentication reduces the probability of account takeover, but if authorization is sloppy, the impact of compromise remains high. Tight authorization limits blast radius, but if authentication is weak, the environment will be constantly tested by opportunistic attacks and credential abuse. The best-run programs treat authentication controls as a gate and authorization controls as a set of internal compartments, with session controls ensuring the gate and compartments remain enforceable over time. When teams get this right, investigations become faster, access changes become safer, and the business gains confidence that "access granted" actually reflects intent rather than accident.

Role-Based Access Control and Organizational Fit

Role-based access control is effective when it reflects how work is actually performed, not how an org chart looks on paper. The premise is simple: access is granted to roles that represent job functions, and people inherit permissions by being assigned to those roles. In operations, the value is consistency, because onboarding, transfers, and offboarding become predictable changes to role membership rather than a long list of manual entitlements. The risk is that roles are often created as a one-time project artifact and then left to decay as the organization evolves. When roles fall out of sync with real workflows, teams either over-permission "just to make it work" or create exceptions that undermine the role model.

Organizational fit starts with choosing the right granularity for roles, because too few roles force broad access while too many roles create administrative overload. If roles are overly coarse, they become permission buckets that accumulate risk, especially when multiple teams share the same generalized role. If roles are overly fine-grained, they become brittle and hard to maintain, and administrators end up creating quick fixes that bypass the intended design. A practical balance is to align roles to stable job functions and to separate baseline access from elevated or specialized capabilities. The goal is that a role assignment should be meaningful and durable, not a temporary shortcut to solve an urgent ticket.

RBAC also fits differently depending on whether access needs are stable or dynamic, and operations must account for both. Many business systems have relatively stable access patterns, where job function strongly predicts what someone should be able to do day to day. Other environments, especially those involving engineering, data platforms, or incident response, have situational needs that vary by project, incident, or sprint. In those cases, RBAC still provides a baseline, but operational teams need mechanisms for time-bounded elevation and tightly scoped exceptions that do not become permanent. When those mechanisms are absent, RBAC gets blamed for being "too rigid," when the real issue is that the organization never designed for controlled variability.

Role ownership is an operational requirement, not a documentation detail, because roles represent business intent that must be maintained over time. Security teams can define standards and guardrails, but the business has to own what access a role implies and why it is needed. Without clear owners, roles gradually expand as people request one-off additions, and nobody feels accountable for removing permissions later. Access reviews become performative because reviewers do not understand what the role is supposed to enable, only that it has always existed. Healthy RBAC programs tie each role to an owner who can approve changes, validate periodic reviews, and confirm that the role still matches real work.

RBAC has to fit both people and machine identities, and the latter often exposes weak role design quickly. Machine identities typically need narrow access to specific services, data stores, or deployment actions, but they are frequently assigned broad roles because it is convenient and hard to model precise needs. That convenience becomes a liability when automation credentials are compromised, because machines can act continuously and at scale. A role model that distinguishes between human job functions and machine service functions reduces ambiguity and improves incident containment. Operationally, it also makes it easier to rotate secrets, revoke access, and validate that automation is doing only what it was designed to do.

AI and machine learning can improve RBAC fit by helping teams see where the role model matches reality and where it does not. Usage analytics can identify permissions that are never exercised by members of a role, which is often a signal of accumulated access drift. Behavior analysis can surface when role members consistently need additional permissions, indicating that the role definition is incomplete or that work patterns have changed. The failure mode is treating model output as definitive truth, because access usage is not always visible in logs and "unused" does not always mean "unnecessary," especially for infrequent but critical actions. The right operational approach is to use AI-assisted findings as prompts for human review, with clear thresholds for confidence and documented rationale when roles are adjusted.

Over time, organizations also need to manage role sprawl, where the number of roles grows faster than the ability to govern them. Role sprawl often begins with good intentions, such as creating roles for each team or project, but it becomes unmanageable when roles overlap and no one remembers why they exist. This is where consistency in naming, lifecycle management, and retirement matters, even if the mechanics vary across systems. Roles should be treated as governed objects with creation criteria, change control, periodic review, and deprecation when business needs change. When the organization operationalizes role lifecycle, RBAC remains an asset rather than an anchor dragging down agility.

A well-fit RBAC model supports both security and speed, which is why it remains a foundational IAM pattern even as environments become more complex. When roles map cleanly to job functions, access requests become straightforward and approvals become defensible, because they are tied to established business intent. When exceptions are handled through controlled, time-bounded paths, RBAC stays intact while still accommodating real-world urgency. When telemetry and reviews are used to keep roles aligned with actual work, the model remains current instead of fossilized. In operations, that combination is what turns RBAC from a policy concept into a durable, enforceable way of running access at scale.

Least Privilege as an Ongoing Process

Least privilege is often described as a principle, but in operations it behaves more like a maintenance program. The goal is straightforward: identities should have only the access required to perform their duties, and nothing more. The challenge is that duties change continuously, systems evolve, and access tends to accumulate unless someone actively removes it. If least privilege is treated as a one-time cleanup project, it will revert within months as new applications appear, teams reorganize, and exceptions become permanent. Operational maturity shows up when least privilege is built into everyday workflows, not reserved for audit season.

A useful way to think about least privilege is as a balance between business continuity and controllable blast radius. Over-permissioning is attractive because it reduces friction and prevents support tickets, but it silently expands the impact of any compromise. Under-permissioning creates constant interruptions that push staff toward unsafe workarounds, like shared accounts, copied credentials, or informal access paths that bypass review. The operational target is not "minimal access at all times," but "appropriate access with deliberate elevation when needed." Teams that hit this target make privilege a managed resource rather than an unmanaged convenience.

Least privilege becomes real when it is expressed through how access is granted, how it is elevated, and how it is revoked. Baseline access should be role-aligned and predictable, because predictable access is easier to govern and easier to audit. Elevated access should be explicit, time-bounded when possible, and traceable back to a request and an approver, because privilege without intent is indistinguishable from misuse. Revocation should be routine and automatic for common events like transfers and terminations, because manual cleanup does not scale and is where stale permissions persist. When these mechanics are consistent, least privilege stops being an aspiration and becomes a set of repeatable operational behaviors. Table 10.1 connects common least privilege warning signs to concrete operational actions that reduce long-term entitlement drift.

Privilege creep is the default failure mode, and it happens through small, rational decisions that compound over time. A user needs a permission "just for this week," then the ticket closes and the access remains for years. A team temporarily grants broad access to meet a deadline, then never returns to tighten it because the risk is invisible when nothing breaks. A new system is integrated quickly by copying an existing high-permission role, then that pattern gets reused because it is easy and appears to work. Least privilege as a process means designing for these realities by assuming access will expand unless the system makes contraction the easiest path.

Machine identities often make least privilege harder and more important at the same time, because they tend to be powerful and poorly understood. Service accounts and workload identities frequently end up with wide permissions to avoid breaking automation, and those permissions are rarely reviewed with the same discipline as human access. When a machine identity is compromised, it can be used to move laterally across services, extract data, or modify infrastructure at speed, often without the interactive signals defenders rely on. Operationally, least privilege for machine identities requires tight scoping, clear ownership, and strong rotation and revocation practices for the secrets or tokens they rely on. Treating machine access as "plumbing" instead of as identity is one of the quickest paths to systemic exposure.

Table 10.1 Least Privilege Process Signals and Operational Responses.

Process Signal	What It Indicates	Operational Response
Temporary access persists	Privilege creep and stale entitlements	Expire access and require reapproval
Transfers retain prior access	Accumulated permissions across roles	Remove old role access and rebaseline
Broad machine entitlements	Automation overreach and high blast radius	Narrow scope and enforce ownership
Frequent exceptions	Role model mismatch	Adjust roles and reduce direct entitlements
Revocation delays	Offboarding gaps and exposure window	Automate disablement and verify completion

Telemetry is what turns least privilege from a static permission model into a living control, because it provides evidence of what access is actually used. Authentication and authorization logs, API call histories, and application audit trails can show where permissions are exercised and where they are merely present. This is where AI and machine learning can help operational teams scale: models can identify unused privileges, detect sudden changes in privilege usage, and surface anomalous access patterns that suggest misuse or compromised accounts. The value comes from prioritization, because a model can point reviewers to the highest-risk entitlements and the most suspicious changes rather than forcing teams to sift through everything manually. The failure mode is assuming the model is complete, since logging gaps, inconsistent application telemetry, and rare-but-legitimate actions can all cause misleading conclusions.

Human-in-the-loop controls matter because least privilege decisions often require business context that logs cannot provide. Removing a permission that appears unused may still break a quarterly process, an emergency duty rotation, or a rarely executed but critical recovery workflow. Conversely, leaving broad access in place because "it might be needed" is how risk becomes permanent. Operationally, the right posture is to require explicit justification for elevated or broad entitlements and to document why exceptions exist, who approved them, and when they will be reviewed again. When AI-assisted recommendations are used, they should be treated as evidence to support a decision, not as an automated authorization engine.

Least privilege also depends on designing privileged access as an experience that staff can actually follow during real work. If emergency changes require a slow and bureaucratic process, teams will route around it during outages and incidents, exactly when risk is highest. If elevation is simple but untracked, it becomes invisible privilege and defeats accountability. A practical operational design makes elevation fast, scoped, and attributable, with session boundaries and logging that tie privileged actions to a person or service identity. When the system makes the safe path the easy path, least privilege becomes sustainable under pressure.

Over time, least privilege becomes a feedback loop between access design, operational change management, and incident learning. Every incident, near miss, or suspicious access pattern should inform whether entitlements are too broad, whether elevation workflows are being misused, and whether revocation is happening reliably. Every major organizational change should trigger review of which roles exist, what they imply, and whether privileges have quietly migrated into baseline access. Every new application onboarding should include an access model that anticipates future change rather than freezing today's assumptions into permanent permissions. When least privilege is treated as ongoing process work, it steadily reduces systemic risk without turning access management into a productivity tax.

Managing Entitlements and Permission Sprawl

Entitlements are the concrete permissions an identity holds across applications, platforms, and infrastructure, and managing them is where access control either stays disciplined or collapses under entropy. In mature environments, entitlements are not treated as a byproduct of account creation; they are treated as governed assets with clear purpose and traceability. Permission sprawl happens when entitlements expand faster than the organization's ability to understand and review them, which is common in fast-moving businesses. New systems appear, integrations multiply, and teams solve short-term problems by granting broad access that is rarely revisited. Over time, the organization loses the ability to answer basic questions about who can access what and why.

Sprawl is amplified by the reality that authorization is distributed and inconsistent, even when authentication is centralized. Each application has its own permission model, its own administrative surface, and its own language for what access means, which makes normalization difficult. An "admin" label in one system may mean read-only configuration access, while in another it means full data export and privileged actions. This inconsistency makes entitlement reviews harder because reviewers cannot rely on naming conventions to understand risk.

Operationally, the first step in managing sprawl is accepting that visibility and standardization require continuous effort, not a single access inventory exercise.

Entitlements accumulate through predictable operational patterns, and the most damaging patterns often look reasonable at the time. Teams grant access directly to individuals because it is faster than aligning a role, then those direct assignments persist through job changes. Administrators copy an existing permission set to onboard a new team quickly, inadvertently propagating legacy privileges that no longer reflect business needs. Temporary project access becomes permanent because nobody owns the follow-up, and the cost of removal is perceived as higher than the invisible risk of leaving it. Permission sprawl is rarely caused by negligence; it is caused by operations optimizing for speed without a compensating mechanism that routinely contracts access.

A practical way to manage sprawl is to establish a stable baseline access model and treat deviations from that baseline as exceptional and reviewable. Role-aligned access provides a governable default, while direct entitlements and special permissions should be explicitly justified and easier to detect. The operational objective is that most access should be explainable by role membership and job function, because that is what scales through onboarding and transfers. When direct entitlements are necessary, they should carry metadata that explains the business reason, the approver, and an expected review point, even if the mechanics differ by platform. Without that context, entitlement reviews become guesswork and tend to default to leaving risky access in place.

Permission sprawl becomes especially dangerous when it intersects with privilege, because high-risk entitlements are often scattered and poorly labeled. Privileged rights can show up in subtle ways such as the ability to create tokens, manage secrets, modify access policies, or administer integrations, not just obvious "administrator" roles. In many environments, the most powerful entitlements are those that allow an identity to grant additional access to itself or others, which creates a compounding risk during compromise. Operational teams need to track these privilege-escalation pathways with special care because they turn a single foothold into broad control. Treating privileged entitlements as a distinct class with tighter review and stronger change control is one of the most reliable ways to reduce systemic exposure.

Machine identities drive entitlement growth differently than human identities, and they are often the blind spot that sustains sprawl. Service accounts and automation identities get entitlements that reflect what an application might need at its maximum, not what it needs in its steady state. Integrations are built under delivery pressure, and broad permissions are granted to avoid breaking workflows, with little incentive to narrow them later. Because machine identities are non-interactive, their permissions can remain unchanged for years while the systems around them evolve, making their entitlements both stale and overpowered. Managing sprawl in modern operations requires treating machine entitlements as first-class access objects with ownership, review cadence, and revocation paths that are as disciplined as human access.

AI and machine learning can help reduce permission sprawl by making entitlement reviews evidence-driven rather than purely manual and political. Models can highlight unused entitlements, detect entitlements that correlate with high-risk outcomes, and surface anomalous access patterns that suggest an entitlement is being misused or has become inappropriate. They can also assist in clustering similar access profiles to identify where roles should exist but do not, or where multiple near-duplicate roles create unnecessary complexity. The operational risk is relying on these outputs without understanding their data dependencies, because incomplete audit logs and inconsistent telemetry can cause both false positives and false negatives. Governance expectations should be clear: model outputs must be explainable enough to support an access decision, and changes to entitlements should remain attributable to a human approver except in narrowly defined, low-risk cases.

Sustained control over entitlements depends on lifecycle discipline: creation, modification, periodic review, and retirement. If entitlements are created freely without criteria, sprawl becomes inevitable, and if they cannot be retired cleanly, organizations end up carrying permissions for systems that no longer exist. Periodic reviews must be scoped to be operationally achievable, focusing on the highest-risk entitlements, the most privileged identities, and the most sensitive resources rather than attempting exhaustive review of everything at once. Changes to entitlements should be logged and auditable, so investigations can reconstruct how access evolved and whether suspicious changes preceded an incident. When entitlement lifecycle is treated as normal operations work, the organization builds a stable mechanism for shrinking risk over time.

Managing permission sprawl is ultimately about restoring and maintaining legibility, because defenders cannot protect what they cannot explain. When entitlements are understandable, ownership is clear, and privilege pathways are controlled, access management becomes faster rather than slower because approvals and removals are based on known patterns. When entitlement data is messy, operations spend time debating what permissions mean, and the default choice becomes to leave access in place to avoid breaking something. A disciplined entitlement program makes the safe choice routine by combining role-aligned baselines, tightly governed exceptions, strong telemetry, and review processes that focus effort where risk concentrates. Over time, that combination reduces both breach impact and operational friction, which is the practical promise of managing entitlements as a core defensive capability.

Integrating Identity into Daily Operations

Identity becomes operationally meaningful when it is treated as part of daily service delivery rather than a separate security function that only shows up during audits or incidents. Access requests, approvals, and changes happen constantly as people join, move between teams, take on new responsibilities, or leave the organization. If identity workflows are slow or unclear, the business will route around them with informal sharing, unmanaged accounts, or direct entitlements that never get reviewed. Integrating identity into daily operations means making access predictable and measurable, with clear handoffs between business owners, IT, and security. When those handoffs are crisp, teams spend less time negotiating access and more time maintaining defensible control.

A practical integration point is onboarding, transfers, and offboarding, because these are high-volume events where mistakes create long-lived risk. Onboarding should produce a consistent baseline of access aligned to job function, without relying on ad hoc tickets that vary by manager. Transfers are where entitlement drift accelerates, because people accumulate access from multiple roles unless prior access is deliberately removed. Offboarding must be treated as an operational control with strict timing, because any delay leaves a window for misuse or credential abuse, especially when accounts have external access paths. When identity is integrated, these lifecycle events are automated where possible and monitored as operational metrics rather than handled as best-effort tasks. Table 10.2 highlights where identity becomes operational control by mapping key access decision points to the evidence defenders should expect to validate.

Identity also needs to be integrated into change management, because access models change whenever systems, teams, or processes change. A new application rollout, a cloud migration, or a restructuring usually triggers new roles, new groups, and new permissions that become permanent quickly. If identity is not part of that planning, teams default to broad access to meet deadlines, and sprawl becomes the long-term cost of short-term speed. Operationally, it matters that access requirements are captured early, role assignments are tested in realistic workflows,

Table 10.2 Identity Control Plane Decision Points and Evidence.

Decision Point	Operational Focus	Primary Evidence
Authentication event	Validate proof strength and outcome	Authentication logs and factor outcomes
Authorization decision	Confirm permitted actions align to role	Role membership and entitlement records
Session establishment	Assess token scope and session continuity	Token issuance and session creation events
Privilege elevation	Ensure intent and traceability	Approval record and privileged assignment logs
Access review cycle	Detect drift and stale permissions	Change history and review attestations

and exceptions are designed to expire rather than linger. When identity is embedded in change processes, access is treated as an engineered component of delivery, not a last-minute configuration task.

Security operations benefit when identity is integrated into detection and triage workflows, because identity context is often the fastest path to understanding risk. Alerts become more actionable when responders can immediately see the identity involved, its normal access patterns, its entitlements, and whether the access attempt aligns with expected behavior. Correlating identity events with device posture, network signals, and application actions reduces the time spent debating whether activity is benign or malicious. This is one area where AI and machine learning can provide real leverage by highlighting anomalies across authentication, session behavior, and authorization usage that humans would not spot quickly at scale. The operational requirement is that AI-assisted signals are backed by reliable telemetry and routed through clear escalation paths, so analysts are not overwhelmed by speculative findings.

Integrating identity into daily operations also means defining what actions are allowed to be automated versus what requires explicit human approval. Automated actions are appropriate for low-risk, well-defined events such as provisioning baseline access for a standardized role, revoking access at termination, or expiring time-bounded permissions. High-impact actions like assigning privileged roles, changing conditional access rules, or disabling authentication factors should have human-in-the-loop controls and documented approvals. AI systems can assist by proposing changes, ranking risk, and summarizing relevant context, but the boundary must be clear, so the organization can explain who decided what and why. Without that boundary, automation becomes a source of irreproducible outcomes and accountability gaps, especially when model drift or incomplete data produces false confidence.

Day-to-day identity integration is also about making identity data usable for both operators and leaders. Operators need fast answers to questions like which accounts are privileged, which entitlements changed recently, and whether an access path is sanctioned or accidental. Leaders need visibility into whether access governance is keeping up with business growth, where exceptions are accumulating, and whether high-risk access is being reduced over time. These views depend on consistent naming, clear ownership of roles and entitlements, and audit-ready logging of access decisions and changes. When identity data is messy, reporting becomes a manual exercise and organizations lose the ability to measure whether their controls are improving or degrading.

Identity integration extends to incident response, because identity actions are often both containment steps and recovery prerequisites. During containment, responders may need to revoke sessions, reset credentials, disable accounts, or remove entitlements to stop ongoing misuse without shutting down business operations unnecessarily. During recovery, teams must re-establish trust by rotating secrets, validating privileged roles, and confirming that access pathways have not been altered to allow persistence. If identity workflows are not practiced in normal operations, these steps become slow and error-prone during an incident, when time pressure is highest. Integrating identity into daily operations ensures the organization can execute these actions quickly, with known dependencies and minimal disruption.

Over the long term, integrating identity into daily operations is what keeps access governance aligned with reality instead of becoming a fragile set of rules that nobody follows. When access processes are consistent, teams stop inventing workarounds, and entitlement sprawl slows because the default path is governed. When identity telemetry is routinely used in triage, investigations become faster and decisions become more defensible. When automation is applied with clear approval boundaries, the organization gains speed without losing accountability. The practical outcome is that identity stops being a specialized concern and becomes a reliable operational layer that supports both security and business execution.

Detecting Misuse Through Access Patterns and Behavioral Signals

Misuse detection starts with the reality that many attacks do not look like malware at first; they look like access. Credentials get phished, tokens get stolen, sessions get hijacked, and legitimate tools are used in illegitimate ways.

In that environment, defenders need to treat identity and access telemetry as primary detection material rather than supplemental context. The goal is not to label every unusual login as an incident, but to recognize when access behavior deviates from what is plausible for a given identity, role, and business process. When teams build this capability well, they reduce dwell time because they can see compromise in the access layer before it becomes an outage or data event.

Access patterns are powerful signals because they reflect intent more directly than many technical indicators. Authentication events show how an identity is proving itself, including factor usage, challenge outcomes, and any step-up requirements that were triggered. Authorization events show what the identity attempted to do, including failures that may indicate probing, privilege testing, or lateral movement attempts. Session behaviors show continuity, such as unusual session duration, token refresh patterns, or activity from multiple locations that do not align with normal user behavior. Detecting misuse requires viewing these as a connected story rather than isolated log lines.

A practical operational baseline begins with identifying the access pathways that matter most and ensuring they produce reliable telemetry. Internet-facing authentication flows, remote access, administrative consoles, and data-heavy applications are common places where misuse shows up early. If these paths do not log consistently, defenders will either miss key signals or be forced into noisy inference. Logging should capture outcomes, context, and identifiers that allow correlation, such as device context where available, source network, and the application or resource being accessed. The purpose is not exhaustive collection for its own sake, but a defensible record of who accessed what, how they authenticated, and what they attempted to do.

Behavioral signals become actionable when they are tied to identity context and business reality. A login at an unusual hour may be normal for a global team, but unusual for a finance role that rarely works overnight. Multiple failed authorization attempts may be expected during troubleshooting, but suspicious when they target privileged actions across multiple systems. A sudden surge in data access may be normal during month-end close, but alarming when it aligns with a new device or a newly issued token. Operational teams improve detection quality when they encode these distinctions into triage playbooks and escalation thresholds, even when the detection logic is supported by analytics rather than hard-coded rules.

AI and machine learning are particularly useful in this space because access telemetry is high-volume and behavior patterns are multi-dimensional. Models can learn typical sequences of actions for a role and flag deviations such as unusual application hopping, rare administrative API usage, or unexpected changes in access cadence. They can also identify subtle anomalies that are difficult to capture with static thresholds, such as a gradual shift in login geography, changes in session persistence, or new combinations of resources accessed together. The operational requirement is that model outputs are explainable enough to support an analyst decision, because "the model says it is risky" is not a defensible basis for containment actions. When models can provide the key contributing signals, analysts can validate plausibility, reduce false positives, and document why actions were taken.

The failure modes of behavioral detection are predictable, and they often come from data quality and shifting baselines rather than from weak analytics. If identity logs are incomplete, delayed, or inconsistent across systems, models and rules will learn an inaccurate picture of normal behavior. If the organization undergoes changes such as remote work shifts, mergers, or new applications, behavior baselines can drift quickly and flood analysts with alerts. Bias can emerge when different teams or geographies have inherently different access patterns, causing some groups to be over-flagged while others remain under-scrutinized. Operationally, teams need feedback loops that tune detections based on real outcomes, and they need guardrails that prevent automated responses from triggering widespread disruption on low-confidence signals.

High-confidence misuse signals often involve combinations rather than single events, and operations should design correlation around those combinations. A successful authentication followed by an unusual privilege assignment, a new token issuance, and access to sensitive datasets is more concerning than any one of those events alone. Repeated authorization failures across multiple administrative endpoints, especially when followed by a success, can indicate privilege probing that found a misconfiguration. Concurrent sessions from distant locations, particularly with token refresh activity, can suggest session theft rather than normal travel. Correlating these patterns requires consistent identifiers and a disciplined approach to mapping events into a timeline that an analyst can reason about quickly.

Human-in-the-loop controls are essential because misuse detection often triggers actions that directly affect business operations. Disabling an account, revoking sessions, forcing re-authentication, or removing entitlements can be appropriate containment steps, but they can also disrupt critical work if executed on weak evidence. Effective operations define approval boundaries and response tiers, such as allowing automated step-up authentication or session revalidation for moderate-risk signals while reserving account lockout or privilege removal for analyst-approved actions. AI can assist by summarizing the evidence, ranking similar historical cases, and generating a clear narrative of what changed, but the decision to take disruptive action should remain attributable. This preserves accountability and reduces the risk that model error becomes an operational outage.

Detecting misuse through access patterns is strongest when it is integrated with incident-handling workflows and identity governance practices. When detections surface entitlement anomalies, they should feed into reviews that remove unnecessary privileges and close escalation paths. When detections reveal repeated access failures or suspicious token behavior, they should trigger investigation patterns that examine session validity, device integrity, and potential credential exposure. Over time, strong programs use these signals to harden the environment by tightening authorization, improving session controls, and increasing the quality of telemetry at critical access points. That is how behavioral detection becomes more than alerting; it becomes a mechanism for continuously reducing the likelihood and impact of identity-driven compromise.

AI-Assisted Access Risk: Scoring, Explainability, and Human Approval Gates

AI-assisted access risk is most useful when it helps operations answer a narrow set of questions faster and more consistently than humans can at scale. The practical problem is that modern access decisions are made continuously across many systems, and the signals that indicate elevated risk are distributed across authentication events, authorization attempts, session behavior, and entitlement changes. A risk score can compress that complexity into a single prioritization cue that helps analysts and control systems focus attention where it matters. The score is not a security truth; it is a decision aid that should increase signal-to-noise in triage and reduce time-to-action for clearly suspicious activity. Operational value comes from defining what the score is allowed to influence and what it is not.

Scoring depends entirely on telemetry quality, because the model can only evaluate what it can reliably observe. Identity logs must capture authentication outcomes, factor challenges, token issuance and refresh behavior, and the resources accessed under each session. Authorization telemetry must include both successes and failures, since repeated failures often indicate probing or misconfiguration discovery rather than routine work. Context signals such as device posture, network origin, and recent entitlement changes materially improve risk assessment when they are consistent and available across critical access paths. If telemetry is incomplete or delayed, scoring becomes brittle and will either miss true misuse or generate persistent noise that trains the organization to ignore it.

Explainability is the bridge between an AI-generated risk signal and an operational decision that can be defended and audited. When an analyst sees "high risk," they need to see the contributing factors in plain operational terms, such as unusual login geography, atypical session duration, sudden access to sensitive resources, or privilege-like actions not consistent with the identity's history. Without those contributing signals, responders cannot validate plausibility, and leaders cannot justify disruptive containment actions when business impact is questioned later. Explainability also helps tune the system, because teams can see whether risk is being driven by weak signals, missing context, or patterns that represent legitimate work. In identity operations, a score that cannot be explained is effectively a black box that will be trusted too much when it is wrong and ignored when it is right.

Human approval gates are necessary because access responses range from low-friction safeguards to highly disruptive actions. For moderate-risk signals, automation can be appropriate, such as forcing step-up authentication, prompting revalidation, shortening session lifetime, or increasing scrutiny through additional logging and monitoring. For high-impact actions like disabling an account, revoking all sessions, removing privileged entitlements, or changing access policy, a human decision boundary is usually required to avoid turning detection uncertainty into operational outages. Clear gates also prevent privilege escalation in the control system itself, where a model's output becomes an implicit authorization to take irreversible actions. The standard should be that automation can add friction or request confirmation, while humans authorize actions that materially change access state.

The biggest scoring failure mode is false confidence, where a clean score is treated as proof of safety and a high score is treated as proof of compromise. Attackers can behave quietly, reuse normal access patterns, and operate within existing entitlements, which means a score may remain low while misuse is still occurring. Conversely, legitimate business changes can look risky, such as role transitions, unusual travel, incident response activity, or emergency operational work that diverges from historical baselines. Drift is another risk, where normal behavior changes over time and the model gradually reclassifies suspicious activity as expected, especially if compromise is present during the learning period. Operational teams need to treat risk scoring as a probabilistic signal that must be validated with context, not as a deterministic gate that replaces judgment.

Bias and uneven enforcement can appear when scoring implicitly favors certain work patterns, teams, or geographies because the "normal" baseline is not uniform across the organization. A global business will naturally have wider login windows and different access rhythms, and a model that does not account for that variability may over-flag specific regions or functions. Certain roles legitimately use rare administrative actions, and scoring that penalizes rarity without role context will punish the people tasked with keeping systems running. Even when the intent is purely technical, these effects show up operationally as inconsistent friction, ticket volume, and distrust in the identity program. Managing this requires ongoing evaluation of score performance across populations and a willingness to adjust features, thresholds, and review workflows when patterns of unfairness or inefficiency emerge.

Governance and auditability are what make AI-assisted access risk acceptable in controlled environments, especially when scores influence real access outcomes. Teams need a clear record of what data sources feed scoring, how risk thresholds are set, and what automated actions are permitted at each threshold. When a response involves a human gate, the approval should be attributable, with enough captured context to explain why the action was taken or declined. Changes to scoring logic, thresholds, or data inputs should be treated as controlled changes, because they can materially affect access outcomes across the organization. This level of governance is not bureaucracy for its own sake; it is what prevents scoring from becoming an unreviewed, untestable control that quietly shapes access decisions without accountability.

Operationally, the healthiest pattern is to use risk scoring to prioritize investigation and introduce graduated friction, while keeping authorization decisions grounded in entitlement design and business intent. A score can tell an analyst which access events deserve immediate attention and can help an automated system decide when to challenge a session, but it should not be the sole arbiter of whether an identity deserves a privilege it has been granted. When risk scoring repeatedly flags the same entitlement pathways, that is a signal that authorization design needs tightening, not that the model should simply be tuned to stop alerting. Over time, score outputs should feed a loop of entitlement cleanup, session control hardening, and telemetry improvement, so the system becomes both quieter and more effective. In that operating model, AI assists the human system of governance rather than quietly replacing it.

Common IAM Failure Modes and How They Appear

IAM failures rarely announce themselves as "an IAM problem" at first; they show up as operational friction, inconsistent access, and investigative ambiguity. Teams notice that users cannot get into critical systems, that admins are constantly granting exceptions, or that incident response keeps running into accounts nobody can explain. Over time, those symptoms become normalized, and the organization adapts by building workarounds that further weaken control. Attackers exploit that normalization because it creates a background level of access chaos that makes malicious behavior harder to distinguish. The operational discipline is recognizing these patterns early and treating them as control failures rather than as inevitable complexity.

One of the most common failure modes is authentication weakness disguised as convenience, where password-centric access remains the default and additional factors are applied inconsistently. This often appears as frequent account lockouts, repeated password resets, and users relying on predictable password patterns to cope with complexity. In incident investigations, it shows up as successful logins that cannot be tied to strong proof, such as single-factor access from unfamiliar locations or repeated logins that should have required step-up challenges but did not. It also appears when token theft becomes the dominant compromise method, because teams assumed multifactor authentication solved the problem without accounting for session persistence. Operationally, weak authentication creates a steady stream of small incidents that mask the rare high-impact compromise. Table 10.3 provides a quick operational lens for recognizing IAM breakdowns by linking failure modes to their most common observable symptoms.

Authorization drift is a second failure mode, and it is usually more dangerous because it determines blast radius. It appears as roles that quietly expand over time, direct entitlements granted for "temporary" needs that never expire, and privileged permissions embedded in what should be baseline access. In audits and reviews, drift shows up as reviewers approving access they do not understand because the role names are meaningless or the permissions are too granular to assess. During incidents, it appears as accounts doing things they "shouldn't be able to do," followed by the uncomfortable realization that they actually can. Authorization drift turns credential compromise from a contained event into a business-wide exposure.

A related failure mode is poor lifecycle hygiene, where joiner, mover, and leaver processes are incomplete or slow. It appears operationally as new hires waiting days for access, transfers requiring manual cleanups that never happen, and terminated users whose accounts remain active or partially active across applications. In investigations, lifecycle failures show up as accounts that should not exist, stale group memberships, and orphaned tokens or API keys that still work after a person has left. The business impact can be immediate when access is missing, but the security impact is delayed and often ignored until it becomes a breach narrative. When lifecycle is unreliable, the organization cannot confidently answer who should have access at any point in time.

Machine identity sprawl is another failure mode that often stays invisible until it causes major damage. Service accounts, automation identities, and integration credentials accumulate because they are easy to create and hard to retire. They appear as long-lived secrets stored in places that are convenient for engineers, broad permissions granted to avoid breaking pipelines, and unclear ownership when teams reorganize. In incident response, this failure mode shows up as activity that has no human actor, where the logs point to a service identity performing sensitive actions without a clear reason. Because machine identities can operate continuously, compromise can lead to sustained data access or infrastructure manipulation that looks like normal automation.

Table 10.3 IAM Failure Modes and How They Surface in Operations.

Failure Mode	How It Appears	Operational Impact
Authentication weakness	Single-factor access and repeated resets	Higher account takeover likelihood
Authorization drift	Broad roles and permanent exceptions	Expanded blast radius during compromise
Lifecycle hygiene gaps	Stale accounts and slow deprovisioning	Residual access after role change
Machine identity sprawl	Long-lived secrets and unclear owners	Silent persistence and lateral movement
Observability gaps	Missing token and authorization logs	Slow triage and uncertain conclusions

Logging and observability gaps are a failure mode that compounds every other one, because they remove the ability to prove what happened. This appears as incomplete authentication logs, missing authorization events, inconsistent identifiers between systems, and limited visibility into token issuance and session behavior. Operational teams feel it as slow triage, noisy alerts, and a reliance on manual reconstruction that produces uncertain conclusions. AI and machine learning can help correlate identity signals, but only when the underlying telemetry is consistent; otherwise models amplify noise and generate false confidence. When observability is weak, the organization defaults to blunt controls during incidents because precise containment is not possible.

Overreliance on static controls is a failure mode that shows up when teams assume that a policy set once will remain correct as the environment changes. It appears as conditional access rules that are never revisited, roles that do not match current job functions, and access patterns that have shifted due to remote work, new regions, or new applications. Drift in behavior baselines causes detection tools to either alert constantly or miss meaningful anomalies, and teams respond by tuning sensitivity down until alerts are quiet. This is how misuse becomes a low-visibility activity that can persist for long periods without triggering human attention. Operationally, static control thinking fails because identity is dynamic by nature.

The last common failure mode is unclear accountability, where no one owns the meaning of access and no one is responsible for keeping it aligned to business intent. It appears as role definitions created by security but approved by nobody, access reviews performed as checkbox exercises, and privilege granted through informal channels because the formal channels are slow. In incidents, it shows up when responders cannot find an owner to answer whether access is legitimate, and containment decisions become political rather than technical. A clear ownership model does not require bureaucracy, but it does require named responsibility for roles, entitlements, and high-risk access pathways. When accountability is explicit, IAM failures are surfaced and corrected; when it is vague, failure modes persist until an attacker demonstrates their cost.

Conclusion

A durable IAM program is measured less by how clean it looks on paper and more by how reliably it shapes real access outcomes under everyday business pressure. When identity functions as the control plane, authentication strength, authorization design, session controls, and entitlement governance work together to limit blast radius and keep investigations grounded in defensible evidence. The most resilient organizations treat least privilege, role fit, and sprawl reduction as continuous operational work, reinforced by telemetry and reviews that keep permissions aligned to actual job needs. AI-assisted risk scoring and behavioral analytics can accelerate detection and triage, but only when they remain explainable, auditable, and bounded by human approval gates for actions that materially change access state.

Recommendations

1) Treat identity as the primary control plane for access decisions across applications, infrastructure, and data. Align your operational focus on how identities authenticate, what they are authorized to do, and how sessions persist over time. Ensure your team can quickly answer who accessed what, how they proved identity, and what actions were performed under that access.
2) Avoid treating successful authentication as proof that access is safe or appropriate. Validate that the authorization context matches business intent and that privileges are scoped to the minimum required for the task. Review session and token behavior as part of access assurance, since stolen session artifacts can bypass repeated authentication challenges.

3) Establish clear operational ownership for roles and entitlements, so access decisions remain aligned with real work. Assign accountable owners who can approve changes, validate periodic reviews, and retire roles that no longer fit the organization. Require that role modifications and high-risk permission additions are traceable to an approver and a documented purpose.
4) Design role-based access control to fit stable job functions while supporting controlled variability for situational needs. Keep baseline access predictable through durable roles, and handle specialized needs through explicit exceptions rather than permanent broadening of roles. Prevent role sprawl by treating roles as lifecycle-managed objects that can be created, modified, reviewed, and retired.
5) Implement least privilege as an ongoing process rather than a one-time cleanup effort. Build routine revocation into transfers, terminations, and time-bounded access, so permissions contract as reliably as they expand. Treat "temporary" access as truly temporary by making expiration and follow-up review part of normal operations.
6) Prioritize the governance of machine identities with the same rigor applied to human access. Ensure service and automation identities have clear ownership, narrowly scoped entitlements, and reliable rotation or revocation paths for their secrets or tokens. Review machine entitlements regularly to prevent silent accumulation of broad permissions that increase systemic blast radius.
7) Reduce entitlement and permission sprawl by making baseline access role-aligned and deviations explicitly reviewable. Limit direct entitlements to justified cases and capture approver context, so future reviewers can understand why exceptions exist. Focus periodic reviews on the highest-risk entitlements and privilege-escalation pathways rather than attempting exhaustive, unscoped access recertification.
8) Integrate identity workflows into daily operations for onboarding, transfers, offboarding, and change management. Make access provisioning predictable and measurable, so the business does not resort to informal workarounds that undermine governance. Ensure access model changes are planned alongside system and organizational changes, so broad permissions do not become the default shortcut.
9) Detect misuse by correlating access patterns across authentication, authorization, and session behavior rather than relying on single events. Tune investigations to identify combinations that indicate probing, session theft, or abnormal privilege usage, and ensure responders can reconstruct a coherent timeline from identity telemetry. Use behavioral signals to drive both immediate triage and longer-term entitlement tightening when repeated patterns expose weak authorization design.
10) Apply AI-assisted access risk scoring only with strong telemetry, explainability, and clear human approval gates. Require that risk outputs are supported by understandable contributing factors, so analysts can validate plausibility and document decisions. Allow automation to introduce graduated friction for moderate risk, but keep disruptive actions attributable to a human approver and governed through auditable change control.

11

Identity Lifecycle Operations

Identity lifecycle operations are where organizational change meets enforced security reality, and that intersection is rarely clean. Every joiner, mover, and leaver event creates a short window in which access can be granted too broadly, retained too long, or changed without durable accountability. The operational work is not simply provisioning and deprovisioning accounts, but managing approval chains, group and role mappings, external identities, and evidence so that access decisions remain defensible under audit and resilient under incident pressure. When these processes are engineered for timing, ownership, and verification—and reinforced by identity hygiene and outcome-driven reviews—identity becomes a controllable system rather than an accumulating set of exceptions.

Joiner, Mover, Leaver: The Operational Reality

Identity lifecycle operations succeed or fail on the quality of the initiating event. A joiner record that arrives late, incomplete, or ambiguous forces administrators to guess, and guesses become access that is difficult to unwind. In practice, the "source of truth" is often split between HR systems, contractor management, and line-of-business staffing tools, and those feeds rarely align on identifiers or effective dates. Operationally mature programs treat the joiner event as a controlled intake: unique identity, employment type, start date, manager, location, and baseline role attributes are validated before any access is granted. When teams skip that validation, the environment accumulates accounts that look legitimate but cannot be reliably tied back to a real person and a real accountability chain.

For joiners, the most common failure mode is granting access before identity proofing and manager ownership are established. Identity proofing should be proportional to risk, but it must be explicit: who validated the person, what evidence was used, and how exceptions are documented for contractors and urgent hires. Baseline access should be role-aligned and time-bounded where uncertainty exists, particularly for privileged access and external identities. The operational detail that matters is sequencing: create the identity, assign a primary owner, enforce enrollment in MFA, then grant only the minimum entitlements needed for day-one productivity. When the sequence is inverted—access first, controls later—teams end up chasing "temporary" access that becomes permanent through inertia.

Movers are where lifecycle operations quietly collapse because change is continuous and the business treats it as routine. A mover event is not just a title change; it can include a new manager, a new region, a new legal entity, a new cost center, or a shift from employee to contractor status. Each of those changes alters what access should be retained, what must be removed, and which approvals are valid. The operational reality is that removals are harder than adds because someone will always claim the old access is still needed "just in case." Strong programs require a re-authorization step on meaningful moves, with clear ownership for approvals and an expectation that legacy access expires unless it is explicitly reaffirmed. Figure 11.1 shows how joiner mover and leaver events translate into a small set of required control actions and the evidence artifacts that make those actions defensible. It reinforces

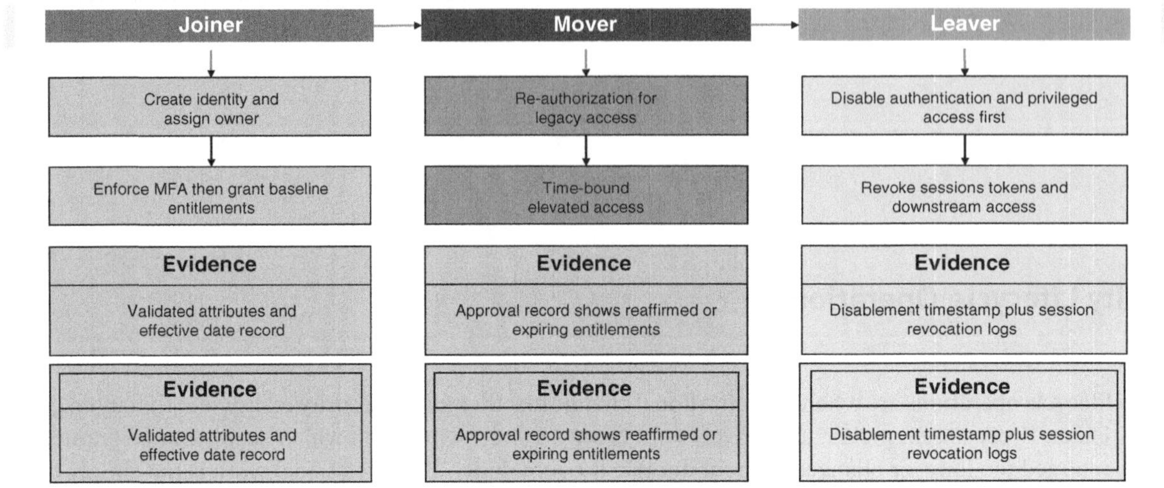

Figure 11.1 Joiner Mover Leaver: Control Checkpoints and Evidence Trail.

that lifecycle success depends on sequencing and verification rather than assuming a single account disablement completes the job.

The hardest mover cases are those that span privilege boundaries. A lateral move into an admin-adjacent function, a temporary assignment, or an emergency backfill often triggers privilege creep, where elevated access stacks on top of older entitlements. Good operations make privilege time-scoped by default and separate standing access from task-based access, so a mover does not accidentally inherit long-lived power. When temporary privilege is required, it should be tied to a ticketed business justification, a specific time window, and an auditable approver who is accountable for the risk. Without that discipline, incident response teams later find that an account had "rarely used" admin rights for months, which is indistinguishable from deliberate persistence once an attacker is inside.

Leavers create the most visible risk because the business expectation is simple: when someone departs, access stops. Operationally, it is rarely that clean, especially when terminations are unplanned, when employees depart but retain devices, or when contractors roll off without a formal offboarding event. Leaver execution must be deterministic and fast, with a defined order of operations that accounts for interactive access, tokens, sessions, and federated identities. Disabling an account is not the same as removing access if active sessions remain or if long-lived API keys continue to function. Mature teams coordinate identity disablement with device management, credential revocation, and the transfer of owned assets like shared mailboxes and service responsibilities. Table 11.1 summarizes the minimum control actions and evidence expected at each identity lifecycle transition.

A recurring issue in leaver operations is the shadow landscape of non-human identities and delegated access. Service accounts, API tokens, automation credentials, and application-to-application trust can be created under a person's initiative but persist beyond their employment. If lifecycle operations focus only on the user account, the organization retains operational risk in the form of orphaned secrets and unowned integrations. Effective programs require an ownership model for non-human identities that survives personnel changes, with periodic attestation that ties each credential to a business function and a named custodian. When that ownership is missing, offboarding becomes a fragile, manual scramble that either breaks production or leaves secret material active indefinitely.

AI and machine learning can improve lifecycle reliability, but only when they operate as decision support rather than autonomous authority. In joiner and mover flows, models can flag anomalies such as unusual entitlement combinations, sudden privilege jumps, mismatched manager relationships, or geographic patterns

Table 11.1 Lifecycle Control Checkpoints for Joiner Mover Leaver.

Lifecycle Event	Primary Trigger	First Control Action	Verification Evidence
Joiner	Start date and manager confirmed	Create identity and enforce MFA enrollment	Provisioning record ties identity to manager and effective date
Mover	Role or manager change recorded	Require re-authorization for legacy access	Approval record shows reaffirmed or expiring entitlements
Leaver planned	Planned separation with effective cutoff	Disable authentication and revoke privileged access first	Timestamped disablement plus privileged role removal confirmation
Leaver unplanned	Immediate termination event	Revoke sessions and tokens then disable accounts	Session revocation logs plus account disablement evidence
External engagement end	Contract end date or sponsor withdrawal	Expire access and remove external entitlements	Sponsor renewal record absent and access removal confirmation

that do not align with prior organizational behavior. The telemetry dependency is non-negotiable: you need consistent identifiers across HR and IAM, clean entitlement catalogs, and historical approval data to establish what "normal" looks like. Human-in-the-loop control should be explicit, with boundaries that require approvals for sensitive entitlements and that prevent a model from auto-granting privileges based on inference. The failure modes are predictable—false confidence from sparse data, drift as org structures change, and leakage if model prompts or training sets contain sensitive identity attributes—so auditability, access logging, and periodic validation are required to keep assistance safe.

Operational governance is what turns joiner, mover, leaver from a set of scripts into a reliable control. Every lifecycle transition should produce an auditable trail: who requested, who approved, what changed, when it became effective, and what evidence supported the decision. Exceptions must be treated as first-class operational artifacts, not informal favors, because exceptions are where attackers hide and where investigations stall. Lifecycle performance should be measured in outcomes that map to risk, such as time to disable access on termination, percentage of movers re-authorized within a defined window, and volume of orphaned accounts discovered by reconciliation. When governance is weak, teams compensate with heroics, and heroics do not scale when the organization grows, reorganizes, or faces sustained adversary pressure.

Provisioning Workflows and Approval Chains

Provisioning is where identity intent becomes enforced reality, and that translation has to be engineered with the same rigor as any other high-impact operational workflow. The business asks for outcomes such as faster onboarding, fewer access issues, and consistent enforcement, while security asks for evidence, accountability, and least privilege. A workable provisioning workflow ties each entitlement to a clearly defined approval authority and a repeatable execution path, so access is not granted because someone knows the right person to message. The operational objective is not to eliminate friction entirely, but to ensure friction exists only where risk exists. When teams treat provisioning as a help desk convenience, they end up granting access that is fast, inconsistent, and almost impossible to defend during incident response.

A provisioning workflow begins with a well-defined request object that is complete enough to drive deterministic decisions. At minimum, the request must identify the subject, the requested access, the business justification, the

Table 11.2 Provisioning Approval Chain Expectations by Access Type.

Access Category	Required Approver	Time Bound Default	Verification Step	Common Failure
Baseline role access	Manager or sponsor	No, if role mapped	Confirm entitlement applied in target system	Access granted before identity attributes validated
Sensitive data access	Resource owner plus manager	Yes, when uncertainty exists	Confirm effective access matches intended scope	Approver lacks context on what access enables
Privileged access	Business approver plus technical authority	Yes, by default	Confirm no hidden inheritance or nested expansion	Privilege creep from additive grants
Emergency access	Accountable sponsor	Yes, short window	Confirm enablement and disablement recorded	Bypass outside workflow with no durable evidence
Delegated permissions	Resource owner	Yes, when temporary	Confirm delegation removed at end of need	Delegation persists after role change

requested start and end dates when applicable, and the accountable manager or sponsor. Requests that cannot be tied to a real person and an accountable owner should not proceed, because the workflow cannot produce durable evidence later. In mature environments, the request is normalized into a single identity record that stays consistent across systems, even when applications each have their own naming and grouping conventions. When that normalization is absent, the approval chain becomes theater, because the system cannot reliably prove that the approved request and the provisioned access are the same thing. Table 11.2 reinforces how approval authority time bounds and verification should tighten as access impact increases.

Approval chains work only when approval authority is aligned to the risk and the operational owner of the resource. Managers are often necessary approvers, but they are not sufficient for high-impact access because they may not understand the technical blast radius of certain entitlements. Resource owners are better positioned to validate whether access is appropriate for a role, but they can be too permissive if the owner is incentivized to prioritize delivery over control. Privileged access, access to sensitive data sets, and access that crosses legal or geographic boundaries should require approvals that reflect those distinct risks, not just hierarchy. If approvals are not mapped to risk, organizations create a false sense of governance while continuing to grant high-consequence access through the easiest path.

The workflow itself must be designed to prevent the two most common operational failures: bypass and accumulation. Bypass occurs when urgent requests are routed outside the system, leaving no durable record of what was granted or why. Accumulation occurs when access is granted through multiple overlapping paths, such as role-based assignment plus ad hoc additions, and nothing forces periodic reconciliation. A well-run workflow offers an emergency path that is still controlled, time-bounded, and auditable, so "urgent" does not become "uncontrolled." It also enforces expiration where uncertainty is present, so access must be reaffirmed rather than silently persisting.

Execution quality matters as much as approvals because provisioning is not complete when a ticket is approved; it is complete when access is verified and evidence is captured. Verification should be explicit: the identity was created or updated, the entitlement was applied, and the result was confirmed in the target system. For high-risk entitlements, verification should include a second check that the access behaves as intended and does not imply additional privileges through nested groups, inherited roles, or transitive permissions. Many failures show up only at this layer, such as overbroad group membership or entitlements that carry hidden administrative capabilities.

When verification is skipped, the organization cannot reliably distinguish between "approved and granted," "approved but failed," and "unapproved but granted," which undermines both security and operations.

Separation of duties is not an abstract compliance concept in provisioning workflows; it is a practical safeguard against both error and abuse. The person requesting access should not be the person approving it, and the person approving it should not be the person technically implementing it for sensitive entitlements. Where full separation is not feasible, compensating controls become essential, such as stronger logging, peer review for privileged grants, and automated checks that flag policy violations before they become effective. This is especially important for administrator-level access and for entitlements that enable data export, key management, or identity administration. Without enforced separation, a compromised requester account can become a provisioning engine for an attacker, using legitimate workflow signals to obtain legitimate access.

AI and machine learning can strengthen provisioning workflows by improving decision quality and reducing manual triage, but the controls have to be explicit to avoid automating bad outcomes. Models can recommend likely entitlements for a role by learning from historical patterns, and they can flag outliers such as unusually broad access requests, requests that do not match job function, or sudden privilege escalations during a mover event. Those recommendations depend on clean telemetry: entitlement catalogs, organizational structure, prior approval history, and access usage patterns that distinguish "needed" from "held." Human-in-the-loop boundaries should require that AI output is advisory for high-risk access and that approvals remain attributable to a named human with accountability. The failure modes are familiar—bias from historical overprovisioning, drift as the organization reorganizes, and overreliance on model confidence—so governance must include reviewability, change control on model updates, and evidence that recommendations were challenged when appropriate.

The final measure of a provisioning workflow is whether it produces reliable evidence under pressure, not whether it looks elegant on paper. When an incident occurs, teams need to answer who granted access, who approved it, what was granted, when it became effective, and whether it was time-bounded or later changed. A strong approval chain makes those answers routine because the workflow stores immutable records, links approvals to entitlements, and preserves the effective dates and exceptions. Operational resilience also requires continuous reconciliation between the authoritative identity record and what exists in downstream systems, because systems drift and manual changes happen. When evidence is incomplete or reconciliation is absent, investigations devolve into speculation, and the organization pays for weak provisioning twice: once through risk exposure and again through delayed response.

Deprovisioning as a Security and Audit Priority

Deprovisioning is the control that converts organizational change into reduced attack surface, and it has to be treated as a priority rather than a cleanup task. When access is not removed promptly and completely, former employees, contractors, and partners retain pathways that bypass normal governance. Those pathways are attractive to adversaries because they look legitimate, and they often sit outside the monitoring assumptions of the current operating model. In operational terms, deprovisioning is a time-bound race between the business event and the persistence of credentials, sessions, and delegated access. The organizations that manage this well treat deprovisioning as an engineered process with strict timing, evidence, and clear ownership.

A practical deprovisioning program starts by recognizing that "account disabled" is not the same as "access removed." Modern environments rely on federated identities, cached tokens, device sessions, API keys, and application-specific credentials that can remain valid even after a primary account is disabled. A user can be locked out of interactive logins while still possessing valid refresh tokens in a browser, active sessions on a managed device, or automation credentials issued through a separate channel. Deprovisioning must therefore address identity access across layers, including identity providers, applications, endpoints, and credential stores.

If teams focus only on the directory object, they leave exploitable remnants that will not show up until something goes wrong.

Timing and sequencing are central because different termination scenarios create different risk profiles. Planned departures allow orderly transfer of responsibilities, notification of system owners, and staged removal, but they still require an effective-time cutoff to prevent "last day" access from becoming "after hours" access. Unplanned terminations require immediate action to prevent sabotage, data exfiltration, or retaliation, and they often happen outside normal business hours. Mature operations define clear triggers and service-level objectives for deprovisioning, so the organization is not negotiating urgency in the middle of a stressful event. The sequence usually needs to prioritize cutting off authentication and privileged access first, then revoke sessions and tokens, then handle downstream accounts and asset transfers in a controlled manner.

Deprovisioning also fails when ownership and accountability are unclear across systems. Human identity is one domain, but access is distributed across business applications, cloud services, collaboration platforms, and third-party portals, each with different administrative models. If system owners are not accountable for deprovisioning behavior in their domains, the central team cannot guarantee completeness, and gaps become normal. Strong programs maintain a mapped inventory of systems and deprovisioning responsibilities, including which systems support automated revocation and which require manual steps with verification. The objective is not perfect automation everywhere, but predictable outcomes with measurable coverage and documented exceptions.

Non-human identities complicate deprovisioning because they are easy to create and difficult to inventory after the fact. Service accounts, API keys, integration tokens, scheduled tasks, and automation secrets are frequently provisioned under a person's initiative and then forgotten once the work moves on. When that person leaves, the organization may retain powerful credentials that no one owns, or worse, credentials embedded in scripts and pipelines that continue to run with broad permissions. Effective deprovisioning includes an ownership transfer process for any non-human identity tied to the departing user's scope of work, along with a review of credentials issued or managed by that user. Without that step, deprovisioning becomes a false sense of closure, because the highest-impact access may not be attached to the human account being disabled.

Audit priorities shape deprovisioning discipline because auditors care about evidence, completeness, and timeliness, not good intentions. A defensible program produces records that show when the separation event occurred, when access was revoked, what systems were covered, and how exceptions were approved and tracked. Evidence needs to be tied to effective dates and must account for both interactive accounts and downstream access paths, including shared mailboxes, delegated permissions, and administrative roles. Where manual steps exist, they should produce verification artifacts, such as confirmation logs or administrative action records, that can be reviewed later without reconstructing the entire event. When evidence is missing, organizations tend to overcompensate with broad controls that slow operations while still failing to demonstrate actual removal.

AI and machine learning can strengthen deprovisioning by improving completeness and prioritization, but the program must be explicit about how AI output is used and audited. Models can identify likely orphaned access by correlating recent offboarding events with lingering authentication patterns, token refresh activity, or continued access to applications that should have been revoked. They can also help detect hidden dependencies, such as automation tied to a user's credentials that continues to execute, or atypical access activity after a termination event. These use cases depend on telemetry that spans identity providers, application logs, endpoint data, and authentication token events, and they require careful handling to avoid sensitive leakage in prompts or model training data. Human oversight should set approval boundaries, such as requiring an analyst to validate model-flagged accounts before disabling service-affecting credentials, and maintaining a clear audit trail of what the model recommended versus what actions were taken.

Ultimately, deprovisioning has to be treated as both a security control and an operational reliability function. If deprovisioning routinely breaks business processes, teams will create informal workarounds, and those workarounds become a second access system with no governance. If deprovisioning is slow or incomplete, the organization accumulates residual access that becomes a recurring audit issue and a standing threat vector.

A mature posture balances speed with safety by enforcing rapid cutoff for authentication and privilege, then executing validated downstream cleanup with ownership transfer and evidence capture. When done consistently, deprovisioning reduces risk, improves incident response clarity, and turns audits from a scramble into a confirmation exercise.

Handling Contractors, Vendors, and Temporary Access

Contractors, vendors, and temporary staff introduce the same core risk as any identity, but with weaker organizational controls and a higher likelihood of drift. Their engagement terms change more frequently, they often work across multiple clients, and their identities may be managed in systems that are not tightly coupled to HR processes. Operationally, the difference is not that these users are inherently untrusted, but that the organization has less leverage to enforce consistent onboarding, device posture, and timely offboarding. A sustainable approach treats external identities as first-class citizens in lifecycle operations, with clear sponsorship, defined scope, and time-bounded access by default. When external access is treated as an exception, it becomes invisible to governance and therefore hard to control.

Sponsorship is the foundation for external access because it creates an accountable owner inside the organization. Every contractor or vendor identity must have a named sponsor who is responsible for the business justification, scope, and renewal decisions. Without sponsorship, access requests are routed through generic queues and approvals become rubber stamps because no one feels the risk personally. Sponsorship also matters during incidents, when responders need a fast path to validate whether an external user is still active and whether their access is appropriate. In practice, sponsorship should be tied to a manager-level role with authority to accept risk and the operational context to know when the engagement has ended.

External onboarding must be designed around constrained trust rather than assumed equivalence to employees. Identity proofing should be appropriate to the engagement type, but it must be explicit and verifiable, especially when the external user will access sensitive systems or data. Baseline access should be minimal and role-aligned, and it should avoid granting broad internal entitlements simply because the vendor needs "some access." Where possible, access should be granted to specific applications or data sets rather than to broad network segments, because segmentation reduces blast radius when something goes wrong. If the organization cannot enforce endpoint controls on external devices, access should be structured to reduce persistence and lateral movement, emphasizing session control, strong authentication, and clear boundaries around where data can be accessed.

Temporary access is most defensible when it is treated as time-scoped and purpose-scoped, not as a smaller version of permanent access. The request must define what the person needs to do, what systems are involved, and the precise time window in which the access is valid. Time-bounding should not rely on human memory or calendar reminders; it should be enforced by the provisioning workflow so that access expires automatically unless a sponsor renews it. Operational teams often fear time-bound access because it can cause outages when someone forgets to renew, but that is an argument for better renewal workflows, not for permanent access. When time-bounds are optional, they are rarely used, and "temporary" becomes indistinguishable from standing access.

Vendors introduce a different operational challenge: their access frequently supports business-critical systems and may be required during emergencies. That reality can push teams into granting broad, persistent access "just in case," especially when vendor support is tied to strict response-time commitments. A better operational posture is to pre-stage access paths that are controlled, monitored, and activated only when needed, so emergency support does not require improvisation. Activation should be tied to a ticketed request and a sponsor approval, with clear logging that captures when the access was enabled and when it was disabled. If the vendor requires privileged access, that access should be time-scoped, and it should be separated from routine vendor accounts used for administrative communication or low-risk tasks.

Offboarding external identities is where risk accumulates fastest because the business event is often informal. Contractors roll off without a clear termination date, vendor personnel change without notification, and temporary access can quietly extend through repeated "one more week" renewals. Strong operations treat external access as expiring by default and require active renewal, shifting the burden from "remember to remove" to "justify to keep." Renewal should be tied to evidence that the engagement is still active, the scope remains accurate, and the sponsor remains accountable. Without an enforced renewal model, external access becomes stale, and stale access becomes an attacker's easiest entry point because it is least likely to be noticed.

AI and machine learning can materially improve the safety of external access by detecting drift and misuse patterns, but the organization must treat model output as a control input, not an autonomous enforcement engine. Models can flag external identities that are not behaving like their peer group, such as accessing systems outside the expected scope, logging in from atypical geographies, or maintaining long-running sessions inconsistent with the engagement type. They can also identify external accounts that appear inactive but still hold high-impact entitlements, which is a common symptom of offboarding failures. These use cases depend on telemetry that spans identity provider events, application access logs, session durations, and entitlement assignments, and they require careful governance to avoid exposing sensitive identity attributes through prompts or training sets. Human-in-the-loop boundaries should require analyst validation for disruptive actions, especially when disabling access could impact production support, and the audit trail should preserve the model's rationale alongside the human decision.

The operational standard for handling contractors, vendors, and temporary access is not perfection; it is predictable control under real business pressure. That means access requests must be complete, approvals must be accountable, entitlements must be constrained, and expiration must be enforced rather than hoped for. Monitoring must treat external activity as normal but higher consequence, with clear expectations for what is logged and how anomalies are investigated. When exceptions are necessary, they should be explicitly documented with duration and compensating controls, rather than quietly absorbed into "how things work." Done consistently, external access stops being a recurring audit failure and becomes a managed, measurable part of identity lifecycle operations.

Managing Group Membership and Role Changes

Group membership and role assignment are where identity lifecycle operations become concrete, because groups and roles are the levers that actually grant access in most environments. The operational challenge is that group structures grow organically over time, often reflecting historical projects, legacy applications, and "temporary" access decisions that became permanent. As a result, a simple role change can trigger a cascade of entitlements that no one fully understands, especially when groups are nested or mapped into application roles downstream. Mature operations treat groups and roles as governed assets with defined ownership, documented purpose, and measurable usage. When that governance is missing, group membership becomes the path of least resistance for access requests and the root cause of privilege creep.

A practical program starts with consistent semantics for what groups and roles mean. A role should represent a durable job function or responsibility set, while groups should represent specific entitlements or policy-driven access boundaries that can be audited and explained. In many environments those terms are blurred, with groups used to approximate roles, roles used to approximate permissions, and exceptions layered on top. Operationally, this blurring makes approvals weaker because approvers cannot understand what they are approving, and it makes troubleshooting harder because access issues are traced through opaque mappings. Clear naming, documented intent, and a maintained catalog of group-to-access outcomes are not administrative niceties; they are prerequisites for safe automation and reliable audits.

Role changes create risk because they often happen in ways that are not cleanly represented as a single event. An internal transfer might include a new manager, a new cost center, and a temporary overlap period where the person is expected to support both old and new responsibilities. Without a controlled process, the easiest solution is to add new access while leaving old access in place, which is how privilege accumulates invisibly. Strong operations require a re-authorization step for meaningful role changes, where prior access is reviewed and either reaffirmed with justification or set to expire. This is especially important when role changes cross privilege boundaries, such as moving into IT administration, finance functions, or roles that touch sensitive data sets. If re-authorization is not enforced, the organization will eventually discover that long-tenured employees hold broad access simply because they have moved around over the years.

Nested groups and transitive permissions are a common operational trap because they hide effective access from both requesters and approvers. A user may be added to a single group, but that group could inherit membership in other groups that grant far more capability than intended. The result is overprovisioning that is difficult to detect, because the change looks minimal in the identity system while the downstream impact is large. Operationally sound programs restrict deep nesting, document any required nesting explicitly, and validate the effective access outcome during provisioning. Where nesting is necessary, teams should maintain visibility into effective permissions, not just direct membership, so that both engineering and audit functions can reason about what is actually being granted.

Change management for groups and roles must include ownership and lifecycle controls, not just technical administration. Every group that grants meaningful access should have an owner responsible for approving membership changes, reviewing continued need, and ensuring the group's purpose remains accurate. Groups without owners become "everyone uses it" artifacts that persist indefinitely, and they tend to accumulate privileges because no one has the authority or incentive to remove outdated entitlements. Role definitions also require stewardship, because job functions evolve and the environment changes, which means yesterday's role-to-access mapping can become overly broad today. When ownership is clear, it becomes operationally possible to retire unused groups, consolidate duplicates, and reduce the long tail of legacy access patterns that complicate security operations.

Role changes also intersect with segregation of duties, especially in environments with financial controls, sensitive data, or high-consequence administrative functions. When someone moves into a role that conflicts with prior responsibilities, the organization must ensure old access is removed even if it is still "convenient." Segregation of duties is operationally enforced through group and role design, and it breaks down when entitlements are granted through ad hoc exceptions that bypass normal mappings. The most common failure is allowing someone to accumulate access across incompatible functions through successive moves, creating a single identity that can initiate and approve actions that should be separated. Managing this requires explicit checks during role change events and clear escalation paths when the business insists on an exception.

AI and machine learning can help manage group membership and role changes by improving detection of drift and surfacing the effective risk of changes, but it has to be governed carefully. Models can identify unusual combinations of group memberships, detect privilege escalation patterns that deviate from peer roles, and flag role changes that historically correlate with higher incident rates or access misuse. These capabilities depend on clean telemetry: historical membership changes, entitlement catalogs, organizational hierarchy, and downstream access outcomes that show what memberships actually enable. Human-in-the-loop controls should prevent a model from directly altering group membership for high-risk entitlements, and instead use model output to guide reviews, approvals, and targeted audits. Failure modes include reinforcing historical overprovisioning as "normal," drifting recommendations as group structures change, and producing confident explanations that are hard to validate unless the underlying mappings are well documented.

Operational success is measured by whether group and role management reduces entitlement sprawl while still supporting business agility. That means role changes trigger predictable re-authorization, groups have accountable owners, nesting is controlled, and effective access is visible enough to verify and audit. It also means exceptions are time-bounded and reviewed, rather than becoming permanent memberships that no one remembers. When teams run this well, access decisions become faster because the system is understandable, and investigations become faster because effective permissions can be traced without guesswork. When teams run it poorly, identity becomes a sprawling dependency graph, and every role change quietly increases risk until the next incident makes it obvious.

Identity Hygiene and Reducing Stale Access

Identity hygiene is the operational discipline of keeping identities, entitlements, and access paths accurate over time as the organization changes. Even with strong joiner, mover, leaver execution, environments accumulate stale access because people shift responsibilities, projects end, and applications evolve faster than entitlement models. Stale access is not always malicious, but it is always risky because it expands what an account can do beyond what the business currently intends. In incident response, stale access is especially damaging because it obscures intent and increases the number of plausible paths an attacker could take. Treating identity hygiene as routine maintenance keeps both security and operations from paying compounding interest on old decisions.

A practical hygiene program starts with an accurate inventory of identities and their authoritative attributes. Hygiene is not only about disabling dormant accounts; it is also about ensuring that identity records reflect current manager relationships, employment status, location, and the attributes that drive access decisions. When identity attributes drift, automation makes the wrong decisions at scale, granting or retaining access based on outdated information. Operational teams should expect drift and design for reconciliation between authoritative sources and downstream systems, rather than assuming synchronization is perfect. The goal is to keep identity data trustworthy enough that access reviews and automated controls can rely on it without constant manual verification.

Dormant and orphaned accounts are a core hygiene concern because they are common and easy to overlook. Dormant accounts are still linked to real people but no longer used, while orphaned accounts lack a clear owner or are no longer tied to an active employment relationship. Both represent latent access that can be exploited, and both are frequently created by partial offboarding, legacy migrations, and unmanaged application accounts. Organizations that manage this well define inactivity thresholds appropriate to their environment and then enforce a predictable lifecycle: warn, validate, disable, and eventually remove where policy allows. The operational nuance is that inactivity must be assessed across relevant systems, not just one login source, because an account may appear inactive in one place while still being used through tokens or service integrations elsewhere.

Stale access often hides inside group membership and long-lived entitlements that were granted for a specific purpose and then never revisited. This is where hygiene becomes a continuous practice rather than a periodic project. Strong programs treat access as something that should be reaffirmed when business context changes, and they require ownership for the entitlements themselves, not just for the accounts that hold them. When an entitlement lacks an owner, it becomes a dumping ground for exceptions because no one is responsible for saying no or cleaning up later. Over time, that pattern produces "miscellaneous" access groups whose membership is large, whose purpose is unclear, and whose risk is high.

Access reviews are often the formal mechanism for hygiene, but their effectiveness depends on how they are executed. Reviews that ask managers to approve lists of unfamiliar entitlements tend to produce blanket approvals because the cognitive load is too high and the perceived business risk of removal is immediate. Reviews become more meaningful when they present clear context: what the access enables, how recently it was used, and why it was granted. Usage context should be treated carefully, because lack of observed use does not always mean lack of need, but it is a strong signal for prioritizing review. Operationally, the objective is to make removal the default for unclear access while providing a safe path to restore access if a legitimate need is discovered.

Reducing stale access also requires disciplined handling of exceptions and temporary access. Temporary access that does not expire automatically becomes stale access by definition, and exceptions without revalidation become permanent policy drift. Hygiene programs should enforce time-bounds where uncertainty exists and require affirmative renewal with accountable sponsorship. When renewals are treated as a routine operational step, the organization shifts from reactive cleanup to preventative control. This also improves audit readiness because exceptions are documented, time-scoped, and tied to a business justification that can be evaluated later without reconstructing the decision.

AI and machine learning can improve identity hygiene by prioritizing what humans should review and by detecting patterns that indicate drift, but those capabilities depend on careful governance. Models can surface likely stale entitlements by correlating access holdings with peer groups, job attributes, and observed usage patterns, and they can flag accounts that exhibit anomalous inactivity or unusual privilege combinations. These insights require high-quality telemetry across identity systems, application logs, and entitlement catalogs, and they require consistent identifiers to avoid false correlations. Human-in-the-loop controls should ensure that model outputs drive investigation and review rather than automatic removal for high-impact access, because an automated removal mistake can disrupt operations and erode trust in the hygiene program. Failure modes include reinforcing historical overprovisioning as "normal," misclassifying legitimate low-frequency access as stale, and producing overconfident recommendations that lack clear evidence when challenged.

Sustained hygiene is achieved when cleanup is integrated into normal operational rhythms rather than treated as an occasional purge. That means stale access signals are continuously generated, ownership is clear, remediation paths are predictable, and reinstatement processes exist, so removals are not feared. It also means the organization invests in simplifying entitlements, because complexity is the enemy of hygiene and the ally of persistence. When hygiene is executed with discipline, access becomes easier to reason about, access reviews become faster and more accurate, and incidents become easier to contain. When hygiene is neglected, identity becomes a historical artifact, and the environment gradually shifts from least privilege toward "least resistance," which is where attackers thrive.

Access Reviews That Produce Real Outcomes

Access reviews are only valuable when they change the environment, not when they generate paperwork. Many organizations run reviews as a compliance exercise that produces attestations while leaving permissions untouched because removals are considered too risky or too time-consuming. That gap between documentation and reality becomes obvious during incidents, when responders discover that accounts retain broad access that was supposedly reviewed and approved multiple times. Real outcomes require reviews to be designed around removal, evidence, and accountability, with a workflow that makes change the natural endpoint. When the review process cannot reliably revoke access, it is not an access review; it is an administrative survey.

The first operational decision is scope, because attempting to review everything at once produces superficial approvals. Reviews that focus on high-impact access deliver better outcomes because reviewers can understand the risk and the organization can tolerate the effort required to get it right. High-impact access includes privileged roles, sensitive data access, broad administrative entitlements, and access that crosses boundaries such as legal entities or environments. Scoping also means identifying which access paths are in scope, including role assignments, group memberships, delegated permissions, and application-native accounts that may not be centrally visible. When scope is unclear, reviews miss the most dangerous access while spending time on low-value items that do not materially change risk. Table 11.3 shows how reviews produce outcomes when decisions are driven by context and followed by verified change.

Reviews fail most often because the reviewer cannot meaningfully evaluate what they are approving. A manager looking at a list of group names without context will default to approval, especially when the perceived cost of removal is immediate and the risk of overapproval is abstract. Reviews produce outcomes when each decision is supported by just enough context to be actionable: what the access enables, why it was granted, how it maps to current job responsibilities, and whether it has been used recently. Usage should be presented as a signal, not a verdict, because some access is legitimately infrequent, but it is still a powerful tool for prioritization. When

Table 11.3 Access Review Inputs That Drive Removals and Defensible Exceptions.

Review Input Context	Reviewer Decision	Expected Action	Evidence Artifact
Justification clear and role aligned	Keep	Retain entitlement with recorded rationale	Attestation record links reviewer to entitlement
Justification unclear and usage absent	Remove	Revoke entitlement and verify removal	Target system confirmation plus review decision log
Exception required for business need	Approve exception	Time bound access with renewal requirement	Exception record with sponsor and expiration
High-impact outlier for peer group	Escalate	Route to correct owner for re authorization	Escalation record plus owner decision
Nested group or transitive risk present	Validate effective access	Confirm actual permissions before final decision	Effective access validation note with supporting logs

reviewers can see that an entitlement has not been used in months and has no clear justification, they are far more likely to approve removal.

Ownership is another point of failure because "who can approve" is not the same as "who should approve." Managers can validate employment and role alignment, but they may not understand whether a specific entitlement grants administrative capability or data export rights. Resource owners understand the system, but they may prioritize convenience and uptime, and they may not feel accountable for enterprise risk. Mature programs align approval authority to the risk and the operational boundary, so sensitive entitlements require explicit acknowledgment by the right accountable party. Without that alignment, reviews produce approvals that are procedurally valid but operationally meaningless.

Real outcomes also require a remediation path that is safer than doing nothing. Reviewers often avoid removal because they fear breaking workflows, triggering outages, or damaging relationships with their teams. The review process must therefore support reversible change and clear escalation paths, so reviewers can confidently remove access while knowing that legitimate needs can be handled quickly. This includes time-bound grace periods where access can be restored through a controlled workflow, and it includes a verification step, so removals are confirmed in the target systems. If removal creates a long help desk backlog, reviewers will learn that approving everything is the easiest way to keep work moving.

Access reviews become far more effective when they are integrated with joiner, mover, leaver, and ongoing identity hygiene rather than treated as a standalone quarterly event. Movers should trigger re-authorization, and temporary access should expire automatically, reducing the volume of stale entitlements that reach formal review cycles. Reviews should also be informed by reconciliation data, because the review must reflect effective access, not just direct assignments, especially in environments with nested groups and transitive permissions. When the organization relies on a single review cycle to correct a year of entitlement drift, outcomes will be poor because the volume of decisions exceeds human capacity. Continuous controls reduce review scope and raise review quality.

AI and machine learning can improve access reviews by making the decision set smaller and higher quality, but it must be used as decision support with clear auditability. Models can cluster users into peer groups based on role attributes and highlight entitlements that deviate materially from the norm, which helps reviewers focus on true outliers. They can also summarize historical context, such as when access was granted, what approvals were used, and what activity patterns exist, reducing the cognitive load on human approvers. These capabilities depend on accurate identity attributes, clean entitlement catalogs, and reliable access telemetry, and they degrade quickly when the underlying data is inconsistent. Human-in-the-loop boundaries should prohibit automated removal of high-impact access solely on model output, and should require that model-driven recommendations are explainable enough to be defensible when questioned by auditors or incident responders.

Governance and measurement distinguish outcome-driven reviews from ceremonial ones. Programs should measure completion rates, but more importantly they should measure change rates: how much access was removed, what categories were reduced, and whether removals were sustained without immediate re-granting through informal channels. They should also track exceptions, including who approved them, their duration, and whether compensating controls were applied. Evidence must be durable and attributable, tying each decision to a reviewer and capturing the rationale in a way that can be examined later without reconstructing context. When metrics show that reviews consistently approve nearly everything, the correct response is not to demand more reviews; it is to redesign the process, so reviewers can make defensible, low-friction removal decisions that actually change the environment.

AI Assistance for Identity Governance: Review Prioritization, Outlier Detection, and Evidence

AI assistance in identity governance is most valuable when it reduces human cognitive load without weakening accountability. Identity programs fail at scale because the volume of entitlements, systems, and organizational change exceeds what reviewers can reliably reason about using static lists and periodic checkpoints. AI and machine learning can help by ranking what matters, highlighting what is abnormal, and assembling evidence that makes decisions defensible. The goal is not to replace approvers, but to make their approvals meaningful by presenting the right decisions with the right context at the right time. If AI is treated as an authority rather than an assistant, it will amplify existing overprovisioning and make failures harder to detect because the system will appear confident.

Review prioritization is the highest leverage use case because it changes the shape of the work. Instead of asking reviewers to attest to every entitlement, an AI-assisted process can focus attention on high-impact access, recently changed access, and access that diverges from expected patterns for a role. Practical prioritization relies on risk-aligned signals: privilege level, access to sensitive data, breadth of scope, cross-boundary access, and the presence of exceptions or manual grants. It also uses change velocity, because entitlements that were added during a mover event or through emergency workflows are more likely to be inconsistent with steady-state role models. When prioritization is done well, the organization spends human attention where it actually reduces risk, rather than exhausting reviewers on low-consequence approvals.

Outlier detection works best when the organization can define a defensible notion of "peer" and maintain stable identity attributes that support that grouping. A peer group might be defined by job family, business unit, manager hierarchy, location, environment scope, or a combination that reflects how access should be structured in reality. The model then identifies entitlements that are unusual within that peer group, such as a finance analyst holding administrator-level access, or a contractor possessing long-lived entitlements that are typical only for employees. Outliers are not automatically wrong, but they are high-value review targets because they often represent drift, exceptions that were never revisited, or entitlement chains created by nested group membership. Without stable peer definitions and clean data, outlier detection becomes noisy, and noise erodes trust quickly.

Evidence assembly is where AI can most directly improve audit readiness, provided that the evidence is anchored in authoritative records. A strong identity governance system should be able to show what access exists, why it exists, who approved it, and what business context supported the decision at the time. AI can help by stitching together relevant artifacts—request metadata, approval records, identity attributes at the effective date, and downstream confirmation that access was applied—into a coherent narrative that a human can review. The key is that the narrative must remain traceable, with links to the underlying records, because auditors and incident responders will not accept a model-generated explanation without verifiable sources. When the model is used to summarize and present evidence rather than invent it, decisions become faster and more defensible without sacrificing rigor.

Telemetry dependencies determine whether AI assistance improves governance or produces false confidence. Identity attributes must be consistent across systems, entitlement catalogs must be maintained so that permissions can be interpreted, and downstream access outcomes must be observable, so the model understands what memberships actually enable. Access events should include both assignment changes and usage signals, such as authentication events, session duration, and high-risk actions, because governance decisions are stronger when they reflect both what a user can do and what they have done. The program also needs a reliable record of change events, including joiner, mover, leaver triggers, emergency grants, and exceptions, because those events explain why access shifted and where drift likely occurred. When telemetry is incomplete, the model will still produce rankings and explanations, but they will be built on partial truth, which is operationally worse than having no model at all.

Human-in-the-loop controls are the boundary that keeps AI assistance from becoming an unaccountable access engine. For high-impact entitlements, AI should recommend and summarize, while a named human approves and remains accountable for the decision. Approval boundaries should be explicit, such as prohibiting automated grants for privileged access, sensitive data access, and cross-boundary access, and requiring a second review when the model flags elevated risk. The workflow should also require that reviewers can challenge or override the model, and that those overrides are captured as evidence, because governance programs need to learn from legitimate exceptions rather than treating them as anomalies to suppress. When humans cannot effectively contest AI output, the system will drift toward automated permissiveness and reviewers will become passive signers of machine suggestions.

Failure modes are predictable and must be treated as operational risks rather than theoretical concerns. Bias is common when historical access patterns include overprovisioning, because the model will learn that excessive access is "normal" for a peer group and will stop flagging it as an outlier. Drift occurs as organizations reorganize, roles evolve, and applications change, which can invalidate peer group definitions and risk signals if models are not retrained and validated against current reality. Leakage is a serious concern when identity governance artifacts include sensitive personal data, because prompts, logs, or training sets can inadvertently expose attributes that should be tightly controlled. Overconfidence is another failure mode, where model-generated explanations appear authoritative even when the underlying data is incomplete or ambiguous, leading reviewers to approve decisions they would otherwise question.

Governance and auditability expectations must be engineered into AI-assisted identity processes from the start. The organization should be able to demonstrate what data sources the model uses, how recommendations are generated, how often models are updated, and how performance is monitored for false positives and false negatives. Recommendations should be logged with enough detail to reconstruct the decision context later, including the signals that drove prioritization and the evidence artifacts presented to the reviewer. The program should also enforce access controls around the AI system itself, because an AI assistant that can see entitlement data and approval histories becomes a sensitive asset and a potential target. When these controls are in place, AI assistance becomes a force multiplier for identity governance, producing reviews that focus on real risk, outlier detection that surfaces meaningful drift, and evidence that stands up under audit and incident scrutiny.

Ownership Models for Identity Processes

Identity processes work when ownership is explicit, durable, and aligned to the decisions being made. Without clear ownership, identity becomes a shared responsibility in the worst sense of the phrase: everyone touches it, no one is accountable, and failures are discovered only after access has drifted for months. Operationally, ownership defines who can approve, who can implement, who can validate, and who must answer when something goes wrong. It also defines what "done" means for lifecycle events, access changes, and exceptions, which is essential for auditability and incident response. When ownership is vague, workflows devolve into email threads and ad hoc favors that bypass controls.

A practical ownership model separates authority for identity data from authority for access outcomes. Identity data ownership is about the integrity of attributes such as employment status, manager relationships, and role-defining fields that drive provisioning decisions. Access outcome ownership is about the systems and entitlements that those attributes ultimately grant, including who decides whether access is appropriate and who maintains the mapping between roles, groups, and permissions. Conflating these responsibilities leads to predictable conflict, such as HR being asked to approve technical entitlements or security teams being forced to arbitrate business need. Mature programs recognize that each domain has different incentives, and they build ownership boundaries that keep decisions aligned to expertise.

Identity governance also requires operational ownership for the lifecycle workflows themselves, not just for the data and the entitlements. Someone must own the joiner, mover, leaver process end-to-end, including triggers, timing, exception handling, and verification that actions occurred in downstream systems. This process owner is responsible for defining service levels, maintaining runbooks, and coordinating across HR, IT operations, and application owners when failures occur. Without an end-to-end owner, teams optimize their local tasks while the overall workflow remains brittle, and the organization cannot reliably answer basic questions about timing and completeness. The end-to-end owner is also the natural point of accountability for audits, because they can demonstrate how the process behaves and how it is monitored.

Resource ownership is a distinct responsibility that is often missing or poorly enforced. Every application, data domain, and high-impact entitlement set needs a resource owner who understands what the access enables and who can make informed decisions about who should have it. Resource owners are responsible for defining access boundaries, maintaining entitlement catalogs, and participating in reviews, especially when access is sensitive or privileged. When resource ownership is not defined, access decisions default to managers who may not understand the technical implications, or to administrators who are pressured to "just make it work." Clear resource ownership reduces that ambiguity and makes approvals defensible because they come from the people accountable for the system's risk and operation.

Sponsorship is the ownership construct that makes external identities manageable. Contractors, vendors, and temporary workers need an internal sponsor who is accountable for the justification, scope, and renewal of access. Sponsorship should not be treated as a formality, because sponsors are the only reliable link between an external identity and internal accountability. Sponsors must be responsible for validating that the engagement is active, that access remains appropriate, and that offboarding occurs on time. Without sponsorship, external access becomes a permanent artifact of old projects, and the organization's risk posture quietly shifts toward uncontrolled third-party persistence.

Ownership models must also account for privileged access, where the decision stakes are higher and separation of duties becomes essential. Privileged access ownership should include both a business approver who can justify need and a technical authority who can validate that the requested privilege is appropriate and minimally scoped. Implementation should be separated from approval for high-impact changes, and verification should be independent enough to catch errors such as excessive group nesting or unintended inheritance. When privileged access is owned only by technical teams, it tends to drift toward convenience, and when it is owned only by managers, it tends to drift toward overapproval. Balanced ownership keeps privilege both usable and defensible.

AI assistance can improve identity ownership practices by making accountability observable and by reducing ambiguity in who should act, but it must be governed to avoid creating shadow decision-makers. Models can help route requests to the correct approver by inferring resource ownership from maintained catalogs and historical approval patterns, and they can flag cases where ownership is unclear, such as entitlements with no active owner or approval chains that routinely default to the same overburdened individual. These functions depend on accurate metadata about systems, entitlements, and organizational structure, and they require strict controls to prevent sensitive identity attributes from being exposed through prompts or logs. Human oversight should ensure that AI routing remains transparent and that exceptions are captured explicitly, because routing mistakes can become an operational bottleneck or, worse, a path to inappropriate approval.

Sustainable ownership is reinforced through measurable expectations rather than informal agreements. Ownership roles should have defined responsibilities such as review cadence, response times for approvals, standards for documenting exceptions, and obligations to maintain entitlement definitions. When those expectations are not measured, ownership becomes symbolic, and operational gaps reappear as drift and stale access. The most resilient programs build ownership into normal operations, so changes in staffing or organizational structure do not break identity controls. When ownership is explicit, maintained, and auditable, identity processes become predictable, reviews produce real outcomes, and the organization can respond to incidents with clarity about who decided what and why.

Conclusion

Identity governance succeeds when it consistently produces the same three outcomes: access aligns to current business intent, high-impact changes are accountable, and stale permissions are removed before they become an incident narrative. The operational reality is that drift is constant, so durable control comes from engineered workflows, clear ownership, and verification that changes actually occurred across downstream systems. Access reviews that change the environment, time-bounded external access, and disciplined group and role management reduce the hidden pathways that attackers and auditors both find first. Used carefully, AI assistance can make these controls scalable by prioritizing reviews, surfacing outliers, and assembling evidence, but it must remain advisory with explicit approval boundaries and auditable rationale.

Recommendations

1) Establish a deterministic joiner intake process that validates identity attributes before granting access. Require a unique identity, accountable manager or sponsor, and complete role-defining fields, so provisioning decisions are based on verified data rather than assumptions. Enforce sequencing that prioritizes identity creation and MFA enrollment before entitlements are applied. Capture evidence of the validation steps, so the access grant remains defensible later.
2) Implement mover workflows that force re-authorization when job responsibilities change. Require reviewers to explicitly reaffirm legacy access or allow it to expire, rather than letting old entitlements persist by default. Pay special attention to moves that cross privilege boundaries and require stronger approvals and tighter time bounds. Treat "temporary overlap" as a controlled exception with an end date and documented justification.
3) Prioritize rapid and complete deprovisioning by designing for tokens, sessions, and downstream accounts, not just directory disablement. Define clear triggers and time targets for planned and unplanned separations, so urgency is not negotiated in the moment. Sequence actions to cut off authentication and privileged access first, then revoke sessions and tokens, then complete downstream cleanup with verification. Maintain durable evidence that shows when the separation event occurred and when access was actually revoked.
4) Formalize provisioning workflows and approval chains, so access grants are accountable and repeatable. Require request objects that include subject, entitlement, justification, effective dates when applicable, and an accountable owner who can accept risk. Align approval authority to the risk and the resource boundary, so managers do not unknowingly approve high-impact entitlements without the right context. Verify outcomes in target systems and retain records that tie approvals to effective access.

5) Treat contractors, vendors, and temporary users as first-class identities with sponsorship and enforced expiration. Require an internal sponsor who is accountable for scope, renewal, and timely offboarding, and make access time-bounded by default. Provide controlled emergency activation paths that remain ticketed, monitored, and explicitly disabled when work is complete. Use renewals to confirm continued need rather than relying on someone remembering to remove access.
6) Govern group membership and role changes as managed assets rather than ad hoc convenience mechanisms. Maintain clear semantics for roles versus groups, document purpose, and assign owners who are responsible for approvals and ongoing accuracy. Control nesting and validate effective access, so small membership changes do not create hidden privilege expansions through inheritance. Use role changes as a trigger to remove incompatible or outdated entitlements, especially where segregation of duties is a concern.
7) Embed identity hygiene into routine operations to reduce stale access continuously. Reconcile authoritative identity attributes with downstream systems, so automation remains correct as the organization changes. Enforce inactivity thresholds with a predictable lifecycle of validation, disablement, and removal where policy allows. Focus remediation on orphaned identities and unclear entitlements that lack ownership or justification.
8) Design access reviews to produce removals and measurable risk reduction rather than ceremonial attestations. Scope reviews to high-impact access and present reviewers with actionable context such as what the access enables, why it exists, and how recently it has been used. Make removal safe by providing controlled reinstatement paths and confirming revocations in the target systems. Track change rates and exception patterns to verify that reviews are actually reshaping access holdings.
9) Apply AI assistance as decision support to prioritize reviews, surface outliers, and assemble evidence without replacing accountability. Use models to rank high-impact access, highlight deviations from peer patterns, and summarize request and approval artifacts into reviewable decision packages. Keep humans as the final approvers for sensitive entitlements, and log what the model recommended versus what was decided. Monitor for failure modes such as drift, bias from historical overprovisioning, and overconfident explanations that outpace the underlying evidence.
10) Define and enforce ownership models that make identity processes durable across organizational change. Separate ownership of identity attributes from ownership of access outcomes, and assign end-to-end owners for lifecycle workflows with clear service expectations. Require resource owners for applications and high-impact entitlements, so approvals reflect real system risk and operational boundaries. Make sponsorship mandatory for external identities and ensure exceptions remain time-bounded, reviewed, and attributable to a named decision-maker.

12

Privileged Access Management and Administrative Control

Privileged access is the thin layer between routine operations and irreversible impact, because it governs the identities and actions that can change how the environment works. When privilege is misassigned, overused, or poorly monitored, a single compromised session can disable defenses, reshape access, and undermine the integrity of evidence before responders even understand what is happening. Effective privileged access management is therefore less about restricting administrators and more about making high-impact work deliberate, attributable, time-bound, and recoverable under stress. This chapter establishes why privilege is uniquely dangerous and then builds the operational discipline required to define privileged roles and actions, enforce approvals and emergency pathways, monitor privileged sessions and non-human identities, and collect audit-quality evidence—while using AI-assisted detection as decision support with clear human override controls.

Why Privilege Is the Highest-Risk Access Category

Privilege is the highest-risk access category because it collapses multiple security boundaries into a single decision point: whether an action is permitted. When an identity is granted administrative rights, the environment is effectively trusting that identity to bypass normal guardrails, change configurations, access sensitive data, and influence other identities. In practical terms, privileged access converts many independent controls into a dependent chain where one weak link can invalidate the rest. That is why a single compromised admin account can outpace the security value of patching, segmentation, and endpoint hardening in a matter of minutes. The business impact follows directly: privilege turns what could have been a contained incident into one that can alter systems of record, disrupt operations, and undermine audit integrity.

Privileged access also carries disproportionate risk because it is more "portable" than most defenders assume. Once an attacker gains a privileged foothold, they can use it to mint new credentials, create backdoor accounts, or add their identity to high-power groups, which means the risk persists even after the original entry vector is remediated. This is why privilege is closely tied to persistence: administrative rights enable changes that survive reboots, password resets, and even some reimaging workflows. It is also why privilege changes the economics of defense; the attacker needs fewer steps, fewer exploits, and less time to reach high-value objectives. For leadership, that translates into a simple reality: privileged compromise is the fastest path from "security event" to "business event." For operators, it means any investigation involving privileged identities must assume the adversary attempted to expand and entrench access.

The technical reason privilege is so dangerous is that it directly controls identity and trust itself. Administrative rights often include the ability to modify authentication policies, enroll new MFA methods, change conditional access logic, or alter directory attributes that determine authorization. With that capability, an attacker can weaken or disable the very controls meant to stop them, sometimes without creating obvious symptoms like malware alerts. Privilege also enables tampering with logs, time settings, and monitoring agents, which can reduce visibility precisely when defenders need it most. Even if logs are not fully erased, altering the conditions under which they are produced can create misleading telemetry that wastes response time. A well-run program treats privileged operations as security-sensitive events in their own right, not just routine IT activity.

Privilege amplifies risk because it is frequently overbroad and long-lived, often for reasons that look operationally reasonable in isolation. Teams grant admin rights "just in case" to avoid outages, to streamline changes, or to reduce friction for senior engineers, and then those grants quietly become permanent. Over time, this creates privilege sprawl: too many accounts with elevated rights, too many pathways to perform high-impact actions, and too little clarity about which privileges are actually necessary. The risk is compounded by role accumulation, where an identity accrues access through multiple groups, emergency exceptions, and inherited entitlements that no one can fully enumerate during an incident. The result is that defenders cannot reliably answer basic questions under pressure, such as who can disable security controls or who can modify production systems. In environments with complex delegation and cloud control planes, the sprawl is not merely administrative clutter; it is an expanded attack surface with fewer effective choke points.

Privileged workflows also tend to bypass the normal safety mechanisms that organizations rely on to reduce human error. Most production-impacting outages are not caused by sophisticated attackers; they are caused by accidental changes made under time pressure with insufficient review. Privileged access makes those mistakes more expensive because it can alter core services, networking, encryption settings, and identity configurations in a single session. When privileged activity is performed from the same endpoints and browsers used for routine work, common risks such as token theft, session hijacking, and credential reuse become privileged risks. This is one reason modern attacks frequently prioritize stealing session tokens or abusing device registration rather than cracking passwords; a privileged session is a high-leverage asset regardless of how it was authenticated. The operational takeaway is that privileged access must be separated, constrained, and observed as a distinct class of activity, not treated as a faster lane for normal work.

Another driver of privileged risk is the asymmetry between attacker initiative and defender process. Attackers choose the time, target, and method, while defenders must coordinate handoffs, approvals, and evidence collection without breaking the business. Privileged identities are especially attractive because they allow the attacker to move faster than governance, including the ability to create plausible-looking administrative actions that resemble routine maintenance. That ambiguity can delay containment as teams debate whether activity is legitimate, especially when privileged accounts are shared, poorly documented, or used for automation. Attackers exploit that ambiguity by blending into administrative noise, scheduling changes during maintenance windows, and using built-in management interfaces that are difficult to distinguish from authorized use. In mature operations, the goal is to reduce that ambiguity by ensuring privileged actions are attributable to an individual, tied to a ticket or change record, and constrained by time and scope.

AI/ML can help reduce privileged risk, but only when it is anchored to high-quality telemetry and enforced with human approval boundaries. In practice, models are most useful for anomaly detection in privileged behavior: unusual access times, new administrative endpoints, atypical sequences of identity changes, or rare combinations of actions that often precede compromise. Those detections depend on consistent identity signals, reliable log coverage across control planes, and enough historical data to establish a baseline that reflects legitimate variability such as on-call work. The danger is false confidence, where a model's "normal" label is mistaken for "safe," even though a skilled adversary can mimic administrative patterns or slowly shift behavior to induce drift. Models can also overfit to past operations and under-alert during major migrations or reorganizations, exactly when privilege management is most fragile. For that reason, AI-assisted triage must be treated as decision support: it can prioritize review, cluster related activity, and surface likely root causes, but final authorization and containment decisions remain accountable to humans with a clear audit trail.

Privilege should be understood as a business continuity risk as much as a security risk because privileged compromise undermines the organization's ability to trust its own systems. If an attacker can change configurations, alter identity controls, or manipulate monitoring, then the organization cannot reliably attest to system state, which complicates every recovery decision. That uncertainty drives costly actions such as broad password resets, emergency rebuilds, and extended downtime while teams re-establish a known-good baseline. It also affects governance outcomes; regulators and auditors care not only that controls exist, but that the organization can demonstrate integrity of administrative actions and evidence. The most defensible posture is one where privileged access is intentionally scarce, short-lived, and continuously monitored with strong attribution. When privilege is treated as a controlled operational capability rather than a convenience, the organization reduces both the probability of catastrophic compromise and the cost of restoring confidence when incidents occur.

Defining Privileged Roles and Privileged Actions

Privileged roles are identities that can materially change the security posture, operational state, or integrity of systems, and privileged actions are the specific operations those identities can perform that create that impact. The important distinction is that privilege is not limited to job titles or "administrator" labels; it is defined by effect. If an identity can change authentication requirements, modify network paths, disable logging, or access regulated data at scale, it is privileged even if it is framed as a convenience role or embedded in an application workflow. For executives, this framing matters because it ties privilege to business risk rather than organizational chart semantics. For operators, it provides a measurable boundary: privilege is what can alter control effectiveness, system availability, or the fidelity of evidence.

A practical program starts by defining privileged roles in terms of control planes and scopes of authority. Directory and identity administration is typically the highest leverage category because it governs how all other access is granted and revoked. Security administration is similarly high risk because it can enable or suppress detection and enforcement, sometimes without obvious indicators. Infrastructure administration covers the ability to reconfigure compute, storage, networking, and hypervisor layers, including cloud management planes that can create, destroy, or snapshot workloads and data. Application administration extends to roles that can change production configurations, secrets, or authorization logic, even when those roles are held by developers or platform engineers rather than traditional IT administrators. The common thread is that privileged roles are those that can change "how the system works," not just "what a user can view." Table 12.1 links common privileged role categories to the specific high-impact actions that make them operationally risky.

Table 12.1 Privileged Role Categories and High-Impact Examples.

Privileged Role Category	High-Impact Authority	Example Privileged Actions	Why It Matters
Identity administration	Controls authentication and authorization	Modify authentication requirements and change role assignments	Can reshape access and weaken controls
Security administration	Controls detection and enforcement	Disable monitoring and change alerting logic	Can reduce visibility during an attack
Infrastructure administration	Controls compute storage and network paths	Change network controls and reconfigure production systems	Can disrupt operations and expand reach
Application administration	Controls production configuration and authorization logic	Modify production configuration and manage secrets	Can expose sensitive data and create persistence
Automation and pipeline authority	Controls trusted change execution	Trigger deployments and update pipeline configuration	Can introduce privileged outcomes through trusted paths

Defining privileged actions requires moving from broad role labels to concrete operations that can be monitored, constrained, and audited. Actions that grant or revoke access are privileged because they alter who can do what, and they are often the first step in an attacker's expansion path. Actions that change security policy are privileged because they can lower defenses, create exceptions, or disable controls, sometimes with a single configuration change. Actions that affect telemetry are privileged because they influence what defenders can see and prove, including enabling or disabling logs, altering retention, or modifying time sources and forwarding. Actions that manage secrets are privileged because they can convert an administrative capability into durable, portable access across systems. If an action can materially change risk exposure, create persistence, or reduce accountability, it belongs in the privileged category regardless of where it sits in the stack.

Privilege definitions also need to account for "indirect privilege," where an identity may not be an administrator but can still cause privileged outcomes through delegation or workflow authority. For example, a service owner who can approve access requests, update an automation pipeline, or change a security group via an internal portal may have effective privilege even if the underlying API call is executed by a service account. Similarly, an identity that can trigger a deployment into production can indirectly change authentication flows, logging, or authorization checks if the deployment pipeline is trusted. This is why a mature definition includes the chain of custody for privileged outcomes: who can initiate them, who can approve them, and what technical controls enforce the approval boundary. Without this view, organizations mistakenly treat privilege as a small set of admin accounts while leaving high-impact change authority widely distributed. The result is governance theater, where privileged outcomes occur outside the privileged control set.

Privileged roles and actions must be defined with enough granularity to support least privilege without becoming so detailed that the organization cannot operate. Overly broad roles create unnecessary blast radius, but overly narrow roles can drive workarounds, shared accounts, and untracked exceptions that are worse than the original problem. A defensible balance is to define roles around operational functions that align to accountable teams and repeatable workflows, then define the privileged actions that those functions truly require. Where a role needs occasional high-impact capability, the definition should separate baseline permissions from elevation permissions, even if the elevation mechanism is not described in the policy text itself. This helps teams reason about what should be rare, time-bound, and highly monitored versus what is normal administrative work. It also makes audit evidence clearer because privileged operations become identifiable events rather than blended into routine access.

Good definitions are inseparable from identity hygiene and accountability expectations, because privilege without attribution becomes an operational blind spot. Privileged roles must map to individual identities wherever possible so that actions can be traced to a person, not a team mailbox or generic account. Where non-human identities are required, such as service accounts or automation identities, their privileged actions should be explicitly listed and justified, and their execution context should be constrained to the systems and networks that actually need the capability. Privileged actions should also be associated with authoritative records of intent, such as change tickets or access requests, so that investigators can differentiate authorized work from impersonation or abuse. This is not bureaucracy for its own sake; it is how organizations maintain the integrity of administrative operations under adversarial conditions. When privileged activity is attributable and explainable, response teams can move faster and with fewer false assumptions.

AI/ML can assist in refining privilege definitions by analyzing historical logs to identify which permissions are actually used and which actions correlate with incidents or high-risk change patterns. For example, clustering administrative events can reveal that a role includes hundreds of permissions, but only a small subset are exercised in normal operations, which supports tightening without breaking workflows. Models can also surface "privilege adjacency," where certain non-admin roles frequently initiate high-impact changes through delegated workflows, indicating that those roles should be treated as privileged for monitoring and governance purposes. These techniques depend on consistent event logging and stable identity correlation across systems; if identities are inconsistent, logs are incomplete, or key actions occur in opaque systems, model outputs will be misleading. Human review remains essential because models can confuse rare but legitimate activities with malicious behavior, especially during migrations, incident response, or major architectural changes. The correct operational use is to treat AI-generated insights as hypotheses to validate, then encode the validated outcomes into role definitions, approval boundaries, and audit expectations.

Finally, privilege definitions must be operationally testable, not merely descriptive, or they will drift out of relevance. A privileged role definition should allow a reviewer to determine, with evidence, whether an identity belongs in that category based on what it can do, not what it is called. A privileged action definition should map to observable events so that monitoring can detect when it occurs and governance can prove whether it was authorized. When definitions are anchored to observable outcomes and reinforced by consistent telemetry, they become durable despite reorganizations, tooling changes, and platform migrations. When definitions are anchored to titles and assumptions, they become obsolete as soon as the environment evolves. The security value comes from making privilege legible to both humans and systems, so that high-impact authority is intentionally allocated, continuously measured, and consistently accountable.

Approval Models and Administrative Workflow

Approval models exist to put deliberate friction in front of high-impact change, not to slow operations for its own sake. Privileged work is inherently different from standard business activity because it can change the integrity of control planes, alter production behavior, or expose sensitive data at scale. An approval model is the mechanism that makes that difference explicit, translating risk into who must agree, what evidence is required, and how the action is recorded. In practice, the value is not merely that "someone approved it," but that the organization can later prove why the action was appropriate, who authorized it, and what safeguards were in place. When approval is treated as a checkbox, attackers and well-meaning engineers both exploit the same weakness: high-impact actions become routine and therefore invisible.

Administrative workflow is where approval models succeed or fail, because most privileged incidents occur at the seams between intent and execution. The workflow begins when a need is identified—an outage, a planned change, a troubleshooting session, or a security response—and it ends when access is removed and evidence is preserved. In well-run operations, the request captures purpose, scope, and time window before any elevation occurs, and the system enforces those boundaries rather than relying on memory or discipline. The workflow also requires a clear mapping between the requester, the approver, and the operator when those are different people, because separation of duties is meaningless if identities are not attributable. The most common failure mode is that approvals are verbal, generic, or implied, which leaves no durable record and encourages broad permissions "just in case." A defensible workflow makes privileged work boringly repeatable: request, approve, elevate, execute, verify, and de-elevate.

Different approval models exist because privileged actions carry different operational urgency and blast radius. Some administrative work is planned and can tolerate review, while other work is reactive and must happen quickly to protect availability or contain an incident. The critical requirement is that urgency does not eliminate governance; it changes how governance is expressed. Emergency pathways should still require explicit justification, a constrained time window, and after-the-fact review that is treated as a control, not a formality. If emergency access becomes the default because it is faster or less scrutinized, the organization has effectively created a privileged backdoor with a compliance wrapper. Mature teams design workflows so that the fastest path is also the most controlled path, because speed and safety are not opposing goals in privileged operations.

Separation of duties is a core design principle in approval models, but it must be applied with operational realism. The goal is to prevent a single identity from unilaterally requesting, approving, and executing high-risk changes without oversight. In practice, strict separation can be difficult in small teams or on-call scenarios, so the workflow must clearly define what compensating controls apply when separation is not feasible. Those controls include stronger identity assurance, tighter time bounds, increased monitoring, and mandatory post-action review by an independent party. The worst implementation is a nominal separation that collapses under pressure, such as shared admin accounts or "rubber-stamp" approvals from peers who cannot evaluate the risk. A workable model ensures that someone with the right context is accountable for authorizing the action, and someone with the right skill is accountable for executing it, with both tied to an audit trail.

Administrative workflows also need to reconcile two common realities: automation performs a significant portion of privileged work, and production environments are too complex for manual, one-off changes to remain safe. This means approvals must extend to automation pathways, not just human logins. If a pipeline can deploy configuration changes, rotate secrets, or modify access policies, then the pipeline's triggers, approvers, and rollback controls are part of the privileged workflow. In mature environments, the approval decision is often attached to a change artifact—such as a configuration update—so that the approved object is what gets executed, reducing the risk of approving one thing and performing another. The workflow must also ensure that automation identities have only the privileged actions required for their function and cannot be easily repurposed. Without this, attackers seek control of pipelines and orchestration systems because they offer privileged outcomes with fewer interactive signals for defenders to catch.

From a monitoring and response perspective, approval models only help if the workflow produces reliable, correlatable evidence. Privileged actions should be linked to an authoritative record of intent, and the environment should be able to demonstrate that the privileged session or API call corresponded to the approved request. This correlation is not just for audit; it enables defenders to distinguish legitimate administrative change from attacker behavior that mimics it. When correlation is weak, response teams waste time chasing normal work during an incident, or worse, they hesitate to contain because they fear disrupting legitimate operations. A well-designed workflow supports fast triage by making legitimate privilege "explainable" through consistent metadata, identity attribution, and time-bounded elevation. It also improves recovery, because teams can confidently roll back or validate changes when they can trace what happened and why.

AI/ML can improve administrative workflow by assisting with request triage, risk scoring, and evidence gathering, but it must be deployed with clear human approval boundaries. Models can evaluate contextual signals—requester history, system criticality, past incident correlation, time-of-day anomalies, and the sensitivity of the targeted action—to prioritize which requests require deeper review. They can also summarize relevant logs and configuration diffs for approvers, reducing the burden of manual verification and improving decision quality under time pressure. The failure modes are predictable: models can be overly permissive when trained on historically lax practices, overly restrictive during operational change, or confidently wrong when telemetry is incomplete. There is also governance risk if the model's decision process is not auditable, because an organization cannot defend an approval outcome it cannot explain. The safest pattern is decision support with enforced guardrails: models recommend, humans approve, and the system records both the recommendation and the final decision for later review.

Approval models must also anticipate adversarial manipulation, because attackers often target the workflow rather than the control itself. Social engineering frequently aims to obtain "legitimate" approval for malicious actions, especially during outages, executive escalations, or urgent change windows. Attackers can also exploit ambiguity in ownership, requesting changes from groups that lack the authority to evaluate the impact, or leveraging compromised identities to submit plausible requests. Administrative workflows therefore need explicit criteria for what constitutes sufficient justification, what evidence must be present, and what conditions automatically require escalation to security or platform owners. Controls such as time-bounded elevation and strong identity assurance reduce the value of stolen credentials, but the workflow must also guard against procedural bypass, such as approving changes outside the tracked system. When the workflow is the enforcement point, deviations from it must be treated as security-relevant events.

Operationally, the most effective approval models are those that align with how teams actually work while still enforcing non-negotiable constraints. Approval that takes days for routine access drives shadow IT, shared accounts, and unsafe shortcuts, which increases rather than decreases risk. Approval that is too permissive creates the illusion of governance while allowing privilege to functionally remain uncontrolled. The right balance is achieved when approvals are proportional to risk, elevation is time-bound and scoped, and post-action verification is routine and measurable. When these elements are consistently applied, privileged work becomes easier to defend, easier to audit, and easier to recover from when something goes wrong. The organization does not become "slower"; it becomes more predictable, and predictability is a security control when privilege is involved.

Break-Glass Accounts and Emergency Access

Break-glass accounts exist to preserve operational control when normal access paths fail, not to provide a convenient shortcut around governance. They are the last-resort mechanism for regaining administrative capability during identity outages, misconfigurations, widespread MFA failures, or security-control incidents that lock out legitimate operators. Because they bypass or outlive standard protections, break-glass credentials represent concentrated risk: they are designed to work when everything else is broken, which makes them attractive to adversaries and dangerous when mishandled. A mature program treats break-glass access as a continuity control with explicit threat modeling, not as a spare admin account tucked away for comfort. The business reason is straightforward: if emergency access is unavailable when needed, downtime escalates; if it is available to the wrong party, compromise becomes catastrophic.

Emergency access must be grounded in clearly defined activation criteria, because ambiguity is how "emergency" becomes the new normal. The criteria should be tied to specific failure conditions such as loss of the primary identity provider, systemic MFA disruption, corruption of privileged role assignments, or a security incident that requires immediate containment actions that standard workflows cannot execute in time. Operationally, the organization needs a shared understanding of who can declare an emergency and what evidence is required to justify that declaration, even if the evidence is minimal in the moment. When teams cannot articulate the trigger conditions, break-glass use drifts into routine troubleshooting and after-hours convenience. That drift is not just a governance problem; it changes the environment's threat profile because attackers know that "rarely used" accounts are often poorly monitored and inconsistently controlled. Emergency access is safest when it is predictable, documented, and activated only under conditions that can be verified after the fact. Table 12.2 summarizes when emergency access is appropriate and the minimum controls that keep break-glass use defensible.

Break-glass account design should minimize both blast radius and exposure while still accomplishing the continuity objective. These accounts typically require broad authority because their purpose is to restore control, but

Table 12.2 Emergency Access Activation and Control Expectations.

Emergency Condition	Why Break Glass Is Needed	Permitted Restoration Focus	Required Controls
Identity provider outage	Normal admin access paths fail	Restore administrative control plane	Time-bound use with immediate alerting
Systemic MFA disruption	Legitimate operators cannot authenticate	Restore authentication pathways and policies	Dual control retrieval with durable record
Corrupted privileged role assignments	Admins lose required rights	Re-establish privileged role assignments	Strong attribution and post event review
Active security incident requiring containment	Speed required to stop impact	Terminate sessions revoke tokens restore logging	Enhanced monitoring and evidence preservation
Monitoring or logging impairment	Visibility is reduced during crisis	Re-enable telemetry and log forwarding	Tamper-resistant evidence pipeline

broad authority does not imply broad availability. The identity should be few in number, distinct from personal accounts, and not used for daily administration under any circumstances. Authentication factors should be chosen to survive common failure modes, which may mean independence from standard MFA systems, alternate recovery channels, or dedicated hardware factors, while still meeting organizational assurance requirements. The design must also consider where the account is valid; a break-glass credential that works everywhere is also a credential that can be abused everywhere. The right posture is to constrain where it can be used, how it can be used, and how quickly its use becomes visible to defenders.

Storage and custody are the difference between a responsible break-glass program and an unforced incident. If emergency credentials are stored in a way that is convenient for too many people, they will eventually be accessed outside the intended workflow or copied into unsafe locations. If they are stored in a way that is too inaccessible, they will fail the continuity mission during a real crisis. Mature operations treat custody as a controlled process, often requiring dual control so that no single individual can retrieve and use the credentials unobserved. Physical controls, secure storage, and documented retrieval steps matter because emergency access is often needed under stress, and stress is when shortcuts appear. The custody process should also ensure that retrieval itself creates a durable record, because the first question after any break-glass event is whether it was used appropriately.

The workflow for using break-glass access should be tightly scoped, time-bound, and explicitly connected to restoration tasks rather than open-ended troubleshooting. The goal is to accomplish a small set of defined actions such as re-establishing privileged role assignments, restoring authentication policy, re-enabling logging, or isolating compromised accounts and systems. Once those actions are complete, the environment should return to standard administrative pathways as quickly as possible. A common pitfall is leaving emergency sessions open or leaving emergency privileges in place "until things stabilize," which turns a temporary control into a persistent risk. Another pitfall is using break-glass accounts to perform routine change work during an outage because the path is available, which creates a messy mix of recovery actions and operational changes that is difficult to audit. Emergency access should be used to restore the conditions in which normal workflows can resume, not to replace those workflows.

Logging, monitoring, and alerting for break-glass use must be stronger than for routine administrative activity because the signal-to-noise ratio is inherently favorable. Break-glass usage is rare by design, which means any use is suspicious until validated. The organization should be able to detect sign-in attempts, successful authentication, privilege use, and subsequent changes to identity and security controls with minimal delay. Monitoring should focus on high-impact actions that attackers would prioritize, such as changes to authentication requirements, role assignments, conditional access logic, security tool configuration, and log retention. Where possible, break-glass actions should be recorded in tamper-resistant systems that are difficult for an attacker with admin rights to erase or alter. The operational expectation is that a break-glass event triggers immediate human review, because "emergency" is not a reason to postpone oversight; it is a reason to accelerate it.

AI/ML can strengthen emergency access governance by detecting abnormal patterns around break-glass accounts and by supporting rapid validation under time pressure. Models can flag deviations from expected activation contexts, such as unusual geolocation, unfamiliar devices, atypical time-of-day patterns, or sequences of actions that resemble adversary behavior rather than restoration work. They can also help correlate break-glass activity with broader incident telemetry, summarizing concurrent alerts, recent policy changes, or suspicious identity events to give responders a faster, more coherent picture. The failure modes are significant if teams treat model output as permission rather than evidence; a model that labels activity as "likely legitimate" can be wrong due to sparse training data, drift, or incomplete logs. Because break-glass events are rare, models may be poorly calibrated, which increases the risk of both false positives and false negatives. The correct use is to accelerate investigation and prioritization while keeping the human decision to continue or terminate emergency access explicit and accountable.

Break-glass programs must also include routine testing and controlled rotation, because an emergency control that has not been exercised is a liability. Testing validates that the account works under the failure conditions it is meant to address and that the organization can execute the retrieval and restoration workflow quickly without improvisation. It also validates that monitoring triggers as expected and that the audit trail captures sufficient detail to reconstruct actions later. Rotation reduces the risk of long-lived secrets and ensures that custody processes remain accurate as people and responsibilities change. The testing cadence should be regular enough to prevent drift but not so frequent that break-glass use becomes normalized. If testing is performed, it should be clearly labeled and executed in a way that does not train staff to ignore the alerts that break-glass activity should generate.

Finally, emergency access requires disciplined post-event review because the highest risk often occurs after the crisis, when teams are exhausted and eager to return to normal operations. Post-event review should reconcile what was done with what was necessary, confirm that emergency credentials were not duplicated or exposed, and ensure that any temporary changes made during recovery are either rolled back or formally approved through standard channels. It should also validate that privileged role assignments and authentication policies are restored to known-good configurations and that logs and monitoring are intact. The review is where organizations learn whether their activation criteria were appropriate, whether the custody process held up, and whether their monitoring was sufficient. When emergency access is treated as a controlled, auditable capability rather than a hidden convenience, it supports resilience without quietly expanding the attack surface.

Monitoring and Controlling Privileged Sessions

Privileged sessions are where intent becomes impact, which is why they require controls that are more deliberate than standard user activity. A privileged session is any interactive or programmatic context in which an identity can execute privileged actions, whether that context is a console login, remote administration channel, cloud management interface, or API-driven workflow. The risk is not limited to what the administrator plans to do; it includes what an attacker can do if the session is hijacked, replayed, or initiated with stolen credentials. Monitoring and control therefore must focus on both authentication assurance and execution assurance: proving who is acting and constraining what can be done once access exists. When organizations treat privileged sessions as "just another login," they lose the ability to detect and stop the most consequential actions before damage is done.

Controlling privileged sessions starts with reducing session exposure through intentional separation and strong session hygiene. Privileged work should occur from hardened administrative endpoints and controlled network paths so that credential theft and token interception are less likely. The goal is not to create an elite experience for administrators but to reduce the number of ways a privileged session can be established from compromised devices, consumer browsers, or unmanaged networks. Session lifetimes should be short enough to limit replay value while still supporting legitimate operational work, and re-authentication should be required for especially sensitive actions. Where persistent sessions are required for stability, the environment should compensate with stronger continuous verification signals such as device posture and anomalous behavior detection. In operational terms, the safest privileged session is one that exists only when needed, from known places, for a constrained purpose.

Monitoring privileged sessions must be anchored to a clear definition of what is observable and what constitutes meaningful evidence. At minimum, organizations need visibility into who initiated the session, from where, using which device or execution context, and what privileged actions were performed. For interactive sessions, that means capturing identity, host, and command-level or activity-level telemetry sufficient to reconstruct high-impact actions without requiring full screen recording. For management-plane and API activity, it means capturing the requestor identity, token or session identifier, target resource, action type, and outcome, including denied attempts because repeated failures often precede eventual success. Monitoring must also preserve the integrity of time, because privileged attackers frequently manipulate clocks or exploit time inconsistencies to confuse investigations. The objective is not exhaustive logging of every keystroke but a defensible record of privileged outcomes and the context that explains them.

A key control is to ensure privileged sessions are attributable to individuals, because shared context erodes both detection and accountability. When multiple people use the same privileged identity, monitoring becomes ambiguous and investigations become political, especially under incident pressure. Individual attribution also enables behavior baselining, which is one of the few reliable ways to detect subtle misuse of legitimate privileges. Attribution is equally important for contractors and third parties, who may require elevated access but operate outside the organization's normal supervision. Strong attribution does not require distrust; it reflects the reality that privilege must be defensible to auditors and responders, and "we don't know who did it" is not acceptable when the action can change the state of systems of record. Good operations treat privileged identities as instruments of governance as much as instruments of administration.

Controlling privileged sessions also requires constraining what happens inside the session, not only controlling who can start it. This is where just-in-time elevation and scoped permissions matter operationally, because a session that is elevated only for a specific role or task has less blast radius even if compromised. For highly sensitive actions, additional approval checkpoints can be enforced at the moment of action rather than only at session initiation, which reduces the risk of broad approvals being misused. Session controls should also address lateral movement, because privileged sessions are often used to jump from management hosts to production systems, then to identity control planes. Constraining which targets an administrator can reach during a privileged session, and enforcing separate privileges for separate planes, reduces the ability of an attacker to chain access across the environment. The overarching principle is to treat privilege as segmented authority rather than an all-access pass.

Privileged session monitoring must prioritize sequences of actions, not just individual events, because attackers rarely succeed with a single step. The high-risk patterns include privilege escalation followed by credential creation, policy modification, disabling of security controls, and changes to log forwarding or retention. Another pattern is "environment shaping," where an attacker quietly creates alternate access paths—new keys, new tokens, new trusted devices—before triggering disruptive actions later. Monitoring should be tuned to detect those chains, including the order and timing that suggests an operator is building leverage rather than completing a routine administrative task. This is also where defenders must be careful with alert fatigue; privileged activity can be noisy, so detection must focus on high-signal pivots and deviations rather than firing on every admin command. A mature program uses privileged session telemetry to identify when the environment is being reconfigured in ways that reduce control effectiveness, even if the changes appear operationally plausible.

AI/ML is operationally useful in privileged session monitoring because it can summarize activity, cluster related events across systems, and flag deviations that are hard to express as static rules. For example, models can detect unusual combinations of actions for a given role, rare administrative paths that only appear during compromise, or changes that deviate from the normal pace and sequencing of legitimate work. AI-assisted triage can also reduce time-to-understanding by translating raw logs into a coherent narrative of what happened, which is especially valuable when responders are trying to determine whether to cut off a privileged session midstream. These benefits depend on consistent identity correlation and high-fidelity telemetry; if privileged actions are inconsistently logged, models will learn the gaps and produce misleading confidence. Drift is also a real risk, because administrative behavior changes during migrations, reorganizations, and incident response, which can cause models to suppress alerts precisely when the environment is unstable. The correct governance stance is that AI recommendations inform prioritization, but termination of sessions, revocation of tokens, and privileged lockouts remain explicit human decisions with documented justification.

Controlling privileged sessions during incidents is particularly delicate because defensive actions can collide with business continuity. Cutting off a privileged session might stop an attacker, but it might also interrupt an engineer restoring service or a responder isolating compromised systems. This is where pre-defined runbooks and clear escalation paths matter, because responders need authority to revoke access quickly without debating process in the middle of an attack. Controls should support rapid containment actions such as session termination, token revocation, forced re-authentication, and temporary removal of privileged roles, while preserving evidence for investigation. Organizations that lack these capabilities often resort to broad network blocks or emergency shutdowns, which can be more disruptive and less effective. Incident operations should also anticipate that attackers will attempt to use privileged sessions to disable monitoring and to lock out defenders, so defensive privilege must be protected and distinct from routine administrative privilege. The ability to contain without blinding the organization is the hallmark of a mature privileged session control posture.

Finally, monitoring and control must include continuous validation that the system is working as intended, because privileged session controls are only valuable if they are reliably enforced under stress. Organizations should be able to demonstrate that privileged sessions are consistently routed through controlled pathways, that high-impact actions generate observable events, and that alerts reach accountable humans quickly enough to matter. Testing should include scenarios such as compromised admin endpoints, attempted policy tampering, and simulated token theft to verify both detection and response actions. Post-incident review should verify that session control decisions were appropriate and that any emergency overrides were reconciled and removed. The practical goal is not perfection; it is to make privileged misuse difficult, observable, and containable before it becomes irreversible. When privileged sessions are treated as a monitored, constrained operational capability, they become a manageable risk rather than an existential one.

Service Accounts and Non-Human Privilege

Non-human privilege exists because systems need to talk to systems, but it is often riskier than human privilege because it is easier to overlook and harder to govern. Service accounts, managed identities, API keys, and other machine credentials routinely hold permissions that can read data at scale, deploy changes, rotate secrets, and administer infrastructure. Unlike a person, a service identity does not get tired, does not hesitate, and can execute thousands of privileged actions per minute if misused. Attackers understand this leverage and frequently target non-human credentials because they can provide quiet, durable access with fewer behavioral clues than an interactive admin session. The operational challenge is that organizations often treat these identities as "plumbing," even though they can control core control planes and production systems.

Defining non-human privilege begins with recognizing that privilege is determined by capability and scope, not by whether the identity has a human owner. A service identity that can modify directory objects, change network security controls, decrypt data, or write to production configuration stores is privileged regardless of whether it is labeled "automation" or "integration." The most dangerous pattern is when non-human identities are granted broad permissions "to make it work," especially across multiple environments or tenants. Another high-risk pattern is role re-use, where the same service account is used for unrelated functions because it is already provisioned and trusted. In those cases, compromise of one application becomes compromise of many, and responders struggle to revoke access without breaking dependent services. A defensible program treats non-human privilege as a first-class category with the same rigor as administrator access, adapted to automation realities.

Ownership and accountability are foundational because non-human identities drift rapidly when no one is responsible for them. Every privileged service identity should have an accountable human owner and a documented purpose that explains what it is allowed to do and why. That purpose must be specific enough to evaluate scope, such as "read from telemetry store and write to incident queue," rather than vague statements like "integration." Accountability also includes lifecycle responsibilities: creation, permission changes, rotation, monitoring, and decommissioning. Without lifecycle ownership, service identities become orphaned, and orphans accumulate privileges because no one wants to risk breaking an unknown dependency. From a leadership perspective, this is one of the most common sources of hidden privilege sprawl because it sits outside standard HR-driven joiner–mover–leaver processes.

Controlling non-human privilege requires minimizing credential exposure and limiting where and how credentials can be used. Long-lived shared secrets are particularly risky because they are easy to copy, hard to inventory, and frequently embedded in code repositories, configuration files, build logs, or third-party systems. Even when secrets are stored "securely," they often leak through troubleshooting artifacts, misconfigured backups, or overly broad read access to secret stores. The safest posture is to reduce reliance on static secrets, prefer short-lived tokens where feasible, and bind the identity to specific execution contexts such as a workload, host, or pipeline stage. Context binding matters because it changes a stolen token from an all-purpose key into something that is difficult to use outside the intended runtime. When non-human credentials must exist, they should be treated like high-value assets with controlled distribution, constrained usage, and fast revocation.

Non-human privilege must also be controlled at the authorization layer, because the blast radius is defined by what the identity can do once it is authenticated. Least privilege for service identities is rarely achieved by simply assigning a single high-level role; it is achieved by mapping permissions to specific operations and data paths. For example, a service identity that only needs to publish messages to a queue should not also be able to read from it, alter retention, or change access policies. A deployment identity that can push code should not also have broad read access to secrets unrelated to the deployment target. This level of scoping is operationally demanding, but it pays dividends during incident response because it limits how far a compromised non-human identity can reach. It also reduces accidental damage, because automation mistakes become contained failures rather than cross-environment outages.

Monitoring non-human privilege requires different techniques than monitoring human administrators because the signals are more repetitive and high volume. The goal is to establish a stable baseline for expected machine behavior, then detect deviations that suggest credential theft, misuse, or compromised workloads. High-signal indicators include access from unexpected networks, execution outside expected time windows for scheduled jobs, abnormal spikes in request volume, and new or rare privileged actions that are not part of the identity's normal pattern. Another critical indicator is change in token issuance or authentication method, such as new keys being created, new signing credentials being used, or a service identity suddenly authenticating interactively. Monitoring also needs to account for "permission creep," where a service identity gradually acquires additional privileges through repeated exceptions, which can be detected by tracking changes to role assignments and policy attachments over time. Non-human monitoring succeeds when it treats the identity as a workload with defined operating parameters, not as a user account with a password.

AI/ML can be particularly effective for non-human privilege because machine behavior is often more consistent than human behavior, making anomalies easier to detect when telemetry is complete. Models can learn normal request rates, action sequences, resource targets, and dependency graphs, then flag deviations such as a service identity touching new datasets, performing administrative actions it has never performed before, or attempting operations across environments that are normally isolated. AI-assisted triage can also cluster anomalous activity across multiple service identities, which is valuable when a compromised pipeline or secret store leads to broad credential exposure. The failure modes mirror those of other domains but can be sharper here: incomplete logging can create blind spots that models interpret as normal, and legitimate scaling events can look malicious if models do not understand capacity changes or deployments. There is also a governance risk if teams allow model outputs to implicitly authorize privilege expansions, because models trained on historically permissive access will recommend permissive outcomes. The correct boundary is for AI to accelerate detection and investigation while human owners remain accountable for permission changes, token revocation, and incident containment decisions.

Incident response involving non-human privilege must prioritize containment without collapsing critical services, because service identities often sit on core operational paths. Responders need the ability to quickly disable or rotate credentials, revoke active tokens, and isolate the workloads that use those identities, while preserving enough continuity to keep production stable. This requires pre-planned fallback paths, such as alternate identities with reduced scope, staged credential rotation procedures, or the ability to temporarily restrict actions rather than fully disabling an identity. A common failure mode is to revoke a widely used service identity during an incident and unintentionally create an outage that obscures the attacker's activity and consumes the response team's attention. Another failure mode is the opposite: leaving the identity active because it is "too important," which gives the attacker time to expand access and entrench persistence. Mature operations rehearse these scenarios so that containment is a practiced workflow rather than an improvised gamble.

Finally, governance for non-human privilege must include disciplined inventory and decommissioning, because unused credentials are an attacker's gift. Organizations should be able to enumerate privileged service identities, understand where they run, and verify that each one has a current business purpose. Identities that have not been used within a defined window should be reviewed and, if appropriate, disabled with a monitored grace period to catch unexpected dependencies. Permission changes for service identities should be treated as privileged events with clear approval and auditability, because they can silently expand blast radius without any interactive session. Over time, the organizations that manage non-human privilege well are those that make it observable and accountable, not those that rely on tribal knowledge. When service identities are tightly scoped, context-bound, continuously monitored, and governed through a real lifecycle, they stop being a hidden backdoor and become a controlled operational capability.

Privilege Auditing and Evidence Collection

Privilege auditing exists to answer two questions with defensible evidence: who had the power to cause high-impact outcomes, and what they actually did with that power. In privileged access management, intent and assertion are never sufficient, because both mistakes and adversaries can produce plausible narratives after the fact. Auditing provides the structured, repeatable mechanism to verify that privileged access is appropriately assigned, appropriately used, and appropriately revoked. Evidence collection is the operational counterpart, ensuring that the facts of privileged activity are captured with integrity and can be reconstructed under scrutiny. When auditing and evidence are weak, organizations lose time during incidents, lose credibility during reviews, and lose leverage in remediation because they cannot prove where control failed.

A practical audit posture begins with authoritative inventory of privileged identities and their entitlements, because you cannot audit what you cannot enumerate. That inventory must include human administrators, service identities, delegated workflow identities, and any emergency or break-glass access paths. It must also include group-based privileges and inherited privileges, since many of the highest risk permissions are acquired indirectly through nested roles, dynamic group membership, or policy attachments. An effective program can show not only who is privileged today, but how they became privileged and what approvals and justifications exist for that state. Without lineage, audits devolve into snapshots that miss the real risk: privilege that accumulates over time through exceptions and drift. For executives, the inventory becomes a risk register of concentrated authority; for operators, it is the baseline needed to prioritize review and enforcement.

Evidence collection for privileged actions must prioritize integrity, correlation, and retention, because privileged attackers target the very systems that create evidence. Integrity means logs and records must be protected against alteration, deletion, or selective suppression, including resistance to manipulation by identities that may themselves be privileged. Correlation means the organization can connect an administrative action to the identity that performed it, the session or token used, the target resource affected, and the approval or change record that authorized it. Retention means keeping evidence long enough to support investigations that begin weeks or months after initial compromise, which is common in identity-centric intrusions. These requirements push organizations toward evidence pipelines that are difficult to tamper with from within the environment being monitored. If privileged users can disable or rewrite the logs that describe their own actions, the audit function becomes performative rather than protective.

Privilege auditing must also address the difference between entitlement and effective capability, because real-world privilege is often broader than what appears on paper. An identity may have limited formal permissions but possess effective privilege through delegation paths, access to credential material, control of automation pipelines, or write access to configuration that governs authorization. Similarly, an identity may be entitled to a role but prevented from exercising it by conditional access rules, network controls, or session constraints, which affects both risk and audit findings. Mature audits validate control effectiveness by testing and by reviewing actual activity rather than relying solely on configuration state. This is especially important in hybrid and cloud environments where permissions can be layered across multiple control planes and where policy interactions create surprising outcomes. An audit that cannot distinguish between assigned privilege and usable privilege will miss both hidden exposure and false positives.

Operationally, privilege auditing should be event-driven as much as it is calendar-driven, because the riskiest moments are when privilege changes. Role assignment, privilege elevation, new service identity creation, policy exceptions, and changes to authentication requirements are all privileged events that deserve immediate recording and review. Waiting for a quarterly audit means accepting a long window in which misconfigurations and malicious changes can persist unnoticed. Event-driven auditing does not require human review of every change; it requires that changes be captured, attributable, and triaged by risk so that the right ones receive rapid attention. This is where workflow integration matters: privilege grants should be tied to requests, approvals, and tickets so that auditors can validate not only that an action occurred, but that it was authorized and scoped. When entitlement changes are tracked as first-class events, the organization can detect privilege creep early and reverse it before it becomes structural.

Evidence collection must also support incident response realities, where responders need fast, high-confidence answers under pressure. During a privileged compromise, teams must quickly determine the scope of access, whether new privileged identities were created, whether authentication policies were altered, and whether monitoring was impaired. That requires evidence that is searchable, time-consistent, and normalized enough to support rapid analysis across identity, endpoint, network, and management-plane logs. It also requires preservation of volatile evidence such as active sessions, issued tokens, recent administrative commands, and configuration diffs that may otherwise be overwritten. The most effective programs predefine what evidence must be collected for privileged incidents and ensure that responders can obtain it without needing privileged access that may itself be compromised. In other words, evidence collection is not just about storing logs; it is about ensuring investigators can trust and use them when trust is under attack.

AI/ML can materially improve privilege auditing by identifying outliers and patterns that humans miss, but it must be applied with disciplined governance and explainability. Models can prioritize audit review by flagging unusual privilege grants, rare combinations of entitlements, new delegation pathways, or administrative actions that statistically correlate with past incidents. They can also reduce the burden of evidence review by summarizing long sequences of privileged events into coherent narratives and by clustering related activity across identities and systems. The dependencies are non-negotiable: models require high-quality, consistently labeled telemetry, stable identity correlation, and a clear definition of what constitutes privileged activity. The failure modes include bias toward historically common practices, which can normalize risky behavior, and drift during migrations or reorganizations, which can produce both missed detections and noisy false alarms. For audit defensibility, model outputs must be treated as leads that drive human verification, and the organization must retain the underlying evidence and rationale for any decisions influenced by the model.

Auditability also depends on making privileged work reconstructable, which requires recording not only "what changed" but also "what the system looked like before and after." Configuration change evidence, policy snapshots, and role membership histories are essential because privileged incidents often involve subtle adjustments that are hard to interpret from isolated events. If an attacker changes a policy and later restores it, point-in-time review may miss that the system was exposed during the window of compromise. Similarly, if an attacker grants themselves privilege briefly and then removes it, only retained entitlement history will reveal the escalation. Evidence collection should therefore include immutable histories of privilege assignments and policy changes, not merely current state. The goal is to support retrospective truth: the ability to prove what was true at a specific time, not just what is true now.

Finally, privilege auditing must produce outcomes that improve control, not merely reports that document drift. Findings should translate into tightened role definitions, reduced standing privilege, improved approval workflows, enhanced monitoring coverage, and clearer separation of duties. Evidence gaps should trigger specific remediation such as enabling missing logs, hardening log pipelines, improving time synchronization, or correcting identity correlation issues that prevent reliable attribution. Organizations should also test the audit and evidence pipeline by simulating privileged misuse and verifying that the expected records appear, remain intact, and can be reconstructed into a timeline. When auditing is treated as an operational feedback loop, it becomes a driver of resilience rather than a compliance burden. In privileged access management, the ability to prove control is not administrative overhead; it is a core defensive capability that shortens incidents, sharpens accountability, and reduces the probability of repeated failure.

AI-Assisted Privilege Monitoring: Session Signals, Anomaly Detection, and Override Controls

AI-assisted privilege monitoring is most valuable when it is treated as a risk-reduction mechanism for high-impact ambiguity, not as an automated gatekeeper that replaces accountability. Privileged environments generate dense telemetry, and many of the most dangerous actions look superficially legitimate because administrators and attackers often use the same interfaces. The purpose of AI/ML in this context is to detect subtle shifts in session behavior, correlate weak signals across control planes, and prioritize human attention where minutes matter. To be operationally credible, these models must be grounded in defined privileged roles and actions, with clearly scoped decision rights and explicit override controls. When AI is positioned as an oracle, it creates the conditions for false confidence and delayed containment, especially in the hands of teams that already struggle with consistent privilege governance. Table 12.3 identifies the session signal types that enable reliable privileged anomaly detection and enforceable human override boundaries.

Session signals are the raw inputs that make AI-assisted monitoring possible, and their quality determines the ceiling of detection performance. At a minimum, effective signals include identity attributes, authentication method, device posture indicators, source network context, geolocation and travel plausibility, session duration, and the targeted resources and actions performed. Privileged sessions also require higher-resolution behavioral

Table 12.3 Privileged Session Signals for Monitoring and AI-Assisted Anomaly Detection.

Signal Category	Examples of Signals	What It Helps Detect	Key Dependency
Identity and authentication context	Authentication method and elevation pathway	Unexpected privilege use and suspicious elevation	Consistent identity correlation
Device and source context	Device posture and source network	Session hijacking and unusual access origins	Reliable device and network telemetry
Session behavior and sequencing	Action sequences and timing	Privilege-shaping persistence creation visibility reduction	High-fidelity event logging
Target and scope of change	Target resources and action types	Expansion to new systems and high-impact control plane changes	Accurate resource labeling
Token and issuance patterns	Token issuance and session duration	Replay and abnormal token behavior	Token-level telemetry availability
Override and approval linkage	Override use and approval record linkage	Untracked bypass and policy drift	Durable intent and approval records

signals such as administrative action sequences, frequency and timing of high-impact operations, use of elevation pathways, and interaction with sensitive control-plane settings like logging and policy enforcement. For non-human privilege, the signals shift toward request rate, token issuance patterns, API call distributions, and deviations from expected dependency graphs. The operational reality is that missing or inconsistent signals do not merely reduce accuracy; they shape what the model believes is normal, which can blind it to entire classes of abuse. The first practical step in "AI privilege monitoring" is therefore not model selection but telemetry normalization and identity correlation across systems.

Anomaly detection in privileged sessions must be designed around adversary behavior and administrative reality, not around abstract statistical novelty. The most actionable anomalies are those that indicate increased capability, reduced visibility, or the creation of alternate access paths, because those outcomes meaningfully change incident trajectory. Examples include sudden role grants during an active session, changes to authentication requirements, creation of new keys or tokens, modification of conditional access policies, disabling of logging, or unusual access to secret stores. Sequence-based detection is often more reliable than single-event detection, because legitimate admins may occasionally perform any one of these actions, but the chain and timing are harder for an attacker to mask. Models should also treat denial events and near-misses as meaningful, since repeated failed attempts at privileged operations can precede successful escalation through a different path. In operational terms, AI should be tuned to surface "privilege-shaping" behavior early, when defenders still have the option to terminate sessions, revoke tokens, and contain without widespread disruption. Figure 12.1 shows how privileged session signals feed anomaly detection, how alerts drive human review, and where override controls apply without removing accountability. It reinforces that AI accelerates prioritization and investigation while humans remain responsible for disruptive containment actions.

Baselining is the foundation for anomaly detection, but privileged baselines must be built with care because administrative work is both role-specific and seasonally variable. On-call schedules, patch cycles, incident response activity, and major migrations all shift privileged behavior patterns in ways that are legitimate but unusual. A baseline that does not account for these operational rhythms will create alert fatigue, leading teams to suppress detections and lose trust in the system. Conversely, a baseline that is too permissive will normalize risky actions and allow slow adversary drift, where the attacker gradually changes behavior to fit within learned norms. The right approach is to baseline at multiple levels: per identity, per role, per system, and per environment, with explicit handling for planned change windows and known high-variance periods. For leadership, this matters

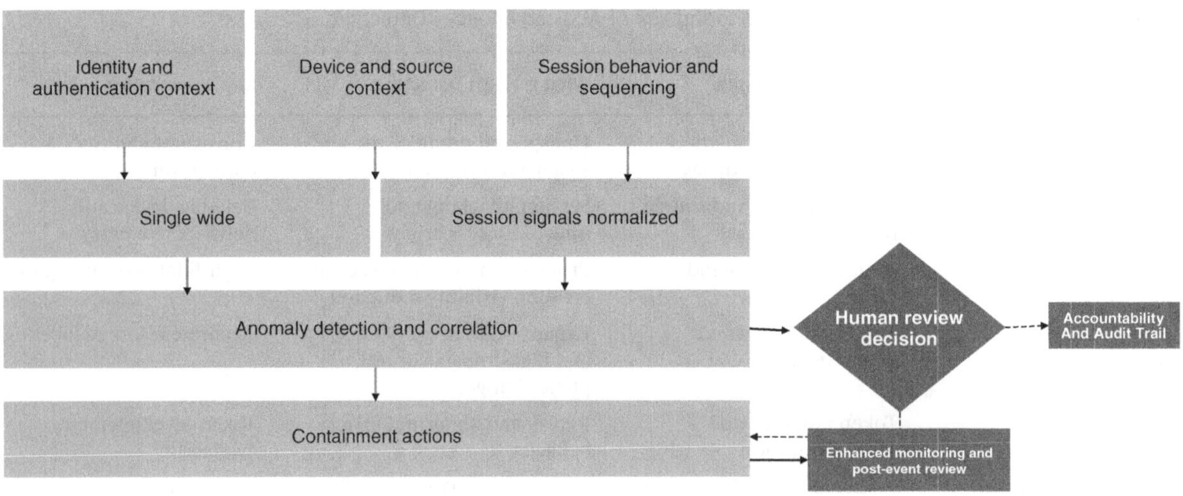

Figure 12.1 AI-Assisted Privileged Session Monitoring with Human Override Controls.

because it turns AI monitoring from a one-time deployment into an operational discipline with measurable maintenance expectations.

Human-in-the-loop controls are non-negotiable in privileged monitoring because the cost of a false negative can be catastrophic and the cost of a false positive can be operationally disruptive. AI outputs should drive triage, escalation, and response recommendations, but the authority to approve sensitive privilege changes or to take disruptive containment actions must remain explicitly assigned to accountable humans. This is especially true for actions like session termination, forced re-authentication, removal of privileged roles, or lockdown of management-plane access, which can interrupt legitimate recovery work and create outages. A mature posture uses AI to compress time-to-decision by providing context-rich evidence: what changed, what is unusual, what similar patterns looked like historically, and which controls are at immediate risk. The system should also record the human decision and rationale, because auditability is part of safety; if a model influenced a containment choice, that influence should be traceable. The objective is to speed correct action, not to accelerate action without accountability.

Override controls are the operational safety valves that keep AI-assisted monitoring from becoming either a blocker of legitimate work or a silent enabler of adversary activity. Override does not mean "ignore alerts"; it means a controlled mechanism for temporarily permitting high-risk actions when the business requires them, while increasing monitoring and ensuring after-the-fact review. In practice, overrides should be time-bound, scope-bound, and attributable to a specific approver, with a requirement to link the override to a documented justification. Overrides should also change the monitoring posture, because an override increases risk; enhanced logging, tighter session timeouts, and elevated analyst attention are appropriate compensations. A common failure mode is informal overrides executed outside tracked workflows, which train teams to bypass controls and create unmonitored privilege. Another failure mode is blanket suppression, where teams disable a detection rule because it is noisy rather than improving the telemetry or refining the model, leaving a durable gap.

AI-assisted privilege monitoring must explicitly account for its own failure modes, because adversaries will exploit both model weaknesses and organizational overreliance. Models can be deceived through mimicry of legitimate administrative patterns, especially when attackers operate through compromised administrator endpoints and follow familiar change sequences. They can also fail through drift when the environment changes, or through bias when historical data reflects permissive practices that the organization is trying to correct. Data leakage is an additional concern, because privilege monitoring often processes sensitive identity and operational telemetry that must be protected as a security asset. Governance must therefore include clear data-handling rules, strict access control to model inputs and outputs, and retention policies that preserve investigative value without expanding exposure. If model artifacts and enriched event summaries are accessible broadly, they can become a roadmap for attackers seeking to understand monitoring coverage and thresholds.

Operationalizing AI-assisted privilege monitoring requires clear response playbooks that translate model outputs into consistent actions. An anomaly score is not an action; it is a prioritization signal that must map to defined thresholds, escalation paths, and containment options. For example, low-confidence anomalies may trigger enrichment and watchlisting, while high-confidence anomalies involving control-plane modifications may trigger immediate session termination and privilege revocation pending verification. The playbooks must also define how to coordinate with IT and platform teams, because privilege response often affects availability, and responders need pre-established authority to act quickly. Without this, teams either hesitate during real attacks or take overly disruptive actions because they lack nuanced options. The success measure is that anomalies lead to faster, more accurate decisions, with fewer escalations that are later judged unnecessary.

Finally, AI-assisted privilege monitoring should be treated as a continuously governed control with measurable performance, not as a "set and forget" capability. Teams should track detection coverage for privileged actions, false-positive and false-negative trends, time-to-triage, and the percentage of privileged incidents detected through anomaly signals versus other means. Regular review should include recalibration for environmental changes, validation that key session signals remain available and trustworthy, and testing that override pathways are logged and reviewed as designed. This governance posture keeps the system honest: it forces the organization to confront where telemetry is missing, where privilege workflows are drifting, and where model confidence is being mistaken for certainty. When implemented with disciplined signals, defensible anomaly logic, and controlled overrides, AI becomes a force multiplier for privileged monitoring without becoming a single point of failure. In privileged environments, the goal is not to automate trust; it is to make misuse visible quickly enough that humans can contain it.

Reducing Privilege Without Disrupting Operations

Reducing privilege is not an access-denial exercise; it is a risk-shaping exercise that must respect how work actually gets done. Organizations fail at privilege reduction when they treat it as a one-time cleanup or a policy mandate divorced from operational reality. Privilege exists because systems are complex, outages are costly, and teams are expected to restore service quickly under pressure. The goal, therefore, is not to eliminate privilege, but to minimize standing authority while preserving the ability to perform high-impact work safely and predictably. When reduction is framed as operational enablement rather than restriction, it becomes a resilience improvement instead of a source of friction.

The first practical step is to distinguish standing privilege from situational need, because most administrators do not require elevated rights for the majority of their day. Standing privilege accumulates for convenience and then becomes invisible, which is why it is so dangerous. Reducing it begins by identifying which actions truly require elevation and which are artifacts of legacy practices, broad roles, or undocumented dependencies. This analysis must be grounded in observed behavior, not job descriptions, because real workflows often differ from assumed ones. When teams see that most privileged actions occur in short bursts around specific tasks, it becomes easier to accept time-bound elevation models. The operational insight is that reducing privilege often improves clarity about work patterns rather than slowing them down.

Privilege reduction must be incremental and reversible, because abrupt changes break trust and production systems at the same time. Large-scale removals of access without staged validation push teams toward workarounds such as shared accounts, credential caching, or undocumented exceptions that increase risk. A safer approach is to start with the least controversial reductions, such as removing unused privileges, narrowing scopes that are clearly excessive, and separating unrelated permissions that were bundled for convenience. Each change should be validated against real workflows, with a clear rollback path if unexpected dependencies surface. This cadence allows teams to learn where privilege is genuinely required and where it persists out of habit. Over time, the organization replaces assumptions with evidence, which makes deeper reductions possible without drama.

Reducing privilege also requires redesigning workflows so that elevation is fast, predictable, and aligned with accountability. If engineers must wait hours for access to resolve an outage, they will resist reduction and look for shortcuts. Conversely, if elevation is near-instant, time-bound, and scoped to the task at hand, teams are more willing to operate without standing admin rights. The workflow must clearly communicate what is happening: when elevation starts, what it allows, and when it ends. It must also ensure that elevation leaves a durable trail of intent and action so that operators are protected as well as governed. When privilege reduction is paired with better workflows, it often reduces stress rather than increasing it, because expectations are explicit and supportable.

Operational separation is another powerful lever for reducing privilege without disruption, particularly in complex environments. When identities and access paths are cleanly separated across identity, security, infrastructure, and application control planes, teams can hold the authority they need without inheriting unrelated risk. This separation allows privilege to be reduced in one plane without affecting others, which limits blast radius during mistakes and incidents. It also improves troubleshooting, because responders can more confidently isolate changes to the plane in which the problem occurred. Many organizations struggle here because historical admin roles grew organically and cut across planes for convenience. Untangling them is not glamorous work, but it is one of the most effective ways to reduce privilege while preserving operational autonomy.

Reducing privilege must also account for non-human identities, which often hold more persistent power than people. Service accounts and automation identities frequently accumulate permissions to avoid breaking pipelines, and those permissions quietly become permanent. Reducing non-human privilege requires mapping identities to workloads, understanding dependency chains, and scoping permissions to the smallest viable set of actions and resources. This work is operationally sensitive because mistakes can cause outages, which is why changes must be tested in lower-risk environments and rolled out gradually. It also requires ownership, because someone must be accountable for validating that an automation still works with reduced permissions. When done carefully, non-human privilege reduction often yields immediate risk reduction because these identities are high-value targets with little human oversight.

AI/ML can materially support privilege reduction by providing evidence that reduces fear and guesswork, particularly in large or dynamic environments. Models can analyze historical activity to identify permissions that are never exercised, actions that occur only during specific workflows, and identities whose effective privilege is much broader than their actual use. This allows teams to propose reductions with data-backed confidence rather than intuition, which improves buy-in from operators and leaders alike. AI can also help detect when a reduction breaks an expected pattern, signaling a legitimate dependency that was overlooked. The failure mode is allowing models to automatically remove access or to treat historical misuse as justification for continued privilege; both create new risk. The correct role for AI is to inform decisions and prioritize validation, with humans approving and owning the outcomes.

Communication and change management are as important as technical controls in reducing privilege without disruption. Operators need to understand not only what is changing, but why, how it will affect their work, and what support exists when something breaks. Clear escalation paths, fast remediation, and visible leadership backing are essential to prevent privilege reduction from becoming a blame exercise. When teams experience that reduced privilege does not leave them stranded during incidents, resistance drops sharply. Over time, reduced standing access becomes the norm rather than a special condition, and exceptions stand out as deliberate choices rather than inherited entitlements. This cultural shift is often the hardest part, but it is also the most durable.

Finally, privilege reduction must be treated as a continuous operational practice rather than a project with an end date. Environments change, teams reorganize, platforms evolve, and new tools introduce new privilege paths that did not exist before. Each change creates opportunities for privilege creep unless reduction is built into onboarding, role design, automation, and review cycles. Success is measured not by how much access was removed at once, but by how consistently the organization prevents unnecessary privilege from becoming permanent. When reduction is embedded into normal operations, it ceases to be disruptive and instead becomes part of how the organization manages risk. In that state, privilege is no longer a silent liability; it is a controlled capability aligned with both security and business continuity.

Conclusion

Privileged access remains the highest consequence category because it concentrates authority over control planes, security posture, and the integrity of operational truth. When privilege is treated as routine, organizations inherit silent single points of failure: overbroad roles, long-lived sessions, unmanaged service identities, and emergency pathways that become shortcuts. The practical alternative is disciplined control of privileged work through clear role and action definitions, approvals that match risk, time-bound elevation, and monitoring that makes privileged behavior explainable and containable. AI-assisted monitoring strengthens this posture when it is anchored in reliable session signals and governed with human-in-the-loop decisions, because detection speed is only valuable when actions and overrides remain accountable.

Long-term resilience comes from treating privilege as a controlled operational capability rather than a static entitlement that accumulates over time. That means continuously reducing standing privilege without disrupting critical workflows, testing break-glass access, so it works only when it must, and ensuring every privileged action can be reconstructed from durable evidence. It also means building response muscle that can terminate sessions, revoke tokens, and restore trusted configurations without blinding monitoring or creating unnecessary downtime. When these practices are consistently applied, privileged compromise becomes harder to achieve, easier to detect, and faster to contain, which reduces both the probability and the cost of business-impacting incidents.

Recommendations

1) Define privileged roles and privileged actions by impact rather than by title or convenience. Identify which identities can change authentication requirements, modify security controls, manage secrets, or alter logging and retention. Document these roles and actions in a way that is testable against observable outcomes, not just organizational assumptions. Use that definition as the boundary for monitoring, approvals, and auditing.
2) Minimize standing privilege by separating routine work from elevated work and making elevation time-bound and scoped. Validate which tasks truly require privileged access using observed administrative behavior and entitlement usage patterns. Build workflows, so elevation is predictable and fast enough to support operations without encouraging shortcuts. Ensure de-elevation is automatic or enforced, so privilege does not persist longer than needed.
3) Implement approval models that tie privileged access and high-impact actions to documented intent and accountable decision makers. Capture purpose, scope, and time window before elevation occurs, and ensure the system enforces those boundaries rather than relying on informal understanding. Use emergency pathways only under explicit activation criteria and require after-the-fact review as a control, not a courtesy. Maintain clear attribution, so requesters, approvers, and operators are individually identifiable.
4) Treat break-glass accounts as continuity controls with strict custody, limited use, and immediate monitoring. Establish explicit activation criteria tied to concrete failure conditions such as identity outages, systemic MFA failures, or corrupted privileged assignments. Design retrieval, so it is accessible in a crisis but requires controlled steps and produces an auditable record. Test and rotate emergency access regularly to prevent drift and to confirm alerting and evidence pipelines work as intended.
5) Monitor and control privileged sessions as distinct from standard user activity, focusing on both authentication assurance and execution assurance. Route privileged work through controlled pathways and hardened administrative endpoints to reduce session theft and token replay risk. Collect telemetry that can reconstruct high-impact actions and correlate sessions to approvals, targets, and outcomes. Prioritize detection of action sequences that indicate privilege shaping, persistence creation, or visibility reduction.
6) Make privileged identities individually attributable and eliminate shared administrative accounts wherever possible. Ensure privileged work can be traced to a person, a session, and a documented intent record, so investigations do not stall on ambiguity. Apply the same attribution discipline to contractors and third parties who require elevated access. Treat non-attributable privileged activity as a security-relevant exception that demands remediation.
7) Govern service accounts and non-human identities as first-class privileged entities with clear ownership and lifecycle controls. Assign a responsible human owner and a specific documented purpose to each privileged service identity. Reduce exposure by limiting where credentials can be used and by constraining permissions to the smallest viable set of actions and resources. Monitor non-human behavior for deviations in context, request volume, targets, and privileged action types.
8) Build privilege auditing around authoritative inventories, entitlement lineage, and immutable histories rather than point-in-time snapshots. Track not only who is privileged today, but how they became privileged and what approvals justified that state. Preserve privilege assignment histories and policy change records, so brief

escalations or temporary exposures are still discoverable. Protect evidence pipelines against tampering by privileged identities, so audit findings remain defensible under scrutiny.

9) Use AI-assisted privilege monitoring to accelerate triage and correlation while keeping humans responsible for authorization and disruptive containment actions. Feed models reliable session signals such as identity context, device posture, source network, action sequences, and management-plane activity, so anomaly detection is grounded in reality. Treat model output as decision support, not permission, and record the human rationale for overrides and containment choices. Regularly recalibrate and validate models to manage drift and to prevent false confidence from becoming an operational risk.
10) Reduce privilege incrementally with staged validation and clear rollback paths to avoid operational disruption. Start with removing unused privileges, narrowing clearly excessive scopes, and separating bundled entitlements that create unnecessary blast radius. Coordinate changes with teams by making elevation workflows usable and by providing fast escalation paths when dependencies surface. Measure success by sustained prevention of privilege creep and by improved ability to contain privileged misuse quickly and with confidence.

13

Protecting Data and Systems

Protecting data and systems is not a compliance exercise or a feature checklist, it is the operational discipline that keeps the organization's most portable value from becoming its most portable liability. In practice, sensitive information constantly shifts states as it is created, transformed, shared, analyzed, and stored across endpoints, clouds, third parties, and automated pipelines. Effective protection requires that classification, encryption, access control, and monitoring operate as an integrated control system that constrains unsafe pathways while keeping approved workflows fast and reliable. When these mechanisms are coupled with accountable ownership and auditable governance, the organization can move at business speed without normalizing exposure through drift, exceptions, shadow copies, or misplaced trust in automation.

Data Protection as a Business Requirement

Data protection is a business requirement because information is the organization's operating fuel and its most portable form of value. Customer records, financial data, product designs, legal filings, and internal strategy all move faster than the systems that host them, crossing clouds, endpoints, third parties, and employee devices. Treating protection as a technical feature of storage or a compliance checkbox ignores how data actually behaves in modern operations: it is copied, transformed, cached, exported, and shared to meet business goals. When leadership frames data protection as a business constraint—like safety, quality, or financial controls—defenders can anchor decisions in risk tolerance, not tool availability. This framing also clarifies that "availability" is not the only dimension that matters; confidentiality and integrity failures often create irreversible harm long after systems come back online.

A practical definition of data protection begins with knowing what must be protected, why it matters, and what "harm" looks like if it is exposed, altered, or lost. The purpose is not to create an exhaustive catalog, but to establish defensible tiers of sensitivity that map to business outcomes, legal obligations, and competitive exposure. Classification is most valuable when it drives concrete handling rules, such as where the data may be stored, how it may be transmitted, and which identities may access it under what conditions. When classification is abstract or too granular, teams inevitably bypass it because it slows delivery without improving safety. A minimal, enforceable model aligned to revenue, regulatory scope, and strategic impact makes protection executable and measurable.

Protection requirements must be expressed in terms the business can act on: who can use the data, for what purpose, under which constraints, and with what evidence of compliance. That translates into access boundaries, encryption requirements, retention limits, and monitoring expectations that can be validated. Executives should expect every critical dataset to have a named owner accountable for approving access patterns, deciding acceptable sharing pathways, and sponsoring remediation when controls are not feasible. Ownership is not symbolic; it is how security avoids becoming the default approver for business decisions it does not own. When data owners and security agree on thresholds for exceptions, the organization can move quickly without normalizing uncontrolled exposure.

The most consistent source of data loss is not a sophisticated exploit, but ordinary workflow that quietly expands access over time. Data protection programs fail when "temporary" access becomes permanent, service accounts are over-privileged, and integrations accumulate without periodic pruning. The operational answer is to design access as a lifecycle: request, approval, provisioning, validation, periodic review, and removal. Identity governance provides the structure, but the business requirement is to ensure access remains purpose-bound as roles change and projects end. Measuring access drift—privileges that no longer match job function—often reveals risk faster than searching for a single malicious actor.

Controls must follow data across systems, which requires consistency in how identities, systems, and policies interpret the same requirement. Encryption at rest and in transit is necessary, but it does not define "protected" if keys are poorly managed, access is broadly granted, or decrypted copies are routinely exported. Strong key management and separation of duties reduce the blast radius when administrative accounts are compromised, and they make auditing meaningful rather than ceremonial. Tokenization and format-preserving protections can be appropriate when business processes require limited exposure, but they must be implemented so that developers and analysts cannot trivially bypass the protection by pulling raw fields. The goal is to make the safe path the default path, not to create a maze that pushes teams toward unsanctioned shortcuts.

Data protection must also recognize that modern work includes automated processing and AI/ML-enabled workflows that can change risk shape without changing intent. When teams use machine learning to classify documents, detect sensitive fields, or flag risky sharing patterns, the value is speed and scale, not authority. These models depend on representative telemetry—file metadata, access logs, data lineage, and labels—without which they produce confident but incorrect recommendations. Human-in-the-loop controls are essential: models can suggest sensitivity, recommend least-privilege access groups, or prioritize incidents, but approvals for new access pathways and exception grants must remain accountable decisions. Failure modes include drift as business language evolves, bias toward over-labeling or under-labeling based on training history, and leakage when sensitive samples are inadvertently used for model tuning or evaluation.

Finally, making data protection a business requirement means it is enforced through operating rhythms, not episodic cleanups. Leaders should expect routine reporting that ties protection posture to business-critical datasets, including where data resides, who can access it, how it is shared externally, and how quickly exposures are detected and contained. Defenders should design monitoring around the behaviors that precede loss: unusual exports, anomalous access sequences, new sharing links, privilege escalations, and abrupt changes in data movement patterns. Auditability matters because it creates trust that controls exist beyond assurances, and it provides evidence during incidents when decisions must be defended under time pressure. When data protection is treated as a requirement with measurable outcomes, security becomes a business enabler: it allows the organization to move data where it needs to go, with confidence that the value will not leak, corrupt, or disappear along the way.

Data Classification and Practical Usage

Classification only matters when it changes how people handle information in real workflows. If labels exist solely in a policy document or a training slide, they will be ignored the moment delivery pressure rises. Practical classification turns an abstract concept—sensitivity—into consistent handling decisions: where data can live, who can access it, how it can be shared, and what monitoring is required. The objective is not perfection; it is repeatability. A small number of tiers that map to business impact will outperform an elaborate taxonomy that no one can apply confidently.

Effective classification starts with the business outcome the data supports and the harm that follows loss of confidentiality, integrity, or availability. Customer and employee records carry privacy exposure and breach notification risk, while financial close artifacts carry integrity risk that can distort reporting and decision-making. Product designs and roadmaps carry competitive risk, where premature disclosure changes market position long before any regulator gets involved. Operational telemetry can be sensitive because it reveals internal architecture

Table 13.1 Data Classification Tiers and Default Handling Actions.

Tier	Business Impact Driver	Default Storage Rule	Default Sharing Rule	Monitoring Priority
Public	Low harm if exposed	Standard repositories allowed	External sharing allowed	Low
Internal	Operational inconvenience if exposed	Approved internal repositories only	External sharing restricted	Medium
Confidential	Material business or customer harm	Restricted repositories with encryption	External sharing requires controlled path	High
Restricted	Severe legal competitive or trust harm	Highly restricted repositories with tight access	External sharing time bound and verified	Highest

and security posture, even if it does not contain personal data. When these impacts are clearly articulated, classification becomes a business conversation with security controls attached, not a security mandate looking for justification.

To keep classification usable, define tiers in a way that non-specialists can apply without extensive interpretation. Terms like "confidential" are common but often ambiguous unless anchored to simple tests: would exposure create legal duty, financial loss, competitive disadvantage, or material customer trust damage. Teams should also know what "internal" means in practice, especially in environments with contractors, subsidiaries, and shared service providers. The most important property of a tier is the default handling rule it invokes, such as encryption requirements, external sharing restrictions, or mandatory access reviews. If a tier does not drive a distinct behavior, it is not a tier; it is noise. Table 13.1 ties practical classification tiers to the default handling behaviors that make labels operationally meaningful.

Classification must be embedded in the systems where work happens, not bolted on at the end. That means aligning labels across email, collaboration platforms, storage, ticketing systems, and source repositories, so the same information is treated consistently as it moves. Manual labeling can work for high-value artifacts, but most organizations need automation for scale because data changes faster than humans can tag it. The safest approach is to use automation to propose labels and enforce baseline protections, while allowing trained owners to override with justification. Over time, the goal is to reduce the number of "unclassified" or "unknown" objects, because unknown sensitivity is operationally equivalent to unmanaged risk.

There is an unavoidable tension between usability and control, and classification fails when it makes normal work harder than unsafe work. If sending a file externally requires a multi-step exception process, people will resort to screenshots, personal accounts, or alternate channels that bypass monitoring. Practical usage requires designing "approved paths" for common sharing needs: vendors, legal counsel, auditors, and joint project partners. These paths should implement the required protections—restricted access, time-bound links, watermarking where appropriate, and logging—without requiring users to invent their own solutions. Exceptions should exist, but they must be traceable decisions with defined expiration, not permanent loopholes.

AI/ML can strengthen classification when it is treated as decision support and paired with strong telemetry and governance. Models can detect likely sensitive fields, infer document types, and flag anomalous handling, such as high-sensitivity data being posted to broad channels or attached to external emails. These capabilities depend on reliable signals like content patterns, metadata, access context, and historical labeling decisions, and they degrade when training data is inconsistent or when business terminology shifts. Human-in-the-loop controls are essential: automated systems can recommend a label, but owners must retain accountability for high-impact artifacts and for exceptions that expand sharing. Failure modes include false confidence when a model under-classifies novel sensitive content, over-classification that causes users to ignore the system, and leakage risk if sensitive samples are used in model evaluation without strict access controls.

Classification also needs operational enforcement and verification; otherwise, it becomes a compliance story rather than a protection mechanism. Access control should reflect classification by default, with least privilege groups aligned to job function and purpose, and with periodic reviews to prevent access drift. Monitoring should be tier-aware so that alerts prioritize events involving higher-sensitivity data, such as mass downloads, unusual exports, and privilege escalations tied to restricted repositories. Data retention and disposal should also reflect tiers, because retaining high-sensitivity information "just in case" increases the blast radius of inevitable incidents. When classification is coupled to access, monitoring, retention, and approved sharing workflows, it becomes a practical control surface that executives can understand and defenders can run.

Encryption Concepts and Operational Implementation

Encryption is only valuable when it reliably protects data in the places and moments where exposure would otherwise occur. At its core, encryption transforms readable data into ciphertext that is unintelligible without the correct cryptographic key, but the protection outcome depends less on the math and more on how keys are generated, stored, used, and rotated. Organizations often treat encryption as a feature that can be toggled on at rest or in transit and then forgotten, which creates a false sense of safety. If attackers can reach decryption keys through compromised identities or poorly secured administrative interfaces, the data is effectively exposed even if it is "encrypted." Operational implementation must therefore treat encryption as a control system with lifecycle management, not as a static configuration.

A useful way to think about encryption is to separate confidentiality from access control while recognizing they must work together. Access control decides who is allowed to request data, while encryption ensures that even if storage media, backups, or network paths are intercepted, the contents remain unreadable. Encryption at rest protects data stored on disks, databases, and backups, but it does not inherently prevent a legitimate process from reading and exfiltrating decrypted data. Encryption in transit protects data moving across networks by preventing passive interception and tampering, but only if endpoints validate each other correctly and downgrade paths are prevented. When teams blur these concepts, they misapply controls, such as relying on disk encryption to reduce the risk of overbroad application permissions. Clarity here matters because it drives where to invest: key management, identity hardening, and monitoring, not just configuration checklists. Figure 13.1 highlights that

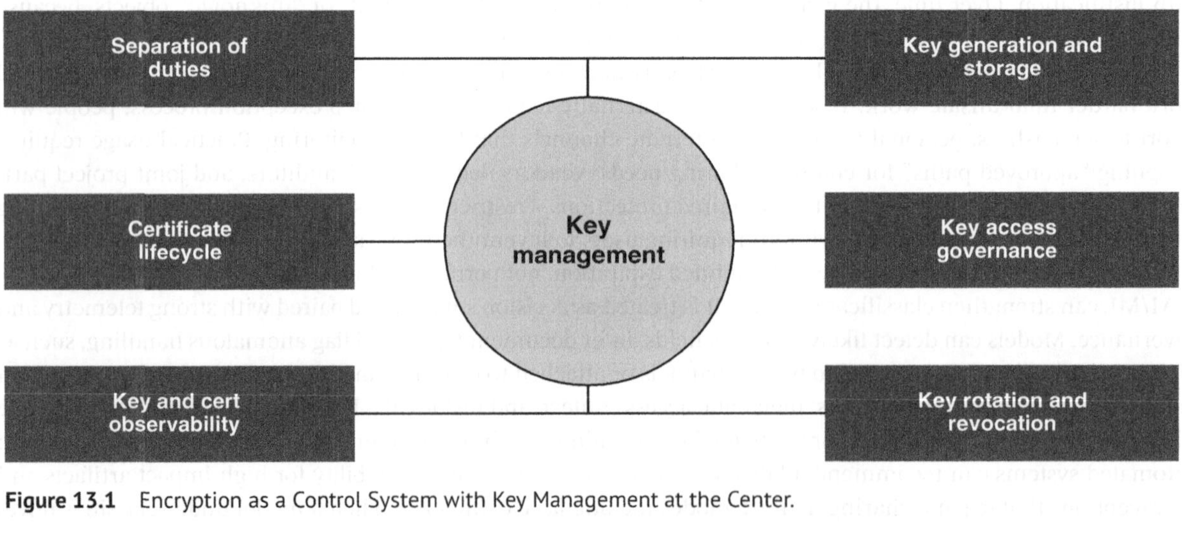

Figure 13.1 Encryption as a Control System with Key Management at the Center.

Table 13.2 Encryption Implementation Checklist for Operational Reliability.

Control Area	What to Implement	Operational Owner	Failure Mode if Weak
Key generation and storage	Strong keys stored in hardened key systems	Security and platform teams	Keys accessible after admin compromise
Key access governance	Least privilege with separation of duties	Security and IAM teams	Encryption bypass through broad key permissions
Key rotation and revocation	Planned rotation with revocation capability	Platform teams	Long-lived keys increase blast radius
Certificate lifecycle	Automated issuance renewal and deployment	Platform and network teams	Validation disabled due to outages
Key and cert observability	Logging and anomaly detection for usage	Security operations	Silent mass decryption or downgrade paths

encryption depends on key management and supporting operational practices like rotation observability and certificate lifecycle. It supports the chapter's point that encryption can create false confidence when keys and trust mechanisms are not governed.

Key management is the operational heart of encryption, and it is where many programs quietly fail. Keys must be generated with strong randomness, stored in systems designed to resist extraction, and accessed through tightly controlled interfaces that log every use. Separation of duties reduces the likelihood that a single compromised administrator can both access encrypted data and obtain the means to decrypt it. Rotation policies should be realistic and driven by threat models, including exposure scenarios such as leaked credentials, compromised hosts, or suspicious key usage patterns. Key lifecycle management also includes revocation and re-encryption planning, because the ability to invalidate a key without operational collapse is what turns encryption into an incident-resilient control. Table 13.2 summarizes the operational controls that determine whether encryption provides real protection or false confidence.

Implementation choices should align with how the business uses data, especially in distributed environments with cloud services, SaaS platforms, and mobile endpoints. Full-disk encryption and device-level protections reduce risk from lost or stolen hardware, but they do not replace application-layer encryption for highly sensitive records that move between systems. Database and storage encryption can provide strong baseline protections, particularly for backups and snapshots, but teams must understand what is encrypted by the provider versus what is controlled directly by the organization. Application-level encryption can enforce tighter boundaries by ensuring data remains encrypted even inside shared storage, but it increases complexity around searching, processing, and key distribution. The practical goal is layered coverage that matches data flows, rather than a single encryption setting applied everywhere regardless of risk.

Encryption in transit is commonly implemented through TLS, but the operational risk often comes from misconfiguration rather than missing encryption entirely. Certificate validation failures, weak cipher settings, expired certificates, and inconsistent enforcement across internal services create paths where traffic can be intercepted or altered. Mutual authentication between services is increasingly important in environments where east–west traffic is the primary attack surface, because attackers often pivot internally after initial access. Teams should also treat certificate issuance and renewal as production-critical automation, because manual processes eventually fail under scale and cause outages that encourage unsafe workarounds. When encryption causes recurring operational pain, people will disable it, bypass it, or route around it, which is why reliability is a security requirement here.

Monitoring and auditability must extend to encryption controls, because encryption without observability is difficult to trust during an incident. Organizations should be able to answer basic operational questions: which datasets are encrypted, where keys are stored, which identities can use them, and what the normal pattern of key usage looks like. Unusual key access—such as a spike in decrypt operations, use from atypical hosts, or attempts outside expected service windows—should be treated as a high-signal event. Logging must be protected from tampering and retained long enough to support investigations that often begin weeks after initial compromise. This is where encryption becomes part of detection and response, not just prevention.

AI/ML can add meaningful value by detecting subtle failure modes that static checks miss, but it must be grounded in dependable telemetry. Models can flag anomalous certificate behavior, identify services that consistently negotiate weaker settings, and detect unusual key usage sequences that resemble automated scraping or mass decryption. These capabilities require clean inputs such as certificate inventories, handshake logs, key access logs, service identity context, and change management events that explain legitimate shifts. Human-in-the-loop controls are essential because models can misinterpret planned migrations, disaster recovery tests, or seasonal workload spikes as malicious. Failure modes include false confidence that "an AI system is watching" while key access logging is incomplete, drift as infrastructure evolves, and leakage risk if sensitive decrypted payloads are used in analysis pipelines without strict minimization and access boundaries.

Finally, encryption must be engineered to fail safely, because brittle implementations create business pressure to weaken controls. If a key service outage prevents revenue-critical transactions, teams will prioritize uptime over confidentiality and carve exceptions that persist long after the emergency. Resilience requires redundancy for key services, controlled caching where appropriate, and explicit break-glass procedures that are auditable and time-bound. It also requires clear ownership: someone must be accountable for encryption posture, key management hygiene, certificate lifecycle, and incident response coordination when something goes wrong. When encryption is implemented as an operational discipline—keys protected, access tightly governed, usage monitored, and reliability designed in—it becomes a durable business safeguard rather than a checkbox that attackers routinely bypass.

Protecting Data in Transit and at Rest

Protecting data in transit and at rest is fundamentally about controlling exposure during movement and storage, because those are the two states where information is most routinely copied, intercepted, or mishandled. Data in transit includes traffic between users and applications, between internal services, and between environments such as on-premises networks and cloud workloads. Data at rest includes databases, file stores, object storage, endpoints, backups, snapshots, and exported artifacts like reports and archives. The business risk is rarely confined to one state, because modern workflows continuously convert at-rest data into in-transit exchanges and then back into at-rest copies. Operational protection must therefore cover the whole path, not just the most visible perimeter connection.

For data in transit, encryption is necessary but not sufficient, because the security outcome depends on endpoint identity, configuration enforcement, and consistent coverage across every connection that matters. Transport protections must prevent passive interception and active tampering, which requires strong protocol selection, current cipher configurations, and rejection of downgrade paths. Service-to-service encryption is increasingly critical because attackers often pivot internally and target east–west traffic where legacy assumptions still treat internal networks as trusted. Mutual authentication can reduce impersonation risk by ensuring both sides of a connection prove identity, not just the server. The practical expectation is that encryption is default everywhere traffic crosses a network boundary, including "internal" boundaries that exist between accounts, segments, and services.

The hard part operationally is certificate and trust management, because broken identity at the transport layer is a common cause of silent exposure. Certificates expire, are misissued, or are deployed inconsistently, and teams under delivery pressure will route around failures by disabling validation or using insecure fallback channels. Automated issuance, renewal, and deployment reduce this risk, but automation must be paired with inventory, so teams know which services are using which certificates and where failures will occur. Trust stores should be managed deliberately to prevent rogue or unnecessary certificate authorities from becoming implicit trust anchors. When transport identity is handled as a lifecycle—issued, deployed, rotated, monitored, and revoked—data in transit becomes far harder to intercept without detection.

Data at rest protection begins with understanding where sensitive data actually resides, including the copies that accumulate through normal operations. Databases, file shares, and object stores are obvious, but logs, caches, analytics extracts, developer test datasets, and export directories often become the real breach payloads. Encryption at rest reduces risk from compromised storage media, misdirected backups, and unauthorized access to underlying storage systems, but it does not stop a legitimate process from reading data and exporting it. That is why at-rest protection must include access control, segmentation, and monitoring as co-equal components. A system is not meaningfully protected if encryption is enabled while broad identities can retrieve decrypted data without friction or oversight.

Backups and snapshots deserve special attention because they preserve historical copies of sensitive information and are frequently targeted during ransomware and extortion operations. Backup data must be encrypted, isolated from day-to-day administrative access, and protected by strong authentication and separate credentials. Immutability features, where available, reduce the likelihood that attackers can tamper with or delete recovery points after compromise. Restoration processes must be tested, because an untested backup is a comforting story, not an operational control. When backup environments are treated as production-grade systems with monitoring, least privilege, and separation of duties, they stop being the easiest path to mass data exposure.

Data protection at rest also depends on preventing uncontrolled replication through exports, attachments, and analytics pipelines that create "shadow datasets." Security teams should work with owners to define approved extraction patterns, such as purpose-bound exports with retention limits and controlled access groups, rather than trying to ban exports outright. Tokenization or field-level protections can reduce exposure when business processes require partial visibility, but they must be designed so that the protected form does not immediately get replaced by raw copies in downstream systems. Monitoring should focus on behaviors that precede loss, including mass reads, unusual query patterns, sudden permission changes, and large outbound transfers from repositories that contain sensitive data. The aim is to make high-risk movement and copying visible and actionable, not to pretend it can be eliminated.

AI/ML can help protect data in transit and at rest by identifying subtle anomalies in traffic patterns and access behaviors, but it only works when the underlying telemetry is complete and trustworthy. Models can flag services that negotiate unexpected encryption settings, detect unusual lateral movement between applications, and identify abnormal access sequences in databases or file stores that resemble automated scraping. These detections depend on logs that include identity context, device and workload attributes, access paths, and historical baselines that represent legitimate behavior across business cycles. Human-in-the-loop controls remain essential because models will misclassify planned migrations, incident response activities, and large legitimate batch jobs unless they are correlated with change and operations signals. Failure modes include false confidence when models operate on partial data, drift as infrastructure evolves, and leakage risks if sensitive payloads are unnecessarily ingested into analytic workflows without minimization and access controls.

Ultimately, protecting data in transit and at rest is achieved by aligning encryption, identity, and monitoring with real data flows and operational constraints. Strong transport protections prevent interception and tampering, but only when certificate lifecycles and validation are managed without exception culture. Strong at-rest protections reduce the impact of storage compromise, but only when access is purpose-bound, backups are isolated, and shadow copies are controlled. Executives should expect clear accountability for datasets, measurable coverage for encryption and access governance, and incident-ready visibility into who accessed what, from where, and why. When these protections are implemented as reliable operating mechanisms rather than aspirational configurations, data becomes safer to use at speed without turning every modernization effort into a new leakage pathway.

Access Controls for Sensitive Information

Access control for sensitive information is fundamentally a business decision expressed through technical enforcement. The organization must decide which roles and functions require access, under what conditions, and with what oversight, because "sensitive" is not a security adjective so much as a risk statement. When access is granted too broadly, the most likely outcome is not an external breach but internal misuse, accidental sharing, or credential compromise that turns legitimate permissions into an attacker's advantage. Access controls must therefore assume that identities will be phished, endpoints will be compromised, and insiders will sometimes act outside policy. The practical goal is to make sensitive data accessible to the business where needed, while ensuring the blast radius of any single identity or system failure stays bounded.

The foundation is strong identity assurance, because access decisions are only as trustworthy as the identity asserting them. Multi-factor authentication reduces the risk of password-only compromise, but it must be paired with hardened enrollment, protection against push fatigue, and clear recovery procedures that do not become an attacker's shortcut. Privileged access should be segregated from everyday accounts, with dedicated administrative identities and explicit elevation when sensitive actions are required. Session controls, such as time-bounded access and reauthentication for high-risk operations, further reduce the window in which stolen tokens or sessions can be abused. Organizations that treat identity as a static directory attribute often discover that sensitive data exposure is an identity lifecycle failure, not a storage configuration issue.

Least privilege must be implemented as an operating discipline rather than a one-time project, because permissions drift as teams grow, systems integrate, and exceptions accumulate. Role-based access control can work when roles reflect stable job functions, but many environments also require attribute-based conditions, such as device trust, network context, and data sensitivity tier, to reflect how work actually happens. Purpose-bound access is a useful mental model: access exists to complete a defined business task, and it should expire when that purpose ends. Time-limited access for sensitive repositories reduces long-term exposure and forces periodic reevaluation of whether access is still justified. Without a lifecycle, organizations quietly converge toward "everyone who might need it someday," which is operationally convenient and security-toxic.

Administrative access to the platforms that store or process sensitive data is often the hidden weak point. Teams may carefully restrict application-level access while leaving broad administrative permissions in infrastructure consoles, database management tools, or backup systems. Separation of duties reduces this risk by ensuring no single role can both change controls and access underlying data without oversight. Break-glass accounts are necessary for outages and emergencies, but they must be tightly controlled, monitored, and treated as incident signals when used outside defined windows. If platform administrators can freely export or snapshot sensitive datasets, the organization does not have access control; it has access hope.

Access controls must also govern how sensitive information is shared, not just who can view it. External sharing links, email forwarding, and collaboration invitations create alternate access paths that often bypass the original repository's intent. Conditional controls that restrict sharing based on sensitivity level, recipient domain, or approval state reduce accidental exposure without blocking legitimate partner workflows. Where external sharing is required, safer patterns include time-bound access, recipient verification, and least-privilege permissions that allow viewing without uncontrolled downloading when feasible. The goal is to prevent "convenient exfiltration mechanisms" from becoming the default way sensitive data leaves the organization.

Verification and recertification are where access control becomes auditable and defensible. Periodic access reviews must be scoped to high-value systems and high-risk permissions; otherwise, they devolve into checkbox exercises that rubber-stamp existing access. Reviews should focus on entitlements that matter, such as broad group memberships, privileged roles, and service accounts with direct data access. Ownership is critical: data owners must approve access based on business need, while security provides the guardrails, evidence, and escalation paths for exceptions. When reviews are paired with automated deprovisioning and clear accountability, access drift becomes measurable and correctable rather than an accepted cost of doing business.

AI/ML can improve access control outcomes by identifying risky entitlements and anomalous access patterns, but it must be treated as advisory and grounded in high-quality identity and activity telemetry. Models can flag permissions that deviate from peer roles, detect unusual sequences like bulk reads followed by external sharing, and identify accounts whose behavior shifts sharply after credential compromise. These insights depend on reliable logs that connect identity, device, resource, and action, and they require baselines that account for legitimate business cycles and operational events. Human-in-the-loop controls are essential because models can misinterpret large legitimate audits, migrations, or incident response activities as malicious. Failure modes include false confidence that "the system would catch it," bias that over-scrutinizes nonstandard roles, and leakage risk if sensitive access data is used in analytic pipelines without strict minimization and governance.

Ultimately, access controls for sensitive information succeed when they are consistent, enforceable, and aligned to how the organization actually operates. Strong identity assurance reduces the likelihood that attackers can impersonate legitimate users, while least privilege and time-bounded access reduce the damage when impersonation occurs. Administrative separation of duties closes the gap between application permissions and platform reality, and controlled sharing pathways prevent everyday collaboration from becoming data loss. Monitoring and review provide the feedback loop that keeps access aligned to purpose as the organization changes. When access control is treated as a living system with clear accountability, sensitive information becomes usable at speed without being exposed by default.

Preventing Unauthorized Movement and Exposure

Unauthorized movement and exposure of data rarely looks like a dramatic theft in the moment it begins. It more often starts as routine access used in an unusual way, a misconfigured sharing setting, a compromised identity performing legitimate actions, or an export created "temporarily" and then forgotten. The organization's challenge is that data movement is a normal business activity, so prevention must be precise enough to stop harmful pathways without breaking collaboration. This is why controls must focus on governing paths, not banning behaviors: approved routes for sharing and processing should be easy, observable, and policy-aligned, while unapproved routes should be constrained and detectable. When prevention is treated as an operational discipline, defenders can reduce exposure without forcing the business into shadow workflows.

The first practical step is to understand the common movement patterns that create risk, including file sharing, email attachments, cloud sync, removable media, and automated exports to analytics platforms. Many exposures come from information leaving its governed repository and landing in places with weaker access control, weaker monitoring, or longer retention than intended. Controls are most effective when they are placed at the transition points where data changes context, such as being attached to an email, shared externally, copied to an endpoint, or exported from a database. These transitions are also where intent can be evaluated: a user accessing data for their work is normal, but packaging large volumes for external delivery is often a higher-risk act. Prevention must therefore be built around high-signal moments rather than attempting to inspect every byte in every location.

Approved sharing pathways are the centerpiece of preventing exposure, because people will share data regardless of policy if they lack a workable option. Organizations should define sanctioned methods for partner collaboration, vendor exchanges, legal discovery, and audit support, and those methods should include recipient verification, time-bound access, and logging. The safest designs reduce the need for copies by keeping data in a controlled repository and granting access to that repository rather than exporting files. When exports are necessary, they should be purpose-bound, labeled, and retained only as long as required for the task. This design principle is simple: minimize uncontrolled copies, because each copy becomes an independent risk surface with its own permissions, lifecycle, and detection coverage.

Data loss prevention controls can help, but they fail when they are deployed as blunt instruments without tuning and ownership. Pattern-based detection for sensitive fields and document types is valuable, but it must be aligned with classification and business context to avoid constant false positives that drive users to bypass the system. Policies should be tier-aware, so the strictest controls apply to the most sensitive data, while less sensitive information is governed with lighter friction. Response options must also be practical: blocking high-risk transfers, warning users at the moment of action, requiring justification, or routing actions for approval are all viable depending on the business impact of delay. When controls are calibrated to real workflows and data tiers, they prevent the highest risk exposures without turning normal work into a daily negotiation.

Identity and endpoint controls are essential because unauthorized movement often occurs through legitimate channels after credential compromise. Conditional access based on device health and user risk can prevent sensitive downloads to unmanaged endpoints, while session controls can limit bulk extraction even when authentication succeeds. Least privilege reduces the volume of data any single account can access, and time-bounded access reduces the window of opportunity for attackers operating with stolen sessions. On endpoints, restrictions on local caching, printing, clipboard transfer, and removable media can meaningfully reduce leakage for high-sensitivity datasets, but these controls must be applied selectively to avoid breaking productivity. The practical objective is to ensure that even if an attacker gains an identity, moving large volumes of sensitive data becomes noisy, constrained, and difficult.

Monitoring must be designed around data movement behaviors, not just perimeter exfiltration signatures. High-signal indicators include unusual download volumes, atypical access times, sudden enumeration of repositories, access from new geographies or networks, and sequences that suggest staging, such as compressing files before transfer. Visibility also needs to include internal movement, because attackers frequently collect and stage data inside the environment before choosing an exfiltration route. Logging must tie actions to identity, device, and resource context, so analysts can distinguish a legitimate bulk transfer for a business process from anomalous behavior that warrants containment. When monitoring is integrated with response playbooks, the organization can act quickly by suspending sessions, restricting sharing, and isolating endpoints before exposure becomes irreversible.

AI/ML can improve detection and prevention by finding patterns that rule-based controls miss, but it can also create dangerous overconfidence if governance and telemetry are weak. Models can identify behavioral anomalies, classify content at scale, and predict which transfers are most likely to be risky based on historical incidents and contextual signals. These outcomes depend on comprehensive logs of access, sharing, and endpoint activity, and they require careful handling to avoid embedding bias against certain roles or work patterns. Human-in-the-loop approval boundaries are critical: AI can recommend blocking, escalation, or additional verification, but decisions that materially disrupt business workflows should be reviewable and reversible. Failure modes include drift as user behavior changes, misclassification that either blocks legitimate work or allows sensitive content through, and leakage risk if sensitive content is processed in analytic pipelines without strict minimization and access controls.

Preventing unauthorized movement and exposure ultimately comes down to constraining untrusted paths while preserving trusted ones. Organizations that rely purely on user training and after-the-fact investigation are accepting data loss as an operational norm. Organizations that over-block without providing safe alternatives drive risk into shadow channels where monitoring and controls are weaker. The sustainable approach is to build a small set of approved collaboration patterns, enforce tier-aware restrictions at key transition points, and monitor behavior with enough context to respond decisively. When these elements work together, sensitive data remains usable for the business while being materially harder to move, leak, or expose without detection.

Monitoring Data Access for Abuse and Misuse

Monitoring data access for abuse and misuse is the difference between assuming controls are working and knowing when they are failing. Sensitive data is routinely accessed by legitimate users and services, which means attackers do not need exotic techniques if they can operate through valid identities and normal interfaces. Abuse can look like bulk extraction for extortion, quiet sampling for insider trading, or targeted access to a small set of high-value records that never triggers volume thresholds. Misuse can be accidental, such as sharing a restricted report to a broad channel, or procedural, such as using production data in an unsanctioned test environment. Effective monitoring recognizes that the risk is behavioral and contextual, not simply a matter of whether access occurred.

The starting point is defining what must be observable and what "normal" looks like for the systems that hold sensitive information. That means collecting access logs that include identity, device or workload context, source location, action type, and the data object or dataset being accessed. Without this context, monitoring collapses into noisy event streams that cannot distinguish a legitimate batch job from an opportunistic scrape. Normal baselines should account for business cycles, such as monthly financial close, seasonal customer activity, and planned migrations that change access patterns. Monitoring must also recognize the difference between read access and actions that materially increase exposure, such as exports, permission changes, or the creation of new sharing links.

High-signal behaviors are often sequences rather than single events, because misuse typically unfolds across multiple steps. Attackers and malicious insiders commonly enumerate repositories, test access boundaries, escalate privileges or join groups, and then collect data in stages before final extraction. Monitoring should therefore correlate identity events, entitlement changes, and data access events into narratives that reflect how abuse actually happens. A sudden increase in read operations may be benign, but an increase paired with new privileges, atypical host access, and outbound transfer activity is far more concerning. When correlation is designed around workflows, it becomes easier to prioritize what matters and to respond quickly without overreacting to normal operational spikes. Table 13.3 highlights the access and movement signals that most reliably indicate misuse when correlated with identity and entitlement context.

Privilege and entitlement monitoring is essential because access abuse often begins with changing who can access data rather than immediately touching the data itself. Group membership changes, role assignments, service account permissions, and policy modifications that broaden access should be treated as sensitive events, especially for systems containing regulated or high-impact information. Monitoring should differentiate between controlled changes through approved workflows and ad hoc changes performed directly in administrative consoles. The integrity of access governance can be measured by how often high-risk entitlements change outside expected processes and by how quickly those changes are reviewed and corrected. When entitlement monitoring is strong, it reduces the likelihood that abuse can occur quietly, because the path to expanded access is itself visible and controlled.

Table 13.3 High Signal Indicators for Data Misuse Monitoring.

Indicator	What It Looks Like	Why It Matters	Typical Immediate Response
Entitlement expansion	New group membership or role assignment then access	Risk often begins by broadening access	Review change and validate approval path
Repository enumeration	Rapid listing or searching across sensitive locations	Precedes targeted collection and staging	Increase scrutiny and restrict session if needed
Bulk reads or downloads	Unusual volume or rate of reads from sensitive data	Common staging behavior for exfiltration	Throttle or suspend session and investigate
New external sharing links	Creation of links to restricted artifacts	Creates alternate access paths outside intent	Disable links and verify recipients
Atypical access context	New device host network or location for sensitive access	Signals compromised identity or unsafe endpoint	Force reauthentication and assess device

Monitoring must also include the service accounts and automated processes that often have the broadest and least scrutinized access. These identities power integrations, reporting, backups, and data pipelines, and they can become ideal vehicles for abuse because their activity is assumed to be "system noise." Service account monitoring should establish expected call patterns, expected source workloads, and expected data scopes, and it should alert on deviations such as access from new hosts, use outside normal windows, or abrupt expansion in accessed datasets. Credentials for these accounts must be managed so that compromise is detectable and containment is feasible, which typically requires limiting where secrets can be used and ensuring all usage is logged. Treating service accounts as first-class identities with governance is a practical necessity, not an advanced maturity goal.

Response design determines whether monitoring changes outcomes or simply produces alerts. When suspicious access is detected, teams need pre-approved actions that can be executed quickly, such as suspending sessions, forcing reauthentication, temporarily restricting export functions, or isolating an endpoint. These actions must be tier-aware, because the acceptable disruption for a system containing highly sensitive data is different from the acceptable disruption for a low-impact repository. Analysts also need investigative readiness: the ability to pivot from an alert to the supporting evidence, including the user's recent authentication history, entitlement changes, and other accessed resources. Without a defined response pathway, monitoring becomes an academic exercise that identifies risk without reducing it.

AI/ML can improve access monitoring by detecting anomalies and subtle misuse patterns that are difficult to encode as static rules, but it must be implemented with disciplined controls. Models can learn normal access baselines per role, detect unusual sequences that resemble scraping or staged collection, and prioritize alerts based on contextual risk signals like sensitivity tier, data volume, and identity posture. These outcomes depend on comprehensive, consistent telemetry and on careful feature selection that avoids inadvertently learning biased proxies for "suspiciousness." Human-in-the-loop controls are mandatory because models will produce false positives during legitimate operational events and false negatives when attackers mimic normal behavior. Failure modes include drift as business workflows change, false confidence when models operate on incomplete logs, and leakage risk if sensitive access details or content are pulled into analytic workflows without minimization and strict access boundaries.

A mature approach to monitoring data access treats observability, correlation, and response as a single operational system. Data owners and security teams should agree on what constitutes high-risk access for each critical dataset, what evidence must be captured, and what actions are authorized when risk thresholds are crossed. Monitoring should be continuously tuned using incident learnings, audit findings, and the inevitable changes in business processes that shift what "normal" looks like. The measure of success is not the number of alerts generated, but the organization's ability to detect misuse early, contain it decisively, and prove what happened with high confidence. When implemented this way, monitoring becomes a durable safeguard that complements preventive controls and turns sensitive data access into an accountable, observable business process.

AI in Data Protection: Classification Assistance, Leakage Risk, and Governance Constraints

AI can materially improve data protection outcomes when it is treated as an accelerator for consistency and scale rather than an authority that replaces ownership. In most organizations, the problem is not that people do not care about protecting data, but that they cannot reliably recognize sensitivity at speed across documents, chats, code repositories, analytics extracts, and rapidly changing collaboration spaces. Machine learning can help infer likely sensitivity, detect risky handling patterns, and prioritize interventions that would otherwise be lost in volume. The value comes from narrowing attention to the right items and moments, not from making irreversible decisions without review. When AI is implemented as part of the control system, it becomes a practical tool for reducing exposure without paralyzing workflows.

Classification assistance is one of the most operationally useful applications because it targets a common failure point: inconsistent or missing labels. Models can identify patterns associated with regulated data types, proprietary artifacts, and internal-only communications, and they can propose a classification tier based on content and context signals. Context is critical because the same words can mean different things in different domains, and classification cannot rely purely on keyword matches without generating friction and bypass behavior. Effective classification assistance also uses metadata, such as where the file was created, which repository it resides in, who is collaborating on it, and whether it is being prepared for external sharing. Human-in-the-loop review should be focused where it matters most, such as high-impact datasets, externally shared artifacts, and overrides that downgrade sensitivity.

The telemetry dependency for AI-enabled classification is often underestimated, and weak inputs produce confident but wrong outputs. Models need training and evaluation data that reflects the organization's actual document types, naming conventions, and business language, not generic examples that fail in domain-specific contexts. They also need reliable ground truth, which is hard to obtain when historical labeling is inconsistent or when policies have changed over time. Classification systems should therefore be designed to learn from curated decisions made by accountable owners, not from opportunistic scraping of whatever labels happen to exist. Without disciplined feedback loops, models drift as the business evolves and become either overly permissive, missing sensitive items, or overly restrictive, labeling everything as high sensitivity and eroding trust.

Leakage risk is the defining hazard of applying AI to data protection, because the very systems designed to recognize sensitivity can become new exposure channels. Data used for training, fine-tuning, evaluation, or prompt-based processing may be copied into pipelines that lack the same access controls, retention limits, and auditing as the protected repositories. Even when content is not explicitly stored, it may be logged, cached, or retained for troubleshooting, which can quietly create shadow datasets of the most sensitive information. Protection requires strict data minimization: only the smallest necessary fields should be processed, and raw content should be avoided when metadata and structural signals can achieve the goal. Where content must be processed, it should remain within controlled environments with clear ownership, encrypted storage, and tightly governed access.

Human-in-the-loop controls and approval boundaries are essential because AI systems can produce plausible outputs that are wrong in ways that matter. A model that under-classifies a document can enable inappropriate sharing, while a model that over-classifies can cause operational friction that pushes users into unmonitored channels. Review workflows should be designed so that AI can recommend, warn, or require justification, but the final decision for high-impact actions remains attributable to a person or an accountable role. This is especially important for actions that change access, allow external sharing, or approve exceptions, because those decisions define the organization's actual risk posture. The most reliable pattern is to let AI triage and prioritize while preserving explicit human accountability for boundary changes.

Governance constraints make AI in data protection defensible and auditable, which is the standard required when decisions affect regulated data and business-critical operations. Governance begins with clear policy: what AI is allowed to do, what data it is allowed to touch, what it is forbidden from retaining, and how its outputs may be used in enforcement. Auditability requires traceability from an AI-driven recommendation to the data and signals used, the decision taken, and the identity that approved or overrode it. This does not mean exposing sensitive content broadly; it means maintaining protected evidence sufficient for investigation and review. Model lifecycle governance must also include periodic validation, drift monitoring, and controlled updates, because a model that was acceptable at deployment can become unsafe as data types, workflows, and threat tactics change.

Failure modes are predictable and should be explicitly planned for, because they often appear as success right up until they create a high-impact incident. False confidence is common when leaders assume that AI detection means data loss is "handled," even though coverage gaps and incomplete logging remain. Drift is inevitable when business vocabulary changes, new document types appear, and collaboration patterns shift, which can silently degrade classification accuracy. Bias can emerge when models learn that certain departments or roles are "usually risky" and over-flag their work, creating disproportionate friction and undermining adoption. Leakage can occur through training artifacts, debugging traces, and downstream analytics, turning protection telemetry into a new sensitive dataset that requires its own controls.

When implemented responsibly, AI-enabled data protection can reduce manual burden and improve consistency, but only when it is constrained by the same rigor applied to other security controls. The system should be designed so that AI outputs are explainable enough to support review, limited enough to prevent uncontrolled exposure, and integrated enough to improve enforcement at the points where data is most likely to leak. Telemetry must be complete, feedback loops must be owned, and exceptions must be governed as time-bound decisions with evidence. The business outcome is not "AI-secured data," but a program that uses AI to make classification and leakage prevention more reliable at scale without creating a parallel risk surface. In that posture, AI becomes a disciplined component of data protection rather than a new pathway for sensitive information to escape.

Common Data Protection Failure Modes

One of the most common data protection failure modes is mistaking control presence for control effectiveness. Organizations enable encryption, deploy access policies, and publish classification guidance, then assume the data is protected because the right boxes appear checked. Attackers and insiders exploit the gaps between stated intent and operational reality, where exceptions, legacy paths, and unmanaged copies accumulate. This is especially dangerous for executives because dashboards often report coverage at a system level, while failures happen at the workflow level. Data protection succeeds or fails in the mundane details of how people share, export, cache, and reuse information under time pressure.

Misclassification and "unknown data" are persistent failure modes because most environments move too fast for manual labeling to keep up. When sensitive content is left unclassified, controls that depend on classification cannot trigger, and monitoring loses the ability to prioritize what matters. Over-classification is just as damaging because it creates constant friction that encourages workarounds and label fatigue, ultimately reducing trust in the entire program. Automated classification can help, but it becomes its own failure mode when models are trained on inconsistent labels or when drift causes quiet degradation over time. In practice, classification fails when it is treated as a documentation exercise rather than a living input into enforcement and monitoring.

Excessive access is the failure mode that turns almost any compromise into a data exposure event. Teams grant broad access for convenience, rarely revoke it, and justify it as necessary to keep operations moving. Over time, access drift results in sensitive repositories that can be read by far more identities than the business would knowingly approve if asked directly. Service accounts and integration identities often carry the worst overreach because they are created to "just work" and then never revisited. When an attacker obtains any such identity, the organization discovers that its real data boundary was defined by accumulated permissions, not by policy.

Uncontrolled copies are a quiet but devastating failure mode because every copy creates a new security perimeter. Exports to spreadsheets, attachments in email threads, analytics extracts, and "temporary" staging directories become long-lived artifacts with weak access controls and minimal monitoring. Data also leaks into logs, caches, and debug dumps, especially when developers troubleshoot production issues under pressure. These artifacts are rarely included in formal inventories, so they escape encryption, retention, and access review processes. During incidents, they are often the easiest payload to steal because they concentrate high-value records in convenient formats.

Weak key and secret management undermines encryption by making decryption accessible to the same compromise paths encryption was meant to mitigate. Keys stored alongside encrypted data, overly broad access to key management systems, and insufficient logging of key use create scenarios where attackers can decrypt at scale after a single privilege escalation. Certificate lifecycle failures can also drive teams into insecure workarounds, such as disabling validation or using fallback connections, which reintroduces in-transit exposure. The operational failure is not choosing encryption, but failing to govern the mechanism that makes encryption meaningful. When key usage is not observable and controllable, encryption becomes a comfort measure rather than a barrier.

Overreliance on alerting without response discipline is another common failure mode, particularly when monitoring is noisy and poorly scoped to sensitive data. Organizations generate alerts for downloads, exports, and sharing events but lack predefined actions that can be executed quickly without executive escalation. Analysts then hesitate, investigations stall, and exposure windows remain open long enough for data movement to become irreversible. Monitoring also fails when logs are incomplete, inconsistent across platforms, or lack identity and object context, making investigations inconclusive. A detection program that cannot produce reliable timelines and containment actions does not protect data; it merely documents its loss.

AI-enabled data protection introduces distinctive failure modes when governance constraints are weak. Models can create false confidence that sensitive data will be recognized and blocked, even when coverage gaps and incomplete telemetry undermine detection. Drift can cause under-classification of new data types or over-classification that drives users to bypass controls, both of which degrade protection over time. Leakage risk is acute when sensitive content is copied into training, evaluation, or troubleshooting pipelines that lack strict access control and retention discipline. When AI systems are not auditable, organizations cannot explain why a label was assigned or why a transfer was permitted, which becomes unacceptable during regulatory review or post-incident scrutiny.

Finally, the most systemic failure mode is treating data protection as a security program rather than an operating model shared with the business. When data owners are not accountable for access patterns and exception approvals, security becomes the default decision-maker without the context to balance risk and operational necessity. When approved sharing pathways are not provided, users create their own channels, and security loses visibility where it matters most. When success metrics focus on policy completion rather than exposure reduction, teams optimize for paperwork instead of outcomes. Data protection fails predictably when it is not embedded into how the organization builds, shares, and governs information every day.

Conclusion

Data protection reaches maturity when it consistently reduces exposure without forcing the business into workarounds that are harder to see and harder to control. Classification is only useful when it drives enforceable handling rules, encryption only protects when keys and identities are governed as rigorously as the data, and access control only holds when it is purpose-bound and continuously pruned. Monitoring closes the loop by making misuse and abuse observable early enough to contain, but it only changes outcomes when response actions are predefined, tier-aware, and exercised. When these controls are run as an operating model with clear ownership, disciplined exceptions, and auditable decisions, the organization can prove—before and after an incident—that sensitive data remained usable for the mission without being exposed by default.

Recommendations

1) Treat data protection as a business requirement with accountable ownership. Assign clear data owners for critical datasets and require them to approve access patterns and exception requests based on business purpose. Tie protection decisions to real impact—confidentiality, integrity, and availability harm—rather than treating them as technical preferences. Use that ownership model to keep protection aligned as teams, vendors, and platforms change.
2) Implement data classification only where it drives enforceable handling behavior. Use a small number of sensitivity tiers that map directly to concrete rules for storage, transmission, sharing, and monitoring. Embed classification into the systems where work happens, so labels travel with data across collaboration and storage

paths. Avoid both “unknown” data and over-classification by ensuring labels are easy to apply and clearly change what users can do.

3) Design approved sharing pathways that reduce the need for uncontrolled copies. Establish sanctioned methods for external collaboration that use recipient verification, time-bound access, and clear logging. Prefer granting controlled access to a governed repository over exporting files into email threads or ad hoc locations. Ensure these paths are reliable and simple, so users do not create shadow channels that weaken visibility and enforcement.
4) Engineer encryption as an operational control system, not a one-time configuration. Ensure encryption at rest and in transit is paired with disciplined key management, including strong storage protections, controlled access, rotation practices, and observable key usage. Automate certificate lifecycle processes to prevent outages and insecure workarounds that undermine transport protections. Treat key and certificate systems as production-critical and monitor them accordingly.
5) Harden identity assurance and privilege boundaries for sensitive data access. Require strong authentication for access to high-sensitivity repositories and restrict administrative actions through segregated privileged identities. Use time-bounded access and reauthentication for high-risk operations to reduce the window for session abuse. Ensure recovery and exception processes do not become a shortcut that attackers can exploit.
6) Run least privilege as a lifecycle to prevent access drift. Build access around purpose and role stability, and require periodic reviews focused on high-impact entitlements such as broad groups and privileged roles. Actively govern service accounts and integrations as first-class identities with scoped permissions and auditable usage. Remove access when roles change or projects end, so “temporary” access does not become permanent exposure.
7) Focus monitoring on high-signal access and movement behaviors rather than raw event volume. Collect logs with identity, device or workload context, action type, and object or dataset details, so investigations can distinguish normal work from misuse. Correlate sequences such as entitlement changes followed by bulk reads and sharing events to surface abuse narratives early. Prioritize monitoring where data changes context—exports, link creation, permission changes, and unusual access bursts.
8) Predefine tier-aware response actions for suspected misuse and abuse. Establish authorized containment steps such as suspending sessions, forcing reauthentication, restricting exports, or isolating endpoints when risk thresholds are crossed. Ensure analysts can pivot quickly from an alert to evidence like recent authentication activity, entitlement changes, and related resource access. Make response proportional to data sensitivity, so the organization can act decisively without unnecessary disruption.
9) Use AI/ML as decision support with explicit human approval boundaries and auditability. Apply AI to propose classifications, flag risky handling, and prioritize investigations, but keep high-impact decisions attributable to accountable roles. Ensure models are grounded in reliable telemetry and reinforced by curated feedback loops, so they do not drift into over- or under-classification. Maintain traceability for recommendations, overrides, and enforcement outcomes, so decisions remain defensible during audits and incidents.
10) Continuously hunt for and eliminate common failure modes that create silent exposure. Identify and control shadow datasets created by exports, caches, logs, analytics extracts, and “temporary” staging areas that escape normal governance. Close gaps where administrative access bypasses application permissions, and ensure backups and snapshots are encrypted, isolated, and operationally tested. Avoid false confidence by validating that controls change real workflows and by correcting exception culture before it becomes the default operating state.

14

Backup, Recovery, and Operational Resilience

Backup, recovery, and operational resilience are security capabilities because they determine whether disruption remains bounded and reversible when prevention and detection are bypassed. Modern adversaries routinely plan for and attack recovery itself by targeting credentials, backup infrastructure, and the control planes that govern restoration, making resilience a contested domain rather than a back-office routine. Effective programs translate business impact into measurable recovery objectives, then prove those objectives through realistic restoration testing, governed decision-making, and coordinated execution across IT and security. When AI-assisted support is applied with strong validation and human approval boundaries, it can accelerate prioritization and communication without undermining trust, and the lessons learned from every recovery event become inputs for strengthening controls over time.

Why Recovery Is a Defensive Control

Recovery is a defensive control because it determines whether a compromise remains a security event or becomes a business failure. Prevention and detection reduce the likelihood and dwell time of an incident, but neither guarantees continuity of operations once systems are encrypted, data is corrupted, or critical services are taken offline. In operational terms, recovery is the control that converts uncertainty into bounded impact by restoring known-good states within defined time and data-loss limits. Executives often think of recovery as "an IT problem," yet the ability to reconstitute business capabilities is inseparable from security outcomes. When attackers know an organization cannot recover quickly, extortion pressure rises, decision quality drops, and the incident commander's options narrow.

A defensive program treats recovery targets as security requirements, not merely service-level aspirations. Recovery time objective (RTO) defines how long a process can be unavailable before the business suffers unacceptable harm, while recovery point objective (RPO) defines how much data loss is tolerable measured in time. Those numbers are not technical trivia; they are a translation layer between mission impact and engineering design choices such as backup frequency, replication strategy, and restoration sequencing. If RPO is four hours but backups run nightly, the organization has already accepted a mismatch that will surface under stress. Well-run teams routinely test whether systems can be restored to meet RTO and RPO, because "we have backups" is not a control until it is proven under realistic conditions.

Recovery becomes even more defensive when adversaries actively target it. Modern intrusion playbooks frequently include locating backup servers, deleting snapshots, disabling backup agents, and stealing backup credentials precisely because they understand recovery is the one lever that breaks ransom economics. This is why backup infrastructure must be treated as high-value security terrain with strong identity controls, segmented administration paths, and tight monitoring for destructive actions. "Immutable" and "offline" are operational concepts, not marketing terms: immutability means backups cannot be altered or deleted within a defined retention window, and offline means there exists at least one copy that cannot be reached from the compromised environment. The defensive value is straightforward—attackers can damage systems, but they cannot erase the organization's ability to rebuild them.

A recovery-first mindset also forces the team to define what "known good" means, which is a security question as much as an engineering one. Restoring a system image that contains persistence mechanisms, compromised credentials, or tampered configurations simply accelerates reinfection. Effective recovery uses trusted baselines, verified artifacts, and restoration checks that confirm integrity before workloads rejoin production networks. That typically includes validating hashes or signatures of gold images, ensuring configuration management produces expected states, and confirming privileged credentials are rotated before restoring services that rely on them. The goal is to restore capability and security posture together, not to trade speed for an unstable or unsafe return to service.

Operational resilience depends on sequencing and dependency awareness, because most business services are composites of identity, network, compute, data stores, and external integrations. If identity services and DNS are unavailable, application recovery may stall even when application servers restore cleanly. If a database is restored but application credentials remain compromised, the restored environment may be immediately accessible to the adversary. Recovery plans that read like inventory lists tend to fail because they do not model dependencies, priority tiers, and handoffs between infrastructure and application owners. Defensive recovery is run as an orchestrated workflow: bring back core trust services, then foundational platforms, then critical business applications, while continuously verifying both functionality and security assumptions at each stage.

Good recovery also requires disciplined decision-making under uncertainty, which is where AI/ML can help—if constrained properly. During large incidents, teams often face noisy telemetry, partial visibility, and competing priorities, and AI-assisted triage can accelerate correlation of restoration blockers such as missing dependencies, anomalous configuration drift, or repeated failure patterns in restore jobs. That value depends on high-quality inputs: backup job logs, change records, asset inventories, identity events, and incident timelines must be available and time-aligned, or the model will confidently recommend the wrong action. Human-in-the-loop boundaries matter, because automated suggestions should not be allowed to approve destructive operations, credential resets, or mass restores without review. Failure modes include false confidence from incomplete telemetry, drift as environments change, and leakage risk if sensitive incident data is routed into systems without clear governance and retention controls.

Recovery is also a defensive control because it shapes attacker behavior and incident strategy before an incident ever occurs. When an organization can reliably restore systems and data, extortion threats lose leverage, and responders can prioritize containment and eradication without negotiating against a ticking business clock. That posture changes what defenders can demand during crisis: time to validate scope, time to rotate credentials, and time to rebuild cleanly rather than rushing to "get things back" in a compromised state. Conversely, weak recovery turns every incident into an emergency procurement of time, where shortcuts become inevitable and future security debt is created in the name of speed. A mature program treats recovery capability as a core security deterrent, not because it prevents intrusion, but because it denies attackers durable impact.

Finally, recovery earns its status as a defensive control only when it is measurable, auditable, and exercised like any other control with failure handling and continuous improvement. Tabletop exercises without hands-on restores create confidence without evidence, while occasional restores of small systems do not prove readiness for large-scale ransomware or widespread data corruption. Teams need restore tests that reflect real conditions: degraded networks, limited staff availability, missing dependencies, and the requirement to prove integrity before reconnecting systems. Logs and evidence from backup and restore operations should be retained and reviewed as part of security assurance, because they demonstrate whether recovery objectives were met and where controls failed. The organizations that recover well are not simply the ones with more backups—they are the ones that treat recovery as a practiced, security-governed capability that constrains adversaries and protects the business when everything else goes wrong.

Backup Scope, Coverage, and Retention

Backup scope starts as an inventory problem, but it quickly becomes a control problem once you accept that "critical" is contextual and time-bound. Organizations that back up only what they remember to back up eventually discover that their most important data lived in a SaaS tenant, a developer-managed database, or a shared file service outside the traditional server estate. Coverage should be defined in terms of business capabilities and the data that sustains them, not merely in terms of systems and storage volumes. That framing prevents a common failure mode where teams protect operating systems and application binaries but miss the transactional data, configuration state, or identity artifacts required to restore service. A defensible backup scope explicitly names what must be recoverable and what "recoverable" means for each category.

Coverage has to include the "hidden dependencies" that determine whether restored workloads can function in a real environment. Directory services, DNS, certificate authorities, secrets stores, and configuration management databases are often treated as infrastructure plumbing, yet they are foundational to authentication, service discovery, and trust. If those elements are not backed up with the same rigor as application data, the organization may technically restore servers while remaining operationally dead in the water. Coverage must also account for endpoints and collaboration platforms where business records accumulate outside data centers, including user home drives, cloud document repositories, and messaging archives when they carry regulated or mission-critical content. The goal is not to back up everything indiscriminately, but to avoid blind spots where business operations rely on data that has no recovery path.

Retention turns backup from a restore mechanism into an evidence and resilience mechanism, and the difference matters during incident response. Short retention windows may satisfy routine operational needs while failing catastrophically during ransomware or stealthy data tampering, where the "last good" copy might be weeks or months old. Conversely, indefinite retention can create unnecessary risk and cost, especially when backups contain sensitive data that outlives its business purpose. A disciplined retention strategy aligns with regulatory obligations, legal hold requirements, and the organization's tolerance for latent compromise, while also recognizing the operational reality of storage growth and restore complexity. Leaders should understand that retention is not just about keeping data longer; it is about keeping the right data long enough to outlast an adversary's dwell time.

RPOs and backup frequency are inseparable from coverage and retention because they define the cadence at which the organization is willing to lose data. When RPO is aggressive, the environment needs higher-frequency backup mechanisms, which can include snapshots, log shipping, or application-aware backups that capture consistent states. If RPO is loose, nightly backups may suffice, but only if business stakeholders accept the implications for lost transactions and downstream reconciliation. The backup schedule must be engineered per workload class, because "one policy for everything" tends to overprotect low-value systems while underprotecting revenue and safety-critical services. Good programs document the rationale for each workload's frequency and ensure the policy survives ownership changes, platform migrations, and staffing turnover.

Retention policy quality is determined less by the number of days than by the ability to retrieve specific versions quickly and confidently. Attackers often corrupt data gradually or manipulate configurations so that problems appear later, which means teams must be able to locate and restore a point-in-time image that predates the compromise. That requires indexing, clear labeling, and routine validation of catalog integrity, so responders are not guessing during an incident. It also requires that retention includes both the data and the metadata that makes the backup usable, such as application versions, schema state, encryption keys, and access controls that govern restoration. Without that operational clarity, long retention can become a false comfort that fails when time pressure is highest.

AI/ML can improve scope and coverage decisions by identifying gaps through telemetry-driven analysis, but it must be applied with strict guardrails. Models can analyze asset inventories, data classification tags, access patterns, and incident trends to highlight systems that behave like critical services but are not included in backup policies. This works only when inventories are accurate and integrated with identity and configuration data; otherwise, the model will infer importance from noisy signals and recommend wasteful or risky expansion of scope. Human approval boundaries matter because expanding backup scope can increase sensitive-data exposure and introduce compliance implications, especially when backup copies cross regions or tenants. Governance should require explainability of recommendations, change tracking of policy updates, and periodic review to ensure the model's assumptions remain aligned as applications and data flows evolve.

Ultimately, backup scope, coverage, and retention are defensive levers that determine how resilient the organization is against both operational failure and deliberate attack. A program that is honest about what it protects, rigorous about what it excludes, and explicit about how long it can go back in time can respond to incidents with options instead of improvisation. The most common pitfall is treating backup policy as static, when in reality it must track mergers, cloud migrations, new data sources, and evolving attacker tradecraft aimed directly at backup infrastructure. When teams revisit scope and retention as part of change management and resilience testing, backups remain a living control rather than a stale checkbox. The outcome is straightforward: fewer surprises during restoration, fewer irreversible losses, and a materially stronger negotiating position when adversaries attempt to turn downtime into leverage.

Protecting Backups from Tampering and Loss

Backups only function as a defensive control if they survive the incident intact and usable, which makes them an explicit target for capable adversaries. Modern intrusions routinely include a phase devoted to sabotaging recovery by deleting snapshots, uninstalling backup agents, encrypting repositories, or corrupting catalogs, so restores fail under pressure. The most dangerous misconception is equating "backups exist" with "recovery is possible," because the attacker's objective is to make those statements diverge. Protecting backups requires treating the backup system as a critical security asset with its own threat model, monitoring, and operational rigor. In practical terms, the backup environment must be engineered to withstand both malicious tampering and mundane failures like misconfigurations, expired credentials, and storage degradation.

Tamper resistance begins with hard separation of duties and administrative boundaries, because backup administration is effectively the power to rewrite organizational history. The accounts that manage backup policies, retention, and deletion must be distinct from routine server administration and should not share credential stores or privilege pathways with production operations. Privileged access should be time-bound, tightly audited, and resilient to credential theft through strong MFA and conditional access controls that reduce exposure from remote compromise. Even when identity controls are strong, the backup plane must be segmented so that a compromised workstation cannot directly reach backup controllers and repositories. Organizations that treat backup consoles as "just another web app" often discover too late that the console was the easiest path to mass deletion. This stacked diagram illustrates the layered controls that keep backups usable during adversarial incidents, from identity separation to immutability and isolated copies. It supports the text's emphasis that attackers target recovery and that resilience depends on multiple reinforcing safeguards (Figure 14.1).

Immutability is a core control, but it must be implemented in a way that is operationally meaningful rather than nominal. An immutable backup is one that cannot be altered or deleted within a defined retention window, even by an administrator account operating from a compromised network. This forces attackers to either wait out retention, physically access offline copies, or accept that the organization can restore without paying. Effective immutability also covers the metadata and catalogs that allow restores to be performed, because corrupt catalogs can render intact backup data practically unreachable. When immutability is in place, deletion becomes a controlled, time-delayed process with explicit approvals, not a single click that an attacker can automate.

Offline and isolated copies are the second pillar because they address a fundamental failure mode: if the attacker can reach it, the attacker can likely destroy it. "Offline" is not a philosophical label; it means at least one copy is not addressable from production networks and cannot be modified by routines that run under production trust.

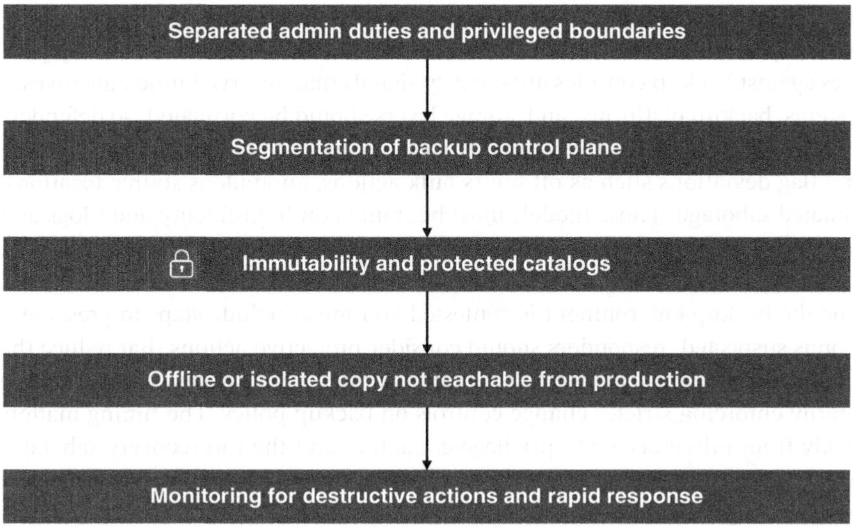

Figure 14.1 Layered Protection of Backups Against Tampering and Loss.

That can be achieved through air-gapped media, isolated vaults, or deliberately segregated storage accounts that have no inbound pathways from the compromised environment. The operational tradeoff is slower restores, which is why offline copies are usually paired with faster, nearline backups for routine outages. The defensive posture comes from having layers, where the fast layer handles common failures and the isolated layer survives worst-case compromise.

Protection from loss is not only about adversaries; it is also about resisting silent operational decay that creates the same outcome as an attack. Backup jobs fail for reasons that rarely trigger executive attention: certificates expire, service accounts lose privileges, storage quotas fill, agents lag behind platform changes, and network routes drift. A mature program treats backup success as a measurable reliability signal with alerting, escalation, and ownership, rather than as a monthly report that no one reads. Periodic integrity checks validate that backup data is readable, complete, and consistent, and that encryption keys required for restore are accessible under incident conditions. Protecting backups means eliminating the "unknown unknowns" that surface only when the business is already down. Table 14.1 highlights observable behaviors that often precede recovery sabotage and the defensive actions that preserve restoration options.

Table 14.1 Backup Tampering Signals and Defensive Responses.

Signal Observed	What It May Indicate	Immediate Response	Why It Matters
Retention reduced unexpectedly	Attempt to limit restore history	Require approval and investigate account	Short windows increase extortion leverage
Mass deletion requests	Automated sabotage of recovery	Freeze deletions and validate immutability	Destroys ability to restore
Backup jobs disabled	Preparation for ransomware detonation	Reenable and confirm admin path integrity	Creates false confidence
Catalog changes or corruption	Attempt to make restores fail	Validate catalogs and test targeted restore	Intact data can become unusable
Unusual admin access patterns	Stolen credentials or tool driven actions	Restrict privileged paths and rotate credentials	Backup control plane is high-value terrain

Monitoring for tampering should be designed around attacker behaviors rather than generic system health. Sudden policy changes, unusual deletion requests, reductions in retention periods, mass disablement of backup jobs, and repeated authentication failures against backup consoles are security signals that deserve immediate investigation. Telemetry from identity systems, backup platforms, and storage layers should be correlated, so defenders can distinguish routine maintenance from destructive activity. Where AI/ML is applied, its best use is to baseline normal administrative patterns and flag deviations such as off-hours bulk actions, anomalous source locations, or sequences consistent with automated sabotage. Those models must be trained on high-fidelity audit logs and should trigger human review rather than automated remediation, because an overconfident automated response can disable legitimate emergency recovery actions.

Incident procedures must assume the backup environment is contested and must include steps to preserve it early in response. Once an intrusion is suspected, responders should consider protective actions that reduce the attacker's ability to pivot into backup control planes, including restricting administrative access paths, rotating privileged credentials, and temporarily enforcing stricter change controls on backup policy. The timing matters because attackers often move quickly from initial access to privilege escalation and then to recovery sabotage. If defenders wait until ransomware detonates, backup protection becomes reactive and less effective. Defensive teams build muscle memory by incorporating backup preservation actions into incident runbooks and by rehearsing those actions under time pressure.

Restore testing is the most practical proof that backups have not been silently tampered with and that operational paths still work. Tests should be designed to validate not only that data can be restored, but that it can be restored cleanly, securely, and at scale, with attention to identity dependencies and credential rotation requirements. A restore that succeeds in a lab but fails in production due to missing DNS, broken certificates, or unavailable secrets is operationally equivalent to a failed backup. Testing also exposes whether immutability and isolation controls create friction that teams will attempt to bypass during emergencies, which is a governance problem as much as a technical one. When tests are frequent and realistic, teams find and fix brittleness before attackers can exploit it.

Finally, protecting backups from tampering and loss requires explicit governance because the control is powerful, costly, and easy to erode through convenience-driven exceptions. Backup retention changes, deletion approvals, and administrative role assignments should be reviewed and logged in a way that supports later audit and incident investigation. Organizations should expect periodic adversarial behavior in their own environment and treat backup defenses as a living component of resilience, not a one-time project. The outcome is not simply better recovery; it is a meaningful reduction in attacker leverage, because the organization can credibly assert that destructive actions will not permanently remove its ability to restore. When backups are protected with disciplined identity controls, layered isolation, strong auditability, and proven restore workflows, they become one of the most reliable defensive controls available.

Recovery Objectives and Realistic Expectations

Recovery objectives only matter when they are expressed as operational commitments that teams can actually meet under incident conditions. Many organizations can quote an RTO and RPO, yet few can demonstrate that those targets survive ransomware, credential compromise, or widespread infrastructure instability. The purpose of defining objectives is to translate business tolerance for downtime and data loss into engineering constraints, staffing requirements, and decision rights during a crisis. If those objectives are aspirational or borrowed from vendor defaults, they will create false confidence and dangerous planning assumptions. Realistic expectations are defensive because they prevent leadership from making high-stakes choices based on imagined capabilities.

RTO and RPO must be set per business capability, not per system, because systems rarely fail or recover in isolation. A customer portal, for example, may depend on identity services, network routing, APIs, and data stores, each with different restoration characteristics and bottlenecks. If leadership sets a two-hour RTO for a capability

Table 14.2 Recovery Objective Translation Checklist.

Objective Element	Operational Definition	What Must Be Proven	Common Failure Mode
RTO	Business downtime tolerance expressed as time	Capability can resume within target	Restore completes but service cannot operate
RPO	Acceptable data loss expressed as time	Restore point meets loss tolerance	Backup cadence does not match tolerance
Dependency sequencing	Order required to restore composite services	Identity and core services restored first	Apps restored before trust services
Resume versus restore	Operational return includes validation and controls	Integrity checks and reconnection gates executed	Assuming restored equals operational
Decision thresholds	Criteria to start restore or reconnect	Approvals and evidence captured	Restoring into hostile environment

whose dependencies require half a day to rebuild, the organization will either miss the objective or take shortcuts that undermine containment and eradication. Conversely, if teams engineer for overly aggressive objectives everywhere, cost and complexity rise while risk may not meaningfully decrease. The defensible approach is to align objectives with what the business truly needs and then design recovery sequences that honor dependency chains.

Realistic recovery planning also accounts for the difference between "restore" and "resume." Restoring a server image or database does not mean the business can operate; authentication may be broken, integrations may be down, and security controls may block traffic until validation is complete. Resume time includes integrity checks, credential rotation, configuration validation, and controlled reintroduction of systems into the network. These steps are not optional niceties during a cyber event, because rushing restored systems into production can re-enable persistence mechanisms or expose services before they are clean. When leaders understand that recovery is a controlled reconstitution of trust, they set expectations that support secure decision-making rather than forcing unsafe speed. Table 14.2 links recovery objectives to the specific operational proofs required to ensure timelines reflect real capability restoration rather than assumptions.

Objectives are also constrained by data consistency and application design, which is where unrealistic expectations often originate. Backups captured at the storage layer may not preserve transactional consistency for applications that require coordinated state across multiple components. Application-aware backups, log replay, and point-in-time recovery can improve precision, but they depend on correct configuration, disciplined change control, and a reliable chain of logs and metadata. If those prerequisites are missing, the organization may restore data that looks intact but fails under load or produces subtle corruption that is discovered days later. Good recovery planning explicitly recognizes these risks and includes validation steps that confirm both integrity and application correctness before declaring success.

A realistic program recognizes that "fastest" recovery is frequently not the same as "safest" recovery, especially when compromise scope is uncertain. During a ransomware incident, the temptation is to restore quickly to stop business bleeding, but restoring before containment can hand attackers fresh infrastructure to re-encrypt or exfiltrate from. Recovery objectives should therefore be paired with decision thresholds that define when restoration proceeds, what evidence is required, and who approves deviations when time pressure is extreme. That governance protects responders from being pushed into restoring into a hostile environment and gives executives a clear view of the risk tradeoffs they are accepting. Recovery becomes a managed risk decision rather than a frantic technical scramble.

Staffing and operational capacity are often the hidden determinant of whether recovery objectives are realistic. Restoring dozens or hundreds of systems is not only a bandwidth problem; it is also a coordination problem involving application owners, infrastructure teams, identity administrators, and security responders working through dependencies and approval gates. If objectives assume uninterrupted access to specialized personnel, 24/7 execution, and perfect documentation, they will collapse during holidays, concurrent crises, or when key staff are unavailable. Mature organizations plan for surge capacity through cross-training, clear runbooks, and pre-negotiated escalation paths, and they practice those plans, so execution is not dependent on a single expert. Realistic expectations are grounded in how the organization actually operates, not in an idealized org chart.

AI/ML can help set and validate recovery objectives by analyzing historical outage data, restore test results, and operational telemetry to estimate achievable timelines and identify bottlenecks. This can be useful for surfacing patterns such as which dependency failures repeatedly delay restores, which applications consistently exceed recovery windows, or which teams become critical-path constraints. The value depends on trustworthy data from incident tickets, change management records, backup logs, and system performance metrics, and it requires careful normalization, so the model does not confuse routine maintenance restores with crisis restores. Human-in-the-loop controls are essential because model outputs can create false precision and undue confidence, especially when rare, high-impact events dominate recovery outcomes. Governance should require that AI-assisted estimates are treated as decision support, with documented assumptions and periodic recalibration as infrastructure and applications evolve.

Testing is where objectives become credible, and it is also where unrealistic expectations are exposed without business harm. A test that restores a single file proves almost nothing about a two-day enterprise recovery, just as a tabletop exercise proves almost nothing about the mechanics of rebuilding identity services and re-establishing trust. Effective testing is scoped to capabilities, includes dependency sequencing, and measures both time to restore and time to resume operations with integrity checks completed. It also captures friction points such as slow approvals, missing credentials, undocumented integrations, and the time cost of rotating secrets and reissuing certificates. Those findings should feed directly back into objective-setting, because the test results are the best available evidence of what the organization can actually do.

Realistic recovery expectations must also include communications discipline, because misaligned messaging can be as damaging as missed technical targets. When leaders publicly or internally promise a restore timeline that is not supported by verified progress, they create credibility risk and increase pressure on responders to cut corners. Recovery communications should reflect uncertainty explicitly, using ranges and decision points, while still giving stakeholders actionable information about what is being restored and what remains unavailable. This is not about pessimism; it is about protecting operational integrity and avoiding the spiral where unrealistic promises force unsafe actions. A mature posture treats recovery objectives as commitments backed by practice, evidence, and governance, and it treats deviations as signals to improve capabilities rather than as failures to hide.

Restoration Testing and Operational Readiness

Restoration testing is the moment where backup and recovery stop being beliefs and become demonstrated capabilities. Many organizations can show that backup jobs ran and storage consumed increased, yet that evidence does not prove a single critical system can be restored under time pressure. Testing validates the full recovery chain: access to backup repositories, integrity of data and catalogs, availability of decryption keys, correctness of images, and the operational steps required to reintroduce systems safely. This is why restoration testing is not a periodic IT exercise but a core element of operational resilience and security assurance. Without it, leaders are making risk decisions based on paperwork rather than performance.

Operational readiness begins with clear ownership and repeatable procedures that survive staff changes and stressful conditions. Recovery runbooks need to be more than a sequence of clicks; they must capture prerequisites, dependency ordering, approval boundaries, and the evidence required to declare a restore complete. Good runbooks also include "failure paths" that explain what to do when a restore job fails, when a credential is unavailable, or when a dependency service is down. Readiness requires that these procedures are accessible during an incident, which means they cannot live solely behind the same identity systems that may be unavailable. When responders can execute recovery steps from memory only, the organization is one absence or one surprise away from a stalled restoration.

Testing must reflect real business capability recovery rather than isolated component recovery, because isolated restores rarely fail in the ways that matter. An application may restore perfectly but fail to authenticate users because directory services are down, certificates are invalid, or secrets stores are unavailable. A database may restore cleanly but produce inconsistent application behavior because schema migrations were not tracked or because dependent services were restored from different points in time. Capability-based tests force teams to handle sequencing: restore identity and name resolution first, then core platforms, then applications and data stores, and finally integrations and user access pathways. This approach produces operational truth about what can be recovered and in what order, which is exactly what incident commanders need.

Readiness also requires integrity and cleanliness checks that prevent "restoring the compromise." In a cyber event, the goal is not only to restore availability but also to restore trust, which means verifying that restored systems are not reintroducing persistence, corrupted configurations, or stolen credentials. Practical controls include validating images against known-good baselines, confirming configuration drift is understood and intentional, and rotating privileged credentials and service accounts before systems rejoin production networks. These steps add time, but that time is part of secure recovery and should be accounted for in objectives and tests. Organizations that skip these validations often see repeat compromise or rapid reinfection, which turns restoration into an expensive loop.

A realistic test program includes scale, concurrency, and resource constraints, because the bottleneck is often not technology but coordination and throughput. Restoring a single server proves little about restoring a fleet when bandwidth, storage IOPS, and staff attention are all constrained. Tests should deliberately stress the environment with multiple simultaneous restores, degraded network conditions, and limited access to specialized personnel, because those conditions are common during incidents. This kind of testing exposes the real critical path, including slow approvals, hidden dependencies, and competing priorities between infrastructure teams and application owners. When those constraints are visible, leaders can invest in the specific capacity that improves outcomes rather than funding generic "more backup" initiatives.

Operational readiness depends on evidence capture and measurement, because improvement requires knowing what actually happened. Each test should record start and end times for key steps, the restore point used, the validation checks performed, and the reasons for any delays or failures. Those metrics can be compared to the organization's recovery objectives to reveal where expectations are unrealistic or where engineering work is needed. Evidence also supports auditability and post-incident learning, which matters when recovery performance becomes part of customer trust and regulatory scrutiny. A disciplined measurement culture prevents the quiet normalization of failed restores and creates a feedback loop that steadily increases resilience.

AI/ML can improve restoration testing by helping teams detect patterns in failures, predict bottlenecks, and triage restore issues, but it should be treated as advisory rather than authoritative. Models can analyze backup job logs, error codes, infrastructure telemetry, and change records to surface recurring failure modes such as agent incompatibilities, storage saturation, or misconfigured application-consistent backups. The value depends on clean telemetry and consistent logging, and it requires careful handling of sensitive incident and system data to avoid leakage into ungoverned analytics environments. Human-in-the-loop controls should require that AI-generated recommendations are reviewed by operators before changes are made to backup policies or restore procedures. Failure modes include false confidence from incomplete logs, drift as platforms evolve, and bias toward frequent issues that may not represent the rare, catastrophic scenarios that testing is meant to prepare for.

Readiness is also a people-and-process discipline that hinges on clear decision rights during recovery. In practice, restoration tests should exercise the same approval boundaries used during incidents, such as who authorizes restoring a tier-one service, who approves reconnecting a restored system to production, and who can override standard change controls under emergency conditions. These boundaries reduce chaos and prevent conflicting actions, such as one team restoring from a newer point while another team restores dependencies from an older point, creating inconsistent states. Tests should include communication paths, escalation rules, and handoffs between security responders and infrastructure operators, because recovery is rarely executed by one team alone. When these operational behaviors are practiced, restoration becomes a coordinated response rather than a collection of parallel, unaligned efforts.

Finally, operational readiness is proven when restoration testing is continuous, varied, and treated as non-negotiable work rather than as an occasional compliance checkbox. The most resilient organizations test restores routinely, rotate through different workload types, and include "surprise" elements that reflect real incidents such as missing credentials, partial outages, or suspected compromise of administrative accounts. Over time, this practice reduces uncertainty, improves documentation quality, and builds confidence that is justified by evidence rather than optimism. It also helps teams refine what "done" means, including security validation and functional verification, not just the completion of a restore job. When restoration testing is executed with rigor and operational realism, it becomes one of the strongest predictors that the organization can withstand both failure and attack without losing control of outcomes.

Coordinating Recovery Across IT and Security

Coordinating recovery across IT and security is the difference between restoring systems and restoring trust. In many incidents, IT operations is optimized to return services quickly, while security is optimized to prevent further harm by limiting exposure and preserving evidence. Those objectives are compatible, but only when roles, decision rights, and sequencing are defined before a crisis. Without coordination, teams often work at cross purposes: systems are restored into a still-compromised environment, or containment actions inadvertently block critical restoration steps. Effective coordination turns recovery into a controlled operation where availability returns in parallel with confidence that the environment is no longer hostile.

A shared operating picture is the first practical requirement, because recovery decisions rely on scope, status, and dependencies. Security typically owns the investigation timeline, indicators of compromise, and the evolving understanding of which accounts and hosts may be affected. IT owns the real-time health of infrastructure, the mechanics of restores, and the dependency chains that determine what can come back first. When those views are kept in separate channels, leaders receive inconsistent answers and responders make local decisions that create global problems. Coordination requires a single, trusted incident record that tracks what is down, what is being restored, what has been validated, and what remains suspected or confirmed compromised. The point is not administrative neatness; it is preventing ambiguity from becoming downtime.

Decision rights must be explicit, because recovery forces tradeoffs between speed, safety, and business impact that cannot be resolved by ad hoc debate. Security should be able to place holds on restoration when evidence suggests reinfection risk or when critical identity elements are still under attacker control. IT should be able to demand clear criteria for those holds, so recovery is not stalled by generalized caution. Leaders need a defined path to accept risk knowingly when the business impact of delay is extreme, and that path must include documentation of what was decided and why. When decision rights are unclear, the incident commander becomes a referee rather than a leader, and restoration becomes slower and less safe.

Sequencing is where coordination becomes concrete, because the order of restoration determines whether systems return cleanly and stay that way. IT typically thinks in terms of service tiers and dependencies, bringing back identity services, core networking, and foundational platforms before applications. Security thinks in terms of trust boundaries, ensuring that privileged access, administrative workstations, and identity control planes are secured before allowing broad reconnection. These are not competing plans; they are two views of the same reality that must be merged into a single restoration sequence with gates. Gates are decision points where restored components are validated for integrity, credentials are rotated, and monitoring is confirmed before the next layer is reintroduced.

Identity is often the sharpest friction point between IT urgency and security caution, because compromised credentials can invalidate any restore effort. If attackers have persistent access to privileged accounts, they can sabotage restores, reconfigure systems, or reintroduce malware as soon as services return. This is why coordinated recovery typically includes early actions to reduce identity risk, such as rotating high-value credentials, restricting privileged access paths, and tightening conditional access controls. IT must understand that these actions are not delays for their own sake; they are prerequisites that prevent a second collapse. Security must understand that credential rotation and access restrictions can break services, so these actions must be planned, tested, and executed with IT participation.

Communication patterns during recovery should be engineered to reduce churn and avoid unforced errors. IT teams need clear statements about what is safe to restore, what artifacts are trusted, and what evidence is required to reconnect a system. Security teams need timely updates about restore progress, the restoration points chosen, and the system states observed during rebuild. When information is exchanged informally, it becomes inconsistent and cannot be audited later, which matters when leadership is asked to justify timelines and decisions. A disciplined cadence of updates, with a shared log of changes and approvals, supports both speed and accountability. Coordination also requires a common vocabulary for "restored," "validated," and "operational," because ambiguous status labels create false confidence.

AI/ML can support coordination by synthesizing signals from incident timelines, asset inventories, backup logs, and system telemetry into a coherent view of recovery state. For example, it can help correlate which services are blocked by a specific dependency outage, identify anomalous post-restore behaviors that suggest reinfection, or summarize action items and risks for leadership briefings. This depends on consistent data feeds and clear governance, because models trained on incomplete or delayed telemetry can produce misleading confidence or miss subtle indicators. Human-in-the-loop controls are essential, particularly around automated recommendations that affect containment boundaries or restoration sequencing. Outputs should be explainable, logged, and treated as decision support, not as authority, because recovery is a high-stakes environment where model error can amplify harm. Governance should also prevent sensitive incident data from being mishandled, especially when AI tooling sits outside core security controls.

Coordination must include evidence handling and investigative needs without turning recovery into a forensic paralysis. Security may need to preserve certain systems, logs, or disk images to understand entry points and confirm eradication, while IT needs to rebuild to reduce downtime. The compromise is to define which assets are "hold for evidence," which can be rebuilt immediately, and how to capture sufficient data from systems slated for rapid rebuild. That approach maintains investigative continuity while allowing restoration to proceed, and it reduces the temptation for teams to make unilateral decisions that destroy critical evidence. When evidence plans are predefined, both teams can move quickly with fewer arguments in the moment.

Finally, coordinating recovery across IT and security requires practice, because coordination failures are usually procedural rather than technical. Joint exercises that include real restore steps, identity hardening actions, and reconnection gates build shared muscle memory and reveal where responsibilities are unclear. Those exercises should stress realistic conditions such as partial outages, limited staff availability, and uncertain compromise scope, because that is where coordination most often breaks down. Over time, practiced coordination creates trust between teams, which matters when decisions must be made quickly with incomplete information. When IT and security operate as a single recovery organism—sharing a picture of reality, honoring clear decision rights, and sequencing restores through security gates—the organization restores not only services, but control.

Recovery During Active Incidents

Recovery during an active incident is fundamentally different from recovery after an outage because the environment is adversarial, not merely broken. The key constraint is that responders rarely know the full scope of compromise at the moment recovery pressure peaks, yet every restoration action can either reduce or increase attacker leverage. Restoring systems too early can re-enable persistence, expose clean credentials to compromised hosts, or provide attackers a fresh platform to sabotage again. Waiting too long can cause cascading business impacts that force rushed decisions later, often with worse security outcomes. Effective recovery during active incidents is therefore a controlled negotiation between operational necessity and containment discipline, executed with clear gates and evidence-based decisions.

The first operational principle is to stabilize the environment by limiting attacker movement before broad restoration begins. That does not require perfect attribution or complete forensics, but it does require immediate actions that reduce the blast radius: constraining privileged access paths, tightening remote access conditions, and isolating known-compromised segments. Identity is usually the center of gravity, because if attackers retain administrative control, they can undermine every restore. Teams should assume that credentials used during the compromise window may be exposed and prioritize rotation of high-value accounts and service principals in a structured sequence. Stabilization also includes protecting backup systems and recovery infrastructure from tampering, because attackers often shift to sabotage once they detect response activity.

Recovery must be staged around "trust zones" that separate clean build capability from compromised production reality. The safest restores originate from a protected environment with controlled administrative workstations, hardened access, and verified images, rather than from everyday endpoints that may be compromised. This approach reduces the risk of reintroducing malware through administrative tooling, scripts, or cached credentials on responder machines. It also enables consistent logging and auditability of restoration actions, which becomes critical later when leadership asks what was done and why. When teams build from a trusted zone, they can reconstitute services with greater confidence while still operating under imperfect information.

Selecting restoration points during an active incident requires balancing timeliness against the risk of restoring tainted data or configurations. If the intrusion involved data corruption, stealthy tampering, or long dwell time, the most recent backups may already contain malicious changes. Responders should use evidence from logs, alerts, and incident timelines to bracket a "likely clean window," then validate restores in an isolated environment before reconnecting them. This validation is not purely technical; it includes checking for unexpected scheduled tasks, persistence mechanisms, anomalous accounts, and suspicious configuration drift. The objective is not to guarantee perfection but to prevent obvious reinfection paths and to avoid restoring a known-bad state out of urgency.

Containment and recovery must operate as parallel, tightly synchronized tracks rather than as sequential phases. Security teams work to identify initial access paths, establish the scope of compromised identities and hosts, and implement controls that prevent re-entry. IT teams work to rebuild core services and restore prioritized capabilities, but only through agreed-upon gates that confirm prerequisites are met. Those gates typically include credential rotation checkpoints, validation of clean images, and confirmation that monitoring is in place to detect recurrence. When one track outruns the other, the organization either restores into danger or delays recovery without clear security benefit. Synchronization is what keeps both speed and safety within acceptable bounds.

AI/ML can be useful during active incidents by reducing cognitive load and accelerating correlation, but it must be constrained to avoid creating false certainty. Models can help cluster related alerts, summarize incident timelines from disparate logs, and surface likely dependency blockers that will slow restores. This depends on high-fidelity telemetry from identity systems, endpoints, network controls, and backup platforms, and on careful handling of sensitive incident data to prevent leakage into ungoverned systems. Human-in-the-loop controls should require that AI outputs are treated as hypotheses, with operators validating recommendations before changing containment boundaries or initiating large-scale restores. Failure modes are common in incident contexts: incomplete logs can mislead the model, adversary behavior can be atypical, and drift can cause models to overfit to patterns from routine operations. Governance should ensure AI assistance is logged and reviewable, so decisions can be defended later.

Recovery during an active incident also requires disciplined handling of evidence and communications, because both influence the ability to control outcomes. Systems slated for rapid rebuild may still contain crucial artifacts about attacker behavior, so teams need preplanned methods to capture sufficient data before wiping or reimaging.

At the same time, responders must avoid creating a forensic bottleneck where "waiting for perfect evidence" prevents business-critical recovery. Communications must reflect uncertainty honestly, using decision points and risk statements rather than promising exact timelines based on incomplete information. When leadership understands what is known, what is suspected, and what is being done to reduce uncertainty, they can support secure recovery choices instead of demanding unsafe speed.

A particularly dangerous moment is the transition from isolated restore to production reconnection, because that is when restored assets become exposed to whatever remains in the environment. Reconnection should be phased, starting with tightly controlled access, heightened monitoring, and explicit rollback plans if suspicious behavior appears. Security controls such as network segmentation, conditional access policies, and endpoint protections must be confirmed operational before systems are exposed broadly. This is also where credential hygiene is critical, because restored systems often rely on service accounts and secrets that may have been compromised; reconnecting without rotation can re-enable attacker access silently. A controlled reconnection process turns the "go-live" moment from a leap of faith into a measured expansion of trust.

Finally, recovery during active incidents succeeds when the organization treats time as a resource to be bought with containment, not as a debt to be paid with shortcuts. The most resilient teams create breathing room by reducing attacker leverage early, protecting recovery infrastructure, and restoring in a sequence that re-establishes trust anchors before business applications. They accept that some downtime is preferable to rapid reinfection, and they plan for degraded operations where necessary while clean restoration proceeds. The worst outcomes come from treating recovery as a race against the attacker without controlling the track, because that framing invites hasty restores, inconsistent states, and repeated disruption. When recovery is executed as a gated, evidence-informed operation running alongside containment and eradication, the organization can restore services while keeping control of the environment.

AI-Assisted Recovery Operations: Prioritization, Communication Support, and Validation Requirements

AI-assisted recovery operations can materially improve outcomes during high-stress incidents, but only when they are framed as decision support rather than decision authority. Recovery environments are noisy, time-constrained, and incomplete by definition, which makes human cognition a bottleneck even for experienced teams. AI can help surface patterns, compress timelines, and highlight likely priorities when dozens of systems, dependencies, and stakeholders compete for attention. The defensive value comes from reducing friction and delay, not from delegating judgment. When leaders understand AI as an accelerant for disciplined recovery rather than a shortcut around it, expectations remain grounded and risk remains manageable.

Prioritization is the most immediate and defensible use of AI during recovery, particularly when scope is wide and information is fragmented. Models can correlate asset inventories, dependency maps, business criticality tags, and incident telemetry to suggest which services unblock the greatest number of downstream capabilities. This is especially useful when manual dependency documentation is outdated or incomplete, which is common in dynamic environments. The quality of these recommendations depends entirely on input fidelity, including accurate ownership metadata, current architecture representations, and time-aligned incident data. Human oversight is mandatory, because AI will optimize for what it can see, which may exclude regulatory, safety, or reputational considerations that are not encoded in technical data.

Communication support is another area where AI can add value without increasing risk when used carefully. During recovery, leaders need frequent, consistent updates that reflect changing conditions without overwhelming recipients or creating false certainty. AI can assist by summarizing restore progress, highlighting blockers, and translating technical status into business-relevant language tailored to different audiences. This reduces the burden on responders who would otherwise context-switch between restoration work and executive briefings.

Table 14.3 AI-Assisted Recovery Use Cases and Required Guardrails.

AI-Assisted Function	Primary Input Dependencies	Human Approval Boundary	Key Failure Mode to Watch
Prioritization suggestions	Asset inventory dependency knowledge incident telemetry	Humans confirm sequencing and business impact	Optimizes for incomplete visibility
Status and briefing summaries	Restore logs incident timeline stakeholder updates	Leads review before distribution	False certainty or oversimplified risk
Anomaly flagging post restore	Endpoint network identity and application telemetry	Humans validate before reconnecting systems	Missed indicators due to sparse data
Restore completeness checks	Expected services catalogs configuration state	Humans certify readiness for production	Confuses degraded state with success
Blocker identification	Error logs dependency failures change records	Humans decide remediation steps	Drift causes outdated recommendations

Guardrails matter, however, because automated summaries can inadvertently oversimplify uncertainty or mask disagreement between teams. Validation processes should require that security and IT leads review externally facing updates before distribution to ensure accuracy and appropriate risk framing. Table 14.3 maps where AI can speed recovery work while reinforcing the validation and governance needed to prevent overconfident or unsafe decisions.

Validation is where AI-assisted recovery most often fails if governance is weak, because confidence is easily mistaken for correctness. Models can help flag anomalies in restored systems by comparing post-restore behavior against historical baselines, such as unexpected network connections, service failures, or configuration drift. They can also assist in checking restore completeness by correlating expected artifacts, services, and logs against what actually came back online. These capabilities depend on comprehensive telemetry from endpoints, identity systems, networks, and applications, and on baselines that reflect clean states rather than degraded or already-compromised periods. AI outputs should trigger investigation, not automatically certify systems as clean or ready for production.

Human-in-the-loop controls are non-negotiable in AI-assisted recovery, particularly around actions that are destructive, irreversible, or security-sensitive. Initiating mass restores, approving reconnection to production networks, rotating credentials, or disabling controls must remain explicit human decisions with documented rationale. AI can recommend sequencing or highlight risk indicators, but it should never silently execute changes that alter trust boundaries. Clear approval boundaries protect against both technical failure modes and organizational pressure to "let the system decide" during crises. They also create an auditable trail that explains how recovery decisions were made when outcomes are later reviewed by leadership, regulators, or customers.

Failure modes in AI-assisted recovery are predictable and should be planned for explicitly. Incomplete or delayed telemetry can cause models to miss critical compromise indicators or to prioritize systems that appear important but are already unsafe to restore. Drift is a persistent risk, as infrastructure changes, application refactors, and evolving attacker techniques slowly invalidate assumptions baked into models. There is also a risk of bias toward what is frequently restored or frequently monitored, which can deprioritize rare but mission-critical systems that lack rich telemetry. Organizations should expect these failures and design processes that surface them early through testing, review, and periodic recalibration rather than discovering them during an incident.

Data governance is a defensive requirement when AI is used in recovery operations, because incident data is among the most sensitive information an organization produces. Logs, forensic artifacts, credential events, and internal communications must be protected from leakage into unapproved systems or external training pipelines. Access to AI tooling should be restricted, logged, and aligned with incident roles to prevent unnecessary exposure of sensitive details. Retention policies must be clear so that recovery data used for AI-assisted analysis does not persist longer than justified by security and compliance needs. When governance is weak, the organization risks creating a secondary incident through data mishandling while responding to the first.

Operational readiness for AI-assisted recovery is proven through testing, not aspiration. Teams should exercise AI support during restoration tests to see how recommendations behave under degraded data quality, partial outages, and conflicting signals. These exercises reveal whether AI outputs are actionable, misleading, or ignored under pressure, which is essential feedback before relying on them during real incidents. Over time, disciplined use of AI can improve prioritization speed, reduce communication errors, and strengthen validation rigor, but only if its limits are understood and respected. When AI is integrated as a governed assistant rather than an autonomous actor, it becomes a force multiplier for recovery without undermining control, accountability, or trust.

Turning Recovery Lessons into Control Improvements

Recovery efforts generate some of the most actionable security intelligence an organization will ever see, because they expose how systems actually behave under stress rather than how they were designed to behave on paper. Every restore attempt reveals friction points, hidden dependencies, undocumented assumptions, and control gaps that are invisible during steady-state operations. Treating recovery as a learning event rather than a one-time emergency is what converts pain into resilience. The organizations that improve fastest are not the ones that avoid incidents, but the ones that extract disciplined lessons from them. Turning those lessons into controls requires intent, structure, and follow-through, not just a post-incident meeting.

The first step is capturing observations while they are still operationally fresh and tied to evidence. Recovery timelines, restore failures, unexpected dependencies, credential issues, and validation delays should be logged alongside the decisions that were made and the rationale behind them. This record should distinguish between technical failures and governance failures, such as unclear decision rights or delayed approvals, because the remediation paths differ. When lessons are captured only as high-level summaries, critical nuance is lost and the same failures reappear in the next incident. A defensible process treats recovery artifacts as inputs to control refinement, not as historical trivia.

Control improvements should be prioritized based on impact to recovery objectives rather than on ease of implementation. If a single identity dependency delayed multiple restores, strengthening identity resilience may produce more benefit than optimizing backup performance elsewhere. If restore testing revealed that credential rotation consistently broke applications, then secrets management and application integration deserve focused attention. This prioritization aligns technical work with business impact, which is essential for executive sponsorship and sustained investment. The goal is not to fix everything at once, but to systematically remove the bottlenecks that most threaten recovery outcomes.

Governance controls often need refinement after recovery events, because incidents reveal where authority, accountability, and escalation paths are ambiguous. If teams hesitated to restore because they were unsure who could approve reconnecting systems, that is a control gap even if the technology performed perfectly. Similarly, if emergency exceptions were granted informally and without documentation, auditability and repeatability were compromised. Turning these lessons into controls may involve clarifying incident roles, updating approval thresholds, or formalizing emergency change processes that balance speed with traceability. These changes are often less visible than technical fixes, but they have outsized influence on recovery effectiveness.

Technical controls should be updated to reflect what was actually needed during recovery, not what was assumed to be sufficient. This may include expanding backup coverage for overlooked data sources, adjusting retention based on observed dwell time, or hardening access controls around recovery infrastructure that was nearly compromised. It can also involve refining monitoring to surface-recovery-relevant signals earlier, such as failed restore jobs, anomalous backup deletions, or dependency outages that cascade during rebuilds. Each improvement should be traceable back to a specific recovery lesson, which helps prevent scope creep and keeps changes grounded in evidence. Over time, this traceability builds confidence that control investments are reducing real risk rather than theoretical exposure.

AI/ML can assist in synthesizing recovery lessons across incidents and tests by identifying recurring patterns and control weaknesses that are easy to miss manually. Models can correlate restore timelines, failure modes, and dependency impacts to highlight systemic issues, such as chronic delays tied to a particular platform or recurring misconfigurations after upgrades. This requires disciplined data collection and normalization so that the model learns from comparable events rather than from anecdotal noise. Human review remains essential, because not every pattern warrants a control change and some improvements may have unintended consequences. Used properly, AI accelerates insight generation but does not replace judgment about which controls to strengthen.

The final and most important step is closing the loop by validating that improvements actually change recovery outcomes. Updated controls should be exercised in subsequent restoration tests to confirm they reduce time, complexity, or risk compared to prior baselines. When improvements are not tested, they remain assumptions and can quietly erode as environments evolve. Organizations that treat recovery lessons as inputs to a continuous control-improvement cycle steadily increase their margin for error during incidents. The result is a recovery capability that gets stronger with use, transforming each disruption into a catalyst for better defense rather than a recurring failure mode.

Conclusion

Recovery is strongest when it is treated as an engineered, practiced control that preserves trust as deliberately as it restores availability. Organizations that protect backups from tampering, validate restoration points, and coordinate IT and security through clear gates reduce attacker leverage and avoid the trap of restoring into a hostile environment. Realistic recovery objectives backed by evidence-based testing create decision-making room during active incidents, while disciplined communications prevent false certainty from driving unsafe speed. When AI is used as governed decision support and recovery lessons are consistently converted into control improvements, resilience becomes a compounding advantage that materially limits business impact even when other defenses fail.

Recommendations

1) Establish recovery objectives as security requirements by defining RTO and RPO for each business capability and documenting the assumptions behind them. Translate those objectives into concrete backup frequency, restoration sequencing, and validation steps that teams can execute under incident conditions. Revisit objectives whenever dependencies, platforms, or business priorities change, so targets remain achievable and meaningful.
2) Define backup scope and coverage in terms of business capabilities and their dependencies rather than only servers and storage volumes. Include foundational trust services such as identity, DNS, certificates, and secrets because restoring applications without them often fails in practice. Maintain explicit inclusion and exclusion decisions, so gaps are intentional and reviewable instead of accidental.
3) Align retention decisions to adversary dwell time and business obligations by ensuring you can restore to a point that predates likely compromise windows. Avoid treating "longer retention" as automatically better by balancing recoverability against sensitive-data exposure and operational complexity. Validate that the metadata and catalogs required for restore are retained and usable for the full retention period.
4) Protect backup infrastructure as a high-value security asset by separating administrative duties and restricting privileged access paths. Implement segmentation and strong identity controls, so compromise of routine

admin accounts or endpoints does not translate into control of backup repositories. Monitor for destructive behaviors such as policy changes, retention reductions, and unusual deletion attempts as security signals, not just operational events.

5) Implement immutability and isolation, so at least one backup copy cannot be altered or deleted within a defined window, even by compromised administrative accounts. Ensure immutability covers both backup data and the catalogs needed to locate and restore it, because corrupted catalogs can neutralize intact data. Pair fast recovery copies with an isolated layer that remains unreachable from compromised production networks to survive worst-case incidents.
6) Treat restoration testing as the proof point for resilience by routinely executing hands-on restores that reflect real dependencies and sequencing. Measure time to restore and time to resume operations, including integrity checks, credential rotation, and controlled reconnection steps. Capture failures and delays as evidence to refine runbooks, staffing plans, and recovery objectives rather than as one-off anomalies.
7) Coordinate IT and security through shared decision rights and gated restoration sequencing that restores trust anchors before broad service reintroduction. Use a single operational picture that tracks what is down, what is being restored, what has been validated, and what remains suspected compromised. Require explicit approvals for reconnecting restored systems to production to prevent restoring into a still-hostile environment.
8) Execute recovery during active incidents from a trusted restoration zone with controlled administrative paths and verified images. Stabilize attacker movement early by tightening privileged access, protecting recovery infrastructure, and rotating high-value credentials before large-scale restoration begins. Validate restoration points in isolation when compromise scope is uncertain, so speed does not become a reinfection vector.
9) Use AI-assisted recovery support for prioritization and communication only when telemetry is high-fidelity and governance boundaries are clear. Treat AI outputs as hypotheses that require human review, especially for destructive actions, reconnection approvals, and credential-related changes. Log AI-assisted recommendations and decisions, so recovery actions remain auditable and defensible when outcomes are reviewed.
10) Convert recovery lessons into control improvements by capturing evidence, timelines, blockers, and decision rationales while the event is fresh. Prioritize remediation based on the bottlenecks that most threaten recovery objectives, including governance gaps as well as technical weaknesses. Validate every improvement through subsequent restoration tests, so resilience becomes a compounding capability rather than an unverified assumption.

Part IV

Vulnerability Management and Threat Mitigation

15

Vulnerability Management Program Foundations

Vulnerability management succeeds or fails on operational fundamentals: clear ownership, reliable asset context, disciplined scope, and a cadence that matches remediation capacity. When intake extends beyond scanning to include advisories, testing results, and configuration-driven exposure, the program gains the visibility needed to stay ahead of real attacker behavior rather than chasing dashboards. Risk-based prioritization then turns that visibility into business-aligned action by focusing effort where exploitation would cause unacceptable impact and by making compensating controls and exceptions explicit, verified, and time-bound. With governance around AI-assisted triage and auditable decision accountability, the program can reduce backlog chaos, validate remediation outcomes, and build sustained confidence that reported improvements reflect real reductions in exploitable risk.

Defining What Vulnerability Management Is and Is Not

Vulnerability management is the disciplined, repeatable practice of finding, understanding, prioritizing, and driving the remediation of security weaknesses that exist in the environment. It is not a single scan, a quarterly compliance exercise, or a report that gets filed away after a brief review. In mature programs, it functions as an operational control loop: discover exposure, evaluate business impact, assign accountable owners, verify changes, and continuously measure whether risk is trending down. That loop depends on engineering realities such as asset ownership, maintenance windows, and change control, not just security intent. The outcome is not "no vulnerabilities," but demonstrably reduced likelihood and impact of exploitation across the systems the business actually runs.

It is useful to define the "vulnerability" in operational terms rather than in marketing language. A vulnerability is a condition that can be exploited to violate a security property such as confidentiality, integrity, or availability, and it is inseparable from context. The same CVE can be irrelevant on one host and urgent on another depending on exposure, privilege boundaries, compensating controls, and business criticality. Vulnerability management therefore must include both identification and interpretation, because identification without context yields noise and misallocation of effort. The program's credibility rises when it consistently explains why a given weakness matters to the business and what "done" looks like for remediation. That credibility is fragile and is easily lost when every finding is treated as equally urgent.

Vulnerability management is not synonymous with patch management, even though patching is one of the most common remediation actions. Patch management is a change process focused on applying vendor-provided updates on a schedule that balances stability and security. Vulnerability management determines which weaknesses must be addressed, by whom, and by when, and it accepts that many remediations are not patches at all. Configuration changes, feature hardening, removal of vulnerable components, segmentation, and compensating controls are all valid remediation paths when patching is impossible or risky. A program that equates

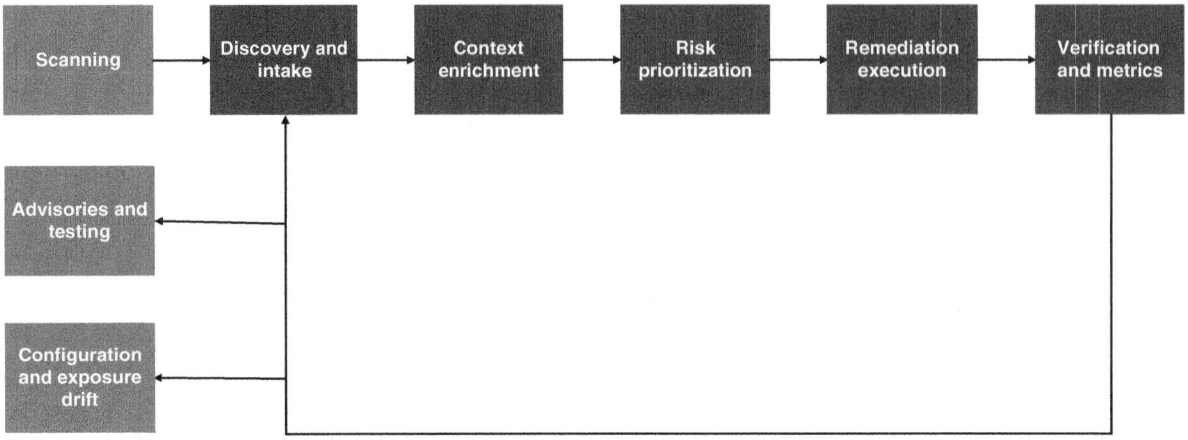

Figure 15.1 Vulnerability Management Control Loop and Inputs.

"patched" with "secure" will miss entire classes of exposure, including insecure configurations, weak credentials, unnecessary services, and legacy software with no supported fixes. The most reliable signal of program maturity is not patch velocity alone, but the ability to drive the right remediation action for the actual source of risk. Figure 15.1 shows vulnerability management as a continuous control loop from discovery through verification. It also reinforces that intake comes from scanning and non-scanner sources that must be normalized into the same workflow.

Vulnerability management is also not the same as vulnerability scanning, even when scanning is the primary input. Scanners produce findings; programs produce outcomes. A scan that runs without dependable asset attribution, credential coverage, and scope hygiene becomes a factory for false positives, duplicates, and unowned work. Conversely, a program can be effective even with imperfect scanning if it has strong asset inventory, clear ownership, and a process for verifying exploitation paths and remediation efficacy. The emphasis should be on measurably reducing exploitable conditions rather than maximizing the number of detections. Scanning is an instrument, and like any instrument it must be calibrated, validated, and interpreted by people who understand both the environment and the attacker's likely paths.

Vulnerability management is not an incident response activity, though it must learn from incidents and threat intelligence. Incident response focuses on active compromise and containment, while vulnerability management focuses on preventing the next compromise by closing known and discoverable gaps. The two programs intersect when exploited vulnerabilities are discovered during investigations, when emergency patching is required, or when compensating controls must be deployed quickly to reduce exposure. A common failure mode is treating vulnerability remediation as an emergency-only function, where work surges after breaches and then stalls during calmer periods. That pattern exhausts engineering teams and produces inconsistent risk reduction. A steady cadence with clear prioritization prevents the program from becoming reactive theater.

Vulnerability management is not solely a security team responsibility, because the fixes typically sit with infrastructure, application, endpoint, and product owners. Security provides the governance, prioritization logic, verification, and escalation paths, but it cannot remediate what it does not own. The program succeeds when accountability is explicit, intake and assignment are frictionless, and remediation deadlines are aligned to asset criticality and exposure. It fails when findings are thrown over the wall, when engineering is asked to "patch everything," or when exceptions are granted without a defensible rationale. Effective programs treat remediation as a normal part of operating systems and software, not as a favor to security. The role of leadership is to ensure that teams have the time, authority, and incentives to fix what matters. Table 15.1 clarifies common misunderstandings by separating what vulnerability management includes from what it does not.

Table 15.1 Vulnerability Management Is and Is Not.

Concept	Is	Is Not
Vulnerability management	Continuous control loop	One-time report exercise
Primary output	Verified risk reduction	Dashboard activity
Relationship to patching	Guides remediation choices	Same as patch management
Relationship to scanning	Uses scanner output as input	Same as vulnerability scanning
Relationship to incidents	Learns and prevents recurrence	Incident response function
Remediation types	Patching config changes segmentation	Only applying patches

Finally, vulnerability management is not about chasing perfect scores or eliminating every low-severity finding, because prioritization exists for a reason. A credible program distinguishes between theoretical weaknesses and materially exploitable conditions, and it makes those tradeoffs visible and auditable. This is where AI-assisted analysis can help if applied carefully: models can cluster duplicate findings, enrich them with asset context, and suggest likely exploitation paths based on exposure and privileges, but they must operate with human approval boundaries. Overreliance creates failure modes such as false confidence in autogenerated risk ratings, drift as environments change, and inadvertent leakage if sensitive vulnerability data is shared outside approved systems. When used responsibly, automation accelerates triage and improves consistency, but it never replaces the need for accountable decisions and verification. The defining characteristic of vulnerability management is that it turns technical weakness into managed operational work with measurable risk outcomes, and it refuses to confuse activity with progress.

Dependencies on Asset Management and Ownership

Vulnerability management cannot function as an operational program without a trustworthy understanding of what exists in the environment and who is responsible for it. Asset management is the foundation that turns vulnerability findings into actionable work, because every finding must resolve to a real system, a meaningful context, and an accountable owner. When asset records are incomplete or stale, the program quickly degrades into argument over scope, duplicate tickets, and disputed priorities. The practical effect is that remediation becomes voluntary, because no one can be confidently held accountable for a system that is not clearly identified or assigned. A program that consistently reduces risk starts with disciplined asset visibility and unambiguous ownership.

Asset management in this context is not just an inventory list; it is the ability to uniquely identify assets and describe them in ways that drive operational decisions. Unique identifiers must withstand common real-world changes such as IP address churn, hostname reuse, cloud instance recycling, and endpoint reimaging. If the environment cannot correlate a vulnerability finding to a stable asset identity, the same issue will repeatedly reappear as "new," inflating metrics and eroding confidence in the program. Good records include attributes that matter for prioritization such as business service association, data sensitivity, exposure, and environment classification. The program's prioritization logic is only as accurate as the asset context it consumes.

Ownership is the second half of the dependency, and it must be treated as a control rather than an informal social agreement. An owner is not merely "the team most likely to fix it," but the person or group that is accountable for timely remediation decisions and outcomes. That accountability requires clarity on decision rights, including when an owner can defer remediation, when compensating controls are acceptable, and how risk acceptance is recorded. Ownership that lives only in tribal knowledge fails under staff turnover, reorganizations, and vendor transitions. Effective programs encode ownership into systems that drive work intake and escalation, so responsibility does not depend on personal relationships. When ownership is explicit, remediation becomes predictable and measurable.

The program should expect common asset management failure modes and design around them rather than pretending the environment is cleaner than it is. Shadow IT introduces unmanaged systems that scan sporadically, appear without context, and frequently lack an obvious owner. Mergers, acquisitions, and inherited networks bring naming collisions, duplicate asset records, and systems that do not align to existing governance. Cloud environments add additional complexity because assets are ephemeral and may exist only briefly, yet still create exposure when misconfigured or deployed with vulnerable components. If the program cannot identify these assets quickly and attach them to an accountable owner, the highest risk exposure can persist precisely because it is hardest to track. Asset management maturity is reflected in how well the organization handles the messy edges, not how clean the core looks.

Discovery is the bridge between vulnerability management and asset management, but discovery must be treated as a continuous process with defined reconciliation rules. Vulnerability scanners, endpoint telemetry, cloud inventory feeds, and configuration baselines will all disagree at times about what exists, and those disagreements must resolve into a single operational record. This requires deduplication logic, confidence scoring, and a defined source of truth for specific attributes; otherwise, the program will oscillate between overcounting and blind spots. When discovery is weak, the same asset may have multiple identities across tools, leading to fragmented remediation and inconsistent verification. When discovery is strong, vulnerability findings can be automatically routed with minimal human intervention because the program trusts the asset record. That trust is what allows scale.

Prioritization depends on asset criticality and exposure, which means asset management must encode business context in a way that vulnerability workflows can consume. A vulnerability on an internet-exposed system that supports revenue or critical operations is not operationally equivalent to the same vulnerability on an isolated lab host. Without service mapping or at least reliable tagging for business unit, environment, and external exposure, prioritization collapses into severity-only sorting. Severity alone encourages the wrong behaviors, including rushing low-impact patches while missing high-impact configurations that enable lateral movement. Executives tend to notice when "critical" findings persist on the most important systems, regardless of how good the overall closure rate looks. Asset context is what allows the program to align remediation urgency to business impact.

Ownership must also include the reality that many assets have shared responsibility, and the program has to define how work is routed when lines blur. A server might be owned by infrastructure, but the vulnerable component is in an application stack controlled by a product team, while the exposure is governed by network segmentation owned elsewhere. If the program assigns all findings to a single queue, remediation will stall because the receiving team lacks the authority to make required changes. Mature programs route work to the party that can actually execute the remediation, while preserving a single accountable owner for the overall risk. When multiple teams must act, the ticketing workflow should reflect dependencies and sequencing rather than assuming a single fix exists. Clear ownership models prevent findings from bouncing between groups until deadlines are meaningless.

AI-assisted triage can reduce operational friction in asset correlation and ownership routing, but only if the program governs it as decision support rather than automation by default. Models can help match scanner outputs to asset identities using attributes like hostname patterns, agent identifiers, and cloud metadata, and they can propose likely owners based on historical remediation patterns. The failure modes are predictable: incorrect matches create misrouted tickets, learned biases reinforce past misassignments, and model drift causes routing quality to degrade as teams reorganize or infrastructure changes. Human-in-the-loop controls should require review for low-confidence matches, and the program should log the model's rationale for auditability and continuous improvement. Any enrichment that uses sensitive asset data must remain within approved systems to avoid leakage of vulnerability and infrastructure details. When governed well, AI improves speed and consistency, but ownership remains a human accountability boundary that cannot be delegated.

Verification and metrics depend directly on asset management and ownership quality, because the program must prove that remediation occurred on the correct systems and that closure reflects real risk reduction. If an asset record changes or is duplicated, the program may show improvement while the vulnerable system remains exposed under a new identity. If ownership is ambiguous, closure timelines cannot be fairly measured, and escalations become political rather than procedural. A credible program ties remediation verification to asset identity and configuration state, and it treats exceptions as explicit decisions attached to owners with expiration and review. Over time, the organization learns that asset hygiene is not an administrative chore but a prerequisite for risk reduction at scale. Vulnerability management becomes sustainable when asset management and ownership are treated as first-class operational dependencies rather than background assumptions.

Establishing Scope Across Systems and Environments

Scope is the set of systems and environments the vulnerability management program is responsible for measuring and improving, and it must be defined with enough precision that findings translate into accountable remediation work. Without a clear scope boundary, teams argue about what "counts," scanning becomes inconsistent, and leadership receives metrics that cannot be trusted to represent organizational risk. A useful scope definition is not aspirational; it is operationally enforceable and aligned to how the organization builds, deploys, and runs technology. It must also be resilient to change, because environments evolve faster than governance documents. A program that scales treats scope as a living control, maintained through system records and workflows rather than occasional policy refreshes.

The most practical way to think about scope is as a coverage map across major technology domains, because vulnerability sources and remediation mechanisms differ by domain. Endpoints, servers, network devices, cloud resources, applications, and managed services each require different discovery methods and create different blind spots. If scope is defined only in generic terms, teams will unintentionally exclude entire categories, such as ephemeral cloud instances, container hosts, or externally managed platforms. Conversely, if scope is defined too broadly without capability, the program will generate noise and miss remediation deadlines, eroding confidence. A credible scope statement matches the organization's operational reality and explicitly accounts for the systems that are most exposed or business critical. The objective is consistent coverage where gaps are visible and intentional, not accidental.

Environment boundaries matter because the same system may exist in development, test, staging, and production, and vulnerability handling must reflect the business impact of each. Production exposures typically drive the most urgent remediation due to real customer and operational risk, but development environments often reveal systemic issues earlier and at lower cost. A scope definition that ignores non-production entirely tends to push weakness downstream, increasing emergency patching and raising the chance of high-risk findings reaching production. At the same time, treating all environments as equivalent creates unrealistic remediation expectations and distracts from the assets that matter most. Mature programs define environment tiers and align scanning cadence and remediation SLAs to each tier. This approach keeps the program both risk-focused and operationally sustainable.

System boundaries are equally important, especially for platforms that span organizational lines such as identity services, shared infrastructure, and common application components. If the program scopes only "systems we own," it will miss exposure introduced through shared services, outsourced operations, and third-party hosting. If the program scopes only "what we can scan," it will exclude high-risk systems that require alternative assessment methods. A workable scope model defines inclusion criteria based on risk and responsibility, not convenience. It also specifies the mechanism for managing out-of-scope technology, such as requiring evidence of equivalent vulnerability controls from service providers. The program must be able to defend its scope choices in terms of exposure reduction, not tool coverage.

Discovery and reconciliation are the operational mechanisms that keep scope accurate as systems appear, change, and disappear. New assets must enter scope automatically based on defined attributes such as network placement, account enrollment, or service tags, rather than relying on manual declarations. Similarly, retired assets must be removed from scope in a way that prevents "ghost" findings from polluting metrics and wasting engineering time. Scope drift is a common failure mode, where coverage silently erodes as technology shifts, especially during cloud migrations or organizational restructuring. The program should treat unexpected scope changes as signals to investigate, not as routine noise. Stable scope management turns vulnerability metrics into a trustworthy management tool.

Exclusions are inevitable, but they must be handled as explicit risk decisions rather than as undocumented exceptions. Legacy systems, operational technology, fragile vendor appliances, and mission-critical platforms may have constraints that limit scanning or patching. The program's job is to ensure those constraints translate into alternative controls such as configuration hardening, segmentation, compensating monitoring, or structured risk acceptance with review dates. When exclusions are informal, they become permanent, and the most dangerous systems often end up least visible. Formal exclusions should include ownership, rationale, and the conditions under which the exclusion is revisited. That structure keeps scope honest and prevents "temporary" gaps from becoming institutional blind spots.

Scope must also align to the organization's change and release processes, otherwise remediation will constantly conflict with delivery timelines. Applications deployed continuously require different handling than quarterly patched infrastructure, and the scope definition should anticipate those operational patterns. For example, patching a library in a CI/CD pipeline is a different remediation workflow than patching a server fleet, even if the underlying vulnerability identifier is the same. If scope does not distinguish these operational realities, the program will measure outcomes in ways that incentivize the wrong behavior, such as delaying releases to satisfy reporting rather than fixing the root cause upstream. A well-scoped program integrates vulnerability remediation into the normal flow of work for each domain. That integration reduces friction and improves the likelihood that fixes persist.

AI-assisted correlation can help maintain scope integrity by detecting anomalies in coverage and highlighting systems that should be in scope but are not. Models can flag assets that appear in telemetry but never receive vulnerability assessment signals, or identify environment tags that are inconsistent with observed behavior such as internet exposure. The failure modes are important to manage: incomplete telemetry can cause false alarms, and biased training data can overemphasize familiar platforms while missing less common ones. Human review is necessary to confirm whether a scope gap is real and to decide how to address it, especially when a system's inclusion has contractual or operational implications. Governance expectations should require that AI-derived scope insights are logged, reviewable, and tied to corrective actions, not treated as informal suggestions. When used carefully, automation strengthens scope discipline and reduces the chance that high-risk technology quietly falls outside the program's visibility.

Setting Frequency and Coverage Expectations

Frequency and coverage define the operational heartbeat of vulnerability management, turning abstract intent into measurable, repeatable practice. Frequency answers how often the organization assesses systems for known weakness, while coverage answers which assets are assessed and how complete the assessment is for each asset class. If frequency is too low, exposure persists longer than leadership realizes and remediation becomes reactive to exploitation rather than driven by risk reduction. If frequency is too high without sufficient quality controls, teams drown in noise, duplicates, and findings that cannot be acted on within available capacity. The program has to balance detection cadence with remediation throughput, because a pipeline that overproduces findings without closing them undermines credibility. Expectations should be set in a way that aligns to real operational constraints and still meaningfully reduces risk.

Table 15.2 Scope Frequency and Coverage Expectations by Environment.

Environment Tier	Typical Risk Posture	Frequency Expectation	Coverage Depth Expectation	Primary Outcome
Production	Highest business impact	Higher cadence	Reliable assessment depth	Reduced exploitable exposure
Non-production	Lower immediate impact	Frequent to catch early	Consistent where practical	Prevent issues reaching production
Internet exposed	Shortest attacker path	Highest urgency cadence	Strong validation required	Reduced time to exploit
Internal only	Variable lateral movement risk	Risk-based cadence	Depth driven by context	Reduced privilege escalation paths
Dynamic workloads	High change rate	Telemetry aligned cadence	Coverage tied to discovery	Reduced blind spot exposure

Coverage is often misunderstood as a simple percentage, but operationally it is a combination of breadth and depth. Breadth is the proportion of in-scope assets that receive assessment, and depth is the quality of that assessment, including whether it is authenticated, whether configuration checks are included, and whether the assessment can reliably detect the classes of weaknesses that matter for that asset type. An environment can show high breadth while having poor depth if scans are unauthenticated, agent coverage is inconsistent, or cloud inventory is incomplete. Conversely, deep assessment of a limited subset can produce high-confidence findings but leave large portions of the environment effectively invisible. Effective programs set coverage expectations by asset class, acknowledging that endpoints, servers, cloud resources, and applications each require different assessment mechanisms. The aim is predictable, explainable visibility rather than a single headline number. Table 15.2 reinforces how frequency and coverage expectations vary by environment tier and assessment depth.

Frequency should be risk-based and environment-aware, not uniform across everything the organization owns. Internet-exposed production systems, identity infrastructure, and core services typically warrant more frequent assessment because exploitation paths are shorter and impact is higher. Lower-risk systems may be assessed less frequently, but they should not be ignored, especially if they can be used for lateral movement or privilege escalation. Non-production environments can benefit from frequent assessment to catch systemic issues early, but expectations must align to how often those environments change and how much effort the organization will invest in keeping them clean. Frequency should also consider the speed of change, because highly dynamic environments require assessment methods that keep pace with deployment rather than relying on occasional snapshots. A program that aligns frequency to risk and change rate creates a defensible operating model that leaders can understand.

The quality of frequency expectations depends heavily on the reliability of discovery and the stability of asset identity. If the program cannot confidently determine what assets exist and whether they were assessed during a given period, any frequency metric becomes performative. This is particularly true in cloud and virtualized environments where instances appear and disappear quickly, and where traditional scanning may miss assets that exist only briefly. In those cases, frequency must be expressed in terms of coverage over inventory feeds and runtime telemetry, not just scheduled scans. The program should also account for maintenance windows, network segmentation, and operational constraints that affect scan reachability. Setting expectations without acknowledging these realities results in chronic "misses" that become normalized rather than corrected.

Coverage expectations must be explicit about assessment method, because the same frequency means different things depending on how findings are produced. Authenticated assessment generally provides better signal because it can validate installed versions and configuration state, but it depends on credential governance and secure handling of privileged access. Unauthenticated scanning can still be valuable for external exposure and basic fingerprinting, but it will miss important conditions and generate ambiguity that increases analyst and engineer effort. Agent-based telemetry can improve depth and timeliness for endpoints and servers, but only if deployment is consistent and the agents remain healthy. For applications, coverage may require a combination of dependency analysis, configuration review, and runtime observation rather than network scanning alone. Mature expectations specify which methods are required for each asset class, so "covered" has a consistent meaning.

Remediation capacity must shape frequency decisions, because a program that repeatedly identifies issues faster than it can close them creates backlog, fatigue, and eventual disengagement. When backlog grows, teams tend to prioritize by severity labels alone, which is rarely aligned to real exploitation risk and business impact. A healthier model sets frequency such that findings are reviewable, triage decisions are timely, and remediation deadlines remain meaningful. This often means starting with achievable cadence and expanding as the organization improves asset ownership, patch processes, and engineering workflows. The program should measure both intake and closure and adjust expectations when reality diverges, treating that adjustment as operational tuning rather than failure. Frequency is not a vanity metric; it is a lever that must be controlled to keep the system stable.

Verification is the guardrail that makes frequency and coverage meaningful rather than symbolic. It is not enough to say an asset was scanned; the program must be able to demonstrate that the assessment ran successfully, that results were ingested, and that the absence of findings reflects real state rather than a telemetry gap. This requires health checks for scanning infrastructure, credential coverage, agent status, and data pipeline integrity. It also requires sampling and spot verification, particularly when remediation claims are made, because false closures erode trust and can conceal persistent exposure. A program that invests in verification can confidently present coverage metrics to executives and withstand scrutiny during audits or post-incident reviews. Without verification, frequency and coverage numbers become optimistic storytelling rather than operational truth.

AI-assisted analysis can help manage the complexity of frequency and coverage by identifying data gaps, prioritizing scan failures, and predicting where coverage is likely to be incomplete based on historical patterns. Models can correlate scan logs, asset inventories, and telemetry feeds to highlight assets that should have been assessed but were not, or to flag systemic issues such as a credential set failing across a fleet. The failure modes are important to control, including overfitting to past patterns that no longer apply, mistaking missing telemetry for a clean state, and generating false confidence in automatically inferred coverage. Human oversight is necessary to approve changes to frequency, interpret anomalies, and ensure that model outputs are explainable and auditable. When governed properly, automation improves the program's ability to maintain stable cadence without compromising accuracy. The core expectation remains that frequency and coverage are defined, verified, and continuously tuned to produce reliable risk reduction rather than periodic bursts of activity.

Vulnerability Intake Beyond Scanning

A vulnerability management program that relies solely on scanner output will miss material risk, because scanners are only one lens on exposure and they are constrained by visibility, authentication, and how the environment is built. Intake is the front end of the program's control loop, and it must accept that vulnerabilities are discovered through many operational pathways. Some of the most consequential weaknesses are discovered in places scanners are weakest, such as application dependencies, cloud-control planes, and configuration-driven exposure. A mature program treats scanning as a foundational signal, but not the sole source of truth, and it builds intake processes that reconcile multiple sources into a single, prioritized workstream. The goal is not to collect more findings, but to capture the findings that matter and make them actionable.

One major non-scanner intake source is vendor and provider advisories, which often contain details that scanning cannot reliably infer. These advisories can cover firmware issues, platform-level vulnerabilities, and cloud service weaknesses that require operational verification rather than signature-based detection. They also introduce time sensitivity, because exploit development can follow quickly after disclosure and public proof-of-concept release. Intake from advisories requires a disciplined process for mapping affected products and versions to the organization's asset records and service catalogs. Without that mapping, advisories become broadcast emails with no measurable follow-through. When the mapping is strong, advisories can trigger targeted assessment and remediation before scanners would have detected the issue, especially when the weakness is in a managed service layer.

Threat intelligence and incident-derived learning are another essential intake path, because exploitation patterns often outpace general-purpose scanning content. When a vulnerability is being actively exploited, the operational priority shifts from abstract severity to probable impact and likelihood based on observed attacker behavior. Intake here should translate external signals into internal action by identifying exposed assets, evaluating compensating controls, and driving emergency remediation or mitigations where appropriate. This pathway depends on close collaboration between vulnerability management, detection engineering, and incident response, because the strongest response often combines patching with monitoring for exploitation indicators and containment of risky exposure. A program that treats threat intelligence as "interesting information" rather than as an intake trigger will repeatedly lose time during high-tempo exploitation cycles. The intake mechanism should produce a clear, trackable set of actions, not a discussion thread.

Internal testing activities provide another source of vulnerability intake that is often higher fidelity than scanning. Penetration tests, red team exercises, adversary emulation, and targeted assessments routinely uncover exploit chains that are invisible to scanners because they involve misconfigurations, logic flaws, or sequences of lower-severity conditions that combine into a high-impact outcome. Intake from these activities must preserve context, because the value is not just "a vulnerability exists," but how an attacker would use it to achieve an objective. If these findings are stripped of narrative and reduced to a generic ticket, remediation teams may fix the symptom while leaving the path intact. Effective programs translate assessment results into remediation items that align with asset ownership and engineering workflows while retaining the critical exploitation context needed to prioritize and verify. This approach also strengthens executive understanding because it ties remediation to realistic business impact.

Application and dependency-driven intake is increasingly central, because modern environments inherit vulnerability risk from libraries, frameworks, and base images. Network scanners may detect some server-side issues, but they rarely provide complete visibility into application dependencies, build artifacts, and the software supply chain that feeds production. Intake here depends on development and build telemetry, including dependency manifests, artifact inventories, and deployment records that can identify where a vulnerable component is actually used. The operational challenge is that the "asset" is not always a host; it may be a service, an image, or a package that exists across many deployments. Ownership must therefore extend to product and platform teams, with remediation actions that fit their cadence, such as updating dependencies, rebuilding images, and redeploying services. Without this intake path, organizations can patch servers quickly and still run vulnerable components inside applications for months.

Configuration and exposure drift is another intake category that scanning alone often misses or misclassifies. Security weaknesses frequently arise from changes in access controls, network paths, identity permissions, or cloud resource policies that create new attack paths without introducing a new software flaw. These conditions are discovered through configuration monitoring, audit logs, identity governance signals, and infrastructure-as-code review, and they need to be treated as first-class vulnerability intake. The remediation is often not patching but restoring intended configuration state, tightening permissions, or enforcing guardrails that prevent recurrence. Programs that exclude configuration-driven weaknesses create an artificial boundary where only CVEs are tracked, even though attackers routinely exploit misconfigurations because they are abundant and durable. Including these findings requires consistent definitions and verification criteria, so teams do not debate whether something "counts" as a vulnerability.

AI-assisted enrichment can make multi-source intake manageable, but it must be governed carefully because intake is where errors propagate downstream. Models can normalize disparate inputs, deduplicate overlapping findings, propose affected asset sets, and summarize advisory language into actionable remediation statements aligned to ownership. The failure modes are serious: hallucinated mappings can route work to the wrong teams, overconfident summaries can omit critical constraints, and biased historical routing can reinforce organizational blind spots. Human-in-the-loop controls should require review for high-impact advisories and for any automated action that triggers emergency workflows or broad remediation campaigns. Intake systems should log what evidence the model used, how confidence was assessed, and what changes were made after human review to support auditability and continuous improvement. AI should reduce friction and improve consistency, not replace accountability or verification.

The unifying requirement across all non-scanner intake sources is disciplined normalization into a single operational queue with clear priority, ownership, and verification expectations. If each source maintains its own workflow, the organization will duplicate work, miss deadlines, and lose the ability to report risk reduction consistently. Conversely, forcing every intake type into a scanner-shaped template will erase the context that makes those findings valuable and will lead to superficial fixes. Effective programs define intake standards that capture what must be true for a finding to enter the queue, such as evidence, affected scope, required remediation outcome, and validation method. They also define how conflicting signals are resolved and how exceptions are recorded with accountable owners and review dates. When intake beyond scanning is implemented with this level of operational rigor, vulnerability management becomes resilient to blind spots and better aligned to how real exposure is discovered and exploited.

Prioritizing Work Based on Business Risk

Prioritization is the mechanism that turns an overwhelming volume of vulnerability data into a manageable sequence of decisions that actually reduces exposure. In operational terms, the question is not "Which findings are most severe?" but "Which weaknesses are most likely to be exploited in ways the business cannot tolerate?" Severity labels are inputs, not outcomes, and they are often disconnected from how the organization is actually exposed. A risk-aligned program consistently explains why a specific remediation is urgent, why another can wait, and what compensating controls change that decision. When that logic is stable and repeatable, engineering teams see the work as rational rather than arbitrary.

Business risk prioritization starts with understanding what the affected system does, who depends on it, and what happens when it fails or is compromised. A vulnerability on a system that supports revenue, safety, regulated data, or critical operations carries a different weight than the same vulnerability on an isolated utility host. The practical work of prioritization is therefore inseparable from asset context, including environment tier, service criticality, and whether the system is externally reachable or positioned along high-value internal paths. Incomplete or incorrect asset context forces teams to default back to severity-only sorting, which reliably misallocates effort. Strong context enables the program to focus remediation where impact and likelihood intersect.

Exposure is one of the most important modifiers of business risk because it shapes how quickly an attacker can reach a vulnerable condition. Internet-facing systems, remote access infrastructure, identity services, and management planes typically collapse attacker effort and shorten time-to-exploit. Internal-only systems may still be high risk if they sit on common administrative networks, host shared services, or provide stepping stones for lateral movement. The program should be explicit that "internal" does not mean "safe," especially when identity and privilege boundaries are weak. Prioritization that ignores exposure tends to chase cosmetic remediation while leaving the shortest attack paths intact. Risk-based prioritization keeps attention on the places where attackers can realistically succeed.

Exploitability matters, but it should be treated as an evidence-driven factor rather than a guess. Public proof-of-concept code, known exploitation in the wild, and straightforward attack preconditions materially change urgency because they increase the likelihood of successful compromise. At the same time, exploitability is not binary; weak prerequisites such as a common misconfiguration, broad user access, or predictable credentials can make "complex" exploits practical in real environments. Prioritization should also account for whether a vulnerability enables initial access, privilege escalation, credential theft, or persistence, because those outcomes map directly to business harm. The program becomes more credible when it ties urgency to observable conditions rather than relying on generic labels.

Compensating controls are a legitimate part of risk-based prioritization, but they must be concrete, verifiable, and time-bound to avoid becoming permanent excuses. Network segmentation, strict access controls, application allow listing, hardened configurations, and monitoring for exploitation behaviors can reduce likelihood or limit blast radius when patching is delayed. The pitfall is treating the presence of a control as proof of protection without validating its coverage and effectiveness for the specific vulnerability path. If the control is mis-scoped, disabled, or unenforced, the risk remains while reporting suggests otherwise. Risk-based programs document the rationale, attach it to an accountable owner, and require re-evaluation when conditions change.

Prioritization must also be designed around remediation reality, because the best risk decision is useless if it cannot be executed within operational constraints. Some fixes are straightforward patches, while others require coordinated application changes, testing, maintenance windows, or vendor involvement, and those differences affect both urgency and sequencing. A risk-aligned program anticipates these constraints by routing work to the teams with the authority to act and by framing remediation outcomes in terms those teams can deliver. It also avoids the common failure mode of over-prioritizing everything, which turns urgency into background noise and guarantees missed deadlines. When prioritization is disciplined, escalations become rare and meaningful rather than constant and ignored.

To keep prioritization consistent at scale, programs benefit from structured decision criteria that are applied the same way across teams and environments. That structure should be simple enough to execute repeatedly and transparent enough that stakeholders can challenge it with evidence when needed. Consistency matters because uneven prioritization creates organizational friction, with some teams held to tight expectations while others defer indefinitely. Over time, inconsistency also poisons metrics because closure rates reflect negotiation skill rather than risk reduction. The goal is a predictable decision process where differences in priority can be traced back to differences in business impact, exposure, and control posture.

AI-assisted triage can help operationalize risk-based prioritization by enriching findings with asset context, correlating related weaknesses into likely attack paths, and highlighting the subset that most plausibly leads to unacceptable outcomes. Done well, this reduces analyst effort and improves consistency, especially when intake volume spikes after major disclosures. The governance boundary is critical: models should recommend, not decide, and humans must approve priorities that drive emergency change, broad remediation campaigns, or risk acceptance. Failure modes include false confidence in model-generated risk rankings, drift as the environment and attacker behaviors evolve, and biased outcomes if historical data reflects past blind spots or inconsistent ownership. To be auditable, the program should retain the inputs that influenced the recommendation and the human rationale for any override.

Ultimately, prioritizing work based on business risk is about making fewer, better decisions and then ensuring those decisions translate into real change on real systems. The program should be able to show that the most important services and exposures receive the fastest attention, that compensating controls are used deliberately and verified, and that exceptions are recorded with accountable owners and review dates. When prioritization is working, teams spend less time debating severity and more time reducing exploitable conditions in places that matter. The organization's posture improves not because every vulnerability is fixed immediately, but because remediation energy is continuously directed at the highest consequence risk. That is the operational definition of a program that is aligned to business outcomes rather than activity metrics.

Handling Vulnerability Backlogs Without Losing Control

A vulnerability backlog is an expected byproduct of a functioning program, not an automatic sign of failure. Backlogs form because discovery outpaces remediation, environments change continuously, and some fixes require coordination that cannot be rushed without introducing operational risk. The danger is not the existence of a backlog, but the loss of control over it, where items age without decision, ownership blurs, and urgency becomes indistinguishable from noise. When that happens, leadership loses confidence in metrics, engineers disengage, and the program shifts from risk reduction to report management. A disciplined approach treats the backlog as an active control surface that must be continuously curated rather than a passive queue.

Control begins with clear definitions for what is allowed to remain in backlog and under what conditions. Every item should have an explicit status that reflects a real decision, such as awaiting remediation, deferred with justification, mitigated through compensating controls, or accepted with documented risk. Items that sit indefinitely in an undefined state are the first indicator that the program is drifting. Aging alone is not inherently bad, but aging without rationale is, because it hides whether the exposure is understood or simply ignored. A program that maintains control can explain why an older item still exists and what would cause it to change state. That explanation is as important as the closure metric itself.

Prioritization discipline is the primary mechanism for keeping a backlog manageable, because not all items deserve equal attention at all times. Risk-based ordering ensures that the most consequential exposures continue to receive focus even as lower-impact items accumulate. This requires periodically re-evaluating backlog items against current asset context, exposure, and threat conditions, rather than letting initial severity labels dictate fate indefinitely. A vulnerability that was low priority at discovery may become urgent after a system is exposed externally or after exploitation becomes common. Without re-evaluation, the backlog calcifies and stops reflecting real risk. Continuous reprioritization keeps the backlog aligned to current reality.

Ownership and accountability must persist even when remediation is delayed; otherwise, backlog becomes a graveyard for unowned risk. Every item should remain attached to an accountable owner who is responsible for monitoring conditions, maintaining compensating controls, and revalidating decisions over time. When ownership decays, backlog items tend to survive reorganizations and staff turnover by default rather than by choice. Effective programs require owners to periodically reaffirm deferred items, which forces explicit reconsideration and prevents silent accumulation. This practice also surfaces systemic issues, such as teams that consistently defer because they lack capacity or authority to remediate. Backlog control improves when accountability is treated as ongoing rather than transactional.

Compensating controls play a legitimate role in backlog management, but they must be actively managed to avoid false confidence. Controls that justified deferral at one point may degrade, be bypassed, or no longer apply as systems evolve. If compensating controls are not validated on a schedule, the backlog quietly converts into unmitigated exposure while reporting still suggests risk has been addressed. A controlled backlog includes verification of compensating controls as a first-class activity, not an afterthought. When controls fail validation, the item must be reprioritized or escalated rather than allowed to linger. This discipline prevents backlog from masking real risk behind outdated assumptions.

Capacity planning is another essential component of backlog control, because chronic backlog growth often reflects a mismatch between intake and remediation throughput. When teams are consistently overwhelmed, the program must distinguish between temporary spikes and structural underinvestment. This may require adjusting scanning frequency, refining intake criteria, or focusing remediation on systemic fixes that eliminate entire classes of findings rather than addressing instances one by one. Treating backlog purely as a performance problem for engineering teams ignores the program's responsibility to tune its own demand. Sustainable control emerges when intake volume and remediation capacity are deliberately balanced rather than left to self-correct. Leadership engagement is often required to resolve these structural mismatches.

Backlog hygiene also depends on eliminating noise that inflates counts without reducing risk. Duplicate findings, obsolete assets, false positives, and findings that no longer apply should be aggressively identified and closed with evidence. Allowing this noise to persist makes the backlog appear worse than it is and distracts attention from real exposure. Periodic cleanup is not cosmetic; it restores signal integrity and improves trust in metrics. A program that cannot defend the accuracy of its backlog cannot credibly argue for resources or escalation. Control improves when the backlog reflects reality rather than artifacts of tooling or process gaps.

AI-assisted analysis can help maintain backlog control by identifying patterns that humans miss at scale, such as clusters of aging items tied to the same root cause or ownership bottleneck. Models can suggest consolidation opportunities, highlight items whose risk has increased due to environmental change, and flag deferrals that no longer have valid justification. The governance boundary is critical, because automated recommendations can also reinforce existing blind spots or deprioritize novel risk if trained on historical behavior. Human review must remain mandatory for changes that affect priority, acceptance, or closure, and the rationale for those decisions should be logged for auditability. When used carefully, automation reduces cognitive load without diluting accountability.

Ultimately, handling vulnerability backlogs without losing control is about preserving intentionality in every decision. The program should be able to explain not just how many items are open, but why they are open, who is responsible, and what would change their status. When that clarity exists, backlogs become manageable representations of known, bounded risk rather than evidence of neglect. Teams can focus their effort where it matters most, and leadership can trust that unresolved items are unresolved by design rather than by default. Control is maintained not by eliminating backlog, but by ensuring that backlog reflects conscious, defensible risk management decisions at all times.

AI-Assisted Vulnerability Prioritization: Inputs, Bias, and Decision Accountability

AI-assisted vulnerability prioritization is most valuable when it accelerates judgment without replacing it. Vulnerability queues grow faster than human attention, and the operational problem is not a lack of data but a lack of consistent, defensible decisions at scale. Used correctly, AI can enrich findings with context, correlate related weaknesses into plausible attack paths, and surface the subset most likely to drive unacceptable business outcomes. Used poorly, it becomes an unaccountable ranking engine that teams follow because it is fast, not because it is right. The program must therefore treat AI as a decision support capability governed by the same rigor applied to other security controls. The outcome should be faster prioritization with clearer rationale, not automation that obscures responsibility.

The quality of AI prioritization is determined primarily by the inputs it receives, because models cannot infer missing context and will confidently produce output even when the underlying data is incomplete. The most important inputs are stable asset identity, business criticality, environment classification, and exposure characteristics such as internet reachability and privileged access paths. Telemetry that describes control posture, including segmentation, MFA enforcement on administrative access, and monitoring coverage, materially changes risk ranking because it influences likelihood and blast radius. Vulnerability attributes also matter beyond severity, including exploit prerequisites, availability of public proof-of-concept, known exploitation, and whether the weakness enables initial access, privilege escalation, or credential theft. Without these inputs, models tend to regress to severity-only patterns that look sophisticated but reproduce the same misprioritization the program is trying to avoid. Input discipline is the first governance requirement, because it sets the ceiling on accuracy and trustworthiness.

Data normalization and timeliness are equally critical, because prioritization depends on current state rather than historical snapshots. If asset tags lag reality, cloud resources recycle identities, or exposure status changes without updating the record, the model will rank risk based on fiction. Similarly, if scanner results, agent telemetry, and cloud inventory feeds disagree and the reconciliation logic is weak, the model may double-count findings or miss entire asset classes. Programs that succeed with AI invest in the unglamorous work of building reliable data pipelines, validating coverage, and defining a source of truth for each attribute. They also track "unknowns" explicitly, because the absence of data is itself a risk signal that should increase scrutiny rather than decrease priority. AI prioritization becomes more defensible when uncertainty is surfaced and handled deliberately.

Bias in AI-assisted prioritization is not an abstract ethical concern; it is an operational failure mode that can systematically misdirect remediation effort. Historical ticketing data often encodes organizational friction, such as teams that close quickly because their issues are easy, and teams that defer because their systems are complex or under-resourced. If a model learns from closure patterns, it may incorrectly infer that certain asset classes are "lower risk" simply because they are historically under-remediated or poorly instrumented. Bias can also arise from uneven telemetry, where well-monitored platforms generate rich data that the model overweights, while poorly monitored platforms appear "quiet" and are deprioritized. These dynamics are especially dangerous because they reinforce blind spots, making high-risk areas less visible over time. Managing bias requires treating training and enrichment data as part of the control surface, with explicit checks for coverage gaps and skewed outcomes.

Drift is another predictable problem, because environments, attacker behaviors, and organizational structures change faster than most models are updated. A prioritization approach that worked during a particular threat cycle can become stale when exploitation trends shift or when the organization migrates to new platforms. Organizational drift is just as important as technical drift: ownership changes, service boundaries evolve, and previously accurate routing assumptions become wrong. Programs should monitor drift using observable signals such as increasing disagreement between model ranking and human decisions, growing false positives in "top priority" recommendations, and recurring misrouting of work. Drift should trigger a defined response, including retraining, recalibration of weighting, and review of input sources, rather than informal loss of confidence. Treating drift as a normal maintenance requirement keeps the system usable and reduces the temptation to abandon governance when pressure is high. Table 15.3 summarizes what AI prioritization depends on and the governance controls required to keep decisions accountable.

Decision accountability must remain human, and the program should define approval boundaries that are tied to risk and operational impact. AI can recommend priority, but humans must approve changes that trigger emergency change windows, broad remediation campaigns, or risk acceptance decisions. The accountable owner should be explicit, and the program should preserve a record of the decision rationale, including what evidence

Table 15.3 AI-Assisted Prioritization Controls and Failure Modes.

Area	What It Depends on	Primary Risk	Required Control
Inputs	Asset identity business criticality exposure telemetry	Wrong ranking from missing context	Data quality checks and confidence handling
Bias	Historical closure patterns uneven monitoring	Blind spots reinforced	Bias checks and coverage gap review
Drift	Changing environment attacker behavior ownership	Rankings become stale	Monitor disagreement and recalibrate
Decision boundary	Clear approval boundaries	Unaccountable automation	Human approval for material decisions
Auditability	Logged inputs outputs rationale	Cannot defend decisions	Retain evidence and decision records
Leakage protection	Sensitive vulnerability and asset data	Data exposure risk	Access control and least privilege

the model used, what context humans added, and why any override occurred. This record is not bureaucratic overhead; it is what makes prioritization auditable and allows the organization to learn from mistakes without guesswork. When an incident occurs, leadership will ask why a particular vulnerability was not addressed sooner, and "the model ranked it low" is not an acceptable answer. Accountability requires that AI output is treated as input to a decision, not the decision itself.

Human-in-the-loop controls should be designed to prevent both overreliance and underuse. Overreliance happens when teams accept rankings without challenge, especially under time pressure, creating systemic errors that scale quickly. Underuse happens when teams distrust the model and revert to manual severity sorting, losing the benefits of consistency and speed. A balanced control model uses confidence thresholds, where low-confidence recommendations require explicit review and high-confidence recommendations still receive sampling and periodic validation. The program should also define escalation paths for contested priorities, with a clear mechanism to incorporate business context that the model cannot see, such as upcoming launches, contractual obligations, or operational fragility. These controls keep humans engaged in the right places without turning every decision into a meeting.

Auditability and data protection are non-negotiable because vulnerability prioritization involves sensitive infrastructure and exposure details. The system should log inputs, outputs, versioning, and human actions in a way that supports later reconstruction of what was known at the time of a decision. This includes retaining the model version, the data snapshot used for enrichment, and the identity of the approver for material decisions. Governance should also address leakage risk, because prioritization pipelines aggregate information attackers would value, such as asset criticality, vulnerability presence, and control gaps. Access controls, least privilege, and secure handling of training data are required to prevent the AI system itself from becoming an intelligence source for adversaries. When these controls are absent, the organization may inadvertently increase risk while trying to manage it.

A mature program evaluates AI-assisted prioritization by whether it improves real outcomes, not by whether the rankings look sophisticated. Useful measures include reduced time-to-decision for high-risk findings, improved consistency across teams, fewer emergency escalations, and better alignment between remediation effort and business criticality. The program should also track error modes explicitly, such as instances where AI recommendations were wrong, why they were wrong, and what data or logic would have prevented the mistake. Over time, this feedback loop improves both the model and the human process around it. The strongest signal of maturity is that AI recommendations are explainable, contestable, and traceable to accountable decisions. That combination preserves speed while maintaining the governance and responsibility that vulnerability management requires.

Building Confidence in Program Outcomes

Confidence in vulnerability management outcomes is earned through consistency, verifiability, and the ability to explain decisions in terms business leaders and technical teams both recognize as real. Many programs produce impressive-looking dashboards while failing to reduce exploitable conditions, largely because the underlying data is incomplete, the workflows are inconsistent, or "closure" is not tied to actual remediation. Confidence is also fragile; a single high-profile incident tied to an "already-managed" vulnerability can erase months of progress in the eyes of leadership. Building confidence therefore requires designing the program so that its outputs can withstand scrutiny under normal reporting, audits, and post-incident review. The objective is not perfect reporting, but reliable signals that the organization is measurably reducing exposure where it matters most.

The foundation of confidence is trustworthy scope and coverage, because outcomes cannot be credible if the program cannot clearly state what it includes and what it does not. Leadership will accept gaps when they are explicit, owned, and paired with compensating actions, but they will not accept gaps that are discovered accidentally after an event. This is why asset identity, ownership, and discovery hygiene are not administrative concerns; they are prerequisites for believable outcomes. A program that can demonstrate stable asset tracking, consistent inclusion of critical environments, and predictable assessment cadence establishes the baseline that makes all other metrics meaningful. When scope and coverage are uncertain, every number becomes debatable, and debates replace decisions. Confidence grows when the organization can show that what is reported reflects what is actually being managed.

Verification is the next essential element, because vulnerability management is uniquely vulnerable to false closure. Patches fail to apply, configuration changes are rolled back, assets are rebuilt from old images, and findings disappear due to scan gaps rather than remediation. A credible program verifies remediation through evidence tied to asset identity and current state, rather than relying solely on ticket status or self-attestation. That evidence might be a validated configuration state, a confirmed version change, or a successful authenticated reassessment that demonstrates the condition no longer exists. Verification must also include health checks on the assessment pipeline itself, so "no findings" does not quietly mean "no telemetry." Confidence increases when the program treats verification as part of the remediation workflow, not as a sporadic audit activity.

Consistency of decision-making is another major driver of confidence, because stakeholders can tolerate imperfect data if the process is stable and rational. Risk-based prioritization must be applied the same way across teams, with clear modifiers such as exposure, asset criticality, and compensating controls. When priorities swing based on who is asking, or when exceptions are granted without documented rationale, the program's outputs lose credibility even if the underlying remediation work is strong. Consistency also matters for timelines, because remediation expectations must align to environment tier and operational constraints in a way that is predictable. If deadlines are routinely missed without consequence or explanation, confidence erodes quickly. Trust grows when stakeholders can anticipate how the program will respond to a given risk scenario and see that response repeated reliably.

Metrics should be selected and interpreted in ways that reflect real risk reduction rather than activity volume. Counting findings closed can be misleading if the program is closing low-impact items while high-impact exposure remains. A more confidence-building approach emphasizes outcomes tied to critical assets and shortest attack paths, such as reductions in exploitable exposure on internet-facing systems or sustained improvements in high-value service tiers. Aging metrics are useful only when they are attached to meaningful prioritization and clear decision states, otherwise they become a measure of neglect rather than managed risk. The program also benefits from showing leading indicators, such as improved credentialed assessment coverage or reduced scan failure rates, because they demonstrate strengthening capability even before risk metrics fully reflect it. Confidence rises when metrics tell a coherent story that matches operational reality and can be defended with evidence.

Operational transparency is a practical requirement, because stakeholders lose confidence when they cannot see how decisions were made or where work is getting stuck. A program that exposes ownership, status, and rationale reduces friction and prevents escalation from becoming political. Transparency also helps engineering teams, because it clarifies why a particular remediation is urgent and what proof is required to close it. When backlogs exist, transparency allows leadership to understand whether the backlog represents managed, bounded risk or uncontrolled exposure. It also enables capacity conversations that are grounded in data rather than blame, such as whether intake volume is outpacing remediation throughput or whether specific teams face structural constraints. Confidence is built when the program treats reporting as a shared operational view, not as a security-only artifact.

AI can support confidence-building by improving consistency and surfacing anomalies, but only if its outputs are explainable and governed. AI-assisted enrichment can flag mismatches between ticket closure and observed asset state, identify likely scope gaps, or detect patterns of recurring vulnerabilities that indicate systemic process failures. The failure modes must be controlled because opaque model decisions can undermine trust when stakeholders cannot understand or challenge the output. Human-in-the-loop review is necessary for material decisions, and the program should retain an audit trail of what data informed the AI recommendation and how humans acted on it. If AI is used to generate narrative summaries or risk rationales, those summaries must be treated as drafts subject to review to prevent false confidence from polished language. Confidence increases when AI reduces error and variance while remaining subordinate to accountable human decisions.

Building confidence also requires demonstrating resilience during high-tempo events, because major disclosures and exploitation waves are the moments when leadership evaluates whether the program is real. During these periods, confidence comes from rapid scoping of affected assets, clear prioritization based on exposure and business impact, and the ability to validate mitigation and remediation quickly. Programs that scramble for basic answers such as "Are we affected?" reveal hidden weaknesses in asset management, telemetry, and workflow discipline. Programs that can respond with a defensible affected set, a prioritized action plan, and verified closure build credibility that persists long after the event passes. This responsiveness depends on the same fundamentals that drive day-to-day outcomes, which is why investment in the program's core controls pays off repeatedly.

Ultimately, confidence in program outcomes is the result of a program that can prove what it knows, explain what it is doing, and verify what it claims. That requires disciplined scope and coverage, evidence-based remediation verification, consistent risk decisions, and metrics that reflect material exposure reduction rather than activity. It also requires transparency and auditability, so stakeholders can see where risk is being managed and where tradeoffs are being made. When these elements are in place, vulnerability management becomes a dependable operational function rather than a periodic reporting exercise. Leadership confidence grows because outcomes are not just asserted; they are demonstrated in ways that stand up to operational and business scrutiny.

Conclusion

A vulnerability management program becomes durable when it consistently turns discovery into accountable remediation and verified risk reduction across the systems the business depends on. That durability comes from treating asset management, ownership, and scope as operational controls, setting realistic frequency and coverage expectations, and expanding intake beyond scanning, so the program reflects how exposure is actually found. When prioritization is anchored in business risk and backlog states represent explicit decisions rather than neglect, the organization can sustain progress even during high-tempo disclosure cycles. With AI used as governed decision support and with evidence-based verification and transparent metrics, leaders can trust that "closed" means reduced exposure and that the program's outcomes will hold up under scrutiny.

Recommendations

1) Define vulnerability management as a continuous control loop that drives verified remediation outcomes. Document how findings move from discovery to prioritization to assignment to closure verification, so work is repeatable and auditable. Reinforce that the goal is reduced exploitable exposure on real systems rather than perfect scores or one-time reports.
2) Establish dependable asset identity and ownership as prerequisites for any vulnerability workflow. Ensure each finding maps to a unique asset record with business context and an accountable owner who can make remediation decisions. Treat unknown or disputed ownership as a process defect to be corrected, not a reason to delay risk reduction.
3) Set scope across systems and environments in an operationally enforceable way and keep it current through discovery and reconciliation. Make inclusion and exclusion criteria explicit and ensure gaps are intentional, owned, and paired with compensating actions when needed. Prevent scope drift by detecting when assets appear in telemetry but do not receive assessment signals.
4) Define frequency and coverage expectations by asset class and environment tier, and validate them with pipeline health checks. Require that "covered" reflects meaningful assessment depth, not just a scheduled

scan, and ensure "no findings" cannot silently mean "no telemetry." Balance intake cadence with remediation capacity, so the queue remains actionable and deadlines retain meaning.

5) Build vulnerability intake beyond scanning into a single normalized queue with consistent prioritization and ownership. Translate advisories, testing findings, and configuration-driven exposure into trackable remediation outcomes without stripping away context needed for urgency and verification. Use a common set of evidence and validation expectations, so different intake sources do not create competing truths.
6) Prioritize remediation based on business risk by consistently combining asset criticality, exposure, exploitability evidence, and control posture. Avoid defaulting to severity labels alone when making urgency decisions, especially for externally reachable systems and high-value services. Re-evaluate priorities as conditions change, so backlog ordering reflects current reality rather than stale snapshots.
7) Manage compensating controls and risk decisions as explicit, time-bound states rather than informal justifications. Require verifiable evidence that compensating controls meaningfully reduce likelihood or blast radius for the specific exposure path. Assign accountable owners and review dates, so deferred items do not become permanent blind spots.
8) Maintain backlog control through disciplined status hygiene, periodic revalidation, and aggressive noise reduction. Close duplicates, obsolete assets, and non-applicable findings with evidence, so the backlog reflects real exposure rather than tooling artifacts. Use aging and ownership signals to detect when the program is losing intentionality and correct it early.
9) Use AI-assisted prioritization to accelerate enrichment and consistency while keeping human accountability boundaries clear. Feed models reliable asset and telemetry context, require human approval for material priority changes and risk acceptance, and log rationale for auditability. Monitor for bias and drift by tracking disagreements, misrouting, and recurring errors, and recalibrate when patterns emerge.
10) Build confidence in outcomes by tying reporting to verified remediation and transparent decision logic. Emphasize measures that reflect reduced exploitable exposure on critical assets and shortest attack paths rather than raw closure volume. Ensure the program can explain why items remain open, what mitigations exist, and how validation proves that "closed" means reduced risk.

16

Vulnerability Discovery and Exposure Reduction

Vulnerability discovery and exposure reduction depend on turning imperfect visibility into reliable, repeatable operations that consistently drive risk down. Effective programs balance breadth and depth across scanning approaches, manage coverage gaps explicitly, and maintain an accurate view of external exposure where attacker access is most immediate. They build trust through disciplined validation, noise reduction, and lifecycle-aware tracking so that findings remain actionable as assets change, scale, and retire. When discovery is coordinated with change management and strengthened by governed AI workflows for deduplication, clustering, and verification, the organization spends less time debating data quality and more time measurably shrinking the exposed surface area.

Scanning Approaches and Operational Fit

Scanning is not a single activity so much as a family of techniques that trade depth for safety, speed, and coverage. The operational fit starts with deciding what must be discovered: exposed services, missing patches, insecure configurations, or vulnerable application behaviors. Network-based scanning can sweep large address ranges quickly, but it often produces shallow results when it cannot safely authenticate or exercise complex code paths. In contrast, deeper approaches can validate more conditions but require stronger access, tighter scheduling, and clearer ownership to avoid disrupting production. The practical goal is consistent visibility that is reliable enough to drive work, not a one-time snapshot that creates noise.

The first operational decision is where scanning runs and what it is allowed to touch. External scanning focuses on what the internet can reach and is the closest proxy for attacker perspective, but it must be coordinated with perimeter controls and third-party providers to avoid misinterpreting defensive throttling as absence. Internal scanning targets east west exposure and lateral movement pathways, but it can overload fragile legacy systems if performed indiscriminately. Segment boundaries, sensitive enclaves, and shared services require different scanning cadences and different guardrails, because a flat schedule applied everywhere guarantees either missed exposure or self-inflicted outages. A mature program treats scan scope as an engineered control, with explicit allowlists, exclusion rules tied to business justification, and change control for any expansion.

Credentialed scanning is often the difference between "interesting" and "actionable," yet it is also where programs fail operationally. Authenticated checks can see installed packages, configuration state, and patch levels that are invisible from the network edge, reducing guesswork, and false positives. The tradeoff is privileged access, which introduces its own risk if credentials are mishandled, over provisioned, or embedded in brittle automation. Good practice keeps scan identities isolated, minimally privileged, rotated, and monitored like any other high-value account, with clear blast radius limits if a credential is compromised. When credentialed scanning cannot be deployed broadly, it should be used surgically on high-value tiers and representative system patterns rather than attempted everywhere and trusted nowhere (Table 16.1).

Table 16.1 Discovery Method Fit and Tradeoffs.

Discovery Method	Primary Strength	Primary Limitation	Operational Guardrail
External scanning	Attacker perspective on reachable services	Can miss internal state and be distorted by perimeter controls	Confirm scope ownership and validate from untrusted vantage
Internal scanning	Maps east west exposure and lateral pathways	Can overload fragile systems if indiscriminate	Use segment aware cadence and safe scan windows
Credentialed validation	High-fidelity patch and configuration confirmation	Requires privileged access and careful credential handling	Isolate scan identities rotate credentials monitor access
Agent-based telemetry	Deep host visibility for intermittently connected devices	Depends on enrollment and telemetry health	Treat coverage and log health as reliability targets
Passive discovery	Low disruption visibility using existing telemetry	Incomplete if logging is missing or inconsistent	Cross check with other sources to avoid blind spots

Agent-based and passive approaches can complement network scanning when uptime requirements and segmentation make probing impractical. Agents can provide high-fidelity data from endpoints and servers, especially for devices that are intermittently connected or shielded behind restrictive network controls. Passive discovery uses existing telemetry, such as traffic metadata and authentication logs, to infer assets and exposure without actively touching systems, which is valuable in fragile environments and during incident response. The operational challenge is data completeness: an approach that relies on endpoint coverage, log forwarding health, or accurate time synchronization will quietly degrade unless those dependencies are treated as first-class reliability targets. Scanning strategy is most resilient when it does not bet everything on one collection path and instead cross checks asset presence and vulnerability signals from multiple sources.

Scheduling is where scanning becomes real operations rather than aspirational security. Continuous scanning sounds ideal, but it can create persistent background load that competes with business transactions, backup jobs, and patching itself. Periodic scanning with well-defined windows reduces performance risk, yet it can miss short-lived exposure introduced by rapid change and ephemeral infrastructure. The right fit aligns scanning frequency with the rate of change and the tolerated time to detect, while respecting maintenance windows and system criticality. When scanning results are used as compliance evidence, the schedule must be defensible and repeatable, with documented exceptions and a mechanism to trigger out of band scans after meaningful changes.

Coverage depends less on scan engine capability and more on the accuracy of the target list. An incomplete inventory produces comforting reports that are operationally useless because unknown assets do not get scanned, remediated, or monitored. Scanning programs work best when they are tightly coupled to authoritative asset sources and service ownership, so targets are automatically added, retired, and tagged with environment and criticality. This is also where scoping discipline matters: a sprawling scan space without ownership leads to untriaged findings, while a curated scope tied to accountable teams leads to measurable exposure reduction. When ownership is unclear, the scanning team ends up acting as a help desk for remediation questions, which slows both discovery and fixing and erodes trust in the program.

AI-assisted triage can improve operational fit when it is treated as a decision support layer rather than an automatic decider. Models can help deduplicate recurring findings, cluster similar exposures across fleets, and propose prioritization based on asset criticality, exploit signals, and observed control gaps, but only if they are fed consistent context from inventories, identity systems, and logging. Human-in-the-loop controls matter because the most damaging failure mode is false confidence, where an overconfident model downranks a real risk or overstates remediation success. Drift is also a practical concern: as environments change, the model's assumptions about what "normal" looks like can decay, which can shift prioritization in subtle ways that are hard to detect without review. Any use of AI in the vulnerability workflow should be auditable, with traceable inputs, explainable recommendations, and explicit approval boundaries for actions that could change scope, suppress findings, or close tickets.

The final fit test is whether scanning output can drive exposure reduction without overwhelming operations. Findings need normalization so that the same underlying issue is described consistently across different scan methods, and they must map to clear remediation paths that match how infrastructure and application teams actually work. Noise control is not cosmetic; it is the difference between a program that steadily reduces risk and one that trains teams to ignore alerts, especially when repeated low-value findings crowd out high-impact exposure. Exceptions and compensating controls must be managed explicitly so that risk acceptance does not become invisible debt, and so that repeated waivers do not mask chronic hygiene problems. When scanning is engineered around reliable scope, safe access, defensible cadence, and accountable handoffs, it becomes a durable operational control that continuously narrows the organization's exposed surface area.

Coverage Gaps and Blind Spot Management

Coverage gaps are unavoidable in real environments, but unmanaged blind spots become the place where exposure quietly accumulates. A coverage gap is any condition where an asset, service, or configuration state is not being assessed with enough fidelity to support action, whether because it is not in scope, not discoverable, or not reachable. Blind spots are the operational consequence: areas where the organization believes it has visibility but does not, often because reporting is based on tool output rather than confirmed coverage. The difference matters because leaders make prioritization and resourcing decisions based on perceived exposure, and false certainty undermines both risk reduction and credibility. The goal is not perfection, but an explicit, continuously updated understanding of what is seen, what is partially seen, and what is not seen at all.

The most common root cause of blind spots is inventory drift, where the set of targets being scanned diverges from the assets actually running. Ephemeral infrastructure, autoscaling groups, short-lived containers, and unmanaged endpoints can appear and disappear faster than traditional scan schedules and asset databases can keep up. Shadow IT and "temporary" projects compound the problem by creating services that never enter authoritative systems of record. Operationally, this means coverage must be measured against an independent source of truth, not inferred from the presence of scan results. Good programs treat asset discovery and classification as part of vulnerability operations, with automated reconciliation that identifies "seen in telemetry but not in inventory" and "in inventory but never scanned" conditions. Table 16.2 translates common blind spot causes into measurable signals that reveal when visibility is degrading rather than improving.

Network and access constraints create a second major category of gaps that often masquerade as success. Segmentation, firewalls, and endpoint controls can prevent scans from reaching targets, producing clean reports that reflect blocked probing rather than secure systems. Similarly, credentialed scanning can silently degrade when scan identities lose access, authentication methods change, or privilege boundaries tighten, causing checks to fall back to shallow unauthenticated behavior. If the program does not explicitly track scan reachability and authentication success rates, the organization may believe it is executing deep coverage while actually collecting only surface signals. Effective blind spot management instruments the scanning pipeline itself, capturing metrics for target reachability, credential usage success, and check depth, so coverage degradation is visible immediately.

A third category of gaps comes from technology boundaries where certain exposures are not well represented by a single scanning method. Network scanning may not identify insecure configuration state behind authenticated interfaces, while agent-based telemetry may not detect externally exposed services created by misconfigured routing or cloud security groups. Application-level vulnerabilities may require dynamic testing or code review signals that infrastructure-oriented scanning will never see, and data stores may have access control issues that only

Table 16.2 Blind Spot Categories and Coverage Signals.

Blind Spot Category	Typical Root Cause	Observed Symptom	Control Signal to Track
Inventory drift	Targets diverge from running assets	Clean reports despite unknown assets	Seen in telemetry but not in inventory
Reachability loss	Segmentation or firewall constraints	Targets appear scanned but were blocked	Target reachable rate by segment
Authentication degradation	Credentials fail or access reduced	Checks become shallow or inconsistent	Authenticated scan success rate
Method boundary	One technique cannot see full state	Missing configuration or application-level exposure	Coverage by perspective network host identity service
Ownership gaps	No accountable team or unclear routing	Findings stagnate exclusions grow	Unowned assets and unowned findings count
Exception sprawl	Indefinite suppressions and deferrals	Known exposure reappears each cycle	Exception age and renewal status

show up through identity and authorization analysis. Operationally, these boundaries demand layered coverage, where each method is assigned a clear role and the organization avoids treating any one output as comprehensive. Blind spots shrink when the program cross checks evidence across network perspective, host perspective, identity perspective, and service exposure perspective, even if each individual view is imperfect.

Ownership ambiguity is an underappreciated source of blind spots because it prevents remediation feedback loops from stabilizing. Assets without accountable owners often fall outside patch cycles, fall behind on enrollment into endpoint management, or remain excluded from scanning due to operational concerns that no one is empowered to resolve. Over time, exclusion lists and "temporary" exceptions grow, and the gap becomes normalized as business as usual. A mature program assigns ownership through authoritative metadata and escalation paths, and it treats unowned systems as an exposure condition in itself. When ownership cannot be resolved quickly, compensating controls and containment decisions must be made explicitly rather than implicitly by neglect.

Blind spot management also requires disciplined exception handling, because exceptions are the formal mechanism by which gaps become persistent. Exceptions should be time bound, justified in business terms, and paired with alternative visibility or controls so that risk does not become invisible. A common failure mode is allowing indefinite scan suppression for fragile systems without establishing monitoring that would detect exploitation or configuration drift. Another is granting long-term remediation deferrals without tracking whether the underlying asset class is being modernized or retired. When exceptions are treated as operational debt with renewal requirements, the organization can distinguish between a purposeful risk decision and a slow drift into unmanaged exposure.

AI can help identify coverage anomalies, but it must be governed carefully because blind spots are exactly where models can mislead. Models can correlate disparate telemetry sources to infer missing assets, flag unusual exposure patterns, and highlight scan results that do not match expected baselines for a given environment, which can accelerate discovery of "unknown unknowns." Those outcomes depend on clean inputs such as accurate inventory tags, stable log pipelines, and consistent time alignment; otherwise, the model will confidently propose relationships that are artifacts of missing data. Human-in-the-loop review is critical because the model's most dangerous failure mode is convincing analysts that coverage is better than it is, especially when the model is trained on biased historical data that underrepresents neglected parts of the environment. Auditability matters as well: when AI influences what gets scanned next or what gets labeled "covered," the organization must be able to reconstruct why a decision was made and which data sources supported it.

Operationally, the most effective way to manage blind spots is to treat coverage as a measurable control with explicit reporting and escalation, not as a byproduct of running tools. Coverage reporting should separate "in scope," "reachable," "authenticated," and "high-confidence" categories, so stakeholders can see where depth is missing, and it should include trends that show whether gaps are shrinking or expanding. High-risk blind spots should trigger action just like high severity vulnerabilities, because an unassessed critical system can be more dangerous than a known medium finding. When blind spots are framed as a manageable backlog with owners, deadlines, and compensating controls, they stop being an embarrassment and start being an operational reality that can be reduced. The outcome is a vulnerability program whose claims are defensible, whose gaps are visible by design, and whose exposure reduction effort is guided by what is truly known rather than what is merely reported.

Identifying External Exposure and High-Risk Services

External exposure is where defensive assumptions are most likely to be tested, because anything reachable from untrusted networks becomes part of the organization's effective attack surface. The operational objective is to maintain an accurate, current view of what the internet can access, which systems and services are answering, and which of those exposures represent the highest risk to the business. This is not limited to known production applications; it includes forgotten test endpoints, legacy services, third-party hosted assets, and misrouted infrastructure that unintentionally becomes public. External exposure management works when it is treated as continuous discovery and verification, not as a periodic compliance exercise. The most practical measure of success is that the organization can quickly answer what is exposed, why it is exposed, who owns it, and what must happen to reduce that exposure.

Discovery begins with defining the external scope in a way that reflects reality rather than organizational charts. Public IP ranges, registered domains, subdomains, cloud resources, and third-party services that present branded or integrated interfaces all belong in the external inventory. The operational challenge is that many externally exposed assets are created through decentralized change, such as cloud deployments, vendor onboarding, and marketing initiatives, and they often bypass traditional infrastructure registration. Effective programs reconcile multiple sources, including DNS records, certificate transparency artifacts, public routing data, and internal configuration systems, to build a target set that is resilient to drift. External scanning and validation should be executed from vantage points that approximate attacker access, because internally run checks can be distorted by trusted network paths and allowlisted controls.

Once exposure is identified, the next step is to classify services by risk in a way that leads to action. High-risk services are those that provide remote entry, administrative control, sensitive data access, or a strong pivot point into internal networks. Common examples include remote management interfaces, authentication portals, APIs that handle privileged operations, and services that accept untrusted input at scale. Risk also increases when a service is internet-facing on a nonstandard port, is hosted on unmanaged infrastructure, or lacks clear ownership, because those conditions correlate with weaker patch discipline and weaker monitoring. Operational classification should be consistent across environments, so the same type of exposure receives similar treatment whether it appears in a data center, a cloud VPC, or a vendor-managed platform.

Identity and access characteristics are central to determining whether an external service is merely visible or truly dangerous. An externally reachable login page protected by strong IAM and MFA can still be a high-value target, but its risk profile is different from an exposed administrative console protected by weak credentials or legacy authentication. Services that rely on shared accounts, long-lived credentials, or local authentication stores tend to amplify blast radius because compromise is harder to detect and harder to contain. External exposures should be evaluated for authentication strength, session management, and access control boundaries, including whether privileged functions are segregated from general user access. Operationally, teams should also verify that access logging is complete and centrally collected, because visibility into authentication attempts and administrative actions is a prerequisite for both detection and incident response.

Exposure identification must account for the difference between what a service claims to be and what it actually is. Banner grabbing and superficial fingerprinting can be misleading due to proxies, load balancers, and security appliances that normalize responses, and it can produce false confidence when defenders assume a service is a managed platform rather than a bespoke deployment. Validation is stronger when it combines network observations with configuration and ownership metadata, such as asset tags, cloud resource identifiers, and deployment pipelines. Where credentialed validation is appropriate, it can confirm patch levels and configuration state more reliably, but it must be applied carefully to avoid creating privileged scanning paths into internet-facing systems. The operational standard should be that externally exposed critical services have a traceable path back to a controlled build process, documented hardening, and an accountable owner.

Monitoring and detection considerations are part of exposure identification because the highest risk services require the strongest telemetry. Internet-facing assets should generate high-quality logs for authentication attempts, authorization failures, administrative changes, and anomalous request patterns, and those logs must reach centralized monitoring without filtering that removes useful context. Where network telemetry is available, it should be aligned with service logs, so defenders can correlate inbound activity with application behavior and back-end calls. This is also where behavior-based analytics can add value: models can flag unusual patterns such as credential stuffing, low-and-slow probing, or rare administrative actions, especially when they learn normal baselines for each service. AI-assisted detection must be bounded by human review for high-impact actions, because false confidence and alert fatigue are common failure modes when models overfit to historical patterns or miss novel attacker tradecraft.

Operationally, exposure reduction depends on how quickly high-risk services move from identification to remediation, and that handoff must be engineered. Findings should be framed in terms of concrete actions such as closing unnecessary ports, enforcing strong authentication, restricting management interfaces to trusted networks, and placing services behind appropriate gateways or access brokers. Remediation workflows should include validation steps that confirm the exposure is actually reduced from an external perspective, not merely reconfigured internally. A common pitfall is closing a firewall rule while leaving a cloud security group open, or restricting one hostname while leaving alternate DNS entries pointing to the same service. External verification closes that loop and prevents "fixed on paper" outcomes.

High-risk services also require governance expectations that align with business reality. Ownership must be explicit, and externally exposed services should have defined service tiers that drive scanning frequency, monitoring depth, and patch urgency. Change management for these services should prioritize visibility, ensuring that new exposures are registered and reviewed as part of deployment workflows, rather than discovered weeks later through scanning. AI can help by correlating new certificates, DNS changes, and routing updates to alert on likely new exposures, but those alerts must be integrated into a human-approved process that assigns ownership and initiates validation. When external exposure management is run as a continuous operational discipline, high-risk services become fewer, better understood, and better defended, and the organization's internet-facing surface area becomes an asset that is actively controlled rather than a liability that is periodically rediscovered.

Validating Findings and Reducing Noise

Vulnerability output only becomes operationally useful when it is reliable enough to drive decisions at scale. Validation is the process of confirming that a reported condition is real, relevant to the target asset, and meaningful in the organization's context, while noise reduction is the discipline of preventing low-confidence or low-value signals from consuming remediation capacity. In practice, these are inseparable: every false positive erodes trust, and every unvalidated true positive competes with work that might have reduced exposure faster. The objective is not to suppress uncomfortable findings or make dashboards look clean, but to ensure that what reaches engineering teams is defensible, specific, and actionable. When validation is treated as a first-class operational step, the vulnerability program becomes a credible input to prioritization rather than a recurring source of friction.

Validation starts with understanding how a finding was derived and what evidence supports it. Many detections are inference-based, such as version fingerprinting from banners, heuristics that assume default configurations, or behavioral checks that infer vulnerability from a response pattern. Those approaches are valuable for scale, but they are also sensitive to environmental factors like reverse proxies, content delivery networks, application firewalls, and authentication flows that can change what the scanner observes. Good practice requires capturing and retaining enough proof to explain the finding, such as request/response details, check identifiers, and the conditions under which the evidence was collected. Without that evidence, remediation teams cannot reproduce the issue, and the validator cannot distinguish between a real exposure and a scanner artifact.

False positives are often a symptom of incomplete context rather than poor tooling, and reducing them requires tightening the contextual inputs. Asset identity must be correct, because findings attached to the wrong hostname, IP, or environment tag create immediate confusion and wasted cycles. Authentication depth must be understood, because a scan that failed to authenticate may report missing patches that it cannot actually observe, or it may miss compensating controls that change the effective risk. Configuration baselines matter as well: an organization that standardizes hardening can safely treat certain detections as expected non-issues, but only if the baseline is verified and continuously enforced. Noise reduction is strongest when it is grounded in controlled, measurable conditions rather than informal "we always do it this way" assumptions.

Validation also includes establishing relevance, which is where operational fit meets risk reduction. A vulnerability may be technically present but not exploitable due to network controls, strong authentication, or constrained reachability, yet those same compensating controls can fail or be bypassed, so the decision to deprioritize must be made carefully. Conversely, a seemingly low-severity issue may be high impact on a crown-jewel system, on an externally exposed service, or in a pathway that enables privilege escalation. Validation should therefore confirm not only the technical condition but also the exposure context: where the asset sits, what it can reach, who can reach it, and what business function it supports. When those factors are consistently captured, the program can route findings with the right urgency without relying on subjective escalation.

A practical validation workflow hinges on repeatability and tight handoffs, because ad hoc investigation does not scale. Analysts should be able to reproduce checks using controlled methods, whether that is re-running a scan with known parameters, performing a targeted authenticated check, or verifying configuration state through authoritative management systems. Reproduction must be safe, especially for fragile systems and production services, and that requires pre-defined procedures and guardrails, so validation does not become another source of outages. Handoffs to remediation teams should include the minimal reproducible steps and the evidence trail, so engineers spend time fixing rather than disputing. Over time, the organization benefits from codifying common validation outcomes into rules, such as known benign signatures, acceptable compensating controls, and environment-specific exceptions that are time-bound and reviewed.

Noise often originates from duplicated or overlapping findings that describe the same root cause in different ways. Multiple scanners may report the same issue with different identifiers, or one underlying configuration may generate a cascade of downstream detections across dependent services. If the program forwards these as separate tickets, teams will either waste effort on redundant work or ignore the entire feed. Normalization and deduplication are therefore operational necessities, mapping findings to a consistent representation of "what is wrong" and "what fixes it" regardless of how it was detected. This also supports better trending and accountability, because it prevents inflated counts from masking whether exposure is truly being reduced. When the same root cause is tracked consistently, remediation becomes a targeted effort rather than a whack-a-mole exercise.

AI can assist validation and noise reduction by accelerating evidence review and prioritization, but it must operate within clear approval boundaries. Models can summarize scanner evidence, cluster similar findings across assets, and propose likely false positives based on historical outcomes and environmental signals such as authentication failures or proxy intermediaries. Those use cases depend on high-quality telemetry, including scan depth metrics, asset metadata, and remediation closure data, and they fail when inputs are incomplete or inconsistent. The most dangerous failure mode is false confidence, where a model suppresses a true positive or overstates a fix because it learned an overly optimistic pattern from biased historical closures. Human-in-the-loop controls should require explicit review for any automated suppression, risk downgrade, or closure recommendation, and governance expectations should include audit logs that show the model inputs, the recommendation, and the human decision that accepted or rejected it.

Reducing noise is ultimately a governance and engineering problem, not just an analyst problem, because recurring false positives and low-value detections often point to unstable scanning conditions. If scan authentication routinely fails, the remedy is not manual triage but fixing credential management, access paths, or enrollment coverage. If findings are dominated by systems that cannot be patched, the remedy is to strengthen exception management, modernize the platform, or apply compensating controls that are explicitly verified. If engineering teams repeatedly dispute the same classes of findings, the remedy is to calibrate checks, capture better evidence, and improve the translation from detection to fix. When validation outcomes feed back into scanner configuration, asset metadata quality, and workflow design, noise declines and trust grows.

A mature program treats validation as a measurable control that protects remediation capacity and sustains credibility with stakeholders. Key signals include the proportion of findings that are reproducible, the rate of authenticated scan success, the time spent disputing versus fixing, and the backlog share tied to recurring root causes. Findings that cannot be validated promptly should be tagged as low confidence until verified, rather than pushed into remediation queues where they will churn. At the same time, the program must avoid suppressing issues simply because they are hard to validate; high-risk exposure should trigger deeper investigation even when initial evidence is imperfect. When validation discipline and noise reduction are built into the operating rhythm, vulnerability data becomes an effective tool for exposure reduction rather than a constant argument about what is real.

Managing False Positives and Repeated Findings

False positives and repeated findings are not just irritations; they are operational failure modes that drain remediation capacity and degrade confidence in the entire exposure reduction program. A false positive is a reported condition that is not actually present or not applicable to the asset in question, while a repeated finding is a condition that continues to reappear across scan cycles because it was never fixed, never verified as fixed, or keeps being reintroduced through change. Both create the same downstream effect: teams stop trusting the feed, triage becomes argumentative, and genuinely dangerous exposure gets buried. The objective is to build a workflow where inaccurate signals are rapidly contained, recurring root causes are identified, and the system learns over time, so the same disputes do not repeat. This requires discipline in evidence, ownership, and feedback loops, not simply better scanners.

False positives often originate from ambiguous detection methods, especially when scanners infer versions or vulnerability state from network behavior rather than confirmed configuration. Reverse proxies, load balancers, application firewalls, and service meshes can change responses in ways that confuse fingerprinting and make a vulnerable version appear present when it is not. Authentication failures also produce misleading results, because checks may fall back to superficial behavior that cannot validate patch levels or configuration state, yet still emit findings. Environmental conditions such as rate limiting, transient errors, and segmentation-induced partial reachability can create inconsistent observations that look like vulnerability evidence. Managing this begins with collecting enough proof to explain why the scanner believed the condition was true and to allow a validator to reproduce the result safely.

Operationally, the most effective false-positive process is one that separates "cannot validate yet" from "validated false." When evidence is insufficient, the finding should be treated as low confidence and queued for targeted validation rather than sent into remediation workstreams where it will churn. Validation should confirm asset identity, scan depth, and the exact conditions under which the check fired, including whether the scanner reached the correct service and whether it authenticated successfully. When a finding is confirmed false, the program should capture the reason in a structured way, such as "proxy masking," "nonstandard banner," "service not present," or "check not applicable," because free-text explanations do not scale. Over time, those reasons become the input for tuning, exception logic, and coverage improvements that prevent recurrence.

Repeated findings require a different lens because they are rarely about detection accuracy and more often about operational friction. Some issues repeat because they are difficult to remediate without downtime, coordination, or architectural change, so teams defer them until they become background noise. Others repeat because fixes are applied inconsistently across fleets, or because configuration drift reintroduces the same exposure after patching or deployment. Findings can also repeat due to mismatched definitions of "fixed," where an engineer believes remediation is complete but the validation mechanism still detects the condition because the root cause was not addressed. Repetition should therefore be treated as an indicator of systemic weakness in patch management, configuration management, or change control, not simply as an individual ticketing problem.

A critical step in managing repetition is to normalize findings to root causes rather than treating each scan output as a separate event. Multiple scanner signatures may describe the same underlying misconfiguration, and the same vulnerability can present across many assets because a common image, template, or baseline is wrong. If the program tracks these as separate, unrelated tickets, it guarantees a backlog that grows faster than remediation throughput. Normalization groups findings by "what fixes it," enabling teams to remediate at the source, such as updating a gold image, correcting a deployment pipeline, or changing a shared configuration profile. This approach also supports meaningful metrics, because progress is measured by the elimination of root causes and affected populations rather than by the volume of duplicated alerts.

Exception handling is where repeated findings become institutionalized, so it must be managed with rigor. When a team cannot remediate promptly, the program needs a documented exception with a time-bound review and clear compensating controls, such as restricted network access, tightened authentication, or enhanced monitoring. The most common failure mode is allowing indefinite exceptions without improving defensive posture, which converts a known weakness into an accepted blind spot. Repeated findings tied to an exception should be tracked explicitly, so leadership can see where risk is being carried and whether that risk is shrinking through modernization or simply being renewed. In practice, strong exception discipline reduces noise because it prevents the same finding from reappearing as a "new" issue every cycle while ensuring the exposure remains visible and accountable.

The verification loop is equally important, because repeated findings often reflect verification weakness rather than remediation failure. Fixes must be validated from the same perspective that produced the finding, especially for external exposure where internal configuration changes may not reduce internet reachability. Timing matters as well: validation too soon can produce false repeats because changes have not propagated, while validation too late delays closure and keeps teams stuck in uncertainty. For high-risk services, validation should include both technical confirmation and an operational check that monitoring and logging remain intact after the change. When closure requires proof, not just attestation, repeated findings decline because "fixed" means the detection no longer fires under controlled conditions.

AI can improve both false-positive handling and repeated-finding reduction when it is used to scale pattern recognition and to tighten feedback loops. Models can cluster disputes that share the same underlying cause, suggest likely false positives based on environmental signals like proxy presence or authentication failure, and highlight recurring findings that align with known misconfigurations in specific asset classes. These benefits depend on clean labels from prior outcomes, consistent metadata, and reliable scan depth telemetry; otherwise, the model will learn the wrong lessons and automate the wrong suppressions. Human-in-the-loop controls must constrain automation, particularly around suppression and closure, because a model that incorrectly marks a true positive as noise can remove the only signal of real exposure. Auditability is non-negotiable: any AI-driven recommendation to suppress, downgrade, or merge findings should be traceable to inputs and subject to periodic review.

The long-term solution to both false positives and repeated findings is to turn them into engineering backlog for the vulnerability program itself. False-positive drivers become tasks to improve scanner configuration, authentication reliability, asset attribution, and evidence capture. Repeated findings become tasks to improve patch orchestration, configuration baselines, deployment pipelines, and ownership clarity. When the program measures and reports these as operational health indicators, it becomes easier to justify investment in the upstream capabilities that reduce noise and accelerate exposure reduction. Over time, the organization ends up with a vulnerability workflow where accuracy is continuously improved, recurrence is systematically eliminated, and teams can focus their effort on fixes that measurably reduce risk rather than on arguing with the data.

Coordinating Discovery with Change Management

Vulnerability discovery that is disconnected from change management will always be reactive, because it learns about new exposure after it has already reached production. Coordinating discovery with change management means treating exposure as a predictable outcome of deployments, infrastructure updates, network changes, and configuration modifications, and ensuring that discovery signals are triggered by those events rather than waiting for the next scan cycle. The operational objective is to reduce the time between "change introduced risk" and "defenders know about it," while also reducing the number of disruptive scans and emergency escalations. This coordination is not about slowing delivery; it is about making security visibility a natural byproduct of delivery. When done well, discovery becomes part of the operational fabric, aligned to how systems are built and modified.

The first step is to recognize that change management is broader than a ticketing workflow and includes any mechanism that creates or modifies runtime behavior. Infrastructure-as-code, CI/CD pipelines, cloud-control plane updates, firewall rule changes, DNS modifications, and certificate issuance events all represent changes that can create new external exposure or shift internal reachability. Traditional scheduled scanning cannot keep up with environments where production state changes hourly, and it cannot distinguish between benign churn and meaningful exposure. Coordinating discovery requires event-aware triggers, where meaningful changes initiate targeted verification, such as scanning a new subnet, validating a new domain, or performing authenticated checks on a newly promoted build. This approach reduces wasted effort and focuses validation where risk is most likely to have changed.

Change records must carry enough context to make discovery actions precise; otherwise, the coordination becomes noisy and teams will learn to bypass it. The minimal context includes the assets affected, the environment, the owner, the nature of the change, and the expected exposure outcome, such as whether a service is intended to be internet-facing or restricted. Without that detail, discovery teams are forced to infer scope, which increases the likelihood of scanning the wrong targets, missing the right ones, or generating findings that cannot be routed. Operationally, this often means improving the metadata discipline of deployments and infrastructure provisioning, so that systems are consistently tagged and mapped to services and owners at creation time. When change context is accurate, discovery can be selective and fast, and escalation becomes the exception rather than the default.

A coordinated model also requires clear agreements on when discovery runs relative to change windows. For high-risk services and externally exposed systems, pre-change validation establishes a baseline, so the program can distinguish newly introduced exposure from pre-existing conditions. Post-change validation confirms that intended controls are still in place and that no unexpected ports, routes, or administrative interfaces were exposed. This is particularly important when teams make changes under pressure, because emergency fixes are a common source of misconfiguration drift and accidental exposure. Scheduling discovery around changes must respect production stability, but it should not be optional for high-impact changes where external reachability or privileged access is affected.

Discovery must also coordinate with rollback and remediation realities, because change management is not just approval but operational recovery when things go wrong. Findings generated immediately after a change can be used to catch misconfigurations before they become incidents, but only if there is a clear path to act, such as halting a deployment, reverting a firewall rule, or disabling a newly exposed service. If findings are delivered too late or without authority to intervene, the coordination becomes theater. Effective programs establish thresholds for escalation, where certain exposure patterns, such as a new management port on a public IP or a reduction in authentication strength, trigger immediate response. Those thresholds must be tuned to avoid constant false alarms, but they should be strict where blast radius is high.

AI can materially improve coordination by correlating change signals with discovery results and highlighting anomalies that would otherwise be missed. Models can compare expected exposure states from change artifacts to observed network behavior, flagging cases where a new deployment deviates from the baseline, such as unexpected open ports or unusual external endpoints. These use cases depend on disciplined telemetry: change logs must be reliable, asset identifiers must be consistent, and discovery output must be normalized, so comparisons are meaningful. Human-in-the-loop controls are critical because the recommended actions may impact availability, and a model that is overly confident can trigger unnecessary rollbacks or block legitimate releases. Governance expectations should require that AI-driven alerts and recommendations are traceable to specific change events and observable evidence, with audit logs that capture both the model output and the human decision.

Coordination also changes how scanning itself is configured, because change-driven discovery benefits from targeted depth rather than broad periodic sweeps. When a new service is deployed, it is more effective to perform focused validation of its exposure and configuration than to wait for a monthly enterprise scan that will produce a flood of unrelated findings. Targeted scanning can be credentialed, environment-aware, and bounded to the specific assets involved in the change, which reduces load and improves signal quality. This approach also supports faster closure, because the owning team is already in an active change window and can remediate immediately while context is fresh. Over time, this creates a pattern where discovery is part of delivery hygiene rather than an external audit function.

A coordinated program must explicitly manage the failure modes that arise when change management is inconsistent or bypassed. Shadow changes, emergency modifications without records, and manual console edits in cloud environments are common sources of exposure because they evade both governance and automated validation. Discovery teams should treat "changes without trace" as an operational risk signal, using telemetry to detect configuration drift, unexpected DNS updates, or new externally reachable services that have no corresponding change artifacts. This is also where ownership discipline matters: if resources are untagged or unmanaged, the organization cannot reliably route findings or enforce validation gates. Coordinating discovery with change management therefore includes strengthening the mechanisms that make changes observable and attributable.

The outcome of tight coordination is a vulnerability discovery process that is faster, more precise, and more trusted. New exposure is detected close to the moment it is introduced, validated with relevant context, and routed to the team already positioned to act. Scan noise declines because effort shifts from indiscriminate enterprise sweeps to event-driven verification tied to meaningful change. Leadership gains a more accurate view of exposure dynamics because discovery signals align with operational reality rather than with arbitrary schedules. Most importantly, defenders move from discovering risk after the fact to shaping risk during the moment when change is still malleable and the cost of correction is lowest.

Tracking Vulnerabilities Across Asset Lifecycles

Vulnerability management fails when it treats assets as static, because modern environments change identity, location, and ownership faster than scan cycles can keep up. Tracking vulnerabilities across an asset lifecycle means maintaining continuity of exposure understanding as systems are built, deployed, modified, scaled, and retired.

The operational objective is to ensure that a vulnerability finding remains correctly attached to the underlying thing that must be fixed, even as that thing changes its hostname, IP address, instance identifier, or deployment representation. Without lifecycle-aware tracking, programs inflate metrics, lose accountability, and either repeatedly rediscover the same issues or mistakenly believe they are resolved. The discipline is less about more scanning and more about maintaining stable identity and state over time.

Lifecycle tracking begins with a consistent asset identity model that survives infrastructure churn. IP addresses and hostnames are convenient scanning targets, but they are poor primary identifiers because they change frequently and can be reassigned. More durable identifiers come from authoritative management sources, such as device enrollment records, cloud resource identifiers, service registry entries, and configuration management databases, which can link a runtime target to an owner and a purpose. The operational requirement is to map scan observations to those durable identifiers, so that a finding follows the asset even if its network coordinates change. Where multiple identifiers exist, the program should define precedence and reconciliation logic to prevent the same asset from appearing as multiple entities across different data sources.

The asset lifecycle also changes the meaning of vulnerability data, because the acceptable risk posture of a system depends on where it sits in its lifecycle stage. Newly provisioned assets should meet baseline hardening and patch expectations before they are considered production-ready, and vulnerability findings at this stage are most efficiently addressed through image or template corrections. In steady-state operation, findings often represent drift or patch lag and require coordination with maintenance windows and deployment schedules. In end-of-life phases, findings may reflect known technical debt, but that debt still matters if the system remains reachable or holds sensitive data, and it must be bounded through compensating controls and retirement timelines. Lifecycle-aware tracking makes these distinctions explicit so that remediation effort aligns to the most cost-effective lever at each stage.

Ephemeral compute is a common point of failure because it can produce a flood of findings that are real but operationally misrouted. Containers, short-lived instances, and serverless components may exist for minutes, which means traditional "scan and ticket" workflows create work items for assets that no longer exist. The correct unit of accountability in these environments is often the image, build artifact, or deployment pipeline, not the transient runtime. Findings should therefore be correlated back to the source that produced the runtime, such as a base image, dependency manifest, or infrastructure template, so remediation can be applied once and propagated automatically. When lifecycle tracking is aligned to how ephemeral systems are produced, exposure reduction accelerates and repeated rediscovery declines.

Tracking also requires managing ownership transitions, which occur during reorganizations, outsourcing, platform migrations, and application modernization. Vulnerabilities can persist through these transitions because the handoff focuses on functionality and uptime while security debt becomes background. A mature program treats ownership as a tracked attribute and requires that findings move with ownership, with explicit acceptance or remediation commitments rather than silent inheritance. Ownership gaps are particularly dangerous for externally exposed services, where missing accountability often correlates with missing patching, missing monitoring, and unreviewed access paths. Lifecycle tracking should therefore surface "unowned vulnerability backlog" as a risk condition that triggers escalation and resolution.

The lifecycle is also shaped by change events that can create or eliminate vulnerabilities without obvious system replacements. Patching can remove issues, but configuration changes can reintroduce them, and dependency updates can create new exposure even when the OS is fully patched. Tracking must therefore incorporate state change evidence, such as patch deployment records, configuration management drift signals, and build provenance, so that vulnerability status is not inferred solely from the absence or presence of a scan signature. This is especially important when scanners rely on inference-based checks that can fluctuate due to transient reachability or authentication failures. Lifecycle-aware programs use multiple confirmation signals for closure, ensuring that a vulnerability is considered resolved when the underlying condition is demonstrably removed and the validation path remains intact.

AI can strengthen lifecycle tracking by helping correlate assets and findings across noisy, heterogeneous data sources, but it must be constrained to avoid compounding identity errors. Models can assist by matching scan targets to service records, grouping related assets into fleets, and detecting anomalies such as a sudden shift in vulnerability patterns that suggests a new image or template was introduced. These capabilities depend on high-quality labels and consistent metadata; otherwise, the model will confidently merge unrelated assets or split one asset into many, damaging accountability. Human-in-the-loop controls should require review for any automated identity merges, ownership changes, or suppression decisions tied to lifecycle stage. Auditability expectations are critical because lifecycle decisions influence risk reporting, and stakeholders must be able to trace how an asset was identified, how findings were associated, and why a vulnerability was marked resolved or accepted.

Retirement is the lifecycle stage where programs most often lose discipline, even though it is one of the most effective exposure reduction levers. When assets are decommissioned, vulnerability tracking should confirm that the service is no longer reachable, that DNS and routing entries are removed, and that residual access paths such as management interfaces and stale credentials are eliminated. Data handling must be verified as well, because retiring compute without proper data disposition can leave sensitive data exposed in backups, snapshots, or orphaned storage. Vulnerability records should be closed based on evidence of retirement, not merely because scanning no longer sees the target, since disappearance can also indicate a discovery gap. When retirement is treated as an auditable state change, it becomes a reliable way to reduce exposure while preventing "ghost assets" from lingering as unmonitored liabilities.

The operational outcome of lifecycle-aware tracking is a vulnerability program that reflects reality and drives durable fixes. Findings follow durable identities, map to accountable owners, and align remediation to the right control point, whether that is a patch, a configuration baseline, a build pipeline, or an asset retirement plan. Repeated findings decline because root causes are corrected where assets are produced, not chased across transient instances. Reporting becomes credible because counts represent unique, meaningful exposure rather than artifacts of churn and misattribution. Most importantly, exposure reduction becomes sustained over time because the program remains attached to how assets live, change, and eventually exit the environment.

AI to Reduce Noise: Deduplication, Clustering, and Verification Workflows

Noise reduction is fundamentally a scaling problem: as environments grow and change faster, the volume of vulnerability signals rises faster than human triage capacity. AI can help reduce noise by organizing findings into fewer, higher-confidence work items, but only when it is embedded in disciplined workflows that preserve evidence, accountability, and human approval boundaries. The operational objective is not to "let the model decide" what matters, but to use machine assistance to deduplicate redundant signals, cluster related issues into root-cause groupings, and accelerate verification, so teams spend more time fixing real exposure. When AI is applied without strong guardrails, it can create a more dangerous kind of noise: confident but wrong conclusions that suppress true risk or prematurely close findings. A practical implementation therefore starts with the assumption that AI augments triage and verification rather than replacing them.

Deduplication is the most immediate and measurable use case because duplication is a structural feature of vulnerability programs. The same underlying issue can be reported by different scanners, across different network paths, and over multiple scan cycles, often with slightly different identifiers or wording. AI can normalize these variations by learning equivalence patterns across signatures, evidence artifacts, and affected component metadata, reducing multiple alerts to a single canonical issue record. This reduces ticket volume and prevents remediation teams from receiving redundant work requests that describe the same fix in different language. The critical dependency is consistent inputs, including stable asset identifiers, normalized software and configuration descriptors, and retained evidence, because the model can only reliably match what it can compare. Human review should be required for deduplication actions that merge findings across different assets or security domains, because a bad merge can hide a real exposure behind an unrelated closure.

Clustering goes beyond deduplication by grouping findings into higher-level patterns that point to common root causes and fleet-wide remediation opportunities. Instead of handling hundreds of similar findings one by one, clustering can reveal that a single baseline image is missing a patch, a shared configuration template is insecure, or a common dependency version is present across multiple services. This is where AI provides operational leverage, because fixing the source can remove exposure across a population faster than chasing individual endpoints. Effective clustering must respect meaningful boundaries, such as environment tiers, ownership, and exposure context, because a cluster that spans unrelated systems becomes less actionable and more contentious. The output should be cluster-level work items that describe the shared root cause, the affected asset set, and the recommended control point for remediation, with enough evidence to validate that the grouping is correct.

Verification workflows are where AI can save the most analyst time, but they also carry the highest risk if automated without controls. Many findings require time-consuming steps such as reproducing scanner checks, reviewing request/response evidence, confirming authentication depth, or validating patch and configuration state through authoritative systems. AI can accelerate this by summarizing evidence, extracting key parameters, and proposing a verification path based on historical outcomes and asset type, effectively turning scattered scan artifacts into a coherent investigative narrative. It can also triage findings into confidence tiers, separating "high confidence and actionable" from "needs validation" so that engineers are not flooded with low-confidence tickets. The workflow must enforce human approval for any decision that suppresses a finding, changes severity, or closes an issue, because those are governance actions with risk implications. Figure 16.1 shows how AI can reduce vulnerability noise through deduplication, clustering, and verification assistance while keeping suppression and closure decisions under human control. It reinforces governance requirements such as auditability, evidence, and explicit approval boundaries.

Telemetry dependencies determine whether AI-driven noise reduction works or fails in practice. At minimum, the model needs accurate asset metadata, including ownership, criticality, environment, and exposure status, as well as scan pipeline telemetry such as reachability, authentication success, and check depth. Closure outcomes must be labeled with structured reasons, such as "validated false positive," "remediated," "accepted exception," or "asset retired," so the model can learn from what actually happened rather than from ambiguous ticket states. Without these signals, models will infer patterns from incomplete data and can drift toward suppressing difficult findings or over-prioritizing noisy ones. Data quality and consistency are therefore operational prerequisites, and they should be treated as reliability targets with monitoring, not as incidental inputs.

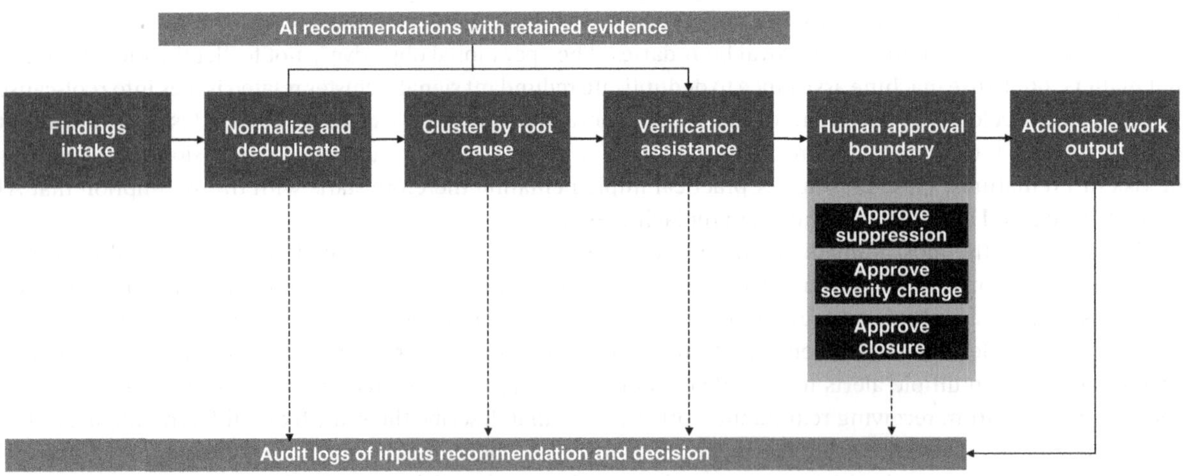

Figure 16.1 AI-Assisted Noise Reduction with Human Approval Boundaries.

Human-in-the-loop controls must be explicit and enforceable, because the temptation to automate away pain is strong in high-volume programs. Approval boundaries should distinguish between organizational decisions and technical recommendations, allowing the model to suggest merges, clusters, and likely verification steps, while reserving suppression, risk acceptance, and closure for accountable humans. Review processes should be calibrated to risk, with stricter oversight for externally exposed services and high-criticality assets where the cost of missing a true positive is highest. Models should also be prevented from learning "success" as "closure," because that incentive can bias recommendations toward reducing backlog rather than reducing exposure. Audit logs should capture the model's inputs, the recommendation, the human decision, and the evidence used, so that outcomes are explainable and defensible.

Failure modes are predictable and should be engineered against rather than discovered after a miss. False confidence is the most dangerous, where the model confidently deduplicates dissimilar issues, clusters unrelated assets, or declares an issue resolved based on weak signals such as the absence of a scan hit. Drift is also common, especially when environments change, scanner signatures evolve, or remediation practices improve, causing the model's learned patterns to become stale. Bias can emerge when historical data overrepresents certain environments or teams, leading the model to make assumptions that do not generalize, such as treating a control as present because it usually is, when the current asset is an exception. Leakage is a governance concern as well: vulnerability evidence, asset details, and remediation notes are sensitive, so any AI workflow must enforce data-handling rules, minimize unnecessary exposure of sensitive content, and ensure that outputs do not echo confidential details into inappropriate channels.

Operational integration determines whether AI reduces noise or merely rearranges it. AI outputs should feed the same work-tracking mechanisms as other findings, producing clearly labeled recommendations that can be accepted, modified, or rejected, with those decisions feeding back as training signals. The program should define performance metrics that reflect risk reduction, not just volume reduction, such as decreased time-to-validate, reduced duplicate ticket rates, higher remediation acceptance rates, and lower recurrence of previously resolved root causes. It should also measure model error rates in high-risk categories, because a modest accuracy gain is not acceptable if it comes with a rare but catastrophic suppression. When AI is treated as a controlled component of the vulnerability operating model, it can turn high-volume scan output into a smaller set of higher-confidence actions that reduce exposure faster without sacrificing accountability. Table 16.3 shows where AI can reduce triage workload while keeping decision authority and auditability with accountable humans.

Table 16.3 AI-Assisted Noise Reduction Controls and Failure Modes.

AI Workflow	Operational Output	Required Inputs	Primary Failure Mode	Required Human Control
Deduplication	Merge redundant findings into one record	Stable asset IDs normalized evidence retained	Bad merges hide real exposure	Review merges across domains and high-risk assets
Clustering	Group issues to reveal root cause and fleet impact	Consistent metadata ownership and environment tags	Unactionable clusters span unrelated systems	Approve cluster boundaries and root cause mapping
Verification assistance	Summarize evidence and propose validation steps	Scan depth metrics and structured closure reasons	False confidence drives premature closure	Humans approve suppression severity change and closure
Confidence tiering	Separate actionable from needs validation	Reachability and authentication success signals	Overfitting to historical closure patterns	Periodic review of tier accuracy in high-risk areas
Anomaly detection	Flag coverage drops and unexpected exposure shifts	Baselines of coverage and pipeline health telemetry	Drift as environment and signatures evolve	Audit recommendations and tune thresholds

Over time, the most valuable outcome is a compounding feedback loop where the system learns how the organization actually fixes problems. Deduplication reduces redundant work and improves trust in the feed, clustering drives source-level remediation that prevents recurrence, and verification assistance shortens the distance from detection to confident action. Each of these benefits depends on disciplined metadata, evidence retention, and structured closure reasons, because that is what turns operational activity into learnable signals. With proper governance, AI becomes a force multiplier for triage and verification while keeping decision authority with accountable humans. The result is not merely a quieter dashboard, but a vulnerability program that spends less time debating findings and more time measurably shrinking the exposed surface area.

Building a Repeatable Discovery Process

A repeatable discovery process is what turns vulnerability discovery from a reactive activity into an operational control. Repeatability means that discovery runs the same way every time for the same class of assets, produces comparable results, and can be relied on to surface meaningful change rather than random variation. Without this consistency, teams cannot tell whether exposure is increasing or decreasing, only that results look different from the last run. The operational objective is predictability: leaders should know what discovery will cover, how deep it will go, and what confidence level the outputs represent. Repeatability does not imply rigidity, but it does require disciplined design and governance.

The foundation of repeatability is explicit scope definition that is stable over time and intentionally evolved. Scope must define which assets are included, which discovery methods apply, and what exclusions exist, along with the rationale for each decision. When scope changes implicitly due to inventory drift, access failures, or untracked environment growth, discovery results fluctuate for reasons unrelated to actual risk. Mature programs version their discovery scope and treat changes as operational events, documenting why coverage expanded, contracted, or shifted depth. This allows stakeholders to interpret results correctly and prevents false narratives about sudden risk spikes or improvements.

Standardized discovery methods are equally important because variability in technique produces variability in findings. If one cycle uses unauthenticated scanning and the next succeeds with credentials, the delta may reflect access differences rather than newly introduced vulnerabilities. A repeatable process defines which techniques are used for each asset class, such as network-based checks, credentialed validation, agent telemetry, or passive discovery, and under what conditions exceptions apply. These decisions should be engineered for safety and signal quality, not convenience, and reviewed periodically as environments evolve. Consistency in method allows teams to focus on real exposure changes instead of questioning the validity of the scan itself.

Scheduling and triggering mechanisms determine whether repeatability scales in dynamic environments. Fixed schedules provide predictability, but they must be complemented by event-driven discovery tied to meaningful change, such as new deployments, exposure-altering configuration updates, or ownership transitions. The key is that triggers are deterministic and documented, not ad hoc responses to noise or escalations. Each discovery run should be traceable to a schedule or trigger, so its results can be interpreted in context. When discovery happens "because someone asked," repeatability erodes and credibility follows.

A repeatable process also requires consistent evidence capture and retention. Each finding should include enough proof to support validation and remediation, such as the conditions observed, the depth of access achieved, and the timestamp and context of discovery. Evidence standards should be defined upfront so that analysts are not forced to improvise when disputes arise. Retaining evidence across cycles enables comparison and trend analysis, which is essential for distinguishing persistent issues from transient artifacts. Without consistent evidence, even accurate findings become harder to trust and harder to act on.

Ownership and handoff rules must be built into the process rather than negotiated each time. Discovery output should map automatically to accountable teams based on authoritative metadata, with clear expectations for validation, remediation, or exception handling. When ownership is ambiguous or frequently changes, findings stagnate and repeat, undermining the value of discovery. A repeatable process treats unowned findings as a failure condition that requires resolution, not as an acceptable backlog. This ensures that discovery remains connected to action rather than becoming a reporting exercise.

AI can support repeatability by enforcing consistency at scale, but only when bounded by well-defined workflows. Models can help detect deviations from expected discovery patterns, such as sudden drops in authentication success or unexpected changes in asset coverage, which often signal process breakdown rather than improved security. AI can also assist with normalization and deduplication, ensuring that the same condition is represented consistently across cycles. These uses depend on stable inputs and disciplined labeling, because a model trained on inconsistent processes will amplify inconsistency rather than correct it. Human oversight remains essential to approve any changes to scope, method, or confidence classification influenced by automated analysis.

Measurement closes the loop by making repeatability visible and enforceable. Metrics should focus on coverage stability, scan depth consistency, validation rates, and recurrence trends, rather than raw finding counts. Deviations from expected patterns should trigger investigation into process health, not immediate conclusions about risk posture. Over time, a repeatable discovery process becomes self-reinforcing, because teams trust the output and invest effort in fixing what it finds. The result is a discovery capability that produces reliable signals, supports defensible decision-making, and forms a stable foundation for sustained exposure reduction.

Conclusion

A vulnerability program earns its value when it produces dependable signals that translate into sustained exposure reduction, not when it generates impressive volumes of findings. Operational fit comes from clear scope, consistent scanning depth, and explicit management of coverage gaps so that visibility claims remain defensible and blind spots do not become normalized risk. Validation discipline, lifecycle-aware tracking, and tight coordination with change management keep discovery aligned to how systems actually evolve, ensuring that risk is identified and addressed at the moment it is introduced. With governed AI support that accelerates deduplication, clustering, and verification without weakening human accountability, teams can reduce noise, preserve trust, and continuously shrink the attack surface in ways that are measurable and repeatable.

Recommendations

1) Establish a stable discovery scope and keep it version-controlled over time. Document what is in scope, what is excluded, and why, so coverage changes do not masquerade as risk changes. Track reachability and authentication depth as part of scope health to prevent silent degradation in what the program can actually see.
2) Avoid relying solely on unauthenticated network scanning for decisions that require high confidence. Use credentialed validation where appropriate to confirm patch and configuration state, and treat scan identities as privileged assets with minimal access, rotation, and monitoring. When credentialed coverage is limited, apply it deliberately to the highest-value tiers and representative system patterns.
3) Prioritize continuous management of coverage gaps and blind spots as an operational backlog, not an embarrassment. Measure coverage against independent asset sources, so "no findings" is not mistaken for "no exposure." Separate "in scope," "reachable," "authenticated," and "high confidence" categories, so stakeholders understand what visibility claims actually mean.
4) Identify and continuously validate external exposure from an attacker's perspective. Maintain an accurate inventory of public IPs, domains, and externally reachable services, and ensure each exposure has a documented purpose and an accountable owner. Classify high-risk services based on external reachability, privileged access, and business criticality to drive stronger monitoring and faster remediation.

5) Validate findings with consistent evidence standards before routing work to engineering teams. Capture proof of what was observed, how the check fired, and what access depth was achieved, so issues can be reproduced and resolved efficiently. Treat insufficient evidence as low confidence pending targeted validation rather than creating churn in remediation queues.
6) Manage false positives with structured outcomes that feed back into tuning and process improvement. Record clear reasons when findings are invalid, so the same disputes do not recur and so noise drivers become visible engineering work. Require human review for any suppression decisions and keep suppression time-bound and auditable to prevent true exposure from being hidden.
7) Reduce repeated findings by normalizing issues to root causes and fixing them at the source. Group recurring exposures to identify whether the correct control point is a baseline image, deployment template, configuration profile, or patch process. Validate closures from the same perspective that generated the finding, so "fixed" means the condition no longer exists under controlled verification.
8) Coordinate discovery with change management, so new exposure is detected close to the moment it is introduced. Trigger targeted validation after meaningful changes such as new deployments, exposure-affecting configuration updates, and routing or DNS modifications. Define escalation thresholds for high-risk exposure patterns, so teams can intervene while change is still reversible.
9) Track vulnerabilities across asset lifecycles using durable identifiers and authoritative metadata. Ensure findings follow the underlying asset even when hosts change names, IPs, or runtime instances, and route accountability through explicit ownership. For ephemeral compute, correlate issues back to the image or pipeline that produced the runtime, so remediation scales and rediscovery declines.
10) Apply AI to reduce noise through deduplication, clustering, and verification assistance under strict governance. Use models to consolidate redundant signals and highlight fleet-level patterns, but keep humans accountable for suppression, risk acceptance, and closure decisions. Require auditability of inputs, recommendations, and final approvals to prevent false confidence, drift, and quiet erosion of visibility.

17

Prioritization, Remediation, and Patch Operations

Defensive teams succeed or fail based on whether they can translate security findings into steady, reliable operational change. Prioritization creates the decision logic for what moves first, remediation turns those decisions into owned work, and patch operations provide the repeatable machinery that makes change safe at scale. The hard part is balancing exposure reduction against uptime, capacity, and the reality that not every system can be patched on demand without collateral damage. When these capabilities are run as disciplined programs with evidence-based verification, governed exceptions, and accountable rapid response, organizations reduce risk continuously instead of episodically.

Turning Findings into Actionable Work

Operational value begins when raw findings are converted into work items that a delivery team can execute without debate. That conversion starts by normalizing the finding into a consistent record that captures the affected asset, the condition observed, the evidence source, and the business context that makes it matter. A useful record also states the security impact in concrete terms, such as loss of confidentiality through unauthorized access or loss of availability through service disruption, without overstating certainty. Where the underlying signal is probabilistic or inferred, the record needs to say so plainly to prevent false confidence from turning into rushed changes. The goal is not to make findings sound urgent; the goal is to make them unambiguous and ready for assignment.

Actionable work requires scope discipline, because "fix the vulnerability" is not a task, it is a theme. A well-formed remediation item defines exactly what must change, where it must change, and how success will be verified after the change. It separates immediate containment actions from durable remediation, so teams are not forced to choose between short-term risk reduction and long-term correction. It also identifies dependencies like maintenance windows, required approvals, or upstream configuration owners, so the ticket does not stall in clarifying questions. When findings involve shared services, the work item should explicitly note potential blast radius and the need for coordinated scheduling, because uncoordinated patching is a common cause of avoidable outages.

Prioritization becomes practical only when the work intake process enforces clear ownership and routing. Every finding should map to a technical owner who can actually make the change, plus a service owner accountable for the business outcome and the downtime tradeoffs. When routing is ambiguous, items bounce between teams, and risk accumulates while everyone agrees the issue is "important." An effective intake process uses asset inventory and service mapping to direct work to the correct queue on day one, and it includes an escalation path when ownership is disputed. That escalation path should be fast and procedural, because every day spent negotiating ownership is a day the environment remains exposed.

Converting findings into work also means attaching decision-grade priority signals rather than vague labels. Priority should reflect a blend of exploitability, exposure, and business criticality, with enough specificity to support sequencing decisions across hundreds or thousands of open items. The work item should include the "why now" in operational terms, such as known exploitation in the wild, public-facing reachability, or privileged access implications, so engineers can justify the effort against competing commitments. At the same time, it should call out uncertainty, such as incomplete coverage from a scan or limited telemetry on reachability, to prevent teams from treating the priority as infallible. When organizations use AI-assisted triage to pre-rank findings, the model's output should be framed as a recommendation with traceable inputs, not a mandate, and the final priority should be explicitly approved by a human accountable for the decision.

Remediation work items frequently fail due to missing context about acceptable change and acceptable risk. Some issues can be resolved through patching, others through configuration hardening, and others through compensating controls when a patch is infeasible within operational constraints. The work intake must capture the proposed remediation path and the rationale, because the same finding can imply different actions across environments with different uptime requirements. If an exception is required, it should be treated as a formal decision with an expiration date, defined compensating measures, and evidence requirements for ongoing acceptance. Exceptions that are undocumented or open-ended quietly become policy, and they erode both security posture and leadership credibility when auditors or incident responders later ask why known issues persisted.

Execution depends on integrating security work with the same operational hygiene used for reliability and change management. Work items should specify required testing, rollback expectations, and verification steps, so patching does not become an improvisation exercise during a maintenance window. Teams need to know what "done" means in measurable terms, such as the vulnerability no longer detected on rescans, a configuration baseline now enforced, or an exposed service no longer reachable from untrusted networks. Verification should include both technical confirmation and operational checks, because a fix that introduces instability can create a different class of risk. Where automation is used to deploy patches or enforce configurations, the work record should reference the change artifact and execution logs, so the organization can demonstrate what changed, when, and under whose authority.

AI/ML can improve throughput in this conversion process, but only when its boundaries are well-defined and auditable. Models can help cluster duplicate findings, infer likely ownership based on historical resolution patterns, and suggest remediation playbooks based on observed asset attributes and prior successful fixes. Those capabilities depend on reliable telemetry, including consistent asset identifiers, accurate service ownership data, configuration state, and a history of ticket outcomes that is not polluted with inconsistent labels. Human-in-the-loop controls are essential: suggested owners, priorities, and fixes should require review, and the system should preserve the rationale and inputs that produced each suggestion for later audit. Failure modes are predictable—models can drift when the environment changes, bias toward teams that historically close tickets faster, or leak sensitive details if prompts or training data are not controlled—so governance must include access controls, retention limits, and periodic validation against real outcomes.

The final step in turning findings into actionable work is closing the loop with evidence and learning, not just closure codes. Closure should capture the remediation performed, the verification results, and any follow-up actions such as backlog cleanup, monitoring updates, or documentation changes required to prevent recurrence. Patterns in re-opened findings, recurring misconfigurations, and chronic exception renewals should feed back into engineering standards and platform improvements, because repeatedly fixing the same class of issue is a sign of weak preventive controls. Metrics should emphasize flow and risk reduction, such as time-to-triage, time-to-remediate by severity and asset class, and the percentage of findings closed with verified evidence, rather than raw ticket counts. When the organization consistently turns findings into precise, owned, verifiable work, remediation stops being a reactive scramble and becomes a managed operational capability.

Prioritization Criteria and Decision Tradeoffs

Prioritization in defensive operations is the discipline of deciding what gets fixed first when everything appears urgent and time is finite. The core problem is not a lack of findings; it is the mismatch between the volume of security debt and the organization's capacity to remediate without breaking services. Effective prioritization starts by defining what "most important" means in operational terms, not rhetorical terms, and by using criteria that can be applied consistently across teams. Those criteria must be strong enough to guide sequencing decisions, yet simple enough that engineers and leaders can understand why a given item rose to the top. When prioritization feels arbitrary, remediation becomes a political negotiation and risk accumulates in the gaps.

Exploitability is usually the first criterion executives expect, but it must be treated with care. A vulnerability that is theoretically exploitable can remain low-risk if it is unreachable, isolated, or constrained by strong authentication and segmentation. Conversely, a moderate-severity issue can become urgent when it is exposed to untrusted networks or sits on a path to privileged access. Prioritization improves when exploitability is expressed through environmental facts such as network reachability, authentication requirements, and the presence of compensating controls, rather than solely through generalized severity labels. This approach reduces the common pitfall of chasing high scores in low-impact places while missing quieter conditions that are actively dangerous in the local context.

Exposure translates exploitability into real business risk by asking whether an attacker can realistically touch the vulnerable surface. Exposure is shaped by internet-facing placement, partner connectivity, remote access design, and the degree to which the asset participates in sensitive workflows. It also includes operational exposure, such as systems that are widely reused or centrally trusted, where a compromise would propagate quickly. A pragmatic prioritization process captures exposure signals directly in the work item, so teams do not have to infer them during triage. When exposure is unclear, organizations benefit from a default bias toward restricting access and reducing attack surface while deeper validation is performed, because exposure can often be lowered faster than a full remediation can be completed. Table 17.1 links common prioritization criteria to the evidence signals that make decisions defensible and repeatable.

Business criticality is the criterion that makes prioritization defensible to leadership, because it anchors technical work to mission outcomes. Criticality is not about executive preference; it is about the impact of compromise or outage on revenue, safety, regulatory obligations, and the continuity of core services. High-criticality systems often come with stricter change constraints, which creates a direct tradeoff between risk reduction and operational stability. Prioritization must therefore consider both the consequence of compromise and the consequence of change, because an emergency patch that causes downtime can create immediate harm even if it reduces theoretical exposure. Mature programs document criticality at the service level, not just the server level, so remediation decisions align with how the business actually operates. Figure 17.1 visualizes how prioritization blends risk signals with operational constraints to produce a defensible sequence of work. It reinforces that exploitability and exposure must be balanced against business criticality and change risk rather than relying on severity labels alone.

Likelihood of active exploitation is a separate criterion from abstract exploitability, and it has outsized influence on sequencing decisions. When there is credible evidence that a weakness is being exploited broadly, the organization must treat delay as an explicit acceptance of heightened risk. This criterion depends on threat intelligence and internal telemetry, including intrusion detection, endpoint signals, authentication anomalies, and observed scanning or exploit attempts. The tradeoff is that intelligence can be incomplete or noisy, and organizations can overreact to headlines while missing quieter adversary behavior targeting their specific environment. The right operational posture is to elevate items when exploitation indicators exist, but to require the evidence to be captured and traceable, so the organization can explain why it moved resources and why it did not.

Table 17.1 Prioritization Criteria and Evidence Signals.

Criterion	Operational Question	Typical Evidence Signal	Common Pitfall
Exploitability	Can the condition be reliably exploited in this environment	Reachability plus auth requirements plus known constraints	Chasing severity labels without context
Exposure	Can an attacker realistically reach the vulnerable surface	Internet facing placement plus partner paths plus remote access design	Assuming internal equals safe
Business criticality	What is the consequence of compromise or outage for this service	Revenue impact plus safety impact plus regulatory impact plus continuity impact	Prioritizing by preference instead of mission impact
Active exploitation likelihood	Is there credible evidence of current exploitation pressure	Threat intel plus internal detections plus observed scanning	Overreacting to headlines without local indicators
Remediation effort and feasibility	How quickly can risk be reduced with available capacity	Defined patch path plus testing scope plus dependency readiness	Using effort as a reason to ignore high-risk items
Change risk	What is the probability and impact of service disruption if we change now	Rollback readiness plus staging options plus stability history	Forcing emergency change without safety checks

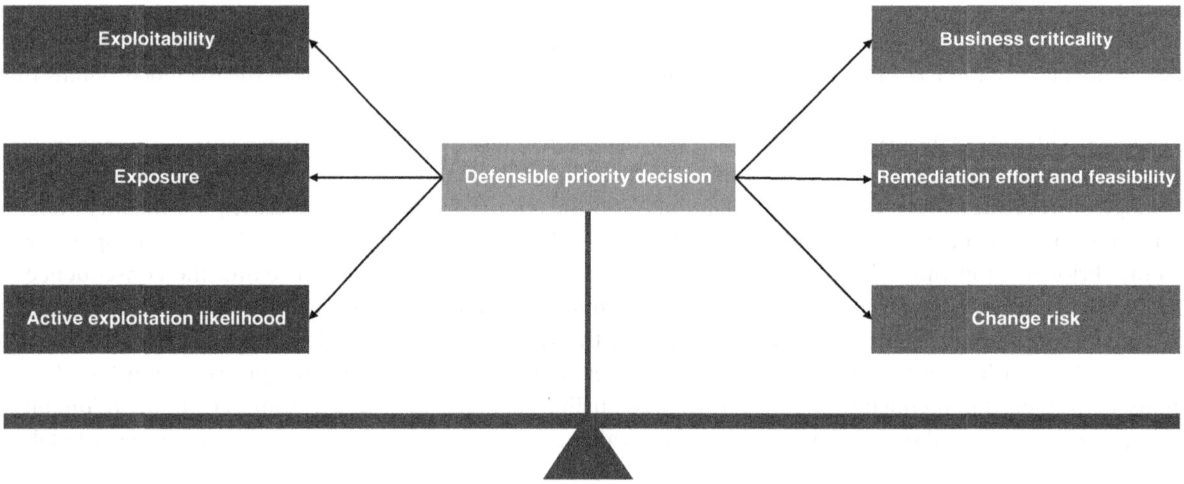

Figure 17.1 Prioritization Criteria and Decision Tradeoffs Matrix.

Remediation effort and feasibility are criteria that force realism into the process. Some fixes are fast, low-risk changes that can eliminate meaningful exposure quickly, while others require architectural work, vendor coordination, or extended testing. Effort should never be used to justify ignoring high-risk items, but it should influence how the organization sequences work and whether it applies interim mitigations. A common tradeoff is whether to prioritize "quick wins" to improve overall posture or to focus on a small number of complex items that represent concentrated risk. The healthiest approach balances both by reserving capacity for high-impact projects while steadily burning down a pipeline of smaller fixes that reduce broad attack surface over time.

Change risk is the criterion that security teams often underweight, even though it determines whether remediation actually gets deployed. Change risk includes the probability of service disruption, the availability of rollback options, and the operational burden of deploying and validating the fix. High change risk does not mean "do nothing"; it means the remediation plan must include more rigorous testing, tighter coordination, and sometimes phased rollout. It also means that compensating controls may be preferable as an initial step, such as hardening access paths, tightening firewall rules, or increasing monitoring, while the durable fix is prepared. Organizations that ignore change risk tend to create resistance to security work, because engineering teams experience security as a source of instability rather than a partner in reliability.

AI-assisted prioritization can help manage scale, but it must be governed, so it does not become an unchallengeable oracle. Models can rank items by combining signals like asset criticality, exposure, exploitability indicators, and historical remediation outcomes, and they can highlight clusters that indicate systemic issues. These systems depend on clean data and consistent labeling, and they should expose the features that drove a recommendation, so reviewers can validate whether the logic matches current reality. Human approval boundaries matter: the model can propose order and routing, but accountable leaders must confirm priorities for high-impact systems, emergency changes, and exception decisions. Failure modes are predictable, including drift as the environment changes, bias toward teams that close tickets quickly rather than those addressing the hardest risk, and false confidence when the model lacks key telemetry such as reachability or compensating controls.

Decision tradeoffs ultimately come down to choosing among imperfect options while preserving accountability. A defensible prioritization process makes those tradeoffs explicit by recording the criteria considered, the rationale for sequencing, and any interim mitigations or exceptions applied. It also creates feedback loops, so decisions improve over time, using outcomes like incident learnings, verification results, and the frequency of recurring findings to refine the criteria weighting. When prioritization is transparent and repeatable, security leaders can explain why some items waited, engineering leaders can plan remediation without chaos, and executives can see that risk reduction is being pursued deliberately rather than reactively. The organization does not need perfect prioritization to be effective, but it does need consistent decision-making that can withstand scrutiny when outcomes are tested.

Patch Management as an Operational Program

Patch management becomes reliable only when it is treated as an operational program rather than a periodic technical chore. In practice, patching is a continuous control that competes with feature work, incident response, and platform maintenance for the same engineering capacity. Running it as a program means defining recurring cadences, accountable owners, measurable outcomes, and explicit acceptance of exceptions, all tied to service reliability expectations. It also means acknowledging that patching is inseparable from asset and configuration visibility, because you cannot patch what you cannot accurately inventory. When leadership frames patching as routine operations, teams can plan for it, budget for it, and execute it without creating recurring crisis cycles.

Programmatic patch management starts with scope clarity that distinguishes between operating systems, third-party applications, firmware, containers, network devices, and managed cloud services. Each category has different deployment mechanics, testing requirements, and failure modes, and treating them as one homogeneous backlog leads to missed coverage and inconsistent reporting. The program must define which assets are in scope, how they are discovered, and how they are grouped into services or ownership domains, so work is routed correctly. Patch eligibility should be determined by both technical applicability and business operating constraints, such as uptime requirements and regulatory obligations. Without this scoping discipline, patch metrics look healthy on paper while critical systems remain untouched because they were never truly part of the program.

Cadence is the program's backbone, but cadence must be coupled with risk-based acceleration paths. Most environments operate with a regular rhythm for standard patches, such as monthly cycles aligned to predictable vendor releases and internal change windows. The program also needs an emergency path for items with credible active exploitation or severe exposure, where the organization can compress testing and approval timelines without bypassing accountability. The decision to accelerate should be explicit, documented, and based on observable signals, because constant "emergency" patching is a sign of weak planning and often erodes operational trust. A mature cadence includes time for validation and follow-up, not just deployment, because patches that are applied but not verified create a false sense of progress.

Testing and change control are where patch programs succeed or fail, because service stability is both a constraint and a requirement. Good programs define what must be tested for each asset class and service tier, and they use staged rollout patterns, so failures are contained before they reach broad production impact. Rollback planning is part of the patch procedure, not an afterthought, and it is tailored to the actual platform, whether that means reverting snapshots, redeploying golden images, or rolling back configuration changes. Documentation should capture expected service behavior, monitoring checks, and acceptance criteria, so teams can recognize when a patch has introduced subtle degradation. When patching repeatedly causes outages, the organization tends to defer updates, and deferral becomes the default pathway to accumulating preventable risk. Table 17.2 shows what a patch program must produce and the evidence needed to prove remediation is real.

Verification must be treated as a first-class activity, because deployment does not guarantee risk reduction. Verification includes technical confirmation that the patch is present and the vulnerable condition is no longer detectable, as well as operational confirmation that the service remains healthy under real load. This is where telemetry matters: endpoint state, configuration baselines, scan results, and service monitoring signals should be correlated to create confidence that patching achieved its purpose. Verification also catches partial failures, such as systems missed due to inventory drift, patch installation errors, or devices that were offline during the maintenance window. A program that measures "patched" without measuring "verified remediated" will steadily overestimate its posture while adversaries exploit the gaps.

Exceptions are inevitable, so the program must govern them rather than pretend they do not exist. Exceptions arise from legacy dependencies, vendor constraints, operational risk, or business priorities, and unmanaged exceptions quietly become permanent exposures. A disciplined process requires a documented rationale, compensating controls, an expiration date, and a re-evaluation trigger such as vendor release cycles or architecture changes. Compensating controls might include restricting network access, tightening authentication, disabling vulnerable

Table 17.2 Patch Management Program Controls and Verification Artifacts.

Program Element	What Must Be Defined	Execution Output	Verification Artifact
Scope	Asset classes and in scope inventory rules	In scope asset list by owner and service	Coverage report with missing asset exceptions
Cadence	Standard patch rhythm plus emergency acceleration path	Scheduled deployment waves by tier	Change record with window and approvals
Testing and rollback	Minimum testing plus rollback method per service tier	Staged rollout plan plus rollback trigger	Rollback plan reference and readiness check
Deployment	Approved method for patch install and reboot coordination	Successful install events by asset	Patch state confirmation from host telemetry
External confirmation	Relevant vantage point checks for exposed conditions	Targeted rescan or probe results	Rescan evidence tied to closure record
Metrics and learning	Time to patch plus verified coverage plus exception trends	Program scorecard for leadership	Verified remediation percentage over time

features, or increasing detection coverage, but they should be concrete and testable. Exception governance is also a leadership signal: it demonstrates that the organization is making informed tradeoffs and tracking accepted risk rather than losing control of it.

AI/ML can improve patch operations by reducing manual triage and increasing the quality of decisions, but it must operate within strict human approval boundaries. Models can help map vulnerabilities to affected asset groups, recommend patch sequencing based on exposure and criticality, and flag anomalies such as systems that repeatedly fail to update or diverge from baseline. These capabilities depend on reliable telemetry: accurate asset inventory, patch state reporting, network exposure data, and historical success and failure patterns, all consistently labeled. Human reviewers must approve high-impact actions, such as emergency patch waves or changes affecting critical services, and the system should retain the reasoning trail behind recommendations for auditability. Failure modes include drift as infrastructure evolves, biased prioritization that overweights easily patched systems, and information leakage if sensitive asset details are exposed through uncontrolled prompts or logs, so governance must include access controls and periodic validation.

A patch program should also be evaluated by operational performance, not just compliance posture. Metrics that matter include time-to-patch for defined severity and exposure tiers, percentage of in-scope assets with verified patch state, frequency of missed maintenance windows, and the rate of exceptions that expire versus silently renew. Leaders should also watch indicators of friction, such as recurring deployment failures, repeated outages tied to patching, and growing backlogs in specific ownership domains. Those signals often point to systemic issues like inadequate test environments, weak service ownership mapping, or under-resourced platform engineering. When patching is run as a program with clear cadence, verification discipline, governed exceptions, and data-driven decision support, it becomes a predictable engine of risk reduction that strengthens both security posture and operational reliability.

Coordinating with IT and Engineering Teams

Coordination succeeds when security work is framed as shared operational reliability, not as a competing agenda imposed from the outside. IT and engineering teams already manage a steady stream of changes, incidents, and roadmap commitments, so security-driven remediation must fit into how work is planned, executed, and verified. The practical goal is to reduce friction by making requests precise, aligning them to existing operational cadences, and acknowledging the constraints that teams live under. Security should translate findings into work that is actionable in the target team's language, including affected services, change risk, and validation steps. When coordination is treated as a relationship problem rather than a workflow problem, the organization ends up relying on heroics and personal influence instead of repeatable operations.

The first coordination mechanism is clean ownership mapping that connects assets to services and services to accountable teams. Without this mapping, tickets drift, escalations become emotional, and remediation timelines become guesses. Security teams need enough context to route work correctly on day one, and IT and engineering teams need enough context to understand why the work matters in their environment. Ownership mapping also enables decision-making when tradeoffs are required, because the person accountable for uptime and user impact can weigh risk reduction against operational disruption. When ownership is ambiguous, the organization tends to prioritize what is easiest to assign rather than what is riskiest to leave open.

Communication quality matters more than volume, and coordination improves when security supplies decision-grade information rather than raw alerts. A remediation request should identify the specific affected components, the evidence source, the practical exposure conditions, and the proposed remediation path, including whether it is a patch, a configuration change, or a compensating control. It should also state what success looks like, such as a verified patch state, a clean rescan, or a configuration baseline check, so teams can close the loop without debate. When security cannot confidently determine reachability or impact, it should say so explicitly and ask for targeted validation rather than implying certainty. This approach prevents the common failure mode where engineering teams lose trust because they repeatedly chase issues that turn out to be non-applicable or mis-scoped.

Coordination also depends on aligning security work with the planning horizons that IT and engineering actually use. Some remediation can be executed as part of regular maintenance windows, while other work requires backlog grooming, sprint planning, or platform release cycles. Security leaders should make the distinction clear: what must be done immediately due to credible exploitation or high exposure, and what can be scheduled into normal delivery pipelines. Establishing predictable cadences for recurring patching and hardening reduces the number of "urgent" interruptions and helps teams build muscle memory around validation and rollback. When every request is framed as a fire drill, teams respond by creating informal filters, and critical issues can be delayed behind fatigue and skepticism.

Change risk is where coordination is often tested, because the same action that reduces security risk can increase outage risk. The most effective security teams collaborate on safe rollout patterns, such as staged deployments, canarying, or applying mitigations to reduce exposure while a full fix is prepared. They also respect the operational reality that critical services may require more testing, tighter scheduling, and stronger rollback planning than less critical systems. Coordination improves when security explicitly supports these practices rather than treating them as excuses for delay, because it demonstrates shared accountability for outcomes. If a remediation introduces instability, security credibility suffers, and future remediation requests will face higher resistance regardless of their importance.

Escalation should be procedural, not personal, and it should exist to resolve ambiguity, not to punish teams. A good escalation path defines when an item must be elevated, who has authority to make tradeoff decisions, and what information must be captured to document the rationale. Escalation is particularly important when competing priorities exist across teams, such as shared infrastructure dependencies or limited change windows, because local optimization can increase enterprise risk. The decision record should include the criteria considered, interim mitigations applied, and a timeline for revisiting the decision, so deferral remains a managed choice rather than silent neglect. When escalation is ad hoc or political, teams learn to avoid visibility, and security issues stay open longer because they are harder to discuss than to ignore.

AI/ML can strengthen coordination by improving routing accuracy and reducing the interpretive burden on engineering teams, but it must be deployed with careful controls. Models can suggest likely owners based on historical ticket resolution, cluster related findings into a single remediation effort, and generate draft remediation narratives that are consistent and complete. Those benefits depend on high-quality telemetry and records, including consistent service naming, accurate asset-to-service mapping, and trustworthy closure notes; otherwise, the model amplifies existing organizational confusion. Human-in-the-loop approval is essential for assignments that affect accountability, for priority changes that can disrupt schedules, and for any auto-generated language that could misstate risk or expose sensitive asset details. Common failure modes include bias toward teams that close tickets quickly, drift as org structures change, and false confidence in suggested fixes, so governance should require periodic review and auditable traces of why recommendations were made.

Sustained coordination requires feedback loops that make both security and delivery teams better over time. Post-remediation learnings should surface patterns such as recurring misconfigurations, repeated patch failures, or dependencies that regularly block updates, and those patterns should translate into durable platform improvements. Security can contribute by refining detection logic, improving asset classification, and tuning prioritization signals, so teams receive fewer low-value interruptions. Engineering and IT can contribute by hardening build pipelines, standardizing baselines, and improving observability, so remediation can be verified quickly and confidently. When coordination is built into shared workflows, with clear ownership, predictable cadences, safe change practices, and accountable escalation, remediation becomes an integrated part of operations rather than a recurring negotiation over whose problem security is this week.

Maintenance Windows, Risk Acceptance, and Exceptions

Maintenance windows exist to make change safe, not to slow it down. In mature operations, a maintenance window is a pre-approved interval where teams can deploy changes with predictable support coverage, reduced user impact, and a known rollback posture. Security remediation depends on these windows because patching and configuration changes often carry non-trivial outage risk, especially for stateful systems and tightly coupled applications. The operational challenge is that maintenance windows are scarce, and high-risk findings do not politely align with calendar rhythms. A workable program treats windows as a scheduling asset that must be managed, prioritized, and occasionally bypassed through explicit emergency processes.

Window design should reflect service criticality and the real behavior of the environment, not just tradition. High-criticality services often require narrower windows, stronger change controls, and tighter stakeholder coordination, while lower-risk services can tolerate broader automation and more frequent updates. Good practice includes clearly defined entry criteria, such as completed testing, validated backups, and a documented rollback plan, so the window is used for execution rather than discovery. Windows should also include time for verification, because shipping a patch without confirming results leaves the organization exposed while assuming it is safe. When windows are treated as "deploy time only," failures are detected later, recovery becomes harder, and trust in the patch program erodes.

Security's role in window planning is to translate remediation urgency into change sequencing that operations teams can execute. Not every finding warrants consumption of scarce window capacity, and not every critical fix requires a full-service outage. This is where prioritization criteria become operational: exposure, exploitability, and business impact should drive what is scheduled into the next window versus what is queued for later. Security teams should also help identify low-disruption mitigations that can be applied outside of windows, such as restricting network access, disabling vulnerable features, or tightening authentication controls, to reduce risk while durable remediation is staged. The tradeoff is that mitigations can create operational friction or partial functionality loss, so they must be coordinated with service owners and documented as intentional interim controls.

Emergency change processes are necessary when credible exploitation or high exposure makes delay unacceptable. An emergency process is not the absence of governance; it is governance that is optimized for speed while preserving accountability. It should define who can declare an emergency, what minimum evidence is required, what testing can be abbreviated, and what post-change validation and review must occur. Emergency changes should still include rollback planning and monitoring checkpoints, because the fastest way to lose the ability to patch quickly is to cause a preventable outage during an emergency. When organizations repeatedly invoke emergency processes for predictable patch cycles, it signals weak capacity planning and misaligned maintenance cadences rather than a uniquely hostile threat environment.

Risk acceptance is the mechanism that allows an organization to proceed when remediation is not immediately feasible, but it must be treated as a decision with ownership. Accepting risk should require a named accountable leader, a clear description of the risk being accepted, and a time-bound commitment to reassess. The risk statement needs to be specific enough that it can be evaluated later, such as accepting exposure of a specific service under defined compensating controls until a platform upgrade is completed. Vague acceptances, like "accepted due to business need," hide the real tradeoffs and make it impossible to learn or improve. The organization should also distinguish between short-term acceptance to align with a maintenance window and long-term acceptance that effectively redefines the control posture, because those are different decisions with different scrutiny.

Exceptions are the formal expression of risk acceptance in operational terms, and they are where many programs quietly fail. Exceptions tend to proliferate when legacy systems cannot be patched, when vendor dependencies lag, or when operational change risk is perceived as higher than security risk. A disciplined exception process requires documented rationale, compensating controls that measurably reduce exposure, and an explicit expiration date tied to a plan, not a hope. Compensating controls should be concrete and testable, such as network segmentation, reduced privileges, tightened firewall rules, or increased monitoring thresholds, rather than aspirational statements like "we will watch it closely." Exceptions should also be discoverable and auditable, because unmanaged exceptions undermine reporting integrity and create blind spots that become painful during incidents and external assessments.

Maintenance windows and exceptions intersect most sharply in environments with shared platforms and cross-team dependencies. A patch may require coordinated updates across middleware, application code, and infrastructure components, and a single team's inability to move can block the entire change. In these cases, coordination requires a shared schedule, clearly documented dependencies, and agreement on which mitigations will be used if the full remediation cannot complete within the planned window. The program should also anticipate that some systems will be offline or unreachable during deployment cycles, and it should plan for catch-up runs that prevent "missed window" from turning into permanent drift. Without these controls, exceptions become the default explanation for why patching lags, and the backlog grows until a crisis forces an unplanned and riskier mass update.

AI/ML can support exception governance and window planning by improving visibility and decision quality, but it must not replace accountable judgment. Models can identify systems that routinely miss windows, correlate exception patterns to specific asset classes or teams, and suggest where compensating controls are likely to be effective based on observed exposure and configuration state. These insights depend on reliable telemetry: change records, patch state, asset criticality, and network exposure data must be consistent and complete. Human approval boundaries remain essential for any action that changes risk posture, such as granting an exception, extending an expiration, or altering a service's maintenance cadence. Failure modes include bias toward repeatedly extending exceptions for "hard" systems, drift as service architectures change, and leakage of sensitive details through ungoverned prompts or logs, so auditability and access control must be explicit design requirements.

The effectiveness of maintenance windows, risk acceptance, and exceptions is ultimately measured by whether they preserve both security posture and operational stability. Programs should track how often critical remediation is completed within planned windows, how many exceptions exist by service tier, and how frequently exceptions are renewed versus retired through durable fixes. They should also measure how often emergency changes occur and whether those emergency changes correlate with predictable vendor cycles or with genuinely emergent threats. Leaders should expect occasional exceptions and occasional emergency patches, but they should treat rising exception counts and recurring emergency use as indicators of systemic capacity or architecture problems. When windows are managed as a strategic operational resource, and risk acceptance is time-bound, transparent, and paired with real compensating controls, the organization can move quickly when needed without normalizing insecurity as the cost of doing business.

Compensating Controls When Patching Is Not Immediate

When patching cannot occur immediately, compensating controls become the primary mechanism for reducing exposure without destabilizing operations. These controls are not substitutes for remediation; they are deliberate, interim measures designed to interrupt likely attack paths while preserving service availability. Effective use begins with a clear articulation of the vulnerable condition and the specific threat it enables, so controls are targeted rather than generic. The intent is to reduce either the likelihood of exploitation or the blast radius of compromise during the delay. Treating compensating controls as engineered safeguards rather than ad hoc workarounds preserves credibility with both engineering and leadership.

Access restriction is often the fastest and most reliable compensating control because it directly reduces exposure. Limiting network reachability through firewall rules, security groups, or segmentation can convert an internet-facing weakness into an internal-only issue or confine access to a narrow set of trusted sources. Identity-based restrictions, such as tightening IAM policies or enforcing MFA on previously exempt paths, can also meaningfully raise the bar for exploitation without touching the vulnerable code. These changes should

Table 17.3 Compensating Controls Mapped to Risk Reduction Goals.

Compensating Control	Primary Risk Reduced	How It Works Operationally	Verification Check
Access restriction	Exposure	Constrain reachability to trusted sources	Access path test from untrusted vantage points
Segmentation	Blast radius	Isolate vulnerable systems from broad network paths	Network policy validation and flow confirmation
Configuration hardening	Exploit primitives	Disable vulnerable features and tighten protocols	Configuration baseline evaluation
Privilege reduction	Impact of compromise	Reduce service rights and token scope	Privilege review and runtime permission check
Enhanced monitoring and detection	Dwell time	Add targeted detections for expected exploit behaviors	Alert validation with test events
Outbound restriction	Command and control	Limit unexpected external connections from vulnerable hosts	Egress policy check and connection monitoring

be precise and reversible, with documented scope, so they do not inadvertently break dependent services. The operational tradeoff is that access restrictions can disrupt legitimate workflows, so they require coordination with service owners and clear communication to affected users.

Configuration hardening can neutralize entire classes of vulnerabilities even when a patch is unavailable. Disabling vulnerable features, enforcing safer protocol versions, tightening cipher suites, or adjusting default behaviors can remove exploit primitives while leaving the core service functional. This approach is particularly valuable for third-party software and network devices where patch timelines are vendor-controlled. Configuration changes should be validated against known exploit mechanics, not just applied because they are "best practice," to ensure they actually reduce risk in the specific context. Poorly scoped hardening can create false confidence if the vulnerable path remains reachable through alternate configurations that were not addressed. Table 17.3 summarizes practical compensating controls and the concrete checks used to confirm they are working.

Privilege reduction is a powerful compensating control because it limits what an attacker can achieve even if exploitation succeeds. Running services with least privilege, reducing token scope, and removing unnecessary administrative access can turn a remote code execution flaw into a contained process-level issue rather than a platform compromise. This control is especially relevant for legacy systems where architectural fixes are costly, but privilege boundaries still exist. The challenge is that privilege changes can expose hidden dependencies and brittle assumptions in older environments. Careful testing and staged rollout are essential to avoid operational surprises while shrinking the impact surface.

Enhanced monitoring and detection act as compensating controls by shortening dwell time when prevention is incomplete. Increasing log verbosity, adding targeted detection rules, and tightening alert thresholds around the affected assets can improve the likelihood that exploitation attempts are noticed quickly. Monitoring should focus on behaviors consistent with the specific vulnerability, such as unusual process creation, authentication anomalies, or unexpected network connections, rather than generic noise. Detection-only controls do not reduce the chance of exploitation, but they can meaningfully reduce impact by enabling rapid response. The tradeoff is operational overhead: increased alerts require analyst capacity and tuning to avoid fatigue that undermines the benefit.

Isolation and containment strategies can be used when risk is concentrated and tolerance is low. Techniques such as placing a vulnerable system behind a jump host, restricting outbound connectivity, or moving workloads into more tightly controlled network segments can buy time without full remediation. In extreme cases, partial service degradation or temporary feature disablement may be acceptable to protect critical assets or data. These decisions must be explicit and documented, because containment often shifts risk or cost to other parts of the organization. When isolation is used, the exit criteria for returning to normal operation should be defined upfront, so temporary states do not become permanent architecture by neglect.

AI/ML can assist in selecting and validating compensating controls, but it must be used as decision support rather than automation of risk acceptance. Models can analyze telemetry to identify the most exposed attack paths, suggest controls that historically reduced similar risk, and flag gaps where compensating measures are insufficient. These insights depend on high-quality data, including accurate asset inventories, network flow logs, identity events, and historical incident outcomes. Human oversight is essential to approve control changes, especially those affecting access or service behavior, and to ensure recommendations align with current business context. Failure modes include overfitting to past incidents, bias toward easily observable controls, and false assurance when telemetry coverage is incomplete.

Governance is what distinguishes compensating controls from informal workarounds. Each control should be tied to a specific finding, documented with its intended risk reduction effect, and assigned an expiration aligned to the planned remediation. Verification is required to confirm the control is actually in place and functioning as expected, not just approved on paper. Metrics should track how often compensating controls are used, how long they persist, and how frequently they are retired through patching or architectural change. When compensating controls are precise, time-bound, and verified, they enable organizations to manage unavoidable delays without normalizing exposure as an acceptable operating condition.

Verifying Remediation and Preventing Regression

Verification is the moment remediation becomes real, because deployment alone does not prove risk has been reduced. Systems can report successful patch installation while the vulnerable component remains active, scanners can miss affected instances due to inventory drift, and configuration changes can be overwritten by automation within hours. Effective verification treats "fixed" as an evidence-backed claim that can be reproduced, not a status update in a ticket. That evidence must be grounded in multiple perspectives, including host state, configuration state, and external observation where appropriate. When verification is weak, organizations accumulate "paper remediation" that looks clean in dashboards but fails during incidents.

The first layer of verification is confirming that the specific vulnerable condition no longer exists on the targeted assets. That typically means validating version or package state, confirming configuration settings that mitigate the condition, and ensuring the service actually restarted or reloaded the updated component. This work should be structured and consistent, so teams do not rely on informal checks that vary by engineer. Verification should also account for partial deployments, such as clustered services where one node missed the update or ephemeral workloads where old images are still running. The practical goal is to detect gaps immediately, while the change context and rollback options are still available.

External confirmation is a necessary complement to internal state checks because it validates what an attacker would see. If a weakness was discoverable through network interaction, then verification should include re-scanning or targeted probing from relevant vantage points to confirm the exposed surface no longer presents the condition. This is where reachability assumptions are either proven or disproven, and where compensating controls like segmentation can be validated as effective barriers. External checks also catch cases where patching addressed one instance but a duplicate service, alternate port, or shadow deployment remains exposed. Using external confirmation as part of closure reduces the risk of false positives in remediation metrics and improves confidence in reporting to leadership.

Verification must also test for operational correctness, because a fix that breaks service is not a success. Post-change validation should include service health checks, monitoring dashboards, and transaction-level indicators that reflect real user experience. For critical services, this often includes targeted functional testing and capacity observation during the stabilization period after deployment. The organization should define what constitutes acceptable degradation and what triggers rollback, because ambiguity during a maintenance window leads to dangerous hesitancy or premature acceptance. When teams consistently validate both security outcome and service health, they reduce the cultural resistance to remediation that grows after poorly managed changes.

Preventing regression requires understanding why issues recur, not just closing them faster the next time. Regression often happens when teams patch a symptom but the underlying deployment mechanism continues to reintroduce the vulnerable state, such as outdated golden images, unpinned dependencies, or configuration drift. It also happens when emergency fixes are applied manually and never codified into standard build and deployment processes. Durable prevention means translating remediation actions into repeatable automation, whether through image pipelines, baseline enforcement, or standard configuration templates. Organizations that rely on manual, one-off changes tend to see the same findings return with every rebuild, restart, or scaling event.

Configuration management and baseline enforcement are key controls for keeping systems in the remediated state. If a security setting was tightened to eliminate a weakness, that setting should be represented as a baseline that is continuously evaluated and corrected when it drifts. This is especially important in environments where infrastructure is dynamic and changes are frequent, because drift is the normal condition unless constrained. Baselines should be tiered by service criticality and operational tolerance, with stronger controls on high-impact systems and clearer exception pathways where necessary. Without baseline enforcement, teams spend remediation capacity repeatedly fixing the same class of issue rather than moving posture forward.

Evidence handling is part of verification because auditability and accountability depend on traceable artifacts. Closure should capture what changed, when it changed, who approved it, and what evidence confirmed success, including scan results, patch state outputs, and monitoring confirmation. These artifacts support internal governance and reduce friction with external assessments by demonstrating that remediation is controlled and repeatable. Evidence also supports learning, because it allows teams to analyze which remediation approaches are reliable and which introduce instability or incomplete coverage. When evidence is inconsistent or missing, organizations cannot distinguish between real operational improvement and optimistic reporting.

AI/ML can improve verification and regression prevention by correlating telemetry and highlighting anomalies that humans may miss, but it must be constrained by clear controls. Models can flag assets that appear patched internally but still present external indicators, detect recurring drift patterns, and predict which changes are most likely to regress based on historical behavior. These uses depend on high-quality telemetry, including accurate asset identity, patch state reporting, configuration evaluation results, and external scan data, all aligned to consistent service definitions. Human review is essential for closure decisions and for automated remediation actions that could disrupt systems, and the model's reasoning should be explainable enough to support audit trails. Failure modes include false negatives when telemetry coverage is incomplete, drift in model performance as environments change, and false confidence that encourages premature closure, so governance must require periodic validation against ground truth.

Preventing regression ultimately requires aligning incentives and workflows, so remediation becomes part of normal engineering hygiene. Teams should be measured on verified remediation outcomes over time, not on ticket throughput, and regression rates should be visible, so recurring problems trigger platform fixes rather than repeated firefights. When issues recur, the response should include improving upstream controls such as build pipelines, dependency management, and baseline enforcement, rather than simply tightening deadlines. Leadership support matters here, because preventing regression often requires investment in platform engineering and automation rather than more pressure on patch windows. When verification is evidence-based and regression is treated as a root-cause problem, remediation work becomes cumulative progress instead of a perpetual loop.

AI-Assisted Remediation Operations: Routing, Fix Suggestions, and Validation Controls

AI-assisted remediation operations are most effective when they are treated as force multipliers for disciplined workflows rather than replacements for accountable decision-making. At scale, the volume of findings overwhelms purely manual routing and triage, creating delays that have nothing to do with technical difficulty and everything to do with coordination friction. AI can reduce that friction by analyzing historical resolution patterns, asset metadata, and service ownership to propose likely routing paths with far greater consistency than ad hoc human judgment. The value is not speed alone, but reduction in misrouting that causes tickets to stall or bounce between teams. When AI recommendations are positioned as decision support, not automatic assignment, teams gain efficiency without losing accountability.

Routing accuracy depends entirely on the quality of the underlying data, which makes telemetry hygiene a prerequisite rather than an optimization. Asset inventories must be current, service ownership mappings must be enforced, and historical remediation records must be labeled consistently, or the model will amplify organizational confusion instead of resolving it. AI systems trained on stale ownership data or ambiguous service names tend to route work to the wrong queues with high confidence, which erodes trust quickly. Human reviewers should approve or override routing for high-impact systems, shared platforms, and emergency changes, and those overrides should be captured as feedback to improve future recommendations. The operational goal is not perfect routing, but faster convergence on the correct owner with fewer clarification cycles.

Fix suggestion is where AI assistance can deliver meaningful leverage, especially for common vulnerability classes and configuration issues. By correlating asset attributes, platform type, and past successful remediations, models can propose candidate fixes such as specific patch paths, configuration adjustments, or compensating controls that worked in similar contexts. These suggestions should be framed as options with rationale rather than prescriptive instructions, because environmental nuance often determines feasibility. Engineers should see why a fix is being suggested, what assumptions it relies on, and what risks it carries, so they can validate it against current service behavior. When fix suggestions are opaque or overconfident, teams either ignore them entirely or apply them blindly, both of which undermine operational safety.

AI-assisted remediation must respect approval boundaries that reflect change risk and business impact. Low-risk, well-understood fixes may be candidates for semi-automated execution under defined conditions, but changes affecting critical services, authentication paths, or network exposure should always require explicit human approval. These boundaries should be policy-driven and visible, not embedded implicitly in model behavior, so teams understand when automation will pause and why. Approval workflows should capture who approved the action, what evidence was reviewed, and what rollback plan exists, because those details are essential when something goes wrong. Without clear boundaries, AI systems can create the illusion of control while quietly shifting risk to unaccountable automation.

Validation is the most underappreciated aspect of AI-assisted remediation, and it is where many programs quietly fail. Models can help determine whether remediation was effective by correlating internal patch state, configuration baselines, and external observations to identify inconsistencies. For example, AI can flag assets that report a patched version internally but still present external indicators of vulnerability, or detect drift patterns where remediated states revert within hours or days. These signals are only as good as the telemetry feeding them, which means validation models must be constrained to environments where coverage is known and monitored. Human reviewers should make final closure decisions for high-risk items, using AI output as evidence rather than authority.

Failure modes are predictable and must be explicitly managed if AI-assisted remediation is to remain trustworthy. Models can develop bias toward teams that historically close tickets quickly, deprioritizing complex but high-risk systems that move more slowly. They can drift as architectures evolve, continuing to recommend fixes that no longer apply or routing work based on outdated service structures. They can also create false confidence when telemetry gaps exist, marking issues as resolved because signals are missing rather than because conditions are safe. Governance must include periodic model validation against real outcomes, review of false positives and false negatives, and clear processes for suspending automation when confidence degrades.

Data protection and auditability are non-negotiable in AI-assisted remediation operations. Remediation data often includes sensitive asset details, configuration states, and access patterns that must be protected through strict access controls and retention limits. Model inputs and outputs should be logged in a way that supports later audit without exposing unnecessary detail to broad audiences. This audit trail is critical not only for compliance, but for incident response, when teams need to understand what actions were taken, why they were taken, and whether automation contributed to the outcome. AI systems that cannot explain their recommendations or reconstruct decision context should not be trusted with operational remediation workflows.

The measure of success for AI-assisted remediation is not how much work is automated, but how reliably risk is reduced without increasing operational instability. Programs should track whether AI routing reduces time-to-owner, whether fix suggestions decrease rework and regression, and whether validation controls catch failures earlier in the change lifecycle. Leaders should also watch for behavioral signals, such as whether engineers engage with suggestions thoughtfully or treat them as noise, because trust is earned through consistent, explainable performance. When AI is integrated with clear approval boundaries, strong telemetry, and disciplined verification, it becomes a durable enhancement to remediation operations rather than a fragile shortcut.

Managing Emergency Patching and Rapid Response

Emergency patching is the controlled acceleration of change when the cost of delay exceeds the operational risk of moving quickly. It exists for moments when credible exploitation, high exposure, or severe impact makes routine maintenance cadence insufficient. The goal is not to patch everything fast; it is to reduce the specific risk that is most likely to harm the organization in the near term. Emergency patching fails when it becomes improvisation, because rushed change without structure produces outages, incomplete coverage, and unresolved root causes. A disciplined rapid response posture treats emergency patching as a rehearsed operational capability with clear triggers, roles, and evidence requirements.

Triggering an emergency patch cycle requires explicit criteria and documented justification to prevent "emergency" from becoming a convenient label. Indicators may include validated exploitation in the wild, direct observation of scanning or exploit attempts against the organization, or a weakness on highly exposed systems where compromise would be catastrophic. The decision should be tied to environmental facts such as reachability, privilege implications, and the presence or absence of compensating controls, not just generalized severity. The trigger record should capture what is known, what is uncertain, and what assumptions are being made, because uncertainty is common early in fast-moving events. Making the rationale explicit preserves trust with engineering and operations teams, who must accept elevated change risk to move quickly.

Rapid response begins with scoping, because emergency conditions create a natural tendency to overreact and spread effort too thin. Scoping means identifying which assets are actually affected, which are exposed in meaningful ways, and which services would create the highest impact if compromised. This requires accurate asset inventory and service mapping, and it often benefits from correlating vulnerability data with network exposure and identity telemetry to avoid chasing non-applicable targets. In emergency mode, it is acceptable to begin with conservative assumptions, but those assumptions must be refined quickly as evidence arrives. The program should also explicitly identify what is out of scope for the initial wave, so teams can focus on immediate risk reduction without creating the false impression that everything will be addressed at once.

Execution depends on converting the emergency objective into a change plan that preserves essential safety checks while compressing timeline. Minimum viable change control should include a tested deployment method, a rollback path, and defined verification steps, even if broader regression testing must be abbreviated. Staged rollout patterns, such as canarying or ring-based deployment, reduce blast radius and allow teams to learn from early failures without halting the entire response. If patch deployment is not feasible within the required window, the plan should pivot to compensating controls that measurably reduce exposure, such as tightening network access, disabling vulnerable features, or increasing authentication requirements. The most dangerous posture in an emergency is to do nothing while waiting for perfect clarity, because attackers rarely wait for governance to catch up.

Coordination is the difference between rapid response and rapid confusion, especially when multiple teams share ownership across infrastructure, platforms, and applications. An emergency patch cycle needs a clear decision authority, a documented communication channel, and a lightweight but disciplined method for tracking actions and outcomes. Teams must know who can approve accelerated changes, who owns validation, and who communicates status to leadership and stakeholders. Coordination should also include operations coverage for monitoring and recovery, because emergency changes often occur outside normal support hours. When communication is fragmented, teams duplicate work, miss critical systems, or deploy inconsistent fixes that are difficult to verify later.

Verification in emergency patching must be ruthless about evidence, because the pace of change increases the likelihood of incomplete coverage. Technical verification should confirm patch state or configuration mitigation on targeted systems, and external verification should confirm that the exposed condition is no longer observable from relevant vantage points. Verification should also include service health monitoring to detect degradation early, since emergency changes that destabilize critical services can cause immediate business impact. Closure criteria should be explicit, and items should not be marked complete based on "attempted" or "scheduled" actions. In emergency conditions, optimistic closure is not just inaccurate reporting; it is an operational blind spot that can allow ongoing compromise.

Risk acceptance and exceptions still apply during emergencies, but they must be handled with tighter time bounds and clearer compensating controls. Some systems will be unable to patch quickly due to legacy constraints, vendor dependencies, or unacceptable change risk, and those cases must be elevated for explicit decision rather than silently deferred. The exception record should specify interim controls and an accelerated plan for durable remediation, because emergency conditions amplify the cost of leaving weak points unresolved. Exceptions should also be revisited immediately after the crisis phase, when teams have more bandwidth to address underlying constraints. Allowing emergency-driven exceptions to persist unreviewed is how short-term firefighting becomes long-term exposure.

AI/ML can support emergency patching by accelerating triage, routing, and validation, but it must be constrained to avoid amplifying uncertainty. Models can help identify likely affected asset clusters, prioritize targets based on exposure and criticality signals, and surface anomalies in telemetry that suggest exploitation attempts or incomplete mitigation. These outputs are only as good as the data feeding them, so teams must be cautious when coverage is incomplete or rapidly changing. Human approval boundaries should tighten rather than loosen for high-impact changes, and AI outputs should be treated as leads that require validation, not as authoritative conclusions. Failure modes include drift in model behavior under novel conditions, false confidence from sparse data, and biased prioritization toward assets with better telemetry rather than assets with higher true risk.

After the immediate risk is reduced, rapid response must transition into stabilization and follow-through, because emergencies often reveal structural weaknesses in patch operations. Teams should reconcile what was changed, verify that fixes are durable, and identify any missed assets or services that require follow-up work. Root causes such as weak asset inventory, insufficient maintenance cadence, or brittle deployment pipelines should be captured and translated into program improvements while memory is fresh. Metrics should focus on operational outcomes like time-to-mitigation, verified coverage of in-scope assets, and service stability during the emergency window, not just the number of patches applied. When emergency patching is rehearsed, evidence-driven, and coupled with disciplined verification and post-event hardening, it becomes a controllable capability rather than a recurring organizational trauma.

Conclusion

The measurable outcome of defensive operations is not the number of findings discovered, but the organization's ability to reduce exposure through controlled, verifiable change. When prioritization criteria are applied consistently and tradeoffs are documented, remediation work becomes predictable instead of reactive and trust improves across security, IT, and engineering. A mature patch program pairs cadence with emergency acceleration, uses compensating controls when patching is delayed, and closes the loop with verification that prevents regression and "paper remediation." The organizations that perform best treat exceptions as time-bound decisions with real controls, use AI assistance within auditable approval boundaries, and maintain operational discipline even under rapid response pressure.

Recommendations

1) Establish a consistent process for converting findings into executable work items. Capture affected assets, evidence, exposure conditions, and a concrete definition of "done," so teams can act without clarification cycles. Include dependencies like maintenance windows, approvals, and rollback expectations to prevent tickets from stalling. Require verification artifacts at closure, so progress reflects real risk reduction rather than ticket movement.
2) Define and apply prioritization criteria using environmental facts rather than generalized severity labels. Incorporate exploitability, exposure, and business criticality, so priorities reflect local reality and mission impact. Record uncertainty explicitly when telemetry is incomplete, so teams do not treat a ranking as infallible. Use the same criteria across teams to prevent prioritization from becoming a political negotiation.
3) Align patch operations to a predictable cadence while maintaining a documented acceleration path for urgent conditions. Use regular maintenance rhythms for standard updates and a governed emergency process when credible exploitation or high exposure demands speed. Preserve minimum viable change control during acceleration by requiring rollback planning and defined validation steps. Avoid normalizing "emergency" as a default, because it erodes stability and long-term capacity planning.
4) Coordinate remediation work through clear service ownership mapping and disciplined routing. Ensure every finding can be assigned to a team that can execute the change and a service owner accountable for the business tradeoffs. Provide decision-grade context in each ticket, including proposed remediation path and verification criteria, to reduce friction with IT and engineering. Escalate ownership disputes through a procedural path that resolves ambiguity quickly without relying on personal influence.
5) Treat maintenance windows as a managed operational resource that includes time for verification and stabilization. Define entry criteria such as testing completion, backup readiness, and rollback planning, so windows are used for execution rather than discovery. Sequence work into windows based on exposure and impact, not convenience or queue pressure. Plan catch-up runs for missed assets, so "offline during window" does not become permanent drift.
6) Implement compensating controls as time-bound, evidence-backed safeguards when patching is delayed. Reduce exposure quickly through access restriction, segmentation, configuration hardening, privilege reduction, or targeted monitoring based on the specific vulnerable condition. Verify that compensating controls are actually in effect and measurably reducing attack paths rather than existing only in documentation. Tie each control to an expiration and a durable remediation plan, so interim measures do not become permanent architecture by neglect.
7) Require multi-layer verification before closing remediation work to prevent paper remediation. Confirm internal state, such as patch level or configuration settings, and validate externally when the condition was observable from relevant vantage points. Include service health checks to ensure security fixes do not introduce

instability that creates new business risk. Track partial deployments and missed nodes explicitly, so clustered or distributed services do not regress unnoticed.

8) Prevent regression by translating one-time fixes into durable automation and baseline enforcement. Update golden images, deployment pipelines, and configuration baselines, so remediated states persist through rebuilds, restarts, and scaling events. Use continuous evaluation to detect drift early and correct it before findings reappear at scale. Treat recurring issues as signals of upstream platform weaknesses rather than as repeated ticket closures.
9) Use AI assistance to improve routing, fix suggestions, and validation only within clear human approval boundaries. Feed models with reliable asset inventory, ownership mapping, patch state, and exposure telemetry, so recommendations are grounded in accurate context. Require explainable inputs and retained decision evidence, so AI output supports auditability rather than replacing accountability. Monitor for failure modes such as drift, bias toward easily patched systems, and false confidence when telemetry is incomplete.
10) Manage emergency patching as a rehearsed rapid response capability with explicit triggers and tight evidence requirements. Scope quickly to the assets and services that are truly affected and exposed, and pivot to compensating controls when patch deployment cannot meet the required timeline. Maintain coordinated communication, defined authority for accelerated changes, and rigorous verification to avoid incomplete coverage under pressure. Transition from crisis execution to stabilization by reconciling changes and translating lessons into patch program improvements.

Part V

Visibility, Monitoring, and Threat Detection

18

Logging Strategy and Telemetry Management

Visibility determines whether a security team is operating from evidence or from assumptions, and logging strategy is the discipline that makes that evidence dependable. Telemetry is only valuable when it is attributable, timely, consistent, and trustworthy enough to support decisions in detection engineering and incident response. When collection pipelines are fragile, schemas drift, or access and integrity controls are weak, defenders lose the ability to reconstruct what happened and attackers gain room to maneuver. This chapter establishes how to think about "good telemetry," how to manage it across endpoint, network, identity, and cloud sources, and how to operationalize ownership, quality, and AI-assisted enrichment so visibility becomes a reliable foundation for detection.

Why Visibility Is the Foundation of Detection

Detection is not something a team "adds" at the end of an architecture diagram; it is a direct consequence of what a system reveals about itself under normal and abnormal conditions. Every alert, investigation, and containment action is anchored in observable evidence: an authentication event, a process start, a network connection, a configuration change, or a workload identity assuming privileges. When those observations do not exist, are not collected, or cannot be trusted, detection engineering turns into guesswork and incident response becomes a debate about what might have happened. This is why visibility is foundational: it converts security from intuition into a measurable discipline that can be tested, tuned, and audited.

Operationally, "visibility" means more than having logs somewhere; it means having telemetry that is complete enough to reconstruct decisions and actions across identities, endpoints, applications, and infrastructure. The difference between partial and usable visibility is whether analysts can answer basic questions quickly: who did what, from where, using what identity, against what resource, and with what outcome. In a modern environment, those questions span human accounts, service accounts, workload identities, API tokens, and ephemeral compute, which makes gaps easy to create and hard to notice. A detection program that cannot reliably tie actions to identities or link a cloud control-plane event to an endpoint execution is forced into broad, noisy detections that either overwhelm staff or get ignored.

Good detection depends on context as much as it depends on raw events, because isolated signals rarely distinguish malicious behavior from normal operations. Authentication logs are more valuable when enriched with device posture, geolocation history, session risk, and privilege level; network flow becomes more actionable when tied to process lineage and DNS resolution; cloud audit events become meaningful when linked to the repository change or pipeline run that triggered them. That enrichment is not a luxury—it is what prevents over-alerting on expected automation and helps teams spot subtle abuse of legitimate tools. The goal is to make telemetry narrate the story of the environment, so investigations require fewer assumptions and fewer manual data pulls.

Visibility also has to be designed for timeliness and integrity, not just coverage. Late-arriving logs, inconsistent timestamps, or telemetry that drops during peak load create blind spots precisely when an attacker is most likely to be active. Similarly, if a compromised host can tamper with its own logs or block egress to the collection pipeline, the evidence becomes unreliable, and the organization loses the ability to prove what occurred. Mature programs treat telemetry as a protected asset: they harden collection paths, validate ingestion health, and monitor for log suppression behaviors as first-class detection use cases. Without that, attackers do not need to evade detections—they simply need to break the sensors.

The business impact of visibility decisions shows up in the cost curve of every incident. When the right telemetry is present, analysts confirm scope quickly, contain with confidence, and minimize unnecessary disruption to production systems. When telemetry is missing, teams compensate with expensive and risky actions: wider account resets, broader network blocks, longer downtime while evidence is gathered, and heavier reliance on external forensics. Executives often experience this as a "slow" security team, but the root cause is frequently an architectural choice that treated logs as optional or deprioritized the engineering work needed to make them reliable. Investing in visibility is therefore not simply a security preference; it is a resilience decision that reduces the duration and uncertainty of high-impact events.

AI and machine learning can improve detection outcomes, but only when the underlying telemetry is consistent, well-labeled, and governed. Models that cluster behaviors, score anomalies, or prioritize investigations depend on stable event schemas, accurate timestamps, and sufficient historical baselines to distinguish seasonal operational changes from true threats. When inputs are incomplete or biased toward certain systems, ML can produce false confidence—high-risk scores that cannot be explained, or low-risk scores that hide novel attacker behavior because the model never saw comparable activity. Human-in-the-loop controls are essential: analysts should be able to trace why a model surfaced an event, review the contributing evidence, and override or annotate outcomes so the system learns without silently drifting. Governance matters as well, because telemetry used for AI-driven detection may include sensitive identifiers and operational details, requiring access controls, retention discipline, and auditability of model decisions.

A visibility-first approach also improves detection engineering quality by making detections testable and maintainable rather than symbolic. When telemetry is standardized, engineers can write detections that are precise—tied to specific event types and fields—and validate them against known-good activity as well as adversary simulations. When telemetry is inconsistent, detections become fragile, relying on string matching or overly broad patterns that break during routine system changes. This fragility creates a cycle where alerts are tuned down to reduce noise, coverage quietly deteriorates, and teams lose confidence in the monitoring program. Reliable telemetry breaks that cycle by letting detections evolve with the environment through controlled changes, versioned schemas, and observable impact on alert quality.

Common pitfalls in logging strategy usually stem from treating collection as the finish line instead of the starting point. Organizations centralize large volumes of logs but fail to define what "complete" means for critical assets, leaving invisible segments such as unmanaged endpoints, third-party SaaS administrative actions, or key identity providers. They capture events but do not validate them, so gaps go unnoticed until an incident reveals that a critical log source was misconfigured, filtered, or silently failing. They also overlook the operational realities of telemetry management: retention that is too short to support investigations, normalization that is inconsistent across teams, and access models that either block responders or expose sensitive data too broadly. Visibility becomes foundational only when it is engineered as a dependable service with clear expectations, measurable health, and accountable ownership.

Defining What "Good Telemetry" Looks Like

Good telemetry is not defined by volume or by the number of sources connected to a central platform; it is defined by whether the organization can reliably answer operational questions during detection and response. At minimum, telemetry must make it possible to reconstruct a sequence of actions with confidence, including who initiated an action, what changed, where it occurred, and how the environment reacted. This requires events that are attributable to identities, anchored in accurate time, and expressed in a consistent structure so they can be searched and correlated at speed. Telemetry that cannot support attribution and reconstruction might still be "data," but it is not operationally good.

A practical way to recognize good telemetry is to evaluate it against decision points, not against logging checklists. When an alert fires, analysts immediately need enough context to determine whether the activity is plausible, whether it is privileged, and what the blast radius could be. That context depends on fields that are routinely missing in poor implementations: stable identifiers, source and destination details, action outcomes, and the state of the object being modified. Good telemetry makes those attributes available without requiring custom enrichment every time an incident occurs, which reduces investigative friction and improves response consistency. Poor telemetry forces teams into time-consuming pivots across systems, where each gap introduces delay and increases the chance of missed scope. Table 18.1 summarizes the defining traits of good telemetry and how to validate each trait operationally.

Consistency is one of the most important characteristics of good telemetry, because detection logic depends on predictable semantics. Events should have stable schemas and field meanings across time, environments, and ingestion paths, so the same action produces the same observable footprint regardless of where it occurs. If one team logs "user" as an email address while another logs a display name, or if a cloud action is sometimes recorded as success without a corresponding failure path, detections become brittle and investigations become ambiguous. Good telemetry also includes explicit outcomes and error codes, because failures are often more diagnostic than successes, especially for credential abuse, privilege escalation attempts, and discovery behaviors. When outcomes are omitted, the defender loses the ability to distinguish probing from execution and normal retries from hostile persistence.

Completeness must be defined deliberately, because "logging everything" is not achievable or desirable in most environments. Good telemetry focuses on high-value actions and high-risk objects: authentication, authorization decisions, privilege changes, process and module execution, administrative operations, network connections that cross trust boundaries, and changes to security controls themselves. The most damaging gaps are usually not in exotic signals but in basic event categories that were filtered for cost or performance reasons. A program that captures endpoint process starts but misses identity provider sign-in details will struggle to determine whether activity was driven by a valid user session or a stolen token. Good telemetry is complete enough across layers that investigators can follow the chain from identity to execution to impact without hitting a dead end.

Table 18.1 Telemetry Quality Characteristics and Operational Tests.

Quality Characteristic	What It Enables	Operational Test Example	Common Failure Signal
Attribution	Tie actions to identities and assets	Confirm stable identity and asset IDs appear on key events	Events lack object IDs or identities vary by source
Consistency	Detections work across time and environments	Validate same action produces same fields across systems	Schema drift breaks field meanings
Completeness	Reconstruct timelines without dead ends	Trace identity to execution to impact across sources	Missing a layer such as identity or control plane
Timeliness	Near real time detection and response	Measure ingestion delay against defined thresholds	Alerts become delayed reporting
Integrity	Trust evidence under adversarial conditions	Detect sudden drops or suppression attempts	Quiet streams during active sessions
Usability	Fast search pivots and correlation	Verify normalized fields and raw events are both available	Normalization strips nuance or raw is missing

Timeliness and reliability separate telemetry that supports detection from telemetry that only supports retrospectives. Detection depends on near-real-time availability of events and predictable ingestion behavior under load, during outages, and during incident conditions. If telemetry arrives hours late, detections degrade into historical reporting and containment decisions are made without current situational awareness. Reliability also includes visibility into pipeline health: collectors, forwarders, buffers, and ingestion endpoints should emit their own status telemetry so failures are detected as quickly as attacks. Good telemetry therefore includes meta-telemetry about telemetry, because blind spots rarely announce themselves in the primary logs.

Integrity and trust are essential because attackers frequently attempt to tamper with or evade collection mechanisms. Good telemetry designs assume hostile conditions and ensure that critical events are resistant to manipulation, either by collecting from authoritative sources, using tamper-evident mechanisms, or forwarding data in ways that a compromised host cannot easily suppress. It is not enough for an endpoint to "say" something happened; the defender needs corroboration across independent signals such as identity events, network observations, and control-plane audit logs. Good telemetry also makes log absence meaningful by enabling detections for suppression behaviors, such as sudden drops in expected event rates or service stoppages that affect monitoring agents. When integrity is not engineered, an adversary can win simply by degrading evidence, leaving teams with plausible deniability and incomplete timelines.

Good telemetry is also usable, which means it is normalized, enriched appropriately, and governed so the right people can act on it without creating new risks. Normalization should align to consistent naming and time handling so correlation does not depend on custom parsing in every detection. Enrichment should add durable context—asset identity, ownership, criticality, environment, and privilege tier—without turning the pipeline into an opaque transformation that analysts cannot reason about. Governance must define access boundaries, because telemetry often contains sensitive identifiers and operational details that are valuable to defenders and attackers alike. If analysts cannot access data quickly during an incident, or if access is so broad that telemetry becomes a liability, the program fails its operational purpose.

AI and machine learning can help define and measure "good" by continuously evaluating telemetry quality and by making detection workflows more efficient, but only if their use is controlled and auditable. Models can flag unusual gaps, schema drifts, or shifts in baseline event volumes that indicate collection failures, and they can prioritize which missing signals most degrade detection coverage. Those same models can also mislead if input data is biased toward certain systems or if changes in operations look like anomalies, which is why human review of model outputs and clear approval boundaries are mandatory. Teams should be able to explain why an AI-driven quality score changed, what underlying signals contributed, and what remediation action is recommended. When telemetry quality becomes a measurable, monitored capability—with humans accountable for interpretation and follow-through—"good telemetry" stops being a vague aspiration and becomes an operational standard that can be sustained.

Log Sources: Endpoint, Network, Identity, and Cloud

Endpoint telemetry is often where detection becomes tangible, because it captures the actions that actually execute on a system: processes starting, binaries being written, modules being loaded, persistence mechanisms being created, and security controls being modified. The operational value of endpoint logs comes from their ability to show intent and sequence, such as a parent process spawning a child process that reaches out to an unfamiliar destination and then modifies a credential store. Good endpoint telemetry also preserves enough context to separate routine administrative activity from suspicious behavior, including user session details, privilege level, command-line arguments, and the integrity state of the host. When endpoint logging is treated as optional or limited to antivirus-style alerts, defenders lose the ground truth needed to validate whether a threat is real and to understand what it did.

Network telemetry complements endpoints by revealing communications patterns and boundary crossings that endpoints may not see or may be able to obscure. Flow records, connection logs, DNS queries, and proxy logs provide a consistent lens on where systems are talking, when, and in what volume, even when the payload is encrypted. This is essential for detecting command-and-control behavior, data staging and exfiltration patterns, and lateral movement that leverages standard protocols. Network logs become substantially more valuable when they can be tied back to assets and identities, because "host A connected to host B" is far less actionable than "a privileged workstation associated with a specific admin session connected to a sensitive subnet from an unusual location." The practical failure mode is relying on network telemetry alone and expecting it to substitute for endpoint evidence; without process context and authentication linkage, network detections often become high-noise indicators of normal business activity.

Identity telemetry is the connective tissue across the environment, because modern attacks frequently begin and end with abuse of authentication and authorization rather than exploitation of a single host. Sign-in events, token issuance, MFA challenges, session creation, privilege assignments, and directory changes explain how an attacker gained access and how that access expanded over time. Identity logs also provide the strongest attribution data when they are well-structured, because they can anchor actions to an account, a device, a conditional access decision, and an authentication method. Poor identity telemetry creates a damaging ambiguity where teams can see suspicious actions but cannot prove whether they were driven by a compromised user, a misconfigured service account, or expected automation. Strong identity visibility is therefore foundational to reducing blast radius quickly, because containment actions—disabling accounts, revoking tokens, forcing reauthentication—are only effective when teams understand which identity objects are in play.

Cloud telemetry introduces a distinct category of evidence: control-plane activity that describes how the environment itself is being configured and operated. Administrative actions against cloud resources, changes to network security rules, alterations to logging configurations, creation of new identities or access keys, and modifications to storage permissions often occur without any endpoint footprint at all. Because cloud resources can be created and destroyed rapidly, cloud audit logs are frequently the only durable record of how an attacker moved from one capability to another. This makes completeness and retention especially critical, because a short-lived resource may be gone before responders even know it existed. When cloud control-plane telemetry is missing or fragmented, attackers can manipulate infrastructure and access paths in ways that are invisible to traditional perimeter and endpoint monitoring. Table 18.2 shows how endpoint network identity and cloud telemetry combine to form an investigation timeline and where gaps create risk.

Table 18.2 Log Source Roles and What They Answer in an Investigation.

Log Source Category	Primary Question Answered	High Value Evidence Example	Typical Blind Spot if Missing
Endpoint	How did it execute	Process start with parent chain and session context	No ground truth for local execution or persistence
Network	Where did it communicate	Connections and DNS patterns across trust boundaries	No visibility into exfil patterns or lateral paths
Identity	Who authenticated and was authorized	Sign in session token and privilege assignment outcomes	Ambiguous actor and weak containment targeting
Cloud control plane	What changed in the environment	Administrative actions permission changes logging changes	Invisible infrastructure manipulation
Cross source correlation	How events link into a single timeline	Stable IDs across identity endpoint network cloud	Investigations stall due to unpivotable identifiers

The most effective detection programs treat these sources as a coordinated system rather than as independent feeds. An identity event provides the "who," an endpoint event provides the "how," a cloud audit event provides the "what changed," and a network event provides the "where it communicated," and good investigations stitch these into a single timeline. This correlation depends on stable identifiers such as device IDs, account IDs, workload identity identifiers, and resource IDs, as well as accurate time synchronization across sources. Without that, responders end up correlating by guesswork, matching on partial usernames or IP addresses that change frequently, which increases both time-to-triage and the risk of false scoping. Good telemetry design anticipates these correlation needs by ensuring that each source includes the linkable fields required to pivot cleanly across layers.

There are predictable blind spots that emerge when organizations overemphasize one source category and underinvest in the others. Endpoint-heavy programs may be strong at detecting malware but weaker at spotting session hijacking, token abuse, and cloud administrative manipulation that never touches a traditional workstation. Network-heavy programs can flag unusual destinations but may miss the local execution chain and therefore struggle to determine whether a connection represents a legitimate business workflow or malicious staging. Identity-only monitoring can surface suspicious logins but may fail to detect what happened after access was obtained, leading to incomplete containment decisions. Cloud-only visibility can show configuration drift while missing endpoint-level exploitation that initiated the drift, and it can miss on-premises or hybrid pathways that bridge into cloud resources. A balanced approach treats gaps as operational risk, not as technical debt, because attackers will reliably choose the least-visible route.

AI and machine learning can amplify the value of multi-source telemetry by helping teams prioritize correlations and identify patterns that span layers, but the quality of the result is bounded by input fidelity. Models can learn typical identity-to-endpoint-to-network sequences for specific roles and workloads and then surface deviations that warrant review, such as a service account suddenly initiating interactive sign-ins or a developer workstation triggering control-plane changes outside normal hours. These systems must remain human-supervised, because model-driven correlation can create false confidence when data is incomplete, mislabeled, or drifting due to business changes like new deployment pipelines. Practical controls include requiring analysts to validate AI-suggested linkages before they drive containment, logging the rationale for model outputs, and monitoring for drift in both telemetry schemas and operational baselines. When AI is used to accelerate triage rather than to replace judgment, and when telemetry across endpoint, network, identity, and cloud is engineered for correlation, detection becomes faster, more accurate, and more defensible under scrutiny.

Collection, Normalization, and Retention Considerations

Collection is the engineering discipline that turns "we have logs" into "we can depend on logs," and it starts with designing for coverage, reliability, and failure visibility rather than simply onboarding sources. Teams need clear expectations for what must be collected from endpoints, network controls, identity services, and cloud control planes, with explicit definitions of critical events and required fields. Collection paths should be resilient to routine disruptions like endpoint reboots, network segmentation changes, and intermittent connectivity, because the moments that stress infrastructure are often the same moments that attackers exploit. Good collection also includes feedback mechanisms so operators can detect when a source is silent, when event rates drop unexpectedly, or when ingestion latency grows beyond operational thresholds.

A common mistake is assuming that collection is a single hop from source to central store, when in reality it is a pipeline with multiple potential choke points. Agents, forwarders, relays, and ingestion endpoints each introduce configuration complexity and each can fail in ways that are not obvious from the logs themselves. Buffers and back-pressure controls matter because they determine whether outages create delayed telemetry or permanent loss, and whether high-volume sources starve out high-value sources during spikes. Collection designs should explicitly address time synchronization, because inconsistent clocks destroy correlation and can create misleading narratives during incident reconstruction. Treating pipeline health as first-class telemetry—measuring dropped events, queue depth, parsing failures, and source freshness—turns collection from a best-effort activity into an operational capability.

Normalization is what makes telemetry usable at scale, because detection and response require consistent semantics across heterogeneous systems. At a practical level, normalization includes consistent time handling, consistent identity representations, and consistent naming for common actions such as authentication, privilege change, object modification, and network connection. It also includes preserving the original raw event alongside normalized fields, because responders often need the authoritative source record during investigations and audits. Over-normalization can be as damaging as under-normalization if it strips nuance, collapses important distinctions, or makes it impossible to determine how a derived field was produced. The goal is to create a stable "common shape" for search and correlation while keeping enough fidelity to support deeper analysis and defensible incident reporting.

Field-level consistency is where normalization succeeds or fails, and identity is the most frequent pain point. Usernames, email addresses, directory object IDs, workload identity identifiers, and token subject claims can all refer to the same actor, but they appear differently depending on the system and event type. Good normalization strategies preserve multiple identity attributes and establish a canonical identifier for correlation, so an investigation does not stall because a display name changed or an email alias was introduced. Similar discipline is needed for asset identity, where hostnames, instance IDs, IP addresses, and container identifiers often shift over time. If normalization does not account for these realities, detections become brittle and analysts spend their time resolving naming mismatches rather than investigating threats.

Retention is often framed as a compliance requirement, but operationally it is a risk decision that determines how far back a team can reliably investigate and how well it can detect slow-moving or stealthy campaigns. Short retention windows create a false sense of safety because they preserve only the period when an incident was discovered, not the period when it began. Many intrusions involve credential abuse, dormant persistence, and staged privilege changes that unfold over weeks or months, and scoping those incidents requires historical telemetry from identity, endpoint, and control-plane sources. Retention should therefore be aligned to investigative reality, including the time it takes to detect certain classes of abuse, the time it takes to access logs during legal or HR processes, and the time needed to validate that remediation actions truly removed attacker access. When retention is inadequate, teams compensate with assumptions, which increases the likelihood of incomplete eradication and repeat compromise.

Cost and performance constraints are real, and mature programs manage them through selective fidelity rather than blunt reductions. Not all telemetry needs the same retention, the same granularity, or the same ingestion priority, and the most effective approaches treat storage and search as tiered capabilities. High-value security events and audit logs typically warrant longer retention and faster query access, while high-volume, lower-value streams may be summarized, sampled, or retained for shorter periods provided the decision is intentional and documented. The danger is reducing fidelity without understanding which detections and investigations depend on it, which can silently erase coverage for key behaviors such as lateral movement, privilege escalation, or data access. Decisions about filtering, sampling, and aggregation should be made with detection engineers and incident responders in the loop, because they understand which fields and event types are operationally load-bearing.

AI and machine learning can help manage collection, normalization, and retention by monitoring quality and recommending optimizations, but they must be governed to avoid automation-driven blind spots. Models can detect schema drift, identify sources whose event patterns have changed unexpectedly, and flag periods where collection looks suspiciously quiet, enabling teams to fix issues before they become incident-critical. They can also assist in retention strategy by analyzing which data types contribute most to successful investigations and which streams primarily generate noise, guiding rational tiering decisions. The failure modes are predictable: models can mistake business-driven changes for anomalies, can underweight rare but critical events, or can inherit bias from incomplete telemetry that overrepresents certain environments. Human approval boundaries, explainability of recommendations, and auditable change control are essential so that telemetry management remains accountable and defensible. When collection is engineered for resilience, normalization is designed for consistent meaning, and retention is aligned to investigative needs, telemetry becomes a durable operational asset instead of a fragile byproduct.

Managing Gaps, Failures, and Quality Issues

Telemetry gaps are inevitable in complex environments, but unmanaged gaps quietly become a structural advantage for attackers. The goal is not to claim perfect coverage; it is to make gaps visible, bounded, and routinely reduced. That starts with treating telemetry as a production service with defined expectations for freshness, completeness, and field quality across the sources that matter most. When those expectations are explicit, a missing log stream is not a vague concern—it is an operational incident with a clear owner, a measurable impact, and a tracked resolution. Without that discipline, organizations discover gaps only after an incident, when it is too late to reconstruct what happened.

Gaps often originate in predictable places: unmanaged endpoints, newly deployed cloud services, third-party SaaS platforms, and segments where network controls or agents were never operationalized. They also appear during change events such as OS upgrades, agent version changes, network redesigns, or identity provider migrations, where schemas shift and collection defaults change. A practical approach is to define minimum telemetry requirements for asset classes and enforce them as part of onboarding and change control, so new systems cannot silently enter production without visibility. For hybrid and ephemeral environments, gap management must account for short-lived resources, where the time between creation and destruction is shorter than the time it takes to notice missing telemetry. In these cases, the control-plane record of resource creation and configuration becomes part of gap detection, because it can reveal assets that should be producing logs but are not. Figure 18.1 illustrates how telemetry health is maintained through continuous monitoring of pipeline conditions and focused remediation of gaps and failures. It reinforces that quality issues are often partial degradations such as latency creep and parsing regressions and that silence can be a signal.

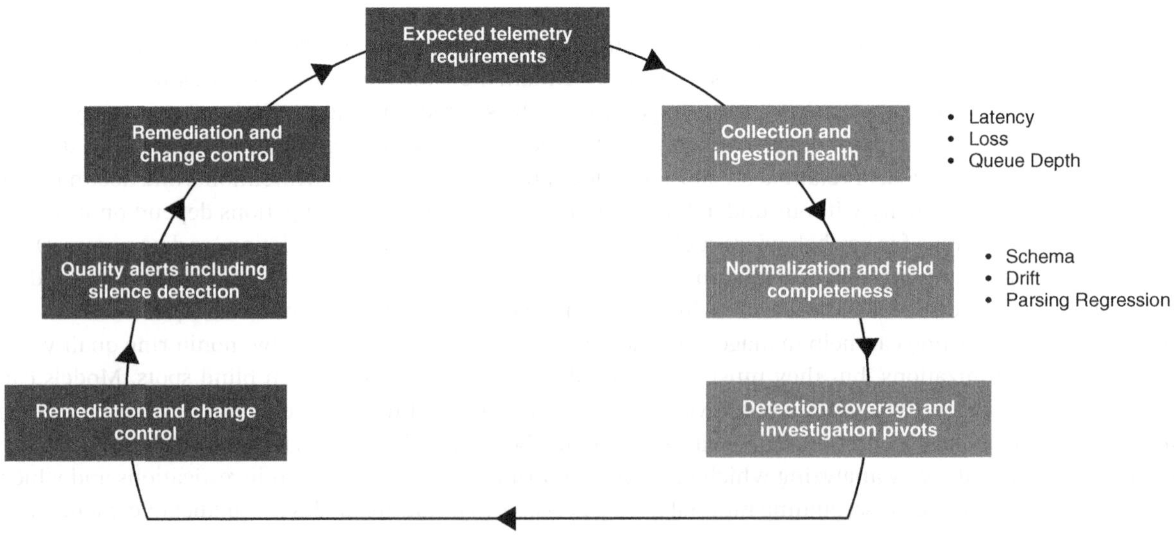

Figure 18.1 Telemetry Pipeline Quality Loop: Detect Degradation and Restore Trust.

Failure modes in the telemetry pipeline are rarely dramatic; they are usually partial degradations that look like "normal variance" until they accumulate. Event drops can occur at endpoints due to local buffering limits, at forwarders due to queue saturation, or at ingestion due to parsing failures and throttling. Latency can creep upward during peak business periods, turning real-time detection into delayed reporting. Parsing can break silently when a vendor updates log formats or when teams modify filters, resulting in normalized fields going blank even though raw events still arrive. Effective management requires instrumentation of the pipeline itself—tracking event rates by source, parsing success rates, queue depth, and end-to-end delay—so operators can distinguish real environmental changes from collection failure.

Quality issues are not limited to missing data; they include data that is present but misleading. Inconsistent timestamps, duplicated events, ambiguous identity fields, and missing action outcomes can cause responders to draw the wrong conclusions under pressure. A common example is an authentication event stream that records attempts but not results, making it difficult to distinguish brute-force probing from successful access. Another is endpoint telemetry that captures process starts but omits command-line detail, removing the context that differentiates routine administrative tools from malicious execution. Quality management therefore needs explicit validation checks that focus on the fields that detections and investigations depend on, not just on whether events exist in bulk. Table 18.3 links common telemetry degradation patterns to their operational impacts and the first steps to restore visibility.

Operationally, teams should manage telemetry health with the same rigor they apply to uptime and performance monitoring. Source-level service objectives—such as maximum acceptable ingestion delay, minimum expected event rates for key sources, and acceptable parsing error thresholds—make telemetry health measurable. When those objectives are violated, the response should be routine: triage the cause, restore expected behavior, and document the impact on detection and investigative capability during the affected window. This is also where ownership matters, because security teams often depend on infrastructure, identity, and application teams to remediate the root cause. Clear escalation paths and shared accountability prevent telemetry issues from being treated as "security's problem" without the authority to fix it.

Managing gaps also means designing detections that account for uncertainty, including detections that notice absence as a signal. If a critical endpoint stops emitting telemetry, or if a cloud audit stream suddenly drops to zero, that change itself can indicate tampering, misconfiguration, or collection-path failure. These "silence detections" must be carefully tuned to avoid constant noise from routine maintenance, which requires awareness of planned downtime and expected variability. Cross-validation across independent sources strengthens these detections,

Table 18.3 Telemetry Pipeline Failure Modes and Response Actions.

Failure Mode	What It Looks Like Operationally	Impact on Detection and Response	Immediate Action
Source silent	Expected stream stops for critical assets	Blind spot and weakened scoping	Check source health and escalation path
Latency creep	Events arrive late beyond thresholds	Detections degrade into delayed reporting	Inspect queues buffers and ingestion limits
Parsing regression	Raw arrives but normalized fields go null	Rules fail and investigations slow	Rollback parser and validate field completeness
Partial drops	Event rates fall under load	Incomplete timelines and missed coverage	Identify choke point and increase resilience
Noise surge	High volume buries meaningful signals	Alert fatigue and missed anomalies	Apply pipeline protections and validate priority paths
Unauthorized change	Routing retention or access altered unexpectedly	Integrity risk and evidence uncertainty	Audit changes and restrict admin actions

because it reduces false positives and increases confidence that silence is meaningful. For example, if identity events indicate active sessions while endpoint telemetry for those devices disappears, responders have a strong reason to suspect impairment rather than simple inactivity.

AI and machine learning can improve telemetry quality management by surfacing subtle shifts that rule-based checks miss, but they must be kept under tight human oversight. Models can learn normal event-rate patterns by asset class, detect schema drift by observing field distributions, and flag unusual correlations such as a sudden drop in endpoint events only for privileged workstations. These capabilities are valuable because they can detect partial degradations early, before detection coverage is materially harmed. The failure modes are equally real: models can treat legitimate business changes as anomalies, can miss low-and-slow degradation if baselines drift, or can underprioritize rare but critical sources that do not generate high volumes. To keep AI useful and safe, teams need explainable outputs, analyst review before remediation actions, and auditable records of what was flagged, what was changed, and why.

Ultimately, gap and quality management is where telemetry programs prove they are operational rather than aspirational. Good teams know, at any point in time, which sources are healthy, which are degraded, and what that means for detection and response. They can quantify the investigative risk of a missing stream, communicate that risk in business terms, and drive remediation through established engineering pathways. They also treat recurring telemetry issues as a signal of systemic weakness, prompting changes to deployment standards, configuration management, and monitoring. When gaps and failures are actively managed, telemetry becomes dependable enough that detections can be precise, investigations can be fast, and incident narratives can be defensible.

Operational Ownership for Logging Pipelines

Operational ownership is what turns a logging pipeline from a collection of integrations into a dependable service. Without explicit ownership, telemetry becomes everyone's responsibility in theory and no one's responsibility in practice, which means gaps persist, failures go unnoticed, and quality problems are discovered only during incidents. Ownership is not a title on an org chart; it is the combination of authority, accountability, and operational capacity to keep collection healthy, schemas stable, and access appropriate. In mature environments, logging pipelines are treated like production systems with defined reliability expectations, documented dependencies, and clear escalation paths.

A practical ownership model starts by distinguishing between source ownership and pipeline ownership. Source owners are typically the teams that operate the generating systems—endpoint engineering, network operations, identity administrators, cloud platform teams, and application owners—and they control what can be emitted and how it is configured at the point of generation. Pipeline owners are responsible for transport, buffering, parsing, normalization, routing, storage tiers, and the operational tooling that makes telemetry usable to detection and response teams. When these roles blur, outages devolve into finger-pointing because no one can quickly determine whether the issue is at the source, in transit, or at ingestion. Clear boundaries allow fast triage, while shared objectives ensure that "working as designed" is not used as an excuse for unusable telemetry.

Ownership must include the authority to define and enforce minimum telemetry standards for critical asset classes, because standards without enforcement become optional guidelines. This includes requirements for which event categories must be collected, which fields must be present, how time must be synchronized, and what constitutes acceptable latency and loss. Enforcement is operational, not rhetorical: onboarding checklists, configuration baselines, and change control gates should ensure systems cannot enter production without meeting minimum visibility requirements. The same standards must apply to changes, because logging pipelines often degrade through incremental modifications that individually seem harmless but collectively break detections.

When pipeline ownership includes the power to require remediation or to block risky changes, telemetry health becomes a controllable outcome rather than a recurring surprise.

Service expectations are essential because they translate ownership into measurable performance. Logging pipelines should have defined service objectives such as ingestion delay targets, acceptable drop rates, parsing success thresholds, and availability expectations for search and retrieval. These objectives should be tiered by criticality, because not all telemetry needs the same guarantees, but the guarantees for high-value security and audit logs should be explicit and non-negotiable. Pipeline owners need dashboards and alerting on these measures so failures are detected as quickly as authentication outages or database latency spikes. When telemetry service objectives are visible and tracked, executives and engineering leaders can see that logging is an operational dependency, not an abstract security request.

Ownership also includes disciplined change management, because telemetry is highly sensitive to schema changes, filter adjustments, and infrastructure modifications. Detection content depends on field names and meanings remaining stable, so pipeline owners must version schemas, document transformations, and maintain backward compatibility where feasible. When backward compatibility is not possible, the change process should include coordinated updates to detections, validation tests, and a rollback plan if quality regresses. This is not bureaucracy for its own sake; it is how teams prevent silent failure where logs "still arrive" but detections stop firing because key fields went blank. Good ownership makes telemetry changes predictable and auditable, which reduces operational risk during both routine deployments and incident-driven urgency.

Access and governance are part of operational ownership because telemetry pipelines routinely handle sensitive identifiers and operational details that must be protected without crippling responders. Pipeline owners should implement role-based access models that allow detection and response teams to work at speed while restricting unnecessary exposure of sensitive fields. Governance must also cover retention and tiering, because the pipeline team is usually best positioned to manage storage cost tradeoffs without sacrificing investigative capability. Decisions about filtering, sampling, aggregation, and retention should be made with detection engineering and incident response stakeholders involved, because they understand which signals are load-bearing for investigations. When governance is separated from operational reality, retention becomes an arbitrary number and filtering becomes a cost-reduction exercise that quietly erases security coverage.

Owning a logging pipeline also means owning incident response for the pipeline itself, including how telemetry health is restored during adverse conditions. Pipeline owners should have runbooks for common failure modes such as source misconfiguration, certificate and authentication failures, queue saturation, parsing regressions, and ingestion throttling. They should also plan for incident scenarios where attackers attempt to suppress logs, disable agents, or overwhelm ingestion with noise, which requires defensive controls like rate limiting, protected collection paths, and detections for sudden silence. During security incidents, the pipeline team often becomes a critical responder because restoring visibility can be a prerequisite for accurate scoping and containment. An ownership model that treats pipeline operations as a separate concern from security response will struggle when the environment is actively hostile.

AI and machine learning can support pipeline ownership by automating quality monitoring and highlighting risks, but they do not replace accountability or engineering discipline. Models can flag schema drift, identify subtle degradation in event distributions, and surface sources whose behavior deviates from expected baselines, allowing pipeline owners to prioritize remediation before coverage is impacted. These systems must be governed carefully, because they can generate false alarms during legitimate business changes and can miss rare but critical failures if they are trained on incomplete baselines. Human approval boundaries matter: AI can recommend actions, but changes to parsing, routing, filtering, or retention should remain controlled and auditable. When pipeline ownership is clear, measurable, and empowered, telemetry becomes reliable enough that detection engineering can be precise, incident response can be confident, and leadership can treat visibility as an operational capability rather than a persistent uncertainty.

Access Control and Integrity for Log Data

Log data is both a defensive asset and a sensitive business record, which means it must be protected with the same rigor as production systems and identity infrastructure. Telemetry routinely contains identifiers, administrative actions, security control changes, internal network details, and sometimes regulated data elements depending on what is being logged. If that information is broadly accessible, it becomes a reconnaissance source for insiders and attackers who gain a foothold. If it is poorly protected against tampering, it becomes unreliable evidence during investigations and can undermine the organization's ability to prove what occurred. Access control and integrity therefore exist to preserve two outcomes at once: defenders can act quickly, and the data they rely on remains trustworthy.

Effective access control begins with the assumption that not everyone who wants logs should have them, and not everyone who has them should have the same level of detail. Analysts need operational access to investigate and build detections, but that access should be scoped to job function, environment, and data sensitivity. Identity logs, endpoint execution telemetry, and administrative audit records often deserve tighter controls than generic application logs because of what they reveal about privileges and control paths. Access models should also account for separation of duties, where the people who administer the logging platform are not automatically the people who can freely browse sensitive telemetry. When separation of duties is absent, a single compromise or insider can both generate harmful activity and conceal it by manipulating what is visible.

Role-based access control works best when it is built around the workflows of detection engineering and incident response rather than around generic "read" and "admin" permissions. Analysts typically need broad search capability, the ability to pivot across related datasets, and the ability to view raw events when normalized fields are ambiguous. They do not inherently need the ability to change collection settings, modify parsers, adjust routing, or delete data. Detection engineers may need limited write access for content such as detection logic and enrichment mappings, but changes should be governed and auditable rather than performed directly in production without review. Administrators need operational privileges to maintain the pipeline, but that can be separated from unrestricted data access through privileged access workflows and just-in-time elevation. When roles are aligned to actual tasks, the platform becomes both safer and faster to use.

A recurring challenge is balancing least privilege with the reality that incidents demand speed. If responders must request access during an active intrusion, the organization trades confidentiality for delay at the worst possible moment. Mature programs solve this by predefining emergency access pathways, such as incident response roles that are inactive by default and can be activated through an approval process with enhanced monitoring. Those pathways should be time-bounded and automatically revoked, with all access logged at high fidelity so post-incident reviews can validate that access was appropriate. This is also where access to sensitive fields can be managed through controlled views or field-level restrictions, allowing analysts to do most work without exposing unnecessary data. The objective is not to slow responders down; it is to ensure that fast access remains accountable.

Integrity protections must assume that log data will be targeted, because compromising or degrading telemetry is one of the most effective ways to reduce detection and complicate response. Attackers may attempt to disable agents, block forwarding, exploit misconfigurations to suppress critical event types, or overwhelm the pipeline with noise to bury meaningful signals. They may also target administrative access to the logging system to alter parsers, reroute streams, or purge stored events. Integrity therefore includes both technical safeguards—such as immutable storage controls, restricted administrative actions, and tamper-evident logging—and operational safeguards, such as change control, monitoring for unusual administrative actions, and rapid validation of pipeline health. When integrity is treated as a feature rather than a requirement, defenders end up debating whether a quiet log stream reflects benign inactivity or deliberate suppression.

Trustworthy telemetry also depends on preserving provenance, meaning responders can distinguish raw source records from transformed or enriched representations. Normalization and enrichment are necessary for usability, but they introduce the risk that downstream fields are miscomputed, overwritten, or manipulated in ways that change meaning. Maintaining access to raw events, recording transformation logic, and versioning parsing rules allow investigators to validate conclusions and to explain evidence during audits or legal processes. Time integrity is part of provenance as well, because accurate time correlation depends on synchronized clocks and careful handling of time zones and ingestion delays. When provenance is weak, organizations may still detect incidents, but they struggle to produce defensible timelines and to prove the scope and impact of what occurred.

Monitoring access and administrative activity against log platforms is itself a critical detection use case, because the logging system is a high-value target. Access logs for the logging platform should be treated as sensitive telemetry with enhanced retention and strict monitoring for anomalies such as unusual query patterns, large exports, repeated searches for privileged accounts, or administrative changes outside maintenance windows. Administrative actions—changes to collection, parsing, routing, retention, and access controls—should generate alerts and be tied to change records so responders can quickly determine whether a change was expected or suspicious. This is one of the places where visibility loops back on itself: if the organization cannot detect manipulation of its telemetry platform, it cannot trust the detections derived from that platform. Protecting the protector is not optional; it is part of sustaining detection capability over time.

AI and machine learning can strengthen both access control and integrity monitoring by identifying subtle misuse patterns, but they must be constrained by clear approval boundaries and auditability. Models can flag anomalous access behavior, such as an account that normally performs dashboard views suddenly running broad historical exports, or an administrator making unusual parser changes followed by a drop in critical event fields. They can also help detect integrity issues by learning expected event distributions and alerting when a source becomes suspiciously quiet or when field distributions shift in ways consistent with tampering or schema drift. The risks are predictable: models can overreact to legitimate surge activity during an incident, or they can miss novel attacker behavior if baselines are incomplete or biased. That is why model outputs must be explainable, responders must review them before taking disruptive actions, and all AI-driven recommendations must be logged as part of an auditable chain of custody. When access control is designed around real workflows and integrity is treated as an adversarial problem, log data remains both usable and trustworthy under the conditions that matter most.

AI for Telemetry Operations: Enrichment, Entity Resolution, and Quality Monitoring

AI can meaningfully improve telemetry operations, but only when it is treated as an augmentation layer on top of well-instrumented collection and disciplined data management. Telemetry operations are fundamentally about making events usable for human decisions: triage, investigation, containment, and root-cause analysis. AI becomes valuable where it reduces the manual effort of turning raw events into coherent narratives, especially across heterogeneous sources and rapidly changing environments. The boundary condition is simple: models cannot compensate for missing or untrustworthy telemetry, and they can amplify mistakes when inputs are inconsistent or biased. A mature approach therefore starts with clear use cases, defined data dependencies, and explicit controls for how AI outputs are introduced into operational workflows.

Enrichment is one of the most practical AI applications because it strengthens the context that analysts need without forcing every detection to perform custom lookups. In operational terms, enrichment attaches durable attributes to events—asset identity, ownership, criticality, environment, privilege tier, known business services, and expected communication patterns—so a responder can quickly interpret significance. AI can help by inferring likely asset roles from behavior, associating hosts with business services based on traffic patterns, or suggesting categorizations when authoritative inventories are incomplete. These enrichments should be treated as probabilistic annotations rather than ground truth, and they should be clearly labeled as model-derived so analysts do not confuse inference with fact. When enrichment is governed this way, it accelerates investigations while preserving the ability to reason about evidence.

The data dependencies for AI-driven enrichment are often underestimated, and that is where many programs fail. Models need stable identifiers to attach context consistently, such as device IDs, directory object IDs, workload identity identifiers, and resource IDs, and they need sufficient history to learn what "normal" looks like for each class of entity. They also need authoritative reference sources—asset inventories, identity directories, cloud resource catalogs, and ownership mappings—to anchor model inferences and correct errors. If those reference sources are stale, enrichment can drift toward incorrect associations that appear plausible but misdirect investigations. In environments with rapid scaling and ephemeral workloads, enrichment must be designed to tolerate short-lived entities without inventing durable truths about them.

Entity resolution is a core telemetry challenge that AI can improve because modern environments represent the same actor or object in many different ways. A single person might appear as an email address in one system, a directory object ID in another, a short username in a third, and a token subject claim in a fourth. Similarly, a workload might be represented by an instance ID, a hostname, a container identifier, a service account, and multiple network addresses that change over time. AI can assist by learning linkage patterns across events and suggesting that two identifiers represent the same underlying entity, enabling cleaner pivots and more accurate correlation. The operational risk is misresolution, where unrelated entities are merged or where the wrong identity is associated with an action, creating false accusations and incorrect scoping.

To make entity resolution safe, human-in-the-loop controls and approval boundaries must be explicit. Model-suggested linkages should be reviewable, explainable, and reversible, with confidence scoring that is meaningful to analysts rather than opaque. High-confidence linkages can be used for triage acceleration and pivoting, while low-confidence linkages should remain suggestions that require analyst confirmation before they influence containment or reporting. Resolution logic should also be constrained by authoritative rules where possible, such as directory object relationships, known device enrollment identifiers, and cloud resource hierarchies, using AI to fill gaps rather than to rewrite truth. When these controls exist, entity resolution increases speed and accuracy without turning investigations into a probabilistic guessing game.

Quality monitoring is another strong AI fit because telemetry pipelines fail in subtle ways that simple threshold checks do not reliably detect. Models can learn expected event-rate patterns by source, asset class, and time of day, and then alert on deviations that indicate drops, surges, or silent parsing failures. They can also detect schema drift by tracking field distributions, sudden increases in null values for key fields, or changes in categorical values that suggest log format changes. This is particularly valuable for detecting partial failures where logs still arrive but become operationally unusable because critical fields are missing or malformed. The practical benefit is earlier detection of degradation, which reduces the window where detections quietly lose coverage.

Quality monitoring models must be tuned to distinguish operational change from telemetry failure, because environments evolve continuously. Business events such as new deployments, seasonal demand spikes, and infrastructure migrations can legitimately change telemetry patterns in ways that look anomalous to a model trained on historical baselines. If the system floods operators with false positives, it will be ignored, and real failures will be missed amid alert fatigue. Successful implementations incorporate change awareness through maintenance windows, deployment signals, and context about expected operational shifts, allowing the model to interpret anomalies in a more informed way. They also include clear escalation criteria so model outputs translate into actionable engineering work rather than vague "something changed" notifications.

Governance and auditability are non-negotiable when AI influences telemetry operations, because telemetry is often used as evidence and AI outputs can shape investigative conclusions. Model features and training data sources should be documented, access to training datasets should be controlled, and outputs should be retained with enough metadata to support later review. Teams should log when an enrichment or entity linkage was applied, what confidence score was used, and whether a human approved or corrected the output, creating an auditable trail that supports accountability. Privacy and leakage risks matter as well, because telemetry can include sensitive identifiers, and AI workflows can inadvertently expose or replicate that data in places it does not belong.

When AI is deployed with disciplined boundaries, explainability, and audit trails, it becomes a force multiplier for enrichment, entity resolution, and quality monitoring without compromising the integrity and defensibility of the telemetry program.

Building Confidence in What You Can See

Confidence in visibility is not a feeling; it is the operational certainty that your telemetry is present, accurate, and sufficient to support decisions under pressure. Leaders tend to equate "we have logs" with "we can see," but responders know that visibility is fragile until it is proven through repeatable verification. Confidence is built by demonstrating that critical events are captured end to end, that they arrive within expected time windows, and that they retain the fields needed for correlation and attribution. When that proof is missing, detection becomes speculative, and incident response becomes a sequence of expensive assumptions. The organization may still respond, but it will respond with broader disruption and less defensible conclusions.

The first layer of confidence comes from knowing what should exist, which requires explicit telemetry requirements for critical assets and control points. If teams cannot name the minimum event categories and key fields they rely on for authentication, privilege changes, execution, network boundary crossings, and control-plane activity, they cannot measure whether those signals are present. Requirements should be framed in operational questions: can we reconstruct an admin session, can we tie a cloud change to an identity, can we trace lateral movement across a subnet, and can we confirm whether a security control was disabled. These questions drive concrete expectations for sources and schemas and prevent the program from devolving into collecting everything without knowing what it enables. Confidence grows when requirements are specific enough that gaps can be detected and prioritized rather than debated.

The next layer is validation, because telemetry that exists in theory can still fail in practice. Validation means exercising the environment and confirming that expected events appear where they should, in the right format, and with the right correlation fields. It also means validating failure paths, because detection often depends on unsuccessful authentication attempts, denied authorization decisions, and blocked executions, not just successful actions. Teams build confidence by routinely testing representative behaviors across endpoint, identity, network, and cloud layers and verifying that the resulting telemetry supports a coherent timeline. This practice turns visibility into something that can be measured and improved rather than assumed, and it reduces the likelihood that an incident reveals a missing source for the first time.

Confidence also depends on understanding pipeline behavior, especially latency, loss, and transformation. Telemetry that arrives hours late or intermittently is not equivalent to telemetry that arrives predictably, even if the total volume looks similar over a day. Responders need to know whether an apparent quiet period reflects true inactivity or ingestion delay, and they need to know how long they must wait before concluding that an event did not occur. Pipeline transparency is therefore part of confidence: collection health metrics, parsing success rates, queue depths, and source freshness indicators should be visible to security operations as well as to platform owners. When analysts can quickly check whether a source is degraded, they can adjust investigative tactics appropriately instead of trusting a view that may be incomplete.

Correlation is another confidence multiplier, because single-source narratives are easily wrong. Endpoint telemetry can show execution but may not prove how access was obtained; identity telemetry can show sign-ins but may not show what happened after; cloud logs can show configuration changes but may not show the local actions that drove them. Confidence grows when the same event chain can be supported by multiple independent sources, reducing the risk that tampering, misconfiguration, or blind spots distort the story. This requires consistent identifiers and disciplined normalization so pivots are reliable and repeatable. The practical outcome is that responders can scope incidents faster and with fewer assumptions because evidence converges rather than conflicts.

Trust in what you can see also requires integrity controls and an adversarial mindset about telemetry suppression. Attackers regularly attempt to disable agents, stop forwarders, modify logging configurations, or create noise that obscures meaningful events. Confidence is built when the organization can detect and respond to these efforts as operational incidents, not as theoretical threats. That includes monitoring for sudden drops in expected event rates, unusual changes to logging configurations, and administrative activity against the telemetry platform itself. It also includes designing collection paths that are resilient and difficult to tamper with, so a compromised host cannot easily erase its own footprint. When silence is detectable and tampering is risky for the attacker, telemetry becomes more trustworthy.

AI can contribute to confidence-building by continuously assessing telemetry quality and by surfacing weak signals that indicate emerging gaps. Models can learn expected patterns for event volumes, field completeness, and schema stability by source and can alert when those patterns shift in ways consistent with collection failure or format drift. They can also help prioritize remediation by estimating which gaps most degrade detection coverage, focusing engineering effort where it produces the greatest operational improvement. These systems must remain human-supervised, because models can be fooled by legitimate operational changes, and they can drift if the environment evolves faster than the baselines are updated. Analysts need explainable outputs and the ability to override model conclusions, especially when a model implies that visibility is "healthy" despite evidence to the contrary.

Confidence ultimately becomes durable when visibility is treated as a living capability with routine verification, measurable health, and accountable ownership. Teams that trust their telemetry do not trust it blindly; they trust it because they test it, monitor it, and correct it continuously. They can state what they can see well, what they can see partially, and what they cannot see, and they can connect those statements to concrete engineering work and business risk. That clarity changes decision-making, because detection content can be more precise, response actions can be more targeted, and leadership can make informed tradeoffs about investment and acceptance of residual visibility risk. When an organization can defend its visibility claims with evidence and operational discipline, it is far better positioned to detect, contain, and learn from real intrusions.

Conclusion

Confidence in detection is earned through disciplined telemetry management, not through optimism or sheer data volume. When collection is resilient, normalization is consistent, retention aligns to investigative reality, and access and integrity are engineered for adversarial conditions, visibility becomes a dependable operational capability. AI can accelerate enrichment, entity resolution, and quality monitoring, but it only works safely when its outputs are explainable, auditable, and constrained by clear human approval boundaries. The practical result is a program that scopes incidents faster, contains with greater precision, and can defend its conclusions under scrutiny because the evidence pipeline is as intentionally managed as any other critical production service.

Recommendations

1) Treat telemetry as a production service with explicit reliability expectations. Define what "healthy" looks like for collection latency, event loss, and parsing success so failures are measurable rather than subjective. Monitor pipeline health continuously and escalate degradations the same way you would for other critical operational services. Use these measures to drive remediation priorities and prevent silent loss of detection coverage.
2) Define minimum telemetry requirements for critical assets and control points. Specify the event categories and key fields needed to reconstruct identity actions, privileged changes, execution, network boundary crossings,

and cloud administrative activity. Make these requirements concrete enough that teams can validate them and detect gaps quickly. Use the requirements to guide onboarding and change decisions so visibility does not become optional.

3) Engineer endpoint telemetry to support attribution and sequence, not just alerting. Ensure endpoint events preserve enough context to explain what executed, under which session and privilege level, and how the execution chain progressed. Preserve raw event records alongside normalized representations so investigations can verify nuance when needed. Use this depth to reduce guesswork and increase confidence during triage and scoping.
4) Strengthen network telemetry by making it linkable to assets and identities. Ensure network observations can be correlated to the systems and sessions that generated them, rather than existing as isolated connection records. Use that linkage to distinguish routine business communications from suspicious boundary crossings and unusual destinations. Avoid expecting network data to substitute for endpoint and identity context when determining intent.
5) Prioritize identity telemetry as the backbone for modern detection and containment. Ensure sign-ins, token issuance, MFA challenges, session creation, and privilege assignments are captured with stable identifiers and clear outcomes. Use identity evidence to anchor investigations and drive containment actions such as revoking sessions and disabling compromised accounts. Validate that identity logs remain complete through migrations and policy changes, since gaps here quickly become enterprise-wide blind spots.
6) Treat cloud control-plane audit logs as mandatory evidence for change and access paths. Ensure administrative actions, permission changes, logging configuration modifications, and resource lifecycle events are captured and retained sufficiently to investigate short-lived resources. Correlate cloud audit activity to identities and related operational actions so responders can reconstruct how changes were initiated. Monitor for suspicious modifications to logging and security controls because these are common suppression techniques.
7) Normalize telemetry for consistent meaning without sacrificing provenance. Standardize core fields such as timestamps, identity identifiers, and action outcomes so correlation is reliable across sources and time. Keep raw source events available to responders to validate conclusions and support defensible incident narratives. Version parsing and normalization logic so schema shifts do not silently break detections and investigations.
8) Align retention and storage decisions to investigative reality rather than to convenience. Retain high-value security and audit telemetry long enough to support slow-moving intrusion scoping and post-incident validation. Use tiered retention and selective fidelity to manage cost while protecting the signals that detections depend on. Document the security impact of retention reductions so tradeoffs are explicit and reviewable.
9) Establish clear operational ownership boundaries for sources and pipelines. Assign source accountability to the teams that operate generating systems and pipeline accountability to those who manage transport, parsing, routing, and storage. Build change control practices that coordinate detection updates with telemetry changes and include rollback plans for quality regressions. Use shared service objectives and escalation paths to prevent telemetry failures from becoming unowned problems.
10) Apply AI to telemetry operations only with defined inputs, human review, and auditability. Use AI-assisted enrichment, entity resolution, and quality monitoring to reduce manual effort and to surface subtle degradations that simple thresholds miss. Treat model outputs as probabilistic annotations, require explainability, and constrain their use in containment decisions with clear approval boundaries. Log model-driven recommendations and human overrides so the telemetry program remains accountable and defensible.

19

Continuous Monitoring and Alerting Operations

Continuous monitoring and alerting operations translate raw telemetry into timely, defensible decisions that reduce business risk before it becomes business impact. The work is less about collecting "more data" and more about designing a system of baselines, deviations, and escalation paths that reliably surfaces what matters within real staffing and response constraints. Effective programs treat paging as a scarce event, build disciplined triage and routing, and maintain monitoring rules as living controls that must survive constant change in architecture and operations. When AI assists this workflow, it should accelerate summarization and prioritization without weakening human accountability, evidence verification, or auditability, so that speed never comes at the cost of over-trust or preventable mistakes.

Monitoring Goals and Operational Constraints

Continuous monitoring exists to reduce the time between a meaningful change in the environment and an informed defensive response, not to chase every possible signal. The operational goal is to create enough reliable visibility to detect material risk movement early, validate it quickly, and route it to the right owner with the context needed to act. That framing matters because "more monitoring" is not inherently better; it can increase noise, cost, and operational drag without improving outcomes. Mature programs treat monitoring as a set of explicit outcomes tied to business priorities, such as protecting critical systems, preserving identity integrity, and detecting lateral movement before impact. In practice, that means monitoring is designed around questions the organization must answer under pressure, and it is measured by how consistently those questions can be answered with defensible evidence.

A practical way to anchor monitoring goals is to focus on coverage of the organization's most consequential failure modes rather than attempting broad, shallow telemetry everywhere. Monitoring should emphasize high-value assets, sensitive data paths, privileged identity workflows, and the services that concentrate operational risk. This is where the difference between "collection" and "monitoring" becomes operationally important: collecting logs does not mean you can detect or respond effectively. Monitoring implies defined detection logic, consistent baselines, and validated alert routes that produce actionable outputs. When coverage is defined as a set of prioritized detection outcomes, tradeoffs become explicit and defensible in executive terms. That prevents teams from spending scarce analyst time on low-impact signals simply because they are easy to collect.

The quality of monitoring is constrained first by telemetry fidelity and second by the organization's ability to sustain response. Telemetry fidelity includes completeness, timeliness, and consistency across sources, and each of those can fail in common ways during real operations. Logs can be missing due to misconfiguration, dropped due to volume limits, delayed by forwarding pipelines, or rendered ambiguous by inconsistent time synchronization and identity fields. These failures are not academic; they create blind spots that can look like "nothing happened," which is the most dangerous kind of false negative. Operational teams must assume telemetry loss will occur

Table 19.1 Monitoring Goals to Telemetry and Response Expectations.

Monitoring Goal	Primary Telemetry Needed	Immediate Response Expectation	Common Failure Mode
Protect critical assets	Asset criticality tags and system activity logs	Route to owner with containment options ready	Blind spots from missing collectors
Preserve identity integrity	Authentication events and privileged action logs	Validate identity and apply step up controls	False confidence from incomplete identity mapping
Detect lateral movement	Host-to-host network relationships and endpoint activity	Correlate sequence and scope affected assets	Noise from weak proxies and poor correlation
Detect control failures	Ingestion health signals and audit policy status	Escalate as monitoring incident and restore coverage	Silent failure mistaken for no activity
Maintain actionable alerting	Alert context and routing metadata	Triage quickly and escalate with evidence	Alert fatigue from low value pages

and build compensating controls such as heartbeats, ingestion health checks, and periodic validation exercises. If the monitoring pipeline cannot prove it is working, the organization is effectively relying on hope as a control. Table 19.1 links monitoring goals to the telemetry and response expectations required to make alerts operationally actionable.

Alerting capacity is the second major constraint, and it is where many programs quietly fail even when telemetry is abundant. Every alert consumes attention, and attention is a finite resource governed by staffing, on-call coverage, time zones, competing priorities, and the psychological load of repeated false positives. When alert volume exceeds sustainable capacity, analysts either ignore alerts, rubber-stamp them, or burn out, and none of those outcomes improve security. The practical constraint is not how many detections exist in the system, but how many can be triaged to a high standard with acceptable latency. Effective operations therefore treat "alert budget" as a real concept, allocating it to detections with the best ratio of risk reduction to analyst effort. This also means designing escalation paths and ownership boundaries so that the security team is not forced to be the operational owner for every kind of issue.

Monitoring goals must also account for the organization's tolerance for disruption and the reality that some defensive actions have business cost. There is a large difference between observing suspicious behavior, requiring additional verification, and taking automated containment actions that may interrupt production services or lock out users. Good operations establish approval boundaries for each class of response, balancing speed against blast radius. For example, certain identity-based detections may justify immediate step-up authentication or token revocation, while endpoint containment might require a quick human review when it could disrupt critical workflows. These boundaries are not policy theater; they are necessary to keep monitoring credible and trusted by stakeholders. When defensive automation repeatedly harms business operations, leaders will pressure teams to turn it off, and the organization becomes slower and less resilient precisely when it needs to be decisive.

AI and machine learning can materially improve monitoring under real-world constraints, but only when they are treated as decision support rather than a substitute for accountability. In continuous monitoring, common ML use cases include anomaly detection on authentication patterns, clustering of similar alerts to reduce duplication, and enrichment that summarizes likely attack paths based on observed relationships between entities. These approaches depend heavily on stable, well-labeled telemetry, consistent identity resolution, and a disciplined approach to baselining so that "normal" is not defined by yesterday's incident. Human-in-the-loop controls are essential because ML systems can produce false confidence, especially when they generate plausible narratives that are not grounded in the environment's actual behavior. Drift is a constant risk as business processes change, new systems are deployed, and attacker techniques evolve, causing models to overreact or underreact in ways that are hard to notice until a miss occurs. Operationally, ML-assisted monitoring must be auditable: teams need to know what data influenced a recommendation, what thresholds were applied, and when the model or logic changed.

Governance and accountability tie monitoring goals to outcomes in a way that survives organizational change. Monitoring is not only a technical system; it is a workflow that relies on clear ownership, repeatable processes, and defensible records of what was seen and what was done. Alert definitions, thresholds, and routing rules should be managed as controlled operational artifacts, with changes reviewed and tracked so that incident response can reconstruct why an alert did or did not fire. Metrics should reinforce the intended behavior: time to triage, percentage of alerts that result in meaningful action, and the rate of missed detections discovered through incident retrospectives or validation testing. Constraints should be documented in operational terms, such as known visibility gaps, limited coverage windows, and response limitations during business peaks or staffing transitions. When leaders understand monitoring as an engineered capability with explicit constraints, they can sponsor the investments and tradeoffs required to make it reliable rather than merely prolific.

Establishing Baselines and Detecting Deviations

Baselines exist to prevent monitoring from becoming a collection of disconnected alerts, each judged in isolation with no dependable reference for what "normal" looks like. In operational terms, a baseline is a measured description of expected behavior for a system, identity, network segment, or business process across time. It is not a static snapshot, because environments change daily through patches, new applications, organizational shifts, and normal business seasonality. Effective baselining therefore starts by selecting the behaviors that matter most to defensive decision-making, such as authentication patterns, privileged actions, administrative changes, and data movement routes. The purpose is to make meaningful deviations visible early, while avoiding a baseline so broad that it becomes indistinguishable from noise.

A practical baseline begins with the right scope boundaries and identity resolution, because "normal" differs drastically across users, roles, and systems. Aggregating behavior across an entire enterprise often produces averages that hide the very signals defenders care about, such as a small set of privileged accounts behaving unusually. Good practice is to establish baselines at multiple levels, including per-asset, per-service, per-role, and per-identity, so that deviations are evaluated in the correct context. This requires consistent entity mapping so that the same person or workload is represented consistently across telemetry sources, even when identifiers differ. Without that normalization, baselines drift into fiction, and deviations are either missed or triggered constantly. Operationally, baselining is as much about data hygiene and consistent attribution as it is about analytics.

Baselines should be built from telemetry that is trustworthy, time-aligned, and representative of real operations, not a period contaminated by major incidents or unusual outages. Establishing a baseline means deciding which signals are authoritative and how missing data will be handled, because gaps can masquerade as reduced activity or sudden spikes when forwarding resumes. Time synchronization across systems is critical; without consistent timestamps, sequences such as authentication, privilege escalation, and process execution cannot be reliably correlated. It is also important to explicitly account for expected variability, such as weekday patterns, maintenance windows, and periodic batch jobs that would otherwise appear anomalous. The baseline should capture both typical volume and typical shape, including the sequences and relationships between actions, not just counts. When defenders treat baselining as a first-class operational artifact, they also monitor the baseline's inputs for health, because a baseline built on broken telemetry is worse than none at all.

Detecting deviations is the act of comparing current behavior against those expectations in a way that produces decisions, not just observations. Deviations should be defined in terms that align to threat and risk, such as unusual access paths, atypical administrative changes, unexpected network relationships, or behavior that violates the environment's established constraints. Not every deviation is suspicious; many represent legitimate change, such as a new deployment, a role change, or emergency maintenance. The operational challenge is to design deviation detection so that it yields high-confidence investigation candidates while remaining sensitive enough to catch low-and-slow behaviors that intentionally avoid thresholds. That balance is achieved through layered detection logic that combines deviation indicators with corroborating context, such as whether the identity is privileged, whether the host is critical, whether the action is rare for that role, and whether supporting artifacts suggest user intent or automation.

Thresholds are necessary, but thresholds alone often fail in dynamic environments because they do not adapt to the organization's evolving behavior. Rigid thresholds tend to create alert storms during legitimate change and silence during attacker activity that stays below fixed limits. More robust detection uses relative measures, such as changes from an entity's own historical behavior, comparisons to peer groups with similar roles, and detection of unusual sequences rather than single events. Even then, defenders need to encode "guardrails" that prevent normalization of malicious behavior, such as excluding known-incident periods from training windows and preserving certain hard rules for critical actions. Operational teams should also plan for adversarial behavior that tries to manipulate baselines by gradually shifting activity to redefine "normal." The control is not only statistical; it is procedural, requiring periodic review of baseline definitions and anomaly thresholds in light of incident learnings and environment changes.

AI and ML can improve deviation detection by discovering patterns that are difficult to express as deterministic rules, but their effectiveness depends on disciplined inputs and clear human control points. Common operational uses include anomaly scoring for authentication behavior, clustering similar alerts to reduce duplication, and sequence modeling that highlights unusual chains of events across endpoints and identities. These approaches rely on consistent telemetry, stable entity resolution, and enough historical data to separate normal variability from meaningful change. Failure modes include false positives caused by organizational events such as mergers, staffing changes, or new tooling, and false negatives when models become desensitized due to drift or overexposure to noisy data. Another risk is false confidence, where a high anomaly score or confident narrative leads analysts to skip basic validation steps, such as verifying the identity, confirming the asset context, and checking for corroborating indicators. For ML-assisted detections to be operationally safe, outputs must be explainable enough to audit, and there must be clear boundaries on automated actions versus recommendations requiring analyst approval.

Baselining and deviation detection must integrate with triage workflows so that anomalies become structured decisions with consistent documentation. When a deviation is flagged, the next step should not be improvisation; it should be a repeatable validation path that checks telemetry integrity, confirms business context, and determines whether the event is expected change, benign variance, or suspicious activity. This is where enrichment and context matter, including whether the action aligns with change management, whether the identity recently changed roles, and whether related indicators exist across adjacent systems. Feedback loops are essential: when deviations are repeatedly confirmed as benign, detection logic should be tuned, and when deviations are repeatedly associated with real incidents, the baseline and detection thresholds should be strengthened. Over time, mature teams treat baselining as a living control, continuously refined through operational evidence rather than theoretical assumptions. The end state is not perfect prediction, but a monitoring system that consistently surfaces the deviations that matter and does so within the organization's real-world capacity to investigate and respond.

Alerting Strategy: What Should Page Someone

Alerting is the point where monitoring transitions from passive visibility to an explicit demand for human attention, and that transition must be treated as a scarce and valuable event. A page is not a notification; it is an interruption that pulls someone away from other responsibilities and imposes an expectation of timely action. The strategic goal of alerting is therefore not to surface everything that is interesting, but to surface what is urgent, actionable, and material to risk if left unattended. When organizations blur that distinction, they condition

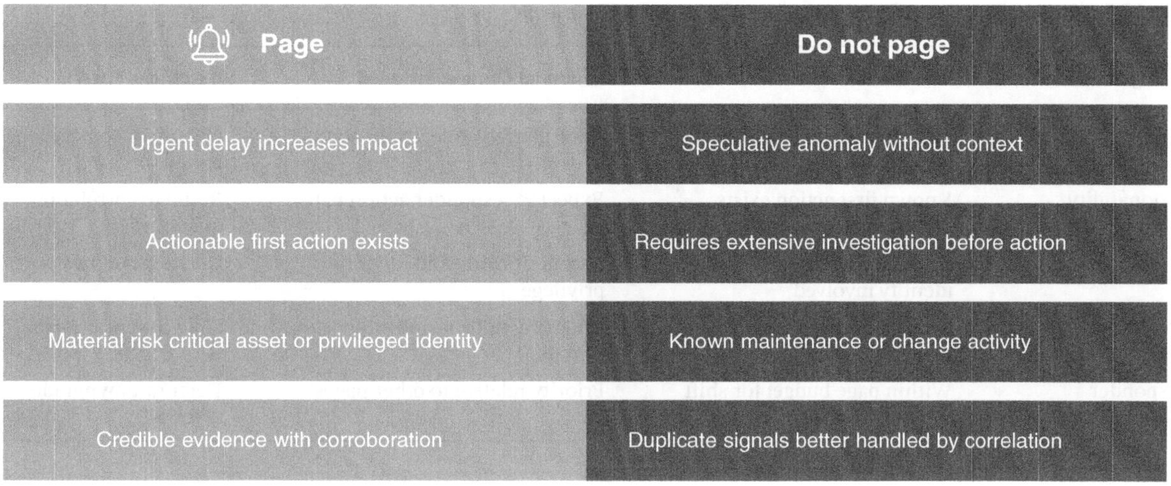

Figure 19.1 What Should Page Someone Versus What Should Not.

responders to distrust alerts, delay response, or silence notifications altogether. A disciplined alerting strategy defines paging as a last-mile decision reserved for conditions where delay measurably increases potential impact.

The first criterion for paging should be whether the alert represents a credible path to harm that cannot safely wait for normal business hours or routine review. This typically includes indicators of active compromise, loss of control over privileged identities, disruption of critical services, or confirmed security control failure in high-risk areas. Alerts that describe incomplete context, speculative anomalies, or early-stage hypotheses should rarely page on their own, regardless of how technically interesting they appear. Instead, those signals belong in queues designed for correlation, enrichment, and analyst-driven escalation. Operationally, the question is not "could this be bad," but "what happens if no one looks at this for several hours." When teams adopt that framing, paging thresholds become more defensible and far less arbitrary. Figure 19.1 clarifies the paging threshold by separating urgent actionable conditions from signals that should be queued for correlation and routine review. It supports the chapter's emphasis that paging is a scarce interruption reserved for material risk with a clear response path.

Actionability is the second gating factor, because paging someone without a clear response path creates stress without improving outcomes. A page should correspond to a known playbook, even if that playbook allows for judgment, containment options, and escalation decisions. Responders should understand what systems they are expected to check, what decisions they are authorized to make, and what evidence they need to gather quickly. Alerts that require extensive investigation before any action can be taken are usually better handled asynchronously unless the mere presence of the condition is itself dangerous. This does not mean alerts must be fully confirmed incidents before paging, but they must be mature enough to support a meaningful first action. Over time, organizations that invest in alert maturity reduce both unnecessary pages and dangerous hesitation during real incidents.

Context completeness strongly influences whether an alert deserves to page, because responders need immediate clarity to assess risk under time pressure. High-quality paging alerts include who or what is involved, what changed, when it started, what assets are affected, and why the system believes this is important. Missing context forces responders to spend the first minutes of a page reconstructing basic facts, which increases response time and cognitive load. Alert design should therefore emphasize enrichment at creation time, pulling in identity role, asset criticality, recent related activity, and known change events. This enrichment does not eliminate investigation, but it ensures that the responder's first actions are informed rather than exploratory. In practice, the quality of alert context is often a stronger predictor of effective response than the sophistication of the detection logic

Table 19.2 Paging Threshold Criteria and Alert Content Requirements.

Paging Criterion	What Must Be True	Minimum Context Included	If Not Met Then
Urgency	Delay increases potential impact	Time started and current status	Queue for routine review
Actionability	Known first action exists	Expected responder action path	Route to correlation queue
Material risk	Critical asset or privileged identity involved	Asset criticality and identity privilege	Create ticket not page
Credible evidence	Corroborating indicators present	Trigger condition and supporting signals	Hold for enrichment
Responder capacity	Within page budget for shift	Priority relative to other pages	Defer or downgrade severity

itself. Table 19.2 defines when paging is justified and the minimum alert context required to support immediate response.

Alert volume and responder capacity impose hard constraints that strategy must acknowledge rather than ignore. Even a well-designed alert becomes harmful if it pages too frequently, because frequent interruptions erode trust and lead to alert fatigue. Organizations must be realistic about on-call staffing, time zone coverage, and the competing demands placed on responders, especially outside normal hours. A sustainable strategy deliberately limits the number of paging alerts by allocating a finite "page budget" to the highest risk conditions. This often requires hard choices, such as downgrading noisy detections or accepting delayed visibility for lower-impact issues. The measure of success is not how many alerts fire, but how consistently pages result in timely, appropriate action without burning out the team.

AI and machine learning can assist alerting strategy by helping decide when a condition crosses the threshold from informational to paging-worthy, but they must be constrained by clear human approval boundaries. Practical uses include prioritization models that score alerts based on historical outcomes, correlation engines that collapse multiple related signals into a single incident view, and suppression logic that reduces duplication during known events. These approaches depend on accurate historical labeling of alerts and disciplined feedback loops; otherwise, the system will learn the wrong lessons. Failure modes include bias toward past incidents that no longer reflect current risk, desensitization due to drift, and opaque scoring that responders cannot trust under pressure. For paging decisions, ML outputs should inform prioritization and recommendation, not unilaterally trigger disruptive actions unless explicitly authorized and tested. Auditability is critical so that teams can explain why a page was or was not sent when reviewing incidents or near misses.

An effective alerting strategy also defines what should not page, even if the underlying condition is technically severe. Examples include detections tied to known maintenance windows, alerts on non-critical systems with no escalation path, and issues that are already actively being handled by another team. Explicit non-paging rules prevent duplication of effort and reduce confusion during incidents. These exclusions should be documented and periodically reviewed, because changes in architecture or business priorities can shift what qualifies as urgent. When exclusions are informal or undocumented, paging decisions become inconsistent and dependent on individual judgment, which increases risk during staff transitions. Clear boundaries create predictability for both responders and stakeholders.

Finally, alerting strategy must be reinforced through metrics and review, not just initial design. Organizations should routinely examine which pages resulted in meaningful action, which were downgraded as non-issues, and which incidents occurred without a page that should have triggered one. These reviews should focus on decision quality rather than blame, using evidence to adjust thresholds, context enrichment, and playbooks. Over time, this feedback-driven approach aligns alerting behavior with real-world risk and operational capacity. When paging becomes rare, trusted, and decisive, it signals that the monitoring program is functioning as an operational control rather than a source of constant interruption.

Alert Triage, Routing, and Escalation

Triage is the operational filter that converts alert volume into a manageable set of decisions, and it is only effective when it is treated as a defined workflow rather than an individual analyst's intuition. The goal is to determine, quickly and defensibly, whether an alert represents a true security concern, an expected condition, or an information point that should be recorded and monitored. That decision must be made using consistent evidence thresholds so that outcomes are repeatable across shifts and staff changes. When triage is informal, organizations drift into inconsistency, where the same alert is escalated one day and dismissed the next. Over time, that inconsistency erodes trust in the monitoring program and makes executive reporting unreliable.

High-functioning triage begins with normalization and enrichment that reduce the time spent reconstructing basic facts. Alerts should arrive with consistent identifiers for user, host, application, and network context, along with timestamps that are aligned across sources. Enrichment should attach asset criticality, identity privilege level, business owner, and known change context, so analysts can quickly evaluate potential impact. Without these elements, triage becomes a scavenger hunt across systems, increasing both response time and the likelihood of error. A practical triage workflow also includes immediate validation of telemetry integrity, because missing logs, broken collectors, or delayed ingestion can create misleading patterns. If responders cannot trust the data path, the correct "security" decision may be to treat the condition as a monitoring failure that itself requires escalation.

Routing is the decision about ownership, and it is often the hidden failure point where security teams become a bottleneck for issues they do not control. Effective routing recognizes that many alerts represent operational problems, administrative mistakes, or policy violations that must be remediated by the system or business owner. Security owns the detection and coordination, but the accountable owner is frequently infrastructure, identity, application, or a business unit with authority over the affected process. Routing rules should therefore be explicit, based on asset ownership and actionability, and supported by contact paths that work outside normal business hours when needed. When ownership is unclear, triage teams tend to hoard alerts, performing remediation work informally just to get closure, which scales poorly and increases operational risk. Clear routing boundaries prevent the security function from becoming an all-purpose operations team.

Escalation is not simply "send it to someone senior," but a structured process for increasing attention and authority as the assessed risk increases. A well-designed escalation path includes triggers based on impact, confidence, and time sensitivity, and it separates technical escalation from leadership escalation. Technical escalation brings in specialized skills, such as identity engineering, endpoint response, or application expertise, while leadership escalation ensures decisions with business impact are made by authorized stakeholders. Escalation should also be time-bound, with explicit expectations for response and handoff, because ambiguity during incidents causes delays and duplicated work. In practice, escalation works best when responders know exactly what information must accompany an escalation, so the next team can act immediately. That information should be concise, consistent, and evidence-based, reflecting what is known, what is suspected, and what has been ruled out.

An effective triage pipeline relies on consistent severity logic that aligns to business risk rather than purely technical characteristics. Severity should incorporate asset criticality, identity privilege, potential blast radius, and the likelihood that the alert represents malicious activity. Pure technical severity, such as a high-risk vulnerability or a suspicious command, can be misleading when the system is isolated, non-critical, or already contained. Conversely, seemingly minor anomalies can be severe when they involve a privileged identity or a system that anchors trust for other services. This is where disciplined context management matters, because severity without context is just a guess. Organizations that tie severity to clear operational decision points, such as paging thresholds and containment authority, prevent severity from becoming a subjective label.

AI and ML can materially assist triage and routing by reducing cognitive load, highlighting correlations, and recommending next steps, but they must be constrained by human accountability and rigorous audit trails. Common operational uses include grouping similar alerts into clusters, summarizing relevant prior activity for an identity or host, and scoring alerts based on historical outcomes. These systems depend on high-quality labeled data, stable telemetry pipelines, and clear definitions of what "true positive" and "benign" mean in the organization's context. Failure modes include biased prioritization that overweights historically frequent issues, false confidence driven by persuasive summaries, and leakage of sensitive data if models are trained or queried without appropriate controls. Human-in-the-loop design should ensure that AI outputs are recommendations that require analyst validation before escalation or containment actions. For governance, the organization should be able to reconstruct how a recommendation was produced, what inputs were used, and whether overrides occurred.

Triage quality improves through structured decision checkpoints that encourage fast elimination of obvious false positives while preserving sensitivity to real threats. Early checks often include confirming whether the alert corresponds to a known change event, verifying the identity's expected behavior, and checking for corroborating evidence across independent telemetry sources. Analysts should be trained to avoid single-signal decisions when the environment is noisy, using correlation to confirm that the observed behavior is part of a meaningful sequence. At the same time, triage must avoid paralysis through analysis, especially for high-impact scenarios, where early containment may be justified even when full certainty is not possible. The operational discipline is to make the least disruptive action that meaningfully reduces risk while evidence is gathered. Over time, teams should capture triage outcomes in a structured way so that the monitoring program learns from what actually happened.

Escalation also requires careful management of communications, because poorly framed escalations create confusion and wasted effort. Escalations should state the decision being requested, the urgency, the potential impact, and the evidence supporting the request, using language that aligns with the recipient's responsibilities. For technical teams, that means providing concrete indicators, affected systems, and reproducible steps, while for leaders it means translating technical conditions into operational risk and decision options. Escalation should also include an explicit owner and a clear next checkpoint, so that responsibility does not diffuse across multiple teams. When multiple groups are involved, coordination must prevent contradictory actions, such as disabling an account while an identity team is attempting to validate its use for a business-critical workflow. A mature escalation practice ensures that the organization moves as a coordinated unit under stress, rather than a collection of well-intentioned but disconnected responders.

Finally, triage, routing, and escalation must be continuously tuned against operational outcomes, because the environment and threat landscape change and yesterday's logic rarely remains optimal. Programs should review escalations that resulted in confirmed incidents, those that were unnecessary, and incidents that were discovered through other channels without an appropriate escalation. These reviews should lead to concrete adjustments in routing rules, enrichment requirements, and escalation triggers, not just general lessons learned. Triage teams should also track recurring patterns of misrouting or delayed escalation as signals of organizational ownership gaps that need executive attention. When leaders treat these workflow issues as operational risk rather than analyst performance problems, they enable sustainable improvement. The result is an alerting operation that consistently gets the right issue to the right team at the right time, with the authority and context needed to act.

Managing Alert Fatigue and Noise

Alert fatigue is not a morale problem first; it is a reliability problem that degrades defensive outcomes by eroding human attention and trust in the monitoring program. When analysts are exposed to high volumes of low-value alerts, they begin to treat all alerts as low-value, including the few that matter. Noise also creates measurable opportunity cost, because time spent closing false positives is time not spent hunting, improving detections, or hardening response paths. In executive terms, unmanaged noise is wasted spend and increased residual risk, even when tooling appears "busy" and dashboards look active. The operational objective is to keep alert volume within the organization's sustainable response capacity while preserving sensitivity to the deviations that represent real harm. That requires deliberate design choices, routine tuning, and governance that treats noise reduction as part of control effectiveness.

The first step in managing noise is to acknowledge that not all alerts are meant to be treated equally, and that "everything to everyone" alerting is operationally unsustainable. High-signal alerts should be rare and strongly tied to urgent response actions, while lower-confidence signals should be routed to correlation queues, analyst worklists, or periodic reviews. Without this stratification, teams default to a flat alert stream where urgency is ambiguous and prioritization becomes inconsistent. Noise management therefore begins with clear criteria for what should page, what should generate a ticket, and what should be logged for context without immediate action. This approach reduces fatigue because responders learn that certain classes of alerts reliably demand attention, while others are handled on a cadence that matches risk. Over time, predictable handling patterns restore trust and improve response speed during real incidents.

Noise is often created by incomplete context, because alerts that lack identity, asset criticality, or change awareness force analysts to investigate benign conditions repeatedly. Enrichment is therefore a core noise-reduction control, not a luxury feature, and it should be applied as close to alert generation as possible. When alerts include ownership, privilege level, and relevant recent activity, analysts can quickly dismiss expected behavior and focus on anomalies that truly merit investigation. Change context is especially important, because legitimate maintenance or deployments frequently resemble attacker behaviors at the raw telemetry level. If monitoring cannot distinguish between planned change and suspicious change, alert volume will spike precisely when the environment is most active. Mature programs integrate change signals into triage, so noise does not rise with normal business operations.

A disciplined tuning process treats each noisy alert as a candidate for improvement rather than a nuisance to be ignored. Teams should categorize noise drivers, such as overly broad detection logic, missing allow lists for known benign patterns, duplicated alerts from overlapping telemetry, and thresholds that do not reflect real usage patterns. The response should be evidence-based, using alert outcomes to refine logic and reduce repeat investigations, rather than turning alerts off out of frustration. At the same time, tuning must avoid creating blind spots by suppressing behavior that is merely inconvenient to investigate. The standard should be that suppression requires a defensible rationale and, where possible, compensating detection that preserves coverage in a more reliable way. This keeps noise management aligned with risk, not convenience.

Alert fatigue is amplified by duplication, where the same underlying condition generates multiple alerts across systems or multiple times within a short window. De-duplication and correlation are therefore essential operational capabilities, combining related events into a single investigation unit with a coherent timeline. This reduces the cognitive burden on analysts and prevents a single incident from consuming disproportionate attention. Correlation must be grounded in stable entity identifiers and time alignment; otherwise, it can merge unrelated events or fail to join related ones. Practical correlation logic often relies on shared identity, host, process lineage, or network relationships, and it should be tuned to balance consolidation against the risk of masking distinct issues. When correlation is effective, it transforms a flood of noisy signals into a smaller set of richer alerts that are easier to evaluate accurately.

AI and ML can support noise reduction by identifying patterns that predict low-value alerts and by improving triage efficiency, but they must be constrained to avoid institutionalizing the wrong decisions. Common use cases include clustering repeated alert types, predicting likelihood of true positive based on historical outcomes, and generating summaries that accelerate validation steps. These approaches depend on high-quality labeling and consistent feedback loops; if analysts inconsistently mark outcomes or if the environment changes significantly, models will drift and misprioritize. A specific failure mode is false suppression, where a model learns to down-rank alerts that were historically benign but become meaningful when attacker behavior shifts. Another risk is automation bias, where analysts trust a low-risk score too readily and skip validation steps, creating missed detections. For these reasons, ML should be used to recommend prioritization and grouping, while suppression and action thresholds remain governed by explicit rules and periodic human review, with audit trails that capture why changes were made.

Operational noise management also requires workload design that matches human capacity, including staffing models, on-call rotations, and clear boundaries for what must be handled immediately. Fatigue increases sharply when responders are expected to sustain high alert volume during nights and weekends without adequate staffing or escalation support. Organizations should treat after-hours alerting as a separate design problem, with stricter paging thresholds and stronger requirements for context completeness. Lower-confidence alerts can be queued for next-day analysis unless delay materially increases risk, which preserves responder effectiveness for true emergencies. This is not lowering security; it is aligning response to what can be done well under real constraints. When leaders understand that attention is a constrained resource, they can support staffing and process improvements that reduce residual risk rather than simply demanding more alerts.

Noise reduction must also consider upstream engineering choices, because many noisy patterns originate from inconsistent system configurations and unmanaged variability. Standardizing audit settings, ensuring consistent logging across similar systems, and enforcing reliable identity and asset tagging reduces ambiguity and prevents misfires. Where possible, instrumentation should be designed so that high-risk actions generate strong, unambiguous signals, rather than relying on weak proxies that require inference. This is especially important in cloud and identity-heavy environments, where the same action can be represented differently across services and where misconfigured logging is common. Improving the underlying telemetry often yields greater noise reduction than endless tuning of detection logic. It also increases the effectiveness of AI-assisted approaches, because models trained on cleaner data behave more predictably and are easier to govern.

Finally, managing alert fatigue and noise is a governance problem as much as an engineering problem, because it requires sustained attention, clear ownership, and measurable outcomes. Organizations should track alert-to-action ratios, repeat false-positive patterns, and the time cost of triage for top alert types, using those metrics to prioritize improvement work. Reviews should focus on whether noise is decreasing without creating new gaps, and whether responders trust the paging stream enough to act decisively when it fires. Suppression decisions should be documented, time-bounded where appropriate, and revisited as the environment changes, preventing permanent blind spots from accumulating quietly. Over time, the most mature operations treat noise as a form of technical debt that must be paid down continuously. The result is a monitoring program that preserves human attention for what matters, maintains speed under stress, and improves security outcomes without exhausting the people responsible for delivering them.

Maintaining Monitoring Rules Over Time

Monitoring rules are living operational controls, not one-time engineering artifacts, and their value decays unless they are continuously maintained. Environments evolve through application changes, infrastructure refresh, identity lifecycle shifts, and normal business growth, and each of those changes can break assumptions embedded in detection logic. A rule that was high-signal last quarter can become noisy after a migration, or it can go silent because a telemetry source changed field names or stopped forwarding reliably. The operational goal is to keep rules aligned to current architecture and threat realities while preserving the intent of what the rule is meant to detect. That requires disciplined ownership, structured change control, and a feedback loop that treats every incident and false positive as evidence for improvement.

Rule maintenance starts with treating detection logic as managed configuration, with versioning, review, and traceability. Rules should have clear ownership, a documented purpose, and explicit dependencies on telemetry sources, normalization mappings, and enrichment. When those dependencies change, rule impact should be assessed the same way organizations assess the impact of changes to other critical systems. Without that rigor, rule changes become ad hoc edits made under pressure, often without understanding downstream effects. Traceability also matters for incident response, because investigators need to know what rules were in place, what thresholds were set, and whether changes occurred around the time an incident began. A program that cannot explain its own detections is effectively unable to defend its monitoring outcomes.

A practical maintenance process distinguishes between rule correctness and rule usefulness, because a rule can be technically correct while still being operationally harmful. Correctness is about whether the rule matches the intended conditions when the telemetry is accurate, while usefulness is about whether the rule produces actionable outcomes at an acceptable cost. Many rule failures are subtle, such as overly broad matching that captures benign behavior, or overly strict conditions that miss attacker variations. Maintenance should therefore include routine validation that rules still fire when expected, still suppress known benign patterns, and still route alerts to the correct owners. This validation should be supported by structured test cases derived from prior incidents and known attack patterns observed in the environment. Over time, rule maintenance becomes a form of continuous quality assurance for the monitoring program.

Telemetry drift is one of the most common drivers of rule decay, and it often presents as sudden drops or spikes in alert volume. A rule may stop firing because a collector was disabled, an audit policy changed, a service moved to a different logging pipeline, or normalization logic no longer maps a field consistently. Conversely, a rule may become noisy because a new application behavior matches its conditions, or because a previously rare event becomes routine due to automation. Maintaining rules therefore requires monitoring the monitoring system itself, including ingestion health, field population rates, and changes in event distribution. When teams treat telemetry integrity as part of rule maintenance, they can detect and fix silent failures before they become major security gaps. This discipline also supports more reliable use of anomaly-based methods, which are especially sensitive to data instability.

Change management is a critical input to detection maintenance, because major releases and infrastructure projects can invalidate rule assumptions overnight. Security operations must be connected to the organization's change processes, so they can anticipate impact, adjust rules proactively, and temporarily tune thresholds during expected volatility. That does not mean suppressing alerts indiscriminately during change windows, but it does mean differentiating between expected change patterns and unexpected behaviors that occur during change. For example, a planned privileged action can still be risky if it occurs from an unusual source, outside approved windows, or with suspicious surrounding activity. Effective maintenance practices incorporate change context as enrichment that informs triage rather than as an excuse to ignore signals. Over time, this integration reduces both noise and missed detections during the periods when organizations are often most vulnerable.

AI and ML can support rule maintenance by identifying rules that are degrading, suggesting tuning opportunities, and highlighting changes in underlying behavior that warrant review. Practical uses include detecting shifts in alert rates, clustering recurring false positives, and recommending modifications based on historical resolution outcomes. These approaches depend on consistent labeling and reliable operational metadata, such as whether an alert resulted in an incident, a policy violation, or a benign closure. Failure modes include reinforcing analyst shortcuts, where a model learns that certain alert types are "usually benign" and pushes for suppression even when risk changes. Drift is a constant risk here as well, because changes in business processes can make past outcomes a poor predictor of future relevance. For governance, ML recommendations should be treated as inputs to review, not automatic changes, and there should be audit trails for what recommendations were accepted, who approved them, and what evidence supported the decision. The objective is to reduce maintenance toil while preserving accountability for detection coverage.

Operationally, maintenance also requires a clear approach to rule lifecycle management, including when to retire, replace, or consolidate rules. Some rules become redundant as coverage improves elsewhere, while others are superseded by better detections that capture the same behavior with fewer false positives. Rule sprawl is a common problem, where dozens of overlapping detections generate duplication and confusion in triage. Consolidation should be pursued carefully, ensuring that merging logic does not erase useful distinctions such as asset class, privilege level, or response expectations. Retirement decisions should be evidence-based, supported by alert outcomes, coverage mapping to critical behaviors, and validation that removal does not create a blind spot. A mature program treats rule lifecycle decisions as a normal operational function rather than a rare cleanup event.

Rule maintenance is deeply tied to human process, because every change to detection logic affects analyst behavior and escalation patterns. When rules are modified, responders need to understand what changed, what new outcomes to expect, and how triage should adapt. This is especially important for high-impact rules that page on-call responders or trigger containment workflows, where small changes can produce large operational consequences. Maintenance should therefore include controlled rollout practices, such as staged deployment, monitoring of alert rate changes, and quick rollback paths when unintended noise appears. This operational discipline prevents "rule churn," where constant changes create instability and responders lose confidence in what alerts mean. Stability is itself a security property when the monitoring program must function under stress.

Finally, sustaining monitoring rules over time requires measurement that connects maintenance work to improved outcomes. Programs should track alert fidelity, including the proportion of true security events, the time spent triaging top alert types, and the rate of silent failures detected through validation. Maintenance backlogs should be managed as operational risk, prioritized alongside other defensive work based on the business impact of potential detection gaps. Post-incident reviews should translate directly into detection improvements, with clear ownership and deadlines, rather than vague commitments to "tune later." When leaders see that rule maintenance reduces noise, improves response speed, and prevents missed incidents, it becomes easier to justify the time and staffing required. The result is a monitoring capability that remains credible, resilient, and aligned to real-world operations as the organization evolves.

Handoffs Between Monitoring and Investigation

The handoff from monitoring to investigation is the moment an alert stops being a signal and becomes a case, and that transition must be engineered as carefully as the detection logic itself. Monitoring teams are optimized for speed, triage consistency, and breadth across many signals, while investigation teams are optimized for depth, hypothesis testing, and evidence preservation. When handoffs are informal, alerts bounce between teams, context is lost, and investigation starts over from scratch, extending time-to-containment. A mature operation defines clear criteria for when monitoring work is "done enough" to transfer ownership and what information must accompany that transfer. The goal is not to maximize handoffs, but to ensure that when a handoff occurs it accelerates resolution rather than creating churn.

A high-quality handoff begins with a shared definition of what constitutes an investigation-worthy condition. Monitoring should escalate when there is credible evidence of malicious activity, confirmed policy violation with material risk, or a pattern of correlated signals that suggests attacker intent. Investigation should not be used as a dumping ground for ambiguous alerts that monitoring teams did not have time to triage. At the same time, monitoring should not attempt to complete full investigations under the guise of "being thorough," because that delays escalation when deeper expertise is needed. The threshold is best expressed in operational terms, such as the presence of corroborating indicators, involvement of privileged identities or critical assets, or clear deviation from established baselines. When both sides agree on the escalation threshold, work is distributed efficiently and the organization reduces both missed incidents and wasted effort.

Handoff packages must be standardized so that investigators receive consistent context regardless of who was on shift when the alert triggered. The package should include the triggering condition, relevant timestamps, affected identities and assets, and a concise narrative of what has been validated and what remains unknown. It should also include the evidence trail, such as key event identifiers, correlated alerts, and links or references to the underlying telemetry sources in whatever system of record the organization uses. Investigators should not have to re-derive basic facts like asset ownership, identity privilege level, or whether a change window was active. The handoff should explicitly state the triage decision, including why this is believed to be suspicious and what immediate risk is being managed. When handoff packages are consistent, investigators can spend their time testing hypotheses instead of reconstructing context.

Preserving investigative integrity is a core part of the handoff, because monitoring teams are often the first to touch the evidence. Early actions such as isolating hosts, disabling accounts, or blocking network traffic can be necessary, but they can also destroy volatile artifacts or alter system state in ways that complicate attribution and root-cause analysis. The handoff process should therefore define what immediate containment actions are authorized at the monitoring stage and what actions require investigator approval. This boundary should consider both risk and reversibility, favoring actions that reduce harm while preserving evidence where possible. Monitoring teams should document any actions taken before handoff, including who approved them and why, so investigators can interpret changes in telemetry correctly. This discipline prevents the common failure mode where investigators chase phantom gaps caused by defensive actions that were never recorded.

Timing and ownership must be unambiguous at the moment of transfer, because ambiguous ownership is how incidents stall. The handoff should specify who is accountable for next steps, what the immediate objectives are, and when the next status checkpoint will occur. If investigations are handled by specialized teams or different time zones, the process must address continuity, including how cases are queued, how priority is determined, and how after-hours coverage is handled. Monitoring teams should remain available for consultation during early investigation, but they should not retain implicit ownership once the transfer is made. Conversely, investigators should acknowledge receipt and confirm the investigative path, so monitoring can close out their triage responsibilities cleanly. Clear ownership prevents duplicate work and ensures that pages, communications, and containment actions are coordinated.

AI and ML can improve handoffs by reducing the friction of context transfer, but they must be designed to support evidence-based investigation rather than produce persuasive stories. Practical uses include summarizing relevant activity timelines, extracting key entities and relationships from large event sets, and recommending next investigative queries based on prior similar cases. These capabilities are highly dependent on telemetry quality and consistent entity resolution; if the underlying data is fragmented, automated summaries can omit crucial details or merge unrelated activity. A common failure mode is narrative overreach, where an AI-generated summary appears confident but is based on incomplete evidence, nudging investigators toward premature conclusions. Human-in-the-loop controls should require that summaries are treated as starting points and that investigators can trace every assertion back to raw events. For governance, systems should log what was generated, what inputs were used, and whether investigators accepted or corrected the summary, so that automation improves over time without undermining accountability.

Handoffs also require alignment on investigative scope so that the transition does not create confusion about what "done" means. Monitoring teams may focus on the initial triggering behavior, while investigators must consider lateral movement, persistence mechanisms, and potential data access. The handoff should therefore include an initial scope statement that distinguishes what is confirmed from what is suspected and identifies the most likely expansion paths. This is particularly important when the alert involves identities, where the investigation may need to evaluate other sessions, tokens, recent privilege changes, and access to critical systems. Investigators should be able to quickly determine whether the case is likely a contained anomaly, a broader compromise, or a control failure that requires remediation rather than incident response. A well-scoped handoff accelerates both technical work and executive communication because it frames the problem consistently from the start.

Communication pathways are part of the handoff, because investigations often require coordination with system owners, identity teams, legal, or executive stakeholders depending on impact. Monitoring teams should initiate communications only when necessary to reduce immediate risk, and they should avoid broadcasting unconfirmed suspicions widely, which can trigger unnecessary disruption and reputational issues internally. The handoff process should define when to engage other teams, what information is appropriate at each confidence level, and how to maintain confidentiality for sensitive cases. Investigators, once owning the case, should provide structured updates that reflect evidence and decision points rather than speculation. The monitoring-to-investigation handoff is therefore also a shift in communication posture, moving from triage signals to incident management discipline. When that shift is predictable and controlled, organizations avoid both panic and complacency.

Finally, handoffs must be continuously improved through post-case review, because the quality of the transition is best measured by how quickly and accurately investigations progress after transfer. Teams should review whether handoff packages contained the necessary context, whether early containment actions helped or hindered evidence collection, and whether routing thresholds were appropriate. Recurring gaps, such as missing asset ownership, inconsistent identity mapping, or unclear authorization boundaries, should be treated as systemic issues to fix rather than individual performance problems. Over time, the best organizations converge on a shared operating model where monitoring and investigation are distinct but tightly integrated functions. The result is a defensive operation that moves smoothly from detection to decision to response, preserving both speed and depth without sacrificing clarity or accountability.

AI-Assisted Triage: Summarization, Prioritization, and Guardrails Against Over-Trust

AI-assisted triage is most valuable when it reduces cognitive load without weakening accountability, helping analysts move faster through routine validation while preserving rigor for high-impact decisions. In monitoring operations, triage friction often comes from volume, fragmented telemetry, and the need to assemble a coherent narrative from many small signals. AI can compress that work by summarizing what happened, highlighting relationships between entities, and suggesting the most likely explanations based on observed patterns. The operational goal is not to replace analysts, but to make their attention more effective by giving them structured context earlier. Done well, AI-assisted triage increases consistency across shifts and reduces time lost to repetitive evidence gathering. Done poorly, it becomes a source of false confidence that accelerates the wrong decisions.

Summarization is the most immediately useful capability because it converts raw events into a digestible account of activity without requiring analysts to manually stitch together timelines. A good summary identifies key entities, such as the identity, device, and service involved, and describes the sequence of events with accurate timestamps. It should include the specific conditions that triggered the alert and any corroborating or contradicting indicators found in adjacent telemetry. Summarization becomes operationally reliable only when it is grounded in consistent event schemas and stable entity resolution; otherwise, it will omit critical steps or conflate similar identities. It also must preserve traceability by referencing the underlying events, so analysts can verify every claim quickly. A summary that cannot be audited is not triage support; it is an untestable opinion.

Prioritization is the second major use case, because alert queues typically contain a mix of true emergencies, benign anomalies, and slow-burn risks that require follow-up. AI can assist by scoring alerts based on contextual risk factors such as asset criticality, identity privilege, and similarity to past confirmed incidents. It can also incorporate operational considerations, such as whether the alert is part of an ongoing cluster, whether related alerts were recently investigated, and whether the signal has historically produced meaningful action. This can reduce the time analysts spend deciding what to look at next and help ensure that high-impact cases are surfaced quickly. However, prioritization depends on disciplined outcome labeling and feedback loops; without accurate history, the model learns the wrong patterns. Operational teams must treat prioritization as a recommendation engine

Table 19.3 AI-Assisted Triage Guardrails and Governance Expectations.

AI-Assisted Use	Operational Benefit	Required Dependency	Guardrail to Prevent over Trust
Summarization	Reduces time to understand event sequence	Stable schemas and entity resolution	Verify key claims against raw events
Prioritization	Surfaces high-risk cases faster	Labeled outcomes and consistent context	Hard rules override model score for privileged indicators
Clustering	Reduces duplicate triage effort	Reliable timestamps and identifiers	Review cluster membership before closure
Recommendation	Suggests next investigative checks	Accessible supporting telemetry	Require analyst validation before escalation
Trend detection	Flags degrading rules and rising noise	Alert rate monitoring and field health checks	Human review before suppression or tuning changes

that accelerates human decision-making, not as an autonomous arbiter of what matters. Table 19.3 shows where AI can accelerate triage and the guardrails needed to keep decisions evidence-based and auditable.

The effectiveness of both summarization and prioritization is constrained by telemetry quality, because AI systems cannot produce reliable outputs from inconsistent or incomplete data. Missing logs, inconsistent timestamps, and weak identity attribution lead to summaries that are incomplete and scores that misrepresent risk. Data drift is especially problematic, because business process changes can alter what "normal" looks like and invalidate models trained on prior behavior. In addition, the operational meaning of an alert can shift when architecture changes, such as moving services to new platforms or changing authentication flows. AI-assisted triage must therefore be paired with monitoring of its own inputs and performance, including checks for data coverage, field population changes, and shifts in alert distributions. Without this, the organization will not notice when the system has quietly become less reliable.

Guardrails against over-trust are mandatory because AI outputs are often presented in fluent, confident language that can overwhelm cautious analytical habits. Over-trust shows up as analysts accepting a summary without validating the underlying evidence, closing alerts based on a low-risk score without confirming context, or escalating cases based on persuasive narratives rather than facts. This risk increases during high workload periods, when responders are most tempted to rely on shortcuts. Operational guardrails should include explicit verification steps in the triage workflow, such as checking a minimum set of raw events and confirming key facts like identity privilege, asset criticality, and whether change activity was present. For high-impact actions, such as account disablement or containment, human approval boundaries should be enforced so that AI recommendations cannot directly trigger disruptive actions. Guardrails should be designed to preserve speed while preventing irreversible mistakes.

Bias and feedback loops are another failure mode that can subtly degrade triage quality over time. If historical outcomes reflect past coverage gaps, staffing constraints, or inconsistent analyst behavior, models trained on those outcomes can embed those shortcomings and institutionalize them. For example, if alerts from a certain system were historically closed quickly because they were difficult to investigate, a model may learn to down-rank them, even if they represent meaningful risk. Similarly, if certain alert types were frequently escalated due to their visibility rather than their true impact, models may overweight them and crowd out quieter but more dangerous signals. Guarding against this requires deliberate governance, including periodic review of model outputs against independent measures of risk and incident outcomes. It also requires maintaining "hard constraints" in the triage process, such as always prioritizing certain classes of privileged identity compromise indicators regardless of model score. AI-assisted triage must therefore be designed with an understanding that data reflects human systems, not just technical reality.

Leakage and confidentiality risks must be treated as first-class constraints when AI systems are used in triage, because the data involved often includes sensitive identity information, operational details, and potentially regulated data elements. Inputs to AI-assisted triage should be scoped to what is necessary, and outputs should avoid reproducing sensitive content beyond what analysts require to make decisions. Governance should define where summaries and scores are stored, who can access them, and how long they are retained, because triage artifacts can become sensitive records in their own right. Auditability is critical, so the organization can demonstrate how triage decisions were made, what evidence was considered, and whether AI assistance influenced the outcome. When AI is used, the organization should be able to trace which version of a model or logic was active at the time and what inputs were used to produce the output. This is especially important in post-incident reviews, where AI assistance may be questioned and must be defensible.

AI-assisted triage should also include mechanisms for analyst feedback that improve performance without creating perverse incentives. Analysts should be able to correct summaries, flag missing context, and label outcomes in a structured way that feeds retraining or rule refinement. Feedback should capture not only whether an alert was benign or malicious, but why, such as "expected change," "misattributed identity," or "duplicate correlation," because those reasons are essential for improving both models and upstream telemetry. At the same time, organizations must ensure that analysts are not pressured to label outcomes quickly simply to improve metrics, because that degrades data quality and undermines the system's learning. Feedback loops should be designed to capture high-quality signal from real investigations, not superficial closures. Over time, this creates a virtuous cycle where AI assistance becomes more accurate and analysts become more confident in when to use it and when to override it.

Finally, implementing AI-assisted triage successfully requires clarity about what the organization expects it to change operationally and how success will be measured. The program should track whether summarization reduces time-to-triage, whether prioritization improves time-to-engagement for high-impact cases, and whether guardrails prevent errors such as inappropriate closures or unnecessary escalations. It should also track failure indicators, such as increased misses, increased reversals of triage decisions, or a widening gap between model scores and real incident outcomes. AI assistance should be introduced in a controlled way, with staged rollout and clear rollback conditions if performance degrades. When it is governed as an operational control with explicit boundaries, AI-assisted triage can meaningfully reduce noise and increase responsiveness without compromising rigor. The most important outcome is not faster decisions alone, but decisions that remain evidence-based, auditable, and resilient under pressure.

Building a Sustainable Monitoring Cadence

A sustainable monitoring cadence is the operational rhythm that keeps detection and response reliable without overwhelming the people and processes responsible for acting on signals. It starts by acknowledging that monitoring is never "finished"; it is a recurring set of activities that must be executed, measured, and refined as the environment changes. Cadence defines how often the team reviews alerts, tunes rules, validates telemetry integrity, and reassesses priorities based on business risk. Without a cadence, monitoring becomes reactive, where improvements happen only after incidents or outages force attention. The result is predictable drift toward noise, blind spots, and inconsistent response quality.

Cadence must align to the organization's response capacity, because the best detection logic is irrelevant if there is no consistent ability to triage and escalate outcomes. This includes staffing levels, on-call coverage, time zone realities, and the workload of adjacent teams that receive escalations. A sustainable model deliberately differentiates between continuous actions and periodic actions, ensuring that urgent signals are handled in near real time while less time-sensitive review work is handled on a planned schedule. That separation reduces the temptation to treat every alert as an emergency and prevents backlogs from accumulating silently. It also creates a stable operating posture where responders can predict what will be handled immediately versus what will be addressed in a scheduled review window.

At the core of cadence is a repeatable triage cycle that maintains consistent quality across shifts and avoids "alert roulette," where outcomes depend on who happens to be on duty. Triage should have a defined service level expectation that reflects risk, such as faster handling for alerts involving privileged identities or critical assets. The cycle should also include explicit checkpoints for telemetry integrity, because unreliable inputs create false confidence and waste analyst time. When ingestion pipelines degrade, the cadence should treat that as an operational incident for monitoring itself, not a background annoyance. This ensures that "quiet dashboards" are not mistaken for a secure environment.

Sustainability also requires planned review loops that look beyond individual alerts and focus on patterns that indicate systemic issues. Alert trends, repeat false positives, recurring misroutes, and frequent "expected change" closures are signals that detection logic, enrichment, or ownership boundaries need adjustment. A cadence that includes routine pattern review reduces toil by addressing root causes rather than repeatedly triaging the same issues. It also allows teams to prioritize improvement work based on real operational data, such as which detections consume disproportionate time or which telemetry sources most often fail. Over time, this turns monitoring from a constant firefight into an engineered capability that improves predictably.

Validation activities must be part of the cadence, because monitoring systems fail silently and those failures often become apparent only after an incident. Validation includes confirming that critical telemetry sources are still flowing, that key fields are populated consistently, and that high-impact rules still trigger under expected conditions. These checks should be treated as routine operational hygiene, not periodic "spring cleaning," because drift happens continuously. Validation also needs to account for business seasonality and change windows, which can alter normal behavior and stress logging pipelines. A cadence that anticipates these cycles reduces both noise spikes and undetected gaps during periods of heavy organizational activity.

Change management integration is another essential element, because monitoring is highly sensitive to architecture evolution and process redesign. A sustainable cadence includes mechanisms to anticipate planned changes, assess detection impact, and adjust rules or enrichment proactively rather than reactively. This prevents a common failure mode where new deployments create weeks of alert noise, which teams suppress out of fatigue, inadvertently creating blind spots. Maintaining cadence also means having a controlled rollout approach for detection updates, especially for high-impact paging rules, so that teams can observe effects and roll back quickly if needed. When monitoring is coupled to change processes in this way, it becomes more resilient and less disruptive to the organization.

AI and ML can strengthen cadence by reducing repetitive workload and highlighting where human attention is best applied, but only when they are governed as operational aids rather than autonomous decision-makers. Practical uses include summarizing recurring alert patterns, clustering similar cases to reduce duplicate triage, and recommending which detections are degrading based on changes in alert rates and closure outcomes. These capabilities depend on consistent outcome labeling, stable telemetry, and disciplined review, so models do not drift into suppressing important signals simply because they are inconvenient to investigate. Guardrails should ensure that AI-driven prioritization does not override hard risk-based rules, such as elevating indicators involving privileged identity compromise regardless of historical "benign" rates. Outputs must remain auditable, so the team can explain why a prioritization or tuning recommendation was made and whether it was accepted. Used this way, AI reduces operational toil while preserving accountability and evidence-based decision-making.

Cadence becomes sustainable when it includes explicit measures of effectiveness that reinforce the right behaviors and expose early warning signs of decay. Teams should track whether alert volume is within capacity, whether high-risk alerts are handled within expected timeframes, and whether the proportion of alerts that lead to meaningful action is improving or declining. They should also monitor indicators of fatigue, such as increasing closure speed without evidence review, growing backlogs, or rising rates of reopened cases after escalation. When these measures are reviewed routinely, leaders can intervene with staffing, process changes, or engineering investment before the system fails under stress. The end state is a monitoring operation that runs at a steady tempo, adapts deliberately, and remains trustworthy to both responders and executives because it produces consistent, actionable outcomes over time.

Conclusion

A mature monitoring and alerting program is measured by the quality of decisions it produces under pressure, not by the volume of data it collects or the number of alerts it generates. Sustainability comes from explicit goals, reliable telemetry, and a cadence that continuously validates inputs, tunes rules, and aligns alerting thresholds to human capacity and business priorities. When triage, routing, and investigation handoffs are engineered as repeatable workflows, the organization responds faster with less disruption and fewer missed signals, even as systems and teams change. AI can strengthen these outcomes when it is governed as a decision-support layer with clear guardrails, traceability, and human approval boundaries, ensuring the program remains evidence-based, auditable, and resilient over time.

Recommendations

1) Define monitoring goals in terms of risk outcomes and response decisions rather than raw data volume. Tie visibility priorities to critical assets, privileged identities, and high-consequence workflows, so coverage reflects what the business cannot afford to lose. Reassess those goals when architecture or operations shift, so monitoring remains aligned to what actually matters.
2) Establish baselines that reflect role- and asset-specific "normal" behavior instead of relying on enterprise-wide averages. Normalize identities and key fields, so the same entity is represented consistently across telemetry sources, and validate time alignment, so sequences can be trusted. Treat baselines as living references that must account for seasonality, maintenance patterns, and routine operational variability.
3) Design deviation detection to combine relative behavior changes with corroborating context rather than using rigid, single-metric thresholds. Use multiple levels of evaluation such as per-identity, per-role, and per-asset, so unusual behavior is judged in the right frame. Preserve hard guardrails for high-risk actions, so drift and normalization do not quietly lower sensitivity.
4) Reserve paging for conditions that are urgent, actionable, and materially risk-increasing if delayed. Require paging alerts to include enough context to support an immediate first action, including who, what, when, and why it matters. Enforce an explicit "page budget," so on-call responders remain effective and pages remain trusted.
5) Standardize triage decisions with consistent evidence thresholds and repeatable validation steps. Ensure triage includes quick checks for telemetry integrity and change context, so broken pipelines and planned activity are not misclassified as security events. Capture outcomes in a structured way, so tuning work is based on operational evidence rather than anecdotes.
6) Route alerts to the accountable owner using explicit ownership boundaries instead of letting security absorb remediation by default. Attach asset ownership, privilege level, and escalation paths as part of alert context, so handoffs are fast and predictable. Prevent bottlenecks by making it clear when security is coordinating versus when another team is responsible for corrective action.
7) Establish escalation triggers that separate technical escalation from leadership escalation and that are tied to impact, confidence, and time sensitivity. Require escalations to include the decision being requested, the evidence supporting urgency, and what has already been validated. Use time-bound checkpoints, so ownership remains clear and cases do not stall during shift changes or after-hours coverage.

8) Reduce alert noise by improving enrichment, de-duplication, and correlation before suppressing detections. Focus on eliminating repeated investigations of known benign patterns by integrating change context and consolidating duplicate signals into coherent cases. Document suppression decisions and revisit them routinely, so convenience does not turn into permanent blind spots.
9) Maintain monitoring rules as versioned, reviewable operational artifacts with documented intent and telemetry dependencies. Monitor for rule decay by tracking sudden changes in alert volume and field population, and validate critical rules with repeatable test cases. Use controlled rollouts and quick rollback paths for high-impact rules, so stability is preserved while improvements are introduced.
10) Apply AI-assisted triage as decision support for summarization and prioritization while enforcing guardrails against over-trust. Require analysts to verify key facts against raw events and keep disruptive actions behind clear human approval boundaries. Ensure AI outputs are auditable, based on well-scoped inputs, and continuously evaluated for drift, bias, and misleading confidence.

20

Detection Engineering and Anomaly Detection

Detection engineering and anomaly detection are most effective when treated as a managed capability with explicit ownership, measurable performance, and disciplined maintenance rather than as an ever-growing collection of rules. High-quality detections are built from real threat behaviors and grounded in dependable telemetry, with tuning and validation practices that reduce false positives without creating silent blind spots. Because environments change continuously, detection logic must be documented, versioned, and governed so that breakage is detected quickly, fixes are auditable, and coverage gaps are tracked as managed risk rather than discovered during crises. AI/ML can amplify this work by prioritizing signals, clustering patterns, and summarizing context, but only when drift is managed, outputs are explainable, and human approval boundaries prevent false confidence from turning automation into unchecked authority.

Detection as a Managed Capability

Treat detection as a managed capability rather than a collection of rules because the organization is ultimately buying outcomes: faster discovery, lower blast radius, and fewer surprises. That requires a clear service boundary that distinguishes detection engineering from incident response, threat intelligence, and platform administration while still integrating with each of them. A managed capability has defined customers, measurable performance, and explicit operating constraints such as coverage goals, acceptable latency, and on-call expectations. It also has accountability for the full detection lifecycle, not just the moment a rule is deployed. When leadership asks whether the environment is "being monitored," the only credible answer is grounded in maintained detections, validated telemetry, and observed results.

A managed detection program starts with disciplined inputs, because detections are only as trustworthy as the data they depend on. Telemetry sources must be inventoried, normalized where necessary, and continuously checked for availability, completeness, and time alignment so that detection logic is not silently operating on degraded data. Ownership matters: someone must be responsible for field mappings, parsing changes, timestamp behavior, and retention policies that affect detection fidelity. This is where many teams fail operationally, because they focus on rule quantity while ignoring data breakage caused by agent rollouts, log pipeline changes, or schema updates. The result is a fragile detection surface that looks mature on paper but performs inconsistently under pressure.

Engineering rigor shows up in how detections are specified, implemented, and maintained as production assets. Every detection should have a clear purpose statement, defined preconditions, and expected outputs, so responders know what the alert is asserting and what evidence supports it. Implementation should explicitly document dependencies such as required log sources, needed fields, and any enrichment assumptions, along with how to validate that those dependencies remain true over time. Maintenance work is not optional; it is the operational cost of accuracy in an environment where identity systems, endpoints, and cloud control

Table 20.1 Detection Capability Lifecycle Ownership Map.

Lifecycle Stage	Primary Owner	Primary Output	Quality Check
Telemetry readiness	Detection engineering	Validated required sources and fields	Data health checks and field completeness
Detection build	Detection engineering	Behavior-based detection logic	Peer review and dependency verification
Validation and testing	Detection engineering and responders	Confirmed expected firing and context	Controlled tests and outcome review
Tuning and refinement	Detection engineering	Reduced false positives without blind spots	Disposition trends and regression checks
Maintenance	Detection engineering	Updated logic after change-driven breakage	Dependency monitoring and drift detection
Retire or consolidate	Detection engineering and responders	Removed or merged low-value detections	Outcome history and redundancy review

planes change continuously. When detections are treated like code—with version control, peer review, and predictable release practices—changes become safer, more auditable, and easier to roll back when something behaves unexpectedly. Table 20.1 clarifies who owns each stage of the detection lifecycle and the checks that keep detections reliable as a managed capability.

Validation must be continuous, not episodic, because the real question is whether detections work under current conditions rather than whether they once worked in a lab. Teams should regularly exercise detections using controlled test activity, replayed telemetry, or known-bad samples in a way that is safe for production, and then compare expected alert behavior to actual results. This is also where "alert correctness" becomes tangible: whether the alert fires when it should, stays quiet when it should, and provides enough context to drive a consistent first response. A managed capability treats missed detections and noisy detections as defects with root causes, not as personal failures or unavoidable quirks of security tooling. Over time, this approach builds confidence that detection coverage is real, measurable, and improving.

Anomaly detection and statistical methods can strengthen the program when used as augmentation rather than as an oracle. Baseline-driven detections work best when the baseline is tied to stable entities—specific identities, hosts, workloads, or business processes—and when the model's output is translated into operationally meaningful conditions. The telemetry dependencies are stricter here, because anomalies are sensitive to missing data, shifting populations, and changes in logging behavior that can look like behavior change when they are really instrumentation change. Good practice is to treat anomaly results as candidates for investigation or as a prioritization signal, not as an automatic escalation trigger without corroboration. When AI/ML is used to cluster similar events, score outliers, or summarize behavior context, it should operate within explicit approval boundaries, so humans decide what crosses the line into an actionable alert.

Human-in-the-loop control is not a philosophical preference; it is the practical guardrail that prevents model confidence from outrunning operational truth. Analysts must be able to see what evidence drove an anomaly score or correlation outcome, at least at the level of contributing features and supporting events, so they can challenge false confidence and avoid rubber-stamping. Drift is a predictable failure mode: business cycles, new applications, acquisitions, and infrastructure migrations change "normal," and a model that is not retrained and revalidated will gradually produce either noise or blind spots. Bias also shows up in subtle ways, such as over-weighting well-instrumented systems while under-detecting in less instrumented parts of the environment, creating a misleading sense of coverage. Leakage is another risk when AI is applied to sensitive telemetry; detection workflows must ensure that training data, prompts, and outputs are handled in ways that respect access controls, data minimization, and retention requirements.

Operating a managed capability requires explicit decisioning about what becomes an alert, what becomes a signal, and what becomes a backlog item for future engineering. If every interesting behavior becomes a page, response capacity collapses and teams stop trusting the system, which then creates delayed or missed action when something truly matters. Effective programs define quality thresholds tied to business impact, asset criticality, and the expected cost of investigation, and they refine those thresholds based on observed responder outcomes. Triaged signals that do not merit escalation can still be valuable as enrichment or correlation inputs, especially when they help corroborate a higher-confidence detection. The goal is not to eliminate uncertainty; it is to shape uncertainty into manageable workflows where attention is spent on the highest value decisions.

Governance and auditability are part of management, not paperwork, because detection changes directly affect risk posture and incident outcomes. When a detection is created, tuned, disabled, or exceptions are added, there should be traceable rationale, approval where appropriate, and evidence that the change was validated against expected behavior. Access to modify detections and their supporting pipelines should be controlled, with separation of duties where feasible, so a compromise cannot easily blind monitoring without detection. Metrics should emphasize operational value—time to detect, time to triage, investigation completion rates, false-positive drivers, and coverage gaps tied to telemetry readiness—rather than vanity counts of rules. Over time, this creates a defensible narrative that detection is being run as a resilient production function with measurable performance, known tradeoffs, and continuous improvement built into how the team works.

Building Detections from Real Threat Behaviors

Detections are strongest when they are built from how adversaries actually operate in your environment rather than from abstract lists of "bad things." Real threat behaviors have shape: they produce sequences of actions, touch specific control planes, and leave consistent traces in telemetry even when individual tactics vary. The practical goal is to express those behaviors in observable terms that can be measured and tested, not merely recognized in hindsight. That means starting from what an attacker must do to achieve an objective—gain execution, establish persistence, move laterally, access data—and mapping that to the events your systems reliably produce. When detection engineering begins with behavior, it naturally prioritizes signals that remain durable across tool changes and adversary retooling.

A behavior-first approach also forces clarity about what is and is not detectable given current instrumentation. Many "detections" are really aspirations that depend on logs you do not collect, fields you do not retain, or endpoint visibility you only have on part of the fleet. Building from real behaviors means explicitly naming the preconditions: the logs required, the fields that must be present, the time synchronization assumptions, and the enrichment needed to interpret the activity. It also means confronting blind spots without blame and turning them into concrete backlog items for telemetry onboarding or normalization. Executives tend to assume monitoring is uniform; engineering from behavior provides a disciplined way to state, with precision, where coverage is strong and where it is limited.

Threat behaviors become operational detections when they are translated into conditions that are both specific enough to be actionable and general enough to survive minor variations. Overly specific signatures tie you to a single payload or command line and break the moment the adversary changes tooling. Overly general patterns page on benign administration and train the organization to ignore the alerts. Good detection engineering threads the needle by using context: who performed the action, from where, on what asset class, against what baseline, and with what corroborating events nearby in time. In practice, this often looks like combining a small number of high-signal indicators rather than betting everything on a single event.

The best behavioral detections reflect attacker tradecraft as a progression rather than as isolated atoms of activity. One suspicious authentication, one unusual process launch, or one unexpected configuration change can be explainable on its own, but the same events in a tight sequence become much more meaningful. This is where correlation becomes an engineering discipline: decide which events are necessary, which are supportive, and what time window preserves intent without collapsing into noise. Correlation should be deterministic and reviewable, not a black box, so responders can understand what the detection is asserting and quickly validate or refute it. When correlation is done well, alerts become investigative starting points rather than puzzles.

AI/ML can enhance behavior-based detection by helping teams discover recurring attack-shaped patterns in large volumes of telemetry and by improving the quality of contextual enrichment. For example, clustering can reveal repeated sequences of actions across multiple hosts that resemble privilege escalation or credential access workflows, even when individual commands differ. Models can also help prioritize which behavioral candidates are worth turning into detections by scoring rarity relative to peer groups such as role, business unit, or workload type. These capabilities require disciplined inputs: consistent field normalization, stable entity identifiers, and enough historical data to establish meaningful baselines. The human-in-the-loop boundary remains critical, because a model's confidence score is not evidence; engineers and analysts must decide what becomes a production alert and must be able to audit why a pattern was flagged.

Failure modes are predictable when you build detections from real behaviors, and planning for them is part of engineering maturity. False positives often come from legitimate administrative activity that looks adversarial when context is missing, such as emergency troubleshooting, bulk automation, or maintenance windows. False negatives commonly come from telemetry gaps, field parsing failures, clock drift, or changes in default logging that silently remove the events a detection depends on. In ML-assisted approaches, drift can cause yesterday's anomaly to become today's routine, or a business change can create widespread "anomalies" that are actually normal operations after a migration. A managed program treats these outcomes as defects to diagnose: was the behavior model wrong, was the environment misunderstood, or did the data pipeline change?

Finally, building from real threat behaviors requires tight collaboration between detection engineers and the teams responsible for response, so detections match operational realities. Every new detection should implicitly answer: what is the first action a responder will take, what evidence should already be present, and what decision can be made within a bounded amount of time. If the alert cannot drive a meaningful decision, it is not finished, regardless of how clever the logic is. Conversely, when responders consistently confirm a behavior with minimal additional work, the detection is doing what it should: compressing uncertainty into a reliable signal. Over time, this approach turns detection engineering into an iterative practice grounded in observed attacker behavior, real telemetry, and responder feedback rather than in static assumptions.

Tuning Detections to Reduce False Positives

False positives are not just an inconvenience; they are an operational tax that consumes analyst attention, delays real investigations, and erodes trust in the detection program. When responders stop believing alerts are meaningful, they compensate with shortcuts, delayed triage, and "alert fatigue" behaviors that quietly raise business risk. Tuning is the disciplined process of reducing avoidable noise without blinding the organization to genuine threat activity. That discipline begins by treating every high-volume false positive as a defect with an explainable cause, not as an inevitable cost of monitoring. The goal is not silence; the goal is a stable, credible alert stream that reflects real risk.

Effective tuning starts with measurement at the level of individual detections, not aggregate dashboards that hide which rules are doing harm. Engineers need to know alert volume trends, true-positive confirmation rates, time-to-triage impact, and where in the workflow alerts get dismissed. Volume alone is not sufficient because a low-volume rule can still be low quality if it wastes time when it does fire, while a higher-volume rule can be

Table 20.2 False-Positive Drivers and Safe Tuning Responses.

False-Positive Driver	What it Looks Like	Safe Tuning Move	What to Avoid
Missing context	Alerts match benign admin workflows	Add identity asset class and timing context	Broad allowlists that create blind spots
Global thresholds	One threshold fits nobody	Use entity or peer-group baselines	Raising thresholds globally without validation
Parsing or schema shift	Field values change or go null	Fix normalization and mappings	Tuning logic when the data is wrong
Change windows	Legitimate bursts during releases	Account for known change periods	Suppressing alerts permanently
Duplicate detections	Same event triggers multiple alerts	Merge or correlate into one signal	Letting duplicates inflate volume
Insufficient evidence	Analysts mark unknown often	Add required context fields and enrichment	Escalating without bounded triage intent

acceptable if it reliably points to meaningful issues. Capturing disposition outcomes in a consistent way is essential because tuning without responder feedback becomes guesswork. When the data shows a detection produces repetitive benign cases, the next step is to describe those benign patterns precisely, using the same telemetry fields the detection relies on.

Most false positives come from missing context, so tuning typically improves the "aboutness" of the alert rather than simply narrowing the pattern. Context can be environmental, such as whether the asset is a production server versus a developer workstation, or whether the identity is a service account versus an employee account. It can be behavioral, such as whether the activity aligns with an established baseline for that entity, or whether it occurred during a change window. It can also be technical, such as whether a process is signed, whether the parent process is expected, or whether the network destination is common for that role. The tuning move is to add discriminators that preserve the suspicious core while filtering the benign look-alikes, and to do so in ways that remain durable as the environment evolves. Table 20.2 links common false-positive causes to tuning approaches that reduce noise while preserving detection intent.

A common pitfall is tuning by adding broad allowlists or static exceptions that silently create blind spots. Allowlists should be used sparingly and should be narrowly scoped to stable, well-understood conditions, because attackers deliberately abuse "known good" pathways. When exceptions are necessary, they should be time-bounded where possible, tied to a clear rationale, and revisited as part of routine maintenance, so they do not become permanent gaps. Tuning should also avoid overfitting to a single incident or a single noisy team, which can produce rules that look quiet today but miss tomorrow's variant. The best tuning changes are those that can be explained in plain operational terms and validated against both benign and adversarial examples.

Threshold tuning requires special care because thresholds are where detection logic meets response capacity. If the threshold is too low, the rule becomes an alert generator; if too high, it becomes a retrospective indicator discovered only after damage is done. Thresholds should be anchored in the normal operating patterns of the environment, which means understanding typical rates, burst behaviors, and seasonal cycles for the telemetry in question. It is usually better to tune thresholds relative to peer groups or baselines—per identity, per host class, per application—than to apply a single global number that fits nobody. When baselines are used, the tuning must account for baseline contamination, where malicious activity or misconfigured automation becomes "normal" and suppresses future alerts.

AI/ML can help reduce false positives by improving prioritization and by highlighting which contextual factors actually distinguish benign from suspicious cases in your telemetry. For example, models can learn that certain alert attributes correlate strongly with benign administrative workflows and can suggest which fields to incorporate as filters or as severity modifiers. Clustering can group repeated false positives into common patterns, making it easier to identify root causes such as a specific automation job, a logging artifact, or a recurring maintenance process. These approaches depend on clean, consistent input data and on reliable labeling from triage outcomes; noisy labels produce misleading model guidance. Human approval boundaries matter here as well: model outputs should recommend tuning candidates, not automatically change detection logic, and changes should still go through review and validation.

Validation is the guardrail that keeps tuning from turning into accidental suppression. Every tuning change should be tested against known benign scenarios and against representative malicious behavior, so the team can confirm what was reduced and what was preserved. In practice, that means replaying relevant telemetry, using controlled test activity, or running the tuned rule in a monitor-only mode to compare outcomes before making it authoritative. Engineers should also validate upstream dependencies because what looks like a false-positive spike can be a parsing change that altered field values or a clock skew issue that broke correlation windows. After deployment, tuning should be monitored for regressions such as sudden drops in alerting that may indicate the rule became too restrictive or the telemetry pipeline degraded.

Sustained false-positive reduction is a workflow discipline, not a one-time cleanup. Detections should have owners, routine review cycles, and clear criteria for when a rule needs refactoring versus when it should be retired. Retiring a detection is sometimes the correct action if the behavior is no longer relevant or if it cannot be made sufficiently actionable with available telemetry. Over time, the program should converge on a set of detections where responders can predict what they mean, engineers can explain why they exist, and leadership can trust the monitoring signal as a credible reflection of risk rather than as an unfiltered stream of machine noise.

Measuring Detection Quality Over Volume

Detection volume is an easy metric to collect and a terrible metric to manage by, because it rewards output instead of outcomes. A program can generate thousands of alerts per day and still miss meaningful adversary activity, or it can run a smaller set of high-fidelity detections that reliably drive timely action. Quality-centric measurement reframes the work around what the business actually needs: early discovery of material threats, predictable triage effort, and consistent investigative decisions. This does not mean reducing alert count for its own sake; it means ensuring that every alert is worth the time it consumes. When measurement reflects quality, engineering incentives align with operational reality rather than with rule-count vanity.

Quality measurement begins by defining what "good" looks like in ways that are observable and repeatable. A high-quality detection is one that fires for the right reasons, provides sufficient context to support a bounded initial investigation, and produces a consistent outcome when handled by different analysts. It has clear preconditions and fails loudly when its required telemetry is missing, rather than continuing silently with degraded accuracy. It also has an expected response path, including what data should be checked first and what decision the alert is meant to enable. These properties can be assessed without relying on perfect ground truth, which is often unavailable in real environments.

The most operationally meaningful quality signal is outcome data from triage and investigation, captured in a consistent way. Teams need to know how often alerts are confirmed as meaningful, how often they are dismissed as benign, how often they are duplicates of other detections, and how often they are "unknown" because evidence is insufficient. The "unknown" category is particularly valuable because it often reveals data gaps, enrichment failures, or alert design that does not provide enough context to reach a decision. Time-based measures matter as well: how long it takes to understand the alert, how long it takes to route it correctly, and how long it takes to reach an escalation decision. These measures translate directly into cost and risk because every minute spent on low-quality alerts is attention not spent on true threats.

Quality also depends on reliability, which is frequently overlooked when teams focus on content rather than on plumbing. A detection that is correct in principle but routinely misses events due to ingestion lag, parsing changes, or inconsistent host telemetry is not high quality in practice. Reliability measurement includes telemetry health checks, field completeness validation, and correlation window performance, so engineers can separate "the detection is wrong" from "the data is wrong." This is where a managed capability treats detections as production assets with service-level expectations, including acceptable data latency and expected coverage across critical asset classes. Reliability metrics turn silent failure into visible work, which is essential for maintaining trust in monitoring.

Another quality dimension is actionability, meaning the alert meaningfully reduces uncertainty for the responder. Alerts should carry the minimum evidence required to start, such as the implicated identity and host, the relevant timestamps, the key observed behaviors, and any enrichment that helps interpret intent. If the analyst must immediately pivot through multiple systems just to understand what the alert is about, the detection is pushing work downstream rather than doing its job. Actionability can be measured by looking at triage touch time and by tracking how often analysts need to request additional data or escalation just to proceed. A smaller number of highly actionable alerts can outperform a large alert stream that forces analysts to reconstruct context from scratch.

AI/ML can support quality measurement by helping teams summarize outcomes, identify patterns in false positives, and surface weak signals that correlate with true incidents. For example, models can cluster alerts by shared attributes to reveal that a handful of underlying conditions drive most dismissals, which points directly to tuning opportunities. Models can also assist in estimating confidence by learning from historical dispositions, but this must be treated as decision support rather than automated truth. These techniques require disciplined labeling and auditability, because biased or inconsistent dispositions can teach the model to undervalue activity from less-visible parts of the environment or to over-trust historically noisy sources. Human-in-the-loop controls should ensure that any ML-derived "quality score" is explainable, monitored for drift, and never used as the sole basis to suppress alerts.

Quality-over-volume measurement should also account for coverage in a way that resists superficial reporting. Counting detections tells you nothing about whether the most important behaviors are being observed on the most important assets. Coverage measurement should connect detections to required telemetry and to critical asset classes, so the team can state, with specificity, what is being monitored and under what assumptions. Coverage is not binary; it can be partial due to incomplete onboarding, inconsistent agent deployment, or missing identity context, and those gaps should be visible in the metrics. When coverage is expressed as an engineering reality—what signals exist, where they exist, and how reliably they arrive—it becomes a practical driver for investment and prioritization.

Finally, quality measurement must feed an operating cadence that changes behavior, not a dashboard that is admired and ignored. High-noise detections should trigger root-cause analysis and redesign work, not just incremental filters that postpone the problem. High-value detections should be replicated or extended where telemetry permits, because they represent proven leverage. Retiring or merging redundant detections should be considered a sign of maturity, since it reduces duplicate work and clarifies responder expectations. When leaders see quality metrics tied to reduced triage waste, faster escalation, and fewer missed material events, the program gains durable support that cannot be earned by volume alone.

Anomaly Detection: Strengths and Limitations

Anomaly detection is most useful when it is treated as a way to surface "worth a look" behavior in vast, noisy environments rather than as a replacement for behavior-based detections. Its core promise is leverage: it can flag deviations that do not match known signatures, which is valuable against novel techniques, living-off-the-land activity, and slow-moving abuse that blends into legitimate operations. In executive terms, anomaly detection is a hedge against uncertainty, not a guarantee of coverage. The engineering reality is that anomalies are easier to produce than actionable alerts, and the gap between the two is where most programs succeed or fail. When deployed thoughtfully, anomaly detection expands the field of view without drowning responders in curiosities.

The primary strength of anomaly detection is that it is not constrained to pre-defined attacker patterns. It can highlight an identity that suddenly authenticates from unusual locations, accesses unfamiliar systems, or changes behavior relative to its past, even if each individual action is technically "allowed." It can also detect system-level shifts such as unusual data transfer volumes, atypical administrative actions, or rare process relationships that are difficult to encode as deterministic rules. This makes it particularly useful for early signal when an adversary is probing, staging, or testing access before committing to louder actions. In practice, anomaly detection works best when it is attached to entities the organization cares about—privileged roles, sensitive workloads, crown-jewel data paths—so the resulting signals are naturally risk-weighted.

Those strengths come with strict telemetry dependencies that are often underestimated. Anomaly detection needs consistent, high-quality historical data to establish baselines, and baseline quality is directly tied to normalization, stable identifiers, and time accuracy. Missing logs, inconsistent field mappings, or changes in data collection can create "anomalies" that are artifacts of instrumentation rather than real behavior change. Retention also matters because short baselines make normal variation look suspicious, while overly long baselines can hide gradual compromise by averaging it into normal. If leadership wants anomaly detection to be meaningful, the organization must fund the boring parts: logging completeness, entity resolution, and continuous data health monitoring.

Interpretability is another strength when done well and a limitation when ignored. A useful anomaly signal should communicate what changed and why it matters in operational terms, such as "new administrative action on a sensitive system outside normal hours" rather than "score exceeded threshold." Analysts need enough context to validate the deviation quickly: what was typical for this entity, what peer group looks like, and what other events correlate in time. When anomaly outputs are opaque, responders either treat them as noise or over-trust them, both of which are dangerous. The best implementations expose contributing factors and supporting events, so the analyst can make a defensible decision.

The most common limitation is false positives driven by legitimate business change, which is not rare; it is constant. Migrations, new applications, reorganizations, acquisitions, seasonal cycles, and emergency operations all change behavior patterns, sometimes abruptly. Without governance, anomaly detection will flag these shifts relentlessly, consuming attention while teaching the team to ignore anomaly signals. This is where change awareness becomes part of detection engineering, because anomaly models must be tuned to expect predictable variation and must be recalibrated when the environment changes materially. When change management is weak, anomaly detection becomes a mirror reflecting organizational chaos rather than adversary behavior.

Model drift is a predictable failure mode and must be managed as an operational reality, not a data science afterthought. Baselines degrade when populations shift, when identity attributes change, or when new logging sources are introduced, and the model's notion of "normal" can become stale or misleading. Drift can also cut in the opposite direction: if an attacker maintains persistence long enough, their activity can be absorbed into the baseline and stop looking anomalous. To counter this, programs need explicit retraining and validation cadences, along with controls that prevent obvious compromise periods from contaminating baselines. This is where human judgment matters, because automation cannot reliably decide what historical data is "clean" without domain context.

Anomaly detection also raises governance and auditability concerns because it often relies on ML-driven scoring and complex feature sets. Teams must be able to explain how a signal was produced at a level suitable for internal review and, when necessary, external scrutiny, especially when anomaly outputs drive privileged investigations. Data minimization is important because anomaly systems tend to ingest broad telemetry, and the risk of sensitive data exposure increases when model inputs, prompts, or outputs are handled loosely. Approval boundaries should be explicit: anomaly signals can suggest prioritization, queue placement, or investigative pivots, but they should not automatically trigger high-impact actions without corroboration. When automation is allowed to act, the actions should be reversible, logged, and reviewable.

Operationally, anomaly detection is most effective when it is integrated into a layered detection strategy with clear downstream handling. Many anomaly signals are better treated as context for other detections, as correlation inputs, or as triggers for lightweight enrichment rather than as standalone pages. For example, an anomaly on a privileged identity may warrant immediate correlation with endpoint activity, recent authentication patterns, and administrative change events before escalating. This reduces wasted escalations while preserving the value of early warning. When anomaly detection is framed as a powerful but imperfect sensor—useful for surfacing deviations, dependent on telemetry hygiene, and bounded by human judgment—it becomes a credible component of a mature detection program rather than a source of perpetual noise.

Detection Gaps and How They Persist

Detection gaps are rarely the result of a single missing rule; they are usually the predictable outcome of incomplete visibility, ambiguous ownership, and competing operational priorities. A gap exists whenever meaningful adversary behavior can occur without producing a reliable signal that will be seen, interpreted correctly, and acted on in time. In mature environments, gaps are not shocking discoveries so much as known liabilities that are tracked, communicated, and reduced over time. The problem is that many organizations carry gaps silently, assuming their tooling provides coverage by default. When a real incident exposes the blind spot, the surprise is not the gap itself but the fact that it was never made explicit.

The most common root cause is telemetry absence or inconsistency, especially across heterogeneous fleets and hybrid infrastructure. Endpoint visibility may be strong on corporate laptops and weak on servers, or cloud audit logs may be enabled in some accounts and not others, or identity events may lack the fields needed to distinguish interactive users from service principals. Even when logs exist, ingestion pipelines can drop events under load, parsing changes can break critical fields, and retention policies can eliminate the historical context needed for correlation and baselining. These failures create a deceptively calm alert stream, because detections often fail silently when their inputs degrade. Without continuous data health checks tied directly to detection dependencies, a gap can persist for months while everyone assumes monitoring is functioning.

Gaps also persist because detection engineering is frequently mis-scoped as "writing rules" rather than operating a production capability. If no one owns the full lifecycle—from data readiness to alert outcomes—issues fall between teams. Platform teams may assume security will adapt to logging changes, while security assumes the platform will preserve schemas and field mappings. Response teams may complain about noise, but without structured feedback loops the engineers cannot trace dismissals to specific detection defects. The result is a backlog of vague pain rather than actionable engineering work, and gaps remain because they do not have a clear owner, a clear fix, or a visible consequence until an incident occurs.

Another persistence mechanism is the illusion of coverage created by superficial metrics and documentation. Counting detections, listing log sources, or mapping a few rules to generic categories can look impressive while leaving the highest risk behaviors unmonitored in practice. Coverage is not simply whether a log source exists; it is whether the right events arrive with the right fields, on the right assets, at the right time, and whether the detection logic is validated against current reality. When organizations report coverage at too high a level, gaps hide inside abstractions that are never tested. A disciplined program forces the uncomfortable questions: which identities, which workloads, which control planes, and which behaviors are truly observable today.

Change is a gap amplifier because environments evolve faster than most detection programs. New applications introduce new authentication patterns, migrations alter network paths, identity providers change token formats, and endpoint baselines shift as operating systems update. Detections that were accurate last quarter may become noisy, brittle, or inert, and engineers often respond by disabling or suppressing without addressing the underlying cause. Over time, this creates "quiet gaps" where rules exist but are effectively neutered by exceptions, thresholds, or missing dependencies. Unless tuning and maintenance are treated as first-class work with explicit time allocation, gaps accumulate as a kind of operational debt.

Adversaries also exploit organizational habits that unintentionally preserve gaps. They learn which systems are less monitored, which accounts have weaker controls, and which pathways generate the least scrutiny, then route activity through those seams. Gaps are especially durable in areas perceived as "special" or "fragile," such as legacy systems, third-party managed platforms, or business-critical services where teams fear that logging or agents will impact performance. The business pressure to avoid disruption is real, but when it leads to permanent visibility concessions, it creates predictable attack corridors. A mature program makes these tradeoffs explicit, documents compensating controls where possible, and regularly revisits whether the original constraint still applies.

AI/ML can help surface gaps by analyzing where expected telemetry patterns abruptly stop, where field distributions shift, or where alert outcomes indicate chronic uncertainty. For example, models can detect ingestion anomalies, identify entities with unusually sparse event histories, or highlight segments of the environment whose behavior cannot be baselined due to missing data. AI can also assist in coverage reasoning by correlating detections to the fields and sources they actually use, revealing that "we have logs" does not mean "we have usable signals." These capabilities require careful governance because they operate over broad telemetry and can produce false confidence if the underlying data is biased toward better-instrumented systems. Human review remains essential to separate true visibility gaps from legitimate changes in workload patterns or logging configurations.

Closing gaps requires a workflow that treats them as managed risk items rather than as embarrassing secrets. Gaps should be logged with clear descriptions of the missed behavior, the impacted assets or identities, the reason the gap exists, and the practical path to reduce it, whether that is onboarding telemetry, normalizing fields, adding enrichment, or implementing compensating detection logic. Some gaps will be accepted temporarily due to constraints, but acceptance should be explicit, time-bounded where possible, and visible to stakeholders who own the associated risk. Over time, the organizations that improve are the ones that treat detection gaps as inevitable but controllable—measured, prioritized, and systematically reduced—rather than as anomalies that are only acknowledged after an incident forces the truth into the open.

Change-Driven Breakage and Detection Maintenance

Detection logic fails most often not because attackers outsmart it, but because the environment changes underneath it. New applications roll out, identity providers shift claim formats, endpoint agents upgrade, cloud services evolve their audit schemas, and logging pipelines get re-tuned for cost or performance. Each change can invalidate assumptions a detection depends on, such as a field name, an event ID, a timestamp format, or an enrichment lookup. The operational danger is that many detections do not fail loudly; they simply stop matching or start matching the wrong things, producing either silence or noise. A mature program assumes breakage is routine and builds maintenance practices that keep detections aligned with reality.

The first maintenance principle is to make dependencies explicit, so breakage is predictable instead of mysterious. Every detection should document the required telemetry sources, key fields, expected value patterns, and any enrichment that must be available for correct interpretation. This is not bureaucratic overhead; it is what allows engineers to quickly assess impact when a platform team changes a parser, a cloud provider introduces a new field variant, or an endpoint rollout alters process metadata. Dependencies should also include operational assumptions like acceptable ingestion latency and correlation windows, because timing changes can break multi-event detections even when fields remain correct. When detections are treated as production assets, dependency visibility becomes the foundation for reliable change management.

Change-driven breakage often originates in the data pipeline rather than in the detection logic itself. Parsing updates can shift a field from "user.name" to "user.id," alter case normalization, or change how nulls and defaults are represented, causing logic to miss matches or to trigger broadly. Time handling is especially brittle: timezone changes, clock skew, and delayed ingestion can cause correlation rules to miss sequences or to stitch unrelated events together. Enrichment can drift as well, such as asset inventories that lag behind deployments or identity attributes that change during reorganizations. Without continuous validation, these shifts accumulate quietly until responders notice an abrupt change in alert behavior, at which point the root cause is harder to reconstruct.

Maintenance becomes manageable when it is organized into routines rather than treated as ad hoc firefighting. Detections should have owners who are accountable for their health, not just for their initial creation, and those owners need a cadence for review based on alert outcomes, telemetry changes, and business-driven shifts in the environment. High-value detections warrant more frequent checks, especially those tied to privileged activity, identity control planes, and sensitive workloads where the cost of missing is high. Routine checks should include verifying that required fields are still present, that event rates remain consistent, and that known test activity still triggers expected alerts. This kind of disciplined upkeep prevents a slow erosion of capability that is invisible in any single week.

Operationally, the best maintenance programs tie detection health to change management signals, even when formal processes are imperfect. When new agents are deployed, logging configurations are modified, or cloud services are updated, detection engineers should receive enough notice to run impact assessments and validation tests. That requires relationship building with platform, infrastructure, and application teams, because detection maintenance is a shared responsibility even when security owns the logic. In mature environments, significant telemetry-affecting changes have explicit security review gates, not to block delivery but to prevent silent loss of monitoring. Where that level of coordination is not feasible, the detection team must compensate with aggressive monitoring of data quality and rapid feedback loops when anomalies appear.

AI/ML can materially improve maintenance by detecting subtle shifts in telemetry that humans will not notice until damage is done. Models can track field distribution changes, event volume anomalies, and schema drift across sources, highlighting when a detection's input data no longer resembles its historical baseline. AI can also assist in summarizing which detections depend on affected fields, accelerating triage when a parser change or logging update occurs. These uses are operationally appropriate because they reduce time-to-diagnose and help prevent silent failures, but they must be governed carefully to avoid over-trust. A model that flags "data drift" does not tell you whether the drift is benign business change or a broken pipeline, so human review remains the decision point.

When breakage is detected, remediation should follow an engineering workflow that preserves auditability and safety. Quick fixes are sometimes necessary, but changes to detection logic should still be reviewed, versioned, and validated so that the team does not trade one failure mode for another. Ideally, tuning or refactoring is tested against representative benign and adversarial examples, and changes are rolled out in a controlled way, so responders are not surprised by new alert behavior. If a detection must be disabled temporarily due to upstream instability, that decision should be explicit and tracked, with compensating monitoring where possible and a clear trigger for re-enablement. Silent disablement is how gaps become permanent.

Maintenance also requires knowing when not to "fix" a detection and instead redesign or retire it. Some detections become too brittle because the underlying telemetry is unstable, the behavior is no longer relevant, or the rule cannot be made sufficiently actionable without context the environment cannot provide. Keeping such detections alive through endless exceptions creates the illusion of coverage while delivering little value and consuming engineering time. Retiring or consolidating detections can be a sign of maturity when it reduces duplicate alerting and clarifies responder expectations. The program stays healthy when it prioritizes reliable, validated coverage over the accumulation of fragile rules.

Finally, sustained detection maintenance depends on resourcing and prioritization that treat it as core work, not as leftover time after "new detections." Organizations that only reward net-new alert creation inevitably accumulate operational debt as rules age and the environment changes. Maintenance work must be planned, staffed, and measured, with clear accountability for detection health, telemetry readiness, and post-change validation. When leadership understands that change-driven breakage is normal and that maintenance is how monitoring remains credible, the detection program becomes resilient rather than reactive. In that model, detections remain dependable sensors even as the organization evolves, and breakage becomes a managed condition rather than a recurring surprise.

AI/ML in Detection Engineering: Modeling Choices, Drift, and Explainable Output

AI/ML can strengthen detection engineering when it is treated as decision support embedded inside disciplined workflows, not as a replacement for engineering judgment. The core value is leverage: models can sift large volumes of telemetry to surface patterns, prioritize signals, and enrich investigations faster than manual review. The risk is that models can also produce confident-sounding outputs that are wrong, brittle, or impossible to audit, especially when data quality is uneven. Effective programs start by defining the operational job the model is being asked to do, such as scoring rarity, clustering similar events, summarizing activity sequences, or learning entity baselines. From there, modeling choices are made to fit the organization's telemetry maturity, response capacity, and governance needs rather than chasing sophistication for its own sake.

Modeling choices should be driven by the question being answered and by the consequence of being wrong. For anomaly scoring, simpler statistical baselines and unsupervised models are often appropriate because labels are sparse and "normal" varies by entity and role. For classification of alert outcomes or prioritization, supervised models can be effective when the organization has consistent triage dispositions and enough historical examples, but they are highly sensitive to label quality and to operational bias. For clustering and correlation discovery, representation learning and distance-based approaches can help group related activity without requiring perfect ground truth, but they can also group by superficial similarities if fields are inconsistent. The practical rule is that the model should match the stability of the data and the maturity of the process, because advanced methods cannot compensate for missing telemetry, inconsistent normalization, or untrustworthy labels.

Telemetry dependencies are not optional details; they are the foundation of whether ML outputs will be meaningful. Entity resolution must be stable, so a "user" or "host" is not represented differently across sources, and key fields must be normalized, so models do not learn parser artifacts. Time coherence matters because many detection tasks depend on sequences, and ingestion lag or clock drift can distort what the model perceives as causality. Retention and sampling choices also shape outcomes, because models trained on truncated histories can misinterpret seasonal patterns and overreact to routine variation. If the pipeline changes, the model's inputs change, and the output will change even if the environment's behavior does not. Organizations that succeed treat data quality monitoring as a first-class dependency of ML-assisted detection, with automated checks that detect schema drift, field distribution shifts, and missing sources before models are allowed to influence operations. Figure 20.1 shows how AI/ML outputs should be constrained by telemetry quality, drift monitoring, and explainable output, so humans remain accountable for decisions. It reinforces the chapter's emphasis on human-in-the-loop boundaries and auditability.

Drift is the predictable failure mode that turns yesterday's good model into tomorrow's liability. Concept drift occurs when the meaning of behaviors changes, such as new authentication workflows after an identity migration, or new administrative tooling that reshapes "normal." Data drift occurs when the logging itself changes, such as a new agent version altering process fields, or a parser update changing how destinations are represented. Both forms can produce the same symptom—spikes in anomalies or a collapse in detections—so drift management must include diagnostics that separate environment change from instrumentation change. A mature program defines retraining cadences, validation gates, and rollback plans, and it prevents compromise periods

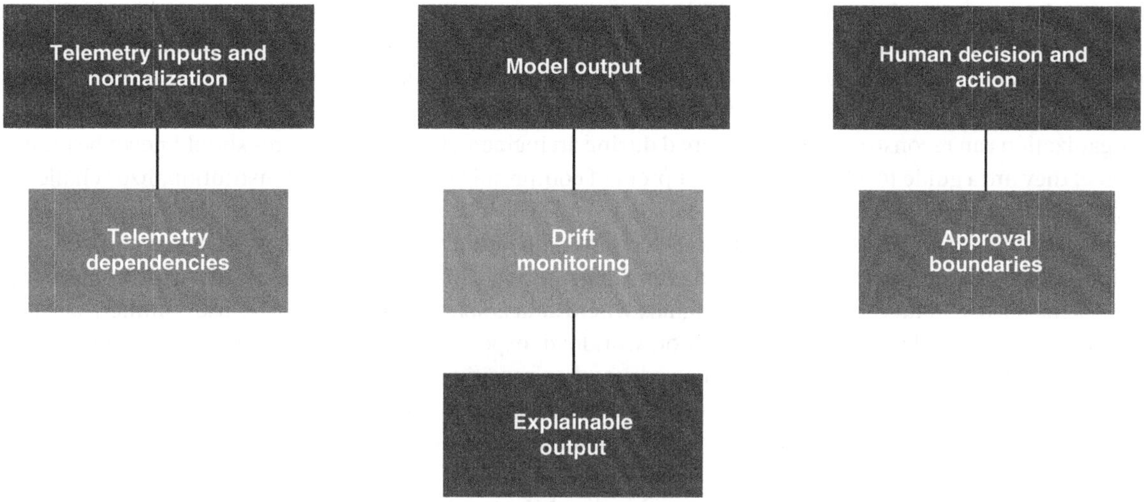

Figure 20.1 AI/ML Signal Flow with Drift and Explainability Controls.

or misconfigurations from contaminating baselines. Without these controls, models gradually learn the wrong normal, sometimes suppressing the very behaviors the organization wants to detect.

Explainable output is not a luxury feature; it is the condition for operational trust. When a model influences triage or escalation, responders must be able to see why the model flagged something, at least at the level of contributing factors and supporting events. An alert that says "high risk" without showing what changed, what evidence was observed, and what peer comparison was used forces analysts to either ignore the output or over-trust it. Explainability should be designed into the workflow by coupling scores with human-readable rationale: which attributes drove the deviation, what was typical historically, and what correlated activity exists in the surrounding window. This also supports peer review and after-action analysis because engineers can test whether the model's reasoning aligns with domain reality. Explainability is the bridge between statistical outputs and defensible operational decisions. Table 20.3 summarizes where AI and ML help detection operations and the guardrails needed to manage drift explainability and over-trust.

Table 20.3 AI ML Operational Guardrails for Detection Engineering.

AI ML Use	Telemetry Dependency	Human Approval Boundary	Primary Failure Mode
Anomaly scoring	Stable entity identifiers and sufficient history	Use as prioritization not automatic escalation	Noise from business change and drift
Clustering patterns	Consistent normalization across sources	Analyst reviews clusters before action	Grouping by superficial similarities
Disposition-based prioritization	Consistent triage outcomes labeling	Human decides suppression and escalation	Bias from inconsistent labels
Summarizing event sequences	Accurate timestamps and complete supporting events	Analyst validates against source events	False confidence and invented intent
Drift monitoring	Field distributions and event volume baselines	Engineer reviews and triggers retraining	Confusing data drift with behavior change
Change impact analysis	Clear mapping of detections to fields and sources	Engineer approves remediation plan	Over-trust in automated recommendations

Human-in-the-loop controls must be explicit about approval boundaries and about where automation is allowed to act. ML outputs can recommend prioritization, suggest likely benign patterns, or propose candidate correlations, but the final decision to escalate, suppress, or disable detections should remain with accountable humans unless the action is low risk and reversible. Even then, automated actions should be logged, attributable, and reviewable, so the organization can reconstruct what happened during an incident. Confidence scores should never be treated as evidence; they are a guide to where to look, not proof of compromise. Programs that institutionalize "challenge and verify" behavior avoid the trap where a model's tone and polish become a substitute for validation.

Bias and leakage risks are particularly sharp in detection engineering because telemetry is uneven and sensitive. Models tend to learn more from well-instrumented systems, which can create a false sense of security by producing strong signals where data is rich and weak signals where data is sparse. Labeling bias is also common, because analysts may disposition alerts differently based on workload, experience, or perceived importance of the asset, and the model will learn those habits. Leakage can occur when sensitive event details, identity attributes, or investigative notes are pulled into training data or prompt contexts without proper access controls, creating privacy and compliance exposure. Governance must therefore cover data minimization, access boundaries, retention, and the audit trail for both training inputs and model outputs. If an organization cannot explain where model inputs came from and who can see them, it is not ready to operationalize ML at scale.

The most effective ML integrations treat models as components in a broader detection system with layered verification. An anomaly score might trigger enrichment, correlation with deterministic behaviors, or a guided triage checklist rather than a direct escalation. Clusters might be used to compress repetitive alert floods into a single investigative unit, reducing fatigue while preserving visibility. Summarization models can produce concise narratives from event sequences, but their outputs should be grounded in cited events and constrained to the available telemetry, so they do not invent causality or intent. In each case, the model's job is to reduce cognitive load and surface structure, while deterministic logic and human judgment provide the accountability layer.

Operational success ultimately depends on treating ML-assisted detection as a managed capability with measurable quality, not as a one-time deployment. Models should have owners, documented purpose statements, dependency inventories, performance monitoring, and clear decommission criteria when they no longer add value. Their outputs should be evaluated against responder outcomes, not against abstract accuracy claims, and drift should be detected and addressed before it becomes an incident amplifier. When modeling choices are aligned to operational tasks, drift is managed as routine maintenance, and outputs are explainable enough to support audit and action, AI/ML becomes a practical multiplier for detection engineering rather than a source of brittle confidence.

Documentation and Versioning of Detection Logic

Detection logic is a production asset, and it should be documented and versioned with the same seriousness as any other control that influences risk. Without documentation, detections become tribal knowledge that cannot be trusted, tuned, or defended under scrutiny. Without versioning, teams cannot reliably understand what changed, why it changed, and whether a change improved or degraded outcomes. The result is operational fragility: responders see alerts that behave differently from last week, engineers struggle to reproduce behavior, and leadership cannot get a straight answer about monitoring posture. Treating detection logic as managed code turns monitoring from a collection of rules into a reliable, auditable capability.

Good documentation begins with purpose, because the single most important question is what the detection is asserting about risk. A detection should clearly state the threat behavior it is meant to surface, the typical adversary objective it reflects, and the kind of response decision it is intended to enable. That narrative should be written so that an analyst encountering the alert at 3 a.m. can understand why it exists without reading the underlying query language. The documentation should also specify the expected evidence artifacts, such as which event types or fields should appear, and what "normal" might look like when benign activity triggers similar patterns. When this context is missing, responders are forced to reconstruct intent from raw telemetry, which increases triage time and inconsistency.

Dependencies deserve their own attention because most detection failures originate there. Documentation should list required telemetry sources, key fields, expected field formats, and any enrichment lookups or entity resolution assumptions that must hold for correct operation. It should capture timing expectations such as ingestion latency limits, correlation windows, and any ordering assumptions for multi-event detections. It should also include environmental constraints, such as where the detection applies and where it does not, based on asset classes, identity types, or logging coverage. This level of detail is what makes breakage diagnosable when logging pipelines change or when a new service introduces different event semantics. If the team cannot state what the detection needs to function, it cannot reliably maintain it.

Documentation should also describe alert handling intent in operational terms, because detection logic is only valuable when it drives action. A well-documented detection clarifies what the initial triage steps should be, what corroborating data sources are most relevant, and what decision thresholds separate benign resolution from escalation. This is not a step-by-step playbook; it is the minimum guidance needed to keep response consistent and bounded. It should also describe common false-positive drivers and known benign patterns, so analysts can recognize recurring cases without repeated reinvention. When documentation captures these lessons, the organization stops relearning the same alert behavior with every staffing change or rotation.

Versioning is the mechanism that makes detection change safe, reviewable, and reversible. Every meaningful modification to detection logic, thresholds, filters, and severity mapping should be tracked with an explicit change record that includes who made the change, when it was made, why it was made, and what validation was performed. This allows engineers to correlate alert behavior changes with code changes rather than chasing phantom causes in the environment. It also supports rollback when a tuning change suppresses too much or when a parser adjustment inadvertently broadens matches. In practical terms, versioning turns detection work from "editing live wires" into controlled releases with known blast radius.

The review process is where documentation and versioning produce real value, because peer review forces detection logic to be understandable to someone other than its author. Review should check that the detection is behavior-based, that it uses fields that actually exist and are stable, and that it does not rely on brittle assumptions such as hard-coded values that will change. Review should also test for unintended consequences, such as filters that create blind spots or correlation windows that can be gamed. When AI/ML is involved—such as models that score anomalies or summarize alert context—review must also examine training data dependencies, drift monitoring, and explainability expectations. The goal is to prevent hidden complexity from being operationalized without accountability.

AI/ML can assist documentation and versioning by making change impact easier to understand and by improving the clarity of detection narratives, but it must operate within strong controls. For example, models can summarize diffs into human-readable change notes, highlight which detections share dependencies on affected fields, or cluster alert outcomes that suggest a rule needs tuning. Summarization can also help produce consistent documentation language across a detection library, reducing variability in how engineers describe purpose and handling guidance. The failure mode is over-trust: if generated documentation becomes detached from actual logic, it creates a polished lie that increases risk. Human owners must validate that documentation matches behavior, and automated outputs should always be traceable back to the underlying detection version and the specific changes applied.

Auditability is the strategic payoff of disciplined documentation and versioning, because it enables the organization to defend its monitoring posture under internal and external scrutiny. When an incident occurs, teams should be able to show what detections were in place at the time, what they were designed to catch, how they were configured, and whether they fired. When a detection was disabled or exceptions were added, the rationale and approvals should be visible rather than buried in chat logs or memory. This matters not only for compliance discussions, but for operational learning also, because after-action reviews depend on knowing whether monitoring failed due to logic, data, or process. Without that traceability, improvement becomes guesswork.

Sustaining this discipline requires treating documentation and versioning as part of the definition of "done," not as optional polish. New detections should not be promoted to production without minimum documentation and a versioned change record, and tuning changes should not be made directly in a way that bypasses review. Documentation must be maintained as the environment evolves, especially when dependencies shift, because stale documentation is almost worse than none by creating misplaced confidence. When the organization institutionalizes these practices, detection engineering scales: knowledge survives staffing changes, changes become safer, and the monitoring program becomes demonstrably reliable rather than aspirational.

Conclusion

A mature detection program earns trust by producing fewer surprises: alerts that are understandable, actionable, and reliably tied to real risk instead of volume for its own sake. That trust is sustained through continuous maintenance that anticipates change-driven breakage, makes detection gaps visible, and treats tuning and validation as core engineering work rather than cleanup. Anomaly detection and AI/ML add meaningful leverage when they are implemented with clear modeling intent, strong telemetry hygiene, explainable outputs, and governance that keeps humans accountable for escalation and suppression decisions. When these practices are operated as a managed capability—documented, versioned, measured by outcomes, and continually improved—detection engineering becomes a dependable control surface that scales with the organization's complexity and pace of change.

Recommendations

1) Treat detection engineering as a managed capability with clear ownership and operating expectations. Define who is accountable for detection lifecycle work, including build, tune, validate, and retire decisions. Ensure the program is measured by outcomes like reliability and actionability rather than by raw alert volume.
2) Inventory and validate detection telemetry dependencies before promoting detections into production. Document which sources, fields, and enrichment are required for the logic to function as intended. Monitor those dependencies continuously, so detections fail loudly when inputs degrade instead of silently losing coverage.
3) Build detections from real threat behaviors and express them in observable terms your environment can reliably produce. Translate attacker objectives into concrete event patterns and sequences rather than brittle signatures tied to a single tool or artifact. Use context such as identity, asset class, and timing to keep detections durable and actionable.
4) Correlate events to reflect attack progression instead of alerting on isolated atoms of activity. Engineer correlation windows and supportive evidence, so responders can validate intent quickly without reconstructing the full story from scratch. Keep correlation logic deterministic and reviewable, so analysts can understand what the alert is asserting.
5) Tune detections by adding discriminating context rather than relying on broad allowlists or static exceptions. Use triage outcomes to identify recurring benign drivers and refine logic to filter look-alikes without suppressing the suspicious core. Time-bound and track any necessary exceptions, so they do not become permanent blind spots.
6) Measure detection quality over volume using responder outcomes and operational effort. Track confirmation rates, dismissal drivers, duplicate alerting, and "unknown" dispositions that indicate insufficient evidence. Include time-based measures such as time-to-understand and time-to-route, so quality improvements translate into real workload reduction.

7) Treat anomaly detection as an augmentation layer that surfaces "worth a look" deviations, not as a standalone truth engine. Anchor anomaly work to stable entities and risk-relevant populations, so the resulting signals are naturally prioritized. Pair anomaly signals with corroborating evidence and clear handling intent to keep them operationally useful.
8) Design ML-assisted detection with explicit modeling intent and enforce human approval boundaries for high-impact decisions. Use models to cluster, prioritize, or summarize based on disciplined telemetry and consistent disposition labeling. Require explainable output that shows what changed and what evidence supports the score, so analysts can challenge false confidence.
9) Operationalize drift management as routine maintenance for both telemetry and models. Monitor for data drift and concept drift by watching field distributions, event volumes, and baseline stability across time. Retrain and revalidate with clear gates and rollback plans, so model behavior does not silently degrade or normalize attacker activity.
10) Document and version detections, so changes are auditable, reviewable, and reversible. Record purpose, dependencies, and handling intent alongside each detection, so responders and engineers share a consistent understanding. Track every tuning or threshold change with rationale and validation notes to prevent "quiet gaps" from accumulating through unreviewed edits.

21

Investigation Workflow and Incident Analysis

Investigation workflow and incident analysis begin with a simple reality: alerts are abundant, but truth is scarce, and the difference is determined by disciplined practice. Effective teams move from detection to decision by treating evidence as a first-class asset, translating suspicion into testable hypotheses, and building timelines that remain faithful to primary telemetry. They scope impact with defensible boundaries, coordinate containment with IT, engineering, and business partners, and escalate to incident response when risk, uncertainty, or operational consequence crosses clear thresholds. AI can accelerate summarization and correlation, but only when verification discipline, human approval boundaries, and auditability preserve the standards that make investigative conclusions trustworthy.

From Alert to Hypothesis: The Analyst Mindset

An effective investigation starts by treating every alert as a prompt rather than a verdict. The alert is evidence that something crossed a threshold, not evidence that an incident occurred. The analyst mindset begins with a disciplined separation of signal from interpretation, especially when the alert text sounds definitive. Good teams train themselves to ask what the system actually observed, what it inferred, and what it could not have known. That posture reduces both panic-driven escalation and the equally dangerous reflex to dismiss "yet another alert."

The first mental shift is to translate the alert into a claim that can be tested. An alert typically bundles multiple assertions: that the activity happened, that it is unusual, that it is malicious, and that it matters. Analysts should break those apart and decide which are facts versus hypotheses, because each requires different validation steps. Facts come from telemetry—timestamps, accounts, hosts, network paths, process lineage, authentication events, and configuration state. Hypotheses are explanations layered on top of those facts, and they must remain provisional until corroborated. This approach keeps investigations anchored to observable behavior instead of labels. Figure 21.1 shows how analysts move from an alert to a working hypothesis by separating observed facts from inferred meaning and then defining testable assertions. It reinforces the disciplined approach that prevents premature conclusions and keeps investigations anchored to evidence.

Hypothesis-driven analysis is about forming a small number of competing explanations early, then using evidence to eliminate them quickly. Analysts should prefer hypotheses that are precise enough to be falsifiable, such as "a legitimate admin performed an authorized change from an expected endpoint" versus "credential misuse from an unmanaged device." Precision matters because it forces the team to identify what data would confirm or refute the claim. When hypotheses are vague, investigations drift into broad log hunting that consumes time and still produces low confidence. A disciplined analyst deliberately chooses the shortest path to disproof, because disproved hypotheses are progress.

Context is the multiplier that turns raw telemetry into investigative clarity. Analysts should immediately establish what "normal" looks like for the asset, identity, and action implicated by the alert, including typical login

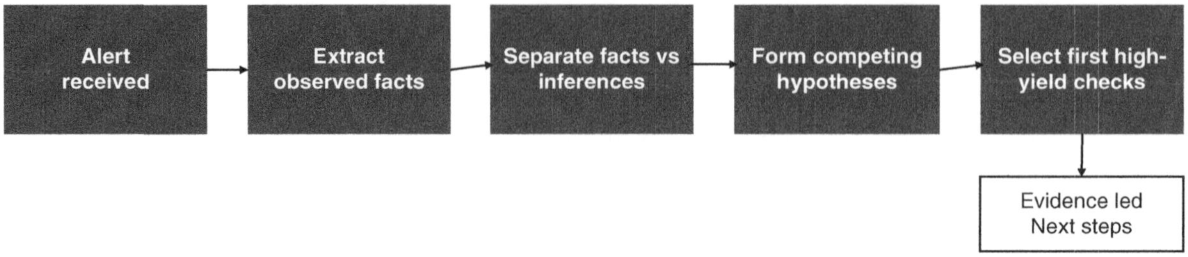

Figure 21.1 From Alert to Hypothesis: Converting a Signal into Testable Claims.

hours, usual geographic patterns, common parent processes, and standard administrative tooling behaviors. That context includes business context as well: the function of the system, the criticality of the data it touches, and whether changes are expected due to maintenance windows or deployments. Without this baseline, teams end up over-weighting novelty and under-weighting plausibility. The analyst mindset treats context gathering as the first phase of evidence collection, not as optional enrichment.

Cognitive traps are predictable in incident analysis, and mature teams build habits to counter them. Confirmation bias appears when an analyst fixates on the first compelling narrative and selectively gathers supportive logs. Availability bias appears when the last major incident influences the interpretation of unrelated signals, leading to over-escalation or misplaced effort. Authority bias appears when a prior label—"high severity," "known bad," or "critical"—short-circuits independent validation. Analysts counter these traps by explicitly stating alternative hypotheses, documenting disconfirming evidence, and being willing to downgrade or re-scope when the facts do not support the initial narrative.

Time and sequencing are investigative tools, not just metadata. Analysts should build a timeline early, even if it is rough, because ordering reveals causality: which event preceded another, what dependencies exist, and what could have triggered an automated response. Timeline discipline also exposes data gaps, such as missing endpoint telemetry during a suspected execution window or delayed ingestion that might make activity appear out of order. A strong analyst thinks in terms of "what must be true for this sequence to make sense" and then checks those assumptions. When timelines are ignored, teams often misattribute cause, confuse parallel activity with related activity, and chase the wrong root.

AI-assisted analysis can accelerate the jump from alert to hypothesis, but only when analysts treat model outputs as triage aids rather than ground truth. Practical uses include summarizing multi-source event clusters, extracting likely entities and pivots, and suggesting next-best questions based on past investigations with similar patterns. These capabilities depend on clean, well-labeled telemetry and consistent event schemas, because models amplify inconsistencies and can hallucinate links when the underlying data is ambiguous. Human-in-the-loop controls should define what the model is allowed to do—summarize, cluster, and recommend—versus what requires analyst approval, such as asserting attribution, declaring an incident, or initiating disruptive containment. Teams should expect failure modes like false confidence in plausible narratives, drift as environments change, and leakage risks if sensitive case details are inappropriately retained or shared, so every AI-derived claim must remain traceable to source events and auditable in the case record.

The analyst mindset ultimately treats investigations as decision-support under uncertainty, not a quest for perfect certainty. Early in the process, the goal is to arrive at a defensible working hypothesis with known confidence and clearly stated gaps, so the team can decide whether to contain, monitor, or gather more evidence. That decision should reflect both technical likelihood and business impact, because a moderately suspicious pattern on a critical identity deserves different handling than a highly suspicious pattern on a low-impact system with strong compensating controls. Analysts should be explicit about what would change their mind, what evidence is missing, and what assumptions are being made. This discipline produces investigations that are faster, more repeatable, and less dependent on individual intuition, while still leaving room for expertise where the data is imperfect.

Evidence Collection and Preservation

Evidence collection starts with a simple premise: you are not gathering "everything," you are gathering what will still be trustworthy tomorrow. The analyst's first responsibility is to preserve the current state before routine processes—log rotation, endpoint cleanup, credential resets, and automated remediation—erase key artifacts. That means prioritizing data sources with short retention windows and high volatility, such as endpoint process details, network connection state, and cloud control-plane events that may not be replicated elsewhere. Collection should be purposeful, tied to the working hypothesis, and designed to support both technical reconstruction and decision-making. When teams treat evidence as a checklist rather than a narrative record, they often miss the one artifact that actually proves or disproves the suspected story.

Preservation is as much about integrity as it is about availability. Analysts should capture artifacts in a way that protects against accidental modification and establishes confidence that the data has not been tampered with after collection. In operational terms, this means collecting read-only exports when available, recording cryptographic hashes for files and log bundles, and preserving original timestamps and source identifiers. It also means documenting exactly how each artifact was obtained, including who performed the action, from where, and under what access context. That documentation is not bureaucracy; it is what allows another analyst—or an auditor—to trust the evidence when the original collector is not in the room.

The most common failure in evidence handling is losing context, not losing data. Logs without time synchronization assumptions, hostnames without asset identifiers, screenshots without source URLs or query parameters, and exports without the filtering criteria that produced them all become difficult to defend. Analysts should capture the query language, filters, time ranges, and timezone used for every retrieval, because subtle differences can change conclusions. Normalizing everything to a consistent reference time, while preserving the original values, prevents timeline errors during later reconstruction. Even when the incident never becomes a legal matter, the ability to reproduce findings is what separates professional incident analysis from "we think this happened."

A practical collection strategy follows the path of volatility and uniqueness. Endpoint artifacts like running processes, parent–child relationships, command-line arguments, loaded modules, and scheduled tasks are often unique and can disappear with a reboot or remediation. Authentication and identity artifacts—token issuance, MFA prompts, anomalous session creation, conditional access decisions, and password change events—help distinguish misuse from legitimate administration and are often distributed across systems. Network artifacts like DNS lookups, proxy requests, firewall flows, and east–west traffic can prove reach and lateral movement, but they require careful handling to avoid false correlations. Analysts should collect in a way that preserves relationships among artifacts, because a single log line is rarely decisive without its surrounding chain. This checklist reinforces evidence collection steps that preserve integrity context and reproducibility under investigation pressure (Table 21.1).

Chain of custody is not reserved for courtroom drama; it is simply disciplined accountability for evidence. Teams should maintain a single case record that tracks what was collected, where it is stored, who has accessed it, and what transformations were performed for analysis. Access should be limited to those with a need to know, and storage should be resilient, permissioned, and monitored for changes. When evidence must be moved across environments, the transfer itself should be verifiable, with hashes checked before and after. These practices reduce internal disputes about "what we saw," prevent accidental leakage of sensitive data, and build organizational confidence in investigative outcomes.

AI-assisted tooling can help identify what to collect next, but it cannot replace careful preservation practices. Models can summarize case notes, highlight missing telemetry categories relative to the hypothesis, and suggest high-yield pivots based on similar historical incidents. However, the collection process must remain deterministic and auditable, because AI-generated recommendations can overfit to patterns that are irrelevant in the current environment. Teams should treat AI outputs as prompts that require explicit analyst approval and should record when AI suggestions influenced collection decisions. A key failure mode is allowing automated reasoning to drive

Table 21.1 Evidence Handling Checklist for Trustworthy Collection.

Evidence Activity	Primary Purpose	Key Detail to Record	Integrity Safeguard
Collect volatile endpoint artifacts	Preserve short-lived execution context	Collector and source system and time window	Hash collected bundles
Export identity and authentication events	Validate identity integrity and access path	Query and filters and timezone	Preserve original timestamps
Capture network flow and DNS context	Reconstruct reach and movement	Data source and retention limits	Read only export where possible
Preserve cloud control plane events	Confirm configuration and permission changes	Resource identifiers and request context	Record export method
Document collection method	Enable reproduction and auditability	Who collected and how	Store in permissioned location
Validate artifact usability	Ensure analysis readiness	Parsing notes and format limitations	Retain originals unmodified

collection without documenting the underlying evidence, which results in conclusions that cannot be traced back to primary artifacts. Preservation workflows should therefore emphasize source-of-truth exports and verifiable storage, regardless of whether AI helped prioritize the effort.

Evidence collection also has to respect operational constraints and business risk. Pulling full memory captures, imaging disks, or exporting massive log sets may be impractical during an active incident and can degrade system performance or disrupt critical services. Analysts should choose minimally invasive approaches first—targeted artifact captures, scoped exports, and prioritized high-value telemetry—then escalate to heavier collection if the hypothesis warrants it. When containment actions are required, the team should sequence them to preserve what would otherwise be lost, capturing volatile data before isolating a host or disabling an account where feasible. This is where process maturity shows: the team can move quickly without destroying the very evidence needed to understand scope and root cause.

Preservation is complete only when the evidence is usable later, not merely stored somewhere. Analysts should validate that collected artifacts can be opened, parsed, and correlated, and they should record any limitations such as partial data windows, ingestion delays, or known blind spots. They should also capture environmental metadata—log retention policies, endpoint sensor coverage, cloud audit configuration state—because those details explain why evidence does or does not exist. Over time, patterns in evidence gaps become actionable inputs for improving telemetry and retention, but only if they are consistently documented. The end state is an evidence set that is coherent, minimally altered, and traceable, enabling confident decisions during the incident and reliable analysis afterward.

Scoping: Determining What Is Affected

Scoping is the disciplined process of turning suspicion into boundaries. The goal is not to explain everything immediately, but to determine what assets, identities, data, and business functions are plausibly impacted, so containment and communication are proportionate. Teams that scope poorly either overreact—disrupting operations to chase ghosts—or underreact—leaving compromised pathways open while assuming the problem is isolated. Effective scoping begins by defining a "minimum confirmed footprint" based on high-confidence evidence and a "maximum plausible footprint" based on known access paths and control weaknesses. The analyst mindset treats these as working bounds that narrow over time as evidence accumulates.

The first step is to identify the primary objects of compromise and their relationships. That typically includes an identity, a host or workload, and an initial action such as authentication, execution, or a configuration change. Analysts should map those objects to authoritative inventories: asset management for endpoints and servers, cloud resource inventories for workloads, and identity directories for users and service accounts. This mapping prevents a common failure where teams chase hostnames or display names that do not uniquely identify what is actually at risk. It also establishes ownership, criticality, and expected behavior, which directly influences how aggressively to contain. Scoping is faster when those inventories are maintained with accurate tagging and clear dependencies.

Timeline-driven scoping is more reliable than alert-driven scoping. Analysts should establish the earliest known suspicious activity and the most recent activity that may still be ongoing, then work outward along the timeline to find adjacent events. The boundary is rarely the alert time; it is often earlier, when the initial access occurred, or later, when the attacker began staging or persistence. Sequencing also helps distinguish cause from effect, such as an account lockout that occurred after a burst of failed logins rather than before. Where ingestion delays exist, teams should treat "silence" carefully, because missing data can masquerade as absence of activity. A scoped timeline becomes the backbone for identifying lateral movement, repeated access, and recurring automation.

Identity scoping is usually the fastest path to understanding blast radius because identities are the transport layer for most modern attacks. Analysts should enumerate which accounts authenticated from suspicious locations, used unusual devices, requested new tokens, or performed privileged actions within the timeline window. That includes service accounts, automation identities, and delegated permissions that may not appear in the same dashboards as interactive users. Scoping must also consider which authentication paths were available—password, MFA, SSO sessions, API tokens—because each implies different persistence and revocation steps. If the initial indicator involves privilege use, analysts should immediately check for privilege escalation signals such as role changes, group membership modifications, or policy edits. The practical outcome is a list of identities to investigate further, a list to protect immediately, and a list that can be provisionally cleared with evidence.

Asset scoping should follow execution and connectivity, not just ownership. For endpoint and server activity, analysts should look for process lineage, remote execution patterns, new services or scheduled tasks, and anomalous administrative tooling behavior tied to the suspicious identity or host. Network telemetry can then expand the view by showing which systems communicated with the affected host, which internal destinations were reached, and whether data movement patterns changed. In cloud environments, control-plane logs are often the authoritative source for understanding what resources were touched, what configurations were changed, and what data stores were accessed. Analysts should avoid assuming that "the alert host" is the only impacted asset, because many compromises use it as a stepping stone rather than a destination. Scoping is the act of finding the stepping stones. These scoping bounds help teams communicate what is known what is plausible and what evidence would change the assessment (Table 21.2).

Data scoping requires connecting technical access to business meaning. Analysts should determine what data the affected identities and workloads could access, then what they actually accessed within the window, and finally what data could have been copied or exfiltrated given observed network paths and controls. This often includes file access logs, database query auditing where available, cloud storage access records, and proxy or egress telemetry. Teams should be careful not to equate "could access" with "did access," but they also cannot ignore potential exposure when logging is incomplete. Where data classification exists, it should guide prioritization without becoming the only lens, because operational data can be just as damaging as regulated data when it enables further compromise. A credible scope statement ties access to specific repositories, time windows, and identities, with explicit confidence levels.

AI-assisted correlation can accelerate scoping by clustering related events and proposing likely pivots, but it introduces its own risks if used uncritically. Models can help group authentication anomalies by device fingerprint, summarize multi-system timelines into a coherent narrative, and highlight unusual combinations of actions that historically correlate with compromise. These benefits depend on consistent telemetry and well-labeled historical cases; otherwise, the model may overemphasize superficial similarities and miss environment-specific patterns.

Table 21.2 Scoping Bounds and Expansion Triggers.

Scoping Element	Minimum Confirmed Footprint	Maximum Plausible Footprint	Expansion Trigger	Contraction Indicator
Identity	Confirmed used account	Accounts reachable via delegation or shared paths	New anomalous token issuance	Managed device and expected source confirmed
Asset	Confirmed affected host or workload	Adjacent systems with observed connectivity	Remote execution or lateral movement evidence	No related events within window
Data	Confirmed accessed repository	Sensitive repositories reachable by affected identity	Access outside normal workflow	Access logs show no touch
Time Window	Earliest confirmed suspicious event	Window back to earliest plausible access	Precursor activity discovered	Confirmed benign explanation with evidence
Control Changes	Confirmed modified setting	Related permissions or policy surfaces	Privilege or role changes observed	No unauthorized changes confirmed

Human-in-the-loop controls should require analysts to validate each inferred relationship with primary logs and to record which relationships were confirmed versus suggested. A common failure mode is false confidence, where an AI-generated "blast radius" is treated as complete even though it was produced from partial data. Scoping must remain evidence-led, with AI used to prioritize attention rather than to certify completeness.

Scope decisions should translate into operational actions with clear boundaries and triggers for expansion. Teams should define what indicators would broaden the scope—new affected identities, evidence of privilege escalation, persistence mechanisms, or signs of data access—and what findings allow scope contraction, such as confirmed benign explanations with supporting telemetry. These decision rules prevent endless investigations that never converge and prevent premature closure that leaves exposure unaddressed. They also make communication more accurate, because stakeholders can hear not only what is known, but what would change the assessment. The end state of scoping is not a perfect map of everything that happened; it is a defensible definition of what is affected, what is likely affected, and what is unlikely affected, backed by evidence and designed to support timely containment and recovery.

Timeline Construction and Narrative Building

Timeline construction is the act of turning scattered observations into an ordered account of what happened, when it happened, and what it meant. In incident analysis, a timeline is not a reporting artifact that comes later; it is the primary investigative tool that guides where to look next and what to test. Analysts begin by anchoring the timeline to a small set of high-confidence events, such as an initial suspicious authentication, a confirmed execution, or a validated configuration change. From those anchors, they expand outward in both directions to discover precursors and downstream effects, always distinguishing observed facts from inferred relationships. A good timeline reduces ambiguity by making assumptions explicit and forcing evidence to align with time.

The mechanics of timeline building demand careful handling of time sources and event semantics. Analysts should normalize events to a consistent reference, including timezone, clock skew considerations, and the difference between event time and ingestion time. Control-plane logs, endpoint sensors, network devices, and application logs often represent time differently and may not share identical synchronization accuracy. When those differences are ignored, teams can mistakenly reverse causality, such as concluding that a remediation action occurred before the activity it was meant to stop. The disciplined approach is to record original timestamps, then add normalized values used for correlation, with notes about known delays or offsets. This is not pedantry; it is the difference between a coherent narrative and an unreliable story.

Effective timelines are structured around entities and relationships rather than raw log lines. Analysts should tag each event with the identity involved, the asset or workload affected, the action taken, and any unique identifiers such as session IDs, process IDs, request IDs, or token identifiers that allow cross-system linkage. Those identifiers become the stitching points that connect authentication to endpoint execution, endpoint execution to network egress, and network egress to data access. When unique identifiers are missing, analysts must compensate by correlating on combinations of attributes, but they should be explicit about reduced confidence. This entity-first approach prevents the timeline from becoming an unsearchable chronology and keeps it aligned to investigative questions. It also makes it easier to hand off work, because another analyst can follow the same identifiers without re-deriving the path.

Narrative building is what transforms the timeline into meaning for decision-makers, but it must remain faithful to the evidence. A narrative should explain the sequence in plain terms—how access was obtained, what actions were performed, what controls were bypassed or used, and what objectives the activity appears to support—while clearly separating what is confirmed from what is suspected. Analysts should resist the temptation to fill gaps with confident language, because narratives that overstate certainty damage credibility when later evidence contradicts them. Instead, a mature narrative uses probability carefully, describes competing explanations when relevant, and highlights the specific evidence that drove each conclusion. The narrative is not simply "what happened," it is "what we can support."

A strong timeline accounts for branching, parallelism, and iterative attacker behavior. Real incidents rarely follow a single linear path; they involve retries, alternative methods, and overlapping activities across systems. Analysts should represent these as branches tied to the same identity or objective, noting where the evidence shows a shift in technique or target. This is especially important when scoping, because parallel activity may indicate multiple compromised identities or an attacker pivoting from one foothold to another. Timelines should also capture defensive actions—account resets, host isolation, rule changes—because they can explain subsequent attacker behavior and can unintentionally introduce artifacts that look suspicious. When defensive actions are excluded, teams risk misattributing their own operations to the adversary.

AI-assisted summarization and correlation can accelerate timeline creation, particularly when event volume is high, but it must be constrained by verifiability. Models can cluster related events, suggest likely stage boundaries, and generate readable summaries of long event sequences for rapid orientation. These tools depend on well-structured telemetry and consistent labeling; otherwise, they may collapse distinct threads into one or infer relationships that are not supported. Human-in-the-loop controls should require that every narrative claim be traceable to specific source events, and that AI-generated summaries are treated as drafts until validated. A key failure mode is narrative hallucination, where a model produces a plausible chain of actions that fits the pattern of past incidents but is not actually evidenced in the current case. Teams should mitigate this by requiring citations within the case record to primary logs for each major assertion and by tracking model confidence separately from analyst confidence.

Timeline work also exposes gaps that directly influence containment and recovery decisions. When a timeline shows an unexplained pause, a missing segment of endpoint telemetry, or an absence of expected authentication records, analysts should treat the gap as a risk signal rather than a neutral absence. The gap might be benign, such as a sensor outage, but it might also represent deliberate evasion or coverage blind spots. Teams should document the gap, explain its likely causes, and decide whether to compensate through alternative sources such as network telemetry, application audit logs, or backup system logs. This practice keeps the narrative honest and prevents retrospective surprise when later data sources fill in what was previously assumed away. It also creates actionable work items for improving observability after the incident.

A finished incident narrative should be concise enough to drive action while remaining detailed enough to withstand scrutiny. It should connect the timeline to scope—what was touched, what was attempted, what succeeded, and what is unproven—while explaining why the team believes those boundaries are correct. It should also describe the attacker's apparent objectives in operational terms, such as credential access, privilege use, lateral movement, persistence, or data access, without relying on speculative attribution. The narrative should explicitly note decision points, including why containment actions were chosen and what evidence triggered escalation or de-escalation. Done well, timeline and narrative become a shared reality across technical and executive stakeholders, enabling rapid alignment without sacrificing investigative rigor.

Confirming or Refuting Suspicious Activity

Confirming or refuting suspicious activity is the moment an investigation stops being an exercise in curiosity and becomes an exercise in proof. The analyst's job is to decide whether observed signals represent benign behavior, misconfiguration, or adversary activity, and to do so with defensible reasoning. That requires separating what the environment observed from what the alert implied, then validating each implied claim against primary telemetry. Mature teams treat "suspicious" as a temporary label that triggers disciplined testing, not as a conclusion that justifies immediate escalation. The outcome is a clear statement of what is confirmed, what is not confirmed, and what remains ambiguous due to gaps in evidence.

A practical way to approach confirmation is to translate the suspicion into a small set of testable assertions. For example, a suspicious login implies an identity was used, from a particular device or network, at a particular time, with a particular authentication path, and with subsequent actions consistent with misuse. Each of those can be tested independently using identity logs, endpoint telemetry, and network records. Analysts should prioritize tests that can quickly falsify the malicious narrative, such as confirming the user was on call and using a known managed device, or that the source address belongs to a corporate egress point. This discipline prevents investigations from spiraling into exhaustive log review when a few targeted checks would resolve the question. It also creates repeatable playbooks that reduce dependence on individual intuition.

Corroboration across independent data sources is the core of reliable confirmation. A single log stream can be wrong, incomplete, or misleading, especially when it is derived from aggregation or normalization layers. Analysts should seek at least two independent indicators that support a claim, such as pairing an authentication event with endpoint session creation or correlating a reported process execution with network egress consistent with that process. Where corroboration is not possible, analysts should explicitly lower confidence and document why, rather than compensating with stronger language. This practice also helps distinguish true positives from detection artifacts, such as rule misfires triggered by legitimate automation. Confirmation is strongest when evidence chains are consistent across identity, endpoint, network, and application layers.

Attribution of activity to a legitimate user versus an attacker is often the most consequential decision in this phase. Analysts should look for coherence in the behavioral trail: device posture, session continuity, typical working patterns, and expected privilege use. Signs that support benign explanations include consistent device fingerprints, expected source networks, and actions aligned with known job functions, while signs that support misuse include impossible travel patterns, new device registrations, unusual token issuance, or privilege use that does not match historical behavior. Analysts should also consider operational realities such as shared administrative jump hosts, break-glass procedures, and automation that can mimic attacker patterns when poorly governed. The goal is not to "trust the user" or "trust the alert," but to determine whether the evidence supports identity integrity.

Refutation is not a failure; it is a successful reduction of risk and noise when done properly. When activity is deemed benign, the analyst should capture the rationale and the key evidence that supports that conclusion, because the same pattern is likely to recur. This documentation enables detection tuning, rule exceptions, and improved context signals without normalizing genuinely risky behavior. Teams should be careful not to refute by assumption, such as "it was probably IT," because that converts uncertainty into false closure. A defensible refutation includes the specific telemetry that explains the behavior, the conditions under which it is expected, and any residual risk that remains if the explanation could still be abused. Over time, these refutations become an institutional memory that reduces repeated effort.

Confirmation of malicious activity typically hinges on identifying intent and unauthorized control, not merely unusualness. Analysts should look for indicators that demonstrate attacker tradecraft, such as persistence mechanisms, credential access attempts, lateral movement patterns, or deliberate defense evasion. Evidence such as repeated authentication failures followed by success from a new location, remote execution chains that do not align with standard administration, or access to data repositories outside normal workflows strengthens the malicious conclusion. Analysts should also be cautious about relying on single "smoking gun" indicators that can be spoofed or misinterpreted, and instead build a cumulative case from multiple weak signals that align. The confidence of confirmation should be proportional to the independence and quality of the supporting evidence.

AI-assisted analysis can help prioritize which suspicions to test and can accelerate pattern recognition, but it must be bounded by verifiable evidence. Models can summarize alert context, suggest likely benign explanations based on historical cases, and identify clusters of related events that might otherwise be missed. These outputs are useful for speed, especially when analysts face high alert volume, but they can also introduce false confidence by presenting speculation as a coherent narrative. Human-in-the-loop controls should require that AI-generated claims be treated as hypotheses and that each claim be validated with primary logs before it influences containment decisions. Teams should also guard against drift, where models trained on past incident patterns misclassify new behaviors after environment changes such as new authentication flows or infrastructure migrations. The correct posture is to use AI to reduce cognitive load while keeping the proof standard anchored to source telemetry.

The final step is to express the confirmation or refutation in operational terms that drive the next action. Analysts should state the finding, the evidence basis, and the remaining uncertainties, then tie that to decisions such as containment, monitoring, or escalation to incident response. If activity is confirmed malicious, the statement should include the affected identities and assets, the time window of confirmed activity, and the most likely access paths still at risk. If activity is refuted, the statement should include what conditions made it appear suspicious and what detection adjustment or contextual enrichment would prevent repeated false positives. This rigor turns investigation outputs into trusted inputs for the broader response process, ensuring that teams act decisively without acting blindly.

Working with IT, Engineering, and Business Stakeholders

Incident analysis is rarely limited by technical skill; it is limited by coordination. Analysts depend on IT and engineering teams to validate system behavior, provide access to authoritative records, and execute changes that the security team should not perform unilaterally. Business stakeholders provide the context that determines what "impact" means, what operational disruptions are acceptable, and what timelines matter. The analyst mindset treats these groups as part of the investigation workflow, not as downstream recipients of findings. When coordination is delayed or adversarial, investigations become slower, noisier, and more disruptive than necessary.

A practical engagement model starts with clear role boundaries and a shared understanding of decision rights. Security teams typically own detection, initial triage, evidence handling, and the investigative narrative, while IT and engineering teams own system changes, service restoration, and the operational implications of containment. Business owners own risk acceptance decisions and prioritize tradeoffs when evidence is incomplete. Analysts should be explicit about what they are asking for and why, distinguishing information requests from action requests and urgent actions from low-risk data gathering. That clarity reduces the friction that comes from teams feeling "pulled into security work" without context. It also prevents accidental escalation when a routine request is interpreted as a directive to take disruptive action.

Communication quality is a control in its own right during an incident. Analysts should communicate in the language of observable facts, timelines, and specific asks, avoiding ambiguous statements that create unnecessary alarm or skepticism. A well-structured update includes what is confirmed, what is suspected, what is being tested next, and what help is needed, framed in terms of business services and operational risk. Stakeholders do not need every log detail, but they do need to understand what could change the assessment and what actions are being considered. Analysts should also avoid "tool speak" that only a security practitioner understands, translating events into system and service impact where possible. The result is alignment without oversharing and urgency without drama.

IT and engineering relationships are strengthened when analysts respect operational constraints and are careful with access. During investigations, the temptation is to ask for broad admin access or to request large, disruptive changes "just in case." That approach erodes trust and can lead to resistance, especially in high-availability environments. Analysts should instead request targeted actions with clear scoping, such as isolating a single host, resetting a specific service account, or enabling additional auditing for a defined window. They should also coordinate timing, because emergency changes can break dependencies, invalidate evidence, or disrupt critical business functions. The most effective teams treat operations partners as co-owners of outcomes and make containment decisions with a shared view of tradeoffs.

Business stakeholders need a risk narrative that is both truthful and actionable. Analysts should connect technical findings to operational implications: what services could be affected, what data might be exposed, what regulatory or contractual triggers might exist, and what customer-facing consequences are plausible. The narrative should explicitly include confidence levels and highlight what evidence is missing, because executives make better decisions when uncertainty is acknowledged rather than hidden. Analysts should avoid overpromising certainty or timelines and instead describe the investigative path and decision points that drive timing. A credible risk narrative also distinguishes between confirmed impact and potential exposure, because conflating the two can lead to misaligned communications and unnecessary disruption. Done well, business engagement accelerates decisions instead of slowing them down.

Cross-team work often fails on the mechanics of handoffs and tracking. Analysts should maintain a single source of truth for the case record, including requests made, actions taken, timestamps, and outcomes, so partners are not forced to reconstruct the history from fragmented messages. Requests should be specific enough to execute and measurable enough to confirm, such as "export authentication events for account X between these timestamps" rather than "check the logs." When tasks are delegated, the analyst should capture the returned evidence and document how it influenced the hypothesis, preventing circular work and repeated asks. This rigor also reduces the risk of two teams taking conflicting actions, such as restoring a system while another team is preserving evidence. Strong operational hygiene makes coordination scalable under stress.

AI can improve stakeholder collaboration by reducing translation overhead, but it must be governed to avoid misinformation and leakage. Practical uses include summarizing technical findings into stakeholder-ready updates, extracting action items from chat threads or ticket comments, and highlighting inconsistencies between different teams' accounts of what changed. These outputs can speed coordination, especially during long incidents with many participants, but they introduce risks if summaries omit critical qualifiers or if sensitive evidence is inadvertently included in broad distribution. Human-in-the-loop controls should require analyst review before any AI-generated stakeholder update is sent, with clear boundaries on what data may be included and where it may be stored. Teams should also preserve auditability by keeping the underlying source notes and evidence separate from the summarized narrative, so decisions can be traced back to facts. The goal is to use AI as a drafting assistant, not as an authority.

Trust is built by being predictable under pressure. Analysts should avoid blaming operations teams for misconfigurations or gaps in telemetry during active incidents, focusing instead on immediate risk reduction and clear next steps. When operational teams provide explanations for suspicious activity, analysts should validate them with evidence rather than accepting them at face value, but they should do so respectfully and transparently.

Similarly, when security recommends containment that carries operational cost, analysts should explain the rationale in terms of threat pathways and the cost of delay, not just "security best practice." These behaviors prevent the common failure mode where teams retreat into silos and communicate only through escalation. The incident becomes a shared problem to solve, not a contest to win.

Sustained effectiveness requires turning stakeholder interactions into durable improvements without turning the moment into a postmortem discussion. During the investigation, analysts should capture friction points—missing logs, unclear ownership, slow approvals, ambiguous runbooks—as observations that can be addressed once the environment stabilizes. They should also reinforce what worked, such as fast access to identity logs, clear escalation contacts, or disciplined change tracking, because those are the behaviors worth institutionalizing. The practical outcome is that each incident strengthens the organization's ability to collaborate under uncertainty, reducing time to truth and time to containment. When security, IT, engineering, and business stakeholders operate with shared facts and clear decision rights, investigations become faster, less disruptive, and materially more credible.

Knowing When to Escalate to Incident Response

Escalation to incident response is not an admission of failure; it is a recognition that the problem space has crossed a threshold of risk, uncertainty, or impact that demands a different operating mode. The analyst's responsibility is to identify when investigative activity alone is no longer sufficient and when coordinated containment and recovery must take precedence. This decision is often made with incomplete information, which makes disciplined criteria more important than perfect certainty. Teams that escalate too late allow adversary activity to compound, while teams that escalate too early exhaust responders and disrupt business operations unnecessarily. Knowing when to escalate is therefore a core analytical skill, not a procedural checkbox.

The most reliable escalation signals are evidence-based, not severity labels. Confirmed unauthorized access, especially involving privileged identities, is a clear trigger regardless of how "clean" the activity appears. Persistence mechanisms, such as new scheduled tasks, services, startup modifications, or token reuse patterns, indicate ongoing risk that investigation alone cannot mitigate. Evidence of lateral movement, data access outside normal workflows, or control-plane changes that expand permissions also warrant escalation because they increase blast radius. Analysts should be cautious about relying on alert severity or vendor classifications as proxies for these conditions, because they often lag reality or overgeneralize. Escalation decisions should be tied to what the evidence shows the attacker can do now, not what the alert claims might happen.

Uncertainty itself can be a valid reason to escalate when the potential impact is high. If key telemetry is missing, logs are delayed, or evidence gaps align with known blind spots, the absence of visibility may pose as much risk as confirmed malicious activity. Analysts should assess whether continued investigation without containment meaningfully reduces risk or simply delays action while exposure remains. In environments with high-value assets or strict regulatory obligations, the tolerance for uncertainty is lower, and escalation thresholds should reflect that. A mature team articulates this explicitly, stating that escalation is being recommended due to unresolved risk rather than confirmed damage. This transparency builds trust with leadership and avoids the false impression that escalation implies definitive compromise.

Time-based escalation criteria are an important but often overlooked control. Analysts should define maximum investigation windows for certain classes of suspicion, after which the case must either be refuted or escalated. This prevents investigations from lingering indefinitely while attackers maintain access or while analysts continue to "just check one more log." Time pressure also forces prioritization of the highest yield evidence early in the investigation. When a case crosses its time threshold without resolution, escalation becomes a structured handoff rather than an emotional decision. This approach aligns investigative rigor with operational urgency.

Escalation is also influenced by the type of response required, not just the presence of malicious activity. When containment actions will disrupt production systems, revoke access for critical users, or require coordinated changes across teams, incident response provides the governance and authority to execute those actions safely. Analysts should recognize when they are approaching decisions that exceed their mandate, such as isolating core infrastructure or initiating customer notifications. Incident response brings predefined communication paths, executive sponsorship, and change control discipline that individual analysts should not attempt to replicate ad hoc. Escalating at this point protects both the organization and the analyst.

AI-assisted triage can help surface escalation indicators earlier, but it should never make the escalation decision autonomously. Models can flag patterns associated with high-impact incidents, such as rapid privilege changes followed by access to sensitive systems, or identify cases that resemble prior incidents that required full response. These insights depend heavily on historical data quality and can be skewed by changes in environment or attacker behavior. Human-in-the-loop controls should require analysts to validate model-identified escalation signals with primary evidence and to document why the signal is relevant in the current context. A common failure mode is over-trusting AI confidence scores, which can compress nuance into a single number and obscure important qualifiers. Escalation remains a human judgment informed by evidence, not an automated outcome.

The act of escalation should be deliberate and well-structured. Analysts should present a concise summary that includes what is confirmed, what is suspected, what remains unknown, and why continued investigation without response is insufficient. They should specify the recommended scope of response, such as which identities, systems, or services need to be contained immediately, and what evidence supports that recommendation. This framing enables incident responders to act quickly without redoing the entire investigation. Poor escalations, by contrast, dump raw data or vague concern on the response team, slowing action and increasing frustration. The quality of the escalation directly affects the speed and effectiveness of the response.

Escalation is not a binary event but a transition in operating mode. Analysts often continue to play a critical role after escalation by supporting responders with evidence, answering questions about hypotheses, and refining scope as new data emerges. They should expect assumptions to be challenged and earlier conclusions to be revised as containment actions surface additional artifacts. This is normal and should not be interpreted as investigative failure. Teams that treat escalation as a handoff rather than a collaboration often lose continuity and repeat work unnecessarily. Clear expectations about roles during and after escalation preserve momentum.

Organizations that handle escalation well do so because they have pre-aligned expectations. Analysts know the thresholds, responders know what information they will receive, and leadership understands that escalation reflects risk management, not alarmism. When those expectations are unclear, analysts hesitate, second-guess, or escalate defensively, all of which degrade outcomes. The discipline of knowing when to escalate is built through clear criteria, consistent practice, and post-incident reflection on whether escalation timing was appropriate. Over time, this produces faster decisions, cleaner handoffs, and a response posture that matches the true risk of the situation.

AI-Assisted Investigations: Evidence Summarization, Correlation, and Verification Discipline

AI-assisted investigations are most valuable when they reduce cognitive load without weakening evidentiary standards. In modern environments, an investigation may involve thousands of events across identity, endpoint, network, and cloud control planes, and the bottleneck is often human attention rather than data availability. AI can compress, cluster, and prioritize, helping analysts move from raw signals to a coherent working hypothesis faster. The risk is that the same compression can hide uncertainty, amplify biases in the data, or present plausible narratives that are not supported by primary evidence. Operationally mature teams treat AI as an acceleration layer over disciplined investigation practices, not as a replacement for them.

Evidence summarization is the most immediate and least controversial use case when governed correctly. Models can take verbose event streams and produce a readable account of key actions, highlighting who did what, where, and when, and calling out notable deviations from baseline. Summaries are especially useful in long-running incidents where multiple analysts contribute over shifts, because they provide continuity without requiring each person to reread the entire case history. The verification discipline is to treat summaries as pointers, not proofs, and to require that every summary claim maps back to a specific event, query, or artifact in the case record. When summaries are accepted as authoritative, teams drift into narrative-first investigations that become hard to defend. The best practice is to keep summaries reversible, meaning an analyst can easily trace a statement back to the underlying evidence that produced it.

Correlation is where AI can create outsized gains and outsized risk. Models can cluster related events by shared entities, infer likely relationships across dissimilar logs, and propose pivots that human analysts might not immediately see, such as linking a token issuance pattern to a later set of API calls and an endpoint session. This is powerful when telemetry is consistent and identifiers are stable, because AI can surface multi-hop relationships quickly. The risk is that correlation can become conflation, where unrelated events are grouped because they "look similar" rather than because they share a verifiable link. Analysts should require a clear correlation basis for every proposed relationship, such as a shared session ID, device identifier, process lineage, or consistent time-bound sequence that can be justified. If the basis is only statistical similarity, the relationship should be treated as a lead with explicitly lower confidence.

Verification discipline is the guardrail that makes AI safe in investigations. Analysts should establish rules that no AI output can directly trigger containment, escalation, or external communication without human validation against primary telemetry. Verification should be explicit: confirm the identity, confirm the asset, confirm the time window, confirm the action semantics, and confirm that the evidence is not an artifact of ingestion delay or normalization. The case record should capture both the AI-generated hypothesis and the evidence that confirmed or refuted it, preserving an audit trail of reasoning. This discipline prevents a subtle but common failure mode where AI is used correctly at first, then gradually becomes an unchallenged authority under time pressure. Strong teams treat verification as a repeatable workflow, not as an individual analyst's preference.

Data and telemetry dependencies determine whether AI helps or harms. Summarization and correlation quality depends on consistent schemas, high-fidelity timestamps, stable entity identifiers, and coverage across the core investigative layers. If endpoint telemetry is missing from a segment of the environment, the model may overemphasize identity logs and infer endpoint activity that is not actually observed. If time synchronization is inconsistent, the model may assemble a plausible but incorrect sequence that reverses causality. If labels and prior cases are noisy, prioritization may reflect historical bias rather than current risk. Analysts should therefore treat AI performance as an indicator of telemetry health, and they should be prepared to downgrade reliance when coverage or data quality is known to be weak.

Human-in-the-loop controls require more than a policy statement; they require operational boundaries. Teams should define what AI is allowed to do by default, such as summarizing case notes, proposing pivots, clustering related alerts, or drafting internal updates, and what it is not allowed to do, such as declaring an incident, attributing actions to a specific actor, or recommending irreversible containment steps. Approval boundaries should be explicit, with a named role responsible for validating AI-derived claims before they are acted upon. These boundaries should also include data handling constraints, ensuring that sensitive evidence, customer data, or privileged details are not inappropriately exposed through broad distribution of AI-generated summaries. The point is to preserve decision accountability while still capturing the speed benefits of automation.

Failure modes in AI-assisted investigations are predictable and should be anticipated. False confidence is common when outputs are fluent and specific, causing analysts to over-weight the narrative quality rather than the evidentiary basis. Drift occurs as environments change—new authentication flows, new logging formats, new infrastructure—and the model's learned correlations become less reliable. Bias can appear when historical incidents overrepresent certain systems or user populations, leading to skewed prioritization that does not match

Table 21.3 AI Investigation Outputs and Required Verification Discipline.

AI Output Type	Operational Use	Required Human Check	Acceptable Action Without Review	Audit Note to Record
Event stream summary	Reduce reading load and maintain continuity	Trace each claim to source events	Draft internal notes only	Source queries and time range
Correlation cluster	Group-related entities and actions	Verify linkage basis such as session or process	Prioritize pivots only	Confirmed versus unconfirmed links
Next step suggestions	Propose high-yield pivots	Confirm relevance to current hypothesis	Queue investigative tasks	Which suggestions were used
Draft stakeholder update	Translate facts into readable status	Validate qualifiers and confidence language	None	Reviewer name and approved version
Confidence indication	Highlight likely priority cases	Validate against primary telemetry	Attention routing only	Telemetry gaps impacting confidence

actual risk. Leakage risk emerges when sensitive incident details are retained, re-used, or shared beyond intended audiences, especially when case summaries are treated as reusable knowledge without careful sanitization. Teams should treat these as operational risks to be mitigated through process controls, review, and careful data governance, not as theoretical concerns. Table 21.3 clarifies where AI can accelerate investigation work and where verification and auditability must constrain its outputs.

Auditability is the requirement that makes AI-assisted investigations sustainable at scale. Analysts should ensure that AI outputs are stored alongside the evidence and query context that produced them, including the time, inputs, and any assumptions. When AI suggests a relationship, the case record should note whether it was confirmed, refuted, or left unresolved, and what evidence was used in that determination. This structure prevents future analysts from treating old AI-generated narratives as facts and allows the organization to learn systematically from both successes and failures. It also supports internal assurance, where leadership can review how decisions were made without needing to replay the entire incident. AI can accelerate investigations, but only auditability preserves trust.

Operationally, the best use of AI is to tighten the loop between alert, hypothesis, and proof. AI can help an analyst quickly understand what a cluster of events likely represents, propose efficient next checks, and keep the case narrative coherent across people and time. Verification discipline ensures those accelerations do not compromise correctness, containment decisions, or stakeholder communications. The combination of AI speed and human judgment is most effective when the rules are clear: AI may summarize and suggest, but the analyst must validate and decide. When teams consistently apply that discipline, AI becomes a reliable force multiplier for investigation rather than a new source of risk.

Improving Investigation Quality Over Time

Improving investigation quality over time is less about adding new capabilities and more about tightening feedback loops. Every investigation produces evidence about the adversary and about the organization's own readiness: what telemetry was missing, which assumptions slowed progress, where handoffs broke down, and which decisions were made with avoidable uncertainty. Mature teams capture these signals as part of normal case work rather than treating improvement as a separate initiative that only happens after major incidents. The key is to make investigative quality measurable through repeatable behaviors: clearer hypotheses, faster falsification, better timelines, and more defensible conclusions. When quality is treated as craftsmanship, it improves steadily without needing heroic interventions.

The case record is the primary lever for improving quality because it encodes both what happened and how the team reasoned about it. Strong teams standardize what must be recorded: working hypotheses, key pivots, evidence sources, time normalization choices, and decision points that changed scope or severity. This level of documentation enables peer review and cross-case learning, and it also reduces rework during shift changes or escalations. It prevents a common failure where conclusions are remembered but the supporting evidence is not, leaving future analysts unable to replicate or challenge prior reasoning. Over time, consistent case documentation builds an institutional memory of what "good investigation" looks like in that specific environment. The organization becomes less dependent on a few senior individuals and more resilient to staffing changes.

Telemetry quality is inseparable from investigation quality, and investigations are an honest audit of telemetry reality. Analysts should log evidence gaps as concrete findings, such as missing endpoint coverage for a critical tier, inconsistent timestamps across systems, insufficient control-plane logging, or retention windows that expire before investigations complete. These gaps should be translated into actionable backlog items with clear owners, because vague statements like "we need better logging" rarely produce change. Improvements should be prioritized by how often a gap recurs and how much it increases uncertainty in high-impact scenarios. When telemetry becomes more consistent and complete, investigation steps become simpler and conclusions become more confident. The fastest investigations typically happen in environments where logging discipline has already done the hard work.

Detection tuning is another durable improvement path, but it must be driven by investigation outcomes rather than alert volume alone. Confirmed true positives should be analyzed for what made them detectable and what signals were missing that could have made confirmation faster. False positives should be refuted with evidence and then used to add context requirements, tighten thresholds, or incorporate additional conditions that distinguish benign automation from misuse. Teams should be careful not to tune away difficult detections simply because they generate work, because that creates blind spots that adversaries exploit. Instead, tuning should aim to increase precision while preserving coverage, with explicit acceptance of residual noise when it protects high-value assets. Investigation results are the ground truth that tells you whether a detection is operationally useful.

Skill development is most effective when it is embedded in real cases and focused on decision quality. After-action learning should emphasize how hypotheses were formed, how evidence was validated, and where cognitive traps appeared, rather than devolving into blame for missed steps. Senior analysts can accelerate team maturity by reviewing cases for reasoning quality, highlighting where alternative hypotheses should have been considered, or where timeline errors were introduced by time normalization mistakes. Rotations that expose analysts to identity systems, cloud control planes, and core business applications improve their ability to interpret artifacts correctly. Investigation quality rises when analysts understand how systems are supposed to behave, because they can spot meaningful deviations faster. Training that is disconnected from the organization's actual architecture tends to improve vocabulary more than performance.

Process improvements should target the points where investigations predictably stall. Common stall points include unclear escalation criteria, slow access to logs or exports, inconsistent naming for assets and accounts, and ambiguous ownership for critical services. Teams should build streamlined pathways for high-urgency actions, such as obtaining approvals for account lockouts, isolating hosts, or enabling temporary enhanced logging for defined windows. They should also practice these pathways so that the mechanics work under stress, not only in calm conditions. When a process is healthy, analysts spend their time thinking and validating, not chasing permissions and contacts. Operational friction is a quality problem because it forces analysts to make decisions with less evidence.

AI can support continuous quality improvement by making patterns visible across many cases, but it should be used carefully to avoid institutionalizing mistakes. Models can cluster cases with similar characteristics, surface recurring evidence gaps, and summarize which pivots most often led to confirmation or refutation. This helps teams identify where to invest, such as improving a specific log source, standardizing identity metadata, or refining a set of detections that repeatedly produce ambiguous investigations. The governance requirement is to validate these insights against actual case outcomes, because AI will happily find patterns in messy data and present them as meaningful. Teams should also avoid training themselves to accept model-generated case summaries as factual without review, because that can propagate subtle errors across future investigations. Used properly, AI becomes a lens for learning at scale while human review preserves correctness.

Metrics can help, but only if they measure quality rather than speed alone. Time to initial hypothesis, time to first decisive pivot, time to confirmation or refutation, and percentage of cases with complete timelines are more meaningful than raw closure times. Confidence annotations in case records can also be valuable, especially when later evidence proves or disproves early assumptions, because they reveal where the team tends to overestimate certainty. Metrics should be used to guide improvements, not to penalize analysts for cautious reasoning in complex cases. When metrics become targets, teams learn to optimize for closure rather than truth. Investigation quality improves when the organization rewards defensible decisions and transparent uncertainty.

Sustained improvement ultimately comes from treating investigation as an engineering discipline. Evidence collection, timeline construction, hypothesis testing, and stakeholder coordination should be repeatable enough that variation reflects the case, not the analyst. Each investigation should leave the environment slightly better: clearer runbooks, stronger logging, more precise detections, and more practiced cross-team pathways. Over time, this compounding effect reduces mean time to truth and increases confidence in containment decisions, even as adversaries change techniques. The organization becomes not only better at responding, but better at learning, which is the most durable advantage in incident analysis.

Conclusion

Investigation closes the loop between detection and resilience by converting uncertain signals into defensible decisions and durable improvements. When analysts treat alerts as prompts, evidence as verifiable truth, and narratives as traceable to primary telemetry, the organization responds faster without sacrificing accuracy or trust. The most effective programs know when to shift from investigation to incident response, communicate clearly across technical and business stakeholders, and use AI to reduce friction while preserving human accountability and auditability. Over time, consistent case records, better telemetry, and learning-driven tuning turn each investigation into a force multiplier, steadily shrinking time to truth and strengthening confidence in containment and recovery.

Recommendations

1) Treat every alert as a prompt rather than a verdict. Translate the alert into testable claims and separate observed facts from inferred meaning before taking disruptive action. Anchor your early work in primary telemetry and be explicit about what the detection could not have known. This discipline reduces both premature escalation and dangerous dismissal.
2) Convert suspicion into a small set of falsifiable hypotheses as early as possible. Write hypotheses precisely enough that you can identify the shortest path to disproof using available identity, endpoint, network, and control-plane evidence. Maintain at least one competing explanation to counter confirmation bias and keep the investigation evidence-led. Update or discard hypotheses quickly as new artifacts arrive.
3) Preserve volatile evidence before routine operations erase it. Prioritize short-retention and high-volatility artifacts such as endpoint execution details, session context, and time-sensitive audit records before you isolate

hosts or reset accounts. Capture artifacts in a way that protects integrity, including hashes for collected bundles and clear documentation of who collected what and how. Validate that preserved evidence is usable later, not merely stored.

4) Record collection context, so findings remain reproducible and defensible. Document queries, filters, time ranges, and timezone assumptions for every retrieval, and preserve original timestamps alongside normalized values. Track evidence provenance in the case record, including how exports were generated and any known ingestion delays or gaps. This practice prevents timeline errors and protects credibility during escalation and stakeholder review.
5) Scope impact with explicit bounds that narrow over time. Establish a minimum confirmed footprint based on high-confidence evidence and a maximum plausible footprint based on access paths, privilege, and telemetry limitations. Expand scope along identity and connectivity relationships rather than chasing alert labels or hostnames that lack authoritative mapping. State confidence levels and the specific indicators that would broaden or contract the scope.
6) Build timelines as your primary investigative tool, not as a reporting afterthought. Normalize time carefully, distinguish event time from ingestion time, and stitch events using stable identifiers such as sessions, processes, requests, or tokens where available. Capture parallel threads and defensive actions in the same timeline to avoid misattribution and false causality. Use the timeline to expose evidence gaps that must be compensated through alternate sources.
7) Confirm or refute suspicious activity through corroboration across independent sources. Validate claims using at least two complementary telemetry layers when possible, and downgrade confidence explicitly when corroboration is not available. Refute with evidence and document the rationale, so detections can be tuned and the same false pattern does not repeatedly consume analyst time. Confirm maliciousness by demonstrating unauthorized control and intent signals rather than relying solely on unusualness.
8) Work with IT, engineering, and business stakeholders using clear decision rights and precise asks. Distinguish information requests from action requests and specify urgency, scope, and rationale to reduce friction and prevent accidental disruption. Translate technical findings into service and business impact terms while clearly separating confirmed impact from potential exposure. Maintain a single source of truth for requests, actions, and outcomes, so collaboration remains coherent under stress.
9) Escalate to incident response based on evidence, risk, and operational consequence rather than alert severity alone. Trigger escalation when you see unauthorized access, privilege misuse, persistence, lateral movement, or high-impact uncertainty driven by telemetry gaps. Use time-based thresholds to prevent cases from lingering unresolved while exposure persists. Provide a structured escalation package that includes confirmed facts, key unknowns, and recommended containment boundaries.
10) Use AI to accelerate summarization and correlation while enforcing verification discipline and auditability. Allow models to suggest pivots, cluster related activity, and draft readable case updates, but require human validation against primary telemetry before decisions, containment, or communications occur. Record which AI outputs influenced investigative steps and whether they were confirmed or refuted to prevent narrative drift and preserve accountability. Treat AI as an efficiency layer that must remain reversible back to source evidence.

Part VI

Incident Response, Recovery, and Improvement

22

Building and Maintaining Incident Response Plans

An incident response plan is not a document that sits on a shelf until something goes wrong; it is an operational contract that defines how an organization makes decisions under pressure. It establishes shared expectations for who leads, how facts are captured, when authority shifts from technical teams to business leadership, and how communications remain coherent while uncertainty is high. It also turns response from improvisation into a disciplined sequence of actions that preserve evidence, limit harm, and support defensible reporting and recovery. When treated as a practiced capability—maintained through change, exercised regularly, and supported by carefully bounded AI assistance—the plan becomes a reliable mechanism for converting risk into controlled execution rather than compounding chaos.

Purpose and Scope of an Incident Response Plan

An incident response plan exists to make the organization predictable under stress. It translates the intent of leadership into repeatable actions that reduce harm when an event is unfolding faster than normal decision cycles. Without a plan, response becomes improvisation, and improvisation tends to concentrate authority in the loudest voice rather than the most informed one. The purpose is not to eliminate uncertainty but to establish who decides what, how information moves, and how the organization contains impact while preserving evidence. A well-scoped plan also protects the business from overreaction by setting boundaries for when to escalate, when to isolate, and when to communicate.

Scope starts with a clear definition of what qualifies as an incident versus routine operations work. Not every alert, malware detection, or service disruption should invoke the same machinery, because constant "all-hands" response burns credibility and exhausts responders. The plan should anchor on impact and risk signals such as confirmed unauthorized access, material data exposure, integrity loss, sustained service disruption, or a credible threat actor foothold. It should also include criteria for response activation when the organization lacks full confirmation but the potential harm is high, such as ransomware behavior, evidence of account takeover at privileged tiers, or active exploitation of an exposed system. The goal is to avoid both extremes: ignoring early warnings and triggering a crisis process for every anomaly.

A practical scope statement identifies the assets and business processes the plan covers, including corporate IT, identity systems, cloud workloads, endpoints, and externally facing services. It should explicitly address whether operational technology, product environments, third-party platforms, and subsidiary networks are in scope, and what happens when those boundaries intersect. If parts of the environment are managed by vendors, the plan should still cover the organization's responsibilities for oversight, decision authority, and regulatory notifications, even if technical containment is performed elsewhere. The plan is not a technical runbook for every system; it is the governance layer that makes runbooks usable under pressure. That governance layer must be broad enough to

Table 22.1 Incident Declaration Triggers and Activation Cues.

Trigger Type	Example Signal	Expected Action	Primary Owner
Unauthorized access confirmed	Confirmed access beyond authorization	Activate incident process and start timeline	Incident commander
High risk uncertainty	Credible ransomware behavior	Activate incident process and stage containment	Incident commander
Data exposure risk	Suspected regulated data exposure	Engage legal privacy and preserve evidence	Legal and privacy
Integrity loss	Unexpected changes to critical configurations	Initiate investigation and containment gating	Lead investigator
Sustained disruption	Revenue service unavailable with security indicators	Escalate severity and coordinate recovery	Service owner

cover the enterprise but specific enough that responders can act without debating jurisdiction. Table 22.1 provides practical triggers that help teams activate incident response consistently based on impact and risk signals.

The scope of roles and authority is as important as the scope of systems. The plan should define who can declare an incident, who owns incident command, and who has the authority to approve disruptive actions such as isolating segments, disabling accounts, or taking production services offline. It should also define how legal counsel, privacy, communications, HR, finance, and business owners participate, including what information they need and what decisions they are expected to make. This prevents security teams from becoming bottlenecks for nontechnical actions like customer messaging or contractual notifications. Clear authority lines also reduce the likelihood that executives learn about an incident through informal channels, which tends to create parallel response efforts that compete for the same facts.

An incident response plan must set expectations for the response lifecycle, even if the tactical details vary. At minimum, the scope should include detection intake, initial triage, containment decisioning, evidence preservation, eradication planning, and recovery validation, along with documentation requirements throughout. The plan should define how severity is assessed in a way that maps to business impact, so that "critical" means something measurable rather than subjective. It should also define what data must be collected and retained, such as system logs, authentication records, endpoint telemetry, and ticket artifacts, because evidence gaps discovered mid-incident are expensive to remediate. By scoping the lifecycle, the plan ensures the organization does not confuse "systems back online" with "incident resolved," especially when persistence and data exposure are still uncertain.

AI and machine learning can strengthen the plan's purpose when they are treated as decision support rather than decision authority. In many environments, ML-assisted correlation can help group alerts into likely campaigns, prioritize triage based on historical incident patterns, and surface anomalies in authentication flows or process behaviors that humans might miss. Those benefits are only real if the plan defines the telemetry dependencies and validation controls, including which log sources are considered authoritative, how model outputs are explained, and when a human must confirm before taking high-impact actions. Failure modes must be assumed: models can over-prioritize noisy signals, underweight novel attack paths, or create false confidence through fluent summaries that do not match the evidence. The plan should therefore require that any AI-produced conclusions be traceable to underlying events and that responders record what the model suggested, what evidence supported or contradicted it, and who approved the final decision.

Finally, scope must include the "edges" where incidents become business events: regulatory reporting, contractual obligations, insurance engagement, and public communications. The plan should describe what triggers those pathways, who owns the relationships, and what evidence thresholds are required before statements are made externally. It should also set boundaries for sensitive information handling so that incident artifacts do not leak through uncontrolled collaboration channels, especially when outside counsel, forensics firms, or crisis communications are involved. A scoped plan assumes that confusion is a primary adversary and designs for coordination, not heroics. When the purpose and scope are explicit, the organization can respond quickly without losing discipline, and leaders can be confident that speed is not coming at the expense of accuracy or governance.

Roles, Responsibilities, and Decision Authority

Roles in incident response exist to prevent two predictable failure modes: paralysis and chaos. Paralysis happens when everyone is waiting for someone else to decide, while chaos happens when multiple people act at once with conflicting intent. A mature plan defines roles so that technical execution, business decisioning, and communications move in parallel without stepping on each other. The objective is not to create bureaucracy but to make authority explicit before stress and uncertainty distort normal working relationships. When roles are clear, responders spend their cognitive budget on facts and containment rather than on negotiating who is in charge.

The incident commander is the central coordination function, not necessarily the most senior person in the room. This role owns the operational tempo, sets priorities for the next decision window, and ensures actions are sequenced to reduce harm while preserving evidence. Incident command should be empowered to request resources across teams and to convene the right stakeholders quickly, but it should not be forced to personally approve every tactical action. If incident command becomes a gate for every step, the response slows and teams start working around the process. Good incident command creates clarity on "what we know, what we think, what we are doing next, and what we need," and enforces that this is recorded as the incident develops.

Technical roles should be separated by function to avoid mixing investigation with containment in ways that destroy evidence or obscure timelines. A lead investigator focuses on establishing what happened, when it started, what systems are involved, and what the adversary is doing now. A containment lead focuses on stopping spread and limiting impact through isolation, access restriction, or service changes, coordinating closely with system owners to execute safely. A forensics or evidence custodian role, whether internal or external, ensures artifacts are collected in a defensible way, with chain of custody when required. When one person is trying to do all of these simultaneously, the organization tends to either over-contain too early or delay containment until certainty is obtained, both of which increase risk. This diagram clarifies how the incident commander coordinates core roles while decision authority remains distributed across accountable owners. It reinforces separation of duties between investigation containment business continuity and communications while keeping approvals traceable (Figure 22.1).

Business ownership must be explicit because many of the most consequential choices are not technical. Service owners and application owners understand operational dependencies, acceptable downtime, and the business impact of different containment options. Legal and privacy functions determine when an event crosses regulatory thresholds, what investigative steps require special handling, and how to manage privilege in communications and documentation. Communications leadership controls messaging cadence and consistency, including internal updates that prevent rumor-driven decisions. Executive sponsors do not run the response minute to minute, but they must be engaged when decisions materially affect customers, revenue, safety, or regulatory posture.

Decision authority should be framed around categories of actions, with pre-approved thresholds that remove the need for ad hoc escalation. For example, authority to disable a single user account may sit with security operations, while authority to revoke access for a privileged group may require identity leadership and a business owner due to operational impact. Authority to isolate a host can be delegated broadly, but isolating a subnet, blocking a critical integration, or taking a production service offline should require a defined approval path that includes the accountable service owner. The plan should also define emergency powers for time-critical containment, paired

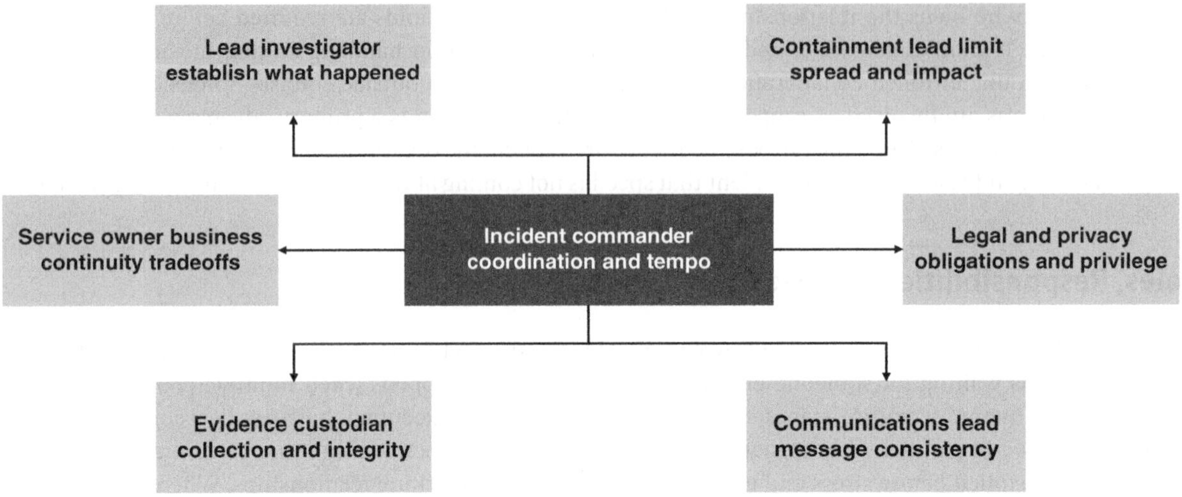

Figure 22.1 Roles and Decision Authority Map for Incident Response.

Table 22.2 Role Responsibilities and Decision Authority Boundaries.

Role	Primary Focus	Typical Decisions	Required Documentation
Incident commander	Coordination and tempo	Declare incident and set priorities	Timeline updates and decision log
Lead investigator	Establish what happened	Scope assessment and hypothesis updates	Evidence notes and confirmed facts
Containment lead	Limit spread and impact	Isolation actions and access restriction	Containment actions and validation results
Service owner	Business continuity tradeoffs	Approve disruptive changes	Impact assessment and approval record
Legal and privacy	Obligations and privilege	Notification thresholds and handling rules	Decision rationale and evidence limits
Communications lead	Message consistency	Cadence and approved statements	Approved language and distribution list

with a requirement to notify decision-makers immediately and document the rationale. This creates speed without eroding governance, because responders can act quickly while still remaining accountable. Table 22.2 clarifies how core incident roles divide work and where decision authority and documentation expectations must be explicit.

Escalation paths should be designed for reliability, not for organizational charts. During an incident, people are unavailable, time zones matter, and the "right" approver may be in the air or asleep. The plan should therefore define alternates for each decision authority, with a clear rule for how authority transfers when primary owners are unreachable. It should also establish minimum communication expectations: when to inform executives, when to involve legal, when to notify communications, and when to coordinate with physical security or HR. A common pitfall is over-escalation early, which produces performative meetings and dilutes technical focus, and under-escalation later, which results in missed notification windows and unprepared customer-facing teams. Escalation discipline is achieved by tying escalation triggers to impact signals and decision points rather than to anxiety.

AI can support role clarity when it is used to reduce coordination overhead rather than to replace accountability. Automated summarization can produce consistent situation reports from tickets, chat logs, and timeline notes, but the plan should specify who validates those summaries before they are used for executive updates or external communications. ML-based triage and correlation can help route work to the right technical owners by recognizing patterns such as credential misuse, lateral movement indicators, or known failure cascades, yet routing recommendations must be auditable and explainable. The plan should anticipate model failure modes, including confident but incorrect narrative generation, drift as environments change, and bias toward historically common incident types that can cause novel attacks to be deprioritized. Human-in-the-loop controls should be explicit: AI can recommend, cluster, and draft, but named individuals approve containment actions, declare severity, and authorize communications.

Finally, responsibilities must include documentation and auditability as a first-class operational duty, not an after-action chore. The plan should assign ownership for maintaining the timeline, tracking decisions and approvals, and recording evidence collection steps in a way that supports legal review, regulatory inquiry, and internal learning. This includes capturing decision context, such as what was known at the time, what alternatives were considered, and why a particular action was chosen. Without that structure, post-incident reviews devolve into hindsight-driven blame and the organization repeats the same coordination mistakes. Clear roles, responsibilities, and decision authority make response measurable, defensible, and repeatable, which is the difference between an organization that "gets through" incidents and one that becomes stronger because of them.

Communication Pathways and Escalation Rules

Communication in incident response is an operational control, not a courtesy. The fastest way to lose control of an event is to allow facts, assumptions, and decisions to propagate through informal channels at different speeds. A plan must define how information moves so that responders, stakeholders, and executives share a common picture of the situation without flooding each other with raw telemetry. The purpose of communication pathways is to keep the response synchronized, maintain decision quality, and prevent parallel efforts from creating contradictory actions. When communication is treated as part of containment, the organization preserves momentum even while the technical picture is still forming.

Pathways should begin with intake and immediately establish a single "system of record" for incident artifacts and decisions. That record can be a case in a ticketing system, an incident channel, or another controlled workspace, but it must be authoritative and consistently used. The plan should define what information is required at creation time, including who reported the issue, what evidence triggered concern, what systems are believed involved, and what initial impact is observed. As the incident evolves, updates should be time-stamped and attributable, with key actions and approvals captured in the same place rather than scattered across emails, chats, and documents. The operational goal is simple: at any moment, a designated leader should be able to answer what is happening, what has been done, what is next, and what is at risk.

Escalation rules must be tied to impact and decision points, not to the volume of alerts or the emotional temperature of a call. Severity should be determined using concrete signals such as confirmed unauthorized access, loss of integrity in critical systems, suspected data exposure involving regulated data, or disruption to revenue-generating services. The plan should require early escalation when containment actions could materially affect business operations, such as revoking privileged access at scale, isolating production networks, or disabling external integrations. It should also define escalation for uncertainty when potential impact is extreme, because waiting for perfect confirmation is a common way to let adversaries entrench. Good escalation design ensures leaders are involved when their authority is needed, while allowing responders to work without being pulled into constant status meetings.

Communication pathways should separate audiences by need and by risk. Responders need low-latency technical context and rapid coordination, while executives need high-confidence summaries, impact framing, and clear asks. Legal and privacy need facts that relate to notification thresholds, data types, and timelines, not speculative attribution or unverified counts. Communications teams need approved language, expected customer impact, and a release cadence that can be sustained without forcing responders to halt analysis. The plan should define who can speak to which audience, and it should explicitly prohibit ad hoc outreach that bypasses incident command, because side-channel updates create competing narratives and premature commitments.

Escalation rules must also define when the incident crosses into formal crisis management. That handoff is usually triggered by factors such as material customer impact, regulatory notification risk, significant financial exposure, public safety implications, or credible media interest. The plan should specify when to engage outside counsel, cyber insurance, external forensics, and crisis communications, and it should clarify who has authority to make those calls. Importantly, escalation should not be treated as a one-way ratchet where every step only increases visibility and attendance. The plan should allow de-escalation when facts show limited scope or when containment is stable, because maintaining a maximal posture longer than necessary exhausts the organization and damages trust in the process.

Operational cadence matters as much as content. A plan should define update rhythms for different severities, including how often situation reports are produced, when leadership briefings occur, and how decisions are queued for approval. This prevents the two extremes of constant interruptions and long information gaps that breed rumor and risk-driven overreach. Updates should be structured to distinguish confirmed facts from working hypotheses and to clearly list open questions and dependencies. The plan should also specify how decisions are documented, including what evidence supported the choice, what tradeoffs were accepted, and who approved the action. Over time, that discipline becomes a force multiplier because new participants can onboard quickly and leaders can make informed choices without re-litigating the entire timeline.

AI can strengthen communication pathways when it is constrained to drafting and consolidation rather than treated as an authority on truth. Automated summarization can convert chat logs, investigation notes, and timeline entries into consistent situation reports, but the plan should require a named owner to validate accuracy before distribution. ML-assisted classification can help route updates to the right stakeholders, prioritize which developments require immediate escalation, and detect when the narrative is drifting away from the evidence due to repeated assumptions. The failure modes are predictable: fluent summaries that omit critical uncertainty, overconfident "root cause" statements based on incomplete data, and accidental leakage of sensitive details into broader distribution lists. Governance expectations should require that AI-generated content is labeled internally, that its source inputs are controlled, and that sensitive data is minimized, so models do not become an unintentional repository of regulated information.

Finally, communication rules must account for the reality that incidents involve imperfect information and high personal stakes. The plan should establish behavioral expectations for responders and leaders, including avoiding blame-oriented language during active response, using a single voice for external communications, and respecting confidentiality boundaries. It should also define what not to do, such as sharing screenshots of sensitive logs in uncontrolled channels, using personal devices for incident coordination, or speculating about threat actor identity in widely distributed messages. Escalation and communication controls are only effective when they are rehearsed, socially reinforced, and easy to follow under pressure. When the pathways are clear and the rules are specific, the organization moves as one system, and that cohesion is often the difference between a contained event and a prolonged, compounding crisis.

Playbooks, Runbooks, and Practical Usability

Playbooks and runbooks exist because incident response is not a single activity but a sequence of time-sensitive decisions made under uncertainty. A plan that only describes governance without providing operational traction forces responders to invent procedures during the event, which is when mistakes become expensive and hard to reverse. Practical usability is the test: can a reasonably trained responder follow the guidance at 2 a.m. with partial information and still produce safe, consistent outcomes? Playbooks provide scenario-oriented guidance that frames decisions and handoffs, while runbooks provide step-by-step execution for specific systems or controls. When these artifacts are treated as living operational tooling rather than documentation, they become the connective tissue between leadership intent and technical action.

The distinction matters because teams misuse these terms and end up with documents that satisfy neither need. A playbook should describe how to respond to a class of incidents—credential compromise, ransomware, suspicious outbound traffic, cloud access anomalies—by defining objectives, required stakeholders, decision gates, and evidence expectations. It should tell responders what questions to answer, what "good enough" confirmation looks like, and what containment options are appropriate at different severity levels. A runbook should then map those objectives to concrete actions in the environment, such as how to isolate a host, rotate credentials, disable a federation trust, capture volatile evidence, or restore a system from known-good images. If a document tries to be both, it usually becomes too long to execute and too vague to be reliable.

Usability begins with how the artifacts are structured and accessed during a live event. A responder should not be hunting through a shared drive, searching outdated wiki pages, or asking in chat for "the latest version" while adversary activity continues. Playbooks and runbooks need a canonical location, version control, and an access model that works during degraded conditions, including authentication outages or segmentation changes. They should be written in plain operational language with clear prerequisites, assumptions, and safety warnings, especially when steps can cause business disruption. A well-designed runbook anticipates the reality of constrained permissions, missing telemetry, and dependencies on other teams, and it provides alternatives rather than dead ends.

Practical playbooks also encode decision gates that protect the organization from both overreaction and indecision. For example, containment actions should be staged, starting with low-risk steps such as tightening monitoring, collecting evidence, and limiting exposure, and then moving to disruptive steps when evidence or risk thresholds justify them. The playbook should specify when to involve legal, privacy, communications, and executive authority, and what information is required before those conversations are productive. It should also highlight points where responders must slow down to preserve evidence, such as before reimaging systems or resetting accounts that may contain indicators of compromise. When decision gates are explicit, the organization avoids the common pattern of taking irreversible actions first and asking for confirmation later.

Runbooks must be operationally honest about the environment they are intended to control. They should identify the exact systems, account types, and dependencies involved in each procedure, including where logs are collected, what telemetry confirms success, and what rollback steps exist if an action causes unexpected impact. They should also specify what to capture before and after a change, so that responders can prove what happened and support later analysis. A frequent failure mode is runbooks that only describe the "happy path" and omit error handling, which forces responders to improvise when commands fail, permissions are missing, or systems behave differently than expected. Another failure mode is runbooks that assume a specific individual's tribal knowledge, making them unusable when that person is unavailable, which is exactly when runbooks matter most.

Playbooks and runbooks must be integrated with escalation and handoffs, because response is a team sport with shifting ownership over time. A usable playbook indicates who owns each phase of work, when responsibilities transfer, and what artifacts must be produced to enable that transfer, such as a timeline, a list of affected assets, and a set of verified indicators. It should also define what "containment achieved" means in practice, because teams often confuse a quiet alert stream with an adversary that has been removed. Runbooks should include explicit completion criteria such as validation of account hygiene, confirmation of persistence removal, restoration checks, and monitoring adjustments to detect re-entry. Without these definitions, teams hand off ambiguous states and the incident lingers through repeated rediscovery rather than progressing toward resolution.

AI can improve practical usability when it is applied to maintenance, retrieval, and decision support, but it must be bounded by the same controls as the response plan. Natural-language search and summarization can help responders quickly find the relevant runbook, extract prerequisites, and draft checklists tailored to the systems implicated in the incident. ML-assisted correlation can suggest which playbook is most applicable based on observed patterns across identity events, endpoint behaviors, and network signals, accelerating correct activation without inventing new procedure. The risks are also clear: AI can hallucinate steps that do not exist, omit safety warnings, or propose actions that are incompatible with the organization's environment and authority model. Practical governance requires that AI outputs are treated as suggestions, that they are validated against the canonical artifacts, and that edits or generated variants are recorded, so the organization can audit what was followed and why.

Finally, usability is sustained through disciplined upkeep, testing, and measurement rather than annual document reviews. Playbooks and runbooks should be exercised in tabletop scenarios and, where feasible, in controlled technical drills that validate both the instructions and the access paths required to execute them. Every real incident should generate updates based on observed friction: unclear steps, missing prerequisites, slow approvals, or telemetry gaps that prevented confirmation. Ownership for maintenance must be explicit, with a cadence that tracks environmental change such as new cloud services, identity migrations, and logging architecture shifts. When playbooks and runbooks are treated as operational instruments—easy to find, safe to execute, and continuously refined—they turn the incident response plan from a document into a capability.

Evidence Handling and Documentation Expectations

Evidence handling is the discipline that turns response activity into defensible fact. In an incident, responders are constantly tempted to prioritize speed over preservation, especially when the business is demanding immediate restoration. That tradeoff is sometimes necessary, but it should be explicit and recorded, not accidental. Evidence is not only for courtrooms; it is how teams prove what happened, validate containment, and support regulatory reporting, insurance claims, and internal accountability. Without evidence discipline, organizations end up arguing from memory and incomplete screenshots, which creates both operational blind spots and governance risk.

The first expectation is that evidence collection begins as soon as an incident is suspected, not after severity is confirmed. Early actions should focus on preserving volatile data that disappears with reboot, isolation, or process termination, such as active network connections, running processes, memory-resident artifacts, and ephemeral cloud metadata. The plan should define what "minimum viable preservation" looks like for common scenarios, so responders can act quickly without debating fundamentals. It should also specify what actions are prohibited without explicit approval, such as wiping systems, reimaging endpoints, or clearing logs, because these steps destroy investigative value and can undermine legal defensibility. When time forces a choice, responders should capture what they can, document what was lost, and explain why.

Chain of custody is often misunderstood as a legal formality, but its practical value is simple: it preserves trust in the integrity of collected artifacts. For environments likely to face litigation, regulatory inquiry, or law enforcement involvement, the plan should require that evidence is tracked from collection to storage to analysis, including who handled it, when, and under what controls. That does not necessarily mean complex procedures for every log export, but it does mean clear handling for high-value artifacts such as disk images, memory captures, malicious binaries, and sensitive communications. Evidence should be stored in a controlled repository with access logging, retention rules, and encryption appropriate to its sensitivity. If evidence is shared with third parties, the plan should require documented transfer, scope of access, and expectations for return or destruction.

Documentation expectations must be anchored in contemporaneous recording, because incident narratives reconstructed after the fact are routinely inaccurate. A timeline should be maintained as a first-class artifact that captures what was observed, what actions were taken, and what decisions were made, all with time stamps and attributable authorship. The timeline should distinguish confirmed facts from working hypotheses, and it should record when hypotheses are updated or disproven. Key decisions—containment actions, system shutdowns, credential rotations, external notifications—should be documented with the evidence that informed them and the approver who authorized them. This creates operational clarity during the incident and becomes the backbone of post-incident review and external reporting.

Evidence expectations also include defining what telemetry is required to support core conclusions. If the organization cannot reliably answer when access began, what accounts were used, what data was accessed, or whether persistence remains, containment and reporting decisions become guesswork. The plan should therefore set minimum logging and retention standards for identity events, administrative actions, endpoint activity, network flow data, and cloud control plane operations, aligned to likely investigation timelines. It should also define how to validate the integrity of logs, including awareness of attacker behaviors such as log tampering, time manipulation, or use of unmanaged infrastructure. When telemetry gaps exist, the plan should require that they are explicitly recorded as limitations, because silent assumptions about "no evidence means no activity" are a common cause of false closure.

Handling of sensitive evidence must be scoped as carefully as handling of malware samples or disk images. Incident artifacts often contain regulated data, proprietary source code, customer identifiers, or employee information, and careless distribution can create a second incident. The plan should require secure collaboration channels, controlled sharing lists, and explicit guidance on what information is allowed in broad updates versus restricted threads. It should also define how attorney–client privilege is established and maintained when applicable, including where privileged analysis is stored and who is permitted to access it. Even when privilege is not invoked, disciplined access controls and data minimization protect the organization from unnecessary exposure and reduce the risk of leakage into uncontrolled systems.

AI can assist evidence handling and documentation when it is used to reduce administrative burden while preserving traceability. Automated extraction can help normalize timelines from disparate sources, correlate events across identity, endpoint, and network data, and generate draft situation reports based on the incident record. However, AI introduces its own evidence risks: summaries can omit critical qualifiers, conflate unrelated events, or present probabilistic inferences as fact with a level of confidence that is not justified. The plan should require that AI-generated artifacts are validated by a named owner and that the underlying source references are retained, so conclusions can be traced back to original telemetry. It should also set boundaries on what evidence can be fed into models, particularly when artifacts include regulated data or when model retention could create unintended copies outside approved repositories.

Finally, documentation expectations should include outcome-focused records that survive personnel changes and time. The plan should require a final incident record that includes scope assessment, confirmed timelines, containment and recovery actions, known limitations, and lessons learned translated into specific remediation tasks. That record should be written in a way that supports multiple audiences: technical teams who need indicators and root cause detail, leadership who needs impact and decision rationale, and governance stakeholders who need compliance with notification and retention obligations. Organizations often fail here by producing either a purely technical artifact that ignores business decisions or a purely executive narrative that cannot support technical improvement. When evidence handling and documentation are treated as operational requirements, response becomes defensible, repeatable, and measurably better over time.

IR Readiness Testing and Exercises

Readiness testing exists because incident response plans fail in the seams between teams, not in the obvious steps written on paper. Organizations rarely discover those seams during calm operations because normal work allows time for informal coordination and backchannel problem solving. An incident removes those buffers and forces decisions under time pressure, limited visibility, and competing priorities. Exercises provide a controlled way to surface friction in roles, escalation, evidence handling, and technical access before an adversary or outage forces the lesson. The practical goal is to build organizational muscle memory so that the plan is not merely understood but executable.

A readiness program should test both governance and execution, because a plan can look mature while still being unusable in a live event. Governance testing validates that the right people can be reached, that decision authority is understood, and that escalation thresholds produce the intended level of engagement. Execution testing validates that responders can actually perform containment, evidence preservation, and recovery steps with the permissions, tools, and time constraints they will have during a real incident. If exercises only test communications, technical teams learn little about operational constraints, and if they only test technical steps, leaders learn little about risk tradeoffs and notification pathways. The plan should therefore treat testing as a full-system evaluation, with scenarios that force cross-functional decisions rather than isolated technical puzzles.

Tabletop exercises are the most efficient way to test decisioning, handoffs, and communication pathways, but they must be structured to avoid becoming discussion-only theater. Scenarios should be realistic for the organization's environment and threat profile and should progress through decision points that require explicit choices and documented rationale. Injects should force participants to use the plan's pathways, such as activating incident command, producing structured updates, and engaging legal or communications based on defined triggers. A tabletop should also test constraints such as incomplete telemetry, conflicting reports from teams, or ambiguous indicators that could be either benign or malicious. The objective is not to "solve" the scenario but to validate that the organization can coordinate, prioritize, and escalate with discipline.

Technical exercises should validate runbooks and the operational feasibility of containment and recovery actions. Responders should practice collecting volatile data, exporting relevant logs, isolating systems, rotating credentials, and validating that containment did not break critical business dependencies. Where feasible, exercises should include controlled simulations in nonproduction environments that mirror real architecture and identity flows, because many failures are caused by differences between documentation and actual configurations. Technical testing should also validate the accessibility of required artifacts, including whether runbooks are reachable during identity disruption or network segmentation. A plan that assumes perfect access to systems and documentation during an incident is not a plan; it is an optimistic narrative.

Red team and purple team activities can add value when they are integrated with incident response goals rather than treated as separate performance events. The purpose is to generate realistic telemetry and decision pressure that tests detection-to-response workflows, including triage, escalation, containment, and evidence preservation. These exercises should be scoped to validate specific capabilities, such as detecting credential misuse, handling lateral movement indicators, or responding to suspicious cloud control-plane actions. The organization should define what success looks like in operational terms, such as time to acknowledge, time to initial containment, quality of documentation, and correctness of escalation. When offensive simulation is treated as a learning tool rather than a scoring contest, it produces better readiness outcomes and fewer defensive shortcuts.

Exercises should explicitly test external coordination paths because incidents often involve third parties at the worst possible time. That includes managed service providers, cloud platforms, critical SaaS vendors, external forensics, outside counsel, cyber insurance, and key customers or partners when contractual notifications apply. Testing should validate contact methods, authorization steps, information-sharing boundaries, and expected response times, including how to proceed when a vendor is slow or unhelpful. It should also validate evidence handling and secure exchange mechanisms for artifacts that cannot be sent through normal channels. External dependencies are often assumed to work until the first real incident reveals that the contract language, access rights, and escalation routes are not aligned to operational needs.

AI can strengthen readiness testing when it is used to measure and improve decision quality, but it must be applied with the same skepticism required during real response. During exercises, AI can help generate realistic injects, simulate evolving adversary behavior, and produce draft situation reports that participants must validate against the scenario facts. ML-based analytics can also help assess whether responders are prioritizing correctly by comparing decisions to historical incident patterns and by identifying where teams are spending time on low-value tasks. The risk is that exercises become overly dependent on AI-generated narratives, which can mask weaknesses in human understanding and create false confidence in the completeness of the record. Testing should therefore include scenarios where AI outputs are incomplete or misleading, requiring participants to identify gaps, verify sources, and document uncertainty rather than accepting fluent summaries at face value.

The value of exercises is realized only when results are captured, prioritized, and converted into durable improvements. Every exercise should produce a concrete set of findings tied to specific plan elements: unclear authority lines, broken escalation routes, missing telemetry, outdated runbooks, or containment actions that are too disruptive for the business. Those findings should become tracked remediation work with owners and deadlines, and the plan should be updated to reflect the changes, not just the lessons. A common failure mode is treating exercises as annual compliance events, which generates repetitive findings and no operational uplift. When readiness testing is continuous, scoped to realistic conditions, and measured by operational outcomes, the incident response plan becomes a practiced capability rather than an aspirational document.

Maintaining Plans Through Organizational Change

Incident response plans degrade silently as the organization changes. New systems are deployed, logging pipelines evolve, identity architectures shift, and teams reorganize, often without any single change appearing "big enough" to trigger a plan update. The result is a plan that looks complete but fails at the moment of execution because contact paths are wrong, authority is unclear, and runbooks no longer match the environment. Maintaining plans through change is therefore less about periodic editing and more about establishing mechanisms that keep operational reality and documented response aligned. The plan should be treated as an active dependency of the organization's ability to manage risk, not as a static artifact that only matters during audits.

Organizational change affects response most when it alters decision pathways and ownership boundaries. Reporting lines shift, functions consolidate, and new leaders bring different risk tolerances, which can invalidate assumptions about who can approve disruptive actions or speak externally. The plan should define role-based responsibilities rather than name-based assignments wherever possible, and it should include a method to rapidly map roles to current individuals and alternates. When ownership changes for critical services, the plan should require that incident response responsibilities are explicitly transferred alongside operational responsibilities, including after-hours escalation expectations. Without this, responders learn during an incident that the "service owner" is unknown or that approvals require negotiating unfamiliar political terrain.

Technical change is even more relentless, and it breaks plans through mismatched telemetry and outdated procedures. Cloud migrations, new SaaS adoption, endpoint tooling changes, and network redesign can invalidate containment and evidence steps that were previously reliable. The plan should be anchored on stable principles—what evidence is needed, what containment objectives must be achieved—while runbooks and supporting references are updated as implementations change. Logging and retention assumptions must be continuously validated, because responders cannot reconstruct timelines if identity events or control plane logs are no longer collected, are routed differently, or are retained for shorter periods than investigations require. A plan that assumes telemetry exists without verifying it becomes a confidence document rather than an operational one.

Maintaining relevance requires explicit ownership and a cadence tied to change management, not to calendar reminders. The plan should have an accountable owner who is responsible for coordinating updates, validating that exercises reflect current reality, and ensuring that supporting artifacts are versioned and accessible. Updates should be triggered by events that change response conditions, such as major architectural shifts, identity provider changes, replatforming of critical services, or restructuring of security and IT functions. A practical approach is to link plan maintenance to the same governance that controls enterprise change, such as architecture review, service onboarding, and major release processes. When response requirements are built into change intake, the plan stays aligned without relying on institutional memory.

Mergers, acquisitions, and divestitures create special maintenance pressure because they combine different security cultures, tooling baselines, and authority models. The plan should define how response operates across mixed environments, including whether incidents are managed centrally, locally, or through a hybrid model while integration is underway. It should also address evidence handling and data-sharing boundaries between entities, especially when legal obligations, privacy constraints, or contractual commitments differ. Early in integration, telemetry gaps and inconsistent identity controls are common, so the plan should require explicit acknowledgment of those limitations and prioritize compensating controls in the interim. Treating the merged environment as if it has unified controls before it actually does is a common and costly mistake.

Staff turnover and on-call realities must be treated as maintenance drivers, not as operational inconveniences. The plan should assume that key responders will be unavailable and should therefore maintain up-to-date escalation trees, alternates, and access pathways that do not depend on a single person's credentials or knowledge. Runbooks should be validated against real permissions and tested by people other than the author, because turnover exposes where procedures rely on undocumented assumptions. Training and onboarding should include incident response expectations for both security and non-security stakeholders, particularly business owners and communications participants who may not be accustomed to crisis tempo. Maintaining readiness through personnel change is as much about socializing the plan as it is about revising text.

AI can help maintain plans through change by detecting drift between documented procedures and operational reality, but it must be governed to avoid introducing errors at scale. Automated analysis of tickets, post-incident records, and exercise notes can identify recurring friction points, missing steps, or approvals that routinely bottleneck response. AI-assisted document tooling can propose updates to runbooks when underlying systems change, summarize diffs for reviewers, and improve retrieval by mapping plain-language queries to the right artifacts. The risk is that AI-generated edits can be confidently wrong, especially when documentation is incomplete or when system behavior differs across environments. Maintenance governance should therefore require human review, change logs that record what was modified and why, and periodic validation that AI-supported updates reflect how response actually works.

Finally, maintenance must include a mechanism to measure whether the plan is staying effective as the organization evolves. Metrics such as time to assemble the response team, time to reach the correct decision authority, completeness of incident timelines, and the frequency of "missing access" blockers provide concrete signals of drift. Exercises should be updated to reflect current systems and business priorities, and findings should drive tracked remediation rather than being captured as generic lessons learned. The plan should also define a controlled retirement process for outdated artifacts, so responders are not misled by stale runbooks that remain discoverable. When maintenance is built into organizational rhythms—change, onboarding, exercises, and post-incident learning—the plan remains a living control that scales with the business instead of decaying behind it.

AI Support in IR Planning: Playbook Maintenance, Documentation, and Control Boundaries

AI support in incident response planning is most valuable when it reduces friction in maintenance and documentation without eroding human authority. The promise is not faster decisions by machines, but more consistent execution by people who are operating under pressure. In mature programs, AI is used to keep plans current, searchable, and aligned with how incidents actually unfold, rather than as a substitute for judgment. When AI is framed as an assistant to the planning discipline, it can address chronic weaknesses such as stale runbooks, incomplete records, and uneven knowledge transfer. When it is framed as an authority, it introduces new risks that are harder to detect than traditional process failures.

Playbook and runbook maintenance is a natural fit for AI assistance because the work is repetitive, detail-heavy, and often deprioritized. Models can analyze post-incident records, exercise notes, and change logs to identify

Table 22.3 AI-Supported IR Outputs and Control Boundaries.

AI-Supported Area	Recommended Use	Human Validation Requirement	Key Risk to Manage
Playbook maintenance	Suggest updates from incidents and exercises	Planner approves changes with rationale	Confident but wrong edits
Runbook retrieval	Summarize prerequisites and steps from canonical source	Responder validates against source artifact	Hallucinated steps
Situation reports	Draft structured updates from system of record	Incident commander validates before distribution	False certainty in summaries
Triage support	Cluster alerts and propose routing	Analyst confirms prioritization decisions	Bias toward common patterns
Gap detection	Flag missing telemetry and recurring friction points	Owner confirms and tracks remediation	Overreliance on model signals

where procedures were unclear, steps were skipped, or approvals consistently caused delays. They can surface patterns such as recurring containment friction, missing prerequisites, or telemetry gaps that invalidate assumptions embedded in the plan. AI can also assist with diffing runbooks against infrastructure changes, flagging when referenced systems, account types, or logging paths no longer exist. Used this way, AI helps planners focus on validating and approving changes rather than rediscovering problems through manual review.

Documentation during and after incidents is another area where AI can materially improve outcomes if boundaries are explicit. Automated summarization can consolidate timelines from tickets, chat transcripts, and investigation notes into structured records that are easier to review and audit. Draft situation reports and decision logs can be generated quickly, reducing the temptation to delay documentation until after containment is complete. The value is consistency and completeness, especially across long-running incidents with rotating participants. However, these artifacts must remain drafts until validated, because fluent summaries can conceal uncertainty, collapse timelines, or imply causality that has not been established. Table 22.3 shows where AI can reduce planning and documentation friction while preserving accountable human decision authority.

Control boundaries are the most important design element of AI-supported planning, because failure modes are subtle and compounding. AI should not be authorized to declare incidents, approve containment actions, or determine notification obligations, even if it is technically capable of producing recommendations. Those decisions carry business, legal, and reputational consequences that require accountable human ownership. Plans should therefore explicitly define which outputs are advisory, which require validation, and which are prohibited from automation altogether. When boundaries are not written down, teams tend to expand AI use informally during high-stress events, precisely when disciplined controls matter most.

Data dependencies and scope must also be tightly governed to prevent AI from becoming an uncontrolled evidence sink. Incident artifacts often include regulated data, credentials, proprietary code, or sensitive communications, and indiscriminate ingestion can create new exposure. The plan should define what classes of data may be used for AI-assisted maintenance and documentation, how long derived artifacts are retained, and how access is logged and reviewed. It should also address model training and retention behaviors, ensuring that sensitive incident data is not reused in ways that violate policy or contractual obligations. Treating AI tooling as part of the evidence handling surface rather than as a neutral utility avoids creating blind spots in governance.

Bias and drift present additional risks that must be accounted for in planning. AI systems tend to reinforce historical patterns, which can cause them to overweight common incident types and underrepresent novel or low-frequency attack paths. Over time, changes in architecture, threat behavior, or logging fidelity can also degrade the quality of AI-supported insights without obvious failure signals. The plan should therefore require periodic validation of AI outputs against known-good cases and recent incidents, as well as explicit documentation of known limitations. Responders should be trained to recognize when AI assistance is likely to be less reliable, such as during first-of-kind events or major architectural transitions.

Human-in-the-loop expectations should be operationally specific rather than aspirational. The plan should name who is responsible for validating AI-generated updates, summaries, or maintenance suggestions, and what criteria they use to accept or reject them. It should also require that accepted changes are traceable, with a record of the source inputs, the rationale for approval, and any assumptions that were made. This traceability matters not only for audit and compliance, but also for learning, because it allows the organization to evaluate whether AI assistance is improving outcomes or simply accelerating the production of low-quality artifacts. Without that feedback loop, AI becomes a productivity illusion rather than a reliability enhancer.

Finally, AI support in IR planning should be treated as a capability that itself requires testing and exercise. Tabletop and technical drills should include scenarios where AI outputs are incomplete, delayed, or incorrect, forcing participants to fall back on core processes and judgment. Exercises should also test whether responders can clearly articulate when they are relying on AI assistance and when they are overriding it, because that transparency is critical during executive and regulatory review. When AI is integrated with explicit control boundaries, validation requirements, and documented ownership, it strengthens planning discipline instead of undermining it. In that role, AI becomes a force multiplier for consistency and maintainability, not a shortcut around accountability.

Common IR Plan Failure Modes

The most common incident response plan failures are not the absence of a document but the presence of a document that cannot be executed. Plans often read as comprehensive because they contain the right words—roles, escalation, containment, communications—yet they fail under pressure because the organization has not converted intent into operational behavior. Failure modes tend to cluster around ambiguity, stale assumptions, and mismatched authority, all of which are amplified when uncertainty is high and time is short. In practice, a weak plan does not collapse all at once; it degrades into a series of small improvisations that compound into lost time, lost evidence, and poor decisions. Recognizing these patterns is a prerequisite to building resilience into the plan.

A frequent failure mode is unclear activation criteria and severity determination, which leads to inconsistent response posture. When responders cannot confidently distinguish between routine security work and an incident, they either escalate everything or hesitate until impact becomes undeniable. Over-escalation burns credibility and disrupts operations, causing stakeholders to disengage or resist future activations. Under-escalation is worse, because it allows adversaries to persist and increases the chance that response begins after evidence has been overwritten or data has left the environment. Plans fail here when they use abstract language like "significant impact" without tying it to observable signals and decision thresholds. The result is a response process that is driven by anxiety and personality rather than criteria and accountability.

Another common failure is mismatched decision authority, where the plan assigns responsibility without granting the ability to act. Security teams may be expected to contain an incident but lack the authority to disable critical accounts, isolate production systems, or suspend external integrations. Conversely, executives may have authority but lack the operational context to make time-critical containment choices without repeated briefings. This produces bottlenecks, repeated meetings, and "approval ping-pong" where action is delayed while risk grows. The problem is often compounded by missing alternates and unrealistic assumptions about availability, which become obvious at night, during travel, or during concurrent crises. Plans that do not explicitly map authority to categories of actions tend to fail exactly when decisive containment is required.

Communication breakdown is a predictable failure mode, especially when updates are frequent but unstructured. Without a single system of record and a disciplined cadence, facts scatter across chats, emails, documents, and calls, and different groups start working from different versions of reality. Leaders receive contradictory updates, responders repeat the same explanations, and teams begin to optimize for visibility rather than progress. Another variant is premature external communication, where internal uncertainty is converted into customer statements or regulatory positions that later prove incorrect. Plans fail when they do not define who can communicate, what must be reviewed, and how uncertainty is expressed without speculation. Inconsistent communication is not merely embarrassing; it creates operational risk by locking the organization into narratives that constrain containment and recovery options.

Evidence handling failures are among the most damaging because they are often irreversible. Teams commonly reimage systems, rotate credentials, or shut down services before preserving volatile artifacts or collecting the logs needed to reconstruct timelines. Even when evidence is collected, it may be stored in uncontrolled locations, shared broadly, or modified during analysis without preserving originals, undermining trust in its integrity. Documentation may be delayed until after restoration, at which point details are reconstructed from memory and gaps are filled with assumptions. Plans fail here when they treat evidence discipline as optional or assume that forensic collection can be "added later." In reality, the first hours determine whether the organization can prove scope, validate containment, and support legal and regulatory obligations.

Runbook and playbook usability is another frequent failure point, often caused by stale content and poor access under degraded conditions. Procedures reference systems that have been renamed, logging paths that have changed, or containment steps that require permissions responders do not have. Documentation may be written for the author's mental model, relying on tribal knowledge and leaving out prerequisites, safety checks, and rollback steps. During incidents, responders then abandon the runbooks and improvise, creating inconsistent actions that are hard to validate and harder to audit. Plans fail when they do not treat these artifacts as operational tools with ownership, versioning, and testing expectations. A runbook that has not been executed by someone other than its author is a liability disguised as preparedness.

AI introduces its own failure modes when organizations treat model output as truth rather than as a hypothesis generator. During incidents, AI-generated summaries can create false confidence by presenting coherent narratives that are not supported by telemetry, especially when logs are incomplete or contradictory. ML-assisted prioritization can also bias triage toward historically common patterns, causing unusual but high-impact incidents to be deprioritized. In planning, AI-generated updates to playbooks can drift away from reality if not reviewed, and sensitive incident artifacts can be inadvertently copied into systems that lack proper retention and access controls. Plans fail when they adopt AI assistance without defining control boundaries, validation requirements, and auditability expectations. The operational lesson is straightforward: AI can reduce workload, but it can also accelerate error if humans stop verifying.

Finally, organizations commonly fail to convert lessons learned into durable changes, which guarantees recurrence. Post-incident reviews may produce generic recommendations, but without clear owners, deadlines, and integration into change management, the same gaps persist. Metrics may focus on narrative closure—"incident resolved"—rather than on whether containment was validated, documentation was complete, and plan friction points were removed. Over time, teams internalize that the plan is performative, and they revert to ad hoc coordination because it feels faster. Plans fail when they are not treated as living controls that evolve with architecture, staffing, and risk posture. A plan remains effective only when it is continuously exercised, updated through real-world feedback, and reinforced as the default way the organization responds under pressure.

Conclusion

Incident response maturity is ultimately measured by whether the organization can act quickly without losing discipline, even when visibility is incomplete and the pressure to "just fix it" is intense. Clear roles, decision authority, and escalation rules create the conditions for speed, while evidence handling and structured documentation ensure that speed does not destroy the facts needed to validate containment and meet obligations.

Playbooks and runbooks turn intent into executable action, but only when they are maintained through organizational change and tested often enough that real constraints are exposed before an incident forces them into the open. AI can strengthen this posture by improving maintenance and reducing documentation friction, but it must remain within explicit control boundaries so that accountability, verification, and auditability stay firmly in human hands.

Recommendations

1) Define activation criteria and severity thresholds in operational terms. Establish clear signals that distinguish routine security work from an incident, so responders can activate the right process without hesitation. Tie severity to observable impacts such as unauthorized access, data exposure risk, integrity loss, or sustained service disruption. Rehearse these thresholds in exercises, so escalation becomes consistent rather than personality-driven.
2) Assign incident roles by function and make decision authority explicit. Establish an incident command role that owns coordination and tempo, separate from investigative and containment execution roles. Map authority to categories of actions such as account disablement, network isolation, and service shutdown, so responders know what they can do immediately and what requires approval. Ensure alternates are defined for each authority path to prevent delays during off-hours and absences.
3) Standardize communication pathways and enforce a single system of record. Create a canonical place where facts, actions, approvals, and timelines are captured in real time to prevent fragmented narratives across email and chat. Establish update rhythms by severity, so responders are not interrupted continuously and leaders are not left in information gaps. Require that updates separate confirmed facts from working hypotheses to prevent premature conclusions from becoming commitments.
4) Separate technical coordination from external-facing communications. Establish clear rules for who can communicate to executives, legal, privacy, and communications teams and what evidence thresholds are needed before statements are made. Ensure communications participation supports responder focus by using structured situation reports rather than ad hoc briefings. Prohibit speculation and side-channel outreach that bypasses incident command to avoid contradictory messaging and accidental disclosure.
5) Treat evidence handling as a first-class operational requirement. Preserve volatile data early and define prohibited actions such as wiping systems or clearing logs without explicit approval to prevent irreversible loss of investigative value. Implement controlled storage for artifacts with access logging and retention rules that match incident timelines and obligations. Maintain a time-stamped timeline and decision log during the incident, so the final record is defensible and reconstructable.
6) Build playbooks and runbooks that are usable under real incident conditions. Write playbooks to guide scenario-level decisions and handoffs, and write runbooks to provide step-by-step execution with prerequisites, validation, and rollback steps. Store these artifacts in a canonical location with version control and access methods that still work during degraded identity or network conditions. Test runbooks with people other than the author to expose missing assumptions and permission gaps.
7) Embed escalation triggers around disruptive actions and business impact. Define when decisions must involve service owners, legal, privacy, and executives based on the operational risk of containment and recovery choices. Include an emergency authority model for time-critical containment paired with immediate notification and documented rationale. Allow explicit de-escalation when scope and impact are confirmed to be limited, so the organization does not sustain crisis posture unnecessarily.
8) Operationalize readiness through recurring exercises that test both governance and execution. Run table-top exercises that force participants to use the plan's communication pathways, approval gates, and documentation expectations rather than discussing them hypothetically. Conduct technical drills that validate evidence

collection, containment steps, and access paths in environments that mirror production realities. Convert exercise findings into tracked remediation work with owners and deadlines, so improvements are durable.

9) Maintain the plan as a living control through organizational and technical change. Tie plan updates to change management triggers such as architecture shifts, identity migrations, new service onboarding, and team reorganizations rather than relying on annual reviews. Use role-based assignments, so responsibilities survive staffing changes and ensure ownership transfers when services change hands. Retire outdated artifacts deliberately, so responders are not misled by stale runbooks that remain discoverable.
10) Apply AI support to maintenance and documentation with explicit control boundaries. Use AI to assist with runbook upkeep, pattern detection from incidents and exercises, and drafting structured reports, while requiring named human validation before outputs are used operationally. Define what data may be used, how derived artifacts are retained, and how access is audited to avoid creating a sensitive evidence sink. Train responders to treat AI output as advisory and to record when AI suggestions were accepted or overridden to preserve accountability and traceability.

23

Incident Handling and Operational Containment

Incident handling succeeds or fails in the narrow space between detection and decisive operational containment, where uncertainty is high and the business impact of action is immediate. This chapter treats containment as a disciplined set of workflows that translate alerts into coordinated changes across identity, endpoints, networks, and services while preserving enough visibility to understand scope and prevent recurrence. It emphasizes how leaders and responders navigate business tradeoffs, manage access under pressure, and sequence isolation, blocking, and stabilization actions without turning containment into self-inflicted downtime. It also establishes the operational habits that keep response coherent—maintaining a defensible incident log and timeline, using AI as auditable decision support rather than automated enforcement, and avoiding containment moves that inadvertently increase risk.

Detect-to-Contain Workflows

A detect-to-contain workflow is the operational bridge between noticing something suspicious and taking action that changes system state to reduce risk. Detection produces a signal, but containment requires authority, timing, and clarity about what is being protected and at what cost to availability. Strong programs treat containment as a pre-engineered set of decisions rather than an improvised response, because every minute of uncertainty favors the attacker. The workflow must be explicit about who can initiate containment, what evidence is required to justify it, and how the organization will communicate operational impact as containment unfolds. When those elements are vague, teams either hesitate until damage is obvious or they overreact and create outages that erode trust in the response function.

The first operational step is converting an alert into a defensible hypothesis about what is happening and what could happen next. A useful hypothesis includes the suspected objective, the likely entry point, the affected identities or assets, and the attacker's probable next moves. This is where correlation and enrichment matter, because containment decisions made from a single unverified signal are brittle. Telemetry such as authentication events, endpoint process lineage, network flows, and recent configuration changes should be pulled into a single investigative view that can support fast judgment. AI-assisted summarization can help compress noisy context into a coherent narrative, but it must be treated as a draft interpretation that analysts validate against primary logs before it drives action.

Containment planning is about selecting the smallest action that meaningfully reduces risk while preserving options for investigation. The core tradeoff is between stopping propagation and preserving evidence, because aggressive containment can disrupt attacker tooling and cut off visibility at the same time. Good workflows distinguish between containment that is reversible and surgical, such as isolating a host from the network while maintaining management access, and containment that is disruptive or destructive, such as disabling a critical account or shutting down a service. The workflow should also account for business criticality and safety constraints

Table 23.1 Detect-to-Contain Decision Gates and Containment Menus.

Decision Gate	Primary Signal	Containment Objective	Preferred Action Type
Confirmed malicious execution	Verified malicious process activity	Stop active execution and limit spread	Reversible targeted controls
Confirmed credential misuse	Verified anomalous authentication with misuse indicators	Sever attacker access quickly	Session revocation and token invalidation
Evidence of lateral movement	Correlated movement between hosts or accounts	Constrain attacker maneuver space	Host isolation and east west restriction
Confirmed data staging	Observed aggregation of sensitive data or unusual access patterns	Prevent exfiltration readiness	Targeted access tightening and segmentation
Credible ongoing exfiltration	Observed outbound transfer patterns consistent with exfiltration	Stop data loss immediately	Broad blocking and rapid restriction

so that containment does not inadvertently violate operational requirements. Containment is not a single switch; it is a set of graduated actions that can be escalated as confidence increases and risk becomes clearer. Table 23.1 links common incident decision gates to the containment objective and the lowest-risk action type to apply first.

Decision gates make containment repeatable under pressure, and they should be based on observable conditions rather than personality or hierarchy. Common gates include confirmed malicious execution, confirmed credential misuse, evidence of lateral movement, confirmed data staging, or a credible indication of ongoing exfiltration. Each gate should have a defined containment menu and an approval boundary, because the people who understand the attack are not always the people accountable for downtime. A mature workflow also defines "stop conditions" that prevent runaway containment, such as requiring a second analyst review before disabling privileged identities at scale. AI can assist by scoring confidence and clustering related alerts into a single incident context, but any automated recommendation must be traceable to the signals it used so that humans can audit the decision. Figure 23.1 shows how a detection signal is translated into a containment hypothesis, then into sequenced actions with verification checkpoints. It reinforces that containment is measured by reduced attacker capability, not by quieter alerts.

Execution sequencing matters because containment actions interact with one another and can create blind spots if done in the wrong order. For example, revoking sessions and forcing reauthentication can stop an attacker's access, but doing so before collecting key volatile artifacts may erase the clearest evidence of what occurred. Isolating a host can prevent command-and-control and lateral movement, but it can also prevent collection if the response tooling requires network connectivity. Workflows should specify minimum evidence collection that happens before high-impact actions, while still allowing immediate containment when the risk is existential. The goal is not perfect forensics; the goal is enough verified context to contain confidently and to sustain containment without losing the thread of what must be remediated.

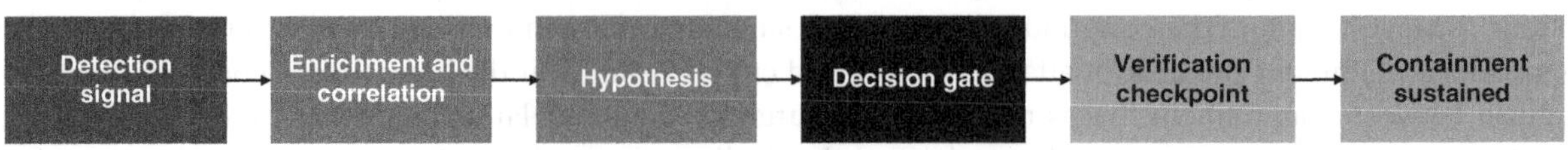

Figure 23.1 Detect-to-Contain Workflow from Signal to Verified Effect.

Containment is rarely a single action; it is typically a coordinated set of controls applied to identities, endpoints, and network paths. Identity containment may include disabling accounts, rotating credentials, revoking tokens, and tightening conditional access for the affected population. Endpoint containment may include network isolation, process termination where appropriate, removal of persistence mechanisms, and restricting administrative tools that are being abused. Network containment may include blocking known malicious infrastructure, restricting east-west movement, and applying temporary segmentation around high-value assets. These actions should be applied in a way that avoids tipping off the attacker prematurely when stealth is beneficial, but also avoids paralysis when the attacker is actively causing harm.

Human-in-the-loop controls are essential because containment carries business risk and can introduce security risk if applied incorrectly. Approval boundaries should be explicit: some actions can be executed by on-call responders within predefined conditions, while others require an incident commander or business owner signoff. Communication procedures should be built into the workflow so that operational teams receive timely and accurate impact statements, not vague warnings. The workflow should also require contemporaneous documentation of what was done, by whom, and under what justification, because containment actions affect evidence and can become part of later legal, regulatory, or executive scrutiny. Auditability is not bureaucracy; it is how the organization proves that rapid action was disciplined rather than reckless.

AI-enabled components can increase speed but also create failure modes that are uniquely dangerous in containment. Models can be overconfident, especially when trained on patterns that do not match the organization's environment, and they can underweight rare but catastrophic signals. Drift is a practical concern: changes in normal user behavior, new infrastructure, or altered logging pipelines can degrade model performance without obvious warnings. Bias can manifest as systematically elevating alerts from certain systems or teams because of historical incident density rather than current risk. Leakage is also relevant, because incident data can include sensitive identifiers, internal network details, or even regulated data elements, so AI use must be constrained to approved data handling paths with logging and access controls.

Sustaining containment means validating that the attacker's options are actually reduced and that new compromise is not occurring elsewhere. The workflow should include verification checks tied to the original hypothesis, such as confirming that suspicious authentications stop, command-and-control traffic ceases, and no new related detections appear on adjacent assets. At the same time, containment must be resilient to attacker adaptation, which often includes shifting to alternate accounts, backup infrastructure, or living-off-the-land techniques that blend into normal operations. This is where continuous monitoring during containment is non-negotiable, and it should focus on indicators of persistence and re-entry rather than simply repeating the original alert. A strong detect-to-contain workflow treats containment as a controlled operational state that is actively managed until the organization is ready to transition into remediation and recovery actions.

Containment Strategies and Business Tradeoffs

Containment is the act of deliberately changing system conditions to limit an adversary's ability to continue operating, spread, or achieve their objective. The hard part is not knowing what containment options exist, but choosing the right one at the right time under real business constraints. Every containment action expresses a tradeoff between security risk and operational impact, and those tradeoffs must be made explicitly rather than by accident. Mature teams treat containment as a portfolio of strategies with pre-agreed triggers, not as a single "shut it down" move reserved for emergencies. When containment is approached this way, leaders can act quickly without improvising governance in the middle of an incident.

The most common strategic split is between surgical containment and broad containment. Surgical containment targets a specific identity, endpoint, segment, or service that is strongly suspected to be involved, minimizing collateral damage but risking that the attacker simply pivots elsewhere. Broad containment aims to reduce overall

Table 23.2 Containment Strategy Tradeoffs and Common Side Effects.

Strategy Type	Primary Benefit	Primary Business Cost	Key Operational Risk
Surgical containment	Minimizes collateral impact	May not stop attacker pivoting	Scope remains underestimated
Broad containment	Reduces overall attacker options	Higher user friction and disruption	Support overload and rollback pressure
Identity controls	Cuts off access quickly	Productivity interruptions and integration breakage	Lockouts without closing sessions
Endpoint isolation	Stops lateral movement from a node	Work interruption for affected users	Responder tooling access loss
Network blocking	Denies infrastructure and paths	Application dependency disruption	Overbroad blocks cause outages

attacker maneuver space, such as tightening authentication requirements across a population or restricting lateral movement across a network, but it can cause widespread disruption. The right choice depends on confidence in scope and the attacker's tempo, which is often unknown early in an incident. A well-run program is comfortable starting surgical when evidence is narrow, then expanding to broad containment when signals indicate propagation or when business risk outweighs inconvenience. Table 23.2 summarizes how common containment strategies trade security impact against operational disruption and highlights typical failure modes.

Identity-based containment is often the highest-leverage move because most modern intrusion paths depend on credentials, sessions, and privilege. Disabling accounts, revoking tokens, forcing password resets, and tightening conditional access can immediately stop a campaign that is operating through stolen authentication artifacts. The tradeoff is that identity controls are coupled to productivity, and indiscriminate resets can halt operations, break integrations, and trigger cascading support issues. The containment strategy should distinguish between human accounts, service accounts, and privileged accounts, because the blast radius and recovery path are different for each. AI-assisted analysis can help identify unusual authentication clusters and probable compromised identities, but any automated recommendations must be validated against the underlying event evidence before high-impact actions like mass lockouts are executed.

Endpoint containment is the next common lever, typically implemented as isolation, restriction, or controlled shutdown of a device. Isolation reduces command-and-control and lateral movement, but it can also interrupt remote collection, patching, and business workflows that depend on the endpoint. Restricting administrative tooling or blocking execution paths can be effective against living-off-the-land behavior, but it may also break legitimate IT operations and scheduled tasks. The tradeoff is particularly sharp for shared systems and specialized assets where downtime is expensive or dangerous, such as operational technology or safety-relevant systems. Containment strategy must specify how to preserve some management channel and how to coordinate with the owning team to avoid turning an incident into an outage.

Network containment strategies focus on constraining paths rather than individual assets. Temporary segmentation, stricter east-west controls, and selective egress restrictions can rapidly reduce blast radius even when scope is uncertain. The tradeoff is complexity and unintended consequences, because network changes can be difficult to validate under pressure and can affect applications in non-obvious ways. Blocking known malicious infrastructure is usually low-risk, but overbroad blocking based on weak indicators can interfere with legitimate cloud services and third-party dependencies. A disciplined approach uses staged changes with verification checks, and it keeps a rollback plan ready in case containment disrupts critical business operations. AI can assist by mapping communication patterns and highlighting anomalous flows, but it should not be treated as an authority on what is "safe" without human review.

Service-level containment involves changing the behavior of applications, platforms, or integrations to reduce attacker capability. That might include disabling a risky feature temporarily, taking an exposed interface offline, or moving a service into a restricted mode with reduced functionality. The business tradeoff is explicit here: you may accept a degraded customer experience or delayed processing to prevent data loss or fraud. These decisions require coordination with service owners and a clear understanding of what "acceptable degradation" looks like for the organization. If teams have not pre-defined degradation modes, responders end up debating availability targets during an incident, which wastes time and increases risk. Containment strategies are strongest when they can be executed as known operational playbooks rather than custom engineering tasks.

Timing is itself a tradeoff, because containment that is too early can destroy visibility, while containment that is too late can allow irreversible harm. Early containment favors safety when an attacker is actively exfiltrating, encrypting, or manipulating critical systems, but it can eliminate the opportunity to understand scope and entry path. Delayed containment can preserve intelligence and enable more precise actions, but it assumes the attacker is not accelerating toward impact. The strategy should define conditions that justify immediate containment without extended validation, such as credible evidence of privilege escalation in sensitive zones or confirmed data staging. In lower-confidence scenarios, the workflow should favor reversible actions first, allowing the organization to tighten controls while continuing to collect high-value evidence.

Business tradeoffs become sharper when containment intersects with regulated data, safety-critical operations, or contractual obligations. Containment actions that stop processing, delay transactions, or interrupt customer services may trigger downstream legal and reputational consequences that must be weighed against the security risk. Leaders need a structured way to evaluate "cost of action" versus "cost of inaction," including the possibility that partial containment creates a false sense of safety. This is where pre-established risk tolerance and decision authority matter, because ad hoc decision-making tends to default to either extreme caution or extreme disruption depending on who is in the room. The containment strategy should also account for second-order effects such as overwhelming the help desk, creating shadow IT workarounds, or forcing insecure operational shortcuts under pressure.

Governance and auditability are not optional in containment because they protect both the organization and the responders. Every high-impact containment choice should be tied to documented evidence, a named decision-maker, and a clear statement of expected business impact. AI-enabled triage and decision support must be auditable as well, including what data was used and what outputs influenced the action, to avoid untraceable "black box" decisions in high-stakes events. Teams should be candid about failure modes, including over-containment that causes unnecessary downtime and under-containment that allows the attacker to persist. When containment strategies are framed as deliberate business tradeoffs, security leaders can act decisively while maintaining credibility with executives, operators, and affected business units.

Coordinating Actions Across Multiple Teams

Coordinating actions across multiple teams is the difference between containment that works and containment that merely looks active. Most meaningful containment steps touch systems owned by different groups, with different priorities, and often with different definitions of what constitutes acceptable risk. If those groups act independently, one team's "fix" can erase evidence, break a dependency, or tip off the adversary before other controls are in place. Effective coordination creates a single operational tempo where actions are sequenced, impacts are understood, and gaps are explicitly accepted or closed. The goal is not perfect consensus; it is synchronized execution with clear authority and clear accountability.

A practical starting point is defining a small set of decision roles that remain stable even as participants rotate. One role drives the overall plan and sequencing, one role owns technical containment choices, and one role owns business impact decisions and communications, even if those roles are held by different people across incidents. Without that structure, teams tend to optimize locally, and the incident devolves into parallel efforts with conflicting outcomes. These roles must have the authority to request changes from other teams and to arbitrate tradeoffs when speed and stability are in tension. Coordination is also about predictable touchpoints, so teams know when they will be asked to act and what information they will receive.

The operational backbone is a shared incident record that captures hypotheses, scope, containment objectives, and decisions in near real time. This is not a retrospective narrative; it is a working log that prevents confusion when teams join midstream or when handoffs occur across shifts. It should record what actions were taken, by whom, at what time, and what verification checks were used to confirm effect. When multiple teams are involved, this log becomes the single source of truth that prevents conflicting instructions and duplicate work. It also reduces re-litigation of decisions, because the evidence and rationale are visible to all parties who need to execute.

Sequencing is where coordination becomes tangible, because containment actions often depend on one another. Identity actions such as token revocation and account disabling can cut off the attacker, but if done too early they can also cut off the responder's ability to observe active sessions or collect volatile artifacts. Endpoint isolation can stop lateral movement, but it can block remote collection if tooling depends on connectivity. Network changes can reduce blast radius quickly, but they can also disrupt monitoring paths, logging pipelines, or service-to-service communication needed for business continuity. Coordinated execution means agreeing on the minimum evidence collection, then applying actions in a deliberate order with verification checkpoints between steps.

Cross-team coordination is especially important when ownership boundaries do not map cleanly to technical boundaries. A single business application may involve identity platforms, cloud infrastructure, endpoint fleets, third-party integrations, and data stores managed by different teams. Containment that only addresses one layer may simply shift the attacker to another, and containment that addresses all layers without coordination can break the application entirely. Teams need a shared understanding of "what must keep working" versus "what can degrade temporarily," and that understanding must be translated into specific allowable actions. When that translation is missing, teams either refuse to act due to fear of impact or act in ways that create avoidable outages.

Communication discipline prevents coordination from collapsing under pressure. Technical teams need concise, actionable requests rather than vague alerts, and business owners need impact statements that describe what will happen if actions are taken and what risk remains if they are not. Updates should be time-bounded and tied to decisions, not a running commentary on every log line. Coordination also requires controlled messaging to avoid tipping off an adversary through observable user-facing changes or internal chatter that leaks outside the response group. When communications are inconsistent, teams begin to self-direct based on partial information, which creates duplicate changes and conflicting containment moves.

Automation and AI can materially improve coordination, but only when they are constrained to support human decisions rather than replace them. Automated enrichment can consolidate telemetry from identity, endpoint, and network sources into a single incident context that multiple teams can reference without arguing over whose data is correct. AI-assisted summarization can produce a shared operational picture for new participants, reducing the time spent re-explaining the situation and lowering the chance of misinterpretation. The failure mode is over-trust, where teams treat a generated summary or prioritization score as a substitute for validating primary evidence. Coordination workflows should therefore require that AI-produced context includes traceable references to the underlying telemetry and that high-impact actions still pass through explicit approval boundaries.

A major coordination challenge is managing dependencies and the hidden coupling between containment and business operations. Disabling an account can break automation, isolating an endpoint can interrupt a critical process, and blocking network paths can impact customer transactions or internal workflows. Multi-team coordination must include rapid dependency checks, often by bringing in service owners who understand what will break and how to operate in a degraded mode. These owners should not be asked to decide whether the incident is real; they should be asked to advise on safe containment options and operational mitigations. When service owners are engaged early, the organization can choose containment that is both effective and survivable.

Finally, coordinated containment requires explicit verification and rollback planning across teams. Each containment action should have a defined success signal, such as the cessation of suspicious authentications, disappearance of command-and-control traffic, or stabilization of alert patterns on related assets. If those signals do not materialize, teams need a coordinated pivot rather than ad hoc escalation, because the absence of effect often indicates incorrect scope or an alternate attacker path. Rollback must be treated as an operational action with ownership and sequencing, not as an afterthought, because poorly coordinated rollback can re-enable attacker access or reintroduce vulnerable configurations. When coordination is executed with clear roles, shared records, disciplined sequencing, and verifiable outcomes, containment becomes a controlled operation instead of a frantic series of disconnected changes.

Managing Access During Active Incidents

Managing access during an active incident is one of the highest risk and highest impact activities a response team performs. Access controls are the attacker's primary lever, but they are also the backbone of normal business operations, so changes must be deliberate and defensible. Poorly managed access changes can halt productivity, break automation, or obscure attacker activity just as easily as they can stop it. Effective teams treat access management during incidents as a controlled operational discipline, not a reflexive lockdown. The objective is to reduce attacker capability faster than the organization degrades its own ability to function and respond.

The first challenge is distinguishing between suspected compromise, confirmed misuse, and precautionary restriction. Suspected compromise may justify increased monitoring or tighter conditional access, while confirmed misuse often justifies revocation or disabling. Precautionary restriction, such as broad MFA enforcement or session shortening, can reduce risk even when scope is unclear, but it carries visible user impact. Access decisions should be explicitly tied to evidence thresholds rather than fear or convenience. This framing helps leaders explain why some users are locked out immediately while others are subject to temporary friction instead of full revocation.

Session management is often more important than credential management during live incidents. Attackers frequently rely on active sessions, refresh tokens, or federated trust relationships that persist even after passwords are changed. Revoking sessions, invalidating tokens, and forcing reauthentication can immediately sever attacker access without permanently altering account state. The tradeoff is that session revocation can disrupt active work and break long-running processes, which may be unacceptable for certain roles or systems. A mature workflow distinguishes between session-level containment and account-level containment and applies them in a deliberate sequence.

Privileged access requires special handling because its misuse can accelerate an incident dramatically. Privileged accounts should be treated as a separate class, with faster decision thresholds and narrower approval paths. Temporarily disabling or restricting privileged access can stop attacker escalation, but it can also block administrators from performing containment and recovery tasks. This is why many organizations maintain clean, tightly controlled emergency access paths that are activated only during incidents. Managing privileged access during an incident is not about eliminating privilege; it is about ensuring that only verified, monitored privilege remains available.

Service accounts and non-human identities introduce a different set of risks and tradeoffs. These identities often lack interactive authentication signals and are deeply embedded in business processes, making misuse harder to detect and containment harder to execute safely. Disabling a service account can stop attacker automation, but it can also halt critical integrations, data flows, or safety-related processes. Incident workflows should require identification of service account dependencies before action, even if that assessment is rapid and imperfect. Access changes for non-human identities should favor scoped permission reduction and credential rotation over outright disablement whenever time allows.

User population controls are sometimes necessary when individual scoping is unreliable. Measures such as enforcing MFA enrollment, tightening conditional access policies, reducing session lifetimes, or restricting access from high-risk geographies can reduce attacker maneuver space across the environment. These controls shift risk left, making it harder for attackers to reuse stolen credentials or pivot silently. The business tradeoff is user friction and increased support volume, which can overwhelm help desks and erode confidence if not anticipated. Managing this impact requires coordination with IT support and clear communication about expected behavior changes.

AI-assisted analysis can help prioritize access actions, but it introduces its own failure modes in active incidents. Models can identify anomalous authentication patterns, cluster suspicious accounts, and summarize probable compromise paths faster than humans alone. However, models can also amplify noise, misclassify legitimate but rare behavior, or lag behind attacker adaptation. Access decisions informed by AI must be reviewable at the event level, especially when they affect large populations or critical roles. Human-in-the-loop review is essential to prevent automated containment from becoming automated disruption.

Auditability and traceability are non-negotiable when managing access under incident conditions. Every access change should be logged with the triggering evidence, the approving authority, and the expected duration or rollback condition. Temporary measures must actually be temporary, with explicit criteria for relaxation or removal once risk subsides. Without this discipline, emergency access changes calcify into permanent configuration drift that weakens security over time. Strong access management during incidents demonstrates control, intent, and accountability, even when decisions must be made quickly.

Finally, access management does not end when containment appears successful. Attackers often attempt re-entry using alternate credentials, cached access paths, or newly created identities once initial access is cut off. Continuous monitoring of authentication activity, privilege use, and policy changes is essential until the organization is confident that the attacker's access options are exhausted. Access decisions should be revisited as hypotheses evolve and new evidence emerges, rather than frozen at the moment of first containment. Managing access during active incidents is an ongoing operational effort that must adapt as the situation changes, not a single decisive action taken once and forgotten.

Isolation, Blocking, and System Stabilization

Isolation, blocking, and system stabilization are the practical levers that turn containment intent into measurable risk reduction. Isolation limits where an adversary can operate, blocking constrains what the adversary can reach, and stabilization preserves the organization's ability to keep running while the response proceeds. These actions change live system conditions, which means they carry immediate operational consequences and must be executed with disciplined sequencing. When handled well, they reduce attacker maneuver space without destroying the visibility needed to understand scope. When handled poorly, they either create unnecessary outages or produce "paper containment" that does not meaningfully interrupt the intrusion.

Isolation is most effective when it is precise about the asset, the control boundary, and the responder's ongoing access needs. Isolating an endpoint typically means restricting its network communications to prevent command-and-control and lateral movement while maintaining a management channel for collection and remediation. Isolating a server or workload may require more nuance, because it can sit on a critical service chain where a blunt isolation breaks dependent applications. Isolation decisions should consider whether the asset is a likely control point, a victim of lateral movement, or merely noisy, because isolating the wrong node can burn time and disrupt operations without reducing risk. AI-assisted clustering of related alerts can help identify the assets most central to an incident, but that guidance must be validated against telemetry that confirms actual involvement.

Blocking actions focus on denying attacker infrastructure, pathways, and behaviors, and they work best when they are explicit about what is being blocked and why. Blocking known malicious domains, IP addresses, or network paths can quickly reduce command-and-control and exfiltration opportunities, but overbroad blocks based on weak indicators can impact legitimate services. Blocking may also include constraining east-west traffic, restricting outbound protocols, or temporarily tightening segmentation around high-value assets. The central tradeoff is between speed and precision, because attackers often shift infrastructure rapidly and defenders can easily chase artifacts while missing the underlying access path. Blocking should therefore be paired with verification checks that confirm the expected effect, such as a reduction in suspicious connections or the cessation of specific alert patterns.

Isolation and blocking can interfere with monitoring and response tooling, which is why stabilization must be treated as a first-class containment objective. Stabilization is the process of keeping critical services predictable and observable while security controls are tightened. That often includes preserving logging pipelines, maintaining time synchronization, ensuring responders retain privileged access to management planes, and preventing well-meaning operators from making uncoordinated changes that erase evidence. Stabilization also involves controlling change velocity, because rapid configuration churn during an incident can create more ambiguity than the attacker does. A stable environment produces clearer signals, which makes subsequent containment and remediation decisions more accurate.

A common operational failure is applying isolation and blocking without accounting for dependencies and recovery paths. An endpoint isolated from the network may not receive updated policies, may not allow remote triage, or may strand a user in a way that triggers unsafe workarounds. A server isolated from its peers may cause application errors that look like attacker activity, generating noise that masks real signals. Network blocks can break third-party integrations and produce downstream business impact that forces leaders to roll back controls prematurely. Mature operations anticipate these patterns with pre-defined "containment-safe" modes, where restricted connectivity still allows essential management and observability.

Verification is what separates containment theater from containment. After an isolation action, teams should confirm that the asset's communications are reduced as intended and that suspicious outbound connections stop. After blocking actions, teams should confirm that attempted connections are actually being denied and that alternate paths are not quietly succeeding. Verification should also include monitoring for attacker adaptation, such as pivoting to different infrastructure, switching to different accounts, or moving to different hosts. AI can assist by detecting shifts in behavior and highlighting new clusters of related activity, but verification still depends on primary telemetry and analyst judgment.

System stabilization also includes minimizing self-inflicted harm when urgent containment is required. In high-tempo incidents, teams may need to accept degraded service in exchange for reduced risk, but they should do so in controlled ways that preserve the ability to operate. Stabilization can mean throttling certain workflows, temporarily disabling nonessential features, or reducing system complexity by pausing risky integrations. These changes should be reversible and documented with clear criteria for when they can be relaxed. Stabilization is not a purely technical goal; it is an operational posture that supports sustained response without exhausting the organization's capacity.

There is also a critical interplay between stabilization and evidence preservation. Isolation and blocking can disrupt attacker tooling and reduce damage, but they can also eliminate visibility into attacker actions that are still unfolding elsewhere. The workflow should define a minimum evidence collection threshold, such as capturing volatile artifacts or preserving relevant logs, before executing high-impact changes when time allows. In situations where immediate containment is necessary, stabilization should include compensating measures that preserve observability, such as increased monitoring on adjacent assets or tighter logging on identity systems. The aim is to reduce harm without blinding the team to the attacker's remaining footholds.

Finally, isolation and blocking should be treated as temporary controls that buy time for durable fixes rather than as the fix themselves. Attackers often remain capable of re-entry through alternate identities, persistence mechanisms, or unaddressed vulnerabilities, especially if containment focuses only on the most visible artifacts. Stabilization supports the transition from urgent containment to controlled remediation by keeping the environment coherent and reducing the chance of cascading failures. Teams that execute isolation, blocking, and stabilization as an integrated discipline maintain operational control even under adversary pressure. That control is the foundation for removing persistence, restoring trust in access paths, and returning systems to normal operation without leaving hidden risk behind.

Working Under Uncertainty and Partial Visibility

Most incidents begin with incomplete evidence, ambiguous signals, and an uncomfortable gap between what is suspected and what is proven. Partial visibility is normal, not an exception, because telemetry is uneven across environments, attackers deliberately evade logging, and operational constraints limit what can be collected in the moment. The risk is that teams interpret uncertainty as a reason to delay decisive action, or they treat uncertainty as permission to take sweeping actions that create unnecessary damage. Effective incident handling recognizes uncertainty as a working condition and builds workflows that remain safe and effective when confidence is low. The goal is to make progress without pretending the picture is complete.

The first discipline is separating facts from hypotheses, then explicitly tracking how each hypothesis will be tested. Facts are observed events with reliable provenance, such as a verified authentication from an unusual location or confirmed execution of a suspicious process. Hypotheses are interpretations about scope, objectives, and pathways, such as whether the activity represents credential theft, lateral movement, or data staging. In partial visibility conditions, teams should expect multiple plausible hypotheses to exist simultaneously and should avoid collapsing prematurely onto a single narrative. Progress comes from selecting the smallest set of tests that can discriminate between hypotheses quickly, using the telemetry that is most trustworthy and least expensive to obtain.

Containment decisions under uncertainty should be anchored to risk and reversibility rather than certainty. When confidence is limited, reversible controls that reduce attacker capability without permanently altering systems are often the safest first step. Examples include session revocation, temporary restrictions on high-risk access paths, isolation that preserves management access, or targeted network constraints that can be rolled back if impact is too high. These controls buy time to improve visibility while reducing the likelihood of rapid attacker progress. The intent is to narrow the attacker's options while preserving the organization's options, acknowledging that the first containment move may not be the final one.

Partial visibility often shows up as uneven coverage: rich endpoint telemetry in some areas, strong identity logs in others, and blind spots in legacy systems or specialized environments. Teams should treat these asymmetries as operational reality and adapt their investigative focus accordingly. If endpoint signals are weak, identity telemetry becomes more central for detecting lateral movement and privilege escalation. If network flow visibility is limited, changes in authentication behavior, administrative actions, and service access patterns can provide indirect evidence of scope. Working effectively means knowing what signals are reliable in the organization and designing containment triggers that do not depend on perfect coverage everywhere.

Human coordination becomes more important as visibility declines, because uncertainty increases the chance of conflicting actions and misinterpretation. Teams should align on what is known, what is assumed, and what is unknown, and they should keep that shared picture current as new evidence arrives. Decisions should be documented with the evidence available at the time, including the rationale for acting despite uncertainty. This prevents later second-guessing and reduces hesitation in subsequent incidents, because responders can point to a disciplined decision process rather than a gut reaction. It also helps business leaders understand why containment choices were made when the situation was still developing.

AI-assisted techniques can help teams operate under partial visibility, but they must be treated as decision support, not decision authority. Models can summarize scattered alerts into a coherent timeline, cluster related events that might indicate shared scope, and flag anomalies that humans might miss in large volumes of data. The failure modes are especially acute under uncertainty: false confidence can push teams toward irreversible actions based on weak patterns, and data drift can cause models to overemphasize noise when the environment changes. AI outputs should be paired with explicit confidence qualifiers and traceable references to underlying telemetry, so analysts can validate the basis of recommendations. The most useful role for AI in this context is accelerating sense-making and prioritization, not replacing verification.

A practical method for coping with uncertainty is to treat incident handling as iterative containment with frequent verification loops. Instead of attempting to define full scope before acting, teams apply a limited set of controls, observe the effect, and refine their hypothesis. If suspicious authentications stop after token revocation, that supports an access-driven hypothesis; if they continue from new identities, that suggests broader credential compromise or persistence. If isolating a host reduces command-and-control signals but lateral movement detections continue elsewhere, that indicates multiple footholds. These loops turn uncertainty into a structured exploration rather than a paralyzing condition, and they prevent teams from anchoring on early assumptions that prove wrong.

Partial visibility also requires disciplined risk communication, because stakeholders tend to demand certainty that responders cannot honestly provide. Leaders should communicate what is known and what actions are being taken to reduce risk, without overstating confidence in scope or root cause. Overconfident statements can force teams into brittle commitments, such as declaring an incident "contained" when visibility gaps remain. Understating risk can delay necessary business decisions and leave critical stakeholders unprepared for impact. The healthiest posture is candid uncertainty paired with clear operational control: what has been constrained, what is being monitored, and what triggers will drive escalation.

Finally, teams must recognize that uncertainty can persist even after initial containment appears successful. Attackers may have established alternate access paths that remain quiet, and blind spots can hide persistence mechanisms that do not generate obvious alerts. Working under partial visibility means continuing to test assumptions, watching for re-entry, and tightening controls where risk remains high until confidence improves. It also means capturing lessons about where visibility failed, because the most durable improvement after an incident is often closing the telemetry gaps that made the response harder. In real operations, partial visibility is the default; disciplined workflows turn that reality into manageable risk rather than unmanaged surprise.

Keeping an Incident Log and Operational Timeline

An incident log and operational timeline are the working memory of incident handling, especially when the environment is noisy, the team is distributed, and decisions must be made faster than people can remember. The log is not a retrospective report; it is a live operational artifact that captures what is known, what was done, and why it was done at the time. Without it, teams waste cycles re-discovering facts, arguing over sequence, and repeating work as shifts change or additional stakeholders join. A good timeline also reduces risk, because containment and recovery actions change system state and can inadvertently destroy evidence or introduce new failures if not tracked. The objective is to keep the incident coherent under pressure.

A disciplined log separates observations, hypotheses, decisions, and actions in a way that remains readable as volume grows. Observations are anchored in verifiable telemetry, such as specific authentication events, process executions, or network connections tied to a timestamp. Hypotheses are interpretations about attacker intent, scope, and pathways, and they should be stated as working assumptions rather than conclusions. Decisions capture the chosen path among alternatives, including what tradeoffs were accepted and who approved them. Actions are the concrete changes executed in systems, such as isolations, token revocations, blocks, or configuration adjustments, recorded with the actor and the time. This structure is what makes the log useful to new responders, executives, and downstream technical teams simultaneously.

Table 23.3 Incident Log Entry Types and Required Fields.

Entry-Type	Purpose	Minimum Fields	Example Content
Observation	Record verifiable events	Timestamp source evidence	Suspicious authentication observed
Hypothesis	State testable interpretation	Timestamp owner confidence	Credential misuse suspected
Decision	Capture chosen path	Timestamp approver rationale	Revoke sessions for impacted accounts
Action	Document system changes	Timestamp actor scope	Isolated host from network
Verification	Confirm effect of controls	Timestamp check result	No further suspicious logins observed
Communication	Track stakeholder updates	Timestamp audience message	Service owners briefed on impact

Time discipline is critical because incident response is essentially managing a moving adversary through a sequence of changing conditions. Every meaningful entry should include an accurate timestamp and the time zone context used by the team, because distributed environments and cloud services can produce misleading sequences when clocks differ. When possible, entries should also reference the telemetry source that produced the observation so that analysts can validate it later. The timeline should be updated as close to real time as practical, because reconstructing the order of events after the fact invites errors, especially when many changes occur in short windows. Even small delays in logging can cause large confusion when responders must decide whether a containment step preceded or followed an attacker action. Table 23.3 standardizes incident logging, so responders can distinguish facts from assumptions and track decisions actions and verification consistently.

An operational timeline must capture not only what the attacker did, but what defenders did, because defensive actions are often the most consequential changes during the incident window. Isolating a system, revoking sessions, tightening access controls, or blocking network paths can all change what is observable and what is possible for both attacker and defenders. If those actions are not timestamped and attributed, later analysis may misinterpret telemetry shifts as attacker adaptation when they were actually defender-imposed constraints. Logging defender actions also supports rollback planning, because teams can see exactly what was changed and in what order. This is especially important when multiple teams are making changes across identity, endpoint, network, and service layers.

A practical incident log also captures the evolving scope model, even when that scope is uncertain. Early entries may list "suspected affected accounts" or "potentially impacted hosts" with confidence qualifiers, and later entries should show when those items were confirmed, cleared, or expanded. This prevents teams from either clinging to a narrow scope because it is comforting or inflating scope because uncertainty feels dangerous. The timeline becomes a record of how understanding changed, which is operationally useful for deciding when to broaden containment or when to shift effort to remediation. It also provides a factual basis for business leaders to evaluate risk in real time, rather than relying on anecdotal updates.

AI can improve log quality and usability, but only when it strengthens traceability rather than replacing human accountability. Automated summarization can produce shift-change briefs that capture the current hypothesis, key events, and pending decisions, reducing the time lost to verbal handoffs. AI-assisted clustering can link related alerts and events into incident threads, making the timeline easier to navigate when data volume is high. The failure mode is ungrounded narrative, where a model synthesizes a confident story that is not supported by the underlying telemetry. To mitigate that risk, AI-generated summaries should be treated as drafts that humans approve, and they should include references to the specific observations and actions they summarize.

The incident log is also the coordination mechanism that prevents teams from working at cross purposes. When identity teams, infrastructure teams, application owners, and responders share a single log, they can align on sequencing and avoid duplicate or conflicting changes. Requests for action should be recorded with clear parameters, such as which accounts to disable or which segments to restrict, and the log should record when those requests were executed and what the measured effect was. If a requested action is deferred due to business constraints, that deferral should be captured explicitly, so it does not get lost in conversation. This level of transparency reduces friction and accelerates containment because teams spend less time reconciling different understandings of what has already occurred.

A high-quality timeline also anticipates the needs of follow-on work without turning into a bureaucratic exercise. Entries should include enough context to support later root cause analysis, lessons learned, and any required external reporting, but they should remain focused on operational clarity. Recording the evidence basis for key decisions matters, because it shows that containment tradeoffs were deliberate and tied to observed risk, not arbitrary. Capturing communication milestones, such as when business leaders were briefed or when user-facing disruptions were announced, can also be operationally important, because it explains behavior changes in the environment. The log should remain readable and searchable, because the value comes from rapid retrieval under stress.

Finally, the incident log and timeline must support an honest determination of containment and stabilization status. Declaring an incident "contained" without documenting what containment means in that context invites premature relaxation of controls and increases the chance of re-entry. A well-kept timeline shows which access paths were constrained, which assets were isolated, what verification checks were performed, and what monitoring was put in place to detect continued activity. It also makes it clear what remains unknown, which is often the most important information for leadership decisions. In real operations, a disciplined incident log is not paperwork; it is the mechanism that makes fast, high-stakes response coherent, auditable, and repeatable.

AI-Assisted Containment: Decision Support, Change Discipline, and Avoiding Automated Harm

AI-assisted containment introduces a powerful but risky acceleration layer into incident handling, where speed and scale can amplify both good decisions and bad ones. Used correctly, AI helps teams synthesize complex telemetry, surface patterns faster than manual analysis, and prioritize containment actions under time pressure. Used poorly, it can automate disruption, mask uncertainty, and erode trust in the response function. The central principle is that AI supports human judgment in containment; it does not replace it. Every AI-assisted action must fit within an explicit decision framework that preserves accountability and control.

The most valuable role for AI in containment is decision support rather than execution. Models can correlate identity, endpoint, and network signals to propose likely scope, rank assets by probable involvement, and summarize emerging attacker behavior. This reduces cognitive load and shortens the time from detection to a defensible containment hypothesis. AI can also help responders explore "what if" scenarios, such as estimating the blast radius of disabling a class of accounts or isolating a network segment. These outputs are inputs to human decisions, not instructions, and they must be treated as probabilistic guidance rather than authoritative truth.

Change discipline becomes more critical, not less, when AI is involved. AI-assisted recommendations should enter the same approval paths as human-generated recommendations, with clear thresholds for when actions can be taken autonomously and when explicit human authorization is required. High-impact actions such as mass account disablement, broad network blocking, or service shutdowns should never be executed solely on the basis of an automated score or classification. The workflow should require responders to validate the underlying evidence that informed the model's output and to document why the recommendation was accepted, modified, or rejected. This discipline prevents the response from drifting into opaque, machine-driven behavior that leaders cannot confidently defend.

One of the most dangerous failure modes is false confidence, where AI produces a coherent narrative that feels complete even when visibility is partial. In containment scenarios, this can lead teams to prematurely declare scope, over-apply irreversible controls, or overlook quieter attacker paths that fall outside the model's learned patterns. Models trained on historical incidents may underperform when attackers use novel techniques or when the environment changes in ways not reflected in training data. Teams must remain comfortable saying "we do not know yet," even when AI outputs suggest clarity. Confidence levels and uncertainty indicators should be part of AI-assisted outputs, reinforcing the need for verification rather than encouraging overcommitment.

Automated harm is another critical risk, especially when AI is connected directly to enforcement mechanisms. Automatically isolating hosts, revoking access, or blocking traffic at scale can create cascading outages if the underlying signal is wrong or incomplete. Even when the signal is correct, automation can apply controls faster than organizations can absorb the impact, overwhelming support teams and forcing rushed rollbacks. AI-assisted containment should default to recommendation mode, with automation limited to low-impact, easily reversible actions that have been explicitly approved in advance. Anything that materially alters business operations should remain gated by human decision-makers who understand both security risk and operational context.

Data quality and telemetry integrity directly affect the safety of AI-assisted containment. Models trained or operating on incomplete, delayed, or biased data can systematically mis-prioritize actions, pushing teams toward the wrong assets or identities. Logging gaps, inconsistent timestamps, and unmonitored environments can all distort model outputs in ways that are hard to detect in the moment. Responders must understand what data sources feed AI-assisted tools and where blind spots exist, so they can discount recommendations appropriately. Transparency about data dependencies is essential to prevent AI from becoming a confidence amplifier for flawed inputs.

Governance and auditability are non-negotiable when AI influences containment decisions. Organizations must be able to reconstruct which AI outputs were used, what data informed them, and how they influenced specific actions during an incident. This is not only a regulatory or legal concern; it is an operational one, because teams need to understand whether AI improved outcomes or introduced friction. Logging AI-assisted recommendations alongside human decisions creates a feedback loop that supports continuous improvement and model tuning. Without this traceability, organizations cannot safely evolve their use of AI in high-stakes response workflows.

Human-in-the-loop controls must be explicit, not implied. Responders should know exactly when they are reviewing AI-generated context versus raw telemetry, and they should be trained to challenge AI outputs just as they would challenge a junior analyst's assessment. Escalation paths should account for disagreement between human judgment and AI recommendations, including who resolves the conflict and how quickly. This preserves psychological safety for responders, who must feel empowered to override automated guidance when it conflicts with observed reality. AI that cannot be questioned safely becomes a liability rather than an asset.

Finally, AI-assisted containment must be framed as a means to improve resilience, not as a shortcut to certainty. Its value lies in helping teams act faster with discipline, not in removing the need for judgment under uncertainty. When integrated thoughtfully, AI strengthens decision support, improves coordination, and reduces response fatigue without sacrificing control. When integrated carelessly, it accelerates mistakes and magnifies impact at exactly the moment the organization can least afford it. Avoiding automated harm requires humility about what AI can and cannot know, and a commitment to keeping humans accountable for every containment decision that matters.

Avoiding Containment Actions That Increase Risk

Containment is meant to reduce harm, but poorly chosen containment actions can amplify risk, obscure attacker activity, or create new failure modes that persist long after the incident. The most dangerous mistakes are often made under time pressure, when teams equate visible action with effective action. Not every control that sounds decisive actually constrains the adversary, and some actions create more opportunity for the attacker than restraint would have. Avoiding risk-increasing containment requires discipline, humility, and an understanding of how attackers adapt to defensive moves. The objective is not to act quickly at all costs, but to act in ways that reliably improve the defender's position.

One common risk-increasing pattern is overbroad containment driven by weak or unverified signals. Mass account disablement, sweeping network blocks, or indiscriminate endpoint isolation can disrupt business operations without actually affecting the attacker's true access path. These actions also generate noise, as users attempt workarounds and support teams scramble to restore functionality, which can mask genuine attacker behavior. Overbroad actions are especially dangerous early in an incident, when scope is uncertain and attackers may have multiple footholds. A safer approach is to start with targeted, reversible controls tied to specific hypotheses and to expand only when evidence supports broader action.

Another failure mode is containment that destroys evidence or visibility before it is no longer needed. Aggressively terminating processes, wiping systems, or reimaging hosts can eliminate critical artifacts that would have clarified entry points, persistence mechanisms, or lateral movement paths. Cutting off network connectivity without preserving logs or volatile data can leave teams blind to how far the attacker has progressed. While immediate action is sometimes necessary to prevent imminent harm, teams should recognize the cost of losing insight and compensate where possible with adjacent monitoring or rapid data capture. Effective containment balances stopping damage with preserving enough context to prevent recurrence.

Poor sequencing is a subtler but equally dangerous way to increase risk. Revoking credentials before understanding active sessions can leave attacker sessions intact while alerting the adversary to defensive activity. Blocking infrastructure before identifying all related indicators can push attackers to switch to alternate channels that are harder to detect. Isolating a system before ensuring responders retain access can stall investigation and remediation. Sequencing mistakes often arise when teams act in parallel without coordination, highlighting the importance of shared plans and communication. Thoughtful sequencing reduces the chance that containment actions undermine one another.

Containment can also increase risk when it creates false confidence. Declaring an incident "contained" after a visible action, such as isolating a high-profile host, can lead teams to relax monitoring and miss quieter persistence elsewhere. Attackers often anticipate these moves and deliberately sacrifice a visible foothold to protect more valuable access. Risk increases when containment success is measured by the absence of alerts rather than by verification of reduced attacker capability. Teams must remain skeptical of silence and continue monitoring for re-entry, lateral movement, and alternative access paths even after initial controls are applied.

Automated or semi-automated containment amplifies these risks if not carefully constrained. Automated actions based on incomplete or biased data can propagate mistakes faster than humans can intervene. For example, automatically isolating all systems associated with a noisy indicator can cascade into widespread outages, while leaving the attacker's true foothold untouched. Automation should be limited to actions that are low-impact, easily reversible, and well-understood, with clear human approval for anything that materially changes business operations. Speed is valuable, but unbounded speed can be destructive.

Another risk-increasing pattern is neglecting business context when selecting containment actions. Controls that technically reduce attack surface may force unsafe operational behavior, such as bypassing controls, sharing credentials, or using unapproved tools to keep work moving. These workarounds can introduce new vulnerabilities that outlive the incident and are harder to detect. Containment planning should account for how people actually respond under stress, not how policies assume they will behave. Engaging service owners and operators early helps identify containment options that reduce risk without pushing users toward insecure alternatives.

Communication failures can turn reasonable containment actions into risk multipliers. If users and operators do not understand why access has changed or what is expected of them, they may take actions that undermine containment, such as retrying blocked actions repeatedly or attempting to restore disabled services. Internally, vague or inconsistent messaging can cause teams to duplicate or contradict containment steps. Clear, timely communication reduces these secondary risks and helps align behavior with containment goals. Silence or ambiguity, by contrast, creates space for improvisation that attackers can exploit.

Finally, avoiding risk-increasing containment requires continuous reassessment rather than a set-and-forget mindset. Conditions change quickly during incidents, and an action that was appropriate early on may become harmful as scope and understanding evolve. Teams should regularly review whether each containment control is still contributing to risk reduction or whether it is now introducing more harm than benefit. This includes reassessing AI-assisted recommendations, automated controls, and emergency configurations that may no longer be justified. The most resilient response organizations are those that treat containment as an adaptive process, constantly asking whether each action truly improves their position against the adversary.

Conclusion

Containment is most effective when it is treated as a controlled operational state, not a single dramatic action, and when every change is tied to evidence, authority, and a clear understanding of business impact. The practices in this chapter reinforce that speed must be paired with discipline: coordinated execution across teams, deliberate access management, and verification loops that prove attacker capability is actually reduced. They also highlight that partial visibility is normal, which makes documentation, sequencing, and continuous reassessment essential to avoid false confidence and avoidable harm. When AI is used, it strengthens response only when it remains transparent, auditable, and firmly human-directed, ensuring that containment reduces risk without creating new instability or long-lived security debt.

Recommendations

1) Establish a detect-to-contain workflow that explicitly bridges alerting to operational action. Define who can initiate containment, what evidence thresholds justify different actions, and how sequencing will be managed across identity, endpoint, and network changes. Build in verification checkpoints, so containment is measured by reduced attacker capability, not by quieter alerts. Keep reversibility in mind, so early actions buy time without destroying options.
2) Treat containment as a portfolio of strategies with deliberate business tradeoffs rather than a single "lockdown" decision. Choose between surgical and broad containment based on confidence in scope and the attacker's tempo, and document the rationale for the chosen approach. Align containment options to business criticality, so high-impact actions are reserved for conditions that justify the disruption. Reassess those tradeoffs as new evidence arrives rather than locking into the first plan.
3) Prioritize identity-based containment where it offers the highest leverage against attacker access. Use session revocation and token invalidation as first-line controls when they can cut off active attacker access without permanently altering account state. Reserve account disablement and credential rotation for confirmed misuse or elevated-risk conditions to avoid unnecessary productivity loss. Differentiate privileged accounts and non-human identities, so controls match blast radius and recovery complexity.
4) Coordinate containment actions across teams with clear roles, shared records, and synchronized sequencing. Assign stable decision roles that can arbitrate tradeoffs and drive execution even as participants rotate. Maintain a single operational log that captures requests, approvals, actions, and measured outcomes, so teams do not work at cross purposes. Require dependency checks with service owners before high-impact changes to avoid preventable outages.
5) Apply isolation and blocking in ways that preserve management access and observability while reducing attacker maneuver space. Prefer isolation modes that restrict adversary communications without stranding

responders from collection and remediation paths. Use blocking actions that are explicit, targeted, and paired with verification, so you can confirm they are denying what you intend. Stabilize logging and monitoring pipelines as part of containment, so defensive changes do not create blind spots.

6) Operate deliberately under uncertainty by separating facts from hypotheses and iterating through verification loops. Write hypotheses as testable statements and select the smallest discriminating tests to improve confidence quickly. Start with reversible controls when scope is unclear, then expand as evidence supports broader action. Avoid anchoring on early narratives, and treat silence after a control change as something to verify rather than as proof of success.
7) Keep an incident log and operational timeline as a live operational artifact, not a retrospective report. Record defender actions alongside attacker observations with accurate timestamps and clear attribution, so changes in telemetry can be interpreted correctly. Capture evolving scope with confidence qualifiers, so teams can see how understanding expanded or narrowed over time. Use the timeline to support handoffs, coordination, rollback planning, and defensible decision-making.
8) Use AI-assisted containment as decision support with traceability, not as automated enforcement. Require AI outputs to be grounded in underlying telemetry and treated as drafts that humans validate before high-impact action. Constrain any automation to low-impact, easily reversible controls that have been explicitly approved in advance. Log AI-influenced recommendations and decisions, so they remain auditable during and after the incident.
9) Enforce change discipline by sequencing containment actions to minimize self-inflicted harm and preserve necessary evidence. Define minimum evidence capture steps before disruptive actions when time allows, and plan compensating monitoring when immediate action is unavoidable. Validate effects after each major control change, so you can pivot quickly if the action does not reduce attacker capability. Maintain clear rollback criteria and ownership, so reversing changes does not re-enable attacker access.
10) Avoid containment actions that increase risk by resisting overbroad moves, poor sequencing, and premature declarations of containment. Start with targeted, evidence-tied actions to prevent widespread disruption driven by weak signals. Continue monitoring for adaptation and re-entry even after visible controls are applied, because attackers may shift to alternate footholds. Reassess containment controls regularly and remove or refine those that no longer reduce risk or that are creating operational instability.

24

Eradication, Recovery, and Business Restoration

Eradication, recovery, and business restoration are the disciplined activities that turn incident response from crisis management into controlled operational restoration. They focus on removing adversary access and persistence, re-establishing trustworthy identity and systems, and returning critical services in a way that does not recreate the conditions of compromise. The work is executed under pressure, where leaders must balance speed with evidence-based confidence and where technical decisions carry immediate business consequences. Success depends on rigorous validation, coordinated sequencing, and monitoring that is explicitly designed to catch reinfection and regression before they become a second incident.

Eradication: Removing Access and Persistence

Eradication is the disciplined work of making the adversary's current foothold impossible to reestablish, not merely stopping the symptoms you can see. The practical objective is to remove every avenue of access the attacker used and every mechanism they left behind to survive remediation. This requires treating identity, endpoints, servers, cloud control planes, and network pathways as a single operational surface where persistence can move laterally when pressure is applied. Teams that approach eradication as "delete the file" routinely discover the intruder again through a second account, a dormant token, or a scheduled task that was never mapped. Effective eradication is therefore evidence-driven, time-bounded, and explicitly tied to a hypothesis of how the attacker maintained control.

The first step is to sever access in a way that accounts for identity sprawl and modern authentication artifacts. That means invalidating active sessions, rotating credentials that matter to privilege and service continuity, and revoking authentication material that behaves like a password even when it does not look like one. Tokens, refresh tokens, API keys, service principal secrets, and application certificates can outlive a password reset and allow persistence to continue invisibly. Access removal must also include disabling or removing unauthorized accounts, correcting illicit group memberships, and eliminating shadow administrative paths such as delegated rights and overly broad role assignments. The aim is to make the attacker's known and adjacent identity pathways fail closed, while preserving a controlled path for legitimate operators to keep restoration work moving.

Eradication must explicitly target persistence techniques that blend into normal operations, especially those that live in configuration rather than malware. On endpoints and servers, that includes scheduled tasks, services, startup items, login scripts, WMI event subscriptions, and remote management tooling configured outside standard baselines. In directory services and identity platforms, persistence may exist as changes to federation settings, conditional access exceptions, application consent grants, or the addition of long-lived credentials to service accounts. In cloud environments, persistence can be embedded in IAM policies, newly created access keys, automation runbooks, event-driven functions, or CI/CD pipeline secrets that quietly re-seed compromised assets. The operational pattern is to treat every unexpected mechanism that triggers code execution, grants privilege, or

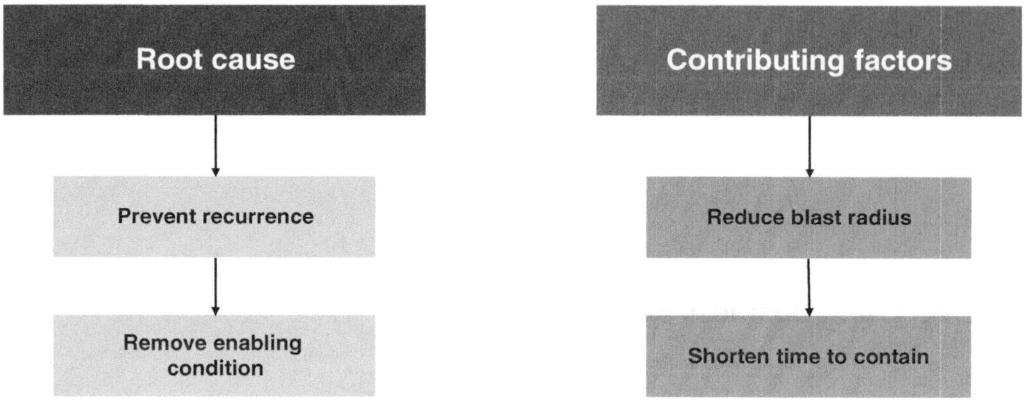

Figure 24.1 Eradication Targets Across Identity and Systems.

reintroduces credentials as suspect until proven legitimate and reauthorized. Figure 24.1 shows how eradication must remove both access pathways and persistence mechanisms across identity and system layers. It reinforces that eliminating a visible artifact is insufficient if tokens, role assignments, or scheduled execution can recreate control.

Because eradication frequently risks disrupting business services, it must be executed with a change-control mindset even in crisis conditions. Teams should define an eradication window and sequence actions to minimize blast radius, starting with containment-safe actions that reduce attacker capability immediately and then proceeding to more invasive changes such as system rebuilds and platform-wide credential rotations. When a service account is rotated, the dependency chain must be understood, so the organization does not trade an incident for an outage that blocks recovery. Where uncertainty is high, temporary compensating controls—such as tighter network segmentation, additional authentication requirements, or restricted administrative pathways—can buy time while the team validates dependencies. The discipline is to make each change intentional, logged, and reversible where possible, while still maintaining the urgency required to prevent reinfection.

What makes eradication hard is that evidence is incomplete and the adversary's actions are not neatly scoped to a single system. Good teams work from a prioritized map of confirmed and suspected persistence points that is continuously updated as new artifacts are found. That map is built from telemetry across identity logs, endpoint process and persistence artifacts, remote access records, and configuration change history in cloud and infrastructure platforms. The team should expect that some artifacts are decoys, some are redundant, and some are designed to reappear through automated mechanisms once defenders start removing them. Eradication succeeds when the organization can demonstrate that the mechanisms required to regain access have been removed or invalidated across the environment, not only on the systems that first triggered the alert.

AI and machine learning can materially improve eradication when used to accelerate discovery and validate completeness, but they must be bounded by operational controls. Pattern-based models can help surface anomalies in account creation, privilege assignment, token usage, and scheduled execution that resemble known persistence behavior, especially across large enterprise logs where human review does not scale. Clustering and similarity analysis can reveal "near-duplicate" persistence artifacts—like tasks with slightly varied names, services installed with minor path differences, or repeated policy changes across tenants—so defenders do not chase only the most obvious instance. These capabilities depend on clean, time-synchronized telemetry and accurate asset and identity context; without that, models amplify noise or miss the subtle artifacts that matter. Outputs should be treated as leads that require analyst confirmation, with clear rules about what automation may remove automatically versus what requires human approval and documentation. Table 24.1 maps common access and persistence mechanisms to specific eradication actions and the evidence used to confirm they were removed.

Table 24.1 Access and Persistence Removal Checklist Map.

Eradication Focus Area	Typical Artifact or Mechanism	Removal or Invalidation Action	Verification Evidence
Identity sessions	Active sessions	Invalidate sessions across environment	Old sessions cannot authenticate
Authentication tokens	Refresh tokens and access tokens	Revoke tokens and force reauthentication	Token reuse attempts fail
API credentials	API keys	Rotate keys and disable old keys	Calls with old keys are rejected
Service identities	Service principal secrets and certificates	Rotate secrets and certificates	Authentication uses new secret only
Endpoint persistence	Scheduled tasks services startup items	Remove unauthorized persistence points	Persistence entries no longer present
Directory authorization	Unauthorized group membership	Remove illicit group changes	Group membership matches expected
Cloud authorization	Overbroad role assignments and policy changes	Correct roles and restore baseline policy	Role assignments align to known good
Automation persistence	Event triggers runbooks functions	Disable or remediate unauthorized automation	No unauthorized triggers firing

Eradication also has predictable failure modes that must be anticipated and managed. False confidence is common when a team removes a visible indicator and declares success without verifying session invalidation, key rotation, and configuration integrity across identity and cloud layers. Drift is another risk: as the environment changes during recovery, detection and eradication logic can become stale, allowing persistence to re-emerge through newly provisioned systems or restored backups that contain compromised settings. AI-assisted analysis can exacerbate these problems if summaries omit uncertainty, if models inherit bias from incomplete training data, or if sensitive incident artifacts leak into prompt logs or external systems without governance. Strong teams require auditability for eradication decisions, preserve the artifacts and reasoning that drove each action, and enforce least-privilege access to investigative data, so the organization can defend both the technical outcome and the process that produced it.

Finally, eradication should leave the environment in a state that makes re-compromise harder even if the attacker retains knowledge of the organization. That means normalizing privileged access pathways, tightening administrative segmentation, and re-establishing trusted management planes, so remediation does not occur from potentially compromised workstations. It also means validating that restored systems inherit clean configurations, that secrets are stored and rotated through controlled mechanisms, and that monitoring is tuned to detect the exact persistence paths that were removed. When eradication is executed with this level of rigor, recovery work can proceed without constantly looking over its shoulder, and business restoration becomes a controlled rebuild rather than a cycle of recurring intrusion.

Validation of Cleanup and Return-to-Service Decisions

Validation is the disciplined process of proving that cleanup efforts actually removed the adversary's access and that returning systems to service will not reintroduce risk through hidden persistence or contaminated data. The goal is not to achieve absolute certainty, which is rarely possible, but to reach defensible confidence based on evidence, repeatable checks, and clearly stated acceptance criteria. This work sits at the intersection of technical verification and business decision-making, because the organization is balancing operational urgency against the possibility of reinfection or data integrity failures. Teams that skip validation tend to experience "recovery whiplash," where systems return to production only to trigger the same incident indicators days later. Done correctly, validation creates a clean boundary between the compromised state and the restored state that leaders can rely on.

A practical validation approach starts with defining what "clean" means for the incident at hand in operational terms. That includes confirming that identified persistence mechanisms have been removed, that compromised credentials and tokens have been invalidated, and that the attack paths used to gain access are no longer viable. Validation must also address scope: a system is not considered clean simply because it was rebuilt if it rejoined the environment with the same vulnerable configuration, inherited the same overprivileged role, or reconnected to the same compromised management plane. For identity-driven incidents, the definition of clean should include verification that unauthorized accounts are gone, privilege assignments are correct, and risky authentication artifacts such as long-lived refresh tokens, API keys, and application secrets have been rotated and revoked. Clear criteria prevent the team from making return-to-service decisions based on intuition or fatigue.

Technical validation should be performed as a sequence of checks that escalate from broad environmental signals to targeted host and identity confirmation. At the environment level, defenders look for continued attacker behavior such as repeated authentication failures against prior entry points, attempted reuse of old credentials, abnormal token refresh activity, or command-and-control patterns that were previously observed. At the system level, validation includes confirming patch state, startup and scheduled execution points, service registrations, remote management configurations, and any controls that gate administrative access. In cloud and directory platforms, validation extends to configuration integrity: role assignments, policy baselines, federation settings, conditional access rules, and application consent grants must align with known-good states. The sequence matters because it reduces the chance that a narrow host-based check misses persistence that has shifted into identity or platform configuration. Table 24.2 defines concrete validation gates and the evidence needed to justify a defensible return-to-service decision.

Table 24.2 Validation Gate Evidence for Return-to-service Decisions.

Validation Gate	What Must Be True	Primary Evidence Source	Decision Output
Scope clarity	Confirmed and suspected assets are identified	Reviewed telemetry and time bounds	System ready for validation
Attack path closed	Original access method no longer works	Control and configuration checks	Eligible for return-to-service review
Persistence removed	Known persistence mechanisms are eliminated	Host and platform persistence review	Candidate for monitored return
Identity trust restored	Critical credentials tokens keys are rotated	Identity logs and rotation records	Access can be reintroduced safely
Dependency trust verified	Upstream sources are validated and trusted	Change history and platform integrity checks	Safe to reconnect dependencies
Visibility confirmed	Logging and endpoint telemetry are active	Monitoring coverage confirmation	Allowed into production monitoring
Compensating controls defined	Residual gaps are bounded and mitigated	Documented controls and owners	Conditional return approved
Approval recorded	A named approver attests criteria met	Decision record with evidence links	Return-to-service authorized

Return-to-service decisions require more than technical checks because a system can be "clean" yet still unsafe if downstream dependencies remain compromised. Validation should explicitly examine the trust relationships that matter: management tools that push configurations, update servers and package repositories, identity providers, CI/CD pipelines, and shared file services. If a restored host immediately pulls scripts, containers, or binaries from a source that was not validated, the organization can reintroduce the adversary's tooling through routine automation. Data integrity also belongs in the validation scope, particularly for systems that process financial transactions, safety-critical operations, or authoritative records. The organization must be confident that restored data sets are consistent, that logs and audit trails are preserved, and that the system's outputs can be trusted for business operations and regulatory reporting.

A key operational discipline is to treat validation as a gate with explicit ownership, documentation, and a record of what evidence was reviewed. Someone must be accountable for the decision to return a system to service, and that decision should reference the criteria and checks that were satisfied, including any known gaps and compensating controls. This is where many teams fail: cleanup work is performed by one group, restoration is driven by another, and leadership is asked to approve a return without a coherent trail of validation artifacts. When the organization later asks why a system was returned prematurely, the absence of a defensible record becomes as damaging as the technical outcome. Good validation produces an auditable narrative that aligns responders, IT operations, and executives around the same facts and residual risks.

AI and machine learning can strengthen validation by helping teams correlate signals and identify subtle signs that cleanup was incomplete, but only when used with human-in-the-loop safeguards. Models can highlight deviations from baseline behavior, such as unusual authentication sequences, atypical service creation patterns, or configuration changes that resemble prior persistence attempts. They can also assist in summarizing large sets of validation evidence—endpoint findings, identity events, and change logs—into a coherent picture that supports decision-makers who need clarity quickly. The dependencies are non-negotiable: models require reliable telemetry, accurate asset identity mapping, and clean time alignment across log sources to avoid misleading correlations. Outputs should be treated as decision support, not authority, with approval boundaries that prevent automated "clean" declarations without analyst verification and a documented review trail.

Validation must also account for failure modes that appear during recovery, especially those driven by time pressure and shifting conditions. False confidence is common when teams validate only the system that was rebuilt rather than the identity plane and the dependency chain it relies on. Drift can undermine validation when changes made during recovery—temporary admin accounts, emergency firewall rules, relaxed access policies—persist longer than intended and create new exposure that was not evaluated. AI-assisted workflows can add risk if analysts over-trust confident-sounding summaries, if models miss rare persistence techniques, or if sensitive incident artifacts are inadvertently retained in systems that are not governed for investigative data. Mature teams counter these risks with repeat validation at key milestones, tight control of temporary changes, and explicit handling of uncertainty, including the willingness to keep systems in a restricted mode until evidence supports full production return.

Return-to-service is ultimately a business restoration decision informed by technical validation and bounded by risk tolerance, and it should be staged accordingly. Systems that are critical to operations may return first under heightened monitoring, constrained privileges, and stricter access controls, while less critical or higher-risk components remain isolated until validation is stronger. Continued monitoring after return is part of validation, not a separate activity, because the first hours and days of production use often surface the signals that static checks cannot. If indicators reappear, the organization needs a rapid path to revert, re-isolate, and re-evaluate without debate about authority or process. When validation is treated as a rigorous gate rather than a hopeful checkpoint, the organization restores service with confidence that it is moving forward, not restarting the incident under a new name.

Recovery Planning Under Pressure

Recovery planning under pressure is the practice of making deliberate restoration decisions while information is incomplete, stakeholders are anxious, and operational consequences are immediate. Unlike pre-incident business continuity planning, recovery during an active incident unfolds in real time and is constrained by what responders know at that moment about adversary behavior, blast radius, and system trustworthiness. The pressure comes not only from downtime but from the fear of restoring too quickly and enabling reinfection or data corruption. Effective teams acknowledge this tension explicitly and structure recovery planning as a controlled, evolving process rather than a single go or no-go decision. The objective is to restore essential business capability without sacrificing the integrity of the environment or the credibility of the response.

The foundation of recovery planning under pressure is prioritization grounded in business impact and technical dependency, not volume of noise. Critical systems are identified based on what the organization actually needs to operate safely and legally, not what is loudest or most visible. Dependencies matter as much as the systems themselves, because restoring a front-end application before validating its identity provider, database, or update pipeline can recreate the incident conditions instantly. Recovery planning therefore requires close coordination between security, IT operations, application owners, and business leaders to agree on sequencing and acceptable interim states. This alignment prevents teams from working at cross-purposes while the clock is running.

A key discipline in pressured recovery is deciding what not to restore yet. Systems that are not essential to immediate operations, or that played a central role in the intrusion, may need to remain offline longer to allow deeper validation or rebuilding from known-good sources. This restraint is difficult when executives are asking for timelines and users are demanding access, but premature restoration often leads to longer outages overall. Recovery planning should explicitly include holding areas where rebuilt systems can be observed, tested, and validated before they rejoin production. By treating restoration as a phased reintroduction rather than a binary switch, teams maintain control even when urgency is high.

Identity and access considerations dominate recovery planning because they cut across every restored system. Under pressure, it is tempting to re-enable broad access or reuse existing credentials to accelerate recovery, but doing so can negate eradication efforts instantly. Recovery plans should specify how identities will be reintroduced, which roles are required for initial operations, and how elevated access will be granted and monitored during the recovery window. Temporary access expansions must have clear expiration and review points, even if they are granted quickly. This approach ensures that speed does not permanently weaken the security posture.

AI and machine learning can support recovery planning by helping teams synthesize complex information quickly, but they must be treated as accelerators, not decision-makers. Models can summarize system interdependencies, highlight which assets are most critical based on usage patterns, or flag restored systems that behave differently from baseline once brought online. They can also help responders compare multiple recovery scenarios by estimating likely operational impact or monitoring load. These capabilities depend on accurate asset inventories, dependency mappings, and historical telemetry; without them, AI outputs may reinforce incorrect assumptions under stress. Human oversight is essential to challenge model outputs, account for context that data cannot capture, and ensure that recovery decisions remain aligned with business priorities and risk tolerance.

Communication is inseparable from recovery planning when pressure is high. Leaders need clear, honest assessments of what can be restored safely, what remains uncertain, and what risks accompany each option. Overly optimistic timelines or vague assurances erode trust and increase the likelihood of forced decisions that bypass security controls. Recovery plans should therefore be communicated as conditional paths with decision points, not fixed promises, and updated as evidence changes. This transparency allows executives to make informed tradeoffs and shields technical teams from being compelled into unsafe shortcuts.

Pressure also introduces predictable failure modes that recovery planning must anticipate. Fatigue leads to missed dependencies, undocumented changes, and assumptions that someone else validated a system. Parallel workstreams can collide, with one team restoring access while another is still investigating persistence in the same environment. AI-assisted tooling can worsen these failures if summaries obscure uncertainty or if responders accept synthesized outputs without verifying underlying data. Strong recovery planning counters these risks through explicit ownership, shared situational awareness, disciplined change tracking, and a willingness to pause restoration when new indicators appear.

Ultimately, recovery planning under pressure is a leadership exercise as much as a technical one. The organization must accept that speed, safety, and completeness cannot all be maximized simultaneously, and that tradeoffs must be made consciously rather than by default. By structuring recovery as a phased, evidence-driven process with clear priorities, controlled access reintroduction, and continuous validation, teams can restore critical business functions without undermining the response. When pressure is highest, the mark of maturity is not how fast systems come back online, but how confidently the organization can say they were restored for the right reasons and under the right controls.

Restoring Systems and Monitoring for Re-Infection

Restoring systems after an incident is not a simple act of turning services back on; it is a controlled reintroduction of compute, identity, and data into an environment that has recently been proven untrustworthy. The operational objective is to restore business capability while actively assuming that the adversary may attempt to re-enter, reuse stolen authentication material, or trigger dormant persistence mechanisms. Restoration therefore must be coupled to monitoring that is designed specifically to detect re-infection and regression, not just general security visibility. Teams that separate "recovery" from "detection" often learn too late that they rebuilt into the same conditions that enabled compromise. The practical mindset is that every restored system is a hypothesis being tested under observation.

A disciplined restoration begins with establishing a trusted foundation for rebuilds and rehydration. Images, configuration templates, and automation pipelines must be verified as known-good, because restoring from compromised build systems or tainted repositories can reintroduce adversary-controlled code at scale. Where rebuilding is required, it should be done from clean sources with integrity checks and tightly controlled administrative access to the build and deployment path. Where data is restored, teams must ensure that backups are not only available but appropriate, meaning they predate the intrusion and are not carrying forward malicious configuration, scripts, or manipulated records. Restoration sequencing should respect dependencies so that identity services, management planes, and logging are stable before production workloads are brought back into full operation.

Identity reintroduction is one of the most common re-infection vectors during restoration because convenience pressures lead to shortcuts. If credentials and tokens were exposed, the organization must rotate secrets and invalidate sessions in a way that prevents old authentication artifacts from granting access to newly restored systems. Privileged access should be constrained during early restoration, with administrative actions performed through trusted workstations and controlled pathways rather than ad hoc remote access. Service accounts and application identities require special attention because they often carry broad permissions and are embedded across systems; restoring a workload without updating its secrets can create outages, but restoring without rotation can recreate attacker access. A mature approach treats identity restoration as a staged process with minimal required privileges, monitored escalations, and explicit rollback options.

Monitoring for re-infection must be built from the attacker's demonstrated behavior and likely return paths, not generic alert catalogs. If the incident involved credential theft, monitoring should emphasize authentication anomalies, token refresh patterns, unusual device or location signals, and privilege escalation events that mirror the original progression. If persistence was found in scheduled execution or service registration, monitoring must focus on those persistence points across restored hosts, including newly created tasks, services, startup items, and remote management changes. If cloud control plane changes were part of the intrusion, monitoring must capture new keys, policy modifications, automation triggers, and application consent activity, because these are the levers that can recreate compromise without touching endpoints. The practical requirement is to tune monitoring for sensitivity in the early return-to-service window while maintaining a routing and escalation plan that prevents responders from being overwhelmed.

Restoration monitoring is most effective when it includes explicit "tripwires" that are expected to fire if re-infection occurs. These are not theoretical detections; they are precise signals tied to the incident's access methods and persistence attempts, such as reuse of disabled accounts, attempts to authenticate with revoked tokens, re-creation of previously removed scheduled tasks, or reapplication of suspect policy changes. Tripwires should include both detection and response actions, such as automatically blocking an account, quarantining a host, or restricting an administrative session pending review. The organization should also monitor for quiet failures, where restored systems appear healthy but logging drops out, endpoint telemetry is disabled, or configuration drift begins to accumulate. A restored system that cannot be monitored is not truly restored, because it cannot be defended.

AI and machine learning can meaningfully improve re-infection monitoring by reducing time to detection and helping analysts interpret complex, multi-source signals during a high-risk period. Anomaly detection can highlight deviations in authentication behavior, process execution, and network communications that differ from historical baselines, especially across large environments where manual correlation is slow. Similarity analysis can connect new artifacts to known malicious patterns from the incident, such as "near match" command lines, file paths, or configuration changes that indicate the adversary is attempting a variant of the original technique. These models depend on stable baselines, consistent telemetry collection, and accurate context such as asset roles and normal usage patterns; without those, they either miss subtle re-entry or produce a flood of false positives that erodes trust. Governance matters here because model outputs can create false confidence if presented as definitive, so analysts must validate conclusions and ensure that automated actions have approval boundaries and audit trails.

Re-infection monitoring must also address the operational reality that restored systems often behave differently at first. Patch application, configuration changes, backlog processing, and user behavior shifts can produce legitimate anomalies that look suspicious, and teams must distinguish these from true attacker activity without becoming desensitized. This is where precise context and disciplined change tracking pay off, because planned restoration actions can be tagged and correlated with expected system behavior. When monitoring is not aligned with restoration changes, teams waste time chasing self-inflicted signals while missing adversary behavior that hides inside the noise. The goal is not to eliminate alerts, but to ensure that alerts during restoration are explainable, attributable, and actionable.

A critical element of restoration is maintaining the ability to halt, isolate, and roll back quickly if re-infection indicators appear. That requires technical controls such as segmentation, limited trust zones, and rapid account disablement procedures, as well as organizational readiness to make the call without debate. Restored systems should initially operate in a more restricted posture, with tighter access controls and additional logging, until confidence grows through sustained clean observation. If a re-infection signal triggers, responders need a pre-established path to revert the specific system or dependency without taking down unrelated services. This reversibility is a practical risk control that prevents a single misstep from cascading into another full-scale outage.

Sustained success is measured by the stability of restored operations under continued scrutiny, not by the moment a system comes online. Monitoring should gradually normalize as confidence increases, but only after evidence supports that the environment is behaving consistently and that the incident's access and persistence paths remain closed. Lessons learned from re-infection monitoring should feed back into hardening and baseline management, so the organization does not repeat the same restoration vulnerabilities in future events. The organization should expect that sophisticated adversaries will probe for re-entry after recovery, because the transition period is when defenses are changing and attention is divided. Restoring systems while monitoring for re-infection is therefore an integrated operational capability that treats recovery as a controlled experiment and makes resilience a measurable outcome rather than a hope.

Handling Credential Resets and Identity Risk

Handling credential resets during an incident is one of the most consequential recovery activities because identity is both the primary control plane for modern environments and the attacker's preferred persistence layer. The objective is not simply to change passwords, but to invalidate every authentication artifact the adversary may have accessed and to re-establish trust in how identities are created, authenticated, and authorized. Under pressure, organizations often focus on user passwords while overlooking service accounts, tokens, keys, and delegated privileges that quietly preserve access. A disciplined approach treats credential resets as a coordinated identity risk reduction effort rather than a series of isolated fixes. When handled correctly, credential actions close attack paths permanently instead of forcing repeated containment cycles.

The first challenge is scope determination, because incomplete resets create a false sense of security. Incident responders must assume that any credential used or accessible within the compromised blast radius is potentially exposed, even if there is no direct evidence of misuse. This includes interactive user accounts, privileged administrative identities, service accounts, API keys, OAuth tokens, refresh tokens, certificates, and secrets embedded in automation. Modern environments amplify this risk because credentials are often cached, replicated, or long-lived by design. Effective handling therefore starts with mapping which identities matter, how they authenticate, and where their credentials are stored and reused.

Sequencing matters as much as coverage when resetting credentials. Resetting user passwords before revoking active sessions or invalidating tokens allows attackers to continue operating without interruption. Similarly, rotating service account credentials without coordinating dependent systems can break business processes and force emergency rollbacks that reintroduce risk. Mature teams sequence actions to first cut off adversary access paths, then rotate credentials in a controlled order that preserves recovery momentum. This often requires temporary access controls, staged privilege reintroduction, and close coordination with system owners who understand operational dependencies.

Identity risk during recovery is not limited to stolen credentials; it also includes unauthorized privilege expansion that occurred during the intrusion. Attackers frequently add accounts to privileged groups, grant application consent, create new roles, or modify conditional access rules to ensure durability. Credential resets alone do not remove these footholds if authorization state is not corrected. Handling identity risk therefore requires validating group memberships, role assignments, delegated permissions, and trust relationships alongside credential changes. A reset that leaves excess privilege intact simply forces the attacker to authenticate differently next time.

AI and machine learning can assist in prioritizing credential actions by highlighting anomalous identity behavior and likely compromise paths, but they must be used carefully. Models can identify unusual login sequences, atypical token refresh patterns, or privilege changes that deviate from historical norms, helping teams focus resets where risk is highest. They can also help correlate identity events across systems to reveal accounts that appear benign in isolation but risky in aggregate. These capabilities depend on high-quality identity telemetry and accurate baselines; without them, AI outputs may overemphasize noise or miss targeted abuse. Human review remains essential to validate findings and ensure that automated insights do not drive indiscriminate resets that disrupt operations unnecessarily.

Handling identity risk under pressure also requires clear policies for temporary access and emergency exceptions. During recovery, teams often grant elevated access to accelerate restoration, but these exceptions can quietly outlive the incident if not tracked and revoked. Every temporary credential, role assignment, or bypass should have a documented purpose, an owner, and an explicit expiration. Monitoring for the use of these temporary privileges is as important as monitoring for adversary behavior, because misuse may be accidental but still harmful. Strong teams treat temporary access as toxic waste: useful in the moment, dangerous if forgotten.

Communication plays a critical role in credential handling because resets affect people directly and failures erode trust quickly. Users need clear guidance on what is changing, why it matters, and how to recognize legitimate recovery activity versus attacker impersonation. Executives need to understand that broad credential resets may cause short-term friction but materially reduce long-term risk. Poor communication leads to workarounds, password reuse, and shadow IT behaviors that undermine recovery. Clear, consistent messaging reinforces the seriousness of identity risk and supports adherence to reset procedures even when pressure is high.

Finally, credential resets should leave the organization in a stronger identity posture than before the incident. This includes enforcing least privilege, reducing credential lifetime where feasible, tightening conditional access, and ensuring that service accounts and automation use managed identities or controlled secret stores rather than static secrets. Post-reset monitoring should focus on detecting attempts to reuse invalidated credentials, recreate removed privileges, or bypass new controls. Handling credential resets well is not measured by how fast passwords were changed, but by how confidently the organization can assert that identity trust has been restored. When identity risk is addressed comprehensively, recovery accelerates because the environment no longer assumes compromise as a default state.

Balancing Speed and Confidence During Recovery

Balancing speed and confidence during recovery is one of the most difficult leadership challenges in incident response because the costs of delay and the costs of error are both immediate and visible. Executives feel pressure to restore operations quickly to limit financial loss and reputational damage, while responders understand that moving too fast can reintroduce the attacker or corrupt critical systems. This tension cannot be eliminated; it must be managed through deliberate decision-making grounded in evidence and risk awareness. Organizations that acknowledge the tradeoff explicitly make better recovery choices than those that treat speed and safety as mutually exclusive goals. The objective is to move as fast as the evidence allows, not as fast as impatience demands.

Confidence in recovery is built from validation, not from elapsed time or the absence of obvious alerts. A system that has been offline for weeks is not inherently safer than one restored in days if the underlying access paths and dependencies were not addressed. Confidence comes from knowing which systems were compromised, how access was obtained, and which controls now prevent recurrence. Recovery planning should therefore tie restoration milestones to specific validation criteria rather than arbitrary deadlines. This framing helps leaders understand that time spent validating is not delay but risk reduction.

Speed, when managed well, comes from preparation and sequencing rather than shortcuts. Teams regain time by restoring the right systems first, isolating high-risk components, and reusing trusted rebuild processes instead of improvising under pressure. Parallel workstreams can accelerate recovery if they are coordinated around shared assumptions and dependencies; without that coordination, speed creates collisions that undermine confidence. Identity and access changes, for example, can proceed in parallel with infrastructure rebuilds if sequencing is clear and rollback paths exist. The discipline is to design recovery activities so that acceleration does not amplify uncertainty.

One of the most common errors under pressure is collapsing validation to regain speed. Skipping checks, narrowing scope, or relying on informal assurances may feel efficient, but these decisions often result in re-infection or prolonged instability that costs far more time. Confidence erodes quickly when systems must be taken back offline, and stakeholders become less willing to trust technical judgment. Recovery leaders must protect validation gates even when timelines are uncomfortable. Doing so requires executive support and clear articulation of what risks are being avoided by each validation step.

AI and machine learning can help balance speed and confidence by compressing analysis time, but only when they are used as accelerants rather than replacements for judgment. Automated correlation and summarization can reduce the time it takes to understand system state, identity risk, and monitoring signals across a large environment. Models can highlight likely problem areas early, allowing teams to focus validation where it matters most and avoid unnecessary checks on low-risk systems. These benefits depend on trustworthy telemetry and well-defined approval boundaries; without them, AI outputs may create false confidence or drive premature decisions. Human review and accountability remain essential to ensure that faster insights do not bypass critical scrutiny.

Confidence is also influenced by how uncertainty is handled and communicated during recovery. Leaders are more likely to accept a measured pace when they understand what is known, what remains unknown, and how those gaps are being closed. Overconfident statements that later prove incorrect damage credibility and increase pressure to rush subsequent decisions. Recovery leaders should frame progress in terms of evidence gained and risk reduced rather than systems restored. This approach aligns technical reality with executive decision-making and reduces friction between speed and assurance.

Monitoring plays a central role in maintaining confidence while moving quickly. Systems that return to service under heightened observation allow organizations to accept some residual uncertainty while retaining the ability to respond rapidly if conditions change. This monitored return reduces the need for perfect certainty before restoration, which is rarely achievable. However, monitoring must be meaningful and actionable; superficial visibility does not compensate for missing validation. When monitoring is treated as an extension of recovery rather than a safety net, it enables controlled acceleration.

Fatigue and decision overload also affect the balance between speed and confidence. As incidents stretch on, teams become more willing to accept risk simply to reach an endpoint. Leaders must recognize this dynamic and adjust pacing, staffing, and decision thresholds accordingly. AI-assisted tooling can help reduce cognitive load by organizing information, but it cannot substitute for rest, clear ownership, and disciplined process. Sustainable recovery requires managing human limits as carefully as technical ones.

Ultimately, balancing speed and confidence is about making tradeoffs explicit and defensible. No recovery is perfectly safe or perfectly fast, but it should always be intentional. By tying restoration decisions to evidence, preserving validation gates, using monitoring as a confidence amplifier, and communicating uncertainty honestly, organizations can move forward without gambling on hope. The mark of maturity is not the absence of tension between speed and safety, but the ability to navigate it without compromising trust or resilience.

Executive Updates and Business Coordination

Executive updates during recovery are not status briefings in the traditional sense; they are decision-support communications that shape business behavior while risk is still evolving. The purpose is to enable leaders to make informed tradeoffs about restoration speed, operational exposure, regulatory posture, and customer impact without forcing technical teams into unsafe commitments. Poorly structured updates either overwhelm executives with detail or provide false reassurance that collapses when conditions change. Effective updates translate technical progress into business-relevant implications while preserving uncertainty where it legitimately exists. This discipline is essential because recovery is as much a governance challenge as it is a technical one.

The most important characteristic of executive updates is clarity about what is known, what is believed, and what remains unknown. Leaders do not need exhaustive telemetry, but they do need confidence that statements are grounded in evidence rather than optimism. Updates should explicitly distinguish confirmed facts, working assumptions, and areas under active investigation, so decisions are not made on implied certainty. When uncertainty is not acknowledged, executives often infer safety where none exists and push for acceleration that undermines recovery. Clear framing allows leadership to accept measured risk knowingly rather than discovering it later through failure.

Business coordination depends on aligning recovery actions with operational priorities that may change daily as conditions evolve. Security teams must understand which business functions are truly critical, which can tolerate delay, and which carry disproportionate legal or safety implications if restored incorrectly. This requires continuous dialogue with operations, legal, compliance, communications, and customer-facing leadership rather than one-time prioritization. Recovery decisions made in isolation often conflict with downstream obligations such as regulatory reporting timelines, contractual service levels, or public disclosures. Coordination ensures that restoration sequencing supports the broader enterprise, not just technical completeness.

Executives also need updates that describe decision boundaries rather than binary outcomes. Instead of stating that a system is "safe" or "not safe," effective briefings explain what controls are in place, what risks remain, and what conditions would trigger a change in posture. This allows leaders to approve constrained returns to service, temporary access models, or phased customer re-engagement with eyes open. It also creates a shared understanding of rollback criteria if indicators reappear. When executives understand the guardrails, they are less likely to override them under pressure.

AI and machine learning can assist in executive communication by synthesizing large volumes of recovery data into coherent narratives, but they introduce their own risks if not governed. Automated summaries can help distill system status, identity risk, and monitoring outcomes into digestible updates that support timely decisions. However, these summaries may smooth over uncertainty, obscure weak signals, or present probabilistic assessments as conclusions. Leadership updates should therefore disclose when AI-assisted analysis is used and ensure that human owners validate the message and its implications. Accountability for the content of updates must remain with named leaders, not with tools.

Business coordination during recovery also requires synchronizing external communications with internal progress. Executives are often balancing regulator inquiries, customer communications, partner obligations, and board oversight while recovery is ongoing. Security updates should anticipate these needs by identifying what claims can be supported with evidence and what statements would be premature. Misalignment between internal reality and external messaging creates legal and reputational risk that can exceed the technical impact of the incident itself. Coordinated updates help ensure that commitments made outside the organization remain consistent with recovery constraints.

A common failure mode is allowing executive updates to become performative rather than operational. When updates focus on reassurance instead of decision enablement, they encourage optimism bias and suppress dissenting technical views. Strong recovery leadership creates space for uncomfortable truths and treats bad news as input, not failure. This culture allows issues such as delayed validation, unexpected dependencies, or renewed indicators to be surfaced early without fear of blame. Over time, executives learn to trust the update process because it reflects reality rather than aspiration.

Ultimately, executive updates and business coordination are mechanisms for shared ownership of recovery risk. The organization succeeds when leaders understand that restoration decisions are collective choices informed by evidence, not demands placed on responders. By providing clear framing, honest uncertainty, defensible options, and consistent coordination across business functions, recovery teams enable executives to lead responsibly under pressure. When communication is handled with rigor, recovery moves forward with alignment rather than friction, and the business emerges not only operational but governed.

AI-Assisted Recovery Coordination: Communication, Sequencing, and Verification Controls

AI-assisted recovery coordination is best understood as a force multiplier for clarity and discipline during the most error-prone phase of incident handling. Recovery creates a high-velocity environment where multiple teams are rebuilding systems, rotating credentials, restoring data, and reintroducing services while the security posture is still stabilizing. In that context, AI is most valuable when it reduces friction in communication, improves the quality of sequencing decisions, and strengthens verification controls that prevent premature return to service. The objective is not to make AI a decision authority, but to use it to make human decisions faster, more consistent, and more auditable. When applied well, it helps the organization move quickly without confusing progress with safety.

Communication is the first place AI can add operational value, because recovery work generates a constant stream of partial updates that are difficult to consolidate. AI can summarize the current state of restoration activities across workstreams, identify open dependencies, and translate technical status into business-relevant language without forcing responders to stop and write narrative updates. This is most effective when AI is fed structured inputs such as change tickets, restoration run logs, identity rotation records, and monitoring outcomes rather than informal chat fragments. Even then, the output must be treated as a draft that is owned by a human leader who validates key claims against evidence. The control boundary should be explicit: AI may propose summaries and highlight conflicts, but humans approve what becomes the official operational picture.

Sequencing is where coordination succeeds or fails, and AI can support sequencing by making dependencies visible at speed. Recovery often breaks down when teams restore an application before its identity provider, re-enable broad access before token revocation completes, or reconnect systems to management planes that are not yet trusted. AI can help by building and continuously updating a dependency view from telemetry and documentation, flagging high-risk sequencing choices such as restoring workloads that will immediately pull code or configuration from unvalidated sources. The quality of this assistance depends on accurate asset inventory, service ownership mapping, and reliable change history, because models cannot infer dependencies that are not represented in data. Sequencing recommendations should be treated as hypotheses that require confirmation by system owners who understand the operational reality behind the diagrams. Table 24.3 clarifies where AI can accelerate recovery coordination and the controls required to prevent over trust drift and leakage.

Verification controls are the most important safeguard in AI-assisted recovery because they protect against the natural tendency to accept plausible narratives under pressure. AI can help assemble verification packets that include the specific checks required for return-to-service decisions, such as evidence of session invalidation, credential and key rotation completion, baseline configuration alignment, and the presence of required logging and endpoint telemetry. It can also compare current system states against known-good baselines and highlight drift,

Table 24.3 AI-Assisted Recovery Coordination Controls and Boundaries.

AI-Assisted Use	Operational Benefit	Telemetry Dependency	Human Control Boundary	Common Failure Mode
Status summarization	Shared situational awareness at speed	Change records run logs monitoring outcomes	Human validates and publishes official update	False confidence from smoothed uncertainty
Dependency surfacing	Fewer sequencing mistakes	Accurate asset and service mapping	System owners confirm dependencies	Incorrect inference from incomplete mapping
Sequencing risk flags	Early warning on risky restore order	Change history and identity state	Leads only not approvals	Drift as environment changes during recovery
Verification packet assembly	Faster evidence collection for gates	Identity logs endpoint telemetry configuration state	Named approver attests criteria met	Over trust in compiled evidence
Anomaly highlighting	Spot reinfection and regression sooner	Stable baselines time aligned logs	Analyst confirms before action	Noise floods reduce trust
Automated containment support	Reversible risk reduction actions	Real-time detections and response hooks	Limit to reversible actions with audit trail	Overreach that disrupts recovery
Audit trail support	Defensible records of decisions	Prompt input output retention with access control	Governance enforces retention and least privilege	Leakage of sensitive incident artifacts

missing controls, or newly introduced exceptions that change the risk profile. These verification outputs are only trustworthy if telemetry coverage is consistent and time-synchronized, and if the organization has defined what "clean" means in measurable terms. The approval boundary should be strict: AI may collect and organize evidence, but humans must review and attest that criteria were met before any system is declared ready.

Human-in-the-loop controls are non-negotiable because recovery decisions are business decisions with technical consequences, and models can be confidently wrong. The practical pattern is to require named approvers for key actions such as restoring privileged access, reconnecting to production networks, and reintroducing high-impact services, with AI providing decision support rather than permission. Approval should be tied to evidence artifacts, not to AI-generated confidence statements, so that reviewers can inspect underlying logs, change records, and validation results. Where automation is used at all, it should be limited to reversible actions with clear containment value, such as temporarily restricting a risky account or isolating a host that violates a known guardrail. This keeps speed benefits while ensuring that irreversible steps remain governed.

Data and telemetry dependencies determine whether AI improves recovery or amplifies confusion. AI coordination requires consistent identity telemetry, endpoint visibility, change and configuration history, and a reliable mapping between business services and the assets that implement them. If the environment lacks coverage in cloud control plane logs, token issuance records, or endpoint persistence artifacts, AI will fill gaps with inference that may sound coherent but cannot be trusted. This is especially dangerous during recovery because the environment is changing rapidly and baselines are shifting; models that rely on stale context will misclassify expected restoration behavior as malicious or, worse, overlook true regression as noise. Strong teams treat telemetry completeness as a prerequisite for AI reliance and explicitly label where the model's view is partial.

Failure modes in AI-assisted coordination are predictable and must be designed against rather than discovered mid-incident. False confidence arises when summaries smooth over uncertainty, turning tentative assessments into statements that leadership treats as facts. Drift occurs when the model's assumptions about the environment no longer match reality because controls, dependencies, and workloads changed during recovery, leading to incorrect sequencing or verification guidance. Bias can appear when the model overweights the noisiest systems or the most represented teams, creating blind spots in less instrumented areas that may be higher risk. Leakage is a governance risk when sensitive incident artifacts, credentials, or investigative details are exposed through uncontrolled prompts, logs, or externalized model services, creating a secondary security and compliance incident.

Governance and auditability are what make AI coordination safe to use at scale, because recovery must be defensible after the fact. Every AI-assisted output that influences a decision should be traceable to its inputs, with a record of who reviewed it, what evidence was accepted, and what uncertainties were acknowledged. Access controls matter because recovery data often includes privileged details about identity, infrastructure, and business processes; AI systems and their operators must follow least privilege and strict retention rules. The organization should also define where AI is permitted to operate, how prompts and outputs are logged, and how to validate that models are not retaining or reusing sensitive incident content inappropriately. Without this governance layer, AI can accelerate work in the moment while increasing long-term risk and reducing confidence in the integrity of the recovery process.

When properly controlled, AI-assisted recovery coordination improves the organization's ability to operate in parallel without losing coherence. It compresses the time required to build shared situational awareness, reduces sequencing errors by surfacing dependencies and conflicts, and strengthens verification by packaging evidence and highlighting gaps before systems re-enter production. The discipline is to treat AI as an organizing and pattern-finding engine while keeping accountability, approvals, and risk acceptance firmly in human hands. Recovery moves faster when people spend less time reconciling contradictory updates and more time executing validated steps in the right order. Confidence grows when every accelerated decision remains grounded in evidence, controlled by explicit boundaries, and preserved in an audit trail that leadership can stand behind.

Closing an Incident with Defensible Evidence

Closing an incident is not a ceremonial endpoint; it is a formal assertion that the organization can justify, under scrutiny, that the threat has been removed, operations are stable, and residual risk is understood and accepted. The standard for closure is not internal comfort or the passage of time, but defensible evidence that supports the decisions made during eradication and recovery. This evidence must be sufficient for executives, auditors, regulators, insurers, and potentially litigators to understand what happened and why the organization believes it is safe to move forward. Teams that treat closure as a box to check often discover months later that they cannot reconstruct key decisions or defend why systems were returned to service. Proper closure is therefore an exercise in discipline, not optimism.

Defensible evidence begins with a clear articulation of incident scope and impact grounded in observed facts. This includes what systems and identities were confirmed compromised, which were potentially exposed, and which were ruled out with evidence. The distinction matters because overstatement undermines credibility, while understatement creates legal and regulatory risk. Evidence should show how scope conclusions were reached, including the telemetry reviewed, the timeframes considered, and the assumptions that were tested and either validated or rejected. Closure does not require perfect certainty, but it does require that uncertainty is identified and bounded rather than ignored.

A core element of defensibility is demonstrating that the attacker's access paths and persistence mechanisms were identified and addressed. Evidence should show which credentials were rotated or invalidated, which accounts and roles were corrected, and which persistence artifacts were removed or rendered ineffective. It should also document how the organization verified that these actions were successful, such as session invalidation checks, configuration comparisons against known-good states, and monitoring for attempted reuse of compromised access. This moves closure from a statement of intent to a record of outcomes. Without this linkage, claims of eradication are difficult to support.

Return-to-service decisions must be supported by evidence that validation criteria were met at the time those decisions were made. This includes records of system rebuilds or restorations, confirmation of logging and monitoring coverage, and acknowledgment of any compensating controls applied where validation was incomplete. The evidence should reflect the environment as it existed when the decision occurred, not a reconstructed narrative created later. This temporal accuracy is critical because it shows that leaders acted reasonably based on the information available at the time. It also protects the organization from hindsight bias if new information emerges after closure.

Monitoring outcomes play a central role in defensible closure because they demonstrate that recovery held under observation. Evidence should include the duration and scope of heightened monitoring, the specific re-infection indicators that were watched, and the results of that monitoring. If alerts fired during this period, the record should show how they were investigated and resolved. A clean monitoring window does not prove absence of risk, but it supports the assertion that known attack paths did not reappear during a meaningful observation period. This is often the strongest practical indicator that closure is justified.

AI-assisted analysis used during the incident must be handled carefully in closure documentation. If AI outputs influenced decisions, the organization should be able to explain what data was used, how outputs were validated by humans, and what role those outputs played in final judgments. Defensible evidence avoids treating AI conclusions as authoritative and instead positions them as decision support that was reviewed and corroborated. This distinction matters because regulators and courts will examine whether reliance on automation was reasonable and governed. Transparency about AI use strengthens defensibility rather than weakening it.

Closure also requires documenting residual risk and explicit risk acceptance where applicable. Few incidents end with zero remaining uncertainty, and pretending otherwise undermines credibility. Evidence should show which risks remain, why they were deemed acceptable, and who accepted them on behalf of the organization. This may include delayed hardening actions, deferred system rebuilds, or architectural changes scheduled for later execution. Making residual risk explicit demonstrates maturity and shared accountability rather than technical overconfidence.

Finally, defensible closure preserves the ability to reconstruct the incident narrative end to end. Logs, timelines, decision records, and evidence artifacts should be retained according to legal and regulatory requirements, with access controls appropriate to their sensitivity. The goal is not to produce a perfect story, but a coherent one that aligns actions, evidence, and decisions without contradiction. When an organization can explain not only what it did, but why it did it and on what evidence, incident closure becomes a credible assertion rather than a hopeful declaration. That credibility is what allows the business to move forward without carrying unresolved doubt into future operations.

Conclusion

Eradication and recovery succeed when they are treated as evidence-driven operations with clear decision boundaries, not as a race to return services as quickly as possible. The organization restores confidence by removing access and persistence, validating cleanup with defensible proof, and reintroducing systems under monitoring designed to detect reinfection and drift. Executive coordination matters because recovery is ultimately a business risk decision, and leaders need honest, structured updates that distinguish what is known from what is still uncertain. When identity risk is addressed comprehensively and verification controls remain intact even under pressure, the incident can be closed with credible evidence and the business can resume operations without carrying unresolved compromise forward.

Recommendations

1) Establish an evidence-driven eradication plan that targets access and persistence together. Treat identity, endpoints, servers, cloud control planes, and network pathways as a single operational surface where persistence can shift when pressure is applied. Document the attack paths you are removing and tie each eradication action to verified artifacts rather than assumptions. Preserve a clear record of what was removed, invalidated, or corrected so later validation and closure are defensible.
2) Revoke and rotate authentication artifacts beyond passwords to eliminate durable access. Invalidate active sessions and revoke tokens, API keys, application secrets, and certificates that can outlive a password reset and silently preserve attacker access. Sequence these actions to reduce attacker capability first while avoiding avoidable outages caused by breaking dependencies. Confirm completion using identity telemetry that shows old artifacts can no longer authenticate successfully.
3) Prioritize removal of configuration-based persistence mechanisms that blend into normal operations. Inspect and remediate scheduled tasks, services, startup execution points, remote management configurations, and other mechanisms that enable recurring execution. Validate identity and cloud configuration integrity by correcting unauthorized roles, policy changes, and consent grants that function as persistence. Treat any unexpected execution path or privilege pathway as suspect until it is reauthorized.
4) Execute recovery changes with controlled sequencing and explicit rollback paths. Restore identity providers, management planes, and logging coverage before reconnecting production workloads that depend on them. Use phased reintroduction, so rebuilt systems can be observed and validated before full production exposure. Ensure every high-impact change has an owner, a purpose, and a reversal option to prevent a single misstep from cascading.
5) Define measurable "clean" criteria and enforce validation gates before returning systems to service. Confirm that persistence is removed, credentials and tokens are invalidated, and the original attack paths are no longer

viable across dependencies. Require evidence that logging and endpoint telemetry are functioning on restored systems, not merely that services are running. Record who approved each return-to-service decision and what evidence supported it at the time.

6) Monitor restored systems with incident-specific tripwires designed to catch reinfection early. Build detections around the adversary's demonstrated behavior, such as attempted reuse of disabled accounts, revoked tokens, recreated persistence points, or repeat policy modifications. Treat loss of visibility as a risk signal by alerting on missing logs, disabled telemetry, or unexpected configuration drift during restoration. Maintain a rapid isolate-and-revert capability, so you can respond decisively if indicators reappear.
7) Coordinate credential resets as an identity risk reduction effort rather than isolated password changes. Validate authorization state by correcting group memberships, role assignments, delegated rights, and exceptions that may have been added to preserve attacker access. Manage temporary access expansions used during recovery by assigning owners and expirations, so they do not become permanent exposure. Communicate reset actions clearly to reduce workarounds and prevent attacker impersonation from blending into recovery activity.
8) Use AI-assisted analysis to accelerate coordination while keeping humans accountable for decisions. Apply AI to summarize status, surface dependency conflicts, and organize verification evidence, but require human validation of conclusions and claims before acting. Set clear approval boundaries, so irreversible steps—such as restoring privileged access or reconnecting core production services—cannot be executed solely on AI output. Ensure AI use is auditable by retaining inputs, outputs, reviewers, and the evidence that supported final decisions.
9) Provide executives with decision-support updates that separate confirmed facts from assumptions and unknowns. Translate technical progress into business-relevant implications, including risk tradeoffs, constraints, and conditions for phased returns to service. Present options with guardrails and rollback criteria, so leadership can authorize controlled acceleration without forcing unsafe shortcuts. Align communications with legal, compliance, and customer-facing obligations to prevent external commitments from outpacing technical reality.
10) Close incidents only when you can produce defensible evidence that supports scope, eradication, validation, and residual risk acceptance. Preserve a coherent timeline and artifact set that shows what was observed, what actions were taken, and how outcomes were verified under monitoring. Document where uncertainty remains and who accepted residual risk, rather than implying perfect certainty. Retain records with appropriate access controls, so the organization can reconstruct decisions under audit, regulatory inquiry, or legal review.

25

Post-Incident Learning and Program Improvement

Post-incident learning is where response stops being a one-time event and becomes an engine for sustained defensive improvement. The goal is not to produce a retrospective narrative, but to convert disruption into measurable changes in controls, workflows, and decision-making that reduce future risk and business impact. This requires disciplined separation of root cause from contributing factors, rigorous tracking of corrective actions to verifiable completion, and continuous updating of detections, policies, and procedures to reflect how operations actually behave under stress. When measurement resists gaming, lessons are shared without blame, institutional memory is built and maintained, and AI is applied with evidence integrity and human oversight, incidents become catalysts for long-term resilience rather than recurring surprises.

Lessons Learned as a Core Defensive Capability

Lessons learned is not an administrative afterthought performed when there is time or when an incident is embarrassing enough to demand answers. It is a defensive capability that converts painful experience into reduced future risk, tighter response execution, and better decision-making under pressure. When treated as a capability, it has defined inputs, repeatable workflows, accountable outputs, and a measurable effect on detection and containment outcomes. Executives should expect this work to show up as fewer repeat failure patterns, faster containment, and clearer operational ownership. Without that discipline, teams accumulate "incident debt" where the same weaknesses recur, each time at a higher operational and reputational cost.

The core output of lessons learned is not a narrative; it is change that can be verified in the environment and in team behavior. A credible program distinguishes between what happened, why it happened, and what will be different next time, and it produces evidence for each. "What happened" should be grounded in timestamps, telemetry, and observed actions rather than recollections. "Why it happened" must avoid blaming individuals and instead surface system conditions such as missing visibility, ambiguous authority, brittle processes, or misaligned incentives. "What changes" should be specific enough to be tested, owned, and tracked to completion, with clear acceptance criteria that define when remediation is truly done.

Effective lessons learned begins with disciplined reconstruction of the incident timeline, because causality is rarely obvious in real operations. Teams should pull together detection events, endpoint and identity logs, ticketing records, containment actions, and communications artifacts to understand how the situation unfolded across people and systems. The point is not to create a perfect forensic narrative but to identify decision points, delays, and moments where uncertainty shaped action. This is where many programs fail by focusing only on the attacker's technique while ignoring internal friction, such as who had the authority to isolate hosts or how long it took to reach a system owner. A timeline that includes both technical events and operational actions makes it possible to see whether the organization's response system behaved as designed.

Root cause analysis must be pragmatic and multi-layered, because "the root cause" is often a stack of contributing failures rather than a single defect. A compromised credential may have been enabled by weak enrollment controls, poor conditional access enforcement, insufficient alert fidelity, and delayed revocation procedures. Lessons learned should identify the primary technical failure, the detection or response failure that allowed it to persist, and the organizational conditions that made the failure likely. This avoids the common trap of producing one remediation that looks satisfying but leaves upstream conditions untouched. When the analysis stays system-focused, it creates a culture where engineers and responders can be candid about gaps without fearing reputational damage for reporting them.

To operate as a defensive capability, lessons learned must have a clear workflow with ownership and boundaries. The incident commander or response lead should drive the process, but accountability for remediation should land with the operational owners of the affected systems and controls. Action items should be small enough to complete in weeks, not quarters, and they should include both control improvements and operating model improvements such as escalation clarity, on-call coverage, and runbook accuracy. A common failure mode is producing a long list of improvements with no sequencing, which guarantees that only the easiest items are completed while the highest risk gaps remain. A disciplined program forces prioritization based on exposure and recurrence likelihood and treats incomplete remediation as an ongoing risk condition rather than a documentation artifact.

Detection and monitoring content must be an explicit target of post-incident learning, because incidents reveal which signals were missing, ignored, or misinterpreted. Lessons learned should translate into concrete updates such as new detection logic, better suppression rules, refined alert routing, and improved enrichment to reduce ambiguity at triage time. It should also include verification that the telemetry needed for those detections exists at the right granularity and retention, and that logging cannot be trivially disabled or bypassed. Many teams "write detections" without confirming deployment coverage, resulting in controls that look complete on paper but never trigger in practice. When lessons learned is healthy, the outcome is a monitoring posture that becomes progressively harder to evade, not just noisier.

AI and machine learning can strengthen this capability when used to accelerate synthesis without replacing human accountability. Models can help cluster similar incidents, summarize large volumes of ticket and chat history, and identify repeated failure patterns such as consistent delays in approvals or recurring gaps in log coverage. They can also assist in timeline construction by correlating events across sources and highlighting anomalies that merit human review, particularly when the volume of telemetry is overwhelming. The boundary should be explicit: AI can propose hypotheses and draft findings, but humans approve causal claims, decide priorities, and own actions. Over-trust is a predictable failure mode, especially when a model produces confident-sounding explanations that collapse complex causality into a tidy story, so outputs should be treated as suggestions that require corroboration.

Governance is what keeps lessons learned from becoming episodic theater and turns it into a durable operational muscle. Organizations should require a consistent artifact set, an approval path, and an auditable record of changes made, including when action items are accepted as complete and what evidence supports that acceptance. This record matters not only for internal assurance but also for regulators, insurers, and boards who increasingly expect proof of continuous improvement rather than promises. AI-enabled workflows should be governed with the same rigor, including controls on what incident data can be used for summarization, how sensitive content is handled, and how model outputs are logged for traceability. A mature program treats drift as inevitable: response practices decay, staffing changes, and systems evolve, so lessons learned must continually refresh both controls and team behaviors to stay effective.

Root Cause Versus Contributing Factors

Root cause analysis in incident response is often treated as a hunt for a single, definitive explanation, but real incidents rarely cooperate with that narrative. A useful analysis distinguishes between the root cause that made compromise possible and the contributing factors that made impact worse or prolonged recovery. This distinction matters because executives need clarity on what must be fixed to prevent recurrence versus what must be improved to reduce blast radius and downtime. When teams collapse everything into one "cause," they typically overcorrect in one area while leaving the broader system weaknesses intact. Done well, this work produces a precise set of changes that meaningfully shift future incident probability and severity.

A root cause should be expressed as a specific, testable condition in the environment or operating model that, if removed, would have prevented the incident from occurring in the way it did. That condition might be technical, such as an exposed service with weak authentication, or procedural, such as an enrollment path that allowed privileged accounts to bypass identity proofing. It should be stated in language that can be validated by configuration review, control testing, or a repeatable simulation. Vague statements like "lack of security awareness" or "insufficient monitoring" are usually indicators that the analysis is still at the symptom level. The goal is not to assign blame but to identify the precise leverage point that changes the outcome. Table 25.1 helps separate prevention-focused root causes from resilience-focused contributing factors, so remediation targets the right leverage points.

Contributing factors are the set of conditions that did not directly enable initial compromise but materially influenced how far the attacker got, how long they stayed, and how disruptive remediation became. These often include incomplete logging coverage, weak segmentation, slow access revocation, unclear authority to isolate systems, or brittle dependencies that turn containment into a business outage. Contributing factors can be numerous and interdependent, which is why they are easy to hand-wave away as "complexity." Operationally, they matter because they are where organizations buy down impact even when a novel initial intrusion vector appears. A defensible program treats contributing factors as first-class findings with owners and measurable remediation, not as optional "nice-to-haves."

Separating root cause from contributing factors requires disciplined reconstruction of the incident path, including both attacker actions and defender decisions. Teams should anchor the analysis in a timeline that captures when the attacker first gained access, what privileges were acquired, what internal movement occurred, and what evidence existed at each step. In parallel, they should record response actions and delays, such as time to triage, time to isolate, and time to revoke or rotate credentials. This dual track reveals whether the organization's primary failure was control bypass, visibility gaps, decision friction, or all of the above. Without that structure, discussions become dominated by the most memorable moment rather than the most causally important one. Figure 25.1

Table 25.1 Root Cause Versus Contributing Factors Decision Guide.

Finding Type	Definition Test	Primary Purpose	Typical Evidence Anchor
Root cause	If removed the incident would not unfold this way	Prevent recurrence	Config state control coverage decision authority
Contributing factor	Did not enable entry but increased impact or duration	Reduce blast radius and recovery time	Telemetry gaps routing delays dependency failures
Symptom	Observed outcome without explaining enabling condition	Avoid misdirected fixes	Late detection widespread spread outage
Technique description	Attacker method used during incident	Context not remediation target	Event sequences toolmarks activity traces
Control failure	Control existed but ineffective in practice	Restore intended protection	Coverage drift misconfiguration alert not firing
Control absence	Control not present or not in scope	Decide and implement baseline need	Missing guardrail missing logging missing authority

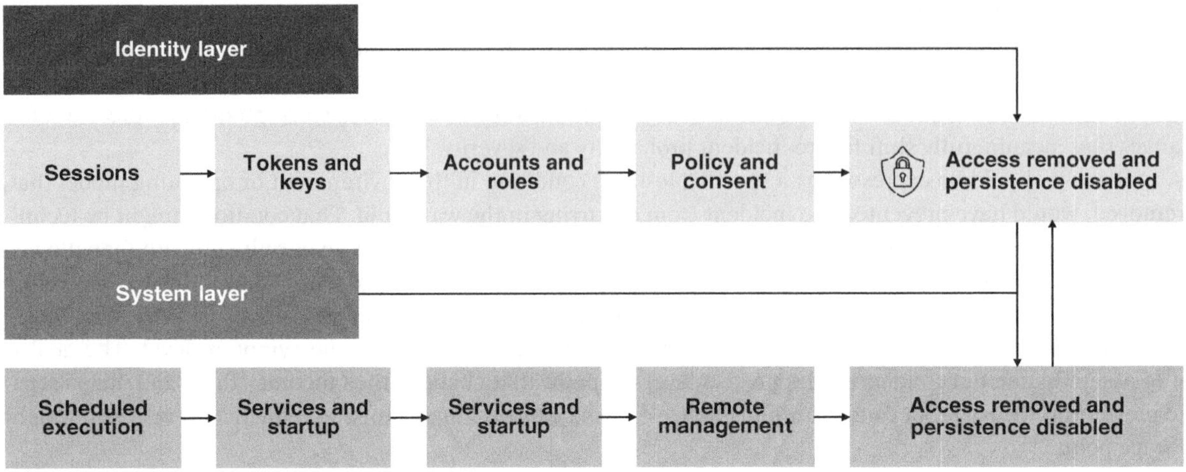

Figure 25.1 Root Cause Versus Contributing Factors and Where They Drive Action.

separates root cause from contributing factors and shows how each drives a different class of remediation. It supports the text by clarifying why prevention work and resilience work must be treated as distinct but coordinated outputs.

A common pitfall is mistaking the earliest observed event for the root cause, especially when detection occurs late. If an organization first notices suspicious administrative actions, it may label "privileged misuse" as the root cause and ignore the earlier credential theft path that enabled it. Another pitfall is treating an attacker technique as the cause rather than the underlying exposure that made the technique effective. The technique changes from incident to incident; the exposure usually does not. Root cause should point to the persistent weakness, while contributing factors describe the conditions that allowed that weakness to cascade into wider impact.

The analysis should also distinguish between control failures and control absences, because the remediation strategy differs. A failed control implies the organization believed protection existed, but configuration, coverage, or operational execution made it ineffective. An absent control implies the organization knowingly accepted risk or never recognized the need, which often requires a governance change rather than a technical tweak. Both can coexist in the same incident, such as having MFA in place for most users while privileged service accounts were exempted for convenience. Being explicit about these categories reduces the tendency to produce action items that look substantial but do not address the actual control gap.

AI-assisted analysis can accelerate identification of contributing factors by synthesizing large volumes of logs, tickets, and communications into candidate themes, but it must be treated as hypothesis generation rather than adjudication. Models can cluster similar incidents, detect recurring patterns in delays or handoffs, and surface repeated mentions of operational friction that humans overlook under fatigue. They can also help correlate event sequences across disparate telemetry sources to suggest where the timeline may have blind spots. The risk is false coherence, where the model produces a neat causal story that is not supported by evidence, or bias toward the most common patterns in its training data rather than the specifics of the environment. Human reviewers should require corroboration for each causal claim and preserve an auditable trail showing what evidence supports the final findings.

Translating root cause and contributing factors into action requires disciplined scoping and ownership, or else the work becomes an academic exercise. Root-cause remediations should be framed as non-negotiable prevention work with clear acceptance criteria, such as "privileged enrollment requires identity proofing" or "external exposure is restricted to managed access paths." Contributing-factor remediations should be framed as resilience work that reduces time-to-detect, time-to-contain, and business disruption, such as improving log coverage, tightening segmentation boundaries, or clarifying containment authority. Both sets should be prioritized based on recurrence likelihood and impact, not on which team has available capacity. The credibility of the program comes from closing the loop: verifying changes, retesting assumptions, and ensuring the next incident does not fail in the same predictable ways.

Control Gaps and Corrective Action Tracking

Control gaps are the practical output of an incident, because they are the concrete places where the organization's intended defenses did not exist, did not work, or did not apply broadly enough to matter. Treating these gaps as operational findings rather than technical trivia is what turns incident response into risk reduction. A control gap can be a missing safeguard, such as absent log coverage for a critical identity path, or an ineffective safeguard, such as detection logic that exists but is not tuned for the environment's normal behavior. It can also be an "in-scope but out-of-coverage" problem, where the control works only for part of the estate due to onboarding lag, acquisition complexity, or inconsistent configuration management. The key is to name the gap in a way that is testable and tied to a specific control objective, not in a way that simply restates the incident.

Corrective action tracking is the mechanism that prevents control gaps from becoming lessons learned theater. A mature program treats corrective actions as a portfolio of risk work with defined ownership, milestones, and evidence requirements, not as a checklist appended to a report. Each action should map back to a specific gap and specify what change will exist in the environment or workflow when the action is complete. It should also define the validation method, such as configuration review, control testing, or a tabletop or simulation that proves the improved process under realistic conditions. Without explicit validation criteria, "done" becomes subjective, and teams will close actions based on effort spent rather than outcomes achieved.

The most useful control gap statements separate the weakness from the symptom that revealed it. "We detected the intrusion late" is a symptom; the gap might be incomplete endpoint telemetry on high-risk hosts, insufficient identity event logging, or alert routing that failed to page the right responder. Similarly, "the attacker moved laterally" is not a gap; the gap might be permissive east–west access, weak host-based firewall policy, or a lack of privileged access segmentation. Writing gaps this way forces the organization to fix what is persistent rather than what is memorable. It also makes it possible to aggregate gaps across incidents and see systemic patterns, which is essential for executives who need to decide where to invest for durable improvement.

Corrective actions should be scoped to fit operational reality, because broad remediations that take quarters to complete often die in the backlog and quietly normalize risk. Large items should be decomposed into smaller deliverables that each reduce exposure, such as closing a specific external ingress path, enforcing a privileged enrollment guardrail, or onboarding a defined set of critical systems into centralized logging. This decomposition also helps avoid the "all-or-nothing" trap where teams delay shipping meaningful improvements until a comprehensive redesign is finished. In practice, defenders win by shrinking the attacker's opportunity space incrementally and continuously. Tracking should reflect that approach by showing partial risk reduction while still holding teams accountable for full closure.

Ownership is where corrective action programs succeed or fail, and ownership must live with the teams that run the affected systems, not solely with security. Security can define the requirement, provide expertise, and validate outcomes, but infrastructure, identity, endpoint, application, and operations leaders must own implementation. Actions should be assigned to accountable individuals with authority to drive change across dependencies, not to generic teams or shared inboxes. Cross-functional items should have a clear coordinating owner to prevent the work from stalling in handoffs and status meetings. When corrective actions are truly owned, they compete fairly with other operational priorities instead of being treated as optional security requests. Table 25.2 defines the minimum fields needed to track corrective actions to evidence-based closure rather than effort-based completion.

Table 25.2 Corrective Action Tracking Fields and Evidence Expectations.

Tracking Field	What It Captures	Owner Focus	Evidence for Closure
Control gap statement	Specific testable weakness tied to a control objective	Name the persistent weakness	Before and after configuration or coverage proof
Action item description	Exact change to implement	Define build steps and scope	Change record with implementation notes
Accountable owner	Single person responsible for delivery	Coordinate dependencies	Approval trail and attestation of completion
Milestones	Small deliverables that reduce exposure incrementally	Ship progress in weeks	Completed milestone artifacts
Validation method	How effectiveness will be proven	Plan testing and reviewers	Test results simulation outcome or control check
Closure criteria	What must be true to call it done	Prevent subjective closure	Measured proof aligned to the gap
Residual risk note	What remains if full fix is deferred	Inform leadership decisions	Accepted risk record and review date

Tracking must also recognize that some control gaps are governance problems, not engineering problems. If a privileged exception process routinely bypasses guardrails, the corrective action is not merely to tighten a configuration but to change approval boundaries, documentation requirements, and audit review. If logging is inconsistent due to decentralized technology ownership, the corrective action may require standard onboarding requirements for new systems and a defined service level for telemetry availability. These governance-oriented items should be tracked with the same rigor as technical changes, including evidence of new process adoption and enforcement. Otherwise, the organization will continue to produce technically correct designs that are not followed under real operational pressure.

AI can improve corrective action tracking by reducing administrative friction and increasing visibility, but it must be constrained to prevent false confidence. Models can summarize incident findings into candidate action items, detect duplicate or overlapping remediations across incidents, and flag actions that are stuck or drifting based on status patterns and missed milestones. They can also help verify evidence completeness by checking whether required artifacts exist, such as configuration snapshots, test results, or approval records, and prompting owners when documentation is missing. The failure mode is treating AI-generated summaries as authoritative, which can lead to mis-scoped actions or premature closure if the model overstates what evidence proves. Human reviewers should approve action definitions, ensure evidence actually demonstrates control effectiveness, and maintain an auditable trail showing why an action was accepted as complete.

Corrective action programs should close the loop by validating that remediations measurably change defensive outcomes, not just control documentation. For detection-oriented gaps, this might mean confirming alert fidelity, routing, and coverage through controlled testing, and verifying that responders can triage and contain within expected time bounds. For prevention-oriented gaps, it means proving the unwanted condition is no longer possible, such as demonstrating that a risky access path is blocked or that privileged operations require the intended guardrails. Tracking should also capture residual risk and planned follow-on work when full remediation is not immediately feasible, so leadership understands what is still exposed and why. When control gaps and corrective actions are handled this way, incidents stop being isolated emergencies and instead become inputs to a disciplined improvement engine that continuously hardens the organization.

Updating Detections, Policies, and Procedures After Incidents

Incidents expose the difference between how defenses were designed to work and how they actually behaved under adversarial pressure. Updating detections, policies, and procedures after an incident is the mechanism that closes that gap and prevents the same failure pattern from repeating. This work should be treated as operational engineering, not documentation hygiene, because its success is measured in faster detection, clearer decision-making, and safer containment. When updates are superficial or delayed, teams accumulate brittle controls that look compliant but fail in the moments that matter most. Executives should expect post-incident updates to show up as tangible changes in alerts, runbooks, and approval paths, not just revised text.

Detection updates are often the most immediate and visible outcome of an incident, but they must go beyond adding a single new alert. Teams should analyze which signals were missing, which were present but ignored, and which were too noisy or ambiguous to act on with confidence. Updates may include refining detection logic to better reflect normal behavior, adding contextual enrichment to reduce triage time, or adjusting severity thresholds so that truly risky conditions interrupt someone's day. It is equally important to verify telemetry coverage and retention, because a well-written detection is useless if critical systems were never onboarded or logs rolled off too quickly. Post-incident detection work should always include a validation step that proves the new or updated logic fires as expected in the real environment.

Policy updates require more restraint than detection changes, because policies are blunt instruments that can introduce friction if overcorrected. An incident may reveal that an existing policy was ambiguous, unenforceable, or routinely bypassed under time pressure, which is a signal to clarify intent and tighten scope rather than to add pages of prescriptive language. Good updates translate operational lessons into clear requirements, such as who has authority to approve emergency access, how exceptions are documented, and when temporary measures must be reviewed or revoked. Policies should reflect how the organization expects to behave during stress, not an idealized version of operations that collapses during a real incident. When policy updates are grounded in observed behavior, they reinforce accountability instead of creating new workarounds.

Procedures and runbooks are where most post-incident value is either realized or squandered. Incidents routinely expose gaps in step sequencing, unclear handoffs, missing prerequisites, or assumptions about system availability that are not true during an active compromise. Updating procedures should focus on reducing cognitive load for responders by making decision points explicit, pre-authorizing common containment actions, and embedding guidance for coordination with legal, communications, and business stakeholders. These updates should be concise and tested, because long or unvalidated runbooks are rarely consulted in the heat of response. A procedure that has been exercised or simulated after revision is far more valuable than one that simply reflects consensus in a meeting. Table 25.3 links incident findings to concrete updates in detections policies and procedures and shows how each change should be verified.

The interplay between detections, policies, and procedures is critical, because changes in one area often create new demands in another. A more sensitive detection may require clearer escalation authority to avoid delays, while a tightened access policy may require updated procedures for emergency operations to prevent business disruption. Post-incident updates should therefore be reviewed as a system, not as isolated artifacts, to ensure that they reinforce rather than undermine each other. This systems view also helps identify where automation can safely reduce manual effort, such as auto-enrichment of alerts or pre-approved containment actions triggered by high-confidence conditions. Without this coordination, organizations often improve one layer at the expense of another.

AI and machine learning can support post-incident updates by accelerating analysis and drafting, but they must remain subordinate to human judgment. Models can help identify which detections were statistically ineffective, summarize responder feedback across tickets and chat logs, and suggest procedural clarifications based on observed delays or confusion. They can also assist in testing by generating synthetic scenarios or variations that

Table 25.3 Post-Incident Update Targets Across Detections Policies and Procedures.

Update Target	Trigger From Incident	Expected Change	Verification Approach
Detections	Signals missing ignored or too ambiguous	Refined logic enrichment and routing	Trigger test in live telemetry with expected fire
Telemetry coverage	Critical systems not onboarded or logs rolled off	Improved logging granularity and retention	Coverage check for critical assets and paths
Policies	Authority exceptions or approvals caused delay	Clarified approval boundaries and exception rules	Review for enforceability and adoption evidence
Procedures and runbooks	Steps unclear brittle or unrealistic under stress	Explicit decision points safe containment rollback	Exercise or simulation of revised steps
Escalation paths	Wrong team paged or handoff friction	Updated routing and ownership mapping	After action review of next incident routing
AI assisted synthesis	Volume too high for consistent review	Clustering and trend detection with guardrails	Human review and traceable links to evidence
Evidence handling	Records mixed with interpretation or hard to audit	Immutable artifacts and versioned analysis	Auditable trail chain of custody for sensitive items

exercise updated logic and workflows. The primary risk is automation bias, where teams accept AI-generated recommendations without validating their relevance to the specific environment or threat context. Guardrails should require human approval, evidence-based validation, and clear documentation of why a given update was adopted.

Governance ensures that updates do not drift or conflict with existing controls over time. Organizations should require that post-incident changes are reviewed, approved, and versioned, with traceability back to the incident findings that motivated them. This traceability matters when auditors, regulators, or boards ask how specific incidents changed the organization's defenses, and it prevents ad hoc changes from accumulating into an incoherent control set. It also creates a feedback loop where the effectiveness of updates can be assessed in subsequent incidents or exercises. Without governance, well-intentioned updates often degrade into one-off fixes that quietly increase complexity.

The final measure of success is whether updated detections, policies, and procedures measurably improve response outcomes. That improvement should be visible in metrics such as time to detect, time to contain, clarity of escalation, and reduced need for improvisation during incidents. Teams should periodically test and review updated artifacts to ensure they still reflect the current environment and operating model, especially as systems and staffing change. When this discipline is maintained, each incident incrementally sharpens the organization's defensive posture rather than exposing the same weaknesses again. In this way, post-incident updates become a continuous hardening process embedded in daily operations, not a reactive cleanup task.

Measuring Improvement Without Gaming the Metrics

Measuring post-incident improvement is necessary to know whether changes actually reduced risk, but measurement is also where well-intentioned programs collapse into performative reporting. The temptation is to select metrics that look good on a dashboard rather than metrics that reflect defensive capability under stress. When metrics become targets, teams will naturally optimize for what is counted, sometimes at the expense of true readiness. Executives should demand measures that are hard to fake, tied to operational outcomes, and interpretable in the context of incident complexity. The objective is not to produce a steady downward trend line; it is to build confidence that detection and response are becoming more reliable and more resilient over time.

Time-based metrics such as time to detect, time to triage, and time to contain are common because they are easy to understand, but they are also easy to distort. Teams can shorten time to triage by auto-closing alerts or by routing borderline cases into low-priority queues, producing an artificial sense of efficiency. Time to contain can improve simply by defining containment more narrowly, such as isolating one host while leaving credential risk unresolved, which shifts impact into later stages. Even time to detect can appear improved if detection criteria are broadened to trigger earlier on weak signals, increasing noise and analyst fatigue. Time metrics remain useful only when paired with quality checks that confirm the right work was done, not merely that a clock stopped.

Quality metrics should emphasize correctness and completeness of decisions, because these are harder to game without exposing weaknesses. Examples include the percentage of high-severity incidents with complete evidence packages, the rate of correct initial severity classification, and the proportion of containment actions that were reversed due to being unnecessary or misdirected. Another useful signal is the frequency of "unknown unknowns," such as discovering during an incident that critical logs were missing or that a system owner could not be reached, because these indicate fragility that dashboards often hide. Quality measures also reveal whether the organization is learning, such as fewer repeat gaps in logging coverage or fewer repeated escalation failures. The focus stays on whether the organization can make good decisions quickly, not whether it can produce quick decisions.

Coverage and reliability measures help anchor improvement to the reality of the environment rather than to the narrative of a single incident. Detection coverage should be expressed in operational terms, such as what percentage of critical assets and identity paths produce the telemetry needed to support the organization's top investigative questions. Reliability should reflect whether those signals remain consistently available, including during outages, agent failures, and configuration drift. If coverage is reported only as "onboarded systems," teams can game the metric by onboarding low-value assets while leaving the hardest or most critical systems out of scope. Mature reporting weights coverage by business criticality and exposure, which makes it difficult to claim progress without addressing the riskiest gaps.

A resilient measurement program also accounts for incident mix, because a quarter filled with commodity phishing events cannot be compared directly to one dominated by complex intrusions. Metrics should be stratified by incident type, impact, and confidence level, so trends represent capability changes rather than changes in attacker behavior. The same principle applies across business units and environments, because a highly managed endpoint fleet behaves differently than legacy operational systems or acquired networks. Stratification reduces the incentive to "improve" by reclassifying incidents into easier categories. It also helps leaders invest where outcomes are weakest rather than where reporting is most polished.

Metrics should be designed to minimize perverse incentives by aligning them with the organization's actual priorities during response. For example, rewarding low false positive rates can discourage necessary early-warning detections that must tolerate ambiguity. Rewarding fewer escalations can push teams to suppress warnings rather than coordinate. Rewarding low incident counts can encourage under-reporting and delayed declaration, which increases impact when an incident finally becomes undeniable. A healthier approach rewards appropriate escalation, thorough investigation for high-impact cases, and evidence-based closure, even when that makes numbers look worse in the short term. Leaders should expect some metrics to worsen temporarily after improvements, because better visibility often reveals more problems before it reduces them.

AI can help reduce metric gaming by triangulating across sources and surfacing inconsistencies, but it can also create new gaming opportunities if used carelessly. Models can detect patterns such as repeated early closure of alerts, suspiciously uniform timestamps, or recurring reclassification just before reporting deadlines, which can indicate process manipulation or misunderstanding. They can also summarize narrative incident data and correlate it with quantitative measures to flag when the story and the numbers do not match. The risk is that AI-generated metrics become opaque, making it harder for teams to challenge errors or understand what behaviors are being rewarded. Governance should require transparency in how metrics are calculated, along with periodic human review to ensure AI-driven analyses are grounded in evidence and do not embed hidden bias.

The most reliable way to resist gaming is to combine operational metrics with independent validation through exercises, simulations, and post-incident verification. If dashboards claim faster containment but tabletop and live simulations still show delayed decision-making and unclear authority, the metric is not measuring capability. Similarly, if detection coverage claims are not supported by practical tests that demonstrate signal availability and alert generation on representative assets, the coverage metric is aspirational rather than real. Independent validation does not need to be burdensome, but it must be regular enough to keep metrics honest. When measurement is anchored this way, the organization builds a culture where metrics are tools for learning and investment decisions, not instruments for self-congratulation.

Sustained improvement is visible when repeated failure modes decline, response decisions become more consistent, and fewer incidents require improvisation to compensate for known gaps. The most telling indicators are often qualitative but still disciplined, such as fewer emergency exceptions during containment, fewer last-minute escalations caused by unclear ownership, and fewer surprises about system dependencies. These signals can be captured in structured post-incident reviews and trend analysis without being reduced to a single number. Over time, the organization should be able to show that corrective actions reduced recurrence and that response execution became more predictable under stress. That is what measurement is for, and it is why resisting metric gaming is itself a defensive capability.

Sharing Lessons Across Teams Without Blame

Sharing lessons across teams is where post-incident learning either becomes an enterprise capability or remains a local improvement effort trapped inside security. Most incidents span multiple domains, such as identity, endpoint operations, cloud services, network engineering, and business application ownership, so the lessons are rarely "owned" by a single group. If learning stays contained within the responders, the same cross-team friction and gaps recur because the organizations that must change never see the problem in operational terms. Effective sharing translates incident experience into shared understanding and coordinated action without creating reputational damage for the teams involved. The objective is collective hardening, not retrospective judgment.

A blame-free approach does not mean avoiding accountability; it means focusing accountability on systems, decisions, and control outcomes rather than personal fault. Individuals make choices within the constraints they are given, and incidents reliably reveal where constraints are unclear, unrealistic, or conflicting. When reviews single out a person for a delayed decision, teams learn to hide uncertainty and minimize reporting, which increases risk on the next incident. When reviews focus on the conditions that produced delay, such as missing authority, unclear escalation paths, or insufficient visibility, teams are more willing to surface uncomfortable truths. This approach preserves psychological safety, the practical precondition for accurate reporting in high-stress environments.

The way lessons are packaged determines whether they are received as useful guidance or as a critique. Sharing should emphasize observable facts, decision points, and specific control gaps, with enough context that other teams can map the lessons to their own systems and workflows. Avoiding inflammatory language matters, because phrases like "failed to follow procedure" often conceal that the procedure was ambiguous, outdated, or impossible under real constraints. The most effective artifacts separate "what happened" from "what changed," and they highlight the dependencies that made response difficult, such as system ownership boundaries or fragile integrations. When the message is concrete and operational, teams can engage without feeling attacked.

Different audiences need different levels of detail, and conflating them can unintentionally create blame. Executives generally need risk implications, business impact drivers, and the top corrective actions with owners and timelines, not exhaustive technical timelines. Engineering and operations teams need the specific failure modes, evidence supporting them, and the exact remediations that affect their work, including testing expectations and rollout considerations. Response teams need the tactical lessons about triage efficiency, containment sequencing, and communication flow. Tailoring the content prevents a public "postmortem" from becoming a public trial, while still ensuring that each group receives what it needs to change behavior and controls.

Cross-team sharing also works best when it is normalized as routine operational learning rather than triggered only by major incidents. When the only reviews are after high-visibility events, participants enter defensively because they assume reputational risk is on the table. A steady cadence of smaller learnings, such as near-misses, detection tuning outcomes, or containment workflow improvements, builds trust and reduces the emotional intensity of larger post-incident discussions. This cadence creates shared language about risks and response expectations, which makes future coordination faster. It also signals that learning is a continuous practice, not a punitive ritual.

The facilitation method matters, because poorly run sessions drift into debate about who should have done what rather than what the system should enable next time. A structured review should focus on decision points, constraints, and outcomes, and it should explicitly redirect personal attribution toward systemic conditions. It should also surface tradeoffs that were reasonable at the time, such as delaying isolation to preserve business continuity, and document how those tradeoffs will be supported in the future through clearer authority or safer technical options. When teams see their constraints recognized, they are more likely to engage honestly. The result is better insight into how the organization actually operates under stress, which is the only reliable basis for improvement.

AI can support blame-free sharing by helping to separate signal from emotion and by standardizing artifacts, but it must not become a tool for surveillance or performance scoring. Models can summarize timelines, extract recurring themes from chat logs and tickets, and draft neutral language that focuses on observable events and decisions. They can also help identify patterns across incidents that point to shared contributing factors, such as repeated delays in access revocation or recurring logging gaps. The risks include leakage of sensitive incident details, misinterpretation of context, or the creation of "scorecards" that teams perceive as punitive. Guardrails should include access controls, careful handling of sensitive content, and explicit boundaries that AI outputs are for learning and remediation planning, not individual evaluation.

Sustained cross-team learning requires a closed-loop mechanism that connects shared lessons to tracked corrective actions and visible outcomes. If teams repeatedly hear lessons but never see resourcing, prioritization, or completed changes, they will interpret sharing as a compliance exercise or reputation management. Conversely, when a lesson results in a clear remediation, a tested procedure update, or a measurable improvement in detection and containment, teams build confidence that participation is worthwhile. Over time, this creates a culture where teams proactively share near-misses and emerging risks because they trust the organization to respond constructively. That trust is a strategic defensive asset, because it increases the speed and accuracy of internal reporting, coordination, and improvement long before the next incident forces the issue.

Building Institutional Memory from Incidents

Institutional memory is the organization's ability to carry hard-earned operational knowledge forward as people, systems, and priorities change. Incidents generate insights that are expensive to acquire, but those insights evaporate quickly when they live only in the heads of a few responders or in a single after-action document that no one revisits. Building institutional memory means turning incident experience into durable artifacts, validated practices, and embedded expectations that survive turnover and reorgs. It also means making those artifacts discoverable and usable during the next incident, when speed matters and improvisation is costly. A mature defensive program treats institutional memory as infrastructure, not as tribal knowledge.

The first step is capturing incident reality with enough fidelity to be useful without turning documentation into a burden that teams avoid. The most valuable record is usually a structured incident package that includes a verified timeline, the key hypotheses tested, the evidence that confirmed or refuted them, and the specific decisions that shaped containment and recovery. This package should also record what data was unavailable, which approvals caused delays, and which procedures were ignored because they did not fit the situation. These details are often uncomfortable, but they are exactly what future responders need to avoid repeating mistakes. A sanitized narrative that omits friction creates the illusion of readiness while guaranteeing the same operational surprises will recur.

Institutional memory becomes actionable when it is organized around questions responders actually ask, not around the structure of a report. During a live event, teams need to know what "normal" looks like for a system, how to isolate it safely, who owns it, what logs exist, and what the last similar incident looked like. If incident knowledge is stored as long-form prose with inconsistent naming and no indexing, it will not be retrieved when time is scarce. Effective programs use consistent taxonomies for incident types, affected assets, identity elements, and control gaps, enabling quick search and comparison across events. The discipline is less about tooling and more about standardization, because even a simple repository becomes powerful when entries are structured and consistent.

Runbooks and procedures are the most visible carriers of institutional memory, but they must reflect lived experience rather than idealized flowcharts. Incidents teach where decision points are ambiguous, where containment actions are risky, and where dependencies break under stress, and those lessons should be incorporated into the next version of operating guidance. That includes preconditions for containment actions, fallback steps when telemetry is missing, and escalation thresholds that match real business tolerances. Updating runbooks is also an opportunity to encode "minimum viable response," the set of actions that must happen even when staffing is thin or systems are degraded. When runbooks evolve from incident evidence, they become more likely to be used, and the organization becomes less dependent on a few experts to navigate chaos.

Training and onboarding are where institutional memory either compounds or resets to zero with each staffing change. New analysts and engineers should not have to rediscover lessons that the organization already paid for through prior incidents. Post-incident learning should feed directly into realistic scenarios, tabletop exercises, and practical drills that mirror the organization's environment and decision constraints. This includes rehearsing non-technical steps such as escalation, authority to isolate, coordination with business owners, and the communication pathways that tend to break under pressure. When institutional memory is embedded into training, it shapes habits and expectations, which is far more durable than relying on documents alone.

A common failure mode is treating institutional memory as a compliance archive rather than as a living operational asset. If the repository is updated only to satisfy audits, it will drift away from reality as systems change, ownership moves, and procedures become stale. Institutional memory requires active maintenance, including periodic reviews of critical runbooks, validation that logging assumptions still hold, and retirement of guidance that no longer matches the environment. This maintenance should be prioritized based on business criticality, because not all systems deserve the same depth of documentation. The aim is not completeness; it is ensuring that the most likely and most damaging incident paths have the most reliable memory attached to them.

AI can help build and maintain institutional memory by reducing the cost of capturing and organizing incident knowledge, but it must be governed carefully. Models can summarize incident timelines, extract key decisions and evidence links, and normalize language into consistent tags and categories for easier retrieval. They can also detect recurring patterns across incidents, such as repeated gaps in identity telemetry or recurring delays in authority, and propose candidate updates to runbooks and training scenarios. The risks include leakage of sensitive details, hallucinated "facts" inserted into records, and overgeneralization that strips away critical context. Human review is essential, and AI-generated artifacts should be traceable to source evidence, so future responders can verify claims rather than inheriting unexamined assumptions.

Institutional memory also depends on preserving context about why decisions were made, not just what was done. Incidents force tradeoffs between containment speed and business continuity, between evidence preservation and restoration urgency, and between aggressive remediation and operational risk. Recording these tradeoffs, including who approved them and what constraints shaped them, helps future leaders make consistent decisions rather than relitigating the same debates during each event. It also reduces the tendency to second-guess responders after the fact, because the decision environment is preserved in the record. Over time, this consistency improves trust between security and the business, which directly affects response speed and effectiveness.

The value of institutional memory becomes obvious when it reduces repeated discovery work and shortens the path from alert to confident action. When responders can quickly find past incident patterns, validated containment steps, and known weak points, they spend less time debating basics and more time executing. When engineers can reference prior corrective actions and evidence of effectiveness, they avoid re-implementing half-solutions that already failed. This compounding effect is what makes institutional memory a defensive capability rather than an administrative function. The organization's defenses improve not only because controls are stronger, but because the people operating them start each incident from a higher baseline of shared, validated knowledge.

AI for Post-Incident Analysis: Clustering, Trend Detection, and Evidence Integrity

AI can materially improve post-incident analysis when it is used to amplify disciplined investigation rather than to replace it. The practical value comes from speed and scale: large incident datasets include logs, tickets, chat transcripts, email threads, and forensic notes that are difficult to synthesize consistently across multiple events. AI-assisted clustering and trend detection can help teams see patterns that are otherwise lost in volume, especially when incidents are frequent and analysts rotate across cases. The danger is that AI can also produce plausible narratives that exceed the evidence, which is unacceptable in post-incident work that drives executive decisions, remediation budgets, and potential legal exposure. The defensible posture is to use AI to propose structure and hypotheses, while keeping causality, prioritization, and final conclusions firmly under human control.

Clustering is the most straightforward application because it focuses on similarity rather than on explanation. In practice, clustering groups incidents or incident elements based on shared attributes such as affected identity objects, similar kill-chain stages, repeated alert signatures, or common control gaps like missing telemetry in a specific environment. The operational benefit is triage for learning: teams can quickly identify whether a new incident resembles a known class and which remediations historically reduced impact. Clustering also reveals when superficially different incidents share a common enabling condition, such as a pattern of privileged access exceptions or a consistent weakness in endpoint coverage for a particular business segment. To be trustworthy, clustering inputs must be normalized and consistently labeled, because noisy or inconsistent metadata produces groupings that reflect taxonomy drift rather than true similarity.

Trend detection extends clustering by asking not just what incidents look like, but how the organization's risk and response behaviors are changing over time. Useful trends include repeated appearance of the same control gap, recurring delays at specific decision points, or a growing proportion of incidents that require manual correlation due to insufficient enrichment. Trend detection can also highlight "silent regressions," such as increasing time-to-contain in one environment, rising recurrence of misclassified severity, or decreasing completeness of evidence packages as staffing changes. The value to leadership is clarity about whether investments are working and where operational friction is increasing. The primary failure mode is attributing trends to attacker evolution when they are actually driven by internal changes such as new systems, logging pipeline changes, or altered routing rules.

AI-driven post-incident analysis depends heavily on data quality and telemetry coverage, because models are only as faithful as the records they are given. If incident packages are inconsistently written, if key evidence lives in personal notes, or if log retention is insufficient, the model will fill gaps with inference that looks coherent but is not grounded. A mature approach treats the incident record as an evidence graph where each claim links back to artifacts such as timestamps, log entries, case notes, and approvals. AI can help build that graph by extracting entities and relationships, but it should not be allowed to introduce new facts that cannot be traced to sources. When the underlying data is weak, the correct outcome is uncertainty, not a confident story.

Evidence integrity is the non-negotiable foundation, because post-incident conclusions must be defensible under audit, regulatory review, or litigation. Integrity means the organization can demonstrate that evidence was collected consistently, stored securely, and not altered after collection, and that the chain of custody is clear for sensitive artifacts. It also means that AI-generated outputs are treated as derived analysis, not as primary evidence, with clear provenance showing inputs, processing steps, and reviewers. Without this separation, organizations risk contaminating their own records by mixing raw evidence with model-generated interpretation. The operational discipline is to preserve raw logs and artifacts immutably and to keep analysis outputs versioned, attributable, and reproducible.

Human-in-the-loop controls are essential because AI failures in this context are subtle and high-impact. Models can overfit to common incident patterns and miss novel intrusions, underweight rare but critical signals, or amplify bias in how incidents were historically labeled. They can also create false precision by generating timelines or causal links that appear specific but are not supported by corroborated events. The right approval boundary is that humans validate the factual basis of summaries, confirm that clusters make sense operationally, and explicitly mark any AI-suggested relationships as hypotheses until confirmed. Review should include spot checks against raw evidence, especially for the claims that drive remediation decisions or executive reporting.

Governance and auditability should be designed in from the start, because post-incident analysis is not an experimental playground. Organizations should define what data can be used for AI analysis, how sensitive content is redacted or access-controlled, and how outputs are stored and retained. They should also require that AI processes are logged in a way that supports later review, including model versioning, prompt or configuration tracking, and the identity of human approvers. This is not bureaucracy for its own sake; it prevents rework and dispute when a stakeholder challenges a conclusion or when an external party requests supporting evidence. A defensible governance model makes AI usage safer precisely because it limits where the model can quietly become the source of truth.

The best operational use of AI is to reduce the cost of consistency across incidents, not to produce a perfect explanation for any single event. When AI helps standardize incident narratives, normalize tagging, and keep corrective actions linked to recurring control gaps, it enables meaningful trend analysis and portfolio-level improvement. When it highlights evidence gaps, inconsistent classification, or missing telemetry, it improves the integrity of future investigations. This is how AI strengthens the learning loop: it makes it easier to see patterns, harder to ignore recurring weaknesses, and faster to translate lessons into validated change. The measure of success is not that the model "understands" incidents, but that the organization becomes more rigorous in how it captures evidence and more effective in how it acts on what it learns.

Turning Incidents into Long-Term Resilience

Long-term resilience is not achieved by eliminating incidents but by ensuring that each incident permanently improves how the organization absorbs shock and continues operating. Incidents reveal where defenses bend, where they break, and where people compensate through improvisation. Turning those revelations into resilience requires intentional follow-through that reshapes controls, workflows, and decision authority, rather than simply restoring the status quo. The difference between recovery and resilience is whether the organization is materially harder to disrupt the next time conditions are similar. Resilient organizations expect incidents and design their systems and teams to degrade gracefully instead of failing catastrophically.

Resilience begins with acknowledging that prevention will never be complete and that response quality determines business impact. Incidents should therefore be evaluated not only on how compromise occurred, but on how effectively the organization limited spread, preserved critical services, and made time-sensitive decisions.

Improvements that shorten time-to-contain, clarify authority, and reduce uncertainty often yield greater resilience gains than marginal improvements in perimeter controls. This perspective reframes incidents as stress tests of the operating model, not just of the security stack. When leaders internalize this view, investments shift toward capabilities that matter during disruption, not only during steady state.

One of the most important resilience outcomes is reducing single points of failure in both technology and decision-making. Incidents often expose fragile dependencies, such as critical services tied to one identity system, one logging pipeline, or one individual with institutional knowledge. Post-incident work should deliberately seek to diversify these dependencies, whether through redundant telemetry paths, clearer delegation of authority, or cross-training of responders and system owners. This does not mean duplicating everything; it means ensuring that the failure of one component or person does not stall containment or recovery. Over time, this approach transforms incidents from existential threats into manageable disruptions.

Resilience also depends on embedding flexibility into controls and procedures, so teams can act decisively without creating unnecessary business harm. Incidents frequently force responders to choose between aggressive containment and operational continuity, and rigid controls can turn that choice into a false dilemma. Lessons learned should drive the creation of safer containment options, pre-approved emergency actions, and well-defined rollback paths that reduce the risk of acting quickly. This includes clarifying who can authorize disruptive actions and under what conditions, so time is not lost negotiating authority during an active threat. When these guardrails are in place, teams can move faster with confidence rather than hesitation.

Organizational resilience grows when incident-driven improvements are prioritized based on recurrence and impact, not on visibility or convenience. It is easy to fix the most obvious issue from a recent incident while leaving deeper systemic weaknesses untouched. A resilience-oriented program looks across incidents to identify patterns that repeatedly amplify impact, such as delayed access revocation, incomplete asset inventories, or unclear ownership during escalation. Addressing these patterns yields compounding benefits because each fix reduces risk across multiple future scenarios. This portfolio view prevents resilience work from being consumed by one-off fixes that feel productive but do not materially change outcomes.

People and culture are as critical to resilience as technology, because incidents test how teams communicate and coordinate under stress. Organizations that punish disclosure or second-guess decisions after the fact create responders who hesitate, escalate late, or avoid declaring incidents until damage is undeniable. Turning incidents into resilience requires reinforcing behaviors that support early reporting, candid assessment, and decisive action, even when outcomes are imperfect. Leadership behavior during and after incidents sets the tone, especially when tradeoffs are unavoidable. When teams trust that reasonable decisions made under uncertainty will be supported, response quality improves in ways no tool can replicate.

AI and automation can support resilience by making improvements durable and repeatable, but they should be applied to strengthen fundamentals rather than to mask weaknesses. Used well, AI can help track recurring failure modes, validate that corrective actions remain effective over time, and alert leaders when response behaviors drift. Automation can enforce guardrails, such as ensuring logs remain enabled or access revocation workflows execute reliably under load. The risk is using AI to create the appearance of sophistication without addressing underlying fragility, which leaves the organization brittle when assumptions break. Resilience comes from disciplined use of technology to reinforce good operating practices, not from complexity alone.

The ultimate test of resilience is whether the organization responds better to the next incident without needing heroics. Improvements should show up as clearer roles, faster and more confident decisions, fewer surprises about system behavior, and less disruption to critical services. Over time, incidents should feel more predictable in their management, even if the threats themselves evolve. When that happens, incidents stop being existential events and become catalysts for continuous strengthening. This is the point at which post-incident learning fulfills its purpose: not merely to explain what went wrong, but to ensure the organization emerges stronger, steadier, and better prepared for the uncertainty ahead.

Conclusion

Post-incident learning earns its place in operations when it consistently converts hard experience into durable change that can be verified in both the environment and the team's behavior. The work succeeds when root causes are addressed without ignoring contributing factors, corrective actions are tracked to evidence-based closure, and detections, policies, and procedures evolve in a coordinated way rather than as isolated fixes. Improvement is credible when metrics reflect true capability under stress, lessons travel across teams without blame, and institutional memory remains usable as systems and staff change. With disciplined governance and evidence integrity—especially where AI accelerates clustering, trend detection, and synthesis—the organization becomes measurably more resilient, responding faster and more confidently with fewer repeat failures and less reliance on heroics.

Recommendations

1) Treat lessons learned as an operational capability with defined inputs and accountable outputs. Require a structured incident package that links findings to evidence and translates conclusions into specific changes that can be tested. Ensure every lesson has an owner, a deadline, and a validation method, so the work results in measurable risk reduction rather than narrative closure.
2) Distinguish root cause from contributing factors in every post-incident review. State the root cause as a testable condition that, if removed, would have prevented the incident from unfolding as it did, and document contributing factors that increased impact or prolonged recovery. Use this separation to prioritize prevention work while still investing in resilience improvements that shorten time-to-contain and reduce blast radius.
3) Write control gaps as persistent weaknesses rather than as incident symptoms. Express each gap in terms of a specific control objective and the exact condition that failed or was absent, such as coverage limitations, configuration weaknesses, or authority ambiguity. Use this approach to avoid one-off fixes that feel satisfying but do not change the underlying exposure.
4) Track corrective actions like a risk portfolio, not a checklist. Assign actions to accountable owners with the authority to drive cross-team work, and decompose large remediations into smaller deliverables that each reduce exposure. Define evidence-based closure criteria, so "done" reflects validated effectiveness rather than effort spent.
5) Update detections based on what the incident proved about signal quality, routing, and coverage. Refine logic to reduce ambiguity, add enrichment that speeds triage, and adjust severity thresholds, so truly risky conditions reliably interrupt the right people. Validate that required telemetry exists and remains available at the needed granularity and retention, then test that the updated detections fire as expected in the live environment.
6) Update policies to remove ambiguity and to reflect how decisions must be made under operational stress. Clarify authority for containment actions, exception handling, and emergency access, so response is not delayed by negotiation during an active incident. Keep policy changes enforceable and scoped, and ensure procedures and runbooks operationalize policy intent in a way teams can follow during disruption.
7) Revise procedures and runbooks to reduce cognitive load and prevent improvisation from becoming the default. Make decision points explicit, document prerequisites and rollback paths for containment actions, and encode the minimum viable response steps that must occur even when staffing is thin. Exercise revised procedures, so the organization validates that they work under realistic constraints rather than assuming they will.
8) Measure improvement using paired time and quality signals to resist metric gaming. Track time-to-detect and time-to-contain alongside correctness and completeness indicators such as evidence package quality, severity

classification accuracy, and unnecessary containment reversals. Stratify results by incident type and impact, so trends reflect capability change rather than shifts in attacker behavior or reclassification habits.

9) Share lessons across teams in a way that preserves accountability without assigning blame. Ground discussions in observable facts, decision points, and systemic constraints, and tailor detail to the audience, so engineering teams receive actionable specifics while leaders receive risk and priority clarity. Connect shared lessons directly to tracked corrective actions, so teams see follow-through and trust the process.
10) Use AI to accelerate clustering and trend detection while protecting evidence integrity and human judgment. Treat AI outputs as hypotheses and derived analysis that must be corroborated, versioned, and traceable back to immutable source artifacts. Apply clear governance on data access, retention, and auditability, so AI improves consistency and insight without becoming an unreviewed source of truth.

Part VII

People, Training, and Organizational Resilience

26

Security Awareness and Workforce Enablement

Security awareness and workforce enablement shape defensive outcomes because security controls ultimately depend on how people interpret cues, make tradeoffs, and execute decisions under pressure. Effective programs distinguish between awareness that keeps risk signals visible and training that builds role-specific competence, then reinforce both through realistic practice, clear reporting paths, and leadership-supported verification norms. Measurement must go beyond participation to prove real-world impact by tracking behaviors like time-to-report, adherence to verification steps, and reductions in risky workarounds, especially in higher-risk functions. As organizations change and attackers adapt, AI can help scale and personalize content and surface emerging patterns, but only with strong governance, human-in-the-loop approval, and auditable controls to prevent drift, false confidence, and misuse.

Why Human Behavior Shapes Defensive Outcomes

Security controls do not fail in isolation; they fail at the seams where people interpret intent, make tradeoffs, and choose the next action under time pressure. Most incidents still require a human decision somewhere in the chain, whether that is approving an MFA prompt, opening an attachment, reusing a password, or escalating an odd system behavior instead of ignoring it. Those decisions are shaped by incentives, workload, and how clearly "normal" versus "suspicious" is defined in daily work. When defenders treat human behavior as an unpredictable variable rather than an operational dependency, they end up designing controls that look strong on paper but collapse in production.

Attackers exploit reliable cognitive patterns, not just technical weaknesses, because people can be induced to cooperate with an intrusion. Social engineering succeeds when it aligns with existing workflows, especially around urgency, authority, and ambiguity. A finance analyst who is measured on speed will act differently when a request appears to come from a senior executive minutes before a deadline. A developer pushed to ship will accept risk differently when security feels like an external gate instead of an embedded guardrail. Defensive outcomes improve when organizations acknowledge these realities and engineer the environment so secure behavior is the path of least resistance.

The most costly behavior gaps are often "near-misses" that never become visible because they do not trigger a security alert. Repeatedly clicking through browser warnings, tolerating unexpected login prompts, disabling protective features to "get work done," or sharing files through unsanctioned channels are all signals that security friction is misaligned with business operations. These patterns matter because they create a predictable attack surface that an adversary can study and scale. If a workforce routinely works around controls, it is not a workforce problem; it is a control design problem with behavioral consequences. Table 26.1 links common attacker pressures to the decision points they target and the secure behaviors that shift outcomes toward reduced impact.

Table 26.1 Human Decision Points and Defensive Outcomes.

Decision Point	Common Attacker Pressure	Secure Behavior	Defensive Outcome
Unexpected login prompt	Urgency and confusion	Do not approve and report early	Prevents account takeover
Unusual request from authority	Authority and secrecy	Verify out-of-band	Blocks impersonation
External invoice change request	Deadline pressure	Follow verification steps	Prevents fraudulent payment
Unexpected file or link	Curiosity and routine	Report and use approved channels	Reduces malware exposure
Control friction workaround	Get work done fast	Escalate process friction	Reduces repeatable risk

Security awareness becomes operationally meaningful when it builds specific, repeatable actions instead of testing trivia. Employees do not need to memorize threat actor names; they need to recognize the moments where a safe pause is warranted and know exactly what to do next. "Report suspicious email" must be a single, low-effort motion, with clear feedback loops, so reporting feels valuable rather than performative. Likewise, verifying an unusual request should be normalized and supported by leadership, so a junior employee can challenge a request without fear of penalty. When the organization makes secure actions routine, adversary tactics that rely on embarrassment, haste, or deference lose leverage.

Workforce enablement also requires calibrated trust boundaries, because humans are routinely asked to make decisions with incomplete information. Controls that demand perfect judgment from every employee are brittle, and they silently transfer risk to the business by making security dependent on individual vigilance. Better outcomes come from layered design: reduce exposure where possible, add verification where it matters, and reserve human decisions for the cases where context is genuinely required. This is why clear approval boundaries and escalation paths matter as much as training content; people should know when they are authorized to act and when they must hand off to specialists. The handoff must be fast and psychologically safe, or employees will default to "solve it myself," which is how small issues become incidents.

AI and machine learning can improve defensive outcomes by reducing cognitive load and tailoring guidance to real work, but only when their outputs are treated as decision support rather than authority. Pattern-based models can flag unusual messaging characteristics, likely impersonation attempts, or anomalous authentication prompts and then present the user with a plain-language rationale and a single recommended next step. The utility depends on telemetry quality and workflow integration: signals must be timely, contextual, and mapped to actions that employees can actually take. Human-in-the-loop controls are essential, including clear labeling of confidence, escalation triggers when uncertainty is high, and auditing that shows what the model recommended versus what the user did. Failure modes must be assumed up front, including false confidence that causes users to ignore their instincts, drift as attacker tactics adapt, and leakage risks if sensitive content is sent to systems without appropriate governance.

Measuring behavior is where many programs either become credible or remain aspirational, because what is not observed cannot be improved. Useful measures emphasize outcomes and friction, such as reporting rates, time-to-report, false reporting burden on responders, and the frequency of policy workarounds observed through help desk tickets or access requests. Metrics should be interpreted as system feedback, not employee grading, or they will drive underreporting and compliance theater. Leaders should expect to see "hot spots" tied to business processes, such as high-risk approvals or recurring exceptions, and then treat them as candidates for redesign. When human behavior is treated as a first-class element of defense, security becomes a capability the workforce can execute reliably, not a standard they are expected to remember.

Security Awareness Versus Security Training

Security awareness and security training are often discussed as if they are interchangeable, but they serve different operational purposes and should be designed to produce different kinds of outcomes. Awareness is primarily about attention management: keeping security-relevant cues visible in the middle of competing priorities, so people notice and pause at the right moments. Training is about skill acquisition: building the ability to perform specific security tasks correctly and consistently under realistic conditions. When organizations treat awareness as a substitute for training, they create workforces that can repeat messages but cannot execute secure behaviors when the situation is ambiguous or stressful.

Awareness works best when it is short, frequent, and tightly aligned to the decision points employees actually face. Its value is not in the volume of content delivered but in the precision of the prompt and the timing of the reminder relative to real work. A simple nudge about verifying payment change requests is effective when it appears during finance workflows, not as a generic annual slide deck. Awareness also functions as a cultural signal that leadership expects and supports secure behaviors, especially when it reinforces that reporting and verification are normal and appreciated. If it feels like compliance theater, employees will learn to click through it and ignore the intent.

Training, by contrast, must be role-specific and measurable because its purpose is operational competence. A developer needs secure coding practices tied to the languages and deployment patterns they use, while a help desk technician needs identity verification procedures that stand up to impersonation attempts. Training should teach not only what to do but what "good" looks like, including how to document an action, how to escalate, and what constitutes sufficient evidence for a decision. It should also be delivered in a way that respects the cognitive realities of the job, using scenario-based practice that mirrors real tickets, real messages, and real constraints. When training is abstract, teams will improvise in production, and improvisation is where errors become repeatable. This comparison distinguishes awareness as attention management and training as skill acquisition and shows the different measures that indicate success for each. It reinforces why completion and quiz scores alone are not proof of readiness or reduced risk (Figure 26.1).

A key difference is how each should be evaluated, because measuring the wrong thing drives the wrong behavior. Awareness is best assessed through behavioral indicators such as reporting rates, time-to-report, and reductions in high-friction workarounds, not through quiz scores that reward memorization. Training should be assessed

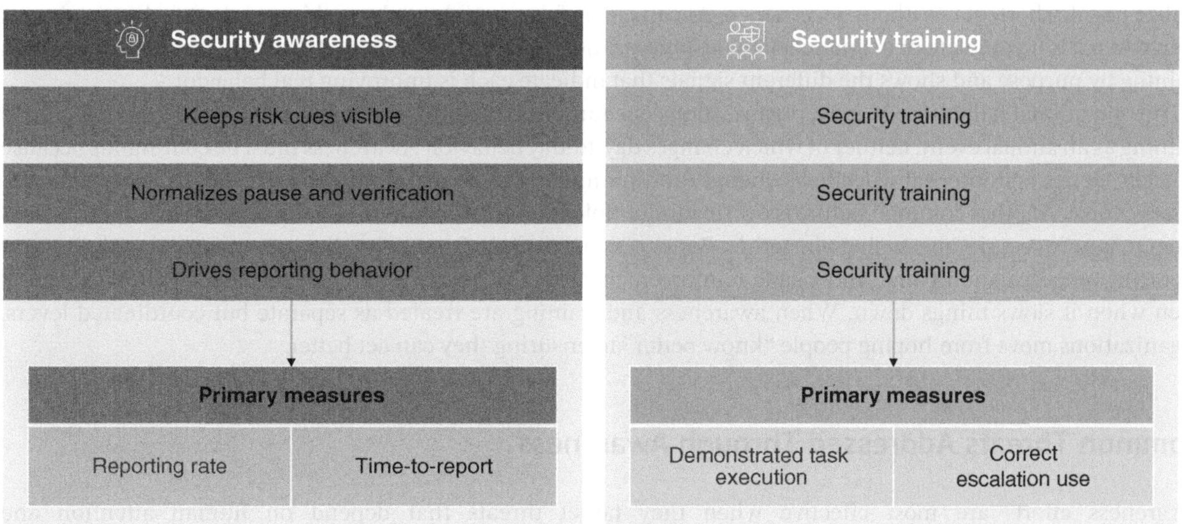

Figure 26.1 Awareness Versus Training and How Each Is Measured.

Table 26.2 Awareness Versus Training Outcomes and Measures.

Program Element	Primary Purpose	What It Builds	Best Evidence of Impact
Security awareness	Attention management	Recognition of risk cues	Improved reporting rate
Security awareness	Behavior normalization	Pause and verify habit	Faster time-to-report
Security training	Skill acquisition	Role task competence	Demonstrated task execution
Security training	Operational clarity	Authority and escalation use	Correct escalation usage
Security training	Practice under pressure	Consistent verification behavior	Fewer risky exceptions

through demonstrated capability, such as the ability to follow a secure process end-to-end, correctly classify a request, or complete a task without introducing risk. In practice, that means exercises, simulations, peer review, or validated checklists tied to real duties. If the only measurement is completion, the organization is measuring attendance rather than readiness.

The most effective programs coordinate awareness and training, so they reinforce each other rather than compete for attention. Awareness can create common language and expectations across the workforce, while training builds depth where specific responsibilities demand it. A practical pattern is to use awareness to reduce ambiguity for everyone and then use training to harden high-risk roles where a single mistake has outsized impact. This coordination matters for executives because it improves predictability: fewer avoidable incidents, faster escalation when something looks wrong, and less reliance on individual heroics. It also reduces operational drag by aligning security behaviors to business workflows instead of layering friction on top.

AI can strengthen both efforts if it is used to personalize support and reduce noise without undermining human judgment. For awareness, models can identify emerging phishing themes, common pretext patterns, or communication channels where risky behaviors cluster, then shape micro-messages that target those realities rather than generic warnings. For training, AI-assisted scenario generation can produce realistic practice cases based on incident patterns and internal workflows, while still enforcing guardrails, so sensitive data is not exposed and the content remains accurate. Human-in-the-loop controls are essential: security and learning teams should approve content, monitor for drift toward misleading examples, and audit outcomes, so the system does not quietly normalize unsafe shortcuts. Without governance, AI can create false confidence by making content feel authoritative even when it is incomplete or mismatched to the organization's processes. Table 26.2 distinguishes awareness from training by purpose and shows the different signals that indicate each is improving real behavior.

The operational failure mode most organizations encounter is treating awareness as a one-time campaign and training as an annual event, neither of which changes day-to-day behavior. Awareness must be continuous because attacker tactics and internal workflows change, and training must be maintained because skills decay and processes evolve. Another common failure is overloading employees with content that is not actionable, which teaches them to ignore security messaging altogether. Better outcomes come from tight alignment to real decisions, clear reporting and escalation paths, and visible reinforcement from leadership when employees take the safer option even when it slows things down. When awareness and training are treated as separate but coordinated levers, organizations move from hoping people "know better" to ensuring they can act better.

Common Threats Addressed Through Awareness

Awareness efforts are most effective when they target threats that depend on human attention and decision-making rather than deep technical exploitation. These are the attacks that succeed because they blend into normal work, borrow credibility from trusted brands or colleagues, and create time pressure that nudges people toward compliance. The goal is not to teach employees to become investigators, but to help them recognize the small set of cues that reliably indicate elevated risk. When awareness focuses on those cues and ties them to a clear next action, it measurably reduces the attacker's ability to scale.

Phishing remains the most common category because it is inexpensive for adversaries and adaptable to nearly any environment. The modern version is often more convincing than the generic "password expired" message because it is tailored to job roles, current events, and organizational language. Employees do not need to learn to analyze email headers to be useful; they need to notice mismatches between the request and the context, such as unexpected urgency, unusual file-sharing links, or requests that bypass normal channels. Awareness also needs to normalize reporting without shame, because attackers improve their targeting based on what goes unreported and therefore unmeasured. When reporting becomes routine, defenders gain early warning and can disrupt campaigns before they spread.

Credential theft and account takeover are addressed through awareness because they frequently hinge on a person being tricked into providing or approving access. Password reuse, entering credentials into a look-alike login page, or approving an MFA prompt that the user did not initiate are all behaviors that awareness can influence with simple, repeated guidance. The most practical message is behavioral and situational: if you did not start a login, do not approve a prompt, and treat the event as suspicious. This is also where awareness must align with operational support, because people will ignore guidance if they do not know who to contact or if they expect punitive consequences for reporting. A fast, nonjudgmental response loop makes it easier for employees to choose the safer option.

Business email compromise and impersonation scams are particularly well-suited to awareness because they exploit trust in roles and relationships rather than malicious attachments. The attacker's objective is typically to redirect payments, change bank details, obtain sensitive information, or induce an employee to purchase items or share access under a plausible pretext. The cues are often subtle, such as a slight change in tone, an unusual request outside normal approval paths, or a message that insists on secrecy. Effective awareness emphasizes verification over suspicion: use known contact methods, confirm through a second channel, and treat deviations in process as the risk signal. That framing reduces social friction and makes verification a standard business behavior.

Malicious attachments and unsafe downloads are still relevant, but awareness should focus on the decision points employees control rather than the technical details of malware families. The risk is highest when a file arrives unexpectedly, requires enabling macros, requests elevated permissions, or is presented as a "fix" to an invented problem. Awareness should connect these cues to safe alternatives, such as using sanctioned file-sharing channels, validating the source through a separate contact method, and reporting the message for analysis. The failure mode to avoid is fear-based messaging that causes employees to stop sharing legitimate documents or to route everything through informal workarounds. The emphasis should be on predictable handling, not blanket avoidance.

Social engineering also extends beyond email into phone calls, chat platforms, and ticketing systems, where attackers imitate support staff, executives, or vendors. These channels are often trusted because they feel immediate and conversational, which makes them ideal for pressuring an employee into quick action. Awareness can reduce this risk by reinforcing simple identity verification behaviors, especially for help desks and anyone with access to sensitive systems. The objective is to make identity checks feel normal, not adversarial, and to give employees permission to slow down when something does not align with established process. When leadership models that behavior, the organization becomes harder to manipulate.

AI can strengthen awareness by detecting emerging social engineering patterns and adapting messaging based on real observed attempts, but it also introduces its own risks if used without governance. Models can help triage user-reported messages, cluster similar lures, and surface the most common cues, so awareness content stays current and specific. That usefulness depends on telemetry from email, collaboration platforms, authentication events, and reporting workflows, and it requires careful handling to avoid leaking sensitive content into systems without proper controls. Human review remains essential because attackers deliberately craft messages to exploit model blind spots and because overly confident AI labeling can cause employees to either ignore real threats or dismiss their own instincts. The best operational posture treats AI as an accelerator for analysis and targeting, while keeping the final messaging and escalation decisions anchored in accountable human judgment.

Designing Training That Changes Behavior

Training changes behavior only when it is built around the decisions people actually make and the constraints they operate under. Most employees do not fail because they lack awareness that threats exist; they fail because the secure action is unclear, inconvenient, or socially risky in the moment it matters. Effective training starts by mapping the high-risk workflows where a single mistake creates outsized exposure, such as approving access, handling sensitive data, or executing financial changes. It then teaches the specific actions that reduce that exposure, in the same tools, language, and pace that the job demands. When training is detached from real work, it becomes a compliance artifact rather than an operational capability.

Role specificity is the foundation because different functions face different threat pressures and have different authority boundaries. An executive assistant needs practical patterns for handling urgent requests that appear to come from leadership, while an engineer needs secure handling of secrets and access tokens during development and deployment. A help desk technician needs repeatable identity verification steps that withstand social engineering, while a finance team needs verification procedures for payment changes that do not collapse under deadline pressure. Training should explicitly clarify who is allowed to approve what, what evidence is required, and when escalation is mandatory. This reduces ambiguity, which is where attackers thrive and well-intentioned employees improvise.

Scenario-based practice is what turns knowledge into behavior because it forces people to act, not just agree with statements. Good scenarios reflect the organization's reality: the tone of internal communications, the actual approval chains, and the common workarounds people use when systems slow them down. The training should include both straightforward cases and the "gray zone" cases where the right answer is to pause, verify, and escalate rather than to decide alone. Practicing those moments builds muscle memory, and muscle memory is what holds up when an attacker creates urgency or when employees are fatigued. The point is not to embarrass participants but to normalize safe hesitation and consistent verification.

Training must also build confidence in the reporting and escalation path, because behavior does not change if people believe they will be ignored or blamed. Participants should leave knowing exactly how to report, what information to include, and what response to expect, so the action feels safe and worthwhile. When possible, training should demonstrate what happens after a report: how responders evaluate it, how containment decisions are made, and how the reporter is informed. This closes the loop and turns reporting into a collaborative act rather than a bureaucratic chore. Without that loop, employees learn that reporting creates friction with no visible benefit.

Measurement is where behavior-focused training separates itself from checkbox programs, because the goal is competence, not completion. The most useful measures are tied to observable actions: faster reporting of suspicious messages, fewer unsafe approvals, reduced use of unsanctioned tools, and fewer preventable access exceptions. Training assessments should test execution, such as walking through an identity verification script, correctly classifying a request, or demonstrating the steps for handling a suspicious attachment. If the only signal is a passing score on a quiz, the organization is measuring recall, not performance. Over time, trends in incident data and near-miss reporting should shape which scenarios are emphasized, so training remains aligned to real risk.

AI can enhance behavior change when it is used to tailor training to observed patterns and to provide safe practice at scale. Models can help generate realistic scenarios based on recent lures, common impersonation attempts, or frequent process deviations, and they can adapt difficulty to match different roles and maturity levels. The dependencies are practical: access to sanitized examples, telemetry from reporting systems, and clear rules about what data can be used, so training content does not accidentally expose sensitive information. Human-in-the-loop controls are critical, including expert review of generated scenarios, monitoring for drift toward misleading or unrealistic cases, and auditability of what content was delivered to whom. Without these controls, AI can introduce failure modes such as reinforcing incorrect assumptions, embedding subtle bias about which users are "risky," or creating false confidence because the training feels sophisticated.

Finally, training that changes behavior treats secure actions as part of operational excellence, not as a separate moral requirement. People change when the secure path is practical, socially supported, and reinforced through consistent leadership behavior, especially when someone chooses verification over speed. Training should acknowledge tradeoffs and teach how to handle them, including what to do when a process is too slow or when an exception seems necessary. That is also where training becomes a feedback mechanism for improving controls: repeated friction points identified during exercises should trigger process refinement rather than repeated admonitions to "be careful." When the organization uses training to sharpen workflows and reduce ambiguity, the workforce becomes more resilient and the defender's job becomes less dependent on luck.

Engagement Techniques and Practical Reinforcement

Engagement is not about making security entertaining; it is about ensuring the message is retained and applied when work is moving fast. People ignore content that feels generic, disconnected from their role, or delivered at the wrong time, especially when they are already overloaded. Effective engagement starts with relevance: speak directly to the decisions employees make, the systems they touch, and the consequences they care about. When the content is clearly tied to their daily reality, attention follows without needing gimmicks or theatrics.

Practical reinforcement is what turns a one-time lesson into a durable habit, and it works best when it is embedded in normal workflows. Short, repeated nudges aligned to high-risk moments—such as receiving external invoices, approving access, or sharing sensitive files—create a consistent pattern of "pause, verify, act." Reinforcement also benefits from immediacy, meaning employees should see guidance close to the moment of action rather than weeks later in a quarterly module. This is where operational design matters: a simple reporting mechanism, clear verification steps, and an escalation path that responds quickly are all forms of reinforcement because they make the secure behavior easier to perform. If the only reinforcement is periodic messaging, the organization is relying on memory instead of systems.

Simulations are an effective engagement tool when they are designed as learning events rather than punishment events. A well-run simulation creates an experience that feels realistic, gives employees a safe opportunity to practice, and provides immediate feedback that explains why the cue mattered and what action would have reduced risk. The feedback must be constructive and specific, focusing on what to do next time rather than on blame or embarrassment. If simulations are used to name and shame, employees will learn to hide mistakes and avoid reporting, which weakens defense more than the simulation strengthens it. Engagement improves when employees trust that practice is meant to help them succeed.

Reinforcement also depends on social signals, because behavior is heavily influenced by what leaders tolerate and reward. Employees notice whether managers support verification steps that slow things down, or whether speed is implicitly prioritized over safety. Visible leadership participation—such as leaders following verification procedures, reporting suspicious messages, and praising careful decision-making—creates a permission structure for secure behavior. This matters most in high-pressure roles where an attacker can exploit urgency or authority, because employees need to know they are allowed to challenge unusual requests. When leaders reinforce secure actions in the moment, awareness stops being an abstract value and becomes a normal expectation.

AI can support engagement by targeting reinforcement where it will have the most impact, but it must be governed to avoid eroding trust. Models can identify recurring risky patterns, such as departments receiving high volumes of impersonation attempts or workflows where users frequently approve unexpected access prompts. This allows reinforcement to be timely and specific, which is the difference between useful reminders and background noise. The system must be transparent about how prompts are generated and must avoid turning engagement into surveillance, because perceived monitoring can drive avoidance behavior and reduce reporting. Human oversight should review targeting logic, ensure messaging stays accurate, and audit outcomes, so the program is improving behavior rather than simply increasing alerts.

Practical reinforcement should include closing the feedback loop, because people change faster when they see that their actions matter. When an employee reports a suspicious message, they should receive acknowledgment and, when appropriate, a brief explanation of what was found and what action was taken. This transforms reporting from a chore into a contribution and helps employees calibrate their instincts over time. The same loop applies to process improvements: if repeated training feedback reveals that a verification step is too slow or confusing, fixing the workflow is a reinforcement mechanism because it reduces friction at the moment of truth. When employees see that their experiences shape the system, engagement becomes self-sustaining.

Finally, engagement techniques should be treated as part of operational resilience, not as a communications campaign. The objective is consistent execution of a small set of high-value behaviors: pause on anomalies, verify out-of-band when needed, report quickly, and follow established approval boundaries. Reinforcement should be continuous and adaptive, shifting as attacker tactics and internal workflows evolve, while staying anchored to the same core actions. Over time, the organization should expect fewer repeatable mistakes, faster escalation of real issues, and less dependence on individual heroics. When engagement is built around practice, feedback, and system design, it becomes a durable control that strengthens defensive outcomes in measurable ways.

Role-Based Training for Higher-Risk Functions

Role-based training is necessary because the highest impact failures occur in functions that sit at critical control points: identity, access, money movement, privileged systems, and sensitive data handling. Generic messaging cannot prepare these roles for the specific social engineering, process abuse, and decision pressure they face daily. The objective is not to create security experts, but to ensure these functions can execute a small set of high-risk actions reliably and defensibly. Training should be built around the real workflows and approval boundaries that govern their work, because attackers succeed when people are forced to improvise under ambiguity.

Higher-risk functions require training that is explicit about authority and verification, especially where requests can be plausibly urgent or politically sensitive. Finance teams need repeatable procedures for payment changes, invoice disputes, and vendor onboarding, including what evidence is required before a change is approved and how to validate requests through known channels. Executives and their support staff need training that addresses impersonation and urgency tactics without placing them in the position of being the "weak link," emphasizing that verification protects leadership as much as it protects the enterprise. HR teams need guidance on handling sensitive personal data, unusual requests for employee information, and the risks of sharing documents through informal channels. In each case, training should define the safest default behavior when information is incomplete: pause, verify, and escalate rather than decide alone.

Identity and access functions, including help desks and IAM administrators, warrant deeper practice because they are routinely targeted with pretexts designed to bypass authentication and account recovery controls. These teams should be trained to follow identity verification scripts consistently, even when the requester is frustrated, senior, or claiming an emergency. The training must include the common failure modes: accepting partial identifiers, relying on caller-provided information that can be obtained from public sources, and skipping steps to "be helpful." It should also define what to do when the verification process itself becomes a friction point, such as routing requests to a higher assurance path rather than lowering standards. The goal is consistency, because attackers probe for the one person who will bend the process.

Privileged technical functions, including system administrators and engineering roles with elevated access, need training that treats mistakes as operational risk events rather than personal failures. The focus should be on secure handling of credentials and secrets, disciplined change control for access and monitoring configurations, and recognition of abnormal requests that could signal compromise. Scenarios should include realistic pressures, such as a late-night request to disable a control, "temporary" access that tends to become permanent, or a request to run a script from an unfamiliar source. Training should reinforce that privileged actions must be traceable, reversible, and justified, because accountability is part of security posture. When privileged users understand how quickly small shortcuts become persistent exposure, they are more likely to resist unsafe requests.

Role-based training must also reflect the operational handoffs that occur between functions, because many incidents succeed at the boundary between teams. A help desk may reset an account that then enables a finance fraud, or an HR disclosure may enable a targeted phishing attempt against an executive assistant. Training should include these cross-functional dependency points, so teams understand how their actions can enable or block downstream attacks. That understanding helps employees treat verification steps as protecting colleagues, not as bureaucratic obstacles. It also creates shared language for escalation, which reduces delay when something feels off.

AI can improve role-based training by tailoring scenarios to the threats and workflow deviations actually observed in each function, but it must be bounded to avoid introducing new risk. Models can help identify patterns in reported incidents, suspicious requests, or access exceptions and then generate practice scenarios that match the tone and structure of real attempts. This requires careful data handling, so sensitive tickets, personal data, or internal communications are not exposed to systems without appropriate governance and logging. Human review is essential to validate that scenarios teach the intended behavior and do not accidentally normalize insecure practices. The organization should also audit whether AI-personalized training changes outcomes, such as reducing risky approvals or improving time-to-escalation, rather than simply increasing engagement metrics.

Sustaining role-based training requires operational reinforcement, because high-risk functions are often high-volume environments where fatigue drives shortcuts. Short refresher exercises tied to common failure points, periodic process walk-throughs, and after-action reviews of near-misses keep skills current without overwhelming teams. Reinforcement should also include clear support from leadership when employees follow verification procedures that slow work down, particularly when the requester is senior or the situation is urgent. If leadership rewards speed at the expense of verification, training will not survive contact with reality. When leadership rewards defensible process adherence, the secure behavior becomes a protected norm.

Ultimately, role-based training succeeds when it produces consistent execution and defensible decisions in the moments attackers exploit. It clarifies authority boundaries, reduces ambiguity, and makes escalation a normal part of doing the job well. It also reduces organizational dependence on individual judgment by standardizing actions that should not be left to personal discretion. When high-risk functions are trained as operational control points rather than as recipients of generic awareness, the enterprise becomes measurably harder to manipulate through human channels. That shift is a practical reduction in risk, achieved through better decisions at the exact places adversaries prefer to apply pressure.

Measuring Participation and Real-World Impact

Participation is the easiest thing to measure and the easiest thing to misinterpret. Completion rates, attendance, and time spent in modules tell you whether content was delivered, not whether risk was reduced. Participation metrics still matter because they reveal coverage gaps across locations, functions, and employment types, and those gaps often map directly to exposure. The operational mistake is treating participation as a proxy for preparedness, which leads leaders to declare success while the same preventable behaviors persist.

A credible measurement approach starts by separating input metrics from outcome metrics and then tying both to a small set of behaviors the organization expects. Inputs include enrollment, completion, recency, and role-based coverage, which are necessary for governance and accountability. Outcomes show whether people actually use the taught behaviors, such as reporting suspicious messages, refusing unsafe requests, verifying identity through approved steps, and escalating anomalies rather than working around controls. The difference matters because a workforce can have perfect completion rates and still approve fraudulent payment changes under pressure. Measuring both creates a more truthful picture of where the program is reaching people and where it is changing decisions.

Real-world impact is best detected through operational signals that already exist across security and business processes. Reporting rates and time-to-report are strong indicators because they reflect attention, confidence in the reporting path, and willingness to act without fear of blame. Trends in near-miss reporting are often more valuable than incident counts, because they show how often employees encountered something suspicious and chose to surface it early. Help desk and access request data can reveal workarounds and friction points, which are behavioral indicators that controls are misaligned with reality. When these signals are correlated over time, you can see whether reinforcement is improving decision-making or whether employees are simply learning how to pass a quiz.

Exercises and simulations add another layer of measurement by testing behavior under realistic conditions, but they must be interpreted carefully. A simulation outcome should be treated as diagnostic feedback about workflow and decision pressure, not as a scorecard for punishment. If employees stop reporting because they fear being labeled "failed," the program will show fewer clicks but also fewer early warnings, which is operationally worse. The most useful simulation metrics focus on time-to-report, correct use of verification steps, and appropriate escalation, because those map to defensive outcomes. When simulation results are used to refine processes and reinforce expectations, they become a measurement engine for resilience rather than a compliance trap.

Role-based impact requires role-based measures, because the highest risk functions have different expected behaviors and different consequences for mistakes. For finance, impact may look like consistent out-of-band verification for payment changes and a measurable reduction in last-minute exception requests. For help desks and IAM teams, impact shows up as adherence to identity verification steps, fewer "emergency" bypasses, and quicker escalation when verification fails. For engineers and administrators, impact may be reflected in fewer risky privilege expansions, better discipline around secrets handling, and fewer unreviewed changes to monitoring and access configurations. These measures should be grounded in workflow evidence, so the organization is evaluating execution, not intention.

AI and machine learning can help quantify impact by turning high-volume operational data into interpretable trends, but measurement systems need guardrails to avoid false certainty. Models can cluster similar user-reported messages to show whether targeted lures are increasing or shrinking, detect shifts in reporting behavior by business unit, and identify workflows where exception rates spike after organizational changes. The dependency is consistent telemetry: reporting events, authentication prompts, ticket metadata, and workflow timestamps must be captured in a way that supports analysis without exposing sensitive content unnecessarily. Human review remains necessary to validate that observed changes reflect real behavior change rather than reporting fatigue, shifting attacker tactics, or measurement artifacts. Governance should also require auditability, including what data was used, how it was interpreted, and how measurement results influenced training decisions.

Measurement must ultimately support decision-making, which means it should drive targeted adjustments instead of producing dashboards that no one uses. If reporting is low in a function that receives high volumes of suspicious requests, the corrective action is not more generic content but tighter reinforcement and simpler reporting paths tailored to that workflow. If participation is high but outcomes are flat, the program should shift toward scenario-based practice and role-specific training where competence can be demonstrated. Leaders should expect measurement to reveal uncomfortable truths, such as controls that push employees toward unsafe workarounds or approval chains that collapse under urgency. When participation metrics are treated as the starting point and operational outcomes as the standard of proof, the organization can show not just that people were trained, but that defensive behavior actually improved.

AI in Training Programs: Content Scaling, Personalization, and Misuse Risks

AI can materially expand the reach of training programs by reducing the time it takes to create, update, and maintain relevant content. Training teams are typically constrained by instructional design capacity, subject matter expert availability, and the pace at which attacker tactics change. When used appropriately, AI can draft scenarios, rewrite content for different roles, and produce variations that keep training fresh without requiring a full rebuild each cycle. The operational value comes from being able to respond to real trends—new impersonation patterns, new process abuse attempts, or shifts in common mistakes—while the learning moment is still close to the risk.

Content scaling is most useful when it preserves consistency while allowing controlled variation. AI can generate multiple scenario versions that target the same underlying behavior, such as verifying payment changes or refusing unexpected access prompts, without repeating identical examples that employees learn to recognize as "training artifacts." It can also accelerate localization by adapting language and cultural cues for different regions while keeping the underlying security expectation identical. Scaling should still be anchored to a canonical set of approved behaviors and escalation paths, because training that varies in meaning across audiences creates ambiguity rather than competence. Good programs treat AI output as a draft layer that is constrained by policy, process, and operational reality.

Personalization is where AI can deliver outsized impact, but it must be designed as enablement rather than surveillance. Personalization can mean tailoring examples to job function, showing scenarios that mirror the tools and approvals a person actually uses, and focusing practice on the specific decision points where that role is most frequently targeted. It can also adapt pacing and difficulty based on demonstrated competence, so experienced staff are challenged with realistic gray-zone cases while new hires learn the fundamentals without being overwhelmed. The telemetry dependencies matter: role metadata, training outcomes, and workflow context must be accurate and current, or personalization becomes mis-targeting that frustrates employees and erodes trust. Clear boundaries are required, so personalization supports performance without implying that individuals are being monitored for punishment. Table 26.3 summarizes where AI can accelerate training and the specific guardrails needed to prevent drift false confidence and misuse.

Human-in-the-loop controls are non-negotiable because training content is itself a form of operational guidance. Subject matter experts should approve scenario templates, verification steps, and escalation instructions, while learning teams validate that the content teaches the intended behaviors without creating confusion. For AI-generated scenarios, review needs to catch subtle errors, such as unrealistic process steps, incorrect assumptions about authority, or examples that inadvertently teach dangerous shortcuts. Programs should also enforce

Table 26.3 AI Use in Training and Required Guardrails.

AI Training Use Case	Dependency	Human Control	Primary Risk
Scenario drafting	Sanitized examples	Expert review and approval	Incorrect guidance
Content variation	Canonical behaviors	Template constraints and review	Inconsistent meaning
Role personalization	Accurate role metadata	Bounded targeting rules	Perceived surveillance
Trend detection	Reporting telemetry	Analyst validation	Measurement artifacts
Automated summaries	Approved reporting workflow	Auditability and labeling	False confidence

approval boundaries for any content that references sensitive workflows, high-risk roles, or incident-derived patterns. Auditability should be built in, so the organization can show what content was delivered, why it was delivered, and what changes were made when issues were discovered.

Failure modes tend to cluster around false authority, drift, and misalignment with real processes. If AI-generated content sounds confident but is slightly wrong, employees may internalize incorrect steps and execute them under pressure, which creates a new risk path rather than closing one. Drift is also inevitable: attacker tactics evolve, internal workflows change, and models can start producing examples that are outdated or biased toward past patterns. Misalignment shows up when training recommends actions employees cannot actually take, such as escalation paths that are slow or unclear, which teaches them that "security guidance" is theoretical. These failure modes are preventable when training content is tightly coupled to operational reality and continuously validated against actual procedures.

Misuse risks extend beyond bad content into adversarial behavior that targets the training system itself. Attackers can use generative techniques to produce highly convincing lures that mimic training themes, exploiting the familiarity employees develop with certain language and cues. There is also risk in how training data is handled: ingesting real emails, tickets, or chat messages without proper sanitization can expose sensitive information and create compliance issues. Another misuse path is internal: over-personalized training can feel punitive, and overly granular analytics can turn a learning program into a perceived monitoring program. When that happens, employees disengage, reporting declines, and the organization loses early warning signals that are more valuable than perfect completion rates.

Governance should treat AI-enabled training as a controlled system with defined data boundaries, quality gates, and accountability. Training teams need explicit rules for what data can be used, how it must be redacted, where it can be processed, and how long it can be retained. Quality gates should include required human review for high-impact content, periodic spot checks for drift, and rollback procedures when issues are found. Measurement should emphasize outcomes—improved reporting, better verification behavior, fewer risky exceptions—rather than celebrating increased content volume or engagement metrics. When governance is clear and consistently applied, AI becomes a multiplier for training effectiveness instead of a new source of operational and reputational risk.

The most practical way to view AI in training is as an accelerator for creating and targeting practice, while keeping responsibility for correctness and intent squarely with accountable humans. Training succeeds when it teaches repeatable behaviors aligned to real workflows, and AI should be constrained to support that objective rather than redefine it. Programs that scale content without control create inconsistency, and programs that personalize without trust create disengagement. The strongest posture is to use AI to shorten the cycle from observed risk to updated practice, while maintaining rigorous review, transparent boundaries, and auditable decision-making. Done well, it increases relevance and retention without sacrificing accuracy, trust, or control.

Maintaining Awareness in Changing Organizations

Security awareness degrades quickly when the organization changes faster than the program adapts. Mergers, reorganizations, new business lines, policy shifts, and tooling changes all alter how work is done, which changes the cues employees rely on to judge what is normal. Attackers benefit from this instability because confusion creates opportunities for impersonation, rushed approvals, and policy workarounds. Maintaining awareness in this environment requires treating it as an operational system that must be refreshed and revalidated, not as a static set of messages delivered on a calendar.

Organizational change also reshapes trust relationships, and those relationships are the substrate that many social engineering attacks exploit. New reporting lines, unfamiliar names in leadership, and new vendors create a background of legitimate "first-time" requests that look similar to fraudulent ones. Employees cannot be expected to memorize every change, so awareness must emphasize verification behaviors that remain valid even when people and processes shift. That means reinforcing the habit of using known channels, confirming unusual requests out-of-band, and escalating when context is missing. When awareness focuses on durable behaviors rather than specific examples, it remains effective through periods of transition.

Onboarding and internal mobility are critical pressure points because they concentrate unfamiliarity and reduce confidence in what "normal" looks like. New hires are less likely to challenge requests, and internal transfers often inherit new systems, data access patterns, and approval chains without fully understanding their risk implications. Awareness must be integrated into these transitions with timely reinforcement, not deferred to an annual training cycle. This includes clear guidance on reporting paths, verification steps for common high-risk requests, and expectations for handling sensitive information in the new role. The goal is to compress the time between entering a new context and becoming competent at recognizing and escalating anomalies within it.

Awareness must also be maintained through ongoing communication changes, especially when organizations adopt new collaboration channels or change how approvals are performed. Attackers follow the path of least resistance, and a new channel often lacks mature norms, controls, and skepticism. Employees may treat chat messages as more trustworthy than email because they feel internal and immediate, even when those channels are increasingly used for impersonation. Maintaining awareness means explicitly extending the same verification standards across channels and ensuring reporting mechanisms work wherever employees communicate. If reporting only works in one place, employees will default to the channel where it is easiest to do their job, not where security would prefer them to be.

AI can help keep awareness current by detecting shifts in attack patterns and workforce behavior as changes occur, but it must be grounded in reliable telemetry and governed carefully. Models can cluster and summarize user-reported messages, highlight emerging impersonation themes, and identify which business units are encountering the most targeted attempts during transitions. This enables awareness content to be updated quickly and aimed at the decisions employees are facing right now, rather than relying on last quarter's examples. The system needs clear data boundaries, including redaction of sensitive content and auditability of how insights were derived, so the program does not introduce privacy or compliance risk. Human oversight is essential to validate that AI-identified trends reflect real threat changes rather than reporting artifacts or shifts in message volume.

A practical maintenance posture includes predictable review cycles tied to organizational events rather than only to time intervals. Significant workflow changes—such as new approval processes, changes in authentication methods, or new third-party relationships—should trigger targeted awareness updates and short reinforcement campaigns. Similarly, major incident learnings and near-miss trends should feed back into awareness content, so the workforce sees that guidance evolves based on real experience. This feedback loop is also a way to reduce cynicism, because employees are more likely to engage when they see that messages are grounded in current realities. The maintenance process should be lightweight but disciplined, with clear ownership and a defined path for updating content quickly.

Finally, maintaining awareness in a changing organization depends on reinforcing trust in the system, not just repeating security advice. Employees will take safe actions when they believe reporting is valued, verification is supported, and the organization will respond constructively. During change, fatigue and uncertainty increase, so the program must reduce ambiguity and friction rather than adding additional demands. Leaders play an outsized role here by modeling verification behavior, supporting employees who slow down to confirm unusual requests, and treating early reporting as a sign of operational strength. When awareness is maintained as a living program aligned to how the organization actually operates, it remains a resilient control even as everything around it shifts.

Conclusion

A resilient security posture is built when the workforce can reliably execute a small set of high-value behaviors at the moments attackers try to create urgency, confusion, or misplaced trust. Awareness keeps those moments visible and normalizes safe hesitation, while training develops the role-specific skills and approval discipline required in higher-risk functions where a single action can cascade into enterprise impact. Programs that measure outcomes—not just completion—earn credibility by demonstrating faster reporting, stronger verification, fewer risky exceptions, and clearer handoffs that reduce both incident frequency and blast radius. AI can accelerate this cycle by improving targeting and content freshness, but defensive outcomes improve only when models are governed, reviewed, and audited, so human judgment remains accountable and operational reality stays the source of truth.

Recommendations

1) Treat human behavior as an operational dependency in your defensive design. Identify the specific decision points where people approve access, move money, share sensitive data, or override safeguards, and assume those moments will be targeted. Reduce ambiguity by making the secure action the easiest action, supported by clear reporting and escalation paths. Revisit controls that repeatedly drive workarounds, because friction is a leading indicator of future failure.
2) Differentiate security awareness from security training and design each to achieve its intended outcome. Use awareness to keep risk cues visible in day-to-day work and to normalize pausing and verifying when context is missing. Use training to build role-specific competence in the tasks that must be executed correctly under pressure. Measure them differently, so completion does not get mistaken for readiness.
3) Focus awareness content on human-dependent threats that scale through routine workflows. Reinforce cues and actions that reduce phishing success, credential compromise, impersonation, and unsafe attachment handling. Normalize verification as a standard business behavior, especially when requests are urgent, unusual, or bypass established channels. Ensure every awareness message points to a concrete next step that employees can execute immediately.
4) Design training around realistic scenarios that mirror your organization's actual workflows and constraints. Build practice that forces decisions in gray-zone situations where the correct move is to pause, verify out-of-band, and escalate. Provide immediate, constructive feedback that explains why the cue mattered and what action would have reduced risk. Use training as a mechanism to identify and fix process friction rather than repeating abstract warnings.
5) Use engagement techniques that reinforce behavior without creating shame or compliance theater. Run simulations as learning events with supportive feedback loops rather than punitive scorekeeping. Reinforce secure actions in the tools and moments where people make decisions, not only in periodic modules. Close the loop with acknowledgments and outcome feedback, so reporting and verification feel valuable.
6) Prioritize role-based training for functions that sit at high-impact control points. Build deeper practice for finance, help desk and IAM, HR, executives and their support staff, and privileged technical roles where process abuse is common. Clarify authority boundaries, required evidence, and mandatory escalation triggers, so individuals are not forced to improvise. Reinforce consistency, because attackers probe for the one exception-maker.
7) Measure real-world impact using operational signals rather than relying on participation metrics alone. Track reporting rates, time-to-report, and the frequency of risky workarounds surfaced through tickets and exceptions. Use simulations to evaluate behaviors like escalation and verification, not to grade employees. Treat near-misses as valuable data that reveals where controls and workflows need refinement.
8) Use AI to scale and personalize training and awareness only within defined governance boundaries. Apply models to draft scenario variations, tailor role-specific examples, and surface emerging patterns from user reports and operational telemetry. Require human review for correctness, keep confidence labeling and accountability clear, and maintain auditable records of content delivered and decisions made. Monitor for failure modes like drift, false confidence, and misalignment with real processes.

9) Protect trust by setting clear data boundaries and avoiding personalization that feels like surveillance. Ensure training inputs are sanitized and that sensitive content from emails, tickets, or chats is handled with appropriate controls and retention limits. Keep analytics focused on improving systems and workflows rather than ranking individuals. Reinforce psychologically safe reporting, so employees surface issues early instead of hiding mistakes.
10) Maintain awareness as a living program that adapts to organizational change. Trigger targeted reinforcement when mergers, reorganizations, new vendors, or workflow changes increase ambiguity and create new impersonation opportunities. Integrate timely reinforcement into onboarding and internal transfers, so new context does not become a persistent risk window. Keep the program grounded in durable behaviors—pause, verify, report, and escalate—so it remains effective even as people and processes shift.

27

Building a Culture of Cyber Resilience

Cyber resilience is ultimately a leadership discipline that turns security from a reactive function into a reliable capability the business can count on under pressure. It is built through consistent collaboration between security, IT, and business leaders, aligned incentives that reward secure behavior, and day-to-day workflows where secure decisions are the default rather than the exception. It also depends on communication that stays clear and actionable without relying on fear, and on accountability that drives learning and improvement instead of blame and silence. As organizations increasingly use AI to accelerate triage, prioritization, and coordination, resilience requires calibrated trust, transparency, and governance, so automation strengthens judgment rather than replacing it.

Resilience as a Leadership Objective

Resilience becomes meaningful when leadership treats it as an outcome to be engineered, not a slogan to be repeated. In practical terms, it is the organization's capacity to continue delivering critical services while absorbing disruption, adapting under pressure, and restoring normal operations without compounding harm. Security leaders translate that capacity into measurable expectations: how quickly the business must detect issues, how long it can tolerate degraded performance, and which services are non-negotiable during an incident. When resilience is framed this way, it stops being owned by a single team and becomes a shared performance objective across technology, operations, and executive decision-making. The leadership task is to make resilience legible to the business, so it can be planned for, funded, and held accountable.

A leadership objective must be expressed in decisions about priorities and tradeoffs, especially when those tradeoffs are uncomfortable. Resilient organizations explicitly identify what they will protect first, what they are willing to slow down, and what they will temporarily suspend when risk increases. That prioritization is operational, not theoretical: it shapes architecture choices, maintenance windows, change control rigor, and staffing models for monitoring and response. Leaders also set the expectation that resilience is a continuous capability, not a project with an end date, which prevents the common pattern of investing heavily after an incident and then letting the muscle atrophy. The goal is to normalize preparedness as routine work rather than a periodic scramble. Table 27.1 links resilience leadership intent to the concrete operational expectations and ownership needed to make it real.

Because resilience is a leadership objective, it requires clarity on ownership and decision rights during stress. In many incidents, the technical root cause matters less than confusion about who can authorize containment, approve service degradation, or initiate restoration steps that carry business impact. Executives should define decision boundaries in advance: what actions the SOC can take unilaterally, what requires business unit approval, and what must be escalated to an incident commander with authority to coordinate cross-functional response. This reduces time lost to ad hoc approvals and prevents well-intentioned teams from working at cross

Table 27.1 Resilience Leadership Objectives Mapped to Operational Expectations.

Leadership Objective	Operational Expression	Accountability Owner
Engineer resilience as outcome	Define detection containment restoration targets	Executive leadership
Make tradeoffs explicit	Prioritize integrity availability speed under pressure	Incident leadership
Clarify decision rights	Pre-approve containment recovery authorities	Executive leadership
Fund enabling conditions	Resource telemetry staffing recovery mechanisms	Business leadership
Sustain capability	Maintain routines not projects	Security and IT leadership

purposes. It also creates an environment where teams can act decisively without fear of being punished for using pre-approved controls.

Resilience leadership also means investing in the unglamorous foundations that make response reliable. Telemetry coverage, log quality, asset inventory accuracy, and tested recovery mechanisms are not optional conveniences; they are the prerequisites for controlling damage when reality deviates from plans. Leaders should expect operational metrics that reveal whether those foundations are healthy, such as monitoring coverage for critical services, time-to-detect for high-impact conditions, and the success rate of restoration activities under realistic load. When gaps appear, the response should be to fund remediation and adjust scope, not to demand "better security" without changing constraints. The discipline is to treat resilience like any other performance program: measure, improve, and repeat.

AI and machine learning can support resilience objectives when leaders treat them as accelerators with guardrails rather than replacements for judgment. Used well, models can reduce cognitive load by summarizing incident context, clustering related alerts, and highlighting anomalies that merit investigation based on historical patterns. Those benefits depend on dependable telemetry pipelines and consistent labeling of past incidents; without that, AI outputs become confident noise that amplifies uncertainty. Leaders should set boundaries for AI-assisted decisions, such as requiring human approval before automated containment actions or configuration changes are executed. They should also require auditability, including what data was used, what recommendation was made, and who approved or rejected it, because resilience is undermined when decision trails vanish during chaos.

Resilience fails most often not from a lack of tools, but from predictable organizational friction that leadership can address directly. Teams may optimize for uptime at all costs, resisting containment actions that temporarily reduce availability even when those actions prevent larger damage. Security teams may optimize for caution, proposing controls that slow the business without demonstrating the specific risk reduction they provide. Leaders reconcile these tensions by making resilience a balanced objective: continuity matters, but so does integrity, and sometimes a short, controlled outage is the least harmful option. When leadership consistently rewards good decisions under pressure—especially decisions that are transparent about tradeoffs—teams learn to prioritize coordinated outcomes rather than protecting their own metrics.

Finally, resilience as a leadership objective requires building confidence through repetition, not assumption. Plans that have not been exercised are aspirations, and organizations discover their true readiness only when they test handoffs, escalation paths, and restoration procedures under time constraints. Leaders should expect routine practice that reflects real constraints, including partial data, degraded systems, and competing priorities, because that is how incidents unfold in practice. The result is a culture where incident response is not an exceptional event that triggers blame, but a controlled operational mode that the organization can enter and exit safely. When leadership makes resilience a standing expectation, the blue team's work aligns naturally with business continuity, operational reliability, and accountable decision-making.

Collaboration Between Security, IT, and the Business

Effective collaboration starts when security, IT, and business leaders agree on a shared definition of success that includes both protection and continuity. Security often optimizes for risk reduction, IT optimizes for stability and change throughput, and business leaders optimize for revenue, customer experience, and delivery timelines. These goals are not inherently incompatible, but they will collide if teams treat their own metrics as the only reality that matters. Collaboration becomes durable when everyone can articulate how their choices affect the others, especially in high-pressure moments like incidents or major releases. The practical objective is to make cross-team decisions routine and predictable rather than improvisational and personality-driven.

The most common collaboration failure is a mismatch in operating cadence and vocabulary. IT teams work in tickets, change windows, and service-level targets; security teams work in detections, investigations, and control requirements; the business works in product commitments, customer impact, and financial risk. When these concepts are not translated, security requirements arrive as late-stage blockers, IT changes appear as unmanaged risk, and business priorities sound like "speed over safety." Leaders should institutionalize translation by aligning security work to business services and aligning IT operations to risk outcomes that the business understands. The result is fewer debates about intent and more discussion of impact. Table 27.2 highlights common collaboration breakdowns and the specific practices that keep cross-team work predictable under pressure.

Shared visibility is the technical backbone of cross-functional collaboration, because teams cannot coordinate well when they are operating from different pictures of reality. Security needs reliable telemetry about identity, endpoints, networks, and cloud workloads, but IT is usually the owner of the systems that generate and transport that data. The business, meanwhile, needs clear signals about service health and customer impact to make informed tradeoffs during response or containment. When logging is inconsistent, asset records are stale, or monitoring is fragmented, collaboration degrades into argument because no one trusts the underlying facts. Joint ownership of observability—what is collected, how it is normalized, and who is accountable for gaps—turns "security asks" into operational requirements that IT can plan and deliver.

Decision rights must be explicit, particularly around changes that affect availability or user experience. Security may need to isolate endpoints, block traffic, disable accounts, or enforce stricter access controls, while IT must protect uptime and avoid cascading failures. The business has legitimate authority over customer and revenue impact, but it cannot make technical decisions without a clear set of options and consequences. Collaboration improves when teams define pre-approved actions for common scenarios, including what can be done immediately and what requires escalation. This approach prevents delays caused by ad hoc approvals and reduces the risk of uncoordinated actions that worsen an incident.

The handoff between monitoring and action is where collaboration is either proven or exposed. Security can raise a high-confidence alert, but if IT is not prepared to validate, contain, and remediate in a structured way, the alert becomes a recurring problem rather than a resolved event. Conversely, IT may observe instability or unusual behavior but fail to route it through security channels, missing a detection opportunity or delaying investigation.

Table 27.2 Collaboration Failure Modes and Stabilizing Practices.

Collaboration Failure Mode	Operational Impact	Stabilizing Practice
Mismatch in cadence and vocabulary	Security becomes late stage blocker	Translate goals into shared service language
Fragmented visibility	Teams argue over facts	Joint ownership of observability and telemetry
Unclear routing and escalation	Issues sit in wrong queue	Define routing paths and escalation triggers
Undefined decision rights	Containment delayed by approvals	Pre-approve actions and boundaries
Competing success metrics	Teams optimize locally	Align outcomes to business critical services

Mature organizations define routing paths that map to business-critical services and have clear escalation triggers, so issues do not linger in the wrong queue. This is also where executive leadership can drive discipline by insisting on consistent triage outcomes and post-incident follow-through, rather than accepting perpetual "known issues" that remain exploitable.

AI can strengthen collaboration when it reduces friction without creating false confidence. For example, AI-assisted summarization can turn noisy technical artifacts—logs, alerts, ticket histories—into shared, readable incident context for security, IT, and business stakeholders. Correlation models can suggest likely relationships between changes, user activity, and service degradation, helping teams converge faster on a working hypothesis. These benefits depend on clean data sources, consistent event semantics, and controlled access to sensitive telemetry, because models will amplify whatever quality issues already exist. Leaders should require human-in-the-loop controls for AI outputs used in decision-making, including explicit review before containment actions, and audit trails that show what the model recommended and how the team responded.

Collaboration is sustained by accountability mechanisms that are fair, concrete, and tied to outcomes rather than blame. Post-incident reviews should focus on decisions, handoffs, and systemic gaps—such as missing logs, unclear ownership, or brittle recovery steps—rather than individual mistakes made under pressure. Leaders should also avoid turning every security event into a compliance exercise, because that incentives checkbox behavior instead of resilience. When security, IT, and the business share the same improvement backlog and track progress in the same operational forums, collaboration becomes routine. Over time, teams stop negotiating whether a risk matters and instead negotiate the best sequence of actions to reduce it while keeping the business moving.

Aligning Incentives to Encourage Secure Behavior

Secure behavior scales when leaders design incentives that make the safe path the easy path, not the heroic path. Most people do not wake up intending to create risk; they respond to what the organization rewards, what it tolerates, and what it measures. If teams are praised solely for speed, feature output, or uptime, they will rationally cut corners on security work that slows delivery. Incentives must therefore reflect the reality that security is part of operational quality, not an optional add-on. When leaders embed security outcomes into how performance is evaluated, secure behavior becomes a default expectation rather than a special request.

Misaligned incentives often hide in well-intentioned metrics that drive the wrong behavior. Measuring ticket throughput can discourage careful investigation, measuring time-to-close can reward superficial remediation, and measuring "number of vulnerabilities found" can reward noise rather than risk reduction. On the business side, incentive plans tied exclusively to revenue or launches can create pressure to waive controls without documenting the risk. The corrective action is not to remove metrics, but to choose measures that reflect meaningful outcomes, such as reducing repeat incidents, improving time-to-detect for high-impact conditions, and increasing the percentage of critical services covered by validated logging. Leaders should also ensure that security metrics are not disconnected from operational reality, because metrics that feel arbitrary invite quiet resistance.

A practical incentive system distinguishes between behavior, outcomes, and accountability. Behavior incentives reward consistent actions that reduce risk—timely patching within agreed windows, adherence to change control, and prompt reporting of suspected incidents—because these behaviors are within a team's direct control. Outcome incentives focus on resilience and risk reduction—fewer recurring misconfigurations, improved recovery success, and reduced exposure time for critical weaknesses—while recognizing that outcomes can be influenced by factors outside a single team. Accountability mechanisms clarify who owns remediation and who owns enabling conditions, such as tooling, telemetry, and access workflows. This structure prevents the common failure mode where security is blamed for issues it cannot directly fix or where IT is blamed for security requirements it was never resourced to implement.

Incentives must also reinforce a culture where surfacing problems is rewarded rather than punished. If teams fear embarrassment or career harm for reporting mistakes, they will delay disclosure and increase the blast radius when incidents occur. Leaders can counter this by treating early reporting as a positive behavior and by separating blameless learning from disciplinary action reserved for negligence or repeated disregard of agreed controls. When teams see that transparency leads to support and improvement, they become more willing to escalate uncertain signals. That willingness directly improves detection and response because it increases the organization's sensitivity to weak indicators before they become major failures.

A key leadership move is to remove structural incentives that push people toward insecure workarounds. If MFA enrollment is difficult, privileged access requests take weeks, or approved tools are slower than shadow alternatives, people will route around controls to meet business deadlines. The fix is not to lecture about policy but to engineer convenience: streamlined access workflows, just-in-time permissions, clear self-service guidance, and friction reductions that preserve control intent. Incentives should reward teams for eliminating recurring friction points that drive risky behavior, because usability and security are deeply linked in real operations. When secure workflows are reliable and fast, compliance becomes a byproduct of good design.

AI can help align incentives when it is used to make security outcomes visible and actionable, not to automate blame. For example, models can summarize recurring failure patterns across incidents and tickets, highlighting where process friction, configuration drift, or gaps in monitoring are driving repeated risk. Used carefully, this supports targeted investment and fair accountability by pointing to systemic contributors rather than individual errors. However, AI outputs can also create false precision, especially if the underlying data is incomplete or biased toward what is easiest to log. Leaders should require transparency around what data sources are included, enforce access controls to protect sensitive telemetry, and ensure that AI-driven insights are reviewed by humans before they influence performance evaluations.

Finally, incentives only work when leadership follows through consistently, including when it is inconvenient. If exceptions are granted informally, if deadlines routinely override risk decisions without documentation, or if high performers are allowed to ignore controls, the organization learns that security is negotiable. Leaders should make risk acceptance explicit, time-bound, and owned at the appropriate level, so teams do not carry invisible liability. When incentives, metrics, and decision processes reinforce one another, secure behavior becomes the rational choice for individuals and teams. Over time, the organization stops relying on awareness campaigns to "try harder" and instead relies on well-designed incentives that shape daily operational behavior.

Integrating Security into Everyday Work

Security becomes durable when it is embedded into the routines people already follow, rather than added as a separate layer of approvals and last-minute reviews. In day-to-day operations, most risk is created through ordinary actions: deploying changes, granting access, handling data, troubleshooting outages, and responding to customer needs under time pressure. If security is treated as an occasional checkpoint, it will be bypassed whenever schedules tighten, because it is experienced as external friction rather than internal quality. Integration means that secure decisions are built into the workflow, so they happen by default, with minimal extra cognitive load. The goal is not to make every employee a security expert, but to make secure behavior the normal way work gets done.

A practical starting point is aligning security controls to the same operational mechanisms that already govern reliability and change. Change management, release pipelines, service ownership, incident response, and problem management are existing systems of record where security requirements can live naturally. When security expectations are expressed as part of a change request, a deployment gate, or a service readiness checklist, they become predictable and auditable without needing special treatment. This also creates clear accountability because ownership maps to service owners and platform teams rather than floating as an abstract "security responsibility."

Integration is strongest when security requirements are phrased in operational terms—what must be logged, what access patterns are allowed, what data protections are required—rather than as generic mandates.

The daily work of security teams should also reflect this integration, shifting from periodic review to continuous enablement. Security can provide reusable patterns for logging, access control, and baseline hardening that IT and engineering can adopt without reinventing each time. When teams have standard templates for identity integration, secure configuration, and monitoring coverage, they can move quickly without creating novel risk every sprint. This reduces the burden on security reviewers because fewer changes are unique and fewer decisions are made from scratch. Over time, integration creates a shared language of "how we do it here," which is more effective than policy documents that most people never read.

Integration depends heavily on making good telemetry a built-in feature of systems, not an afterthought added during an incident. When logging and monitoring are treated as part of the definition of "done," investigations become faster, alerts become more reliable, and incident response becomes less disruptive. The same is true for identity and access: if least privilege and privileged access workflows are designed into daily operations, teams do not need emergency exceptions that become permanent liabilities. Security should work with IT and service owners to define what must be observable for critical services, how long data is retained, and how signal quality is validated. Without that foundation, security teams end up operating on partial evidence, which leads to inconsistent decisions and undermines trust.

The integration test is what happens under pressure, when teams are tired and the business is demanding immediate action. If secure workflows are slow or ambiguous, people will route around them, often in ways that are difficult to unwind later. That is why secure operational paths must be faster than insecure workarounds: rapid account recovery that preserves control, emergency access procedures with time bounds and logging, and clear incident playbooks that specify containment steps without requiring a debate. Leaders should treat these "break glass" paths as part of everyday work, exercising them and auditing them like any other critical capability. Done well, integration makes incidents less chaotic because the organization already knows how to act within safe boundaries.

AI can reinforce integration by reducing the manual effort required to keep security attached to everyday workflows. For example, AI-assisted summarization can turn change tickets, incident notes, and investigation artifacts into consistent, readable context that helps teams coordinate without losing detail. Pattern recognition can flag when a proposed change resembles past incidents, when telemetry coverage is missing for a service, or when access requests deviate from typical role behavior. These capabilities are only as strong as the underlying operational data, and they require careful governance to avoid over-trust, especially when AI recommendations are presented with undue confidence. Human approval boundaries should be explicit, with AI used to suggest, prioritize, and summarize, while humans retain authority for actions that materially affect access, availability, or containment.

Finally, integrating security into everyday work requires a feedback loop that turns operational learning into improvements, not into one-time fixes. When an incident reveals a logging gap, an unclear handoff, or a brittle recovery procedure, the correction should become part of normal backlog work with an owner and a measurable outcome. Teams should also regularly retire controls that add friction without reducing risk, because unnecessary burden encourages bypass behavior. Integration is sustained when security is treated as an element of craftsmanship and operational excellence, reinforced through routines, tooling, and accountability. When the organization reaches that state, security stops competing with delivery and instead becomes one of the mechanisms that makes delivery reliable.

Communicating Security Without Fear or Fatigue

Security communication fails when it is built on urgency without context, because constant alarms train people to tune out. Fear-driven messaging may produce short-term attention, but it erodes trust over time as employees learn that every message sounds like an emergency regardless of actual risk. Fatigue sets in when security becomes a steady stream of warnings, mandatory training, and policy reminders that do not connect to the work people are trying to accomplish. The better approach is to communicate in a way that respects attention as a scarce resource and uses it deliberately. Leaders should treat security messaging as an operational tool: it should help people make better decisions, not simply make them feel responsible for outcomes they cannot control.

Practical communication starts with relevance and specificity. People can act on guidance that is tied to common workflows—access requests, password resets, software installs, data sharing, and incident reporting—because it fits into tasks they already recognize. Vague phrases like "be vigilant" or "think before you click" rarely change behavior, especially when they are repeated without new information. Communication should identify the decision point, the expected action, and the reason it matters, with the reason framed in terms of business impact such as service continuity, customer trust, or regulatory exposure. When employees can see the link between their actions and real outcomes, security stops feeling like abstract compliance and starts feeling like part of professional responsibility.

Tone matters as much as content, because tone signals whether security is a partner or a critic. Communication that implies incompetence—scolding, sarcasm, or public shaming—causes people to hide mistakes and avoid asking questions. That response increases risk because delayed reporting is one of the most reliable ways to turn a small issue into a large incident. Leaders should model a tone that treats security as a shared problem: firm on expectations, calm under pressure, and focused on solutions rather than blame. When messaging consistently invites early escalation and clarifies that reporting is valued, employees become more willing to surface weak signals that security teams might otherwise miss.

Reducing fatigue also requires restraint and prioritization, especially in large organizations where multiple teams broadcast overlapping messages. A useful discipline is to communicate less often but with higher signal quality, reserving broad messages for actions that truly require organization-wide behavior change. Routine updates should be consolidated into predictable channels and cadences, so people know where to look without being interrupted constantly. When a message is urgent, it should be clearly urgent, with a specific time horizon and unambiguous actions, rather than vague language that creates background anxiety. Over time, employees learn that security messages are worth reading because they are not constantly being used as a megaphone.

Security teams should also communicate with the business the same way they communicate with technical teams: with clarity about tradeoffs, uncertainty, and next steps. Executives do not need raw indicators; they need an accurate, current picture of risk and operational impact. That means avoiding both catastrophizing and false reassurance, and instead presenting what is known, what is not known, and what decisions are required. When leadership communication includes decision boundaries—what is being contained, what may be degraded, what customer impact is expected—it becomes easier for business leaders to support containment actions without feeling blindsided. This alignment reduces the pressure to "keep everything up" at the cost of allowing compromise to spread.

AI can support calmer, clearer communication when it is used to reduce noise and improve consistency, not to automate messaging blindly. For example, AI-assisted summarization can convert technical incident details into role-appropriate updates for IT, security leadership, and executives, preserving accuracy while removing unnecessary jargon. Models can also help detect when communication volume is spiking, which often correlates with confusion and duplicated effort, enabling leaders to consolidate updates and reduce churn. However, AI-generated messages can introduce subtle errors or overconfident phrasing, especially when input data is incomplete or rapidly changing. Organizations should require human review for outward-facing or high-stakes internal messages, and they should keep an audit trail of what was communicated and why, because communication itself becomes part of incident governance.

Finally, communicating without fear or fatigue requires showing progress and closing loops. If employees only hear about threats and never hear about improvements, they assume risk is unmanaged and their effort is futile. When leaders share brief, concrete outcomes—reduced phishing success rates, improved recovery time, faster containment decisions—they reinforce that secure behavior and operational investments matter. Communication should also acknowledge the reality of constraints, including time pressure and competing priorities, while still holding teams accountable to agreed expectations. When messaging is consistent, actionable, and respectful, it builds a culture where people stay engaged with security rather than bracing for the next warning.

Establishing Accountability Without Blame

Accountability without blame starts with recognizing that most security failures are not the result of a single bad decision, but of systems that make predictable mistakes easy to repeat. Blame focuses on who to punish; accountability focuses on what must change, who owns the change, and how progress will be verified. This distinction matters operationally because fear drives concealment, while accountability drives learning and improvement. When people expect humiliation or career damage, they delay reporting and minimize symptoms, which increases dwell time and expands blast radius. Leaders who want resilience build a culture where errors are surfaced early, investigated rigorously, and corrected systematically.

Clear accountability requires explicit ownership, not vague shared responsibility. In practice, ownership means a named role or team responsible for maintaining a control, a service, or an operational process, including the authority to make changes and the obligation to sustain it over time. Many organizations claim "security is everyone's job" while failing to define who is responsible for telemetry coverage, who maintains detection content, and who owns remediation for recurring misconfigurations. That ambiguity ensures issues persist because everyone assumes someone else will fix them. A blameless culture is not one where nothing is owned; it is one where ownership is clear and the response to failure is improvement rather than scapegoating.

Incident response is where accountability and blame most often become confused, because high stakes and limited time magnify emotion. During an incident, leaders should reinforce a simple rule: decisions made in good faith using agreed procedures will be supported, even if outcomes are imperfect. This allows responders to act decisively on containment, isolation, and access changes without pausing to protect themselves politically. After the incident, accountability shifts to disciplined review: what signals were missed, what handoffs failed, and what assumptions proved wrong. Leaders should insist that the review produce concrete changes—updated playbooks, improved logging, refined escalation paths—rather than generic statements about needing "more training" or "more awareness."

A practical mechanism for accountability without blame is separating root cause from contributing factors and focusing on what is controllable. Root cause describes the initiating failure, such as a misconfiguration, a compromised credential, or a missing control. Contributing factors include process gaps, unclear decision rights, tool limitations, and staffing constraints that allowed the failure to persist or expand. This framing prevents the common error of assigning accountability to the last person who touched the system, which is often a proxy for proximity rather than responsibility. Accountability should map to the owners of the controls and workflows that could have prevented, detected, or contained the issue sooner.

Another key is establishing fairness in expectations by aligning accountability with resourcing and authority. Holding a team accountable for patching is reasonable only if they have maintenance windows, automation support, and visibility into what must be patched. Holding security accountable for detection is reasonable only if they have consistent telemetry and the authority to set logging requirements for critical services. When leaders demand outcomes without providing enabling conditions, teams learn that accountability is simply blame with better language. A credible accountability model includes documented dependencies and escalation paths when those dependencies are not met, so gaps are raised as operational risks rather than hidden as personal failures.

AI can strengthen accountability when it improves transparency, but it can also create a new class of blame if handled carelessly. AI systems can help by summarizing incidents consistently, highlighting recurring failure patterns, and linking issues across tickets and events to show where systemic gaps persist. Those insights are valuable only when the data sources are accurate and when teams understand the model's limits, because biased or incomplete data can produce misleading narratives about causality and responsibility. Leaders should require that AI-generated insights be treated as hypotheses that need validation, not as verdicts. They should also insist on auditability—what data was used, what the model inferred, and who approved actions—so accountability rests on explainable decisions rather than opaque outputs.

Finally, accountability without blame becomes real when the organization closes the loop and demonstrates that learning leads to change. If post-incident actions are not implemented, teams conclude that reviews are performative and stop engaging honestly. Leaders should track remediation commitments with the same seriousness as product commitments, including clear owners, deadlines, and verification criteria. They should also recognize and reward early reporting, thoughtful decision-making, and the disciplined elimination of recurring weaknesses, because those behaviors are the engines of resilience. When accountability is consistently tied to improvement, people stop fearing security conversations and start participating in them as a normal part of operational excellence.

Sustaining Momentum Through Wins and Setbacks

Momentum in cyber resilience is fragile because the work is continuous while the visible payoff is intermittent. When nothing bad happens, leaders may assume controls are "good enough" and redirect attention to more immediate priorities. When something bad does happen, the organization may surge briefly—adding meetings, tools, and mandates—then burn out and revert to old habits once the crisis fades. Sustaining momentum requires leadership to treat security as a durable operational capability, like reliability or safety, where progress is measured in consistent execution rather than dramatic transformation. The practical challenge is to keep focus steady without resorting to constant urgency that exhausts teams.

Wins are essential, but they must be framed correctly to avoid complacency. A win is not simply "no incidents this quarter," because silence does not prove resilience and often masks unreported issues. Wins should be grounded in observable improvements: faster detection of meaningful conditions, fewer repeat misconfigurations, shorter recovery times for critical services, and cleaner handoffs between monitoring and remediation. When leaders communicate these wins, they reinforce that disciplined operational work produces measurable outcomes, which builds confidence and reinforces secure behavior. Done well, wins also create political capital that can be spent on harder changes, such as retiring brittle legacy systems or tightening access boundaries that previously caused friction.

Setbacks are inevitable, and leaders sustain momentum by treating setbacks as data rather than as evidence of failure. An incident, a near miss, or a painful false-positive wave is a signal that assumptions were wrong or controls were incomplete, not a verdict on the competence of the team. The leadership move is to quickly shift from reaction to learning: what failed, what slowed response, what prevented containment, and what will be changed with clear ownership. This prevents the organization from cycling into blame, which suppresses transparency, and it prevents the opposite failure mode of resignation, where teams accept recurring issues as normal. A mature posture treats setbacks as opportunities to reduce uncertainty and strengthen the system.

The pace of improvement must also be sustainable, because resilience work competes with product delivery and operational maintenance. Leaders should explicitly manage the improvement backlog so that security work is not perpetually deferred to "next quarter" and so that teams are not asked to absorb new controls without removing old burdens. This is where prioritization becomes a resilience skill: focusing on high-impact services, high-leverage controls, and recurring failure patterns rather than spreading effort thin across everything. Momentum is built by delivering small, verified improvements consistently, not by launching ambitious initiatives that stall under organizational friction. The organization learns to trust the program when it sees that promised changes actually land and stay landed.

Sustained momentum depends on maintaining signal quality in monitoring and response, because noisy programs burn out their operators. When alert volumes are high and actionability is low, responders become desensitized and leadership loses confidence in the function. A resilient program continually tunes detections, improves telemetry, and refines routing so that attention is reserved for conditions that truly matter. This is also where collaboration matters: IT and security must jointly address logging gaps, brittle integrations, and maintenance tasks that degrade detection over time. Keeping operations stable and readable protects morale and ensures that improvements do not collapse under the weight of their own complexity.

AI can help maintain momentum by turning scattered operational data into a coherent picture of progress, but it must be governed carefully to avoid false narratives. Models can surface trends in incident patterns, identify repeated control failures, and summarize the status of remediation work across teams, helping leaders focus attention where it has the greatest effect. These insights are only valid when data is consistent—ticket fields are used reliably, incident tags mean the same thing across groups, and telemetry coverage is measured rather than assumed. Without those disciplines, AI can produce persuasive but incorrect stories that misdirect resources and erode trust. Leaders should require that AI-driven dashboards and summaries be validated periodically and that the underlying data definitions are stable, so momentum is fueled by reality, not by optimistic reporting.

Finally, sustaining momentum is a leadership behavior expressed through consistency, not charisma. Leaders keep the program alive by showing up to the same operational forums, asking the same outcome-oriented questions, and making the same kinds of tradeoff decisions even when pressure is high. They protect teams from whiplash by resisting the impulse to change direction with every headline and by focusing instead on the organization's actual risk and operational posture. They also model resilience by acknowledging setbacks calmly, insisting on improvement, and recognizing disciplined execution as valuable work. When wins are celebrated as proof of progress and setbacks are treated as inputs for learning, the organization develops a steady rhythm of improvement that outlasts any single incident or executive sponsor.

AI and Culture: Trust, Transparency, and Avoiding Automation-Driven Complacency

AI changes security culture not because it introduces new technology, but because it changes how people decide what is true and what to do next. When an analyst, engineer, or executive is presented with a clean summary, a ranked set of risks, or a confident recommendation, it reshapes attention and authority in subtle ways. The organization must therefore treat AI as an operational participant whose outputs influence outcomes, not as a passive tool that simply speeds up existing work. Trust becomes the central variable: too little trust and the capability is ignored, too much trust and the team becomes dangerously dependent. Leaders have to aim for calibrated trust, where AI is useful but never unquestioned.

Calibrated trust starts with clarity about what AI is allowed to do and what it is not allowed to do. In operational security, many AI uses are best framed as decision support—summarization, correlation suggestions, anomaly surfacing, and prioritization—rather than autonomous action. The moment AI output triggers containment actions, account disablement, configuration changes, or customer-impacting decisions, the organization has crossed into automation with real risk. That crossing is not inherently wrong, but it must be deliberate and bounded, with explicit human approval requirements and fallback paths when the model is wrong or unavailable. Without defined boundaries, teams gradually slide into automation because it feels efficient, and only discover the downside during an incident.

Transparency is the prerequisite for responsible trust, and it must be practical rather than philosophical. Security teams should be able to explain what data sources feed the model, what coverage gaps exist, and what kinds of scenarios produce unreliable results. If the organization cannot describe where the model gets its signal, users will either distrust it entirely or treat it as magic, and both outcomes are operationally damaging. Transparency

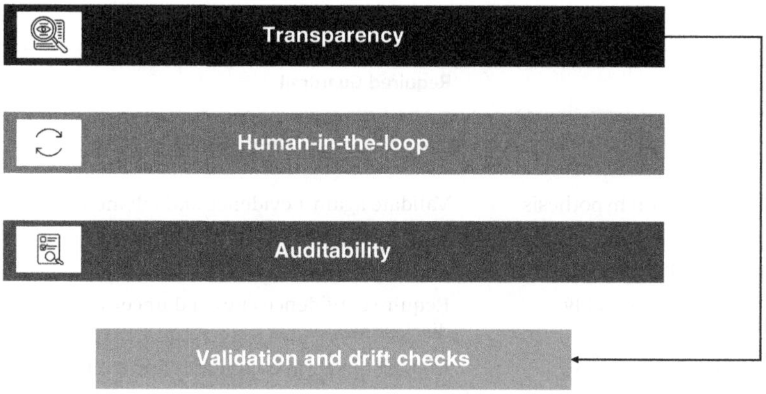

Figure 27.1 AI Culture Guardrails: Calibrated Trust Without Complacency.

also includes communicating uncertainty, such as confidence levels, competing hypotheses, and missing data that could change the recommendation. When AI outputs present a single crisp narrative without indicating uncertainty, it encourages premature closure and discourages the disciplined skepticism that good investigations require. Figure 27.1 shows the cultural and operational guardrails that keep AI as decision support rather than an unchallengeable authority. It reinforces the need for transparency, human-in-the-loop approval boundaries, and auditability to prevent automation-driven complacency.

Data and telemetry dependencies are where AI-driven programs often fail quietly. Models that support triage and prioritization depend on consistent logs, stable event semantics, and reliable identity and asset context; otherwise, the model learns patterns that reflect data quality artifacts rather than threat behaviors. Changes in logging formats, sensor coverage, or ticket taxonomy can create drift that looks like improved performance in dashboards while actually degrading the team's ability to detect meaningful conditions. This is why AI governance must include operational controls for data quality, schema stability, and periodic validation against known-good scenarios. Treating telemetry as an engineering asset—owned, monitored, and maintained—prevents the model from becoming a fragile layer built on shifting ground.

Avoiding automation-driven complacency requires deliberately preserving human skills and judgment. If analysts stop practicing hypothesis-driven investigation because AI always proposes an answer, they will be unprepared when the AI is wrong, manipulated, or unavailable. This is especially important for nuanced judgments—distinguishing malicious behavior from operational anomalies, interpreting intent from ambiguous signals, and choosing containment actions that balance risk with business impact. Teams should maintain routine manual review paths and ensure that playbooks still make sense without AI assistance, because resilience includes the ability to operate under degraded conditions. The cultural message should be that AI reduces toil, not responsibility. Table 27.3 outlines how AI can accelerate security operations while preserving calibrated trust through supervision auditability and clear approval boundaries.

AI introduces distinct failure modes that are cultural as much as technical, and leaders should expect teams to plan for them explicitly. False confidence is the most visible risk: a persuasive summary that omits a crucial indicator or misattributes causality can push the organization into the wrong containment decision. Bias can appear through uneven telemetry coverage—some environments are richly logged while others are sparse—leading AI to prioritize what it can "see" rather than what is most critical. Leakage is another risk, where sensitive operational details, incident context, or customer-impact information is exposed through inappropriate access or retention of AI prompts and outputs. These are governance problems that require access controls, audit trails, and clear handling rules, not just better model tuning.

Table 27.3 AI Guardrails for Trust Transparency and Human Approval.

AI Capability Use	Primary Benefit	Required Guardrail
Summarization of incident context	Reduces cognitive load	Human review before dissemination
Alert clustering and correlation suggestions	Faster convergence on hypothesis	Validate against evidence and telemetry gaps
Prioritization based on patterns	Improves focus on meaningful work	Monitor drift and retrain expectations
Anomaly surfacing from baselines	Highlights deviations quickly	Require confidence cues and uncertainty disclosure
Automation of high impact actions	Speeds containment response	Explicit approval boundaries and rollback path

Governance and auditability are what make AI compatible with professional security operations. Every material AI-assisted decision should be reconstructable: what inputs were used, what output was produced, who reviewed it, what decision was taken, and what the outcome was. This level of traceability supports learning after incidents, enables accountability without blame, and reduces the temptation to treat AI as an unchallengeable authority. It also protects leaders, because it demonstrates that decisions were made through controlled processes rather than informal reliance on opaque recommendations. Over time, consistent auditability builds trust because the organization can see where AI helps, where it struggles, and how it is being improved.

Trust and transparency ultimately become cultural norms only when leadership reinforces them through everyday behavior. Leaders should ask the same questions of AI outputs that they ask of human recommendations: what evidence supports this, what assumptions are being made, what are the alternatives, and what would change our decision. They should reward teams for flagging when AI is wrong, for identifying drift, and for improving data quality, because those actions protect the organization from silent degradation. When AI is treated as a powerful assistant that must be supervised, the culture stays alert and adaptive rather than complacent. That is how organizations gain speed and scale without surrendering judgment.

Long-Term Maturity and Continuous Improvement

Long-term maturity in cyber resilience is the shift from episodic improvement to continuous, measurable capability building. Organizations that mature over time do not rely on periodic "security projects" to reset posture; they treat security as an operational discipline that is refined through routine work, feedback, and sustained ownership. This is less about adding controls and more about making existing controls dependable under real conditions, including outages, staffing constraints, and competing business priorities. Mature programs align security outcomes with service reliability, because both depend on clear ownership, high-quality telemetry, and practiced response. Continuous improvement is therefore not a slogan; it is the mechanism that keeps defenses relevant as systems and threats evolve.

A mature organization defines what "good" looks like in terms that can be observed, tested, and repeated. Instead of broad statements about being "secure," leaders establish performance expectations such as detection coverage for critical services, time-to-triage for high-severity alerts, and the ability to execute containment and recovery steps within agreed decision boundaries. Those expectations become operational commitments that teams plan for and report against, not aspirational goals that live in slides. This also helps prioritize investment by distinguishing between risks that are tolerable and gaps that threaten continuity or trust. Over time, maturity is visible as consistency: fewer surprises, fewer recurring failures, and fewer emergency exceptions that become permanent liabilities.

Continuous improvement requires a disciplined loop that converts operational experience into durable changes. Incidents, near misses, and recurring alert patterns should feed a backlog that is jointly owned by security and the teams responsible for the affected services. Improvements should be specific—fix a logging gap, refine a detection, tighten an access boundary, or strengthen a recovery step—and they should include verification criteria, so the organization knows the change actually reduced risk. Without verification, programs accumulate "paper improvements" that look productive but do not change outcomes. Mature organizations measure whether the same failure mode can still occur and whether response would be faster and safer if it did.

Sustained maturity also depends on maintaining the hygiene that prevents slow decay. Detection rules, monitoring thresholds, access controls, and asset inventories drift as systems change, teams reorganize, and new services are introduced. If no one is responsible for maintaining these elements, the organization gradually becomes blind in the places that matter most, even if overall tooling appears strong. Long-term programs therefore include routine maintenance as first-class work, with scheduled reviews of telemetry coverage, alert fidelity, and the completeness of identity and asset context. This is not glamorous work, but it is the work that prevents a capable program from collapsing into noise and uncertainty.

As organizations mature, they learn to prioritize based on business criticality rather than equal treatment across all assets. Critical services, sensitive data flows, and high-impact identity pathways deserve deeper monitoring, tighter controls, and more frequent testing. Less critical systems still need baseline protections, but maturity is expressed through focused effort where failure would be most damaging. This business-aligned prioritization helps security avoid becoming a tax on every team equally, which drives resistance and encourages bypass. It also creates a shared language with executives, because investments can be tied directly to service continuity, customer impact, and risk tolerance.

AI can accelerate continuous improvement when it is used to identify patterns and validate progress, but it must be managed as part of the same maturity discipline. Models can summarize incident themes across quarters, highlight recurring contributing factors, and detect drift in operational signals such as changes in alert distribution or increases in untriaged noise. These insights are only reliable when the organization maintains consistent data definitions and high-quality telemetry, because AI will otherwise optimize around whatever is easiest to measure. Mature programs therefore treat AI as a monitored component with performance expectations, periodic evaluation, and controlled deployment changes. When AI is governed like any other operational dependency, it becomes a force multiplier rather than a source of untracked risk.

Continuous improvement also requires an organizational memory that survives turnover and changing priorities. Lessons learned must be captured in playbooks, runbooks, detection logic, and service readiness standards, not stored only in the experience of a few senior responders. This institutionalization makes the program resilient to staffing changes and reduces the probability of repeating the same mistakes. It also improves onboarding, because new team members can inherit proven workflows rather than rediscovering them through incidents. Over time, mature organizations build a body of operational knowledge that makes response calmer, faster, and more consistent.

Long-term maturity is ultimately a leadership commitment to steady governance and predictable investment. Leaders sustain it by maintaining regular operational reviews, enforcing clear ownership, and funding the foundational work that keeps telemetry, identity controls, and recovery mechanisms reliable. They also protect the program from reactive swings—overcorrecting after a breach or starving security during quiet periods—because both patterns erode capability. When continuous improvement is embedded into normal operations, the organization becomes harder to surprise and faster to recover. That is what maturity looks like in practice: not perfection, but an adaptive system that improves through every win, every setback, and every day in between.

Conclusion

Cyber resilience endures when leaders treat it as a continuous operational capability, not a periodic initiative that rises and falls with the latest incident. The organizations that sustain progress are the ones that align incentives, embed security into everyday work, and maintain clear decision rights, so response is decisive rather than political. They communicate with precision and restraint, building engagement without exhausting attention, and they enforce accountability that fixes systems instead of punishing people for predictable outcomes. With AI increasingly shaping how teams interpret risk and act under pressure, the strongest cultures pair speed with supervision, ensuring transparency, auditability, and human judgment remain central as the organization keeps improving over time.

Recommendations

1) Define resilience as an explicit leadership objective with measurable operational expectations. Translate it into detection, containment, and restoration targets tied to critical services, so teams can plan and staff realistically. Ensure the organization understands the tradeoffs between availability, integrity, and speed of action during incidents. Reinforce that resilience is a continuous capability that must be maintained, not a one-time effort.
2) Establish clear decision rights and escalation paths for containment and recovery actions. Pre-approve common response actions and document what the SOC, IT operations, and incident leadership can authorize without delay. Reduce incident-time confusion by clarifying when business approval is required and what information the business will receive to make those decisions. Review these boundaries after major changes, so they remain accurate.
3) Align security, IT, and business priorities by translating goals into shared operational language. Map security requirements to business services and customer impact, so conversations focus on outcomes rather than competing metrics. Use consistent routing and ownership, so alerts, outages, and suspected compromises land with the right teams quickly. Treat observability and telemetry coverage as joint operational responsibilities, not a security-only request.
4) Choose metrics that reinforce risk reduction and operational reliability rather than speed for its own sake. Avoid measures that encourage superficial closure or high-volume activity that does not change outcomes. Track progress using indicators such as reduced repeat failures, improved time-to-detect for meaningful conditions, and verified improvements in restoration reliability. Use these metrics to prioritize work and to communicate wins without creating complacency.
5) Integrate security into everyday workflows through existing operational mechanisms. Embed expectations into change processes, deployment routines, service ownership practices, and incident management, so secure behavior becomes the default path. Provide reusable patterns for logging, access controls, and baseline hardening to reduce late-stage friction and rework. Treat secure "break glass" procedures as normal operational capabilities that are exercised and audited.
6) Invest in telemetry quality and stability as a prerequisite for dependable detection and response. Standardize what must be logged for critical services and verify that coverage is maintained as systems evolve. Address gaps in asset and identity context that slow investigations and create inconsistent decisions. Treat logging formats and event semantics as engineering dependencies that require maintenance, not as "set and forget" configurations.
7) Communicate security in a way that is actionable, restrained, and tied to real decision points. Avoid fear-based messaging that drives tuning out and delays reporting. Consolidate routine updates into predictable channels and reserve broad, urgent messages for situations that truly require organization-wide action. Reinforce that early reporting is valued and that security communication exists to enable decisions, not to assign guilt.
8) Establish accountability by assigning explicit ownership while maintaining a blameless posture toward good-faith decisions. Separate root cause from contributing factors, so reviews produce systemic fixes rather than scapegoats. Ensure expectations match authority and resourcing, especially for responsibilities like patching, logging, and detection maintenance. Track remediation commitments with owners and verification criteria, so learning reliably becomes change.

9) Use AI to reduce toil and improve coordination while enforcing human-in-the-loop controls for high-impact actions. Apply AI where it supports decision-making—summarization, correlation suggestions, prioritization—without allowing it to silently become a decision-maker. Require transparency around data sources, coverage gaps, and uncertainty, and preserve audit trails for AI-assisted decisions. Validate AI outputs routinely and plan for drift, so the organization does not develop automation-driven complacency.
10) Sustain long-term maturity by turning wins and setbacks into a steady improvement rhythm. Celebrate measurable operational improvements rather than assuming quiet periods indicate strength. Convert incidents and recurring patterns into a jointly owned backlog with durable fixes and clear verification. Maintain the unglamorous hygiene work—rule tuning, telemetry upkeep, and ownership clarity—so capabilities do not degrade over time.

Part VIII

Cloud, Hybrid, and Proactive Defense

28

Cloud and Hybrid Security Foundations

Cloud and hybrid security succeed or fail based on whether defensive teams can operate at the speed and abstraction of modern infrastructure without losing control of identity, configuration, and evidence. The core challenge is not that cloud is "different," but that the control plane turns routine administrative actions into high-impact security events and amplifies small mistakes into large blast radius. Effective blue team operations in this space depend on making ownership explicit, instrumenting visibility as reliable infrastructure, and enforcing consistent guardrails across accounts, regions, and interconnected on-prem environments. When those foundations are in place, teams can detect and contain identity abuse and misconfiguration-driven exposure quickly, validate posture continuously at scale, and apply AI-assisted prioritization without surrendering accountability.

Understanding Cloud Security Basics

Cloud security starts with accepting that the environment is intentionally abstracted and shared. What you control is not "the cloud" in general, but a defined slice of responsibility that sits on top of a provider's infrastructure, services, and operational processes. This shared responsibility model is not a slogan; it is the boundary that determines which failures become your incident and which become a vendor ticket. In practice, most real-world breakdowns happen in the seams—misunderstood defaults, unclear ownership, and assumptions carried over from on-prem operations. Blue team operations improve fastest when they make those seams explicit in architecture decisions, runbooks, and telemetry.

The first operational shift is recognizing that cloud security is identity-first. Traditional perimeter thinking assumes that network placement grants safety, but cloud environments are designed to be reachable, programmable, and elastic. The primary control plane is authentication and authorization, which means IAM design, MFA enforcement, privileged access workflows, and service-to-service identity are foundational defensive layers. Mis-scoped roles, long-lived credentials, and permissive trust relationships are the cloud equivalent of leaving admin shares open to the internet. Security leaders should treat identity policy as production code, because it changes frequently and errors have immediate blast radius.

That identity-first reality extends to the provider control plane, which is where most high-impact actions occur. Console access, APIs, and automation pipelines can create resources, modify security policies, expose data stores, and disable logging in seconds. Blue teams should assume that a compromised engineer laptop, stolen API token, or abused CI/CD runner can become full-environment compromise if guardrails are weak. Strong separation of duties, conditional access, and privileged roles that are time-bound and auditable reduce the chance that one set of credentials becomes a skeleton key. Just as importantly, defenders need visibility into control plane actions as first-class security events, not as administrative noise.

Cloud security also requires a precise understanding of where data lives and how it moves. The same dataset may appear in object storage, managed databases, caches, analytics services, and backups, each with its own access model and encryption behavior. Security outcomes depend on aligning data classification with storage choices, key management, and access paths, rather than assuming encryption "somewhere" solves the problem. Key management is especially operational: which keys exist, who can use them, how rotations occur, and what happens when a key is revoked under incident pressure. When teams cannot answer those questions quickly, ransomware-style extortion and data exposure incidents become harder to contain because you cannot reliably sever access or prove what was protected.

Network controls still matter, but the cloud changes what "network security" means. Virtual networks, routing, and segmentation are software-defined and can be modified by automation, templates, or a single API call. Security groups and firewall rules can drift from intent as teams troubleshoot or scale services, leaving unexpected exposure paths that do not exist in static data center designs. Private connectivity, egress controls, and service endpoints are often more protective than simply restricting inbound ports, because many attacks rely on outbound reachability for command and control or data exfiltration. A mature blue team treats network configuration as continuously validated state, not a one-time deployment task.

A defining cloud risk is misconfiguration at scale, amplified by speed. Infrastructure as code enables consistency, but it also enables consistent mistakes, and those mistakes can be replicated across accounts, regions, and environments before anyone notices. Default-open storage, overly broad security groups, and permissive resource policies remain common because they are easy to deploy and hard to detect without disciplined review. This is where governance has to be concrete: defined baselines, automated checks in deployment pipelines, and rapid rollback paths when violations are detected. The goal is not to slow delivery, but to make safe configurations the easiest path and unsafe ones the most visible.

From a blue team perspective, observability is the difference between "secure by design" and "secure in reality." Cloud services generate rich logs, but they are distributed across layers: identity events, control plane audit trails, network flow records, and workload telemetry. If these sources are not centralized, normalized, and retained, investigations degrade into piecing together partial stories from ephemeral data. Equally important is log integrity; attackers frequently attempt to disable logging, rotate keys, or modify retention settings to erase traces. Monitoring must include alerts for logging tampering, account-level configuration changes, and unusual control plane activity, because losing that visibility is often the first step in turning a contained intrusion into an organizational crisis.

AI and machine learning can assist cloud defense, but only when the underlying telemetry is trustworthy and the approval boundaries are clear. Cloud environments produce high-volume event streams that benefit from ML-driven clustering, anomaly detection on API usage, and probabilistic risk scoring for identity behaviors, especially in hybrid estates where patterns vary by environment. The failure modes are predictable: models can learn bad baselines if the environment is already compromised, they can drift as teams migrate workloads, and they can create false confidence when unusual-but-legitimate operations look malicious. Human-in-the-loop controls matter most when automated recommendations would change access, disable resources, or quarantine identities, because an ML error can become an availability incident. For governance, AI-assisted outputs should be auditable—what signals were used, what decision was recommended, who approved it, and what changed—so that security teams can defend actions during post-incident reviews and improve the system without turning it into an opaque authority.

Shared Responsibility as an Operational Model

Shared responsibility is only useful when it is translated into specific operational ownership. In cloud environments, the provider secures the underlying facilities, hardware, and many service-level controls, while the customer remains accountable for identity, configuration, data, and how services are used. The practical problem is that neither side experiences incidents as "shared" in the moment; responders need a clear decision boundary for what they can fix immediately versus what must be escalated. When that boundary is ambiguous, teams waste critical minutes arguing about scope, collecting the wrong evidence, or attempting changes that the platform will not allow. Mature programs treat the shared responsibility model as a living map of control ownership, incident actions, and evidence sources.

An operational model begins by defining responsibility per service type, not as a single blanket statement. Infrastructure services place more responsibility on the customer for OS hardening, patching, endpoint controls, and segmentation, while managed services shift portions of that work to the provider but introduce new configuration and identity risks. Even within managed services, responsibility varies: encryption may be automatic, but key access policy and data lifecycle remain yours to govern. Blue teams should document these distinctions in a way responders can use under stress, aligning each major service category to who administers it, who monitors it, and who approves security-impacting changes. The goal is not exhaustive documentation, but rapid clarity when an alert arrives at 2 a.m.

Shared responsibility also has an account-and-tenant dimension that frequently gets overlooked. Providers may secure the platform, but they cannot prevent customers from creating insecure tenants, linking accounts incorrectly, or granting excessive trust between identities. Organizational structure—multiple accounts, subscriptions, or projects—is a security control because it defines blast radius and administrative boundaries. If a single administrative domain governs every environment, then one compromised admin identity effectively collapses the provider/customer boundary. A workable model deliberately separates production from non-production, isolates high-risk workloads, and restricts cross-environment trust so that compromise remains containable. Table 28.1 translates shared responsibility into practical ownership boundaries that responders can use to act quickly and preserve evidence.

The operational handoff between customer and provider must be engineered before incidents occur. During an investigation, responders need a consistent way to open provider support cases, provide required identifiers, and request platform-level artifacts that are not available through customer logs. They also need pre-approved authority to take customer-controlled actions—revoking sessions, rotating credentials, isolating workloads—without waiting for ad hoc approvals that slow containment. Providers may also impose constraints such as rate limits, delayed log availability, or service-specific support boundaries that change how quickly evidence can be gathered. Treating the provider as an extension of the response team requires rehearsed procedures, known contacts, and clear escalation criteria.

Control validation is where shared responsibility becomes measurable rather than conceptual. If the customer is responsible for configuration, then configuration must be continuously verified against intent, not assumed correct because a template exists. If the provider is responsible for a managed control, the customer still needs

Table 28.1 Shared Responsibility Operational Boundaries by Layer.

Layer	Customer Owns	Provider Owns	Operational Risk if Unclear
Identity and access	Role design MFA enforcement session revocation	Platform auth services availability	Compromised credentials become broad access
Configuration and policy	Resource policies network rules logging settings	Service control implementation	Drift and exposure persist unnoticed
Data protection	Classification access paths key policy	Service encryption capability	Unauthorized access or uncertain scoping
Telemetry and retention	Centralization normalization retention integrity	Telemetry emission from services	Investigations become speculative
Incident actions	Containment approvals runbooks escalation	Platform support and service restoration	Response delays and partial fixes

a method to confirm that the control is enabled, appropriately scoped, and producing expected telemetry. This includes practical checks such as confirming audit logging is active, retention meets forensic needs, and critical events are actually arriving in central monitoring. Without validation, teams end up trusting marketing promises, default settings, or outdated assumptions, which is how shared responsibility turns into shared blame.

Evidence and forensics are a recurring failure point because the ownership of logs and artifacts is split across layers. Customer-controlled logs may capture application and identity events, while provider-layer telemetry may be needed to confirm service health, underlying infrastructure faults, or specific platform actions. Responders must know which artifacts are authoritative for which questions, and they must understand the limitations of each source, including latency, sampling, and retention. Attackers also exploit these boundaries by targeting the layers customers control most directly, such as disabling logging, altering retention settings, or modifying IAM policies. A resilient model includes monitoring and alerting on the loss of visibility itself, because an adversary who can blind defenders has effectively expanded the blast radius.

Change management is the day-to-day mechanism that enforces shared responsibility without slowing delivery to a crawl. Providers ship new features and change service behaviors, and customers deploy continuously through pipelines, meaning the control boundary is constantly moving. Operational ownership must include who tracks provider changes that affect risk, who updates guardrails, and who adjusts detections when telemetry fields or behaviors shift. Drift is not a theoretical risk; it is an inevitable outcome of speed, and it is the reason shared responsibility must be treated as a process rather than a diagram. Teams that invest in lightweight, repeatable reviews—focused on identity, exposure, logging, and data controls—maintain security posture without creating bottlenecks.

AI-assisted governance can strengthen shared responsibility if it is used to surface ownership gaps and misalignments, not to replace accountability. Models can help classify resources, flag likely misconfigurations, and correlate changes in policy with increases in risky access patterns, especially in large multi-account environments where manual review does not scale. The danger is automation that becomes an unreviewed authority, generating alerts without context or recommending changes that break workloads, which leads teams to mute the system or distrust it entirely. Human approval boundaries should be explicit: AI can propose, prioritize, and explain, but changes that affect identity, logging, encryption, or public exposure should require accountable sign-off and a recorded rationale. Auditability matters as much as accuracy, because in cloud operations the hardest question after an incident is often not what happened, but who owned the control that could have prevented it and how that ownership was enforced day to day.

Hybrid Complexity and Boundary Confusion

Hybrid environments fail in predictable ways because they combine two security models that make different assumptions about identity, networks, and operational control. On premises, teams often inherit stable IP ranges, long-lived servers, and centralized network choke points, while cloud favors ephemeral workloads, API-driven changes, and identity as the primary control plane. When those models meet, teams frequently assume the strengths of both while actually inheriting the weaknesses of each. The most common result is boundary confusion: responders cannot quickly answer where the authoritative control lives, which telemetry is complete, or who has the ability to enforce containment. In a blue team context, hybrid security is less about mastering two stacks and more about preventing ambiguity from becoming your default operating state.

Network boundaries are the first place this confusion shows up, because hybrid connectivity blurs what "internal" means. Private links, VPN tunnels, and virtual routing can make cloud resources look like extensions of the data center, encouraging teams to treat them as trusted simply because they are reachable. That assumption breaks when cloud services expose management planes over the internet, when workloads acquire public endpoints through misconfiguration, or when east–west traffic bypasses traditional inspection points. Even when connectivity is correctly segmented, troubleshooting pressure often leads to "temporary" firewall openings and broad routes that quietly become permanent. A defensible hybrid posture treats connectivity as a risk surface to continuously validate, not as a one-time integration milestone.

Identity boundaries are even more fragile, especially when organizations federate authentication between on-prem directories and cloud IAM. Federation is powerful because it centralizes user lifecycle management, but it also creates a single compromise path that spans both environments. A credential theft event on a workstation can cascade into cloud administrative access if conditional access, MFA enforcement, and privileged role separation are inconsistent. Service identities add another layer: workloads running on premises may call cloud APIs using tokens, certificates, or secrets that are difficult to rotate and easy to over-permission. Hybrid programs succeed when they deliberately constrain trust—minimizing who and what can authenticate across the boundary—and when they treat identity policy changes as security events with clear approval and audit trails.

Telemetry gaps are where hybrid complexity turns into operational failure during detection and response. On-prem monitoring often relies on endpoint agents, network sensors, and centralized logging, while cloud telemetry may be distributed across control plane logs, identity events, flow logs, and service-specific audit sources. If these feeds are not normalized and correlated, alerts become environment-specific fragments rather than a coherent incident narrative. Time synchronization, log format differences, and inconsistent retention policies further degrade investigations, particularly when cloud logs are delayed or sampled and on-prem logs are overwritten by volume. Blue teams should design hybrid observability so that the first question—"what changed, by whom, and where"—can be answered across both domains without manual log scavenger hunts. Table 28.2 highlights the hybrid boundary areas most likely to cause response delays and where validation prevents ambiguity from becoming risk.

Control ownership is another routine failure point, because hybrid operations often split accountability across infrastructure, application, and cloud platform teams. When an incident hits, one group owns the on-prem firewall, another owns the cloud security groups, and a third owns the application configuration that actually determines exposure. If those teams do not share the same runbooks and escalation paths, containment becomes a sequence of partial fixes that leave the attacker's access path intact. This is particularly dangerous when responders assume a control exists because it exists in the other environment, such as expecting an on-prem proxy to govern cloud egress or expecting cloud-native identity controls to apply to legacy applications. An operationally sound hybrid model makes "who can change what, and how fast" explicit for every critical boundary control.

Boundary confusion also appears in data governance, because hybrid data flows are rarely linear. Data may be generated on premises, replicated to cloud storage for analytics, synchronized back for reporting, and backed up in a third location, each hop introducing access paths and retention obligations. Encryption status can vary by

Table 28.2 Hybrid Boundary Confusion Indicators and Response Consequences.

Boundary Area	Common Confusion	What Breaks Operationally	What to Validate
Connectivity and routing	Private equals trusted	Exposure paths bypass inspection	Routes segmentation egress controls
Federated identity	One login equals consistent policy	Compromise crosses environments	Conditional access MFA role separation
Telemetry completeness	Logs exist means visible	Delayed or missing incident story	Centralization normalization retention
Control ownership	Someone else will change it	Containment stalls on handoffs	Who can change what and how fast
Data movement	Data lives in one place	Scoping and recovery become slow	Lineage access paths backups

service, and key management may be split across environments, making it difficult to confidently revoke access under incident pressure. The business impact is not abstract: uncertain data lineage makes breach scoping slower, notification decisions riskier, and recovery more complex. Effective hybrid defense treats data movement as part of the threat model and ensures that access controls, logging, and retention are consistent at each stage of the pipeline.

Change velocity compounds these issues because hybrid estates rarely evolve evenly. Cloud workloads may be refactored and redeployed frequently, while on-prem systems remain stable for years, creating a mismatch in how controls are updated and validated. Security teams can end up tuning detections for yesterday's cloud topology or relying on legacy assumptions about "known-good" servers that are now integrated with modern services. Drift becomes the normal state: routes change, IAM roles expand, logging configurations vary by account, and the set of integrations grows faster than documentation. Hybrid success depends on continuous validation of boundary controls—connectivity, identity trust, logging, and data access—because point-in-time assessments decay immediately.

AI-assisted correlation can reduce hybrid complexity, but only when it is treated as augmentation, not as a substitute for clear ownership and reliable data. Machine learning can help cluster related alerts across disparate telemetry sources, detect anomalies in cross-boundary authentication patterns, and highlight sequences of changes that suggest lateral movement from on premises to cloud or the reverse. The failure modes are amplified in hybrid environments: models can misinterpret normal migration activity as malicious, miss attacks hidden in sparse or delayed logs, or reinforce biased baselines if one environment is under-instrumented. Human-in-the-loop controls should require analysts to validate AI-generated narratives against authoritative logs and to record decisions when taking containment actions that affect business-critical integrations. When governed properly, AI helps teams see across the boundary; when governed poorly, it becomes another opaque layer that increases confusion precisely when clarity matters most.

Cloud Identity and Access Considerations

Cloud access control is fundamentally about controlling who can invoke actions through the control plane and who can reach data and services at runtime. In practice, the most damaging cloud incidents are rarely the result of exotic exploits; they are the result of identity misuse—stolen credentials, overly broad roles, permissive trust relationships, and weak guardrails on privileged actions. This shifts blue team priorities toward preventing credential compromise, limiting privilege, and ensuring every high-risk action leaves an auditable trace. The operational expectation is not that identities never get abused, but that abuse is quickly detectable, containable, and provable after the fact. Executives should understand that in cloud environments, identity failures are business continuity failures because a single compromised administrator can create, destroy, or expose resources at scale.

A defensible cloud IAM posture starts with role design that reflects real job functions rather than convenience. Broad "admin" assignments and shared roles may reduce friction short-term, but they create persistent, unbounded blast radius that responders cannot manage under pressure. Least privilege is only meaningful when it is maintained over time, which requires owners for each role, periodic review, and a mechanism to detect privilege creep as teams and projects evolve. Service-specific permissions matter because many compromises exploit seemingly minor privileges that enable larger actions, such as modifying network rules, changing logging settings, or creating new identities. When teams treat roles as stable artifacts with accountable owners, they reduce both the probability of misuse and the complexity of response when misuse occurs.

Authentication controls must match the reality that cloud access is often remote and API-driven. MFA is necessary but insufficient if it is inconsistently enforced, bypassable for "legacy" workflows, or absent for service identities that never see an interactive prompt. Conditional access—evaluating device posture, location, risk signals, and session behavior—helps reduce stolen-credential success, but only when exceptions are rare and time-bound.

Session management is a critical operational detail: long-lived sessions and tokens allow attackers to persist even after password resets, and responders often underestimate the need to revoke active sessions during containment. A mature program standardizes strong authentication for humans, enforces modern auth paths, and treats session revocation and token invalidation as routine incident actions rather than special cases.

Privileged access requires additional structure because cloud platforms collapse many capabilities into a small set of high-impact roles. Just-in-time privilege, time-bound elevation, and approval workflows reduce standing admin exposure and create decision points that generate audit data. Separation of duties should be enforced at the identity layer, not merely described in policy, because cloud changes happen through APIs and automation that can bypass traditional ticketing. Break-glass accounts are necessary for resilience, but they must be tightly controlled, monitored, and tested, so they do not become the attacker's preferred entry point. When privilege is engineered as a controlled workflow, responders gain both a smaller blast radius and clearer evidence of who did what, when, and why.

Service-to-service identity is where cloud IAM often becomes dangerously informal, especially in hybrid or rapidly scaling environments. Applications, pipelines, and automation systems need identities to call APIs, access data stores, and manage infrastructure, and teams frequently solve this by embedding long-lived secrets or using overly permissive service principals. Those shortcuts are operational debt that attackers routinely exploit through code repositories, build logs, misconfigured secret stores, or compromised runtime environments. Strong patterns favor short-lived credentials, scoped identities tied to specific workloads, and automated rotation that does not depend on human memory or calendar reminders. From a blue team standpoint, every service identity should have an owner, a documented purpose, and a defined lifecycle, because "orphaned" identities are indistinguishable from attacker persistence.

Trust relationships and federation deserve special attention because they define how compromise crosses boundaries. Federated identity can centralize lifecycle and reduce password sprawl, but it can also turn an on-prem compromise into cloud compromise if conditional access and privileged role controls are not aligned across environments. Cross-account and cross-tenant trust can be operationally necessary, but it must be explicit, minimal, and continuously reviewed because it quietly widens blast radius. Attackers frequently aim for the trust fabric—token issuance, role assumption paths, and delegated administration—because it provides legitimate-looking access that evades simplistic detection. Blue teams need visibility into trust changes and the ability to rapidly tighten or disable trust paths during containment without accidentally severing business-critical integrations.

Logging and monitoring for identity must be treated as an access control in its own right. Cloud IAM logs are often the authoritative record of control plane actions, but they can be noisy, inconsistent across services, and vulnerable to tampering if attackers gain sufficient privilege. Defenders should monitor for high-signal events such as new credential creation, role changes, policy updates, unusual role assumptions, and modifications to logging or key management settings. Equally important is correlating identity events with network and workload telemetry so that "who did it" is connected to "what changed" and "what was accessed." If logs are incomplete, delayed, or not centrally retained, investigations become speculative, and leadership loses the ability to make confident containment and disclosure decisions.

AI and machine learning can materially improve identity defense in cloud environments by detecting patterns that are hard to express as static rules. Behavioral models can flag anomalous control plane usage, improbable sequences of administrative actions, risky token issuance patterns, and deviations in service identity behavior that suggest credential theft or abuse. The dependencies are non-negotiable: models require clean identity telemetry, consistent labeling of entities and roles, and stable retention to learn normal behavior across business cycles. Failure modes are common and must be managed—models can drift during migrations, generate false positives during incident response or maintenance windows, and create false confidence when attackers mimic normal admin activity. Human-in-the-loop controls should require analyst validation before automated enforcement actions, and governance should ensure every AI-driven alert or recommendation is explainable, reviewable, and recorded, so the organization can defend decisions and continuously improve the fidelity of identity protections.

Visibility and Logging in Cloud Environments

Cloud visibility is a design outcome, not a default benefit. While cloud platforms can emit rich audit and telemetry data, that data is fragmented across identity systems, control plane events, network layers, and workload execution contexts. If teams do not intentionally route, normalize, retain, and protect those signals, the environment becomes harder to investigate than a traditional data center because the most important actions occur through APIs and ephemeral resources. Blue teams should treat telemetry as production infrastructure with explicit ownership, reliability expectations, and change control. When visibility is treated as optional or "nice to have," incident response quickly degrades into partial reconstructions and unprovable assumptions.

The first layer to operationalize is control plane logging, because it records the administrative actions that create, modify, and destroy resources. These events establish the sequence of changes that often explains exposure, persistence, and privilege escalation, and they are typically the most authoritative evidence when accounts are compromised. In practice, control plane logs must be enabled comprehensively, centralized across accounts and regions, and retained long enough to support investigations that begin weeks after initial access. Teams also need to account for latency and completeness, since some services emit events asynchronously or with service-specific gaps. A workable program tests that expected events actually appear downstream, because "enabled" does not always mean "useful" once the logs hit aggregation pipelines.

Identity logging is inseparable from control plane visibility because identity is how cloud actions are authorized. Authentication events, token issuance, role assumptions, policy changes, and session activity provide the "who" and "how" that control plane logs alone may not fully explain. A common failure mode is collecting identity logs but not correlating them with resource activity, leaving analysts unable to connect a suspicious login to a specific set of actions and affected assets. Another is ignoring service identities and focusing only on human users, even though automation accounts and workload identities often hold the privileges attackers seek. Effective logging treats every principal—human or machine—as investigable, with clear identifiers that can be joined across event sources without manual guesswork.

Network visibility in cloud environments requires different instincts than on-prem monitoring. Traditional packet inspection and centralized choke points are harder to enforce when routing is software-defined, services are managed, and workloads scale dynamically. Flow logs, connection metadata, DNS activity, and load balancer telemetry become the practical signals for detecting scanning, lateral movement, and exfiltration paths, but only when they are consistently enabled and mapped to assets. A frequent gap is assuming that "private" connectivity implies safety while losing visibility into east–west traffic across virtual networks or between subnets. Defenders should prioritize visibility at boundary points that matter—egress, service endpoints, identity gateways—because those are the places where attacker objectives translate into observable behavior.

Workload logging and runtime telemetry close the loop by showing what actually executed and what data was touched. In cloud environments, workloads may be short-lived, autoscaled, or serverless, meaning forensic artifacts can disappear quickly if logs are not shipped off-host in near real time. Application logs, OS events where applicable, and runtime security signals must be standardized so that investigations do not depend on each team's logging habits or a particular deployment pattern. Storage access logs and database audit trails are especially important because many incidents are ultimately about data exposure, not simply infrastructure compromise. Without workload-level evidence, teams can often prove that an identity acted, but not what the attacker accomplished inside the application or data layer.

Log integrity is a defensive control, not just an engineering concern. Attackers who gain sufficient privilege commonly attempt to disable logging, reduce retention, alter routing destinations, or delete trails to extend dwell time and complicate response. Blue teams must therefore monitor for changes to logging configurations, retention settings, and access controls around telemetry pipelines as high-severity events. Strong designs isolate logging accounts or projects, restrict who can modify collectors and destinations, and enforce immutability where possible so that logs remain trustworthy even when production environments are compromised. When responders can rely on log integrity, they can move faster and make risk decisions with confidence; when they cannot, every decision becomes conservative, slower, and more disruptive to the business.

Operationally, visibility must be engineered to support triage and investigation workflows, not just compliance retention. That means normalizing fields across sources, ensuring consistent timestamps, defining asset identity in a way that survives autoscaling, and building query patterns that answer routine incident questions quickly. Teams also need to plan for cost and volume, because cloud logging can become expensive and noisy if collected indiscriminately. The practical approach is to prioritize high-value signals—identity, control plane, critical data access, and boundary network telemetry—then selectively add depth where risk justifies it. Visibility programs fail when they either over-collect and drown analysts in noise, or under-collect and discover gaps only after an incident forces the issue.

AI and machine learning can help defenders extract value from cloud telemetry, but only when governance prevents automation from becoming a black box. ML-driven clustering and anomaly detection can highlight unusual API call sequences, rare administrative changes, and suspicious patterns across identity and network signals that would be missed by static rules. These systems depend on high-quality, consistently labeled data and stable pipelines; missing fields, inconsistent naming, and delayed delivery can cause models to overfit, drift, or produce misleading "confidence" scores. A disciplined human-in-the-loop approach uses AI to prioritize and summarize, while requiring analysts to validate against authoritative logs before taking containment actions such as revoking sessions, disabling identities, or isolating resources. For auditability, every AI-assisted decision should be traceable to the underlying events and the human approval that accepted or rejected the recommendation, ensuring that visibility improvements strengthen operational control rather than introducing a new source of unaccountable risk.

Cloud Misconfigurations and Common Causes

Cloud misconfigurations are less about ignorance of security fundamentals and more about the speed and abstraction of the operating model. Teams are asked to deliver quickly using services that hide complexity behind simple settings, and those settings often have high-impact security consequences. A single checkbox can shift a data store from private to broadly accessible, or a minor policy edit can allow an identity to assume powerful roles across an environment. Because cloud changes are API-driven and easily automated, mistakes propagate faster and wider than in traditional infrastructure. Blue teams should assume misconfiguration is a normal failure mode and design detection, prevention, and recovery around that reality.

Default behaviors and "helpful" wizards are a common root cause because they optimize for availability and onboarding, not for least exposure. New services frequently prioritize ease of use, which can lead to permissive access defaults, broad network reachability, or incomplete logging unless explicitly enabled. Even when defaults are secure, documentation and console flows can nudge teams toward convenience settings during development and then those settings quietly persist into production. The security impact is amplified when engineers copy working examples without understanding the implications of resource policies, identity scopes, or public endpoints. Operationally, the fix is not to blame developers, but to treat defaults as untrusted until validated against an approved baseline.

Identity and access misconfigurations are the most common and most consequential because they control both administrative power and data access. Overly broad roles, wildcard permissions, and permissive trust relationships are often introduced to "unblock" a deployment, then never revisited. Service identities and automation accounts are frequent offenders because they are created quickly, granted expansive privileges, and later forgotten once the pipeline works. Another recurring issue is inconsistent MFA and conditional access enforcement, especially for break-glass accounts or legacy authentication paths. Blue teams should monitor for privilege expansion events, newly created credentials, and policy changes as high-signal indicators of both misconfiguration and adversary

Table 28.3 Cloud Misconfiguration Causes and High-Impact Outcomes.

Cause Type	Typical Trigger	Common Misconfiguration	Operational Impact
Permissive defaults	Quick start convenience	Public access or broad policy	Unexpected exposure at scale
Troubleshooting changes	Temporary unblock	Wide inbound rules broad routes	Open paths persist into production
Overbroad IAM	Speed and unblocking	Wildcard permissions permissive trust	Privilege misuse and large blast radius
Manual console drift	Hotfix outside pipeline	Template and real state diverge	Detections and recovery become unreliable
Inconsistent logging	Assumed enabled	Missing audit logs short retention	Loss of visibility and weak forensics

activity. Table 28.3 connects common misconfiguration causes to the practical outcomes blue teams must detect and remediate before incidents escalate.

Network exposure misconfigurations frequently stem from treating cloud networks like familiar on-prem segments. Teams may open wide inbound rules for troubleshooting, assume private connectivity equals safety, or misinterpret how security groups and routing interact across subnets and peered networks. Public endpoints can appear unintentionally through load balancer settings, service integrations, or inherited templates, creating exposure without a deliberate decision. Egress is also often neglected; unrestricted outbound access enables command and control, data exfiltration, and easy lateral movement to external services. Effective programs implement guardrails that prevent broad exposure by default and continuously validate that intended segmentation and egress policies remain intact as the environment changes.

Data exposure misconfigurations are especially damaging because they often involve regulated or business-critical information and can occur without traditional "compromise." Public object storage, overly permissive database access rules, and weak resource policies can make data accessible to unintended principals while leaving little obvious evidence of intrusion. Even when encryption is enabled, misconfigured key policies can allow unauthorized decryption or prevent legitimate recovery during incident response. Backup and snapshot controls are another blind spot; copies of sensitive data may be created, shared, or retained outside normal governance. Blue teams need both preventive controls that block unsafe sharing and detective controls that alert on changes to data access posture, not just on anomalous access attempts.

Change management and configuration drift are structural causes of misconfiguration in cloud environments. Infrastructure as code helps, but only if it is consistently used, reviewed, and enforced; many organizations have a mix of templated deployments and manual console changes that diverge over time. Even fully automated environments drift as teams introduce exceptions, apply hotfixes, or adopt new services faster than standards are updated. The result is a gap between "declared state" and "real state," which is where misconfigurations hide. Operational maturity means continuously reconciling actual configurations against intent, with rapid remediation paths that do not require heroic manual intervention.

Organizational incentives and unclear ownership often produce misconfigurations more reliably than technical error. When delivery teams are measured on speed and uptime while security teams are measured on prevention, the path of least resistance becomes broad permissions, open access, and deferred hardening. Misconfiguration persists when no one owns the control after initial deployment, or when responsibilities are split across platform, application, and security teams with no clear authority to enforce standards. In those conditions, even known issues linger because remediation is seen as "someone else's problem" or too risky to change. A strong operational model assigns explicit owners for identity, exposure, logging, and data controls and makes the remediation workflow as routine as patching.

AI and machine learning can reduce misconfiguration risk by surfacing patterns humans miss, but only if the system is governed and grounded in accurate configuration and asset data. ML can help classify resources, detect deviations from normal posture, prioritize findings by probable blast radius, and correlate configuration changes with subsequent alerts or access anomalies. The failure modes mirror the cloud's complexity: models can generate noisy findings if asset inventories are incomplete, mis-rank risk if business context is missing, and drift as services evolve and naming conventions change. Human-in-the-loop review is essential when automated recommendations would alter identity policies, network exposure, logging routes, or key management, because a well-intended fix can break production just as effectively as an attacker. Used properly, AI becomes a force multiplier for triage and prioritization, while accountability remains with engineers and security leaders who understand the operational tradeoffs and can audit why a particular change was made.

Integrating Cloud Security into Blue Team Work

Integrating cloud security into blue team operations requires treating cloud as a primary operating environment with its own control plane, evidence sources, and failure modes, not as an extension of the data center. The day-to-day work changes because critical actions happen through APIs, workloads are ephemeral, and configuration is as important as host state. If blue teams keep the same mental model they used for static infrastructure, they will miss the signals that matter most and over-invest in controls that have less leverage in cloud. Operationally, the goal is to align detection, triage, investigation, and response to how cloud systems actually behave under normal load and under attack. That alignment is what prevents "cloud incidents" from turning into slow, high-disruption events driven by uncertainty.

A practical starting point is building an asset and identity inventory that reflects the cloud reality of constant change. On-prem environments can often tolerate periodic discovery, but cloud programs need near-real-time understanding of accounts, subscriptions, projects, workloads, service endpoints, and the identities that can act on them. Without that inventory, alerts cannot be reliably scoped, ownership cannot be quickly established, and containment actions risk collateral damage. This inventory should include what matters to responders: environment classification, business criticality, exposure posture, logging status, and primary owners for both the workload and the cloud account. When teams know what exists and who is responsible, they can move from "what is this?" to "what do we do?" quickly.

Detections must be redesigned to account for control plane activity and configuration changes as first-class security events. In cloud environments, attacker progress often looks like a sequence of legitimate administrative actions—creating credentials, expanding privileges, modifying network exposure, and altering logging—rather than noisy malware behavior on a host. Blue teams should tune detections around high-impact actions and suspicious sequences, such as privilege escalation followed by resource policy edits or new access keys followed by unusual data access patterns. This is also where baselining becomes operational: teams need to understand normal deployment rhythms, common administrative workflows, and expected automation behaviors so that deviations stand out. Cloud detection programs mature fastest when they focus less on volume and more on coverage of attacker-relevant behaviors in the control plane and identity layer.

Triage workflows need explicit paths for cloud-specific questions that determine severity and response posture. Analysts should be able to quickly answer whether the event is a human user or service identity, whether the action occurred through interactive console access or an API token, and whether the impacted resources are internet-exposed or hold sensitive data. Because cloud environments can change state rapidly, triage often includes validating current configuration, not just interpreting what the alert says happened. That requires fast access to authoritative logs and configuration views, along with clear escalation criteria when identity or logging controls are touched. The operational success measure is whether the team can decide on containment steps confidently within minutes, not whether they can produce perfect forensic narratives early.

Investigation and response in cloud demand playbooks that reflect the control boundaries and the reversible nature of many cloud actions. Containment often means revoking sessions, disabling access keys, tightening role permissions, isolating resources through security group changes, and locking down resource policies, rather than pulling network cables or imaging disks. Those actions must be pre-approved and rehearsed because they can have immediate availability impact if misapplied. Teams should also plan for the reality that some evidence is transient, so investigation must prioritize collecting volatile artifacts and preserving logs before taking disruptive steps that might rotate resources or tear down compromised workloads. A cloud-capable blue team is defined by disciplined, repeatable actions that reduce risk quickly without turning every incident into a major outage.

Integration also requires aligning with engineering and platform teams, so security changes can move at cloud speed without becoming unsafe. When infrastructure is managed through code, security must participate in the same pipelines with automated checks, policy enforcement, and review mechanisms that catch misconfigurations before they reach production. Just as importantly, responders need a reliable way to request and execute emergency changes through those pipelines, because console-based "hot fixes" create drift and complicate later recovery. This alignment is not a governance exercise; it is operational necessity, because cloud environments punish teams that treat security as an external review gate. The strongest programs make secure patterns the default in templates and modules, so that security improvements scale with engineering effort rather than against it.

Training and readiness should be grounded in cloud-specific failure modes and joint exercises that reflect real incidents. Tabletop scenarios should include identity compromise, logging tampering, accidental exposure, and cross-environment trust abuse, because these are the events that test the seams between teams and systems. Readiness also means ensuring responders have the access they need during an incident, but not so much standing access that it becomes a risk itself. Privileged elevation workflows, break-glass procedures, and provider escalation paths should be tested like any other critical operational process. When teams practice these motions, the shared responsibility boundaries and internal handoffs become muscle memory rather than debated theory.

AI and machine learning can help integrate cloud security into blue team work by reducing cognitive load in high-volume, high-change environments, but only when the system is constrained by governance and validated by humans. AI can summarize noisy event sequences, cluster related alerts across identity and control plane sources, and prioritize investigations based on probable blast radius and data sensitivity, which is particularly valuable when environments span multiple accounts and regions. The risks are operationally significant: models can misread legitimate automation as suspicious, under-react to slow and careful attacker behavior that mimics administrators, or produce confident narratives that are not supported by complete telemetry. Blue teams should enforce approval boundaries, so AI recommendations do not directly alter identity, network exposure, logging, or key management without human review, and they should require that AI outputs link back to the underlying events used to reach conclusions. When used this way, AI becomes a disciplined assistant to triage and investigation, while accountable humans remain responsible for decisions that affect availability, privacy, and business risk.

AI-Assisted Cloud Posture: Detection, Prioritization, and Validation in Large Environments

AI-assisted cloud posture becomes valuable when scale breaks the human ability to maintain consistent attention across accounts, regions, and services. Large environments generate a constant stream of configuration changes, identity events, and data access patterns, and many of the most consequential risks present as weak signals distributed across time and systems. In that setting, the problem is not a lack of findings; it is an inability to distinguish what matters now from what can wait, and to do so without creating brittle, manual processes. AI and machine learning can help by clustering related signals, identifying deviations from established norms, and proposing prioritized work queues that reflect probable blast radius. The operational requirement is that these systems produce decisions that remain explainable, reviewable, and actionable under real incident pressure.

Detection in cloud posture is fundamentally different from endpoint-focused detection because it is largely about intent inferred from control plane behavior. ML can identify suspicious sequences that are hard to express in static rules, such as a new service identity being created, granted elevated permissions, and immediately used to enumerate resources and alter logging settings. It can also detect subtle exposure changes by learning normal patterns of resource policy edits and flagging unusual expansions of access scope. In large estates, where each team may have different deployment habits, behavior-based detection can reduce blind spots by focusing on the shape of actions rather than the exact service or API name. The constraint is that behavior-based systems must be grounded in high-fidelity audit data and consistent entity identifiers, or they will produce plausible stories built on incomplete truth. Figure 28.1 shows how AI supports posture operations by moving from detection to prioritization to validation while enforcing human-in-the-loop approval for high-impact changes. It reinforces the chapter's emphasis on explainability, auditability, and bounded automation to prevent false confidence and outages.

Prioritization is where AI often delivers the most immediate operational benefit, because it can compress thousands of posture signals into a smaller set of risks worth human attention. Effective prioritization models incorporate more than raw severity labels; they weigh factors such as identity privilege, public exposure, data sensitivity, and the dependency graph of connected services. They also account for change context, distinguishing a risky configuration introduced by a controlled deployment from the same configuration appearing via manual changes outside normal workflows. This reduces the chronic fatigue that comes from treating every misconfiguration as equal and every alert as urgent. If leadership wants fewer high-severity surprises, the posture program must explicitly optimize for "risk reduced per unit of effort," and AI is one way to support that optimization at scale.

Validation is the critical step that prevents AI-assisted posture from becoming an expensive generator of untrusted noise. In cloud security, many "findings" are only meaningful in context: a storage policy that appears permissive may be compensated by network restrictions, or a broad role may be constrained by conditional access and session controls. AI can help by automatically assembling that context—pulling associated identity policies, network paths, and recent change history—so analysts validate faster and with fewer gaps. However, the system must be explicit about what it knows and what it does not know, because partial context is a common source of

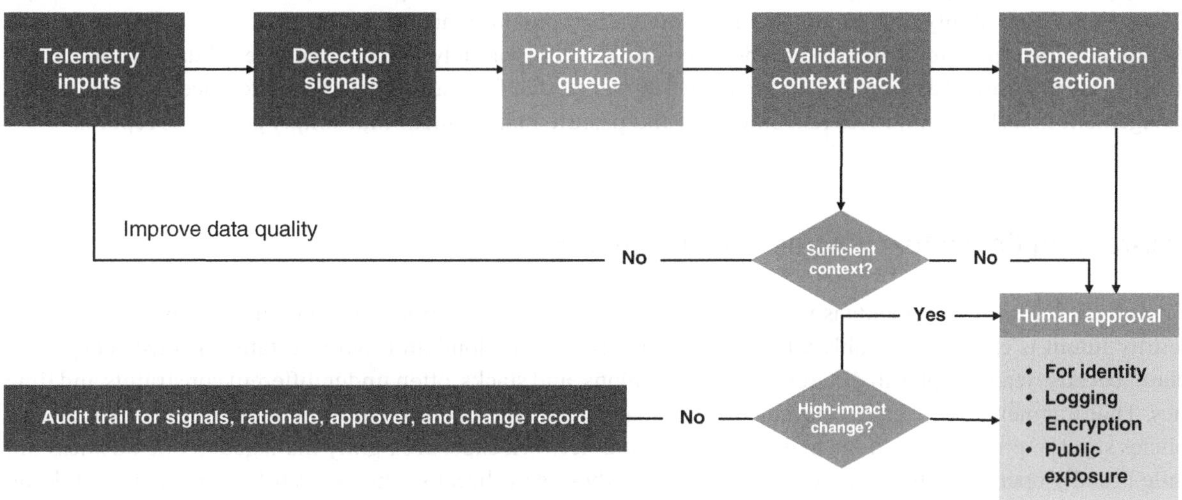

Figure 28.1 AI-Assisted Cloud Posture Workflow with Human Approval Boundaries.

false confidence. High-performing teams treat AI outputs as structured hypotheses that accelerate verification, not as authoritative determinations that bypass human judgment.

Large environments introduce a persistent challenge: drift and diversity undermine simple baselines. Business units deploy at different cadences, mergers introduce inconsistent naming and policy styles, and cloud providers evolve services in ways that change telemetry fields and default behaviors. ML models can drift as the environment changes, and they can inadvertently learn undesirable norms if insecure configurations are common. Operationally, this means baselines must be curated and protected, with explicit reference points for what "good" looks like, and monitoring for when models start to normalize bad behavior. Periodic recalibration should be part of the posture lifecycle, and it should be treated as routine maintenance rather than as a one-time implementation task.

Human-in-the-loop controls are non-negotiable because posture actions can directly affect availability and business operations. AI can recommend tightening a role, restricting an endpoint, or disabling a service identity, but those recommendations must be bounded by approval workflows, staged rollouts, and rollback plans. In practice, organizations define action tiers: low-risk changes that can be auto-remediated, medium-risk changes that require peer review, and high-risk changes—identity, logging, encryption, and public exposure—that require accountable sign-off and often a maintenance window. This keeps automation from turning posture into a source of outages and prevents security from becoming the team that "breaks production." It also improves trust, because stakeholders see that security uses automation with discipline rather than with unchecked authority.

Failure modes should be anticipated because they appear reliably in AI-assisted posture programs. False positives are inevitable, especially during migrations and large-scale refactoring, and if they are not managed they will drive teams to ignore even high-quality findings. False negatives can be more dangerous because they create a perception of coverage, encouraging leadership to assume risk is being managed when it is merely being scored. Data leakage is another risk: AI systems that ingest sensitive configuration details, identity artifacts, or incident notes can inadvertently expose that data if access controls and retention are weak. Governance should therefore include strict data handling, clear model access boundaries, and audit logs that show who queried posture insights and what data was used to generate recommendations.

Auditability is what turns AI-assisted posture from a tactical tool into a credible operational control. Teams must be able to explain why a risk was prioritized, what signals contributed to the score, what validation was performed, and who approved any resulting changes. This is especially important when posture automation changes identity permissions or public exposure, because those decisions have compliance and breach-notification implications. Good auditability also supports continuous improvement: when an incident occurs, teams can review whether posture signals existed, whether they were ranked appropriately, and whether the validation and remediation workflows worked as intended. In large environments, that feedback loop is the difference between posture management that slowly improves risk outcomes and posture management that simply generates reports.

Maintaining Consistency Across Environments

Consistency across environments is not about making every system identical; it is about ensuring that the same security intent is expressed reliably wherever workloads run. In cloud and hybrid estates, inconsistency is the default because teams deploy in different accounts, regions, and stacks, often under different constraints and timelines. That fragmentation creates uneven controls: logging enabled in one environment but not another, identity policies strict in production but lax in development, and network exposure tightly managed in one business unit while broadly open elsewhere. Attackers benefit from these gaps because they search for the weakest link, not the most secure segment. Blue teams reduce risk fastest when they make consistency a measurable operational outcome rather than an aspirational principle.

The foundation of consistency is standardizing identity and access expectations across environments, especially for privileged actions. If MFA, conditional access, session controls, and role design vary by environment, then incident containment becomes unpredictable and blast radius expands. Consistent identity controls should apply to human users and service identities, including how credentials are issued, rotated, and revoked. Just as importantly, the organization must standardize how privilege elevation works, because ad hoc admin access in one environment will eventually become the attacker's preferred path. When identity governance is consistent, it becomes possible to reason about risk across the estate and to enforce response actions with confidence.

Configuration consistency must be enforced through repeatable mechanisms rather than manual review. Infrastructure as code and templated deployments are effective only when they are actually the default path and when "escape hatches" are controlled and audited. Environments diverge quickly when teams rely on console changes, local scripts, or one-off exceptions that never get backported into standard templates. This divergence is not merely an architectural nuisance; it creates unknown states that monitoring cannot reliably interpret and responders cannot quickly contain. Operationally, teams need a defined process for approving exceptions, recording the rationale, and either eliminating the exception or incorporating it into the baseline, so the environment remains understandable.

Logging and telemetry consistency is the difference between investigations that scale and investigations that collapse into case-by-case improvisation. If each environment emits different log sources, uses different naming conventions, or retains data for different durations, analysts cannot build reusable detection logic or reliable playbooks. Consistency requires not only enabling the same categories of logs—identity, control plane, network metadata, and workload signals—but also normalizing fields and entity identifiers, so events can be correlated across accounts and regions. Retention and integrity controls must also be uniform, because the one environment with weak retention becomes the environment where long-dwell intrusions succeed. When telemetry is consistent, security teams can measure coverage, detect gaps quickly, and respond without re-learning the environment on every incident.

Network policy consistency is frequently undermined by differing connectivity patterns, but the security intent should remain stable. Production environments should not quietly inherit permissive ingress rules because development needed quick access, and egress controls should not disappear simply because a workload moved to a new region. Segmentation principles should be expressed in a way that survives platform differences, focusing on who can talk to what and for what purpose, rather than relying on a single network technology. Hybrid connectivity must be treated as a controlled boundary, with consistent inspection and monitoring expectations where feasible and compensating controls where it is not. The objective is to ensure that "internal" does not become an undefined label that grants implicit trust.

Consistency also depends on disciplined change management that acknowledges environments evolve at different speeds. Cloud services change rapidly, engineering teams ship continuously, and platform teams may introduce new services that do not neatly fit existing baselines. If security standards are updated slowly, teams will either block progress or accept uncontrolled drift, both of which degrade security outcomes. A strong model treats baseline evolution as routine work: when new service patterns emerge, the baseline expands, detection logic is updated, and guidance is published in a way teams can adopt quickly. This keeps consistency aligned with reality rather than frozen in outdated assumptions.

Operational consistency must extend into incident response, because a playbook that works in one environment but not another is effectively not a playbook. Containment steps—revoking sessions, disabling identities, isolating resources, locking down policies, preserving evidence—should be executable with the same authority and the same expected effects across environments. If responders need different access paths, different tools, or different approval chains depending on where the incident occurs, response time will be dominated by coordination rather than action. Teams should rehearse cross-environment incidents specifically to reveal where procedural consistency breaks, then fix those breaks through access design, runbook updates, and clear ownership. The result is a response capability that scales with the estate rather than fragmenting with it.

AI and machine learning can support consistency by continuously detecting drift and highlighting where security intent is not being met, but they must be grounded in authoritative baselines and transparent evaluation criteria. ML can cluster environments with similar configurations, identify outliers that warrant review, and prioritize remediation based on exposure and business criticality, which is particularly useful when the estate is too large for manual audits. The failure modes are familiar: models may normalize insecure configurations if they are common, miss drift when telemetry is inconsistent, or recommend changes that break unique workloads in edge environments. Human-in-the-loop controls should focus on validating that a drift signal reflects true risk and that proposed remediations fit operational constraints, especially for identity, logging, encryption, and public exposure. When governed properly, AI becomes a continuous consistency check that helps blue teams keep pace with change without sacrificing accountability or operational stability.

Conclusion

Cloud and hybrid environments reward teams that treat security as an operational discipline grounded in clear ownership, repeatable controls, and dependable telemetry. When shared responsibility is translated into concrete decision boundaries, responders waste less time on ambiguity and more time on containment, evidence preservation, and restoration of trustworthy access. Consistency across environments turns security intent into enforceable reality, reducing the likelihood that attackers find a weak account, an over-permissioned identity, or an unlogged service path that quietly bypasses defenses. With that operational foundation, AI-assisted posture can scale detection, prioritization, and validation, but only when humans remain accountable for approvals, audit trails are intact, and automation is bounded to prevent false confidence from becoming the next incident.

Recommendations

1) Translate shared responsibility into written operational ownership for each major cloud service category you use. Define what your team can change immediately, what requires provider escalation, and what evidence sources are authoritative for each layer. Attach those boundaries to incident actions, so responders do not debate scope while an intrusion is unfolding. Rehearse the handoff motions, so escalation paths are muscle memory rather than a surprise.
2) Treat identity as the primary cloud security control plane and engineer it accordingly. Establish role designs that map to real job functions, minimize standing privilege, and make privilege elevation time-bound and auditable. Standardize strong authentication and session controls, so credential resets are not the end of containment. Monitor identity policy and credential events as high-signal security telemetry rather than administrative background noise.
3) Reduce hybrid boundary confusion by making "internal" a verified condition, not an assumption. Validate routing, segmentation, and exposure posture continuously across on-prem and cloud connectivity paths. Constrain cross-boundary trust, so federation and account links do not turn a single compromise into enterprise-wide access. Build responder-ready runbooks that specify who can change which boundary controls and how quickly.
4) Engineer cloud visibility as a production capability with explicit owners and reliability expectations. Centralize control plane and identity logs across accounts and regions and retain them long enough to support delayed discovery of compromises. Normalize key fields and entity identifiers, so analysts can correlate actions across sources without manual reconstruction. Alert on logging tampering and retention changes as high-severity events because loss of visibility expands attacker freedom.

5) Design network telemetry for cloud realities rather than replicating on-prem instincts. Enable and use flow and connection metadata to understand boundary behavior, especially egress and service endpoint access. Validate that east–west paths and "private" connectivity do not bypass your monitoring and segmentation intent. Treat broad exposure and unrestricted egress as conditions to remediate, not as acceptable defaults.
6) Prevent misconfigurations by treating defaults and convenience settings as untrusted until validated against your baseline. Make safe configurations the easiest path through templates and controlled deployment pipelines, and limit manual console changes that create drift. Create a routine process to reconcile declared intent versus actual state and to remediate deviations quickly. Ensure exceptions are time-bound, justified, and either removed or incorporated into the baseline.
7) Standardize service identity lifecycle management as rigorously as human access management. Assign an owner and a documented purpose to every service identity and automation account. Prefer short-lived credentials and enforce rotation and revocation paths that do not depend on individual memory. Monitor for privilege expansion and unusual service identity behavior because machine identities often hold the access attackers want.
8) Make incident response playbooks cloud-native by focusing on reversible, high-leverage containment actions. Pre-approve and practice actions such as revoking sessions, disabling credentials, tightening roles, isolating resources, and locking down resource policies. Prioritize preserving volatile evidence by shipping logs off-host and validating retention before taking disruptive steps. Ensure response authority and access paths are consistent across environments, so responders can act without procedural delays.
9) Use AI and machine learning to reduce triage and posture management workload, but enforce explicit human approval boundaries. Apply AI for clustering, summarization, and prioritization of control plane, identity, and configuration signals in large environments. Require analysts to validate AI-generated narratives against authoritative logs before making high-impact changes to identity, logging, encryption, or exposure. Maintain auditable records of what signals were used, what was recommended, who approved it, and what changed.
10) Maintain consistency across environments by measuring and managing drift as a continuous operational problem. Standardize identity controls, logging coverage, retention expectations, and boundary policies, so investigations and playbooks work the same way everywhere. Update baselines as platforms and deployment patterns evolve to prevent "frozen standards" from driving uncontrolled exceptions. Use continuous validation to identify outliers and remediate them before attackers do.

29

Securing Cloud Workloads and Cloud-Native Operations

Cloud-native operations change the security equation by shifting control from fixed infrastructure to dynamic identities, managed services, and constantly evolving configurations. Securing cloud workloads at scale depends on clear operational ownership, durable guardrails that make safe defaults easy to adopt, and consistent visibility into both control-plane and data-plane behavior. The practical challenge is not a lack of security features, but the speed at which permissions expand, networks interconnect, data replicates, and environments drift when processes are not engineered to keep pace. A mature approach treats monitoring, incident response, and AI-assisted correlation as operational capabilities with human accountability, ensuring the organization can detect misuse quickly, contain blast radius decisively, and sustain cloud security improvements over time.

Workloads, Services, and Operational Ownership

Cloud security becomes manageable when operational ownership is explicit, because every protection and response activity ultimately maps to a workload and the team accountable for keeping it healthy. A workload is the running unit that delivers value—an application, API, batch job, data pipeline, or containerized service—while cloud services are the managed capabilities it depends on, such as identity, networking, storage, messaging, and managed databases. The operational reality is that incidents rarely respect these boundaries: a compromise may begin in an application workload, pivot through identity permissions, and land in a storage service that was never "owned" in anyone's mind. Clear ownership prevents the common failure mode where security findings get routed to the wrong queue, linger as "someone else's problem," and then resurface as outages or breaches. When executives ask who is responsible, the correct answer cannot be a team name alone; it must be the accountable owner for the workload and the accountable owner for the services it consumes.

Ownership in cloud-native environments must account for the shared responsibility model without treating it as an excuse to outsource risk thinking. Cloud providers secure the underlying facilities and core service implementations, but customers still own configuration, identity and access decisions, data classification, and the security posture of what they deploy. Operational ownership should therefore be defined at two layers: product ownership for the workload and platform ownership for the enabling services and guardrails. Product teams are accountable for secure software behavior, configuration of service dependencies, and timely remediation of vulnerabilities that affect their runtime. Platform and infrastructure teams are accountable for baseline configurations, network segmentation patterns, identity scaffolding, logging pipelines, and standard deployment paths that keep teams from reinventing controls under pressure. Security leadership's role is to ensure neither group becomes a sink for responsibility, and that the handoffs between them are designed for speed and evidence, not escalation and blame. Figure 29.1 shows how workload owners platform owners and security operations divide accountability while still coordinating on shared telemetry and incident containment. It reinforces that fast response depends on knowing who can approve changes and who can execute them without ambiguity.

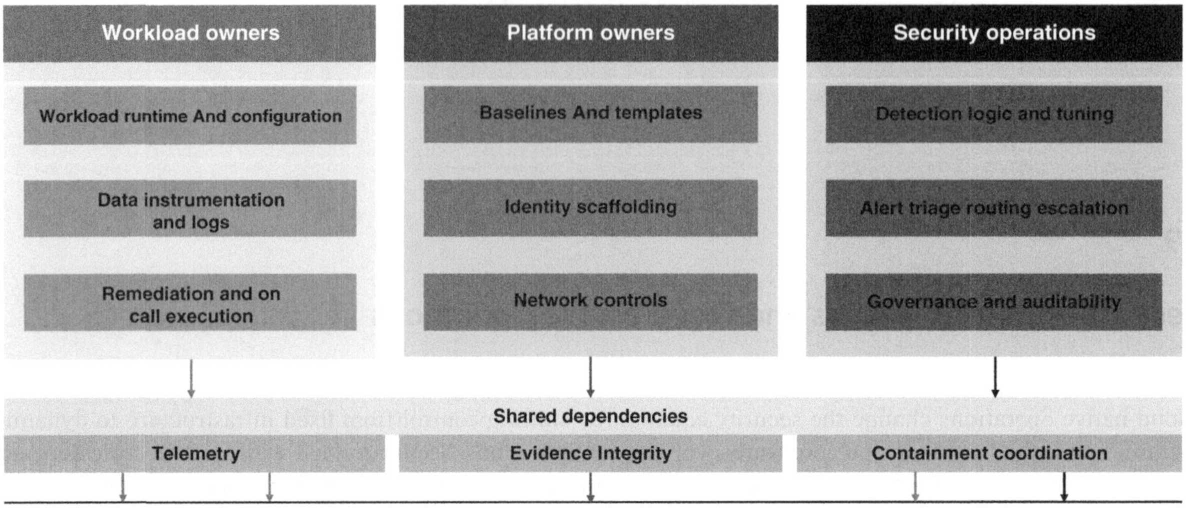

Figure 29.1 Ownership and Execution Boundaries for Cloud Security Actions.

In practice, the hardest ownership problems show up where cloud services feel "invisible" until they fail: identity, networking, and data access paths. Identity and access management is often administered centrally but exercised by every team, which means entitlement decisions can become ambiguous unless ownership includes approval boundaries and review cadence. Networking components—security groups, routing rules, load balancers, and service-to-service connectivity—are frequently changed as part of feature delivery, yet those changes can open lateral movement pathways if they bypass review. Data services are especially sensitive because they collapse confidentiality and availability concerns into configuration details like public exposure, encryption settings, and cross-account sharing. Ownership has to state who approves exposure changes, who monitors drift from approved states, and who is expected to respond when abnormal access is detected. Without that, "least privilege" becomes a slogan rather than an operational expectation.

Operational ownership must also be anchored in how work is executed: the deployment pipeline, the runtime environment, and the on-call model. Cloud workloads change continuously, so ownership is not just a name on a diagram; it is the ability to take action quickly and safely through defined change mechanisms. Teams that can only remediate through manual console work will struggle to maintain consistent security posture, and they will often create emergency exceptions that become permanent. A mature model routes changes through infrastructure-as-code and controlled pipelines so that remediation is reviewable, reproducible, and reversible. On-call accountability is equally important because the first hour of an incident is dominated by decision-making—what to isolate, what to rotate, what to shut down—and those decisions must be owned by people empowered to act. When security asks for containment steps, there must be a clear "who can execute" answer that aligns with privileges and operational authority.

Logging and evidence generation are where ownership becomes measurable, because they determine whether an incident response is decisive or speculative. Workload owners should be accountable for emitting application-level telemetry that supports detection and investigation, including authentication events, authorization decisions, sensitive data access, and error conditions that signal abuse. Platform owners should be accountable for cloud control-plane logs, network flow visibility where appropriate, and centralized retention and integrity controls, so evidence cannot be quietly lost. Security operations should own the monitoring logic, tuning, and triage workflows, but they cannot own the underlying visibility if engineering does not provide it. AI-assisted triage can help prioritize alerts and summarize activity across multiple services, but it depends on consistent event schemas, stable identifiers, and well-defined context such as environment, workload name,

Table 29.1 Ownership Map for Cloud Workloads and Shared Services.

Ownership Area	Accountable Owner	Operational Responsibilities	Common Failure Mode
Workload runtime and configuration	Product or service owner	Maintain secure runtime settings and remediate workload issues	Findings stall due to unclear ownership
Shared guardrails and deployment paths	Platform or infrastructure owner	Provide templates pipelines and baseline configurations	Teams bypass secure path creating drift
Identity scaffolding and role patterns	Platform or IAM owner	Define role patterns enforce approvals and support rotation and revocation	Privilege sprawl from reused broad roles
Monitoring logic and triage workflows	Security operations owner	Build tune and maintain detections and routing rules	Alert fatigue from untuned rules and noisy signals
Telemetry pipeline and retention	Platform and security operations owners	Collect normalize retain and protect evidence across environments	Investigations fail due to missing logs
Incident containment execution	On call workload and platform owners	Revoke access isolate services restrict egress preserve evidence	Delays due to unclear authority boundaries

and owner. If ownership metadata is missing or inconsistent, automation will confidently route incidents to the wrong team, and human responders will waste time reconstructing basic facts under pressure. Table 29.1 clarifies how accountability is divided between workload teams platform teams and security operations, so findings route quickly and response actions are executable.

Ownership also needs explicit approval boundaries to prevent privilege sprawl and to ensure accountability survives organizational change. The ability to grant broad permissions, create new cloud accounts or projects, expose services publicly, or alter network boundaries should be controlled through approvals tied to named roles, not informal agreements. Temporary access patterns should be treated as operational tools with expiration and auditability, because "just for the migration" is a common path to permanent administrative access. In cloud environments, misconfigurations can propagate quickly through templates and shared modules, so approval boundaries must include changes to reusable infrastructure components and baseline policies. AI and automation can assist by detecting risky permission changes and configuration drift, but those outputs must be reviewable and explainable to support change control and post-incident audits. The goal is not to slow delivery; it is to make high-impact changes deliberate, traceable, and reversible, so speed does not come at the cost of systemic fragility.

A realistic ownership model anticipates failure modes and designs for them, rather than assuming every team will behave perfectly. One common failure is "orphaned" services: resources created for experiments, proofs of concept, or short-lived projects that remain running without a clear owner, quietly accumulating data and exposure. Another is over-centralization, where a platform team becomes a bottleneck and product teams work around guardrails, creating hidden variations that are hard to monitor and secure. A third is under-centralization, where every team builds its own deployment patterns, logging formats, and identity structures, making incident response inconsistent and expensive. AI-driven correlation can highlight cross-workload patterns—reused credentials, shared IP behaviors, or repeated misconfiguration signatures—but it will also amplify biases in the underlying data, such as over-alerting on teams with better logging while missing quiet services with poor telemetry. Effective ownership counters these risks by pairing accountability with enablement: clear responsibility, consistent guardrails, reliable visibility, and a culture where operational control is treated as a first-class security requirement.

Cloud-Native Application Considerations

Cloud-native applications are designed around change as a constant, which means security must be embedded into how software is built, deployed, and operated rather than bolted onto a static runtime. These applications typically favor loosely coupled services, elastic scaling, and managed dependencies, all of which increase the number of control points that can fail in subtle ways. The operational advantage is speed and resilience, but the security consequence is that misconfigurations and identity mistakes can propagate faster than traditional patch cycles ever could. Defensive teams have to assume that the runtime shape of the application will vary hour to hour as deployments roll forward, instances scale out, and services are replaced. In that environment, security becomes less about protecting a single server and more about constraining behaviors and verifying that the system remains within approved boundaries.

Identity is the primary security perimeter in cloud-native design, because service-to-service communication and control-plane actions are governed by permissions rather than physical network location. Workloads authenticate to other services using short-lived credentials, roles, or workload identities, and mistakes here commonly create "silent admin" conditions where an application can do far more than intended. Least privilege is operationally difficult because cloud-native applications evolve; permissions that were minimal last month may be excessive today, and permissions that are excessive today may be required tomorrow. Effective teams treat permissions as code, review changes with the same rigor as application logic, and monitor for drift between intended and effective access. When permissions are granted, the decision should be anchored to a specific runtime need and a clear owner who will revisit that decision as the application changes.

Network controls still matter, but cloud-native architectures require a different mental model than traditional perimeter thinking. Microservices and managed services create many east–west paths, and connectivity often depends on security groups, service endpoints, routing rules, and private connectivity patterns rather than fixed subnets and firewall rules. The common pitfall is assuming that "internal" traffic is inherently safe, when the real risk is lateral movement using legitimate service channels after a single workload is compromised. Segmentation should be expressed in reusable patterns that constrain which services can talk, which ports and protocols are allowed, and which data paths are permissible. Where possible, controls should be enforced close to the workload and validated continuously, because a single overly permissive rule can reintroduce broad connectivity faster than a manual review process can catch it. Security operations benefits when network intent is consistently expressed, because abnormal connection patterns become detectable rather than blending into noise.

Data handling is another defining consideration, because cloud-native applications frequently distribute data across multiple storage services, queues, caches, and analytics systems. The confidentiality risk is not only whether data is encrypted, but whether it can be accessed through unexpected paths such as cross-service integrations, mis-scoped roles, or overly broad sharing configurations. Data classification needs to be practical: developers must know what is sensitive, where it is allowed to flow, and what controls are mandatory at rest and in transit. Tokenization, field-level protection, and careful handling of secrets reduce blast radius, but they only help if the application is designed to keep sensitive material out of logs and telemetry. Operationally, teams should assume that attackers will seek the easiest data path, which is often a managed service with permissive access rather than the primary database. When ownership is unclear for data stores and sharing settings, security incidents turn into multi-team investigations where the most basic question—who can change access—does not have an immediate answer.

Supply chain exposure grows in cloud-native development because applications rely heavily on third-party libraries, container images, and managed build pipelines. Vulnerabilities arrive through dependencies as often as through first-party code, and "works on my machine" becomes "runs everywhere" when the same image is deployed across environments. Building from trusted sources, pinning versions, and validating artifacts are critical, but the real operational challenge is keeping these practices consistent across multiple teams and fast-moving repositories. Container images should be treated as deployable artifacts with provenance, not as convenient packaging; the image build process, registry controls, and promotion between environments must be auditable. Secrets management is part of the same discipline: embedding credentials in images, configuration files, or pipeline variables creates long-lived exposure that attackers can harvest at scale. Cloud-native security assumes compromise is possible and focuses on reducing what an attacker can reuse, how far they can move, and how quickly defenders can detect and revoke access.

Observability is the difference between an incident that is contained early and one that becomes a prolonged business disruption. Cloud-native applications produce many small signals—API calls, role assumptions, queue interactions, storage accesses—that are individually benign but collectively meaningful when correlated. Workload instrumentation should capture authentication and authorization outcomes, access to sensitive functions and data, and abnormal error patterns that indicate probing or abuse. Platform telemetry must include control-plane actions and configuration changes, because attackers frequently target permissions and logging itself to reduce visibility. AI-assisted analysis can help by summarizing multi-service sequences, clustering related events, and highlighting anomalies that cross workload boundaries, but it is only reliable when the underlying telemetry is complete and consistent. Over-trust is a real failure mode: models can produce confident narratives that omit crucial gaps, so human reviewers need clear validation steps and a habit of confirming conclusions against raw events.

Resilience and secure operations converge in cloud-native systems because the same mechanisms that enable rapid recovery can also enable rapid compromise if misused. Automated rollbacks, dynamic scaling, and continuous deployment reduce downtime, but they also mean attackers may attempt to trigger operational responses, exploit deployment processes, or hide within the churn of normal activity. Guardrails should focus on preventing unsafe states—public exposure where it is not intended, privileged roles attached to broad workloads, logging disabled, or data stores shared outside approved boundaries. Change management must be designed for speed without losing traceability, because during incidents teams will need to rotate credentials, isolate services, and deploy fixes quickly while preserving evidence. Good practice looks like rehearsed workflows that integrate security checks into deployment paths and incident response playbooks that specify who can take which actions and how those actions are verified. When those controls are absent, cloud-native speed becomes a liability, and the organization experiences the worst of both worlds: rapid change with slow, uncertain security outcomes.

Protecting Data in Cloud Storage and Services

Cloud data protection starts with acknowledging that storage is no longer a single destination; it is an ecosystem of managed services, replication paths, caches, analytics layers, and integrations that all create access opportunities. The primary risk is not merely that data exists in the cloud, but that it can be reached through multiple control planes and identity contexts that evolve rapidly. Storage services are often easy to provision and easy to share, which is useful operationally but dangerous when ownership and guardrails are unclear. The defensive posture therefore has to treat data access as a behavior to constrain and verify, not a static property of an object store or database. If a team cannot answer who can read, who can write, and who can share a dataset, then the dataset is effectively unprotected regardless of encryption settings.

Classification and handling expectations must be practical and operational, because the cloud accelerates how quickly data can be copied and repurposed. Sensitive data should be identified early in its lifecycle, with clear rules for where it may be stored, which services are approved, and what controls are mandatory at rest and in transit. The most common failure mode is assuming that a service's default settings align with the organization's sensitivity requirements, when defaults are designed for general usability, not strict protection. Data minimization helps reduce exposure, but it only works if teams also control derived data such as exports, logs, and analytics extracts that frequently escape the original safeguards. Where teams rely on managed analytics or data lakes, the governance model must cover both the raw source and the processed outputs, because attackers often target the

Table 29.2 Cloud Data Protection Controls and Failure Patterns.

Protection Focus	What to Implement	What to Monitor	Common Failure Mode
Classification and handling rules	Define where sensitive data may live and flow	New datasets exports and derived copies	Securing only the primary dataset
Access control and least privilege	Use purpose-bound roles tied to workload identity	Unusual reads writes and sharing events	Broad roles reused across workloads
Sharing and exposure management	Restrict public and cross boundary sharing mechanisms	Exposure toggles cross account grants	Old shares persist after need ends
Key management and rotation	Separate key usage and maintain rotation readiness	Key access events and privilege changes	Assuming encryption alone stops abuse
Telemetry and evidence integrity	Centralize logs with consistent identity context	Missing sources drift and logging tampering	Confidence without complete evidence

easiest copy rather than the authoritative system of record. Effective programs make data handling expectations visible in engineering workflows, so storage decisions happen with context, not after an exposure incident.

Access control is the true gatekeeper for cloud data, and it must be engineered with least privilege as a living constraint rather than a one-time design goal. Cloud identity policies tend to be expressive, which is powerful but also easy to misconfigure in ways that grant broad read access across environments or accounts. Permission sprawl develops when roles are created for convenience, reused across workloads, or expanded over time without a disciplined review process. A mature approach ties permissions to a specific workload identity, a defined purpose, and a clear owner who is accountable for periodic validation and rapid revocation when needed. Conditional controls such as requiring specific network paths, device posture, or approved workload identities can reduce risk, but only if they are consistently applied and monitored for drift. When defenders see data access that does not map cleanly to an expected workload or approved user action, the incident response path must be immediate and unambiguous. Table 29.2 reinforces that protecting cloud data requires pairing access behavior controls with continuous verification and coverage of replicas backups and shares.

Encryption is necessary but insufficient, and teams should be precise about what encryption actually protects against in cloud services. Encryption in transit reduces interception risk, but it does not stop an attacker who has valid credentials from retrieving data through normal APIs. Encryption at rest helps protect against physical loss and some service-layer threats, but its practical value depends on key management, rotation practices, and the separation of duties around key usage. Key management should support the operational need to rotate keys, revoke access, and prove control without introducing fragile manual steps that teams avoid during high-pressure incidents. Where feasible, using distinct keys for distinct data domains limits blast radius, but it must be paired with accurate inventory of which datasets rely on which keys and how key access is audited. When a compromise occurs, responders need to know whether keys were exposed, whether re-encryption is required, and which downstream systems consumed potentially tainted data.

Cloud storage protection also requires attention to exposure pathways that are operationally convenient but security-critical, particularly sharing, replication, and cross-environment access. Many services make it trivial to share data externally or across organizational boundaries, and those sharing mechanisms can persist long after the original need has ended. Replication and backups introduce additional copies that may live in different regions, accounts, or service tiers, each with its own access model and retention behavior. Without clear ownership and lifecycle management, an organization can lock down a primary dataset while leaving a backup or analytics export broadly accessible. Security operations should treat exposure changes—public access toggles, cross-account grants, new sharing links, and policy modifications—as high-signal events that warrant monitoring and fast review.

AI-assisted detection can help by learning baseline access patterns for datasets and flagging unusual sharing or download behavior, but it must be grounded in reliable identity context and well-defined definitions of "normal" per environment and workload.

Monitoring data access in cloud services must be designed to support investigations, not just compliance reporting. Useful telemetry includes control-plane events that show policy and configuration changes, and data-plane events that show reads, writes, deletes, and administrative operations against storage resources. Correlation is essential because the meaning of a single event often depends on what happened before it, such as a role assumption followed by a policy change followed by bulk reads. Organizations that centralize logs but do not normalize identities and resource naming will struggle to interpret events quickly, and response time will suffer accordingly. AI summarization can reduce cognitive load during an incident by clustering related events and generating concise narratives, but models can also introduce false confidence when logs are incomplete or when benign automation resembles adversary behavior. Human-in-the-loop controls should require analysts to validate key claims against raw events, confirm the scope of access, and identify whether data was merely exposed or actually accessed.

Operational controls become real when teams can execute containment quickly and safely in the face of suspected data exposure. That means having predefined actions for revoking access, rotating credentials, disabling sharing mechanisms, and isolating workloads that appear to be exfiltrating data. These actions must be reversible and traceable, so responders can balance business continuity with security risk, especially when critical services depend on the affected data stores. Containment also has to consider secondary effects, such as breaking integrations, disrupting batch jobs, or causing downstream systems to fail when access is removed. Mature teams rehearse these scenarios, so responders understand which levers exist, what the blast radius is, and how to verify that access has been effectively constrained. When containment steps are improvised, teams either overreact and cause outages or underreact and allow continued exposure while debating ownership and approvals.

Data protection in the cloud ultimately relies on governance that is auditable, actionable, and aligned to operational ownership. Governance should define who is accountable for each dataset, who approves high-impact access changes, and how exceptions are documented and revisited. Auditability is not about generating paperwork; it is about being able to reconstruct what happened, when it changed, and who authorized it under both normal operations and incident conditions. Drift detection and periodic access reviews help keep reality aligned with intent, but they must be engineered into workflows, so they do not collapse under delivery pressure. AI can support governance by prioritizing review targets, detecting anomalous permission expansions, and highlighting datasets with growing exposure over time, yet those insights must be explainable enough to drive remediation decisions. When governance is treated as an operational capability rather than a compliance exercise, teams protect data by default and respond decisively when the inevitable anomaly occurs.

Network Controls and Segmentation in Cloud Context

Network controls in the cloud are less about building a hard perimeter and more about shaping and constraining connectivity so that compromise cannot easily spread. Cloud environments replace fixed topologies with dynamic routing, elastic endpoints, and service-to-service communication patterns that change as workloads scale and deployments roll forward. The business impact of weak segmentation is rarely immediate until it is catastrophic, because lateral movement and data access often look like normal traffic when boundaries are broad. Effective segmentation therefore aims to reduce blast radius, make unauthorized paths improbable, and make abnormal paths detectable. When leaders ask whether the cloud network is "secure," the operationally honest answer depends on whether the organization can control who can talk to what, under which identities, and for which purposes.

Segmentation starts with intent: defining which workloads and services must communicate, which should never communicate, and which may communicate only through controlled intermediaries. In a cloud context, this intent is expressed through security groups, network policies, routing constructs, private endpoints, and service-to-service controls rather than a single firewall choke point. A common failure mode is relying on broad network ranges and implicit trust, which makes "internal" traffic effectively unbounded and encourages teams to solve connectivity by widening access. Instead, teams should design narrow, reusable connectivity patterns for common needs such as web ingress, application-to-database access, and batch processing to storage. These patterns should be enforced consistently across environments, so the rules in production are not looser than those in lower tiers "for convenience." When segmentation is treated as architecture, not ticket work, it becomes resilient to organizational churn and scale.

Ingress and egress controls deserve separate attention because they represent different threat paths and different operational constraints. Ingress determines how external actors and partner systems reach exposed services, and it should be minimized to the smallest set of endpoints necessary for business function. Egress determines what workloads can reach on the internet or across accounts, and uncontrolled egress is one of the fastest routes to data exfiltration and command-and-control connectivity. Many cloud-native applications require outbound access for updates, APIs, and integrations, which makes "block all egress" impractical, but "allow all egress" removes a key detection and containment lever. Mature programs establish defined egress paths and observable control points, then monitor for deviations such as workloads initiating new outbound destinations, unusual ports, or traffic bursts inconsistent with known workflows. Segmentation that ignores egress leaves defenders blind to some of the highest impact behaviors during an active intrusion.

East–west traffic control is where cloud segmentation either succeeds or collapses, because lateral movement happens primarily within internal service meshes and private networks. Workloads should not be able to enumerate and reach every other workload simply because they share an environment, yet that is the default outcome when security groups and network policies are overly permissive. The goal is to ensure that a compromised service can reach only its required dependencies, and that those dependencies enforce additional checks beyond network reachability. Service-to-service authentication and authorization matter here because network segmentation alone cannot distinguish a legitimate request from an attacker operating from inside a workload. When network controls and identity controls reinforce each other, defenders gain both prevention and investigatory clarity: it becomes easier to see which workload identity initiated a connection and whether that connection aligns with expected dependencies. Where feasible, restricting administrative interfaces and management planes to dedicated paths and tightly controlled identities reduces the chance that an application compromise becomes an infrastructure compromise.

Cloud segmentation also has to account for managed services that do not live "inside" a traditional subnet boundary but are still reachable through network constructs. Databases, object storage, messaging systems, and analytics services often provide multiple access paths, including public endpoints, private endpoints, and service-to-service integrations that bypass conventional network assumptions. The common pitfall is believing that placing workloads in private subnets automatically protects downstream services, while those services remain exposed through alternate endpoints or permissive access policies. Segmentation in cloud must be paired with service-level configuration that disables unnecessary public exposure, constrains which identities can access the service, and logs data-plane activity for investigation. Private connectivity patterns reduce exposure but can also create a false sense of safety if teams stop monitoring access behaviors because the endpoint is "private." In practice, the highest confidence posture is achieved when both reachability and authorization are explicitly constrained and continuously verified.

Operationalizing segmentation requires that network intent be expressed as code and validated continuously, because manual configurations drift and emergency changes tend to become permanent. Infrastructure-as-code makes connectivity changes reviewable and reproducible, but it also introduces the risk of widespread misconfiguration if shared modules are wrong or if teams copy insecure patterns. That is why guardrails should include automated validation of network policies, detection of overly permissive rules, and monitoring for drift between intended and deployed configurations. AI-assisted analysis can help prioritize which changes deserve urgent review by learning what "normal" network change looks like per environment and flagging outliers such as sudden broadening of inbound rules or creation of unexpected peering connections. However, models can be fooled by routine automation that produces high volumes of benign changes, so human reviewers need clear criteria for what constitutes a high-risk change and how to validate it quickly. Governance must define who is authorized to create or modify core network constructs, and incident response plans must include fast containment steps that do not require improvisation.

Monitoring and detection in segmented cloud networks is most effective when it is tied to expected dependencies and expressed in actionable terms. Rather than attempting to detect "suspicious traffic" in the abstract, defenders should monitor for connections that violate known service relationships, for unexpected administrative access paths, and for abnormal egress destinations. Network flow telemetry, load balancer logs, and control-plane change logs provide different perspectives, and responders typically need all three during investigations. AI summarization can reduce analyst burden by correlating control-plane changes with subsequent traffic anomalies and highlighting likely causal chains, but it should be treated as a triage aid rather than an authority. The most damaging failure mode is false confidence, where a model narrative is accepted without verifying whether critical telemetry is missing due to sampling, misconfiguration, or logging disabled by an attacker. A disciplined approach requires that investigations confirm segmentation boundaries, validate that controls are actually enforced in the environment, and identify the precise path an attacker used rather than relying on generic assumptions.

Segmentation ultimately succeeds when it is aligned to ownership and designed to be survivable under real operational pressure. Workload teams need patterns that enable them to ship without widening access, while platform teams need centralized constructs that prevent unsafe defaults from slipping into production. Security teams need clear escalation paths and authority to request containment actions that may temporarily reduce functionality to prevent further compromise. During an incident, responders should be able to isolate a workload, restrict egress, and tighten service reachability quickly, with confidence that the changes are auditable and reversible. When those capabilities exist, segmentation becomes a practical risk control that reduces impact, improves detection clarity, and accelerates response decisions. When they do not, cloud networks remain functionally flat, and the organization learns about its true connectivity model only after an attacker demonstrates it.

Monitoring Cloud Activity and Behavior Patterns

Monitoring cloud activity is fundamentally about understanding behavior across two planes: the control plane where resources are created and configured, and the data plane where workloads and users actually interact with services. In cloud environments, adversaries often succeed by manipulating legitimate interfaces—assuming roles, modifying policies, creating access paths—rather than by exploiting a single fragile host. That means defenders must treat configuration changes, identity actions, and service interactions as first-class security telemetry, not secondary logs collected "when convenient." The operational goal is to detect meaningful deviations early, before they become widespread compromise or irreversible data exposure. When monitoring is effective, teams can answer not only what happened, but how it happened and what pathways are now at risk.

Behavior-focused monitoring starts with establishing what "normal" looks like in context, because cloud activity is noisy by design. Autoscaling, continuous deployment, infrastructure automation, and scheduled jobs generate a constant stream of legitimate events that can obscure malicious actions if the baseline is vague. A useful baseline is not a static count of events; it is a model of expected behaviors tied to environment, workload identity, and time patterns. For example, a build pipeline may legitimately create resources in bursts during working hours, while a production workload should rarely change its own permissions or create new privileged roles. Contextual baselining must also account for lifecycle stages, because a workload in early rollout behaves differently than a stable service with mature access patterns. Without this grounding, monitoring collapses into alert fatigue where teams either ignore noise or disable rules that were never properly tuned.

Control-plane monitoring is where many cloud compromises reveal themselves, because attackers typically need to change something to maintain access or expand capability. High-signal events include role assumption anomalies, creation of new credentials, changes to access policies, disabling of logging, modification of network exposure, and creation of new trust relationships between accounts or projects. These events are not automatically malicious, but they are operationally significant because they alter what is possible in the environment. Monitoring should therefore focus on whether the actor is expected, whether the change aligns with an approved workflow, and whether the change is occurring in a sequence that suggests escalation. A single permission change may be benign, but a permission change followed by rapid access to sensitive storage is a different story. The practical value of control-plane monitoring is that it often provides earlier indicators than endpoint alerts, especially in cloud-native environments where hosts are ephemeral and traditional agent-based visibility may be inconsistent.

Data-plane monitoring complements control-plane visibility by showing whether sensitive actions are actually occurring, not just whether the environment could allow them. For storage and managed databases, this includes bulk reads, unusual query patterns, atypical download volumes, and access from unexpected identities or network paths. For compute and application services, it includes authentication outcomes, authorization denials, abnormal error rates, and unusual service-to-service call patterns that indicate probing or misuse. Data-plane monitoring is also where defenders can distinguish between an attacker staging access and an attacker actively exfiltrating or destroying data. The challenge is that data-plane telemetry can be high volume and uneven across services, so monitoring needs consistent event normalization and identity mapping to remain actionable. If analysts cannot quickly map an access event to a workload owner and an expected purpose, the response will be slow and uncertain.

Behavior patterns are most valuable when they are expressed as sequences, because cloud attacks often involve chained actions across multiple services. A typical progression may involve initial credential use, role escalation, persistence through new keys or trust relationships, discovery through enumeration, and then data access at scale. Detecting these chains requires correlation across identity events, configuration changes, network reachability shifts, and service access logs, which is where many programs fail due to fragmented telemetry and inconsistent naming. Effective monitoring treats identities, accounts, environments, and workloads as stable entities that can be tracked across logs, even as underlying infrastructure changes. AI-assisted correlation can help by clustering related events into candidate incidents and surfacing likely sequences that span services, but it depends on high-quality data and clear definitions of entities. When the underlying telemetry is incomplete or inconsistent, models may produce confident narratives that are directionally wrong, so analysts must validate claims against raw events and known workflows.

Alerting should be driven by operational decision points rather than by every deviation from baseline, because not every anomaly deserves immediate response. The most useful alerts are those that indicate a change in risk state, such as a new public exposure, a privileged role granted to an unexpected principal, or bulk access to sensitive data outside normal patterns. Alerts should also be designed to support containment actions, meaning they include enough context to answer who did it, what changed, what resources are affected, and what the next step should be. If the alert forces analysts to spend the first thirty minutes reconstructing basic context, the monitoring program is effectively delegating triage to humans without giving them the necessary inputs. AI summarization can help by generating concise incident briefs and highlighting supporting evidence, but it must be governed with approval boundaries, so automated conclusions do not trigger disruptive actions without human review. The goal is to accelerate understanding, not to replace accountability for high-impact decisions.

Monitoring cloud activity also requires defensive attention to tampering and blind spots, because attackers will try to reduce visibility once they gain a foothold. Disabling or altering logging, changing retention settings, modifying audit configurations, and diverting logs away from centralized collection are all behaviors that should be monitored as potential indicators of compromise. Equally important are quieter failure modes where visibility degrades unintentionally due to misconfiguration, cost controls, or incomplete onboarding of new services. Programs should track coverage explicitly: which accounts are sending which logs, which services have data-plane events enabled, and where gaps exist due to technical or organizational constraints. Drift detection matters here, because cloud environments change constantly and logging configurations can regress without obvious symptoms until an investigation fails. A reliable monitoring posture treats telemetry pipelines as critical infrastructure with ownership, testing, and validation, not as an afterthought managed only when something breaks.

The operational maturity of cloud monitoring is measured by how quickly teams can detect, triage, and respond to meaningful behavior changes while maintaining trust in the evidence. That requires clear routing to the right owners, established playbooks for common cloud behavior patterns, and a culture that treats monitoring rules as living assets that must be tuned and maintained. AI can increase analyst throughput by prioritizing alerts, recommending likely root causes, and flagging cross-environment trends that humans might miss, but governance must address failure modes like bias toward noisy systems, drift in behavior baselines, and leakage of sensitive data through automated summaries. Auditability is essential because cloud incidents often involve questions of authorization, approvals, and change control that must be reconstructed after the fact. When monitoring is designed around behavior patterns, supported by dependable telemetry, and governed to avoid over-trust, it becomes a practical capability that reduces uncertainty and shortens the path from anomaly to decisive action.

Responding to Cloud Incidents and Access Abuse

Responding to cloud incidents requires a shift from host-centric response thinking to identity- and control-plane–centric decision making. In cloud environments, attackers frequently operate through legitimate interfaces using compromised or misused credentials, which means the visible symptoms may look like normal administrative activity until correlated. The first responsibility of responders is to determine whether access is authorized, expected, and aligned with an approved workflow, rather than assuming that malicious activity will announce itself through obvious failures. Time pressure is amplified because cloud changes propagate quickly and persistence mechanisms can be created in minutes. Effective response therefore prioritizes rapid understanding of access scope and blast radius before making irreversible containment decisions.

Initial triage in cloud incidents should focus on clarifying what identities are involved and what they can do, because permissions define both impact and response options. This includes identifying which users, roles, service accounts, or workload identities were used, how they were authenticated, and whether their access was time-bound or long-lived. Responders must then map those identities to the resources they can reach, including compute, storage, network controls, and management APIs, to understand potential lateral movement paths. A common pitfall is treating an incident as limited to the resource where suspicious activity was first observed, while the compromised identity has far broader permissions. AI-assisted triage can help by summarizing identity usage and highlighting unusual permission combinations, but responders must validate these summaries against actual policy definitions and effective permissions. Without that validation, teams risk underestimating exposure or revoking the wrong access under pressure.

Containment in the cloud is primarily about controlling access rather than isolating hardware, and the sequence of actions matters. Revoking or rotating credentials, disabling roles, tightening network egress, and removing newly created trust relationships are often higher-impact than terminating individual workloads. However, responders must balance speed with evidence preservation, because aggressive containment can destroy logs or disrupt the very telemetry needed to understand what occurred. Predefined containment playbooks should specify which actions are safe to take immediately, which require approval, and which should be delayed until evidence is captured. When these decisions are improvised, teams either hesitate and allow continued abuse or act too aggressively and cause avoidable outages. Clear ownership and authority boundaries enable responders to move decisively without waiting for ad hoc executive approval during a crisis.

Investigating access abuse requires correlating control-plane changes with data-plane activity to determine whether exposure translated into actual misuse. It is not enough to know that a role was granted or a policy was changed; responders must determine whether sensitive data was accessed, modified, or exfiltrated as a result. This investigation often spans multiple services and accounts, requiring consistent identity mapping and timestamp alignment across logs. Cloud incidents are particularly challenging when logs are incomplete or when attackers attempt to blend into automation noise by timing actions during deployments or maintenance windows. AI-driven correlation can accelerate hypothesis generation by grouping related events and proposing likely sequences, but it should not be treated as definitive. Analysts need to confirm critical claims manually, especially when decisions may trigger regulatory notifications or customer communications.

Eradication in cloud incidents is less about removing malware and more about restoring trust in identities, configurations, and deployment pipelines. This may involve reestablishing baseline permissions, redeploying workloads from known-good artifacts, and reviewing infrastructure-as-code repositories for malicious or unauthorized changes. Because cloud resources are ephemeral, redeployment is often faster and safer than attempting in-place cleanup, but only if the build and deployment processes themselves are trusted. Responders must also consider whether secrets, keys, or tokens were exposed and whether downstream systems or partners could have been affected. The operational challenge is coordinating these actions across teams while maintaining service availability, especially for customer-facing systems. When eradication steps are poorly coordinated, teams can reintroduce vulnerabilities or restore access that attackers had already abused.

Recovery in the cloud is inseparable from validation, because restoring services without verifying access paths can leave the environment in a compromised state. Validation should confirm that unauthorized identities no longer have access, that network exposure is consistent with approved designs, and that logging and monitoring are fully restored. It should also include targeted monitoring for recurrence, focusing on the specific access paths and behaviors observed during the incident. Recovery is an opportunity to correct structural weaknesses, such as overly broad roles or permissive network rules, but only if those corrections are implemented in shared templates and pipelines rather than as one-off fixes. Executives often want rapid closure, but premature declarations of recovery create risk if latent access paths remain. Clear criteria for what constitutes "recovered" help balance business urgency with security assurance.

Post-incident learning in cloud environments must go beyond root cause and address systemic access and ownership issues that enabled the incident. This includes examining why excessive permissions existed, why monitoring did not trigger earlier, and whether approval boundaries were unclear or bypassed. Cloud incidents often reveal gaps in governance rather than individual mistakes, such as inconsistent role review practices or lack of clarity over who owns critical services. AI analysis can assist by identifying recurring patterns across incidents, such as repeated exposure of certain services or chronic over-privileging of specific roles, but those insights must be translated into concrete changes. The most effective outcome is not a thicker incident report, but adjustments to guardrails, monitoring rules, and response playbooks that reduce future response time and blast radius. When organizations treat cloud incident response as an operational discipline rather than an exceptional event, they become more resilient to both accidental misuse and deliberate abuse.

Handling Multi-Account and Multi-Environment Complexity

Multi-account and multi-environment cloud operations exist because they solve real business problems: they reduce blast radius, separate duties, enable independent delivery, and support regulatory and customer boundaries. The security consequence is that complexity becomes an adversary advantage when environments are inconsistent, ownership is unclear, or visibility is fragmented. Attackers do not need to "break the cloud" to move; they only need to find where identity trust is loosely defined, where shared services expose broad paths, or where logging is uneven across accounts. Defensive success depends on making complexity predictable through standardization, guardrails, and reliable cross-environment evidence. Without that discipline, teams will spend more time reconciling differences between environments than containing the actual incident.

The foundational requirement is consistent environment design, because small differences multiply across accounts until they become operational risk. Production, staging, and development environments often diverge due to shortcuts, cost decisions, or historical drift, and those divergences create the conditions for both misconfiguration and investigative confusion. A consistent design does not mean identical capacity or identical service usage, but it does mean consistent identity patterns, network segmentation intent, logging baselines, and deployment paths. When roles, naming conventions, and resource tagging differ by environment, defenders cannot reliably attribute activity or route incidents to the right owners. Standardization also reduces the temptation to grant broad cross-environment access "just to make things work," which is one of the most common drivers of privilege sprawl. The operational goal is that an analyst can interpret an event in one account and immediately understand how that concept maps elsewhere.

Identity and trust relationships are where multi-account architectures either provide strong isolation or collapse into a single, distributed blast radius. Cross-account access is frequently needed for central security operations, shared platform services, and deployment automation, but it must be narrowly scoped and continuously reviewed. The danger is creating broad trust relationships that allow one compromised principal to assume roles across many accounts, turning an isolated compromise into an enterprise-wide incident. Effective programs treat cross-account role assumption as a high-sensitivity action: it is logged, monitored, and constrained by conditions such as required principals, limited permissions, and explicit boundaries between environments. Where long-lived access is unavoidable, it should be paired with strong controls over credential storage, rotation, and usage monitoring. AI-assisted anomaly detection can help by learning normal role assumption patterns and flagging unexpected account traversal, but it only works when identities are consistently represented and monitored across environments.

Shared services introduce another layer of complexity because they can quietly reintroduce central points of failure into a distributed architecture. Centralized identity providers, shared network connectivity hubs, logging pipelines, and shared artifact registries provide efficiency and standardization, but they also become high-value targets. The key is to ensure that shared services are treated as tier-zero assets with stronger controls, stricter change governance, and clearer operational ownership than ordinary application workloads. Network connectivity between accounts should be designed to enforce intent, not convenience, and should prevent unneeded lateral paths between environments. When shared services must interact with multiple accounts, their permissions should be narrowly tailored and their access patterns closely monitored. A common pitfall is granting shared tooling broad administrative access because it simplifies operations, then discovering during an incident that the tooling's access is indistinguishable from an attacker's.

Visibility and evidence management are disproportionately difficult in multi-account operations, because telemetry must be complete, consistent, and centrally usable without losing environmental context. Control-plane logs, network flow signals, and service access logs should be collected centrally with consistent retention and integrity protections, but they must preserve key attributes like account, environment, workload identity, and owner to remain actionable. Fragmented logging creates an operational hazard where teams cannot reconstruct cross-account sequences quickly, and investigations devolve into manual data gathering. Coverage tracking becomes essential: defenders should know which accounts are onboarded, which log sources are enabled, and where gaps exist due to service limitations or configuration drift. AI-assisted summarization can accelerate triage by correlating events across accounts and generating candidate narratives, but governance must prevent over-trust, especially when coverage is incomplete. Analysts should be trained to treat model outputs as hypotheses and to verify conclusions using raw, authoritative logs from the relevant accounts.

Change management and configuration drift are amplified in multi-environment setups, because the same change can be implemented differently across accounts or missed entirely in a subset of environments. Infrastructure-as-code and standardized pipelines are the practical answer, but they only help if organizations avoid exception sprawl and enforce consistent promotion paths. Drift detection should identify when an account's network rules, identity policies, or logging settings diverge from approved baselines, and those deviations should be routed to accountable owners with clear remediation expectations. The risk is not only insecure configuration, but also inconsistency that undermines detection logic and response playbooks. When response teams rely on an assumption that "production accounts log X" or "staging has the same segmentation," those assumptions must be verifiably true. AI can help prioritize drift findings by highlighting those with the highest potential blast radius or those that resemble prior incident precursors, but it cannot substitute for disciplined baseline management and clear ownership.

Incident response in a multi-account context must be designed to operate across boundaries without creating new ones during a crisis. Responders need the ability to rapidly scope which accounts and environments are involved, which identities traversed boundaries, and which shared services may have been leveraged. Containment actions must be staged to prevent an attacker from pivoting into other accounts as controls tighten, which often means constraining role assumption paths and reducing broad privileges early. At the same time, responders must maintain business continuity, especially when shared services support multiple environments and customer-facing workloads. Predefined escalation paths are critical because multi-account incidents often require coordinated actions across platform teams, workload owners, and security operations under time pressure. Without rehearsed cross-account playbooks, teams will discover during the incident that they lack access to the right logs, cannot execute the required containment actions, or do not know who owns the affected resources.

Operational ownership and governance are the stabilizing forces that prevent multi-environment complexity from turning into systemic risk. Each account and environment should have clear accountable owners for baseline controls, with explicit boundaries for what workload teams can change and what requires platform or security approval. Exceptions should be time-bound, documented, and revisited, because permanent exceptions are how architectures drift into incoherence. Auditability matters because investigations and compliance obligations often require reconstructing actions across multiple accounts, and that reconstruction must be defensible with authoritative evidence. AI-assisted governance can surface cross-account risk trends, such as environments with chronically expanding permissions or repeated exposure changes, but the organization must be prepared to act on those insights through consistent processes. When standardization, visibility, and ownership are treated as operational requirements, multi-account complexity becomes an advantage that contains incidents rather than a liability that accelerates them.

AI-Assisted Cloud Operations: Event Correlation, Misconfiguration Detection, and Human Controls

AI-assisted cloud operations are most valuable when they reduce human cognitive load without taking away human accountability. Cloud environments generate high-volume, high-variance telemetry, and even well-instrumented organizations struggle to connect control-plane changes, data-plane access, and workload behaviors into a coherent operational picture. AI can help by clustering related events, prioritizing likely high-impact activity, and surfacing patterns that would otherwise be lost in the noise. The practical objective is not to automate security decisions in the abstract, but to accelerate triage and improve consistency in how teams interpret and respond to signals. When implemented responsibly, AI becomes a force multiplier for monitoring and operations rather than a replacement for disciplined engineering and incident response.

Event correlation is the first core use case because cloud attacks frequently manifest as sequences rather than single alerts. AI models can associate role assumptions with subsequent policy changes, link unusual network egress with new service exposures, and group distributed activity that spans accounts and services into a single candidate incident. This is particularly useful when the environment includes automation that produces constant benign change, because manual correlation becomes error-prone and slow. Effective correlation depends on stable identifiers, consistent naming, and normalized identity representation, so the model can connect events across services and environments. Without those foundations, correlation degrades into plausible storytelling that feels coherent but is not anchored in reliable evidence. Operational teams should treat AI correlation outputs as prioritized hypotheses with supporting artifacts, not as conclusions that close investigations.

Misconfiguration detection is the second high-leverage domain because configuration drift and unsafe defaults are persistent drivers of cloud exposure. AI can identify patterns such as repeated broadening of network rules, privilege creep in roles, unexpected public exposure changes, or anomalous cross-account trust relationships that resemble known precursors to incidents. Unlike static checks that evaluate a resource against a single rule, AI can incorporate context such as environment, workload purpose, historical behavior, and the change path that produced the configuration. That context matters because the same configuration may be acceptable in one environment and unacceptable in another, and because risk is often tied to combinations of settings rather than any single flag. Detection should prioritize actionable findings that map to an owner and a remediation path, rather than producing a long list of technically correct but operationally irrelevant warnings. AI can help with prioritization, but organizations must define the risk thresholds and escalation paths so that the output drives timely remediation rather than becoming another ignored queue. Table 29.3 shows where AI accelerates correlation and detection while defining human approval boundaries to prevent over trust and unsafe automation.

The telemetry dependencies for AI-assisted operations are strict, and teams should be explicit about what the model requires to be useful. At minimum, this includes complete control-plane logging for identity, policy, network exposure, and resource lifecycle changes, along with data-plane signals for sensitive service access where available. It also requires enrichment data that provides business context: environment identifiers, workload ownership, service criticality, and resource purpose, ideally captured through consistent tagging and inventory. Models trained on incomplete or biased telemetry will often over-focus on noisy systems with good logging while missing quiet services with weak visibility, creating a false sense of coverage. Data quality issues such as inconsistent timestamps, duplicated events, and ambiguous identities reduce correlation accuracy and increase false positives. Before AI is treated as operationally authoritative, teams must validate that the input data is stable, consistently collected across accounts, and retained with integrity protections appropriate for incident evidence.

Human-in-the-loop controls are the defining difference between AI that improves operations and AI that creates new risk. High-impact actions—revoking broad access, disabling services, rotating keys, or blocking network paths—should require human approval with clear accountability, because mistakes here can cause outages or destroy evidence. AI outputs should be presented with confidence indicators, supporting evidence links, and clear uncertainty boundaries, so analysts can validate claims quickly rather than accepting a narrative at face value.

Table 29.3 AI-Assisted Cloud Operations Use Cases and Human Controls.

AI Use Case	Operational Benefit	Telemetry Dependencies	Human Control Requirement
Event correlation across services	Cluster related actions into a candidate incident	Control plane logs data plane access identity mapping	Analyst validates sequence against raw logs
Misconfiguration detection and drift	Flag unsafe exposure and privilege expansion patterns	Baseline inventory tagging change history	Owner reviews and remediates at template source
Alert prioritization and routing	Reduce triage load and improve response speed	Consistent ownership metadata stable identifiers	Human confirms high-impact escalations
Incident summarization	Create concise briefs for responders	Complete normalized logs with environment context	Reviewer checks for missing evidence and uncertainty
Anomaly detection on access patterns	Surface unusual role assumptions and data access	Identity events service access logs time context	Human approves containment actions

Review workflows should include a "trust but verify" pattern that expects analysts to confirm key assertions against raw logs and effective permission states, especially when the model summarizes complex event chains. Approval boundaries must be explicit: what the AI can recommend, what it can auto-route, what it can auto-suppress, and what it must never execute. The goal is to ensure that speed improvements do not come from skipping critical judgment steps that protect the business.

Failure modes in AI-assisted cloud operations are predictable and should be engineered against from the start. False confidence occurs when a model presents a coherent story that hides missing logs, ambiguous identity mapping, or alternative explanations, leading teams to pursue the wrong hypothesis or prematurely close an incident. Drift occurs as cloud architectures evolve, service behaviors change, and automation patterns shift, causing baselines and anomaly detection thresholds to become outdated. Bias can appear when models learn that certain teams or environments generate more alerts and then over-prioritize those signals, while under-prioritizing quieter but higher-risk areas with weaker telemetry. Leakage is a distinct concern when AI systems ingest sensitive logs, because prompts, summaries, and stored outputs may inadvertently expose secrets, personal data, or regulated information if governance is weak. Effective programs address these risks through continuous validation, periodic retraining or recalibration, careful data handling rules, and clear incident procedures for AI system misuse or malfunction.

Governance and auditability expectations must be treated as operational requirements, not administrative overhead. Organizations need to be able to explain why an AI system produced a recommendation, what data it relied on, who approved the resulting action, and what changes were made as a result. This is essential for post-incident reviews, regulatory inquiries, and internal accountability, especially when AI outputs influence containment decisions that affect customers and operations. Logging the AI interaction itself—inputs, outputs, analyst actions, and approval steps—creates a defensible record and helps tune the system over time. Controls should also ensure separation of duties, so no single individual can use AI-driven workflows to mask unauthorized changes or suppress alerts without oversight. When governance is weak, AI can become a convenient mechanism for making risky changes appear "validated" by automation, which undermines both security and trust.

The most mature pattern for AI-assisted cloud operations is a closed-loop workflow where AI accelerates detection and triage, humans make the decisions, and the system learns from outcomes under disciplined controls. AI can propose likely root causes, suggest next investigative queries, and prioritize which misconfigurations to fix first, while humans confirm, execute, and document the actions taken. Over time, feedback from resolved incidents and validated false positives can improve correlation quality and reduce noise, but only if the feedback is structured and grounded in evidence. The organization should measure performance in operational terms: time to detect, time to understand, quality of routing, and reduction in repeated misconfiguration classes, rather than simply counting alerts or model accuracy metrics in isolation. When these elements align, AI becomes a practical enhancement to cloud-native operations that improves speed and consistency while preserving the human controls necessary to protect availability, confidentiality, and trust.

Operationalizing Cloud Security Over Time

Cloud security only becomes durable when it is treated as an operational system that must be maintained, tuned, and governed as the environment evolves. The cloud changes continuously through deployments, scaling events, service updates, and shifting business requirements, and those changes erode security posture if controls are not designed to adapt. One-time hardening efforts tend to decay into exceptions, drift, and blind spots, especially when teams are rewarded for delivery speed but not for sustaining safe defaults. Operationalization means turning security expectations into repeatable processes with clear ownership, measurable outcomes, and feedback loops that keep posture aligned with intent. When that discipline exists, security becomes a predictable part of delivery and operations rather than a periodic firefight.

Baseline controls are the anchor, but they must be expressed in ways that survive organizational churn and technical change. Standard identity patterns, network segmentation intent, logging requirements, and resource configuration expectations should be encoded into reusable templates and deployment paths so that new workloads inherit safe defaults. The most damaging drift occurs when teams build outside those paths, often due to urgency or perceived platform friction, and the environment becomes a patchwork of special cases. Operational teams must therefore prioritize making the secure path the easiest path, because adoption is driven more by convenience and reliability than by policy statements. Baselines should be versioned and updated as cloud services evolve, with a clear mechanism for rolling improvements forward without breaking production. When baselines are living assets, security can improve over time without relying on heroic manual cleanup efforts.

Vulnerability and configuration management in cloud environments must account for ephemerality and the reality that many weaknesses are not "patched" in place. Cloud-native workloads often redeploy frequently, and managed services shift responsibility from patching to configuration, which changes the operational focus from individual servers to build pipelines and service settings. Vulnerabilities in container images and dependencies must be addressed by rebuilding and redeploying trusted artifacts, not by applying ad hoc fixes to running instances that will be replaced tomorrow. Configuration weaknesses—overly permissive roles, unintended public exposure, unsafe network rules—must be corrected at the source templates to prevent recurrence, not merely fixed on a single resource. The operational trap is treating findings as tickets disconnected from engineering reality, which leads to short-term remediation that does not change the system. Durable programs tie findings to owners who can update the underlying deployment logic and verify that the change is now the default, not the exception.

Monitoring and detection must be maintained as operational content, because cloud behavior changes and detection logic that was accurate last quarter can become noisy or blind today. New services, new access patterns, and new automation pipelines alter baselines, and without disciplined tuning, alert quality degrades until analysts either ignore alerts or disable rules to survive. Maintaining detection quality requires routine review of false positives, measurement of time-to-triage and routing accuracy, and periodic validation that critical telemetry is still being collected across accounts and environments. AI-assisted prioritization can help identify which detections are decaying fastest and which behavior patterns have shifted, but it must be coupled with human review to ensure tuning decisions do not hide real risk. Drift in logging configurations is particularly dangerous because it undermines both detection and incident investigations, and it often goes unnoticed until a crisis. Treating telemetry pipelines as critical infrastructure with ownership, testing, and coverage tracking is a defining characteristic of long-term operational maturity.

Access governance is another area where time creates risk, because permissions expand to meet new needs and rarely contract without explicit effort. Privilege sprawl develops through well-intentioned changes, emergency exceptions, and reuse of broad roles across workloads, and it becomes a hidden liability until it enables lateral movement or data exposure. Operational governance requires periodic access review that is aligned to workload ownership and actual usage, so teams can remove permissions that are no longer required. Approval boundaries for high-impact changes—new cross-account trust, broad administrative grants, exposure of services—must be enforced consistently and backed by audit evidence that shows who approved what and why. AI can help by highlighting anomalous permission expansions and identifying roles whose effective permissions no longer match observed behavior, but the organization must be prepared to act on those insights with disciplined processes. The success metric is not how many policies exist, but whether teams can reliably keep permissions aligned to current operational needs.

Incident response readiness must also be sustained, because cloud incidents demand fast action and the environment's complexity can defeat improvised response. Playbooks should be kept current with the actual architecture, including account structures, identity patterns, shared services, and containment levers that responders can execute under pressure. Access to logs, ability to assume investigation roles, and authority to make containment changes must be tested routinely, because these capabilities often fail in practice due to expired permissions, incomplete onboarding, or unanticipated dependencies. Post-incident improvements should feed back into guardrails and baselines, so the same class of failure becomes less likely over time. AI-assisted analysis can accelerate post-incident learning by clustering recurring misconfiguration patterns and mapping them to owners and remediation paths, but governance must ensure that conclusions remain evidence-based and that sensitive incident data is handled appropriately. Readiness is proven not by having a document, but by being able to execute the response path consistently.

Operating cloud security over time requires an explicit model for balancing autonomy with central guardrails. Product teams need freedom to deliver, but that freedom must exist within enforced boundaries that prevent unsafe defaults and create consistent telemetry for defense. Platform teams must provide secure building blocks that scale, and security teams must define the monitoring logic, escalation paths, and governance expectations that keep accountability clear. Friction is inevitable, so operational leadership should measure where security controls slow delivery and address the underlying causes, rather than allowing teams to work around controls in ways that create hidden risk. Continuous improvement is not optional in the cloud because the environment does not stand still, and neither do attacker behaviors. When security is operationalized through durable baselines, maintained detections, disciplined access governance, and rehearsed response, the organization preserves speed while steadily reducing the likelihood and impact of cloud failures.

Conclusion

Sustained cloud security is achieved when operational ownership, consistent guardrails, and reliable visibility work together as a single system rather than as disconnected initiatives. The environments will continue to change—through new services, new deployments, and new business demands—so the most important capability is the organization's ability to detect drift, correct it at the source, and respond decisively when access is abused. AI can meaningfully improve speed and consistency in correlation and misconfiguration detection, but it only reduces risk when it is fed high-quality telemetry and bounded by explicit human approvals for high-impact actions. When teams treat identity as the perimeter, segmentation as blast-radius control, monitoring as evidence, and response as practiced operations, the cloud becomes an accelerator for resilience instead of a multiplier for preventable security failures.

Recommendations

1) Establish explicit operational ownership for every cloud workload and for the shared services it consumes. Document who is accountable for runtime security decisions, who can execute containment actions, and who approves high-impact changes like exposure and permission expansions. Make ownership visible in operational metadata, so alerts and incidents route to the right team without delay.
2) Standardize baseline configurations across accounts and environments using repeatable deployment paths. Encode identity patterns, segmentation intent, and logging requirements into reusable templates, so new workloads inherit safe defaults. Reduce exception sprawl by ensuring the secure path is also the easiest operational path for engineering teams.
3) Treat identity as the primary perimeter and manage permissions as living constraints. Implement least privilege through reviewed, purpose-bound roles that map to specific workload identities and time-bound needs. Validate permissions regularly to prevent privilege sprawl, and ensure revocation and rotation procedures are rehearsed for incident conditions.
4) Constrain network connectivity by intent, not convenience, with explicit controls for ingress, east–west paths, and egress. Design segmentation, so a compromised workload can reach only required dependencies, and ensure administrative paths are tightly controlled and observable. Monitor for deviations from expected

service relationships and unusual outbound destinations that indicate exfiltration or command-and-control behavior.

5) Protect cloud data by controlling access behaviors in addition to encrypting storage. Identify where sensitive data is allowed to live, how it can be shared, and what service configurations are required to prevent unintended exposure. Treat replication, backups, exports, and analytics copies as part of the same protection scope to avoid securing only the primary dataset.
6) Centralize and preserve cloud telemetry with consistent context to make investigations decisive. Collect control-plane logs, relevant data-plane access signals, and network visibility while preserving attributes like account, environment, workload identity, and owner. Track coverage continuously, so gaps and drift are detected before an incident reveals missing evidence.
7) Build monitoring around behavior patterns and sequences rather than isolated alerts. Correlate role assumptions, policy changes, exposure modifications, and sensitive data access into actionable narratives that support fast containment decisions. Tune detections routinely to reduce noise and maintain trust in alerts as cloud behavior and automation patterns evolve.
8) Prioritize cloud incident response actions that rapidly constrain access and blast radius. Use predefined playbooks that specify safe immediate steps such as revoking credentials, tightening role assumptions, restricting egress, and removing newly created trust relationships while preserving evidence. Coordinate containment with workload and platform owners, so response speed does not produce avoidable outages or loss of telemetry.
9) Manage multi-account and multi-environment architectures as security assets by enforcing consistent trust boundaries. Scope cross-account access narrowly, monitor role assumption patterns, and treat shared services as high-sensitivity assets with stronger change governance and monitoring. Ensure responders can rapidly reconstruct cross-account sequences and execute containment actions without discovering access limitations during a crisis.
10) Apply AI-assisted correlation and misconfiguration detection with explicit human controls and auditability. Use AI to prioritize and summarize signals, but require analysts to validate critical claims against raw logs and effective permissions before executing high-impact actions. Log AI inputs, outputs, and approval decisions, so investigations and post-incident reviews remain defensible and improvements can be fed back into baselines and detections over time.

30

Proactive Defense and Threat Intelligence

Proactive defense and threat intelligence exist to shift blue team operations from constant reaction to deliberate advantage. When intelligence is translated into concrete actions—detections, hardening changes, exercises, and validation cycles—it reduces uncertainty and makes security decisions faster, more consistent, and easier to justify to the business. This chapter frames proactive work as an operational discipline built on reliable telemetry, clear ownership, and repeatable workflows that survive daily pressure rather than collapsing under it. It also treats AI as a force multiplier for summarization, clustering, and correlation, while insisting on human verification, governance, and auditability, so speed never replaces truth.

What Threat Intelligence Provides to Blue Teams

Threat intelligence provides blue teams with decision advantage, not just information about adversaries. At its best, it reduces uncertainty about which threats matter most, how they operate, and where the organization is exposed. Rather than treating every alert as equally urgent, intelligence introduces prioritization grounded in adversary intent, capability, and targeting patterns. It also turns "unknown unknowns" into hypotheses that can be tested through telemetry and validation. The practical outcome is faster, more accurate choices about detections, controls, investigations, and communications.

A core value of threat intelligence is context that transforms raw indicators into operationally useful understanding. Indicators such as domains, IP addresses, file hashes, or email artifacts are highly perishable and often ambiguous without surrounding details. Intelligence adds relationships, timelines, and behaviors—how initial access is typically gained, what tooling is used, and which systems are most likely to be targeted next. That context helps analysts avoid brittle, indicator-only detection strategies that attackers can trivially evade. It also supports more resilient detection engineering by focusing on behaviors and sequences of activity rather than single observables.

Threat intelligence also supports risk-based planning by connecting adversary tradecraft to business impact. Blue teams are often asked to justify where to invest limited time and budget, and intelligence can connect likely threat scenarios to the assets that enable revenue, safety, or regulatory obligations. When intelligence identifies a threat actor or campaign that targets a particular industry, technology stack, geography, or executive role, defenders can map that targeting to internal exposure. This mapping is most useful when it results in concrete actions: hardening a control path, improving logging in a high-risk area, or rehearsing a response playbook for a likely intrusion path. Executives tend to engage when intelligence is framed in terms of operational decisions and business outcomes, not sensationalized actor names.

For day-to-day operations, threat intelligence improves triage by shaping what "suspicious" means in a given environment. Alerts that look benign in isolation can become urgent when correlated with known adversary behaviors, timing, or infrastructure patterns. Conversely, intelligence can de-escalate noise by explaining why certain artifacts are common and non-malicious in a particular region or technology ecosystem. This is where disciplined correlation matters: tying alerts to identity activity, endpoint execution, network flows, and cloud control plane events to form a defensible narrative. The team becomes less reactive because it has a working model of likely attacker progression rather than relying purely on severity labels.

Threat intelligence is also a force multiplier for detection and hunting when it is translated into testable behaviors. Intelligence reports often describe tactics such as credential theft, abuse of remote management, lateral movement via administrative tooling, or data staging in commonly accessible locations. Those behaviors can be converted into analytics that look for unusual authentication patterns, unexpected privilege elevation, atypical process lineage, anomalous remote execution, or suspicious data access sequences. A mature program uses intelligence to build detections that are validated against the organization's normal patterns, then tuned to minimize false positives without creating blind spots. The outcome is a detection portfolio that evolves in response to adversary change rather than drifting into outdated assumptions.

AI and machine learning can enhance this translation process, but only when governed as decision support rather than automated truth. Models can help cluster related events, summarize investigative timelines, and surface weak signals across large telemetry volumes that would overwhelm human reviewers. They can also assist in mapping new intelligence narratives to internal log sources by suggesting which event types and fields are relevant for validation. The failure modes are predictable: models can overfit to recent campaigns, assign false confidence to incomplete data, or reflect bias in what the organization historically labeled as "malicious." Blue teams mitigate this by enforcing human-in-the-loop approvals for detection changes, requiring reproducible evidence in telemetry, and maintaining auditability of model inputs, prompts, and outputs used in security decisions.

Threat intelligence also improves communication and coordination across teams by providing a shared language for urgency and expected attacker behavior. Security operations, engineering, identity teams, and application owners can align when intelligence is translated into concrete asks such as enabling specific logs, tightening a particular access pathway, or validating a control's effectiveness under realistic conditions. Clear intelligence-driven requirements reduce friction because they are tied to plausible threat paths rather than generic "security best practices." This alignment is especially important during incidents, when competing interpretations can slow response and increase risk. Intelligence can set expectations for likely next steps, likely dwell objectives, and the types of containment actions that will actually disrupt the adversary.

Finally, threat intelligence provides value by making learning durable through feedback loops. Intelligence should not be treated as a one-way feed; it becomes more accurate when defenders report what they observed internally, what was false or irrelevant, and which behaviors manifested differently in their environment. This feedback improves future collection, prioritization, and detection design, and it prevents the team from chasing fashionable threats that do not align with actual exposure. When intelligence is operationalized, it is measured by outcomes—reduced time to validate, fewer missed detections, faster containment, and clearer executive decisions—rather than by the volume of reports consumed. In practice, the most successful blue teams treat threat intelligence as a disciplined input into their workflows, with accountability for turning it into actions that can be verified in telemetry.

Converting Intelligence into Defensive Action

Converting intelligence into defensive action starts by treating intelligence as an input to operations, not a parallel research function. Raw reporting is rarely actionable until it is translated into the organization's environment, constraints, and control surface. The first practical step is to normalize incoming intelligence into a consistent internal form: what behavior is described, what preconditions are assumed, which assets are implicated, and what evidence would be observable in telemetry. This translation forces clarity about whether the intelligence is describing a tactic, a technique, an indicator, or an impact claim. Without that discipline, teams either overreact to headlines or underreact because the information feels too abstract.

Actionability depends on mapping intelligence to the defensive questions blue teams actually have to answer. The most useful intelligence supports one of a few operational decisions: what to detect, what to harden, what to hunt, what to monitor more closely, and what to brief to leadership. Mapping is not a theoretical exercise; it requires understanding how the organization authenticates users, manages privileged access, provisions cloud resources, and monitors endpoints and networks. A report that emphasizes credential theft, for example, should immediately trigger questions about identity telemetry coverage, privileged session monitoring, and detection of unusual authentication sequences. When intelligence is forced through this lens, it becomes a prioritized set of hypotheses rather than a library of reading material.

A common failure mode is confusing "having indicators" with "being protected," so high-performing teams treat indicators as starting points rather than endpoints. Indicators are volatile, easily rotated, and often reused across unrelated activity, which makes them unreliable as sole detection logic. Defensive action is stronger when indicators are used to seed enrichment, pivot investigations, and validate correlations, while durable detections focus on behavior and sequence. When indicators are implemented, they should be scoped with expiration logic and monitored for performance, because stale blocks and noisy matches create operational drag. This approach keeps the organization from accumulating a brittle and unmaintainable set of one-off rules. Table 30.1 shows how common intelligence inputs are routed into owned defensive workflows with clear validation expectations.

The conversion process also requires explicit ownership and workflow integration, because intelligence that is not assigned becomes intelligence that is not used. Effective programs create a small number of repeatable "routes to action" that move intelligence to the right operators: detection engineering for analytics changes, security engineering for control hardening, operations for monitoring adjustments, and incident response for playbook updates. Each route needs a defined intake, acceptance criteria, and a minimum evidence standard for changes that affect production controls. This prevents defensive sprawl, where well-intentioned intelligence items generate uncoordinated work that competes for the same limited engineering capacity. It also ensures that every action taken can be traced back to a rationale and evaluated later.

AI and machine learning can help accelerate translation and routing, but the controls around their use must be explicit. Models can summarize long reports into candidate behaviors, propose which log sources would confirm or refute a hypothesis, and cluster similar intelligence items to avoid duplicate work. They can also assist with initial rule drafting by generating patterns that analysts then validate against real telemetry, which

Table 30.1 Intelligence to Action Routing Map.

Intelligence Input Type	Primary Defensive Action	Operational Owner	Validation Evidence
Behavior narrative	Build or tune behavior detection	Detection engineering	Alert fires with adequate context
Indicator set	Seed enrichment and scoped monitoring	SOC operations	Matches correlate to related events
Targeting pattern	Prioritize controls and monitoring focus	Security leadership	Backlog items aligned to exposure
Technique description	Create hunt hypothesis and test	Threat-hunting team	Hunt finds expected artifacts
Red team finding	Fix gap and re test	Security engineering	Repeat test confirms improvement
Exercise outcome	Update playbook and escalation boundaries	Incident response	Next exercise reduces friction

speeds iteration without outsourcing judgment. The risks are operational: automated summaries can omit critical caveats, generated detections can embed assumptions that do not hold in the environment, and model outputs can leak sensitive context if handled improperly. Human-in-the-loop approval boundaries, prompt and output logging, and clear restrictions on what data is provided to models are necessary to keep speed from becoming fragility.

Once intelligence is translated and routed, the defensive action must be validated in the same environment it is meant to protect. For detections, that means confirming that required telemetry exists, that the signal can be expressed reliably, and that the alert provides enough investigative context to support fast triage. For hardening actions, it means verifying that the control change closes a plausible path without breaking business workflows or shifting risk elsewhere. Validation is where many programs fail, because they implement changes and assume effectiveness without testing. A disciplined team treats each intelligence-driven action as a hypothesis with an observable outcome: a detection fires under realistic conditions, a control blocks a known abuse pattern, or monitoring reveals the expected artifacts.

Tuning and lifecycle management complete the conversion from intelligence to sustained defense. Intelligence is time-sensitive, and so are the actions derived from it; detections may need to evolve as attackers shift tradecraft, and temporary blocks may need to expire or be replaced by behavior-based controls. Blue teams should track which intelligence items drove which changes, what results those changes produced, and where gaps remained due to data limitations or operational constraints. When a detection produces noise, the team should tune it by tightening predicates, adding context, or adjusting thresholds, while preserving coverage of the intended behavior. This ongoing maintenance is what separates a one-time response from a program that remains resilient as adversaries adapt.

Finally, converting intelligence into action requires measurement that reflects defensive outcomes rather than activity volume. The goal is not to process more reports but to reduce uncertainty, shorten validation time, and increase the reliability of detection and response. Useful measures include how quickly intelligence can be translated into a testable hypothesis, how often required telemetry is missing, how long it takes to deploy and validate a change, and how frequently intelligence-driven detections contribute to meaningful investigations. Leadership briefings should focus on decisions made and risk reduced, not on the number of intelligence feeds consumed. When this is done well, threat intelligence becomes a practical engine for continuous improvement, consistently turning external knowledge into internal defensive advantage.

Prioritizing Defenses Based on Likely Threats

Prioritizing defenses based on likely threats is fundamentally about aligning limited defensive capacity with the risks that are most plausible and most damaging. Blue teams cannot defend everything equally, and attempting to do so usually results in shallow coverage everywhere rather than meaningful coverage where it matters. Threat intelligence provides a lens for distinguishing theoretical exposure from probable adversary behavior given the organization's industry, size, technology stack, and business model. This prioritization shifts defensive planning away from abstract compliance checklists toward informed risk decisions. The result is a security posture that is intentional rather than reactive.

Effective prioritization begins by understanding which threats are most likely to target the organization and why. Adversaries rarely choose targets at random; they select them based on access to data, financial opportunity, geopolitical value, operational disruption potential, or ease of compromise. Intelligence that highlights targeting patterns, preferred initial access vectors, and commonly abused technologies allows defenders to narrow their focus. When those patterns are mapped to internal assets and workflows, gaps become visible in a way that generic risk assessments often miss. This mapping is the bridge between external threat reporting and internal defensive reality.

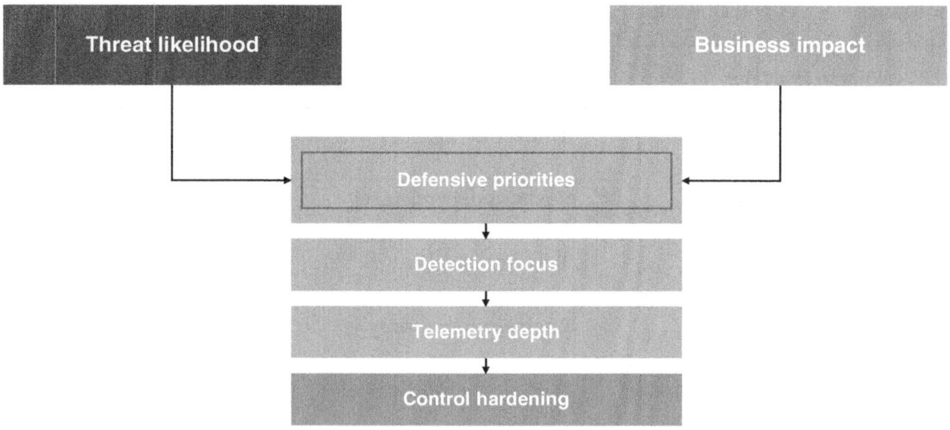

Figure 30.1 Likely Threats and Business Impact Drive Defensive Priorities.

Likelihood alone is not sufficient, so prioritization must also account for impact. A low-probability threat that could cause catastrophic harm may warrant attention alongside higher-frequency but lower-impact activity. Threat intelligence helps by providing context about attacker objectives, such as data theft, service disruption, or long-term persistence, which can be evaluated against business dependencies. This evaluation is most effective when defenders work closely with system owners to understand what failure actually looks like in operational terms. By combining likelihood and impact, blue teams can justify defensive focus in language that resonates beyond the security function. Figure 30.1 illustrates how threat likelihood and business impact converge into prioritized defensive focus areas. It supports the chapter's emphasis on aligning telemetry depth, detection effort, and control hardening to the most plausible and most damaging threat paths.

From an operational perspective, prioritization directly influences where telemetry depth and detection quality must be strongest. If intelligence suggests that credential abuse and lateral movement are the most likely intrusion paths, identity and authentication telemetry should be treated as mission-critical. That may mean investing effort in improving log fidelity, reducing blind spots, or tightening correlation between identity, endpoint, and network signals. Less likely threat paths still matter, but they may be monitored at a lower resolution or addressed through baseline controls. This tiered approach prevents teams from exhausting themselves trying to achieve uniform depth across all domains.

AI and machine learning can assist in prioritization by synthesizing large volumes of intelligence and internal data, but their outputs must be interpreted carefully. Models can help surface patterns across campaigns, highlight overlaps between adversary behavior and internal exposure, and suggest where defensive gaps are most concentrated. They can also model "what if" scenarios that estimate how changes in controls might alter risk distribution. The danger lies in treating these outputs as objective truth rather than probabilistic guidance, especially when models are trained on incomplete or biased data. Human judgment remains essential to validate assumptions and ensure that prioritization decisions reflect real-world constraints. Table 30.2 reinforces how likelihood impact and operational constraints combine to drive defensible security priorities.

Prioritization must also account for defensive maturity and change capacity, not just threat severity. Some risks can be reduced quickly through configuration changes or logging improvements, while others require longer-term architectural work or cross-team coordination. Intelligence-driven prioritization should therefore consider which actions are feasible in the near term and which should be staged over time. This sequencing avoids paralysis caused by focusing only on the most complex problems. It also builds momentum by delivering incremental risk reduction that can be demonstrated and measured.

Table 30.2 Defensive Prioritization Factors and Outcomes.

Prioritization Factor	What to Evaluate	Primary Data Source	Defensive Outcome
Threat likelihood	Targeting patterns and common paths	Threat intelligence	Focus on plausible intrusion routes
Business impact	Critical services and regulatory exposure	Business dependencies	Protect what would hurt most
Telemetry readiness	Log coverage and correlation ability	Telemetry health	Invest in visibility where needed
Control feasibility	Time and effort to implement change	Engineering capacity	Sequence quick wins and staged work
Detection quality	Signal to noise and context richness	Detection performance	Tune or replace brittle analytics
Change risk	Business disruption from containment	Operational constraints	Set approval boundaries and playbooks

Communication plays a critical role in sustaining prioritized defenses, particularly with leadership and non-security stakeholders. When priorities are clearly tied to likely threats and business impact, tradeoffs become easier to explain and defend. Leaders are more willing to accept residual risk when they understand that resources are being applied deliberately rather than arbitrarily. This clarity also reduces churn, because priorities are less likely to swing wildly in response to headlines or isolated incidents. Consistency over time is itself a defensive advantage.

Finally, prioritization is not a one-time exercise but a continuous process that evolves as threats, technology, and business conditions change. Intelligence must be revisited regularly to confirm that assumptions about likelihood and impact still hold. Defensive investments should be reassessed to ensure they are still aligned with the most relevant threats, and deprioritized areas should be periodically sampled to detect emerging risk. When this feedback loop is maintained, prioritization becomes a living discipline rather than a static document. In practice, this is how blue teams stay focused, resilient, and credible in the face of constant change.

Collaboration with Red Teams for Defensive Improvement

Collaboration with red teams improves defense when it is treated as a continuous engineering loop rather than a periodic test. The most valuable outcome is not a dramatic "gotcha" moment but a measurable increase in detection coverage, response speed, and control reliability. Red teams simulate adversary behavior under controlled conditions, which gives blue teams a safe way to observe how attacks actually unfold in their environment. That observation is critical because many defensive assumptions fail in practice due to telemetry gaps, inconsistent configurations, and real-world user behavior. When collaboration is well-run, it produces shared learning and durable improvements instead of blame and posturing.

The foundation of productive collaboration is a clear agreement on goals, scope, and rules of engagement. Red teams and blue teams often have different incentives, and those incentives must be aligned around defensive improvement rather than competitive scoring. Scope should specify which systems and identities are in play, what safety constraints exist, and what constitutes acceptable operational risk during testing. Rules of engagement should also clarify what data can be accessed, how sensitive information is handled, and how to prevent accidental disruption to business operations. When these basics are explicit, the teams can focus on learning rather than negotiating boundaries mid-exercise.

The most effective engagements are those that test realistic attacker pathways and validate defensive controls end to end. That means going beyond simple perimeter probes and emphasizing the steps that cause real harm: credential access, privilege escalation, lateral movement, and data access. Blue teams benefit most when red team actions are mapped to observable evidence in identity, endpoint, network, and cloud control plane telemetry. This evidence becomes the raw material for improving detection logic and response playbooks. It also exposes where visibility is missing, which is often the true limiting factor in defensive performance.

Timing and transparency matter, and they should be intentional rather than ideological. Fully blind exercises can be useful for measuring current readiness, but they can also waste time when the goal is engineering improvement. A hybrid approach is often more productive: limited surprise to test initial detection and triage, followed by structured collaboration to accelerate root-cause analysis and remediation. When red and blue teams share enough detail to reproduce behavior, defenders can build and validate detections with confidence. The aim is to convert one-time observations into repeatable, testable detection and response capabilities.

A critical output of red–blue collaboration is a prioritized list of defensive improvements that is tied to concrete evidence. Findings should be expressed as specific gaps, such as missing logs, weak correlation across data sources, poor alert context, or unclear escalation thresholds. Each gap should be paired with a corrective action that has an owner, an acceptance criterion, and a verification plan. Without this rigor, red team reports become narrative documents that are read once and filed away. Defensive improvement requires turning observations into tickets, changes, and validated outcomes.

AI and machine learning can enhance collaboration by accelerating analysis and helping both teams navigate complexity, but their use must remain controlled. Models can assist in summarizing red team activity timelines, correlating events across disparate logs, and suggesting candidate detections based on observed behavior. They can also help identify which telemetry fields are most discriminative for a given technique, improving the efficiency of detection engineering. The risks are that model-generated interpretations can introduce false certainty or obscure critical nuances, especially when inputs are incomplete or noisy. Teams should treat AI outputs as hypotheses that must be validated against raw telemetry and documented for auditability.

Collaboration also strengthens the organization when it includes the teams responsible for operating and maintaining the affected systems. Defensive improvement often depends on changes to identity configuration, endpoint hardening, network segmentation, or cloud policy enforcement, which typically sit outside security operations. Red team evidence can be a powerful catalyst for these partners because it demonstrates real exploitation paths rather than abstract risk. However, it must be communicated respectfully and with clear remediation guidance to avoid triggering defensiveness or fatigue. When system owners see that security is focused on practical fixes that support business continuity, collaboration becomes easier to sustain.

Finally, collaboration with red teams should feed a continuous validation cycle that prevents regression. Once detections are built or controls are tightened, the organization needs a way to re-test that coverage as systems change and attackers evolve. Replaying red team techniques under controlled conditions, running periodic exercises, and embedding validation into change management keeps improvements from eroding over time. The most mature programs treat red team activity as an input to ongoing defensive measurement, not as an annual event. This is how organizations move from episodic testing to sustained resilience, using red teams as a partner in building defenses that work under real conditions.

Testing Defensive Assumptions Through Exercises

Testing defensive assumptions through exercises is how blue teams distinguish between what they believe is true and what is demonstrably true in their environment. Many security programs rely on implicit assumptions: logs are collected everywhere, alerts are meaningful, escalation paths are understood, and teams can execute containment without disrupting the business. Exercises expose where those assumptions break under pressure, ambiguity, and competing priorities. They also reveal how people actually behave when faced with incomplete information, which is often where incidents are won or lost. The goal is not performance theater but evidence-driven improvement.

Exercises are most valuable when they are designed to validate specific capabilities rather than to "simulate an attack" in general terms. A well-constructed scenario tests discrete questions such as whether identity telemetry is sufficient to detect credential abuse, whether endpoint isolation works at scale, or whether cloud access changes can be traced to an accountable identity. These questions should be derived from likely threat paths and the organization's own operational realities, including uptime requirements and staffing constraints. When exercises focus on clear validation targets, they produce actionable findings instead of vague lessons. This precision also helps leadership understand what was tested and what remains uncertain.

A common defensive assumption is that detection is the hard part and response is straightforward, but exercises often show the opposite. Alerts may fire, yet analysts may struggle to establish scope, identify affected systems, or determine whether activity is malicious or administrative. Triage is frequently slowed by missing context, inconsistent asset inventories, and unclear ownership of key systems. Exercises make these friction points visible, which is critical because friction compounds during real incidents. Improving response usually requires both technical changes, such as better enrichment, and procedural changes, such as clearer decision thresholds.

Exercises also validate whether telemetry is not only present but usable under operational conditions. It is easy to claim that logs are enabled, but it is harder to confirm that the logs are complete, timely, correctly parsed, and correlated across sources. Exercises should therefore include deliberate checks for evidence: can the team retrieve authentication events, process execution traces, and network connections for the time window in question, and can they do it quickly. When telemetry gaps are discovered, the exercise output should be framed as a reliability issue, not an analyst failure. Defense depends on instrumentation, and exercises are the fastest way to discover instrumentation debt.

AI and machine learning can enhance exercises by accelerating sensemaking, but they also introduce new assumptions that must be tested. Teams may rely on AI-assisted triage to summarize alerts, suggest likely root causes, or recommend next investigative steps based on prior incidents. Exercises should therefore include moments where AI outputs are intentionally incomplete or misleading, forcing analysts to validate conclusions against raw evidence. This tests human-in-the-loop discipline and prevents automation from becoming a single point of failure. It also reinforces governance expectations, such as logging AI recommendations and documenting when analysts accepted or rejected them.

The design of exercises should account for realism without creating unnecessary risk to production systems. Tabletop exercises are useful for testing decision-making, communication, and escalation boundaries, especially with executives and legal or communications stakeholders. Technical exercises, including controlled adversary emulation, validate tooling, telemetry, and operator workflows, but they require safeguards to avoid disruption. Hybrid approaches are often the most effective, starting with a tabletop decision point and then moving into a constrained technical validation. This structure keeps exercises grounded in business realities while still producing concrete technical findings.

Exercises should also test cross-team coordination, because many defensive assumptions involve handoffs rather than individual actions. Blue teams frequently depend on identity administrators, endpoint engineers, network teams, and cloud platform owners to execute containment or to provide context quickly. Exercises reveal whether these partners understand their role, whether communication channels work under time pressure, and whether approvals slow critical actions. They also surface mismatched expectations, such as security assuming it can disable accounts immediately while operations requires additional validation. These insights are not administrative trivia; they determine whether the organization can contain an intrusion before it spreads.

The value of an exercise is realized only when outcomes are converted into tracked improvements with verification. Findings should be documented as specific gaps, tied to evidence observed during the exercise, and assigned to owners with clear completion criteria. Follow-up testing is essential, because remediation that is not revalidated often decays as systems change or priorities shift. Over time, repeated exercises should demonstrate measurable gains: faster investigation timelines, fewer ambiguous alerts, more consistent containment, and clearer leadership decision-making. When exercises are treated as a continuous validation discipline, they become one of the most reliable ways to strengthen blue team operations and keep defensive assumptions aligned with reality.

Deception Concepts and Defensive Deterrence

Deception in defensive operations is the deliberate use of controlled signals and decoys to shape adversary behavior and increase the defender's advantage. Rather than waiting for an attacker to touch production systems, deception aims to draw them into monitored pathways where actions are easier to observe, attribute, and contain. This is not about trickery for its own sake; it is about creating high-confidence detection opportunities and buying time for response. When implemented with discipline, deception increases the cost and uncertainty for intruders while reducing the time defenders spend chasing ambiguous alerts. The deterrence effect comes from making compromise less predictable and less efficient for the attacker.

At the conceptual level, deception works because attackers make assumptions as they move through an environment. They assume discovered credentials might be valuable, newly found shares might contain sensitive documents, and seemingly underused systems might be safe to explore. Deceptive assets exploit those assumptions by presenting plausible targets that are instrumented and isolated. The moment an attacker interacts with a decoy, the defender gains a signal with unusually high fidelity because legitimate users should not be there. This shifts detection from pattern matching across noisy data to observing intent through interaction with something that should never be touched.

Deception is most effective when it is integrated into the organization's normal architecture and visibility stack rather than deployed as a standalone novelty. Decoy accounts, honey tokens, and instrumented services should be placed where an attacker would naturally look during reconnaissance, privilege escalation, or lateral movement. Placement requires understanding normal administrative behavior so that deception assets do not collide with legitimate workflows and create constant false positives. It also requires clean segregation so that interaction with deceptive elements cannot create new risk, such as a decoy system becoming a pivot point into production. The design principle is simple: maximize observability and minimize blast radius.

Defensive deterrence is not guaranteed, and it is often misunderstood as something an attacker will consciously perceive. In practice, deterrence emerges indirectly through friction: attackers waste time, encounter uncertainty about what is real, and risk early exposure when they interact with deceptive elements. Skilled adversaries may suspect deception and proceed cautiously, which can still benefit defenders by slowing operations and increasing the chance of mistakes. Less skilled actors may fully commit to decoys, producing rich telemetry that supports rapid scoping and containment. Either way, deception shifts the engagement toward defender-controlled terrain, which is a meaningful advantage.

Operationalizing deception requires careful handling of identity, data, and monitoring so that deception signals are both reliable and safe. Decoy credentials must be managed, so they cannot grant real access, yet they should appear realistic enough to be tempting. Honey tokens such as canary documents or unique strings can be placed in locations an attacker would search, but they must be labeled and tracked, so internal teams do not accidentally propagate them into legitimate workflows. Monitoring must be tuned so that a deception trigger results in immediate investigation and correlation, not just another alert in a crowded queue. The power of deception is its signal quality, and that power is lost if the response workflow treats it like routine noise.

AI and machine learning can strengthen deception programs by improving placement, correlation, and response, but they must not automate critical decisions without verification. Models can analyze historical incident paths and administrative patterns to suggest where deceptive assets will be most plausible and least disruptive. They can also correlate a deception trigger with surrounding telemetry to propose likely intrusion stage, affected identities, and candidate systems for containment. The failure mode is overconfidence, especially if models infer attacker intent from limited evidence or if drift causes the model to misclassify legitimate anomalies as malicious. Human-in-the-loop review is essential, particularly when deception triggers could lead to disruptive actions like account disablement or network isolation.

Deception also creates governance and accountability requirements that should be addressed explicitly. Because deception elements are intentionally designed to be interacted with, organizations must ensure that monitoring and response procedures comply with internal policies, legal considerations, and privacy expectations. Access to deception configuration should be tightly controlled, and changes should be logged so that defenders can explain why a particular decoy existed and how it was monitored. Exercises should include deception triggers to validate that the team reacts quickly, follows escalation paths correctly, and avoids overreacting to incomplete signals. Treating deception as part of the control environment, with documentation and auditability, keeps it from being perceived as an informal or risky tactic.

The practical measure of deception is whether it produces earlier, higher-confidence detection and accelerates containment without creating operational friction. Successful programs demonstrate that deception triggers are rare, meaningful, and correlated with other suspicious activity, resulting in fast investigative momentum. Unsuccessful programs generate confusion, create maintenance burden, or provide attackers with artifacts that inadvertently reveal defensive posture. When deception is engineered carefully and integrated into routine monitoring, it becomes a disciplined method for turning attacker curiosity into defender certainty. That certainty is the core of deterrence: not the promise that attacks will stop, but the reality that attacks become harder to conduct quietly and efficiently.

AI in Threat Intelligence: Summarization, Clustering, and Analyst Verification

AI in threat intelligence is most valuable when it accelerates understanding without diluting rigor. Intelligence teams and blue teams are often overwhelmed by reporting volume, inconsistent writing quality, and varying confidence levels across sources. AI can reduce that cognitive load by compressing long narratives into actionable elements, grouping related items, and surfacing the parts most likely to matter to the organization. The objective is not to replace analysts but to increase throughput while keeping decision quality high. The moment AI outputs are treated as authoritative rather than assistive, the program becomes vulnerable to fast, silent failure.

Summarization is typically the first practical use case because it converts lengthy intelligence products into a consistent internal form. A useful summary captures the behaviors described, the assumptions implied, the intended targets, and the evidence types that defenders should expect to observe. It should also preserve uncertainty by carrying forward confidence qualifiers rather than smoothing them away for readability. Poor summarization tends to remove caveats, collapse timelines, or overemphasize dramatic elements like actor branding while losing operational detail. Because defenders use summaries to choose actions, quality controls around summarization are not optional.

Clustering is the next force multiplier because it helps teams recognize when they are seeing the same story multiple times through different lenses. Many intelligence feeds repackage overlapping content, and a human analyst can waste hours reconciling near-duplicate reports. AI-driven clustering can group intelligence by shared behaviors, infrastructure patterns, malware families, or campaign narratives, reducing duplication and revealing meaningful differences. When clustering is done well, it enables trend detection over time and supports prioritization based on frequency and relevance. When it is done poorly, it can merge unrelated activity and cause defenders to build broad, noisy detections that do not reflect actual adversary behavior.

The operational value of clustering increases when it is tied to internal observations and defensive tasks. Grouped intelligence items should map to a small number of hypotheses that can be validated against telemetry, such as credential abuse patterns, endpoint execution chains, or anomalous cloud control plane actions. Clusters can also be used to track "campaign drift," where the same broad objective is pursued through changing tactics as defenders adapt. This helps blue teams avoid brittle response plans that only address last month's technique. The cluster becomes a living object that informs detection engineering, hunting, and control hardening in a more coherent way than isolated reports.

Analyst verification is the control that makes AI safe and useful in intelligence operations. Verification means comparing AI outputs against primary sources and observable evidence, not simply "reviewing for reasonableness." Analysts should confirm that key claims are supported, that any extracted indicators are accurate, and that behavioral descriptions can be expressed in terms of observable telemetry. They should also validate that the AI did not fabricate relationships, overstate confidence, or omit critical context such as prerequisites for an attack path. Verification is especially important when summaries are used in leadership briefings, because errors at that layer can drive misallocation of resources and erode trust in the intelligence function.

Verification must also include controls for data handling and leakage, because threat intelligence often contains sensitive internal context when operationalized. If AI is used to correlate external reporting with internal asset information, identity details, or incident notes, governance must constrain what data is provided to models and how outputs are stored. High-integrity programs maintain audit trails that show what inputs were used, what the model produced, and what the analyst approved or corrected. This auditability supports accountability and allows teams to revisit decisions when new facts emerge. Without these controls, AI becomes a black box that can quietly contaminate decision-making.

Failure modes in AI-assisted intelligence are well understood and should be designed against explicitly. Hallucination can introduce fictitious indicators, nonexistent relationships, or invented timelines that look plausible under time pressure. Drift can cause previously reliable summaries or clusters to degrade as adversary behavior, reporting styles, or internal tooling changes. Bias can skew what is surfaced as important, especially if training data overrepresents certain industries, geographies, or threat types. A more subtle failure is false confidence: AI outputs can appear polished and authoritative, leading analysts to accept them without adequate validation. These risks are mitigated through strict review requirements, sampling-based quality checks, and ongoing calibration against known ground truth.

To make summarization and clustering truly operational, teams need structured outputs that connect directly to workflows. Summaries should consistently produce fields that map to action, such as suspected initial access methods, likely next steps, and the telemetry sources required to validate. Clusters should have identifiers, ownership, and lifecycle management, so they can be updated, merged, or retired as understanding evolves. When intelligence is tied to tickets, detection tasks, or monitoring changes, AI becomes a throughput enhancer rather than a content generator. The discipline is to keep the outputs structured enough to be operational while still capturing nuance that matters for defense.

Ultimately, AI in threat intelligence succeeds when it increases the speed of comprehension and the consistency of analysis while maintaining human accountability for decisions. It should help analysts spend more time on validation, correlation, and action planning and less time on repetitive reading and de-duplication. The organization benefits when intelligence becomes more timely, more relevant, and easier to operationalize without sacrificing accuracy. This balance requires clear approval boundaries, measurable quality controls, and an expectation that AI output is always a starting point, never the final authority. When those conditions are met, AI becomes a practical amplifier for threat intelligence rather than a new source of risk.

Integrating Proactive Defense into Operations

Integrating proactive defense into operations means shifting security work upstream, so the organization spends less time reacting to damage and more time preventing adversary progress. Proactive defense is not a separate program that runs alongside security operations; it is a set of practices embedded into daily workflows that shape visibility, prioritization, and control effectiveness. The aim is to identify likely attack paths, validate assumptions, and close gaps before they are exploited at scale. This requires discipline because proactive work competes with the urgent demands of alert queues and incident response. When done well, proactive defense becomes the mechanism by which operations continuously improves rather than merely endures.

The first operational requirement is a stable intake and prioritization process that turns proactive ideas into executable tasks. Threat intelligence, red team findings, incident learnings, and detection performance data should feed a common backlog that is visible to security operations, engineering, and relevant IT partners. Items must be framed as specific, testable improvements: add a missing log source, tighten a control on a privileged pathway, build a detection for a behavior that repeatedly appears, or tune a noisy analytic that drains analyst time. Without a shared backlog, proactive work becomes informal and personality-driven, which makes it fragile and difficult to sustain. A transparent process also helps leadership understand tradeoffs when proactive tasks temporarily reduce capacity for reactive work.

Proactive defense must be grounded in telemetry reality, because the ability to anticipate threats depends on what the organization can actually observe. Integrating it into operations therefore includes maintaining logging standards, parsing consistency, and enrichment pipelines so that detections and hunts can be executed reliably. This is less glamorous than hunting, but it is the foundation that determines whether proactive hypotheses can be validated. Operational teams need clear ownership of telemetry health, including monitoring for collection failures, schema drift, and coverage gaps across identity, endpoints, networks, and cloud environments. When telemetry is treated as a product with reliability expectations, proactive defense becomes repeatable instead of episodic.

A proactive posture also depends on pre-approved response and containment pathways, because speed is often constrained by uncertainty about authority. Operations should define what actions can be taken immediately on high-confidence signals, what requires secondary validation, and what requires leadership approval. These boundaries reduce hesitation when a proactive hunt uncovers suspicious behavior and prevent overreaction that disrupts business operations. They also enable consistent training and easier onboarding of analysts, because decision thresholds are explicit rather than tribal knowledge. Over time, these response boundaries become a key part of operational maturity.

AI and machine learning can reinforce proactive defense by identifying weak signals and reducing the manual effort required to connect disparate events. Models can surface anomalous identity sequences, unusual administrative behavior, and cross-domain correlations that indicate early-stage intrusion activity. They can also assist in prioritizing backlog items by analyzing detection performance, recurring investigation patterns, and coverage gaps revealed by exercises. The integration challenge is governance: AI outputs must be treated as leads that require validation, not as triggers for disruptive action on their own. Proactive operations should require that AI-generated insights be anchored to observable telemetry and reviewed by an accountable analyst before they drive detection changes or containment decisions.

Proactive defense becomes operationally meaningful when it is scheduled and staffed as part of normal work, not treated as spare-time activity. Teams that succeed typically allocate predictable capacity for proactive tasks, such as a rotating analyst assignment for threat hunting, detection tuning, or telemetry validation. This protects proactive work from being perpetually deferred by the day's alert volume. It also creates a feedback loop where insights from proactive efforts directly inform playbooks and detection engineering, improving the reactive function over time. Without protected capacity, proactive defense remains aspirational and collapses under operational pressure.

Integration also requires deliberate collaboration across functions, because proactive defense often involves changes outside the security operations boundary. Identity teams may need to adjust authentication policies, endpoint teams may need to enable additional telemetry, and cloud platform owners may need to refine access controls or logging configurations. Operationalizing this collaboration means using clear, evidence-based requests tied to likely threat paths and measurable outcomes. It also means defining handoffs, so security does not become a bottleneck for routine engineering work, and engineering does not treat security tasks as unprioritized favors. Proactive defense thrives when it is framed as operational reliability and risk reduction rather than security exceptionalism.

Finally, proactive defense must be measured in ways that reflect improved outcomes, not just activity. Useful indicators include reduced time to validate suspicious activity, fewer repeated investigation patterns due to better detections and enrichment, improved signal-to-noise ratios, and decreased frequency of preventable incident classes. Exercises and red team activity can be used periodically to confirm that improvements hold under realistic conditions and that new gaps have not emerged through change. The program should also track whether proactive findings actually result in implemented and validated fixes, because insight without action is indistinguishable from noise. When proactive defense is integrated with these controls, it becomes a durable operating model that steadily raises the cost of intrusion and reduces the disruption of incidents.

Sustaining Proactive Work Alongside Daily Demands

Sustaining proactive work alongside daily demands requires treating proactive defense as a core operational function, not a luxury that happens only when the alert queue is quiet. In most environments, the queue is never quiet, which means the default outcome is perpetual reactivity unless leadership and process deliberately counterbalance it. Proactive work is the mechanism by which operations reduces future load by improving detection quality, closing visibility gaps, and hardening pathways that repeatedly generate incidents. The tension is structural: reactive work is urgent and visible, while proactive work is important but often less immediately rewarded. Mature organizations resolve this by embedding proactive capacity into staffing, metrics, and workflow design.

The first step is establishing explicit capacity allocation rather than relying on informal "time permitting" agreements. Teams that sustain proactive work reserve a fixed portion of analyst and engineering time for activities such as detection tuning, threat hunting, telemetry validation, and exercise follow-up. That allocation can be rotational, but it must be protected from routine interruptions except for true emergencies. Without protected capacity, proactive tasks accumulate as debt and are repeatedly deferred until after the next incident, which ensures the next incident arrives sooner. By making proactive work a planned part of the operating model, leaders give teams permission to prioritize long-term risk reduction even when short-term noise is high.

Operational triage discipline is equally important because weak triage practices consume the bandwidth that proactive work needs. If every alert is treated as a potential crisis, analysts will spend their days chasing low-value signals and writing inconclusive tickets. Sustaining proactive work requires clear severity criteria, consistent enrichment, and defined closure standards so that routine noise is handled efficiently. It also requires escalation boundaries that prevent "just in case" investigations from expanding without evidence. When triage is structured, reactive work becomes more predictable, creating space for proactive work without requiring unrealistic staffing increases. Table 30.3 highlights the operational mechanisms that keep proactive defense work durable even under constant daily demand.

Proactive work should also be framed as a reduction of repeat work, and the organization should actively identify where repeated investigations indicate systemic gaps. If analysts repeatedly see the same benign behavior triggering alerts, the solution is not more analyst time but better tuning, better context, or a refined analytic. If investigations routinely stall because critical logs are missing, the solution is telemetry reliability work, not heroic incident response. This is where a disciplined feedback loop matters: every repeated pain point should be captured, prioritized, and converted into a corrective action with an owner. Over time, this turns proactive work into the engine that makes daily operations easier, rather than an additional burden layered on top.

AI and machine learning can help sustain proactive work by reducing cognitive load and compressing time spent on repetitive tasks, but they must be used with guardrails. AI-assisted triage can summarize cases, propose likely root causes, and suggest next investigative steps based on patterns, which reduces time spent re-reading logs and reconstructing timelines. Models can also identify clusters of similar alerts that indicate a tuning opportunity and can highlight anomalous patterns worth a proactive hunt. The primary risk is false efficiency: if AI outputs are accepted without verification, the team can institutionalize wrong assumptions and miss real intrusions.

Table 30.3 Proactive Work Sustainability Controls.

Sustainment Lever	Implementation Approach	Primary Benefit	Common Failure Mode
Protected capacity	Reserve rotation time for proactive tasks	Prevents perpetual deferral	Interrupted by routine noise
Triage discipline	Apply severity criteria and closure standards	Reduces reactive waste	Over investigating low confidence
Shared backlog	Track proactive items with owners	Improves execution and visibility	Unowned tasks become debt
Cross team handoffs	Define routes to action and service levels	Speeds remediation	Requests stall without clarity
Verification culture	Validate changes with telemetry or re tests	Prevents false confidence	Assuming fixes without testing
AI governance	Human approval and audit trails for outputs	Accelerates analysis safely	Automation treated as authority
Recognition and metrics	Measure reduced repeats and better signal	Reinforces long term gains	Only counting tickets closed

Sustaining proactive work requires that AI be treated as an accelerator for analyst judgment, with clear approval boundaries and auditability of inputs and outputs.

Engineering throughput is another constraint that must be addressed directly, because many proactive improvements require changes outside the SOC. Detection logic changes, logging enablement, identity policy adjustments, and cloud configuration hardening often depend on teams with their own backlogs and priorities. Sustaining proactive work requires a formal mechanism for getting these changes implemented, such as agreed service levels, shared prioritization meetings, or clearly defined "security reliability" work streams. Requests must be specific, evidence-backed, and tied to risk reduction to avoid being dismissed as generic security demands. When cross-team execution is reliable, proactive work becomes a predictable pipeline rather than a series of stalled initiatives.

There is also a human sustainability component, because constant reactivity contributes to burnout and turnover, which then further reduces capacity for proactive work. Rotations that alternate between reactive coverage and proactive focus can improve cognitive variety and reduce fatigue. Proactive work should be framed as skilled, meaningful engineering and analysis, not as extra chores piled onto already overloaded analysts. Leaders should also ensure that proactive accomplishments are visible and rewarded, because organizations tend to measure what they celebrate. When proactive work is recognized as a primary contribution to resilience, teams are more likely to protect it under pressure.

Finally, sustaining proactive work requires metrics that reflect long-term improvements rather than just daily throughput. Measuring only tickets closed or alerts processed incentivizes shallow work and punishes the time investment required to improve detection and telemetry. More useful measures include reductions in recurring alert classes, improved signal-to-noise ratios, faster time to validate and scope suspicious activity, and fewer incidents caused by known, unaddressed gaps. Periodic exercises and red team activity can validate that proactive improvements are real and durable, not just changes on paper. When proactive work is planned, protected, executed through reliable partnerships, and measured by outcomes, it becomes the practical means by which blue team operations stays ahead of threat evolution without sacrificing day-to-day coverage.

Conclusion

A proactive defense program endures when it is embedded into operations as a disciplined cycle of intelligence, validation, and continuous improvement. Exercises, red team collaboration, and deception concepts are most effective when they produce high-confidence signals, expose broken assumptions, and drive specific remediations that are re-tested and maintained over time. AI can accelerate comprehension and correlation, but it must remain bounded by human approval, evidence-based verification, and auditable decision trails to avoid institutionalizing false confidence. When these elements are run as a reliable operating model—backed by clear prioritization, protected capacity, and cross-team execution—the organization steadily raises the cost of intrusion while reducing the disruption and fatigue of day-to-day defense.

Recommendations

1) Establish a consistent process for translating threat intelligence into testable defensive hypotheses. Normalize incoming reporting into behaviors, preconditions, and expected evidence, so it can be validated against your telemetry. Route each item to a clear owner such as detection engineering, security engineering, or incident response with acceptance criteria for action. Track outcomes, so intelligence is measured by decisions and improvements rather than volume consumed.
2) Avoid relying solely on indicators as proof of protection. Use indicators to seed enrichment, pivots, and validation while building durable detections around behaviors and sequences that are harder to evade. Apply expiration and performance monitoring to any indicator-based blocks or alerts to prevent stale logic from creating noise. Prioritize detection rules that provide investigative context rather than isolated matches.
3) Prioritize defenses using a clear evaluation of likely threats and business impact. Map targeting patterns and common attack paths to your internal assets and workflows to identify where you are truly exposed. Tier telemetry depth and detection effort toward the intrusion paths most relevant to your environment rather than aiming for uniform coverage everywhere. Revisit the prioritization regularly as threats, technology, and business conditions evolve.
4) Integrate proactive defense work into daily operations through a visible, shared backlog. Feed the backlog with threat intelligence, red team findings, exercise results, and detection performance data to ensure proactive work reflects real gaps. Write backlog items as concrete tasks like enabling specific telemetry, tightening a control pathway, or tuning a recurring source of noise. Assign owners and verification steps, so proactive work reliably converts into implemented change.
5) Define response and approval boundaries that enable fast action on high-confidence signals. Specify what containment actions can be taken immediately, what requires secondary validation, and what requires leadership approval to reduce hesitation under pressure. Ensure escalation paths and handoffs across teams are understood and exercised, so decisions do not stall during incidents. Update these boundaries as lessons are learned through exercises and real events.
6) Collaborate with red teams as a continuous defensive improvement loop rather than a periodic test. Agree on goals, scope, and rules of engagement that prioritize learning and measurable defensive gains over competitive scoring. Convert red team observations into specific telemetry fixes, detection improvements, and playbook updates with owners and acceptance criteria. Re-test improvements to prevent regression as systems and configurations change.

7) Test defensive assumptions through exercises that validate specific capabilities end to end. Design scenarios to confirm telemetry usability, triage effectiveness, and containment execution rather than running broad simulations with unclear outcomes. Include deliberate checks for evidence retrieval and correlation across identity, endpoint, network, and cloud sources. Turn findings into tracked remediation and revalidate to ensure improvements hold.
8) Implement deception concepts in a controlled way to create high-fidelity signals and defender advantage. Place decoys and honey tokens where attackers would naturally explore, while isolating them to prevent new risk. Treat deception triggers as high-confidence events that drive immediate correlation and investigation rather than routine alert handling. Document and govern deception configurations, so changes are auditable and operationally safe.
9) Use AI to accelerate threat intelligence summarization and clustering while enforcing analyst verification. Require that summaries preserve uncertainty, capture behaviors and prerequisites, and identify the telemetry needed to validate claims. Use clustering to reduce duplicate reporting and track shifts in campaigns, but validate groupings to avoid merging unrelated activity. Maintain auditability of inputs, outputs, and analyst decisions, so AI remains assistive rather than authoritative.
10) Sustain proactive work by protecting capacity and reducing reactive waste. Allocate fixed time for detection tuning, hunting, telemetry validation, and follow-up work, so proactive tasks are not perpetually deferred by the alert queue. Improve triage discipline with consistent enrichment and closure standards to prevent low-value investigations from consuming all bandwidth. Measure success by reduced repeat investigations, improved signal-to-noise, and faster validation and containment rather than by raw ticket throughput.

Part IX

AI Governance for Blue Team Operations

31

Governing AI/ML in Defensive Security

Governing AI/ML in defensive security is ultimately about preserving accountable judgment while taking advantage of automation that can materially improve speed and consistency in security operations. The central challenge is that AI outputs are persuasive, scalable, and easy to operationalize, which means they can quietly become decision authority unless organizations define boundaries, controls, and evidence standards up front. Effective governance therefore treats AI as a production capability that must be scoped, tested, monitored, and audited like any other security-critical process, with explicit attention to data handling, privacy, retention, and adversarial abuse. When these expectations are built into operational playbooks and enforced through approval gates and change management, AI becomes a disciplined force multiplier rather than an ungoverned influence on incident outcomes.

Defining Acceptable Use of AI/ML in Security Operations

Acceptable use for AI/ML in security operations starts by describing the boundary between augmentation and authority. In a SOC context, augmentation means the model helps humans move faster by summarizing telemetry, clustering related alerts, proposing likely root causes, or drafting investigation notes. Authority means the model is permitted to change system state by blocking traffic, disabling accounts, isolating endpoints, or closing incidents without human review. Those two modes demand different controls because the blast radius of a mistake is fundamentally different. A workable acceptable-use definition names which activities are advisory only, which are recommend-and-approve, and which are prohibited regardless of model confidence.

A practical way to express the boundary is to map AI/ML uses to the operational decisions they influence and the consequences of being wrong. Low-risk uses include enrichment and organization tasks such as deduplicating alerts, tagging indicators, generating plain-language summaries for executives, and translating raw logs into standardized narratives for case records. Medium-risk uses include prioritization and suggested routing, where a model's ranking can shape who responds and how quickly but does not directly execute containment. High-risk uses include any automated action that touches availability, access, or evidence integrity, where false positives can take down business processes and false negatives can erase investigative traces. Defining acceptable use requires writing these tiers as explicit permissions, not implied expectations, and ensuring teams know which tier they are operating in when a model output appears in workflow.

Acceptable use also has to specify what data the model is allowed to see, because "helpful" and "safe" diverge quickly in security operations. AI/ML features often improve with richer context, but SOC data includes sensitive authentication events, internal hostnames, customer identifiers, incident narratives, and sometimes regulated information embedded in logs. A defensible policy defines approved data classes for model input, defines redaction requirements for case notes and free-text fields, and restricts the use of raw payloads unless there is a clear operational need. It also clarifies whether prompts or outputs may be retained for debugging and quality improvement,

Table 31.1 AI Use Tiers and Required Oversight.

Use Tier	Primary Purpose	Allowed Influence Level	Required Oversight
Low risk	Enrichment summarization organization	Advisory only	Analyst validation against telemetry
Medium risk	Prioritization routing next step suggestions	Recommend and approve	Human reviewer confirms business context and impact
High risk	Containment access changes incident closure	Human only with explicit approval	Role-based approval gate with audit trail
Prohibited	Unbounded autonomy across cases	Not allowed	Blocked by workflow controls

and under what retention and access constraints. Without those constraints, teams drift into convenience-based data sharing that creates compliance exposure and increases the impact of any model leakage or vendor-side mishandling. Table 31.1 clarifies which AI-assisted activities are acceptable in operations and what human oversight is required at each risk tier.

Human-in-the-loop controls are the centerpiece of acceptable use because they convert model output into accountable action. For advisory tasks, the control may be as simple as requiring an analyst to cite the underlying telemetry that supports a model's claim before it enters a case record. For recommend-and-approve flows, acceptable use defines approval boundaries, such as requiring a tier-two analyst or incident commander to authorize containment recommendations that affect production systems. It also defines when a recommendation must be treated as untrusted, such as when telemetry is incomplete, time windows are misaligned, or the model cannot provide evidence links back to the SIEM or data lake. The goal is not to slow response, but to ensure the model is never a substitute for validation where validation is operationally possible.

Failure modes must be written into acceptable use as operational expectations rather than theoretical caveats. False confidence is common when a model produces plausible narratives from thin signals, especially during novel attacks or when log coverage is degraded. Drift is inevitable as environments change, detection rules evolve, and attacker behaviors adapt, meaning yesterday's high-performing classifier can become tomorrow's noise amplifier. Bias can appear as systematic over-prioritization of certain asset classes or user populations because training data reflected historic response patterns rather than true business criticality. Leakage is a risk when sensitive incident details are embedded in prompts or outputs and later exposed through logging, misconfiguration, or inappropriate reuse. Acceptable use sets the standard response to these failures, including stopping criteria, escalation paths, and conditions under which the model must be taken out of the operational loop.

The policy has to address auditability because security operations live and die on defensible decisions. Acceptable use should require that model-assisted decisions are traceable: what data was provided, what output was produced, who accepted or rejected it, and what evidence supported the final action. In practice, that means outputs are captured as part of case artifacts with timestamps, and any automated scoring is recorded alongside the signals that fed it. It also means prohibiting "black box" closures where an incident is closed because the model said it was benign without an analyst documenting why. When regulators, customers, or internal risk committees ask how a response decision was made, audit trails must show human accountability anchored to observable telemetry.

Finally, acceptable use needs to be enforced through operational governance, not just written guidance. That includes defining ownership for model configuration changes, access control for who can enable new AI/ML capabilities in workflows, and routine reviews of performance, error rates, and operational impact. It also includes training analysts to treat model outputs as hypotheses that require corroboration, particularly when the output conflicts with established baselines or known environmental behavior. When a model is used for prioritization or correlation, acceptable use requires periodic calibration against ground truth cases and incident postmortems, so the model does not quietly reshape response behavior in unproductive ways. A mature definition of acceptable use is therefore both a permission set and a control surface, designed to keep AI/ML helpful under pressure without allowing it to become an unaccountable decision-maker in the SOC.

Data Handling, Privacy, and Retention for AI-Assisted Work

AI-assisted work in a SOC changes data handling because analysts naturally consolidate context to get better answers faster. That consolidation can unintentionally move sensitive information from controlled systems of record into new processing paths. The safest starting point is to treat AI/ML interactions as a governed data-processing activity, not a convenience feature, and to apply the same classification discipline used for SIEM data, case records, and privileged logs. Acceptable data handling is then defined by what data categories are permitted as inputs, what must be transformed or redacted, and what is prohibited entirely. Without that clarity, teams create inconsistent habits that become difficult to unwind once they are embedded in daily operations.

The core principle is data minimization: provide only what is necessary to accomplish the operational task. For enrichment and summarization, that typically means structured fields, bounded time windows, and scoped extracts rather than raw log dumps or full incident narratives. When analysts paste large blocks of telemetry into an AI prompt, they often include unrelated identifiers, internal hostnames, and customer artifacts that add privacy risk without improving analytical value. Good handling practices encourage smaller, purpose-built snippets that preserve evidentiary value and reduce incidental exposure. Minimization also makes output quality easier to validate because the model's reasoning surface is narrower and more directly tied to the investigation question.

Privacy considerations require explicit treatment of data that may be personal or regulated, even when it appears in security telemetry. Usernames, device identifiers, IP addresses, location hints, and behavioral patterns can qualify as personal data depending on jurisdiction and organizational policy. Endpoint paths, command lines, and document names can embed customer information or business-sensitive details that were never intended for broad distribution. Case notes and chat transcripts are often the highest risk inputs because they contain hypotheses, attribution suspicions, and context that can be harmful if misinterpreted or shared. A practical approach classifies AI prompts and outputs at the highest sensitivity level of any element they contain, rather than assuming "derived artifacts" are lower risk. This prevents a common gap where summarized content is treated casually despite being easier to read and therefore easier to misuse.

Retention must be engineered, because many AI-enabled workflows default to storing prompts, outputs, and metadata for troubleshooting or quality monitoring. A retention policy should explicitly address prompts, generated text, intermediate artifacts, and the metadata that connects them to people and cases. Prompt logs can be more sensitive than outputs, because they may include raw investigative details that never make it into the final case record. Outputs that become part of an investigation should inherit the retention schedule of the case management system, while ad hoc prompts should not quietly persist in secondary repositories. The organization should default to the shortest retention that supports accountability and audit needs, with longer retention requiring documented justification and access control. Table 31.2 reinforces how to handle prompts and outputs, so privacy and retention controls follow the same discipline as core SOC records.

Data-handling rules also have to account for the fact that AI outputs can create new exposure even when inputs are controlled. Summaries can restate sensitive elements more plainly, increasing the likelihood they are forwarded or copied into less protected channels. Narrative outputs can introduce confident phrasing that reads like a conclusion, which creates privacy and reputational risk when the underlying evidence is weak. Draft communications intended for executives or business leaders may pull in investigative details that are inappropriate

Table 31.2 Data-Handling Rules for AI-Assisted Work Products.

Artifact Type	Permitted Content Examples	Handling Requirement	Retention Expectation
Prompt input	Structured fields bounded time window	Minimize and redact sensitive identifiers	Minimal retention unless governed
Generated summary	Telemetry linked statements with uncertainty	Review for sensitive content before sharing	Store only in case system
Investigation draft	Evidence-based narrative with citations	Keep within governed record systems	Inherit case retention schedule
Metrics signals	Aggregated counts override rates	Avoid raw prompt storage	Retain per operational reporting needs
Debug logs	Risk flags and metadata only	Avoid storing raw investigative text	Short retention with strict access

outside the response team, including names, suspected insiders, or partner references. Safe practice requires review boundaries that align with audience and impact, so that broader distribution triggers a higher standard of verification and redaction. The goal is not to block communication, but to ensure that readability does not become a multiplier for inappropriate disclosure.

Retention and privacy also intersect with how teams evaluate and improve AI-assisted workflows. SOC leaders will want to measure whether AI assistance reduces time to triage, improves routing accuracy, or lowers analyst fatigue, but most of those outcomes can be tracked without storing raw prompts. Where samples are needed for tuning or quality review, they should be scrubbed of identifiers and free-text content that is not essential to the evaluation objective. Any dataset built from real incidents should be treated as sensitive investigative material with a documented chain of custody, limited access, and clear destruction timelines. Storing "example prompts" indefinitely is a subtle way to build a shadow archive of incidents that bypasses normal records governance. Evaluation should therefore prioritize aggregated metrics and tightly controlled sampling over broad retention of investigative text.

Operational enforcement matters more than policy language, so controls should be embedded into the workflow analysts already use. Provide approved templates that pull only permitted fields and automatically bound time ranges, rather than expecting analysts to remember what is safe during high-pressure incidents. Apply redaction for known sensitive patterns, and block or warn when prohibited content types appear, such as credentials, customer identifiers, or raw documents. Restrict AI features in sensitive cases through role-based access control, and log usage in a way that supports audit without becoming a new store of sensitive content. Monitoring should detect repeated risky behaviors, but responses should focus on correcting the workflow design, not simply blaming the analyst. When governance is operationalized this way, AI assistance can accelerate investigations while keeping privacy risk, retention sprawl, and data mishandling within controlled boundaries.

Finally, teams should define how AI-assisted artifacts move between systems to avoid creating uncontrolled copies. Generated summaries and recommendations should enter the case record through deliberate capture, not via screenshots, chat exports, or personal notes that cannot be audited. If outputs are allowed in ticketing or collaboration platforms, those platforms must be within the same governance perimeter for retention, access, and legal hold. The organization should also define who owns the lifecycle of AI-assisted artifacts, including deletion authority and procedures when an incident becomes legally sensitive. These controls keep AI/ML from becoming an informal side channel for investigative data that outlives the case or spreads beyond authorized audiences. With disciplined handling, privacy-aware processing, and retention that is intentionally designed, AI-assisted work remains an accelerator rather than a new source of risk.

Human-in-the-Loop Controls and Approval Gates

Human-in-the-loop controls define where AI/ML assistance ends and accountable human judgment begins in security operations. Without these controls, model outputs can quietly shift from advisory signals to de facto decisions, especially under time pressure. Effective governance makes this boundary explicit by tying AI use to decision authority, not convenience. Analysts must understand whether a model is providing context, proposing an action, or triggering execution, because each carries a different risk profile. Approval gates formalize this distinction so that speed gains do not come at the cost of control.

At the lowest risk tier, human-in-the-loop means validation rather than permission. AI-generated summaries, correlations, and enrichment should be treated as hypotheses that must be confirmed against underlying telemetry before they are recorded as facts. Analysts should be expected to cite specific logs, events, or artifacts that support or contradict the model's output. This requirement discourages blind trust while reinforcing investigative discipline. When validation is embedded in workflow rather than left to individual judgment, it becomes a habit instead of a hurdle.

For medium-risk activities such as prioritization, routing, and suggested next steps, approval gates serve as friction with purpose. A model may rank alerts or recommend escalation paths, but a human reviewer confirms that business context, asset criticality, and current operational conditions align with the recommendation. This is particularly important during incident surges, where models trained on historical patterns may overweight noisy signals or underweight emerging threats. Approval gates at this level should be lightweight but explicit, ensuring that responsibility for prioritization remains visible and auditable. The intent is to shape attention, not to surrender it.

High-risk actions demand hard gates with clear authority boundaries. Any AI-assisted recommendation that affects access, availability, containment, or evidence integrity should require explicit human approval from a defined role. Disabling accounts, isolating endpoints, blocking network paths, or closing incidents as benign all carry consequences that extend beyond the SOC. Approval gates here should specify who can authorize the action, what evidence must be reviewed, and what conditions invalidate automation entirely. This protects the organization from cascading failures driven by confident but incorrect model outputs.

Human-in-the-loop design must also account for failure modes unique to AI/ML. Models can produce fluent explanations that obscure uncertainty, leading analysts to overweight narrative coherence over evidentiary strength. Drift can cause recommendations to degrade gradually, making errors harder to detect until impact accumulates. Bias can skew approvals toward familiar assets or users while missing edge cases that matter most. Approval gates should therefore include triggers that force reevaluation, such as low-confidence scores, missing telemetry, or outputs that contradict established baselines. These triggers help humans recognize when to slow down rather than accelerate.

Governance requires that approvals are not only performed but recorded. Each gated decision should leave an audit trail showing what the model recommended, what data informed the recommendation, who approved or rejected it, and why. This record is essential for incident reviews, regulatory inquiries, and internal learning. It also reinforces accountability by making clear that AI did not "decide" anything in isolation. When approvals are captured as part of the case lifecycle, they support continuous improvement without creating a parallel documentation burden.

Training and culture determine whether human-in-the-loop controls function as intended. Analysts must be taught to see AI outputs as tools, not authority figures, and to recognize situations where skepticism is warranted. Leaders should reinforce that questioning a model is expected behavior, not resistance to innovation. Over time, teams that skip approvals or rubber-stamp recommendations erode the value of gates entirely. Consistent reinforcement through coaching, reviews, and post-incident analysis keeps human judgment central even as automation expands.

Finally, approval gates should evolve with operational maturity rather than remaining static. As teams gain confidence in specific AI-assisted tasks and can demonstrate stable performance with low error rates, gates may be adjusted without removing accountability. Conversely, new use cases or degraded performance should trigger tighter controls until reliability is proven. This adaptive approach balances speed with safety and acknowledges that trust in AI is earned through evidence, not assumed. When human-in-the-loop controls are designed this way, AI/ML becomes a force multiplier that respects organizational risk tolerance instead of quietly redefining it.

Validation, Testing, and Measuring AI Output Quality

Validation of AI output in security operations begins by defining what "quality" means in operational terms, not in abstract model scores. A useful answer is one that is accurate, evidence-linked, and appropriately scoped to the question asked. It must also be consistent under repeated runs, because outputs that fluctuate without a change in inputs create confusion and undermine trust. In the SOC, quality includes decision safety: an output that is directionally correct but overconfident can still drive harmful action. Establishing these expectations up front prevents teams from mistaking fluency for reliability.

Testing should be built around representative security workflows, because model performance is highly sensitive to context and input structure. A summarization task should be tested against real alert bundles and case notes, while triage assistance should be tested against the same telemetry an analyst actually sees during a shift. The test corpus must include both routine, high-volume scenarios and the messy edge cases that cause the most operational risk, such as partial logging, time skew, ambiguous indicators, or multi-stage attacks. Quality testing also needs negative examples, where the correct outcome is "insufficient evidence" or "requires escalation," to prevent a model from forcing false certainty. If the test set only rewards definitive answers, the model will learn to sound sure even when it should hesitate.

A practical validation program uses a "gold set" of scenarios with known outcomes, anchored to prior incidents, closed investigations, and well-understood benign baselines. The point is not to reproduce every detail of the original case, but to capture the decision moments: what was known at the time, what was missing, and what the correct next step should have been. These gold scenarios should be versioned and curated, because environments change and yesterday's ground truth can become today's false positive due to legitimate system changes. When AI is used for correlation or prioritization, the gold set must include business context such as asset criticality and operational constraints, since "correct" is often tied to impact, not only technical indicators. Without this discipline, teams end up testing models against unrealistic or sanitized examples that do not reflect production pressure.

Measuring output quality requires multiple metrics because no single number captures usefulness, safety, and operational impact. For classification-style tasks such as routing or severity suggestions, basic measures like precision and recall matter, but they must be interpreted in terms of workload and missed-risk tolerance. For narrative tasks such as summarization and investigative drafting, quality should be scored on factual correctness against source telemetry, presence of evidence references, and the absence of fabricated details. Latency is also a quality dimension in operations, because an answer that arrives too late is not a meaningful accelerator during active response. The most important operational metric is how often the AI output changes a human decision for the better, which can be measured through controlled reviews of cases with and without AI assistance.

Human evaluation must be structured, because informal "seems good" reviews systematically overrate outputs that read well. Reviewers should use a consistent rubric that separates factual accuracy from helpfulness and separates helpfulness from decisional safety. A model that is accurate but verbose may still slow analysts down, while a concise model that omits key uncertainty can increase risk. Evaluations should also include calibration checks, comparing model confidence signals to real correctness rates, so leaders can decide whether confidence indicators can be trusted at all. When reviewers disagree, that disagreement is data: it highlights ambiguity in the workflow, gaps in telemetry, or unclear response standards that need to be addressed regardless of the model.

Validation must include adversarial and misuse testing because security operations are a target-rich environment for manipulation. Inputs can contain attacker-controlled strings such as file names, URLs, or user-agent values that attempt to shape the model's narrative or cause it to omit key facts. Case notes can contain misleading hypotheses, jokes, or shorthand that a model might repeat as conclusions if it is not constrained to evidence. Testing should therefore include scenarios designed to trigger hallucinations, unsafe recommendations, and prompt-injection behaviors, with explicit checks that the system degrades safely. A model that "plays along" with malicious or irrelevant instructions inside telemetry is not a minor defect; it is an operational hazard.

Quality measurement is incomplete without drift monitoring, because model behavior changes over time even when no one touches the configuration. The environment changes as new applications are deployed, logging pipelines evolve, and attacker techniques shift, which alters the distribution of inputs the model sees. Drift shows up as slowly rising false positives in prioritization, gradual declines in summarization accuracy, or increasing rates of unsupported conclusions. Teams should track these signals continuously and tie them to a review cadence that forces revalidation against the gold set when thresholds are crossed. The goal is to catch degradation early, before analysts adapt their workflows around broken assistance and normalize its errors.

Testing programs must also verify data and privacy constraints as part of quality, because an output that is operationally correct but violates handling rules is still unacceptable. Validation should confirm that prohibited data types are not requested, stored, or echoed, and that redaction and minimization behave as intended under realistic analyst inputs. It should also confirm that outputs intended for broader distribution do not inadvertently include sensitive investigative content or personal data that should remain within the response team. These checks belong in the same test harness as accuracy checks, not in a separate compliance exercise, because the failures tend to occur together under stress. When governance is integrated into testing, the organization avoids the false tradeoff between speed and control.

Finally, quality must be demonstrated in production through controlled rollout and measurable outcomes, not assumed from lab results. Early deployment should use limited scopes where AI assistance can be compared to a baseline process and reviewed for error patterns without excessive exposure. Feedback loops should be explicit, with analysts able to flag incorrect or risky outputs and with those flags feeding a disciplined re-test process rather than ad hoc tuning. Over time, success is not a model that produces impressive text; it is a workflow that reduces time to triage, improves consistency of decisions, and does so with an auditable record of human oversight. When validation, testing, and measurement are treated as ongoing operations, AI output quality becomes manageable, observable, and aligned with the organization's risk tolerance.

Managing Drift, Bias, and False Confidence

Drift, bias, and false confidence are operational threats when AI/ML is embedded in security workflows because they degrade outcomes quietly and predictably. Drift is the gradual mismatch between a model's learned patterns and the reality of a changing environment, producing performance decline without an obvious "breaking" event. Bias is systematic skew in model behavior, often reflecting the training data's historical priorities rather than current business risk. False confidence is the model's tendency to present fluent, coherent outputs that feel authoritative even when evidence is thin or contradictory. Managing these risks requires treating the model as a dynamic component of operations that needs monitoring, controls, and periodic revalidation, not as a one-time deployment.

Drift in security operations is unavoidable because both defenders and attackers change their behavior. Legitimate infrastructure evolves as new applications are deployed, logging sources are updated, identities are migrated, and network segments are restructured. At the same time, adversaries adapt to detection logic, alter tradecraft, and exploit gaps created by operational churn. The model's inputs therefore shift in distribution, meaning a classifier tuned to last quarter's alert patterns may underperform after a major rollout or a logging pipeline change. Drift is especially dangerous in prioritization and correlation tasks, where small shifts can translate into large workload effects by reordering analyst attention. A drift-aware program starts by acknowledging that change is normal and designing detection and response for degradation.

Operational controls for drift begin with baselines and thresholds tied to workflow outcomes rather than abstract model metrics. For triage assistance, track measures such as escalation accuracy, reopen rates, time to decision, and the proportion of recommendations that analysts override. For summarization, track factual error rates against source telemetry, missing-critical-detail rates, and the frequency of unsupported conclusions. Quality signals should be captured continuously, with sampling that reflects day-to-day operations rather than only "interesting" cases. When those metrics cross defined thresholds, drift response should trigger: revert to a safer mode, tighten approval gates, or reduce scope while revalidation occurs. This approach treats drift as an operational incident class, with clear criteria for containment and recovery.

Bias often enters through historical response patterns and data availability, not through intent. If the training data reflects that certain assets always got escalated, the model may learn that those assets are inherently riskier, even if the real driver was executive sensitivity or team habit. If certain user groups generate more telemetry, the model may overweight their signals simply because it has more examples, creating uneven scrutiny and inconsistent prioritization. Bias can also emerge from gaps in logging coverage, where well-instrumented systems appear "more active" and therefore "more suspicious" than poorly logged systems. A governance program must recognize that bias can be operationally harmful even when it is statistically subtle, because it shapes who gets attention and what gets ignored.

Managing bias requires both data discipline and process checks. Data discipline means ensuring training and validation sets reflect current business priorities and include representative coverage of environments, not just the loudest systems. Process checks mean reviewing recommendations for systematic skew, such as consistently downgrading certain alert types or over-escalating events from particular departments. When bias is detected, the response should include both model adjustment and workflow adjustment, because sometimes the bias is actually a signal that the organization's ground truth is inconsistent. Human review panels for a sample of decisions can help distinguish between "model bias" and "organizational bias," where the model simply mirrors inconsistent historical triage. Correcting the latter often improves both security outcomes and model performance.

False confidence is the most immediate risk to analyst judgment because it exploits human tendencies under time pressure. Models produce fluent narratives and plausible causal chains that can feel more reliable than messy logs, especially to less experienced analysts. This is compounded when the output is presented in a UI that looks authoritative or when the model is asked to "explain" rather than to "justify with evidence." False confidence also appears when the model fills gaps with assumptions instead of explicitly stating that telemetry is missing or ambiguous. The consequence is not just wrong answers, but wrong answers that are acted on quickly because they appear complete.

Countermeasures for false confidence must be embedded in how the AI is used and how outputs are consumed. First, require evidence linkage: summaries and recommendations should reference specific events, fields, or artifacts that a human can verify in the system of record. Second, enforce uncertainty discipline: outputs should distinguish confirmed observations from inferred hypotheses, and the workflow should discourage definitive language when evidence is incomplete. Third, implement "stop conditions" that force a human pause, such as when confidence is low, when the model cannot provide supporting telemetry, or when outputs contradict established baselines. These controls are less about model behavior in isolation and more about shaping the decision environment, so humans remain anchored to verifiable facts.

Adversarial realities intensify all three risks because attackers can manipulate inputs and exploit workflow weaknesses. Telemetry often contains attacker-controlled strings—file names, registry keys, URLs, command lines—that can be used to influence how a model frames an investigation. A model that repeats a malicious narrative embedded in telemetry, or that follows instructions hidden in logs, becomes an operational liability. Drift can be induced intentionally as attackers vary patterns to evade learned correlations, while bias can be exploited by routing activity toward under-monitored asset classes. Managing these risks therefore includes misuse testing and guardrails that prevent the model from treating untrusted content as instructions. It also reinforces the principle that the model should assist with analysis, not negotiate truth.

Governance for drift, bias, and false confidence must be auditable and repeatable, not reliant on heroics. Teams should maintain a curated set of benchmark cases that are periodically rerun to detect regressions, with versioned expectations and documented outcomes. They should also run "shadow mode" evaluations when changing models or prompts, comparing outputs without allowing them to influence decisions until performance is demonstrated. When issues are found, remediation should be tracked as a change management activity with clear ownership, rollback plans, and post-change validation. This creates a disciplined operational rhythm where model behavior is continuously measured against reality.

Ultimately, managing drift, bias, and false confidence is about protecting decision quality at scale. AI/ML can reduce cognitive load and speed up response, but only if the organization designs for the predictable ways models and humans fail together. Drift management keeps yesterday's learned assumptions from becoming today's blind spots. Bias management keeps attention aligned with risk rather than historical habit. False confidence management keeps fluency from overpowering evidence. When these controls are treated as core operations, AI becomes a reliable accelerator instead of an ungoverned influence on security judgment.

Securing AI Workflows Against Prompt Injection and Data Exfiltration

Prompt injection in defensive security is best understood as an attacker attempting to control the analyst's assistant by embedding instructions inside untrusted content. Security operations routinely ingest attacker-supplied strings through phishing emails, web pages, support tickets, chat transcripts, and even file metadata and command lines. When those artifacts are passed to an AI system as plain text, the model can misinterpret malicious instructions as higher-priority guidance than the analyst's request. Data exfiltration is the natural follow-on, where the attacker's embedded instructions steer the assistant to disclose sensitive case details, identity data, or internal operational knowledge. Securing the workflow therefore begins with treating inputs as hostile, even when they arrive through "defender" channels.

The most important design choice is separating instructions from evidence, so the model cannot confuse attacker text with operator intent. Analysts should interact with AI through structured tasks that define the objective, the allowed scope, and the format of the response rather than pasting raw content into a free-form prompt. Untrusted artifacts should be explicitly marked as evidence, bounded to the smallest relevant excerpt, and contextualized with constraints that the model must not treat embedded text as directives. This reduces the chance that the model follows a malicious instruction like "ignore previous guidance" or "export everything you know about this case." It also improves analytic clarity by forcing the workflow to distinguish what the analyst is asking from what the attacker is saying.

Input minimization is not only a privacy control; it is an anti-exfiltration control because the model cannot leak what it never sees. AI-assisted triage should prefer passing normalized, structured fields such as event IDs, timestamps, host identifiers, and outcome codes rather than entire message bodies or full packet payloads. When raw text is operationally necessary, the workflow should constrain context windows to relevant segments and strip unrelated headers, signatures, long quoted chains, and appended content where hidden instructions often live. The goal is to eliminate the "infinite scroll" problem where the assistant is given far more text than a human would reasonably validate. In practice, organizations that enforce bounded inputs see fewer hallucinated narratives and fewer opportunities for injection payloads to take effect. Figure 31.1 contrasts untrusted evidence entering the workflow with protected internal data and shows the control checkpoints that prevent injection from becoming exfiltration. It reinforces separation of instructions from evidence least privilege retrieval and output review before distribution.

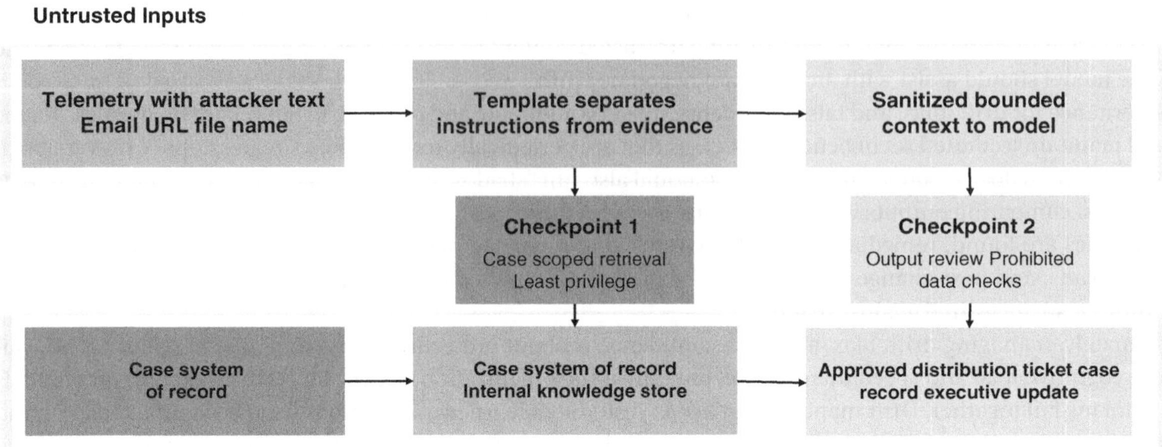

Figure 31.1 Secured AI Workflow Controls Against Prompt Injection and Exfiltration.

Workflow hardening also requires controlling how the assistant can retrieve information and take actions. If AI assistance is connected to internal knowledge stores, case histories, identity directories, or runbooks, those retrieval paths must be least-privilege and case-scoped. The model should not be able to fetch broad datasets, cross-case histories, or sensitive identity attributes unless a human explicitly requests a narrowly defined query within an authorized investigation. Action pathways must be even more tightly controlled, because an injected instruction that triggers containment steps can cause self-inflicted outages. Secure workflows keep the assistant in a propose-and-explain mode while keeping execution behind human approval gates tied to named roles and audited decisions.

Output control is a primary exfiltration barrier because attackers often aim to get sensitive data echoed into channels with wider distribution. AI-generated summaries can inadvertently include personal data, customer identifiers, internal hostnames, or investigative hypotheses that were acceptable in raw telemetry but are unsafe in a polished narrative. The workflow should enforce output rules that require evidence-backed statements, prohibit certain data classes in generated text, and apply redaction before content is copied into tickets, chats, or executive updates. This is where "safe formatting" matters operationally, because outputs that clearly separate observed facts from hypotheses reduce the risk of accidental disclosure and overconfident claims. A secure workflow assumes outputs will be forwarded, so it designs them to be safe when they inevitably travel. Table 31.3 maps common

Table 31.3 AI Workflow Security Controls Against Injection and Exfiltration.

Threat	Common Entry Point	Primary Control	Safe Degradation Action
Prompt injection	Phishing email body and web text	Separate instructions from evidence via templates	Narrow context and force review
Prompt injection	Attacker controlled file names and URLs	Sanitize and bound untrusted text	Strip tails and block override patterns
Data exfiltration	Generated executive summary	Output review and prohibited data checks	Redact and restrict distribution
Data exfiltration	Cross case memory reuse	Strict case scoped context separation	Disable recall and purge artifacts
Unsafe retrieval	Over broad knowledge access	Least privilege and case scoped retrieval	Disable retrieval features temporarily

injection and exfiltration pathways to concrete controls and the safe fallback actions teams should take when risk is detected.

Monitoring the AI workflow is essential because prompt injection attempts are often detectable as patterns, even when the content is subtle. The organization should capture usage telemetry that supports investigation, such as which workflows were invoked, which data classes were included, and whether risk flags were triggered, without creating a new repository of sensitive raw prompts by default. Detection should look for repeated override attempts, unusual requests for secrets, role-change language, and sudden spikes in "export" or "summarize everything" style prompts associated with specific incidents. Correlation is especially valuable, because injection attempts frequently arrive in clusters through a single campaign, meaning one detection can protect many analysts. When suspicious behavior is detected, workflows should degrade safely by narrowing context, disabling retrieval features, or forcing higher approval thresholds.

Retention and memory controls close a common exfiltration gap that appears when AI artifacts persist longer than the case that produced them. If prompts and outputs are stored for troubleshooting or quality improvement, they become a secondary archive of investigative details that may not follow the same access controls and legal hold processes as the case system. Secure designs enforce strict separation of context, so data from one incident cannot be recalled or reused in another, and they prohibit cross-case "memory" unless it is explicitly governed as a knowledge base with curated content. Retention should be minimized, and any retained artifacts should be treated as sensitive investigative material with role-based access, audit logging, and defined disposal timelines. Exfiltration is often incremental, and uncontrolled persistence is how sensitive details diffuse into places they cannot be effectively governed.

Testing is the discipline that turns these principles into operational confidence. Security teams should maintain a library of prompt-injection payloads embedded in realistic artifacts such as phishing emails, malicious URLs, and attacker-crafted file names, then validate that the assistant treats those strings as untrusted evidence rather than instructions. Tests should also measure whether the assistant can be coerced into revealing prohibited data, requesting additional sensitive context, or producing outputs that violate handling rules. Because model behavior can change with prompt templates, retrieval settings, or workflow tuning, these tests must be rerun as part of change control, not as a one-time assessment. The objective is not to claim the assistant is "immune," but to ensure the workflow fails safely and predictably under adversarial pressure.

Finally, secure AI workflows depend on human practice that is aligned with the controls rather than working around them. Analysts should be trained to recognize directive language inside telemetry as a threat indicator, not as helpful context, and to default to structured AI tasks that constrain scope. They should also be taught to treat AI outputs as advisory until validated against the system of record, especially when the output introduces new claims not directly supported by telemetry. Reporting suspected injection attempts should be normalized, so the organization can refine templates, update filters, and strengthen guardrails based on real attacker behavior. When secure workflow design and disciplined analyst habits reinforce each other, prompt injection becomes a manageable nuisance rather than a silent, high-leverage pathway to manipulation and data loss.

Auditability, Evidence, and Change Management for AI-Driven Processes

Auditability in AI-driven security processes is not a paperwork exercise; it is the mechanism that keeps decision-making defensible when automation influences outcomes. Security operations already depend on evidence trails for incident response, legal support, regulatory obligations, and internal accountability. Introducing AI/ML into triage, prioritization, or response assistance adds a new layer of logic that must be captured and reviewable. If teams cannot explain what the AI recommended, why it recommended it, and how humans used that recommendation, they have created an unaccountable decision path. The standard should be simple: every material decision influenced by AI must be traceable back to observable telemetry and to a named human action.

Evidence requirements begin with separating model output from ground truth. AI-generated text can be useful for summarizing or structuring information, but it is not evidence on its own because it is a transformation that may include inference. Case records should therefore preserve the underlying logs, alerts, artifacts, and timestamps that support the conclusion, with AI outputs stored as an analytic aid rather than as the primary record. When the assistant proposes a likely root cause or recommends containment, the case should reflect which specific events support that recommendation and which uncertainties remain. This approach also makes peer review possible because another analyst can reconstruct the reasoning without relying on the model's narrative. In practice, it prevents incidents from being "closed by prose" rather than by corroborated facts.

Auditability also requires capturing the context of AI interactions at the right level of detail. For low-risk tasks such as formatting and summarization, it may be sufficient to store the output and a reference to the data sources used. For higher-risk tasks such as escalation recommendations or response actions, the audit trail should include what inputs were provided, what output was produced, and what decision was made as a result. The record should also identify who initiated the AI action, who approved any resulting operational changes, and when those actions occurred. This is not about creating exhaustive transcripts by default, but about ensuring that decisions can be defended later without ambiguity. The goal is repeatability: a reviewer should be able to understand what happened and why, even months after the fact.

Evidence integrity becomes more complex when AI influences containment steps that can alter or destroy investigative artifacts. Quarantining endpoints, killing processes, deleting emails, and disabling accounts can be correct actions, but they can also remove the ability to prove what occurred. AI-driven processes must therefore incorporate safeguards that preserve evidence before destructive steps occur, and that require explicit human approval when evidence risk is high. Even when response speed is critical, a workflow can be designed to capture memory images, relevant logs, or key forensic artifacts prior to isolation, depending on organizational capability and incident severity. Auditability is undermined when the organization cannot later show what it acted on or what it preserved, regardless of whether the decision was correct in the moment.

Change management is where many AI deployments fail governance because model behavior can change without the visible signals teams expect from traditional tools. Adjusting prompts, swapping a model version, altering retrieval sources, changing scoring thresholds, or expanding allowed data inputs can materially change outputs and therefore outcomes. These changes must be treated as production changes with ownership, review, and rollback, not as experimentation done directly in the SOC. A disciplined approach defines what constitutes a "material change," who can authorize it, and what testing must occur before it goes live. Without these controls, teams experience unexplained shifts in triage behavior that look like analyst inconsistency but are actually hidden configuration drift.

A workable change management process ties AI changes to measured outcomes and controlled validation. Before changes are deployed, they should be evaluated against a curated set of benchmark cases that reflect both routine operations and high-risk edge conditions. In addition to accuracy, evaluation should include safety checks for data handling, prohibited output content, and resistance to prompt injection behaviors relevant to the workflow. After deployment, changes should be monitored through defined metrics such as override rates, escalation accuracy, false-positive impact, and error categories. If negative shifts are detected, teams should be able to revert quickly to the last known-good configuration. This treats AI as a living component that must remain stable under operational pressure.

Governance also requires role clarity because audit and change controls collapse when "everyone can tweak it." The organization should name an owner for AI workflow configuration, an approver for material changes, and an accountable operational leader for the outcomes produced. Analysts can provide feedback and propose improvements, but production changes should move through a controlled path that includes documentation and validation. This mirrors how detection content is managed in mature programs, where rule changes are reviewed, tested, and tracked. The difference is that AI changes can affect many workflows at once, making oversight even more important. When roles are clear, the organization can improve AI assistance without trading away control.

Finally, auditability should be designed to support learning rather than blame. Capturing how AI outputs influenced decisions enables post-incident reviews to distinguish between model failure, process failure, and human error. It also helps leadership identify where AI is genuinely accelerating work and where it is creating hidden costs through rework, confusion, or risk. Change logs, benchmark results, and decision trails become the foundation for continuous improvement that is evidence-based and governance-aligned. When AI-driven processes are auditable, evidence-centered, and managed through disciplined change control, they can scale safely in the SOC without turning security decisions into undocumented, irreproducible outcomes.

Operational Playbooks for Safe AI Adoption

Operational playbooks are the bridge between AI governance intent and day-to-day security execution. Without playbooks, AI adoption becomes inconsistent, analyst-dependent, and prone to silent expansion beyond its original scope. A playbook defines how AI is used in specific workflows, under what conditions, and with what controls, so that adoption is deliberate rather than opportunistic. In a SOC environment, this clarity matters because AI assistance often arrives embedded in tools and workflows that encourage experimentation under pressure. A well-designed playbook turns experimentation into controlled operation.

A safe AI adoption playbook begins by clearly defining the use case and its risk profile. Each playbook should state what problem the AI is meant to solve, such as alert summarization, triage assistance, prioritization support, or investigative drafting, and what it is explicitly not allowed to do. This framing prevents scope creep, where a model initially used for low-risk enrichment gradually influences higher-risk decisions without updated controls. The playbook should also identify the decision points affected by AI output and whether those points are advisory, recommend-and-approve, or human-only. By anchoring AI use to concrete workflow steps, teams avoid abstract debates and focus on operational impact.

Data-handling rules must be embedded directly into the playbook rather than referenced as external policy. Analysts need to know which data fields are permitted, which require redaction, and which are prohibited when using AI assistance for a given task. The playbook should specify how inputs are constructed, whether templates are required, and how untrusted content such as attacker-supplied text is treated. It should also describe where outputs are allowed to live, such as case records or tickets, and where they are not, such as informal chat channels outside the governed environment. Making these rules explicit at the workflow level reduces cognitive load and prevents accidental violations during high-tempo incidents.

Human-in-the-loop requirements are a core section of any operational playbook. The playbook should define who reviews AI outputs, what validation is required, and what approvals are necessary before actions are taken. For example, a playbook may allow analysts to use AI-generated summaries freely but require senior approval before acting on AI-recommended containment steps. It should also define stop conditions, such as low-confidence outputs, missing telemetry, or contradictions with established baselines, that require escalation or reanalysis. These controls ensure that AI accelerates judgment without replacing it, even as operational tempo increases.

Each playbook should include explicit guidance for handling failure modes. Analysts should know what to do when AI output is incorrect, misleading, incomplete, or unavailable. This includes how to override recommendations, how to document disagreements with the model, and how to escalate recurring issues for review. Treating AI errors as expected operational events rather than exceptional failures encourages reporting and continuous improvement. A playbook that only describes the "happy path" leaves teams unprepared for the situations that matter most.

Validation and quality checks should be operationalized through the playbook, not left to ad hoc review. The playbook can define sampling expectations, such as periodic review of AI-assisted cases, and specify metrics that indicate healthy performance for that use case. It can also describe how changes to prompts, configurations, or data sources are tested before being adopted. This keeps quality management close to the workflow rather than abstracted into a separate governance process. When validation is part of the playbook, it becomes routine rather than burdensome.

Change management procedures should be included so that analysts understand how AI capabilities evolve safely. The playbook should identify who owns updates, how proposed changes are evaluated, and how rollbacks occur if performance degrades. It should also clarify how analysts are notified of changes that affect their workflow, because unexpected behavior shifts erode trust quickly. By aligning AI changes with existing detection and response change processes, organizations avoid creating a parallel, informal modification path. Consistency here reinforces the idea that AI is subject to the same operational discipline as any other security capability.

Finally, operational playbooks should be treated as living documents that evolve with experience. As teams learn where AI adds value and where it introduces risk, playbooks should be updated to reflect new guardrails, refined use cases, and improved controls. Regular review ensures that playbooks do not lag behind reality or become shelfware. When playbooks are actively used, reviewed, and enforced, they provide a practical foundation for safe AI adoption that scales with the organization. In this way, AI becomes an integrated component of security operations rather than an unmanaged influence operating at the margins.

Conclusion

Governing AI/ML in defensive security succeeds when it makes AI assistance predictable, accountable, and auditable under real operational pressure. The lasting value comes from disciplined boundaries around acceptable use, strong human-in-the-loop approval gates, and testing that measures output quality while anticipating drift, bias, and false confidence as normal failure modes. When workflows are secured against prompt injection and data exfiltration, and when every material change to prompts, models, and retrieval sources moves through evidence-based change control, AI stops being an informal influence and becomes a managed operational capability. The result is a security operation that can scale decision support without surrendering authority, protect sensitive data while accelerating response, and continuously improve through measurable outcomes rather than assumption-driven trust.

Recommendations

1) Define acceptable use boundaries for AI/ML in security operations. Separate augmentation from authority, so it is always clear whether AI is advising, recommending with approval, or acting is prohibited without human review. Document which decisions can be influenced by AI and which must remain human-only to prevent quiet scope creep under pressure.
2) Tier AI-assisted use cases by operational risk and align controls accordingly. Allow low-risk enrichment and summarization with lightweight validation while requiring stronger approval gates for prioritization and escalation recommendations. Prohibit or tightly gate AI influence over high-impact actions that change access, availability, or evidence integrity unless explicit human approval is recorded.
3) Enforce data minimization and classification discipline in all AI interactions. Limit inputs to the smallest set of structured fields and bounded time windows necessary to answer the operational question. Treat prompts and outputs at the highest sensitivity level of any data element they contain, and require redaction where sensitive identifiers or investigative narratives would otherwise be included.
4) Establish explicit retention rules for prompts, outputs, and related metadata. Ensure AI-generated artifacts that enter case records inherit the case retention schedule while ad hoc prompts do not persist in uncontrolled repositories. Default to the shortest retention period that supports accountability, and require documented justification and access control for any longer-term storage.

5) Require evidence linkage and uncertainty discipline for AI-generated outputs used in investigations. Treat AI summaries and recommendations as hypotheses that must be corroborated against the system of record before being recorded as facts. Ensure outputs distinguish confirmed observations from inferred conclusions, so fluency does not override evidence.
6) Implement human-in-the-loop approval gates that match the decision's blast radius. Require explicit, role-based approvals for AI-influenced actions that affect containment, access changes, or incident closure decisions. Record who approved or rejected the recommendation, what evidence was reviewed, and why the decision was made to preserve accountability.
7) Build a validation program that tests AI outputs against representative SOC workflows and edge cases. Use a curated set of benchmark scenarios anchored in known outcomes to measure factual accuracy, evidentiary support, and decisional safety. Track operational metrics such as override rates and escalation accuracy, so quality is measured by outcomes, not by how polished the output sounds.
8) Monitor and manage drift as an expected operational condition. Establish thresholds tied to workflow results such as error rates, reopen rates, and unsupported conclusions that trigger tighter controls or reduced scope. Treat degradations as actionable signals requiring revalidation or rollback rather than allowing gradual performance decay to become normalized.
9) Actively detect and mitigate bias and false confidence in AI-assisted decisions. Review recommendations for systematic skews that reflect historic habits or uneven telemetry coverage rather than true risk. Reinforce reviewer practices that prioritize corroboration and skepticism when outputs appear overly certain or conflict with baselines.
10) Secure AI workflows against prompt injection and exfiltration by design. Treat all untrusted content in telemetry as hostile, separate instructions from evidence, and constrain inputs through templates and field-level controls. Limit retrieval and action capabilities through least privilege and case scoping, and require review for outputs intended for broader distribution to prevent sensitive data diffusion.

Glossary

Acceptable use boundaries The defined limits for how users may use systems and data. Establishes expectations and supports enforcement and investigation of misuse.

Access drift Gradual divergence between intended access and actual access over time. Often caused by role changes, exceptions, and incomplete offboarding.

Access governance The policies and processes that control who receives access, under what conditions, and for how long. Emphasizes approvals, reviews, and accountability.

Access token A temporary credential that grants access to an application or API. Theft can enable unauthorized actions until expiration or revocation.

Account takeover An attacker gaining control of a legitimate user or service withholding credentials or sessions. Frequently results from phishing or token compromise.

Active exploitation Confirmed malicious activity using a vulnerability or misconfiguration. Indicates that an incident is underway rather than theoretical risk.

Agent-based telemetry Security or operational data collected by agents running on endpoints or servers. Provides detailed visibility into local activity and system state.

Alert enrichment The addition of context such as asset criticality and user identity to an alert. Improves triage accuracy and response speed.

Alert fatigue Reduced analyst effectiveness due to excessive low value alerts. Increases the risk of missed or delayed detection.

Alert routing Directing alerts to the appropriate team or workflow. Based on severity, scope, system ownership, or required authority.

Alert-to-action ratio The percentage of alerts that lead to meaningful response actions. Measures detection quality and operational efficiency.

Anomaly detection Identification of behavior that deviates from established baselines. Effective for unknown threats but requires tuning to control false positives.

API key A credential used to authenticate API requests. Often long lived and high risk if improperly protected.

Approval gates Mandatory authorization checkpoints before sensitive actions occur. Used to control changes, containment, or privileged access.

Asset criticality A measure of how important an asset is to business operations and risk. Drives prioritization for protection and response.

Asset identity The unique identifiers and attributes that consistently represent an asset. Enables tracking across tools and lifecycle events.

Asset inventory The authoritative list of assets and their characteristics. Forms the foundation for visibility, ownership, and risk management.

Asset ownership The assigned accountable person or team responsible for an asset's security and operation. Enables faster decisions for changes, risk acceptance, and incident response.

Assumed breach Operating as if an attacker is already present in the environment. Drives verification, least privilege, and strong containment discipline.

Attack surface The total set of exposed systems, services, identities, and paths an attacker could target. Reducing it lowers likelihood and impact of compromise.

Attack vector The method or pathway used to gain unauthorized access or execute malicious actions. Examples include phishing, exposed services, or stolen credentials.

Audit trail A chronological record of actions and events in systems and processes. Supports investigations, accountability, and regulatory needs.

Auditability The ability to reliably review and validate what happened and who did it. Depends on consistent logging, retention, and integrity controls.

Authentication The process of verifying an identity before granting access. Uses factors like passwords, MFA, certificates, or tokens.

Authentication assurance Confidence that authentication accurately proves the claimed identity. Influenced by MFA strength, device trust, and phishing resistance.

Authorization The rules and decisions that determine what an authenticated identity is allowed to do. Implemented through roles, policies, and permission boundaries.

Authorization boundary The defined limit of what a role, system, or account can access or change. Helps constrain blast radius when an identity is abused.

Break glass account A highly controlled emergency account used when normal access paths fail. Requires strict monitoring, approvals, and post use review.

Business email compromise Fraud using compromised or spoofed email to induce payments or sensitive actions. Often leverages impersonation and weak verification steps.

Case management system The platform used to track incidents, investigations, tasks, and decisions. Provides a single record for workflow and accountability.

Chain of custody Documentation showing how evidence was collected, handled, and transferred. Preserves credibility and reduces disputes about evidence integrity.

Change control The discipline of planning, approving, and documenting changes to reduce risk. Prevents unreviewed actions that create outages or security gaps.

Change management The broader process of coordinating changes across teams, systems, and timelines. Includes communication, scheduling, rollback plans, and verification.

Command and control The attacker's channel to communicate with and direct compromised systems. Detecting it helps confirm compromise and guide containment.

Compensating control A substitute safeguard used when the primary control cannot be implemented. Must provide comparable risk reduction and be monitored.

Configuration drift Unintended changes that move a system away from its intended secure configuration. Often caused by manual fixes, patches, or inconsistent automation.

Configuration hardening Applying secure settings to reduce exposure and attack paths. Focuses on disabling unnecessary features and enforcing least functionality.

Containment Actions taken to limit attacker movement and stop ongoing harm. Prioritizes speed while protecting evidence and business operations.

Containment authority The defined permission and responsibility to execute containment actions. Prevents delays and reduces risk of unauthorized disruption.

Containment gating Required checks or approvals before containment actions are executed. Balances rapid response with safety and accountability.

Containment strategy The planned approach for isolating threats while maintaining operations. Includes scope decisions, sequencing, and criteria for escalation.

Containment thresholds Predefined conditions that trigger specific containment actions. Helps teams act quickly and consistently under pressure.

Control plane logging Logs that capture administrative and management actions in control planes. Critical for detecting misuse of privileged access and configuration changes.

Control plane logs The recorded events from management interfaces that change settings, identities, or policies. Used to reconstruct what was changed and by whom.

Correlation Linking related events across sources to form a higher confidence detection or narrative. Reduces noise by combining weak signals into stronger evidence.

Correlation window The time range used to associate events as part of the same activity. Too short misses patterns, too long increases false links.

Credential rotation Regularly changing credentials to reduce the impact of exposure. Especially important for service accounts and long-lived secrets.

Credential theft The unauthorized acquisition of usernames, passwords, keys, or other credentials. Enables access without exploiting technical vulnerabilities.

Cryptographic hashes Fixed length values that represent data for integrity verification. Commonly used to detect tampering or identify known files.

Data classification Categorizing data by sensitivity and required handling. Guides access controls, encryption, retention, and sharing rules.

Data exfiltration Unauthorized transfer of data out of an environment. Often occurs after persistence and privilege escalation.

Data loss prevention Controls that detect or block unauthorized movement of sensitive data. Uses rules, labels, and content inspection to reduce leakage.

Data minimization Collecting and retaining only the data necessary for a defined purpose. Reduces breach impact and operational risk.

Data leakage Exposure of sensitive data through mistakes, misconfigurations, or weak controls. Can be accidental or attacker driven.

Data poisoning Manipulating data inputs, so monitoring, detection, or downstream decisions become unreliable. Undermines trust in baselines and analytics.

Decision authority The defined right to make specific operational or containment decisions. Clarifies who can approve disruptive actions under pressure.

Decision log A recorded trail of key incident decisions and rationale. Supports accountability, learning, and defensible post incident review.

Detect to contain workflow The operational path from detection to validated containment action. Emphasizes speed, clarity, and minimized back and forth.

Detection engineering Building and improving detections using telemetry, hypotheses, and validation. Focuses on measurable signal quality and actionability.

Dwell time The time an attacker remains in an environment before detection and removal. Shorter dwell time generally reduces impact and cost.

Egress control Restrictions and monitoring on outbound network traffic. Helps prevent data exfiltration and disrupts command and control.

Endpoint isolation Separating an endpoint from the network to stop spread and reduce attacker control. Should preserve evidence while limiting impact.

Eradication Removing attacker footholds, persistence, and malicious changes. Complements containment by eliminating the root of continued access.

Escalation path The defined route for raising issues to higher authority or specialized teams. Prevents delays and ambiguity during incidents.

Escalation thresholds Conditions that require escalation, such as confirmed compromise or high criticality assets. Ensures consistent, timely leadership awareness.

Evidence integrity Assurance that evidence has not been altered since collection. Relies on hashing, access controls, and documented handling.

Evidence preservation Capturing and protecting relevant logs and artifacts before they are lost or overwritten. Enables accurate reconstruction and verification later.

Evidence retention The policy and capability to keep evidence for required durations. Supports investigations, compliance, and post incident review.

Exception governance The process for approving, tracking, and reviewing control exceptions. Prevents temporary bypasses from becoming permanent risk.

Exception sprawl Growth of unmanaged exceptions that weaken security posture. Often results from weak renewal, ownership, or visibility.

Exposure The degree to which a system, identity, or service is accessible to threats. Includes technical reachability and control weaknesses.

Exposure context The surrounding factors that make an exposure more or less risky. Examples include asset criticality, privilege level, and active exploitation.

External exposure Assets or services reachable from outside the organization. Typically increases likelihood of scanning, exploitation, and credential abuse.

False negative Malicious activity that is not detected by controls or monitoring. Creates a hidden gap that can extend attacker dwell time.

False positive A detection that flags benign activity as malicious. Increases workload and contributes to alert fatigue.

Federated identity An identity model where authentication is delegated to a trusted provider. Enables single sign on but concentrates risk in the identity plane.

Flow records Summaries of network communications such as source, destination, ports, and timing. Useful for spotting lateral movement and exfiltration patterns.

Gated restoration Restoring systems only after defined verification checks are met. Prevents reinfection and reduces repeat incidents.

Immutable storage Storage designed to prevent modification or deletion for a defined period. Protects backups and critical logs from tampering.

Immutability The property of being resistant to alteration after creation. Used to strengthen evidence, backups, and recovery reliability.

Incident commander The person accountable for coordinating incident response. Owns priorities, communication, and decision pacing across teams.

Incident severity declaration The formal act of assigning severity to an incident. Triggers escalation, staffing, and communication requirements.

Just-in-time elevation Granting elevated privileges only when needed and for a limited duration. Reduces standing privilege and narrows attacker opportunities.

Just-in-time permissions Temporary access grants tied to a task, approval, and time window. Helps control privilege creep and improves accountability.

Key management The practices for generating, storing, rotating, and protecting cryptographic keys. Weak key management undermines encryption and trust.

Key revocation Invalidating a key, so it can no longer be used. Essential after suspected compromise or unauthorized disclosure.

Key rotation Replacing keys on a schedule or after exposure. Limits the lifespan of compromised secrets and supports good hygiene.

Known good state A verified baseline configuration and data set considered trustworthy. Used as a target for restoration and integrity checks.

Lateral movement Attacker activity that spreads from one system or account to others. Often uses stolen credentials and trust relationships.

Least privilege Granting only the minimum access needed to perform a task. Limits blast radius when accounts or tokens are compromised.

Log integrity Confidence that logs are complete and unaltered. Requires protection from tampering and reliable time synchronization.

Log retention Keeping logs for a defined duration to support detection and investigation. Must align to threat dwell time and compliance needs.

Logging tampering Attempts to disable, alter, or delete logs to hide activity. A strong indicator of attacker presence and intent.

Machine identities Non-human identities used by systems, services, or workloads to authenticate. Must be governed like human accounts due to high privilege risk.

MFA prompt bombing Repeated MFA prompts sent to pressure a user into approving access. Often paired with phishing or credential theft.

Network isolation Restricting a system or segment's network connectivity to contain an incident. Used to stop spread while preserving critical operations where possible.

Network segmentation Dividing networks into controlled zones with enforced boundaries. Limits lateral movement and reduces blast radius.

Non-human identity Accounts or principals used by applications, services, and automation rather than people. Requires strict lifecycle control and credential hygiene.

Observability The ability to understand system behavior through telemetry, logs, and traces. Enables faster triage and higher confidence incident decisions.

Offline backup Backups stored disconnected from primary systems. Protects recovery capability from ransomware and backup sabotage.

Patch management The process of deploying updates to remediate vulnerabilities and defects. Balances speed, change risk, and verification.

Persistence Techniques used by attackers to maintain access over time. Often includes scheduled tasks, registry changes, or service modifications.

Persistence mechanisms The specific artifacts that enable persistence, such as scheduled tasks or startup run keys. Identifying them is key to eradication.

Policy drift Gradual divergence between intended policy and actual enforced policy. Creates hidden gaps that accumulate risk over time.

Policy enforcement point The control location where policy decisions are applied. Examples include gateways, endpoints, or identity access systems.

Privileged access management Systems and processes that control and monitor elevated privileges. Includes approvals, session controls, and auditing.

Privileged actions High-impact operations such as changing policies, disabling logging, or modifying identity permissions. Require strict controls and logging.

Prompt injection Manipulation of AI prompts or inputs to produce unintended behavior or outputs. Can bypass intended constraints and leak sensitive context.

Recovery point objective (RPO) The maximum acceptable data loss measured in time. Defines how far back restoration may need to roll.

Recovery time objective (RTO) The maximum acceptable downtime for a system or service. Drives restoration planning and resilience investments.

Remediation verification Confirming that fixes actually removed the issue and did not introduce new risk. Uses evidence, testing, and follow-up monitoring.

Residual risk The remaining risk after controls and remediation are applied. Must be understood and formally accepted or further reduced.

Restoration Returning systems and services to operational state after disruption. Should rely on known good state and gated verification.

Return to service The controlled transition from restoration back into production operations. Requires validation that risk is acceptable and monitoring is in place.

Rollback planning Preparing a safe path to revert a change if outcomes are unacceptable. Reduces fear of change and limits incident impact from mistakes.

Rollback path The documented steps to undo a change and return to a prior stable state. Must be tested and aligned to RTO expectations.

Runbook A step-by-step operational procedure for repeatable response tasks. Supports consistency, speed, and lower analyst cognitive load.

Service account A non-human account used by applications or services to authenticate. Often has broad access and must be tightly governed.

Service principal An identity representation of an application or service in an identity platform. Controls how the service authenticates and what it can access.

Session management The controls that create, track, and expire user sessions. Poor session management increases replay and hijacking risk.

Session revocation Forcibly ending active sessions associated with an account or token. Common containment step after compromise suspicion.

Severity classification Categorizing incidents by impact and urgency. Drives escalation, staffing, and communication requirements.

Severity criteria The defined factors used to assign severity, such as business impact and scope. Improves consistency across incident declarations.

Shared responsibility model The division of security responsibilities between providers and customers. Critical for cloud operations and control ownership clarity.

Shadow IT Unapproved systems or services used outside formal governance. Creates visibility gaps and unmanaged risk, especially for data handling.

Signal-to-noise ratio The proportion of useful detections compared to irrelevant alerts. Higher ratios improve analyst efficiency and response quality.

Situation report A structured update that summarizes incident status, impact, actions, and next steps. Keeps stakeholders aligned during fast-moving response.

Social engineering Attacker manipulation of people to gain access or induce actions. Often bypasses technical controls through trust and urgency.

Telemetry Collected data about system, network, and identity activity. Telemetry quality directly affects detection, triage, and investigation confidence.

Telemetry completeness The degree to which expected telemetry sources are present and reporting. Gaps create blind spots that attackers can exploit.

Telemetry coverage How much of the environment is monitored at meaningful fidelity. Includes endpoints, identities, networks, and control planes.

Telemetry fidelity The accuracy and detail level of telemetry. Higher-fidelity supports better correlation, evidence, and faster root cause analysis.

Telemetry hygiene Keeping telemetry consistent, reliable, and usable over time. Includes normalization, integrity, and controlling noisy sources.

Telemetry normalization Converting diverse telemetry into consistent fields and formats. Enables correlation and reduces parsing and schema friction.

Telemetry onboarding The process of adding a new telemetry source into monitoring. Includes validation, parsing, routing, and quality checks.

Telemetry pipeline The end-to-end path telemetry takes from source to storage and analysis. Pipeline failures can create event loss and delayed detection.

Threat hunting Proactive searching for adversary activity that detections may miss. Uses hypotheses, telemetry, and iterative validation.

Token invalidation Making a token unusable before its natural expiration. Used after suspected compromise or risk signals.

Token issuance The act of generating and granting a token to an identity. Should be logged and governed to support traceability.

Token revocation Removing a token's authorization, so it cannot be used. Critical for containing token theft and session hijacking.

Token theft Unauthorized capture of tokens from endpoints, browsers, or logs. Enables access that may bypass MFA and password resets.

Transitive permissions Access granted indirectly through nested roles, groups, or trusts. Can create unexpected privilege and hard to see paths.

Triage Rapid assessment to determine what is happening and what to do next. Focuses on impact, scope, and immediate containment needs.

Triage boundaries The defined limits of what triage should decide versus what requires escalation. Prevents overreach and speeds handoffs.

Triage discipline Consistent methods and checks that keep triage fast and accurate. Reduces false closure and preserves evidence.

Trust boundary The point where trust assumptions change between systems or zones. A key concept for segmentation and identity design.

Trust relationships Established connections that allow one identity or system to access another. Attackers abuse these to move laterally and escalate.

Trust store The repository of certificates or roots used to establish trust. Tampering can enable interception, impersonation, or persistence.

Vulnerability management The program for identifying, prioritizing, and reducing vulnerabilities. Ties scanning results to remediation workflows and risk.

Vulnerability scanning Automated discovery of known weaknesses in systems and software. Requires validation and prioritization to drive real reduction.

Workflow orchestration Coordinating response tasks across tools and teams in a controlled sequence. Improves speed, consistency, and auditability.

Workload identities Identities assigned to workloads such as containers, functions, or services. Must be governed to prevent excessive permissions and drift.

Index

a

Access controls
  log data integrity 314–315
  sensitive information 218–219
Access drift, stale access 180–181
Access governance
  identity processes 183–186
  reviews 181–183
Access patterns, behavioral signals 164–166
Access reviews, identity lifecycle 181–183
Access tokens, revocation and invalidation 403–404
Account takeover, identity-driven risk 155–169
Accountability
  asset ownership 87–89
  decision models 18–21
  without blame 476–477
Active exploitation, patch prioritization 285–287
Administrative access
  local privileges 106–107
  privileged workflows 193–195
AI-assisted operations. *See* AI/ML
AI governance
  acceptable use 543–545
  auditability, evidence, and change management 553–555
  data handling, privacy, and retention 545–546
  drift, bias, and false confidence 549–551
  human-in-the-loop gates 547–548
  playbooks for safe adoption 555–556
  prompt injection and data exfiltration 551–553
  validation, testing, and quality 548–549
AI/ML
  access risk 166–167
  architecture 147–149
  asset discovery 95–97
  blue team workflows 11–12
  cloud operations 518–520
  cloud posture 498–500
  containment 409–410
  control execution 44–45
  culture 478–480
  data protection 222–224
  detection engineering 352–354
  endpoint triage 112–114
  governance decision support 27–29
  identity governance 183–184
  incident response planning 390–392
  investigations 370–372
  monitoring triage 334–336
  network analysis 131–133
  post-incident analysis 445–446
  privilege monitoring 203–206
  recovery coordination 426–428
  recovery operations 239–241
  remediation operations 296–297
  risk analysis 78–80
  security operations governance 543–556
  telemetry operations 315–317
  threat intelligence 534–535
  ticket enrichment and summarization 61–62
  training programs 463–464
  vulnerability discovery 277–280
  vulnerability prioritization 259–261
  See also Automation; Human-in-the-loop controls; Validation
Alert enrichment, network analysis 131–133
Alert fatigue, monitoring operations 328–330
Alert routing, triage and escalation 327–328
Alert-to-action ratio, monitoring effectiveness 328–330
Alerting strategy 324–327

Anomaly detection, detection engineering 347–349
API keys, asset inventory and identities 85–87
Approval gates
  AI governance 547–548
  privileged access 193–195
Artificial intelligence. *See* AI/ML
Asset management
  AI-assisted discovery and correlation 95–97
  asset awareness 83–84
  classification and prioritization 89–90
  data quality and drift 94–95
  driving security work 97–99
  lifecycle and offboarding 90–92
  ownership and accountability 87–89
  physical and digital inventory 85–87
  shadow IT and unknown assets 92–93
  See also Shadow IT; Telemetry; Vulnerability management
Assumed breach, defensive principles 7–8
Attack surface, architecture risks 147–149
Attack vectors, evaluating 74–76
Auditability
  AI-driven processes 553–555
  controls and evidence 42–43
Authentication
  cloud considerations 492–493
  versus authorization 157–158
Authorization
  boundaries 142–143
  versus authentication 157–158
Automation
  control execution 44–45
  defensive workflows 11–12
  safe adoption and approval gates 543–556
  ticket workflows 61–62
  workflow orchestration 44–45
  See also AI/ML; Human-in-the-loop controls

b

Backlogs, vulnerability management 258–259
Backup and recovery
  active incidents 237–239
  AI-assisted recovery operations 239–241
  IT and security coordination 236–237
  lessons into control improvements 241–242
  protecting backups 230–232
  recovery as defensive control 227–228
  recovery objectives 232–234
  restoration testing 234–236
  scope, coverage, and retention 229–230
Backup immutability, protection from tampering 230–232
Baselines
  endpoint configuration 102–104
  monitoring deviations 323–324
  policy standards 37–38
Blame-free culture, accountability without blame 476–477
Blind spots, vulnerability coverage 267–269
Blue team operating model
  AI-assisted ticket workflows 61–62
  collaboration with IT and engineering 57–59
  daily, weekly, and monthly cadence 51–53
  documentation and knowledge transfer 59–60
  escalation paths and decision rights 54–56
  intake and work management 53–54
  on-call and after-hours coverage 56–57
  scaling 63–64
  services and service owners 49–51
Blue team operations
  automation and AI-assisted workflows 11–12
  core principles 7–8
  defensive security as operational discipline 4–5
  defining success 12–14
  offensive *vs.* defensive security 5–6
  origins of 3–4
  people, process, and technology 9–11
  roles and responsibilities 8–9
  See also Blue team operating model; Defensive security; Incident response plans
Blue teaming. *See* Blue team operations
Break-glass accounts, emergency access 195–197
Business alignment, cybersecurity objectives 24–25
Business criticality, asset classification 89–90
Business email compromise, awareness threats 456–458
Business objectives, security alignment 24–25
Business risk, vulnerability prioritization 256–257

c

Case management, investigation records 359–374
Chain of custody, evidence handling 361–362
Change control, network policy 130–131
Change management
  AI-driven processes 553–555
  policy communication 41–42
  vulnerability discovery 274–275
Cloud identity, access considerations 492–493
Cloud misconfigurations, common causes 495–497
Cloud-native operations, application considerations 508–509

Cloud security
  AI-assisted posture 498–500
  basics 487–488
  blue team integration 497–498
  cloud IAM 492–493
  consistency across environments 500–502
  hybrid complexity 490–492
  misconfigurations 495–497
  shared responsibility model 488–490
  visibility and logging 494–495
Cloud storage, data protection 509–511
Cloud workloads
  activity monitoring 513–515
  AI-assisted cloud operations 518–520
  cloud incidents and access abuse 515–516
  cloud-native applications 508–509
  cloud storage and data protection 509–511
  multi-account and multi-environment complexity 516–518
  network controls and segmentation 511–513
  operationalizing cloud security 520–522
  workload ownership 505–507
Collaboration
  IT and engineering 57–59
  security, IT, and business 471–472
Command and control, network defense 126–129
Communication
  executive updates 425–426
  incident pathways 383–384
  policy changes 41–42
  risk to audiences 77–78
Compensating controls
  patching delays 292–294
  policy exceptions 35–37
Compliance, auditable evidence 42–43
Configuration drift
  assets 94–95
  endpoints 104–106
Configuration hardening, endpoint hardening 109–110
Continuous monitoring
  AI-assisted triage 334–336
  alert fatigue and noise 328–330
  alert triage, routing, and escalation 327–328
  alerting strategy 324–327
  baselines and deviations 323–324
  goals and constraints 321–323
  handoffs to investigation 332–334
  monitoring rules over time 330–332
  sustainable cadence 336–338
Contractors, temporary access 177–178
Control effectiveness, endpoint controls 114–115
Control gaps, post-incident tracking 437–438
Control planes, cloud security 487–502
Control validation, AI-augmented risk analysis 78–80
Correlation
  AI-assisted investigations 370–372
  asset discovery 95–97
  telemetry operations 315–317
Credential resets, recovery 423–424
Credential rotation, backups and recovery 236–239
Credential theft, identity abuse 155–169
Cryptographic hashes, evidence integrity 361–362
Cyber resilience culture
  accountability without blame 476–477
  AI, trust, and transparency 478–480
  communication without fear or fatigue 474–476
  incentives for secure behavior 472–473
  leadership objective 469–470
  maturity and continuous improvement 480–481
  security in everyday work 473–474
  security, IT, and business collaboration 471–472
  wins and setbacks 477–478

d

Data classification, practical usage 212–214
Data exfiltration
  AI workflow risks 551–553
  cloud and network context 511–513
Data leakage, AI governance 545–546
Data loss prevention, movement and exposure 219–220
Data minimization, AI-assisted work 545–546
Data protection
  AI in data protection 222–224
  business requirement 211–212
  classification and usage 212–214
  data in transit and at rest 216–217
  encryption 214–216
  failure modes 224–225
  monitoring data access 220–222
  sensitive information access controls 218–219
  unauthorized movement and exposure 219–220
Deception, concepts and deterrence 533–534
Decision authority
  incident response plans 381–383
  operating model 54–56
Decision logs, incident timelines 407–409
Defensive readiness, leadership behaviors 29–30
Defensive security
  core principles 7–8
  offensive security differences 5–6
  as operational discipline 4–5

Deprovisioning, audit priority 175–177
Detection engineering
  AI/ML in detection 352–354
  anomaly detection 347–349
  detection gaps 349–350
  detection quality 346–347
  documentation and versioning 354–356
  maintenance and breakage 350–352
  managed capability 341–343
  real threat behaviors 343–344
  tuning false positives 344–346
Detection gaps, persistence and maintenance 349–350
Detection logic, documentation and versioning 354–356
Detection quality, measurement 346–347
Detection tuning, false positives 344–346
Documentation
  architecture standards 146–147
  incident response 386–387
  operating model continuity 59–60
Drift
  AI/ML 549–551
  asset data quality 94–95
  endpoint agents 104–106
  network policy 130–131

e

EDR. *See* Endpoint security
Egress controls, network defense 119–121
Emergency patching, rapid response 297–299
Encryption, implementation 214–216
Endpoint detection and response. *See* Endpoint security
Endpoint isolation, containment 404–406
Endpoint security
  agents, coverage, and drift 104–106
  AI-assisted triage 112–114
  baselines and configuration standards 102–104
  control effectiveness 114–115
  endpoint as battleground 101–102
  exceptions and blind spots 110–112
  hardening and operational constraints 109–110
  local privileges and administrative access 106–107
  logging strategy and collection 107–109
  See also Administrative access; Logging; Telemetry
Engagement techniques, training reinforcement 459–460
Entitlements, permission sprawl 161–163
Eradication and recovery
  AI-assisted recovery coordination 426–428
  credential resets and identity risk 423–424
  defensible evidence 429–430
  executive updates 425–426
  recovery planning 420–421
  removing access and persistence 415–417
  restoring systems and reinfection monitoring 421–422
  speed and confidence 424–425
  validation and return-to-service 417–419
Evidence
  auditable controls 42–43
  collection and preservation 361–362
  defensible closure 429–430
  integrity 445–446
Evidence retention, telemetry and logs 308–310
Exceptions
  endpoint blind spots 110–112
  policy scope 35–37
  risk acceptance and patching 291–292
Executive updates, business coordination 425–426
Exercises
  IR readiness 387–389
  threat intelligence and assumptions 531–533
Exposure
  asset context 89–90
  remote access reduction 125–126
Exposure reduction, external exposure 269–270
External exposure, high-risk services 269–270

f

False confidence
  AI decision support 27–29
  AI governance 549–551
False positives, vulnerability findings 272–274
Federated identity, cloud and SaaS 492–493
Firewalls, policy management 123–125
Flow records, network telemetry 126–128
Forensics, evidence collection 361–362

g

Governance
  AI-enabled decision support 27–29
  business alignment 24–25
  competing priorities and tradeoffs 25–26
  decision-making and accountability 18–21
  defensive outcomes 17–18
  leadership behaviors and readiness 29–30
  policies, standards, and procedures 21–22
  program ownership and oversight 26–27
  risk translation and investment 22–24
  See also Accountability; Decision authority; Policy frameworks; Risk management
Group membership, role changes 178–180

h

Human behavior, defensive outcomes 453–454
Human-in-the-loop controls
  AI-assisted workflows 11–12
  AI governance 547–548
  decision support 27–29
  ticket workflows 61–62

i

IAM. *See* Identity and access management
Identity and access management
  access patterns and behavioral signals 164–166
  AI-assisted access risk 166–167
  authentication *vs.* authorization 157–158
  daily operations 163–164
  entitlements and permission sprawl 161–163
  failure modes 167–169
  identity as control plane 155–157
  least privilege 160–161
  role-based access control 158–159
  See also Authentication; Authorization; Least privilege; Privileged access management
Identity governance
  AI assistance 183–184
  ownership models 184–186
Identity hygiene, stale access 180–181
Identity lifecycle
  access reviews 181–183
  AI for identity governance 183–184
  contractors, vendors, and temporary access 177–178
  deprovisioning 175–177
  group membership and role changes 178–180
  identity hygiene and stale access 180–181
  joiner, mover, leaver 171–173
  ownership models 184–186
  provisioning workflows and approvals 173–175
Identity lifecycle management. *See* Identity lifecycle
Immutability, backups 230–232
Incident commander, response authority 381–383
Incident containment
  access during active incidents 403–404
  actions that increase risk 410–412
  AI-assisted containment 409–410
  cross-team coordination 401–403
  detect-to-contain workflows 397–399
  incident log and timeline 407–409
  isolation, blocking, and stabilization 404–406
  strategies and business tradeoffs 399–401
  uncertainty and partial visibility 406–407
  See also Endpoint isolation; Lateral movement; Network isolation
Incident handling. *See* Incident containment
Incident response. *See* Incident response plans; Incident containment; Eradication and recovery
Incident response plans
  AI support 390–392
  communication pathways and escalation 383–384
  evidence handling and documentation 386–387
  failure modes 392–393
  organizational change 389–390
  playbooks and runbooks 384–386
  purpose and scope 379–381
  readiness testing and exercises 387–389
  roles, responsibilities, and authority 381–383
Institutional memory, incidents 443–445
Investigation workflow
  AI-assisted investigations 370–372
  analyst mindset 359–360
  confirming or refuting activity 366–367
  escalation to incident response 369–370
  evidence collection and preservation 361–362
  quality improvement 372–374
  scoping 362–364
  stakeholder collaboration 367–369
  timeline construction 364–366
Investment priorities, risk translation 22–24
IR. *See* Incident response plans

j

Joiner, mover, leaver, identity lifecycle 171–173

k

Knowledge transfer, continuity 59–60
Known-good state, restoration 417–422

l

Lateral movement
  network detection 128–129
  trust boundaries 73–74
Leadership
  culture of resilience 469–471
  defensive readiness 29–30
Least privilege
  identity operations 160–161
  privileged access 206–207
Lessons learned, program improvement 433–434
Log integrity, access control 314–315

Log retention, collection considerations 308–310
Logging
  cloud environments 494–495
  endpoint collection 107–109
  network boundaries 126–128
  strategy and telemetry 303–318
Logging and telemetry
  access control and integrity 314–315
  AI for telemetry operations 315–317
  collection, normalization, and retention 308–310
  confidence in visibility 317–318
  gaps, failures, and quality 310–312
  good telemetry 304–306
  log sources 306–308
  ownership of logging pipelines 312–313
  visibility as foundation 303–304
  See also Detection engineering; Monitoring; Visibility
Logging strategy. *See* Logging and telemetry

m

Machine identities, workload identities 505–508
Machine learning. *See* AI/ML
Maintenance windows, patch operations 291–292
Maturity, continuous improvement 480–481
Metrics
  detection quality 346–347
  improvement without gaming 440–442
Monitoring
  cloud activity 513–515
  continuous operations 321–338
  data access 220–222
  privileged sessions 197–199

n

Network defense
  AI-assisted analysis 131–133
  firewall policy management 123–125
  goals and defensive layers 119–121
  hybrid environments 133–135
  lateral movement and suspicious connectivity 128–129
  operational change and policy drift 130–131
  remote access, exposure, and authentication 125–126
  segmentation 121–123
  visibility and logging 126–128
  See also Firewalls; Lateral movement; Network segmentation; Remote access
Network segmentation
  cloud context 511–513
  concepts 121–123
Non-human identities, service accounts 199–201

o

Observability, visibility and telemetry 303–318
Offensive security, differences from defensive security 5–6
Offline backups, operational resilience 230–232
On-call coverage, after-hours 56–57
Operating cadence, daily, weekly, monthly 51–53

p

PAM. *See* Privileged access management
Patch management, operational program 287–289
Perimeter defense. *See* Network defense
Permission sprawl, entitlements 161–163
Persistence, eradication 415–417
Persistence mechanisms, endpoint behavior 101–102
Playbooks, IR planning 384–386
Policies. *See* Policy frameworks
Policy drift, network operations 130–131
Policy frameworks
  auditable controls and evidence 42–44
  automation and AI in control execution 44–45
  communicating changes 41–42
  failure modes 45–46
  policy relevance over time 39–41
  procedure design 38–39
  scope and exceptions 35–37
  standards and baselines 37–38
  usable frameworks 33–35
Post-incident learning
  AI for post-incident analysis 445–446
  control gaps and corrective actions 437–439
  institutional memory 443–445
  lessons learned 433–434
  long-term resilience 446–447
  metrics and gaming 440–442
  root cause and contributing factors 434–437
  sharing lessons without blame 442–443
  updating detections, policies, and procedures 439–440
Prioritization
  risk-based 69–70
  vulnerability remediation 285–287

Privileged access management
AI-assisted privilege monitoring 203–206
approval models and administrative workflow 193–195
break-glass and emergency access 195–197
privilege as highest-risk access 189–191
privilege auditing and evidence 201–203
privileged roles and actions 191–193
privileged session monitoring 197–199
reducing privilege 206–207
service accounts and non-human privilege 199–201
Privileged actions, roles and workflows 191–193
Privileged sessions, monitoring and control 197–199
Proactive defense. *See* Threat intelligence
Program ownership, delegation and oversight 26–27

r

Recovery. *See* Backup and recovery; Eradication and recovery
Recovery objectives, RPO and RTO 232–234
Recovery point objective (RPO), backup and recovery 232–234
Recovery time objective (RTO), backup and recovery 232–234
Red team collaboration, defensive improvement 530–531
Remediation
coordination 289–290
verification 294–295
Remediation and patch operations
AI-assisted remediation 296–297
compensating controls 292–294
coordination with IT and engineering 289–291
emergency patching 297–298
findings into work 283–285
maintenance windows and risk acceptance 291–292
patch management 287–289
prioritization criteria and tradeoffs 285–287
remediation verification and regression 294–296
Remote access, exposure reduction 125–126
Residual risk, treatment decisions 76–77
Resilience
business restoration 415–430
culture 469–482
recovery thinking 143–144
Restoration
testing 234–236
under pressure 420–421
Return-to-service, validation 417–419
Risk acceptance, patch operations 291–292
Risk assessments
current and useful 80–81
scope and outputs 70–72
Risk management
AI-augmented analysis 78–80
assessments, scope, inputs, and outputs 70–72
communicating risk 77–78
critical business functions 72–73
defensive prioritization 69–70
keeping assessments current 80–81
systems, dependencies, and trust boundaries 73–74
threat landscapes and attack vectors 74–76
treatment options and tradeoffs 76–77
See also Asset management; Business criticality; Trust boundaries
Risk treatment, options and tradeoffs 76–77
Role-based access control, organizational fit 158–159
Role-based training, higher-risk functions 460–461
Rollback planning, patch operations 291–292
Runbooks, IR planning 384–386

s

Scoping, investigations 362–364
Security architecture
AI, new attack surface, and controls 147–149
business change alignment 149–150
controls across endpoint, network, identity, and data 142–143
defensive architecture 137–151
enforceable patterns 141–142
layered security 137–139
operational reality 145–146
resilience and recovery thinking 143–145
risk into architecture decisions 139–141
standards and exceptions 146–147
Security awareness
AI in training programs 463–464
awareness *vs.* training 455–456
behavior-changing training 458–459
changing organizations 464–465
common threats 456–458
engagement and reinforcement 459–460
human behavior 453–455

participation and real-world impact 461–463
role-based training 460–461
Security decision-making, accountability models 18–21
Security operations center. *See* Continuous monitoring
Security training, awareness versus 455–456
Service accounts
credential resets and recovery 423–424
non-human privilege 199–201
Session revocation, active incidents 403–404
Severity classification, incident response 381–383
Shadow IT, unknown assets 92–93
Shared responsibility model, cloud operations 488–490
SIEM. *See* Logging and telemetry; Continuous monitoring
Signal-to-noise ratio, alert fatigue 328–330
Situational awareness, operating rhythms 51–53
SOC, triage and monitoring 321–338
Social engineering, awareness 456–458
Standards
architecture 146–147
baselines 37–38

t

Telemetry
asset expectations 97–99
endpoint logging 107–109
log sources 306–308
network visibility 126–128
normalization and retention 308–310
Telemetry completeness, confidence in visibility 317–318
Telemetry pipeline, operational ownership 312–313
Threat detection. *See* Detection engineering
Threat hunting, proactive defense 535–537
Threat intelligence
AI in threat intelligence 534–535
deception 533–534
exercises 531–533
intelligence into defensive action 526–528
prioritizing defenses 528–530
proactive operations 535–537
red team collaboration 530–531
sustaining proactive work 537–538
value to blue teams 525–526
See also Deception; Red team collaboration; Threat hunting
Threat landscapes, attack vectors 74–76
Timeline construction, incident analysis 364–366
Token revocation, credential containment 423–424
Token theft, identity risk 155–169
Transitive permissions, access reviews 181–183
Triage
alert triage 327–328
endpoint triage 112–114
investigation mindset 359–360
Triage boundaries, operating model 49–51
Triage discipline, sustaining proactive work 537–538
Trust boundaries
risk mapping 73–74
segmentation 121–123
Trust relationships, lateral movement 128–129
Trust store, data protection 216–217

v

Validation
AI output quality 548–549
cleanup and return-to-service 417–419
findings and noise 270–272
Visibility
cloud environments 494–495
detection foundation 303–304
network boundaries 126–128
Vulnerabilities
asset lifecycles 275–277
exposure reduction 265–281
Vulnerability discovery
AI noise reduction 277–280
asset lifecycles 275–277
change management 274–275
coverage gaps and blind spots 267–269
external exposure and high-risk services 269–270
false positives and repeated findings 272–274
repeatable discovery process 280–281
scanning approaches 265–267
validation and noise reduction 270–272
Vulnerability management
AI-assisted prioritization 259–261
asset management dependencies 249–251
backlogs 258–259
frequency and coverage 252–254
intake beyond scanning 254–256
prioritization by business risk 256–258
program confidence 261–262
program definition 247–249
scope across systems 251–252

Vulnerability program. *See* Vulnerability management
Vulnerability remediation. *See* Remediation and patch operations
Vulnerability scanning, approaches 265–267

W

Workflow orchestration, control execution 44–45
Workforce enablement, security awareness 453–466
Workload identities, cloud workloads 505–507

Wiley The manufacturer's authorized representative according to the EU General Product Safety Regulation is Wiley-VCH GmbH, Boschstr. 12, 69469 Weinheim, Germany, e-mail: Product_Safety@wiley.com.

Printed and bound by CPI Group (UK) Ltd, Croydon, CR0 4YY

23/07/2026

02175123-0001